ABOUT THE EDITORS

Anne Commire developed and edited Gale's *Something About the Author* series (volumes 1–64) and *Yesterday's Authors of Books for Children* (2 volumes) and helped develop and edit *Authors and Artists for Young Adults* (volumes 1–6). As a playwright, she has written *Shay,* first produced in New York City at Playwrights' Horizons; *Put Them All Together* (cited in *Best Plays of 1978–79),* first produced at the McCarter Theatre in Princeton; "Melody Sisters," first produced at the L.A. Public Theatre; and *Starting Monday* (nominated for the Outer-Critics' Circle John Gassner Award), first produced at the Yale Repertory Theatre. All four plays were initially presented at the Eugene O'Neill Playwright's Conference. Commire directed and co-wrote "The NOW Show" at the Dorothy Chandler Pavilion; she also co-wrote, with actress Mariette Hartley, *Breaking the Silence,* and is the recipient of a New York State CAPS grant and a Rockefeller grant in playwrighting.

Deborah Klezmer is a freelance author and editor who has been a frequent contributor to Gale's *Something About the Author* series and *Authors and Artists for Young Adults.* A graduate of New York University's Dramatic Writing Program, she is the author of the plays *Man-of-War* and *Underneath the Apple Tree* and has studied at Circle in the Square and Playwrights' Horizons.

HISTORIC WORLD LEADERS

HISTORIC WORLD LEADERS

3

EUROPE
L-Z

Anne Commire, Editor

Deborah Klezmer, Associate Editor

 **Gale Research Inc.**

DETROIT • WASHINGTON DC • LONDON

Anne Commire, *Editor*
Deborah Klezmer, *Associate Editor*

Gale Research Inc. Staff

Lawrence W. Baker, *Senior Developmental Editor*
Peg Bessette, Jane Hoehner, Leslie Joseph, Allison McNeill, Rebecca Nelson, *Contributing Editors*
Kelle Sisung, *Associate Developmental Editor*

Mary Beth Trimper, *Production Director*
Evi Seoud, *Assistant Production Manager*
Mary Kelley, *Production Assistant*

Benita L. Spight, *Manager, Data Entry Services*
Gwendolyn S. Tucker, *Data Entry Supervisor*
Beverly Jendrowski, *Senior Data Entry Associate*
Nancy Jakubiak, *Data Entry Associate*

Cynthia Baldwin, *Art Director*
Barbara J. Yarrow, *Graphic Services Supervisor*
Mary Krzewinski, *Cover and Page Designer*
Willie F. Mathis, *Camera Operator*

Front cover photographs: (left to right): Volume 1: Confucius, Mohandas (Mahatma) Gandhi, Nnamdi Azikiwe, Moshe Dayan; Volume 2: Winston Churchill, Augustus Caesar, Mikhail Gorbachev, Elizabeth I; Volume 3: Cardinal Richelieu, Margaret Thatcher, Napoleon, Nicholas II; Volume 4: Clara Barton, José Batlle, Frederick Douglass, Dwight D. Eisenhower; Volume 5: Sitting Bull, Abraham Lincoln, Pancho Villa, Malcolm X.

The trademark ITP is used under license.
10 9 8 7 6 5 4 3 2 1

CONTENTS—VOLUMES 2 & 3

CONTENTS—VOLUME 1

CONTENTS—VOLUMES 4 & 5

HISTORIC WORLD LEADERS

Marquis de Lafayette

(1757–1834)

French aristocrat, who was highly influential in three revolutions of the 18th and 19th centuries: one in America and two in France.

Commonly referred to as the "Hero of Two Worlds," the Marquis de Lafayette deeply respected the concepts of liberty and freedom as extolled by the writers of the Enlightenment. He not only witnessed but actively participated in arguably the most dramatic events in modern history: the American and French Revolutions. Even though an aristocrat by birth, Lafayette exhibited extraordinary compassion for all people, and he sought to reform the Old Regime in which only the most privileged classes enjoyed economic and political freedoms.

By 1757, the La Fayettes were a well known and respected family in France. As members of the feudal Nobility of the Sword, most male members of the family served in the military; a large number were killed on the battlefield. But military service, especially for the firstborn son, was the only acceptable occupation for men of their social standing. During the early 1750s, Michel de La Fayette entered the service of the king, earned a commission, and trained in complex military maneuvers. In 1755, he married Julie de la Rivière, a young woman from an aristocratic family. He

Name variations: signed most personal letters "Gilbert." Born Marie Joseph Paul Yves Roch Gilbert du Motier de La Fayette on September 6, 1757, at the family estate in the Auvergne, Château de Chavagnac, about 400 miles southeast of Paris; died in Paris on May 20, 1834; son of Michel de La Fayette and Julie de la Rivière; married: Marie-Adrienne-Françoise de Noailles; children: Henriette, Anastasie, Georges Washington, and Virginie.

Contributed by Robert Saunders, Jr., Ph.D. in History, Auburn University, Auburn, Alabama

1768	Entered College du Plessis at Paris
1776–79	Fought in the American Revolutionary War; commissioned major general in the army of the U.S.; served in the Battle of Brandywine; wounded
1788–92	Prominent in political activities during French Revolution; commanded the National Guard of Paris; lost political favor
1792–97	Captured by Austrians and imprisoned at Olmütz
1799	Returned to Paris; opposed Napoleon's government
1815	Active in French politics after Battle of Waterloo
1824–25	Made a triumphant tour of America
1826–30	Commandant general of the French National Guard; active in the Revolution of 1830
1834	Died in Paris; buried next to his wife at Picpus Cemetery

later described his new bride as "no beauty, but neither is she ugly."

On September 6, 1757, Gilbert (known historically as Lafayette) was born while his father fought in the Seven Years' War. But Michel de La Fayette never saw his son. At the age of 27, after being needlessly exposed to English artillery fire, he was struck and killed during the Battle of Minden. After her husband's death, Julie La Fayette spent most of her time in the fashionable salons of Paris, seeing her son only during the summer months. Lafayette was thus raised mostly by his grandmother.

At the age of five, his schooling began under the care of a Jesuit priest named Abbé Fayon who taught his young pupil to read French and Latin. Fayon's tutorials also included many hours of heraldic history, grand tales of heroic knights, and the chivalric codes most aristocrats were sworn to abide. Lafayette remained under the watchful eye of his tutor for the next 15 years. Even when the boy was summoned to Paris by his mother at the age of 11, Fayon accompanied him and continued as his tutor and closest friend. Lafayette later remembered their relationship as strained, but he received a solid foundation for his university training nonetheless.

Upon his arrival in Paris in 1768, Lafayette's mother enrolled him at the Collège du Plessis, one of the most expensive and exclusive schools in the capital. While there, he was taught theology, law, rhetoric, and history. Though he excelled in Latin,

he preferred reading history; his personal hero was Vercingetorix, a Gallic chief who successfully defended his territory against **Julius Caesar**'s invasions during the first century B.C. Life for Lafayette was structured and closely supervised. Showing an air of independence even at such an early age, he once tried to organize a revolt on behalf of one his classmates whom he felt had been mistreated. The "revolt" failed and the entire class was severely punished. Perhaps, however, this episode demonstrated Lafayette's keen sense of fairness which was so much a part of his later years.

When he was 13, tragedy struck when his mother died of a sudden illness. Just a few weeks later, his grandfather died. Orphaned in Paris, he was forced to look after himself until the arrival of his great-grandfather, the Comte de la Rivière. He had, however, inherited the family fortune and remained relatively wealthy for most of his life.

Soon after graduation, his great-grandfather purchased a commission for him in the Black Musketeers, an elite but somewhat rowdy company which enjoyed the privilege of parading past the king in full regimental dress. He then attended the Académie de Versailles, an exclusive school devoted to training officer candidates, where he excelled in horsemanship and field maneuvers.

While undergoing military training, Lafayette read Abbé Raynal's *A Philosophical and Political History of the Institutions and Trade of the Europeans in the Indies.* One of the many French writers who were extremely popular among Paris's elite (called philosophes), Raynal extolled the virtues of reason, freedom, and religious toleration; he also believed that America had the potential for a wondrous promised land where men could live freely regardless of their economic status. In Paris, America was idealized for the tolerant democratic principles that were slowly evolving there. During his several trips to France, **Benjamin Franklin** was lionized and adored by Parisians for his wit and self-sufficiency, and for the plain values he was believed to represent. Donning his coonskin cap, Franklin stood in sharp contrast to the well-dressed and powdered Parisians. Although intrigued by America, Lafayette, who had recently married Adrienne de Noailles, was fully engaged in Paris's social environment. But the high life in Paris disturbed him. War was his one and only business; without it he became extremely bored.

Meanwhile, England's relationship with its colonies along the eastern seaboard of North America rapidly eroded. In 1776, when Lafayette learned that a revolution was under way in America, he actively sought a commission from King

Louis XVI to fight with the Americans. Although the French government remained for the present reluctant to become involved in the struggle across the Atlantic, Lafayette was determined to achieve military glory; so he crossed the Spanish frontier, purchased the French clipper *Victorie*, sailed for America, and landed near Georgetown, South Carolina, in June 1777.

Traveling to Philadelphia, Lafayette met with leaders of Congress and offered his services to the American government. Congress issued the following decree:

> Whereas the Marquis de Lafayette, out of his great zeal to the cause of liberty... has left his family and his connections, and, at his own expense, comes over to offer his service to the United States, without pension or particular allowance, and is anxious to risk his life in our cause. *Resolved,* that... he have the rank and commission of major-general in the army of the United States.

While in Philadelphia, Lafayette was introduced to **George Washington** who praised the 20-year-old Frenchman for his commitment to the American cause and invited him to his headquarters. But Lafayette was altogether unimpressed with the American army which he later described as, "About eleven thousand, poorly armed, and worst dressed, [which] offered a singular sight. In a motley state, and often naked, their best garments were hunting shirts." The condition of the American army was certainly far removed from that which he had known in the French army. Nonetheless, he quickly developed a keen sense of commitment to the American cause.

While in America, he began to realize that the freedoms and liberties often extolled by the French philosophes were being put into practice. Although he had sailed across the Atlantic Ocean seeking personal fame and glory, at the conclusion of the war he left deeply affected by the American experiment and hoped that Europeans too could enjoy the liberty and freedom so much a part of the fledgling United States. But he also felt that Europe was much different from America, and that if reforms were to occur in France, they would have to evolve slowly and methodically.

Lafayette Receives Hero's Welcome

When Lafayette returned to France in 1785, he was given a hero's welcome by the people of Paris. Apart from being a star attraction throughout the salons of Paris and at numerous dinner parties, he concentrated on representing America's interests in the French court. Considering himself somewhat educated in government, he sought to initiate liberal reforms. That was not to say that he considered himself a radical. Like the American Founding Fathers, Lafayette was first and foremost a patriot who strongly believed in the defense of one's country. Furthermore, personal liberties for each individual were to be granted sparingly and sporadically so as not to produce internal discord. Education was, in his mind, the best means of reforming society, rather than a violent revolution which could destroy that society's foundation.

Between 1785 and 1787, many great honors were bestowed upon him. Traveling throughout Europe, he visited the different courts and conversed with such legendary figures as **Frederick the Great** of Prussia. All was not well in France, however. During the American Revolutionary War, France had contributed huge sums to supply the French forces fighting with the Americans. These expenditures had all but drained the royal treasury and seriously jeopardized France's international credit stability. Furthermore, the French internal tax structure was totally inadequate to meet the country's expenditures.

As a result, Louis XVI's government was rapidly heading toward bankruptcy. Several of the king's economic advisors had attempted to reform the tax system, only to be stymied by the aristocrats who paid little taxes and preferred to keep it that way. During the summer of 1788, with the country tottering on the brink of financial disaster, the king was forced to summon the Estates General into session. To many historians, this signaled the start of the French Revolution.

On May 5, 1789, the Estates General convened in Paris; it was comprised of the First Estate (clergy), the Second Estate (nobility), and the Third Estate. The First and Second Estates included less than ten percent of the French population, but they held most of the political power. The Third Estate, made up of the middle class, the city workers, and the peasants, more than 90% of the population, held no political power. Elected as one of the representatives of the Second Estate, Lafayette watched with growing anxiety as the Third Estate defied traditional protocol and tried to gain an equal voice. After the members of the Third Estate had been locked out of the meeting hall on January 20, they reconvened at a nearby tennis court and swore not to disband until they had drafted a new constitution for France.

Lafayette immediately set out to draft a document to slow what he saw as an active threat to

France's security. In what became the foundation for the *Declaration of the Rights of Man and Citizen* and served as the preamble to France's Constitution of 1791, he declared that all men are created equal. Some men, however, are the natural leaders and thus should control the actual governing process. Lafayette's document further explained that all sovereignty resided in the nation, and that government's primary goal was to protect the common good. This meant that the powers of government should be separated into executive, legislative, and judicial branches to ensure that no one political body could grow too powerful and despotic.

Meanwhile, Parisians grew increasingly volatile as bread prices and unemployment soared, and the government appeared unable to handle the crisis. On July 14, 1789, mobs attacked the Bastille in Paris. Upon gaining entry, they killed and decapitated the mayor of Paris and the commander of the Bastille's small militia force. When Louis XVI was awakened with the news, he reportedly asked, "Is it a revolt?" An attendant nearby answered, "No, Sire, it is a revolution." The king, finally realizing that his position in the country was growing more and more tenuous, decided that he had to give in to many of the revolutionary leaders' demands. Announcing that Paris would be guarded by a citizen militia manned by Parisians, instead of royal troops, Louis named Lafayette to head the new Paris National Guard. At this position, Lafayette was in essence the ruler of Paris.

For the next several weeks, Lafayette recruited soldiers to maintain peace and tranquility in the city. However, the mob that gathered on October 5 soon became uncontrollable. Many of Lafayette's own men joined a mob demanding that the king and the National Assembly be moved from Versailles to Paris. By noon, several thousand Parisians were marching to Versailles to fetch the king. Lafayette determined that the mob had to be stopped, but he departed Paris too late to quell the crisis. The crowd arrived at Versailles ahead of Lafayette's forces, but as they were exhausted after the 12-mile march, nothing happened until the following morning. On October 6, the mob demanded that the king move to Paris. Greatly concerned for the monarch's safety, Lafayette convinced Louis to accept the crowd's demands. But soon after the king and the assembly arrived in Paris, national affairs were increasingly controlled by the revolutionaries. The French Revolution was quickly becoming far more radical than Lafayette had ever envisioned.

France Adopts New Constitution

For the next two years, Lafayette worked within the National Assembly to complete the new constitution. In 1791, the final draft was adopted after a tremendous amount of debate and compromises. Louis was genuinely rankled, however, that his powers had been diminished. On June 20, he determined to leave France, join with the growing number of émigrés (mostly aristocrats who had fled the Revolution), and build an army to march triumphantly back to Paris. But his plans were quickly foiled, and he was returned to Paris basically as a prisoner of the Revolution.

Meanwhile, Leopold II of Austria and Frederick William II of Prussia grew concerned that the French Revolution would spread throughout Europe and threaten their kingdoms. At a secret conference, they signed the Declaration of Pillnitz stating their dissatisfaction with events in France. In response to this perceived threat, radical members of the National Assembly insisted war was necessary to prevent any reversal of the Revolution. Thus, a whole series of wars in Europe erupted in the spring of 1792, and Lafayette was placed at the head of an army charged with halting an expected Austrian/Prussian invasion.

While out of the capital, Lafayette continued to try to prevent the radicals in Paris from controlling events. But he was quickly losing his ability to do so as Parisians became more receptive to their proposals. During the next several months, members of Paris's Jacobin Club began assuming a much more dominant position in the National Assembly, and they soon gained the support of a large portion of the Paris population. The most outspoken leader of this faction was **Maximilian Robespierre,** a man whose plans for the Revolution far exceeded Lafayette's conservative proposals. Despondent but not undaunted, Lafayette fled France, hopeful that he could seek refuge in a neutral country. Soon after he crossed into Austrian-controlled territory, however, he was apprehended by the Austrians and imprisoned in Westphalia at the fortress of Wesel.

After being moved to an old Jesuit monastery converted into a prison at Olmütz, Austria, Lafayette suffered from a lack of food, water, and fresh air. Most of the time he was kept in solitary confinement and referred to only by his assigned number. That he did not know the condition of his wife and four children greatly compounded his misery. Having learned of the Reign of Terror while in prison, he feared that his family had perished at the hands of the radicals. Indeed, Adrienne Lafayette had been imprisoned, and her grandmother, mother, and sister executed at the guillotine. Released shortly after Robespierre's execution in July 1794, she traveled to Austria with two of the children and was allowed to stay with her husband. Finally, in 1797, after five years of imprisonment and numerous, almost unspeakable, hardships, he was released.

In 1799, Lafayette returned to France and engaged in farming on his country estate, content to remain out of politics. But that November, when Napoleon staged his successful coup d'état, Lafayette became a vocal critic of the new regime and steadfastly refused to accept several positions in the imperial government which were offered by Napoleon. Even though Lafayette was skilled in the art of warfare, he also refused active service in the emperor's armies. After the Battle of Waterloo in 1815 and the emperor's subsequent abdication and exile, Lafayette once again entered public service and was soon elected vice-president of the Chamber of Deputies. Proving that he had not lost faith in liberal government, Lafayette defended the rights of the individual, spoke out against censorship of the press, and pleaded for an end to all political oppression.

Americans Hail Lafayette

In February 1824, after receiving a personal invitation from President **James Monroe,** Lafayette and his son Georges Washington returned to America. It was a triumphant journey: he was warmly greeted in every city he visited—thousands of people lined the roads, shouted his name, and hailed one of the heros of the Revolutionary War. In a display of gratitude, Congress awarded him 11,000 acres in the Louisiana Territory. The year-long journey to America was at least some consolation for nearly 35 years of hardship.

In 1830, with the Bourbon Charles X reversing much of the legislation which had been enacted during the French Revolution, Parisians once again erected barricades throughout the city. The Revolution of 1830, which brought about Charles's abdication and the election of Louis-Philippe as the constitutional monarch, was largely directed by Lafayette, proving once again that he was a champion of liberty and a strong advocate of constitutional government by the consent of the governed. The Revolution of 1830, however, was the last major event of his life. Between 1832 and 1834, he spent leisurely hours on his country estate writing memoirs and letters to old acquaintances. He died on May 20, 1834.

Rarely in history has any person had the opportunity to play an instrumental role in so many dramatic and far-reaching events. As true testament of his strong convictions, he never swayed from his heartfelt commitment to liberty. He is remembered and honored by such place names as Lafayette Square in Washington, D.C., and by numerous small towns throughout America. He was indeed the hero of two worlds.

SOURCES:

Buckman, Peter. *Lafayette, A Biography.* Paddington Press, 1977.

de Lafayette, Marquis. *Memoirs of General La Fayette, Embracing Details of His Private and Public Life, Sketches of the American Revolution, the French Revolution, the Downfall of Bonaparte, and the Restoration of the Bourbons.* Barber and Robinson, 1825.

Whitlock, Brand. *La Fayette.* Appleton, 1929.

FURTHER READING:

Gottschalk, Louis R. *Lafayette in the French Revolution: Through the October Days.* University of Chicago Press, 1969.

———. *Lafayette in the French Revolution: From the October Days Through the Federation.* University of Chicago Press, 1973.

Pierre Laval

(1883–1945)

Prime minister of France and open collaborator with the Germans.

Born Pierre-Jean-Marie Laval on June 28, 1883, at Châteldon, France; died by firing squad on October 15, 1945, at Fresnes prison; son of Baptiste (a village innkeeper and butcher) and Claudine Laval; married: Eugenie Claussat, October 20, 1909; children: (daughter) Josée.

From the point of view of both morality and politics, Pierre Laval is one of the most intriguing figures of 20th-century history. Some find him the archvillain of Vichy France, a man who consciously betrayed his nation in the hour of its greatest humiliation. Others claim he always played a double game, giving formal allegiance to Nazi Germany while doing all he could to preserve French interests. Laval would be neither the first leader nor the last who had to choose between morality and expediency, the judgment of posterity and immediate self-preservation.

On June 28, 1883, Pierre Laval was born in the village of Châteldon, lying at the foot of the northern slopes of central France's Auvergne mountains. The fourth and last child of Baptiste and Claudine Laval, Pierre grew up in modest comfort. His father was village innkeeper and butcher; he also ran the mountain mail coach. At age 12, Pierre quit school to drive his father's carrier cart. Such a childhood implanted in him a deep love of the countryside, a sense of thrift bordering on miserliness, and a peasant's suspicion of the outside world.

"If I succeed, there will not be enough stones in this country to raise statues to me. If I fail, I shall be shot."

PIERRE LAVAL

Contributed by Justus D. Doenecke, Professor of History, New College of the University of South Florida, Sarasota, Florida

Thanks to the encouragement of several townspeople, he continued his education in a somewhat nomadic and eclectic fashion, at such places as Lyons (where the superior of his school, Edouard Herriot, was later premier), Autun, Saint-Etienne, Dijon, and Paris. He earned his way as a tutor, taking degrees first in geology and then in law. He spent a brief time in military service, but bad varicose veins led to his discharge. Disliking the experience, he sought to replace a standing army with a citizens' militia.

In 1903, at Saint-Etienne, Laval joined the Socialist Party. In 1909, he was admitted to the Paris bar. That October, he married the daughter of Châteldon's mayor, Eugenie Claussat, commencing a union of lasting and mutual devotion. Laval's first great courtroom success involved defending an anarchist accused of cutting telegraph wires. He soon became the attorney for the Confederation General du Travail, France's national trade union confederation, and he wrote a daily legal column for the trade-union newspaper *La Bataille Syndicaliste*. By this time, as biographer Hubert Cole notes:

> He was a striking young man… with a sense of smouldering fire behind the near-Asiatic features, a black moustache drooping down on either side of his very thick lips, fierce dark eyes above the full, slightly curved nose, a dark swathe of oily hair hanging over his left temple.

In 1914, Laval was elected to the Chamber of Deputies as a Socialist of the extreme left. His district of Aubervilliers was a working-class area less then ten miles northwest of Paris.

During World War I, Laval's reputation as an antimilitarist was strong enough to include him in *Carnet B,* a list of those the interior ministry thought likely to interfere with conscription, though he was never arrested. For two years, he was aligned with Joseph Caillaux, who advocated a negotiated peace with Germany, though in 1917 he supported the return to power of the intensely prowar **Georges Clemenceau.** When on November 2, 1919, the Chamber of Deputies voted on the Versailles treaty with Germany, Laval was one of 53 Socialists who opposed it, claiming that the terms were too severe and the means of enforcement too weak. By this time, Laval had taken on the appearance of a slovenly burger: cigarette drooping out of his mouth, the ubiquitous white tie. An acquaintance of his daughter Josée said to her: "I do wish your father would reverse things: wear a black tie and white teeth."

CHRONOLOGY

1914	Elected as Socialist to Chamber of Deputies from Aubervilliers; remained until November 11, 1919
1923	Elected mayor of Aubervilliers
1924	Re-elected to Chamber of Deputies as independent
1925–26	Appointed minister of public works; under-secretary of State; and minister of justice
1930	Became minister of labor in cabinet of André Tardieu
1931	Laval prime minister until February 16, also interior minister
1934	Chosen foreign minister
1935	Ministry of Laval until January 22, 1936; Hoare-Laval proposals concerning Ethiopia drafted, leading to fall of Laval government
1938	Germany occupied Austria; Munich agreement
1940	Germans invaded Paris; Laval chosen minister of state and deputy prime minister; France and Germany concluded armistice; French government at Vichy; Laval nominated as Pétain's successor; dismissed, arrested
1941	Wounded at Versailles
1942	Laval "head of the government"
1944	Taken under escort to Belfort, then Sigmaringen
1945	Brought to trial before high court; condemned to death

In 1919, in the election sweep of the rightist *Bloc National,* Laval lost his deputy's seat. Now out of office, he amassed a substantial fortune in banking, publishing, radio, and real estate. Indeed, during the interwar years, he was unquestionably one of the wealthiest figures in French politics. In 1923, running as an independent socialist, that is, affiliated with neither the Communists nor the mainline Socialist Party, he was elected mayor of Aubervilliers, a post he held until he was deposed by the Liberation in 1944. A year later, he was re-elected to the Chamber of Deputies, again as an independent but belonging to the left coalition *Cartel des Gauches.*

In 1925, Laval began his long cabinet career directing public works in the ministry of Paul Painlevé. When Aristide Briand became prime minister, he first appointed Laval under-secretary of state, then minister of justice (1925–26). Laval admired Briand's oratory and negotiating skills; Briand respected "the Auvernat's" tenacity. But Laval made little impact in any of these posts, which were simply routine steps of political advancement.

When the left coalition fell in 1926, Raymond Poincaré came to power, and Laval deserted the moderate left for the rightist National Republican Union. Pundits quipped that L-A-V-A-L spelled the same thing from right to left as from left to right. In January 1927, he was elected to the senate from the Department of the Seine. In 1930, the rightist prime minister André Tardieu appointed him minister of labor and social security.

On January 27, 1931, when Laval became prime minister (technically president of the Council), France was at the peak of its power, possessing a highly influential national bank, a strong navy, and the world's best army and air force. During his ministry, he hoped to secure his political position at home by extensive travel abroad. By no means as rigid as the extreme right, Laval advocated rapprochement with Germany, called the Polish corridor "a monstrosity," and warned against an eventual attack on Europe by the Russians and Chinese. Impressed by his diplomatic skill, *Time* magazine named him "man of the year" for 1931. But on February 16, 1932, as a result of parliamentary intrigue, Laval lost his majority. Several governments passed him over, though in February 1934 Prime Minister Gaston Doumergue made him minister of colonies.

Laval Negotiates with Mussolini

In October, one of the most controversial and crowded periods in Laval's career began. In the wake of the assassination of Foreign Minister Louis Barthou by a Croatian terrorist, Laval was appointed minister of foreign affairs. Trouble was obviously brewing, for the vehemently anti-French **Adolf Hitler** had assumed the chancellorship of Germany. At the time, Laval said, "There are five or six men in the world upon whom peace depends. I am one of them." For a while he was successful, smoothing tensions between Yugoslavia and Hungary, and between Yugoslavia and Italy, in the wake of the assassination of King Alexander of Yugoslavia. Meeting with **Benito Mussolini** in January 1935, Laval ceded 800 square kilometers of French Somaliland, plus even more barren land on the southern border of Libya. In return, the Italian dictator recognized French rights in Tunisia, a land where many Italian nationals had settled. When Mussolini complained that he was only being given desert, Laval rejoined, "Oh, there's bound to be a few villages; though, of course, they won't be Rome—or Aubervilliers." In April 1935, at Stresa, Italy, Laval obtained Italian and British condemnation of "any unilateral repudiation of treaties which may endanger the peace of Europe," a move that revealed obvious alarm over such recent Hitler announcements as the existence of a German air force, the introduction of military conscription, and the formation of a 36-division army corps. Though Laval had hoped to co-opt Germany into a four-power directorate of Europe—which would include France, Britain, and Italy—a panicky French cabinet forced him to play the Soviet card. Hence, on May 14, 1935, he journeyed to Moscow, where he negotiated the Franco-Russian pact of mutual assistance, an agreement obviously aimed at Germany. Yet he continually deferred crucial staff talks with the Soviets (they never took place), and the treaty was ratified only after he had left office.

From June 7, 1935, to January 22, 1936, Laval was again prime minister while keeping the foreign ministry. Chosen because of a run on gold from the Bank of France, he was given plenary power to issue provisional decrees; in other words, the previous consent of Parliament was not needed. On July 16, he mercilessly fostered deflation by levying a ten percent cut on most government expenses, including the salaries of all public employees. After violent labor clashes at Brest and Toulon, on August 8 his government instituted loans for public works. Foreign policy troubles began, however, with the Anglo-German naval agreement of June 1935, by which Hitler agreed to limit his surface fleet to 35% of England's. That December, Laval, together with British foreign secretary Sir Samuel Hoare, devised a plan that ceded to Mussolini two-thirds of Ethiopia, a land that Italy had invaded just two months earlier. The remnant would become an Italian sphere of influence. But the terms were prematurely leaked to the press and advocates of collective security saw their entire cause undercut. When the British government repudiated the agreement, Laval in turn felt betrayed. For the rest of his life, he was determined to exact his revenge on the English.

Laval remained in power until January 1936, when protests against the Hoare-Laval agreement, his "poverty" decrees, and the failure to have the Russian pact ratified led, on January 23, 1936, to the termination of his ministry—the 99th government of the Third Republic. As noted by Laval biographer Geoffrey Warner, Laval's impulsive diplomacy had thrown the League of Nations into disarray, brought Anglo-French relations to a low point, neglected the eastern allies, and broken close ties to the linchpin of his diplomacy—Italy. More significant, he was falling victim to a belief in his own infallibility.

Returning to the Senate, Laval remained in the political wilderness during the time that Hitler gained control of the Rhineland, Austria, and Czechoslovakia. France's only hope, he believed, lay in a "Latin bloc," saying in March 1938, "I consider agreement between Italy and France, that is to say the Latin countries, including Nationalist Spain as well, as my life's mission." Laval attacked the government of **Léon Blum** for allowing arms to reach the Spanish Loyalists, abstained from giving Prime Minister Edouard Daladier a vote of confidence concerning the Munich agreement, and called Hitler's seizure of Prague "abominable."

On September 3, 1939, France declared war on Germany, thereby honoring its longtime alliance with Poland. Laval sat in the Senate that unanimously voted for war credit, though he publicly decried the absence of any alliance with Italy. In March 1940, he spoke against a compromise peace, endorsed a quick victory on fiscal grounds, and deplored the fact that France had not sent troops to aid Finland. After several months of "phony war," on May 10, 1940, Germany invaded the low countries and on June 13 occupied Paris itself. On June 22, France and Germany concluded an armistice. Under its terms, three-fifths of France, including Paris and the whole of the Channel and Atlantic coasts, was to be directly occupied by German troops, whose maintenance France was to pay. The rest of France was to remain unoccupied and under direct French administration. The French army faced demobilization, the fleet (the third largest in the world) internment in French ports under Axis (Germany and Italy's) supervision. The French Empire was left untouched. Although in principle the French governed the entire nation, in the occupied zones the Germans could make decrees on the grounds of military necessity. The demarcation lines between occupied and unoccupied zones became a kind of iron curtain, with the passage of people and goods virtually impossible.

He Rises to Leadership in Vichy Government

Meanwhile the French government experienced radical changes. On June 16, 1940, Marshal **Philippe Pétain,** the "Hero of Verdun," became prime minister and on July 12 he became chief of state of an entirely new regime, officially called "État Français" and informally named for its capital—the southern resort town of Vichy. On June 23, Laval became minister of state, on June 27 deputy prime minister, on July 12 the designated successor of Pétain, and on October 24, 1941, foreign minister.

In June, on the eve of French surrender, Laval had opposed the establishment of a French government-in-exile in North Africa. Divided authority, he claimed, would deprive the part remaining in France of its legality and authority. He had also revealed how crucial anti-Bolshevism had become to his thinking. Even if Germany eventually lost the war, he said, "The only possible basis for world equilibrium would still be the Franco-German entente, for a Germany which remained smashed after her defeat would put the Russians on the Rhine and therefore in Paris."

On July 3, the British had shelled that part of the French fleet lying at Mers-el-Kabir, just outside of Oran, and killed 1,300 French sailors. Laval responded to the event: "France has never had, and never will have, a more rabid enemy than Great Britain. All our history is there to prove it." He was instrumental in convincing Parliament to grant full constituent powers to Pétain, telling a dissenting Socialist deputy on July 5:

> We are here to rebuild France. We desire to destroy everything that now exists. Then… we shall create something entirely different from what has been…. [E]ither you accept what we ask and come into line with the German and Italian constitutions—or Hitler will impose it on you.

In a major speech given on July 10, just as the National Assembly—composed of both the Senate and Chamber of Deputies—was voting to dissolve the Third Republic, Laval condemned the declaration of war against Germany as "the greatest crime which has been perpetrated in our country in a long time." Deploring the ideological basis of the conflict, he said, "I heard talk of democracy, but little of France." Calling for a revival of discipline and patriotism, he declared, "It is the excesses of liberty which have led us where we are."

Meeting Hitler at the obscure medieval village of Montoire-sur-Loire on October 22, 1940, Laval endorsed a policy of collaboration. Writes biographer Warner, "Laval knew what he wanted: full participation in a European new order at Britain's expense." His fellow ministers saw him usurping authority and on December 13, he was ousted in a palace revolt. Referring to Laval's meetings with German ambassador Otto Abenz, Pétain said to him:

> I know nothing of what you do in Paris. Every time you go there, I wonder with what new disaster we are going to pay for your journey. You do not have the confidence of the French people. You do not have mine.

There was always personal tension between Laval and Pétain. As noted by historian Gordon Wright, "Laval thought of Pétain as a successor to the presidents of the Third Republic, dignified but powerless, while Pétain thought of Laval as a chief of staff, who ought to be totally dependent on orders from his commander-in-chief." Laval, who often blew smoke in the marshal's face, once said of Pétain:

> He wants everybody at his feet: the French, the German General Staff, Churchill, Roosevelt—probably Stalin as well. He doesn't want to soil his hands. Well, you'll never get anywhere if you're afraid of soiling your hands.

Yet despite fundamental differences in style, background, and thought, Laval and the marshal usually wound up favoring many of the same policies.

Hitler called Laval "nothing but a parliamentary hack," claiming that Laval sought to gain by cunning what **Charles de Gaulle,** leader of the Free French forces, was trying to obtain by force. Admiral Jean-François Darlan was Laval's successor, holding such offices as deputy premier, foreign minster, minister of the interior, and most important of all, heir apparent to Pétain. Darlan appeared even more pro-German than Laval. In August 1941, Laval was shot by an obscure 21-year-old ex-sailor from Normandy. As a bullet was lodged half a centimeter from his heart, the former premier was close to death. On April 18, 1942, after some petty intrigue of Darlan had failed, Pétain restored Laval to power. Laval's posts: the portfolios of foreign affairs, interior, information, and a new title—"head of the government." In the process, he had identified himself more with the Vichy regime than had Pétain himself. Notes biographer Warner:

> Laval was animated by a blinding faith in his own capabilities and there is no reason to doubt that he was at least partially motivated by the conviction that he alone could prevent the awful fate which faced his country.

When General Maxime Weygand, Vichy's representative in North Africa, told him, "Ninety-five per cent of the French people do not think as you do," Laval replied with a grin, "You are mistaken—it's ninety-eight percent." Always opposing the cultist idolatry of Pétain, Laval scorned the high-flown emptiness of his so-called National Revolution. In returning to office, he was able to curb some of the more dangerous stupidity of the marshal, suspending the fascist-oriented National Council and reinstating some dismissed Freemasons. Yet on June 22, 1942, in a radio address, Laval's collaborationism took on an extreme form. Expressing his desire for France to hold a "worthy" place in the new Europe that would arise after the war, he said:

> To construct that Europe, Germany is at the moment engaged in gigantic battles. With others, she must accept immense sacrifices and she is not sparing of the blood of her young men…. I wish for German victory because, without it, communism will establish itself everywhere.

With this stark call for German victory, Laval might well have written his epitaph. No Vichy leader had gone this far. Pétain was horrified, the French public outraged, and even Laval was soon admitting that his endorsement of German victory fell "like a drop of acid on the open wounds of France." Only Darlan sent congratulations.

Laval's record in Hitler's "final solution" has recently been subject to intense scrutiny. Defenders of Laval note that the French politician protected individual Jews, was never personally anti-Semitic, and opposed Vichy's strong discrimination law of October 3, 1940 (though he later signed it). Yet as historian Robert O. Paxton notes, the price of saving French Jews involved the deportation of recently arrived refugees, toward whom Laval was singularly callous.

Such facts lead Paxton to make a wider claim: namely that Laval's brand of collaboration did not—as Laval claimed during his trial in 1945—serve as a "screen" between the German conqueror and the French population. By any criterion—inflation, caloric intake, or general living standards—conditions were just as bad in France as in occupied Europe. Alsace and Lorraine were administered as part of the Reich, and German settlers were sent to colonize the "Speerzone" of northeastern France. In 1943, at Laval's command, more workers were sent to Germany from France than from Poland. Laval claimed to institute a much vaunted 3:1 ratio of exchange, with three French factory workers sent to Germany for each French prisoner of war allowed to return home. Yet, in reality, the ratio turned out to be 8:1, and it remains questionable whether the refurbishment of French farms, from which many of the young troops originally sprang, was worth the valuable industrial skills that Germany suddenly received.

The Germans Occupy France

On November 11, 1942, the Allies landed in North Africa, and on the 27th, the French scuttled their fleet at Toulon. The Germans responded by occupying all of France. The fiction of Vichy autonomy was over. On November 17, Laval forced the 86-year-old Pétain to give him dictatorial powers: "the right to command and take action." If the marshal was relegated to a status akin to a constitutional monarch, Laval found the Germans making increasingly strong demands, ranging from increased labor levies to the incorporation of outright Nationalist Socialists in his cabinet. Although subject to several more assassination attempts, Laval showed some sympathy with the Free French, saying:

> If the Germans are beaten, de Gaulle will come back. I have no illusions: eighty percent or ninety percent of the population will be for him, and I shall be hanged. Why should that worry me? There are two men at this moment who can save our country, and if I were not Laval I should wish to be de Gaulle.

Until the very eve of the Allied invasion of Western Europe, Laval did not think the Germans could be defeated. Yet, ever fearful of the Soviet Union, he personally offered himself to Hitler as mediator between Germany and the Soviet Union. Once the D-Day invasion took place on June 6, 1944, the Liberation was only a matter of time. In a radio broadcast given that day, he told the French people:

> We are not in the war. You must not take part in the fighting. If you do not observe this rule, if you show proof of indiscipline, you will provoke reprisals the harshness of which the government would be powerless to moderate.

Upon hearing of the 20th of July plot on Hitler's life, Laval sent the dictator a cable that he called "reasonably warm." At the same time he privately commented, "The only pity is that he wasn't killed. What a lot of things could have been arranged." He sought to reinstate the National Assembly under the leadership of Edouard Herriot (who had confined himself to a sanatorium), doing so to block rule by the Resistance. The maneuver, feeble at best, was unsuccessful.

On August 17, the retreating *Wehrmacht* took Laval first to Belfort, then to the vast Danube castle of the Hohenzollerns in Sigmaringen, and finally to a farm in nearly Wilflingen. In April 1945, amid the general breakdown of political authority, he fled to Barcelona. The Spaniards immediately turned him over to the Allies and on August 1, he arrived at Paris's Le Bourget airport. By then, writes biographer Hubert Cole, "He was the most hated man in France, the focal point of the nation's shame and revulsion, its evil genius."

On October 4, 1945, de Gaulle's Provisional Government launched Laval's trial. The charge: treason. Even for a political tribunal, the proceedings were embarrassing. The jury screamed obscenities at the defendant. The accused was given no opportunity to introduce evidence. The prosecutor, several years previously, had volunteered to serve on Vichy's Denaturalization Commission, a vehicle for the deportation of the Jews. After Laval's conviction, de Gaulle refused to order a retrial. On October 15, 1945, Laval nearly escaped Gaullist justice by swallowing poison in prison. Revived by a team of frantic doctors, he was executed by a firing squad several hours later.

During World War II, Laval appeared to be approaching the bitter end with the logic of a sleepwalker. Though he always had the option of resigning from the Vichy government, he chose to remain an active servant of the regime, as historian Tony Judt notes, "taking a perverse pleasure in playing what he increasingly understood to be a tragedy."

SOURCES:

Cole, Hubert. *Laval: A Biography.* Putnam, 1963.

Warner, Geoffrey. *Pierre Laval and the Eclipse of France.* Macmillan.

FURTHER READING:

Paxton, Robert O. *Vichy France: Old Guard and New Order, 1940–1944.* Norton, 1972.

Shirer, William L. *The Collapse of the Third Republic: An Inquiry into the Fall of France in 1940.* Simon & Schuster, 1969.

Werth, Alexander. *France, 1940–1955.* Robert Hale, 1956.

Leaders of the German Resistance to Hitler

Ernst Niekisch, Hans Scholl, Sophie Scholl,
Dietrich Bonhoeffer, Claus von Stauffenberg, Ludwig Beck,
Karl Gördeler

During the 12-year reign of Adolf Hitler and the National Socialists in Germany (1933–45), much of the world fought against him. Since Hitler drew his armies, his factory workers, and his death camp guards from among the German people, it is easy—too easy—to lump all Germans together as supporters of or at least passive collaborators with the Nazi dictatorship. This view is not accurate. From the very first days of the National Socialist Party in Bavaria in the early 1920s, through its rise to power in the early 1930s, and then during its rule of Germany until 1945, Germans of many different political and religious persuasions engaged in active and passive opposition to the regime. After 1933, opposition to the Nazis was severely punished, and the absolute number of resistance figures within the overall German population was small. But by their actions, sacrifice, and martyrdom they proved that the assumption of the world about the "bad German" did not always hold true.

In the 1920s, Hitler's Nazis were struggling for voter approval like all other parties. Their main opposition came from the organized left wing of German politics—the Communist and Social

"It is infinitely easier to suffer through risking one's bodily life rather than the spiritual one."

DIETRICH BONHOEFFER

Contributed by Daniel Emmett Rogers, Assistant Professor of History, University of South Alabama, Mobile, Alabama

Democratic parties. Paramilitary groups of Communists and Social Democrats often engaged in street brawls and riots with the storm troopers of the Nazi Party, the S.A. The onset of the Great Depression in 1929 radicalized the German electorate and led to increasing support for Hitler, who promised great changes, increased national pride, and recovery from misery. The Nazi Party became too large for President **Paul von Hindenburg** to ignore; in a period of political stalemate in early 1933, he reluctantly turned to Hitler to lead the government as chancellor. Hindenburg thought he had hemmed in Hitler by not allowing the Nazis many cabinet positions, but he had underestimated the Nazi leader. Quickly using his office to call new elections, Hitler hoped the German public would give the Nazi Party an electoral victory, allowing it to remake Germany unhindered by cooperation with other political parties.

The results of these elections of March 1933 can be taken as the first sign of resistance to his leadership. Despite controlling the government and much of the police, despite the suspension of civil rights and roundup of Communist leaders, the Nazis polled just under 44% of the vote. These last semifree elections failed to give Hitler a popular mandate and meant that his quick takeover of total power would lack the legitimacy only a free election could offer it.

CHRONOLOGY

1914   Germany entered the First World War

1919   Germany forced to sign Treaty of Versailles which most Germans regarded as humiliating; Hitler joined the German Workers' Party, which became the National Socialist (Nazi) Party

1929   Great Depression hit Germany

1933   Hitler named chancellor of Germany; all opposition parties banned; civil rights suspended

1936   Hitler remilitarized the Rhineland

1938   Hitler won the Czechoslovak Sudetenland at the Munich Conference

1939   Hitler began WWII by attacking Poland

1943   "White Rose" student conspiracy in Munich failed; its student leaders executed; Dietrich Bonhoeffer arrested

1944   Attempt on Hitler's life narrowly failed on July 20; plotter Stauffenberg executed; plotter Beck committed suicide

1945   Germany invaded by Allied armies; plotter Gördeler executed; Bonhoeffer executed; Hitler committed suicide; Niekisch freed from Brandenburg prison

Ernst Niekisch

(1889–1967)

German opposition to Hitler had to move underground or out of the country. Open opposition was courageous, but ultimately futile, as was illustrated by the fate of **Ernst Niekisch**. In the early days of the ill-fated Weimar Republic that preceded Hitler's regime, Niekisch had been a leading figure in left-wing politics, and in 1922 began serving as deputy chairman of the Social Democratic Party section of the Bavarian state legislature. He left the party in 1926, however, and began publishing a newspaper called *Resistance*. Niekisch did not yet mean to imply resistance to Hitler, then an insignificant fringe politician in Bavaria, but to the Weimar Republic itself, for which few in Germany harbored any real affection. Niekisch instead pushed for orienting Germany firmly to the east, toward the system of the Soviet Union.

This "national bolshevism" led Niekisch to begin attacking Hitler as the Nazis became more popular in the early 1930s. In 1932, Niekisch published a pamphlet entitled "Hitler: A German Disaster," which marked him as an outspoken foe of Nazism. He continued publishing *Resistance* even after Hitler came to power in early 1933. He survived the Nazi bloodbath of June 1934, the "Night of the Long Knives," in which Hitler dealt severely with all manner of political opponents, thanks to friends who hid him. Niekisch's attacks finally forced the Nazi secret police, the Gestapo, to ban *Resistance* at the end of 1934. The Gestapo did not imprison Niekisch then, but waited until 1937, when he was finally tried for treason and sentenced to life imprisonment.

Ironically, it was Niekisch's early resistance which probably saved his life, since his imprisonment precluded participation in any of the serious schemes to kill or overthrow Hitler. Niekisch therefore lived out the war in the harsh conditions of a political prisoner but survived nonetheless to take up left-wing politics again after 1945. Ever the disillusioned prophet, he joined the East German communist-dominated Socialist Unity Party in 1946 and then, disenchanted, left it in 1954. Niekisch died in relative obscurity in Berlin in 1967.

Hans Scholl
(1918–1943)

Sophie Scholl
(1921–1943)

Hitler's successes in reviving the German economy, in defying the powers (especially France) that had long sought to restrain Germany, and in rearming Germany probably won him the passive support of a majority of Germans. Grand military success from 1939 to 1941 only added to his allure. Consequently, nothing did more to further the cause of resistance than the turning of the tide of war against Germany after 1942. The German catastrophe at Stalingrad in January 1943 drove a group of university students in Munich, gathered together in a clandestine resistance group called the "White Rose," to immediate, ultimately fatal action. The leaders of this group were the **Scholl** siblings, **Hans** and **Sophie.** They were born in southern Germany, children of the man who was mayor of the town of Forchtenberg until 1930. Their youth was as normal as any child's until the Hitler takeover in early 1933. Hans was then 14, Sophie 11, and both were in school in the city of Ulm on the Danube River. Hitler's long-term aims included indoctrinating the youth of Germany with the spirit of National Socialism. At first, Hans and Sophie were willing participants, since they loved their land and with youthful enthusiasm saw in Hitler a man who might make it great again. Hans belonged to the Hitler Youth, Sophie to the League of German Girls, the Nazi youth group for young women.

Both became disillusioned before Hitler began World War II in 1939, Hans after one of his favorite authors was put on a Nazi blacklist, Sophie under the influence of her brother and father. Hans began studying medicine in 1939 and continued in this status even while in the army after 1941. At the University of Munich, Hans made the acquaintance of such like-minded colleagues as fellow medical student Christoph Probst. They formed the "White Rose" group (whose name, Hans would later tell the Gestapo, had been chosen at random from a Spanish novel); their goal was to express their resistance to the Nazi regime to as many Germans as possible. In the summer of 1942, they printed leaflets urging resistance to the lawless, uncivilized government. They distributed the broadsides, sometimes using the mail, sometimes—dangerously—by leaving them in public places. Sophie, newly at the university, discovered her brother's part in the group and asked to join.

In 1942, Hans was sent to the eastern front to serve as a medical aide, while at about the same time, Scholl's father was sentenced to four months' imprisonment for incautiously expressing his hatred of the regime to a fellow employee. His front experiences, his long hostility to Nazi ideals, and his father's ordeal galvanized Hans into further action upon his return. At the end of January and the beginning of February 1943, the Scholls, along with Probst and others, drafted and distributed thousands of anti-Nazi leaflets in the mail and in the halls of the university itself. Hans and coconspirator Alexander Schmorell painted anti-Nazi slogans such as "Down with Hitler" and canceled swastikas on Munich walls. While they hoped to encourage others to follow their example, the immediate effect was to make their capture inevitable. The entire student group, along with Professor Kurt Huber, a philosopher, fellow anti-Hitlerite, and favorite teacher of the students, was arrested. Hans, Sophie, and Christoph Probst went quickly to "trial," were convicted by a special "People's Court" established to deal with such opposition, and were executed by guillotine on February 22, 1943. Huber, Schmorell, and others were executed in the following months.

Dietrich Bonhoeffer
(1906–1945)

From the beginning of Hitler's reign, a few German church leaders worked within the opposition movement. Lutheran clerics refusing to participate in the Nazi takeover of church doctrine, such as Pastor Martin Niemöller, who publicly challenged Gestapo agents sent to listen to his sermons, sometimes paid for their audacity with imprisonment (in Niemöller's case, from 1937 to 1945). But foremost among the resisters in the Lutheran clergy was **Dietrich Bonhoeffer.** The son of a leading psychiatrist, Bonhoeffer had studied theology at the University of Berlin and received his doctorate in 1927. He traveled widely in the succeeding years, including trips to Spain and the United States. From 1933 to 1935, he had led the German Lutheran congregation in London, a stay which would lead to contacts with the English during the war. Rather than flee Germany in 1939 and lose all chance for changing it, he practiced "inner emigration," which in his case meant avoiding active military service by joining the *Abwehr*, or German military intelligence, a center of resistance leadership throughout much of the war. Bonhoeffer's concern for the plight of the Jews led him to consider politically active, instead of solely philosophical, resistance. His Abwehr friends sent him on missions to Switzerland in 1941, during which he urged his church contacts to work for a quick cease-fire when an anticipated coup against Hitler took place. In May 1942, Bonhoeffer traveled to Stockholm, Sweden, to meet with the British bishop of Chichester; here Bonhoeffer hoped to get word to the Allies of German plans for the period that immediately followed a successful coup against the Nazi state.

Hitler's National Socialist state teemed with bureaucracies in rivalry with one another. In the spring of 1943, the Reich Main Security Office began investigating the Abwehr, with the result that some of the chief conspirators against Hitler were uncovered, Bonhoeffer included. Further action by the Abwehr now looked impossible, and Bonhoeffer would remain in prison after April 1943, without trial, until just before his execution by hanging in April 1945.

Bonhoeffer's greatest contribution to the resistance probably came during his captivity. He used the two years of imprisonment to write his family letters that would survive the war, showing Germans how to combine Christianity, love, and patriotism into a "civil courage" that demanded not only action against injustice, but forgiveness for its perpetrators. The fact that the Nazis executed him less than a month before the war ended illustrated just how powerful a moral force they feared Bonhoeffer could be in reconstructing Germany after National Socialism.

Claus Schenk Graf Von Stauffenberg

(1907–1944)

Claus Schenk Graf von Stauffenberg was born into a Catholic family of nobility in Swabia in southern Germany. With his brothers, he attended a high school in Stuttgart that stressed classical subjects. At first, he thought of becoming an architect but soon resolved upon a military career. He was commissioned an officer in a cavalry regiment in 1930. In 1938, his unit participated in the occupation of the Sudetenland part of western Czechoslovakia that Hitler won at the Munich Conference. In 1939, he fought in the war against Poland, in 1940 against France. Then he was assigned to the army General Staff, where he remained until 1943. From February to April 1943, he fought in North Africa in the twilight of the German war effort there. He was seriously wounded in an air attack, losing his right hand, two fingers of his left hand, and his left eye. Upon recovery months later, he was assigned to the General Army Office as chief of staff.

In his early days in the army, Stauffenberg had been attracted by the strongly nationalist bent of the National Socialist party platform. But he never joined or participated actively in Nazi functions, and indeed the Greek philosophy and other classical learning imbibed in high school would have worked against the appeal of many of the cruder, simplistic Nazi aims. He admired Hitler's successes in the early days of the war and concentrated on soldiering while all went well for Germany from 1939 to 1942. When the war began to turn against Hitler and Germany, Stauffenberg began to see the Führer as an obstacle to victory. He spoke privately of the need to kill him to ensure military success. During his convalescence in 1943, he began to take the lead in a movement to assassinate Hitler. He thought destiny had somehow spared him in Africa for something greater: ending the war and thereby saving German lives and honor. His contacts to others in the resistance movement increased throughout early 1944, and while he could never agree with some of them about the necessity of a social reordering of Germany to the left after Hitler was dead, he did participate in active planning for a post-Nazi government.

After the successful Allied invasion of France in June 1944, the need to dispatch Hitler appeared even greater if Germany were to be spared the rigors of defeat in total war. Conspirators made plans to seize radio and telegraph facilities, to usurp command of vital units of the armed forces, and to take over important government offices in Berlin once Hitler had been killed. Several attempts failed, but because his staff position gave him personal access to Hitler, Stauffenberg succeeded in smuggling a bomb in a briefcase into Hitler's remote headquarters in East Prussia on July 20, 1944. The bomb exploded in Hitler's presence—all according to plan. But Stauffenberg erred in thinking Hitler had not survived the blast, which by extraordinary fortune he had. Thus the attempted coup d'état was initiated in Berlin and in Paris, where other conspirators held important army posts, even though Hitler was still very much alive. Stauffenberg himself raced back to Berlin after bluffing his way out of Hitler's East Prussian command center.

Key officials in Berlin remained loyal to Hitler, however, and upon return to the city, Stauffenberg was arrested and summarily executed by firing squad on the evening of July 20. Hitler delivered a radio address to the German people at 1:00 A.M. on July 21 to assure them he had survived. During the speech, he placed Stauffenberg at the head of a "very small clique of ambitious, dishonorable and at the same time criminally stupid officers [who] conspired to remove me and at the same time to overturn the staff leadership of the German armed forces." Like Stauffenberg in North Africa, Hitler saw his narrow escape from death as a sign that "Providence" had spared him for greater glory. While Stauffenberg might ultimately have been correct about his own fate, Hitler was not. He survived another nine months to complete the destruction of Germany he had begun in 1939.

Ludwig Beck

(1880–1944)

Karl Gördeler

(1884–1945)

Another feat Hitler would live to accomplish was rooting out the conspiracy against him. Among those associated in the plot of July 20 and who lost their lives in its aftermath were General **Ludwig Beck** and **Karl Gördeler**. Each illustrates yet another tendency of thought behind the broadly-based resistance movement. Beck came from a family in the Rhineland that had traditionally provided army officers from among its sons, but Beck's father had ended that tradition. Ludwig Beck restored it and entered the army, serving as a staff officer in the First World War. He remained in the army through the rise of Hitler in 1933, at which time he served as head of the troop office in the defense ministry. In 1935, when the troop office received the name "General Staff of the Army," Beck became chief of the General Staff, a position he held until his resignation in August 1938. Although not the top army commander, Beck exercised important influence in German army circles during the 1930s.

After Hitler's takeover of the chancellery in January 1933, Beck supported a steady increase in the size of the army but did not wish to involve Germany in the international complications an excessively hasty buildup might cause. Beck believed that most of Germany's goals could be achieved by the patient course of diplomacy, rather than through the march to war Hitler was intent upon. For Beck, war could only be the last resort in national self-defense, not a means to diplomatic ends. After late 1937, when Hitler's timetable for war became clear, Beck's opposition increased. He participated in the annexation of Austria in March 1938 only because it was less a military invasion than a use of the German army to support a Nazi coup from within Austria.

Thereafter, Hitler's designs were firmly on Czechoslovakia, a new state allied to France, Germany's chief enemy from the First World War. Beck felt certain war with France and Britain would result from Hitler's scheme to take Czechoslovakia. When he tried to rally top generals to confront Hitler en masse with their objections, it was clear from his appeal to his army superior that he meant this protest to be the beginning of the end of the Nazi dictatorship. Hitler, however, knew that among his top generals few besides Beck had the courage to back up their beliefs by directly challenging the Nazi leader. Isolated, Beck submitted his resignation on August 18, 1938. He established contacts in England to attempt to forge a solid bloc of foreign opposition to Hitler; these failed when the leaders of Britain and France yielded the Sudetenland portion of Czechoslovakia to Hitler at the Munich Conference.

Beck then became one of the de facto leaders of the German opposition to Hitler. Another, with whom Beck worked closely, was Karl Gördeler. A lawyer by training, a social conservative by inclination, Gördeler had been active in local politics in several German cities through the beginning of the Nazi period. He had also served as National Price Commissioner in 1931–32 and 1934–35. He resigned from his post as mayor of the eastern German city of Leipzig in 1937 when in his absence his deputy removed a statue of Jewish composer Felix Mendelssohn from its prominent place. Gördeler had long tried to protect Jews in Leipzig from steadily increasing Nazi terror. He traveled abroad and urged foreigners to oppose Hitler actively, but with little success, since as a nationalist he wanted many of the same revisions to the Treaty of Versailles that Hitler demanded. During the war, Gördeler wrote long reports on the future of Germany after Hitler. His vision was a conservative one, but grounded in basic liberties. He nurtured contacts with other resistance figures, including the "Kreisau Circle" of relatively young resisters who met at the estate (in Kreisau) of Helmuth James Count von Moltke and discussed how to make Christianity the basis for a new German political life. Gördeler was scheduled to be the prime minister of the post-Hitler government had Stauffenberg's assassination attempt succeeded.

After Stauffenberg failed, Beck was arrested for his part in the immediate attempt to take power (he was named as head of state on lists prepared by the resistance for the post-Hitler government). He attempted suicide that very night, but a soldier loyal to Hitler had to administer the final, fatal shot to finish him. Gördeler was arrested, imprisoned, "tried," and finally hanged in February 1945 for his complicity in the resistance movement. Thousands of others directly or indirectly involved were arrested, with hundreds facing death for their parts. In strictly practical terms, their actions had made no difference in the war effort. Neither Germany's loss in May 1945 nor the Allies' victories were hastened by plotting for Hitler's death, planning for the future, or the brave walks to gallows, scaffolds, or firing squads that followed July 20, 1944. Rather, the chief contribution of the resistance leaders came with their willingness to serve as examples of virtue, to prove to the German people that one could honorably resist a tyranny in one's midst, and to show the world that not all Germans had removed themselves from the mainstream of civilization.

SOURCES:

Hoffmann, Peter. *German Resistance to Hitler.* Harvard University Press, 1988.
———. *The History of the German Resistance 1933–1945.* Harvard University Press, 1977.
Scholl, Inge. *Students Against Tyranny.* Wesleyan University Press, 1977.

FURTHER READING:

Bonhoeffer, Dietrich. *Letters and Papers from Prison.* Macmillan, 1967.
Rothfels, Hans. *The German Opposition to Hitler.* Regnery, 1962.
Zimmermann, Erich, and Hans-Adolf Jacobsen. *Germans Against Hitler: July 20, 1944.* Press and Information Office of the Federal Government of Germany, 1964.

V. I. Lenin

(1870–1924)

Bolshevik leader, who used the opportunity presented by the collapse of the Russian monarchy in World War I to found a radically new political system that influenced the entire course of the 20th century.

Name variations: Nicolai. Born Vladimir Ilyich Ulyanov in Simbirsk, a city in the Russian Empire, on April 22, 1870; died in January 1924; son of Ilya Ulyanov (a school administrator) and Maria Alexandrovna Blank Ulyanova; married: Nadezhda Krupskaya (a fellow revolutionary); no children. Predecessor: Alexander Kerensky, prime minister of the Provisional Government of 1917. Successor: Joseph Stalin emerged as the key leader of revolutionary Russia by 1929, five years after Lenin's death.

V ladimir Ilyich Lenin was the founder of the Russian Communist Party and the moving force behind the November 1917 Russian Revolution. His Soviet Union, the first state controlled by Marxist revolutionaries, deeply influenced the history of Europe, the United States, and the entire modern world.

Ironically, Lenin held a lonely position on the extreme left wing of European Marxism in the early years of the 20th century. Even within Russian Marxism, he was an isolated figure during this period with a relatively small following. But the chaos of World War I and the collapse of the old political order in Russia at the start of 1917 created an opportunity that he used skillfully to take power. When his Bolshevik Party seized control of Russia's capital city Petrograd in November 1917, it marked a dramatic breakthrough for the Marxist revolutionary movement.

Vladimir Ulyanov ("Lenin" was a revolutionary name that he adopted as an adult) was born in Simbirsk, a city on the Volga River, on April 22, 1870. He was the son of Ilya Ulyanov, a high-ranking school administrator and Maria Blank, a doctor's daughter of German descent. Paradoxi-

Contributed by Neil Heyman, Professor of History, San Diego State University, San Diego, California

"There is not another man who for twenty-four hours of the day is taken up with the revolution,… and who even in his sleep, dreams of nothing but revolution."

PAVEL AXELROD

cally, the father of the future revolutionary attained the rank of a Russian nobleman.

Lenin's early life was uneventful and happy, but his teenage years brought two tragedies. His 54-year-old father died of a cerebral hemorrhage in 1886 (the same illness that probably caused Lenin's early death). Shortly after, Lenin's older brother Alexander, a biology student at the University of St. Petersburg, was arrested for plotting to murder Tsar Alexander III. Although his mother pleaded with government officials for clemency, Lenin's brother was executed by hanging in 1887.

That same year, despite the black mark on the family name, Lenin received important assistance from Fedor Kerensky, the principal of his school, enabling him to enroll as a law student at the University of Kazan. Fedor's son **Alexander Kerensky**, whom Lenin did not know at this time, would later become one of his key opponents in 1917.

Although Lenin was soon drawn into student politics and expelled from the university, he continued to study on his own and passed his examinations to become an attorney in 1891. The young law student read widely during those years; he was influenced by Nicholas Chernyshevsky, a writer of the 1860s who called for opponents of the existing political order in Russia to become professional revolutionaries. Lenin also found himself attracted by the theories of **Karl Marx** and Russian Marxists. These ideas focused on revolutions that would occur inevitably as a society developed economically. Marxists anticipated a revolution in Europe, and possibly Russia as well, that would be carried out by factory workers.

As the young lawyer settled in the Russian capital of St. Petersburg in 1893, he already had a beard and balding head—physical features that would mark his appearance in later years as a successful revolutionary. There he became involved with the Marxist movement and met a fellow revolutionary, Nadezhda Krupskaya. His serious manner and his single-minded interest in revolution impressed other members of his political circle: they began to refer to him as Starik, "the old one."

Lenin was arrested in 1895. Along with dozens of other members of his revolutionary circle, he spent the next years in prison and then in exile in Siberia. While in Siberia, he married Nadezhda Krupskaya in 1898; two years later, the couple settled in Switzerland after both had finished their terms of Siberian exile.

Lenin made his mark on the Marxist movement in 1903 when a variety of Russian Marxists

CHRONOLOGY

1887	Execution of Lenin's brother
1897	Lenin arrested and exiled to Siberia
1902	Wrote *What is to be Done?*
1903	Gathering of Second Congress of Russian Social Democrats
1905	Revolution in Russia
1912	Prague Congress
1914	Start of World War I; Lenin moved to Switzerland
1915	Zimmerwald Conference
1916	Kienthal Conference
1917	March Revolution; Lenin returned to Russia; July uprising; November Revolution
1918	Treaty of Brest-Litovsk; start of Civil War
1921	End of Civil War; Lenin espoused New Economic Policy
1922	Had first stroke; wrote "Testament"

met at Brussels to set up a unified political party. After the Belgian police broke up the gathering, the delegates reconvened in London. This Second Congress of Russian Social Democrats debated the key issue of Party organization and membership. Lenin advocated a position he had set down the previous year in a pamphlet entitled *What is to be Done?* There he claimed that the factory workers, following their own ambitions and desires, would not choose to promote revolution. Instead, they would be satisfied with better wages and working conditions. Therefore, a revolutionary movement had to consist of professional full-time revolutionaries; the workers themselves could play only an auxiliary role.

Lenin's other innovation was to call for a Russian revolutionary movement that included the peasantry. Karl Marx had always counted the peasants of Western and Central Europe as a conservative force who would stand in the way of revolution. Lenin looked at the impoverished Russian peasantry as a mass of angry and discontented individuals who would fight as effective allies in a workers' revolution.

As Russia faced military defeats by Japan in the Far East and rising opposition at home, revolution broke out in 1905. But Lenin reached Russia late in the year and did not play a significant part in events. Returning to Switzerland following the revolution's failure, he began a new period of foreign exile that lasted until 1917.

Lenin quarreled with other leaders of Russian Marxism over numerous issues. For example, there was sharp disagreement on the question of participating in elections for the *Duma*, the new Russian parliament set up in the aftermath of the 1905 Revolution. In early 1912, at a conference of Russian Marxists that Lenin brought together in Prague, he formally broke with his opponents and formed an independent Bolshevik Party.

World War I provided Lenin with his opportunity to take power. At first, his prospects for success seemed slim. True to his reputation, he took a position on the war that isolated him from most Marxists both inside and outside Russia. As many Marxists decided to join in their country's war efforts—or to remain neutral—Lenin declared that the war offered an opportunity for successful revolution. To the shock of most of his fellow Russian Marxists, he declared that military defeat for Russia was a desirable step in bringing on revolution.

At congresses of European Marxists held in Switzerland during the war, Lenin tried without success to win support for his position. At Zimmerwald in 1915, he was voted down decisively, but he convinced a stronger minority to back him at Kienthal in 1916. Nonetheless, by the start of the revolutionary year 1917, even Lenin was discouraged about the prospects for a revolutionary breakthrough. In a speech that he gave to young Swiss sympathizers in January 1917, he declared that the revolution might come only in their generation. Just a few weeks later, news reached Lenin of "bread riots" in Petrograd. (St. Petersburg had been renamed Petrograd at the start of World War I.) Those riots quickly developed to become the spontaneous March Revolution.

The March Revolution led to the abolition of the monarchy and the establishment of a Provisional Government made up of members of the Fourth *Duma*. Though political exiles in Siberia and abroad were free to come home, Lenin found that a difficult task. Neither France nor Italy would let him pass through. As Russia's allies, they saw only danger in allowing Lenin, a declared opponent of the war, to return to Petrograd. On the other hand, since Germany had tried to promote political unrest in Russia since the start of the war, the government in Berlin permitted Lenin and a party of his followers to cross German territory en route to Russia. To protect German soldiers and workers from Lenin's antiwar message,

they insisted that the Russians travel in isolation: the famous "sealed train" of 1917.

Once back in Russia, Lenin called for the overthrow of the Provisional Government, led by Alexander Kerensky. Making a broad appeal for change, he insisted that power be given, not to his Bolshevik Party, but to the *soviets* (organizations of workers, peasants, and soldiers). From March 1917 onward, *soviets* sprang up in many parts of the Russian Empire. They came to look to the *soviet* in the capital city of Petrograd for leadership.

Following an unsuccessful offensive by the Russian army against the Austrians and Germans in July 1917, street demonstrations broke out. The government brought in reliable troops to put down this event of the "July Days," and officials released documents that appeared to show that Lenin and his fellow Bolsheviks were German spies. **Leon Trotsky** and other leading members of Lenin's party were arrested, while Lenin himself went into hiding in Finland.

Lenin's Party Takes Control

By the fall, however, Lenin found himself in a more favorable position. Kerensky's government had become discredited. For example, it had failed to produce land reform, and it had insisted on remaining in the war. In a spectacular example of leadership, Lenin convinced the other Bolshevik Party leaders to launch a coup in early November. This "November Revolution" easily succeeded in taking control of Petrograd with the help of the Red Guard, a militia formed from factory workers. Moscow fell into Bolshevik hands with more difficulty: Lenin's followers took control there only after a week of bloody fighting.

Lenin's new government moved quickly to end the war with Germany. This had been a key promise the Bolsheviks—now renamed the Communists—had made throughout 1917. In another example of hardheaded and effective leadership, Lenin persuaded key members of his Party to accept the brutal Treaty of Brest-Litovsk in March 1918. Although this gave huge chunks of the old Russian Empire to Germany, Lenin was convinced that even this unfair treaty had to be accepted in order to end the war.

By the close of 1918, Lenin's Party had established a dictatorship based upon a new secret police, the *Cheka*. Opponents of the Communists—many of them motivated by a desire to continue the war against Germany—had formed "White" armies to fight against Lenin's "Reds." When Lenin had been nearly assassinated by a political opponent in September 1918, his colleagues had launched a "Red Terror," in which thousands of enemies of the new government were executed.

By the start of 1921, Lenin's Communists had defeated their White opponents in Russia's Civil War. Even intervention by foreign countries, including a full-scale Polish invasion of the Ukraine in 1920, had failed to weaken the revolutionary system Lenin had erected. Now, however, Lenin gave still another example of his political flexibility and his power over the Communist Party. Abandoning the radical economic program developed during the Civil War that had included government control over most of Russian industry and the confiscation of peasants' crops, Lenin called for a "New Economic Policy" (*NEP*) in which much of Russian economic life was to be returned to private ownership. Only in this way could the country hope to recover from seven years of war, revolution, and Civil War dating from 1914.

In international affairs, Lenin also shifted direction. In 1917, he had hoped that the Bolshevik Revolution in Russia would quickly spread to the industrially advanced countries of Europe—to Germany, in particular. While he continued to hope for new revolutionary outbreaks, Lenin promoted a policy of restoring regular diplomatic relations with other major countries. In April 1922, for example, at the Genoa economic conference, Russia and Germany signed a crucial treaty, giving the new Russian government its first official diplomatic recognition by a foreign power.

Another side of the *NEP* policy, however, was a harsh crackdown on anti-Communist political factions in Communist Russia. Leaders of rival groups were put on trial and sentenced to exile. Moreover, Lenin accompanied the moderation of *NEP* in economic affairs with a crackdown on factions within the Communist Party. In a system called "democratic centralism," once the Party had adopted a policy, no group within the Party could continue to oppose it.

Lenin's career as a political leader was cut short by illness. In May 1922, at the age of 52, he suffered the first of a series of strokes. Even more severely disabled by a second stroke in December, he lived out the rest of his life as an invalid.

In his last years, rival leaders like Trotsky and **Joseph Stalin** began to maneuver for power. Lenin became increasingly mistrustful of Stalin, whom he had made secretary-general of the Communist Party in 1922. From this position, and other Party and government posts he had collected, Stalin began to put his followers in key positions. Troubled by Stalin's policies toward non-Russian groups, as well as Stalin's brutal manner, Lenin wrote a blistering attack on him in a final "Testament." Some historians like Moshe Lewin have even argued that Lenin began to have doubts about the nature of the dictatorship he had established.

But Lenin died in January 1924 without being able to block Stalin's continuing rise, and any doubts that he had about the Party's dictatorial rule were never translated into action. The death of the great revolutionary leader quickly led to the creation of a "Lenin cult." He would likely have been appalled to see how the story of his life was rewritten to make him appear a flawless revolutionary leader. From 1924 onward, Communist leaders claimed to be following Lenin's guidelines at all times. The sharpest shifts in policy were justified by ransacking Lenin's huge set of writings for an appropriate quotation.

SOURCES:

Lewin, Moshe. *Lenin's Last Struggle.* Pantheon, 1968.

Tumarkin, Nina. *Lenin Lives!: The Lenin Cult in Soviet Russia.* Harvard University Press, 1983.

Ulam, Adam. *The Bolsheviks: The Intellectual, Personal, and Political History of the Triumph of Communism in Russia.* Macmillan, 1965.

Warth, Robert D. *Lenin.* Twayne, 1973.

FURTHER READING:

McNeal, Robert H. *The Bolshevik Tradition: Lenin, Stalin, Khrushchev, Brezhnev.* 2nd ed. Prentice-Hall, 1975.

Pipes, Richard. T*he Russian Revolution.* Knopf, 1990.

Schapiro, Leonard, and Peter Reddaway, eds. *Lenin: The Man, the Theorist, the Leader.* Praeger, 1967.

Theen, Rolf. *Lenin: Genesis and Development of a Revolutionary.* Princeton University Press, 1973.

Leonidas I

(?–480 B.C.)

Spartan king immortalized in Greek literature and legend because of his heroic last stand against Persian invaders.

Pronunciation: LEE-on-ED-es; name probably means "lion's son." Born in the southern Greek state of Sparta on the Peloponnesian Peninsula, date not recorded, possibly between the years 530–500 B.C.; died in 480 B.C. at Thermopylae in northcentral Greece; son of Anaxandrides, King of Sparta; married: Cleomenes (daughter of his half-brother).

Leonidas is a legend without a biographer. Almost nothing is known of his life. The exact date of his birth is as unknown as the particulars of his childhood. Even the spectacular events surrounding his epic struggle in 480 B.C. are shrouded in mystery and open to controversy. The chief source is the famous Greek historian, Herodotus, but even here Leonidas is given relatively scant attention, and modern scholars have been forced to critically reexamine each of Herodotus's sentences to reconstruct more telling and at times more accurate detail.

Leonidas was born on Spartan territory in the Peloponnesian Peninsula in southern Greece probably between the years 530–500 B.C. He was the son of the Spartan king Anaxandrides and was descended from the Greek cult hero Heracles. However, during his youth and early manhood, Leonidas could not have expected to become king because of a peculiar set of circumstances.

When Anaxandrides' first wife did not conceive during the early years of the marriage, Spartan elders compelled him to take a second wife (contrary to Spartan custom). The firstborn—and only—child of Anaxandrides' second union was a

"Go tell the Spartans, stranger passing by, that here obedient to their words we lie."

INSCRIPTION
AT THE PASS OF THERMOPYLAE

Contributed by David L. Bullock, Ph.D. candidate, Kansas State University, Manhattan, Kansas

male, Cleomenes, who became heir to the throne. In the meantime, the first wife conceived three sons; Dorieus, Leonidas, and Cleombrotus, respectively.

The fates were ironical. Cleomenes was at least mentally disturbed if not mentally retarded, while Dorieus, who would have been heir apparent under more normal circumstances, excelled in "manly quality." Nevertheless, when Anaxandrides died, Cleomenes mounted the throne. Unable to live under his brother's rule, Dorieus set sail for distant lands and embarked on a series of adventures, resulting in his death.

When Cleomenes himself died, probably in 487 B.C., he left no male issue. The line of succession suddenly fell on Leonidas who had married Cleomenes' daughter and, consequently, his own half-niece. Leonidas was only one of Sparta's kings; customarily, this Greek city-state had two. During Cleomenes' reign, the second king had been Demaratus, but they had engaged in a feud and Demaratus had deserted to the Persian Empire. Leotychides succeeded Demaratus. Thus, Leonidas ruled, according to Spartan tradition, in partnership.

According to custom, Leonidas assumed an important position in the priesthood of his state, but his most significant role was as commander of the Spartan army. In matters of war, a Spartan king was expected to be the "first in the march and the last to retreat." In his youth and early manhood, Leonidas would have received very strenuous physical conditioning, along with many years of military training, to hone his warrior's skills to the peak of martial perfection. This was the mandatory agenda of the Spartan male and a regimen which would last, in varying and lessening degrees of severity and discipline, until age 60.

The product of this conditioning was the finest warrior and army in ancient Greece and most probably the world. The Spartan heavy warrior or *hoplite* carried a long, thrusting spear; a short, stabbing sword; and a dagger. His defensive accoutrements included a bronze, crested helmet; a large, round shield; and sometimes a breastplate and leg-greaves ("armor"). Traditionally, the Spartan hoplite wore a bright red cloak which was considered the most manly of colors.

These warriors fought grouped together, shoulder-to-shoulder, in a tactical unit called a *phalanx*. Presenting a forest of spears and shields, the phalanx may be likened, not too unreasonably, as the "tank" of the ancient world. From the front, the phalanx was well-nigh unstoppable, but it was vulnerable in the flanks and rear. In order to limit

CHRONOLOGY

530?–480 B.C.	Raised in the city state of Sparta; married his half-niece; became king of Sparta and commander of the army
490 B.C.	Greeks defeated King Darius' Persian army at Marathon
486 B.C.	Xerxes accession as Persian king
480 B.C.	Leonidas became the advance guard and defender of the Greeks at the Pass of Thermopylae; killed and dismembered by the Persians; passed from history into legend

their vulnerability, the Spartans deployed more lightly-armed javelin troops. In this form of infantry warfare, the Spartans were unequalled. There is no evidence that they employed archers or slingers. Nor did they employ cavalry in significant numbers, for the terrain of Greece is such as to limit the utility of mounted action. Naval matters were, for the most part, left to Sparta's allies.

Despite his impressive war machinery, Leonidas might have been recorded as no more than a name on the scroll of Sparta's kings had it not been for the epic events of 480 B.C. which thrust him center stage. King **Xerxes** and his Persian Empire invaded Greece.

The roots of the Greco-Persian conflict had begun 20 years previously when several small ethnic-Greek states in Asia Minor rebelled against Persian rule. Many Greek states including Athens supported their rebellious cousins, and through skill and good fortune the Greeks managed to defeat King **Darius**'s Persian army at Marathon in 490 B.C.

Ten years later, Darius's son and Persia's king, Xerxes, determined to settle the Greek problem once and for all. As he assembled his mighty army, which even modern scholarship concedes may have totaled 25 million, he dispatched a fifth column of spies and diplomats to demand the submission of the Greeks. This army was well-stocked with cavalry and had at its core the 10,000-man elite body known as the Immortals. A powerful navy significantly larger than anything the Greeks could muster anchored the seaward flank of the army as it marched. The Persian force was centralized and ably led; its only flaw, perhaps, was the preponderance of ethnic units subject to the Empire who might be counted on to fight with varying degrees of enthusiasm.

The immensity of the Persian threat compelled Athens and Sparta to set aside former rivalries and work together. Athens, with her mighty fleet, placed herself under Spartan command. Feuding was endemic among the Greek states, however, and would disrupt Greek ability to react, especially in the first months. In particular, Greek indecision about holding the strategic Pass of Tempe resulted in its early abandonment to the Persians. As Xerxes crossed the Hellespont from Asia Minor, several of the northern Greek states began to defect.

Within the Spartan Council of Elders there was much debate over which of two basic strategies was best. Most dear to the Spartan heart was a stout defense of the Corinth Isthmus, the chokepoint that led into the Peloponnesian Peninsula. But this act would have surrendered northern and central Greece and thereby greatly reduced the chance for a more united stand. The second option was to block the Persian advance at the Pass of Thermopylae.

The Fateful Battle of Thermopylae

Thermopylae, so named because of its hot springs (*therm* in Greek means heat), controlled the vital coast road into central Greece. To the east was the Island of Euboea, the north of which could be used to block the advance of a hostile fleet and thereby protect the right flank of a Greek army at Thermopylae even as the inland mountains served to protect the left.

At length, the preponderance of Spartan opinion elected to send an advance guard to the Pass to be followed by a larger army when the religious festival of *Karneia* was over. Leonidas selected 300 citizen warriors, a customary number when embarking on a special mission, but he only chose among the best who had sons so that no family line would become extinct through the death of the father. In all, 4,000 troops from the Peloponnesian states accompanied Leonidas north in that fateful August of 480 B.C.

While en route to Thermopylae, Leonidas was joined by 700 Thespians, 400 Thebans, 1,000 Phocians, and 1,000 Locrians so that his small army totaled about 7,000. Simultaneously, the allied Greek state navy took position at Artemision at the northern end of Euboea Island. Evidence suggests that many Greeks considered these measures sufficient and that no major action would occur before a larger force could be dispatched to reinforce Leonidas.

Having reached Thermopylae, scouts and informants revealed the immensity of the approaching Persian army. Leonidas held a council at which several Greek contingents expressed an interest in retreating to Corinth. The Phocians and Locrians argued vehemently for holding the Pass, probably because their lands would be the first ravaged by the invader. Leonidas decided to stand and fight. At the same time, he sent messengers to several cities to ask for help.

The Pass of Thermopylae ran west to east, mountains rose sharply to the left or southern side, and the Aegean Sea washed the right or northern side. Leonidas set his main position in the center and began rebuilding the old Phocian wall which had been the scene of many an ancient martial drama. His disposition was well-chosen, for the Persian army would have to disrupt their formations to enter the mouth of the Pass and once inside would have to face the Greeks on more equal terms. The wall itself could serve as a defense, or as a rallying point for a counterattack.

Leonidas seems to have learned about the "Achilles heel" of Thermopylae only after arriving in the Pass. A circuitous mountain route existed, known as the Anapaea Path, by which an enterprising enemy might enter in the rear of Thermopylae, trapping the defenders inside. During a council, the Phocians volunteered to defend this path as they were used to the local terrain and local area. Leonidas accepted.

In the meantime, one of King Xerxes' scouts rode into the pass. As an act of defiance, the Spartans, aware of the scout, continued to play athletic games and leisurely dressed their hair for battle. Unmolested, the scout reported to Xerxes. The Persian King immediately called on the exiled Spartan king, Demaratus, for advice. Demaratus explained the Persians were facing the flower of the Greeks.

Xerxes delayed four days after this reconnaissance to enjoin battle. During this period, he probably waited for his logistics train to arrive and coordinated strategic plans with his navy. On the fifth day, he attacked.

Xerxes' Mede and Cissian divisions moved in first, fighting inside the Pass for several hours. These units were mauled by the better armed and more skillful Greeks. During the second half of the day, Xerxes called on his elite guard, the Immortals, led by the able Hydarnes. Once inside Thermopylae, however, they could not make their superior numbers felt. Time and again the Greeks drove them back and the Persian King was said to have leapt from his throne out of concern thrice that day.

During the course of the second day's battles, the Persians fared no better. Herodotus relates that the Greek territorial units fought in rotation to relieve each other, and that some units feigned retreat in order to draw out the enemy, then suddenly turned and counterattacked their disordered pursuers.

On that second day, however, the Persian King received an extraordinary windfall. A local Greek by the name of Ephialtes offered to guide the Persians over the Anapaea Path for a reward. That evening, Hydarnes and his Immortals entered the mountainous forest of oak trees near the Asopus River and climbed to the summit where they caught the Phocian Greeks off guard. Pelting the Phocians with arrows, the Immortals bypassed them and continued along the path, the end of which would place them at the village of Alpenoi at the eastern end of Thermopylae directly at Leonidas's rear.

On the final, fatal dawn, Leonidas heard from scout runners that they would soon be surrounded. He called a council and once again the opinion was divided. Leonidas declared it would be dishonorable for the Spartans to retreat. The leader of the Thespians, Demophilus, said it would be dishonorable to desert the Spartans. Nevertheless, the other Greek contingents withdrew except for the Thebans, whom Herodotus claimed were forced to stay by Leonidas because they were suspected of dealings with the Persians. As they ate their last meal, Leonidas is reputed to have said: "Eat hearty, lads, for today we dine in Hades."

Mid-morning of the third day, fresh Persian waves came into the Pass. Realizing they would soon be hit by Hydarnes' Immortals from the rear, Leonidas advanced past the Phocian wall into a wider part of the Pass in order to more fully deploy and inflict maximum damage on the enemy while there was still time.

According to Herodotus, the Persians had to drive their leading regiments on with whips against Leonidas's *hoplites*. Ranks and files were trampled to death by their comrades and many were driven into the sea to drown.

> [T]he Greeks, knowing that their own death was coming to them from the men who had circled the mountain, put forth their very utmost strength against the barbarians; they fought in a frenzy, with no regard to their lives.

Most of the *hoplites* had their spears broken in these intense encounters. In order to encourage his troops, Xerxes had sent two of his brothers into the fray to lead by example. Both of them were killed. At this point Leonidas fell, fighting no doubt, from the front rank in the tradition of a Spartan king. Immediately, a struggle ensued over possession of his body. After pushing back four Persian attacks, the Greeks successfully claimed their King's remains.

At this juncture the Immortals were seen inside Thermopylae and closing. Herodotus claimed that the bravest Greek warrior left was Dieneces, who had said at the start of the campaign that if the Persians darkened the sky with arrows he would be pleased to fight in the shade. If not Dieneces, it is certain that some Spartan notable bore, or ordered warriors to bear, Leonidas's body to the hill overlooking the wall that was to be the place of the last stand. As the Spartans and Thespians took their positions, the Thebans deserted to the Persians, who were deploying their regiments to fully surround the last of the Greeks.

> In that spot the Greeks defended themselves with daggers—those who had any left—yes, and with their hands and teeth, and the barbarians buried them in missiles.

The remains of the Greeks were eventually buried at or near the hillock of the last stand. It is possible the body of Leonidas was never found. It is certain he was beheaded and the head impaled by the Persians as an example. In ancient times a lion statue was erected to Leonidas and three inscriptions were placed at the scene of battle, two of which are worthy of note: "Here is the place they fought, four thousand from Peloponesus, And here, on the other side, three hundred ten thousands against." And as a specific tribute to the 300 Spartans who gave their culture devotion's full measure: "Go tell the Spartans, stranger passing by, that here obedient to words we lie."

In the 1930s, archaeological excavations unearthed hundreds of Persian arrowheads at the hill of the last stand. The lion statue and inscriptions were gone, but in 1992 a statue of a Greek *hoplite* stands, spear upraised, against Xerxes' order for the Greeks to surrender their weapons. The inscription reads: "Come and get them."

In the months after Thermopylae, the Persian navy was defeated at Salamis and their mighty army at Plataea. After the battle of Plataea, the nephew of Leonidas, one Pausanius, was urged by a warrior to dismember the body of the Persian commander in the fashion done to his uncle. Pausanius replied:

> For Leonidas, whom you bid me avenge, I tell you he has been greatly avenged; he has found great honor in these countless souls here—both he himself and the others who died at Thermopylae.

SOURCES:

Burn, A. R. *Persia and the Greeks: The Defence of the West, c. 546–478 B.C.* Duckworth, 1984.

Herodotus. *The History.* University of Chicago Press, 1987.

Hignett, C. *Xerxes' Invasion of Greece.* Oxford University Press, 1963.

Lazenby, J. F. *The Spartan Army.* Aris and Phillips, 1985.

Connolly, Peter. *Greece and Rome at War.* Macdonald Pheobus, 1981.

Hooker, J. F. *The Ancient Spartans.* J. M. Dent, 1980.

Michell, H. *Sparta.* Cambridge University Press, 1964.

Warry, John. *Warfare in the Classical World.* St. Martin's Press, 1980.

FURTHER READING:

Bury, J. B. *A History of Greece to the Death of Alexander the Great.* Macmillan, 1917.

Leopold II

(1835–1909)

Second king of the new country of Belgium, who played a crucial role in the development of European imperialism in Africa.

"I have no other desire than to leave Belgium greater, stronger and more beautiful."

LEOPOLD II

Leopold II of Belgium was one of the most colorful, ambitious, and successful European monarchs of the 19th century. A bold and imaginative figure, he never ceased to look beyond his tiny country for economic and political opportunities. His acquisition of the Congo Free State was only the most successful of a series of undertakings designed to bring vast areas of the non-Western world under Belgian control. As far as Leopold was concerned, despite its remarkable prosperity and industrial power, Belgium was a vulnerable part of the European continent whose very existence was in danger. Even though his countrymen were unable to see the value of his expansionist designs, he wished to acquire part of the outside world for them. Moreover, he was uncomfortable in the role of constitutional monarch. By acquiring vast wealth for himself and his heirs, he hoped to carve out special powers for the holders of the Belgian crown. With these resources, Belgian monarchs could guide and manipulate Parliament.

Belgium was a newly created country, a product of the wave of revolutions that struck parts of Europe in the early 1830s. The Belgians broke

Born in Brussels on April 9, 1835; died at Laeken, the royal palace outside Brussels on December 17, 1909; son of Leopold I (first king of the Belgians) and Marie-Louise (daughter of French king Louis-Philippe); married: Archduchess Marie-Henriette of Austria-Hungary (died 1902); married: Caroline Lacroix; children: (first marriage) three daughters, and a son who died at the age of nine; (second marriage) two sons. Predecessor: His father Leopold I. Successor: His nephew, Albert I.

Contributed by Neil Heyman, Professor of History, San Diego State University, San Diego, California

away from the Kingdom of Holland, which had been set up in 1815 as part of the Vienna settlement following the Napoleonic wars. Outside powers like Britain helped the Belgians get their independence, and the Great Powers of Europe guaranteed Belgian neutrality in 1839. In the next decades, Belgium became one of the most industrialized parts of Europe. Its government was a constitutional monarchy under Leopold I, a German prince from Coburg. The country was inward looking, and the major issues in national life were the conflict between the Liberal and the Catholic parties over control of the school system and the debate over how much attention to devote to military defense.

Leopold was born in 1835. His mother Marie Louise was the daughter of the French king Louis-Philippe. A sickly child who was thought to have a "weak chest" (meaning tuberculosis), Leopold walked with a limp due to a defect in his sciatic nerve. He was lazy and undisciplined, and his relations with his father Leopold I, first king of the Belgians, were particularly strained. Given a military education, including receiving the rank of a lieutenant in the Belgian army at the age of ten, his icy relationship with his father featured the need for the young prince to make an appointment to see the king. In 1853, Leopold was married to Archduchess Marie-Henriette of Austria-Hungary. The marriage was made for diplomatic purposes; with the Crimean War approaching, King Leopold I wanted the support of the Habsburg dynasty in case Belgium was threatened with invasion from France.

From the 1850s onward, Leopold began a series of wide-ranging trips outside Europe, visiting Egypt three times to see the construction of the Suez canal, and, in the early 1860s, touring the Far East. Fascinated by the idea of European footholds in the outside world, he joined geographic societies and read their publications with fervor. As early as 1859, he probably collaborated with government officials who were publishing anonymous pamphlets advocating Belgian expansion. By the time he became king in 1865, Leopold was convinced that Belgium could thrive only if it grew but realized his subjects did not share such views. "I am king of a small country and small-minded people," as he put it. Nonetheless, the young king remembered that small states like Carthage and the Dutch Republic of the 17th century had been able to form great empires. Following his trip to Turkey and the Far East in 1864 and 1865, he sent back a marble statue to a Belgian cabinet minister with the inscription: "Belgium must have a colony."

West Africa caught Leopold's eye early, but he had a long list of regions outside Europe that Belgium might acquire. He was interested in Argentina, China, the Philippines, the Transvaal, and Vietnam. Some historians note that his colonial ambitions grew stronger after the 1869 death of his only son Prince Leopold at the age of nine. The king was devastated by the loss—"The wound never healed," wrote one historian—and deeply resented the fact that he was left only with daughters.

Similarly, the Franco-Prussian War of 1870–1871 reminded him of Belgium's vulnerability. When French and German armies fought near the Belgian border, Leopold mobilized the Belgian army and stood ready to defend his country if the war spread into Belgium—but he quickly saw signs of his country's military weakness.

A colonial empire might also serve to unite his country. Belgians seemed increasingly divided from one another and consumed with their domestic problems. Industrialization led to urban unrest—including bloody riots in the 1860s and again in 1885—and the emergence of a socialist movement. Middle-class Belgians were divided in a bitter battle between Catholics and liberals over control of the school system. In 1879, liberals promoted secular schools. Six years later, with the Catholics in power, the reforms were reversed.

By the 1870s, Leopold saw his opportunity. Most of Africa was scarcely known to Europeans but exploration of the great Congo Basin, at the center of the continent, was now beginning. The Belgian public and its political leaders showed no interest in colonial adventures, and thus Leopold had to find a way to seize a colony without involving them. At the same time, Belgium faced the competition of more powerful countries already holding huge empires and likely to expand them.

Stanley Explores the Congo

Leopold operated behind the facade of a philanthropist, scientist, and humanitarian. He began by sponsoring a congress on Africa in Brussels in 1876. This led to a series of international organizations supposedly intended to promote the exploration of Central Africa and the suppression of the slave trade. Leopold found that if he became chairman of such organizations, he could dominate them and use them for his own purposes. He brought to the task "all his bewildering energy, perseverance, and inexhaustible cunning." Under this guise, Leopold established his most important colonial relationship: an agreement with the American explorer Henry Stanley. Stanley had already made a name for himself exploring the Congo Basin when Leopold contacted him in 1877. Although Stanley was supposedly hired by one of the international organizations Leopold had set up, he worked in the interest of the Belgian king. Making treaties with hundreds of native chiefs "in exchange for gin, bits of cloth and discarded uniforms," Stanley brought the vast Congo Basin under European control. This was to become Leopold's Congo Free State.

In late 1884 and early 1885, the Berlin Conference of the Great Powers met to deal with African questions. By playing the British and French against one another, Leopold obtained recognition of his Congo Free State. It would be a neutral state in Central Africa, open to free trade and intended to bring order and civilization to the native population. In fact, the Free State became Leopold's personal colony. He intended to pass it to Belgium at some time in the future, but he found his countrymen were reluctant to see him engaged there. He had difficulty getting the Belgian Parliament to grant him the authority to take the crown of the Free State in 1885. In 1889, he had similar difficulty in obtaining a loan from the Belgian government to help him run his colony. Part of the agreement he made in 1889 stipulated that in ten years he would repay the loan or pass the colony over to the government in Brussels.

Leopold never visited the Congo, but he became an important figure in Africa's history. By the 1890s, the Congo Free State was developing in dangerous and ugly ways. Using a private army to wipe out African resistance, Leopold sponsored expeditions along the borders of the Free State. His representatives also entered territory, like the Sudan, in which Britain and other countries were interested. Here Leopold had to back down in the face of British opposition. Most important of all, his agents, often acting in a brutal manner, tapped the wealth of the Free State for his use. First ivory and then rubber provided a stream of profits. Leopold took much of the Congo in the form of a crown estate (*Domaine de la Couronne*) that was ten times the size of Belgium.

Even in the 1890s, reports from missionaries and foreign visitors to the Congo spoke of mistreatment of the native population. In order to make the Congolese work, they were presented with a "labor tax." In practice, this meant that the Africans were forced to work most days of the month for Europeans, for example, in gathering rubber. Villages were destroyed, Africans fled into the jungle, and—most horrifying of all to public opinion back in Europe—reluctant workers and their families were physically mutilated. Hideous pictures of Africans with hands and feet cut off reached Europe.

Congo Free State Transferred to Belgium

By the start of the 20th century, reports from English observers like the journalist Edmund D. Morel and the diplomat **Roger Casement** had created a storm of protest over the so-called "Congo Horrors." Writers like Mark Twain and Joseph Conrad joined in condemning the king. Ironically, it was a commission of inquiry appointed by Leopold himself that decided the issue. Their report in 1905 was so critical that the king reluctantly bowed to pressure and decided to hand the Congo over to Belgium.

The last chapter in the Congo episode brought a political crisis to Belgium. Negotiations over the transfer went on for years, with the king in a political war with his Parliament over the details. Leopold fought hard to reserve his personal territory and personal wealth.

Belgium took direct control over the Congo in 1908. But long after his death, officials of the Belgian government were still discovering secret funds he had hidden away. In all, the negotiations opened the question whether the king could really be controlled by the provisions of the Belgian constitution.

Remaining one of the most colorful personalities of the era, Leopold became fascinated with motorcycles and fast cars, and spent much of his time on a yacht off the southern coast of France. Morbidly afraid of disease, he would read his copy of the *London Times* only after it had been ironed by his servants to kill germs. During rainy weather, he covered his large beard in a leather case. After numerous love affairs, Leopold became involved in the last years of his life with a young Parisian prostitute, Caroline Lacroix. After siring two illegitimate children with her, he married the young woman only a few days before his death.

Although his imperialist efforts were his greatest interest, Leopold was concerned with one chief domestic reform: military expansion and modernization. In a series of visits to Emperor **Wilhelm II** of Germany after 1904, Leopold became convinced of the danger of invasion. The king rejected the views of many Belgians that the country was protected by the neutrality established by the Great Powers in 1839. In the face of strong domestic opposition, he pushed for two measures. One was the construction of powerful fortifications, especially along the bridges of the river Meuse. He got what he wanted as early as 1887. The second reform was harder to achieve. Leopold wanted to require most Belgian young men to serve in person in the military instead of hiring substitutes. In a dramatic scene in the closing hours of his life, Leopold got word of his success in changing the military service law.

Leopold's ambitions, energy, and political initiative have made historians regard him as an exceptional figure. During his time, many European rulers were becoming largely figureheads. But, as one historian put it, "Leopold had discovered a way to reverse the historical victory of the middle classes over their kings," and he blazed "a new path to absolutism." Another describes the king who turned entrepreneur as someone who created "a form of autocracy probably closer to that of an American millionaire than to that of an Eastern despot or a Renaissance prince."

SOURCES:

Theo Aronson. *Defiant Dynasty: The Coburgs of Belgium.* 1968, Bobbs-Merrill,.

Ascherson, Neal. T*he King Incorporated: Leopold II in the Age of Trusts.* Doubleday, 1963.

Emerson, Barbara. *Leopold II of the Belgians: King of Colonialism.* St. Martin's Press, 1979.

Kossmann, E. H. *The Low Countries, 1780–1940.* Clarendon Press, 1978.

FURTHER READING:

Hallett, Robin. *Africa since 1875: A Modern History.* University of Michigan Press, 1974.

Helmreich, Jonathan E. *Belgium and Europe: A Study in Small Power Diplomacy.* Mouton, 1976.

Huggett, Frank E. *Modern Belgium.* Frederick A. Praeger, 1969.

Pakenham, Thomas. *The Scramble for Africa, 1876–1912.* Random House, 1991.

Trygve Lie

(1896–1968)

Distinguished Norwegian politician who became the first secretary-general of the United Nations, and guided it through the stormy early years of the Cold War between 1946 and 1953.

"Trygve Lie had transformed the United Nations, in his seven years of service, from a paper document into a living political institution."

JAMES AVERY JOYCE

T rygve Lie was the first secretary-general of the United Nations. An unenviable position at any time (he often referred to it as "the world's most impossible job"), it was particularly fraught in the late 1940s and early 1950s when deteriorating relations between the superpowers culminated in the Korean War. The Americans and the Soviets each wanted a secretary-general sympathetic to their own outlook, and by pleasing one superpower Lie was certain to annoy the other. But he was cool-headed and conciliatory, and early recognized that he must take abusive criticism as part of the job. In his book *In the Cause of Peace*, he wrote:

> I have been criticized from all directions. As long as this situation continues I feel I am doing an impartial job. I have been called a reactionary. I have been labeled a Red devil. I don't care so long as the attacks come from all sides.

Although his earlier life in Norway had prepared Lie for the great responsibility he took on with the U.N., no prior experience could have made his tenure there an unqualified success.

Contributed by Patrick Allitt, Assistant Professor of History, Emory University, Atlanta, Georgia

Pronunciation: TRIG–veh LEE. Born in Oslo in 1896; died in 1968; son of Martin and Hulda Lie; married: Hjordis Jorgensen, 1921; children: (three daughters) Sissel, Guri, Mette. Successor: Dag Hammarskjöld.

Lie was born in Oslo, Norway, in 1896. His father was a carpenter, who died while Trygve was still a child; his mother opened a boardinghouse to keep the family going and to raise money for her son's education. With the help of family friends he acquired a part-time job, while still in school, as office boy in the central headquarters of the Norwegian Labor Party, and kept this post right through school and college. In consequence, he was able to see the practical workings of a political organization from the ground up: invaluable experience for his later career. He studied law at the University of Oslo between 1914 and 1919 and was elected head of his local branch of the Labor Party before graduating. As soon as he finished college he was made the Labor Party's administrative secretary, though he was only 23. In this position, he became a delegate to the Soviet Union for one of the first conferences of the newborn Communist International, and shared with other young European leftists the intense feeling of excitement generated by the Russian Revolution. But unlike some of them who veered into utopianism, Lie always remained politically realistic and hard-headed.

Putting his legal training at the service of his convictions, Lie worked as legal advisor to the Norwegian Trade Unions Federation between 1922 and 1935. The unions were growing rapidly in this era, and he was able to restrain them from disorderly industrial action. He preferred to persuade employers to grant better wages and conditions by using the veiled threat of strikes rather than provoking confrontations, and he established important legal protections for the unions in a succession of test cases during these 13 years. In 1926, with an ever-growing reputation among the Norwegian Left, he was appointed to the National Council of the Labor Party, at a time when the Party was enjoying a period of rapid growth. The socialist radicalism of the first Labor government, in 1928, caused a panic among Norwegian businessmen, and capital began to drain out of the country. The government was forced to make a coalition with its Liberal rivals after only two weeks, to restore financial confidence. Observing this failure from outside Parliament, Lie recognized the need for Labor to be more cautious in the future. He and his Party got a second opportunity in 1935, the year Lie entered Parliament, when Prime Minister Johan Nygaardsvold took office and at once appointed the freshman Lie as his minister of justice. Lie held the post for three years and then became minister of commerce in 1939.

The rhythms of everyday political life in Norway, as throughout Europe, were shattered by the outbreak of the Second World War in September 1939. In the First World War, an allied powers' naval blockade and German submarine action had starved Norway of necessary imports. Lie now gained the important post of shipping and supply minister, and tried to stockpile supplies in an effort to avoid comparable shortages in this new war. But his work was cut short when **Hitler**'s armies invaded Norway, quickly overpowering the small Norwegian army. Lie was able to order most Norwegian shipping out of port before resistance ended, enabling it to take cover in Britain rather than fall into enemy hands. But in June 1940, in the company of the other cabinet ministers and Norway's King Haakon VII, he fled to England. In their absence, Hitler set up a collaborationist regime of Nazi sympathizers led by the infamous **Vidkun Quisling**. Soon after his arrival in England with the exile government, Lie was again promoted, this time to the position of foreign minister, an office he held throughout the war.

The various European governments in exile which sheltered in Britain during the war were in an uncomfortable position. Beholden to **Winston Churchill,** the British prime minister, they did not always see eye to eye with him in his conduct of the war and his plans for the postwar world. The most famous case of this tension was the mutual dislike between Churchill and France's **Charles de Gaulle.** But the Norwegian socialists also found Churchill, a bellicose conservative and imperialist, difficult to endure. Lie, for example, was far more sympathetic to the plight of the hard-pressed

Soviet Union than Churchill, and was eager to stay on good terms with Soviet leader **Joseph Stalin** in view of the need for postwar conciliation. During the war, Lie made a mission to Washington, D.C., in 1943 and one to Moscow in 1945, where he discussed the joint Soviet-Norwegian liberation of Norway from German occupation.

In May 1945, just before the war ended, Lie returned to Norway and was reconfirmed as foreign minister following another Labor victory at the polls. He also led the Norwegian delegation to the inaugural United Nations conference in San Francisco and chaired its Commission III, which drafted the Charter of the U.N. Security Council. Lie understood that an inner council of this type was imperative: the major powers must have a forum in which they could act concertedly, rather than submitting to the General Assembly, whose size and variety would make rapid decision-making in crises almost impossible. A natural conciliator and a skilled, informal negotiator, he made a favorable impression on many delegates from other countries at this and subsequent meetings, and his name began to circulate as a possible leader for the new organization.

The U.N. delegates were all aware that their precursor, the League of Nations, founded at the end of the First World War, had been a hopeless failure, never able to assert its will over that of belligerent nations because it had no power to take military action and did not include the United States as a member. If the United Nations were to fare any better, it must have more power, including military force. But although the world's great powers, the United States, the Soviet Union, Britain, France, and China, had all fought on the same side against Germany and Japan, tensions between them now that victory was at hand were glaringly obvious. The prospect of cooperation, when their objectives and intentions were so different, seemed bleak. The Americans and the Soviets were sure to look with jaundiced eyes on any United Nations leader who was too closely affiliated with the other's power bloc.

When the voting for a secretary-general took place at the first U.N. Convocation in London in 1946, the British and Americans favored Lester Pearson, the Canadian ambassador to Washington, D.C. (later Canadian prime minister). The Soviets favored a Yugoslavian diplomat, Stanoje Simic, and since each of these men was unacceptable to the backers of the other, Lie emerged as a palatable compromise candidate. Andrei Gromyko of the Soviet Union had in fact nominated Lie in an earlier round of voting, and the Western powers, although far from happy with the choice, decided that the Norwegian was acceptable. Norway was outside the Soviet orbit but had a strong indigenous socialist tradition; the Russians were confident that he would not be a "stooge" of the United States.

Lie's salary was set at $20,000 per year, with as much again for expenses and a house in Queens, New York. In its early years the United Nations had a succession of temporary headquarters, including New York's Hunter College, but finally settled in its permanent home on 41st Street facing the East River, the land being a gift from the Rockefeller family. Lie had commissioned the American architect Wallace Harrison in 1946 to design a headquarters building in the International Style, and the distinctive skyscraper was finished by 1950. Lie also had the task of organizing a permanent staff of over 4,000 highly skilled men and women to run the U.N., recruited from all parts of the world and dedicated to the high standards and political impartiality which he hoped to make the U.N.'s trademark.

As first secretary-general, Lie had no traditions to follow, and no precedents to fall back on other than the negative precedents of the failed League of Nations. He took an assertive view of his role, arguing that tasks not forbidden him in the Charter were implicitly permitted. In particular, he wanted to establish the principle that he could bring to the attention of the General Assembly, and the Security Council, issues from anywhere in the world which he believed deserving of U.N. debate and action. He also believed strongly that every nation of the world should be admitted to the forum. But from the beginning he faced insurmountable obstacles. As U.N. historian Arthur Rovine emphasized:

> Trygve Lie's entire administration coincided with the worst ravages of the cold war, and the UN's first Secretary-General had no political base from which to mediate the conflict beyond his own neutrality as an international civil servant and his skills as a practiced diplomat.

Initial interventions by Lie seemed to favor Soviet interpretations of the Charter, and led Americans to fear that Lie's early Marxist fervor was guiding his actions. Later moves seemed to suggest, however, that he was simply trying to establish the secretary-general's position and procedures while preventing the Security Council from becoming a propaganda forum.

The Crisis of the Berlin Blockade

Lie's first major crisis, an event which could have led to a Soviet-American world war, was the Berlin blockade of 1948. Berlin lay firmly inside the German territory taken by Soviet armies in 1945. But as Hitler's old capital and the traditional hub of German life, it was symbolically important to all the victors in World War II. Accordingly, the city was divided into four zones: Soviet, American, French, and British. By agreement the three Western powers had access roads through East German territory, but in 1948 the Soviets blocked these roads, in the hope of forcing the Western allies out of what was quickly becoming a Western espionage salient.

Britain and the United States were determined not to yield their position in Berlin, but rather than use tanks to force their way in, they began an airlift of supplies into the besieged city and carried it on successfully for nine months, in effect facing down the Soviets by daring them to fire as planes passed overhead. Lie at once set about trying to arrange compromise negotiations to end the crisis, but the Americans took the view that the Soviets had violated international law and that there should be no negotiation until they dismantled their illegal blockade. In the end, the Americans got their way and won a considerable propaganda victory. Although Lie acted as an intermediary between the powers during the crisis, he played only a minor role in its ultimate resolution. The affair suggested that the U.N. could not be decisive in a superpower standoff.

The next year brought another crisis. **Mao Zedong**'s Chinese Communist revolution dislodged **Chiang Kai-Shek** and conquered China. The American government denied the legitimacy of Mao's revolution and took the view that Chiang's Chinese nationalists, now exiled on the tiny island of Taiwan, should still occupy one of the five permanent seats on the U.N. Security Council. That position enraged the Soviet Union, whose delegates staged a walkout over the issue in 1950. By then the use of the General Assembly as a propaganda grandstand, and superpower neglect of the U.N. as a conflict-resolving forum, was bringing it into widespread disrepute, and its future seemed seriously in jeopardy. Lie, like the Soviets, believed that political realities dictated that Communist China should be seated. He responded to the impasse by launching a "Peace Mission," traveling to the major world capitals and appealing for negotiation to reduce world tensions, hoping that the prestige of his position would carry some weight and alter the intransigent governments'

opinions. Everyone greeted him courteously but he found himself powerless to effect real change.

The Soviet boycott of the Security Council had dramatic consequences later in 1950 because the Soviets' absence coincided with the North Korean invasion of South Korea, which triggered a full-scale war. Under intense pressure from the United States, the Security Council, with Lie's approval, unanimously condemned the invasion and ordered a U.N. "police action" to curb it. President **Harry Truman** and the U.S. State Department were pleasantly surprised to find Lie falling in so readily with their own plans, where hitherto he had seemed an obstruction. Although 16 nations ultimately sent troops to Korea, there can be little doubt that the U.N. was simply a legitimator of American policy during the Korean War. "To the Soviets," says historian Rovine, "Lie's efforts demonstrated with absolute clarity his subservience to the West and his hostility toward the small Communist bloc in the U.N." Lie found the North Korean invasion outrageous, and this view led him to abandon his initial pose of neutrality towards all nations; instead, he treated North Korea and its Communist Chinese allies as enemies of the U.N. Charter itself.

On the big question of superpower rivalry, Lie was doomed to frustration. His organization fared slightly better in dealing with the destinies of smaller powers—a theme which has remained true up to the present. Lie presided over the first Arab-Israeli partition in 1947 when Britain surrendered its League of Nations mandate there. A majority in the U.N., including the United States and the Soviet Union, voted in favor of partitioning Palestine and creating the new state of Israel. All the Arab states voted against it, however, and attacked Israel on the day it became a new nation. Lie then had to find a neutral arbiter to restore peace, if possible, and selected the head of the International Red Cross, Count Folke Bernadotte of Sweden, who was able to arrange the first of many cease-fires in 1948. Lie's intervention helped end the brutal Greek civil war which followed World War II, and he brokered the creation of an independent Indonesia from old Dutch colonies, also in 1948. But if a case has to be made for the U.N. in its early years, it would be less for its directly political work and more for its international social welfare and educational work, (UNESCO), health research (WHO), and its aid to refugees (UNRRA), in each of which fields Lie was an active promoter.

To compound his difficulties, Lie was working in New York at the height of the American "Red scare" of the early 1950s. McCarthyism swept through the United Nations as it did through most other politically sensitive institutions in America. Many members of his secretariat were dismayed when Lie permitted FBI investigators to examine the personal and political credentials of American staffers at the U.N., and when he acquiesced in the removal of those the FBI deemed security risks or "subversives." In his view, the generosity of the United States in acting as host nation should be reciprocated with maximum cooperation. Pointedly dissenting, the United Nations Administrative Tribunal, standing on its dignity as an international organization which should be exempt from American domestic pressures, reversed Lie's decision in 12 cases and reinstated the men and women he had let go. Nevertheless, a majority of the member nations held Lie in high esteem, and when his five-year term as secretary-general expired in February 1951, the General Assembly overruled the Soviet Union's objections in a dramatic debate and reappointed him for a further three years.

Hammarskjöld Succeeds Lie

Exhausted by his responsibilities and by the Korean War, Lie submitted his resignation in November 1952 before the end of this second term. "The United Nations," he declared, "has thrown back aggression in Korea. There can be an armistice if the Soviet Union, the Chinese People's Republic, and North Korean authorities are sincere in their wish to end the fighting. If they are sincere, then a new secretary-general, who is the unanimous choice of the five Great Powers, the Security Council, and the General Assembly, may be more helpful than I." He stayed at the helm until the members had agreed on a successor by March 1953, though he did not like the choice they finally made. Dag Hammarskjöld, another Scandinavian, nevertheless took office and tried to restore the prestige of the secretary-general's office, which had been so badly battered by the Korean War. Hammarskjöld was more willing to conduct behind-the-scenes negotiations than Lie, though he too soon discovered that his position was certain to win him enemies whatever he attempted.

For the remaining 15 years of his life, Trygve Lie enjoyed his position as the most distinguished living Norwegian and was soon drawn back into the politics of his home country, being appointed governor of Oslo and its province from 1955 until 1963, and playing a major role in the Labor government of the mid-1960s, in which he held the ministries of industry and commerce. He also found time to write four volumes of memoirs about his varied political experiences, to chain smoke Turkish cigarettes, to play tennis, and to sleep for nine hours every night, whatever crises stormed about him. He died in December 1968, aged 72, at the skiing resort of Geilo.

Although his tenure in the U.N. secretary-general's office was far from being an unqualified success, he had at least assured the organization's continued existence and shown that its prospects were brighter than those of the League of Nations. Trygve Lie established an activist role for the secretary-general, set in motion immense information-gathering systems and instruments of humanitarian aid, and balanced questions of *realpolitik* with questions of morality in his adjudication of infinitely complex international political crises, even though he was powerless to solve them once and for all.

SOURCES:

Jordan, Robert S., ed. *Dag Hammarskjöld Revisited: the UN Secretary General as a Force in World Politics.* Carolina Academic Press, 1983.

Joyce, James Avery. *One Increasing Purpose.* Llandybie, Wales: Christopher Davies, 1984.

Lie, Trygve. *In the Cause of Peace: Seven Years with the United Nations.* Macmillan, 1954.

Rovine, Arthur. *The First Fifty Years: The Secretary General World Politics, 1920–1970.* Leyden, Netherlands: A. W. Sijthoff, 1970.

United Nations Office of Public Information. *Everyman's United Nations.* New York: United Nations, 1968.

Livia

(58 B.C.–A.D. 29)

Influential consort of Augustus, architect of the Roman Empire, who was depicted in imperial propaganda as the embodiment of womanliness and dedication, while her enemies believed her to be a ruthless seeker of power.

Name variations: Livia Drusilla, later Julia Augusta and Livia Augusta. Pronunciation: LIV-ea. Born 58 B.C.; died A.D. 29; daughter of Marcus Livius Drusus Claudianus; married: Tiberius Claudius Nero (her cousin); married: Gaius Julius Caesar Octavianus, later Augustus; children: (first marriage) Tiberius Claudius Nero and Drusus Claudius Nero. Descendants: the Julio-Claudian dynasty, including the emperors Tiberius, Caligula, Claudius, and Nero.

As mistress of the Roman world, Livia's private life was lived in public. Acting as a moral example of her husband's imperial ideology, she served **Augustus** as helpmate, sounding-board, conveyor of messages-off-the-record and as foster mother to his grandchildren and great-grandchildren. She also successfully secured the throne for her own son by a previous marriage.

On both sides of her family, Livia was the descendant of Roman senators. Her father Marcus Livius Drusus Claudianus was, as his name shows, a member of the Claudian family who was adopted by Livians. Such adoption of an adult, or nearly adult, male heir into a line which lacked one was quite common in Rome. The adoption also served as a political bond between two powerful families.

Livia's early life presumably resembled that led by most young girls in the politically and economically elite circles of the Empire. Many of them were acquainted with rhetoric and philosophy, rather than restricted to the rudiments of literacy. Later some had literary interests, or, at least, joined the cultural avant garde of Roman society. But whatever education had been provided Livia, she displayed no later interest in taking up with a racy

"She was a compliant wife but an overbearing mother. Neither her husband's diplomacy nor her son's insincerity could outmaneuvre her."

TACITUS

Contributed by Phyllis Culham, Department of History, United States Naval Academy, Annapolis, Maryland

intellectual or artistic crowd. That helped to safe-guard her reputation for both chastity and Roman traditionalism and made her a striking contrast to women like Augustus's granddaughter Julia.

Livia's marriage to Tiberius Claudius at 15 was typical for Roman women. Marriage to a cousin was also not uncommon. In this case it was even more to be expected, since the marriage of a Livia to a Claudius further cemented the relationship between both families. Aware of the politics of arranged marriage from an early age, Livia would later put this knowledge to good use in positioning her sons within the new royal family.

The young Livia had started her life as a Roman matron in the most conventional fashion, but the civil war which had already begun with **Julius Caesar**'s death threw everything out of kilter. After the battle of Philippi, her father, who had fought for the Republic against the Second Triumvirate (Lepidus, Marc Antony, and Octavian), committed suicide rather than undergo the indignity of flight. But Livia, along with her infant son Tiberius and her husband, who had also fought in the battle, were fugitives. In their flight to join Sextus Pompey's forces in Sicily, they were nearly captured on two occasions when the child began crying and almost betrayed their presence. It must have been terrifying for Livia at 16 to be running for her life and to have her infant son twice snatched from her and stuffed away where his cries could not be heard.

It remains unknown whether or not Livia was surprised to find her husband less dedicated to the survival of the Republican forces than to his own advancement. After Sextus Pompey refused to accord him the position he wanted, the family set out to join the triumvir Mark Antony, when hostilities broke out between the members of the Second Triumvirate. That journey too was traumatic for Livia. With her infant son and a few attendants, she was almost killed in a forest fire in Sparta. She barely escaped with a smoldering cloak and singed hair.

Livia Marries Octavian

In 39 B.C., the triumvirs reached a settlement among themselves, and Livia's family returned to Italy under a general amnesty. There she met the triumvir **Octavian.** We do not know what Livia thought of him, but he was instantly enamored with her. Overcoming his conservative scruples, the elder Tiberius Claudius gave a traditional wedding feast to celebrate the marriage of his newly divorced wife—who was six months pregnant with his second son—to Octavian. Octavian, who had

CHRONOLOGY

58 B.C.	Livia born
44 B.C.	Julius Caesar assassinated; civil war
43 B.C.	Livia married her cousin Tiberius
42 B.C.	Bore her son Tiberius; she and family fled after Republican forces lost the battle of Philippi
38 B.C.	Met and married Octavian while pregnant with Tiberius's son Drusus
31 B.C.	Battle of Actium; Octavian master of the Mediterranean world
A.D. 14	Augustus (earlier Octavian) died; accession of Livia's son Tiberius as Roman emperor

been unwilling to wait for her to deliver, had sought a priestly opinion that Livia was able to remarry while visibly pregnant. The incident foreshadowed the later Augustan government which appeared to defer to propriety and the constraints of tradition while actually accomplishing whatever Augustus (Octavian) wanted.

Little is heard of Livia during the ensuing years, but her former husband died in 33 B.C., presumably disappointed, as he had received no rapid political or military advancement. The young Tiberius, now nine, gave his father's funeral oration. The situation must have been awkward for Livia and her son. Traditional funeral orations celebrated the political career and goals of the deceased. As war between Antony in the eastern Mediterranean and Octavian in the west loomed, it must have been obvious that the winner would dismantle the old Republic permanently. It was presumably a short and carefully worded speech. That same year Tiberius was betrothed to Vipsania, daughter of Octavian's close friend and aide Agrippa, who was probably even younger than he was. Some have seen Livia's hand at work there, strengthening her son's ties to his stepfather and positioning him for the assumption of power.

Given the circumstances of her remarriage, tension between Livia and her son was inevitable, and the relationship between Octavian and Tiberius was edgy at best. Octavian and Livia had a happy marriage, and Livia's younger son Drusus apparently got along well with his stepfather, but Tiberius did not. In the 20s B.C., Octavian (now the emperor Augustus) claimed to be restoring the old ways of the Republic, though he was actually putting together the elements of a new state. As

Tiberius was educated in Roman politics and history, he must have felt increasing disquiet at the discrepancy between what Augustus claimed to be doing and his actual concentration of power in his own hands.

Nonetheless, Livia managed to devote herself wholeheartedly to both Augustus and Tiberius. Augustus's need for male family members to represent the dynasty in the provinces allowed her to serve the interests of her husband, son, and Empire at once. In 20 B.C., Tiberius was sent to deal with an Armenian crisis and handled it creditably. Upon his return, he was married to Vipsania, and Livia's second son Drusus was set out on his political career. Nonetheless, the year ended on a frustrating note for Livia and Tiberius when Julia, Augustus's daughter by a previous marriage, bore the first of her three sons, Gaius. Lucius followed in 17 B.C. Tiberius could look forward only to being used in the interim, until the grandsons of the emperor's blood were old enough to take over.

But the events of 12 B.C. apparently forecast political success for Livia and Tiberius. Agrippa died, leaving Tiberius, at 29, the only adult male in or close to the family whom Augustus could entrust with potentially sensitive assignments. Undertaking the problem of pacifying tribes in the Danube basin, Tiberius handled the situation well. Livia at least agreed to—and was perhaps even enthusiastic about—Augustus's next plan for Tiberius. Forced to divorce his beloved Vipsania, with whom he had enjoyed a tranquil marriage, Tiberius was made to marry Augustus's daughter Julia, Agrippa's widow. At nearly 50, Livia had had to face the fact that she and Augustus could not have children together. Children of Tiberius and Julia would have been the next best thing. Then in 9 B.C., Tiberius as well as Livia felt deeply the loss of Drusus, who died in a fall from his horse.

Livia Advocates for Her Son

The family crisis came in 5 B.C. Tiberius, who had served Augustus and Rome loyally at some personal cost, was distressed to witness popular affection for the two attractive young grandsons as well as a clamor in the streets calling for them to be allowed to hold political offices at an illegally early age. Never having aroused such popular enthusiasm, Tiberius now felt rejection. He understood an assignment in Armenia to be an effort to get him out of Rome and consolidate opinion behind Gaius and Lucius, and perhaps it was. Though his mother appealed to him to relent, Tiberius refused to work for the regime anymore. Infuriated, Augustus

agreed to let him go to Rhodes for postgraduate study in philosophy, but Livia realized, as Tiberius did not, how precarious his position was. A good general was either loyal to the emperor or dead. In 1 B.C., perhaps at his mother's urging, Tiberius did ask Augustus if he might return to Rome, but Augustus's reply was hostile. Desperately afraid for her son, Livia secured an appointment for Tiburius as ambassador to Rhodes to mask from the public his complete estrangement from his imperial stepfather. When Gaius, Augustus's older grandson and heir apparent, began speculating openly about Tiberius's fate, Livia became frantic. Augustus, given to letting Livia have her way in almost everything, drew the line. He said that it was up to Gaius to let Tiberius return. Finally, in A.D. 2, he did, but Tiberius was ordered, as a condition, to withdraw from political life.

Later that year, the younger grandson Lucius died; Gaius died two years after. By this time, Tiberius and Augustus hated each other, but neither had a choice. Augustus was too old and frail to take active field commands himself; his great-grandson Germanicus was too young. Julia's youngest son was a juvenile delinquent. Tiberius could either serve the emperor or break his mother's heart and face execution. Suzanne Dixon's comment that "the royal family sometimes exaggerated its togetherness for propaganda purposes," seems a tremendous understatement.

Extravagant Roman gossip and popular modern novels have suggested that Livia engineered the deaths of Gaius and Lucius, one at the western end of the Mediterranean and the other at the eastern, but this seems highly unlikely. Nor is it likely that she could have been eliminating all of the emperor's current and prospective heirs, with the exception of her own son, and still have retained the affection of Augustus, a subtle and clever man. Suetonius tells us that **Caligula** later remembered his great-grandmother as an "Ulysses in skirts," alluding to the Homeric hero known for his cunning rather than his use of arms, but the demented Caligula also believed that his horse could be a consul of Rome. Given his paranoid fantasies, there is little reason to accept this particular belief that Livia was indulging in Mediterraneanwide skullduggery.

Certainly Augustus came to respect Livia's devotion to her friends and her penchant for political maneuvering. Suetonius is our source for the gossip that she actually helped to procure for Augustus the younger women he wanted. Roman spouses of both genders were often known to be tolerant of even more exotic extramarital adventures, and that is not impossible. What is sure is that their marital union remained solid. As Suetonius says, "Livia remained the one woman whom he truly loved until his death." Perhaps she was the one person, other than himself, whom Augustus had ever really valued; his final words to her would be, "Be mindful of our marriage."

There is no doubt that during Augustus's final illness in A.D. 14 Livia had her eye on the future. She gave the order to seal the house and surround the streets with soldiers, ostensibly to avoid disturbing the dying man, but surely to secure control for herself and her son and to prevent anyone from contesting their version of his wishes. She was also suspected, along with Tiberius, of ordering the execution of Augustus's scapegrace grandson in exile, the young Agrippa Postumus. Perhaps she did; it would certainly have been the wise thing to do to keep him from being used as a pawn by other parties. She was even suspected of having hastened Augustus's end once he had become dangerously incapacitated. It is more likely that Augustus's loving dependence on her during his final weakness led him to accede to her wishes wholeheartedly. As Tacitus commented, "Livia had the aged Augustus firmly under control." It was never quite clear just when Augustus died. Livia did not allow an announcement until Tiberius was on the spot and in command of the Praetorian Guard.

If Livia consoled herself in her widowhood with the thought that there was only smooth sailing ahead, she must have been shocked by Tiberius's subsequent conduct. He had been disappointed too often to accept the responsibility of rule gladly. He still concealed Claudian republican sentiments which he did not enjoy betraying. At 56, he also did not wish to appear to be ordered about by his mother. Livia had been accorded unprecedented public honors by Augustus: he had dedicated a building in her honor, and she had been allowed to restore a temple. Coins in the provinces proclaimed her the mother of her country and even of the world. She had been granted a status previously reserved for vestal virgins. Augustus's will posthumously adopted her into the Julian clan, allowing her to use the name Julia Augusta. Tiberius stopped the flood of honors.

Genuinely against according Romans the sorts of honors previously associated with the hellenistic potentates of the eastern Mediterranean, he kept the Roman senate from proclaiming her mother of the country and refused to let them put up an altar to her adoption or assign her special attendants. Still, the apparent rancor in some of the scenes in the senate recounted by Tacitus also stemmed from a reluctance to be reminded that his own good services had not secured him the throne; his mother's cleverness had. He was particularly piqued by a senatorial move to add "son of Livia" to his own nomenclature.

Still, Livia's influence often counted with Tiberius in times of discord. She was able to persuade him to show clemency to her friend Plancina who was accused of conspiring to assassinate Augustus's great-grandson Germanicus. In another case, Tacitus tells us that Tiberius did not want to deny his mother, so he promised to appear in court to defend a friend of hers, then took a very slow walk to court and arrived too late. Amazingly, Tacitus, who takes a very dim view of Tiberius, thinks this a smart ploy and reports that the Roman populace thought so too. There must have been a contemporary consensus that simply saying no to Livia was not to be contemplated.

Suetonius claims that "Tiberius then complained that his mother Livia vexed him by wanting to be co-ruler of the Empire," and he therefore avoided her. "Although he did occasionally need and follow Livia's advice, he disliked people to think of him as giving it serious consideration." He became especially angry when a blaze broke out near the temple of Vesta, and she took charge of crowd control and firefighting, "directing the populace and soldiery in person, as though Augustus were still alive."

One vignette in Suetonius is particularly telling. Tiberius and Livia began quarreling openly about a man whose name she wanted registered among those of potential jurors. "Tiberius agreed to do so on one condition—that the entry should be marked 'forced upon the emperor by his mother.'" Livia's response was to haul out some of Augustus's letters to her which described Tiberius's "sour and stubborn" character. Her point was presumably to remind Tiberius that he had not earned adoption as Augustus's successor. She had secured it for him.

Supposedly that incident inspired his partial retirement to Capri and his delegation of the government to the vicious Sejanus, which led in turn to Sejanus's plot, its discovery, and the subsequent "reign of terror" which killed so many senators. Among the consequences of the confrontation over the letters, according to Suetonius, was that Tiberius visited Livia only once in the last three years of her life and not at all during her final protracted illness at the age of 86. He did not attend her funeral or probate her will. He vetoed her deification, which was accomplished by a later emperor, **Claudius,** a handicapped grandson for whom she had little regard.

Livia had, nonetheless, secured a peaceful transition between the first and second emperors, no mean feat since there were no precedents, no legal guidance, and plenty of other claimants. It is quite possible that without her Augustus's great accomplishments including the *pax romana,* the Roman peace itself, might otherwise have been lost in another round of the sort of civil war which had racked the Republic for the previous century.

SOURCES:

Dio Cassius. *Dio's Roman History.* Vols. 6 & 7. Harvard University Press, 1960.

Suetonius. *The Twelve Caesars.* Penguin, 1957.

Tacitus. *The Annals of Imperial Rome.* Penguin, 1989.

FURTHER READING:

Balsdon, J. V. P. D. *Roman Women.* Barnes and Noble, 1983.

Dixon, Suzanne. *The Roman Mother.* Oklahoma University Press, 1988.

Hallett, Judith P. *Fathers and Daughters in Roman Society.* Princeton University Press, 1984.

Levick, Barbara. *Tiberius the Politician.* Thames & Hudson, 1976.

Seager, Robin. *Tiberius.* University of California Press, 1972.

David Lloyd George

(1863–1945)

British statesman, prime minister, and one of the most dominant international figures of the early 20th century.

"There was no man so gifted, so eloquent, so forceful, who knew the life of the people so well."

WINSTON S. CHURCHILL

David Lloyd George was born in Manchester, England, on January 17, 1863. His mother Elizabeth was the daughter of David Lloyd, a Welsh Baptist minister. His father William George was a Welshman from Pembrokeshire who had received an appointment as headmaster of a Manchester elementary school. Forced to give up teaching because of ill health, William George returned home to farm and died in June 1864 of consumption. Because his death left Elizabeth nearly penniless, her brother, Richard Lloyd, took his sister and three children into his family home in Llanystumdwy in Carnarvonshire, Wales. David was heavily influenced by Richard Lloyd, a shoemaker and Cambellite Baptist preacher who was a politically active Liberal. From this environment and his remarkable uncle, he absorbed the basic political radicalism and fervent evangelical ethics that were evident throughout his life. Richard Lloyd tutored the boy in French and Latin and had him basically educated in the village school where his favorite courses were history, geography, and Latin. Before he was 16, David Lloyd George had passed his preliminary law examination and was apprenticed in July

Name variations: First Earl of Dwyfor. Born January 17, 1863, in Manchester, England; died at Ty Newydd, near Llanystumdwy, Caernarvonshire, Wales, on March 26, 1945; son of William George (a Welsh farmer) and Elizabeth (Lloyd) George; married: Margaret Owen, 1888 (died 1941); married: Frances Stevenson, 1943; children: (first marriage—two sons and three daughters) Richard, Mair Eiluned (died at age 17), Olwen, Gwilyn (later Viscount Tenby), Megan (a Liberal and later a Labour member of Parliament). Predecessor: Herbert Henry Asquith. Successor: Andrew Bonar Law.

Contributed by Phillip E. Koerper, Professor of History, Jacksonville State University, Jacksonville, Alabama

1890	Elected as a Liberal to Parliament
1899	Delivered pacifist speeches on Boer War policy
1905	Entered Cabinet as president of the Board of Trade
1908	Appointed chancellor of exchequer
1909	Introduced the "People's Budget"
1910	Led campaign to limit power of House of Lords
1915	Appointed minister of munitions
1916	Secretary of state for war in Asquith Government; became prime minister of a new coalition government
1919	Led British delegation to Paris peace talks
1921	Approved Irish Treaty leading to independence
1922	Resigned as prime minister
1926–31	Leader of the Liberal Party
1931	Excluded from Ramsay MacDonald's National Government
1937–39	Criticized appeasement policy of Neville Chamberlain
1940	Declined Churchill's offer to serve in wartime coalition government
1941	Attacked Churchill's war policies
1945	Elevated to the peerage as Earl Lloyd George of Dwyfor; died in Ty Newydd, Wales

1878 to the law firm of Breese, Jones and Carson in the Welsh seaport town of Portmadoc.

The young apprentice solicitor began to write articles and made speeches on temperance, land reform, and religion, occasionally preaching in the chapel. In 1884, after passing the Law Society examination which qualified him as a solicitor, the 22-year-old opened an office in Criccieth in North Wales, gradually developing an extensive legal practice. He also opened branch offices in other villages, and his brother William ran an office in Portmadoc as a partner while still working on his legal studies. During this time, David insisted on being called by the euphonic double name of Lloyd George rather than the usual last name George. Known as the "poachers' lawyer" for defending poor men accused of violating the strict game laws, he also worked to organize the farmer's union and was openly vocal in the anti-tithe movement. He became well known throughout Wales in 1888

when he successfully defended the right of a non-conformist to be buried in the churchyard cemetery in Llanfrothen. As his reputation and competence grew, he was constantly sought for his legal skills and as a political speaker for the Liberal Party.

On January 24, 1888, Lloyd George was married to Margaret Owen of Mynyddednyfed, the daughter of a prosperous Methodist farmer. Theirs was never a happy marriage because his affairs and infidelities were notorious throughout his life. The turbulent marriage produced two sons and three daughters.

Lloyd George was a passionate advocate of the Welsh Home Rule Movement. In 1887, he had founded a newspaper called *Udgorn Rhyddid* (Trumpet of Freedom) with the hope of using it to gain support for a candidacy for Parliament. In December 1888, he was chosen as the parliamentary candidate for Caernarvon Boroughs. Although the next general election was three years away, Lloyd George took control of the district Liberal Party organization and initiated a well-planned campaign. His efforts were rewarded a few months later when he was appointed to the honorific office of alderman in Caernarvon, an office to which he was re-elected until his death.

He Begins 54 Years of Service in Parliament

The death of the Conservative member of Parliament for Caernarvon Boroughs in March 1890 led to a by-election in April. Lloyd George waged an aggressive campaign against his better-financed Conservative opponent, Hugh Ellis Nanney. Embracing the Liberal Party line of **William E. Gladstone,** he even composed his own campaign song "George and Gladstone" to the tune of "Marching Through Georgia." Following a controversial vote count, Lloyd George won by a majority of 18 out of 3,908 votes cast. He would hold the parliamentary seat for Caernarvon Boroughs until he left the House of Commons in 1945.

During his early years in the House of Commons, Lloyd George emphasized Welsh issues concerning temperance, land reform, disestablishment of the Anglican Church in Wales, and home rule for Wales. In 1894–95, he spearheaded a Welsh revolt within the Liberal Party against Prime Minister Rosebery's indecision on the Welsh disestablishments issue. The Welsh rebels, known as "The Four," contributed to the fall of Lord Rosebery's Government in June 1895, but Lloyd George could not unify the spirit of Welsh nationalism and in time larger issues overshadowed the problems of Wales. Following the Conservative victory in the 1895 general election, Lloyd George became a leader in the radical faction of the Liberal Party and was soon viewed as an independent, unorthodox Liberal who decided issues for himself. This reputation was solidified by his unyielding opposition to the Anglo-Boer War (1899–1902) in South Africa. His pacifistic speeches denouncing the Conservative Government in general and Colonial Secretary Joseph Chamberlain in particular won Lloyd George national prominence. In an uncompromising fashion, he maintained that Britain was primarily motivated by financial greed and asked: "What shall it profit a nation if it annex the gold fields of the whole world and lose its own soul?" During the war, Lloyd George was mobbed on several occasions and his life seriously threatened in Birmingham, the political stronghold of Chamberlain.

With the war ended, Lloyd George led the nonconformist opposition against tax-aided grants to church schools in the Conservative Party's Education Act of 1902. He also became one of the most effective opponents of the Tariff Reform Bill in 1903 and was one of the few free trade supporters in Commons who could best Chamberlain on the issue. Lloyd George was at his peak as a Welsh nationalist and independent radical during this period. He had been gradually moving toward a more important role within the leadership of the Liberal Party and into the fellowship of a more respectable, traditional English radicalism.

When the Liberals returned to power in the 1905 election, Prime Minister Sir Henry Campbell-Bannerman appointed Lloyd George as president of the Board of Trade. He proved his ability as an administrator by creating the Port of London Authority, reforming Britain's patent laws, passing merchant shipping reform legislation, and averting a major railway strike in 1907. When Campbell-Bannerman died in 1908 and Herbert H. Asquith succeeded him as prime minister, Lloyd George was made chancellor of the exchequer.

Inspired by the Bismarckian system of insurance benefits that he studied while in Germany in 1908, Lloyd George introduced similar unemployment insurance and health programs in Britain. This program was included in the "People's Budget" (1909) which was drawn up by Lloyd George and his chief ally, **Winston S. Churchill.** Needing new revenue sources, they proposed duties on tobacco, gasoline, beer, spirits, and land. Conservatives, particularly landowning peers, opposed these socialistic intrusions into traditional English life. In late autumn, the House of Lords' defeated the budget. During a speech in the Limehouse parish of London, Lloyd George attacked his opposition so harshly that the term "limehouse" remains in the English language as a synonym for castigating one's political opposition. Two elections in 1910 upheld the Liberal Government, and the budget was finally passed by the House of Lords. The Lords delay in the budget crisis precipitated the passage of the Parliament Act (1911) which deprived the House of Lords of its veto power over financial affairs. The passage of Lloyd George's highly controversial contributory National Health Insurance Act and the National Unemployment Insurance Act in 1911 laid the foundations of the modern welfare state and cemented his reputation in history as a social reformer.

Before World War I, Lloyd George had shown very little interest or concern with foreign policy. The one major exception had been his Mansion House speech during the Agadir crisis of 1911. When Germany sent a warship to Agadir in French-controlled Morocco, Lloyd George broke with his peaceful image by warning Germany that Britain would protect its national interests. This was a remarkable departure because he would return to his pacifist philosophy by advocating disarmament as late as January 1914. When war broke out in August 1914, Asquith's Liberal Cabinet was divided on a war policy. Although Lloyd George wavered on the war, he quickly aligned himself against Germany, following her violation of Belgian neutrality. Social reform, Welsh nationalism, and tax issues were replaced by his energetic and wholehearted support for the war effort.

Lloyd George Becomes Prime Minister

During the first year of the conflict, Lloyd George remained as chancellor of the exchequer, but he realized the importance of munitions and shells. When Asquith formed the first coalition government in May 1915, he placed Lloyd George in charge of the newly created Ministry of Munitions. From this position he pushed hard for a massive production of ammunition and for a major conscription effort. Meanwhile, Asquith's government suffered military defeats in Mesopotamia, the Dardanelles, and Rumania. Heavy troop losses on the Somme River and a rebellion against British authority in Ireland created a crisis of confidence about Asquith's leadership. When **Lord Kitchener** died in June 1916, Lloyd George was chosen to replace him as secretary of state for war. Concerned about the confusion in the government, Lloyd George worked with the Conservative leaders Sir Edward Carson and Andrew Bonar Law to reform the coalition cabinet, but Asquith refused to cooperate and resigned his office. Lloyd George, with the support of the Conservative and Labour parties and many of the Liberals, accepted the office of prime minister on December 7, 1916, at the age of 54.

As prime minister, Lloyd George immediately reduced the unwieldy War Cabinet from 23 to five members. Streamlining decisions, he eliminated the divisiveness that had existed in the larger body, personally directed a complex network of departments and offices outside the cabinet, and inspired the nation to overcome food shortages, military reversals, military service rivalries, disagreements among the Allies, and the horror of submarine warfare. As Churchill would do in the next war, Lloyd George provided the inexhaustible energy, buoyancy, and courage which inspired the British people and ultimately led to victory.

Following the Allied Powers' victory, Lloyd George, despite the defection of Asquith and his Liberal supporters, decided to maintain the wartime coalition. He and Bonar Law, the Conservative leader, agreed to hold a general election in which those candidates supporting the coalition were given a coupon (joint letter) from the two leaders endorsing them. Held on December 14, 1918, this "Coupon Election" was really a vote of confidence on Lloyd George; he—along with his coupon candidates—swept this khaki (wartime) election by winning 80% of the vote and an overwhelming mandate to remain in power.

At the Versailles Peace Conference, Lloyd George, usually on the side of moderation and generosity, helped frame the treaty ending World War I. From 1919 to 1921, Lloyd George's Government was anticlimactic as his support gradually eroded away. His hope to construct a new society was partially fulfilled in the Housing Act of 1919, the creation of a Ministry of Health and a Ministry of Transport, and the extension of unemployment insurance. He ended the centuries of conflict and a current bloody war with the Irish Republicans by granting the Irish Free State Dominion status in 1921. But mounting labor unrest and unemployment, recession, and allegations of selling peerages damaged both his political and personal standing with the public. His spending policies alienated the Conservatives and his austerity programs upset the radicals in the coalition. The Irish treaty was extremely unpopular with the British electorate and the coalition Conservative Party.

It was foreign policy that brought about Lloyd George's political defeat. In the Turkish crisis of 1922, Lloyd George and his coalition partners held opposing views. His pro-Greek policy and its failure led Britain to the brink of an unnecessary war with Turkey. The coalition Conservatives revolted and by a two-to-one vote withdrew their support on October 19, 1922. When Lloyd George resigned that same afternoon, Andrew Bonar Law became prime minister. Lloyd George would never again hold a cabinet-level position.

In the general election of 1922, Lloyd George's Liberals elected only 57 candidates. Following this disastrous election, he and Asquith, whose faction won only 60 seats, reunified the Liberal Party on the issue of free trade. Later they split again, and Lloyd George tried unsuccessfully from 1926 to 1931 to reunite the Liberal Party and to develop policies to challenge its rivals. The Labour Party had replaced the Liberals as the chief opposition party to the Conservatives after 1922. Unable to win back the defections to the Labour Party and unable to convince the public to accept his new social programs, Lloyd George's final break with the Liberals came in 1931. Refusing to serve in **Ramsay MacDonald**'s National (coalition) Government which had been created to fight the depression, he became an independent Liberal and remained in the opposition.

During his remaining years in the House of Commons, Lloyd George's influence was peripheral. Although he remained a forceful parliamentarian, he was listened to but seldom heeded. He also wrote several books about his career, the most important being *The Truth About Reparations and War Debts* (1932); *War Memoirs* (six volumes, 1933–36) and *The Truth About the Peace Treaties* (two volumes, 1938), and continued to criticize the Conservative Party's foreign and domestic policies. He openly attacked the Hoare-Laval Agreement (1935) over Italian aggression in Abyssinia. In 1936, he met Hitler at Berchtesgaden, Germany, and was temporarily taken in by the Nazi dictator. He castigated the government in 1937 for its nonintervention policy in the Spanish Civil War. When **Anthony Eden,** the British foreign secretary, resigned in 1938 in protest of the appeasement policies of Prime Minister **Neville Chamberlain,** Lloyd George, who had been a critic of Eden, demanded that he be reinstated to the office. He joined Eden and Winston Churchill in denouncing the entire Chamberlain foreign policy which had culminated with the Munich Agreement concerning Nazi ambitions in Czechoslovakia. Finally, on May 7, 1940, Lloyd George attacked Chamberlain and requested his resignation:

> The nation is prepared for every sacrifice…. I say solemnly that the Prime Minister should give an example of sacrifice, because there is nothing which can contribute more to victory in this war than that he should sacrifice the seals of office.

When Chamberlain resigned on May 10, Winston Churchill with the aid of his old friend became prime minister. But Lloyd George was also a critic of Churchill's government; he criticized Churchill's policy on food production, cabinet selections, and conduct of the war itself. He twice refused positions in Churchill's War Cabinet, ostensibly on grounds of health and age.

Lloyd George's wife died in January 1941, and in October 1943, he married Frances Louise Stevenson, his personal secretary for 30 years. In December 1944, Lloyd George, acting on the advice of his physician, announced that he would bring his 54 years in the House of Commons to an end. That same month, elevated to the peerage by King George VI, he took his title, First Earl of Dwyfor, from a mountain stream near his farm in Wales. Lloyd George died on March 26, 1945, at Ty Newydd, near Llanystumdwy, Wales.

SOURCES:

Beaverbrook, Lord. *The Decline and Fall of Lloyd George,* Duell, Sloan & Pearce, 1963.

Cregier, Don M. Bounder *From Wales: Lloyd George's Career Before the First War.* University of Missouri Press, 1976.

Cross, Colin, ed. *Life with Lloyd George: The Diary of A.J. Sylvester.* Harper, 1975.

George, W. R. P. *The Making of Lloyd George.* Faber & Faber, 1976.

Gilbert, Martin, ed. *Lloyd George.* Prentice Hall, 1968.

Grigg, John. *Lloyd George: The People's Champion 1902–1911.* Eyre Methuen, 1978.

———. *The Young Lloyd George.* University of California Press, 1973.

Lloyd George, Earl. *My Father, Lloyd George.* Crown, 1961.

FURTHER READING:

Campbell, John. *Lloyd George: The Goat in the Wilderness 1922–1931.* Jonathan Cape, 1977.

Jones, Thomas. *Lloyd George.* Oxford University Press, 1951.

McCormick, Donald. *The Mask of Merlin.* Holt, 1964.

Owen, Frank. *Tempestuous Journey: Lloyd George His Life and Times.* McGraw-Hill, 1955.

Rowland, Peter. *David Lloyd George: A Biography.* Macmillan, 1975.

Taylor, A. J. P., ed. *Lloyd George: A Diary by Frances Stevenson.* Harper, 1971.

Wrigley, Chris. *David Lloyd George and the British Labour Movement.* Harvester Press, 1976.

Louis IX

(1214–1270)

King of France with a reputation for justice, political and diplomatic astuteness, piety, and crusading zeal, who represented the epitome of medieval kingship and was a major force in shaping his nation.

Name variations: Saint Louis. Born on April 25, 1214, at Poissy, France; died on August 25, 1270, near Tunis (North Africa); son of Louis VIII (king of France) and Blanche of Castile; married: Margaret (Marguerite) of Provence, May 27, 1234; children: Blanche, Louis, Isabelle, Philip III, John, John-Tristan, Peter, Robert, Margaret, Agnes. Descendants: the Capetian dynasty until the end of the lineage in 1328, including Philip IV the Fair (1285–1314). Predecessor: Louis VIII, of France (1223–26). Successor: Philip III, of France (1270–85).

Three months after the birth of Louis IX on April 25, 1214, his grandfather, **Philip II Augustus,** won a crucial victory for France at the battle of Bouvines. This famous battle consolidated the territorial growth that Philip had achieved by bringing Normandy, Anjou, Maine, and Touraine under the feudal control of the French monarchy. An enlarged and strengthened France was the legacy that Louis IX would inherit and continue to build upon.

A younger son of the future Louis VIII and his wife **Blanche of Castile,** the infant Louis was not heir to the throne. But when his older brother Philip died in 1218, the four-year-old Louis was put in the direct line of succession.

Although few specifics are known about Louis IX's childhood, clearly the most influential person in his life was his mother Blanche of Castile. Daughter of Alfonso VIII of Castile and Eleanor of England, Blanche's maternal grandparents were the formidable couple, **Henry II** of England and **Eleanor of Aquitaine.** The strength of character that Blanche displayed all her life undoubtedly reflected this heritage through her maternal line.

Contributed by Karen Gould, Ph.D., Consultant in Medieval and Renaissance Manuscripts, Austin, Texas

"He knew how to reconcile the profoundest politics with the strictest justice, and perhaps was the only sovereign who deserved this praise: in council he was prudent and firm, in battle intrepid but not rash, and compassionate, as if he had always been unhappy. In a word, it is not in the power of man to carry virtue to a greater height."

VOLTAIRE

When Louis was young, Blanche instilled in him a keen sense of piety, devotion, and duty. His later leadership in military affairs shows his training as a knight. He was also tutored in letters by a clerical master. While he was not a scholar, he was well versed in basic Christian theology and the proper conduct of princes. Even at a young age, he was serious, studious, and devout.

In 1223, when Louis was nine years old, his grandfather Philip Augustus died and his father became king of France. Having been actively campaigning in southern France against the Albigensian heresy, Louis VIII continued his crusade until the fall of 1226, when he fell mortally ill while returning north from his military exploits in southern France. On his deathbed, he ordered that his heir should be crowned immediately and that his queen, Blanche of Castile, should serve as regent until the 12-year-old Louis reached the age of majority. When Louis VIII died on November 8, 1226, Louis IX was crowned at Rheims on November 29.

Mother and Son Rule France

With a young king and a female regent, the French monarchy faced a difficult situation. Many of the powerful French nobles who resented the increase in royal power during the reign of Philip Augustus seized the opportunity to assert their independence. As regent, Blanche of Castile effectively utilized alliances and military support from loyal vassals to preserve the French royal patrimony. She won over the initially rebellious Theobald IV, count of Champagne. His support helped Blanche and Louis IX contain an alliance of barons from the northern provinces headed by Peter Mauclerc of Brittany. Henry III of England, who wanted to regain the continental territories in France that his father **King John** had lost to Philip Augustus, intermittently supported this coalition.

The French monarchy prevailed during the turbulent period of Louis IX's minority. In May 1234, Louis married Margaret of Provence, the eldest of four daughters of Count Raymond-Berengar. Although this event unofficially marked the end of Blanche of Castile's regency, she continued to exercise great influence on her son, to the dismay of his new wife. From this point, however, Louis IX assumed control of governmental affairs and led French forces in various military engagements. Louis and Margaret seemed to care for each other as husband and wife despite tensions created by Blanche's interference and Margaret's strong-willed character. The royal couple had 10 children, three of whom would be born while Louis and Margaret were on crusade between 1248 and 1254.

CHRONOLOGY

1214	Louis IX born; Battle of Bouvines
1226	Louis VIII died; coronation of Louis IX
1226–34	Regency of Blanche of Castile
1243	Pope Innocent IV elected
1248	Louis IX departed on crusade
1249	Capture of Damietta in Egypt
1250	Battle of Mansourah, Egypt; Louis IX in captivity in Egypt; Emperor Frederick II died
1250–54	Louis IX in Holy Land
1252	Blanche of Castile died
1254	Louis IX returned to Paris; Pope Alexander IV elected
1258	Treaty of Corbeil with James I of Aragon
1259	Treaty of Paris with Henry III of England
1265	Pope Clement IV elected; Charles of Anjou invested with Kingdom of Sicily
1270	Louis departed on crusade; died near Tunis
1297	Canonized

Between 1234 and 1244, during the first decade of Louis IX's reign in his own right, he continued the policies of consolidating and extending royal power and prerogatives in territories ruled by the French monarch. In accordance with his father's will, he installed his brothers in feudal provinces as they came of age. Thus, Robert became count of Artois in 1237, Alfonso (Alphonse) was invested as count of Poitiers in 1241, and Charles became count of Anjou in 1246. This system of appanages (grants to dependent relatives) helped govern and keep these territories within familial control. Louis IX also directed much attention to the unstable situation in southern France where Count Raymond VII of Toulouse in particular often challenged royal interests. In addition, Louis displayed evidence of his religious faith and piety by supporting crusading efforts and religious orders, especially the mendicant Franciscans and Dominicans. In 1239, he acquired the most prestigious relics in Christendom, the crown of thorns and other relics of the passion, for which he built the magnificent Gothic structure, the Sainte-Chapelle which was dedicated in 1248.

Daughter of King Alfonso VIII of Castile and his queen, Eleanor of England, Blanche of Castile was born March 4, 1188, at Palencia in Spanish Castile. Her maternal grandparents were King Henry II of England and Eleanor of Aquitaine. In the winter of 1200, the elderly Eleanor of Aquitaine made the difficult journey to Spain to complete negotiations for the betrothal of Blanche to Prince Louis, heir of King Philip Augustus of France. On May 23, 1200, Blanche married the future Louis VIII, and the couple had 12 children. At her husband's premature death in 1226, Blanche's eldest surviving son Louis IX was crowned. Blanche served as regent of France on two occasions: from 1226–34 during the minority of Louis IX, and from 1248 until her death in November 1252, when Louis IX was on crusade in the Holy Land.

Although Blanche is less

In December 1244, Louis, who had a frail constitution, became so ill that his attendants thought he had died. As he began to recover, he made a vow to go on crusade. From this point, Louis IX's conduct and character as king altered. He became even more concerned with his responsibilities as a Christian ruler to his French subjects and to the larger world community.

Louis Leads Seventh Crusade to Egypt

Preparations for the march, known as the Seventh Crusade, took four years until the crusaders departed in August 1248 from Aigues-Mortes, the Mediterranean seaport that Louis had built in southern France. After spending the winter in Cyprus, the crusading force, composed primarily of French knights and soldiers, began their first stage of conquest by attacking Egypt, a Muslim stronghold that was key to control of the Holy Land itself. After capturing the port of Damietta in the Nile Delta in June 1249, the crusaders proceeded toward Cairo in the winter. Through ineffective tactics, they met defeat at the battle of Mansourah in February 1250. As they retreated, many, including Louis IX, became seriously ill and were captured. After Louis was released, he and his wife, along with some of his forces, remained in the Holy Land helping to fortify coastal towns held by Christians at Acre, Caesarea, Jaffa, and Sidon.

When Blanche of Castile, left as a regent in Louis IX's absence, died in November 1252, Louis began to plan his return to France. When he arrived in 1254, the hardships of crusade had left their mark: he became even more intense and ascetic in his devotional practices. At the same time, he continued his firm rule over France. He improved the system of royal government established by Philip Augustus. He utilized the provincial civil servants known as *baillis* but added *enqueteurs* who were sent to oversee local officials and curtail abuses of power. He was known for his exercise of justice at all levels and consistently enforced royal jurisdiction even over the temporal possessions and privileges of the Church in France.

His power within his kingdom and his reputation for fairness placed Louis IX in a strong position in the conduct of foreign affairs. He finally reached a settlement with the English king, Henry III, over the former Angevin empire. In the Treaty of Paris in 1259, England formally acknowledged Normany, Anjou, and Poitou as French Capetian territories. In 1258, the Treaty of Corbeil with Spanish Aragon provided that Louis IX would give up French claims in Spain while James I of Aragon renounced his interests in Languedoc in south France. Later, in 1265, Louis IX finally gave his support to the acceptance of the Kingdom of Sicily by his brother, Charles of Anjou. He also arbitrated where French interests were not directly involved, as in the Mise of Amiens in 1264 where Louis IX mediated a dispute between Henry III and his barons.

Louis IX had never abandoned his commitment to a crusade in the Holy Land, and his penitential sense of responsibility for the failure of the Seventh Crusade strengthened his resolve. As the situation in the Holy Land grew more precarious, he renewed his crusading vow in 1267 and set a date for departure in 1270. This Eighth Crusade received little support and seemed illfated from its inception. When Louis IX departed in July 1270, his immediate destination was not the Holy Land but Tunisia in north Africa. His tactical motive remains unclear, but he probably hoped to convert Tunisian Muslims by force or persuasion and establish a base for continuing to Egypt and the Holy Land. In the summer heat, however, many of the crusaders, including Louis IX and his son John-Tristan, became ill. After John died on August 3, Louis IX grew weaker and finally died on August 24, 1270. His death effectively ended the crusade, and his remains were interred in the Capetian sepulchre at the royal abbey of Saint-Denis outside Paris.

recognized than her flamboyant grandmother Eleanor of Aquitaine, she displayed the same strength of character and was in many ways more influential on the course of history. Acting as regent during Louis IX's minority, she skillfully maintained the French royal patrimony by containing the initiatives of several rebellious French nobles. Although after 1234 Louis governed independently, he always regarded Blanche as one of his most trusted advisers. His confidence in her abilities and judgment is shown by his designation of Blanche as regent when he departed on crusade in 1248. Blanche of Castile has been criticized for exercising undue influence on her son, but her firm guidance and decisive actions contributed significantly to the development of a strong French monarchy during the 13th century. ■

Soon after his death, miracles began to be associated with his relics. Because of these miracles and his saintly conduct of kingship, he was officially canonized in 1297. Even now, it is difficult to separate an evaluation of King Louis IX from the hagiographical image of Saint Louis. His leadership as king had its successes and failures. He strengthened the Capetian royal patrimony, improved its governance, and extended royal justice throughout his realm. At the same time, his crusading efforts which cost many lives among the French knighthood were unsuccessful and drained French financial and human resources. However, through his conduct and character which exemplified the virtues of a Christian ruler, Louis IX was able to enhance significantly the prestige and power of the French monarchy.

SOURCES:

John of Joinville. *Life of St. Louis.* Translated by R. Hague. 1955.

Labarge, Margaret Wade. *Saint Louis.* Little, Brown, 1968.

Pernoud, Regine. *Blanche of Castile.* Translated by Henry Noel. Coward, 1975.

Richard, Jean. *Saint Louis.* Translated by Jean Birrell. Cambridge University Press, 1992.

FURTHER READING:

Fawtier, Robert. *The Capetian Kings of France.* Translated by Lionel Butler and R. J. Adam. Macmillan, 1960.

Hallam, Elizabeth M. *Capetian France, 987–1328.* Longmans, 1980.

Jordan, William Chester. *Louis IX and the Challenge of Crusade.* Princeton University Press, 1979.

Louis XIV

(1638–1715)

The most famous of all French kings, who epitomized absolute monarchy and led France through an age of cultural and military ascendancy in Europe.

Name variations: the Sun King, Louis de Bourbon, third Bourbon King of France, Louis the God-given, Louis the Great, the Grand Monarch. Born on September 5, 1638; died on September 1, 1715; first child of King Louis XIII and Anne of Austria; married: Maria-Theresa of Spain, 1660; married: Mme de Maintenon. Descendants: the Bourbon monarchies of France and Spain. Predecessor: Louis XIII. Successor: Louis XV.

The long-awaited birth of the first child of King Louis XIII and Anne of Austria on September 5, 1638, provided a direct male heir to the French throne and the monarch who later would lead France through an age of unequaled grandeur and uncontested ascendancy in the Western world. Hailed by a relieved court as *Louis-Dieudonné,* or Louis the God-given, he became Louis XIV, king of France, on May 14, 1643, the day of his father's death.

As a boy less than five years of age, Louis could not assume the task of ruling the most powerful nation in Europe. This responsibility was taken on by his mother Anne as queen regent, aided by the powerful Italian minister, Cardinal **Jules Mazarin.** Yet all his life Louis, and everyone around him, was aware that he had been born to a privileged position; as king of France, he was God's chosen representative on earth. Being worthy of the inheritance of this position was a great responsibility, for a king needed to be a brave soldier, a skilled statesman, and a careful judge. Mazarin felt that the gifted Louis was particularly suited to fulfill his exalted role and to meet this

"L'État c'est moi [I am the state]."

ATTRIBUTED TO LOUIS XIV

Contributed by Alan M. James, Ph.D., University of Manchester, Manchester, England

threefold challenge. "God has given you all the qualities for greatness," he stressed.

While matters of state were being attended to by Mazarin and Queen Anne, young Louis practiced being king, playing with drums and toy soldiers in the courtyard. But at seven years of age, his formal training began. He was instructed by a team of governors headed by Mazarin which provided a strictly Catholic education aimed specifically at teaching him how to be king. Louis learned quickly. At 12, he could write elegantly in French and could converse in Italian, Spanish, and Latin. He also became adept at horsemanship, fencing, dancing, and other refined skills suitable for a monarch of great stature. Most important, however, Mazarin brought the boy into council sessions where matters of state were being discussed to give him a sense of how decisions were made and how power was exercised. Thus at a very early age, Louis considered abstractly the *métier du roi*, or the craft of kingship, and he anticipated the day when he would take on effectively the responsibility of being the ruler of France.

Although he was being groomed to be king, Louis's childhood was not ideal. At nine years of age, he contracted smallpox and nearly died from the disease and the primitive treatments administered by royal doctors. He also experienced political unrest against a monarchical power firsthand. Across the Channel, civil war had been raging since 1642 against Louis's uncle King **Charles I** of England, who was beheaded in 1649. This hardly could have escaped the attention of a boy who would soon be exercising personal authority as king of France.

In August 1648, just short of his tenth birthday, Louis came face-to-face with the horror of civil war in his own realm. From 1648 to 1653, France was threatened by a series of popular rebellions (collectively called the *Fronde*), instigated by various judicial courts and led by the Parlement of Paris. The *frondeurs*, as they were called, hoped to benefit from the weakness of the king and claim more power by appealing to the crowds to rise up against the government of Queen Anne and the hated Mazarin.

From his window at the royal palace, Louis, a virtual prisoner in his own capital, watched Paris mobs fill the streets, erect barricades, and rise in open rebellion. Because Mazarin was preoccupied with the negotiations of the Peace of Westphalia ending the devastating Thirty Years' War against the Austrian branch of the ruling House of Habsburg, he could pay little attention to the appeals of French subjects, and the danger to the royal gov-

CHRONOLOGY

1638	Louis XIV born
1648	Peace of Westphalia; rebellion known as the *Fronde* began
1654	Coronation of Louis XIV
1659	Peace of the Pyrénées
1667	War of Devolution
1682	Government and court moved to Versailles
1685	Revocation of the Edict of Nantes
1688	Glorious Revolution in England
1702	War of the Spanish Succession against the Grand Alliance began
1710	Louis's great-grandson (Louis XV) born
1713	Peace of Utrecht
1715	Louis XIV died

ernment grew. Suddenly, on the night of January 5, 1649, Louis and his mother were spirited out of Paris by Mazarin and taken to safety in a nearby town where the young king spent the rest of the night on a bed of straw. While royal troops were forced to besiege the city to win it back, the boy-king was deprived of many of life's comforts. Because a second phase of the *Fronde* (1651–53) was supported by many discontented and jealous noblemen, Louis not only came to dislike Paris, the Parlement and any popular movement, he did not even trust his own aristocracy. These experiences of disorder and disobedience reaffirmed his resolution to rule effectively over all people and all situations.

Louis Is Crowned as King

On September 5, 1651, Louis turned 13. According to French law, he was no longer in his minority and could rule in his own right. He knew the seriousness of this challenge:

> The smallest moves were important in these first beginnings which were showing France what was to be the character of my reign and of my conduct for the entire future.

Two days later, he went to the Palais de Justice to chastise the Parlement and to announce that he intended to take on the responsibility of governing France himself. He felt, "It was necessary to humble them... for what they might do in the future." Of course, no one in this time of rebellion against the crown believed that the boy would be able to make good on his promise. But by 1652, the *Fronde* was over in Paris, and in 1654, the victorious Louis was solemnly crowned.

In the early years of his reign, the youthful Louis indulged in good-natured fun. He enjoyed ballet, hunting, and—as an immediate result of his gallantry—the opposite sex. At this pleasure, he did not want. Many young women, attracted as much by the prospect of "royal favour" as by the king himself, allowed Louis to indulge himself fully, adding "playboy" to his list of kingly functions. But Louis had one more important lesson to learn: to achieve greatness as a king, he would have to sacrifice his private life. When it came to marriage, the requirements of the state left no room for personal emotion.

In addition to contracting gonorrhea, Louis was afflicted with life-threatening typhoid fever in the summer of 1658. Since this ordeal had endangered his virility, it was now felt essential that the king soon marry to produce a male heir. The prime candidate was Princess Maria-Theresa of Spain. Because the Peace of Westphalia had not ended hostilities with the Spanish branch of the House of Habsburg, such a match would help secure peace between the two great Catholic crowns and ensure the best possible future inheritance for France. Though Louis recognized the importance of this, he was faced with a very difficult dilemma: he had recently fallen in love with one of Mazarin's nieces, Marie Mancini, a woman of considerably less stature.

Mazarin was horrified and forbade any thought of marriage between the two lovers. Reluctantly, Louis renounced his first love to marry another woman for the glory of the crown. The magnitude of this sacrifice was a profound statement and a testament to his seriousness and dedication. In 1659, the Peace of the Pyrénées was signed by Spain and France, and the following year there was an elaborate marriage ceremony and an hours-long entry parade into Paris for Louis and his new Spanish queen-consort.

Mazarin's death in 1661 provided the opportunity for Louis to make himself the only significant political figure in France. Many had been jockeying for royal favor and the opportunity to replace the powerful first minister, but Louis shocked everyone. He chose not to have a first minister at all and to fill Mazarin's role himself. By making a show of the arrest of the powerful and ambitious superintendent of finance, Nicholas Fouquet, for treason and replacing his position with a Council of Finance, Louis made his insistence on obedience and submission to his authority very clear. Henceforth, he was to rely on a number of people in a variety of councils under his direct authority, seeking men of merit rather than relying solely on rank by virtue of birth. In order to take on such an impressive responsibility, Louis recognized two necessities: "very hard work on my part, and a wise choice of persons capable of seconding it."

He Builds Palace, Holds Court at Versailles

In the 17th century, France was a nation deeply divided by class and by region. Louis undertook to overawe the entire country; his grandeur provided a unifying symbol of strength and authority. By 1682, he had moved his court and government to Versailles, the site of an old royal hunting lodge about 13 miles from Paris. There he had built—at great expense—a palace of such magnificence that it became the envy of all other rulers and the cultural center of the Western world. This architectural marvel set among elaborate gardens and 1,400 fountains came to house up to 10,000 people. In this expression of majesty, Louis made a spectacle of his daily life. Every moment was determined by a complex, detailed procedure designed to exalt the mystique of kingship and to reinforce his role as the personification of the state.

Louis was able to keep the aristocracy under strict surveillance by occupying it with the decadent and demeaning life of Versailles. Anybody of any significance longed to live in the majestic presence of the king, and such tasks as handing the king his nightshirt or holding his candle at bedtime were considered great honors. Incredibly, Louis was able to indulge himself in a lifestyle of overeating and self-satisfaction, while at the same time his passion for ostentatious display allowed him to live a life of continual ritual. All the while, Louis dealt with the many details of government. He likened himself the "father of his people," and, indeed, he had a tremendous effect on everyone. His was a radiance like that of the sun, hence his sobriquet: "the Sun King."

To achieve stability and unity in France, Louis pursued the ideal of "One God, One King, One Law." The Huguenots, or Protestants living in France, were an affront to his need for religious conformity. This relatively wealthy and distrusted minority's right to existence was based entirely on the Edict of Nantes of 1598, a royal concession which had put to rest years of religious wars in

France. Louis XIV, however, felt no need to make concessions to anyone, especially to heretics within his own state. The Huguenots were harassed, but by 1685 Louis went further and a period of official intolerance and persecution began with the revocation of the edict. Although the resulting migrations of middle-class Protestants to the Netherlands, Switzerland, Germany, England, South Africa, and America may have stimulated those countries economically, the numbers were too small to have much impact on France. But the revocation was a brave move, revealing Louis's determination to define and control the character of the nation.

As a great king, Louis saw himself as a reformer. With the advice and service of such men as **Jean-Baptiste Colbert,** many initiatives were undertaken in his reign to codify the laws of the realm, guide the economy, encourage the arts—especially painting, literature, and the theater—and to develop colonies all over the world. At this time, France claimed most of North America from Québec to Louisiana (which was named after the great king). But it was the achievement of glory in Europe that appealed most to Louis. As he put it, "at least I should appear glorious in the eyes of all the nations of the earth." He felt that as the embodiment of the state, his glory and the good of the people were one and the same. Thus, in addition to order and obedience in France, Louis actively made war abroad.

To this end, he reorganized the military and brought it under more direct, efficient royal control, replacing private armies under wealthy noblemen. His army was more disciplined, bigger, and more efficiently supplied than ever before. The genius of Sebastien Le Prestre de Vauban, his great engineer and fortress builder, gave the army a technical and tactical advantage that made it even more formidable. War became a controllable expression of state policy which Louis could use to achieve the glory for which he longed.

Louis the Great Moves Against Neighbors

Driven by the dream of achieving the "natural frontiers" of France (an eastern border along the Alps and the Rhine River), the new army made two moves in 1667 and 1672 against neighboring territories, including France's commercial rival, the Dutch Netherlands. Although the Dutch survived the War of Devolution (1667) and the Dutch War (1672), Louis managed to obtain the Spanish-held Free County of Burgundy (or la *Franche-Comté*) between France and Switzerland and some smaller places along the northeast border with the Spanish

Netherlands (present-day Belgium). In this way, Louis established himself as the dominant European power and earned his new sobriquet: "Louis the Great."

Not satisfied with this, Louis began to push weak legal claims to areas within Alsace and Lorraine to justify a series of annexations, including that of the Imperial Free City of Strasbourg in 1681. By 1686, however, the Austrian Habsburg Holy Roman Emperor Leopold I and his Spanish Habsburg cousin Charles II (or Carlos II)—together with Sweden, the Netherlands, a number of smaller German states, and, a few years later, England—all allied in the League of Augsburg to fight Louis. Although the ensuing war (1688–97) was burdensome and neither side achieved much, Louis's military strength had withstood opposition by almost every power in Europe.

At Versailles, Louis's personal life was equally eventful. When his mother Anne of Austria died in 1666, he was able to act more freely at court. The woman with whom he had been having a love affair, Louise de La Vallière, was recognized as his official mistress and their children were legitimized; within two more years, the already married Marquise de Montespan also became his mistress and bore him many children. Although far from faithful, Montespan remained the favorite of Louis until she was implicated in the Affair of the Poisons, which brought charges of witchcraft and murder against a number of prominent people.

When Maria-Theresa died in 1683, Louis pursued the passion of a more mature man for Madame de Maintenon, who had been the governess of his illegitimate children. Soon playing a very special role in Louis's life, she came to have a great effect on the court. Her piety and austere lifestyle better suited the middle-aged Louis and, after they were secretly married, life at Versailles settled down, taking on a greater aspect of decency and propriety.

Possibly Louis's austerity toward the end of his life was also the result of waning international success. For years, all of Europe had been expecting the death of the sickly Spanish king Charles. Since he had no direct heirs, and the Spanish crown's hold on its vast territories in Europe and overseas was weakening, three European monarchs—each related to Charles—were hoping to receive part of his possessions. Louis, as Charles's brother-in-law, hoped that his children would inherit the entire Spanish crown. When Charles died in 1700, his will stipulated that the Empire be kept intact and offered to Louis's 17-year-old grandson, Philip of Anjou. Reacting to this extension of French Bourbon influence, the international community—England, the Netherlands, Holy Roman Emperor Leopold I, and the German states—formed the Grand Alliance in 1701, and once again France was at war.

Louis's passion for glory ultimately strained and impoverished the nation. France suffered miserably both militarily and economically from the War of the Spanish Succession (1702–13). By the Treaty of Utrecht (1713), Louis officially gave up any idea of joining both crowns so long as his grandson was accepted as king of Spain (Philip V). France gave up all designs on Belgium, and surrendered Newfoundland, Acadia (Nova Scotia), and the area around Hudson's Bay to England. Although France was weakened overseas by the terms of the treaty, Louis kept most of his previous conquests in Europe. France remained a great power in the 18th century, along with Britain which benefited greatly from the Peace of Utrecht. Although Louis's accomplishments were impressive, by 1713 the age of glory was over, and Louis's subjects were suffering for his efforts.

For the aging monarch, life was coming to an end. In retrospect, Louis commented: "I have loved war too much." But it would be wrong to suggest that he had reassessed his style of kingship.

Right to the end, Louis faced his death with the composure and dignity of a great king, taking upon himself the responsibility for the weaknesses and failures of France and suffering quietly as gangrene spread through his body. On September 1, 1715, just short of his 77th birthday, Louis XIV died. With him passed the apogee of divine right monarchy and France's era of glory.

SOURCES:

Rule, John C., ed. *Great Lives Observed: Louis XIV.* Prentice-Hall, 1974.

Stoye, John. Europe *Unfolding: 1648–1688.* Fontana Press, 1988.

Wolf, John B. *Louis XIV.* Norton, 1968.

FURTHER READING:

Erlanger, Philippe. *Louis XIV.* Translated by Stephen Cox, Praeger, 1970.

Goubert, Pierre. *Louis XIV and Twenty Million Frenchmen.* Translated by Anne Carter. Vintage Books, 1972.

Rule, John C., ed. *Louis XIV and the Craft of Kingship.* Ohio State University Press, 1969.

Sonnino, Paul, ed. *The Reign of Louis XIV.* Humanities Press International, 1990.

Treasure, G. R. R. *Seventeenth-Century France.* 2nd ed. J. Murray, 1981.

Louis XVI

(1754–1792)

Last of the French Bourbon kings before the great Revolution of 1789, who was tried for treason by the National Convention and guillotined in Paris in 1792.

"I pause before history; remember that it will judge your decision."

DE SEZE
AT THE TRAIL OF LOUIS XVI

Born at the palace of Versailles on August 23, 1754, to little fanfare, Louis-Auguste (titled the Duke of Berry) was the third son of Louis the *dauphin*, son and heir to the throne of Louis XV. Shortly, the second-born boy died and there were fears that Louis-Auguste also would not survive his infancy. Then one day in May 1761, when the eldest boy—the quick-witted and well-beloved duke of Burgundy—died from complications from an accident at play, the feeble Louis suddenly found himself next in line for the throne behind his father. This raised much concern, for the young boy lacked self-confidence and, in turn, earned more pity than respect.

Louis was not a stupid child. On the contrary, he had many talents. He enjoyed working with tools in his shop. In particular, he liked working as a locksmith, at which he gained notable proficiency. Moreover, he had a tremendous memory. His best subjects were history and languages (primarily Latin and English). But, in general, the reclusive and short-sighted Louis was a poor student, preferring to spend time alone or at play exploring the nearby woods. If Louis could be criticized, it could be only to say that he lacked imagi-

Name variations: Louis-Auguste, Duke of Berry, Citizen Capet. Born on August 23, 1754; died at the guillotine on January 21, 1792; son of Louis le dauphin, grandson of Louis XV; married: Marie-Antoinette of Austria, 1770; children: a daughter and two sons.

Contributed by Alan M. James, Ph.D., University of Manchester, Manchester, England

nation. His thinking was simply systematic and well organized.

Although he remained aloof from court politics and cultural activities considered suitable to one in such an exalted position, the young prince had a relatively clear sense of his duties. He felt mentally and emotionally unprepared for the eventual responsibility of being king, but he was principled and took his position seriously. Like his father, he was austere and religious, and he hoped to prepare himself for his future role. As a child, he wrote:

> My greatest fault is a sluggishness of mind which makes all my mental efforts wearisome and painful: I want absolutely to conquer this defect... and I shall cultivate the good things that are said to be in me.

Louis spent much time learning of the reigns of past kings. Ironically, he had an interest in Charles I of England who was executed in the English Civil War in 1649. "As for me," he said, "in the place of Charles I, I should never have drawn the sword against my people." The shy but sincere boy spoke truly, for later, even in the heat of revolution, he remained reluctant to use force to defend his legal position. "All my plans," he declared, "must be directed by the feeling of tender affection for my people."

Late in 1765, his father died, making him the immediate heir to the throne of Louis XV.

Louis was uncomfortable with this position, and upon the death of his mother sometime thereafter he felt entirely isolated and lonely. Despite his efforts to prepare himself, he still preferred the outdoors to the pressures of the court. A foreign ambassador remarked: "He seems to have been born and reared in the forest." Nevertheless, now Louis would be the next king of France and, although he never showed much interest in girls, arrangements were made with the famous **Maria Theresa of Austria** to marry him to her daughter the Habsburg princess **Marie-Antoinette.** Such a match was a necessary part of his princely duties in order to maintain relations with the powerful Habsburg family and to secure the Bourbon dynasty in France.

Louis Marries Marie–Antoinette

Thus, in 1769, when Louis was 15 years of age, final arrangements were made, and the marriage was celebrated the following year in Paris. Yet the event was marred by a sorrowful disaster: fireworks accidentally caught fire and sent the crowd that had filled the square into a stampede in which many were killed. Sympathetic to the innocent victims, Louis contributed to their relief, but many considered this a very bad omen indeed.

Louis's married life was not entirely happy. Frivolous, self-indulgent, and demanding, his bride was embarrassed with his relatively crude habits and his fondness for the outdoors, scolding him for his inability to adapt to life at court. Most humiliating for the couple, however, was Louis's impotence which was the subject of much gossip. On May 10, 1774, life became even more difficult when Louis XV died after a gruesome and painful illness. The tearful prince was now the 20-year-old king of France. "Oh God," he exclaimed, "I am the unhappiest of men!"

Later, with the encouragement of his brother-in-law, the Austrian emperor **Joseph II,** Louis agreed to undergo an operation to correct a phimosis and his sexual problems were relieved. In 1778, Marie-Antoinette gave birth to a girl; then joyously, on October 22, 1781, she gave birth to a boy—a potential heir to the throne. Despite his perceived faults and growing slovenliness which mostly irritated his wife, Louis was a popular figure among the majority of his subjects. In 1786, when he and his family took a trip to the Norman port of Cherbourg, they were greeted by jubilant crowds happy with the apparent security of the Bourbon dynasty.

HISTORIC WORLD LEADERS

Despite his popularity, France was beset with many serious problems, and although Louis was anxious to remedy them and worked hard, he was only dimly aware of what was necessary. There was certainly a growing (though not yet widespread) intellectual disaffection with the institution of absolute monarchy, as there was against the privileged aristocracy by the growing bourgeoisie (middle class). Moreover, bread riots by a hungry population, seen in retrospect, seem to have been portents of danger. Yet it was an acute fiscal crisis and the reaction of the aristocracy against the attempts of a series of ministers who were unable to effect any progressive reforms (such as more equitable taxation of the propertied elites) that led to Revolution.

Like many European countries at the time, France was carrying a huge debt and suffering financial troubles, primarily from war costs. Desperate measures were required. Yet the nobility refused any innovation on its privileges and, rather than submit to the will of the king or his ministers, insisted that an Estates General be called. A moribund legal institution that met only by the invitation of the king, the Estates-General represented each of the three major social groupings of France: the First Estate (clergy), the Second Estate (nobility), and the Third Estate (which included many wealthy professionals, merchants, and all of the commoners). The aristocracy fully expected that with one vote for each of the estates, they would be able to control the outcome of any such meeting, for many clergymen were also nobles. At first, Louis resisted attempts to manipulate his authority in this way but, because of the severity of the financial crisis, he agreed on July 5, 1788, to call the first meeting of the Estates General in France since 1614.

Because an Estates General was not at all common, there was much debate concerning proper procedure. Granting the Third Estate as many deputies as the other two estates combined, Louis invited them to bring a list of grievances, but it was unclear whether the deputies would vote by estate or by head; Louis had granted the Third Estate greater representation but not necessarily greater power. This sparked national interest about the authority those representing the vast majority of the population should have in the upcoming assembly and future government of France. Although the Third Estate was impressed with the king's goodwill, its deputies had no desire to be dominated by the privileged elites. Ominously, the fall of 1788 and the winter of 1789 were especially harsh and many people went hungry.

On May 5, 1789, the Estates met with the question of the vote unresolved, while Louis, distracted by the sudden death of his eight-year-old son, did little to relieve the tension. Insisting that each delegate should have a vote, the frustrated Third Estate declared itself the National Assembly or Constituent Assembly (*Constituante*) on June 17 and invited members of the other estates to join them. Later, when the delegates found the doors to the assembly hall locked by order of the king, they crossed the street to a tennis court and excitedly declared their resolve never to disband until they had written a new constitution for France (Tennis Court Oath). When the assembly remained defiant in the face of further concessions by Louis, he ordered troops to Versailles as a precaution.

In the countryside and in Paris, the dreadful economic conditions led to rioting, and a widespread alarm, or the "Great Fear," arose in 1789; people armed themselves as much as possible in anticipation of general violence. On July 14, a crowd came to the Bastille in search of weapons they believed were being held in the old prison. When the governor refused entry, the mob forced its way and barbarously murdered him along with his guards only to find little of value. In his diary entry for July 14, Louis entered simply that nothing had happened. Yet to be fair, Louis's diary rarely dealt with politics, as it was concerned mostly with his hunting record. Moreover, he could be excused from recognizing the symbolic significance that "Bastille Day" would hold for future generations in France.

Indeed, Louis XVI did respond to the situation. Thinking it prudent to cooperate with the angered delegates who had taken much of his power into their own hands, he ordered the two other estates to join the assembly and legally recognized it. Nevertheless, frenzied extremists and the desperation and hunger of the crowds were powerful forces. Early in October a mob, which included many women, gathered and marched to Versailles in protest. The crowd demanded that Louis and his family leave Versailles for Paris to live in the Tuileries where they were to be watched and held as virtual prisoners of the revolutionary Parisians.

The King Escapes from Paris

Eventually, Louis took bold measures against the growing impudence of his subjects and repudiated the Revolution. After writing a long denunciation of the recent events which was to be read at the assembly, he prepared his family to make a night-

Marie Antoinette

(1755–1793)

"If the people have no bread, let them eat cake..."

STATEMENT ATTRIBUTED IN DERISION TO MARIE-ANTOINETTE

Marie-Antoinette was born in Vienna on November 2, 1755, the day of the great earthquake at Lisbon. She was christened Marie-Antonia by her parents, the Austrian Empress **Maria Theresa** and Francis I. It was to be the role of the princess to foster good relations with the French crown. To this end, she was married to the future Louis XVI of France in 1770, and, in 1774, upon the death of Louis XV, became queen of France.

At first, the attractive and lively young woman made a favorable impression at the French court and with the French people. She came to enjoy giving grand balls (and gambling—to the great irritation of her husband) and often bestowed expensive favors. After the death of her mother in 1780, she led a more extravagant lifestyle of frivolous amusement and eventually became an object of deep resentment. Various scandals and suspicions that she manipulated affairs to the advantage of her native Austria added to her growing unpopularity.

After a worrisome and embarrassing period of childlessness, she finally gave birth to a daughter (1778), and two sons (1781 and 1785), and despite her reputation for frivolity, she proved a dedicated and loving mother. Indeed, it was a strong sense of principles that led to her downfall, not simply a detached carelessness.

Having learned from her time escape from Paris. On the evening of June 20, 1791, Louis and his family in disguise entered a carriage and fled toward the German frontier where he hoped to gather foreign support. Thirty miles from safety, at Varennes, the king was recognized and the carriage was escorted back to a tension-filled Paris on June 25. The flight had been a costly gamble in which Louis lost much of the public's confidence. Debate on his fate lasted through the night until it was decided that the king had in fact broken the law and was to be put under provisional arrest and held at the Tuileries. Now the radical republican voices gathered strength aided by the evident threat of foreign invasion.

Throughout these dramatic events, the assembly prepared a constitution which, it was hoped, would end the Revolution. Upon its completion in September 1791, the National Assembly was dissolved and replaced by the Legislative Assembly (*Législatif*) which would govern France as a constitutional monarchy in which Louis held a suspensive veto. Louis coolly accepted the constitution though his resolve was not entirely trusted.

Many in France favored going to war against Austria in order to strengthen the Revolution. On March 1, 1792, Leopold II of Austria died and was replaced by Francis II who was even more vitriolic against the French Revolution. Thus, in April the French government declared war, and Austrian and Prussian troops were gathered in preparation. For the radicals in the assembly, it was seen as an opportunity to accept a mission to spread the benefits of democratic revolution abroad. For Louis, it provided an indirect hope that a French defeat might reestablish his authority.

With early French losses, a dissatisfaction with the Legislative Assembly and its constitutional monarchy grew. A patriotic fervor began to grip passions. To the worried radicals the greatest traitor to the Revolution had been Louis himself, whose confidence was now growing with French weakness on the field. Indeed, he dismissed a group of appointed ministers in the assembly and replaced them with his own loyal servants. Thus, on June 20, 1792, an armed crowd gathered in protest at the Tuileries palace and some, who forced their way inside, threatened violence against the royal family. Louis faced the intruders alone and with his calm and assured demeanor was able to avert immediate disaster.

Nevertheless, on July 25, 1792, the duke of Brunswick, who commanded the Prussian army, issued a manifesto warning the French that they would be destroyed if the royal family were hurt in any way. Patriotic passions were inflamed, but the assembly was reluctant to concede to growing pressure to remove the head of state as defined in the new constitution upon which their power was based. On the evening of August 9, 1792, the Revolution became violent as the streets of Paris were alive with enraged mobs that attacked the Tuileries. The royal family, fearful for their lives, fled to the assembly for safety where they huddled in an uncomfortable cell listening to the murderous rioting in the streets by the citizens of Paris. Those who remained behind to defend the palace were brutally killed.

Yet the assembly had lost control. Under pressure from the roused crowd and the insurrectionary municipal Paris Commune, the assembly provi-

mother conservative tenets of government, Marie was a staunch absolutist (believing that absolute power should be in the hands of one ruler). After the outbreak of Revolution in 1789, she became more powerful politically by exerting a conservative influence on her husband, Louis XVI. She resisted Louis's attempts at reform and dissuaded him from cooperating at all with the moderate revolutionaries whom she called a "collection of scoundrels, lunatics, and beasts."

Marie longed for foreign intervention against the French Revolution to restore power to the crown. To this end, she was involved in arranging the ill-fated flight to Varennes of 1791 and welcomed the Brunswick Manifesto of 1792. Marie shared none of the popularity of Louis XVI, and when the extravagant, meddlesome foreign queen was brought to trial, her fate was sealed. On October 16, 1793, she was found guilty and sentenced to public execution which she suffered that day. The resentful Marie-Antoinette met her death confident that she was innocent and simply had maintained her dignity and principles throughout an unspeakably horrible Revolution.

SOURCES:

Loomis, Stanley. *The Fatal Friendship: Marie Antoinette, Count Fersen and the Flight to Varennes*. Doubleday, 1972.

Mayer, Dorothy Moulton. *Marie Antoinette: The Tragic Queen*. Coward-McCann, 1968.

FURTHER READING:

Erickson, Carolly. *To the Scaffold: The Life of Marie-Antoinette*. Morrow, 1991.

Haslip, Joan. *Marie Antoinette*. Weidenfeld & Nicolson, 1987.

Seward, Desmond. *Marie Antoinette*. Constable, 1981.

sionally suspended Louis's power on August 10, 1792. With remarkable resignation, Louis was taken through jeering crowds to await his fate. He and his family were imprisoned in the Temple Tower, a dank and filthy dungeon. Meanwhile the fury of the crowds was not abated, and on September 2, French forces fell to an advancing Prussian army at Verdun. A wave of violence again fell upon the city as hundreds of suspected counterrevolutionaries were murdered.

Unfortunately for Louis, on September 20 the National Convention (*Convention Nationale*) replaced the weak Legislative Assembly, the very day the French army won an inspirational victory by checking the Prussian invasion. Its first act was formally to abolish the monarchy on September 22, 1792. France became a republic, and Louis the Last—or Citizen Capet, as he was then called—was in grave danger. In December, he was brought to trial and removed from his family while the convention debated the now deposed king's future. Twice he appeared before the convention in his own defense, responding to the many accusations brought against him with remarkable poise and calm which engendered a surprising degree of sympathy. Although he was declared guilty "of conspiracy against public liberty and the general security of the state," the question of sentencing was much more difficult. Nevertheless, on January 19, with a very slim majority, Louis was sentenced to immediate execution.

The next day, Louis was allowed to speak with his family for the last time before preparing himself with prayer for his death, and in his final night the imperturbable Louis slept soundly, convinced that he had only acted out of concern for his subjects. On January 21, 1793, he was brought to the Place de la Revolution where he demonstrated incredible courage, wishing only to depart with the dignity befitting his position. He removed his own jacket and removed his own shirt in preparation for the blade of the guillotine. In his final act, he yelled to the crowd: "I die innocent of all charges brought against me."

With his death, France lost a beloved king who had wished for nothing more than to do his duty to the subjects whose welfare had been entrusted to him. Soon France would suffer through the most extreme and violent phase of the bloody French Revolution.

SOURCES:

Fay, Bernard. *Louis XVI or the End of a World*. Translated by Patrick O'Brian. Regnery, 1968.

Padover, Saul K. *The Life and Death of Louis XVI*. Taplinger, 1963.

FURTHER READING:

Cronin, Vincent. *Louis and Antoinette*. Collins, 1974.

Jordan, David P. *The King's Trial: The French Revolution vs. Louis XVI*. University of California Press, 1979.

Walzer, Michael. *Regicide and Revolution: Speeches at the Trial of Louis XVI*. Cambridge University Press, 1974.

Ignatius Loyola

(c. 1491–1556)

Former soldier and founder of the Society of Jesus (Jesuits), who lived a life of prodigious self-mortification, created an organization of "Christian soldiers," and played a vital role in the Catholic Counter-Reformation of the 16th Century.

Name variations: Ignatius of Loyola, Ignatius de Loyola, Inigo Lopez de Recalde. Born Inigo (youngest of 13 brothers and sisters) in c. 1491 in Guipuzcoa, Spain, part of the Basque country in the Pyrénées mountains; died in 1556; son of Don Beltran de Loyola and Doña Marina of Azcoitia. Successor: Diego Lainez.

Inigo of Loyola was born in c. 1491, in Guipuzcoa, part of the Basque country on the Spanish side of the Pyrénées mountains. A vain and worldly young soldier who loved courtly romance and a life of adventure, he suffered a traumatic wound at the battle of Pamplona in 1521 and, while recuperating, turned his mind to religion. For the next two decades, he wandered penniless through Europe, made a pilgrimage to Jerusalem, studied for the priesthood in Paris, and spread his spiritual example to a growing number of followers. His *Spiritual Exercises,* containing methods of prayer and religious self-discipline, became the handbook of the Jesuit order, while his frequent visions of Jesus and the Virgin Mary enhanced his reputation for saintliness. The order which he founded in 1540 spread throughout Europe, gained great political and religious influence, and became the intellectual powerhouse of Counter-Reformation Catholicism.

In 1521, the 30-year-old Inigo of Loyola had been defending Pamplona (in northeastern Spain) against French attackers in one of the recurrent Franco-Spanish wars of the 16th century. The other defenders, recognizing their posi-

"He turned the reforming process on its head by translating the Lutheran doctrine of justification by faith into the principle of absolute obedience to the Church; this for him became the credal hinge, and the certain guarantee of salvation."

PAUL JOHNSON

Contributed by Patrick Allitt, Assistant Professor of History, Emory University, Atlanta, Georgia

tion as hopeless, had urged their commander to surrender, but Loyola's passionate appeals for a heroic defense changed his commander's mind. Loyola led the soldiers until a cannonball hit him in the legs, smashing the right and gashing the left. When he fell, the garrison surrendered, but the French victors, knowing Loyola by reputation, took good care of the severely wounded man and did what they could to set his bones, bandage his wounds, and send him home to recover.

Loyola wanted to pass the time of convalescence reading romances and indulging his chivalric dreams, but when he found that only lives of the saints were available, he turned to them for lack of anything more exciting. He remembered later that his worldly daydreams, pleasant enough at the time, had left a bitter aftertaste, whereas his religious reveries had filled him with joy. He concluded that the first pleasures came from the devil, the second from God. This period of enforced meditation had a profound effect on him and led him to conceive the arduous project of making a pilgrimage to Jerusalem. First, however, he learned that his bones were not setting properly. Rather than go through life disfigured and limping, he ordered that the bones be rebroken, a bone spur sawn off, and the bones reset, despite the incredible pain and the risk of infection.

Loyola Begins Life of Asceticism

Recuperating, Loyola began the life of asceticism for which his Jesuit followers later honored him. He sometimes went days at a time without food, walked barefoot in winter, and deliberately neglected his long hair, of which he had earlier been proud, until it was matted and filthy. He wore a hair shirt and sometimes a nail-studded belt turned inward to his body. The effect of these torments was to weaken him and give him a pale and haggard appearance (which terrified both strangers and acquaintances) and to give him a lifelong succession of gastric problems and stomach pains. After a period of time in Manresa, Spain, where he spent six or more hours a day in prayer and a few hours a day begging for alms, he worked in hospitals, caring for the poor. He had sold all his property and given away the proceeds to the poor. As a local nobleman, however, Loyola was still well known, and his status, along with his growing spiritual reputation, led to frequent invitations to other nobles' houses to dine and to give religious instruction. He would no longer stay with the nobility, however, but retired to humble lodgings to sleep.

An intensely introspective man, he tried to confess and do penance for all the sins of his earlier

life but found the act of enumerating them almost impossible. When a confessor suggested writing them out, Loyola worked diligently at this task but found the list lengthening without end. His excessively scrupulous behavior, and his efforts to deal with it, formed part of the background of his *Spiritual Exercises*. This short but influential book, the product of his meditations, is a guide to retreat directors, and outlines a 30-day regimen of prayer and self-abasement, with the understanding that in all one's doings prayer and mindfulness of God must be central. One characteristic passage reads:

> Take O Lord, and receive all my liberty; my memory, my understanding, and all my will; all I have and possess. Thou hast given it all to me; to Thee, 0 Lord, I restore it; all is Thine; dispose of it according to Thy will. Give me Thy love and Thy grace, for this is enough for me.

Loyola now made good on his plan to visit Jerusalem and persuaded a ship's captain to take him on board at Barcelona en route to Italy, though he had no money for his passage. He took food only reluctantly, seeing starvation during the voyage as another opportunity for self-mortification. After begging in Italy, he took a ship from Venice to Cyprus, then Cyprus to Syria, and walked from there to Jerusalem to visit the Holy Places, all of which were in Turkish hands. He asked the handful of Christian guardians of the Holy Places whether they would permit him to remain near the sites of Christ's life and death, but fearful that his militant zeal would antagonize the Turks, they denied his request. After a farewell visit to the Mount of Olives to see what were alleged to be Jesus' footprints, he tried to find passage home, again "for the love of God" rather than for money. A large Venetian ship and a large Turkish ship both refused him and sank a few days later in a Mediterranean storm, whereas the smaller ship he *did* take weathered the storm and returned him safe to Venice. This good fortune on a hazardous voyage, as well as several more visions of Jesus, maintained his confidence and became the basis of legends of his sanctity. Further maltreatment at the hands of soldiers and citizens in Italy set him on his way back to Spain, where his work in hospitals and his simple preaching once more drew attention.

The 1520s were the decade when the Reformation began in earnest, as much of Germany—for both religious and political reasons—turned to **Martin Luther**'s Protestant alternative to Catholicism. Germany and Spain were then ruled by the same man, the emperor **Charles V.** Unable to stop the spread of Protestantism in Germany, Charles and the Inquisition stamped it out early in Spain. Loyola, though he does not appear to have known about Luther, was suspected by some Spanish religious authorities of being a heretic, and on several occasions he was imprisoned without trial or formal accusation. He always sought out his inquisitors and insisted on a judgment; usually he was found blameless despite his unconventional practices.

The Inquisition was powerful and merciless in the Spain of the 16th century. Under its influence, the forced conversion of Moorish Spaniards and the expulsion of the Jews had followed on the reunification of Spain at the end of the 15th century; at autos-da-fe ("acts of the faith"), the Inquisition paraded sinners in penitential clothes and burned at the stake those condemned as heretics.

Loyola was, to say the least, an unconventional prisoner during his several stays in jail; he made no effort to get a lawyer and refused to complain even when his imprisonment was arbitrary. On one occasion, the inmates of the prison broke out, and all but Loyola and one of his followers escaped. Finding them still in their cell with the door wide open the next day, more of the local citizens began to believe in Loyola's reputation for fearlessness and sanctity. Meanwhile a growing number of townspeople in Alcala, Barcelona, and Manresa, the towns he frequented, were learning of his spiritual gifts and his visions of Jesus and were becoming his followers. When several high-born women followed his example of turning to alms-begging, Loyola had to endure allegations that he was a seducer, but in every case he was able to show himself blameless.

Repeated challenges by inquisitors led Loyola to conclude that he ought to be a fully educated priest rather than a marginal hermit and preacher; to gain a belated education, he went to Paris, then the center of Catholic learning in Europe. Again he lived on alms, begged in Flanders and England between academic sessions, and studied continuously, fighting off the religious visions which distracted his attention from lectures. By his example, he soon converted three eminent Spanish students at the college who gave away all their property, even their books, and began begging for alms. Many of the Spaniards in Paris were angered and denounced Ignatius to the College Rector, who ordered him to be flogged. Ignatius, far from shrinking from the ordeal, welcomed it as an opportunity to suffer for Christ but found nevertheless that he was quaking with fear. He steadied himself with a reminder of the need to suffer but still was not sure whether to protest. His autobiography, as told to a fellow Jesuit in 1553, explains why:

> In that hour two spirits were in combat in the soul of Inigo, which, though seemingly contrary, directed him to the same end. The love of God and a burning desire to suffer pains and insults for the sake of the name of Jesus Christ moved him to offer himself joyfully to the infamy and the flogging; on the other hand, the self-same love of God, coupled with love of his neighbor and zeal for souls, told him otherwise. 'It is good for me to suffer thus, he told himself, but how about its effect on those just begun to live a new life? Will the sight of this make them turn back from the road to heaven, they who have gone only a little way?

Finally the second desire won out; he went to the college rector, explained what had happened, and won an apology; in fact, the rector later told King John III of Portugal that the Jesuits, the order created by his former student, should be entrusted with the task of converting the inhabitants of the Americas and the Far East.

He Meets the Men
Who Form the Nucleus of Jesuits

While in Paris, Loyola met six of the men who were to form the nucleus of the Jesuits, among them a skillful Greek scholar named Pierre Favre, and an athlete and reveler named **Francis Xavier,** both two decades his junior. He persuaded them to follow his example of fasting and prayer, as laid out in his *Spiritual Exercises*. Xavier, though he was the last to succumb, was ultimately the most ardent. "He not only fasted severely but trussed his limbs up so tightly, mindful of the pride he took in his former vaulting on the Ile de Paris; so tightly did he tie himself with ropes that he was unable to move and made the meditations thus trussed." Xavier was to be the first Jesuit missionary to India and Japan between 1542 and his death in 1552.

His 14 years of fasting, flagellation, and other self-inflicted sufferings had finally made Loyola so ill that he was told by doctors that only through a return to his home and a complete rest was there any possibility of his survival. Before leaving, he again learned that he was the subject of heresy rumors. When he asked the chief inquisitor of Paris whether or not he was to be tried, the inquisitor reassured him and even asked for a copy of the *Spiritual Exercises* for his own edification. Blessed and relieved, Loyola prepared to travel home. His followers in Paris bought him a donkey, and on it he undertook the 555-mile journey back to the Basque country of Spain, anything but a restful journey. Arriving home at Azpeitia without mishap, he disdained an invitation from his family to stay with them, going instead to the local poorhouse where he again began to preach. His brother, a nobleman to whom Loyola was a source of disappointment and embarrassment, told him that no one would come to listen to him but was soon proven wrong. By the middle of 1535, the year of his homecoming, Loyola had huge crowds listening to him each day. There are detailed records of this period in his life because, in 1595, when the Church was considering making him a saint, it interviewed numerous men and women who, 60 years earlier, had witnessed Loyola's preaching and remembered his work in Azpeitia; several claimed miraculous cures by his intercession, and many recalled that he had had the gift of settling arguments between husbands and wives or fathers and sons. He had even converted the three town prostitutes who pledged themselves to a life of virtue and set off on a pilgrimage to Jerusalem.

Loyola left his home and Spain shortly afterwards, never to return. After visiting the families of his companions from Paris, he boarded a ship to Genoa, despite the risk of the pirate captain Barbarossa, who was then terrorizing the Mediterranean. The ship lost its rudder in a storm and seemed in imminent danger of sinking. Loyola "examined his conscience and prepared himself for death, having neither fear because of his past sins nor dread of the condemnation they deserved, but being filled with great sorrow and confusion for not having employed well the graces and gifts God had given him." In retrospect—for the ship made it to Genoa and offered him more time to reflect—he was ashamed to discover that he had been confident, when death was close, that he *would* go to

Heaven. His pride in this faith, typically, made him penitent and prayerful.

He went from Genoa to Venice and was rejoined by his handful of followers in 1537. They had *walked* from Paris, enduring severe winter storms on their 54-day march, and witnessing, in south Germany and Switzerland, communities of Protestants who had left in disgust the Church to which these men were devoting their lives. En route several had fallen sick; Francis Xavier had again bound ropes around his legs as a penance; they were so tight that they bit into his flesh as he walked and led him to collapse before the others discovered this self-mutilation.

Ignatius Loyola, who changed his given name as a way of honoring one of the early Church martyrs, Saint Ignatius of Antioch, was at last ordained a priest in 1537 and applied to the pope for his group to make a pilgrimage to Jerusalem; he hoped they might remain there as hospital workers. The pope, Paul III, was delighted by the group's zeal and funded their planned journey, though Turkish pirates in the Mediterranean prevented any pilgrim ships from setting sail that year. Since 1537 was the only year for half a century that pilgrim ships did not leave Venice for Syria, the "Company of Jesus"—as they now called themselves—took it as an omen that their future work did not lie in the Holy Land. Apart from short excursions, Loyola spent the rest of his life within Italy.

Rome, like much of Italy, was in need of both material and spiritual reform. The Protestant Reformation was a response to widespread and genuine abuses: the buying and selling of Church offices, indulgences, and relics, and the promotion of family members to high Church positions by influential families, whatever their merits (an abuse known as simony). The popes were members of feuding families: Sforza, Borgia, Farnese, and others. Repeatedly since 1500, Italy had been swept by warring armies which brought famine and plague in their wake. In 1527, Rome itself had been sacked, plundered, and half burned down by a mutinous army of the Holy Roman Emperor Charles V, leading Pope Clement VII to flee for his life from his fellow Catholics. Witnessing the disarray in Italy, Loyola, whose eyes had until now been fixed on a return to the Holy Land, finally realized an opportunity closer to home and called all his companions from around Italy to join him in Rome.

The time had come, he told them, to establish an order "to the end of time," though it was to be one which differed in vital ways from the older orders of the Church (Benedictines, Carthusians, Franciscans, Dominicans, and others). First, it was to be unquestioningly loyal to the papacy; second, it did not plan to live a monastic life with regular hours of prayer and choral singing; and, third, it was to exalt the doctrine of obedience to an extraordinary degree. (One of the oldest Jesuit tales is of the mortally ill novice on his death bed asking the novice-master for permission to die.) The organization's task was to act as "trumpeters of Christ," to undertake varied work throughout Christendom as the pope should require; its individuals were to be made strong and adaptable by their lives of prayer and self-surrender and to be tempered through a very long training period to a life of total obedience.

At first some influential Roman clergy opposed the unfamiliar form of the new order. One cardinal commented that there were already far too many religious orders which squabbled with one another and with the secular clergy, leading the laity to grow impatient with them all and to turn anticlerical. The pope, however, finally agreed with Loyola that the proposal deserved his endorsement, and in his bull *Regimini Militantis Ecclesiae* of 1540, he canonically established the Society of Jesus. Loyola drafted the *Constitutions* of the order the next year but was slow to put them into a finished form, and they did not take final effect until after his death in 1556.

On April 27, 1541, despite his protest of unworthiness, Loyola was made the first superior general of the Jesuits and, with his companions, visited the seven churches of Rome where together they took their vows, which emphasized obedience to the pope, special work in educating children in the Catholic faith, and a willingness to travel anywhere in the world for the sake of the faith.

Society of Jesus Becomes Influential in Church

In the last decade of his life, Loyola saw his order become a significant force in the life of the Catholic Church and grow from his original ten followers to more than a thousand. Several of the highly skilled theologians among the new Jesuits acted as experts at the Council of Trent by which the Catholic Church tried to reform itself and to respond to the Protestant challenge. Pierre Favre, one of his earliest companions, was the first Jesuit to go to Germany, where he advocated reconciliation with Protestants rather than conflict. Some Jesuits became missionaries to the New World and others to Poland, which reverted to Catholicism after a flirtation with Protestantism. The Jesuits also moved early into the field of education, founding colleges in Italy, Portugal, the Netherlands, Spain, Germany, and India; these became the nucleus of an educational apparatus persisting up to the present and transforming the Jesuits from guardians of the poor into educators of the rich and powerful. "In fact," says historian Paul Johnson, "they were rather like a modern multinational company selling expert services. And they brought to the business of international schooling a uniformity, discipline, and organization that was quite new."

By keeping the sympathy of successive popes, Ignatius was also able to improve conditions nearer to home. He set up a house, St. Martha's, in Rome, as a refuge for reforming prostitutes, inspiring several noblewomen to help in the work. As a result, says historian Mary Purcell:

> for months the piazza in front of the Magdalen home was packed each night with a mob yelling threats and obscenities; Loyola and the Companions were vilely calumniated, in particular by one Cassiano, Master of the Pontifical Post, who went so far as to force his way into the chapel of St. Martha's and drag Father de Eguia from the confessional, threatening to use his influence to destroy the house and its work of reform if a certain penitent did not return to him and her former life.

Loyola did not relent and again got a judicial decision in his favor and a threat of excommunication against Cassiano.

Loyola worked a 20-hour day for most of the last 15 years of his life, interrupting it only in the face of increasingly severe illnesses, all made worse by his self-imposed austerities. He finally died after a day of hard work in the summer of 1556. At his postmortem, doctors discovered that he had been suffering for years from cirrhosis of the liver and from gallstones which must have caused constant severe pain, but about which he had almost never complained.

His entire life after his wounding had been devoted to overturning conventional conduct in pursuit of holiness. Self-consciously abandoning the decorous manners and speech with which he had grown up, seeking out hunger, pain, and poverty instead of plenitude, comfort, and wealth, he was nevertheless a severely orthodox man. He tried to *avoid* challenging Catholic dogma and always knew how to stay on the right side of his religious superiors. Ignatius Loyola was made a saint in 1622, by which time his organization had become the single most powerful weapon of the Catholic Counter-Reformation.

SOURCES:

Gonzalez de Camera, Luis. *St. Ignatius' Own Story, As Told to Luis Gonzalez de Camera.* Regnery, 1956.

Johnson, Paul. *History of Christianity. Atheneum,* 1979.

Purcell, Mary. *The First Jesuit: Saint Ignatius of Loyola.* Loyola University Press, 1981.

FURTHER READING:

Brodrick, James, S.J. *The Origin of the Jesuits.* London, 1940.

Thompson, Francis. *St. Ignatius Loyola.* Burns & Oats, 1962.

_____

Erich Ludendorff

(1865–1937)

First quartermaster general of the German army in World War I, who was responsible for Germany's only major victory.

Name variations: Erich von Ludendorff. Pronunciation: LOO'-den-dorf. Born Erich Friedrich Wilhelm Ludendorff in the Polish area of eastern Germany in 1865; died in Munich, Germany, in 1937; son of a cavalry officer and an aristocrat.

Born in 1865 in a largely Polish area of the imperial German province of Posen, Erich Ludendorff was destined to serve in the Prussian army. His father had been a cavalry officer, as had his aristocratic mother's father. There was unhappily little money; Erich's father, after resigning his commission, had been an unsuccessful and eventually bankrupt landlord. While still a boy, Ludendorff won a scholarship to one of the Prussian state military academies, and on his graduation in 1882 entered the army, eventually being commissioned an infantry lieutenant. Considered a promising officer, he was assigned to the General Staff in 1894, and with few interruptions spent the rest of his prewar career there.

A bullnecked, glowering, joyless man of furious energy, Ludendorff lived only for the army, admitting that he had no other interests and unwilling even to read anything that was not martial in subject. He matured into a man of undoubted military competence but also of very limited vision, understanding nothing of economics, politics, or diplomacy. He was convinced that he was capable of leadership, not only of military affairs but of politics and diplomacy as well.

"Every human life is war in miniature. In internal affairs, the political parties fight for power just as in diplomacy the great powers do so. This will always be the case because it is the law of nature. Enlightenment and moral excellence can make the struggle for power more humane but never eliminate it, for to do so would act against human nature itself. Human nature is war."

ERICH LUDENDORFF

Contributed by Lamar Cecil, William R. Kenan, Jr. Professor of History, Washington and Lee University, Lexington, Virginia

Abrupt, unpleasant, autocratic, he was not an easy officer to serve, nor did he gladly take orders from superiors. Ludendorff's technical competence, which could not be questioned, won him many admirers, but he lacked the charismatic gifts necessary in great leaders. For a devoted soldier, Ludendorff was curiously ridden with anxiety, and throughout his life moments of crisis often led to serious nervous prostration, a problem which further complicated his ability to lead.

By 1908, Ludendorff had become head of the mobilization and deployment division of the General Staff, and as such had to develop the army's course of action in the event of war with France. The German plan, which called for a lightning assault on France by means of an invasion of neutral Belgium, had been designed by Field Marshal Count Alfred von Schlieffen, the chief of the General Staff until 1905, a man under whom Ludendorff served for many years and for whom he had vast admiration. When the First World War broke out in August 1914, Ludendorff was serving as the commander of an infantry brigade stationed on the French frontier. He was responsible for the initial victory by Germany in the war, the seizure of the supposedly impregnable Belgian fortress of Liege just four days after the opening of hostilities. This was the first, and as it happened, almost the last, defeat the kaiser's army inflicted on the enemy, and it guaranteed Ludendorff a measure of fame that few other generals won. Overnight Ludendorff became a celebrated man, and it was clear to Field Marshal **Helmuth von Moltke,** Schlieffen's successor as chief of the General Staff, that Ludendorff's talents should be moved to the eastern front.

Although Tsar **Nicholas II**'s army was immense, the German General Staff had underestimated its ability. There was therefore considerable shock when the advancing Russian army penetrated to within a hundred miles of Berlin. On August 21, 1914, Ludendorff was appointed chief of staff to the commander of the 8th army, the major component of the kaiser's effort to turn back the Russians. There was, however, no commanding general under whom Ludendorff was to serve, for one had been dismissed for failing to defeat the invading Russians, and no successor had yet been appointed.

Moltke had been unable to find a suitable figure among the active generals under his command. He needed first of all an aristocrat, for only nobles commanded the kaiser's armies. That meant that Ludendorff himself had to take the secondary position of chief of staff. The second condition was that the commanding general must

permit Ludendorff to issue the army's orders. Moltke decided to call out of retirement General **Paul von Hindenburg,** who was almost 68, a man whose iron nerves were superior to Ludendorff's but who had little desire to be responsible for day-to-day decisions. Hindenburg accepted the appointment and left for the eastern front, meeting Ludendorff for the first time on the train that took them to their destination in eastern Germany.

Germans Defeat Russians at Tannenberg

Ludendorff and Hindenburg proved to be an admirable team, with Ludendorff devising strategy and Hindenburg willingly giving his assent. No sooner had the pair arrived at headquarters than Ludendorff began issuing orders to their army to attack the Russians, a process that started five days later and that resulted in the most spectacular military victory achieved by imperial Germany in the course of the war. This was the celebrated battle of Tannenberg, fought to drive the Russians out of Prussia. This extraordinary victory, which Ludendorff was unable to celebrate because of the state of his nerves, stood in singular contrast to the miserably unsuccessful campaigns being waged by Germany along the western front in France and Belgium, contests that cost hundreds of thousands of lives but that did not allow the Germans to make significant advances. In the East, not only did Tannenberg rid Germany of the Russian occupiers, but the tsar's army was pursued deep into Russia. Hindenburg and Ludendorff, who were celebrated as national heroes after Tannenberg,

were increasingly regarded as the combination that might make victory possible in the West. In 1916, after a disastrous German attempt to take the French fortress of Verdun, Kaiser **Wilhelm II** decided to make Hindenburg, whom he had meanwhile elevated to field marshal, chief of the General Staff and Ludendorff his "first quartermaster general." If Hindenburg carried off the glory, it was Ludendorff who, with the field marshal's permission, ran the show.

In Ludendorff's opinion, Germany needed to be ruthless, for only strength told in war. For pacifists, proponents of a negotiated peace, or the fainthearted, he had pointed contempt. War, he believed, brought out what was humankind's essential character. "Nature is battle!," he proclaimed without embarrassment or concern. It was the civilian government, Ludendorff was persuaded, that prevented his exercising the sort of brutal war that would win. That being the case, it would have to be replaced and more pliable figures put in office. It did not prove difficult for Ludendorff to persuade Hindenburg that this was so. One by one, they toppled statesmen in Berlin who opposed their notion of the conduct of the war, especially the unrestricted employment of submarine warfare, which Ludendorff (following Admiral von Tirpitz's conviction) felt would swiftly "bring England to her knees." The ultimate victim in Ludendorff's campaign was the imperial chancellor, Theobald von Bethmann Hollweg, who had opposed submarines and favored a negotiated peace. In July 1917, Hindenburg and Ludendorff confronted the kaiser, threatening to resign if Bethmann were not immediately dismissed. Wilhelm II capitulated, and a nonentity replaced the chancellor. From that moment until almost the end of the war, imperial Germany was a military dictatorship under Ludendorff, with Hindenburg his compliant associate and the kaiser virtually removed from his traditional position of authority.

Once completely in charge, Ludendorff favored a massive effort in the West to win the war. The eastern theater had been eliminated by the collapse of imperial Russia in March 1917. After Tsar Nicholas II's abdication, a socialist government had attempted to continue Russia's participation in the war. To thwart this opposition, Ludendorff arranged that **Vladimir Lenin,** the Bolshevik leader in exile in Switzerland who insisted on Russia's immediate withdrawal from the war, be allowed to cross Germany and make his way to Russia through Sweden. This Lenin did aboard a sealed train, arriving at Petrograd and seizing power in November 1917. In March 1918, Lenin signed a peace treaty with Germany that surrendered most of southern Russia to the kaiser.

Ludendorff could now concentrate on the West. His position, which he always persuaded Hindenburg to authorize, was the maximum employment of German forces to breach the Allied line, no matter the cost in human lives. Not only did Germany have to have victory, but it had to be accomplished swiftly. The United States, offended by the sinking of ships carrying American citizens by German submarines, had declared war on Germany in April 1917 and was sending increasing numbers of men to join the French and British in the trenches along the western front. In March 1918, the great campaign began and for a month or so appeared likely to succeed, but Germany's capacity for war had been seriously undermined by four years of fighting, and Ludendorff was unable to sustain his advance.

Ludendorff Flees to Sweden

By late September, Ludendorff realized that all was lost. The result was a nervous breakdown serious enough to warrant bringing a psychiatrist to headquarters. Only Ludendorff's discovery of the draconian terms President **Woodrow Wilson** required for an armistice restored his nerve. He insisted that Germany fight on, somehow assembling troops and materiél, although the economy was in ruins and the population on the brink of revolution. The civilian government in Berlin, anxious not to offend Wilson, insisted that the kaiser dismiss Ludendorff but not the more decorous and less volatile Hindenburg, and at the end of October 1918 Ludendorff was relieved. When the armistice came into effect on November 11; Ludendorff, distraught and bitter, fled in disguise to Sweden, where he remained until the spring of 1919.

Ludendorff blamed Germany's disgrace and collapse on everyone but himself. It was the Jews, the Freemasons, the Jesuits, the socialists, the war profiteers, but not the Allied armies who had defeated the Fatherland. The kaiser's army, Ludendorff argued, would have been invincible but for this betrayal and but for the fact that he had been dismissed. He was absolutely certain after 1918 that he had been the kaiser's authentic genius, and that, unlike those who had sold Germany out, he was the embodiment of "Nordic" virtues. With the cooperation of his second wife, like his mother an aristocrat, Ludendorff in the 1920s developed a pseudoreligious cult that was both anti-Christian and anti-Semitic and which at first had some support among Ludendorff's loyal veterans. Gradually, however, Ludendorff's eccentricity and ferocious dictatorial nature made his cult unpopular, and it was increasingly dismissed as little more than an exhibition of vanity and frustration.

Meanwhile, Ludendorff had become involved in a number of movements that were dedicated to the overthrow of the socialist government which had been established on the kaiser's abdication in November 1918. It was Ludendorff's hope that the monarchy might be reestablished, the army rebuilt, and Germany's position as a great power reasserted. After a number of unsuccessful attempts, Ludendorff gravitated into the National Socialist movement, which by 1923 had been taken over by **Adolf Hitler.** Ludendorff saw in Hitler the future führer, the leader who could restore Germany to greatness. At that point a minor figure, Hitler welcomed the support of an authentic military hero, the only one who had thus far gravitated to the Nazi movement. Ludendorff became a highly visible presence in Hitler's stormy public activity, and he was at Hitler's side in the abortive putsch in November 1923 in a Munich beer hall. The Nazis hoped this would be the first step in their ascent to power, but a weakness of nerve on Hitler's part, as well as on Ludendorff's, caused the effort to fail. Hitler was jailed, but Ludendorff, because of his wartime reputation, was not punished. In the following year, the general won election to the Parliament as a Nazi and served with no great distinction until 1928. By this time, Ludendorff's enthusiasm for Hitler had begun to cool. The führer had his own racist ideas and, with his increasing popularity, no longer needed Ludendorff's military reputation or his meager following of devoted Nordic worshippers.

With his resignation from Parliament in 1928, Ludendorff's role in German history ended. Although he survived for another decade writing books and lecturing to shrinking audiences on his Nordic ideas, no one paid much attention—least of all Hitler. In spite of purging many enemies, the German leader left Ludendorff alone, not because he was dangerous but because he was insignificant. Imperial Germany's great military hero, spurned by his fellow Germans who had found a führer who promised them the victory of which Ludendorff felt he had been cheated, died at the end of 1937, unmourned and almost forgotten.

SOURCES:

Gatzke, Hans W. *Germany's Drive to the West.* 1950.
Goodspeed, D. J. *Ludendorff.* 1966.
Ludendorff, Erich. *Kriegführung und Politik.*

FURTHER READING:

Craig, Gordon A. *The Politics of the Prussian Army, 1640–1945.* 1956.
Falls, Cyril. *The Great War, 1914–1918.* 1959.
Tuchman, Barbara. *The Guns of August.* Macmillan, 1962.

Martin Luther

(1483–1546)

German theologian, who suggested that the Bible, not the Church hierarchy, was the final authority on all matters of faith, thereby shattering the unity of the medieval church and triggering a movement that greatly influenced the course of modern educational, social, economic and political thought.

Born on November 10, 1483, in Eisleben, Saxony (modern Germany); died on October 30, 1546, in Eisleben; son of Hans and Margaret Luther; education: B.A. and M.A. degrees from the University of Erfurt; married: Katherine von Bora (a former Cistercian nun), 1525; children: six.

The world into which Martin Luther was born on November 10, 1483, was in great turmoil. The 15th and 16th centuries were a period of transition from the Middle Ages, an "Age of Faith," to the modern era. Medieval man's worldview underwent radical change in response to new discoveries in every area of life. By the end of the 15th century, the Portuguese had rounded the Cape of Good Hope, and Columbus had discovered the New World. Renaissance humanists freed scholarship and the arts from Church sponsorship. In so doing, they not only rediscovered the individual but also challenged the blind acceptance of authority and encouraged the individual search for truth through reason. In 1543, just three years before Luther's death, Nicolaus Copernicus, a Polish astronomer, suggested that the sun, not the earth, was the center of the universe. Man, once the glory of God's creation, was becoming a solitary figure on an insignificant planet revolving around one of an unknowable number of similar suns.

In such an atmosphere of change, the Luthers were a very typical medieval family. They "reared their son," writes historian Peter J. Klassen,

"[Martin Luther] not only changed the map of Europe, he also redirected the way people thought of themselves, their fellows, and the world about them."

WILLIAM FLEMING

Contributed by Paul R. Waibel, Associate Professor of History, Liberty University, Lynchburg, Virginia

824

"in an atmosphere of rigorous discipline, devout piety, and a generous dose of medieval superstition." Pious, uncultivated, and of peasant background, Hans and Margaret Luther had great hopes for their gifted and studious son. Young Martin excelled as a student. In 1501, he enrolled at the University of Erfurt, one of the oldest and most prestigious universities in Germany. Within four years, he earned both the B.A. and M.A. degrees. In 1505, he had just begun the study of law and was on his way to a career in service to the Church or one of the many German princes, when he abandoned the university for the disciplined life of the monastery.

Returning to the university from a visit with his parents on July 2, 1505, Luther was caught in a thunderstorm. Frightened when lightning struck nearby, he cried out to his patron saint: "Save me, Saint Anne, and I will become a monk." Just two weeks later, Luther entered the cloister of the Eremites of St. Augustine in Erfurt, "noted for its strict discipline and academic vigor." Within a year, he took his final vows, was ordained, and performed his first Mass.

But Luther was no ordinary monk. He was a deeply troubled individual. The medieval church taught that the institutional church stood as an intermediary between the individual and God. The Church ministered salvation to repentant sinners through the sacraments, most notably the Mass, or Holy Eucharist. Also, the Church taught that the individual could, indeed must, by his own free will, love and serve God so as to merit (earn) the favor (salvation) of God. In short, the individual participated in his own salvation through good works. Although such teachings brought comfort to many, for Brother Martin, in his words, "day and night there was nothing but horror and despair."

Luther's problem was that no matter how hard he "worked" at earning his salvation, he could not find any peace with God. All his efforts to appease God led only to physical and emotional exhaustion. Later, in 1538, he wrote of his years as a monk:

> I was indeed a pious monk and kept the rules of my order so strictly that I can say: If ever a monk gained heaven through monkery, it should have been I. . . . I would have martyred myself to death with fasting, praying, reading, and other good works had I remained a monk much longer.

Luther found the answer to his spiritual problem sometime during the fall of 1515. By then he was a professor of theology at the University of

CHRONOLOGY

1483	Born in Eisleben, Saxony
1505	Ordained a priest
1512	Became professor at University of Wittenberg
1517	Posted "95 Theses" on church door; Protestant Reformation began
1519	Leipzig debate with Johann Eck
1520	Excommunicated by pope; declared imperial outlaw by Diet of Holy Roman Empire; translated New Testament
1523	Reformation spread to Switzerland
1524–25	Peasants' Revolt in Germany
1527	Reformation spread to Scandinavia
1529	Reformers first referred to as "Protestants"
1530	Augsburg Confession
1531	Reformation spread to England
1534	First complete *Luther Bible* published
1546	Died on October 30 in Eisleben

Wittenberg and the overseer of 11 monasteries. He was studying St. Paul's epistle to the Romans for a series of lectures on the Pauline epistles (letters, or books of the New Testament). According to his own account, Luther was in his study in a tower of the monastery pondering the meaning of Rom. 1:17: "For it is the righteousness of God revealed from faith to faith; as it is written, The just shall live by faith." In that little verse was contained the heart of Luther's spiritual problem, as well as the answer.

Luther was perplexed by the two phrases, "the righteousness of God" and "The just shall live by faith." In accordance with the teaching of the medieval church and the scholastic philosophers, Luther understood "the righteousness of God" as "the formal or active righteousness according to which God is righteous and punishes sinners and the unjust." Such a view of God both terrified Luther and caused him to hate the God he knew he should love. "Not only did I not love," he later wrote, "but I actually hated the righteous God who punishes sinners." Then, as he meditated over the verse, its meaning broke through:

> Then, finally, God had mercy on me, and I began to understand that the righteousness of God is

that gift of God by which a righteous man lives, namely, faith, and that this sentence—The righteousness of God is revealed in the Gospel—is passive, indicating that the merciful God justifies us by faith, as it is written: "The righteous shall live by faith." Now I felt as though I had been reborn altogether and had entered Paradise. In the same moment the face of the whole of Scripture became apparent to me.

Luther's discovery was more revolutionary than the Copernican (i.e., Scientific) revolution that followed in 1543. It was the medieval church and its worldview that held the medieval synthesis together. And if salvation was by faith alone, a truth discovered in the Bible, not the teachings of the Church, then the whole edifice of the institutional church was unnecessary. For if salvation is not dispensed by the priests through the Mass and other sacraments, then the whole clergy, from pope to parish priest, was also unnecessary.

Luther did not immediately challenge the Church hierarchy. What spurred him to action in 1517 was the appearance outside Wittenberg of a monk peddling indulgences. Albert von Hohenzollern, at age 23, the archbishop of Magdeburg and administrator of Halberstadt, had "purchased" the recently vacated archbishopric of Mainz. To pay back the funds that he borrowed from the Fugger bank in Augsburg, Albert was authorized by Pope Leo X to sell indulgences in Germany.

The indulgence system was based upon the belief that Jesus Christ, the Virgin Mary, and the many saints had stored up in heaven a vast treasury of surplus merit. The Church (i.e., the pope), by virtue of possessing the keys to heaven and hell, could draw upon that surplus merit and apply it to repentant sinners. An indulgence was "the remission of part or all of the temporal penalty imposed for sins already forgiven." It meant, in effect, time off from purgatory.

The abuse of the indulgence system was evident in the aggressive sales tactics of John Tetzel, who appeared outside Luther's door in October 1517. He alleged that indulgences could be purchased for relatives already dead, or for sins one might commit in the future. "As soon as the coin in the coffer rings," Tetzel claimed, "the soul from purgatory springs."

Luther Posts His Theses at Wittenberg

Luther felt impelled to respond to the obvious misuse of indulgences. On the eve of All Saints (October 31, 1517), he posted his "95 Theses" on the church door at the University of Wittenberg. He meant them as an invitation to his colleagues to debate the doctrine of indulgences, but they soon appeared throughout Germany, thanks to the recently invented printing press.

Pope Leo X did not move immediately to silence Luther. He was distracted by imperial politics surrounding the choice of a new Holy Roman Emperor. Luther's prince, Frederick the Wise, was one of the seven electors who would choose the next emperor. Leo X wanted Frederick's support for his candidate, and, since Frederick was protecting Luther, Leo X felt it wise not to offend him.

Luther got an opportunity to debate his theses in July 1519 at the University of Leipzig. There he confronted Johann Eck, one of the leading theologians of the day. In the course of the debate, Luther appealed to Scripture as his authority, thus denying the authority of the pope, church councils, or other temporal authorities where they conflicted with Scripture. In so doing, he identified himself with the teachings of **Jan Hus,** condemned as heretical by the Council of Constance a century earlier. Luther in effect admitted that according to the Church, he was a heretic.

During the course of 1520, Luther wrote extensively. In the treatises and commentaries that appeared during that year, the basic doctrines of the Reformation began to emerge: the Bible is the final authority (*Sola Scriptura*); and salvation is by faith (*Sola Fide*) through God's free grace (*Sola Gratia*). Every man or woman was his or her own priest. Thus, the necessity of the institutional church as an intermediary between the individual and God was removed. In its place stood the doctrine of a priesthood of believers.

In June 1520, Pope Leo X issued a papal bull formally condemning Luther as a heretic and excommunicating him. When a copy of the bull reached Wittenberg, Luther publicly burned it. But the most dramatic and significant event in Luther's career, and a turning point in European history, came on April 18, 1521, in the little Rhineland town of Worms.

Luther was summoned to Worms by the newly elected Emperor **Charles V.** Only 19 years old, the emperor yielded to the persuasion of his uncle, Frederick the Wise, to grant Luther a hearing before the assembled princes (Diet) of the Holy Roman Empire. Charles V granted Luther a safe conduct. He wanted only to give Luther the opportunity to recant. Luther meant to defend his views.

Several accounts of what Luther said before the diet have come down to us. No one knows for certain what were his exact words. But scholars agree that the following concluding lines of his speech, taken from Luther's collected writings, are true to the spirit of, if not the very words, he spoke:

Since then your serene Majesty and your lordships request a simple reply, I will give it without horns and hoofs, and say: Unless I am convinced by the testimony of Scripture or by plain reason (for I believe in neither the pope nor in councils alone, for it is well-known, not only that they have erred, but also have contradicted themselves), I am mastered by the passages of Scripture which I have quoted, and my conscience is captive to the Word of God. I cannot and will not recant, for it is neither safe nor honest to violate one's conscience. I can do no other, Here I take my stand, God being my helper. Amen.

Acting in the name of the emperor, the diet declared Luther to be an imperial outlaw and placed him under a sentence of death. Frederick the Wise had Luther kidnapped and hidden at Wartburg castle, one of his residences near Eisenach. There, during the next 11 months, Luther translated the New Testament into German. By 1534, he had completed a translation of the entire Bible.

Protestant Sects Proliferate

The Protestant movement began to fragment almost immediately. The Bible may be the final authority, but every believer is his own priest, his own interpreter of what the Bible says. Hence, the proliferation of Protestant sects that continues, even in our own day.

All that happened after the Diet of Worms was anticlimactic. Upon his return to Wittenberg in March 1522, Luther tried to halt the radicalism of some of his followers. But fragmentation, not unity, was to characterize the future of the Protestant churches. In 1530, Philipp Melanchthon, Luther's closest associate, drafted a confession of faith. Both he and Luther hoped that it might provide a basis for unity between the new faith and the Roman Catholic Church. Rejected by the Diet of Augsburg, the "Augsburg Confession" became the doctrinal statement of the Lutheran churches.

Luther introduced a number of reforms in the form of worship. Many were merely a rediscovery of practices lost by the medieval church. They included an emphasis upon preaching and teaching of the Bible, rather than the sacrament of the altar, or the Mass. Also, Luther, himself a fine musician, reintroduced music and congregational singing. He published a hymnbook in 1524, and even wrote the music and lyrics for one of the best known hymns of Protestantism, "A Mighty Fortress is Our God" (1528).

Although Luther wrote extensively, and on many diverse subjects, he was not a systematic theologian. Some of his pamphlets reflected his peasant background and remain controversial even today. Under imperial ban, and with a price on his head, Luther remained in Wittenberg, where he continued to preach and teach.

In 1525, Luther married Katherine von Bora, a former Cistercian nun. They had six children, some of whom died early, and adopted 11 more. By all accounts, their home was a happy one. "My beloved Katie," as Luther was fond of calling his wife, was a great source of strength for him. Their home, writes Reformation scholar, E.G. Rupp, "became a more effective apologetic for marriage of the clergy than any writing and the prototype of a Christian minister's household."

In January 1546, Luther journeyed to his boyhood home of Mansfeld to arbitrate a dispute between two brothers, the counts of Mansfeld. On his return journey, he stopped off in Eisleben, where he was born, to preach his final sermon on February 14, 1546. Becoming ill afterwards, he died four days later. According to contemporary accounts, he repeated John 3:16 three times: "For God so loved the world, that he gave his only begotten Son, that whosoever believeth in him should not perish, but have everlasting life." He then breathed his last breath. His body was taken to Wittenberg, where it was laid to rest in the church on whose door he had posted his "95 Theses" on October 30, 1517.

SOURCES:

Estep, William R. *Renaissance and Reformation.* Eerdmans, 1986.

Fleming, William. *Arts & Ideas.* Holt, 1986.

Hillerbrand, Hans J. *The Reformation: A Narrative History Relate by Contemporary Observers and Participants.* Baker, 1978.

Jones, R. Tudur. *The Great Reformation.* Inter-Varsity Press, 1985.

Klassen, Peter J. *Europe in the Reformation.* Prentice-Hall, 1979.

The New Cambridge Modern History, Vol.II: The Reformation, 1520–1559. Cambridge University Press, 1962.

FURTHER READING:

Bainton, Roland. *Here I Stand: A Life of Martin Luther.* Abingdon, 1950.

Dillenberger, John, ed. *Martin Luther: Selections From His Writings.* Doubleday, 1961.

Hendrix, Scott H. *Luther and the Papacy: Stages in a Reformation Conflict.* Fortress Press, 1981.

Hillerbrand, Hans J. *Men and Ideas in the Sixteenth Century.* Houghton, 1969.

Kuiper, Barend Klaas. *Martin Luther: The Formative Years.* Eerdmans, 1933.

Rupp, Gordon. *Luther's Progress to the Diet of Worms.* Harper, 1963.

Rosa Luxemburg

(1871–1919)

Brilliant theoretician and socialist party leader, who fearlessly challenged Marx and his disciples, was active in revolutionary movements everywhere in Europe, and died in Berlin in 1919, leading a vain attempt to provoke a communist revolution.

Pronunciation: LOOKS-emboorg. Born at Zamosc in Russian Poland in March 1871; died leading a revolution in Berlin in January 1919; daughter of a middle-class Jewish family; married: (to obtain German citizenship) Gustav Lubeck, 1898 (divorced).

Rosa Luxemburg was born in March 1871 to a middle-class mercantile family in Zamosc, which was then a part of the Russian Empire but had earlier been part of the independent Kingdom of Poland. Her family was Jewish in religion but German in culture; through her mother and father, Luxemburg became familiar with the great classic writers of the Enlightenment, Goethe being always her favorite. She also developed a lifelong love of Russian literature, as well as an enthusiasm for art and music. The Luxemburgs moved to Warsaw when Rosa was a child, and while still in high school she became involved in protests against tsarist authority. A brilliant student, Luxemburg could not attend the University of Warsaw, to which women were not admitted; therefore, in 1887, she moved to Zurich, whose university made no sexual discrimination in admissions.

Zurich in the 1880s and for some years thereafter was the international headquarters for European socialism, for the Swiss government gave asylum to those exiled from Russia, Germany, and elsewhere for political radicalism. Here Luxemburg met and was closely associated with a

"The psyche of the masses, like the eternal sea, always carries all the latent possibilities; the deathly calm and the roaring storm, the lowest cowardice and the wildest heroism. The mass is always that which it must *be according to the circumstances of the time, and the mass is always at the point of becoming something different than what it appears to be."*

ROSA LUXEMBURG

Contributed by Lamar Cecil, William R. Kenan, Jr. Professor of History, Washington and Lee University, Lexington, Virginia

number of prominent European socialists, especially those such as George Plekhanov and Clara Zetkin who had escaped from Russia. Her closest associate was the Polish socialist, Leo Jogiches, who loved her intensely and with whom Luxemburg had a brief affair and a lifelong friendship. The socialists were an argumentative group, and Luxemburg, who had read Marx and commentaries on his work carefully, held her own in the violent discussions that were a constant feature of the group. She also successfully pursued a doctoral degree in economics, writing a dissertation that was later published on the economic dependency of Poland on Russia.

By the time that Luxemburg had taken her degree she was tired of Zurich and longed to move to Berlin, which was the headquarters of the largest and most successful socialist movement in Europe and the scene of the most active intellectual controversy among socialists. Marx had predicted that Germany would be where the revolution of the proletariat (lower class) would someday begin, for it was the most industrialized, capitalist nation in continental Europe. As a Russian citizen, Rosa Luxemburg could not cross the border, and to overcome that difficulty in 1898 she entered into a marriage of convenience with a German named Gustav Lubeck in order to move to Berlin. It was an entirely businesslike arrangement, and once safely in Germany, where she now enjoyed citizenship, she divorced Lubeck. Berlin was never to her taste, although she was to live for 20 years in this "most repulsive place: cold, ugly, massive, a real barracks." Here Luxemburg established her position as one of the foremost commentators in the ranks of European socialists on the works of **Karl Marx.**

One question that polarized socialists in the Berlin of the 1890s was the problem of nationality. A cosmopolite who drew her ideas and her cultural enthusiasms from many sources, Luxemburg was profoundly mistrustful of nationalism, for in her opinion it inevitably distracted the proletariat from pursuing its identity as an object of economic exploitation, not as a citizen of an existing or hoped for national state. Marx's vision of a classless society could not be realized if patriotism got in the way. **Lenin,** however, and a number of his German admirers took the opposing view that national cultures were to be respected, and even encouraged, provided that they were in harmony with the interests of international socialism. There was, he argued contrary to Luxemburg, no inherent opposition between the two. Lenin was intolerant of opposition, and although Luxemburg's views contrary to his own annoyed him, he admitted that she was an intellectual "eagle."

CHRONOLOGY

1871	Born at Zamosc in Russian Poland
1886	Joined Proletariat Party (Polish Socialist Party)
1887	Attended university in Zurich, Switzerland
1893	Established journal *Worker's Voice*
1895	Established Social Democratic Party of the Kingdom of Lithuania and Poland
1898	Married to obtain German citizenship; moved to Berlin
1899	Wrote *Reform or Revolution?*
1905	Participated in the Russian Revolution
1913	Wrote *The Accumulation of Capital*
1907–14	Taught in socialist academy in Berlin
1915–18	Jailed for sedition
1917	Organized Spartacus League
1918	Freed from jail
1919	Died while leading revolution in Berlin

In 1899, a year after Luxemburg moved to Berlin, one of the titans of the German socialist movement, Eduard Bernstein, had published a book entitled *Principles of Socialism* in which he had advanced what became known as socialist "revisionism." This was the view that Marx had erred in holding that capitalism would inevitably become monopolistic and that the anger of the exploited proletariat would constantly increase. That being the case, capitalism's collapse was unlikely and socialists should therefore abandon hope of achieving a classless society by revolution and instead concentrate on obtaining social reforms by working through existing parliamentary institutions. This challenged the official party orthodoxy, which called for revolution as the means of achieving proletarian victory. The leaders of the German socialist party, Karl Kautsky, Wilhelm Liebknecht, and August Bebel, who were ardent Marxists but rather ossified bureaucrats in mentality, condemned Bernstein. But it was Rosa Luxemburg who was at the forefront of the assault. She immediately attacked Bernstein's view in her *Reform or Revolution?* (1899), which argued that parliamentarianism (like trade unionism) was a trap set by the bourgeoisie (middle class) for the proletariat, which should not forsake its vision of revolution. This led Luxemburg into a protracted struggle with the leaders of the German socialist party.

She Teaches, Writes in Berlin

To Rosa Luxemburg, socialism meant revolution but it meant popular revolution. The duty of the party was not to direct and control the revolution by entrusting its destiny to a tiny handful of leaders, which was exactly Lenin's belief, but instead to encourage the rising up of gigantic strikes and revolutionary movements. She was entirely prepared to act on her beliefs, and with the outbreak of revolution in 1905, Luxemburg went at once to Warsaw; she had become convinced that when Marx's prediction of a great proletarian revolution came about, it would not be in Germany but in Russia. She was soon arrested, and after a harrowing few months in jail, which greatly undermined her health, she was released and returned to Berlin. Here from 1907 to 1914, she taught Marxist philosophy in a socialist school and in her spare time wrote extensively. Her most celebrated tract from this period was *The Accumulation of Capital* (1913), in which she argued that capitalism would indeed—as Marx had argued—fall apart, but that he had not lived long enough to see that the cause would be imperialism. Capitalism would have to expand its markets; in order to do this, capitalism would have to take over the world. Since all capitalist powers will be engaged in this, they would come into conflict, thus fatally weakening themselves and advancing the changes of proletarian victory.

The outbreak of the First World War in August 1914 placed all European socialists in a difficult position. Was their loyalty to the country of which they were citizens or to the class to which they belonged, which according to Marx had no national boundaries? Most German socialists elected to see their duty to the Fatherland rather than to an abstract concept of international socialism, and the majority of socialist deputies voted in favor of war credits. Many socialists went off to be slaughtered as loyal soldiers of Kaiser **Wilhelm II.** Rosa Luxemburg was dismayed, for such behavior was the betrayal of all that Marxist socialism stood for. She denounced the war and socialist participation in it, so brazenly that she was soon arrested and thrown once more into jail where she languished with one brief interruption from 1915 until the end of the war. While a prisoner, she consoled herself with art, music, and reading, and she wrote voluminously to those socialists who, like herself, had refused to support the kaiser.

In 1917, by means of letters from her prison cell, she and her friend Karl Liebknecht, the talented son of the party chieftain Wilhelm Liebknecht, who had also refused to support Germany's effort in the war, founded a group known as the Spartacus League. Named after the gallant Greek slave and gladiator who had led a heroic rebellion against the Romans in the first century B.C., the purpose of the league was to end the war by fomenting revolution in Germany, but in the fever of patriotism that gripped Germany, Luxemburg, and Liebknecht were unable to win many followers.

Helps Found Communist Party of Germany

In March 1917, a revolution by a revisionist socialist faction toppled the Russian Tsar **Nicholas,** but eight months later it fell to the Bolsheviks under Lenin, who thereafter tightly controlled the revolution and carried it out with considerable violence. Luxemburg did not approve, for Lenin was too authoritarian and too cruel, too bent on commanding an elitist revolution rather than inspiring one that was truly popular. A year after Lenin's triumph, Luxemburg would have her own chance, for in November 1918 Germany was defeated and signed an armistice. The kaiser abdicated and fled in exile to Holland, and a group of moderate socialists formed a government in Berlin. Luxemburg and Liebknecht were released from jail and immediately attacked the socialist government, which was cautiously working with the army to bring order to the Fatherland, as being insufficiently revolutionary in ardor. As a result, in December 1918, Luxemburg and Liebknecht decided to found a new party, the Communist Party of Germany (KPD) to agitate for a massive strike that would bring about a truly proletarian revolution.

Luxemburg worked with unquenchable energy to galvanize the working class of Berlin into engaging in a total stoppage of work, certain that this would be the prelude to revolution. Her efforts failed, however, because the socialist government, fearful that violence would ruin its attempt to establish a stable, republican regime, cooperated with the aristocratic army to suppress Luxemburg's rebellion. In January 1919, the strife between the communists and the military had reduced Berlin to civil warfare, and the army called on all its available forces to deal with Luxemburg and her allies. She and Liebknecht were captured, beaten, and then taken to separate destinations to be killed. Luxemburg was shot while in an automobile and her body thrown into the Landwehr canal in downtown Berlin. A few weeks later, Leo Jogiches, her ally and once her lover, suffered a similar fate. The revolution collapsed, the socialist regime survived, and later in 1919 the Weimar Republic was established under the presidency of Friedrich Ebert, a revisionist socialist who had little sympathy for the radical ideas for which Rosa Luxemburg had so passionately stood.

Rosa Luxemburg is an admirable but perplexing figure. Brilliant in argument but tyrannical in personality, she did not make friends any more easily than she kept them. Individual people were less important to her than the Marxist idea of revolution, but that idea was to her—as it was not to Lenin—profoundly human. The revolution for which she hoped was to be by the people and for their benefit, the authentic creation of the popular will. It should be established by conviction and not, as to her dismay had been the case in Lenin's Russia after November 1917, by violence. Although some female socialists insisted that socialism have a feminist face, this notion had no appeal for Luxemburg, who thought sexuality was as politically irrelevant as nationality. Her Polishness meant little to her, although she identified with the suffering of the Poles at the hands of the Russians and Germans. But patriotism to a nation had to be rejected because of its incompatibility to the Marxist idea of identity by class rather than by citizenship. Finally, although Jewish, she rejected the claims of Jews to be a people set apart. Like all others, they were victims of capitalism; like all others, they were to be called to participate in the revolution of the people.

Luxemburg's causes failed; her vision was faulty, her prescriptions of little value. But her intelligence, her forcefulness, her absorption in the cause of improving the world, her insistence that socialism have a human face give her today a reputation, and a relevance, that her socialist rivals, more famous and more successful in their own time, no longer enjoy.

SOURCES:

Bronner, Stephen E., ed. *The Letters of Rosa Luxemburg.* 1979.

Flechtheim, Ossip K., ed. *Rosa Luxemburg: Politische Schriften.* 3 vols. 1966–68.

FURTHER READING:

Bronner, Stephen E. *Rosa Luxemburg: Revolutionary for Our Times.* 1987.

Frolich, Paul. *Rosa Luxemburg, Her Life and Work.* 1940.

Nettl, J. P. *Rosa Luxemburg.* 2 vols. 1966.

MacBeth

(c. 1005–1057)

Last great Gaelic king of Scots, who came to the throne through dynastic struggle, went on pilgrimage to Rome, battled the English and Norse, and ruled for 17 years until being killed by his rival.

Name variations: Machethad; Machetad; Machethad (proper Gaelic spelling) means "son of life"; often confused with MacHeth in later sources. Born perhaps A.D. 1000–1005; killed in August 1057; buried on the island of Iona, situated off Scotland's west coast; son of Findlaech Mac Ruaridh, mormaer (ruler) of Moray; married: Gruoch (a granddaughter of either King Kenneth II [971–995] or Kenneth III [997–1005]); children: none. Predecessor: Duncan I. Successors: Lulach, Malcolm III.

Although MacBeth is probably one of the best known of all the Scottish kings, he may also have the worst reputation, due in large measure to the historical and dramatic works of writers who lived four to five hundred years after his death. Shakespeare's tragic play *MacBeth* represented the culmination of an evil reputation for the Gaelic king that had been in the making for over a century, yet the reign of the historical MacBeth bore little resemblance to that depicted by Shakespeare.

The Scotland into which MacBeth was born about A.D. 1000 was very different from present-day Scotland, with society unlike those of other medieval European kingdoms. In the 11th century, much of the territories rested in the hands of the Norsemen or Vikings. In the north, the Orkney Islands—with the large provinces of Caithness and Sutherland on the mainland—formed no part of the Scottish kingdom but were controlled by a Viking dynasty based in the Orkneys, while the Hebrides Islands in the west were controlled by the king of Norway. The remaining areas of Scotland (except Lothian, the region south of Edinburgh) were Celtic in culture and language. The rural pop-

"King MacBeth is one of the greater figures appearing on the horizon of Scottish history.... Unfortunately for his fair name the later romances laid the crimes of others to his charge so that now he stands before the world branded with 'every sin that has a name.'"

JOHN MACBETH

Contributed by Russell Andrew McDonald, Ph.D., University of Guelph, Guelph, Ontario, Canada

ulation was organized into a sophisticated tribal society that subsisted through pastoral and agricultural farming. There were no large cities or towns in MacBeth's Scotland, and with no coinage, cattle provided the main source of wealth. Scotland, known then as Alba, was ruled by a High King, but the administration was decentralized; the country was divided into a number of provinces most of which were ruled by royal officers called *mormaers* who were supposed to act on the king's behalf but who carried a long tradition of acting as rulers in their own right.

Throughout the 10th and 11th centuries, one of the largest and most important of these provinces was Moray. Consisting of a large territory centered on modern Inverness, it extended west to the coast, east to the river Spey, and south along Loch Ness while being separated from the rest of Scotland by a rugged ridge of mountains called the Mounth. Strategically, Moray was important because it acted as a buffer zone between the attacks of the Norsemen in the north and the remainder of the kingdom of Scots in the south.

The rulers of this province had a special importance attached to them. Although often referred to as *mormaers* like the rulers of the other provinces, in many Irish sources the rulers of Moray are called "kings," and sometimes even "king of Scots," suggesting their high status. Modern genealogical research, moreover, has demonstrated that they were descended from one of the three families which first settled on the western coast of Scotland from Ireland in the early sixth century. Since the kings of Scots were regularly drawn from the other two of these families, the rulers of Moray had a legitimate claim to royal status in the 11th century.

This was the background into which Mac-Beth was born. According to later sources which cannot be entirely trusted, the date of his birth was 1005. His father was Findlaech Mac Ruaridh, the mormaer of Moray, and his mother—whose identity cannot be proven—may have been Doada, a sister (or daughter) of King Malcolm II (1005–34). Virtually nothing conclusive is known of Mac-Beth's childhood. In 1020, Tigernach, an Irish writer, recorded that "Findlaech, Ruadri's son, mormaer of Moray, was slain by the sons of his brother Maelbrigte," while another source only stated that he was "killed by his own people." Although this unadorned account does not offer any motivation for the killing of MacBeth's father, it has been suggested that it represented dissatisfaction with the marriage alliance between Findlaech and Doada and the close ties it entailed between these two royal houses. In any event, in

CHRONOLOGY

1005	Malcolm II proclaimed king of Scots
1020	MacBeth's father Findlaech killed by his nephews
1032	MacBeth became mormaer (ruler) of Moray
1034	Malcolm II died; Duncan I became king of Scots
1040	Duncan I killed; MacBeth inaugurated as king of Scots
1045	Duncan's father Crinan revolted against MacBeth and was killed
1050	MacBeth went on pilgrimage to Rome
1054	MacBeth driven from southern Scotland by Malcolm, son of Duncan, and Siward the earl of Northumbria
1057	MacBeth killed by Malcolm at Lumphanan
1058	MacBeth's stepson Lulach killed; Malcolm III's reign formally began

1032, Gillacomgain, one of Findlaech's nephews who had been involved in his killing and who had assumed the title of mormaer, "was burned, along with fifty of his men," according to the Annals of Ulster, another Irish source. Setting fire to an enemy's residence was not then an uncommon means of eliminating one's enemies, and it is possible that MacBeth killed his cousin to avenge his father's death.

Becoming mormaer of Moray, MacBeth also married Gillacomgain's widow, a lady named Gruoch. The historical "Lady MacBeth" (though she would not have been called this) was the daughter of Bodhe (or Boite), who was probably the son of King Kenneth III, and by marrying her MacBeth merged several claims to the kingship of Scots: his own, as the son of Findlaech, and those of his wife through previous kings of Scots. At the same time, he also adopted Gruoch's son Lulach by her former husband Gillacomgain. Although marrying the killer of one's spouse may seem strange, it is found quite frequently in Irish and Scandinavian literature.

Duncan Dies; MacBeth Becomes King

How, then, did MacBeth become king? After a brief reign of six years, King Duncan I met his end in 1040. Neither old nor kindly, as was Shakespeare's "gracious Duncan," he had not been particularly effective as king. Having come to the throne in 1034, aged about 33 years, he had spent much of his reign raiding south into England; these raids proved largely unproductive, and in 1040 he was forced to turn his attention northward to Moray. According to Tigernach, Duncan was killed "by his own subjects" near Elgin. However, Marianus Scottus, an Irish hermit writing in Germany who took an interest in the doings of his fellow Celts, recorded that "Duncan, the king of Scotland, was killed in autumn, by his earl, MacBeth." His account is the only contemporary evidence implicating MacBeth in the murder of Duncan, suggesting that all future accounts of MacBeth's involvement were derived from it. Regardless of whether or not MacBeth was personally involved in Duncan's death, as mormaer of Moray he would still have been held partly responsible for the murder that took place within his province. Yet even so, MacBeth did not murder a kindly old man in his sleep, urged on, as he was in Shakespeare's play, by "vaulting ambition, which o'erleaps itself," and by an equally ambitious Lady MacBeth. To contemporaries, then, he was not an usurper, yet to men of a later age he became one, and a particularly nasty one at that.

An understanding of the unusual system of succession to the throne which operated in 11th-century Scotland is important to an examination of MacBeth's historical portrayal as a usurper. Among the kings of Scots, there were then few formalized "rules" of succession, like that of father to son. While there was a royal house or kin from whom a royal successor would be chosen, the succession to the kingship tended to alternate between two main branches of the royal house. In general, it is safe to say that no king was succeeded directly by his son or even his brother in the tenth century. In the 11th century, however, the balance of this system was upset. Anxious that his grandson Duncan should succeed him, King Malcolm II of Scotland went to great lengths to ensure that potential rivals were eliminated; in fact, he murdered most of them. This meant that the accession of Duncan I in 1034 was contrary to Celtic custom, and so the double claims of MacBeth to the throne in 1040 were, under Celtic succession, probably better than Duncan's own claims had been. Indeed, modern historians are inclined to view MacBeth as acting on behalf of Scottish conservatism in resisting changes to the traditional Celtic method of succession. But to writers of Shakespeare's day, this method of succession seemed not only distant and incomprehensible but also barbaric.

Of MacBeth's 17-year reign little is known, but he faced strife from both inside and outside Scotland. Upon his succession, Duncan's sons

Malcolm and Donald Ban fled Scotland; Malcolm, who would eventually defeat and kill MacBeth, fled to England where he found refuge with King Edward the Confessor, while his brother hid in the western isles of Scotland or Ireland. In 1045, MacBeth faced a rebellion led by Crinan, a churchman and powerful military leader (it was not unusual for a person to be both during this period) and also the father of the late king Duncan. But Crinan's revolt failed and he was killed. According to Tigernach, "a battle was fought between Scots, upon a united expedition, and Crinan, abbot of Dunkeld, was killed in it; and many along with him, namely nine score fighting men." For about 200 years before MacBeth's time, there had been continual warfare between Scots and Norsemen in the northern provinces of Scotland, and in his day, MacBeth probably campaigned against the Norsemen. The most powerful force in the north was then Thorfinn, the earl of Orkney. Thorfinn apparently engaged in several sea battles with MacBeth, who, it has been suggested, appears in the Norse sagas under the name of Karl Hundason. Although the battles were hard fought, the Norse seem to have had the better of MacBeth, as described in the *Orkneyinga* Saga:

> Ships grappled
> together; gore, as foes fell,
> bathed stiff iron, black
> with Scots' blood;
> singing the bows spilt
> blood, steel bit; bright
> though the quick points quaked,
> no quenching Thorfinn.

MacBeth next appears on the record in the year 1050, on a pilgrimage to Rome. Because the world had not ended as expected in A.D. 1000, a number of kings from northern Europe made pilgrimages to the Holy City shortly thereafter; they included King Sitric of Dublin in 1028 and King Cnut of England in 1030. Marianus Scottus took note of MacBeth's visit, writing that "the king of Scotland ... scattered money like seed to the poor, at Rome." This pilgrimage marked an important change because it indicated that after some two centuries of isolation Scotland was again opening up to the wider European stage. That MacBeth was able to leave his country for an extended period of time attests to the stability of his reign and suggests that he was probably more acquainted with the rest of Europe than were his predecessors. Sometime during his reign, likely after he returned from the pilgrimage, MacBeth and his wife made a grant of land to the Culdees or Celtic monks of Lochleven in return for prayers for their souls. This act, like his pilgrimage, is suggestive of MacBeth's piety in an age when religious considerations were of high importance.

MacBeth's return from Rome saw storm clouds gathering on the horizon. Even before his departure, the greatest threat to his realm had come from England. In 1046, an English annal recorded that "Earl Siward with a great army came to Scotland, and expelled king MacBeth, and appointed another; but after his departure MacBeth recovered his kingdom." This Siward was the powerful earl of Northumbria in northern England—"almost a giant in stature, and of strong hand and mind," according to an English writer—and was perhaps a kinsman of Malcolm, Duncan's son. Although Siward's 1046 expedition had clearly failed (and the chronicler probably exaggerated its initial success), in 1054 he launched another attack, leading the *Anglo-Saxon Chronicle* to record the battle of July 27 in which he led a huge army, accompanied by a fleet, into Scotland, "and fought against the Scots, and put to flight the king MacBeth, and slew all that were best there in the land; and brought thence much war-spoil, such as no man obtained before." English sources relate that this expedition was undertaken at the order of King Edward the Confessor of England with the aim of placing Duncan's son, Malcolm, upon the throne of Scotland. Later tradition records that the battle was fought at Dunsinane Hill, made famous by Shakespeare whose apparition predicted: "Macbeth shall never vanquished be until/ Great Birnam Wood to High Dunsinane Hill/ Shall come against him." By the end of a hard-fought battle, Siward's own son had been killed, along with other Northumbrian nobles and many of MacBeth's supporters. MacBeth, however, escaped and fled northward, back to his home province of Moray, and Malcolm became king over at least the south of Scotland.

Duncan's Son Kills MacBeth

But MacBeth was not yet finished. Three years would pass before, on August 15, 1057, Malcolm (III) finally defeated and killed him in battle at Lumphanan near Aberdeen. Tigernach recorded this event with a typically brief entry: "MacBeth, Findlaech's son, sovereign of Scotland, was slain by Malcolm, Duncan's son." It should be noted that MacDuff had no part in the killing of the historical MacBeth, and indeed the contemporary records do not even attest to the existence of anyone named MacDuff in his time.

Because MacBeth had no children of his own, his stepson Lulach was able to gather enough support to rule briefly over part of Scotland, only to be dispatched by Malcolm in an ambush during March of 1058. Tigernach wrote: "Lulach, the king of Scotland, was slain, by Malcolm, Duncan's son, by treachery," and another chronicler recorded: "Alas! through lack of caution, the hapless king perished." According to slightly later sources, both MacBeth and Lulach were buried on the tiny island of Iona, situated off Scotland's west coast.

As a result of misunderstandings regarding the times in which he lived and later traditions about him, MacBeth has acquired an evil reputation with Shakespeare's MacDuff exclaiming, "Not in the legions/ Of horrid hell can come a devil more damned/ In evils to top MacBeth," while Malcolm referred to his predecessor as "bloody/ Luxurious, avaricious, false, deceitful/ Sudden, malicious, smacking of every sin/ That has a name."

Yet despite these traditional perceptions of MacBeth, there is no evidence to suggest that he was viewed in this manner by his contemporaries. In fact, most writers of his day viewed him quite favorably, with one source calling him "MacBeth of renown." Another, *Berchan's Prophecy* (ascribed to the Irish abbot Berchan), called him the "generous king.... The ruddy, pale-yellow haired, tall one, I shall be joyful in him. Scotland will be brimful, in the west and in the east, during the reign of the furious Red one."

His successor Malcolm III and his sons undertook the introduction of foreign influences into Scotland, accounting for the reference to MacBeth as the last truly Gaelic king of Scots. Much of his evil reputation has been derived from chroniclers writing long after his death, who often had dramatic or moral obligations to fulfill. Although accounts of the historical king MacBeth are scarce, it is apparent that his contemporaries found him more deserving of praise then condemnation.

SOURCES:

Anderson, A. O. *Early Sources of Scottish History, A.D. 500–1286.* 2 vols. Oliver & Boyd, 1922. Vol. 1, pp. 550–604.

———. *Scottish Annals from English Chroniclers, A.D. 500–1286.* David Nutt, 1908.

Cowan, E. J. "The Historical MacBeth," in *Scottish Society for Northern Studies,* forthcoming.

Dunbar, Sir A. H. *Scottish Kings. A Revised Chronology of Scottish History, 1005–1625.* David Douglas, 1899.

Shakespeare, William. *MacBeth.* Edited by S. Barnet. Penguin, 1987.

FURTHER READING:

Barrow, G. W. S. *Kingship and Unity: Scotland, 1000–1306.* Edward Arnold, 1981.

Dickinson, W. C. *Scotland from the Earliest Times to 1603.* 3rd ed. Revised and edited by A.a.m. Duncan. Clarendon Press, 1977.

Dunnett, D. "The Real MacBeth," in *The Sunday Mail Story of Scotland.* Vol. 1, pt. 4. R. Maxwell, 1988.

Ellis, P. B. *MacBeth High King of Scotland, 1040–1057.* Frederick Muller, 1980.

Skene, W. F. *Celtic Scotland.* 3 vols. David Douglas, 1876–1880.

Ramsay MacDonald

(1866–1937)

One of the great architects of the British Labour Party, who was prime minister and foreign secretary of the first Labour government in 1924, Labour prime minister again in 1929, and leader of the predominantly Conservative "National" government from 1931 to 1935.

"With all his faults, he was the greatest leader Labour has had, and his name would stand high if he had not outlived his abilities."

A. J. P. TAYLOR

James Ramsay MacDonald has gone down in history either as martyr or traitor, depending on one's politics. At a time when the British Labour Party was as much a "cause" or a "movement" as a political party, MacDonald twice led it to victory, then became subject to its most bitter scorn.

A man of eloquence and presence, with sensitively chiseled features and large, luminous eyes, MacDonald had the face of an artist, not a statesman. Always strikingly handsome, he was particularly so in later life, when his dark wavy hair turned white. Bernard Shaw called him a 17th-century Highlander and, given his pride and bearing, the remark was an apt one. MacDonald once said of himself, "If God were to come to me and say, 'Ramsay, would you rather be a country gentleman than a Prime Minister?, I should reply, 'Please God, a country gentleman.'" Those attracted by his natural eloquence and aristocratic appearance were often unaware of certain less positive qualities: a predilection for intrigue, a jealous streak, hypersensitivity to criticism, and an indifference to unpleasant facts.

Born James Ramsay MacDonald on October 12, 1866, in Lossiemouth, Morayshire; died at sea on November 9, 1937; illegitimate son of John MacDonald (head ploughman) and Anne Ramsay (a farm worker); married: Margaret Ethel Gladstone (a social worker), November 1896; children: Alister, Malcolm (who held several ministerial appointments), David, Joan, Sheila.

Contributed by Justus D. Doenecke, Professor of History, New College of the University of South Florida, Sarasota, Florida

1906	Elected to Parliament from Leicester
1914	England declared war on Germany
1918	British coupon election; MacDonald lost West Leicester seat
1922	Elected to Parliament from Aberavon district of Glamorganshire, Wales
1923	Baldwin replaced Bonar Law as PM
1924	First Labour Cabinet under MacDonald; Geneva Protocol drafted; Zinoviev letter released; Conservatives defeated Labour; second Baldwin ministry formed
1929	Labour Party won election; second MacDonald Cabinet formed
1931	MacDonald Cabinet resigned; National (coalition) Government formed; England forced to abandon gold standard; MacDonald remained prime minister
1935	Reorganization of Cabinet; Baldwin again prime minister
1935–37	MacDonald appointed lord president of the council

"Gentleman Mac" was born on October 12, 1886, in Lossiemouth, a gray, lowland village of fishermen and farm workers on the northern coast of Scotland. The illegitimate child of a passing love between Anne Ramsay, a farm servant, and John MacDonald, a ploughman from the Black Isle of Ross, MacDonald was reared by his grandmother Isabella Ramsay, known for her character, intelligence, and religious conviction.

The young boy attended the Free Kirk School at Drainie, a village four miles away, where, he said, "the machinery was as old as [John] Knox, the education the best ever given to sons and daughters of men." Here he studied Euclid, the ancient languages, and—thanks to a tubercular schoolteacher—the works of Charles Dickens. Before MacDonald was 17, he had done some teaching himself. His salary: seven pounds, ten shillings a year. He used the school library to advantage, delving into the works of William Shakespeare, Thomas Carlyle, John Ruskin, and Henry George, and began his political life as an ardent follower of William E. Gladstone.

In 1885, at age 18, he set out to Bristol, where he aided a local clergyman in establishing a Young Men's Guild. While in a British Workingman's Coffee Tavern, he joined the Bristol branch of the Social Democratic Federation (SDF), founded only four years earlier by England's foremost Marxist H.M. Hyndman. Hyndman stressed class war, the abolition of private productive property, and nationalization of industry on a huge scale. With all the zeal of a convert, MacDonald spoke frequently—if unsuccessfully—for the SDF at street meetings.

As Bristol turned out to be a false start, MacDonald returned briefly to Lossiemouth. Early in 1886, he ventured to London, where he tramped the streets in search of work and survived only on hot water and oatmeal sent from home. He is said to have found employment on the day his very last shilling was spent: he was first hired to address envelopes, at ten shillings a week, for the Cyclists' Touring Club, then took a job at 15 shillings as an invoice clerk in a warehouse. Spending every spare minute in the Guildhall Library, he soon saw his health broken and was compelled to return home.

In 1888, MacDonald was again back in London and again unemployed. From 1888 to 1891, he was private secretary to a Gladstonian parliamentary candidate from the northern suburb of Islington. In 1894, he became a member of the Independent Labour Party (ILP), a group that saw socialism as more of a way of life than as adherence to orthodox Marxist dogma. A year later, MacDonald unsuccessfully stood for Parliament as ILP candidate from Southampton, polling only 886 votes. In 1896, the ILP elected him to its national administrative council.

Other political activity followed. In 1886, he had joined the Fabian Society, organized by middle-class intellectuals to introduce socialism by legislation, not class warfare. From 1894 to 1900, he served on its executive board. The ILP regarded him as too cautious, the Fabians as dangerously intransigent. In 1888, he became secretary of the Scottish Home Rule Association and in 1892, secretary of the Fellowship of the New Life, a group that maintained that a new socialist order needed morally superior humans to inhabit it. By then, he was earning a slender income from journalism. He was also establishing a reputation as a political orator, and here his fine presence, resonant voice, and Morayshire accent stood him in good stead.

In 1896, MacDonald married Margaret Ethel Gladstone, a social worker whose father was a distinguished chemist and active social reformer. She had mailed him money to cover his campaign expenses a month before she met him. Now relieved of financial worries, he could travel widely—going around the world in 1906 and to India in 1909. Their open houses for fellow socialists at Lincoln's Inn Fields became famous in reform circles. He would suffer a great loss with the death of the more outgoing and polished Margaret in 1911, just 18 months after the death of their youngest son. Becoming more introspective and aloof than ever, he would never remarry.

In 1900, MacDonald was unanimously chosen secretary of the Labour Representation Committee (LRC), then treasurer from 1912 to 1924. In an effort to secure Labour representation in Parliament, the LRC sought to unite the traditional liberal-laborism represented by the Trades Union Congress with the "class-war" brand of socialism advocated by the SDF. Yet this body, which in 1906 became the Labour Party, had a difficult time: only about five percent of the unions cooperated; the SDF soon withdraw; the Fabians were cool; and the powerful miners hostile.

By this time, MacDonald was becoming a prolific author. His *What I Saw in South Africa* (1903) revealed why he opposed the Boer War. In *Socialism and Society* (1906), he started with a stark collectivism.

> Throughout our lives, we are but as men feasting at the common table of a bountiful lord, and when we carry in the dishes for the feast or gather up the crumbs from the board, we pride ourselves on our wealth and the magnificent reward which our labor has brought us.

Capitalism, he continued, would disappear, but not because it was doomed to crisis and revolution; rather its success had created an inequality that only socialism could solve. Similarly, his *Socialism and Government* (1909) rejected the doctrine of class war and sought democratic reform. *The Socialist Movement* (1911) talked of "a law of mutual aid." *The Awakening of India* (1910) was called the best short book on India ever written by a tourist, and he expanded his findings in *The Government of India* (1919).

In 1906, MacDonald entered Parliament as Labour representative for Leicester, an industrial city in central Britain. His own election, and that of 28 other Labour candidates, resulted from a secret agreement with the Liberals by which each party agreed not to contest the other for certain seats. Speaking regularly and eloquently in the House of Commons, he was Labour's most effective voice, in the process establishing a reputation—in the words of Lord Balfour—as a "born parliamentarian."

Even more significantly he dominated his party, first in 1906 as chairman of the ILP, then in 1911 as chairman of the Labour Party. He continually maintained that the Party was socialist, not Marxist, and that its methods must be parliamentary and not revolutionary. During the strike wave of 1911–12, he pleaded the cause of the strikers while exhorting them to patience and discipline.

On August 5, 1914, the day after Britain declared war on Germany, MacDonald resigned the chairmanship of his Party. His reason: Labour pledged itself not to oppose the government's demands for a £100 million war credit. Incorrectly accused of being a pacifist and pro-German, he was soon the most hated man in England. The sensationalist editor Horatio Bottomley printed MacDonald's birth certificate in an attempt to discredit him, and his presence at a public meeting could provoke a riot.

MacDonald's position was far more complicated and seldom understood. He claimed that Britain was wrong to enter the war, but that once it had entered, it must win. He said, "Those who can enlist ought to enlist; those who are working in munition factories should do so whole-heartedly." Briefly, in 1914–15, he was part of a British ambulance unit attached to the Belgian army. His foreign policy could be summed up in the Wilsonian platform of the Union for Democratic control, a group he fostered.

MacDonald supported the first Russian revolution, which took place in February 1917 and was soon led by **Alexander Kerensky,** as it appeared to herald democracy, disavow imperialism, and promote a negotiated peace. The February revolution, MacDonald said, was "a sort of spring-tide of joy" bursting over Europe. He repeatedly warned that if the Western Allies were to insist on a military victory on Germany's eastern front, the moderate socialists in Russia would lose power; the incoming Bolsheviks would sign a separate peace that would result in disaster for Europe. When the Bolsheviks did gain control in October, MacDonald futilely called for diplomatic recognition of the new regime. He found the Allied intervention in Russia counterproductive, and believed that if left alone, Russia would return to parliamentary socialism. In 1920, he called the Bolshevik invasion of the Menshevik province of Georgia "a callous political crime," and he kept the ILP from joining the Third International.

In the general election of 1918, MacDonald lost his seat by just over 14,000 votes. In 1921, running for Parliament in a by-election at East Woolwich, a section of London, MacDonald was defeated by a narrow margin. In 1922, however, he was returned as member for the Aberavon division of Glamorganshire in South Wales. Upon election, he was immediately designated chairman of the Parliamentary Labour Party.

He Becomes Britain's
First Socialist Prime Minister

In the election of 1923, the Conservatives won the largest number of seats. However, the Labourites and Liberals together possessed nine more seats than the Conservatives. The Liberals, led by Herbert Asquith, shifted support to Labour, and on January 22, 1924, Ramsay MacDonald became the first socialist prime minister and foreign secretary that Great Britain ever had.

As MacDonald went to Buckingham Palace, there to kiss the hands of the king, George V confided to his diary: "Today 23 years ago dear Grandmama [Victoria] died. I wonder what she would have thought of a Labour Government!" MacDonald's appointment seemed revolutionary, as Labour had pledged itself to a capital levy and the nationalization of industry. Some feared that Labour would tamper with the army, navy, and civil service. A few extremists thought free love would receive official sanction.

Yet MacDonald was the safest of premiers: by instinct and doctrine he was a gradualist, opposing radical moves of any sort; the bulk of his following lay with the trade unionists, who were mildly socialistic at most; and his majority in the Commons, being dependent upon the Liberals, was uncertain. Hence under MacDonald—who almost appeared to be seeking to prove that a Labour government could be respectable—there was no exodus of capital. His greatest interest was foreign policy, which fortunately for him, was his forte. He secured French and British acceptance for the Dawes plan, a method of financing German reparations that expedited the withdrawal of the French from the Ruhr. The only British prime minister ever to attend the League of Nations Assembly, he signed the Geneva Protocol, by which signatory nations agreed to accept compulsory World Court jurisdiction on any question likely to result in war. (The succeeding ministry of Stanley Baldwin turned it down.) MacDonald suspended work on the great naval base at Singapore, doing so to avoid offending Japan. Far from being a dogmatic pacifist, he slightly increased the size of Britain's navy, and he refused to yield to Indian or Egyptian nationalists.

MacDonald's eloquence struck a ready chord in a generation that seldom attended church but craved sermons. If there was an appalling lack of substance, his addresses were delivered with such sincerity that they won him many followers. Trouble for MacDonald came over matters of communism and the Soviet Union. Within ten days after he took office, he announced recognition of Russia. In his desire to increase the sale of British goods overseas, he sought to float a Russian loan in the British market with interest and repayment guaranteed by the British government. In turn, the Soviets were to end all revolutionary propaganda in Britain. With the income tax standing at 25%, his plan to lend millions to the Soviets worked against him.

Then, before Parliament had a chance to vote on the loan, the following announcement appeared in the Communist *Workers Weekly:*

> From committees in every barracks, aerodrome and ship. Let this be the nucleus of an organization that which will prepare the whole of the soldiers, sailors and airmen not merely to refuse to go to war or to refuse to shoot strikers during industrial conflicts but will make it possible for the workers, peasants and soldiers, sailors and airmen to go forward in a common attack upon capitalism.

The editor, J. R. Campbell, was arrested for incitement to mutiny. Yet under MacDonald's orders, the attorney general dropped the charge, declaring that Campbell had merely sought to persuade soldiers and sailors to refuse police duty in strikes.

The final fiasco came with the so-called Zinoviev letter. **Grigori Zinoviev,** Russian president of the Third International, supposedly instructed a British Communist leader on methods for subverting England. Included was the comment:

> [There should be cells] in all units of the troops, particularly among those quartered in large centres … and also among factories working on munitions and at military store depots…. In the event of danger of war, with the aid of the latter and in contact with the transport workers, it is possible to paralyse all the military preparations of the bourgeoisie and make a start in turning an imperialist war into a class war.

The authenticity of the letter is still debated. According to Soviet expert George F. Kennan, it was probably drafted by White Russian and Polish forgers in Berlin. Historian Sibyl Crowe suspects it was genuine. When MacDonald forwarded the letter to the Foreign Office in the hopes that someone there would investigate its authenticity, it appeared to his critics that he was trying to suppress it. Four days before a major election, it was published in the right-wing *Daily Mail,* and the Conservatives returned to power with a huge majority. In addition to raising the issues of Russia and communism, the Tories claimed that MacDonald had injured the economy by repealing the duties that had given preference to dominion products. Moreover, they stressed that hunger, homelessness, and unemployment still remained. Yet it was the Liberal Party's refusal to continue backing the Labour government, and the subsequent defection of many Liberals in the election to Conservative ranks, that led to Labour's defeat. The Communist issue has been overplayed.

MacDonald's personal reputation did not suffer. Indeed, his influence within the Labour Party increased, and it was due to his influence that Labour again repudiated communism. During the general strike of May 1926, he remained true to his belief that such direct action could not bring true socialism. The nation as a whole had to be converted. Yet having done his best to avert this explosion, he felt bound to support the strikers. In 1928, he played a leading part in drafting the Party manifesto *Labour and the Nation* which combined comprehensive reform with a renewed condemnation of communism.

In May 1929, in the midst of worsening unemployment and Conservative inertia, Labour again returned to power. Possessing 287 seats in Parliament, for the first time it was the strongest party in Britain. Yet the Liberals, who again backed Labour, held the balance of power. MacDonald himself represented the Seaham division of county Durham, an industrial area on the North Sea.

MacDonald Focuses on Foreign Affairs

Though no longer holding the office of foreign secretary, Prime Minister MacDonald continued to focus on foreign affairs. He fostered the London Naval Conference of 1930, in which Britain, the U.S., France, Italy, and Japan agreed to limit certain smaller craft. Under MacDonald, Britain supported the Young Plan for German reparations payments, bound itself to submit most disputes to World Court arbitration, reestablished friendly relations with Russia, and sponsored the Indian Round Table Conference of 1930, which MacDonald personally chaired. Yet unemployment continued to rise, reaching over 2.5 million by 1931, the highest sum in eight years. Between 1929 and 1931, Britain's exports were cut in half, and its balance of payments deteriorated. Shipping

had declined; so had overseas investment. With characteristic aplomb, MacDonald said,

> We are not on trial; it is the system under which we live. It has broken down, not only in this little island.... it has broken down everywhere. And the cure, the new path, the new idea, is organization.

Chancellor of the Exchequer Philip Snowden, with MacDonald's concurrence, adhered to a balanced budget, increased taxation, and a freeze on social legislation. The Unemployment Insurance Fund was running in debt at the rate of £1 million a week. Destitution swept England. Heavy gold withdrawals were being made from the Bank of England. American bankers demanded a balanced budget as the price for saving the pound. The cabinet could not agree on a proposal to reduce unemployment payments, a bare majority accepting the bitter pill of a ten percent cut in the dole. The general council of the Trades Union Congress was resolutely opposed, and on August 24, the MacDonald Cabinet resigned.

King George V appealed to MacDonald to stay on, this time as head of a National Government composed strictly of individuals not parties. Such a regime would simply be temporary, an interim administration established for the sole purpose of settling the financial crisis. On August 25, MacDonald became head of such a government. It consisted of Conservatives, Liberals, and the minority of Labourites—called the National Labour group—who would still accept his leadership. The Labour Party expelled the small pro-MacDonald wing and chose Arthur Henderson, who had just been MacDonald's foreign secretary, as its new leader. Overnight Labour's standard-bearer became its fallen leader, and there was no more hated man in its ranks than J. Ramsay MacDonald. Four Labourites, four Conservatives, and two liberals comprised this first National Government, which included such figures as former Conservative prime minister **Stanley Baldwin,** who became lord president of the Council; Liberal Lord Reading, Rufus Isaacs, who became foreign secretary; and Liberal Sir Herbert Samuel, who became home secretary.

Possessing a parliamentary vote of confidence of 311 to 251, the new government set to work. By cutting unemployment insurance ten percent and drastically reducing the salary of all civil servants from policemen to judges, it balanced the budget. But as the level of the pound sterling continued to fall, it eliminated just what it promised to preserve: the gold standard. Henceforth, the Bank of England would no longer redeem, on demand, its paper money with gold.

A New Conservative Coalition Wins

In the election of October 27, 1931, the new coalition won. Out of 556 seats held by the National Government, a record 471 were occupied by Conservatives. MacDonald, the lifelong socialist, no longer appealed to the electorate as chieftain of the Labour Party but as head of a coalition that became increasingly dominated by Conservatives. Claiming that the pound would be worth nothing should Labour win, MacDonald waved worthless German paper, with a face value of millions of marks, before his audiences. If Labour was elected, he warned, a million British pounds could not buy a postage stamp. Seeking sweeping powers, he asked for "a doctor's mandate"—blanket authority for the National Government to make what prescriptions it desired.

As with his previous ministries, he devoted the bulk of his time to foreign policy. He could count one success: the Government of India Act of 1935, which called for an all-India federation and greater autonomy in the provinces. Believing that the European situation was the key to domestic recovery, he fostered the Geneva Disarmament Conference of April 1932; the Four-Power Conference in London that same month; the World Economic Conference held in London beginning June of 1933; and the Stresa Front of April 1935, wherein he, Italian dictator **Benito Mussolini,** and French premier **Pierre Laval** sought to check German rearmament. All such efforts ended up in failure, and soon the growing menace of Germany appeared obvious. Hence he pushed the White Paper on National Defense, which heralded a program of rearmament.

In this, MacDonald's second National Government, domestic policy was determined by Lord President Baldwin and by a new chancellor of the exchequer, **Neville Chamberlain.** Believing that England must abandon free trade if it were to remain a capitalist nation, such Conservatives promoted the Ottawa agreements of 1932. By its terms, dominion nations raised tariffs against nations outside the British Commonwealth and Britain placed a tariff on foreign agricultural products. The Liberals left the coalition in disgust. The second National Government also granted subsidies to shipping and sought to relieve distressed areas by relocating the unemployed.

On June 7, 1935, MacDonald resigned the prime ministership. In a government led by Baldwin, he was made lord president of the council. By then he was an object of much pity. His eyesight had faded, his memory was weakened. He had lost the power to sustain a thought or follow an argument, much less deliver a coherent speech. Once, while speaking in Parliament, he kept looking over his shoulder, fearful that a man in the peers' gallery was about to shoot him in the back. His former Labour supporters continued to harass him mercilessly. His powers were further impaired by prolonged overwork.

Defeated at Seaham in the November election, MacDonald returned to Parliament in January 1936 as member for the Scottish universities. On November 9, 1937, he died at sea on a holiday voyage to South America.

SOURCES:

Barker, Bernard, ed. *Ramsay MacDonald's Political Writings.* St. Martin's Press, 1972.

Elton, Lord. *The Life of James Ramsay MacDonald.* Collins, 1939.

Marquand, David. *Ramsay MacDonald.* Jonathan Cape, 1977.

FURTHER READING:

Taylor, A. J. P. *English History, 1914–1945.* Oxford University Press, 1965.

Harold Macmillan

(1894–1986)

Conservative British statesman, whose 40-year career in public service culminated with a term as prime minister during the period of imperial dissolution, a diminished role in world affairs, and a brief period of unprecedented economic affluence in Britain.

"The wind of change is blowing through this continent, and, whether we like it or not, this growth of national consciousness is a political fact."

HAROLD MACMILLAN
CAPE TOWN, SOUTH AFRICA
(1968)

Maurice Harold Macmillan was born in Chelsea, London, England, on February 10, 1894. He was the son of Maurice Crawford Macmillan, a Scotsman and son of the founder of the Macmillan Publishing Company, and Helen Artie Belles Macmillan, an American who was born in Spencer, Indiana. At age nine, after attending Gladstone's Day School, Macmillan was sent to the exclusive boarding school Summerfields in Oxford. Following a rather undistinguished record at Eton, he entered Balliol College, Oxford, in 1912. Already interested in politics, he joined several university organizations, including the Oxford Union; elected secretary of the union in 1913 and treasurer in 1914, he might have won the presidency but for the outbreak of war.

Macmillan was commissioned in the King's Royal Rifle Corps at the onset of World War I, then transferred to the Grenadier Guards. Promoted to the rank of captain, he was wounded in the head and arm at the battle of Loos in 1915 and hospitalized in London. Returning to France, he fought in the Second Battle of Ypres and in September 1916 had his pelvis shattered during the

Born Maurice Harold Macmillan on February 10, 1894, in Chelsea, London, England; died at Birch Grove House, Sussex, England, on December 29, 1986; son of Maurice Crawford (a Scotsman and son of the founder of the Macmillan Publishing Company) and Helen Artie (Belles) Macmillan (American-born); married: Lady Dorothy Evelyn Cavendish (daughter of the 9th Duke of Devonshire), 1920; children: (one son) Maurice (member of Parliament, economic secretary at the Treasury); (three daughters) Carol, Catherine, and Sarah. Predecessor: Anthony Eden. Successor: Sir Alec Douglas-Home.

Contributed by Phillip E. Koerper, Professor of History, Jacksonville State University, Jacksonville, Alabama

CHRONOLOGY

1894	Born in Chelsea, London, England
1914	Commissioned in the Kings Rifle Corps
1915–16	Wounded at Battle of Loos and at the Somme River
1919–20	Aide-de-camp to the governor-general of Canada
1924–29	Elected to Parliament as a Conservative candidate for Stockton-on-Tees
1931–45	Member of Parliament for Stockton-on-Tees
1940–42	Parliamentary undersecretary to the Ministry of Supply; undersecretary of state for the Colonies
1942–45	Resident Minister at Allied headquarters, Northwest Africa
1945	Secretary for Air
1945–64	Member of Parliament for Bromley, Kent
1951–54	Minister of Defense
1955	Secretary of State for Foreign Affairs
1955–57	Chancellor of the exchequer; prime minister and First Lord of the Treasury
1963	Resigned as prime minister
1986	Died at Birch Grove House, Sussex, England

battle of the Sommes. His wound would not fully heal until 1920, leaving him with a lifetime of pain and a shuffling gait.

In 1919, Macmillan went to Canada as aide-de-camp on the staff of the Ninth Duke of Devonshire, the governor-general of the Dominion. While in Canada, he met and fell in love with the duke's daughter, Lady Dorothy Cavendish. They returned to England and were married on April 21, 1920, at St. Margaret's, Westminster. Among the wedding guests were Queen Alexandra, the prime minister of Wales (later George VI), Rudyard Kipling, and Thomas Hardy.

Following his 1920 return to Britain, Macmillan became a director in the family publishing firm but maintained his interest in politics. Although he would hold political office over the next 20 years, he worked for the Macmillan firm until he joined the Churchill Government in 1940.

In 1923, emphasizing his desire to gain political experience as much as to win an election victory, Macmillan requested that the Conservative Party's central office include him in their list of candidates. He was assigned to campaign in the seemingly hopeless Liberal Party stronghold of Stockton-on-Tees. Although he had little knowledge of that industrial constituency where unemployment was very high, he and his wife campaigned vigorously. In an election that went poorly for the Conservatives, he lost to the Liberal candidate by only 73 votes. In the general election of October 1924, Macmillan won Stockton over the Labour candidate by more than 3,000 votes. With the exception of two years between 1929–31, he would represent Stockton until 1945.

In his first speech in the House of Commons on April 30, 1925, Macmillan verbally supported **Winston Churchill**'s budget resolution. The Labour members' charge that it was a "rich man's budget," Macmillan called a "monstrous statement" made by a party that had failed to make the same proposals for contributory pensions for widows, orphans, and the elderly while they were in office. Although a somewhat controversial speech, it was well received in the Commons and led to speaking and writing invitations.

Macmillan attached himself to a group of young progressive members of the commons known as the Young Conservatives (humorously called the "Y.M.C.A."). Veterans of the war and representatives of industrial constituencies, they were appalled by the nation's working conditions and unemployment. During the General Strike of 1926, Macmillan developed a deeper sympathy for the strikers and a growing resentment toward Prime Minister **Stanley Baldwin**'s failure to keep his promise of providing a better program for industry.

In a national rejection of Baldwin and the Conservative Government's policies, Macmillan was defeated at Stockton in the general election of 1929. During the coalition rule of **Ramsay MacDonald**'s National Government (1931–35), Macmillan called the veteran cabinet members on the front bench "a row of misused slag heaps." Unopposed in Stockton in the general election of 1934, he won by a majority of over 11,000 votes.

Remaining an advocate of social reform and a champion of a planned economy, he was considered a rebel against Conservative Party discipline and ideology. In 1933, he wrote *Reconstruction: A Plea for a National Policy* which urged the government to choose between orderly capitalism or an impending economic and social disaster. His ideas were expanded in *The Middle Way*, which he published in 1938. Having been influenced by the ideas of John Maynard Keynes and **David Lloyd George**, Macmillan, during his first decade in Parliament, became consistently and more permanently influenced by the views of Winston Churchill in the 1930s.

MacMillan Criticizes Party Policy Toward Facisim

During the appeasement of Conservative prime minister Stanley Baldwin (1935–37) and **Neville Chamberlain** (1937–40), Macmillan joined Churchill as one of the early critics of their ministries. He attacked the government for undermining the League of Nations through its ill-directed policy during the Italian invasion of Ethiopia. In 1938, he ridiculed as hypocrisy Chamberlain's statement that the Munich Agreement with Nazi Germany was peace by negotiation. Macmillan again joined Churchill in November 1938, demanding that a Ministry of Supply be established because of the inevitability of war. His often vitriolic speeches referred to Baldwin and Chamberlain as "extinct volcanoes," as he openly criticized his Party's policies toward the Fascist states of Europe.

With the outbreak of war in September 1939, Macmillan was not included in the reorganization of Chamberlain's cabinet and therefore continued, along with other members of Commons, to criticize Chamberlain's failure to act in the Finnish Crisis (1940) and his inadequate leadership of the general war effort. During the debates over Chamberlain's leadership on May 7–8, 1940, Macmillan spoke and voted against the prime minister. On May 10, following Chamberlain's resignation, Churchill formed a wartime cabinet, and Macmillan received his first ministerial position after 16 years in Parliament. He was appointed parliamentary secretary to the Minister of Supply and served in that position from 1940 to 1942. He was Undersecretary of State for Colonies in 1942 and then received his most important wartime office, Minister Resident at Allied headquarters in Northwest Africa from 1942 to 1945. In his latter position, Macmillan worked closely with Churchill and served as a mediating figure between the quarreling political and military officials in the Allied coalition. During this time, he developed a genuine friendship with General **Charles de Gaulle** of France and with the American Allied commander, General **Dwight D. Eisenhower.**

When the war in Europe ended in 1945, Macmillan held a cabinet ministry as Secretary of State for Air in Churchill's "caretaker" Government (May–July 1945), while awaiting results of the general election. Macmillan lost his Stockton seat in the general election on July 5, but a safe Conservative seat was located for him at Bromley, Kent, which he would represent until his 1964 retirement from the Commons. As a member of Churchill's opposition Shadow Cabinet, he was chairman of the Conservative Fuel and Power Committee and a leading spokesman against the Labour Government's nationalization policy. He championed the European postwar reconstruction and was one of the most influential delegates at the 1948 Congress of Europe that laid the groundwork for the Council of Europe (1949). He served as a delegate to the Economic League of European Cooperation and represented the House of Commons at the Assembly of the Council of Europe in 1949 in Strasbourg, France. In 1950, his plan for the development and regulation of a common European coal and steel industry was widely admired by council members. Greatly respected in economic affairs, he headed the British delegation to the Conference of the European League for Economic Cooperation in Brussels and served a third time as delegate to the Assembly of the Council of Europe in 1951.

When the Conservatives won the general election of October 1951, Churchill returned as prime minister and appointed Macmillan to the cabinet as Minister of Housing and Local Government, charging him with the task of building 300,000 houses a year. By selecting capable assistants, reorganizing the ministry, and applying good business methods, he met the construction goal in 1953.

After three years at Housing, in October 1954, Macmillan was appointed to succeed Earl Alexander of Tunis as Minister of Defense in a cabinet reshuffle. He served in that office until **Anthony Eden** succeeded Churchill as prime minister on April 6, 1955, and moved Macmillan to the position of foreign secretary. During his brief tenure in the Foreign Office, Macmillan met the U.S. and French foreign secretaries in Paris in May, went from Paris to Vienna for the signing of the Austrian Treaty, and attended the four-power Summit Conference at Geneva in July. On December 20, 1955, Eden appointed him to succeed Richard Austin Butler as chancellor of the exchequer (Treasury). At the exchequer, he introduced only one budget that was chiefly remembered for the introduction of the Premium Bonds (lottery) scheme. The problems of the British economy and Macmillan's fiscal program were soon overshadowed by the Suez Canal intervention which helped end Eden's Government in early 1957.

MacMillan Forms New Conservative Government

When Eden resigned as prime minister on January 10, 1957, because of poor health and declining public support following the Suez Crisis, Macmillan was called to form a new Conservative Government. Although he had initially supported intervention in Egypt, Macmillan had shifted his stance when he correctly anticipated the international opposition to the policy. His position on the canal issue was questioned by the Opposition but did him no serious harm with Conservatives. It was generally believed that Macmillan would only be a stopgap prime minister. The British people were bitterly divided, the Conservative Party in disarray, and the cabinet in stalemate. To everyone's surprise, Macmillan remained in office for nearly seven years—the longest period held by a prime minister in 40 years.

In foreign affairs, he inherited the aftermath of the Suez debacle and a serious breach in British-American relations. But he quickly restored British prestige and repaired relations with the United States by meeting President Eisenhower in Bermuda in March 1957, and by visiting him in America in June 1958 and March 1959.

Macmillan seemed to enjoy holding power. He used personal diplomacy to enhance his foreign policy credentials, while using television to display his stature and maturity by "fireside chats" with the public. Believing confidence was a major part of economics, he soon effected an upward turn in industrial production, job growth, and salary increases. The public continued to fuel the recovery by massive purchases of appliances, automobiles, and an unprecedented number of homes. After a brief slump, the resumption of the economic boom was great enough for Macmillan to seek an electoral vote of confidence from the country. Running in 1959 on the slogan "You never had it so good," his Conservative Party increased its majority by 21 seats to a 365–258 majority over the Labour Party. Cartoons and shirts were sold with Macmillan affectionately caricatured as "Super-Mac."

In foreign policy, he strove to play the elder statesman and mediator between the American and Soviet superpowers. While standing firm against threats by the Soviets, he continued to work toward establishing a basis for negotiations. His hopes for a 1960 big-power summit conference in Paris were ruined by the U-2 incident shortly before the scheduled conference.

Although his personal relationship with President John F. Kennedy was good, Macmillan was hurt by the appearance of differences between the two leaders. The British public was disappointed in the way that Macmillan and Britain were relegated to the role of spectator during the 1962 Cuban Missile Crisis. Public dissatisfaction with his leadership grew following the Nassau meeting with Kennedy in December 1962; many believed that Macmillan's decision in Nassau to substitute Polaris submarine missiles for the controversial Skybolt missiles damaged British military power.

During his tenure, Britain had joined the European Free Trade Association and had continued economic ties with the British Commonwealth. Anticipating Britain's economic future, Macmillan opened negotiations to obtain membership in the prosperous European Economic Common Market. This break with Britain's traditional independence from the continent encountered strong opposition and a party split, resulting in election setbacks in 1962. In July, he replaced seven cabinet ministers in an effort to end Conservative discontent. Then on January 29, 1963—following the Skybolt decision at Nassau in December—France's enraged Charles de Gaulle vetoed Britain's entry into the Common Market on the grounds that Britain's special relationship with the United States threatened European independence from America.

In addition to his foreign policy setbacks, by 1963 Macmillan had serious domestic problems. His government was embarrassed by an apparent Soviet espionage endeavor that became a scandal involving John Profumo, secretary of state for war, and a London call-girl ring. Macmillan was initially misled by Profumo, who later admitted his guilt and resigned. But the implications of security breaches and negligence were blamed on Macmillan during a time of economic decline and increasing unemployment.

Macmillan did achieve several outstanding successes during his ministry. His 1960 "winds of change" speech in South Africa acknowledged the end of colonialism and the inevitability of African independence. He was also instrumental in producing the Nuclear Test-Ban Treaty in 1963.

Macmillan underwent surgery for prostate cancer on October 8, 1963. After consulting with his conservative colleagues, he resigned on October 18, 1963; two hours later, Queen Elizabeth visited him at the hospital. He retained his seat for Bromley until 1964. Returning to the Macmillan publishing firm, he used his leisure time to write his six-volume memoirs. Though he had previously refused a peerage, the 90-year-old Macmillan relented in 1984 and became the earl of Stockton. He died at Birch Grove, Sussex, on December 29, 1986.

SOURCES:

Fisher, Nigel. *Harold Macmillan: A Biography*. Weidenfeld & Nicolson, 1982.

Macmillan, Harold. *The Winds of Change: 1914–1939* (1966), *The Blast of War: 1939–1945* (1969), *Tides of Fortune: 1945–1955* (1969), *Riding the Storm: 1956–1959* (1971), *Pointing the Way: 1959–1961* (1972), *At the End of the Day: 1961–1963* (1973)—all published by Harper and Row.

Pike, E. Royston. *Britain's Prime Ministers From Walpole to Wilson.* Odhams Books, 1968.

FURTHER READING:

Horne, Alistair. *Harold Macmillan: 1894–1986.* 2 vols. Viking, 1988–89.

Sampson, Anthony. *Macmillan: A Study in Ambiguity.* Simon & Schuster, 1967.

Van Thal, Herbert. *The Prime Ministers From Sir Robert Walpole to Edward Heath.* Stein & Day, 1975.

Karl Gustaf Mannerheim

(1867–1951)

General in the armies of both imperial Russia and republican Finland, president of Finland, epicure and aristocrat, who was an 18th-century cosmopolite condemned to live in the 20th century.

Name variation: Field Marshal Baron Gustaf Mannerheim. Pronunciation: Manner-HYME. Born Karl or Carl Gustaf Emil, Baron von Mannerheim in Swedish Finland in 1867; died in Switzerland in 1951.

Gustaf Mannerheim was the descendant of a distinguished Swedish noble family that had settled in western Finland in the 18th century, acquiring considerable property. Retaining their essentially Swedish identity, the Mannerheims were not properly Finns, the indigenous people, but rather Finlanders. As a youth, Mannerheim decided on a military career, but he had already developed the streak of willfulness that would be prominent in his mature character. He entered a military academy in Helsinki at the age of 15 but was dismissed four years later for being absent without leave.

To the young Mannerheim, Finland was a place lacking both in culture and opportunity. Never really Finnish in disposition, never mastering the difficult language, and always preferring Russia, or Poland, or England, or Switzerland to the land of his birth, he therefore resolved to seek a fuller life elsewhere. Thus began a life of migration, in which he returned to Finland only in times of distress. That Mannerheim emerged as the savior of Finland is thus paradoxical.

On the heels of the cadet academy dismissal, Mannerheim emigrated to Russia, where he found

"I look forward happily to that moment when I can turn my back forever on Finland and leave—God knows where, but at least I can be my own master."

BARON KARL GUSTAF MANNERHEIM
(1883)

Contributed by Lamar Cecil, Professor of History, Washington and Lee University, Lexington, Virginia

great success in a military career. After receiving a commission, he entered an elite regiment that often did duty at the Romanov court of Tsar **Nicholas II.** The exotic court appealed to Mannerheim's sense of drama. A man of punctilious manners, elegant in appearance, conservative in tastes, an expert horseman, a lover of opulence and refinement, he soon established a sure footing at court, was promoted rapidly in rank, and established friendships within the royal family and with the Tsar's courtiers and government officials. He also married the daughter of a noble general who was a descendant of the great poet Pushkin, but since Mannerheim's enthusiasms were conspicuously military rather than domestic, the baroness and their two daughters soon left him.

After serving with distinction in the Russo-Japanese War and traveling extensively through China and Japan on a military inspection trip, Mannerheim assumed a variety of commands in the army, rising to the rank of lieutenant-general. In the First World War, he was an able and popular commander, but the fall of the Tsar in March 1917 soured his once great affection for Russia. To Mannerheim, **Alexander Kerensky** and his socialist government were traitors and savages, and **Lenin**—who succeeded Kerensky in November 1917—was even worse. Deciding to return to Finland, Mannerheim reached Helsinki in May 1918 after a series of narrow escapes.

Finland, which for centuries had been a province of imperial Russia, was taking advantage of the revolution in Russia to proclaim its independence. Voting to establish a monarchy, the parliament—for some uncharacteristic reason—invited a German prince to come and rule over their country as king. Although the German Kaiser offered his brother-in-law, Prince Friederich Karl of Hesse, the German princeling never set foot in Finland. The Finns, therefore, needed a regent, and they turned to Mannerheim. Although virtually unknown in his own country, Mannerheim was the only person with the sort of military experience necessary to defend the new republic. He knew little of the nation, he had very few friends, and his command of the language was so negligible that his orders had sometimes to be conveyed through interpreters. Living in considerable pomp, eating superbly, dressing with equal elegance in uniform or in mufti, he would not partake of the traditional austerity of Finnish life. There was no other Finn quite like him, but therein lay Mannerheim's destiny. Finland, it seemed, was to be ruled by a man who was Finnish only by an accident of birth.

The nation was convulsed in a civil war. On the Left were partisans of Lenin and other social-

CHRONOLOGY

1867	Born in Swedish Finland
1889	Officer in imperial Russian army
1904–05	Served in Russo-Japanese War
1906–08	Traveled in China and Japan
1909–17	Served in Poland; rose to rank of lieutenant-general
1917	Fled from Russia to Finland
1918	Commander in chief of Finnish army; defeated Bolshevik revolution in Finland; named regent
1919	Defeated in presidential elections
1931	Made head of Defense Council
1939	Commander in chief in "Winter War" against Russia
1941	Commander in chief in "Continuation War" against Russia
1944–46	President of Finland
1951	Died in Switzerland

ists who held much of southern Finland, and who, in some cases, proposed joining Finland to Russia as a constituent republic of the U.S.S.R. On the Right were so-called "white Finns," who were violently opposed to Bolshevism, believing that Finland and Germany should cooperate to destroy socialism not only in Finland but in Russia itself. Mannerheim's victorious campaign against the Left won him the gratitude of the Right, but it also alienated many Finns. When a republic was proclaimed in 1919 and Mannerheim ran for president, he was soundly defeated. His aristocratic contempt for parliamentary democracy was well-known, and the Finns, many of whom were still socialists in spite of their defeat at Mannerheim's hands, were suspicious of his allegiance to the republic.

Stung by this rebuff, Mannerheim spent the next 12 years traveling in Europe, cultivating a variety of friends, including **Winston Churchill, Georges Clemenceau,** and **Marshal Pilsudski,** the dictator of Poland. During this period, he attracted a circle of conservative admirers, some of whom were sympathetic with the Nazi movement in Germany. Finland's position by 1930 was very delicate. Lenin and the Bolsheviks claimed that the nation was properly Russian; Sweden, which was neutral, believed that the Swedish-speaking parts of Finland were properly hers. The only power who could render Finland effective aid in such a situation was Germany, and many members of the government argued in favor of a close connection with Berlin, especially after the rabidly anti-Bolshevik **Adolf Hitler** took power in 1933. For that reason, it seemed that Finland needed to be vigilant, and no one but Mannerheim could provide effective military leadership.

The "Mannerheim Line" Defends Against Russia

In 1931, he was named chief of the Council of Defense, and for the remainder of the decade worked effectively to improve Finland's defenses against Russia, constructing the so-called "Mannerheim Line," a series of fortifications across the Karelian Isthmus in the especially vulnerable southern part of the country. Mannerheim's activity was dictated by the increasingly truculent attitude **Joseph Stalin** took toward Finland, demanding—in vain—territory or the stationing of Russian troops in order to better defend himself against any future aggression by Hitler.

At the end of November 1939, Stalin, fortified by his alliance with Hitler and their common victory two months earlier over Poland, attacked Finland. The so-called "Winter War" began with the hopelessly outnumbered Finns taking to their skis to defeat the Russians. "Sublime Finland," Mannerheim's friend Churchill declared, "which shows what free men can do." But this initial success was short-lived, for Stalin was eventually able to draw up his massive artillery against Mannerheim. Pragmatic by nature, Mannerheim decided that Finland had no choice but to negotiate a 1940 peace treaty, by which Finland was required to cede to Russia strategic territory in the south and to pay a massive indemnity.

Since Mannerheim's task was to protect what remained of Finland from future deprivations by Russia, it was clear that only Hitler could help. The aristocratic Finnish leader had no liking for the low-born German tyrant, but Mannerheim overcame that distaste and entered into an agreement with the Führer that improved Hitler's position against Russia. When, in June 1941, Hitler attacked Russia, Stalin replied by declaring war on Finland, claiming that it was an ally of his enemy. Mannerheim, aided by German troops, now invaded southern Finland and successfully reclaimed the territories he had lost. In June 1942, Mannerheim's 75th birthday was celebrated with great panoply, and Hitler, never enthusiastic about traveling outside Germany, flew to Helsinki to offer his congratulations. Returning the honor, Mannerheim traveled to Berlin a few weeks later.

By the end of the year, however, Germany's fortunes had suffered a serious reverse. The Russian's had encircled the German army in its attempt to take Stalingrad. The surrender of Hitler's forces there early in 1943 convinced Mannerheim that Germany would lose the war and that Russia would emerge the victor. Finland's future would be in grave jeopardy if it continued to support the Führer and antagonize Stalin.

The Finnish government recognized that the very existence of the republic was now at stake and that only Mannerheim, with his strong will, military ability, and international connections was equal to this critical moment. In July 1944, he was elected president and proceeded to take the necessary steps to save Finland. The only course of action, unpalatable though it might be, was to break all ties with Berlin, end the war with Russia, and seek as favorable terms as possible from Stalin. The Kremlin's terms were the removal of all German forces from Finland, the return of the territories won by Russia in the "Winter War" of 1939–40, and the payment of a huge indemnity. In June 1944, just as the Allies invaded France, Mannerheim notified Hitler that German troops were to be removed, and three months later he concluded a peace treaty with Russia that essentially fulfilled Stalin's punitive terms. Finland survived, but the country was reduced in size and all but destroyed economically.

Mannerheim continued as president until 1946, when he resigned because of increasing age and ill health. Eager to spend his old age in more comfortable and civilized conditions than Finland could afford, he retired to Switzerland, where he wrote his memoirs and where he died in 1951. Although universally admired for his military prowess in repulsing the Russians at the beginning of the "Winter War," and for salvaging what could be salvaged in the contest between Hitler and Stalin, in which Finland unhappily found itself caught in the middle, Mannerheim's reputation as a statesmen and his identity as a Finn or even a Finlander have rightly been questioned. His pragmatism sometimes veered on opportunism, he had no enthusiasm for parliamentary democracy, and he was contemptuous of the backwardness of the Finns and their cultural isolation from the rest of Europe.

Mannerheim's bravery and ability as a soldier was exemplary, but otherwise he was peculiarly alienated from the time and place of his birth; he was at heart, as one French observer declared, a courtier at the Versailles of Louis XIV. His genius lay in his ability, in moments of crisis, to rally the Finns, who were often set against one another and hostile to Mannerheim as well, in organizing their defense against the Russian giant to the East, and in leading them under unfavorable circumstances to victories that were often only partial or short in duration. Mannerheim was imperfect, but he was also remarkable, and that Finland has managed to survive for almost 50 years after he retired from office is in large measure due to Mannerheim.

SOURCES:

The Memoirs of Marshal Mannerheim. New York, 1954.

Warner, Oliver. *Marshal Mannerheim and the Finns.* London, 1967.

FURTHER READING:

Engle, Eloise, and Lauri Paananen. *The Winter War: The Russo-Finnish Conflict, 1939-40.* New York, 1973.

Rintala, Marvin. *Four Finns: Political Profiles.*

Wuorinen, J. H. *Finland and World War II.* New York, 1948.

Marcus Aurelius

(121–180)

Roman emperor and Stoic philosopher, who secured the borders of the Empire against repeated attack and whose memoirs, *The Meditations*, have inspired generations.

Name variations: (full imperial name) Imperator Caesar Marcus Aurelius Antoninus Augustus; nicknamed Verissimus ("very truthful") by the emperor Hadrian. Born Marcus Annius Verus Catilius Severus on April 26, 121, in Rome; died in Vienna on March 17, 180; married: Faustina (daughter of Antoninus Pius); children: fourteen. Predecessor: Antoninus Pius. Successor: Commodus.

Marcus Aurelius was raised and educated—possibly more than anyone else in Roman history—to rule the Empire. Called a solemn child from earliest infancy, it was precisely his somber, dedicated approach to his studies that impressed the emperor **Hadrian,** who took a keen interest in his childhood development. In the classroom, Marcus was provided with the leading literary and philosophical figures of the day; out of the classroom, he was exposed early to official duty and gradually integrated into the day-to-day running of the Empire. His education was representative of the man he was to become: the last emperor truly at home in classical civilization.

After the death of his father when he was two, Marcus was raised by his grandfather Marcus Annius Verus, who was three times consul–chief magistrate of Rome. According to his later diaries, *The Meditations,* he learned from his grandfather "good character and avoidance of bad temper," from his mother "religious piety, generosity, not only refraining from wrongdoing but even from thoughts of it, simplicity in diet, and to be far removed from the ways of the rich." His grandfather probably began his lessons at home by teach-

"Severe to himself, indulgent to the imperfection of others, just and beneficent to all mankind."

EDWARD GIBBON

Contributed by Steven L. Tuck, Ph.D. candidate in Classical Art and Archaeology, University of Michigan, Ann Arbor, Michigan

ing him the basics of reading and writing, after which, at the age of seven, the boy was turned over to tutors for formal schooling.

His first tutors were for Greek and Latin language, literature, and oratory; as with all Roman boys, however, character was emphasized above all. His own later recollections of childhood included learning not to staunchly support one side or the other at chariot races or gladiatorial contests, "to bear pain and be content with little, to work with my own hands, to mind my own business, to be slow to listen to slander."

At the same time, his education in official duties began. Still only seven, he was enrolled in the priestly College of the Salii, an elite group of 24 priests chosen from senatorial families to perform the ceremonies for the public worship of Mars, the god of war. That he was chosen for this honor by Hadrian indicates the special favor in which Marcus was held.

His secondary education began at the age of 12, at which time he had two Latin tutors and was tutored in Greek by Alexander of Cotiaeum, the leading contemporary authority on Homer. It was considered essential for a civilized Roman to know Greek and the student took to it well, eventually writing even his personal diaries in Greek. Marcus also was introduced to the additional areas of study necessary for the proper education of a member of the senatorial class, Roman law, mathematics, music, and painting among them. Nor was his physical training ignored. He studied riding, boxing, wrestling, and running, while also enjoying fishing and falconry and earning a reputation as a talented ball player.

Perhaps his greatest influence at this time was his tutor Diognetus, the painting-master, from whom Marcus gained his introduction to philosophy. Under Diognetus's instruction he attended his first lectures by prominent philosophers and wrote philosophical dialogues. So serious in fact was Marcus in his devotion to philosophy that he eagerly sought to adopt the austere lifestyle of a philosopher, pursuing his studies clad in a rough Greek cloak and sleeping on the ground when possible.

At the age of 14, Marcus assumed the toga *virilis,* the garment of manhood. Now a full citizen, he received a new honor; he was named prefect (magistrate of the city in the absence of the consuls), during the annual Latin Festival. He was also betrothed, at the wishes of Hadrian, to the daughter of the emperor's chosen successor Ceionius Commodus. This signaled Marcus's acceptance as a possible imperial successor.

CHRONOLOGY

121	Born in Rome
138	Hadrian died; accession of Antoninus Pius as emperor; Aurelius betrothed to Faustina; Hadrian deified
140	At 18, made consul for the first time; attended imperial councils
161	Antoninus Pius died; Aurelius became emperor with Lucius Verus as co-ruler
169	Lucius Verus died
170–71	Romans defeated; Greece and Italy invaded
172	Aurelius defeated invaders; began Roman offensive
175	Rebellion of Cassius in Syria; Aurelius and court headed east
179	Led Roman victory over northern tribes
180	Marcus Aurelius died at age 58 in Vienna

As a result of his new membership in Commodus's household, Marcus met Stoic philosopher Apollonius of Chalcedon, a leading exponent of the then fashionable school of philosophy. The Stoic system was divided into three sections: Logic, including the theory of knowledge and study of languages; Physics, including theology and metaphysics; and Ethics, the ultimate aim. The philosophy as a whole was compared to a body, of which the bones and muscles were Logic, the flesh and blood Physics, and the soul Ethics.

Marcus Is Tutored by Well-Known Orators

Since Marcus's betrothal had been political in nature, it did not survive the changing political climate. In 138, Hadrian was gravely ill and his designated successor, Commodus, died. Hadrian chose Titus Antoninus Pius as his new successor, formally adopting him as his son and heir. Antoninus in turn was made to adopt both Commodus's son, Lucius Verus, and Marcus who became Marcus Aelius Aurelius Verus Caesar. To further show support for Marcus as Antoninus's successor, Hadrian betrothed him to Antoninus's daughter Faustina. During the year of Hadrian's death, Antoninus Pius succeeded peacefully as emperor, and Marcus at last began his higher education. His new tutors were the most famous and influential in his education: Herodes Atticus and Marcus Cornelius Fronto, two of the most distinguished orators, in Greek and Latin respectively, of the age. Herodes Atticus, an Athenian whose father had been consul, was known for his oratorical specialty: elegant, metaphorically-subtle Greek. He was also the wealthiest man in the eastern part of the Empire; he had met Antoninus Pius when they shoved one another aside in a narrow street. Marcus continued his association with his tutor for the rest of his life.

As a legal advocate, Fronto was considered second only to **Cicero**—the first-century B.C. orator whose speeches were the model for hundreds of years. Instructing in the traditional way, he urged his pupils to study the language of classical writers, recommending Cicero and **Julius Caesar.** Marcus continued his association with Fronto as well, providing correspondence which has helped shed light on his early public life as the heir apparent to Antoninus Pius. Their letters trace Marcus's intellectual development, his significant adoption of the Stoic lifestyle, and the inner workings of the imperial court.

During Antoninus Pius's reign, Marcus took on an integral part in governing the Empire, becoming consul at a mere 18 years of age. As the highest elected office in Rome, the consul was usually held by much older men, often as the crowning achievement of a long career in government service. That Marcus held the office so young, in fact below the minimum legal age, exemplified the trust Antoninus Pius placed in his adopted son. Marcus also began to attend meetings of the consilium, the imperial council. In 145, at age 23, Marcus married Faustina and served as consul a second time, but he did not receive his first real power until December 1, 147, the day after the birth of his first child, a daughter. Granted the imperium (authority over the armies and provinces of the emperor), Marcus earned the right to bring one measure before the senate after the four which Antoninus Pius could introduce. In addition, he was granted the *tribunicia potestas* (tribunal power), which included the rights and powers of the tribune of the plebs—the traditional protector of the rights of common Romans. Theoretically, this included the rights of inviolability, of veto, of summoning the Senate, and of bringing bills before the assembly of the plebs.

The years from 146 to 147 also saw Marcus wholeheartedly turn toward philosophy. From his correspondence with Fronto, we know of his decreasing satisfaction with rhetoric and the increasing appeal of the teachings of Epictetus whose Stoic philosophy steadily became the inspiration for Marcus's actions and perspectives. Embracing the teachings of calm acceptance of adversity, sure knowledge of death, and of the duty to conform freely to whatever destiny might bring, his stoicism served him well during the numerous crises of his later reign.

Marcus and Lucius Verus Share Power

Marcus Aurelius was proclaimed emperor on March 7, 161, after the death of Antoninus Pius. Adding Antoninus to his name in tribute to his adoptive father, he immediately petitioned the senate that Lucius Verus also receive the title "Augustus"—previously reserved only for the emperor—as well as the tribunicial and proconsular power. This first occasion of joint authority in the principate served as a model for later emperors. To further secure the bond between them, Lucius Verus was also betrothed to Marcus's daughter, Lucilla. Still, there remained no question as to who was the senior partner. Ten years older than Lucius, Marcus had served as consul once more and for 14 years had shared power, if at a lesser level, with Antoninus Pius. Their early coins proclaimed a sincere *concordia Augustorum*, harmony of the emperors.

Enormously popular from the first, Marcus and Lucius remained so largely throughout their lives. They began their reign with a large donative to the Praetorian Guard, the army troops garrisoned to guard the city and emperor. In the past, the guard had been known to support its own imperial candidates, but the new rulers gave the equivalent of several years' pay to celebrate the occasion of their accession. In return, the guardsmen swore allegiance. The populace of Rome also benefited from the institution of an imperial foundation to support poor children. They also approved of the lack of pomp of the new imperial court and of their dignified but not glorious manner.

All the events of the first year, however, were not so beneficial. When autumn brought a severe flood of the Tiber followed by famine, the new emperors were forced to oversee the use of the city grain supply for famine relief until the crisis passed. The same year, 161, Parthia, then a loosely organized Empire based in what is now Iran, reasserted itself as a threat to the Roman hegemony (dominance). While it did serve as an eastern check to Roman expansion, the border between the two powers varied widely and clashes over territory were frequent. The Parthians invaded the Roman-protected kingdom of Armenia and a member of the Parthian royal family was placed on the throne.

Marcus dispatched Lucius Verus and able generals with a strong force to recover it, and

Armenia was retaken by Statius Priscus during campaigns in 163–64. Avidius Cassius went further, invading Mesopotamia and making it a Roman protectorate in 166. Even though he had not participated actively in the fighting, Lucius Verus took the honorary title *Armeniacus* (conqueror of the Armenians).

The Plague Devastates the Empire

But the victory was not without cost. In 166, Lucius's returning troops carried a plague back with them that swept through the Roman world. Heavily populated areas were the hardest hit, with Rome—the most densely populated place in the Empire—naturally suffering the worst devastation. No one knows the full effect of the plague, but it is clear that the population of the Empire dropped radically and the most famous doctor of the time, the physician Galen, fled Rome unable to help. In spite of the risk, Marcus stayed on, providing public money for funeral ceremonies for common people and relaxing some of the laws against the selling of tombs, but strictly controlling legal burial locations. Further, in his role as *pontifex maximus* (chief priest of Rome), he performed purification ceremonies and public offerings to the gods, necessary duties that delayed his departure for the north where the borders of the Empire were once again under threat.

In 166, German tribes had poured across the Danube and succeeded in pushing their attack into northern Italy. Marcus arranged for the raising of two new legions to meet the threat but plague losses in the army delayed their mustering. Finally in 168, Marcus and an army set out for Aquileia, the ancient predecessor of Venice. Through negotiation, many of the tribes asked for pardon and returned across the frontier. Some, most notably the Marcomanni and Quadi, did not fully retreat but used the negotiations to stall the imperial advance. Marcus reorganized the administration of northern Italy on a war footing by assigning experienced field commanders and military administrators to the most critical regions. He spent the winter of 168–69 in Aquileia planning his offensive for the following spring. By the time the situation had stabilized, the army was wracked by plague, and early in 169 Marcus was persuaded to return to Rome with Lucius who died on the journey.

After arranging for Lucius's burial with all due honor, Marcus had to turn his attention immediately to the state of the Empire. At a time when at least twice the normal number of recruits was needed to replenish existing legions and recruit new ones, the plague had caused a huge shortfall in available manpower. In answer to the challenge, Marcus hired mercenaries, bandits, and gladiators while offering slaves their freedom for enlistment. When the additional expense of recruiting and training these men exacerbated the existing financial crisis, Marcus responded pragmatically with an auction of imperial possessions.

The plague had caused not only increased imperial expenses but a fall in revenue from the loss of taxes. Unwilling to raise taxes to pay for the new armies, in 169, Marcus ordered a two-month auction of imperial property in the Forum of the Deified Trajan, which included clothes, furnishings, drinking vessels, and royal vases—all of precious materials—as well as imperial jewelry, statues, and paintings by great artists. Marcus raised enough to fight the war without additional taxation, and enough to permit anyone who wished to return their purchases to have their money refunded.

But before Marcus could respond, the German tribes renewed their swift assault and in 170 advanced again into Italy to just outside the walls of Aquileia and into Greece just short of Athens. The Romans lost over 20,000 men as they attempted to stem the two tides of invasion flowing into the Empire. The prosecution of the war remains unclear, but by 172 Marcus had determined that the greatest threat came from the Marcomanni and their allies. He launched an offensive and defeated the tribes by 174. Contemplating the permanent subjugation of the area north of the Danube, he was forced to abandon plans when he learned of a revolt in the east. Marcus compromised by settling the area south of the river with semi-Romanized tribesmen loyal to the Empire and turned his attention to internal problems.

He learned in the spring of 175 that Avidius Cassius, the general who had conquered Mesopotamia in 166, had been declared emperor by his troops, posing a grave threat. Cassius was the governor of Syria and by Marcus's order virtual ruler of the entire eastern Empire. He had the support of most of the eastern provinces including Egypt, the breadbasket of the Empire. Panic spread through Rome and Herodes Atticus sent Cassius a letter of one word in Greek: *emanes* (you are mad).

While consolidating power among the army and civil administrators still loyal to him, Marcus received news of the murder of Cassius by a centurion named Antonius, who then sent Marcus his victim's head, though the emperor refused to see it. Though the immediate crisis in the east had passed, Marcus went through with his plans to travel through the eastern Empire, leaving Rome in July 175 to tour the formerly disloyal provinces.

His actions toward the rebellious officials were characterized by his Stoic moderation: none of them were killed; they received instead only light punishment and the records of the cases were burned to deter retribution against Cassius's supporters.

In addition to reconsolidating power, the tour provided an occasion for Marcus to engage in philosophical discussions with some of the most learned men in the Empire. The Talmud records a meeting and correspondence between the emperor and the celebrated rabbi Juda I. The two are represented discussing such manners as the nature of the soul. Despite the pleasures of the tour, he suffered greatly when his wife Faustina died while accompanying him on his travels.

In 176, he returned to Rome and celebrated a triumph for his northern victories. His son Commodus, now 15, was vested with the tribunicial and proconsular power and, although far below the minimum age, stood for election as consul. As joint ruler, no further powers would be necessary to ensure his succession were his father to die.

In 177, the German tribes again crossed over into the Province of Pannonia, and Marcus and Commodus prepared for the military expedition. Before they left Rome, the emperor again tried to lift the financial burden of empire from the citizens, ordering that all debts owed to the state over the past 46 years be canceled as the records for 133–78 were publicly burned in the Forum. Acutely aware of the effect of imperial expenses on the population of the Empire when his soldiers demanded a bonus after a victory, he told them it would have to be wrung from the blood of their parents and kinsmen.

Finally in 178, he set out once more for the northern provinces to stop the invading tribes. It was officially referred to as an *expeditio Germanica*: a German expedition. With the equivalent of six legions, he continuously pressured the German tribes until the winter of 179–80 when German territory was occupied. Marcus contemplated the addition of two new provinces to the Empire but did not live to see his plan completed. He died on March 17, 180, having implored Commodus to consider the completion of the war as a worthy task. Shortly after Marcus's death, however, Commodus negotiated peace with the tribes and returned to Rome.

SOURCES:

Birley, Anthony. *Marcus Aurelius: A Biography.* Yale University Press, 1987.

Farquharson, A. S. L. *Marcus Aurelius: His Life and His World.* Oxford, 1951.

Marcus Aurelius. *Meditations.* Edited by A. S. L. Farquharson. 1944.

Margaret of Denmark

(1353–1412)

Fourteenth-century Danish queen and first medieval queen to rule in Europe, who united three powerful Scandinavian kingdoms.

Born Margaret Valdemarsdottir in 1353; died in 1412; daughter of Waldemar (Valdemar) IV; married: King Haakon VI of Norway in 1363; children: Olaf V. Predecessor: Olaf V in Norway and Denmark; Albrecht of Mecklenburg in Sweden. Successor: Erik of Pomerania.

"In the year 1386 the queen of Norway gained possession of the kingdom of Denmark as completely as her father Valdemar held it.... When this was done, a fear and trembling seized all the nobles of the kingdom, as they saw the wisdom and power of this lady."

MEDIEVAL LÜBECK CHRONICLE
K. GJERSET,
*HISTORY OF THE
NORWEGIAN PEOPLE*

In the 11th century, the kingdoms of Scandinavia were a relatively new feature of medieval Europe. During the earliest phase of Viking attacks on Europe, the area was characterized by disunity; bands of Vikings from various Scandinavian areas looted Western Europe for personal or regional gain. But from the late 9th through the 11th centuries, the Scandinavian rulers had consolidated the area; by 1100 three distinct kingdoms—Norway, Sweden, and Denmark—had been created. By this time, there were significant regional differences in language and in rules of royal succession which ensured the separate development of the kingdoms. Of these northern realms, only Iceland existed without a king; by the mid-13th century, however, the king of Norway claimed jurisdiction there. Notwithstanding the 11th-century achievements of King **Canute** of Norway, Denmark, and England, the Scandinavian kingdoms remained separate realms with separate monarchs until the 14th century. The individual who succeeded in uniting the three was a woman—Margaret Valdemarsdottir.

A glance at the years immediately preceding her reign reveals the enormity of her accomplish-

Contributed by Cathy Jorgensen Itnyre, Instructor, College of the Desert, Joshua Tree, California

ment. Early in the 14th century, Norway and Sweden were joined into one kingdom under Magnus Eriksson. Magnus was three years old, and the only available heir, when his grandfather, Norway's King Haakon V, died in 1319. The boy's father, Swedish prince Erik Magnusson, had died in prison at the hands of his uncle King Birger of Sweden. Thus, when Birger was forced out of his kingdom by dissident nobles, three-year-old Magnus became king of both Norway and Sweden. His mother Ingebjorg exerted great influence over the affairs of her son, and her plans to enlarge the combined kingdom included designs on Denmark. But the war she provoked with the Danes proved to be so costly to Norway that a popular noble, Erling Vidkunnsson, was made viceroy and ruled Norway until Magnus Eriksson came of age in 1332.

Four years later, in 1336, King Magnus married Blanca of Namur, and by 1340, they had two sons. Erik, the elder, was elected king of Sweden in 1344; the younger son, Haakon (VI), became king of Norway. As the brothers grew to manhood and ascended their thrones, relations between Magnus Eriksson and his sons were marked by turbulence, jealousy, and aggression. In 1362, when Erik died, Haakon was named as his brother's successor in Sweden; he was to rule jointly with his father. The two kings then entered into a war with their powerful neighbor, **Waldemar IV** of Denmark, over rights to Skaane. During this war, Magnus and Haakon enlisted the aid of the Hanseatic League, a powerful alliance of German cities with trading interests in northern Europe. The League's presence in Scandinavia would prove a significantly disruptive influence in

the political and economic life of later medieval Scandinavia. Shortly thereafter, in 1363, Magnus and Haakon arrived at an agreement with Waldemar. Their friendship was cemented by the marriage of the 23-year-old Haakon with Waldemar's 10-year-old daughter Margaret.

Soon after the marriage, Waldemar's son Christopher died, and it became apparent that Margaret would succeed her father—not only as queen in Denmark, but as queen of Norway and heir to the throne of Sweden as well. This alarming prospect stiffened the determination of the German Hanseatic League to extend its control over Denmark by military might, and the 1360s witnessed great strife between the two parties.

By 1370, the great power of the united German cities prevailed, forcing Waldemar to sign the humiliating Peace of Stralsund, which awarded enormous commercial concessions to the Hanse (German merchant guild) and placed the fate of the Danish king under German control. According to the terms of this treaty:

> If it should be that our lord and king, Valdemar, desires to abdicate his land of Denmark during his lifetime, we will and shall not suffer it, unless it be that the [Hanse] cities have given their consent, and that he has sealed to them their privileges with his great seal. Thus, too, it shall be if our lord and king Valdemar, be carried off by death.... Then, too, we will accept no ruler but in council with the cities.

Strained relations between German commercial interests and Scandinavian monarchs would continue in the reign of Waldemar's daughter Margaret; indeed, the tension would persist for the rest of the medieval period.

Margaret was one of several children born to Waldemar and his wife Helvig, who was the sister of the Duke of Schleswig. Although little is known of Margaret's childhood, the normal expectation for noble girls of her period was that they would serve as participants in diplomatic marriages. This was an expectation Margaret clearly fulfilled. As Haakon's 10-year-old bride, Margaret lived in Oslo's Akerhus castle, and her guardian, Marta Ulfsdottir, was a daughter of St. Birgitta of Sweden. By the time Margaret was 18, she had borne her only child, Olaf.

When Waldemar died in 1375, Margaret advanced the candidacy of her young son for the throne of Denmark. There was at the time one other possible heir: Albrecht, the son of Margaret's deceased older sister. Though Waldemar IV had arranged for Albrecht to succeed him, two factors helped Margaret's determination to establish Olaf as king: (1) Albrecht offended the Danish nobility by assuming the title of king, thereby violating the elective nature of that office; and (2) in exchange for commercial privileges in Norway and Denmark, Margaret convinced the Hanse towns not to intervene on Albrecht's behalf. Margaret at age 22 demonstrated great charm, according to contemporary chroniclers, and her political maneuvering resulted in the election of her son Olaf (now Olaf V) to Denmark's kingship in May of 1376.

When Margaret's husband King Haakon VI died in 1380, Margaret immediately went to Norway to ensure Olaf's succession to the throne. Thus began a union between Norway and Denmark that was to last for over four centuries until 1814. Although Margaret was given the power of regency, she was to allow a Norwegian council to rule on her son's behalf when she was in Denmark. With the Hanseatic League controlling important areas of Denmark, the situation there required her energetic attention. Contemporary chronicles attest to her ability to provide effective leadership. "It is quite astonishing," said one source, "that a woman … became so powerful in a quarter of a year that she lacked nothing in the whole kingdom."

When Olaf reached the age of 15 in 1385, he declared his intention to rule without a regent. Nevertheless, Margaret remained his chief advisor and convinced him to press for the title of king of Sweden, despite the fact that Albrecht of Mecklenburg (uncle of the Albrecht who claimed the Danish throne in 1375) had ruled there since Magnus Eriksson's death in 1374. As Olaf's father had continually agitated to obtain the Swedish throne right up to his death in 1380, Margaret encouraged her son to carry on Haakon's policy.

She Gains the Swedish Throne

Olaf's sudden death in 1387 did not dissuade Margaret from her determination to acquire the Swedish throne. Swedish nobles, resentful of the favors their King Albrecht granted to Germans, worked with her in their attempt to depose him. Margaret's position in Denmark and Norway was strengthened in 1387 and 1388 when both countries declared her to be Olaf's rightful heir; the Norwegian council declared her their "mighty lady and rightful ruler." Soon after, a council of Swedish nobles followed their example, vowing not only to overthrow Albrecht, but to accept Margaret and anyone she designated as her successor. In 1389, Albrecht was defeated, and most of Sweden was in Margaret's control.

Stockholm, however, presented a problem for the new queen of Sweden. German Hanse merchants controlled the town and were supplied by a notorious gang of pirates known as the Victuals Brothers. Their illegal activities had been encouraged by the Hanseatic League during its frequent altercations with Denmark. The lawless Brothers were responsible for various atrocities throughout Scandinavia, including the brutal sack of Bergen, Norway. By 1398, Margaret was able to subdue Stockholm, although she was forced to confirm privileges to the Hanse towns.

As Margaret's desire to maintain a united Scandinavian kingdom required her to find an acceptable heir, she chose her great-nephew Erik of Pomerania as her successor. In 1389, the Norwegians proclaimed eight-year-old Erik as king; it required several more years, until 1396, for Margaret to see her adopted son proclaimed king in Denmark and Sweden as well. Despite their shared king, each Scandinavian country retained its own separate government.

In 1397, a meeting was held at Kalmar with hopes of firmly establishing a hereditary state. At this gathering, Erik was officially crowned as king of all the Scandinavian countries. While plans for an even more thorough union were drawn up at Kalmar, they appear not to have been adopted officially by the participants. The first provision of the Kalmar document holds that: "The three kingdoms shall henceforth have one king and shall never be parted." But Danish and Norwegian seals were not attached to this document, indicating that the dynastic choice of Erik was intended to be a singular event. The Kingdoms preferred to make case-by-case decisions regarding future rulers.

Though King Erik was recognized as old enough to rule in 1400, Margaret—whose concerns remained both dynastic and political—managed affairs until her death in 1412. To maintain close ties with England and thus ensure protection against the Hanseatic naval power, she arranged for the marriage of King Henry IV's daughter Philippa to her adopted son Erik. Margaret's administrative policy was to increase the centralizing power of the crown, effected by appointing Danish nobles to oversee her interests in Sweden and Norway.

Critics have said that Margaret strengthened Denmark at the expense of Swedish and Norwegian national aspirations; if so, the more strategic location of Denmark and the vastly greater population perhaps provide the rationale for such a policy. By the end of her reign, she came under significant criticism. According to a Swedish monk: "Albrecht

Walde-mar IV

(1320–1375)

Name variations: Valdemar IV Atterdag. Born in c. 1320; died in 1375; son of King Christopher II of Denmark.

King Waldemar IV Atterdag ruled during a tumultuous period in Danish history. His reign (1340–75) was marked by numerous attempts to recover crown lands alienated in the 1330s, when Denmark was controlled by foreign powers; the bubonic plague epidemic of 1348–49 struck, with resulting vast mortality and agricultural crisis, and the power of the German-Hanseatic cities was a growing threat to the economic well-being of the entire North.

Born in 1321 to King Christopher II of Denmark, the Danish prince was sent to the court of the German Emperor Louis IV when he was only seven years old. Waldemar's education in political tactics and military strategy was thorough, and his intimacy with Germans helped establish the diplomatic ties that enabled him to attain the Danish throne. By marrying Helvig, sister of the Duke of Schleswig, Waldemar shrewdly built up his rights to areas of Denmark that had fallen out of the crown's control.

To regain control of Danish royal properties, he initiated military campaigns and purchased lands with royal revenue generated by taxes. His reunification of Denmark was abetted by his policy of centralizing administrative power, as well as by his use of townsmen and peasants in his expanded national army. Such measures naturally provoked the nobles of Denmark, who had grown accustomed to increased power in the anarchic period preceding Waldemar's reign.

Waldemar's interests as king of Denmark often put him at odds with the commercially powerful cities of the Hanseatic League. In 1361, for example, he raided the German city of Visby, and the resulting legend about the attack well illustrates his cunning preparatory tactics. Allegedly, Waldemar disguised himself as a merchant and seduced the daughter of an important Visby burgher who then revealed to him the town's weaknesses and strengths. The following year, Waldemar put this privileged information to good use in his successful sack of the city. The legend includes as well details of the girl's fate. Abandoned by her "merchant" lover after the attack, she was buried alive in the turrets of the town walls by the enraged citizens of Visby.

As the attack on Visby was a direct challenge to the Hanseatic cities, the resulting enmity preoccupied Waldemar for the remainder of his reign. The Hanse towns attempted to coordinate an alliance with Kings Magnus Eriksson and Haakon VI, but when the naval fleet assembled near Copenhagen in the spring of 1362, the two kings failed to appear. Waldemar IV was able to deflect the Hanse attack, and subsequent negotiations demonstrated his skill at duplicitous diplomacy. For example, during a truce with the Hanse towns, he used the opportunity to seize herring fisheries in Skaane.

In 1363, he married his ten-year-old daughter Margaret to his previous adversary, King Haakon, placing her in a position from which she would later oversee a united Scandinavia. He died in 1375. ■

levied heavy taxes, but Margaret made them still heavier. What he left, she took; the peasant's horse, ox, and cow; in short, all his possessions."

In creating a Scandinavian union, Margaret changed the nature of government throughout her realms. Before 1389, each separate Scandinavian country had a system that entailed the sovereign's actual presence in the realm, making rule intensely personal. Margaret, however, ruled Norway and Sweden from Denmark; thus, she could not provide the important personal element that characterized earlier royal practice. Upon her death, probably from plague in 1412, Margaret left her successor a strong, united Scandinavia, but discontent in Norway and Sweden was to be the legacy of the united kingdoms of the North.

SOURCES:

Gjerset, Knut. *History of the Norwegian People.* Macmillan, 1932.

Larsen, Karen. *A History of Norway.* Princeton University Press, 1948.

Zimmern, Helen. *The Hansa Towns.* London: T. Fisher Unwin, 1889.

Maria Theresa

(1717–1780)

Ruler of the Habsburg lands in Central Europe, who defended her kingdoms against a coalition headed by Frederick II of Prussia, that threatened to partition her empire.

"She did honor to her throne and to her sex."

FREDERICK II

A fter Charles VI failed to father any male heirs, he altered the Habsburg family law by the Pragmatic Sanction of 1713, which proclaimed the indivisibility of his lands—united under the scepter of Austria—and designated his eldest daughter Maria Theresa as his heir. Preoccupied with the problems of succession, he frantically attempted to persuade the estates of his realm and the European powers to accept the decree. Although the Pragmatic Sanction insured that Maria Theresa faced no serious domestic opposition after her father's death on October 20, 1740, the external powers, headed by **Frederick II, the Great** of Prussia, soon challenged the 24-year-old novice. The impulsive Frederick launched an invasion of Silesia with its more than one million inhabitants, ore deposits, and flourishing linen trade. As he argued: "When one has the advantage is he to use it or not? ... The passions of rulers have no other curb but the limits of their power." Recovering from their surprise, the Austrians dispatched troops across the mountain passes from Bohemia into Silesia. The subsequent Prussian victory at Mollwitz in April 1742 persuaded the French to ally with Frederick, but Frederick soon

Born in May 1717; died on November 28, 1780; eldest daughter of Emperor Charles VI and Elisabeth Christina of Brunswick-Wolfenbuttel; married: cousin Prince Francis Stephen of Lorraine, grand duke of Tuscany, February 1736; children: sixteen, including Joseph II, Leopold II, and Marie-Antoinette. Predecessor: Charles VI. Successor: Joseph II.

Contributed by Marsha Frey and Linda Frey, Professors of History, Kansas State University and University of Montana

1740	Charles VI died; Silesia invaded by Frederick II, igniting First Silesian War
1740–48	War of Austrian Succession
1741	Battle of Mollwitz; Maria Theresa crowned queen of Hungary
1742	Charles VII crowned at Frankfurt; Treaty of Breslau; Prussia withdrew from war, taking most of Silesia
1744	Second Silesian War; Frederick II invaded Bohemia, captured Prague
1745	Charles VII died; Prussians victorious at Hohenfriedberg; Francis I crowned; Treaty of Dresden ended Second Silesian War
1748	Treaty of Aix-la-Chapelle ended War of Austrian Succession
1756	Austria and France sign Treaty of Versailles, ending Habsburg-Bourbon rivalry; Seven Years' War began with Frederick II's invasion of Saxony
1763	Peace of Hubertusberg concluded by Austria and Prussia; Prussia retained Silesia
1765	Francis I died; Joseph II became emperor and co-regent
1772	First Partition of Poland; Austria acquired Galicia
1778–79	War of Bavarian Succession
1780	Maria Theresa died

Asserting that he had been next in line for the Habsburgs' possessions, Charles Albert, elector of Bavaria, was elected Emperor Charles VII in Frankfurt in January of 1742. Reentering the fray, Frederick II invaded Bohemia and forced Maria Theresa to sign the Treaty of Breslau of June 1742 by which she ceded the whole of Silesia. When that peace freed her to turn against her other enemies, she successfully pursued the war, driving the allies out of Bohemia and Bavaria.

The second Silesian War began when Frederick, concluding another alliance with Charles VII, marched through Saxony into Bohemia in 1744. In June 1745, 58,000 Prussians defeated 85,000 Austrians and Saxons, captured 7,000 prisoners, and killed or wounded 7,000 more. The battle of Hohenfriedberg and other Prussian victories forced Maria Theresa to conclude the Treaty of Dresden in 1745. Fighting, however, continued until the Peace of Aix-la-Chapelle of 1748. The Habsburgs lost not only Silesia, but also Parma, Piacenza, and Guastalla to the infant son of **Philip of Spain** and the Milanese territories west of the Ticino to Savoy.

Maria Theresa Secures Austrian Throne

Maria Theresa, encumbered with enormous debts, an inept administration, and a badly equipped and poorly trained army, was unable to recapture most of Silesia in the first two Silesian wars, but she did manage, through two treaties, to secure the Austrian throne. After the death of Charles VII in January of 1745, his son had surrendered his pretensions to Austria (in the Treaty of Füssen); and Frederick II recognized Maria Theresa's consort as emperor (in the Treaty of Dresden). Thus, when Francis Stephen, duke of Lorraine and duke of Tuscany, and her husband of nine years, became Francis I of Lorraine, the Habsburg-Lorraine dynasty now held the imperial title. The Empire had survived against tremendous odds.

The wars, however, forced the Habsburgs to reconsider their traditional foreign policy. Maria Theresa's belief that Prussia was the most dangerous enemy led her to accept the advice of her able chancellor Prince Wenzel Anton Kaunitz who accomplished a diplomatic revolution by concluding an alliance with Austria's traditional enemy France. Kaunitz managed to isolate Frederick by concluding additional alliances with Saxony and Elizabeth, empress of Russia. Even those alliances and the next war, the Seven Years' War (1756–63), did not enable her to regain Silesia. Still many were surprised by her resilience and courage. At one point during these anxious times she had writ-

came to respect the resolve of his enemy, Maria Theresa, whom he dubbed "that man in Vienna."

Finding herself immersed in the First Silesian War, Maria Theresa later wrote that she was "without money, without credit, without an army, without any experience or knowledge of my own and finally without any kind of advice." Unprepared for the role thrust upon her, she had the intelligence to defer to those more experienced and the courage to continue the war which soon escalated into struggles in Central Europe, Italy, the Netherlands, North America, the Caribbean, and India. Austria allied with Great Britain, the United Provinces, and Piedmont-Sardinia, and fought against France, Prussia, Saxony, Spain, and Bavaria. With the French and Bavarians allied with Frederick, Maria Theresa was forced to cede Lower Silesia to Prussia in the secret Convention of Klein Schnellendorf on October 9, 1741. Shortly thereafter, Austrian troops conquered Bavaria, but another claimant to the Austrian throne appeared.

ten: "Do not spare the country, only hold it…. [F]or the present I close my heart to pity." The death of the Russian empress Elizabeth in 1762 and the accession of Tsar **Peter III,** an admirer of Frederick II, meant Russian withdrawal from the war. The exhaustion of the combatants and the French defeats forced Maria Theresa to sign the Treaty of Hubertusberg in February 1763.

Although Maria Theresa did not share the cynical statecraft mentality of the day, she participated with Prussia and Russia in the first partition of Poland in 1772. Indeed, she had little choice. The alternatives, Poland as a Russian satellite or Poland partitioned between Russia and Prussia, would have considerably weakened the position of the Habsburgs. Frederick II commented that "she cries but she takes." What she took was Galicia with approximately 3 million inhabitants and its famous salt mines. That seizure had been prefigured when Austrian troops occupied the Polish district of Zips as early as 1770. Kaunitz also acquired Bukovina from Turkey in 1775 in exchange for Habsburg mediation at the peace of Kuchuk-Kainarji between Turkey and Russia. The acquisition of Zips, Galicia, and Bukovina, substantially changed the ethnic composition of the Empire and weakened the dominant position of the Germans, raising the specter of national problems which would haunt the Empire until its dissolution.

The loss of the richest province, Silesia, referred to by Maria Theresa as the "rape of Silesia," convinced her and others of the necessity of reform. "I see very well that with us everything happens far too slowly. This will be our ruin." The struggle with Prussia revealed the weakness of the army which was subsequently enlarged and improved. A military academy was founded at Wiener Newstadt and an engineering academy in Vienna, a general staff created, and a general conscription undertaken. In 1748, the government had created a permanent military establishment of 108,000 men, and in 1763 it had raised that number to 300,000. Other reforms had followed. Those reforms were designed to strengthen the state and the monarch's power within the state. Count Friedrich Wilhelm Haugwitz's levying of increased taxes necessitated both a financial and administration reorganization. In the words of Maria Theresa, he "brought the government from confusion into order."

She Increases Power of the State

The demands of war enabled Maria Theresa to undercut the power of the local estates and the provincial nobility and to persuade the diets to grant an increase in taxes for ten years. While introducing a universal income tax and a graduated poll tax, she also increased the power of the central government by creating a state chancery for Foreign Affairs, a Council of State, and a High Court of Justice. She established secularized universities, broke the Jesuit monopoly on education, and developed a complete scheme for primary and secondary education which included technical and grammar schools. As part of the rationalization and consolidation of royal power and in spite of strong religious feelings, she believed that the state should extend its control over the Church by restricting the number and wealth of convents and by limiting the power of the ecclesiastical courts. To increase taxable wealth, she reduced the number of sacred holidays and abolished the tax exemption of the clergy. Although she discriminated against both Protestants and Jews by deporting several hundred of the former and levying heavy indemnities on the latter, she tolerated the Greek Orthodox Ruthenians in Galicia and Bukovina and the Serbs in Hungary.

To foster the productivity of her peoples and to increase the tax revenues of the state, the empress created a large internal market by uniting all the Danubian lands except Hungary, the Tyrol and the free cities of Cracow, Brody, and Triests into a single customs unit. The government protected goods produced within that area by levying high tariffs and prohibiting the import of similar goods and the export of certain raw materials. Fiscal reasons coupled with humanitarian concerns stimulated agrarian reforms. Maria Theresa hoped to increase state control over the peasants, improve their ability to pay taxes, and guarantee them greater justice. "I must answer my conscience. I do not want to be damned for the sake of a few magnates and noblemen." She limited the local lord's judicial and political authority over serfs. The decree of 1751, which forbade the appropriation of the serf's holdings, and that of 1770, which ordered the lord to allow his serfs to buy their holdings, accomplished little, but the reforms on royal domain where freedom of movement, marriage, and profession were granted were significant. The royal land was divided among the peasants on the basis of long-term leases. She also issued a number of Robot patents which limited the labor services of peasants to either a two- or three-day maximum depending on the provinces. The moderate and tentative nature of these reforms assured their success.

Although technically Maria Theresa had ruled jointly with Francis I, she retained all power in her hands. An affectionate wife, who once remarked that she could never be pregnant often enough, she gave birth to 11 daughters and five sons including **Joseph II,** Leopold II, and **Marie-Antoinette.** After the death of Emperor Francis I in 1765, she always wore mourning. "I have lost everything, a loving husband, a perfect friend, who was my only support."

Her love for her family did not, however, influence her inexorable sense of duty. From 1765 on, she ruled jointly and uneasily with her son Joseph, who strove to push through more radical reforms. She particularly disagreed with his policy of religious toleration. A conservative Catholic, she refused to compromise with heretics, remarking that, "Toleration and indifference are the best way to undermining everything." The humane and pragmatic Maria Theresa deplored "a violence and hardness of character" which she saw in her son. Nonetheless, Maria Theresa had laid the groundwork for the later Josephinian reforms. She sought Joseph's advice, particularly in foreign affairs and legal matters.

Joseph II also sought additional land. After the death of the ruler of Maximilian Joseph of the House of Wittelsbach in 1778, he sent troops into Bavaria to enforce inheritance claims. By the compromise peace of 1779 after the War of Bavarian Succession, Austria acquired the Innviertel between Inn and Salzach but not Joseph's objective, Bavaria.

In November of 1780, Maria Theresa was forced to bed with a cold; her condition steadily worsened. On the 28th, she received the last sacrament. When advised to rest, she replied: "I will not sleep, I wish to see death come."

SOURCES:

Arneth, Alfred von. *Geschichte Maria Theresias.* Braumuller, 1863–1879.

Blanning, T. C. W. *Joseph II and Enlightened Despotism.* Harper, 1970.

Crankshaw, Edward. *Maria Theresa.* Atheneum, 1986.

Guglia, Eugen. *Maria Theresia: Ihr Leben und ihre Regierung.* R. Oldenbourg, 1917.

McGill, William J. *Maria Theresa.* Twayne, 1972.

Gooch, George Peabody. *Maria Theresa and Other Studies.* Longmans, Green, 1952.

FURTHER READING:

Kann, Robert. *A History of the Habsburg Empire, 1526–1918.* University of California Press, 1977.

Macartney, C. A. *Maria Theresa and the House of Austria.* Lawrence Verry, 1969.

Pick, Robert. *Empress Maria Theresa, The Earlier Years, 1717–1757.* Harper, 1966.

Wangermann, Ernst. *The Austrian Achievement, 1700–1800.* Harcourt, 1973.

Constance Markievicz

(1868–1927)

Irish nationalist, labor activist, and feminist, who fought against the British in the 1916 Easter Rising but, as a diehard republican, later refused to compromise in the creation of the Irish Free State.

"She gave orders to her soldiers rather in the manner of a mistress ordering her servants, and unselfconsciously used Edwardian slang words.... She was a good shot, and carefully kept a tally of the number of Tommies whom she had brought down."

ULICK O'CONNOR

The Irish Rebellion of 1916–22 was inspired chiefly by Catholic revolutionaries seeking to throw off the yoke of a centuries-old British domination, but the idea of Irish independence attracted a wide variety of enthusiasts and idealists. None was a stranger, or a more unlikely candidate for the role of Irish freedom-fighter than Constance Markievicz, a rich, privileged Protestant woman, who had once dabbled in art, theater, and feminism but who spent the later years of her life as a guerrilla fighter, parliamentarian, prisoner, and fugitive.

Constance was born in 1868 to the Gore-Booth family, one of the largest landowning families in County Sligo on the Irish west coast. Her wealthy Protestant family was part of the Anglo-Irish "Ascendancy," whose control of nearly all Irish farmland was a source of long-standing resentment to the Catholic Irish majority. From his estate at Lissadell, her father supervised his estates and acted the part of a paternalistic despot to his farm tenants, some of them desperately poor. Whereas many Irish landowners did not even live on their estates, treating them solely as sources of income, the Gore-Booths were at least

Name variations: Countess Markievicz. Born in London in 1868; died in 1927; daughter of Henry Gore-Booth and Georgina Tickhill; sister of Eva Gore-Booth; married: Casimir Dunin Markievicz, 1900; children: Maeve Alys.

Contributed by Patrick Allitt, Assistant Professor of History, Emory University, Atlanta, Georgia

1868	Born in London
1895–99	Art student in London and Paris
1909	Founded the Fianna boys' movement in Dublin
1913	Jim Larkin's strike, the lockout, and "Bloody Sunday"
1916	Dublin Easter Rising
1918	Markievicz became Britain's first woman M.P. but never took her seat
1916–21	Imprisoned four times by British authorities
1921	Markievicz rejected the Free State Treaty compromise, fought it, and was imprisoned by Irish authorities
1927	Died

physically present for part of every year. Her father's hobby was Arctic exploration and Constance, the eldest daughter, grew up like him to be adventurous, high spirited, and daring. She loved hunting and shooting and rode well. At 18, she became a debutante and enjoyed several London "seasons" but was unable to attract a husband, possibly because of her abrasive mockery and an inclination toward practical jokes.

By the age of 25, she had become an annoyance to her parents, and she in turn found living with them hard to endure. After months of persuasion, she won their consent to become an art student in the Slade School, London. From that time on, she and her sister Eva began to move in artistic and literary circles, the best known of their literary friends being the poet W.B. Yeats, who knew them well and admired both. After two years in London, Constance moved on to an art school for women in Paris, and there she met Count Casimir Markievicz. He was six years younger than she, a more talented artist who had won several portrait commissions and held the prospect of a distinguished future. The son of Ukrainian landowners, he too had come to Paris to make his career as an artist. He was already married, but his first wife died in 1899 in the Ukraine, just as Markievicz and Constance were beginning an intense relationship—he even fought a duel with swords to defend Constance's honor when a Frenchman insulted her at a ball. They wed the following year, and spent the early years of their marriage moving between Paris, Lissadell, and his family estates at Zywotowka. When Constance gave birth to a daughter, Maeve, she paid her child scant attention, leaving her to be

brought up almost entirely by her grandmother. And when the Markieviczs settled in Dublin in 1903, it was his son Stanislas by his first marriage who moved in with them, while Maeve paid occasional visits before returning to her grandmother.

Dublin was then experiencing a cultural awakening, a widespread revival of the Irish language, and a burst of artistic creativity from Yeats, George Bernard Shaw, James Joyce, Oscar Wilde, J.M. Synge, Padraic Colum, and dozens of other writers, artists, and poets. The Markieviczs joined Yeats and George "AE" Russell in an arts society, wrote and performed plays, painted, and began to show an interest in nationalist politics, to the dismay of Constance's Ascendancy relatives. At first Arthur Griffith, a moderate Irish nationalist and leader of the nationalist group Sinn Fein, assumed she was a spy sent from Dublin Castle to keep watch on potential troublemakers, but gradually both he and the women's branch of the revolutionary movement "Daughters of Ireland" (founded by Yeats's unrequited love **Maud Gonne**), recognized that Constance was sincere and was abandoning her old way of life for the more alien and arduous life of politics. Moreover, Constance Markievicz quickly gravitated to the radical side of the Irish nationalist movement and came to regard Griffith's Sinn Fein, with its policy of parliamentary moderation, irritatingly slow. A member of its council from 1909, she constantly urged Sinn Fein to more direct action and provocation against the British.

Three Convictions Guide Markievicz's Life

Before her marriage, she and her sister Eva had organized a votes for women movement in their home parish; now Markievicz took up the issue of feminism more seriously and began to write for (and illustrate) the Daughters of Ireland journal *Bean na hEirean*. Eva was living in the north of England, agitating for improved working conditions for women and for women's suffrage, cooperating with the famous Pankhurst family in the Women's Social and Political Union. From Eva and from her new acquaintances and experiences in Dublin, Markievicz too began to develop a sympathy for socialism. These three convictions—Irish nationalism, feminism, and socialism—were to guide her through the rest of her life. She began to make speeches on these issues, especially women's rights, and as biographer Diana Norman notes, "she was always in demand as a speaker because she could rouse uneducated or apathetic audiences in a way more sophisticated orators could not."

Unconventional and increasingly impatient with upper-class family life, she and Casimir spent less time together as the years passed, and their marriage appears to have virtually dissolved by 1912. He was a colorful fixture in the life of the Dublin theater between 1907 and 1913 and still spent part of each year with Constance but rarely joined his wife in her political obsessions. He left Ireland for the last time in 1913.

In 1909, she founded the *Na Fianna Eireann,* an Irish nationalist version of the Boy Scouts. Just as Baden-Powell's scouts (founded during the Boer War) cultivated patriotic militarism in English boys, so she aimed to raise Irish patriot soldiers in the *Fianna.* At times, *Fianna* lads from the poor quarters of Dublin would attack Anglo-Irish Boy Scouts from the wealthier areas and fight pitched battles in the streets of Dublin, with her implicit approval. Thinking that a taste of rural life might also benefit boys from the slums, she hired a large country house and for two years ran it as a *Fianna* commune, at a steady financial loss and to the growing irritation of Casimir. One of her assistants, Liam Mellowes, spread the movement to other parts of Ireland and later helped organize the Irish Volunteers during the Easter Rising of 1916; Constance's coaching of the boys in marksmanship prepared some of them for roles in the coming revolution.

When Constance Markievicz and other Irish suffragists realized that John Redmond's Irish Party in the British Parliament intended to exclude women from the vote if they achieved their goal of Home Rule, these women went into open opposition and began to imitate the violent demonstrations of their English sisters, smashing the windows of public buildings and hunger striking in prison. Moderate Irish nationalists, supporters of Redmond, detested the suffragists for threatening their movement in this way, but Markievicz won steady support from the Irish Trade Unions and their mercurial leader Jim Larkin.

She repaid them by supporting the unions and unemployed workers during the massive lockout of summer 1913 in which Dublin employers tried to break the growing unions' power once and for all. Larkin stayed at the Markievicz house on the night before "Bloody Sunday," August 31, 1913, when a huge police contingent, possibly drunk, attacked a large crowd of trade unionists in O'Connell Street, killing two and injuring more than 450. Markievicz herself was severely beaten by the police:

> One hit me a back hand blow across the left side of my face with his baton. I fell back against the corner of a shop, when another policeman started to seize me by the throat, but I was pulled out of the crowd by some men, who took me down Sackville Place and into a house to stop the blood flowing from my nose and mouth.

Despite the shocked public response to this outrage, the lockout continued into the winter and at last the men, hungry and defeated, were forced back to work, their unions in disarray.

Experiences like this made Markievicz implacable; hating industrial exploitation and male domination, she yet believed that British power lay at the root of all Irish evils. The year 1914 witnessed a general arming for battle in Ireland as the prospect of Home Rule increased. Protestant Ulstermen in northern Ireland took up arms to resist the nationalists and fight *against* independence. Republicans in Dublin countered by forming volunteer armies of their own and publishing strident manifestos. Markievicz helped organize the Irish Citizen Army and cooperated as gunrunners brought weapons ashore to arm it. The mounting crisis was interrupted, however, when the First World War began that summer. Redmond, leader of the Home Rule Members of Parliament, pledged the support of Ireland for the British war effort; he felt certain that Home Rule would be its quid pro quo (something received for something given), and thousands of young Irishmen responded to his call by enlisting for service in the trenches. Markievicz and the radical Irish Citizen Army, on the other hand, disdained Redmond's call; they saw themselves fighting *against* Britain, not for it, and did all they could to obstruct the British recruitment drive in Dublin, while carrying on their own drilling and marksmanship practice. She made shrill speeches, expressing the hope that Germany would win the war, and now seemed, to British eyes, a traitor.

Thousands of English and Irish men died in the trench warfare of the following years, and as British resources became thinly stretched to meet the crisis, the Irish militants realized that the perfect moment had come for them to strike a blow for independence. The secret military council of the Irish Republican Brotherhood (IRB), led by Tom Clark and Sean MacDermott, planned the rising for Easter 1916, and gradually drew into their confidence the leaders of the Irish Citizen Army, including Markievicz; the leaders of the Volunteers; and key figures from the trade unions and universities. It was obvious to the British administration in Dublin, led by Augustine Birrell, that some Irish militants were planning revolt—the Volunteers marched in the streets quite openly with their rifles and bayonets. But Birrell, a mild Liberal, maintained a policy of salutary neglect and thought the drilling was more a matter of bluster than serious intent. He was wrong.

Irish Militants Rebel on Easter

Despite a mix-up over timing and deployment, the IRB went into action on Easter Monday, seizing the General Post Office (GPO), the College of Surgeons, the Law Courts, and other prominently placed public buildings, with about a thousand men and women in arms. They raided Dublin Castle, seat of the British administration, and could have taken it since it was then badly understaffed, but decided it was too sprawling to be defensible. They declared themselves the provisional government of the Irish Republic and raised a tricolor flag—orange, green, and white—over the GPO, along with a flag bearing a gold harp on a green background designed and made by Constance Markievicz herself. The poet and activist Padraic Pearse read out the Irish Declaration of Independence from the steps of the GPO to bemused passers-by and Easter strollers.

After their initial amazement, the British retaliated powerfully, moving first troops, then artillery and a gunboat into action. Constance Markievicz, acting as a liaison officer, hurried between the different republican strongholds until the gunfire became too heavy; she spent the latter half of the week pinned down with a small group in the College of Surgeons. She was a crack shot with years of experience and acted as a sniper against British soldiers in the nearby Shelbourne Hotel. Soon she and all the rebels were desperately hungry; food supplies into the city were disrupted by the rising, and the rebels had been forced to retreat from St. Stephen's Green where they had stockpiled several days' supplies.

The rebels knew that much of the Irish population was indifferent to their action, and that some, whose relatives were fighting in the British army, were actively opposed to them. Nevertheless they believed that even if they failed, as seemed almost certain from the start, they would light the spark of revolution for others to follow. Within a week, British bombardment had battered them into submission and the survivors, including Constance Markievicz, surrendered and were marched off to prison. She felt exhilarated that they had held out for as much as a week, longer than any earlier Irish rising against the British, and now awaited her anticipated execution with equanimity. Sure enough, she was found guilty of sedition and sentenced to death, but the military judges, in view of her sex, commuted her sentence to life imprisonment with hard labor. She then had to sit in a lonely prison cell and listen each morning as volleys of shots announced the death by firing squad of nearly all her remaining comrades, some of whom she had known for 15 or 20 years.

As Clark, MacDermott, James Connally and the other leaders had anticipated, what the rebellion failed to achieve, its aftermath created. Public opinion swung around in favor of the rebels, each of whom, by his death, became a martyr to Irish freedom. News that Connally had been so badly wounded that he had to be tied to a chair to be kept upright at his execution and that the British army had killed such innocent bystanders as Constance's friend Francis Sheehy Skeffington (a radical pacifist who deplored the resort to arms) intensified the shift in Irish public opinion. The British retribution, far from ending the Irish Revolution, in effect brought it to life.

Because the British feared she would become the center of a cult if left in a Dublin prison, Constance was moved to a prison in Aylesbury, England. Treated as a regular criminal rather than a political prisoner, she was placed with prostitutes, thieves, and infanticides, and suffered the squalid miseries and perpetual hunger of the prison regimen for the next year and a half. While in prison, however, she converted to Catholicism, the religion of most of her fellow rebels. Meanwhile Irish friends were working to have her status changed to that of a political prisoner. Others were making propaganda tours of the United States, addressing its large Irish population and urging their support for Irish freedom. When the United States entered the First World War in the spring of 1917, the British government conciliated Irish opinion in America by releasing most of the remaining Irish internees from the rising, and in July of that year, Markievicz emerged from jail and returned to a hero's welcome in Ireland.

She Becomes First Woman
Elected to Parliament

She was elected to the Sinn Fein executive council, but now the organization was a mass revolutionary movement with nearly 100,000 members, rather than a tiny cluster of Dublin moderates. It acted as though the Declaration of Independence, and the Irish Republic, were already political facts of life and gained a surge of new members when the British tried to impose military conscription on Irish men in early 1918. In response to Sinn Fein's anticonscription actions, the British arrested the party's leaders, including Constance Markievicz, and she was once more sent to prison in England, but this time granted political status and the company of other Sinn Feiners; one of them was Maud Gonne. Markievicz was still in prison when the First World War ended in November 1918, and Prime Minister **Lloyd George** called a general election. Sinn Fein ran her as its candidate in the St. Patrick division of Dublin and she won, thus becoming the first woman ever elected to the British Parliament.

Markievicz was one of 73 Sinn Fein candidates to win seats. Rather than go to Westminster, however, those who were at liberty met in Dublin and constituted themselves as the *Dail Eireann* (Irish Parliament). **Eamon de Valera,** who had fought in the Easter rising and added luster to his name by a daring prison escape (he had avoided execution because he was an American citizen and not technically guilty of treason), became the first president of the Republic and appointed Markievicz as his Minister of Labor. In March 1919, she was released from jail by a British government which was anxious lest she die in the influenza epidemic; she again received a hero's welcome on her return to Dublin. Throwing herself into political activity once more and trying to make sure that the nascent (budding) government held fast to its pro-Labor pledges, she urged Irish people to boycott everything British and to carry on their guerrilla war against the Royal Irish Constabulary and the notorious "Black and Tans."

She was rearrested for seditious speeches and jailed a third time in County Cork. Released in October 1919, she found that Sinn Fein was now an illegal organization and spent the following months on the run to avoid further imprisonment, moving constantly from place to place. The Dail had to meet covertly, but it made a point of taking over every aspect of administration it could handle, to give itself an image of effectiveness and plausibility in the eyes of the anxious, war-torn population. Meanwhile a fourth arrest led to another long stay at Mountjoy Prison, Dublin, for Markievicz, during which she learned to speak the Irish language.

When she emerged from this term in prison, momentous negotiations were under way in London between Dail representatives and the British government on the status of a self-governing Ireland. Markievicz and Eamon de Valera insisted on a completely self-governing republic, but the British would only grant Ireland "Free State" dominion status within the British Empire. Fearing renewed British hostilities throughout Ireland which they were ill prepared to repel, the Irish negotiators, led by the guerrilla captain **Michael Collins,** miserably accepted the Free State compromise, and then tried to defend it in the Dail debate which followed. Markievicz spoke passionately against the compromise and joined de Valera and the large antitreaty minority by walking out of the assembly. She toured the United States later that year, speaking on behalf of the Republic and against the Free State, but found on her return in 1922 that civil war had broken out between the two factions. Although she was now 54, she once more took to the barricades as a sniper, lived on the run, and was again arrested while speaking from a cart in Dublin. This fifth term of imprisonment was at the hands of some of the men she had fought beside in 1916, a bitterly ironic outcome of her work.

For the last years of her life, Constance Markievicz was a member of the Free State parliament but could not take her seat because she, like all the antitreaty diehards, refused to take the oath to the king of England which it required. She remained personally popular and helped de Valera, in 1926, to found the Fianna Fail, a party aimed at gaining entry to Parliament without taking the oath. But although she held her seat in another election, she never again spoke in Parliament. Constance Markievicz died disappointed at the outcome of her life's labors, dismayed that the Irish Free State was such a prosaic, compromised affair rather than the radical workers' democracy she had dreamed of and worked for throughout her adult life. Truckloads of flowers and thousands of mourners attended her funeral, though the Free State government refused to grant this hero of 1916 official funeral honors.

SOURCES:

Haverty, Anne. *Constance Markievicz: An Independent Life.* London: Pandora, 1988.

Norman, Diana. *Terrible Beauty: A Life of Constance Markievicz, 1868–1927.* London: Hodder & Stoughton, 1987.

O'Connor, Ulick. *The Troubles: Ireland, 1912–1922.* Bobbs-Merrill, 1975.

Sebestyen, Amanda, ed. *Prison Letters of Countess Markievicz.* London: Virago, 1986.

Charles Martel

(c. 690–741)

Christian warrior, who led the Franks against the Muslims at the Battle of Poitiers, a victory which ended the threat of an Islamic conquest of Western Europe.

Name variations: Charles is the French form of the German "Karl" and the Latin "Carolus"; the nickname "Martel" means "Hammer." Born c. 690; died on October 22, 741, at the palace of Quierzy; son of Pepin II (one of the most powerful nobles of the Frankish kingdom) and Alpaida; married: Chrotrud and Sunnichild; children: four sons and a daughter. Descendants: Emperor Charlemagne. Predecessor: Pepin II. Successor: Pepin III.

Charles Martel made the Carolingian dynasty dominant in the Frankish kingdom, which included today's northern France, Belgium, and parts of western Germany. In fact, the dynasty's name, Carolingian, comes from the Latin form of Charles's name, Carolus. His nickname—Martel, or "Hammer"—referred to his ability to "hammer" his enemies into submission. Martel's nickname may be a reference to the biblical Judas Maccabeus, since Maccabeus also means "Hammer," or it may be of popular origin, for he soon became an heroic figure to the Franks.

Two contemporary narratives of Martel's life have survived. The first is called the *Liber Historiae Francorum* (or *Book of the History of the Franks*), a chronicle narrating the major events of his early years, from 714 to 721. The author's name is unknown, but he was probably a monk from the region around Paris. The second source, far more complete as it covers Martel's entire life, is a continuation of *The Chronicle of Fredegar*. The Continuator, as he is called, is anonymous, but he was probably a monk, as well. The Continuator wrote under the supervision of Count Childebrand,

"Charles was named 'Martel,' because of his fierce spirit. Right from the start he was a warlike man, brave and vigorous."

LIFE OF RIGOBERT

Contributed by Mary L. Alberi, Adjunct Associate Professor, Pace University, New York, New York

Martel's half-brother on his mother's side. Thus the Continuator described the early history of the Carolingian family as the family wanted it to be seen. Charles Martel appears in this *Chronicle* as a man of war—bold, decisive, and energetic.

His strong character enabled him to overcome many enemies. He was the son of Pepin II, "duke of the Austrasians," one of the most powerful nobles of the Frankish kingdom. Like many great nobles of his day, Pepin had more than one wife. Martel's mother was a noblewoman named Alpaida, but she had a rival in Pepin's senior wife, Plectrud. Pepin II's family, with its own internal rivalries, was caught up in the political conflicts that troubled the Frankish kingdom in the late seventh and early eighth centuries. These troubles arose out of the Frankish tradition of divided inheritance, which meant that each one of the king's sons inherited the title of king and a portion of the kingdom.

Over the generations, the royal dynasty—the Merovingians—had divided the Frankish kingdom into three subkingdoms: Neustria (northwestern France and Belgium), Austrasia (northeastern France and parts of western Germany), and Burgundy (southeastern France). Each subkingdom had its own king and administration, with its headquarters in the royal palace. In theory, the Frankish kingdom remained a single unit, and the kings and nobles of each subkingdom were supposed to cooperate. But in reality the division encouraged assassinations and civil wars. As a result, the Merovingian kings lost wealth and power to their nobles, who demanded land and government offices in return for their military support. The biggest prize for a noble in each subkingdom was the office of the mayor of the palace, the head of the royal administration and the army. Only a ferociously strong king could overawe the Frankish nobles, but, unfortunately for the Merovingians, in the later seventh century the family produced too many ineffective boy kings. By Pepin II's day, the mayors of the palaces of Neustria and Austrasia were the real rulers of their subkingdoms. Burgundy was in near chaos, because the nobles were involved in perpetual feuds; the Merovingian kings were puppets controlled by the mayors.

Martel's father, Pepin II, was the first nobleman to unite both Neustria and Austrasia under his authority. He accomplished this by defeating the Neustrians at the battle of Tertry (near Saint-Quentin) in 687. In spite of his victory, however, Pepin's grip on Neustria remained insecure because the noble Neustrian families resented him as an outsider, an Austrasian. Pepin managed to

CHRONOLOGY

687	Pepin III's victory at Tertry
714	Charles's struggle to dominate the Frankish kingdom began
721	Charles's control over the kingdom securely established
725	Major campaign in Alemannia and Bavaria (western Germany)
732	Charles victorious at the Battle of Poitiers
733	Campaigns in Aquitaine, Burgundy, and Provence (southern France) began
734	Rebellion suppressed in Frisia (Netherlands)
738	Rebellion suppressed in Saxony (northwestern Germany)
741	Charles died at the palace of Quierzy

control Neustria with the help of his two sons by Plectrud, but serious trouble broke out at the first sign of weakness.

When Pepin fell seriously ill in 714, his only surviving son by Plectrud, Grimoald II, was assassinated in Liège. Pepin tried to provide for the continuation of his family's power by making Grimoald's young son, Theudoald, mayor of the palace of Neustria. After Pepin's death, Theudoald relied on the protection of his powerful grandmother. Plectrud imprisoned Martel in an effort to prevent him from taking his father's place. But Charles Martel escaped from her custody and rebelled, apparently with the support of his own mother's relatives.

At the same time, the Neustrians rebelled against Theudoald and Plectrud. The Neustrians elected their own mayor, named Raganfred, and set up a Merovingian puppet, King Chilperic II. After defeating Theudoald in battle in 715, Raganfred became Martel's chief enemy. To make matters worse, Raganfred allied himself with the pagan Radbod, duke of Frisia (today's Netherlands). These two nearly destroyed Martel. However, after successfully ambushing Raganfred and Radbod at Amblève (near Malmédy) in 715, Martel's fortunes began to turn. His victory won him the support of the Austrasian nobles. After defeating Raganfred again in 717 at Vinchy (near Cambrai), Charles Martel persuaded Plectrud to hand over Pepin II's personal treasure and to accept him as head of the family.

Martel now controlled Austrasia and set up his own Merovingian puppet, Clothar IV. Next he attacked and defeated Radbod the Frisian in 718. When Raganfred saw this, he allied himself with Duke Eudo of Aquitaine (in southern France), but Martel defeated both of them as well. The Continuator of Fredegar's *Chronicle* describes Martel's attitude through all these battles as "steadfast and fearless." Raganfred lost his position as mayor to Martel. Eudo recognized Martel's lordship and handed over the Merovingian Chilperic to him in 721. This assured Martel control of both Neustria and Austrasia. When both Merovingian kings died shortly afterwards, Martel replaced them with Theuderic IV. When Theuderic died in 737, Martel did not bother to replace him: he felt secure enough to rule Neustria and Austrasia by himself, without a Merovingian puppet.

While his military campaigns were important, Martel's success also depended on his control of the Frankish Church. The Church had long been involved in politics, and its vast wealth could be used to equip and maintain soldiers. Charles Martel made sure that his supporters held powerful positions within the Church, but he did not particularly care about the Church's laws or a man's personal qualifications for religious office. His supporters often broke the Church's laws by holding several ecclesiastical offices at the same time, which made it impossible for them to carry out their spiritual duties. For example, in Neustria, Martel's nephew Hugh was abbot of the monasteries of St. Denis, St. Wandrille, and Jumièges at the same time as he was bishop of Rouen, Paris, and Bayeaux. At least Hugh was a clergyman. In Austrasia, Martel's good friend Milo, a layman who preferred hunting and drinking to prayer, was bishop of Trier, Laon, and Reims. Even more notorious was Bishop Gewilib of Mainz, who had love affairs and participated in a bloodfeud. Martel disregarded the scandal, and his tolerance won him much criticism from stricter clergy. The English missionary and reformer Boniface gave a gloomy picture of the Frankish Church in a letter he wrote to Pope Zachary, shortly after Martel's death:

> [I]n many dioceses, the bishop's office has been given to a greedy layman to use as his own property, or to an adulterous clergyman, a fornicator, a publican, to abuse in an ungodly way.... And among them are found some bishops who ... carry weapons and fight with the army. They are accustomed to shed human blood (Christian or pagan, it does not matter to them) with their own hands.

Once he was secure in Neustria and Austrasia, Charles Martel attacked his enemies along the frontiers of the Frankish kingdom. He began this series of wars in Germany, in order to prevent hostile attacks upon the Frankish kingdom by traditional enemies of the Franks. He suppressed a Saxon rebellion in 724 and in the next year, 725, he crossed the Rhine to fight in Alemannia and Bavaria. After securing the frontier in Germany, he crossed the Loire to attack his old enemy, Eudo of Aquitaine.

Martel Defeats Muslims at Poitiers

The Continuator claims that Eudo called upon the Saracens, or Muslims from Spain, to help him against Martel. Muslims from north Africa had conquered Spain in 711 and were ready to explore the possibilities of further conquests in Europe. Instead of help, Eudo got hostile raids. The Muslims provoked a crisis in 732, when they inflicted a serious defeat on Eudo. One Muslim army penetrated into Burgundy. Another plundered the church of St. Hilary in Poitiers and was marching toward Tours. A religious center of great prestige for the Franks, this city on the Loire River offered access to the heart of the Frankish kingdom. Martel caught the Muslim army on the road between Poitiers and Tours at the battle of Poitiers in October 732. The Continuator offers a near contemporary account of this battle:

> Charles the prince boldly drew up his battle line against the enemy. Charles the warrior rushed upon them. With Christ's help, he overthrew their tents. He ran to battle to inflict destructive slaughter. After killing their king Abd-al-Rahman, Charles overthrew them. Treading their army underfoot, he fought and conquered.

This description offers little support for the view that Martel's army at Poitiers was made up of heavily armed cavalrymen, or knights, who charged their enemies with lances at rest. Most Franks were still infantrymen. After this battle, which was their first major defeat in Europe, the Muslims were on the defensive in the West.

His success at Poitiers encouraged Martel to exert his power over Aquitaine, Burgundy, and Provence (in southern France). When Eudo died in 735, Martel occupied the city of Bordeaux and its surrounding territory, the core of Eudo's property. In addition, Martel campaigned actively in Burgundy and Provence to prevent any more Muslim raids and to ruin Burgundian and Provençal nobles, his enemies and potential allies of the Muslims. After campaigning in Burgundy in 733 and 736, he installed his own men as counts to handle judicial, administrative, and military affairs. He confiscated large amounts of land, especially from the Church. Martel often gave this confiscated land to loyal supporters in return for military service, a practice associated with feudalism. This was a political necessity. He looked on the powerful bishops of Burgundy as political and military rivals. In effect, he followed the same policy in Burgundy as in Neustria and Austrasia to break the power of hostile nobles.

The campaigns in Provence were also directed against Muslims and local nobles. In 737, the Muslims crossed the Rhône River and found a collaborator in a duke named Maurontus. Together they captured Avignon and plundered the surrounding territory. Martel sent his brother Count Childebrand to begin the seige of Avignon. When Martel joined the army, the Franks took the city by storm. The Continuator compares the fall of Avignon to the fall of the biblical Jericho under the leadership of Joshua. Then Martel crossed the Rhône River, to besiege the city of Narbonne and attack the Muslim camp. When another Muslim army from Spain tried to stop him, he destroyed it on the banks of the River Berre, near Corbières. Afterwards, Martel attacked and plundered the cities of Nîmes, Agde, and Béziers.

While Martel was fighting these campaigns, he was forced to deal with rebellions among the Frisians in 734 and Saxons in 738. The conquest of Frisia was an especially important matter to the Franks. The Frisians produced woolen cloth of high quality and handled trade between England, Scandinavia, and the Frankish kingdom. The Franks made strenuous efforts to conquer Frisia and convert the pagan Frisians to Christianity. Martel's father, Pepin II, had campaigned actively in Frisia. He supported Willibrord, an English missionary, whom the pope appointed bishop of Utrecht. When Pepin died in 714, the pagan duke Radbod drove Willibrord out of Utrecht. After defeating Radbod, Martel restored Willibrord and supported his missionary work for the rest of his life. When the rebellion of 734 broke out in northern Frisia, Charles Martel attacked the rebels and killed their leader, the pagan Bubo. He also destroyed the rebels' pagan shrines and their idols. However, Frisian resistance to both Frankish rule and Christianity was stubborn and found constant support among the pagan Saxons. Martel dealt ruthlessly with this Germanic tribe in 738. When the Saxons rebelled—apparently they refused to pay the tribute they owed the Franks—Martel crossed the Rhine into Saxony. The Continuator describes Martel's severity:

> Charles the energetic warrior ravaged an extensive portion of this region with most fearful slaughter.

He ordered part of this very savage tribe to pay tribute and took as many hostages as possible from them. And so, with the Lord's help, Charles the conqueror returned home to his own lands.

However, Martel's expeditions to Saxony were preliminary raids. His grandson, **Charlemagne,** would finally subjugate the Saxons and incorporate Saxony into the Frankish kingdom.

Pope Honors Martel

In 739, Pope Gregory III sent ambassadors to Martel. The pope honored him with the Roman title of "consul" or "patrician." This was the first direct contact between Charles Martel and the pope, who needed military aid against the Lombard kings. These kings, whose kingdom was centered on Pavia in the north, wanted to rule all of Italy, including Rome. But Martel refused a military adventure in Italy. The Lombards had been allies of the Franks in the past, and Martel hoped for their continued support against the Muslims. The popes, however, would persist in their efforts to make the Franks their allies. Pepin III's alliance with the papacy would bring about his usurpation of the Frankish throne from the Merovingians in 751. This same alliance would lead Charlemagne to the conquest of the Lombard kingdom of northern Italy and his imperial coronation in 800. This was the only one of Charles Martel's policies that his successors reversed, with momentous consequences.

By 740, when he was about 50 years old, Martel's health was beginning to fail. Accordingly, he made provisions for his two sons, Carloman and Pepin III, to inherit his power. Like a king, he divided his inheritance. He appointed his elder son, Carloman, mayor in Austrasia, Alemannia, and Thuringia. Pepin III was to be mayor of Neustria, Burgundy, and Provence. Charles Martel died on October 22, 741, at the palace of Quierzy and was buried in the monastery of St. Denis in Paris.

To later generations of Franks, Charles Martel was above all a conquering warrior. The Continuator of Fredegar's *Chronicle* and later Frankish historians liked to emphasize the idea that Charles Martel fought against the enemies of the Christian God. This gave special importance to his wars against the Muslims of Spain and the pagans of Frisia and Saxony. During the Middle Ages, Martel seemed to be the leader of God's people, the Christian Franks, in holy wars which were the predecessors of later crusades. His victories in God's name made him the real ruler of the Frankish kingdom and helped to establish the claim of his dynasty to kingship.

SOURCES:

Bachrach, Bernard S. *Merovingian Military Organization, 481–751*. University of Minnesota Press, 1972.

Gerberding, Richard A. *The Rise of the Carolingians and the Liber Historiae Francorum*. Clarendon Press, 1987.

Wallace-Hadrill, J. M., trans. and ed. *The Fourth Book of the Chronicle of Fredegar with its Continuations*. Thomas Nelson, 1960.

———. *The Frankish Church*. Clarendon Press, 1983.

FURTHER READING:

Bachrach, Bernard S. "Charles Martel, Mounted Shock Combat, the Stirrup, and Feudalism," in *Studies in Medieval and Renaissance History*. Vol. 7. 1970, pp. 49–75.

Geary, Patrick J. *Before France and Germany*. Oxford University Press, 1988.

Karl Marx

(1818–1883)

Revolutionary, philosopher, sociologist, historian, and economist, whose ideas formed the basis for the Communist Party, thereby affecting the lives of one-third of the world's population.

Karl Marx confronts us as a thinker of world-historical dimensions.... Our own century has run much of its course in the shadow of his teaching."

EUGENE KAMENKA

Believing that "philosophers have only interpreted the world in various ways; the point, however, is to change it," Karl Marx spent his life dedicated to both understanding and to action. His father Heinrich was greatly influenced by the enlightenment, especially by Kant and Voltaire. In the age of antireligious sentiment and local anti-Semitism, Heinrich relinquished his ties to Judaism, and the year before his son was born he was baptized into the Evangelical Established Church in order to maintain his position as an attorney in the High Court of Appeals. Marx was to be greatly affected by his father; he carried his picture all his life.

Baptized at age six, Marx was taught little about Judaism, which did not seem to bother him then or in future years, yet it is likely that his exposure to the religious prejudice of the day later caused him to question the social value of religion. He attended a Lutheran elementary school and then, from 1830–35, the Friedrich Wilhelm Gymnasium, a high school that was searched and placed under surveillance for the suspected harboring of liberal teachers and pupils. The school emphasized languages, and Marx performed well in Latin and

Name variations: Surname was originally a shortened form of Mordechai, which was later changed to Markus, then to Marx. Born the eldest of nine children on May 5, 1818, in Trier, a Prussian town of 12,000 (now in West Germany); died in London in 1883; son of Heinrich Marx (an attorney); married: Jenny von Westphalen, February, 1842; children: seven, only three lived to adulthood, Jenny, Laura, and Eleanor (the latter two committed suicide). Descendants: As of 1972, only three living survivors known were his great-grandsons, Charles, Frederic, and Paul Longuet.

Contributed by Brian Morley, Assistant Professor of Philosophy, The Master's College, Pine Valley, California

CHRONOLOGY

1836	Marx transferred to University of Berlin
1841	Received doctorate from Jena
1842	Joined staff of *Rheinische Zeitung*
1843–45	Wrote economic and philosophic manuscripts; met Engels
1845–48	Worked with Engels in Brussels
1848	Co-wrote *The Communist Manifesto;* wrote for radical *Neue Rheinische Zeitung*
1850	Hard years in London began
1851–62	Correspondent for the *New York Daily Tribune*
1867	First edition of *Capital*
1883	Died in London

French (later in life he used his language skills for research, and in his mature years could also read Spanish, Italian, Dutch, Scandinavian, Russian, and English—a language he also spoke, but with a heavy accent). Oddly, he did poorly in history. His sisters recalled that though he bullied them mercilessly, he made up for it by reading them wonderful stories.

From an early age, Marx showed signs of Christian devotion and of a longing for self-sacrifice on behalf of humanity; an essay on the Gospel of John 15:1–14 for his graduation examinations spoke of the "reason, nature, necessity, and effects of the union of believers with Christ…. History teaches the necessity of union with Christ," a union that overcomes sin and brings happiness, making for "a finer and more elevated life." At 17, he was the youngest graduating member of his class.

In 1835, he entered the University of Bonn. Although his father urged him to take up law, Marx preferred philosophy and literature, hoping to become a poet and dramatist. He made himself ill from overwork, and after a period of recovery he resumed his studies but with less enthusiasm. Spending summers in Trier, he became secretly engaged to Jenny von Westphalen, an attractive, intelligent girl, four years his senior, who came from a prominent family. While at school, he wrote poetry, joined a poetry club that included some political activists, fought a duel, spent a day in jail for being drunk and disorderly, and piled up debts.

His father was so displeased with his performance that in 1836 he transferred his son to the University of Berlin, which had a more academic

reputation, and Marx studied law and philosophy. He was a romantic idealist with religious leanings, but the philosophical ideas of Hegel were popular there, and the atmosphere was one that challenged accepted ideas. His thinking changed when introduced to the "left" Hegelians, who saw in Hegel grounds for challenging institutions and the traditional Christian separation between God and creation.

Marx became very involved with a hard-drinking, boisterous discussion group called the Doctor's club, which met at a local cafe. Some of the professors in the Club became his friends and influenced him deeply. Bruno Bauer, his closest companion, lectured in theology, teaching that Jesus never existed and that the gospels arose purely from human need. Friedrich Strauss, author of *Life of Jesus,* interpreted the gospels as myths that embodied the aspirations of the early church. Marx also was influenced by Eduard Gans, a law professor who publicized Saint-Simon's ideas that rich and idle factory owners abuse miserable "proletarian" workers, slaves who would be free only with socialism.

Marx's View Becomes "Dialectical Materialism"

Feuerbach's book *The Essence of Christianity* (1841) also influenced Marx and these Young Hegelians. Hegel believed that "Mind" (or Spirit) progressively realizes itself in history and that ideas are more important than physical things (a view known as "idealism"). But Feuerbach said that reality is physical, not spiritual, and people only imagine God's existence; without a spiritual reality, the human condition is affected only by the material world. For Feuerbach, humanity—not Spirit—struggles to realize itself in history. Humanity must overcome self-alienation. Marx accepted this materialism but retained Hegel's dialectic view, which regarded progress in the world as the result of a clash between opposites, with the original condition (the "thesis") giving rise to another condition that opposes it (the "antithesis"), and out of the conflict would come a new condition (the "synthesis"). Marx's view is thus called "dialectical materialism." As the Young Hegelians became more atheistic and talked of political action, the Prussian government (modern Germany) feared their subversive tendencies and tried to drive them from the universities.

Writing to him in March 1837, his father expressed concern that Marx no longer had room in his heart for "softer feelings…. Your soul is obviously animated and ruled by a demon not given to all men…. Will you ever … be able to spread happiness to your immediate surroundings?" After his father died the following year, Marx became aloof from his studies, rarely attending classes but reading extensively and remaining active in the club. Exempted from the military because of an enlarged heart, he worked on a doctoral dissertation that contrasted the natural philosophies of Democritus and Epicurus. It opened with the defiant words of Promethius: "In one word, I hate all the gods." After finishing his studies at Berlin, Marx submitted his dissertation to the University of Jena, which had a reputation for laxity, and received a doctorate in 1841. Moses Hess, a socialist leader, described him during this period in a letter to a friend: "He combines with the deepest philosophical earnestness the most biting wit."

When his desire to teach philosophy at Bonn University was thwarted by the policy of the Prussian government, Marx turned to writing and journalism. In January 1842, he began contributing to a newspaper newly founded in Cologne, the *Rheinische Zeitung*. One of his essays defended freedom of the press and condemned censorship as an evil that amounted to spying on people's minds and hearts. By October, he was made editor and wrote on topics ranging from theft of forest wood by peasants to communism—the view that there should be no private property ("Communism" developed later as the ideology of the Communist Party, a combination of the views of Marx, **Lenin,** and others). The circulation increased but the Prussian government suppressed the publication, ordering it to close early the next year.

The following month, he married Jenny von Westphalen after a seven-year engagement. Her father was a socialist follower of Saint-Simon, and Marx's former tutor. He liked Marx, but the rest of her family opposed the marriage. Rejecting an offer to work in the Prussian civil service, Marx and his bride moved to Paris, a center of socialism where he anticipated more freedom. While there, he used this freedom to contact leaders of the revolutionary workers' movements, shifting from radical democracy to communism.

He co-edited the *German-French Yearbook,* which put out only one issue but included an important work entitled "Toward the Critique of the Hegelian Philosophy of Right," in which Marx called for the working class to rise up. He now viewed religion as both a symptom of humanity's deeper problems and the culprit responsible for perpetuating those problems—a repudiation of whatever piety he may have felt in his youth. "Religion is the sigh of the oppressed creature.... It is the opium of the people. The abolition of religion

as the illusory happiness of men, is a demand for their real happiness."

Through the *Yearbook* he met another contributor, Friedrich Engels. After a ten-day meeting that took place later that year, Engels wrote that they had reached "complete agreement on all theoretical matters." He became Marx's lifelong collaborator, financial supporter, and friend. Although from a devout Calvinist home, he was converted to communism by Moses Hess, known as the "communist rabbi." Engels's father owned successful cotton mills in Prussia and England in which he worked as a clerk, later becoming part owner. While working in the Manchester mill (1843–44), Engels saw some of the abuses of the early industrial revolution. He never married but stayed with his mistress, an Irish factory girl named Mary Burns, for 20 years.

In 1845, under pressure from the Prussian government, the French Ministry of the Interior ordered Marx out of the country. He and his family went to Brussels, followed by Engels, and there Marx made his first concentrated efforts to organize the working class. But he clashed with other leaders of the movement. When Wilhelm Weitling advocated the establishment of communism by a cataclysmic upheaval by the working class—"one violent push" led by a dictatorship of revolutionary elite—Marx jumped up, slammed his fist on the table, and objected that the view was based on ignorance, that society cannot leap into communism by skipping the bourgeoisie phase and bypassing capitalism. In his book *The Poverty of Philosophy* (1847), Marx strongly disagreed with French socialist Pierre Proudhon, who wanted to salvage the good features in existing economic institutions. For Marx, there could be no salvaging of existing institutions—such a view showed an ignorance of the laws of history.

He and Engels collaborated on *The Holy Family,* a critique of the Hegelian idealism of Bruno Bauer, Marx's former teacher and friend. An unpublished work, "The German Ideology" (1845–46), also hypothesized that the main influence on history is the economic relationship between social classes; that the ruling class determines what ideas are accepted by society; and that those who control the production of goods control society for their own ends.

Marx and Engels Draft Communist Manifesto

Asking Marx to join them, German immigrant workers in London soon changed the name of their secret society to the Communist League. At the group's request, Marx and Engels drafted their political program, *The Communist Manifesto,* which appeared as a pamphlet in January 1848. It opened with the ominous words: "A specter is haunting Europe—the specter of communism." Remarkably, in an era of intense nationalism, it proclaimed that national differences were declining and that workingmen "have no country"; it viewed all history as "the history of class struggles," a clash between "oppressor and oppressed." The oppressor was the "bourgeoisie," those who owned the means to produce wealth and who reduced everything to selfish gain; the oppressed were the "proletarians," the urban poor, who often worked in factories. He foresaw that as the workers organized into trade unions the conflict would become more intense until eventually revolution would break out and the workers would justly overthrow the bourgeoisie to establish a communist society.

The *Manifesto* advocated a plan of action that was not intended as a universal blueprint for communism (Marx never published one). It included abolition of private property and rights of inheritance; graduated income tax; confiscation of property of emigrants and rebels; nationalization of banks, communication, transportation, factories, and farmland; laws requiring all to work; equal distribution of population throughout a country; free public schools; and abolition of child labor. It ended with a rousing call: "The proletarians have nothing to lose but their chains. They have a world to win. Workingmen of all countries, unite!"

Uprisings did indeed start in Europe soon after the *Manifesto* was published, but as Francis Randall points out, the revolutionaries were bourgeois liberals, not socialist workingmen. Furthermore, the revolutionary drives had strong themes of national independence and unity. They were soon put down and did not signal a new era.

In March 1848, Marx was ordered out of Belgium within 24 hours but was invited to return to France by the Provisional Government. He and his wife were arrested and escorted with their children to the French border. After attending a meeting of the Communist League in France, he went to Cologne in April and took over the radical newspaper, *Neue Rheinische Zeitung,* urging the establishment of a constitutional democracy in Prussia and a war with Russia on the grounds that they would intervene against a Prussian democracy.

The king dissolved the Prussian Assembly, which responded by declaring taxes illegal. When Marx called on people to resist the collection of taxes and to take up arms, the government indicted him and suppressed the paper. Acting in his own

defense, he delivered a long speech on the conditions in Prussia; not only did the jury acquit him, but the foreman thanked him for an interesting lecture. The government could not reverse his acquittal, but it did expel him from the country. The paper's last issue was printed in red ink.

Marx and Engels moved on to Frankfurt in an unsuccessful attempt to persuade the left-wing members of the National Assembly to start an uprising by bringing in revolutionary forces from Baden and the Pfalz. When Marx left for Paris as a representative of the German revolutionary parties, Engels stayed to participate in a revolutionary campaign, which was later crushed. Again expelled from Paris, Marx made his home in London in August 1849, where he spent the rest of his life as a man without a state. Britain would not grant him citizenship and Prussia refused to renaturalize him.

He immediately became involved in revolutionary affairs by helping to reconstitute the London Central Committee of the Communist League and by joining the German Workers' Educational Association. Because the liberal bourgeoisie had withdrawn their support from him in Prussia, he advocated working without them.

Marx expected the economic situation to become worse and thereby increase popular revolutionary fervor. When it didn't, he clashed in late 1850 with more radical leaders like August von Willich, who wanted revolutionary action. Marx believed that trying to "achieve power immediately" would put the workers in control before they were ready, and saw instead a long struggle to prepare them. A revolution, Marx maintained, would not succeed until the conditions were right and the workers fully class-conscious. Opposing poorly timed acts of terrorism such as those of Jerome Blanqui, Marx's moderation brought ridicule from more militant types who sought immediate violent action; they accused him of being interested only in lecturing. When his attention turned to noneconomic topics, he produced *The Class Struggles in France* (1850) and *The Eighteenth Brumaire of Louis Napoleon* (1852), historical studies on the French Revolution of 1848 and events which led to the Second Empire of Napoleon III.

Personal Difficulties Beset Marx Family

The next 12 years proved to be miserable and lonely for Marx, with journalism his only steady source of earned income. From 1851 to 1862, he served as correspondent for the *New York Daily Tribune* and contributed about 500 articles and editorials (a fourth of which were actually by

Engels), but at two pounds sterling per article, he remained dependent on Engels's meager earnings as a clerk.

In April of 1850, Marx's family was evicted and their belongings confiscated. In November, his one-year-old son Guido died. The following June, their young maid gave birth to an illegitimate son. With Marx's paternity later confirmed by Engels, it was a bitter disappointment to Jenny, who had been, and would remain, loyal to him.

He was sued more than once, and was at times unable to pay rent, taxes, or debts. The family had neither fuel for heat nor shoes for the children to go to school. Marx pawned his coat and could not go out in the cold and, when threatened with eviction, his wife pawned her clothes. Then in April 1852, their one-year-old daughter Franziska died, followed two years later by eight-year-old Edgar. Jenny delivered a stillborn child three years later. Four children had been lost, largely due to their miserable lifestyle. Jenny had several breakdowns and became seriously ill with smallpox.

But Marx could not, except once, bring himself to accept unemployment benefits. During one difficult period, he was willing to accept a job as clerk but lost the position because his handwriting was barely legible. Believing his work to be the writing of his books, he went daily to the reading room of the British Museum, a few blocks from their two-room quarters. He published his first book on economic theory, *A Contribution to the Critique of Political Economy* (1859), and continued on his main work, *Capital,* of which only Volume I was published during his life. His writing was occasionally interrupted by his own ill health: headaches, toothaches, boils, rheumatism, bronchitis, pleurisy, eye infections, lung abscesses, gallbladder attacks, and hemorrhoids. Heavy pipe and cigar smoking, heavy drinking, and a penchant for spicy foods only aggravated his condition.

And, at times, his personality alienated him from his peers. Moses Hess, who had earlier admired him, wrote in 1841 that Marx demanded "a degree of personal submission that I, for one, will never condescend to give to another." Schurz had never "seen a man whose bearing was so provoking and intolerable.... Everyone who contradicted him he treated with abject contempt." Marx called Lassalle, a prominent Jewish labor leader, a "dirty Jew of Negro blood," and once wrote to Engels, "Your old man is a pig." The Russian revolutionary, Mikhail Bakunin, recounted in 1845, "He called me a sentimental Idealist, and he was right; I called him vain, perfidious, and sly, and I was right too." Most damning was a disaffected follower, Techow, who wrote in 1850 that he suspected "the acquisition of personal power was the aim of all his endeavors." But Marx did inspire confidence in his intellectual ability and leadership, with Schurz describing his words as "full of meaning, logical and clear," and a number of people have remarked that he was an affectionate father whose children were devoted to him.

Times improved for Marx when Engels became part owner of the factory and was able to provide him with greater finances; he also received money after the deaths of some of Jenny's relatives. As he influenced and helped unify the International Working Men's Association, the movement grew to 800,000 in 1869. Later, he faced opposition within the organization from the right when labor unionists wanted to cooperate with the Liberal Party to bring political action. On the left, Bakunin thought a Russian revolution would come through the violence of the peasants, not through the elite, civilized workers in industrial centers whom Marx viewed as the key. Thinking that Marx acted like a dictator, Bakunin tried to free the organization from his grip, but Marx forced him and his followers out of the organization which then declined and eventually disbanded in 1876.

Marx spent the last ten years of his life influencing socialist movements but producing no major writings. Troubled with depression and health problems, he traveled to health resorts as far away as North Africa. His wife died in 1881, his eldest daughter in 1883. Grieved, Marx died in his armchair of a lung abscess on March 14, 1883. Fifteen years later, his daughter Eleanor committed suicide, and in 1911 both his daughter Laura and her husband followed suit. Only the maid's son, Frederick, lived to see the Communist revolution in Russia.

Marx never doubted that revolutions would occur, but he did not expect them in nonindustrialized countries where capitalism had not developed and where the socioeconomic dynamics he sought to explain were virtually nonexistent. He had thought that the excesses of capitalism in industrialized nations would become worse and did not foresee the extent of changes in such things as labor laws, the advent of social security systems, and the rising prosperity of the middle class. Believing revolution would bring a transition period of "dictatorship of the proletariat," then a communist society, he foresaw a day of no private ownership (not even marriage, which he considered "a form of exclusive private property"), no religion, no economic classes, no exploitation, and no inequality. The state would wither away and people would become joyous, free producers of goods solely for the benefit of others.

SOURCES:

Berlin, Isaiah. *Karl Marx*. 3rd ed., 1939; Oxford, 1963.
Evans, Michael. *Karl Marx*. Indiana University Press, 1975.
Kamenka, Eugene. *The Portable Karl Marx*. Penguin, 1983.
McLellan, David. *Marx Before Marxism*. Harper, 1970.
Marx, Karl. *Capital*. Modern Library, 1906.
———. *Early Writings*. McGraw-Hill, 1963.
Randall, Francis, introd. *The Communist Manifesto* by Karl Marx and Friedrich Engels. Washington Square, 1964.

FURTHER READING:

Carver, Terrell. *A Marx Dictionary*. Barnes & Noble, 1987.
Lavine, T. Z. *From Socrates to Sartre: the Philosophic Quest*, Bantam, 1984.

Mary, Queen of Scots

(1542–1587)

Scotland's most famous queen, who ruled successfully until her disastrous marriage to the Earl of Bothwell, and was later executed by Elizabeth I.

"In my end is my beginning."

MARY, QUEEN OF SCOTS

According to tradition, upon hearing of the birth of his daughter Mary on December 7, 1542, James V, king of Scotland, declared: "The devil take it. It came with a lass and it will pass with a lass." Seven days later, the 30-year-old king was dead and his infant daughter had succeeded to the throne, throwing Scotland into yet another royal minority. To further complicate matters, the heir was a woman. Echoing the country's dismay, Protestant reformer **John Knox** exclaimed that "all men lamented that the realm was left without a male to succeed." An infant monarch complicated the already divided government of Scotland which was composed of two factions: those who favored a closer union with England, Scotland's traditional enemy, and those who preferred to maintain the "auld alliance" with France. These loyalties were increasingly influenced by the religious atmosphere of the Reformation which pitted the supporters of Protestant England against those of Catholic France.

The young queen's role as a dynastic property was clear from the moment of her birth. Negotiations for the marriage of Mary to **Henry VIII**'s five-year-old son and heir, Edward, were

Contributed by Margaret H. McIntyre, Ph.D. candidate in History, University of Guelph, Guelph, Ontario, Canada

Name variations: Mary Stuart, Queen of Scots. Born Mary Stewart (during her upbringing in France, she adopted the Anglo-French spelling of Stuart) on December 7 or 8, 1542, at the palace of Linlithgow; executed for treason at Fotheringhay Castle, February 8, 1587; only daughter of James V of Scotland and Mary of Guise; married: Francis (dauphin and king of France), April 24, 1558 (died December 5, 1560); married: Henry Stewart, Lord Darnley, July 29, 1565 (murdered March 10, 1566); married: James Hepburn, Earl of Bothwell, May 15, 1567; children: (second marriage) one son, James. Descendants: royal family of Great Britain. Predecessor: James V. Successor: James VI of Scotland and I of England.

1542	James V died; Mary (7 days old) succeeded to throne of Scotland
1545	First Session of Council of Trent
1548	Mary sent to France as condition of Treaty of Haddington
1553	Edward VI died; Mary I crowned queen of England
1558	Mary Stuart married Francis, son of Henry II of France; Mary I died; Elizabeth I crowned
1559	Henry II died; Francis and Mary acceded to throne of France
1560	Reformation Parliament; Francis II died; Charles IX (age 10) crowned king of France
1561	Mary arrived at Leith
1562	Civil War in France began; rebellion of Earl of Huntly
1565	Mary married Lord Darnley; "Chaseabout Raid"
1566	David Rizzio murdered; James born
1567	Darnley murdered; Bothwell acquitted; Mary married Bothwell; forced to abdicate; James (13 months) crowned king of Scotland
1568	Mary defeated at the Battle of Langside
1569	First trial; Mary detained in England
1571	Ridolfi Plot discovered
1586	Babington Plot uncovered; Mary tried for treason; found guilty
1587	Beheaded at age 44

concluded through the Treaties of Greenwich on July 1, 1543. By December, Henry's insistence upon having custody of Mary led the Scottish lords to reject England and renew their alliance with France. Not to be dissuaded from enforcing his marriage plans, Henry VIII authorized the earl of Hertford to lead a series of invasions to southeastern Scotland, which became known as the "Rough Wooing." His orders were explicit: "Sack, burn and subvert, putting man, woman and child to fire and sword without exception, when any resistance shall be made against you." These heavy-handed tactics only served to strengthen Scottish opposition to the marriage and hatred of union with England. Upon his death in January 1547, Henry's attempt to take over Scotland was a failure, in spite of the earl of Hertford's victory over the Scots at the Battle of Pinkie on September 9, 1547. Mary

was moved to the island priory of Inchmahome for three weeks for greater safety.

By February 1548, the Scots were actively seeking French aid and betrothed their young queen to the French dauphin Francis, the son of Henry II, on the condition that Henry send an army to Scotland to drive the English out. French troops duly arrived in June and on July 29, the five-year-old queen left her native land to spend the next 13 years in France.

Speaking in a broken Scots brogue, she soon learned to converse in French which became the language of her choice for the rest of her life. Her playmates were Francis's brothers and sisters—including the future kings of France Charles IX and Henry III—and her most intimate childhood friend Elizabeth, future queen to **Philip II** of Spain. Mary's popularity grew with her marriage to Francis on April 24, 1558, in a magnificent ceremony at Notre Dame Cathedral.

Within months, international events changed Mary Stuart's life dramatically. On November 17, 1558, the queen of England, **Mary I** (Tudor), died and was succeeded by her Protestant half-sister **Elizabeth I**. As granddaughter of Margaret Tudor, Mary Stuart became heir presumptive to the English throne and in the eyes of Catholic Europe, it was she, and not Elizabeth Tudor, the bastard daughter of Henry VIII and Anne Boleyn, who was the lawful claimant to the crown of England. Mary's prestige reached a climax in July 1559 when she became queen of France after Henry II died of wounds inflicted during a jousting tournament. Her happiness was short-lived, however, after she learned of the death of her mother in June 1560. Six months later, her husband King Francis II was also dead. Mary was devastated, her health deteriorated, and she was plagued by a recurring pain in her side. She continued to suffer from gastric troubles for the rest of her life, particularly during times of emotional stress.

Mary Returns to Scotland

In spite of these personal tragedies, Mary chose to return to Scotland although it was a far different country from the one she had left 13 years before. With monetary and military assistance from Elizabeth I, the Scottish nobles had succeeded in breaking the "auld alliance" with France. By the terms of the Treaty of Edinburgh on July 6, 1560, French troops had withdrawn from Scotland, and the Scottish Parliament had declared Scotland a Protestant country by abolishing the authority of the pope and forbidding the celebration of the Mass.

But the queen who returned to this turbulent kingdom had grown very tall—almost six feet—taller than most men of that time period, and had matured into a warm, lively, and vivacious personage. Historian Gordon Donaldson noted that:

Not the least of her charms was a natural kindness—which in a Queen was condescension, though in Mary it was so graciously and naturally given that neither she nor her subjects thought of it as condescension. It was this characteristic which led to an occasional familiarity with servants and other inferiors which some thought indiscreet, but it caused her to stand well with her subjects throughout her realm as well as with her courtiers and advisers.

Mary's French education had taught her to sing, play the lute, and dance with grace and style. She also had what author Antonia Fraser has described as a "positive mania for outdoor pursuits." Thus, hawking, hunting, archery, golf, and croquet were some of her favorite outdoor activities. Indoors, she inherited her grandfather James IV's passion for playing cards late into the night. Intellectually, she was a true Renaissance princess. She could read at least six languages, including Greek, and her personal library contained a large collection of French and Italian verse. She also collected histories of France and Scotland as well as Italy, the Holy Roman Empire, England, and classical Greece and Rome. Having spent so many years in France, her Scottish court was highly influenced by French style and manners.

As a Catholic sovereign in a Protestant country, Mary ruled successfully during the early years in Scotland. She insisted upon having Mass said in her own chapel and, while she did not ratify the acts of the Reformation Parliament of 1560, she issued a proclamation upon her arrival forbidding any "alteration or innovation of that state of religion which her majesty found public and universally standing at her majesty's arrival in this her realm." In 1562, she agreed to an arrangement whereby a proportion of the wealth of the old Church was shared between the crown and the Protestant ministers, and during the same year she led an armed force to suppress a rebellion initiated by her greatest Catholic magnate, the earl of Huntly. In the opinion of Gordon Donaldson "there is little doubt that by personality as well as policy she made herself acceptable to the great majority of her people."

Mary's continued success was dependent upon her choice of a husband and her relations with Elizabeth I. From her arrival in Scotland and largely under the influence of her chief advisors, William Maitland of Lethington and her half-brother James Stewart, earl of Moray, a policy of peaceful union with England was advocated; Mary would be recognized as Elizabeth's heir in return for her renunciation of any claim to the English throne during Elizabeth's life. The greatest obstacle to this policy of mutual recognition and reconciliation was Elizabeth I's refusal to recognize Mary or anyone else as her successor, and her refusal to say once and for all whether or not she intended to marry.

Serious negotiations for Mary's marriage to continental princes were undertaken in 1563, but in February 1565 she fell in love with her first cousin Henry Stewart, Lord Darnley, whom she described as "the lustiest and best-proportioned long man I have seen." Darnley, as a grandson of Margaret Tudor, was next in line after Mary to the English succession and their marriage on July 29, 1565, united the two nearest claimants to the English throne.

Performed by Catholic rites, the marriage provoked fears among the Protestant reformers that a Catholic revival was imminent. It also alienated Maitland of Lethington and Moray who were upset at having been replaced by Darnley as Mary's chief adviser. One month after the marriage, Moray raised an aimless rebellion known as the "Chaseabout Raid." Although it gathered little support from either the Scottish or English nobles, the rebellion signalled the end of Mary's early successes. Her lords began to criticize her for relying on men "of base degree" who had "neither judgment nor experience of the ancient laws and governance of this realm." She also came to realize that Darnley, who was both "morally and mentally worthless," was not fit to be a consort, let alone a king, and she continued to withhold the crown matrimonial from him.

The Murders of Rizzio and Darnley

Resentment by both Darnley and the magnates centered on David Rizzio, who had first come to the royal court as a musician and was later promoted to secretary for Mary's French affairs. Rumors were spread that he was not only a papal agent but also the queen's lover. Neither of these allegations appears to have had any factual basis, but Darnley was easily persuaded that they were true. On a promise of receiving the crown matrimonial, he signed a bond with several nobles in return for a pardon of the men who had participated in the Chaseabout Raid. On March 9, 1566, Rizzio was brutally murdered in the queen's presence, an event which was clearly designed to endanger the life of Mary herself, who was six months pregnant at the time. In her own words, she described the horrible deed: "They dragged David with great cruelty forth from our cabinet and at the entrance of our chamber dealt him 56 dagger wounds."

The Rizzio murder was a significant turning point in Mary's reign, although it did not bring about a collapse of royal government. The queen showed both courage and intelligence by temporarily regaining Darnley's affections and escaping from her captors. Prince James, the future **James VI,** was born on June 19, 1566, but his birth only served to deepen Mary's animosity towards her husband. "My Lord, God has given you and me a son, begotten by none but you," she declared. "Here I protest to God that he is your son and no other man's son. For he is so much your own son, that I fear it will be the worse for him hereafter."

The baptism of the prince by Catholic rites did nothing to strengthen the queen's position, and in her search for a new and powerful ally, Mary turned to James Hepburn, earl of Bothwell. Described by a contemporary as "a glorious, rash and hazardous young man," Bothwell came from a family who were among the most powerful magnates of southeast Scotland, and one which had a long tradition of loyalty to the crown. In spite of her growing affection for Bothwell, Mary feared that an annulment of her marriage to Darnley would threaten her son's legitimacy. Her desire to be rid of her husband was known by the lords, and plans for his elimination by more violent means were circulating.

On February 10, 1567, at two o'clock in the morning, the lodging known as Kirk O'Field where Darnley was recovering from a recent illness was blown up by gunpowder. His body was found in a garden adjoining the house where he had been smothered or strangled. The murder of the 20-year-old Darnley has remained one of the greatest "whodunits" in history. Although there was undoubtedly more than one conspiracy to kill the king, it was commonly believed that Bothwell was the murderer. Mary's involvement was not proven, but her actions following the crime aroused suspicion.

In a farcical trial, Bothwell was acquitted of the murder. Then, granted a quick divorce from his wife, he married Mary by Protestant rites on May 15, 1567. This marriage turned the last of Mary's loyal magnates against her and led to her defeat by the Confederate Lords at Carberry Hill on June 15, 1567. After the bloodless confrontation, a worn-out and travel-stained queen was brought into Edinburgh in disgrace and insulted by the crowds who shouted "Burn the whore." Within 48 hours, she was taken to the island castle of Lochleven where, on July 24, she was forced to abdicate the throne in favor of her infant son, now James VI, with Moray acting as regent on his behalf. This action was unprecedented in the history of the Scottish monarchy. Never before had a faction imprisoned their monarch, forced an abdication, and proclaimed the heir king while the deposed ruler was still living.

Nine months later, Mary escaped from Lochleven on May 2, 1568, and was able to command enough support to raise another army. Her forces, however, were defeated at Langside, near Glasgow, on May 13. Three days later, she made the fateful decision to cross the Solway Firth to England and seek protection from her cousin Elizabeth.

Her arrival in England placed the English government in an awkward position. They could not allow her to go to France where she had been proclaimed queen of England 10 years before, nor would it have been wise to allow her to return to Scotland where her restoration would alienate the pro-English faction. Instead, the English government chose to hold an investigation into Mary's alleged complicity in the murder of Darnley.

Mary Is Investigated

The inquiry, or trial, was held in 1568–69 at York, Westminster and, finally, Hampton Court in front of a board of English commissioners who heard cases put forward by the representatives of Mary and Moray. The most damning testimony against Mary was produced after her representatives had walked out of the proceedings. The evidence was a collection of letters and documents allegedly found in the possession of Bothwell's servant which Mary was supposed to have written to Bothwell and which were said to prove her complicity in the murder of Darnley. The authenticity of the Casket Letters, as they came to be known, has remained yet another unsolved mystery of Queen Mary's reign. None of the original documents have survived, but it is generally believed that some of the letters were either forged or "re-arranged" by Mary's accusers in order to prove her guilt.

In spite of this evidence, the commissioners concluded that nothing could be proven for or against Mary. Moray was allowed to return to Scotland as regent, with a loan of £5,000 in his pocket, while Mary was condemned to spend the rest of her life in captivity. For the next 18 years,

Mary was lodged at various residences in England. From 1569 to 1585, she resided mostly at Sheffield Castle where she was closely guarded by her keepers George Talbot, earl of Shrewsbury and his formidable wife, Bess of Hardwick. Unable to exercise in the open air and exposed to chills and drafts, Mary soon became afflicted with rheumatic gout and dropsy. Confined to her bedchamber for much of the time, she spent as many hours embroidering as she did plotting her escape.

As a symbol of the Catholic cause, her presence in England became the focus of both domestic and international intrigue. In 1571, she and Thomas Howard, duke of Norfolk, were involved in a plan, known as the Ridolfi Plot, to invade England with a Spanish army. When the conspiracy was discovered, Norfolk was executed and Mary was denounced by the English Parliament as an adultress and a murderess. Zealous English Roman Catholics and foreign agents continued to plan Mary's restoration although Elizabeth I hesitated to punish her despite repeated calls for her execution.

In 1586, Elizabeth I's secretary and spymaster Sir Francis Walsingham intercepted Mary's correspondence with a young English Catholic named Anthony Babington. Mary's fate was sealed with the discovery of a letter in which she allegedly consented to Babington's plan to assassinate the English queen. In October, at the castle of Fotheringhay, the second trial of Mary, Queen of Scots, began. Although she defended herself skillfully, she was found guilty of treason and sentenced to death. Elizabeth I, hesitant to condemn a sovereign princess, finally signed the death warrant on February 1, 1587.

One week later, Mary, Queen of Scots, was beheaded in the Great Hall of Fotheringhay Castle in front of her weeping ladies-in-waiting and 300 spectators. Dressed in a blood-red bodice and petticoat, she faced her death, as she had faced so many other adversities in her life, with courage and composure.

SOURCES:

Donaldson, Gordon. *Mary Queen of Scots.* English Universities Press, 1974.

Fraser, Antonia. *Mary Queen of Scots.* Weidenfeld & Nicolson, 1969.

FURTHER READING:

Cowan, Ian. *The Enigma of Mary Stuart.* Gollancz, 1971.

———. *Mary Queen of Scots.* Saltire Society, 1987.

Lynch, Michael, ed. *Mary Stewart: Queen in Three Kingdoms.* Basil Blackwell, 1988.

Mary I, Tudor

(1516–1558)

Queen of England, who tried to turn back the tide of the English Reformation and reestablish the Catholic Church—only to gain the nickname Bloody Mary and a reputation as a cruel, repressive tyrant.

Name variations: Bloody Mary, Mary Tudor, Mary the Catholic. Born in 1516; died in 1558; only surviving child of Henry VIII and Catherine of Aragon (Mary was declared illegitimate after their divorce in 1533); married: Prince Philip (later Philip II) of Spain, 1554; children: none.

When Mary Tudor was born in February 1516, she seemed destined for the life of the typical English princess: she would spend her childhood learning court etiquette, the fine arts, and languages; then, showered with precious gifts and honors, at 15 or 16 she would marry a man deemed by her father to be diplomatically suitable and worthy of her rank. But thanks to the unpredictable twists of dynastic fate, the princess Mary was to face a future both greater and worse than she could have ever imagined.

By the time of Mary's birth, **Henry VIII** and his Spanish queen Catherine of Aragon had been married nearly seven years, and although Catherine had produced many children, none had lived more than a few weeks. As dynastic marriages go, Henry's relationship with Catherine had been unusually happy, despite their inability to produce a male heir to the throne. Mary's birth—though naturally something of a disappointment—was seen as a good omen. Offered condolences regarding the sex of his child, the 24-year-old king cheerfully replied, "We are both young. If it was a daughter this time, by the grace of God the sons will follow." But Henry's optimistic prediction

Contributed by Kimberly K. Estep, Ph.D. in History, Auburn University, Auburn, Alabama

"Perhaps no other reign in English history has seen such a great endeavour made, and so utterly defeated."

H. F. M. PRESCOTT

failed to materialize, and Catherine conceived no more children.

Henry therefore concentrated his hopes and efforts on the upbringing of his beloved daughter. Provided with her own household of 50 persons and a budget of £1,000 per year, Mary's education was of the rigorous, scholarly kind normally reserved for boys. She was placed under the tutelage of learned Spanish humanist Luis Vives, who devised a plan of study for the princess which included the Church Fathers Augustine and Jerome, and the political works of the Roman philosophers Plato, Plutarch, and Cicero. Fluent in French, Mary gained a respectable command of Latin and spoke a smattering of both Spanish and Italian. Vives's primary goal was a curriculum designed to instill Christian virtue and devotion to the Catholic Church; consequently, while encouraged to supplement her academic studies with needlework and music, Mary was not permitted to read poetry or romantic literature—genres considered not only frivolous and worldly but downright dangerous to a woman's fragile mind. Mary's disposition developed in accordance with her training. She matured into a lively, accomplished young woman, whose inclinations tended nonetheless toward the serious and devout.

Despite his having done everything possible to provide Mary with an enlightened Renaissance education, Henry remained uneasy at the prospect of entrusting the throne to a daughter. Only one queen, Matilda, had ruled England since the Norman Conquest in 1066, and her brief reign was generally regarded as a hopeless failure. So, though he bestowed upon Mary the title Princess of Wales, the king began looking for alternatives. Henry's virility was legendary throughout the kingdom and his relationship with Catherine did not preclude frequent dalliances, many of which had produced royal bastards. He bestowed the title duke of Richmond to the eldest of his illegitimate sons, Henry Fitzroy, making him lord admiral at the tender age of six. Henry hoped that he might make Richmond his successor, but while a legitimate heir—albeit a female one—was alive, there would be little chance of England accepting the illegitimate boy as their future monarch.

By the time Mary reached age ten, another factor entered the royal equation when Henry's lustful eye fell upon Anne Boleyn, a young, vivacious court beauty. Anne, unlike Henry's previous love interests, refused to settle for a place as Henry's mistress, and set her sights on the Crown. Henry, unaccustomed to being denied his desire, only grew more infatuated. Seeing the young, healthy Anne as an answer to his problems of suc-

CHRONOLOGY

1509	Henry VIII married Catherine of Aragon
1516	Mary Tudor born
1527	Henry began annulment proceedings against Catherine
1533	Henry split from Roman Catholic Church; divorced Catherine; had Parliament declare Mary illegitimate
1534	Parliament declared Henry VIII "Supreme Head of the Church in England"
1547	Henry VIII died; Edward VI crowned
1553	Edward VI died; brief reign of Jane Grey; Mary I crowned
1554	Mary I married Prince Philip of Spain; restoration of Catholic Church in England; revival of Catholic heresy laws
1558	Mary I died; Elizabeth I crowned

cession, the king believed that were he to rid himself of his barren wife—now 40 and considered past all hope of childbearing—he could begin anew his attempts to produce a legitimate son.

The Pope Excommunicates Henry

In 1527, Henry tentatively began proceedings to dissolve his marriage. With the modern concept of divorce unheard of in the 16th century, he set out to have the marriage annulled on the basis of Catherine's brief marriage to his sickly elder brother Arthur. Countering Henry's charge that this previous marriage made her marriage to him unlawful, even sinful, Catherine claimed that Arthur had died before the marriage could be consummated. The pope, Clement VII, under pressure from Catherine's powerful nephew, the Holy Roman Emperor **Charles V,** refused to decide the issue, and the case dragged on for six years. Finally, in 1533, Henry could wait no longer. Anne was pregnant, and Henry—certain that she carried his long-awaited son—secretly married her and pressured the English Church to rule that his marriage to Catherine had been invalid. The pope excommunicated Henry, who had by this time already decided to break the English Church away from Rome, and in 1534 the Act of Supremacy declared Henry the "Supreme Head of the Church in England."

Needless to say, these events altered Mary's status dramatically. Also passed in 1534 was the Act of Succession, declaring Mary illegitimate.

Privileges were stripped from her and her household dissolved. When Anne Boleyn bore Henry a daughter, **Elizabeth,** in September of 1533, Mary was sent to her half-sister's household to serve as one of her ladies-in-waiting, and Anne Boleyn, jealous of Henry's affection for Mary, persecuted her maliciously. Denied the right to keep even her closest friends and servants with her, Mary was forbidden to exercise outside or to attend Mass. Anne recommended to Lady Shelton, the guardian of Elizabeth's household, that any intransigence be punished with a few slaps across the face, "considering the bastard that she was."

In spite of the tragic change in her circumstances, Mary remained resolute, determined to bear her burden with grace and convinced that in the eyes of God and the world her mother was still queen and she still Princess of Wales. Henry—angry at Catherine's stubborn refusal to retire into a nunnery—refused to allow her to see her daughter, eventually forbidding even correspondence by letter. But Catherine smuggled letters to Mary, encouraging her to stand fast in her faith, as "the time is come that God Almighty will prove you." Thus encouraged, Mary managed to withstand pressure from Henry to take a formal oath to the two acts of Parliament which threatened all she held dear: the Act of Succession formally declaring her a bastard and the Act of Supremacy which declared the king of England to be the sole authority over the church in England. Henry had executed some of his most respected clergymen and advisors for refusing to take the oath supporting these acts—still, neither Catherine nor Mary would assent to the oath. Luckily for them, the king proceeded cautiously, fearing riot at home and war abroad should he summarily condemn them to death.

While Henry continued exerting pressure, Mary lost her strongest ally when Catherine died in January of 1536. Anne Boleyn was executed on dubious charges of adultery in May, but Henry's new marriage to Jane Seymour did not soften his resolve to force Mary to accept the divorce and the new "reformed" English church. In June, a new parliamentary act declared both Mary and her half-sister Elizabeth illegitimate. To force Mary to affirm the act, Henry's ministers placed her in isolation, watching her night and day, besieging her with thinly veiled threats of execution. Alone and grief-stricken, a frail 20-year-old Mary finally relented. Without reading it, she signed the document given her denying the pope, recognizing Henry as head of the English church, and agreeing that her mother's marriage had been "incestuous and unlawful" and Mary herself illegitimate. This denial of her own faith and principles was to haunt her the rest of her life, but the bitter gall of her defeat sparked a resolve to never again compromise her beliefs.

Mary Submits, Returns to Favor

The immediate result of her submission was a return to her father's favor. Henry invited her back to court, showering her with gifts and money. Jane Seymour, whose tragic death would come as a result of birthing Edward, the long-awaited male heir in 1537, treated Mary warmly, and Henry's last three wives—Anne of Cleves, Catherine Howard, and Catherine Parr—likewise had no quarrel with her. In these years, a cautious affection grew between Mary and her aging father, and the last ten years of Henry's life proved relatively peaceful. Henry had no intention of changing the liturgy or theology of the Anglican Church, and Mary carefully avoided becoming involved in political or religious controversy. In his final will, Henry reconfirmed her title, making Mary second in the line of succession after her brother.

When Henry died in January of 1547, Mary faced a new threat from the regency of her nine-year-old brother Edward VI. The new councillors were strict Protestants, determined to reform the English church to distance it further from the Catholic Church in both belief and practice. Mass was replaced with a simple worship service based upon Thomas Cranmer's *Book of Common Prayer,* and Mary's own priests were imprisoned while she was ordered to conform to the practice of the reformed religion. But Mary still clung to her Catholic faith, and when her mother's nephew, the Catholic Holy Roman Emperor Charles V, threatened England with war, the council relented, allowing Mary to hear Mass in private. The fight, however, was not over; throughout Edward's reign, she was repeatedly forced to defend her right to practice the Catholic religion.

Having always been somewhat sickly, in July 1553, 16-year-old Edward succumbed to tuberculosis. According to their father's will, Mary was to succeed him. But Edward's advisors had other ideas. The leader of Edward's council, the duke of Northumberland, had persuaded the ailing king to draw up a new will, making Northumberland's daughter-in-law, Lady Jane Grey, his successor. Ostensibly Northumberland had arranged Jane's succession to preserve the Protestant church in England, but his self-serving manipulations turned many firm Protestants against him. Although Jane had already been crowned in the Tower of London, Mary issued a proclamation declaring her right of succession and gathered around her a loyal army to meet Northumberland's forces. Her daring move paid off—Northumberland's army soon evaporated, and on August 3, 1553, Mary triumphantly entered London. In spite of her Catholic beliefs, she was still the daughter of Henry VIII and so held the loyalties of most Englishmen.

Mary began her reign with the full intention of exercising leniency. To the council she promised:

> that, albeit her Grace's conscience is stayed in matters of religion, yet she meaneth graciously not to compel or constrain other men's consciences, otherwise than God shall (she trusteth) put into their hearts a persuasion of the truth that she is in, through the opening of his word unto them by godly, virtuous and learned preachers.

Indeed, when the ringleaders of the Protestant conspiracy were rounded up, only Northumberland and a handful of others were executed. At first Mary could not bear to carry out the sentence of death against Lady Jane Grey, who Mary was convinced had been used as a pawn. Instead, she left Jane and her husband Guildford Dudley, Northumberland's son, imprisoned in the Tower of London while she debated their fate. It was only in 1554, after a Protestant uprising known as Wyatt's Rebellion, that Mary was persuaded to carry out their sentences.

Although she came to the throne with noble intentions, Mary misjudged the character of her subjects. Her first mistake involved a belief that at heart England was still basically Catholic and would welcome a return to the Holy Mother Church. She misjudged as well the reaction of the xenophobic English to the introduction of foreigners into English government; most resented the power of a foreign pope over the English church.

With her simple, uncomplicated faith in the Catholic Church, the concept of religion as an arm of the state was alien to Mary. Unlike her father Henry VIII or her sister, the future Elizabeth I, Mary was unable to place policy before personal conviction. Most important to her was England's reconciliation with what she believed to be the one true church; almost immediately upon taking the throne she recalled the papal legate, Cardinal Reginald Pole, to assist her in reestablishing Catholicism in England. Weary with the radical Protestants who had dominated Edward's reign and Parliament, most of her subjects readily acquiesced in Mary's November 1554 decision to petition the pope for absolution for all of England. In addition, Parliament agreed to reenact the old heresy laws for nonconformists. Mary fully expected that these measures would produce a voluntary abandonment of the Protestant movement, which—she was convinced—was the invention of a few wild fanatics. Once the ringleaders were removed, reasoned the queen, England would again embrace the one true Church.

She Burns Noncomformists at the Stake

Accordingly, Mary's government began weeding out religious subversives by employing the reenacted heresy laws. The accused were tried and—if they refused to recant—were burned at the stake. Just under 300 nonconformists were publicly burned during Mary's reign, far fewer than the number of people Elizabeth I would execute for treason, but the popularity of many of the victims, combined with the horrible means of their execution, aroused a great public outcry. The popular sympathy created by these public burnings doomed Mary's dream to eventual failure while earning for her the rather unattractive nickname "Bloody Mary."

Her marriage to Prince **Philip of Spain** only served to further alienate her subjects. When Mary ascended to the throne, no one, especially not the queen herself, expected that she would bear the burden of reigning alone. In an age when women were thought incapable of rational thought, it was imperative that England secure an appropriate mate to rule with the new queen. Mary's councillors suggested several English suitors of royal descent, but Mary accepted Philip's proposal soon after her succession. He was, after all, Spanish—as her mother had been; he was well educated and a fervent Catholic; and, finally, he was the son of Charles V, Mary's champion and advisor during the difficult years between her mother's divorce and her own succession. While these qualifications suited the queen, most Englishmen were appalled at the prospect of being ruled by Spain. Having tried to talk her out of the marriage to no avail, Parliament and Mary's council set firm restrictions on Philip's rights as king: he was essentially to be king in name only, enjoying none of the prerogatives or incomes of the Crown; English law was to be upheld in all respects and no Spanish courtiers were to be allowed to hold office; if no children were born of the marriage, or if Mary were to predecease him, Philip would lose any claim to England's crown.

These severe restrictions on his rights dampened Philip's enthusiasm. He put off sailing for

England until the summer of 1554 and then remained in England for barely a year, deeply offended by Parliament's refusal to allow him to be publicly crowned. At their marriage in July 1554, Mary was 38; Philip was but 27. Though Mary optimistically expected to bear a child to be their heir, in her day 38 was almost ridiculously late for any woman to give birth—particularly one with a history of somewhat frail health. Much to her dismay, her young husband showed little attachment to her or to her country, and after sailing for Spain in 1555 only returned for a brief visit in 1557 to ask for men, money, and supplies in his war against France. Regardless of England's own financial difficulties following two years of bad harvests, Mary agreed to send Philip English forces and monetary aid. The only notable result of England's participation in the struggle was the loss of Calais, England's last possession on the Continent, a national humiliation for which England blamed her Spanish husband.

As Mary sensed the failure of her policies associated with religion, politics, and diplomacy, she became ever more rigid in her defense of them. She continued burning heretics to the last, while England grew more hardened against Catholicism than it had ever been. In the final year of her life, Mary has been described as "a tiny, hysterical, sick woman of forty-two." Never supremely healthy, her condition worsened in 1558, and—knowing herself to be near death—she revised her will naming Elizabeth her successor. After a protracted illness, she finally died on November 17, 1558. The Roman Catholic regime came to an abrupt halt, the alliance with Spain was broken off, and Elizabeth I steered the state back into the same channels charted by Henry VIII.

Rather than provide leadership to meet its goals, Mary's government had relied on the suppression of dissident voices, relegating her a place in history as a persecutor. The best-known Tudor monarchs, Henry VIII and Elizabeth I, excelled in the practice of what is today known as public relations. Unlike her father and sister, Mary's view of the monarchy was a throw back to medieval times—when rulers were answerable only to God. With the secular influences of the Renaissance, successful monarchs had to be more dependent on sound policy and public good will. Her primary failure was the inability to accept and make use of the emerging new order in government, and as a result the reign of Mary is usually viewed merely as a brief setback in England's progression into the modern era.

SOURCES:

Foss, Michael. *Tudor Portraits: Success and Failure of an Age.* Harrap, 1973.

Plowden, Alison. *Tudor Women.* Atheneum, 1979.

Prescott, H. F. M. *Mary Tudor.* Macmillan, 1953.

Tittler, Robert. *The Reign of Mary I.* Longman Group, 1983.

FURTHER READING:

Erickson, Carolly. *Bloody Mary.* Doubleday, 1978.

Haller, William. *Fox's Book of Martyrs and the Elect Nation.* Cape, 1963.

Loades, D. M. *The Reign of Mary Tudor: Politics, Government and Religion in England, 1553–1558.* St. Martin's Press, 1979.

Jan Masaryk

(1886–1948)

Son of the founder of Czechoslovakia, whose career as a diplomat and Czech foreign minister made him a significant figure in the Munich Crisis of 1938, World War II, and the transformation of his country into a Soviet satellite after 1945.

"He was mourned for himself and what died with him: liberty in his country and civilized communion between the world's Communist and capitalist societies."

CLAIRE STERLING

Jan Garrigue Masaryk, son of the founder of the Republic of Czechoslovakia, was a key figure in the history of Central Europe in 1930s and 1940s. While ambassador to Great Britain, he saw his small country betrayed to Nazi Germany in the years leading to World War II. Masaryk became foreign minister in his country's government-in-exile in London during the war, and he continued to serve in that post back in Czechoslovakia in the period after 1945. Seen by some observers as "a latter-day Hamlet doomed by his dilemma," Jan Masaryk spent the last years of his life trying to satisfy **Joseph Stalin**'s demands that Czechoslovakia follow the direction set by the Soviet Union in foreign affairs. At the same time, he struggled to maintain a democratic system within his country.

In the end, Masaryk lived just long enough to see his efforts fail: a Communist dictatorship was installed in Czechoslovakia in February 1948, and his homeland became a Soviet satellite. Thus, ten years after witnessing Czechoslovakia's subordination to Nazi Germany, Masaryk participated in his country's second great tragedy. His death came immediately after the Communist takeover. Possibly suicide, possibly murder at the hands of

Pronunciation: Yän MAH-zahr-ik. Born Jan Garrigue Masaryk in Prague, a city in the Austro-Hungarian Empire, on September 14, 1886; died in Prague under mysterious circumstances on March 10, 1948; son of Thomas Garrigue Masaryk (first president of Czechoslovakia) and Charlotte Garrigue Masaryk; married: Frances Crane Leatherbee, 1924 (divorced, 1929); no children.

Contributed by Neil Heyman, Professor of History, San Diego State University, San Diego, California

CHRONOLOGY

1918	Republic of Czechoslovakia formed; WWI ended
1919	Masaryk entered Czechoslovak foreign office
1925	Appointed ambassador to Great Britain
1937	Death of his father
1938	Munich Conference and partition of Czechoslovakia; Masaryk went into exile in U.S.
1939	Start of World War II; Masaryk joined Czechoslovak National Committee in London
1941	British recognition of Czechoslovak National Committee as government-in-exile
1943	Moscow Conference
1945	End of World War II; Masaryk returned to Czechoslovakia
1946	General elections held in Czechoslovakia
1947	Soviets compelled Czechs to refuse participation in Marshall Plan
1948	Communists took over Czech government; death of Masaryk

his political enemies, it remains a subject of controversy.

Jan Masaryk was born in Prague, then one of the major cities of Austria-Hungary (or the Habsburg Empire), on September 14, 1886. His father **Thomas G. Masaryk** was a distinguished scholar who soon emerged as an important political leader. The elder Masaryk, born in 1850 to a poor peasant family in the Habsburg province of Moravia, was a professor of philosophy at the University of Prague. Jan's mother Charlotte Garrigue was an American, the daughter of an insurance company president. His parents met when both were studying in Leipzig in 1877. Adopting his wife's name after his marriage, Thomas Masaryk became known as "Thomas Garrigue Masaryk."

Austria-Hungary consisted of a variety of lands that had come under the control of the Habsburg family in Vienna over the previous 400 years. Continually reorganized and reshaped, the Habsburg Empire had always contained numerous ethnic groups, but its rulers traditionally had governed chiefly with the help of the German minority. After 1867, when the system was reformed once again, the Habsburg Empire (now also called Austria-Hungary) was governed by two ethnic groups. The German minority within the population dom-

inated the western (or Austrian) part of the Empire. And now the Hungarians, also a minority within the Empire, dominated the eastern part of the Empire. Within this structure, other nationalities, including Slavic groups like the Czechs and Slovaks, considered themselves oppressed peoples. By the outbreak of World War I, Jan Masaryk's father was a key figure in the effort to reform the Empire in order to give more freedom to its various nationalities. The elder Masaryk led the fight for Czech freedom.

Jan Masaryk showed none of the ambition and intellectual talent that his father had used to rise from poverty. He was a mediocre student with little interest in academic life and no desire to go on to study at a university. But the young man had musical talent and a gift for languages. From his American mother he had learned excellent English. There were frequent quarrels between father and son, and young Jan often received beatings. In 1904, he received his parents' permission to leave for the United States. He arrived there with about $100, a parting present from his father.

Young Masaryk spent ten years in his mother's homeland. Since he avoided her relatives, there are still questions about what he did during much of that time. Although his father traveled to the United States in 1908 to lecture at the University of Chicago, it is uncertain whether Jan tried to see him. The young visitor worked at a number of jobs: laboring in factories, playing the piano in movie theaters, and teaching English to immigrants. In later years, European friends remembered his long stay in the U.S. and emphasized how he spoke English with an American accent. As his American writer-friend Marcia Davenport put it, "To many Americans Jan seemed like one of themselves."

In 1914, shortly before the outbreak of World War I, the exile returned to Prague. Soon after the hostilities began, Thomas Masaryk went abroad to seek aid for political reform from Austria-Hungary's enemies. Jan Masaryk entered the Austro-Hungarian army and was placed where the authorities could keep him under their surveillance: at a desk job in Poland far away from the fighting front. The reason for his assignment was clear: many Czechs serving in the Habsburg armies deserted to fight for Russia, which they saw as a Slavic country that would welcome them. Jan Masaryk was placed where he had no chance to go over to the Russians like so many of his countrymen.

By the time the war ended, Thomas Masaryk was calling for an independent Czech state to be carved from the former Austro-Hungarian Empire.

The Empire's wartime opponents like Great Britain supported this goal, and a revolution in Prague in the closing days of the war made it possible. The elder Masaryk returned home in late 1918 as the first president of the new Republic of Czechoslovakia. The new state joined the Czechs with their Slavic neighbors, the Slovaks.

Masaryk Enters Diplomatic Service

The President's son soon entered the young country's diplomatic service. There were few Czechoslovaks who had Jan Masaryk's experience living abroad. His skill with languages and, as he put it, the fact that "he chose his father wisely," opened the door for a career as a diplomat.

After serving in France and the United States, in 1925 he was named his country's ambassador to Great Britain. Jan Masaryk was best known for his personal charm and his participation in the usual round of diplomatic parties. One acquaintance called him, after the character in a play by J. M. Synge, "Playboy of the Western World." He was married for a short time to **Frances Crane Leatherbee,** the sister of the American ambassador to Czechoslovakia and the daughter of an old friend of President Thomas Masaryk.

For years the Masaryk family faced a serious crisis as Jan's mother became increasingly disabled by mental disease. She finally died in 1923. Possibly Jan's own troubled personality, combining a cheerful, playful temperament with stretches of deep depression, was inherited from his mother. He also seemed to feel himself overshadowed by his larger-than-life father, and uncertain of his own abilities. As one historian put it, "He did not have the kind of self-confidence that comes of proven and unaided achievement."

The young ambassador represented a country which was in an increasingly dangerous position. When **Adolf Hitler** rose to power in Germany in 1933, the Führer soon made it clear that he intended to rearm his country and expand at the expense of Germany's neighbors. In the summer of 1937, Jan received a warning of future trouble and a clear set of directions from his dying father. The elder Masaryk warned of "very bad times" for Europe and, in particular, for Czechoslovakia. He asked his son never to desert Edvard Benes, Thomas Masaryk's longtime political ally and his successor as the president of Czechoslovakia.

As Czechoslovakia's ambassador to Great Britain in 1938, Jan Masaryk was a helpless witness to the policy of **Neville Chamberlain,** the British prime minister. Chamberlain decided to sacrifice the interests of Czechoslovakia, specifically to award Germany the border region called the Sudetenland, in order to satisfy Adolf Hitler and to avoid a major European war. This meant stripping Czechoslovakia of its main military defenses against Germany.

During the crisis, Masaryk complained about "the senile ambition of Chamberlain to be the peacemaker of Europe." Neville Chamberlain wanted success at all costs and "that will be possible only at our expense." When Czechoslovakia was forced to surrender the Sudetenland following the Munich Conference of September 1938, Jan Masaryk and Benes went into exile. Friends noticed the strain on Masaryk seen in his aged face and tendency to put on weight.

Despite Britain's role in betraying his country, Masaryk continued to admire the British as a people whose ways were the direct opposite of the Germans. Soon after World War II began in 1939, he joined Benes in London. That same year Benes formed a nucleus for a Czechoslovak government-in-exile, calling it the Czechoslovak National Committee; it was finally recognized by the British in 1941, with Benes as president and Masaryk as foreign minister. At the same time, Masaryk emerged as a popular figure in occupied Czechoslovakia. His countrymen risked the death penalty to listen to his dramatic broadcasts over the BBC.

Czechoslovakia's future depended upon the outcome of World War II and the friendship of its wartime allies. As Soviet forces began to advance into Eastern Europe, the Czechoslovak government's relationship with the Soviet Union became crucial. In December 1943, Benes traveled to Moscow to sign a treaty of friendship with the Soviet Union. Benes, who felt a deep sense of betrayal by Britain and France as a result of the Munich Conference of 1938, was more open to close ties to the Russians than was Masaryk. As Masaryk once put it, "For me, the Russians will always remain Asiatics." By the time Soviet troops began to reach Czechoslovak territory in the winter of 1944–45, it became clear that Stalin would insist that the postwar government in Prague contain a strong group of Czechoslovak Communists.

Masaryk and Benes returned to their country in the spring of 1945, traveling via Moscow. There the Russians had promoted a postwar government combining Communists, Communist sympathizers, and non-Communists. Thus Masaryk and Benes remained president and foreign minister—but left-wing Socialist Zdeněk Fierlinger became prime minister while Communist Party leader **Klement Gottwald** was deputy prime minister.

The first three postwar years brought Masaryk to despair, but he stubbornly refused to leave Czechoslovakia. Gottwald became prime minster following the national elections of 1946, although the country remained under a coalition government of Communists and non-Communists. Masaryk himself remained, as he had always been, independent of all political parties.

Soviet influence was clear and harsh in Masaryk's area of responsibility: foreign policy. He was humiliated as he was ordered around at the United Nations by Russian diplomats like Andrei Vishinsky. He was embarrassed when the Russians insisted Czechoslovakia endorse Moscow's criticism of the United States. But Masaryk's greatest defeat in these years came over the Marshall Plan. This was an American offer of economic assistance to hasten Europe's postwar recovery which first appeared in a speech by Secretary of State **George C. Marshall** in June 1947. Masaryk hoped to get his government, with Soviet permission, to apply for such aid. When in July 1947, under pressure from Stalin, Czechoslovakia dropped its move to participate in the Marshall Plan, Masaryk bitterly described himself to friends as "a lackey of the Soviet government."

Czechoslovakia Becomes Soviet Satellite

The end came in early 1948. Non-Communist ministers, outraged by Communist efforts to dominate the police apparatus, threatened to resign from the government. They hoped to bring about new national elections. Instead, President Benes, under pressure from the Russians and from Communist demonstrations inside Czechoslovakia, accepted the resignations. In February 1948 Czechoslovakia had become a Communist satellite of the Soviet Union.

But the one who refused to resign was Jan Masaryk. Three weeks later he was dead. His mysterious death on March 10, 1948, left many questions behind. When his body was found in a courtyard under the window of his office in the foreign ministry, the Czech security police reported the death as a suicide, claiming Masaryk had jumped deliberately. But to many who knew him, his death seemed more like the result of a murder plot. Masaryk had made plans to flee the country, and only days before he had spoken disparagingly of another minister who had tried to kill himself this way. On the other hand, at a final public appearance while visiting his father's grave a few days before, he had seemed deeply shaken and depressed. Thus, some historians consider that he may indeed have taken his own life.

In 1991, Vaclav Havel, president of Czechoslovakia, expressed his personal view that "it was murder." But, he also noted, "I'm afraid that we shall never know the truth."

SOURCES:

Davenport, Marcia. *Too Strong for Fantasy.* Scribner, 1967.

Mayne, Richard. "Prague's Cruel Spring: Masaryk, 1948," in *Encounter.* Vol. LX. No. 5. May 1983.

Sterling, Claire. *The Masaryk Case.* Harper & Row, 1968.

Zeman, Zbyněk. *The Masaryks: The Making of Czechoslovakia.* Weidenfeld & Nicolson, 1976.

FURTHER READING:

Bradley, J. F. N. *Czechoslovakia: A Short History.* Edinburgh, 1971.

Lockhart, R. W. Bruce. *Jan Masaryk.* Dropmore Press, 1951.

Mamatey, Victor S., and Radomír Lůza, eds. *A History of the Czechoslovak Republic, 1918–1948.* Princeton University Press, 1973.

Zinner, Paul E. *Communist Strategy and Tactics in Czechoslovakia, 1918–1948.* Praeger, 1963.

Thomas G. Masaryk

(1850–1937)

Educator, philosopher, sociologist, and leading force behind the creation of a Czecho-Slovak Republic, who lead his country on the path of democracy after WWI while other Central European states became mired in militarism and authoritarian rule.

"We are beginning to realize that the idea of humanity is not opposed to that of nationality—but that nationality, like the individual man, both ought to be and can be human, humanitarian."

T. G. MASARYK

The green valleys and rolling hills of central Moravia have always presented a scene of great beauty. Yet the picturesque appearance of these lands hid an ugly social reality in the 19th century. Traditionally, society there was divided sharply between the German-speaking gentry, who lived in regal splendor on vast estates, and their Czech and Slovak serfs, whose bondage was as old as it was repressive. In 1849, however, the young emperor **Francis Joseph I** issued a decree by which the ancient feudal obligations were abolished and the serfs declared free. In practice, very little changed. But the Emperor's decree did make it possible for some former serfs to rise, ever so slightly, above the station of their fellows.

One such individual was Josef Masaryk, a Slovak coachman and teamster who worked on an estate belonging to the Emperor. He had been granted permission in 1849 to wed Theresie Kropatschek, a woman ten years his senior who was a domestic servant from the town of Hustopece. Their son Thomas was born in March of the following year at Hodonín.

Because of his father's position as an imperial employee, Thomas ranked above other peasant

Contributed by *Thomas Whigham, Associate Professor of History, University of Georgia, Athens, Georgia*

Name variations: Tomás Masaryk. Pronunciation: Mah-ZAHR-ik. Born in the Moravian village of Hodonín on March 7, 1850; died at Lány near Prague on September 14, 1937; son of Josef Masaryk (a coachman employed on imperial domains) and Theresie Kropatschek (a domestic servant); married: Charlotte Garrigue (an American musician), 1878; children: three daughters and two sons, including Jan Masaryk. Predecessor: Emperor Karl of Austria-Hungary.

1882	Awarded a professorship at Charles University in Prague
1885	Published *The Foundations of Concrete Logic*
1891	Elected to the Imperial Diet, representing the liberal Czech nationalists
1893	Left the Diet
1900	Established a Progressive Party; visited Russia, Britain, and the U.S.
1907–11	Further service in the Diet; grew pessimistic about Austrian policy toward minorities in the Balkans
1914	WWI began; Masaryk became a recognized leader among Czech expatriates, especially in the U.S.
1916	Founded the Czechoslovak National Council in Paris
1918	Proclaimed Czechoslovak independence; confirmed as president
1919–35	Worked to consolidate democratic institutions; concluded foreign alliances to protect Czechoslovakia's precarious strategic position
1935–37	Retired

continue on to work for his doctoral degree. The subject he chose was Plato; from that point onward, he considered himself a Platonist.

In the fall of 1876, having completed his doctorate, Masaryk left Vienna for Leipzig. Still penniless, he provided for his meager needs by tutoring, while in his free time he wrote an occasional article on philosophical themes. In Leipzig, he made a number of stimulating acquaintances from all over Europe. More importantly, he met Charlotte Garrigue, a 27-year-old music student from the United States. Daughter of the president of a well-known American insurance company, she had long been friendly with Masaryk's landlady. Masaryk was immediately impressed by her intelligence, urbanity, and wide-ranging knowledge. Two months after they met, he proposed marriage, then followed her to New York where they were married in March 1878. In a gesture unusual for a Central European of his time, Masaryk assumed his wife's maiden name for his own middle name.

The couple made their home in Vienna for four years. In the imperial capital, Masaryk found it impossible to gain a university appointment, and therefore returned to private tutoring to keep himself and his now growing family out of debt. In 1882, good news finally came in the form of a permanent appointment as philosophy professor at Charles University in Prague. Compared to Vienna the Bohemian capital was a provincial place. Still, after a lapse of some years, Masaryk was back among Czech-speakers, and he soon discovered that the limitations of the Prague milieu stimulated him into new endeavors. For instance, he became the editor of a scholarly journal, *The Athenaeum*, which popularized the writings of such foreign scholars as Georges Sorel, leader of the radical syndicalist movement. Masaryk also took his first tentative steps into politics.

At the end of the 1880s, Masaryk joined with a few of his university colleagues to found a "realist" group that sought a moderate course between the extremism of the Czech nationalists and the reaction of the pro-Austrian party. Masaryk met with Czech politicians of various hues, and, after extensive negotiations, merged his realist grouping with the liberal-nationalist Young Czech Party. In 1891, this coalition sent Masaryk to Vienna as a member of the Imperial Diet (he was elected to the Bohemian parliament as well).

As a provincial representative, Masaryk took a moderate stance toward the burning issues then facing the Austro-Hungarian Empire. He pressed for cultural and educational reform, particularly in regard to uplifting the status of the Empire's

children. He played for the most part with sons of estate officials, and when it came time to go to school, he attended the more prestigious German classes. Thanks to his mother's initiative, young Thomas later went on to German school at Hustopece, where he studied geometry, history, physics, biology, and Czech. His parents remained simple people, especially his father, whose outlook never went beyond the concerns of his team. His mother, however, always lent her support even from afar, even after her son had left the district for a life in the greater world.

After several years of intermittent study, punctuated by work at Brno and Vienna, the 22-year-old Masaryk attempted to enter the renowned Oriental Academy in the latter city, but was frustrated to discover that positions in that august institution were reserved for the nobility. He never forgot his disappointment. It fired his anger at the high-born, and, more particularly, at those in the Empire who would suppress the Czechs simply because they were Czechs.

Hiding his anger, Masaryk enrolled at the Viennese faculty of philosophy to major in classical philology with the idea of becoming a high school teacher (though he did not relish the notion). Instead, after some soul-searching, he decided to

minority peoples. Reason dictated, he argued, that Austria-Hungary evolve in the direction of a federation of equal nationalities freely bound to each other by mutual consent. Such a state would be the envy of Europe.

The idealism of this position soon foundered on the rough shoals of Vienna's power politics. Masaryk had encountered more corruption than he had thought possible and inflexibility on all sides. He questioned the leadership of his own Young Czech Party, their uncompromising nationalism, and their windy proclamations on national glory. By 1893, he had had enough. Masaryk resigned his mandates to both parliaments and returned to the university. From there, he argued that Czech political culture needed something more than the sterile polemics of the various parties.

He set out to provide something more in a series of publications designed to awaken Czech consciousness to the dilemmas of the modern age. Between 1894 and 1896 he produced four much-read studies that addressed this issue: *Ceská Otazka (The Czech Question), Nase Nynejsí Krise (Our Present Crisis), Jan Hus,* and *Karel Havlicek.* Two years later, he supplemented these with the publication of *Parackého Idea Naroda Ceského (Palacky's Idea of the Czech Nation).* In still other publications, Masaryk examined the need for a religious faith that would be compatible with modern scientific thought. He borrowed some ideas from Marxism in this quest, but in the main, was interested in promoting a humanitarian approach to life that would well prepare the Czechs for the new century.

In 1900, Masaryk reluctantly established a new political party, first called the "Popular" and then the "Progressive" Party. This grouping sought to defend the rights of minorities within the empire, though it stopped short of favoring independence. Masaryk's role as party chairman permitted him to see various parts of Austria-Hungary, as well as Russia, Britain, and, once again, the United States. Throughout, he was building a reputation among Czechs as a key political figure. Even those who found his approach overly cautious recognized him as a man of great intellect and moral integrity.

Politicians in the imperial capital also began to see him as someone far more formidable than they had realized earlier. Elected to the Diet again in 1907, he immediately became an active parliamentarian. He delivered several fiery speeches on religious, national, and educational questions, insisting on the right of free expression for all subjects of Francis Joseph.

The Balkan Question

By now Masaryk had withdrawn from all university work to dedicate himself exclusively to political matters. Of particular interest to him was the Balkan question. The Austrian annexation of Bosnia-Herzegovina in 1908 had brought a major confrontation with the small country of Serbia, which claimed a good portion of Bosnia by right of national self-determination. Masaryk regarded the Empire's policy on this matter to be pigheaded in the extreme. When his attempt to mediate between the Serbian prime minister and the Austrian government came to naught, he was even accused of treasonous sentiments by the imperial foreign minister.

In fact, Masaryk was deeply disillusioned. His hopes for a peaceful transition to a more democratic Austria-Hungary were being dashed in favor of a jingoist policy of expansionism. With sinking heart, he continued his efforts to reverse the drift of feeling in Vienna. The 1914 assassination of Archduke Franz Ferdinand in Sarajevo proved to be the end for European peace. It was also the end for Masaryk's faith in a future under Austrian rule.

In the early months of the First World War, Masaryk established contacts with Czech emigrés in France, Italy, Russia, and Great Britain; he brought together the Czech deputies to the Diet, whatever their differences, in support of independence. The police were aware of these activities, yet they still allowed Masaryk to depart on a trip to Italy (then still neutral). Once across the border, he gave up on all plans for a return and became instead a roving spokesman for Czech independence.

In mid-1915, Masaryk accepted a professorship of Slavonic studies at the University of London. From this position, he agitated for the creation of a belt of small buffer nations from Finland to Greece. At the time, this seemed impractical, since it depended on the collapse not only of the German and Austro-Hungarian Empires, but on that of Russia as well. Russia was an allied country, however, and the Western powers had misgivings about supporting a general process of dissolution that might weaken resolve on the Eastern Front.

But 1917 brought two revolutions to Russia—the first in March and the second in October—taking that country out of the war. The Russian Revolution also unleashed upon the Siberian interior several tens of thousands of Czech soldiers, many of whom had been prisoners of war. Having seized a quantity of arms, these men now constituted a national army for a country that had yet to come into existence. And they were isolated along many thousands of miles of rails between the Urals and Vladivostok.

The existence of this "Czech Legion" gave Masaryk a great measure of legitimacy among the Allies. He had spent several years building contacts with French, British, and American leaders, and now used these contacts to assume control over the stranded Czech troops. He had visited them in the field in midsummer 1917 to explain his plans for a provisional government; now they recognized him as the future leader of their country and obeyed him when he gave the order to withdraw across the length of Siberia to Vladivostok, there to embark for redeployment on the Western Front.

Masaryk Heads New Czech Republic

This spectacular retreat drew great attention in the Western press and made the establishment of a Czech-Slovak state a certainty. Masaryk became the pivotal figure in this movement. He tirelessly traveled from one American city to another to address Czech and Slovak audiences. Through the European underground, he also influenced events in Bohemia, Moravia, Slovakia, and Ruthenia, areas that stood the most ready to form the new state when Austria-Hungary disintegrated in October 1918. On the 28th of the month, the Czechoslovak Republic was founded in Prague. Two months later, Masaryk arrived from the United States amid universal acclaim and took office as president.

Masaryk was 68. Forgotten were the days when he was easily dismissed as a meddling professor. Now he had built up a large reservoir of moral capital, and Czechs proudly spoke of him as the *stary pán* ("old man"), as the scholar-turned-statesman whom every young person should emulate.

Masaryk himself had little time for such accolades. Although the constitution sharply limited his powers, he nonetheless used the presidency to help promote stability in the new, multiethnic democracy. Political problems were considerable in the new state; after all, though Czechs had come to regard liberty as an inalienable right, few saw that democracy involves responsibilities as well as rights. In consequence, were it not for Masaryk's moderating hand, partisan politics could have torn apart the nascent republic. A cult of personality developed around Masaryk in the 1920s. While the aging President regretted many aspects of this phenomenon, he nonetheless used it to strengthen the hand of democrats in what otherwise would have been a fragile parliamentary regime.

Czechoslovakia faced threats from Poland, Hungary, and particularly Germany throughout these years. As always, Masaryk counseled prudence and a dependence on collective security agreements that he maintained with France and the entente countries. However tragic and mistaken it was in the long run, his faith in the League of Nations was unswerving.

Reelected in 1927 and again in 1934, Masaryk finally began to fade in old age. One year after his final re-election he suffered a stroke, which caused him to resign shortly thereafter. The government granted him the title of President-Liberator and the use of the beautiful Lány castle for his retirement. He died in 1937, thus missing by just two years the shameful outcome of the Munich Agreement, by which his country was sacrificed to Hitler's ambitions.

In his beliefs and actions, Masaryk was set firmly in the mold of the 19th-century progressive. His very being was anchored in the argument that there existed a rational order and harmony in the universe that was accessible to human reasoning, and that society can be improved with greater toleration and understanding. If Czechoslovakia ultimately fell prey to the worst monster produced by 20th-century Europe, it could still claim that in Masaryk it had found a symbol of hope for democracy and a prosperous future.

SOURCES:

Cohen, Victor. *The Life and Times of Masaryk.* John Murray, 1941.

Hajek, Hanus J. *T. G. Masaryk Revisited: A Critical Assessment.* Columbia University Press.

FURTHER READING:

Kovtun, George J., ed. *The Spirit of Thomas G. Masaryk (1850–1937).* St. Martin's Press, 1990.

Szporluk, Roman. *The Political Thought of Thomas G. Masaryk.* Columbia University Press, 1981.

Matilda of Tuscany

(1046–1115)

Strong supporter of the papacy during the Investiture Controversy, who mediated at the famous meeting between Pope Gregory VII and Emperor Henry IV at her ancestral castle of Canossa in 1077.

"Charmed with her grace and regal carriage, dazzled by her beauty, astonished at the variety of her attainments … no wonder that poets and painters have lauded in verse and picture the amiable, pious and generous Matilda, Countess of Tuscany."

MARY HUDDY

With independence and conviction, Matilda, countess of Tuscany, led an unusual life for a woman of medieval days. Her military, financial, cultural, and, above all, spiritual support were instrumental in strengthening the power of the Church, especially the papacy, at a crucial time of conflict between the Church and the state known as the Investiture Controversy.

Matilda was born probably in 1046 in northern Italy, possibly in or near Lucca. Her father was Boniface II of Canossa; her mother was Boniface's second wife Beatrice. Matilda's heritage was illustrative of the political relationships that then connected Germany and Italy. When the Lombard kingdom of northern and central Italy became part of the Carolingian Empire under Emperor **Charlemagne** in the late eighth century, German rulers sought to impose their control over Italian lands. The Canossa were a family of the Lombard nobility whose territorial holdings were built, in part, through patronage and grants from German emperors.

Matilda's father controlled large amounts of land in northern Italy, including counties of Reg-

Name variations: Matilda of Canossa, Matilda the Great Countess, Matilde la Gran Contessa (Italian). Born probably in 1046, in or near Lucca, Italy; died on July 24, 1115, at Bondeno, near Mantua, Italy; daughter of Boniface of Canossa, Count of Tuscany, and Beatrice of Lorraine, his second wife; married: Godfrey the Hunchback, Duke of Upper Lorraine; married: Welf V, Duke of Bavaria and Carinthia; children: (first marriage) one child, died in infancy.

Contributed by Karen Gould, Ph.D., Consultant in Medieval and Renaissance Manuscripts, Austin, Texas

1046	Imperial coronation of Henry III at Rome
1052	Boniface II, margrave of Tuscany, died
1056	Henry III died; Henry IV crowned
1073	Hildebrand elected pope as Gregory VII
1076	Henry IV deposed Gregory VII; Gregory VII excommunicated Henry IV
1077	Henry IV in penitence at Canossa
1084	Henry IV received imperial coronation from antipope Clement III
1085	Gregory VII died at Salerno
1088	Odo of Cluny elected pope as Urban II
1099	Urban II died; succeeded by Paschal II
1106	Henry IV died; Henry V crowned
1111	Henry V and Matilda of Tuscany reconciled

gio, Modena, Mantua, Ferrara, and Brescia. In addition, around 1027, Conrad II, the German emperor, made Boniface margrave (marquis) of Tuscany. Matilda's mother was a niece of Emperor Conrad II which made Matilda directly related to German rulers Henry III and Henry IV, with whom she would eventually struggle.

Although Matilda had an older brother and perhaps another sibling, the six-year-old became sole heir to the family's extensive lands and power base in northern Italy upon the death of her father and brother in 1052. Because female inheritance was difficult to uphold during the Middle Ages, two years after her father's death, Matilda's mother Beatrice married Godfrey, duke of Upper Lorraine, to afford some protection for her daughter's claims. Godfrey, however, was in conflict with German emperor Henry III who took Beatrice and Matilda and held them captive in Germany from 1055 to 1056. Upon their release shortly before Henry III's death, they returned to their Italian homeland.

Matilda's upbringing was somewhat unconventional for a young woman of the 11th century. Greatly influenced by her strong, intelligent, cultured, and pious mother, Matilda's development included not only traditionally feminine pursuits such as needlework and religious training but also literate studies including knowledge of Latin as well as vernacular languages of Italian, German, and French. Matilda's later acquisition of manuscripts, her donations of books, and her patronage of arts connected with religious institutions are evidence of her educated background. In addition, tradition has fostered the impression that she had some skill in the military arts. Her later presence at several armed conflicts between imperial forces and papal supporters lends credence to the suggestion.

Her mother's greatest influence on Matilda was probably in her religious beliefs and support for the Church. Matilda's youth coincided with a strong movement of Church reform headed by the papacy. On the one hand, medieval rulers, especially the German emperors, believed in theocratic kingship which included exercising control over appointments of Church officials; the imperial position was symbolized by the investiture of Church leaders with both sacred and secular insignia. On the other hand, Church reform in the 11th century advocated the separation of affairs of the Church from those of the state; Church reformers, especially the popes, asserted that the spiritual powers of the Church were superior to secular powers. This conflict, known as the Investiture Controversy, would reach its greatest intensity in the second half of the 11th century during Matilda's maturity.

Through her teens, Matilda became an active supporter of the papacy as she defended, along with her mother and stepfather, the canonically elected pope Alexander II against an imperially backed antipope Caladus of Parma, who took the name Honorius II. It is likely that she was also present at several important battles, such as the battle of Aquino in 1066 where her stepfather's forces defeated the antipope's Roman and Norman supporters. She was present as well at several Church councils, beginning with the Council of Sutri in 1059 which she attended at age 13.

Probably in 1069, after the death of her stepfather Duke Godfrey, Matilda married his son, Godfrey the Hunchback, duke of Upper Lorraine, in what appears to have been primarily a political union. After the death of her infant son in 1071, she returned to Italy while her husband remained in Lorraine. Their political views parted ways as well; Godfrey became more closely aligned with the German emperor Henry IV while Matilda continued her strong backing of the reforming papacy. Godfrey died in 1076.

Pope and Emperor Struggle over Investiture

During the decade of the 1070s when Matilda reached maturity, the Investiture Controversy became a dramatic struggle between its two major protagonists: Pope **Gregory VII** and Emperor Henry IV. Matilda and her mother had long been associated with the archdeacon Hildebrand who became Pope Gregory VII in 1073 and with his strong advocacy of Church reform. At the same time, Matilda's familial and feudal relationship to Henry IV brought her into close association with the German imperial cause. After her mother's death in 1076, Matilda became a leading figure in the heated controversy between Church and state.

As a cornerstone of his reform policy, in 1075 Pope Gregory prohibited lay investiture, a practice central to German imperial policy and ideals of kingship. Henry IV countered in 1076 with a declaration renouncing and deposing the pope. In return, Gregory excommunicated Henry. During one of the most famous and pivotal episodes in the Investiture Controversy, Henry, in order to maintain his rule, traveled across the Alps in a bitter winter of 1077 to do penance before the pope. Pope Gregory received him at Matilda's fortress at Canossa only after Henry waited three days in the snow before being admitted. Then Matilda acted as intermediary between her spiritual father Pope Gregory and her relative Henry.

Henry, however, continued to pursue his policies and his opposition to the papacy. After the 1080 death of Rudolf of Swabia, elected king in place of Henry by the German princes, Henry invaded Italy. Although her forces were no match for Henry's, Matilda remained a steadfast supporter of the papacy. Her one major victory was a surprise attack on Henry's army at Sobara, near Modena, in 1084. During this year, however, Henry was able to crown an antipope in Rome while the Normans rescued Gregory VII and took him to south Italy where he died in 1085.

Matilda supported the legitimately elected popes, first Pope Victor III (1086–87) and then Pope Urban II (1088–89). In 1089, probably to add military strength to her cause, 43-year-old Matilda agreed to another political marriage to 17-year-old Welf V of Bavaria. The marriage did little to assist her position since Henry continued to take over cities and territory that had been in Matilda's possession. This marriage ended six years later.

Though neither side abandoned its ideological positions, the intensity of the Investiture Controversy diminished after Pope Gregory's death. During her later years, Matilda therefore turned her attention to governing and administering her territories, to patronage of religious institutions, and to her spiritual life. As a result of Henry's inroads into her holdings and a general movement for independence among northern Italian cities, many of Matilda's estates were less directly under her control. She made numerous donations of land to churches and monasteries within her dominions while supporting building projects and provision of church furnishings for many of these religious foundations. She also was a patron of the developing school of canon law at Bologna under canonists such as Irnerius.

The last years of her life were increasingly spent in quiet and periods of withdrawal to the Benedictine monastery of San Benedetto Polirone which her grandfather had founded. After the death of her nemesis Henry, she became reconciled with his son and heir Emperor Henry V. Matilda died in 1115 and was buried at Polirone. Her remains were later removed for burial at St. Peter's in Rome in 1635 where her tomb in the crossing of the church is marked by a monument by the great Baroque sculptor, Bernini.

Because Matilda died without heirs or successors, the fate of the Canossa holdings remained a point of contention well after her death. Henry V effectively claimed all her territories when she died, leaving the popes to dispute with the emperors about the disposition of Matilda's grant of her freehold (the right to hold lands for life) lands to the Church.

Matilda's life and accomplishments were chronicled and praised in a long heroic poem composed by Donizo, her chaplain at Canossa. With allowances for its laudatory aim and literary stylistics, this poem and other contemporary references reveal her to have been a complex woman of exceptional abilities. She had great strength, displayed in physical terms as a Christian warrior, and steadfast character, witnessed by her unwavering support of the papal cause. At the same time, her compassion was evident: she tended the wounded on the battlefield and was especially generous in the patronage she bestowed on the Church. She was also educated and cultured, with some understanding of the subtleties of the political and theological positions that inspired the controversy between Church and state. During this critical episode in medieval history, her multifaceted support was instrumental in advancing the position of the Church.

SOURCES:

Bellochi, Ugo, and Giovanni Marzi. *Matilde e Canossa. Il Poema di Donizone.* Aedes Muratoriana, 1984.

Duff, Nora. *Matilda of Tuscany.* Methuen, 1909.

Fraser, Antonio. *Boadicea's Chariot: The Warrior Queens.* Weidenfeld & Nicolson, 1988.

Grimaldi, Natale. *La Contessa Matilde e la su stirpe feudale.* Vallechi Editore, 1928.

Huddy, Mary E. *Matilda, Countess of Tuscany*. John Long, 1906.

FURTHER READING:

Blumenthal, Uta-Renate. *The Investiture Controversy*. University of Pennsylvania Press, 1988.

Fuhrmann, Horst. *Germany in the High Middle Ages c. 1050–1200*. Cambridge University Press, 1986.

Rough, Robert H. *The Reformist Illuminations in the Gospels of Matilda, Countess of Tuscany*. Martinus Nijhoff, 1973.

Giacomo Matteotti

(1885–1924)

Leader of the Italian Socialist Party and bitter and effective critic of Mussolini's dictatorship, whose murder by Fascist thugs led to a crisis that nearly overthrew Mussolini.

"Matteotti fought Fascism with facts and conviction."

CHARLES DELZELL

Born in Fratta Polesine, Rovigno Province, Italy, on May 22, 1885; murdered in Rome on June 10, 1924; married.

Giacomo Matteotti, one of the foremost leaders of Italian socialism following World War I, contested the rise of fascism with courage and eloquence. With his death in 1924, Fascist Italy was soon transformed into a full-fledged dictatorship. On the other hand, the murder of the prominent Socialist stimulated the growth of an anti-Fascist movement that lasted until the overthrow of Mussolini in 1945.

Italy at the start of the 20th century was a recently created country suffering from severe social, economic, and political problems. Unified only in 1861, there remained vast economic and cultural differences between the relatively prosperous northern regions and the poor areas south of Rome. With the unrest in the country's cities, a Socialist Party emerged to help Italy's factory workers. There was even more unrest in the countryside as movements of agricultural workers formed to improve wages and working conditions, but they faced harsh resistance by landowners.

While Socialist leaders promoted a program of reform in the name of the workers, prior to 1914 Italian nationalist leaders like Enrico Corradini spoke of the need to link all Italians together and

Contributed by Neil Heyman, Professor of History, San Diego State University, San Diego, California

to carry out a plan of imperial expansion. Universal suffrage was established in 1912, creating a large number of new voters whose future political loyalties were uncertain.

After bitter debate and violent public demonstrations, the Italian government of Giovanni Giolitti entered World War I in the spring of 1915. Both sides in the war bid to attract Italy. Britain and Drance won over the Italians by promising large postwar territorial gains at the expense of Austria-Hungary. But the war brought massive Italian casualties, disrupted the Italian economy, and resulted in only disappointing territorial gains at the 1919 peace conference. Italian Socialists, inspired by the success of Communist revolution in Russia, were speaking about revolution in their own country.

Mussolini Leads Emerging Fascist Movement

At the same time, a movement on the political right—a movement called fascism—emerged under the leadership of **Benito Mussolini.** A former Socialist who had abandoned the Socialist Party in 1914 to lead a movement to bring Italy into World War I, Mussolini now gathered a variety of followers: embittered war veterans, nationalists, opponents of Socialist revolution. The Fascist program mixed calls for radical economic change

with a strong devotion to Italian nationalism and opposition to socialism.

Over the years from 1919 to 1922, its program lost some of its radical character. Fascism became dominated by nationalism and opposition to the political left. The Party was also distinguished by its use of violence against its political opponents: Socialist meetings were broken up by armed Fascist bands; rival political leaders were beaten; leaders of rural workers' groups were assaulted.

By 1922, fascism gained support from even moderate conservatives who hoped it would be a barrier against Socialist revolution. In the face of bitter opposition from the Socialists, Mussolini came to power as prime minister. His rise to power was technically legal, but the threat of violence stood in the background. He had threatened to lead his movement in a "March on Rome" to force his appointment. In the end, the authorities decided to give in to his wishes without armed resistance, and he headed a coalition cabinet starting on October 31, 1922. But Mussolini was openly contemptuous of parliamentary government. He intended to tighten his control over the country pushing aside opponents of fascism and abolishing the parliamentary system he hated. Matteotti emerged as one of his most effective critics.

Giacomo Matteotti was the son of a prosperous hardware merchant and property owner in the Po Valley. Born in the town of Fratta Polesine in Rovigno province on May 22, 1885, he was attracted to the Socialist movement while he was still in secondary school. He studied law at the University of Bologna and traveled widely inside and outside Italy during his school vacations.

The young man was an enthusiastic scholar of criminal law, and in 1910 he wrote his first book on this subject. Even in this work his Socialist convictions were evident, and he stressed the role of social and economic conditions in producing criminal behavior. Abandoning his plans for a career in teaching, he was elected to posts in municipal and then provincial government.

During the war years, Matteotti, an outspoken opponent of Italy's participation in World War I, rose rapidly as an official of the Italian Socialist Party. He made a national reputation for himself in speeches at the 1916 Party Conference on city government, which dealt with the problems of postwar planning. He was also one of the Party's leading figures in dealing with the problems of rural laborers. In 1922, the Italian Socialist Party split, some of its members moving toward the militancy and authoritarian organization of the Russian Communist Party. Matteotti became the leader of the moderate, democratic Socialist faction, the PSU.

The young Socialist leader was horrified to see fascism emerging as a political force in his home region of the Po Valley. As one friend put it, he saw fascism as "agricultural slavery." When Mussolini took over as prime minister, Matteotti quickly challenged the future dictator. In 1922, he interrupted a speech by the new prime minister with the call, "Long Live Parliament."

Mussolini's control over Italian politics remained a shaky one for years after 1922. His most serious weakness was the lack of a Fascist majority in Parliament. To remove this barrier, Mussolini had a new election law passed. The Acerbo Law of 1923 permitted the Fascists to get an overwhelming majority of the seats in Parliament merely by getting the largest number of votes cast for any party. Thus the elections of April 1924 were crucial to the future of fascism.

Matteotti Accuses Government of Election Fraud

The Fascists obtained their majority, but Matteotti immediately challenged the election results when Parliament met on May 30, 1924. In a dramatic speech lasting more than an hour, Matteotti accused the government of committing election fraud. The balloting, especially in northern Italy, had been marred by violence and intimidation, he claimed. With Fascist bullies overseeing the voting, the results were predetermined and they were corrupt. Matteotti maintained his long-standing reputation for precision and accuracy by citing numerous instances of wrongdoing. Interrupted by a storm of protest from Fascist deputies, he called for the election to be declared invalid.

The speech cost Matteotti his life. Aware of the danger, he had remarked to a colleague at the conclusion of his speech: "Now you can prepare my funeral oration."

In early June, Matteotti disappeared. Witnesses in Rome reported seeing a group of men drag someone into a car on June 10; the blood-stained car was quickly found and traced to officials of the Fascist Party. Although Matteotti's body was not discovered until weeks later, the shock of his kidnapping and probable murder had an immediate effect.

The killers acted without direct orders from Mussolini, and it is possible they intended only to kidnap Matteotti. In trying to fight off his attackers, Matteotti may have led them to kill him.

Nonetheless, Mussolini's movement had made a practice of using violence against political opponents, and Mussolini himself had responded to Matteotti's speech by saying that it deserved more than just words in reply.

Outside Italy, protests developed, notably in Britain and France. Inside Italy, it seemed that Mussolini's Fascist government would fall. When many political leaders called for his resignation as prime minister, Mussolini was forced to give up his cabinet position ·as minister of the interior (an office charged with maintaining domestic order), and several other Fascist leaders gave up high-ranking positions in the police. Five Fascist thugs with long records for attacks on opposition political figures were arrested for assaulting and kidnapping Matteotti.

Gradually, however, Mussolini regained his footing, and anti-Fascist groups in Italy let the opportunity to remove him slip away. The most vigorous protest against the crime came when more than 100 deputies boycotted all sessions of the Italian Parliament beginning in late June. Opponents of Mussolini hoped that King **Victor Emmanuel III** would demand the resignation of the Fascist leader, but the king never took this decisive step. Matteotti's killers went unpunished. During 1925, Mussolini moved to consolidate his dictatorship. Socialist leaders were arrested, censorship was tightened, and Mussolini ended parliamentary control over his government.

The significance of Matteotti's life and death continued to reverberate for more than two decades. Matteotti's Socialist colleague Filippo Turati helped to found a coalition of anti-Fascist exile groups. A symbol of Matteotti's memory was a statue of the murdered leader erected in Brussels, Belgium, in 1927. In 1943 in the midst of World War II, Italian Socialist partisan units formed themselves into "Matteotti brigades" to fight the Fascists.

A remarkable sequel to the Matteotti case came in the aftermath of World War II. In 1945, four of the individuals implicated in the murder of the Socialist leader were arrested. Two of them, including Amerigo Dumini, the leader of the group that killed Matteotti, were convicted and sentenced to 30 years in prison.

SOURCES:

Delzell, Charles F. *Mussolini's Enemies: The Italian Anti-Fascist Resistance*. Princeton University Press, 1961.

Lyttelton, Adrian. *The Seizure of Power: Fascism in Italy, 1919–1929*. Scribner, 1973.

Seton-Watson, Christopher. *Italy from Liberalism to Fascism, 1870–1925*. Methuen, 1967.

FURTHER READING:

De Grand, Alexander. *Italian Fascism: Its Origins & Development*. University of Nebraska Press, 1982.

————. *The Italian Left in the Twentieth Century: A History of the Socialist and Communist Parties*, Indiana University Press, 1989.

Tannenbaum, Edward R. *The Fascist Experience: Italian Society and Culture, 1922–1945*. Basic Books, 1972.

Maximilian I

(1459–1519)

Holy Roman Emperor and Habsburg, who, with a minimum of wealth or political power, used marriage alliances to raise his dynasty to a position of political dominance in Europe.

His rosy optimism and utilitarianism, his totally naive amorality in matters political, both unscrupulous and machiavellian; his sensuous and earthy naturalness, his exceptional receptiveness towards anything beautiful ... these properties Maximilian displayed again and again.

ERNST BOCK

Maximilian was born on March 22, 1459, at Weiner Neustadt in the Austrian province of Styria. His father Frederick III was Holy Roman Emperor, a title that had once implied a degree of lordship over all Europe. By this time, the Empire included Germany and northern Italy, a loose collection of over 300 virtually independent states whose elected emperor presided rather than ruled over them. Several of these states in the Alps and east of the Alps, loosely called "Austria," were possessions of the Habsburg family. But the Habsburgs still dreamed of an empire worthy of the Roman name.

Maximilian was spoiled by his mother who gave him sweets instead of milk, but he was terrorized by a stern teacher whose influence is blamed for the speech impediment which plagued him as a child. He received a thorough education that embraced the liberal arts, seven languages, music, painting and drawing, and practical subjects such as mining and carpentry, which remained a life-long hobby.

In those early years, he gained the common touch from playing with the servant children. A charming engraving shows the young boy leading a

Contpibuted by Arthur White, Episcopal School of Acadiana, Breaux Bridge, Louisiana

Name variations: Maxmilian I, King of Germany. Born in Weiner Neustadt, Austria, on March 22, 1459; died in Wels, Austria, in 1519; son of Frederick III, Holy Roman Emperor, and Eleanor of Portugal; married: Mary of Burgundy, 1477 (died 1482); married: Bianca Maria Sforza of Milan; children: (first marriage) Philip the Handsome, Margaret, and 12 illegitimate children. Descendants: Charles V, Ferdinand II, Spanish Habsburgs to 1701, Austrian Habsburgs to 1918. Predecessors: Frederick III, Charles the Bold. Successor: Charles V.

band of urchins in a charge on the ducks in the castle courtyard. All his life he sought the conversation of servants and soldiers and enjoyed dancing with the burghers' wives of Nuremberg. Having also kept a lifelong interest in the hunting, fishing, jousting, weaponry, and swordplay he was taught as a child, Maximilian grew to be a robust, athletic adult.

In 1476, Frederick III arranged his son's marriage to Mary of Burgundy, the richest heiress in Europe and only legitimate child of Charles the Bold. Charles and his predecessors had made Burgundy a mighty state which included most of modern Belgium, the Netherlands, and Luxemburg and extended into northern and eastern France. A marriage alliance with Frederick's family was useful because Charles was locked in a life-and-death struggle with **Louis IX,** king of France. But before the marriage could take place, Charles the Bold was killed in the battle of Nancy and Louis took to conquering Burgundian lands and demanding the heiress as a bride for his son. In great haste, Maximilian concluded the marriage by proxy and then traveled to Ghent to claim his wife.

A recent biographer describes Maximilian as a "vigorously ugly man." He had thick reddish-blond hair, a face dominated by a huge hooked nose, a protruding lower jaw, and a clumsy mouth with the infamous "Habsburg lip" visible in his descendants into the 20th century. But his burly chest and bull neck showed strength, and Maximilian had wit, intelligence, and charm. The bridal

couple, both in their late teens, were "pale as death" when they met, but immediately fell joyously in love.

The people of Ghent hailed Maximilian as "David, the saviour prince who will deliver his people," and begged him to "Defend us, lest we perish." Unfortunately, they expected him to defend them without expense. When Maximilian put an embargo on trade with the enemy, he was met with howling outrage by the merchant cities of Flanders and Holland. He also received no help from his father and had to haggle for men and money with the all-but-rebellious cities in the Netherlands.

The Burgundian knights had already been routed by the forces of Louis XI, of whom Maximilian said, "there is no greater or more cowardly scoundrel in all the world." But, by employing German tactics using foot soldiers and by fighting shoulder to shoulder with his men, Maximilian defeated Louis XI at the battle of Guinegate in 1479.

In 1482, Maximilian's happiness was shattered when Mary of Burgundy fell from her horse and died while they were hunting together, and all her lands passed to their four-year-old son Philip. Many leaders of the Burgundian territories refused to recognize Maximilian as regent for his son, leaving him caught between foreign war and domestic rebellion.

Maximilian's Father Opposes His Election

It did not impress the Flemish cities that the electors of the Holy Roman Empire chose Maximilian as "King of the Romans" in 1486. This title made him heir to his father and, theoretically, joint ruler in the Empire. Old Frederick, however, who thought Maximilian was extravagant and reckless, opposed the election and ignored his co-ruler.

In 1488, when Maximilian was captured and imprisoned in the rebel city of Bruges, he begged his father for help in a letter smuggled out of prison in the sole of a shoe. When no help came, Maximilian negotiated his way out with concessions that his father considered an "eternal disgrace." But the Germans were offended that pro-French rebels had imprisoned their king and co-ruler, and in 1489, while Maximilian attended a meeting of German princes in Frankfort, they offered him 6,000 troops for his Burgundian Wars.

It was now the son's turn to rescue the father. Matthias Corvinus, the king of Hungary, had occupied Vienna and eastern Austria. Corvinus's death without heirs in 1490 gave Maximilian the opportunity to drive the Hungarians back into their own country, demanding that he be given the crown of Hungary. The crown went instead to Vladislav Jagiello, king of Bohemia (present-day Czech Republic), but at the Peace of Pressburg, Vladislav agreed that if he should leave no heirs, his thrones would go to the Habsburgs. After this, Frederick's attitude toward his son softened and the old emperor virtually retired. He still thought Maximilian was a reckless adventurer, however, and gave him no money.

As regent for his son and co-ruler with his father, Maximilian now had responsibility but no income. Desperately needing territory of his own if he were to finance his obligations, in 1490 he succeeded in obtaining by negotiation the alpine County of Tyrol from his bankrupt uncle Sigismund, and the Tyrolean city of Innsbruck became Maximilian's capital.

In 1493, the long war to save the Burgundian inheritance ended. Maximilian defeated Charles VIII, son of Louis XI, at Salins, after which they concluded the Treaty of Senlis. Although France was given the original duchy of Burgundy, Maximilian and his son retained the Netherlands, the largest and richest part of the inheritance, and the Franche-Comte (Free County of Burgundy) which was a fief east of France in the Holy Roman Empire. After this, Maximilian left the Burgundian lands to his son and turned his attention to Germany where the death of Frederick III gave him more freedom of action.

Meanwhile, the Turks were constantly raiding and capturing slaves in the Austrian provinces of Styria and Carniola. Maximilian, who dreamed of driving the Turks out of Europe and restoring the Byzantine Empire, attacked them in 1493, calling his actions a crusade. But his resources permitted little more than a demonstration of force to curb the Turkish slave raids.

This contrast of vast plans with narrow resources bedeviled Maximilian throughout his life. Gerhard Benecke said, "Maximilian was a politician with many schemes, always impatient, always in a hurry, generally over-ambitious." He was a workaholic who conducted business over his meals saying, "I, Maximilian can take upon my shoulders Herculean labours." He was a tireless traveler, seldom spending more than a few months at his court in Innsbruck. "My true home is in the stirrup, the overnight rest and the saddle," he said. But he also kept moving because he and his entourage could quickly exhaust the limited resources of any locality. He frankly acknowledged, "God knows, I am heartily tired of traipsing around from place to place, and I only do it because of my poverty."

Maximilian's ambitions led to wars and the wars kept him poor. The Italians called him *"Massimiliano senza denaro"* (Maximilian the penniless). While his Austrian provinces were rich in silver, copper, iron, lead, and salt mines, their income was constantly in pledge to bankers, principally the Fugger family, to back the loans that paid for the wars. Maximilian relentlessly consumed the taxes of peasants and merchants, turning collection rights over to his creditors. Often blind to economics, his trade embargoes with France, and later with Venice, ruined trade and sent interest rates soaring. The result was a bureaucratic nightmare. As his biographer Benecke describes it:

> Since Maximilian was hardly ever solvent for more than a few weeks or days he was always robbing Peter to pay Paul, which quickly resulted in a bureaucratic muddle that only Maximilian in person could unravel.

In 1494, Charles VIII of France invaded Italy. Having defeated Charles in the Burgundian Wars just the year before, Maximilian was not willing to see the French king establish his power in Italy, much of which was still part of the Empire. Accordingly, Maximilian joined an anti-French league along with Spain, the pope, Milan, and Venice, but poverty kept him from offering effective help.

Family Marriages

As part of the alliance, and as a means of getting financial aid, Maximilian married Bianca Maria Sforza in 1494. Bianca Maria's uncle, Ludovico il Moro, was the ruler of the wealthy city of Milan whose funds permitted Maximilian to undertake a small expedition to Italy in 1496. The marriage was a failure from the beginning. Maximilian found Bianca Maria "nervous, capricious, indulgent, sickly, and gloomy," and his neglect of her made her failings worse. Eventually, he all but confined her to her quarters in the palace at Innsbruck.

The year after his own marriage, Maximilian concluded even more important marriage alliances for his children. Maximilian's daughter Margaret married Juan, the son and heir of **Ferdinand and Isabella** of Spain, while Maximilian's son Philip the Handsome, who was already ruling the Burgundian lands, married Juan's sister Juana. No one could foresee in 1495 that the deaths of Juan and another sister would make Juana and her son

Charles heirs to Spain. It was this marriage that would give the Habsburgs ownership of Spain and its colonies for almost 200 years.

The same year saw Maximilian busy in Germany at the Diet of Worms, a meeting of the German princes which produced constitutional changes that stood for over 300 years. The changes arose from the reform program of Berthold of Henneberg, archbishop elector of Mainz, who wanted the Empire to be controlled by its leading princes. Opposing Maximilian's foreign wars, he would allow money for them only at the cost of constitutional concessions.

The resulting reforms outlawed private wars between the German princes and set up a central supreme court, the *Reichskammergericht* (Imperial Court Chamber), which was dominated by the princes. In exchange, Maximilian got a small permanent tax called the Common Penny; when many princes still refused to pay it, the exasperated Maximilian remarked wryly that he was, truly, "king of kings." In 1498, Maximilian obtained the further concession that the imperial cities, generally less hostile than the princes, would be permanently represented at the diet.

This small success was outweighed in 1499 by a humiliating defeat in battle against Swiss rebels. The Treaty of Basel gave the Swiss virtual independence from the Empire, undermining Maximilian's prestige in Germany and leading to further defeats. The Germans would give Maximilian no forces or funds when the French conquered Milan, his wife's city, and a valuable ally in Italy. Worse came at the Diet of Augsburg in 1500 when Maximilian had to agree to a Council of Regency, set up by the princes to replace Maximilian at the head of the government. Fortunately for Maximilian, the princes lacked the interest to maintain this advantage and made no move to block him when he dissolved it in 1502. The death of Berthold of Henneberg in 1504 ended further efforts to weaken the imperial government.

He Intervenes in War of Succession

Maximilian regained all his lost prestige in 1504 when he intervened in a war of succession in Bavaria and the Palatinate. He was nearly killed at the battle of Regensburg when he was pulled off his horse, but he was rescued and won a major victory. After Maximilian dictated a settlement of the succession, the Venetian ambassador wrote home that, "his imperial majesty is now a true emperor and ruler of Germany."

To complete his triumph, Maximilian planned to go to Rome in 1508 to be crowned Holy Roman Emperor by Pope Julius II. But Venice, which had seized territories belonging to the Empire, had no desire to see a crowned emperor at the head of a rejuvenated state. The Venetians, therefore, blocked Maximilian's journey and forced him to return to Germany. The pope allowed him to take the title Emperor-Elect; then Maximilian and the pontiff joined with France and Spain in a league to crush Venice. The war, which lasted from 1508 to 1516 was the most costly and unpopular of Maximilian's Italian wars since it interfered with essential trade between Germany and Venice. In 1513, when Venice was beaten badly by the French, Maximilian and the pope turned their energies to preventing the French from controlling Italy.

In 1515, **Francis I** of France captured Milan. Although Maximilian borrowed money to retake it, his troops mutinied from inadequate pay and he returned to Germany. His Italian wars ended in 1516 when he recognized French possession of Milan.

Maximilian was always more successful at marital diplomacy than at war. In 1517, he agreed to a double marriage between his family and that of Louis Jagiello, king of Hungary and Bohemia. Maximilian's granddaughter Maria was betrothed to the Hungarian king, while Louis's sister Anna married Maximilian's grandson Ferdinand. When Louis was killed in 1526 at the battle of Mohacs, both Bohemia and Hungary came to Ferdinand and remained under Habsburg rule until 1918.

In his later years, Maximilian harnessed the humanists, poets, and artists of his court in a great propaganda effort to glorify his reign. Limited as always by lack of money, Maximilian used the new printing press and woodcut engravings to produce a magnificence on paper he could not afford in reality. Thus Albrecht Dürer and other artists produced splendid volumes of illustrations for allegorical arches and processions. They also illustrated Maximilian's three books: *Theuerdank*, an allegorical version of his journey to the Netherlands to meet Mary of Burgundy; *Freydal*, an account of tournaments, masques, and festivities; and Maximilian's autobiography *Weisskunig* (White King). Maximilian was also the patron of Heinrich Isaac and Ludwig Senfl, leading composers at the court chapel in Innsbruck.

But the old emperor's burly physique was wearing down. He had had a noticeable attack of syphilis as early as 1497, and in October of 1518, he had an attack that was probably a stroke. Death came on January 12, 1519, due to stomach and intestinal failures. But his marriage alliances had raised his grandchildren to the thrones of Spain, Burgundy, the Empire, Bohemia, and Hungary. It became a motto of the Habsburg house, "Let others make war, you, happy Austria, marry."

SOURCES:

Benecke, Gerhard. *Maximilian I (1459–1519): An Analytical Biography.* Routledge & Kegan Paul, 1982.

Heer, Friedrich. *The Holy Roman Empire.* Translated by Janet Sondheimer. Praeger, 1967.

Waas, Glenn Elwood. *The Legendary Character of Kaiser Maximilian.* Columbia University Press, 1941.

Zophy, Jonothan W., ed. *The Holy Roman Empire, A Dictionary Handbook.* Greenwood Press, 1980.

FURTHER READING:

Bryce, James. *The Holy Roman Empire.* Macmillan, 1904.

Holborn, Hajo. *A History of Modern Germany. Vol. I. The Reformation.* Knopf, 1959.

Maehl, William H. *Germany in Western Civilization.* University of Alabama Press, 1979.

Jules Mazarin

(1602–1661)

Italian-born French Cardinal and statesman, who helped to make Louis XIV all-powerful, and France a major European power.

Pronunciation: MAZ-e-ren. Born Giulio Mazarini in Pescina, Italy, on July 14, 1602; died in Paris on March 9, 1661; son of Pietro Mazarini and Hortensia Bufalini; may have secretly married Anne of Austria, Queen of France, but this speculation has never been proven; no children. Predecessor: Cardinal Richelieu.

Born in 1602, Giulio Mazarini was the son of Pietro Mazarini, a poor gentleman and client of the powerful Colonna family who was allowed to marry the noblewoman Hortensia Bufalini. Giulio grew up in Rome with one younger brother and four sisters. At age seven, he entered the Roman College, a Jesuit school, where his teachers hoped he would become a Jesuit. Instead, he became a worldly young man, addicted to gambling at which he cheated. "Correcting chance," he called it. One who knew him described him as:

> A young man with a charming face, graceful manners, gracious, agile, lively, likeable, polite, with a penetrating mind, a bright humor, clever at dissimulation, in a word, fit for everything…. He spent money freely.

In 1622, Giulio Mazarini traveled to Spain as a companion for Filippo Colonna's son who was attending the University of Alcala de Henares. Returning to Rome after two years, he became a captain in the papal army, and by 1628, was secretary to the Papal Legate in Milan, his introduction

"Here was a shrewd and adroit Minister, restored to office in the face of great opposition, a man who loved me and whom I loved, who had rendered me very great services."

Louis XIV

Contributed by Arthur White, Episcopal School of Acadiana, Breaux Bridge, Louisiana

to the world of diplomacy. In January 1630, Mazarini was sent as papal nuncio to France where he met the great **Cardinal Richelieu,** chief minister to King Louis XIII.

In 1630, when Giulio Mazarini first visited France, Europe was 12 years into the Thirty Years' War which had begun in Germany as a religious conflict but had become the latest episode in a 200-year power struggle between France and the House of Habsburg, rulers of Spain and the Holy Roman Empire. France and Spain were being drawn into a war for which neither was prepared by a dispute over the inheritance of Mantua in northern Italy.

As the two armies were about to collide outside the Mantuan city of Casale, Giulio Mazarini—as Pope Urban VIII's representative— rode back and forth between the armies until he was able to arrange a truce on October 26, 1630. With this success, he won the respect and gratitude of Richelieu and fame across Europe. Although the pope also rewarded him with church offices, Mazarin continued to wear layman's clothes.

He Leaves Rome for France

In 1631 and again in 1632, the pope sent Mazarini to Paris for negotiations that settled the Mantuan dispute. In 1634, returning to Paris as the papal nuncio, he received further church offices and began to wear clerical garments, though he never became a priest. But when France and Spain officially went to war in 1635, the pro-Spanish party, which was predominant in Rome, regarded Mazarini as too favorable to the French. Deprived of his post in 1636, he returned to Rome to learn "in how many feet of water I find myself and what I can hope from the goodwill of patrons." The water was deep. Losing all hope for further diplomatic appointment, he persuaded Louis XIII and Richelieu to take him into French service. Thus, Giulio Mazarini left Rome on December 13, 1639, and became Jules Mazarin, a Frenchman.

In France, Mazarin advanced quickly. Made a cardinal at Louis XIII's request in 1641, he was also one of the godparents at the baptism of the dauphin, the future **Louis XIV.** And, upon the death of Richelieu in 1642, Mazarin filled his seat on the Council of State. But by 1643, Louis XIII was dying, and the four-year-old dauphin would not be of age until he was 13. The obvious regent was the queen, Anne of Austria. But she was a Spanish Habsburg and unlikely to stand up to her brother, Philip IV of Spain. As coauthor of Louis XIII's will in which Anne was named regent,

CHRONOLOGY

1602	Giulio Mazarini born
1628	Made secretary to Papal Nuncio in Milan
1630	Visited France; Truce at Casale
1632–34	Diplomatic missions to France
1636	Recalled to Rome; diplomatic career ruined
1639	Mazarini (Mazarin) entered French service
1641	Made a cardinal
1643	Louis XIII died; Mazarin named chief minister to Anne of Austria; Battle of Rocroi
1648	Fronde of the Parlement; Peace of Westphalia
1650	Arrest of Condé began the Fronde of the Princes
1651–52	Mazarin exiled; Battle of Porte Antoine, Condé's coup
1652–23	Mazarin exiled for a second time
1653	Fronde of the Princes defeated
1659	Peace of the Pyrénées
1661	Mazarin died

Mazarin made sure she would share power equally with the full Council of State. Anne was furious over this insult. Playing both sides, Mazarin sent her secret reassurance that the important thing was to be named regent; the restrictions could be removed later.

Just four days after Louis XIII died on May 14, 1643, Anne of Austria went with her son Louis XIV to the Parlement of Paris, the highest law court in the kingdom, to have her husband's will overturned. New laws, including the king's will, had to be registered in the Parlement before they could be enforced. The Parlement used this privilege to challenge or modify the laws. In the revised regency, the queen could choose her own ministers, and the council was reduced to an advisory role.

The day after these changes were made, the king's cousin, the prince de Condé, won a crushing victory over the Spanish armies at Rocroi. Spain never recovered from the blow and Condé became a national hero.

But Mazarin was now the chief minister of France. His power was based on the extraordinary relationship he developed with Anne of Austria. When Anne became regent, Mazarin used his ingratiating charm to win her over. "He would not stay in France," he told her, "if he came to feel she was using his services merely out of necessity without liking him personally." After Mazarin moved into the Palais Royal with the queen and her two sons, gossips noted that they met every evening in her private room. It is improbable that Anne, a woman of formidable piety whose favorite pastime was visiting convents, would have tolerated an irregular sexual relationship. There has been speculation about a secret marriage, but 300 years have yet to unearth a shred of supporting evidence. Married or not, it is clear that Anne, Mazarin, and her sons functioned as a family, bound together by affection and mutual respect. Like a devoted father, Mazarin supervised the education and development of the young king.

Outside his new "family," Mazarin was intensely unpopular. He was ignorant of French domestic affairs and used patronage "to turn one man against another and to make each beholden to himself." Richelieu had put on a royal air, but Mazarin's cringing manner, coupled with his use of bribery and duplicity, turned hatred into contempt.

Most unpopular was his continuation of Richelieu's policies. Richelieu had carried out a "governmental revolution—in which royal councils and intendants took over many of the functions of judges and officials who bought their offices and passed them on to their children—offices made lucrative by fees and graft. By building up royal power, Richelieu had undercut the power of officials, the courts, and the nobility who had plotted incessantly against him. Anne of Austria had been Richelieu's enemy; now both hereditary officials and nobles looked to her to reverse Richelieu's work.

Anne released all her noble friends from the prison or exile to which Richelieu had consigned them. But, as Mazarin's influence grew, she denied them the power over the government they sought. Some nobles formed the Cabale des Importants to plot Mazarin's murder, but they were discovered and arrested.

Opposition continued to grow out of the ruthless taxation needed to finance the Thirty Years' War. It was led by the Parlement of Paris which spoke for the discontent of the 40,000 judges and officials whose importance had been undermined by Richelieu. In September 1645, young Louis XIV was taken to the Parlement for a lit de justice, a ceremony in which the king by his personal presence could force the Parlement to register his edicts. But this weapon was resented because the French king was a child manipulated by a Spanish queen and her Italian minister.

When another lit de justice had to be held on January 15, 1648, it led to the first of a series of rebellions called Frondes which means "slingshot." The judges greeted the king and regent with speeches protesting that judges were not "galley slaves." At a joint session with the other major courts in Paris, Parlement now demanded sweeping reforms. These included Parlement's right to review financial edicts and abolition of the intendants and of arbitrary arrest. Mazarin replaced the finance minister, reduced some taxes, and sent these offers with the king to another lit de justice on July 31. But when the judges persisted in their discussions, Mazarin arrested three of their leaders. The result was a three-day riot, "the Days of the Barricades," which ended only when the judges were liberated.

Condé's Army Besieges Paris

In the small hours of the morning of January 6, 1649, the royal family secretly left Paris for St. Germain. In the first conspiracy of the Fronde, the gates of Paris were closed and the popular Prince de Condé's army besieged the city. After three months of fighting, a settlement on March 5 ended the siege. All decrees of the Parlement during the siege and its orders banishing Mazarin were revoked. Paris was to disarm and return the Bastille to the king's control. In exchange, there was to be an amnesty for all. The royal family returned on August 18 to triumphal arches and demonstrations of joyful devotion—in spite of the libelous attacks on the cardinal called mazarinades which continued to circulate.

In the midst of the crisis, Mazarin's foreign policy achieved the successful conclusion of the Peace of Westphalia, ending the war in Germany against the Austrian or imperial branch of the House of Habsburg. France gained the bishoprics of Metz, Toul, and Verdun and most of Alsace. Germany was reduced to a welter of independent states over which the emperor had no control. But war continued with Spain, even as civil war erupted at home.

The "Fronde of the Parlement" was followed by the even more dangerous "Fronde of the Princes" (the second conspiracy). Seeking to replace Mazarin as head of the government, Condé began to form alliances with other dissatisfied nobles and with the Parlement. Mazarin countered on January 18, 1650, by arresting Condé and some of his allies. The provinces in which the arrested princes had influence rebelled. Normandy and Burgundy were pacified when the beloved young king was brought to visit there, but Guienne—the area around Bordeaux—broke into full revolt, and on the northern frontier the rebels were backed by Spain. At that time, the present Belgium and Luxembourg were Spanish possessions and the headquarters of the main Spanish army.

Royal armies successfully captured Bordeaux after a month's siege, but the Spanish conquered many key areas in the north and threatened Paris itself until the battle of Somme-Py halted their advance. On February 4, 1651, the Parlement, supported by mobs in the streets, demanded the liberation of the princes and the dismissal of Mazarin. Planning a second siege of Paris, Mazarin went to St. Germain. Although Anne and her sons were supposed to join him, a mob broke into the palace and attacked the coaches to make sure the royal family did not leave. Mazarin fled to Germany. By that time Anne, virtually a prisoner in Paris, had already released Condé.

But Condé insisted on long lists of governorships, commands, and titles for himself, his family and supporters. He refused to visit the king or even to offer him customary respect when they met in the streets. Condé seriously insulted the king by boycotting the ceremony which declared Louis XIV to be of age on his 13th birthday, September 7, 1651. Though Louis played a growing role in the government, that government was still a family committee of which the absent Mazarin was the head. But Condé's selfish arrogance, the popularity of the king, and Mazarin's absence were causing the revolt to fizzle.

Louis XIV Recalls Mazarin to Government

The revolt sprang to new life in December 1651 when Louis XIV recalled Mazarin to head his government. Though Paris was outraged and the Parlement put a price on Mazarin's head, Louis ignored them and welcomed his mentor to Poitiers where the royal armies were headquartered.

Rebellion coupled with Spanish invasion brought disasters in early 1652. The Spanish army moved south as far as Chartres, Orleans rebelled, and Condé nearly captured the royal family at Gien. On July 2, 1652, a major battle was fought at the Porte Antoine in the suburbs of Paris. Royal forces outnumbered Condé and crippled his army, but he kept control of Paris.

In the city, Condé sought to legalize his rebellion in a meeting of all the judges, city officials and other notables at the Hotel de Ville.

When they supported the king, a riot broke out which killed some of the officials and set fire to the hotel. Most members of Parlement fled the city, and Louis XIII's brother, Gaston d'Orleans—a supporter of Condé—was declared ruler of the kingdom.

Violence and treason cost Condé the support of the moderates who were loyal to the king but hated Mazarin. To exploit this lack of support, the king issued a proclamation full of gratitude and praise for Mazarin but announcing that the cardinal would go into voluntary exile to secure peace. On September 16, with Mazarin gone, Louis called on the Parisians to expel the rebels. Condé left the city and joined a Spanish army invading from the north. When the king returned to Paris, he outlawed Parlement's interference in politics or finances.

In 1653, royal forces, accompanied by the young king, inflicted a series of defeats on Condé. Mazarin returned to join the king on campaign. The war was again becoming a war between France and Spain, though Condé now fought on the other side. Loyalty to the king forced the moderates to accept Mazarin. When he accompanied the king back to Paris, one of his enemies wrote:

> This outlaw, this disturber of the public peace, … on whose head a price had been set, came back to this great city, not only without causing any popular disorder, but like a conquering hero covered with glory.

But opposition to exorbitant taxation survived in the Parlement. Mazarin used bribery and threats to elimilate the most outspoken opponents. Yet in April 1655, financial decrees were again being delayed in Parlement. The king rode to Paris without changing out of his hunting clothes, strode into the Parlement, and ordered immediate registration. Parlementary opposition collapsed.

When he was not in exile, Mazarin amassed enormous wealth and did not always distinguish between the state's finanaes and his own. Several of his nieces came to France and were known as the "mazarinettes." All made splendid marriages. One of them, Marie Mancini, would have been queen had Mazarin not intervened. Louis XIV loved her and wanted to marry her, but Mazarin, intent on a diplomatic marriage for the king and fearing the unpopularity of such a match, forbade the marriage and found Marie a husband in Italy.

Condé, fighting for Spain, could not erase the blow to Spanish strength he had himself inflicted at the battle of Rocroi. In 1658, the Spanish frontier in Flanders (Belgium) collapsed. On November 17, 1659, the Peace of the Pyrénées ended 24 years of war and two centuries of rivalry. France kept conquests in Artois, Cerdagne, and Rousillon. Condé was pardoned and returned to France. On June 9, 1660, Louis XIV married Maria Theresa, daughter of the king of Spain.

Mazarin—who had won the wars, defeated rebellion, and established the position of his god-son Louis XIV at home and abroad—hoped Louis would soon govern without a powerful minister. In his last letter to the king, he wrote:

I shall die well pleased and satisfied when I see you in a position to govern by yourself, only asking your ministers for their counsel, acting on it as seems best to you, and then giving orders for them to carry out.

Mazarin died on March 9, 1661, declaring that "he left behind him two immortal daughters: the Treaty of Westphalia and the Treaty of the Pyrénées." After Mazarin's death Louis followed his advice and ruled alone as the absolute monarch of the strongest power in Europe.

SOURCES:

Carré, Henry. *The Early Life of Louis XIV (1608–1661).* Translated by Dorothy Bolton. Hutchinson, 1951.

Dethan, George. *The Young Mazarin.* Thames & Hudson, 1977.

Kleinman, Ruth. *Anne of Austria, Queen of France.* Ohio State University Press, 1985.

Moote, A. Lloyd. *The Revolt of the Judges: The Parlement of Paris and the Fronde.* Princeton University Press, 1971.

FURTHER READING:

Boulenger, Jaaques. *The Seventeenth Century in France,* William Heinemann, 1920.

Doolin, Paul Rice. *The Fronde.* Harvard University Press, 1935,

Perkinq, James Breck. *France Under Mazarin With a Review of the Administration of Richelieu.* Putnam, 1886.

Giuseppe Mazzini

(1805–1872)

Visionary Italian nationalist, who popularized the idea of unifying his native country through revolutions and guerilla action.

"Which of these men did 'make Italy?' The great diplomat [Cavour]? Or the man he undoubtedly regarded as a harebrained fanatic [Mazzini]? The answer is that Mazzini did more than any other single human being to foster in nineteenth-century Italians the urgent determination to achieve independence and unity."

STRINGFELLOW BARR

Name variations: Joseph Mazzini. Pronunciation: Juh-SAY-pay Mats-ZEE-nee. Born June 22, 1805, in Genoa; died on March 10, 1872, in Pisa; son of Giacoma (a physician) and Maria Drago Mazzini; unmarried; no children.

Until 1870, Italians were not unified under a single government. More than eight governments ruled in Italy, and a famous diplomat dismissed Italy as a "geographic expression." The *Risorgimento*, or resurrection of Italy into a single nation was achieved by 1870 largely through the efforts of three men. The first was **Camillo di Cavour,** a statesman whose masterful diplomacy maneuvered the European Great Powers into helping advance the cause of unification. The second was Giuseppe Garibaldi, a peasant whose citizen armies fought for unification. The third was **Giuseppe Mazzini,** a visionary popularizer.

Living most of his life in exile, Mazzini schemed, wrote, and passionately implored his fellow countrymen to work for the unification of Italy. More than any other man, this revolutionary in exile represented the spirit of the *Risorgimento*.

The son of a physician and his wife, Mazzini was a precocious child. His first tutor, a priest named Don Alberto, declared when the child was seven years of age that the boy knew more than he did about history and literature. Mazzini's parents decided to take an active role in the boy's education when one of his mother's cousins predicted

Contributed by Niles R. Holt, Professor of History, Illinois State University, Normal-Bloomington, Illinois

that the young Mazzini was destined to be one day "admired by all of the culture of Europe." Both mother and father spoke fluent French, and they worked to teach him that language. Friends were encouraged to teach him English and German.

Mazzini was only 14 when he matriculated at the University of Genoa. He was remembered as a dark-haired, brooding student with a fiery glance. His black, shoulder-length hair and graceful but energetic walk made him a familiar figure on campus and gathered a crowd of fellow students around him. He vacillated between wanting to study law and wanting to study medicine. Eventually, politics became his major interest.

The adult Mazzini remembered an experience as a child, when his mother gave a contribution to a fierce-looking man who was standing in the street collecting funds for the refugees of Italy. In his mind, the man became part of the "struggle for the liberty of our country." All Italians were refugees, he insisted, because there was no national Italian government.

The books that Mazzini read as a college student, such as the French Enlightenment writers Voltaire and Jean-Jacques Rousseau, fed his hatred of injustice. From the 18th-century German writer Gottfried Herder, he learned that peoples (*Volk*) were a nationality even if they were under the control of other nationalities. To Mazzini, the greatest injustice was the division of Italy—the splintering of the Italian people among many different governments.

Mazzini grew to adulthood during a period that one writer has called a time of collapsed idealism. The French Revolution of 1789 excited revolutionaries everywhere, raising the possibility that monarchies were on their last legs. Even when the Revolution brought to power a new monarch, the French general (and eventual emperor) **Napoleon Bonaparte,** many Europeans saw his armies as simply the revolution on horseback. As Napoleon's armies invaded (and defeated monarchical armies) in much of Europe, hopes were raised that the age of monarchs was at an end.

When Napoleon Bonaparte's troops invaded Italy, many Italian nationalists actively supported their advance, seeing in the French leader the instrument of God's will to create a united Italy. Napoleon's defeat by the traditional monarchies of Europe—first at Leipzig, Germany, in 1814 and second at Waterloo, Belgium, in 1815—seemed to dash such hopes.

The Great Powers which had defeated Napoleon decided, at a diplomatic conclave named the Congress of Vienna (1814–15), to monitor all parts of Europe closely, and pledged to use their armies to guarantee that future revolutions would be halted quickly. It seemed to signal the end of the era of revolutions. All over Europe, monarchs—who had been put off their thrones by Napoleon—were restored to power. It was, said one wit, an era of dead heroes and live lackeys.

In Italy, the defeat of Napoleon gave Austria a special role in Italy. The Congress of Vienna assigned to Austria the role of stabilizing the Italian peninsula, and Austrian troops occupied the northern Italian states of Lombardy and Venetia. The celebrated Austrian foreign minister, **Klemens von Metternich,** devoted his life to combating both revolutions and rising nationalism. The Austrian Empire, an 11-nation empire ruled by the German-speaking Habsburg family, could not afford to allow the spread of either revolutions or nationalist movements. In an attempt to quash revolutions before they started, Metternich instituted strict censorship and police control in much of Central Europe, including northern Italy.

Mazzini predicted that such repressive policies would, in fact, provoke revolution. The years from 1815 through 1848, which saw numerous revolutions in Europe, seemed to prove him correct. The Spanish people revolted (unsuccessfully) against monarchs in 1808, 1811, and 1819; more successful was the Belgian revolution of 1830, in which the Belgian people gained independence from rule by the Netherlands. Many prominent Europeans sympathized with the successful Greek struggle for independence from the Ottoman Empire in the 1820s; several fought alongside the Greeks. Mazzini proclaimed the Belgian and Greek revolutions as models for Italy. Guerilla action, he maintained, would be the best way to unite Italy under a single government. Italy was to be unified not by monarchs but by "citizen action."

When a friend asked Mazzini in 1827 to join the secret revolutionary order the *Carbonari* (meaning, literally, charcoal burners), Mazzini agreed. He was disappointed with the initiation ritual, which mentioned obedience to the order but not the unification of his country. He later complained that the *Carbonari* signified only a war against the government; nothing was said about unification, republicanism, or monarchies.

In Exile, Mazzini Founds Nationalist Group

Within days of the initiation, Mazzini's name was reported to local police by a police spy who had been present at the ceremony. Jailed for several days, he was released from prison on the condition that he go into exile. Establishing residence in the southern French town of Marseilles, he founded an organization named Young Italy, which was committed to unifying Italy by education and insurrection. "Insurrection by means of a guerilla band," he insisted, "is the true method of warfare for all nations desirous of emancipating themselves from the foreign yoke." It was to replace the *Carbonari*, which was a "senile institution" without a constructive program, which would "never awaken the people to a sense of mission."

With branches in Spain and Germany, as well as Italy and France, Young Italy became a republican organization which rejected monarchy as a path to unification. It became the chief Italian nationalist organization, replacing the *Carbonari*. Living in exile most of the rest of life—at first in Marseilles, and then at Lyons, France—Mazzini relied on his family for funds. As a self-proclaimed nationalist in exile, he headed the organization and edited its journal. By the early 1830s, estimates of its membership ranged up to 60,000. Mazzini predicted that "Europe, weary of skepticism and egoism, will accept the new faith with acclamation."

What was needed in Italy, Mazzini proclaimed, was a "Holy Alliance of Peoples to combat the Holy Alliance of monarchs." Through thought and action, Young Italy would attain the "great aim of reconstituting Italy as one independent sovereignty of free and equal men." Unlike

the *Carbonari*, wrote Mazzini, it was "no society like others; there are no mysteries, no hierarchies of rank; no symbols; it is a brotherhood of young men to work together with frankness, sincerity, and confidence."

In 1831, Mazzini issued a challenge to Charles Albert, king of the northern Italian state of Piedmont, urging him to institute constitutional reforms—to "Believe, and unite Italy." The sight of a committed revolutionary appealing to an Italian monarch caused much comment, and Mazzini insisted that he was trying to demonstrate the uselessness of Italian monarchies. He predicted Charles Albert would ignore the call. Instead, the king of Piedmont complained to the French emperor, **Napoleon III.** French police took over Mazzini's headquarters and forced him to leave the country.

For most of the rest of his life, Mazzini chose to play the role of revolutionary in exile in London, establishing a boys' school for the large number of fellow Italian exiles in the city. The intense man made an impression among prominent Londoners; contributors to his school included Lady Carlyle, wife of a prominent 19th-century historian, and the novelist Charles Dickens. One observer described Mazzini as a man with darting, jet black eyes who spoke with a "fascinating power ... with his gestures, his voice, and his whole bearing that was quite irresistible."

During the revolutions of 1848, Mazzini was one of the first prominent Italians to urge the king of Piedmont to take advantage of a revolution in Austria. Now was the time, he wrote, for Piedmont to drive Austrian troops from northern Italy. He personally appeared in central Italy with 500 volunteer soldiers, largely émigrés who lived in Britain and France.

The journey placed him at odds with the foreign minister of Piedmont, Camillo di Cavour, a statesman who sought to unite Italy by diplomatic means rather than revolution. Compared to the intense and idealistic Mazzini, Cavour was a gregarious and shrewd diplomat who moved easily in the circles of the rich and powerful.

Garibaldi's Red Shirts Oppose Monarchy

Relations between Cavour and Mazzini worsened during the revolutions of 1848. Mazzini's main disciple in Italy, Garibaldi, was inspired to begin a long-term struggle against the monarchy which ruled Italy's largest state, the Kingdom of Naples. As Garibaldi's citizen-army—named Red Shirts—approached lands controlled by the pope in central

Italy, with the apparent idea of "liberating" the area from papal control, Mazzini suddenly appeared in central Italy as well.

Alarmed that revolutionaries might take control of a nation directly on France's borders, the French Emperor Napoleon III (a nephew of Napoleon Bonaparte) condemned Mazzini's move as an appeal to rebellion and civil war. Cavour, who had ingratiated himself with the Great Powers of Europe by portraying himself as a bulwark against revolutionaries such as Mazzini, sent the Piedmontese army into the Papal States to block Garibaldi. In doing so, however, he took control of part of the Papal States. Thus, in the guise of controlling revolutionaries, Cavour achieved another step toward uniting the Italian peninsula. The torch of Italian unification was now in the hands of Cavour, rather than Mazzini.

After a brief trip back to Britain, Mazzini reappeared in Italy in 1849, seeking to help revolutionaries in Tuscany and in Rome. Both attempts were unsuccessful. Within a short time, Mazzini was back in Britain, resuming his customary role as revolutionary-in-exile. In 1853, an attempt to reignite the revolution in Lombardy failed miserably.

Even his British friends had noticed the cleverness of Cavour's diplomacy. They were coming to doubt Mazzini, fearing that Mazzini had become mainly a foil for Cavour to scare the Great Powers of Europe. The two men detested each other. To Cavour, Mazzini was the "chief of the assassins"—a perpetual conspirator. To Mazzini, Cavour was an "upholder of the Piedmontese monarchy ... a worshipper of facts rather any sacred eternal principles."

Cavour consistently outmaneuvered Mazzini. When Cavour insisted that different areas of Italy might join a unified state by plebiscite (vote), Mazzini, who feared a Piedmontese trick, opposed plebiscites. He believed that only revolutions would succeed in uniting Italy. He thus gave the public appearance of favoring revolutions over democracy, allowing Cavour, the aristocrat, to appear to be the supporter of democracy.

Declaring "neither priest nor king," Mazzini sought a federation of Italian states, in which each would retain some independence. Italy would be united by a republican assembly. He failed because (1) he sought a weak rather than a strong central government—raising the question of how united a Mazzini Italy would be and because (2) in his lifetime no strong guerilla movement emerged in Italy to support revolutions, such as had happened in France and Spain.

After 1861, when Cavour was able to unite all of Italy except Rome, Mazzini returned to Italy and chose to work within the Italian parliamentary system created by his rival. Several times, he was elected parliamentary representative from Messina; each time, the national government disallowed the elections. He continued to publish his opinions on politics through a newspaper he edited. When he died in 1872, he was working on organizing a workingman's congress.

For most of his life, Mazzini was in exile from his native Italy, and he was bitterly disappointed with the way Italian unification proceeded. Yet he was an essential part of Italian unification. Without Mazzini to organize unrelenting popular pressure on the monarchs of the individual Italian states, unification would have been much more difficult to achieve—and may have been delayed for many years.

SOURCES:

Griffith, Gwilwyn O. *Mazzini: Prophet of Modern Europe.* London: Hodder & Stoughton, 1932.

Rosen Jervis, Alice de, ed. *Mazzini's Letters.* Westport, Conn.

Salvatorelli, Luigi. *The Risorgimento: Thought and Action.* Harper, 1970.

FURTHER READING:

Barr, Stringfellow. *Mazzini: Portrait of an Exile.* Henry Holt, 1935.

Hales, E. E. Y. *Mazzini and the Secret Societies: The Making of Myth.* Kennedy, 1956.

Hamilton-King, Harriet E., ed. *Recollections of Mazzini.* London: Longmans, 1912.

King, Bolton. *The Life of Mazzini.* London: Dent, 1912.

Silone, Ignazio. *Mazzini.* London: Casell, 1946.

Catherine de' Medici

(1519–1589)

Machiavellian politician, wife of Henry II of France, and later regent for her three feeble sons at the twilight of the Valois dynasty, who authorized the killing of French Protestants in the notorious Massacre of St. Bartholomew's Day in 1572.

"Catherine never forgot anything, neither the horror of civil war, nor the anguish which gnawed at her during the first ten years of her married life, ... nor her constant humiliation as wife and queen by the flaunted liaison between Henry II and Diane de Poitiers."

HENRI NOGUERES

Catherine de' Medici was never able to rule France as its monarch because the Salic Law restricted the succession solely to men. But this Machiavellian—whose father was Machiavelli's patron—ruled it as regent for nearly 30 years, and did everything she could to strengthen the position of her three weak sons on its throne. She presided over, and was partly responsible for, many of the horrors of the French Wars of Religion in the 1560s and 1570s, of which the worst was the massacre of Protestants gathered in Paris to witness the marriage of her daughter Marguerite Valois to Duke Henry of Navarre in 1572. Her calculating policies yielded short-term victories, but when she died in 1589 her hopes for her family's long-term future lay in ruins.

Catherine was born in 1519, daughter of a powerful Italian prince from the Medici family. Her mother died within a few days from puerperal fever and her father succumbed to consumption a week later at the age of 27, leaving her an orphan after less than one month of life. Her father's relatives, among them popes Leo X and Clement VII, took over her care, and she grew up in the midst of the stormy Italian Wars in which they were central

Contributed by Patrick Allitt, Assistant Professor of History, Emory University, Atlanta, Georgia

Name variations: Catherine de Médicis. Born in Florence in 1519; died in 1589; daughter of Lorenzo de' Medici, Duke of Urbino, and Madeleine de la Tour d'Auvergne, Countess of Boulogne; married: Henry II Valois, King of France (1547–59); children: (sons) Francis II, Charles IX, Henry III, Hercules (later renamed Francis, Duke of Alençon); (daughters) Claude, Elisabeth, Marguerite. Predecessor: her husband Henry II. Successor: her son Henry III and her son-in-law Henry IV.

CHRONOLOGY

1519	Catherine born in Florence
1527	Sack of Rome; siege of Florence
1533	Married Prince Henry
1547	Henry ascended to the French throne
1559	Henry killed in a joust
1561	Catherine's oldest son, Francis II, died
1562–70	Successive religious civil wars in France
1572	Massacre of Saint Bartholomew's Day—a Catholic coup against Protestant power
1574	Catherine's second son, Charles IX, died
1589	Death of the Duke of Guise, then Catherine, then Henry III; accession of Henry of Navarre (Henry IV) to French throne

actors. When a German army of the Holy Roman Emperor **Charles V** sacked Rome in 1527, the citizens of Florence took advantage of this eclipse of Medici power to restore their republic, and took the eight-year-old Catherine hostage. Escaping from Rome and hiring a group of mercenaries to recapture Florence, her uncle Clement VII was able to rescue her from her refuge in a nunnery.

In pursuit of Pope Clement's dynastic ambitions, 14-year-old Catherine was married in 1533 to 14-year-old Henry, duke of Orleans, younger son of King **Francis I** of France. The elaborate ceremony at Marseilles Cathedral was conducted by the pope himself, but her childlessness for the first ten years of marriage made her unpopular in the French court. With the help, as she believed, of astrologers—she was patroness of the seer Nostradamus and a lifelong dabbler in necromancy, astronomy, and astrology—she overcame this early infertility and gave birth to ten children, beginning in 1543. Few of them were healthy, however, and she, enjoying an iron constitution and great powers of recovery, would outlive all but one, Henry III, who would follow her to the grave in a matter of months. The death of her husband's older brother in 1536 made Henry and Catherine heirs to the throne, but the circumstances of his death increased Catherine's unpopularity. One of her retinue, Count Sebastian Montecuculi, was suspected of poisoning him to promote the interests of Catherine and, possibly, of France's enemy Charles V.

Catherine's husband, now Henry II, had spent several childhood years as a hostage at the Spanish court in Madrid. On his return, at the age of 11, he had been cared for by Diane de Poitiers, who was 20 years his senior. Despite this age difference, they became lovers, and throughout most of Henry's reign, which began in 1547, Diane completely eclipsed Catherine in influence over the king, though her age and her lack of beauty made Henry's attraction and loyalty to her something of a mystery at court. Diane was even given responsibility for raising Catherine's children, and she and Henry arranged the betrothal of the oldest son, Francis, to **Mary, Queen of Scots** in 1548. But in 1557, Catherine's coolness in an emergency won her new respect from Henry. He had lost the battle of St. Quentin to **Philip II** of Spain; when Paris itself was jeopardized, Catherine made a patriotic speech to the Parlement, persuaded it to raise more troops and money to continue the fight, and put to rest the old suspicion that she was more an Italian schemer than a true queen of France.

At the time of Catherine's birth in 1519 the Reformation was beginning with **Martin Luther**'s criticism of the Catholic Church. The challenge to Rome's religious hegemony (dominance) began in Germany but soon spread throughout Europe. The French lawyer and theologian **John Calvin**, living and writing in Geneva, Switzerland, was particularly inspiring to many French men and women, who saw in his version of Christianity a truer form of their faith than that offered by a politicized and often corrupt Catholic Church. In France, for example, appointments and promotions in the Catholic Church were all at the king's disposal; political cronyism rather than piety and administrative skill led to advancement. French Protestants were known as Huguenots, and the rapid growth of their numbers among the nobility and upper classes as well as among ordinary folk soon made them a politically significant force; the Huguenots held their first general French assembly in 1559.

Henry Dies; Teenage Son Succeeds Him

This was an era in which monarchs assumed that the integrity of their kingdoms depended on the religious uniformity of their peoples; religious schism of the kind which beset France by mid-century was unprecedented. The Catholic monarchs of France and Spain made peace at Cateau-Cambrésis in 1559 partly because they were bankrupt but also so that they could unite their forces against Protestantism. The treaty was sealed by the marriage of Philip II of Spain to Elisabeth, the teenaged daughter of Catherine and King Henry. At the joust held to mark the wedding celebrations, however, King Henry was fatally injured by a lance wielded by a Calvinist nobleman, the Comte de Montgomery. It shattered his helmet, pierced his eye, and entered his brain. Henry's death a few days later brought their oldest son, 16-year-old Francis II, to the throne.

France was full of demobilized soldiers, many of them unpaid for months. Tax burdens on the peasants were heavy, and Calvinist preachers with their message of an uncorrupted faith found a receptive audience. Huguenot noblemen took action almost at once, organizing a conspiracy to overthrow or at least dominate the court of Francis II, and winning the active support of England's new Protestant queen, **Elizabeth I**. Then, at the city of Amboise, their military uprising failed, and the royal army arrested the leaders. In the presence of Catherine, her children, and Mary, Queen of Scots, 57 of the Huguenot leaders were hanged or beheaded. This retribution did not end the religious-political conflicts besetting France, however; from this time forward, the Huguenot Navarre family and the Catholic Guises led rival religious and court factions. The death of 16-year-old Francis II the following year made Catherine regent for her second son Charles, who now became King Charles IX at the age of ten.

Herself a lifelong Catholic but always with a degree of religious cynicism, Catherine appears never to have understood the passion with which many of her contemporaries lived their religious lives. For her, religious differences seemed at first to be bargaining chips in court intrigues, which might be smoothed away by tactful diplomacy. She permitted Admiral Gaspard de Coligny, an influential Huguenot, to act as Charles's chief advisor for awhile, provoking three powerful noblemen, the duke of Guise, the cardinal of Lorraine, and the constable of France, to sink their own differences and make a three-way alliance, a triumvirate, for the defense of Catholicism against Coligny.

Catherine's miscalculation of the Reformation's impact on France was evident at the Colloquy of Poissy, 1561, when she tried to conciliate the Catholic faction, under the cardinal of Lorraine, with the Huguenots, under the reform theologian and friend of Calvin, Theodore Beza. Far from coming to an understanding with one another, the two parties hardened their differences. In the poisoned atmosphere of broken negotiation, open hostilities began, marking the first of a succession of religious wars. Interrupted by truces, but marked by fierce vendettas, the conflict raged for a decade.

Charles IX was an unstable character, and as he matured he came to dislike his mother and her favorite, younger son Henry. Charles, says the lively historian Henri Nogueres:

> had the figure of a sickly adolescent, too thin for its size, hollow-chested and with drooping shoulders ... his sallow complexion and bilious eyes betrayed liver trouble; he had a bitter twist at the corners of his mouth and feverish eyes.... He hunted in order to kill, for he soon acquired a taste for blood, and almost every day he needed the bitter sensation, the uneasy satisfaction of seeing the pulsating entrails and the hounds on the quarry.

Catherine found it relatively easy to dominate Charles, despite his growing resentment, and in the face of constant warfare she also tried to carve some order out of the fiscal and administrative chaos of the kingdom, to strengthen it for her sons' reigns. She took Charles on a long royal journey through his kingdom. She incorporated in 1565 a meeting with her son-in-law, Philip II of Spain, to discuss the continuing religious crisis. Philip disliked her apparent willingness to play off Catholics and Protestants against one another; in his view, she should have been doing more to advance the Counter-Reformation. But he also knew that France's weakness was a strategic benefit for Spain. It made French intervention to aid troublesome Dutch rebels against Spain far less likely. When Philip's wife and Catherine's favorite daughter Elisabeth died in childbirth in 1568, Catherine hoped he might marry her younger daughter Marguerite, but Philip was determined to take his French connection no further. Another blow to Catherine's politicking came the same year when her daughter-in-law, Mary, Queen of Scots, was captured by her English enemies and imprisoned, leaving Scotland open to Protestant domination and effectively ending a Franco-Scottish Catholic encirclement of Elizabethan England.

Through much of the 1560s, the two religious factions were at war while Catherine and Charles tried to avoid falling too heavily into either camp. The religious warfare was complicated further by English incursions into France itself, ostensibly in alliance with the Huguenots, but largely in pursuit of traditional English designs on northern France. The war was also complicated by a blood feud among the major families, brought on when the Huguenot leader Admiral Gaspard de Coligny ordered the assassination of the duke of Guise in 1563. As the fighting continued, especially in the third religious war, from 1568 to 1570, Huguenot armies attacked convents and monasteries, torturing and massacring their inhabitants, while Catholic forces, equally merciless, slew the Huguenots of several districts indiscriminately.

The Peace of St. Germain Is Signed

After a decade of war, the Peace of St. Germain in 1570 reconciled the two sides temporarily and led to Admiral Coligny's return to court. Among the treaty's provisions was the specification that Catherine's daughter Marguerite should marry Henry of Navarre, the Huguenot leader, that the Huguenots should be given several strongholds throughout France, and that Coligny could resume his position as a royal councillor. Catherine hoped that, as a moderate Huguenot, he might act to mollify his fellow Huguenots while she played the same role among Catholics. But Coligny quickly and tactlessly reasserted himself at court, becoming a friend and confidante of King Charles IX but arousing suspicions among Catholic courtiers that he was planning another coup. When Coligny discovered that Charles and his mother were at odds, he miscalculated and chose the king's side rather than Catherine's, provoking her furious resentment.

The city of Paris had remained friendly to the ultra-Catholic Guise party throughout these years of war, and most Parisians resented the concessions to Huguenots made at the Treaty of St. Germain. The population was, accordingly, restless and angry when a large Huguenot assembly entered their city in the summer of 1572 to celebrate the wedding. Marguerite Valois, the bride, was herself a stormy personality and an inveterate intriguer. When Catherine had discovered earlier that Marguerite was having an affair with the duke of Guise, she and Charles IX had beaten her senseless. The motive for this marriage alliance was that Henry of Navarre, though a Huguenot, would have a strong claim to the French throne if neither Charles IX nor Catherine's younger son Henry had a living heir. A connection to the Valois family would strengthen Navarre's claim as well as Catherine's prospects of continued influence. Marguerite, still in love with Guise, resisted the planned marriage, says historian Hugh Williamson:

> she and Henry of Navarre had known each other during their growing up at least well enough to be aware that they had no glimmer of sexual attraction for each other and even domestic accommodation was imperilled by such differences as her liking for at least one bath a day and his aversion to more than one a year. Also he always stank of garlic.

She refused to give up her Catholic faith for this marriage, which was in any case imperiled when Henry's mother Jeanne of Navarre died suddenly during the negotiations which preceded it. In the fevered atmosphere of the time, many Huguenots were ready to believe that Catherine de' Medici had poisoned Jeanne, although that seems unlikely.

Catherine decided to dispose of Gaspard de Coligny once and for all. She accepted an offer from the Guise party to assassinate him, hoping that the outcome would be revived power for her own party. The assassin shot Coligny but failed to kill him, and Charles IX rushed to his side, promising a full inquiry and retribution against the assassins. But under interrogation from Catherine and his younger brother Henry, Charles finally accepted their claim that Coligny was manipulating him, that Coligny planned to overthrow the whole Catholic court, and that he and the other Huguenot leaders should now be finished off in a preemptive strike. According to his brother Henry's diary, Charles at last shouted; "Kill the Admiral if you wish; but you must also kill all the Huguenots, so that not one is left alive to reproach me. Kill them all!"

Catholics Massacre Huguenots

By careful prearrangement, church bells began to ring at two in the morning of August 24, Saint Bartholomew's Day, 1572. The bells signaled Catholic troops to begin, and at once they moved to kill the injured Coligny and other Huguenot leaders. The attacks became indiscriminate; all sense of order broke down. As widespread looting and fighting broke out across Paris, over 2,000 men, women, and children (including many people uninvolved in political and religious controversy) were shot or hacked to death. Similar massacres followed in the provinces, as Catholics seized the initiative against their local Huguenot rivals. King Charles feared that he had unleashed a revolution, but Catherine, according to one onlooker, "looks a younger woman by ten years and gives the impression of one who has recovered from a serious illness or escaped a great danger." A fourth civil war at once began, but by a strange turn of circumstances, leadership of the Huguenot party now fell to Catherine's youngest and most unscrupulous son Francis, duke of Alençon. Placing himself at the head of the Protestant forces and dreaming of a crown, he declared that his older brother Henry, who had just been elected to the throne of Poland, was no longer available as heir of France.

Henry, this third son of Catherine, was less easily dominated and manipulated than Charles. He was homosexual and had had a long succession of lovers. His mother tried to "correct" this propensity by ordering a banquet at which the food was served by naked women, but she could not succeed. Henry had spent the 1560s garnering the laurels of a successful general in the wars against the Huguenots. His victories won him the envy of King Charles IX, whose physical frailty forbade campaigning. Catherine tried to marry Henry to Elizabeth I of England, but the "Virgin Queen" tactfully declined the offer and was equally obdurate against the wooing of the pathetic fourth brother, Alençon, whom she called her "frog." The only woman to excite Henry's interest, and to whom he sent ardent love letters signed in his own blood, was already married to the prince of Conde. Henry did not relish the prospect of going to Poland, even though his mother's judicious distribution of bribes to the electors there had secured the throne for him, but at last he set out. His departure prompted another Huguenot uprising, in which Alençon, Henry of Navarre, and Marguerite Valois were all implicated as conspirators. With her usual energy, Catherine coordinated forces to quell it, and with her usual decisiveness, she witnessed the executions of the ringleaders Montgomery, La Mole, and Coconnas. She also witnessed the death of her son King Charles, aged 24. She now recalled her favorite, Henry, to his hereditary kingdom.

Henry III was crowned in 1575 and married in the same year to Louise of Lorraine, but they had no children to carry on the Valois line. From this time on, Catherine entrusted family fortunes more wholeheartedly to the Catholic Guise family, and approved the formation of the Catholic League in 1576 which marched to triumph against the Huguenots. Henry's homosexual favorites predominated at court. When the Guise provoked a duel and killed two of them, Quelus and Saint-Megrim, Henry conceived an implacable hatred against them. Another round of blood feuding began despite Catherine's continued urging that Henry must settle his differences with the Guise for the sake of national and Catholic security.

Catherine remained politically active until the end of her life, touring France on Henry's behalf and trying to assure the loyalty of its many fractured and war-torn provinces. She also amassed a huge collection of books and paintings, built or enlarged some of Paris's finest buildings, including the Tuileries Palace, and carried on to the end her fascination with astrology. She was fat and gouty by 1589 and was taken ill that year from the exertion of dancing at the marriage of one of her granddaughters. She lived just long enough to hear that Henry's bodyguards had murdered Guise; this news, writes Williamson, "destroyed her will to live, for it epitomized her failure. Her idolized son, for whom she had spent her whole life, had destroyed all that she had built and rejected everything she had taught him." Later that year, Henry III in turn died, assassinated by a Dominican friar, Jacques Clement, who regarded him a traitor to the faith for joining Henry of Navarre against the Catholic League. In this way, the Valois dynasty came to an end. Ironically it was the Huguenot prince Henry of Navarre who succeeded to the throne, though he was unable to sit upon it until 1593 when he cynically adopted the Catholic faith with the famous remark, "Paris is worth a Mass."

SOURCES:

Heritier, Jean. *Catherine de Medici*. St. Martin's Press, 1963.

Nogueres, Henri. *The Massacre of Saint Bartholomew*. Macmillan, 1962.

Soman, Alfred. *The Massacre of Saint Bartholomew: Reappraisals and Documents*. Hague: Martinus Nijhoff, 1974.

Strage, Mark. *Women of Power: The, Life and Times of Catherine de Medici*. Harcourt, 1976.

Williamson, Hugh Ros. *Catherine de Medici*. Viking, 1973.

Lorenzo de' Medici

(1449–1492)

Unofficial ruler of republican Florence during the Renaissance period, who was a poet, diplomatist, and celebrated patron of the arts.

Name variations: Lorenzo the Magnificent. Born in Florence on the first day of 1449; died in his country villa of Careggi, near the city, in the spring of 1492; son of Piero (a preeminent figure in Florence) and Lucrezia Tornabuoni (of an ancient aristocratic family); married: Clarice Orsini (daughter of a Roman nobleman), 1469; children: (four daughters) Lucrezia, Maddalena, Luisa and Contessina; (three sons) Piero (who was briefly master of Florence upon his father's death), Giovanni (who became Pope Leo X), and Giuliano (who became Duke of Nemours).

Lorenzo de' Medici was born on January 1, 1449, in Florence, an independent Italian city-state republic famous then as now for its artistic and intellectual achievements during what scholars call the Italian Renaissance. After 1434, his grandfather Cosimo had established the Medici family's dominant position within the oligarchic group which governed this republic, and from birth Lorenzo was destined to assume Cosimo's role. This was made clear at Lorenzo's baptism on January 6, 1449, which was attended not only by so celebrated a figure as the archbishop of Florence, Antoninus (later to be canonized), but by official representatives of several important governmental bodies.

His parents, Piero de' Medici and Lucrezia Tornabuoni (herself from an ancient and powerful Florentine family), brought up Lorenzo conventionally enough, no doubt to avoid arousing envy in the minds of their peers, many of whom were suspicious of Medici political intentions. Like other patrician children, Lorenzo had his own resident tutor, the priest Gentile Becchi, who reported when his charge was only five how splendidly his humanist studies were progressing—a

Contributed by F. W. Kent, Professor of History, Monash University, Clayton, Victoria, Australia

theme he was to repeat as the young Lorenzo worked his way through the masterpieces of Latin literature and history during the 1450s. From an early age, Lorenzo showed exceptional ability and promise, as even one of his severest contemporary critics, Alamanno Rinuccini, was to admit. As boys together, Rinuccini writes, he had seen in Lorenzo:

> an intelligence so pliable and versatile that, in boyish things, whatever he set his mind to he learned and mastered better than did others, dancing, bowmanship, singing, riding, playing games, performing on musical instruments and many other things.

Indeed, as early as 14 or 15, Lorenzo began to write poetry in the Italian vernacular which would still command the respect of literary critics even were its author not the famous public figure, Lorenzo de' Medici. Although these early verses were in a sense exercises, which inevitably adopted the themes and reworked the poetic techniques of such masters as Francesco Petrarca and Dante Alighieri, Lorenzo was a serious writer who throughout his life produced poetry of increasing independence and virtuosity, tinkering with it almost obsessively. (Most of his poetry is very hard to date as a result of this constant reworking). Some of Lorenzo's early verse was set to music, and contemporary correspondence make it clear that music-making, dining and courtship, amidst parties at elegant villas in the country, was a major activity of his youthful company of intimates, which included his brother-in-law Bernardo Rucellai, friends such as Braccio Martelli and the major vernacular poet, Luigi Pulci. It was Pulci who wrote in 1465 that Lorenzo's "genius is quicker than anybody else's."

Lorenzo's precocious brilliance as an adolescent was also manifested in the rapidity with which he learned the ropes of interstate diplomacy and the political management within Florence. He has sometimes been depicted by later historians as a Renaissance playboy with intellectual leanings, at least until his father's death in 1469, but nothing is further from the truth. Certainly after his grandfather Cosimo's death in August 1464, Lorenzo's participation in public affairs is increasingly evident. Since the health of Piero de' Medici was poor, the Medici family seems to have been intent on grooming Lorenzo to replace his father, as Piero had just replaced Cosimo. Piero de' Medici began quite early to send his son on quasi-diplomatic missions, as when in the late spring of 1465 the adolescent Lorenzo visited the Sforza duchy of

CHRONOLOGY

1463–64	Began writing poetry
1464	Grandfather Cosimo died
1469	Took control of Medici regime on father's death
1472	Revolt of Volterra University of Pisa re-established
1478	Escaped assassination in Pazzi Conspiracy
1478–80	Pazzi War with papacy
1482	His mother Lucrezia died
1482–84	War of Ferrara
1489	Son Giovanni made cardinal
1492	Lorenzo died

Milan for the wedding of Ippolita Sforza and Alfonso of Aragon, accompanied by fatherly advice to be "alert, a man and not a boy, and make every effort to be both careful and clever in learning how to undertake even greater tasks, for this outing can show the world what you can do." Early in the next year, Lorenzo visited the court of the Kingdom of Naples, enjoying a papal audience in Rome on the way.

Elected to the Council of One Hundred

Within Florence, Lorenzo began to assume political office, usually by special dispensation because of his extreme youth; so in December 1466 he was elected to the important Council of One Hundred, "notwithstanding his being under age" as the relevant law commented. More informally, he was learning in the 1460s to cultivate political allies and *clients*—*amici* ("friends") as contemporary sources describe them—just as his Medici relations had always done, offering in return for the allegiance of these dependents all sorts of favors, ranging from political office to tax deductions and suitable marriage partners. His first surviving letter, written on November 18, 1460, when he was 11 years old, is addressed to a rural official on behalf of a humble friend involved in litigation. From about 1466 onward, we also find Lorenzo active in several religious confraternities, in which devout laymen met to pray and sing religious songs but also (according to contemporary criticisms) to discuss politics, form factions, and even to plot dissension. If there was indeed a wide and genuine streak of religious fervor in Lorenzo's complicated makeup that would have attracted him to the lay confraternities, there is no doubt that he also found in them a further means of cultivating friends, especially among the youth of Florence, and of watching his family's potential enemies. Lorenzo's formidable mother was almost as much responsible as was his father for setting Lorenzo a good example of how to influence and control events by the cultivation of clients and friends. When she died, many years later in 1482, Lorenzo wrote that Lucrezia had long been "an instrument who relieved me of many burdens.... The sole refuge in my many troubles."

In the summer of 1466, Lorenzo learned how burdensome his political life was likely to be, when some former allies of the Medici, led by such men as Dietisalvi Neroni and Luca Pitti, had moved to oust his father from his preeminent if unofficial position in Florence. In these troubled events, the young Lorenzo played some part in outmaneuvering his family's enemies, whose final defeat was marked by a public assembly of citizens in support of the Medici regime on September 2, to which—a foreign ambassador reported—"Piero sent about 3000 armed men on to the piazza, with his son Lorenzo himself on horseback and armed to the teeth." Threats to his own personal safety were to crop up again in the next year, indeed throughout his life, and it is no wonder that Lorenzo himself looked back on his youth as a difficult and dangerous one. Meanwhile his family continued to prepare him for leadership, arranging a great armed joust in Piazza Santa Croce on February 7, 1469, which, inevitably, Lorenzo won, despite his own later admission that he was too young for his martial blows to have been very hard. The whole affair cost the huge sum of 10,000 florins, money well spent in keeping Lorenzo on the center stage of all Italy. In June of the same year, Lorenzo was married, amid extraordinary splendor and expense, to Clarice Orsini, from a celebrated Roman noble family. Lorenzo, with what a Milanese observer at this time described as his "most supple intellect," was now more than ready to take his place upon Piero's death, which occurred on December 2, 1469. Several years later, Lorenzo wrote that he had been reluctant to do so. Even so, he had spent the weeks in which his father lay dying in preparation for the invitation extended him to by hundreds of Medici supporters, to become the leader of the Medici and therefore of Florence.

Lorenzo's Government Begins

Most contemporaries said that Lorenzo's ascendancy began well, praising his maturity and sure political instincts. The Milanese ambassador reported in July 1470 that Lorenzo, like his grandfather, wanted to govern "as much as possible by constitutional methods," and this adherence to the constitutional letter of the law remained typical of his regime, necessarily so in a city where many people were still wedded to their traditional republican ideology. Nonetheless, it was just as characteristic of Lorenzo to seek to reform or to tinker with the constitution in a way which assured and if possible increased his personal authority, and that of his allies. Lorenzo's managing to have passed legislation in July 1471 that set up a *balìa*, a pro-Medicean special council with considerable authority, was an early and notable victory, one achieved against swelling internal opposition to his rule. Among his family's friends, elder statesmen such as Tommaso Soderini supported the young man while also determined to make his regime a more genuinely oligarchic one than recent Medici pretensions had allowed. Other people were critical of his extreme youth, while still others disapproved of his pro-Milanese foreign policy. His own elder cousin, Pierfrancesco, was said to have been jealous of Lorenzo's preeminence, and to have worked secretly against his authority during this period, which in other respects was fraught with tension.

Already, Lorenzo's problems with the great family banking house had begun. Unable personally to supervise its many branches, inside and outside of Italy, as his grandfather had managed to do, and unprepared by his humanist education for the job, Lorenzo had to rely on managers, several of whom did not serve him well, and to adopt policies at times dictated more by political than by commercial imperatives. In fact, judging from his correspondence, Lorenzo put more time and energy into the bank than scholars have thought, in the end to no avail as it was to continue to decline throughout his ascendancy, and was virtually bankrupt by 1494. Lorenzo was perennially short of liquid capital, despite his family's extensive country estates, mercantile traditions, and reputation for wealth and its magnificent expression, a fact which explains contemporary charges, not all of them illfounded, that he made personal use of state funds. His own investment in the alum industry of Volterra, a hill town southwest of Florence, may in part explain Lorenzo's advocating a punitive expedition against the city, in revolt against Florence in February 1472. On its surrender after a siege, Volterra was subject to a ruthless sack which, while Lorenzo did not personally authorize it, has left his reputation blemished in some historians' eyes.

Throughout the 1470s, Lorenzo's gradual assertion of authority in Florence and in Italy was achieved by more than just constitutional or, occasionally, forceful means. He worked assiduously to perfect the informal and extraconstitutional methods of control practiced by his Medici ancestors, becoming within Florence what contemporaries called a big shot (*gran maestro*), eventually the "boss of the shop" (*maestro della bottega*). Increasingly, Lorenzo intervened in marriage agreements between prominent families—thereby winning grateful friends and forbidding matches which might have created powerful enemies—and otherwise acted as an arbiter in legal or personal disputes, often among the peasantry. For his clients came from all social groups, just as the extensive correspondence he maintained knew no frontiers of social class and few of geography. Some 20,000 letters written to Lorenzo still exist, and his comparatively numerous surviving answers to them, brilliantly expressed, corroborate the contemporary historian Francesco Guicciardini's judgment that "the letters dictated by him are quite as clever as anyone could wish." In his correspondence, Lorenzo's emerging skills and reputation as a diplomatist on the Italian scene are in evidence, as well as his command of patron-client networks. By the late 1470s, to aid him in this often confidential work and to handle the scores of personal petitioners who always followed him, Lorenzo came to rely increasingly upon a group of agents, personal secretaries, and aides such as Niccolò Michelozzi, Agostino Cegia, and Francesco nicknamed "the goldsmith," and Florentine bureaucrats with firm Medicean allegiances such as Bartolommeo Scala, Antonio Miniati, and Giovanni Guidi; the last two became so closely identified with the private interests of Florence's ruling family that in 1494, on the downfall of Lorenzo's son Piero, they were hunted down savagely by angry citizens.

His Patronage of the Arts and Learning

In this first decade of his leadership, Lorenzo's activities as a patron of the arts and of learning began decisively. To the family collection of antiquities—classical medals, jewels, and vases—Lorenzo added expensive and celebrated pieces of his own. He also continued to build up the excellent Medici private library, especially acquiring Greek manuscripts. Lorenzo supervised with an awesome eye for detail the reestablishment of the University of Pisa, from 1472 onward, interfering in every aspect of the enterprise from the appointment of faculty to questions of student discipline. He began to turn his attention to architectural patronage, starting modestly by contributing to the rebuilding of the convent of Le Murate in Florence in 1471–72 and continuing to fund his family's patronage of its neighborhood church of San Lorenzo. In 1474, he acquired a rural estate on a beautiful site at Poggio a Caiano near Pistoia, and seems already to have been planning the great villa, a prototype of the advanced Renaissance style that he in fact began to construct, with his architect Giuliano da San Gallo, a decade later. The chorus of contemporary praise of Lorenzo as a new Maecenas (a famous ancient Roman patron of the arts) began at this time, when he was also busy writing poetry, enjoying discussions with the neo-Platonic philosopher Marsilio Ficino, and coming to appreciate the friendship and learning of Angelo Poliziano, one of the greatest philologists of his day. Lorenzo sincerely loved learning and learned men, and had a decided and original taste in the visual arts. But he also saw that his reputation as a patron and practitioner of the arts consolidated his authority in Florence, and beyond.

This authority was never more seriously challenged than in April 1478, when members of the Pazzi family, a powerful and ancient Florentine clan of bankers, plotted with several confederates (and with the knowledge of Pope Sixtus IV) to overthrow the Medici. There had been subterranean rivalry between the two families, although it is also possible that the Pazzi had motives that were not merely self-interested. In any event, in an attack on the two Medici brothers at mass in the cathedral, Lorenzo escaped with an injury, only to find that his younger brother, Giuliano, had been murdered. In the aftermath, the Pazzi failed to rally popular support, and most of the culprits and their associates suffered cruel deaths at the hands of the Florentines. The truth of a current adage had been proved: "He who sides with the Medici always prospers, who, on the contrary, takes the part of the Pazzi, is destroyed."

However, in the subsequent Pazzi War, 1478–80 (in which Florence was pitted against the papacy and the Kingdom of Naples), things went badly for the Florentines until Lorenzo managed to negotiate a peace settlement by courageously traveling alone to Naples, where he was at the mercy of his enemies. His return to Florence on March 15, 1480, was a triumph, on which he shrewdly capitalized by almost immediately pushing through constitutional reforms: first a new *balìa* and then the creation of a Council of Seventy which, in Nicolai Rubinstein's words, became "the supreme agency of control and, through its committees, the principal organ for all important decisions." Even a Medici supporter, such as their erstwhile spy the chronicler Benedetto Dei, thought that the Seventy stood for a "tyrannical sort of government" rather than a "civil one." Though some scholars would deny that Lorenzo was ever a tyrant, certainly his grip on Florentine politics, while never completely secure, became firmer and more open in this last period of his short life. As a member of another new government body, the Seventeen Reformers, he took a much more direct role in political decision-making than had been his custom. For understandable reasons, too, after the Pazzi conspiracy he went everywhere with an armed bodyguard, and in other ways lived a more princely life, traveling extensively between the great country villas he was building in the later 1480s at Poggio, Agnano (near Pisa) and Spedaletto (near Volterra).

At the same time, he began to put into effect plans for a radical urban renewal in his own quarter of Florence, including a palace for himself which, had it been built, would have been the wonder of Italy. Lorenzo interfered more and more in the artistic patronage of other Florentines, exercising an almost supervisory role over many major projects, and sending Florentine artists hither and thither to foreign patrons in a game of cultural diplomacy. On the diplomatic stage proper, Lorenzo was a very powerful influence for peace on the turbulent Italian peninsula in the 1480s, while managing to secure his own borders with the capture of Sarzana in the summer of 1487. Even in his own lifetime, Lorenzo was attaining an almost mythological status as "our earthly God," as Pierantonio Buondelmonti described him. If, according to another contemporary source, he had been in the 1470s "the first citizen of his republic," he was "more than lord of this regime" by the next decade, in the words of a non-Florentine observer.

Lorenzo died on April 8, 1492, after years of indifferent health, the succession passing smoothly to his eldest son Piero. Gout and related complaints were hereditary in his family, but it is also possible that he suffered from renal tuberculosis. His slow death, bravely endured with Christian stoicism, was not free of the controversy that marked his life and his subsequent image. The doctor who had failed to save Lorenzo was himself found dead in a well the next morning, and all Italy rang with rumors that he had been killed and his patient poisoned. (There is, however, no grounds for believing the latter rumor.) His childhood friend Rinuccini wrote that an obsessively jealous tyrant, who had robbed Florence of its republican liberty, had died. Another citizen said that Florence had lost "a true and living god."

SOURCES:

Ross, Janet. *Lives of the Early Medici as Shown in Their Correspondence.* Chatto & Windus, 1910.

Rubinstein, Nicolai. *The Government of Florence under the Medici (1434–94).* Clarendon, 1966.

FURTHER READING:

Brucker, Gene. *Renaissance Florence.* John Wiley, 1969.

Hale, John. *Florence and the Medici.* Thames & Hudson, 1977.

Hook, Judith. *Lorenzo de' Medici.* Hamish Hamilton, 1984.

Foster, Philip. *A Study of Lorenzo de' Medici's Villa at Poggio a Caiano.* 2 vols. Garland, 1978.

Roover, Raymond de. *The Rise and Decline of the Medici Bank (1397–1494).* Harvard University Press, 1963.

Klemens von Metternich

(1773–1859)

Austrian politician and diplomat, who suppressed nationalistic and democratic trends in Central Europe but was also the architect of a diplomatic system which kept Europe at peace for a century.

"I have come into the world either too soon or too late. I am spending my life propping up moldering buildings. I should have been born in 1900 and had the twentieth century before me."

KLEMENS VON METTERNICH

Today, more than 100 years after his death, Prince Klemens von Metternich remains a controversial figure. Many late 19th-century Europeans detested him as a foe of freedom and an obstructionist who tried to prevent the unification of the powerful nations of Germany and Italy. Yet Europeans in the late 20th century, recovering from the disasters of World War I and II, tend to see him as a perceptive visionary whose diplomatic ideas kept Europe at peace between 1815 and 1914. In this time period, Europe became the dominant economic and military power in the world. By the mid-20th century, even the future American secretary of state, Henry Kissinger, was praising Metternich's diplomacy.

The French Revolution of 1789 and its consequences were referred to by Metternich as the "hateful time." Although much of the French nobility were executed or fled the country, the French monarch **Louis XVI** was allowed to retain his throne as a limited "constitutional" monarch until 1793. Increasingly convinced that the king was conspiring to import a mercenary army to gain back his full power, the revolutionary government decided in 1794 to execute the king and his family.

Pronunciation: MET–er–nik. Born in Koblenz, Germany, on May 15, 1773; died in 1859; son of a count of the Holy Roman Empire and an Austrian countess; married: Eleonore von Kaunitz, 1795 (died 1825); married: Antoinette von Leykam, 1826 (died 1829); married: Melanie Zichy-Ferraris, 1831 (died 1854); children: (first marriage) three sons and four daughters; (second marriage) one son; (third marriage) three sons and one daughter.

Contributed by Niles Holt, Professor of History, Illinois State University, Normal-Bloomington, Illinois

1789	French Revolution began
1793	Louis XVI removed from throne by revolutionary government; executed the following year
1794–95	Reign of Terror in France
1804	Napoleon crowned emperor
1804–07	Napoleon's armies defeated Spain, Prussia, and Austria
1806	Metternich appointed ambassador to France
1812	French invasion of Russia failed
1813	Second defeat of Napoleon at Leipzig by armies of Britain, Prussia, Austria, and Russia
1814	Napoleon escaped from imprisonment on island of Elbe
1815	Napoleon defeated a second time at Waterloo, Belgium
1815–48	The "Age of Metternich"
1830	French monarchy, restored by the Congress, was deposed in "July Revolution"
1848	Revolutions throughout Europe

A period of bloody chaos, named the "Reign of Terror," followed.

As order was slowly restored, one of the army's generals, **Napoleon Bonaparte,** convinced many French citizens that he could both save the Revolution and restore order. In 1804, following a national referendum, Napoleon was crowned emperor of France. The Revolution had destroyed one monarchy; now it had created another.

Yet the rulers of the other great powers of Europe, all monarchs, did not recognize this "elected emperor" as a true monarch. From the first years of the Revolution, the other great powers had plotted to invade France and restore the family of Louis XVI. All failed, but the continuing attacks on revolutionary France gave Napoleon a justification to invade much of the rest of Europe. Between 1804 and 1807, he defeated Spain, Austria, and Prussia (a large state in northern Germany); he also pressured Russian tsar **Alexander I** into signing a nonaggression treaty. Napoleon portrayed such military campaigns as purely defensive—necessary to protect the French Revolution.

Metternich's family was directly affected by both the Revolution and the fighting. His father, a count who held hereditary lands in western Germany near France, was main minister in the Netherlands—which at that time was an Austrian possession. Metternich's childhood in the western German city of Koblenz, a quiet town of about 12,000, brought him into contact with French culture. His mother saw that he was fluent in both German and French; as an adult, he was often happier expressing himself in French.

After an early education by a series of private tutors, Metternich chose to attend the university at Strasbourg, a city which at various times has been part of either France or Germany. Arriving there a year before the French Revolution began, he quickly witnessed one side effect of the coming turmoil; when a mob of Strasbourg citizens attacked the city hall, a repelled Metternich described it as a "drunken mob which considers itself to be the people."

Transferring his university studies to the German city of Mainz, he met members of the French nobility fleeing the Revolution who insisted that the insurrection would quickly fail, and he believed them. But when advancing French armies destroyed much of their property and occupied their lands, Metternich and his family were forced to flee to the Austrian capital city of Vienna. He came to view revolutionaries as tyrants who used the word freedom to justify violence. He wrote that: "The word freedom has for me never had the character of a point of a departure, but a goal…. Order alone can produce freedom. Without order, the appeal to freedom will always in practice lead to tyranny."

Appointed Ambassador to France

Once Metternich was back in Vienna, his career as a statesman and politician advanced rapidly. His marriage in 1795 to Eleonore von Kaunitz, granddaughter of the Austrian state chancellor, gave him access to the highest social and political circles in the Austrian Empire. His wife's contacts and knowledge were important for an ambitious man who had never before lived in Austria's capital city. After serving as Austrian ambassador to Berlin and Dresden, Metternich was appointed ambassador to France in 1806.

In France when Metternich had the opportunity to study Napoleon, whom he termed "the conqueror of the world," he was not overawed; what he saw was a short, squat figure with a "negligent" appearance. In April of 1809, he appealed to the French emperor's vanity (and cemented a temporary French-Austrian alliance) by marrying Napoleon to Marie Louise, daughter of the Austrian emperor Francis I.

While in Paris, the tall, handsome, sociable, and poised Metternich began to acquire his life-long reputation as a man who had "success with the ladies." But diplomatic success did not come as easily. He sent such optimistic reports back to Vienna—portraying a vulnerable Napoleon who was in danger of being overthrown by a resurgent revolutionary movement in France—that the Austrian government went to war against France and lost. Yet when Metternich gained favorable peace terms from Napoleon, he was rewarded by being appointed the Austrian minister of foreign affairs in October 1809. In 1813, he was given the hereditary title of prince.

Metternich was biding his time, preserving "Austria's freedom of action" while accommodating "ourselves to the victor ... extend(ing) our existence until the day of our deliverance." He almost waited too long. When Napoleon's armies invaded Russia in 1812, Metternich ignored calls for help from Tsar Alexander I. But by late 1812, the French army was not only in retreat, pounded by a severe Russian winter, but was being pursued by the Russian army into Germany.

Belatedly, Metternich involved Austria in the struggle against Napoleon, and in 1813 Napoleon was defeated at Leipzig, Germany, by the armies of Britain, Austria, Prussia, and Russia. After Napoleon escaped from imprisonment on the island of Elbe in the Mediterranean Sea, he rallied the French army for a second time but was defeated in 1815 near Waterloo, Belgium.

The year 1815 saw Metternich at the peak of his power and popularity in Austria. In 1810, Napoleon had been master of much of Europe, and Austria had been a virtual puppet of French foreign policy; five years later, Metternich had become a key leader in the coalition of countries which defeated the French emperor twice. Now the victors held the fate of Europe in their hands.

When the victorious countries agreed to hold a diplomatic conference at Vienna (the Congress of Vienna), Metternich saw it as a personal triumph. He believed that since Austria was at the center of the European Continent, it was the logical place to "lay the foundations for a new European order." "I have," he wrote, "for a long time regarded Europe (rather than just Austria) as my homeland."

Metternich Promotes "Concert of Europe"

At the congress, Metternich's mastery of diplomatic maneuvering earned him the title of "the coachman of Europe." More than any other single leader, he seemed to determine the future direction of the Continent. One observer described him as "

not a genius but a great talent; cold, calm, imperturbable, and a supreme calculator." Metternich's main goal at the congress was to promote the idea of the "Concert of Europe": if all the great powers acted together or in "concert," they would be able to prevent the outbreak of any large European war like the Napoleonic Wars. They might also be able to see that "the foundations of a lasting peace are secured as much as possible."

Some rulers, such as Tsar Alexander, wanted the congress to create an international "police system" to prevent future revolutions and block the emergence of new Napoleons. Metternich sympathized with this aim, but he also wanted to discourage any Russian interest in expanding into Europe. He also was determined to frustrate Austria's main rival in Germany, Prussia.

Together with the British representative, Castlereagh, Metternich successfully worked to create a permanent alliance among the victors, envisioning grouped power that would "balance out" the ambitious or aggressive actions of any one country on the Continent. Although the Quadruple Alliance halted only a few revolutions, and Metternich was disappointed when Britain left the alliance in 1822, the "balance of power" system remained in place throughout the rest of the century. No overall European war on the scale of the Napoleonic Wars occurred until the outbreak of World War I in 1914. So influential was Metternich's diplomacy that the era from 1815 to 1848 is often referred to as the "Age of Metternich."

After 1815, Metternich devoted increasing amounts of his time to Austria's severe internal problems. The Austrian Empire was a conglomeration of 11 nationalities which had been forced under the rule of the Habsburg family by military conquests in the 17th century. The French Revolution had proved to be a threat to the multinational Habsburg Empire, since it fanned the nationalism of some groups in the Empire, such as the Hungarians. Metternich saw nationalism and liberalism as serious threats to the survival of the Austrian Empire and tried to suppress both. At the Congress of Vienna, he also worked to create confederations in both Germany (where he succeeded) and Italy (where he failed). In Metternich's time, Italy and Germany were what he called "geographic expressions"—divided into many individual governments with no national central government. Italy had more than ten governments. Until Napoleon's invasion of Germany, there were more than 300 political divisions in that country, each with its own petty monarch; the Congress of Vienna reduced this to 35, of which the two largest and most powerful were Austria and Prussia.

Metternich would have preferred a Germany united under Austrian leadership. With typical self-confidence, he worked to convince the Austrian emperor (Francis II) to allow himself to be made ruler over all of Germany. "The emperor always does what I want," he predicted, "but likewise, I say what only he should do." When the emperor rejected the idea and a loose confederation of all the German states was created instead, Metternich realized that the way was opened for the other powerful German state, Prussia, to unite Germany (which it eventually did, in 1870).

Liberalism—a 19th-century middle-class movement to weaken monarchies and create parliaments or legislatures—also threatened the Austrian monarchy. Metternich saw liberalism as a child of the French Revolution of 1789. Innately suspicious of new political systems or ideas, Metternich proudly said that "everything changes but me." He added that, "I am not one of those who think that the movement is the purpose of life."

Between 1815 and 1820, Metternich watched suspiciously as liberal revolutions weakened monarchs in western Germany. When secret student fraternities at German universities (the *Burschenschaften*) staged patriotic demonstrations, he charged that the demonstrators were really promoting liberal goals. Secret societies were "the gangrene of society," he proclaimed; "as a device for disrupting the peace, fanaticism is one of the oldest things in the world."

He Becomes Symbol of Repression

After a politically conservative German playwright was assassinated by a student in 1819, Metternich convinced Prussia that the two largest German states should intervene. "With God's help," he declared, "I hope to defeat the German revolutionaries as I defeated the conqueror of the world." Through the Carlsbad Decrees of 1819, Austria and Prussia forced the other German states to institute censorship of books, pamphlets, and newspapers; to allow a Central Commission and police spies to identify and hunt "subversives"; and to restrict student societies and professors in universities. For many in Germany, Metternich became a hated symbol of reaction and repression.

What Metternich feared most was that the liberal and national ideas would tear apart the multinational Habsburg Empire, causing each nationality under Habsburg rule to go its own way and establish its own separate government. In the 18th century, the Austrian emperor **Joseph II** had decided that the way to unify the Empire was to centralize the administrative part of the government and standardize the law. Metternich disagreed, believing that the best way to discourage independence movements was to allow each section of the Empire to have its own distinctive rules and laws.

Yet Metternich's ideas regarding Austria were rejected. Although he was appointed Austrian state chancellor in 1821, his influence was restricted to foreign affairs by Count Kolowrat, the minister of state, who had the ear of the new emperor, the mentally retarded Ferdinand. If it were not for Metternich's skills in diplomacy, his career would have been regarded as a virtual failure. At times, he himself thought that way. When word arrived that the French monarchy (which had been restored by the Congress of Vienna) had fallen victim to another revolution in 1830, Metternich collapsed at his desk, exclaiming, "My life's work is destroyed!"

When ultimately unsuccessful revolutions broke out in the Austrian Empire in 1848, Metternich, the "last great master of the principle of balance," became the target of angry mobs. Forced to resign, he went into exile in England before returning to Vienna in 1858. He died there a year later.

Metternich believed he had unfairly become a symbol of reaction and oppression. His real aim, he said, was to avoid the chaos that he believed would follow in the wake of the major political changes demanded by European revolutionaries. "Old Europe is at the beginning of the end," he proclaimed. "New Europe, however, has not as yet even begun its existence, and between the end and the beginning there will be chaos…. In a hundred years, historians will judge me quite differently than do all those who pass judgment on me today."

SOURCES:

von Metternich, Klemens. *Memoirs of Prince Metternich, 1773–1815.* Edited by Prince Richard Metternich. Translated by Mrs. Alexander Napier. Scribner, 1880.

Milne, Andrew. *Metternich.* Rowman & Littlefield, 1975.

Palmer, Alan. *Metternich.* Harper, 1972.

de Sauvigny, G. B. *Metternich and His Times.* Darton, Longman, and Todd, 1962.

FURTHER READING:

Kissinger, Henry A. *A World Restored: Metternich, Castlereagh, and the Problems of Peace, 1812–1822.* Houghton, 1957.

Kraehe, E. E., ed. *The Metternich Controversy.* Krieger Publishing, 1977.

May, Arthur J. *The Age of Metternich, 1814–1848.* H. Holt, 1933.

Schroeder, Paul W. *Metternich's Diplomacy at Its Zenith, 1820–1823.* University of Texas Press, 1962.

Schwarz, H. F. *Metternich, the Coachman of Europe: Statesman or Evil Genius?* Heath, 1962.

HISTORIC WORLD LEADERS

Count Mirabeau

(1749–1791)

French politician and orator, who was a powerful force in the National Assembly during the first two years of the French Revolution, fighting for the establishment of a constitutional monarchy.

"It was Bonaparte who became the instrument of Mirabeau's project, a king of the Revolution. But the price to be paid was more than Mirabeau would have stood for: liberty."

FRANÇOIS FURET

Mirabeau lived a storybook life in a tumultuous age when storybook lives were not rare. From his conception after the freak death of his father's firstborn son, through his mother's tormenting pregnancy and his deformed deliverance, through a near-fatal childhood illness, through a scandalous youth punctuated with prison terms and public trials, Mirabeau's private life was always "dancing with death." Fighting crushing personal handicaps and obstacles, Mirabeau was to be a bridge between the aristocracy and the French people and a bridge between the legislature and the king of France, but his premature death doomed his project to make the king of France, for the sake of stability, also the king of the Revolution. Mirabeau's splendid funeral on April 4, 1791, and the tearing of his body from the grave during the Reign of Terror may indicate that his cause was correct. No one controlled the Revolution until **Napoleon Bonaparte** years later.

Our story must begin with Mirabeau's father, Victor Riqueti, Marquis de Mirabeau (1715–89), who went to extraordinary lengths to mold his sons into the Mirabeau tradition. It is ironic that Mirabeau had the talent but not the

Name variations: Comte de Mirabeau, M. Honoré, "The Tribune of the People," "Hurricane Mirabeau." Pronunciation: Mira-BO; (French) MEE-ra-bo. Born Gabriel-Honoré Riqueti on March 9, 1749; died on April 2, 1791; son of Victor Riqueti, Marquis Mirabeau, and Marie-Geneviève de Vassan; his younger brother André-Boniface-Louis Riqueti, vicomte de Mirabeau, was also in the legislature and was called "Mirabeau-Tonneau" (Barrel Mirabeau) [many indexes confuse the three Mirabeaus]; married: Marie-Marguerite-Émile de Covet de Marignane, June 23, 1772; children: (illegitimate) Sophie-Gabrielle (daughter of Sophie [Marie-Thérèse-Richard de Ruffy], Marquise de Monnier; (adopted) Lucas de Montigny.

Contributed by Frederic M. Crawford, Jr., Professor of History, Middle Tennessee State University, Murfreesboro, Tennessee

1749	Born disfigured and crippled
1753	Began studies with the lawyer Poisson
1766–69	Joined the regiment of Berry-Cavalerie; promoted to second lieutenant; quarreled with commanding officer; imprisoned; served in Corsican campaign
1771	Presented to the Court at Versailles
1772	Negotiated settlement in Provence; defended exiled members of the Law Court of Provence
1774	Imprisoned; Louis XV died; Louis XVI crowned
1775	Published *Essay on Despotist;* fled to Holland; tried in absentia, executed in effigy
1777–80	Arrested in Amsterdam; imprisoned at Vincennes
1784	Lived in England
1786	Mission to Berlin; wrote *Letters on the Administration of M. Necker;* founding member of the *Amis des Noirs* (Friends of Blacks)
1789	Elected deputy to *États généraux* (Estates General); presented a draft of "Declaration of the Rights of Man"; defended the royal veto
1790	Speech to Jacobin Club denouncing slave trade; secret minister to the King
1791	Elected president of the National Assembly; died and was buried at the Pantheon
1793	Corpse snatched from the Pantheon by a mob and thrown on a public dump

willingness to be "a Mirabeau," while his younger brother had the willingness but not opportunity. It is also ironic that these two brothers, opposite in personality and political persuasion, would defend each other during the Revolution.

Mirabeau's father inherited an active mind, a flair for writing, illustrious ancestors, and magnificent feudal property: the Estate of Mirabeau in Provence, the sunny south of France, with a long history of independence dating back to Roman times. Victor Riqueti loved the family property and the life of the well born. His studies were easy for him, and he became more interested in the theories of agriculture, especially those of the Physiocrats ("lovers of the land") than in the details of managing feudal property. In line with family tradition, he entered military service, served without incident, and inherited the marquisate in 1740 at age 25. He then chose to begin a search for a wife who would bring him children and, perhaps someday, an inheritance from her side of the family. In 1743, he married the 16-year-old Marie-Geneviève de Vassan in defiance of evidence, notes Oliver Welch, that "his prospective father-in-law was detestable and his future mother-in-law scarcely sane, and he should not have been surprised that his wife turned out to be slatternly, moody, malicious, and indiscreet." Marquis Mirabeau never realized any financial advantage from the marriage; several lawsuits were costly; and the emotional cost of constant quarrels was incalculable and surely marked their children (in a 1771 quarrel, she discharged a pistol at her husband). Yet she gave the marquis six children and left him to a housekeeper-mistress-friend, Mme de Pailly, in 1762, after just under 20 years of marriage. The three daughters had been sent to a convent, the two surviving sons to school, and in 1767, the marquis's brother Jean-Antoine de Riqueti arrived at the Estates to add stability to the family throughout the Revolution. All these affairs in the young Mirabeau's first 18 years had to mark him as surely as his childhood smallpox, along with his father's continued attempt to manage him until death.

Father's Writing Influences Mirabeau

His father's writing success also influenced Mirabeau. In 1756, the marquis published *Note on the Usefulness of Provincial Estates to the Royal Authority* which praised the type of legislature his son would seek to create in 1789. His *Friend of Mankind or Treatise on Population* (1756) praising agriculture made him famous and probably reinforced his son's preference for the countryside. The marquis's best work, *Theory of Taxation,* was published in 1760. This work attacked financiers and advised the king that his wealth resided in his 20 million subjects and their work on the land. If his subjects were "looted" by tax agents, the marquis warned, the king would become impotent. Since that is exactly what would happen in 1789, it is fitting that the marquis's son would be there to save the king and the royal authority.

Forty years earlier, the wildest novelist could not have guessed such an ending when Mirabeau was born—the huge head, the two teeth, the malformed tongue, and the misshapen foot. This tragedy was intensified three years later when smallpox struck. Its ravages were probably worsened by the nursing of his mother, who bandaged his face. All his life someone would remark that his was the worst case they had ever seen. The scars probably intensified his emotions and affected his career, if not his love life. Reportedly, Queen

Marie Antoinette at first refused to see him because she had heard he was so ugly. When they did meet (July 3, 1790), they discovered a similarity of ideas.

As young Mirabeau grew, though he pleased his father in his eagerness to learn, he also came to resemble the Vassan side of the family. The birth of two normal children, a girl and a boy, who resembled the Mirabeau side of the family, worsened the situation. Nevertheless, the marquis, who bravely pursued his wife's fortune to the last unsuccessful lawsuit, devoted himself to saving his son and heir. Finding an excellent tutor, in 1746 he sent his son to Paris for three years of study with the famed Abbé Choquard, noted for his discipline as well as his intellect; then in 1767, he found the young Mirabeau a position in the regiment of Marquis de Lambert, a Physiocratic friend. A servant named Grévin was dispatched not only to meet Mirabeau's needs but also to report on his master's behavior. Grévin had much to report. While Mirabeau did well in the military, he argued with de Lambert, spent time in the regimental prison, piled up a huge debt at the card table, became involved with a town girl, and fled to Paris. A compromise was finally reached. Mirabeau came to realize the seriousness of the situation—desertion is deadly serious. Perhaps out of friendship with the marquis, perhaps *noblesse oblige*, de Lambert was surprisingly accommodating. When a royal sealed order (the infamous, tyrannical lettre de cachet) was obtained, Mirabeau went into protective custody on the island of Re near La Rochelle. There, Mirabeau made friends with the commanding officer and after six months gained permission to join a mixed expeditionary force, the Legion of Lorraine, soon to be sent to put down insurrection in Corsica. He spent his first day of freedom in La Rochelle by fighting a duel and in Grévin's words, "swearing and fighting and giving vent to such wickedness as you never saw." But Mirabeau acquitted himself well in military action in 1769 and was praised by his superiors.

Returning home in 1770 at the age of 21, he became active in all the details of maintaining feudal property and living the life of a nobleman. Uncharacteristically for his class, he involved himself with the lives of local people, but he also threw himself into the traditional aristocratic pursuit—a suitable marriage. The best "catch" in Provence at that time was the 19-year-old daughter of a Marquis, Marie-Marguerite-Émilie de Covet de Marignane. Emilie, as she was called, was being raised by a watchful grandmother and was half-promised to one of three suitors. How Mirabeau managed to win over the grandmother and Emilie

was the source of many rumors, but Mirabeau and Emilie were married June 23, 1772. Though his parents did not attend the wedding, Mirabeau obtained a reasonable financial settlement from his father and father-in-law. Mirabeau's stormy youth had ended in calm.

His Liaison with Sophie

When the financial settlement proved insufficient, Mirabeau, faced with bankruptcy, was jailed under another lettre de cachet. Although Mirabeau was furious over another confinement, he had enough privileges to read and write extensively and to meet and to fall in love with a married lady, the Sophie his letters would make famous, Thérèse-Richard-Sophie de Ruffy, marquise de Monnier. In 1771, 19-year-old Sophie's wealthy father, a royal official at Dijon, had married her off to the 65-year-old, recently widowed marquis de Monnier. In May 1776, when Mirabeau escaped from prison and fled to the Netherlands with his lady; her husband filed charges. Tried in absentia, Mirabeau was given the death sentence and executed in effigy. Mirabeau and Sophie were happy in Holland, but in May 1777, they were arrested, and Mirabeau was sent to the famous prison at Vincennes. Sophie was two months pregnant; a daughter Sophie-Gabrielle was born at the beginning of 1778 but would die just before her father was released from Vincennes, December 13, 1780.

Mirabeau's most famous works were written in the 1770s. *Essay on Despotism*, which was published in London in 1774, eloquently urged representative government but with a strong executive in the person of the monarch and opposed an upper chamber of aristocrats as in the English system. *Of Lettres de Cachet and of State Prisons*, written at Vincennes and published in 1782, was a more technical work, ranging over French constitutional history and developing the theme that personal liberty is the one liberty essential to all other liberties—not even national security could be invoked to violate it. This work came to be admired in England and reinforced the opinion in France that the monarchy needed restraint.

While complaining that his supply of paper was rationed, Mirabeau wrote many other works in prison: a French grammar and a classical mythology for Sophie (who had not had much education); a treatise on the new inoculation for smallpox; translations of Tacitus, Ovid, Boccaccio, and *The Iliad*; and literature such as *My Confession* and *The Education of Laura* which he hoped might make money and which critics have termed "licentious" or "pornographic." The variety of Mirabeau's work should have qualified him for recognition as a philosophe, but the philosophes had no admissions policy and no admissions committee. Also, with the deaths of Voltaire and Rousseau in 1778, the philosophic movement was fading. Mirabeau's letters in prison reveal a passionate and ambitious person who, although hostile to the church, had confidence in reason, law, and civic virtue.

Back home in Provence, Mirabeau found his vocation, or at least his greatest talent, serving as his own attorney in public law court cases. Both cases were widely publicized. In 1782, he defended himself against the government and won. The death sentence was nullified. In 1583, he lost suits brought by his wife's family in Aix-en-Provence but won the sympathies of the people who crowded the court room. Six years later, he would be elected by enormous margins in two precincts in Provence to the *États généraux* (Estates General) as a deputy of the Third Estate (Commons).

Then Mirabeau took a mistress, Henrietta-Amélie de Nehra. They traveled to England and he adopted her son, Lucas dd Montigly, who would later edit Mirabeau's papers. Mirabeau found faults with the English system. "The greatness of England," he wrote, "must lay in her civil liberties because there is no real political freedom." Americans might have agreed, but Englishmen and French visitors were shocked and offended. Mirabeau returned to Paris in March 1785 where he sought to reduce his debts by writing pamphlets for speculators on the Paris Bourse or Stock Exchange. His clients included famous persons such as Étienne Claviere, later a finance minister in the Revolution; Du Pont de Nemours, later chairman of the finance committee of the National Assembly; and Talleyrand. Mirabeau's pamphlets antagonized many powerful people including Jacques Necker.

Talleyrand helped Mirabeau obtain a paid semiofficial mission to Berlin where he wrote *The Prussian Monarchy under Frederick the Great* (1788). A serious work of history, Mirabeau noticed signs of decline in Berlin which contemporaries, basking in the glory of **Frederick II**, king of Prussia (1740–86), had not. In Berlin, Mirabeau frequented a Jewish salon, became a friend of Moses Mendelssohn, and published *On Moses Mendelssohn and Political Reform of the Jews;* he would later work in the National Assembly for the emancipation of Jews. Around this time, Mirabeau also became a founding member of "The Friends of Blacks." Though never a large organization, the Revolution would abolish slavery. Mirabeau also published the scandalous *Secret History of the Court of Berlin* (1788), in which he revealed too many secrets, most of them more or less true. So the one diplomatic mission in his career failed.

Mirabeau Named to Assemble of Notables

Mirabeau sought appointment as secretary of the Assembly of Notables, a blue-ribbon panel of 144 personages called by Louis XVI at the request of his finance minister Calonne to endorse the king's package of reforms, including a tax on the nobility. But the court refused Mirabeau, though he was appointed to the Assembly of Notables. The Assembly of Notables refused to endorse any of the reforms, and finance minister Calonne was dismissed. When a new finance minister drew up a series of edicts similar to Calonne's, Louis XVI signed and sent them to the law court. The law court, however, refused to register them on the grounds that by taxing privileged classes the French constitution was violated. The edicts, it declared, would have to be approved by the Estates General which represented the three social estates or classes. This was a flimsy and self-serving position because the Estates General had never passed a constitution and because it had not met since 1614. Another finance minister was appointed—Jacques Necker. A commoner and successful banker from Switzerland, he had already served as finance minister (1776–81) and had won acclaim for his public report on finances—the first in French history—in 1781. Necker made arrangements for election by Estate to the Estates General beginning in January 1789. Mirabeau called this "the step of the century—the day when talent will also be a power."

During the spring of 1789, the French nation was absorbed with the elections which included the drafting of petitions called *cahiers* or notebooks of grievances. The participation rate was very high, highest in the Third Estate. Though the petitions reveal a high regard for the king and a high level of expectation of reform, attention was focused on local issues and conditions. Granted that the king had started reforms in 1774 and had invited petitions, it is difficult to call the petitions "revolutionary." Mirabeau won elections in two precincts of the Third Estate overwhelmingly (he could represent only one of them), and he was defeated in a precinct of the Second Estate (Nobility). Leaders of the Third Estate like Mirabeau and Abbé Sieyès, who wrote the famous pamphlet "What is The Third Estate?" realized the problem. The traditional format of the Estates General provided for three votes. Thus, the two privileged classes expected to defeat a new tax on the privileged by a two-to-one vote. So the issue from May 4 through July 23 was the revolution of the three-vote Estates

General into the one-man, one-vote National Assembly. When the deputies were ordered to disperse on June 23, 1789, Mirabeau thundered their response: "Do tell the king that we are here by the will of the people and we will leave only by the points of bayonets!" The Third Estate, with a few crossovers from the nobility (the Second Estate) and good support from the lower clergy in the First Estate, stood firm, but king and court did not give in until the Bastille fell on July 14, 1789. July 14 has been celebrated as Independence Day ever since.

The first action of the new assembly was to draft a bill of rights, stating the kinds of concerns the Americans had added as amendments to their constitution, and then to write their constitution later. It would take them two years. On August 17, Mirabeau presented to the assembly a draft which became "Declaration of the Rights of Man and the Citizen" when enacted August 26, 1789.

Mirabeau lost many battles in the autumn of 1789. He opposed the king's emotional decision to move from Versailles to Paris. He also opposed the Civil Constitution of the Clergy and the issuance of interest bearing bonds (*assignats*) secured by confiscated church property as did Finance Minister Necker. This action may have been the greatest mistake of the National Assembly. In the summer of 1789, the Committee of Thirty—which included Mirabeau, **Lafayette**, Sieyès, and **Robespierre**—had evolved into the *Club Breton*. When the National Assembly moved to Paris in October 1789, club members rented a house on Rue Saint Jacques (Saint James Street) and Mirabeau struggled to make of the club a political party in the English style. Also in the English style, Mirabeau pushed a bill to create a responsible ministry, but on November 7, 1789, the National Assembly adopted a motion prohibiting members from being a minister of the king in spite of Mirabeau's motion that he be excluded from the ministry.

Still, the crown and the assembly needed guidance and Mirabeau's debts were mounting. So Mirabeau began tortuous, top secret negotiations with the court. In March 1790, he met with Mercy-Argenteau and in May 1790, he signed a contract to provide regular reports to the court and to receive an allowance, probably less than he might have received as a non-secret minister. Naturally, Mirabeau saw the allowance as reasonable recompense for services rendered, intending to guide the court into reasonable, workable policies. Naturally, the court saw the payments as buying a servant and buying votes. Though Mirabeau would later be accused of venality, careful reading of his reports show that he only wrote his convictions. Mostly, the court ignored his advice—until it was too late.

The history of the National Assembly through March 28, 1789, can be traced in Mirabeau's speeches. Jean-Sylvain Bailly, the well-known astronomer who had been the presiding officer of the Assembly, said:

> It cannot be denied that Mirabeau was the moving force in The National Assembly…. Whatever may have been his moral character, when he was aroused by some eventuality, his mind became ennobled and refined, and his genius then rose to the heights of courage and virtue.

Mirabeau described himself in his first letter to the king as "the defender of a monarchy limited by law and the apostle of liberty guaranteed by a monarchy." In spite of losing votes on some issues, Mirabeau became president of the Jacobin Club on November 30, 1790, and president of the National Assembly on January 29, 1791, and he was widely praised for his leadership. Then his health failed. His last speech to the assembly was on March 27, 1791. Though the question was a minor one, he was as fierce as ever. Then he took to his bed, wrote his will, arranged his papers, and died April 2, 1791. The assembly unanimously passed a resolution providing for his burial in the new church of Sainte-Geneviève, now to be called the Panthéon, a monument to nation-heros with the inscription over the doors *Aux Grands Hommes La Patrie Reconnaissante*—("To Great Men from their Grateful Country").

The funeral on Monday evening, April 4, 1791, was spectacular—a seven hour, three-mile-long cortege headed by Lafayette with the entire National Assembly, the Jacobin Club, the ministry, and a three-mile line of officials, troops, and ordinary people. What a vote for "The Tribune of the People."

SOURCES:

Aulard, Alphonse. *The French Revolution: A Political History 1789–1804.* Vol I. 4 vols. Russell & Russell, 1965 (first published 1910).

Crawford, Frederic M. "Comte de Mirabeau," in *Great Lives from History, Renaissance to 1900.* Vol. IV. Edited by Frank N. Magill. 5 vols. Salem Press, 1989.

Furet, François. "Mirabeau," in *A Critical Dictionary of the French Revolution.* Edited by François Furet and Mona Ozouf. Translated by Arthur Goldhammer. Belknap Press of Harvard University Press, 1989.

Higgins, Earl L., ed. *The French Revolution As Told By Contemporaries.* Houghton, 1938.

Welch, Oliver J. G. Mirabeau: *A Study of a Democratic Monarchist.* Jonathan Cape, 1951 (reissued by Kennikat Press, 1968).

FURTHER READING:

Chronicle of the French Revolution 1788–1799. London: Chronicle Communications, 1989.

Nezelof, Pierre. *Mirabeau: Lover and Statesman.* Translated by Warren Bradley Wells. London: Robert Hale, 1937.

Schama, Simon. *Citizens: A Chronicle of the French Revolution.* Knopf, 1989.

Helmuth von Moltke

(1800–1891)

Prussian soldier, historian, military genius and theorist, who designed the spectacular victories achieved by Prussia in the so-called wars of unification that resulted in the formation of the German Empire in 1871.

"It is to minds that are investigative rather than creative, that are cool rather than fiery that in times of war we should entrust the welfare of our brothers and children and the honor and security of our fatherland."

CARL VON CLAUSEWITZ

Helmuth von Moltke was born in 1800 into a Mecklenburg noble family more celebrated for its numerous progeny than for its accomplishments, a record that Moltke would forever alter. A failure both as an army officer and as a landlord, his father separated from his mother when his son was a teenager, but by that time Moltke had already been sent away to school.

At the age of 19, Moltke entered the army of nearby Denmark, but three years later transferred to the Prussian cavalry. He spent several years at the War Academy in Berlin, where he showed an aptitude for two lifelong enthusiasms: history and cartography. He studied military history with relish, specializing in the campaigns of **Napoleon Bonaparte** and **Frederick the Great,** forming a belief that a soldier who was not acquainted with the great generals of the past would not easily make his mark on the battlefields of the future. Mapmaking also became a Moltke specialty, and he was soon regarded as an expert, publishing a book on the subject. So exact were his delineations that even as late as World War II Adolf Hitler's generals issued orders based on maps that Moltke had drawn more than 100 years earlier.

Contributed by Lamar Cecil, William R. Kenan, Jr. Professor of History, Washington and Lee University, Lexington, Virginia

Name variatimns: Field Marshal or Baron von Moltke. Pronunciation: HELL-moot fon MOLT-kuh. Born in the grandduchy of Mecklenburg in 1800; died in Berlin in 1891; son of an army officer; married. Descendants: His nephew, Helmuth von Moltke (1848–1916), was chief of the German general staff when World War I began.

In recognition of his talents, Moltke was posted in 1828 to the General Staff of the Prussian army, then a small detachment of well-trained soldiers who occupied a somewhat inferior position within the military establishment: all strategic plans devised by the General Staff could not be communicated directly to the field commanders but instead sent to the minister of war, who in turn transmitted the orders. In 1835, Moltke was sent to Constantinople in order to advise the Ottoman sultan on the reorganization of the Turkish army, a task that consumed the next four years and which provided Moltke a welcome opportunity to indulge his love for travel. He was an accomplished drawer not only of maps but of landscape, and his sketches of ruins and other sights were executed attractively. Moltke also wrote letters of great style and clarity, a reflection of the exactitude with which he phrased his military ideas.

On his return to Berlin in 1839, Moltke rejoined the General Staff, married a woman of English descent, and became a fixture at the Hohenzollern court. In society, Moltke was deferential and courteous, with no trace of flamboyance. He looked, one friend declared, more like a professor of metaphysics than a soldier. Indeed, unlike the typical Prussian officer of his (or any) time, Moltke was a man of wide-ranging culture, an expert in several languages, and a lover of literature and art. Soon ingratiating himself with the royal family, he became an adjutant to the son of Prince Wilhelm, the brother of King Friedrich Wilhelm IV. Prince Wilhelm had a high opinion of Moltke, especially after Moltke took a firm position against the revolutionary movement of 1848 that led the prince to flee to England. (Similar to the revolution in France, Prussian liberals wanted to limit the power of the monarchy.) Moltke himself was determined to emigrate to Australia if the insurrection was not defeated, and he was happy to contribute to the downfall of the revolution in the fall of 1848.

Moltke Named Chief of General Staff

In 1857, King Friedrich Wilhelm IV suffered a stroke, and a regency was created under his brother Prince Wilhelm. Among the regent's first acts was to appoint Moltke chief of the General Staff. Four years later, when Prince Wilhelm succeeded his brother on the throne as King Wilhelm I, Moltke's position in military affairs became unassailable. In personality, Moltke was able to capitalize on his formal powers, for he had an agreeable manner, was personally fearless, and generous in praise when he felt it had been merited. Modest in demeanor and in his manner of life, Moltke cared little for military glory, but he was obdurate when convinced that he was right. He was also taciturn to a fault, often referred to by his officers as "the great silent one."

As chief of the General Staff, Moltke worked arduously and successfully to modernize the Prussian army and to prepare it for the wars of the future that he felt both inevitable and desirable. His first task was to see to it that the General Staff became the primary instance of military power, responsible for giving orders directly to army commanders. With the support of Wilhelm I, Moltke gradually obtained this authority, one which he exercised rigidly.

He also reorganized the Prussian army's educational system, encouraging the use of complicated war games and laying out the rules for field maneuvers. This would ensure that in time of war his army would fight effectively, but to do so would also require mobility. That meant railroads. Moltke was one of the first Germans to recognize the importance of railroads, not only for military but also for civil purposes. In 1841, at a time when Germany was only beginning the construction of a rail network, Moltke had bought stock and had become a director of the Berlin-Hamburg Railway Company; from that moment on, he stressed continually the decisive importance of railway transportation for military mobilization.

Many of Moltke's tactical ideas were derived from the teachings of the great Prussian military theoretician of the early 19th century, Carl von Clausewitz. Clausewitz's treatises were heavy with abstractions, for which Moltke had little use, but Moltke was entirely in agreement that the art of war was to think offensively rather than defensively. Moltke disliked fortresses and sieges, insisting on movement and attack when least expected. Detachments might have their separate leaders, but a nation's military forces had to have a single, acknowledged commander. "March divided, but attack together" was his motto. There was one respect in which Moltke, however, departed from Clausewitz's teaching. This was in Moltke's insistence that although in peacetime the civilian government might hold the reins of power, when war broke out generals and not statesmen were to have the upper hand. "For the conduct of war," he wrote, "military considerations are preponderant."

It was this viewpoint, one to which Moltke stubbornly adhered, that brought him into great difficulties. In 1862, not long after Moltke's appointment as chief of the General Staff, King Wilhelm I appointed the diplomat **Otto von Bismarck** to be minister-president of Prussia. Bismarck was quite as obstinate as Moltke and far more Caesarian, insistent on having his way and determined to bring to ruin anyone who opposed him. Like Moltke, Bismarck believed that, in the lives of nations and peoples, war was inevitable and indeed desirable. Only the strong survived, which meant that as a statesmen he felt compelled to seek expansion for Prussia, a move which only a victorious Prussian army could achieve.

In 1864, in an attempt to unify Germany, Bismarck brought about his first war, a swift campaign against Denmark, in order to obtain the two rich duchies of Schleswig and Holstein. Moltke designed the operational plan and participated in the action, being largely responsible for the major victory at Alsen that led to the capitulation of the Danes. Wilhelm I's admiration for Moltke was now boundless, and he authorized the completion of Moltke's longstanding desire to have the chief of the General Staff be the ultimate authority (save only for the king himself) in Prussian military affairs.

Bismarck, Moltke Disagree on Tactics

In 1866, Bismarck began his second war, this time against Austria. The army again used an operational plan designed by Moltke, one that quickly resulted in a defeat by the Austrian coalition at Königgrätz in Bohemia. At this juncture, Moltke called for pursuing the disarrayed Austrians right into the capital at Vienna, there administering to them a punitive peace. Bismarck, for diplomatic reasons, was opposed, for he wished to be lenient to the Austrians in order to have their neutrality in a future war with France that was already part of his planning. It was on this issue that Moltke and Bismarck had the first of their celebrated quarrels, with Bismarck berating the general as a "hard-headed General Staff creature who doesn't understand anything about politics." Having more influence with Wilhelm I than Moltke, Bismarck managed to have his way, and the Austrians were allowed to make an orderly retreat to Vienna, later signing the generous peace treaty offered by the victorious Bismarck.

Bismarck now concentrated upon his final war, one directed against the Emperor **Napoleon III** of France, who was a vehement opponent of a unified Germany. Unless France could be overcome, the German Empire could not come into existence. In 1870, by the trickery of a distorted telegram (the Ems dispatch), Bismarck provoked the French into declaring the Franco-Prussian War, but the Austrians, thanks to the conciliation with which they had been treated by Bismarck, did not join the French. Once again Moltke's armies, moving with astounding speed thanks to the extensive network of railroad lines long since laid down for strategic purposes, quickly encircled most of France, defeating and taking prisoner Emperor Napoleon at Sedan and then surrounding the city of Paris.

At this juncture, Bismarck and Moltke had a serious disagreement as to what course of action should be pursued. Moltke was opposed to laying siege and bombarding the French capital, for to him war was an act of movement. Bismarck, to the contrary, insisted that Paris be beleaguered, and once again he persuaded the Prussian king to agree. The city was subjected to siege, and the French eventually capitulated, but it was Bismarck rather than Moltke who spelled out the military as well as the political terms of the peace treaty.

King Wilhelm I, who became German emperor in a ceremony held in the palace of Versailles on January 28, 1871, heaped both Bismarck and Moltke with rewards. Bismarck became a prince, Moltke a count and field marshal and the recipient of a grant of money that he used to purchase an estate in Silesia. The two men, who had disagreed, recognized each other's extraordinary talents and the fact that it might in the future be necessary for Germany to go to war again. For that reason, they forgot the differences that had divided them in the past and established a cordial friend-

Helmuth von Moltke in a quiet moment.

two fronts, both endorsed the idea of preventive war. Bismarck's diplomacy was to forestall the opening of such a conflict until a desirable moment had arrived, while Moltke was to devise the military planning that would deliver victory. Although his views changed in the 1870s and 1880s, Moltke—always careful to weigh both the diplomatic and topographical factors involved—believed that in a German war against a Franco-Russian combination, the initial thrust should be against Russia since the likelihood of a swift victory in the east was greater.

Wilhelm I, for 30 years Moltke's patron, died in March 1888, succeeded by his son Friedrich III, whom Moltke had once served as an adjutant. When Friedrich was fatally stricken with throat cancer and died in June, his son **Wilhelm II,** the last German kaiser, inherited the throne. By this time, Moltke was almost 90, still vigorous in mind but too fragile physically to mount a horse. He had a low opinion of the new 29-year-old kaiser, who failed to consult him, and whom Moltke dismissed as a *"Husarenoffizier."* Less than two months after Wilhelm II's ascension, Moltke resigned. He continued to take an active role in politics, speaking in the Reichstag only a few weeks before his death, which occurred suddenly as he was engaged in a game of whist. He was given a heroic funeral, one appropriate for the man who along with Bismarck had been responsible for the creation of the German Empire.

ship that lasted for almost 20 years. Both Bismarck, now imperial chancellor as well as minister-president of Prussia, and Moltke believed that wars would continue to be fought and that in such an eventuality the new German Empire would be particularly vulnerable because of its geographical position between France and Russia, the two greatest military forces in continental Europe. Increasingly concerned about the likelihood of Germany's someday being embroiled in a war on

SOURCES:

Moltke, Helmuth von. *Gesammelte Schriften und Denkwürdigkeiten.* 8 vols. Berlin, 1891–93. *Briefe,* 2 vols. Leipzig, 1922.

FURTHER READING:

Bucholz, Arden. *Moltke, Schlieffen and Prussian War Planning.* New York, 1991.

Kessel, Eberhard. *Moltke.* Stuttgart, 1957.

Bernard Montgomery

(1887–1976)

Charismatic but controversial English field marshal during World War Two, who defeated the Germans in North Africa, Italy, and Northern Europe, and became a national hero in Great Britain.

"I have never been afraid to say what I believed to be right and to stand firm in that belief. This has often got me into trouble."

BERNARD MONTGOMERY

Bernard Law Montgomery was born into a large, middle-class, Victorian family on November 17, 1887, in St. Mark's Vicarage, Kennington Oval, London. His father—a quiet, thoughtful clergyman—was dominated by his young wife, who gave birth to five children before she was 25. In total, the couple had nine children, of whom Bernard was the fourth. Unable to cope with running such a large household, Bernard's mother—as was common in that era—frequently beat her children, demanding that they be obedient to her will.

Bernard was a stubborn and argumentative boy, and so suffered the majority of his mother's beatings. Not surprisingly, he shifted all his love to his father, whom he came to see as "a saint … a poor dear man" trapped in an unhappy marriage. Montgomery's bitterly unhappy childhood, filled with what in the Victorian era was seen as "healthy discipline," was to leave permanent psychological scars, and perhaps explains some of the less pleasant aspects of his adolescent and adult character. He exhibited a clear tendency to be an arrogant bully. His childhood, however, also taught him to be self-reliant, emotionally hardened, and decisive, traits which would serve him in his later career.

Contributed by John A. Hall, Assistant Professor of History, Albion College, Albion, Michigan

Name variations: Bernard Law Montgomery, 1st Viscount Montgomery of Alamein, popularly known as "Monty." Born on November 17, 1887, in St. Mark's Vicarage, Kennington Oval, London; fourth child of nine born to his clergyman father; married: Betty Carver, July 27, 1927 (died October 19, 1937); children: David.

CHRONOLOGY

1907	Entered the Royal Military College, Sandhurst
1908–13	Stationed in India
1914	World War I began; Montgomery severely wounded; awarded the Distinguished Service Order
1916–18	Served as a staff officer
1939	World War II began
1939–40	Montgomery commanded the 3rd Division during the campaign in France
1942	Appointed to head the 8th Army in North Africa; Battle of El Alamein; Africa Corps defeated in desert war
1943	Germans driven from North Africa; Allied invasion of Sicily and Italy
1944	D-Day landings at Normandy; Montgomery in command of all Allied ground forces; promoted to field marshal; commanded 21st Army Group
1945	Received surrender of German forces in Holland, Denmark and Northwest Germany; VE-Day

In 1889, when Bernard was only two, his father was appointed bishop of Tasmania, an island near Australia, and the family lived there until late in 1901. Upon returning to England, the 14-year-old was sent to St. Paul's School in London. In Tasmania, Montgomery's education had been provided by tutors, and he found himself ill prepared for English school life. Considered an "uncultured Colonial" by his peers, barely able to read or write, Montgomery found that he excelled only in sport. He devoted his energies to rugby and cricket, and within three years he had become school captain in each. Scholastically he was poor, particularly in English, where his teachers described his writing style as "feeble." After three years, he was still considered backward for his age and lazy.

Though his father had hoped that his son would become a clergyman, Montgomery dreamed instead of going into the army. Entrance into the Royal Military College, Sandhurst (the training establishment for British officers) was by competitive examination. With his career at stake, he suddenly began to devote himself to his studies and managed to enter Sandhurst in 1907 ranked 72 out of 170 incoming cadets. At 19, he was older than most of the incoming cadets because he had been held back in school. Nevertheless, he was now embarked upon what was to become one of the most remarkable military careers of the 20th century.

Coming from a large and not particularly prosperous family, Montgomery lacked the financial support most students at Sandhurst took for granted. Unable to afford an active social life, he devoted himself to his studies and sport. Soon attracting the attention of the commandant, he was appointed lance-corporal with certain responsibilities over his peers. This official recognition, along with his prowess on the sports' field, resulted in his becoming one of the student leaders. With his ego boosted, and given a degree of official power, the worst side of his character came to the fore. He organized a gang which even he later admitted was "pretty tough and rowdy" in a series of "battles," terrorizing and intimidating other students. The faculty usually turned a blind eye to such rowdy behavior, but Montgomery went too far when he set fire to the shirt of a cadet he was bullying. His victim, though hospitalized with severe burns, refused to break the cadets' honor code and identify Montgomery as his assailant. Nevertheless, Montgomery's reputation resulted in his being demoted from lance-corporal to gentleman-cadet.

Montgomery Begins Military Career in India

Fearful of destroying his future career, Montgomery turned his attention back to his studies and graduated after 18 months ranked 36th in his class. This was a disappointment. Lacking any sort of financial support from his family, Montgomery had decided to pursue a career in India, where living expenses were cheaper, and where even the poorest junior officer could live on salary alone. Because of these financial considerations, commissions in the Indian Army were highly competitive, and his class placement ensured that he would not get one of the coveted appointments. As a result, he took a commission as a junior officer with the Royal Warwickshire Regiment, a unit which had a reputation as solid but inexpensive, and which was temporarily stationed in India. He joined it at Peshawar on the northwest frontier of India, in December 1908, aged 21.

Until the regiment was recalled to England in 1913, Montgomery's time in India was a period of frustration. He quickly became disillusioned with the complacent attitude of his superiors, the way that they prized drinking and socializing above military knowledge and skills. Military maneuvers were carried out as if they were simply a game. Only one year later, this highly regarded professional British army would be effectively destroyed in the opening campaigns of the First World War.

Montgomery was a 26-year-old full lieutenant when war was declared against Germany in August 1914, and the Royal Warwickshire Regiment was sent to France as part of the British Expeditionary Force. Everyone expected the war to be over by Christmas and the "Butcher of Berlin"—the kaiser—suitably punished for his evil aggression. With his sword newly sharpened, Montgomery soon found himself involved in a series of hard-fought battles where British, French, and German soldiers were slaughtered in a way none had anticipated. Though the German advance was finally halted, by the end of 1914 the prewar British regular army had effectively ceased to exist. The bloodshed which resulted from inept and confused leadership made a lasting impression on Montgomery. During an attack on October 13, 1914, with apparent disregard for his safety, he was shot in both the chest and knee while leading his men but still managed to capture a number of prisoners. Though awarded the Distinguished Service Order, a military decoration second only to the Victoria Cross, he had come to realize that bravery of individual soldiers, or even entire regiments, counted for little in modern war if there was poor leadership and planning.

Upon recovering, Montgomery returned to the western front in France early in 1916 with the rank of brigade-major, in time to witness the catastrophic battle of the Somme. On July 1, 1916, largely as a result of inept planning and an underestimation of the enemy defenses, the British army suffered 60,000 casualties in one day, including 20,000 men killed, mowed down by German machine guns which had been sheltered from the heavy British bombardment. British generals had been so confident of a victory that they had instructed their men to walk, not run, towards the German positimns. Many regiments suffered 90% casualties in just a few minutes. As one survivor remembered:

I could see, away to my left and right, long lines of men. Then I heard the "patter, patter" of machine-guns in the distance. By the time I'd gone ten yards there seemed to be only a few men left around me; by the time I had gone twenty yards, I seemed to be on my own. Then I was hit myself,

Yet the British commanders, lacking any system by which they were informed of what was happening, continued to order regiment after regiment into the attack. Each was slaughtered. Ultimately the battle of the Somme lasted three months, resulting in over 1 million casualties.

Montgomery was sickened by what he saw during that battle, and was profoundly distressed by what he continued to see up until war's end in November 1918, by which time he was a staff officer to a divisional commander:

There was little contact between the generals and the soldiers.... The former lived in comfort, which became greater as the distance of their headquarters behind the lines increased.... [T]he doctrine seemed to me to be that the troops existed for the benefit of the staff. My war experiences led me to believe that the staff must be the servants of the troops.

One aspect which particularly disturbed Montgomery was the lack of reliable information available to generals during a battle, and he devoted much time to developing a system of wireless communication whereby such information could be instantly relayed to the senior officers in the rear who could then more effectively change strategies. Though this system did not work particularly well in 1918 due to the primitive nature of wirelesses, it was to form a cornerstone of military communication during the Second World War.

Montgomery was desperate to be chosen for training at the Staff College, Camberley, which was a necessary step for those aspiring to high command. The students at Aamberley studied military theory, the first time that British officers were exposed to anything other than practical military training. Accepted in 1920, he worked hard, but was considered to be outspoken and intolerant.

Upon graduation, Montgomery was appointed to the thankless position of brigade-major of the 17th Infantry Brigade in Cork, Ireland, where until 1922 he was involved in suppressing the nationalist rebellion led by the Catholic group Sinn Fein. This was, Montgomery admitted:

in many ways ... far worse than the Great War.... A murder campaign in which, in the end, the soldiers became very skillful.... Such a war is thoroughly bad for officers and men; it tends to lower their standards of decency and chivalry.

In January 1926, Montgomery, who had gained a reputation as a hard-working, serious-minded officer, was appointed one of the instructors at the Staff College. His years at Camberley were intensely happy ones. In 1927, at the age of 38, he married Betty Carver, widow of a British officer killed at Gallipoli in World War I. The fol-

General Bernard Montgomery attends his first press conference in the field of France, nine days after the invasion at Normandy in June 1944.

lowing year, his son David was born. For the first time, Montgomery had a happy home life, a world other than books and army manuals. His career continued to progress, however, and in 1930 he was selected to join the committee which would rewrite the manual of infantry training. Ultimately he ignored the recommendations from the rest of the committee and produced a revised and updated manual which was widely considered excellent.

From 1931 until 1938, Montgomery earned a series of promotions and commanded forces in England, India, and Palestine. The death of his wife in 1938 shattered his happy personal life, and he threw himself into his work with even more energy and commitment. As a major general, he was sent in October 1938 to northern Palestine to lead the suppression of an Arab rebellion, and to form the 8th Division with headquarters at Haifa. With the outbreak of the World War, Montgomery barely saw his son again until 1948. Sent to boarding school, David lived during vacations with friends of the family. Though Montgomery later declared that this was "unlucky" for his son, it is clear that there was never any question that his

career and service to the nation should come before the demands of family.

He Commands, Retrains 3rd Division

On August 28, 1939, with Europe perched on the edge of war, Montgomery was appointed to command the 3rd Division in England. A few days later, war was declared between Britain and Germany, and he found himself commanding a division which was ill trained, inadequately equipped, and poorly organized; in short, totally unprepared for modern war. He immediately set about retraining his division, forcing his men to undergo a fierce schedule of physical exercises which allowed him to quickly rid his staff of "weak links." By the time his division was sent to France a few months later, Montgomery had forged a strong bond with his men and turned them into well-trained soldiers. Unfortunately, they remained hopelessly lacking in modern weapons, such as effective antitank guns. In addition, few other divisional commanders were as demanding as Montgomery, and the standard of the British army was poor, particularly when compared to the war machine the Germans had created. British politicians, who for many years had failed to fund the army adequately, hopefully proclaimed in 1939 that, "Our Army is as well if not better equipped than any similar Army." This was nonsense, and Montgomery, though extremely proud of his men, was quite certain that they lacked the equipment necessary to be victorious: "It must be said to our shame," he noted, "that we sent our Army into that most modern war with weapons and equipment which were quite inadequate."

Leading his division in France during the campaign of 1939–40, Montgomery saw the more highly skilled and better equipped German armies, supported by hundreds of tanks and dive-bombers, defeat everything in their path. The 3rd Division fought a number of important rearguard actions to cover the British retreat, and Montgomery constantly visited his troops in the frontline, hearing their problems and gauging their morale. He was determined to become someone they would trust, not some distant and uninformed general like many had been in WWI. The British were forced to retreat to Dunkirk, where a large proportion of them were successfully evacuated from the beaches. Though the "miracle of Dunkirk" saved thousands of men to fight another day, the British army lost the great bulk of its equipment, and the military command realized that the campaign in France had met a resounding defeat.

Following Dunkirk, Montgomery set about reforming the 3rd Division. Though equipment was virtually nonexistent, enough was found to supply Montgomery's men. Once reequipped, the 3rd Division was moved to the southcoast of England to defend against the anticipated German invasion, an invasion which never came. Montgomery was soon appointed the commander of 5th Corps, and on December 1, 1941, was placed in command of the entire South Eastern Army in England. By that time it was evident that the threat of invasion had passed, and Montgomery requested that he be transferred to lead an army in combat.

On August 18, 1942, Montgomery was given command of the 8th Army in North Africa. Upon arrival, he found an army which was demoralized by its defeats at the hands of **Erwin Rommel** and the Africa Corps, and had been driven back to positions at El Alamein, only 60 miles from Alexandria in Egypt. Montgomery set about reinvigorating the men under his command, forcing upon them a policy of extensive physical training. "P.T., P.T., and even more bloody P.T.," was the widely heard complaint. One senior officer described Montgomery at this time as being as "quick as a ferret; and about as likeable," but for the majority of the troops his highly visible, energetic style was a breath of fresh air. "Monty," as his men called him, wearing his distinctive beret with two cap badges, was constantly on the move, meeting everyone under his command, giving hundreds of impromptu speeches, instilling in his troops a sense of pride. At the same time, he established an efficient communication and command structure, weeding out those officers he felt were unsuitable, so that by the time he decided to attack, senior officers to privates knew exactly what was expected of them.

Allies Face Rommel at El Alamein

The Axis and Allied armies faced each other on a 30-mile front at El Alamein, with the sea to the north and an impenetrable natural depression to the south, so it would be impossible to outflank the enemy. Instead, the British would have to attack the German and Italian defensive positions head on, much like WWI. To protect his line, Rommel had built a network of minefields four miles deep, as well as a series of strongpoints and other defensive positions. Montgomery was faced with what appeared an almost impossible task.

With his 8th Army strongly reinforced with fresh regiments and many of America's finest new Sherman tanks, Montgomery set about trying to deceive Rommel as to where he would attack. Hundreds of dummy tanks—fabricated from wood, canvas, and rubber—were moved to the southern sector of the line. Behind these dummy positions, he had his men drag 40-gallon oil drums around in the sand to create a dust cloud as if hundreds of vehicles were moving through the desert. While Rommel moved many of his tanks south to counter the anticipated attack, Montgomery collected his men in the northern sector.

The British attacked on the night of October 23, 1942. Montgomery's plan called for specially-trained sappers ("engineers") to clear lanes through the minefield, allowing British tanks to quickly advance. He hoped for a breakthrough to occur within 24 hours, which would then be exploited by sending in his reserves who would sweep around behind the remaining Axis positions and attack them from the flank and rear. The plan, however, quickly began to collapse. Faced with stubborn resistance from the veteran Africa Corps in the north, the sappers failed to clear the necessary lanes through the mines. The tanks, which were to have broken through, were instead halted by mines and heavy artillery fire, and the reserve divisions found only confusion when they tried to move forward. Heavy fighting continued for another day and night, after which a breakthrough had still not been achieved. Rommel, realizing that he had been deceived by Montgomery, quickly recalled his tanks from the south, and launched a series of counteroffensives. The entire outcome of the battle hung in the balance, and Montgomery was forced to abandon his initial plans. This flexibility to adjust strategy in the light of battlefield conditions was exactly what he had been arguing for more than a decade, a flexibility which few WWI generals had exhibited.

After driving off Rommel's counterattacks, Montgomery ordered his men to attack once again, first in one area then, when German reinforcements were sent there, he would shift the main thrust of the attack elsewhere, constantly probing for a weakness in the Axis line. After days of fierce fighting, Rommel became convinced that Montgomery's main assault would come in the far north. As the German divisions began to concentrate there, Montgomery pulled his reserves further south and launched a large attack against Italian positions. Finally, the British achieved a small breakthrough and threatened to split the German army in the north from the Italian army further south. Rommel was forced to try to halt the British, using his Luftwaffe aircraft which he had carefully preserved. The German planes, led by Stuka dive-bombers, did temporarily stop the advance, but were themselves decimated by British planes of the Desert Air Force. From that point on, the British controlled the skies over North Africa.

After 12 days of extremely hard fighting, during which hundreds of tanks were destroyed and the British suffered over 13,000 casualties, German and Italian defenses began to crumble, and a major breakthrough was finally achieved. As British tanks poured into the desert and swung north threatening to encircle the remnants of the Africa Corps, British infantry supported by artillery began to attack the flanks of German positions. His position hopeless, Rommel began a desperate retreat westward along the coast, constantly harassed by British planes. Abandoned without transport, water, or supplies, the Italians surrendered by the tens of thousands, as did many thousand Germans who were cut off in the far north. Only because heavy rain slowed the British tanks did any of the Africa Corps succeed in escaping.

Montgomery had achieved an overwhelming victory. The Africa Corps, which had appeared to be on the verge of sweeping the British out of North Africa and seizing the Suez Canal, were destroyed. Montgomery's victory encouraged the Allies at a time when the Nazis appeared invincible. As **Winston Churchill** said in a broadcast:

> Rommel's army has been defeated. It has been routed. It has been very largely destroyed as a fighting force. We have victory, a remarkable and deathly victory. A bright gleam has caught the helmets of our soldiers and warmed and cheered all our hearts.

El Alamein secured Montgomery's reputation as an extraordinary leader but did nothing to make him any less outspoken or abrasive. He never tolerated those he saw as inefficient or unprofessional, and as the war progressed he found it difficult to work alongside his American allies. He continued to lead British forces in North Africa until the survivors of Rommel's once-proud army were forced to surrender on May 13, 1943, and he was infuriated by what he interpreted as the patronizing attitude exhibited by some American commanders. Montgomery found in General **George Patton** a man who was equally as conceited, aggressive, stubborn, and strong-willed as himself, and they took an instant dislike to each other.

The defeat of the Germans in North Africa allowed the Allies to gather a huge force there for the invasion of Southern Europe. On September 3, 1943, Montgomery led the 8th Army during the Allied invasion of Sicily. From there the Allies would force their way into Italy, which would become a campaign that would drain much-needed German reserves away from Russia and the defense of France. Soon after the Italian campaign was under way, Montgomery was chosen by General **Dwight Eisenhower** to be the assault leader of all the Allied land troops in the coming Normandy invasion. Though Montgomery was undeniably well qualified, his temperament ill suited him for an appointment necessitating political tact. It seems likely that Eisenhower chose the Englishman in large part so that the invasion would be seen as a truly cooperative Allied venture. By this point, however, Montgomery clearly detested working under anyone's supervision and friction quickly developed between him and Eisenhower. Montgomery made few friends in the American camp, an unfortunate trait in the Allied ground forces commander.

He Commands Land Troops at Normandy

The invasion took place on June 6, 1944, and Montgomery remained in command of Allied ground forces until mid-August. His generalship came under some criticism because of his alleged caution and slowness, though in fact his personal unpopularity among the American high command was probably more significant. When Eisenhower reorganized the command structure in mid-August 1944, he replaced Montgomery as Allied ground forces commander. Promoted to field marshal, Montgomery went back to what he did best; given command of the Canadian and British 21st Army Group, he liberated Belgium and drove across Northern Europe toward Germany.

Montgomery was a supporter of what was known as the "narrow-front" strategy (as compared to a "broad-front" approach), which would have involved one major thrust north across the Rhine and on to Berlin. Not coincidentally, he urged Eisenhower that this decisive, war-winning thrust should be carried out by his own 21st Army Group, and should be supplied by gutting the American armies to the south of many of their tanks, supplies, and trucks. Though far from convinced that Montgomery's approach was the correct one, Eisenhower compromised and gave approval to Montgomery's plan to drop Allied paratroops deep into enemy-held territory in Holland where they would hold bridges over the Rhine River until relieved by quickly advancing ground forces. This would, Montgomery hoped, have opened the way for a rapid advance by his Army Group on Berlin. The airborne drop of "Operation Market-Garden" was successful, but the ground troops were delayed by heavy German defenses and failed to link up with the paratroopers in time, 80% of whom were killed or captured. This disaster further clouded Montgomery's image in the eyes of Eisenhower and other American leaders, though his reputation remained strong in Britain. In December 1944, he was temporarily given command of all Allied troops on the northern side of the "Bulge" during the battle of that name, and his leadership was instrumental in halting the Germans there. On May 4, 1945, Montgomery accepted the surrender of the German armies in Holland, Denmark, and Northwest Germany—over half a million soldiers—a great achievement, but not the symbolic one of taking Berlin that he had hoped for. Nevertheless, the defeat of the Nazis was finally achieved, and his role in that victory was great indeed.

On May 22, he was appointed commander in chief of the British Army of Occupation in Germany and the British member of the Allied Control Commission. In 1946, he was created Viscount Montgomery of Alamein, and later that year was appointed chief of the Imperial General Staff. He remained in the army until his retirement in 1958, a period which saw him appointed Deputy Supreme Allied Commander in Europe with the task of training and equipping NATO forces. After his retirement, he became an active member of the House of Lords. He died in Alton, England, on March 24, 1976. There can be no doubt that Montgomery was a great leader. Though frequently abrasive in tone and intolerant of others, he demanded and got the best from those under his command. He was the greatest British military commander of the Second World War, whose victory at El Alamein inspired and encouraged his nation and helped turn the tide against the Nazis.

SOURCES:

Carver, M. *El Alamein.* 1962.

Churchill, W. *Closing the Ring.* 1951.

Montgomery, B. L. *El Alamein to the River Sangro.* 1948.

————. *The Memoirs of the Field-Marshal the Viscount Montgomery of Alamein, K.G.* 1958.

————. *The Path to Leadership.* 1961.

Moorehead, A. *The March to Tunis: The North African War, 1940–1943.* 1967.

————. *Montgomery: A Biography.* 1967.

Pitt, Barrie, ed. *The Military History of World War II.* 1986.

Thompson, R. W. *Churchill and the Montgomery Myth.* 1967.

————. *Montgomery, the Field Marshal: The Campaign in Northwest Europe, 1944/45.* 1970.

Thomas More

(1478–1535)

Leading English scholar and statesman, who was martyred for opposing his king's determination to detach England from the spiritual authority of the Roman Catholic Church.

Born in 1478 in London; died in 1535; son of Sir John More (a lawyer) and Agnes (Granger) More; married: Jane Colt, 1505; married: Alice Middleton, 1511; children: (first marriage) Margaret, Elizabeth, Cecily, John.

The adult life of Sir Thomas More, and the circumstances of his death, were intimately connected with the English Reformation, a dramatic event which severed England's connection with the papacy in Rome and put the country on the path to becoming a Protestant nation. More's response to this momentous shift was conditioned both by his commitment to Catholicism and his experience and perspective as an eminent lawyer.

The institutions of the law and the Roman Catholic Church had in fact figured prominently in More's life from an early date. His father Sir John More, a barrister and judge, was determined that his son should follow in his legal footsteps. He also nurtured Thomas's religious education by placing him at age 13 in the household of Thomas Morton, archbishop of Canterbury and lord chancellor of England. Quickly recognizing the qualities of intellect and personality in his young ward, Morton predicted that he would become "a marvellous man."

To further his education, More was sent at age 14 to study at Oxford University where his father's stingy allowance permitted him few dis-

"More is that rare figure, an Establishment martyr: a man to whom the world and all its promises were open, who had riches and power to hand, which he could have kept if he had been willing to bend to the wind, and who went to his death without bitterness and with a jest."

ANTHONY KENNY

Contributed by John A. Sainsbury, Associate Professor of History, Brock University, St. Catherines, Ontario, Canada

tractions. According to his own account, however, More acquired his dedication to classical learning after he left the university. While completing his legal training in London's Inns of Court at his father's behest, More established friendships with like-minded scholars and began a close study of ancient Greek. He and his friends were known as "humanists"—a term that implies a love of pagan literature, not for its own sake, but as a way of reinforcing Christian values. When the Dutch priest Erasmus, one of the greatest humanist scholars of the European Renaissance, visited England in 1499, a mutually inspirational friendship with More began which would last until More's death.

While a law student, More seems to have gone through a period of intense religious awakening. An admirer of the austere order of Carthusian monks, whose monastic life he shared, he flirted with the idea of joining the priesthood. According to Erasmus, however, since More "could not overcome his desire for a wife, he decided to be a faithful husband rather than an unfaithful priest." But though he threw himself with relish into the secular world—becoming a successful lawyer as well as a devoted family man—More remained a person of profound religiosity. The hairshirt that he habitually wore was one symbol of his spiritual dedication.

In the first two decades of the 16th century, there were few clouds on More's political and domestic horizons. In 1504, he was elected as a member of Parliament and a year later he married. While resistant to More's efforts to make her a classical scholar, his young wife bore him four children before her death six years later. More was remarried within a month to the widow of a rich merchant. Although in More's ungallant phrase his new wife was "neither a pearl nor a girl," she became a devoted stepmother to his children and helped to maintain the exuberant family atmosphere that More cherished.

The accession of **Henry VIII** to the English throne was at first no impediment to More's happiness and ambition. Indeed, More shared in the outpouring of joy that greeted the arrival of the new monarch. The youthful Henry seemed the embodiment of the Renaissance prince: graceful, courageous, and—most important to More—apparently dedicated to the patronage of humanist learning. As yet there was little sign of the bloated, ulcerous despot that posterity would recall.

More Writes His Two-Part Utopia

Under Henry, More's rise to political and literary eminence proceeded steadily. In 1515, he was sent on a diplomatic mission to Flanders, and it was

CHRONOLOGY

1499	Established friendship with Erasmus
1509	Henry VIII became king of England
1516	*Utopia* published
1517	Martin Luther launched Protestant Reformation
1529	Thomas More became lord chancellor; "Reformation Parliament" convened
1533	Henry married Anne Boleyn
1534	More imprisoned
1534	Parliament declared Henry "Supreme Head of Church of England"
1535	More tried and executed
1935	Canonized by Pope Pius XI

there that he began to write *Utopia*, a book consisting of two parts. The first is a ringing indictment of the social, political, and economic ills that were afflicting Europe and especially England. In a famous passage, More denounced greedy landlords who were throwing people off the land to make way for sheep pasture:

> The nobles and gentlemen, not to mention several saintly abbots, have grown dissatisfied with the income that their predecessors got out of their estates. They're no longer content to lead lazy, comfortable lives, which do no good to society— they must actively do it harm, by enclosing all the land they can for pasture, and leaving none for cultivation. They're even tearing down houses and demolishing whole towns.

Though a loyal son of the Church, More was also unsparing in his attacks on the rapacity and corruption of many in the priesthood.

The second part of *Utopia* portrays an imaginary state, whose inhabitants, by dint of their reason, avoided the kind of ills that befell 16th-century England and constructed a society where people lived in harmony not in conflict. Its keynotes were communal responsibility, religious toleration, and the collective ownership of property. The pursuit of wealth was disdained, while genuine pleasures, such as love of music, were encouraged.

Written in an engagingly humorous style, and widely translated from the original Latin, the book is read with delight to the present day. The central message of the second part, however, remains enigmatic. Although modern socialists have claimed it as an early advocacy of their cause, others interpret it as a celebration of traditional monastic values. More, who was very much a realist, probably had no expectation that the precepts in *Utopia* would be widely imitated. Rather his probable intention was to try and shame European society into mending its ways. Look how much the Utopians have achieved without the benefit of revealed religion, he seems to be saying, while Europe lags so far behind in moral development despite its Christian inheritance.

The publication of *Utopia* secured More's reputation as a leading humanist, but his ascendancy to national political stature was only just beginning. Following further diplomatic missions on behalf of Henry VIII, More was appointed Speaker of the House of Commons in 1524 and later replaced his former patron Cardinal Wolsey as lord chancellor, the highest position in the land beneath the king himself. Ironically, the Protestant Reformation, which would perpetuate religious warfare in Europe and create deep religious and political division in England, served initially to strengthen the bond between More and his royal master. When Thomas More assisted Henry in writing a refutation of the doctrines of **Martin Luther,** the leading European reformer, the endeavor earned Henry the title of "Defender of the Faith" from a grateful pope. More also wrote a number of anti-Protestant tracts on his own behalf in which Luther and other reformers were denounced in vehement, and sometimes crude, polemic. Luther, said More, saw the Catholic Church "through a pair of evil spectacles of ire and envy"; he was prompted by "the itch and tickling of vanity and vainglory." Though himself critical of many church abuses, More was staunch in defense of its central tenets, including the miracle of the Catholic Mass and the central authority of the pope, which the Protestant reformers were rejecting.

More also used his legal position, first as a judge and then as lord chancellor, to counter what he feared was the spread of Protestant "heresy" in England. During his chancellorship, a number of Protestants were executed. Despite his apparent advocacy of religious toleration in *Utopia,* More did not subscribe to a notion of the sanctity of individual religious belief, a position ascribed to him in some biographies and in the popular film about his life "A Man for All Seasons." He lived and died as a partisan in the religious controversies of his time.

Henry's Divorce Leads to More's Execution

Though Henry and More were apparently at one over matters of religion, a wedge was driven between them over an issue which illustrates the adage that profound consequences can ensue from apparently trivial causes. Henry, driven by a potent combination of conscience and lust, was determined to secure a divorce from his wife Catherine of Aragon. He became convinced that he had contravened biblical law in marrying Catherine, the widow of his elder brother Arthur. God's punishment, reasoned Henry, was to render Catherine incapable of producing a male heir to the throne. Henry had also set his eye on Anne Boleyn, a court beauty who was young and presumably fertile. Under normal circumstances the pope, under whose jurisdiction such matters lay, would have readily granted an important European monarch such as Henry the divorce that he craved. But Pope Clement VII was constrained by two circumstances: first, the papacy had sanctioned Henry's marriage in the first place; and second, the pope was the virtual prisoner of the most powerful European ruler of his time, **Charles V,** king of Spain and of much of Europe besides, who was also the doting nephew of Catherine of Aragon. So, despite the best efforts of English diplomacy, the papacy refused to grant Henry a divorce.

It was in this circumstance that Henry initiated the severance of England's links with the Catholic Church. If Rome would not grant him a divorce, then Henry would secure one from a national English Church over which he himself presided. A compliant Parliament, summoned in 1529 and guided by Thomas Cromwell, one of the shrewdest and toughest of Henry's ministers, began the legislative proceedings, which would detach England from Rome's religious authority.

Painful though it was for him, More acquiesced in the early stages of this complex process. But in 1532, as the attack on the Church intensified, More resigned his position as lord chancellor and sought refuge in private life. The pressure on him to bend to the king's will increased, however, when Parliament passed an act declaring the king's marriage to Catherine contrary to God's law and fixed the succession on the future offspring of Anne Boleyn, whom the king had just married. All the king's subjects were required to take an oath subscribing to the content of the act. For More, this was the sticking point. "Unto the oath that there was offered me I could not swear without the jeopardizing of my soul to perpetual damnation," he wrote to his daughter Margaret.

For his refusal, More was imprisoned in the Tower of London while the king and his ministers pondered his fate. Despite moving pleas from his family to take the oath and restore his liberty, he remained steadfast. He was buoyed not only by his faith, but by his belief that by remaining silent he could not be charged with the capital offense of treason. During his imprisonment, he continued to write works of religious piety, maintaining the wit and composure that marked his entire adult life. The grisly execution of some Carthusian monks who, in More's words, went "as cheerfully … to their deaths as bridegrooms to their marriage," only served to bolster his resolve.

After months of grueling interrogation, More was finally brought to trial in July 1535 and, after a piece of perjury by a former protégé, found guilty of treason by denying the king's supreme authority over the Church. His fate now sealed, More denounced his indictment as "grounded upon an Act of Parliament directly repugnant to the laws of God and his holy Church." On the execution scaffold a few days later, he declared himself "the King's good servant, but God's first."

Through his martyrdom, More earned a place in history as a symbol of resistance to secular despotism. An early biographer referred to him as "our noble new Christian Socrates." On an immediate and personal note, his friend Erasmus declared: "In More's death I seem to have died myself; we had but one soul between us."

SOURCES:

Chambers, R. W. *Thomas More.* Jonathan Cape, 1935.
Kenny, Anthony. *Thomas More.* Oxford University Press, 1983.
More, Thomas. *Utopia.* Penguin, 1961.

FURTHER READING:

Bolt, Robert. *A Man for All Seasons: A Play in Two Acts.* Vintage, 1960.
Guy, J. A. *The Public Career of Sir Thomas More.* Yale University Press, 1980.
Marius, Richard. *Thomas More.* Knopf, 1984.

Benito Mussolini

(1883–1945)

Italian dictator, who founded the Fascist movement, conquered Ethiopia, and led Italy into a disastrous alliance with Hitler and World War II.

In 1883, Benito Amilcare Andrea Mussolini was born in a small house outside the village of Predappio in the Romagna region of Italy. He was named after three famous revolutionaries, two of whom were anarchists and the third was the great Mexican leader, **Benito Juarez.** It was Mussolini's father who exercised the most influence on his son and whom the son respected and imitated. The elder Mussolini was a blacksmith who worked only intermittently and was often in debt; he had a strong character, subscribing to a mixture of socialist, anarchist, and republican ideas, and took an active part in the politics of his town. He drank to excess and was frequently unfaithful to his wife.

Although Benito admired his father's courage and political idealism and loved his mother, an elementary schoolteacher and a pious Catholic, in later years he complained about the unhappiness of his childhood. Ironically, for someone who was to become one of Europe's greatest orators, as a child Benito had difficulty in learning to speak and for months his parents feared he might never be able to do so. Only after patient attention from his parents and a medical consultation, did Benito begin to talk. In later years, Mus-

"'I don't give a damn,' the proud motto of [a Fascist gang member] scrawled on the bandage of his wound, is not only an act of philosophical stoicism, it sums up a doctrine that is not merely political. It is an education for combat, the acceptance of the risks which combat brings, and a new way of life for Italy."

BENITO MUSSOLINI (1932)

Contributed by Richard B. Jensen, Assistant Professor of History, Skidmore College, Saratoga Springs, New York

solini recalled a lack of tenderness and affection in his family. His father believed in corporal punishment and a thick leather strap was used to discipline the children. Mussolini described his character at this time as embittered and "almost savage."

When he was nine, his mother sent him to a strict Catholic school, which discriminated against him because of his lowly origins. Along with the poorer boys who paid low tuition, Mussolini ate inferior food, such as ant-infested bread. Once, when a teacher tried to punish him with a ruler, the boy exploded in anger, hurling an inkpot at the man. Often disciplined for breaking the school's rules, young Benito was finally expelled for stabbing a fellow student with a penknife (on another occasion he even knifed his girlfriend).

After working at a few odd jobs, including teaching, the 19-year-old Mussolini emigrated to Switzerland. There he experienced rough times. Broke, he once lived in a packing case underneath a bridge. He even had the humiliation of being imprisoned for begging. Eventually, he fell in with a group of Italian revolutionary socialists. It was in their company that the rootless Mussolini found himself. From then on the chief passion in his life was to be political agitation.

He Edits Official Socialist Newspaper

After a few years of working for the socialists by lecturing, writing, and organizing, in 1908 Mussolini's friends obtained for him the editorship of an Italian socialist paper in the Austrian city of Trent. In 1912, he reached the top when he was appointed the editor in chief of *Avanti!*, the official socialist newspaper for all of Italy. Mussolini proved to be an extraordinary journalist. Under his direction *Avanti!*'s readership increased threefold. One reason for this was that Mussolini had a great talent for composing catchy headlines. His editorials, which appeared on the front page were thrilling. He wrote in a way that was, to use his own terms, "electric" and "explosive." Mussolini's rhetoric often swept people off their feet before they had a chance to think about what he was saying. He could be so "electric" and "explosive" because he always adopted the most extreme, revolutionary position on any question. Soon he was the leader of the left-wing socialists, and for a few years after 1912, he was the de facto head of the entire Socialist Party.

Yet despite all his popularity and talent for politics, in 1914 the Socialists dumped him, expelling Mussolini from the Party. The basic reason was that Mussolini took a position diametri-

CHRONOLOGY

1912	Appointed editor of socialist newspaper *Avanti!*
1914	Favored Italian intervention in WWI; expelled from Socialist Party
1915	Italy entered WWI on the side of Britain, France and Russia; Mussolini joined the army
1919	Founded the Fascist movement
1922	Fascist "March on Rome"; Victor Emmanuel III appointed Mussolini prime minister
1924	Murder of socialist Matteotti
1925–26	Non-Fascist parties dissolved; opposition press silenced; secret police and political courts established
1929	Signed Lateran Accords with the Vatican
1935–36	Invaded and conquered Ethiopia
1936	Proclaimed Rome-Berlin Axis
1938	Promulgated anti-Semitic laws
1940	Italy entered World War II
1943	Mussolini arrested; Italy joined Allies; Germans rescued Mussolini
1945	Italian partisans executed Mussolini

cally opposed to the Socialist Party's policy on Italian intervention in World War I. In August 1914, when Germany and Austria-Hungary went to war against Britain, France, and Russia because of nationalist rivalry and disputes in the Balkans, the Italian government decided to proclaim its neutrality. The Italian Socialist Party also favored neutrality. For a man of Mussolini's violent and impulsive temperament, neutrality was boring while war was exciting; it also promised to open up new political opportunities and make for wonderful newspaper stories. When Mussolini wrote an editorial advocating that Italy support France and Britain in the war, even to the point of military intervention, the Socialists threw him out.

Mussolini immediately founded a pro-war newspaper, *The People of Italy*. A few months after the country declared war on Austria in May 1915, he went off to fight and later boasted of his heroic deeds during battle. Nevertheless, he was not highly decorated for his actions; after a grenade-thrower exploded during a practice session, wounding him with 40 fragments, Mussolini was released from the army in June 1917.

By war's end in November of 1918, Mussolini had returned to his position as editor of *The People of Italy* and was casting around for a larger political role. In March 1919, he brought together a motley group of war veterans, Futurists, anarchists, nationalists, and others to form the *Fasci di combattimento* or "fighting leagues" (literally, *fasci* means "groups"). These "fighting leagues" soon revealed themselves to be a total dud as a political movement. Their political program, embodying extreme nationalism with far-left economic and social reforms, garnered only a few thousand votes in the elections of 1919, and Mussolini failed in his bid to enter Parliament.

But Mussolini was a quick learner and a great opportunist. He realized that while the Socialist Party had a hammerlock on the leftist voters, few political leaders were providing dynamic leadership for Italians on the right. Moreover, a powerful offshoot of the *fasci* soon mushroomed in the Italian countryside. This was squadism, a form of right-wing gangsterism that specialized in beating up socialist and other leftist politicians, breaking up strikes, and trashing leftist-controlled newspapers and townhalls. Among the squadists' favorite weapons were clubs and castor oil. Castor oil, when forced down the throat of an opponent in large quantities, not only humiliated the victim, since it served as a powerful laxative, but might also kill him through dehydration. Mussolini did not originate these tactics, but he knew how to take advantage of them. He saw that many middle- and upper-class Italians were desperately afraid that a socialist or even a Bolshevik revolution might soon sweep through Italy. These frightened people, as well as many liberal politicians, now turned to the Fascists for protection and help in stopping the extreme left. The Liberals even included the Fascists in the government electoral coalition, which in May 1921 facilitated the election of Mussolini and 34 other Fascists to Parliament.

This entrance into national political life, rather than domesticating the Fascists as the old-guard politicians had hoped, only increased Mussolini's intransigence and desire to seize power. He noted that, while Italy sank deeper and deeper into a profound social and economic crisis marked by tremendous inflation, incessant strikes, land seizures by the peasants, and escalating political violence, the old political parties and leaders were ineffectual. In this unstable situation, Mussolini showed himself to be a consummate political tactician, maneuvering between the different political groups in such a way that, although few in Parliament really wanted Mussolini in power, his appointment to lead the country increasingly seemed the only solution for Italy's crisis.

Appointed Youngest Prime Minister in Italian History

It was in this situation of violence and chaos in the countryside, and political anarchy at the top, that the famous "March on Rome" took place in October 1922. From his command post in Milan, Mussolini ordered thousands of blackshirted Fascists to descend on Rome and seize power. Unsure of the reliability of the army and after receiving the advice of several prominent politicians, King Victor Emmanuel III yielded to these pressure tactics, hoping to avoid a civil war. On October 29, he appointed Mussolini prime minister at the age of 39, the youngest prime minister in Italian history.

When Mussolini met with Parliament in November, it voted him full powers for a year. Despite Parliament's submissiveness, Mussolini determined to acquire a majority for his Fascist Party at the next elections. These were held in April 1924 in an atmosphere of unparalleled violence and intimidation, returning a Fascist majority of 65% of the vote. In June, Fascist thugs murdered **Giacomo Matteotti,** a prominent Socialist member of Parliament and relentless critic of these electoral abuses. When news of the murder reached the public, a wave of revulsion swept across Italy and threatened to topple Mussolini from power. Mussolini always denied personally ordering the murder, but he was certainly responsible morally, given his encouragement of Fascist thugs and his belief that "a good beating never does any harm." Taken off guard by the sudden change in public opinion, Mussolini remained unsure of what course to follow. His ulcers began to act up and he vomited blood.

But after several months Mussolini regained his confidence and, benefiting from his opponents' inept tactics, in January 1925 he publicly assumed complete responsibility for the Matteotti murder. During the next two years, he consolidated his dictatorship. The opposition press was silenced and all non-Fascist parties were dissolved. Non-Fascist ministers were dismissed from the government, and Fascist control over the government bureaucracy and local government was strengthened. Mussolini established a secret police force, the "OVRA" (a meaningless term intended to frighten people). Later Mussolini acquired a new title, "Head of Government," a rank which made him responsible to no one except the king. Increasingly, he was referred to as *Duce* (Leader).

Mussolini's authority, however, did not spring simply from the machinery of dictatorial control. Besides skills at political maneuvering such as those that had brought him to power and had seen him through the Matteotti crisis, he possessed substantial charisma due to his oratorical abilities and the general force of his personality. When Mussolini spoke, he always gave the impression of absolute sincerity, decisiveness, and toughness. This lent an extraordinary authority to his words and made them sound irrefutable. His speeches were declamatory in style, consisting mainly of short, staccato sentences; the official designation for this style was "lapidary," which literally means "etched in stone." Mussolini used few gestures as he spoke, and if he did gesticulate, he would immediately return to a pose of immobility. By adopting this style, Mussolini deliberately set himself apart from the ordinary, highly animated Italian. The image Mussolini wanted to project was one of rock-solid strength, someone in whom one could place total confidence.

After he became prime minister and later dictator, his favorite site for speechmaking was the balcony outside his office located in the Palazzo Venezia in the heart of Rome. He referred to this balcony as his stage. Standing there he would invite the crowd to answer his rhetorical questions in chorus so as to involve the people actively in his speech. This was a relatively new technique, although Mussolini has been accused of stealing it from the poet-adventurer Gabriele D'Annunzio. Mussolini was a master at inventing catchy slogans and phrases, sometimes even during the middle of public speeches. This verbal cleverness, this inspired spontaneity, charmed the crowds.

Mussolini also possessed a magnetic personality and personal presence. His practice of journalism had sharpened an already excellent memory for facts. European politicians who visited Rome noted Mussolini's economy of words, the clarity with which he expressed his thoughts, and his mastery of the subject under discussion. But the impact of Mussolini's personality came from more than his intelligence and quickness of mind. People who met him were also thrilled by his immense, animal-like vitality. Enhancing his image as one of the greatest sex symbols of his generation was his frequent appearance, particularly for photographers, on horseback. Even dismounted, his presence was exciting, unsettling, and dominating. His white face with its enormous eyes added to the dramatic impact of his appearance, which he could heighten even further by rolling up his eyeballs to show only the whites. As he grew older, Mussolini gained weight and had his head shaven completely bald; these physical characteristics, together with his propensity to appear in public scowling, his lips pursed into a pout as he stared ahead, gave him a ferocious look.

Pope Recognizes Italian State

Following his successful resolution of the Matteotti crisis, Mussolini went from success to success for the next dozen years. One of his greatest triumphs came in February 1929 when he signed the Lateran Accords with the Catholic Church. Previously the Church's relationship with the Italian government had been poor; indeed, Pope **Pius IX** had refused to recognize any Italian government as legitimate after the latter took Rome away from him in 1870.

Mussolini was an odd person to bring about a reconciliation with Catholicism. He had never been a churchgoer, and in his younger days had written heretical and atheistic pamphlets and even a novel about a lecherous cardinal. *Il Duce* was shrewd enough, however, to realize the immense benefits his regime would gain from an agreement with Pope Pius XI, and after long negotiations, a concordat and treaty were signed. In return for one square mile of territory (Vatican City) and other concessions, the pope recognized the official existence of the Italian state and proclaimed that Mussolini was "the man whom God has sent us." After this settlement, Mussolini's prestige soared both at home and abroad.

As his popularity and confidence grew, so did his ambitions. He saw himself as a new Caesar who would refound the Roman Empire. Indeed he proclaimed that the acquisition of "empire" was central to the meaning of fascism and that Italy must expand or decay. Choosing as his victim Ethiopia, one of the last independent countries in Africa, Mussolini invaded in October 1935. Against **Haile Selassie** and the poorly armed Ethiopians, the duce authorized his army to employ ruthless tactics, including a "policy of terror and extermination" and the use of poison gas. The League of Nations, set up in 1919 and a forerunner of the United Nations, condemned this unprovoked aggression and voted for economic sanctions against Italy. This only led to a backlash of patriotic fervor among Italians who rallied around their embattled leader. In May 1936, Mussolini's armies conquered Addis Ababa, the Ethiopian capital.

Mussolini's triumph over Ethiopia and successful resistance to the League's sanctions prompted a new wave of adulation for Italy's leader.

Peasants in the fields knelt before him, women held up their children for him to bless, and hospital patients called upon his name as an anesthetic before operations. Government-controlled newspapers referred to him as "our divine Duce." As Denis Mack Smith points out, this cult of the duce increasingly undermined Mussolini's capacity to make sound decisions. Since "Mussolini" was "always right," as a contemporary slogan went, there was no reason for the duce to take advice, let alone criticism, from lesser mortals.

Rather than making his decisions based on realistic assessments, Mussolini increasingly relied on considerations of ideology and prestige. In November 1936, he proclaimed a "Rome-Berlin Axis," i.e., a vague alliance, between the two Fascist powers that previously had not been notably friendly toward each other (in private Mussolini spoke of **Adolf Hitler** as slightly mad, as "a gramophone with just seven tunes and once he has finished playing them he start[s] all over again"). Italy's intervention (alongside Germany) on behalf of General **Francisco Franco** in the Spanish Civil War (1936–39) further cemented ties with the Nazis but gained Italy nothing except huge losses of men and matériel. The unpopularity of the Fascist regime caused by the war in Spain was deepened by Mussolini's sudden proclamation in 1938 of laws curbing the rights of Italian Jews. There was little support for these laws in Italy; even Mussolini admitted in private: "I don't believe in the least in this stupid anti-Semitic theory. Whatever I am doing is entirely for political reasons."

Mussolini Joins Nazis

Convinced by a trip to Germany in 1937 that Hitler's army was invincible (and believing that Britain and France had the "spines of chocolate eclairs"), Mussolini allied himself closer and closer with his powerful northern neighbor. Nonetheless, when World War II broke out in September 1939, Mussolini, who had been kept in the dark about Hitler's plans and grudgingly realized that Italy was ill prepared for war, proclaimed "non-belligerency" (a word he coined). Only in June 1940, when Germany was well on its way to crushing France, did Mussolini join the Nazis. While Mussolini boasted that he would overwhelm his enemies with a "lightening war" and an army of 8 million men, his rhetoric soon proved hollow. Humiliating defeats followed in Greece and Africa.

By 1943, Mussolini's health was failing. Observers noted that he had lost weight and often looked like a wreck of his former self. He experienced severe and incapacitating stomach pains, often lapsing into lethargy, without his old mental capacity and willpower. This physical and mental collapse, together with the Allied conquest of Sicily in July, convinced leading Fascists and King Victor Emmanuel that Mussolini had to be removed from power. Following a confused meeting of the Fascist Grand Council on July 24–25 that indicated a loss of confidence in the duce, the king dismissed him from office and put him under arrest.

On September 12, 1943, a German commando unit of glider planes rescued Mussolini from his place of captivity atop Mount Gran Sasso. Subsequently, Hitler installed Mussolini as the titular head of the "Italian Social Republic" in northern Italy. While Mussolini and his government took up residence in resort towns along the shores of Lake Garda, true power lay in German hands. Within a year and a half, the Allied armies had fought their way up the peninsula and threatened to overrun all of northern Italy. In this desperate situation, Mussolini tried to escape into Austria by joining a column of retreating German soldiers. Stopped by communist guerilla fighters near the northern tip of Lake Como, the Germans allowed them to search the convoy and seize Mussolini. On April 28, 1945, these partisans machine-gunned to death the 61-year-old Mussolini and his lover, Clara Petacci, who had insisted on joining him in his final moments.

SOURCES:

Cassels, Alan. *Fascist Italy.* AHM Publishing, 1968.

Clark, Martin. *Modern Italy, 1871–1982.* Longmans, 1984.

Felice, Renzo De. *Mussolini il Rivoluzionario.* Turin: 1965.

Finer, Herman. *Mussolini's Italy.* Grosset, 1965.

Kirkpatrick, Ivanoe. *Mussolini: Study of a Demagogue.* London: Oldhams, 1964.

Smith, Denis Mack. *Mussolini.* Vintage, 1982.

Tannenbaum, Edward. *The Fascist Experience: Italian Society and Culture 1922–1945.* New York: 1972.

FURTHER READING:

Knox, MacGregor. *Mussolini Unleashed, 1939–1941: Politics and Strategy in Fascist Italy's Last War.* Cambridge University Press, 1982.

Imre Nagy

(1896–1958)

Hungarian Communist leader who, after attempting to liberalize the system in the post-Stalin "thaw," briefly headed a government free of Soviet influence that was crushed by Moscow during the Hungarian Revolution.

Pronunciation: Nahj. Born on June 7, 1896, at Kaposvar in southwest Hungary; executed after being found guilty of treason and attempting to overthrow "people's democratic state order" on June 16, 1958; son of poor Calvinist peasants; married; children. Predecessor: Enrö Gerö. Successor: János Kádár.

When the history of the decline and fall of Communism in Eastern Europe is written, Hungary's Imre Nagy will very likely be assigned a major role in explaining why this ideology failed to capture the lasting loyalty of that region's people. As Hungarian premier, Nagy attempted to transform the harsh communist system that had been imposed on his country after 1945 into a more humane socialism, first in 1953–55, and again briefly in 1956, when a people's uprising against the Soviet occupation forces was drowned in a sea of blood.

Born into a poor peasant family, Imre Nagy retained to the end of his life a deep empathy with the lives and suffering of his nation's impoverished rural population. Unlike many Communist leaders who lost touch with common people at an early stage in their careers, Nagy was always a good listener, remaining sensitive to the concerns of ordinary folk. As a rural political organizer in the 1920s, he also began to notice the discrepancies between social reality and abstract Marxist theory. At the same time, Nagy was a committed Marxist revolutionary who had spent almost two decades of his life in the Soviet Union and whose published

"I am not guilty. I consider myself a scapegoat."

IMRE NAGY,
DURING SECRET TRIAL (1958)

Contributed by John Haag, Associate Professor of History, University of Georgia, Athens, Georgia

writings indicate a firm belief in the validity of the Marxist revolutionary doctrine, when revised to match the unique conditions of each nation.

Serving as minister of agriculture in Hungary's first post-liberation government, from December 1944 through November 1945, Nagy headed a radical program of property redistribution that gave land to an impoverished peasantry, quickly becoming the most popular of the Communist leaders in Hungary. Although he approved of the "salami tactics" that systematically eroded the political rights of the non-Communist political parties, by 1947 he had become the only member of the ruling Politburo of the Communist Party to argue against an immediate takeover of power. He also disagreed with his fellow Communist leaders on the issue of forcing the peasants into collective farms, advocating a go-slow approach instead of immediate collectivization, which he believed would be self-defeating and undermine the chances for national economic development.

During the years 1949 to 1951, when Hungary found itself in turmoil and several leading Communists were purged and executed for "Titoist" and other anti-Soviet tendencies, Imre Nagy was stripped of power but was otherwise physically unharmed. Even before the death of **Joseph Stalin** in March 1953, Nagy's political star was again on the ascendancy. In the Soviet Union, the new regime of Premier **Georgi Malenkov** embarked on a cautious policy of political and economic reform. In Hungary, the dismal performance of the economy and growing popular discontent led to the replacement in July 1953 of the Stalinist Matyas Rakosi's universally hated government by Imre Nagy and other reform-minded Communists.

Inaugurates Ambitious Renewal Program

Nagy immediately inaugurated a "New Course" program of reform that revealed itself to be the most ambitious renewal agenda in the Eastern Bloc. Realizing how much the peasants hated the agricultural collectives into which they had been dragooned, Nagy gave them a choice of quitting or remaining members of the state farms. Recognizing the waste of resources associated with Hungary's headlong rush to develop heavy industry, the industrialization program was drastically slowed down. While Nagy's good intentions did not result in immediate economic improvements, the Hungarian populace was impressed by his personal integrity and his obvious desire to improve the lot of the ordinary citizenry. Showing his hatred of Stalinism, Nagy instituted a policy of amnesty for those individuals who had been imprisoned or oth-

CHRONOLOGY

1914	Enlisted in Austro-Hungarian army; became prisoner of war on Russian front
1917–18	Joined Bolshevik forces in Russian revolution; became member of Hungarian section of Russian Communist Party
1919	Returned to Hungary; supported short-lived Soviet Republic; fled to Paris after its collapse
1921–28	Returned to Hungary; imprisoned for subversive activities
1929–41	Moved to Soviet Union; studied agronomy at Moscow State University; directed collective farm in Siberia
1941–44	Helped organize propaganda activities in Moscow; broadcast to Hungary on Radio Moscow
1944	Returned to liberated Hungary; served as minister of agriculture
1945–46	Appointed minister of interior; elected to Central Committee and ruling Political Bureau of Hungarian Communist Party
1947	Elected speaker of National Assembly
1950–51	Resumed political career as minister of food supply
1952	Promoted to deputy premier
1953	Became premier
1954	Dismissed as premier; expelled from Hungarian Communist Party
1956	Swept back into office after popular uprising; Soviet forces crushed Hungarian uprising; Nagy arrested
1958	Placed on trial for treason; executed
1989	On the 31st anniversary of his execution, Nagy received a hero's funeral in Budapest

erwise injured during the worst years of Terror, 1949–51.

Despite considerable public support for his reformist policies, Nagy's power was not derived from within Hungary, but was almost entirely dependent on the fate of the ruling clique within the Byzantine Soviet power structure. The fall of Malenkov in early 1955 signaled the onset of a new phase of political instability in the Soviet Union, a situation that permitted the Stalinist forces in Hungary to regroup and return to power. Nagy was removed from the office of premier, as well as expelled from the Communist Party Central Committee and Politburo, becoming a political nonentity. Unlike the years of Terror, however, he was not imprisoned and remained personally unmolested. During the next 18 months, the "old-age pensioner" busily engaged in private debates with reformers both inside and outside the Communist Party and wrote an ideological defense of his reform brand of Communism. (Circulated only in mimeograph format, a copy would be smuggled out of Hungary in the spring of 1957 and published in London and New York under the title, *On Communism: In Defense of the New Course.*)

The tumultuous events of the year 1956 made it clear that the clock could not be turned back, despite the fact that Stalinist forces remained in control in Hungary and elsewhere in Eastern Europe. New winds of change were blowing through the Soviet Union, where a "secret speech" (soon published worldwide) of **Nikita Khrushchev** to the 20th Congress of the Soviet Communist Party initiated the process of enumerating the bloody crimes of Joseph Stalin and his henchmen. Once the gist of the Khrushchev revelations became known in Hungary, a powerful reaction—particularly among the university students and intellectuals—took place. Centering around a dissident group called the Petöfi Circle (named after the great Hungarian Romantic poet of the 19th century), the reformers voiced demands that the hated regime of Matyas Rakosi be immediately replaced by a reformist government. Bloody riots in Poland made it clear to the Soviet leadership that major reforms in Eastern Europe were long overdue.

Khrushchev and the Soviet Politburo, reading the handwriting on the wall, sent the word to Budapest to replace Rakosi. But instead of a reformer like Imre Nagy, the new premier was Enrö Gerö, another Stalinist with a highly unsavory past. Gerö's apparent strategy was to ride out the storm of criticism that accompanied his accession to power by making some symbolic concessions to the reformers while remaining firm on basic issues, including control of the secret police and the state and party bureaucracy. Premier Gerö's "reforms," which included wage increases and a conciliatory trip to Yugoslavia to visit the once-demonized President **Marshal Tito,** did not satisfy a growing and increasingly vociferous reform movement. Imre Nagy watched these events with great interest, but while many of the reformers respected him, few suspected that the veteran Communist would soon lead their nation in a brief, heroic, and ultimately tragic challenge to the entire Soviet system of control in Eastern Europe.

Reform Movement Turns Revolutionary

By October 1956, Poland and Hungary were in political turmoil, with many observers predicting direct Soviet military intervention to crush the rebellious popular spirit. In Hungary, what had throughout the summer been opposition by an intellectual elite turned into mass protest early in October when the remains of Laszlo Rajk, the foreign minister purged and executed in 1949, were reinterred in a public ceremony in Budapest. The full enormity of the arbitrary and brutal nature of the Communist regime was dramatized by this attempt at contrition for past crimes, and the masses now took to the streets to demand sweeping changes in government and economy. Reformers within the Communist Party now believed that a return to power by Imre Nagy was the only hope of averting chaos. Readmitted to membership in the Communist Party on October 13, Nagy had barely returned to public life when the reform movement found itself transformed by events into a revolutionary upheaval.

On October 23, a mass demonstration in Budapest ended in a bloody massacre when members of the AVO security forces fired into an unarmed crowd. On October 24, Imre Nagy became premier of a government pledged to bring sweeping reforms. At this stage, the Soviet government, deeply concerned by events in Poland as well as in Hungary, gave its approval to the Nagy cabinet and its program. In the next few days, it became clear that many Hungarians desired not a reform of Communism but its abolition, and a withdrawal of their nation from the Warsaw Pact as well as a return to a system of multiparty democracy. The extent of these desires among the Hungarian populace alarmed the Soviet leadership, but Nagy was able to convince **Anastas Mikoyan** and Mikhail Suslov, who flew to Budapest for urgent talks with the Hungarian leadership, that the Soviet Union had nothing to fear from developments in Hungary and that a peaceful evolution of the situation could be anticipated.

During the last days of October 1956, it appeared to optimistic observers that the Cold War might be ending and a new era dawning in Europe. In Warsaw, a Polish reform government under **Wladyslaw Gomulka** had come to power without bloodshed or Soviet intervention. In Hungary, even more radical developments were taking place. On October 30, Nagy abolished the political monopoly of the Communist Party, permitting other parties to function. The next day, *Pravda* voiced its approval of events in Hungary, giving rise to optimistic hopes that the Hungarians would be able to smash the Iron Curtain and propel Eastern Europe into a new, post-Cold War era. But Soviet hesitation did not mean approval, and fears of an unraveling of the Communist world meant that military intervention, despite the condemnation of world public opinion, was the only possible policy option for the Kremlin leadership.

With the world news media focusing on events in the Middle East (France, Great Britain, and Israel had invaded Egypt on October 29 in an attempt to overthrow the nationalist regime of **Gamal Abdel Nasser**), Soviet troops entered Hungary in large numbers on November 1. Still hoping to salvage something from the situation, Premier Nagy held several meetings with Soviet ambassador **Yuri Andropov** to try to fathom the intentions of Moscow but received no satisfactory response. That evening, Nagy declared Hungary to be neutral in the East-West conflict and announced her withdrawal from the Warsaw Pact. These moves very likely only served to further infuriate the Soviet Politburo, for on November 4 Soviet troops attacked Budapest and drowned the Hungarian uprising in blood. A new, Soviet-backed government headed by **János Kádár,** a victim of Stalinist torture and a supporter of Nagy, was announced. Besides significant property damage, suppression of the uprising resulted in a tragic loss of life: Soviet losses may have been as high as 7,000 dead, with between 25,000 and 50,000 Hungarians killed.

Nagy Is Executed

During the attack on Budapest, Nagy and several members of his cabinet were given political asylum in the Yugoslav embassy in Budapest. Tricked by a promise of safe passage out of the embassy by Soviet authorities, Nagy and his group were arrested on November 22 and eventually flown to Rumania. Returned to Hungary in June 1958, Nagy and three associates were secretly tried on charges of conspiracy and treason and all were found guilty. Executed on June 16, their bodies were secretly buried in a pauper's plot, Lot 301, in Budapest's Kozma Street cemetery which over the years became a rubbish dump.

The regime of János Kádár, conceived in a bloody national tragedy, evolved to become one of the more liberal governments in Eastern Europe. While banning complete political freedom, Kádár permitted Hungarians to grumble if they did not actively plot against the state, and much more importantly, by the 1960s he permitted significant economic reforms to be instituted, the result being that by 1970 the Hungarian standard of living was one of the highest in the Soviet Bloc.

For three decades, the memory of the 1956 revolt was officially suppressed, and the younger generation neither knew nor cared much about Imre Nagy, who after all had been a Communist albeit a victim of the system as well. By the late 1980s, however, a growing desire on the part of the younger generation of Hungarians to understand their nation's recent history, as well as the inexorable demands for the final liquidation of the remnants of the Communist system unleashed by the **Gorbachev** spirit in the Soviet Union, combined to create a movement to rehabilitate the historical reputation of Imre Nagy and the leaders of the 1956 revolt.

On June 16, 1989, the national funeral and reinterment of Nagy and his three associates became a crucial symbolic event in that breathtaking year, which witnessed the collapse of Communism in Eastern Europe.

SOURCES:

Gati, Charles. *Hungary and the Soviet Bloc.* Duke University Press, 1986.

Meray, Tibor. *Thirteen Days that Shook the World.* Praeger, 1959.

Nagy, Imre. *On Communism: In Defense of the New Course.* Praeger, 1957.

FURTHER READING:

Ashleigh, Benjamin. "The Spirit of Imre Nagy Returns to Hungary," in *Christian Science Monitor.* June 27, 1989, p. 19.

Brzezinski, Zbigniew. *The Grand Failure: The Birth and Death of Communism in the Twentieth Century.* Collier Books, 1990.

Molnar, Miklos. "The Legacy of Imre Nagy," in *Ten Years After: The Hungarian Revolution in the Perspective of History.* Edited by Tamas Aczel. Holt, 1967.

Tokes, Rudolf L. "Polycentrism: Central European and Hungarian Origins" in *Studies in Comparative Communism.* Vol. VI, no. 4, 1973.

Fridtjof Nansen

(1861–1930)

Norwegian scientist, Polar explorer, and politician, who also played a central role in refugee relief after the First World War, helped found the League of Nations, and won the Nobel Peace Prize in 1922.

Pronunciation: FRI(T)CH-of NAN(T)-sen. Born at Store-Froen, near Oslo, Norway, in October 1861; died in May 1930; son of Baldur (a lawyer) and Adelaide Wedel (Jarlsberg) Nansen; married: Evas Sars, 1889 (died 1907); married: Sigrunn Munthe Sandberg, 1919; children: five.

From the 16th to the 19th centuries, European mariners tried to explore and chart the Arctic seas. For some of them, the motive was commercial; they wanted to discover a faster route to replace the slow and dangerous routes around Cape Horn and the Cape of Good Hope to the spice islands of the Far East. For others, the motive was scientific or simply one of curiosity; where was the North Pole, and could men travel to it and live to tell the tale? Norwegians played an active role in this long search for the Northwest Passage and the North Pole, taking up where their Norse ancestors had traveled almost a thousand years before in their frail longships.

In Fridtjof Nansen, Norway found the ideal expedition leader to take the Arctic quest a large step nearer completion. Although he never reached either pole, Nansen paved the way for Robert Peary, the American North Pole adventurer, and for Roald Amundsen, the fellow-Norwegian who was the first traveler to navigate the Northwest Passage and later the first man to reach the South Pole. Nansen was in every way eminent. After his three-year icebound voyage in the *Fram* (1893–96), he went on to lead a distinguished

"He sometimes felt in his later years that there was a lack of unity in his career: he had advanced along so many paths. Yet he accomplished great things in every one of them."

JON SORENSEN

Contributed by Patrick Allitt, Assistant Professor of History, Emory University, Atlanta, Georgia

career as zoologist, oceanographer, and politician. As a refugee coordinator, he was one of the few Europeans to emerge from the First World War with enhanced international prestige.

Nansen's father was a lawyer, descended from a distinguished family of Norwegian and Danish sea captains, and as a boy Nansen enjoyed a privileged upbringing in suburban Oslo. Tall and strong, he soon distinguished himself as a good marksman and as a competitive skier; throughout his life he was extremely fit and strong, qualities which enabled him to endure the physically punishing ordeals of his expeditions. Nansen went to college at Kristiania and then began a doctoral degree in animal physiology, where he specialized in the study of the central nervous systems of simple vertebrates, shellfish, and worms. During most of the 1880s, he was a zoological museum curator in the coastal city of Bergen; he later published a book on whales. He so distinguished himself as an experimental scientist by the age of 21 that he was offered a faculty appointment at Yale University, and another at Indiana University. His thoughts, however, were not on America but on the Arctic, having fallen under the spell of the Swedish pioneer explorer Nils Nordenskiold, whose advice he sought as he prepared for his own expeditions.

Arctic Explorations Begin

Norwegian whaling and seal-hunting ships were already familiar with hazardous navigation in ice-bound waters, and in 1882 Nansen took an Arctic cruise in one of these hunting ships, the *Viking*, from whose deck he first viewed the frozen wastes. Fascinated with his experimental apparatus, which he brought out in all weathers at the risk of frostbite, Nansen amused the crew of the *Viking* by measuring and charting everything, but they soon recognized his skills as a seal hunter and his success in duels with polar bears. Like most men of his generation, Nansen loved to hunt and appears to have had no second thoughts about clubbing seals or shooting bears, walruses, and other Arctic wildlife, despite his immense enthusiasm for the wilderness and his periodic ruminations about its superiority over the civilized world. The *Viking's* cruise was deflected by unfavorable winds and currents and was ultimately carried down the eastern coast of Greenland, giving Nansen further opportunities to study Arctic currents and weather conditions.

After this first taste of the Arctic, Nansen decided to attempt a skiing expedition across Greenland. Several earlier expeditions, including one led by Nordenskiold, had already failed. Each

CHRONOLOGY

1861	Born at Store-Froen, near Oslo
1882–87	Served as curator of Bergen Museum
1888	Awarded Ph.D. from University of Kristiania
1888–89	Went on ski expedition across Greenland
1893–96	Explored North Pole on *Fram*
1897	Appointed professor at University of Kristiania
1905	Norwegian independence
1906–08	Served as ambassador to Britain
1917	Went on mission to United States
1919	Named delegate to League of Nations
1920–23	Took on refugee and displaced persons' relief work
1922	Awarded Nobel Peace Prize
1930	Died at age 69

of them, starting on the more approachable western coast of Greenland, had been driven back by difficult ice conditions and by the almost unendurable cold. Nansen's plan was to travel from the uninhabited east coast to the west, which would make it a one-way journey rather than a round trip but which would cut off all possible escape routes in the event of disaster. Most of the British and Scandinavian exploring authorities whom he consulted doubted the feasibility of the scheme, but by dogged persistence he raised the money, found five hardy volunteers, and hitched a ride to the Greenland shore on another whaling ship.

The expedition began disastrously when one of its small boats, carrying the six men ashore through ice floes, started to broach. Heaving it onto the floating ice, they struggled to repair it in the following days, while a longshore current dragged them far to the south of their intended landfall. Then they had to row laboriously back along the shore to their starting point. But once started, they did just what Nansen had planned, and crossed northern Greenland from east to west. Nansen discovered that after a very mountainous and broken coastal section, full of murderous ice crevasses, the center of the huge island was covered with a sheet-glacier, thousands of feet thick in places, across which they could sail their sleds with makeshift masts and sails. They reached the west coast suffering from frostbite and near-starvation only to find that the last ship back to Europe for the year had already set off. Instead of going home, they had to spend the winter among the Danish and Eskimo people of Godthaab. Undismayed, Nansen spent the winter learning the Eskimos' language. On his return to Norway, now a hero for his feat, he wrote one book about the ski trip and another about the Eskimos.

From this time on Nansen was a celebrity, making long European lecture tours with his new bride in tow. Although he accepted an appointment as a professor of zoology, he began to prepare an even bolder trip. His idea was to approach the North Pole, which was generally recognized as being an ice cap over water rather than a landmass, by taking a ship into the pack ice and using Arctic ocean currents to drift across the polar region. Working with the winds and currents whose patterns he had done much to trace, he believed that a specially designed, ice-proofed ship could make this journey in three or four years. Funding was no problem this time, despite the expedition's high costs—private patrons and the Norwegian and Danish governments both financed him generously, and a Russian nobleman offered him dog teams for expeditions from his ship.

Nansen asked a skilled marine architect, Colin Archer, to build a ship which could resist the enormous pressures of compacted ice, such as had often crushed whaling ships' hulls into matchsticks. Archer's design was for a hull which, instead of sitting in the ice, would be forced up by the freeze and subject to less stress and compression. Immensely strong and fortified inside and out, the *Fram* (Norwegian for "Forward") was loaded up with 13 volunteers and four years' worth of supplies in 1893. The captain, Otto Sverdrup, had been on Nansen's Greenland trip. For the first year everything went well under Nansen's capable supervision. A stickler for details, he had anticipated every contingency, all possible disaster scenarios, and seemed ready for anything. He once wrote: "To foresee all possibilities is precisely the secret of being a leader; nothing must come as a surprise." Keeping his crew busy to avoid the lassitude which had beset other icebound voyagers, he also fed them a scientifically calibrated diet to assure health and avoid scurvy, another curse of earlier Arctic expeditions.

In the end, however, he suffered from boredom, as the endless polar summer day gave way to the endless polar winter night. "Oh! At times this inactivity crushes one's very soul," he wrote at one point.

One's life seems as dark as the winter night outside; there is sunlight on no other part of it except

the past and the far, far distant future. I feel I must break through this deadness, this inertia and find some outlet for my energies.

The currents were not carrying him as directly as he had hoped over the Pole. Instead his course swung back and forth, often inconclusively, until Nansen decided that with one chosen supporter, he would try to make a dash to the Pole with sled and dog team. The going was extremely treacherous, as they had to cross successive pressure ridges of broken ice, sometimes 25 or 30 feet high, which was slow, dangerous, and difficult. They sometimes had to carry the dogs over these ridges one by one. Finally, having got 200 miles closer to the Pole than any earlier attempt, on April 8, 1895, Nansen and his companion, Hjalmar Johansen, called it quits. They retreated not to the *Fram*, whose position they no longer knew, but toward Franz Joszef Land, an archipelago north of Siberia.

Their trip was a nightmare. One by one they had to kill and eat their 27 dogs; the going became more and more difficult because the summer ice was beginning to melt and they had no steady footing. Finally by trudging and kayaking for three months, they reached the northernmost islands as a new winter was setting in. To help their chances of survival, Nansen and Johansen dug a hole in the hard ground, roofed it with rocks and sealskins, and lived in it throughout the whole Arctic winter. With nothing to do and nothing to read, they stayed alive on the meat of polar bears and seals which they killed. Notes Pierre Berton, historian of the Arctic explorers: "Formal to the end in the Norwegian manner, they did not address each other by their Christian names."

The next spring they marched south and at last bumped into another man, Frederick Jackson, an English would-be explorer in a tweed suit who was hoping to prove that the North Pole was land and could be approached from the Franz Joszef islands. When they told Jackson that he was wrong, he obliged them by taking them back to Norway and a hero's welcome. By chance the *Fram*, under the capable handling of Otto Sverdrup, arrived back just a week later, unscathed from its three years in the ice.

Berton has argued that Nansen was much more sensible than the "hidebound" British and American explorers who had preceded him and who seemed reluctant to learn from experience. The Norwegians, says Berton, were:

a subarctic people, used to cold weather and high winds, familiar with skis, sledges, and dogs. They were also immensely practical. Nansen was daring but never rash; bold but never impulsive; fatalistic but never foolhardy; poetic but never naive. A cool professional, he admired the British explorers for their grit, but he also learned from their mistakes and lack of experience.

By purpose-building his vessel, by dressing sensibly for the conditions, and by taking thousands of precautions, all of which earlier Royal Navy expeditions to the Northwest Passage had neglected, Nansen and all his men came home unscathed.

For the rest of his life Nansen was the most famous living Norwegian, virtually an institution. In addition to his many books, which increased his reputation and wealth, and which blended personal adventure tales with genuine scientific insight into the Arctic, he continued his work as a professor of zoology and oceanography. Making many more short voyages and writing prolifically on the seas around Norway, he never again ventured into the pack ice.

In 1905, his attention was distracted from his studies by a crisis. Throughout the 19th century, Sweden and Norway had been politically unified. Growing Norwegian discontent found an ideal mouthpiece in Nansen. He wrote articles for the European press, and a short book, *Norway and the Union with Sweden* (1905), to popularize the Norwegians' cause. Never a radical, he made judicious speeches on behalf of independence, insisted that political differences rather than enmity between the two countries made the separation necessary, and supported a referendum on the question which found Norway's people overwhelmingly in favor of independence. Norway's most influential foreign supporter was Britain, and the new Norwegian government asked Nansen to serve as ambassador to London. He accepted, spent the years 1906 to 1908 there, and helped smooth the arbitration problems which accompanied separation from Sweden, some of which brought the two countries close to war. Nansen's levelheadedness contributed to peaceable conflict-resolution.

During the First World War, Norway was a neutral nation. At first it profited, like the United States, by trading with both sides, sending copper, iron, and fish to both Germany and Britain. Britain soon intervened to prevent or diminish Norway's trade with Germany and made a secret agreement with the Norwegians to buy their surpluses. When the Americans entered the war on the Allied side in 1917, they too demanded a reduction in Norwegian-German trade, but the Norwegians feared reprisals from the Germans, on whom they depended for grain supplies. Traveling to America in the hope of winning trade concessions, and aiming to keep open the American grain export trade to Norway, Nansen was given wide discretionary powers and on one occasion risked signing an agreement with the U.S. government before he had full authorization from Oslo. Widely respected in America, he was the ideal negotiator for his country, whose people were living on ever-tighter rations (such as butter made from whale fat) as the war dragged on. Nansen addressed audiences of Norwegian immigrants in Washington and New York, wearing the order of St. Olav and again winning acclaim as a national hero.

While in the United States, he became an ardent champion of President **Woodrow Wilson**'s plan for a League of Nations, urged its acceptance at the Treaty of Versailles, and by his prestige was influential in its creation as an international peace-keeping force. He then became Norway's representative to the League, which met in Geneva. We know from our vantage point that the League was crippled at birth by the decision of the United States not to participate, by its exclusion of Germany and the Soviet Union, and by the feebleness of its sanctions when it faced successive crises in the 1930s. But to a world devastated by war in 1919, the League appeared to hold great promise of peaceful arbitration. It also became something of a haven for political utopians, but Nansen, to his credit, insisted on confronting hard political realities and taking energetic steps to preserve the peace.

Nansen Aids Refugees for League of Nations

The League of Nations appointed Nansen its high commissioner to try to solve Europe's huge problem of displaced persons, refugees, and prisoners of war. In Russia alone there were still an estimated 2 million prisoners hoping to return to their German and Austrian homes. A famine, caused partly by the Civil War which followed the Russian Revolution and partly by a severe drought, also presented in 1920 the specter of mass starvation throughout the new Soviet Union. Nansen accepted an additional job, offered by the International Red Cross, as head of the International Russian Relief, for which he worked tirelessly. One of his assistants was **Vidkun Quisling**, who was later to become the notorious pro-Nazi Norwegian governor during World War II (and executed for treason at war's end). Nansen found Quisling diplomatic, persuasive, and very useful because Quisling spoke Russian and Nansen did not. In these pre-Stalin days, moreover, Nansen gained a favorable impression of the new Soviet leaders, noting that **Trotsky** had done everything possible to reconstruct the railway system, and that local commissars were usually willing to aid his relief workers in the starving provinces. Nonetheless, his political sympathies lay with the vanquished "White" Russians rather than with the Bolshevik "Reds." "Nansen Kitchens," established at regional centers, fed millions of destitute Russians and Ukrainians, and "Nansen Passports" provided identification papers to millions of refugees and the chance to set about finding new national homes.

In 1922, Nansen arbitrated an exchange of prisoners between Greece and Turkey at the end of their prolonged war, and administered the resettlement of ethnic minorities from these two nations. The patriotic Norwegian historians Halvdan Koht and Sigmund Skard wrote of his work in these postwar years:

> To him all sufferers had the same claim to pity and help, without distinction of creed or politics or nationality. He spent all his persuasive powers, his eloquence and his compassion, even his indignation, to arouse political authorities and public audiences to the necessity of action. After defeats his heart was sad and bleeding, but he could not abandon what he felt to be his duty. His voice was that of the world's conscience and it reverberated through the world even after his death.

In 1922, for his work with prisoners of war, Soviet famine victims, Greek and Turkish refugees, and White Russian refugees, Nansen was awarded the Nobel Peace Prize.

Fridtjof Nansen died in 1930, just short of his 70th birthday. Even then he was planning further Arctic expeditions, now pinning his hopes on airships like the *Graf Zeppelin* as the means of approach. He had had no opportunities for Arctic exploring after his polar trip because his sense of duty, along with his awareness of his value to Norway, had always forced him to postpone further ventures and accept political appointments at home. Roald Amundsen's ventures in the Northwest Passage and to the South Pole (1911) had Nansen's full support. In his long winter in Franz Joszef Land (1895–96), Nansen had mentally worked out all the details of a South Pole journey but now saw a young admirer carry it out. To the Norwegian people he became, and has remained, the embodiment of national independence, purpose, and selfless dignity.

SOURCES:

Berton, Pierre. *The Arctic Grail.* Viking, 1988.

Hayes, Paul M. *Quisling: The Career and Political Ideas of Vidkun Quisling, 1887–1945.* David and Charles, 1971.

Koht, Halvdan, and Sigmund Skard. *The Voice of Norway.* Columbia University Press, 1944.

Popperwell, Ronald G. *Norway.* Praeger, 1972.

Sorensen, Jon. *The Saga of Fridtjof Nansen.* Norton, 1932.

Napoleon I Bonaparte

(1769–1821)

French emperor who rose through sheer ambition, drive, and intelligence to the epitome of power, ruled France, conquered much of Europe, created an empire, and forever changed the course of European history.

"To die is nothing, but to live defeated and without glory is to die every day."

J. CHRISTOPHER HEROLD

Islands figure prominently in the life of Napoleon Bonaparte; he was born on the island of Corsica and died on the remote island of St. Helena in the south Atlantic. His father Charles was a lawyer and prominent Corsican citizen. Napoleon's mother Letizia Ramolino was a strong, beautiful woman who had eight children (five boys and three girls), held her family together after the death of her husband at age 39, and outlived her famous son by 15 years. The fortunes of this tightly knit, traditional Italian family rose along with those of the ambitious Napoleon: his gentle, intellectual brother Joseph was made king of Naples and then king of Spain; Louis married Napoleon's stepdaughter and became king of Holland; the spoiled, self-centered youngest child, Jerome, wed Princess Catherine of Würtemburg and ruled the kingdom of Westphalia. Among the brothers only Lucien was not granted a royal title; he quarreled with Napoleon in 1802 over his marriage which Napoleon considered a "misalliance." The three sisters—Eliza, Pauline, and Caroline—also benefited from the Napoleonic largesse; Eliza became grand duchess of Tuscany. Caroline, married to Joachim Murat, ruled as queen of Naples, and the lovely, sensuous Pauline eventually mar-

Contributed by Jeanne A. Ojala, Professor of History, University of Utah, Salt Lake City, Utah

Born Napoleone Buonaparte in Ajaccio, Corsica, in 1769; died on the island of St. Helena in 1821; son of Charles (lawyer and prominent Corsican citizen) and Letizia (Ramolino) Buonaparte; married: Josephine de Beauharnais; married: Archduchess Marie Louise of Austria; children: (second marriage) one son. Successor: King Louis XVII (Bourbon).

ried an Italian, Prince Borghese, and led a life of voluptuous dissipation. The mother of this disparate brood was called "Madame Mère" when her son was emperor of the French. Family ties and loyalty remained important to Napoleon.

Napoleon's carefree childhood came to an abrupt end in 1778, when he was nine years old; his father enrolled him in school in Autun, France. The next year, he attended military school at Brienne on a royal scholarship. A scrawny, timid boy, teased by his classmates because of his Italian accent, Napoleon became a "loner." But his mathematical ability earned him a place at the prestigious École Militaire in Paris. A voracious reader, he devoured books on history, famous military campaigns, French literature, and the writings of Plato and Aristotle. In 1785, he received his commission as lieutenant in the French army, assigned to the artillery. He received further training at an artillery school in Auxonne (1788–89). When not in school, Napoleon was often on leave in Corsica, involved with local patriots working for Corsican independence.

Napoleon was in Auxonne when the French Revolution broke out in 1789. The Estates General, a kind of representative body, had been summoned by King **Louis XVI** to deal with the financially distressed government; the deputies immediately made demands for far-reaching reforms and came into conflict with the entrenched privilege and power of the nobility and with the king. The educated, ambitious bourgeoisie who served as representatives of the Third Estate (all commoners in France) refused to discuss new taxes and loans until their grievances were addressed. Calling themselves the National Assembly, the middle-class deputies moved from opposition to rebellion. In the next few months, France would be transformed into a constitutional state, and French subjects into French citizens. One act of the assembly changed Napoleon's attitude towards France; Corsica was made an integral part of France, no longer a crown colony. From this point on, Napoleon was in favor of the Revolution and of the Jacobins who organized public opinion through their national network of political clubs.

The Revolution divided Frenchmen, as did radical reforms affecting the monarchy and the Catholic Church in France. Thousands of nobles emigrated, unable to accept the radical changes, the mob violence, and social upheavals. Many army officers went abroad, and young, able officers like Napoleon were rapidly promoted to fill the void. In April 1792, France declared war on Austria; shortly thereafter, Prussia came to Austria's aid. Napoleon was promoted to captain, then two years later made brigadier general, after successfully expelling the British from the port city of Toulon in December 1793. His reputation was bolstered by this well-executed military action, but in July of 1794, his fortunes were in jeopardy when the Jacobins were ousted from power in Paris. Napoleon's close association with some of the Jacobin leaders made him "suspect," and he was imprisoned briefly.

However, when the National Convention was threatened by a large Parisian mob in October 1795, they called on Napoleon to defend the government. Firing cannon into the crowd, he saved the convention and once again demonstrated his loyalty to the Revolution. Napoleon was rewarded by the succeeding government, the Directory, and in March 1796, was appointed commander of the Army of Italy.

Napoleon Marries Josephine

Only two days earlier, Napoleon had married the elegant, beautiful Josephine de Beauharnais, widow of a noble guillotined during the bloody period of the Terror. Her two children, Eugene (age 14) and Hortense (age 12), were much loved by their stepfather: they returned his affection and remained loyal to him, even after his fall from power.

A few days after his marriage, Bonaparte left for Italy to lead his ragged, ill-disciplined troops in a series of brilliant victories over the Austrian army. At first, some of the older generals and the "old moustaches" (seasoned veterans) were not impressed by the 27-year-old, diminutive figure in an army greatcoat. But General Bonaparte promised them glory and riches, and he kept his promise. By October 1797, the French had defeated their formidable foe; Napoleon, on his own cognizance, negotiated the Treaty of Campo Formio by which France acquired Belgium and the west bank of the Rhine. In addition, the French created two Italian Republics from the conquered territories. Napoleon returned to Paris in triumph, lionized by salon society and the common people.

But inaction would, Napoleon decided, erode his newly acquired fame. He was pressed to assume command of an army and invade England, but he doubted the feasibility of such a venture at that time and refused the post. Napoleon had his eyes on the Near East and, with the support of Foreign Minister Talleyrand, he was outfitted for a campaign in Egypt. The plan was to strike at England by seizing Egypt and cutting trade routes to India, thereby disrupting English commerce. Napoleon, with 35,000 troops and a staff of scientists, artists, and men of letters, sailed from France in May 1798, landed in Egypt in July, and defeated the Mamelukes (vassals of the Ottoman Empire who ruled in Egypt) three weeks later. General Bonaparte set about establishing an administration and judicial system modeled on the French. On August 1, a British fleet attacked the French flotilla at Aboukir and destroyed it. The French army was now stranded. Undeterred, Napoleon made preparations to strike against the Turks in Syria. Unable to capture Acre, the French raised the siege and retreated when Napoleon learned the British were planning to transport a Turkish army to Egypt. In July 1799, 7,000 French mauled the numerically superior Turks, driving them into the sea (the Battle of Aboukir).

But nothing could change the fact that the French army was cut off from receiving reinforcements or supplies. Moreover, news reached Napoleon that France was in danger of being invaded from Italy and Holland by the allied forces of the Second Coalition. He reasoned that France needed his services—and he needed to advance his own career. Without fanfare, he and a few close companions sailed for France, leaving the army under the command of General Kléber. On October 9, Napoleon landed at Fréjus in the south of France. The Egyptian venture was not a complete failure; the French savants had laid the foundations for the study of Egyptology and found the Rosetta Stone which provided the key to ancient hieroglyphics. The unfortunate Kléber was murdered in 1801; his successor surrendered the army to the British who returned the troops to France in 1802.

Again, Napoleon returned to France a "hero." *La patrie* (the country) was in danger, both externally and internally. A resurgence of counter-revolution on the political right and of the Jacobins on the left threatened the Directory government, while unemployment and conscription were causing widespread discontent. The Abbé Sieyés, a cautious and wily old revolutionary and one of the five directors, began moving to oust the current government, prepare a new constitution, and strengthen the executive power. But first he needed to secure the cooperation of a military man who could assure the army's loyalty. General Bonaparte was thought to be that man; his brother Lucien, president of the Council of 500, would be a key figure in the proposed coup. He warned Sieyés, however, that Napoleon would not be easy to control.

On the 18th *Brumaire* (November 9), the deputies of the Councils of Elders and of 500 were warned that a Jacobin plot was afoot, and they were directed to move to St. Cloud, a suburb of Paris. Napoleon was given command of troops in the capital. The next day, he addressed the Council of Elders, and they consented to a constitutional revision. But the Council of 500 was not as easily convinced, and Lucien was forced to call in troops to clear the chamber. A rump meeting of the deputies convened to vote executive power to a temporary triumvirate, including Napoleon, charged with writing a new constitution. The coup of Brumaire was met with stoic acceptance by the mass of Frenchmen; ten years of instability, war, and economic hardship had numbed people's reactions. A strong man was needed to restore confidence, impose order, and ensure the gains of the revolution. Napoleon was just such a man.

The constitution submitted to the French people via a plebiscite was "short and obscure," as Napoleon had directed. The new Consulate government (1800–04) inaugurated a period of efficient, authoritarian rule. As first consul, Napoleon created a government open to talent where former nobles, old regime officials, and Jacobins worked together. This was *not* a military government, despite the dual role of Napoleon during his regime; he held executive power and commanded the military. When war with Austria recommenced in the spring of 1800, Napoleon led the French forces into northern Italy, defeating the enemy at the Battle of Marengo in June. Peace with Austria was followed in 1802 by the Treaty of Amiens with Britain.

Napoleon I surveys the land.

The Little General Becomes Emperor

Meanwhile, domestic affairs occupied Napoleon's attention; a concordat was signed with Pope Pius VII, ending the disunity that had plagued the church in France since the early Revolution. Freedom of religion, civil marriage, and divorce were permitted. The Concordat was in effect in France until 1905. The first consul restored law and order by establishing a strong police force. Censorship was strictly applied. Napoleon founded the Legion of Honor which recognized meritorious service to the state; it is still given as a reward to outstanding individuals. His policies were popular with the majority of Frenchmen and, in 1802, Napoleon was overwhelmingly voted consul for life by plebiscite. The final step in the meteoric rise of this unusual man came in May 1804 when the French voted to approve Napoleon's creation of an Empire; the little Corsican general was now Napoleon I, Emperor of the French. His coronation took place on December 2, 1804, in Notre Dame Cathedral in Paris in the presence of the pope. Napoleon himself placed the crown on his head, and then crowned his wife.

Through his popularity with the French masses, the emperor held power and brought victories, glory, and the most effective government France had ever experienced. He was a reformer, and organizer, administrator, and lawmaker. Equality was stressed at the expense of liberty; legal equality and equality of opportunity were guaranteed. Careers were open to all capable men. The middle classes benefitted from the policy of careers open to talent and from Napoleon's protectionist economic programs. He established the Bank of France which stabilized the national financial system. Everyone was obligated to pay taxes, direct and indirect. The state promoted industry, gave grants to new industries, and prizes for inventions. New roads were built, new crops introduced, and employment bureaus set up.

Napoleon centralized the government of France in ways only dreamed of by former monarchs. All officials in the 83 administrative departments were appointed from Paris; a modern bureaucracy was created which has remained to this day. Local autonomy was obliterated. A national police system was directed by a Minister of Police.

One of the greatest achievements of the regime was the codification of law, the Napoleonic Codes. Laid out in seven codes, it has survived with some revision until the present day. The civil code (1804) regulated aspects of society such as individual liberty, equality before the law and in taxation, freedom from arbitrary arrest, divorce, and religious freedom. Women's rights were severely limited, and they were deemed "less equal than men." In the criminal code, the protection of society was paramount; thus, the prosecution had more rights than the defense. The penal code allowed for execution by the guillotine. The codes were a composite of laws from the old regime, the Revolution, and from tradition.

Another lasting legacy of the Age of Napoleon was the education system which established lycées (roughly high schools) which prepared students for university study. Grandes Écoles trained men as engineers, teachers, and scholars in science and the humanities. The entire system was under the control of the Imperial University—an administrative body which determined curricula, chose texts, and oversaw examinations. This centralized system exists today. Little attention was given to the education of women, who were "to believe, not to think," Napoleon declared. Under the Empire, the Bibliothèque Nationale was enlarged, the Archives Nationales was (and still is) housed in a former aristocratic mansion in Paris, and the Louvre palace was made into one of the greatest art museums in Europe. Classical style monuments and public works were begun which served as symbols of the power of the regime.

Between 1804 and 1812, Napoleon forged an empire, the largest since Roman times, by war and diplomacy. With the Grande Armée of about 200,000 men, a professional officer corps, and the ranks filled with volunteers and conscripts, Napoleon defeated the mightiest states in Europe. The emperor was an innovator; he never fought two battles using the same methods. He simply engaged the enemy and made decisions as the situation required. His presence on the field of battle was worth 50,000 men, according to the **Duke of Wellington;** French troops were certain of victory if the "Little Corporal" was with them. Military success allowed Napoleon to crown himself "King of Italy" in 1805. His stepson, Eugène de Beauharnais, was appointed viceroy, and he never disappointed Napoleon.

The English proved to be one of the most implacable enemies of France, and Napoleon was determined to invade and defeat this "nation of shopkeepers." However, he would have to control the channel, which proved to be impossible because of English naval superiority and the destruction of the French fleet at the Battle of Trafalgar in October 1805. But by this time, Napoleon had turned his mighty army against the Austrians and Russians, defeating them at Ulm (October 1805) and at Austerlitz (on December 2, 1805, the anniversary of his coronation as emperor). A month later, he gave the throne of Naples to his brother Joseph; King Joseph initiated enlightened reforms which were beginning to have a beneficial effect when he was made king of Spain in 1808. Holland also received a Bonaparte monarch; Louis and his wife Hortense were accepted by the Dutch as the only alternative to being annexed to France. Napoleon's penchant for organization was particularly evident in the German states. In 1806, he proclaimed himself Protector of the Confederation of the Rhine, and the archaic Holy Roman Empire ceased to exist.

Russian Tsar, French Emperor Make Peace

Prussia grew fearful of Napoleon's future intentions and allied with Russia. The 37-year-old French emperor destroyed the Prussian army under the command of two aged warriors, Prince Hohenlohe and the Duke of Brunswick, at the battles of Jena and Auerstädt. Berlin was occupied and the French army then headed east to confront the Russians. In February 1807, the two powers fought the bloody battle of Eylau in Poland. It was an indecisive contest, but in June, Napoleon's veterans achieved a great victory over the main Russian army at Friedland. Peace was made at Tilsit, on a small island in the middle of a river, by the Tsar of All the Russias (**Alexander I**) and the Emperor of the French. They talked of creating spheres of influence in Europe and dividing up the ailing Ottoman Empire between France and Russia. As a result of Napoleon's military achievements, the duchy of Warsaw, the Kingdom of Westphalia, the grand duchy of Berg, the state of the Illyrian Provinces (in the Balkans), and the duchy of Tuscany came under French control.

Napoleon appeared unstoppable. He had repeatedly defeated the great powers of Europe, one at a time, had rearranged the map of Europe, and imposed French hegemony (dominance) from the Atlantic to the borders of Russia. His ambition seemed limitless—but he was not omnipotent. If England could not be invaded, Napoleon would defeat her by destroying her economy. He instituted the Continental System by the Berlin Decree, whereby he declared all European ports closed to English goods and ships and to ships carrying British products. It failed in its objective but other events proved to be more troubling to the would-be Master of Europe.

Spain, ostensibly an ally of France, was governed by an incompetent and corrupt government. It was not a threat to France, but it was a major leak in the Continental System and a possible site for a British landing on the continent. Portugal was similarly viewed. Napoleon managed to coerce the Spanish minister Godoy to allow a French army to march through Spain to Portugal; Lisbon was taken in November 1807. More French troops poured into Spain, and Murat entered Madrid in March 1808. By autumn, a French army of 300,000 had been sent to conquer the peninsula. But fighting in Spain was not like the war in Germany and Austria or in Italy. For the first time, guerrilla forces were utilized by an adversary. Moreover, the British under the future duke of Wellington were able to dislodge the French from Portugal. For five years, the Spanish armies lost every battle, yet the French could not win a decisive victory. Spain became Napoleon's "bleeding sore," a struggle of hideous atrocities on both sides. Heartened by Spanish resistance, the Austrians embarked on a new campaign; in a series of four battles in the spring and summer of 1809, Napoleon defeated—but could not destroy—the Austrian army. Russia was making hostile murmurings, and in France, conscription was becoming more difficult. Moreover, the pope had excommunicated Napoleon for taking papal lands in Italy.

Napoleon was also concerned about the perpetuation of his new dynasty. He needed a son, an heir. In December 1809, he reluctantly divorced Josephine, and the following March married the 18-year-old Habsburg archduchess Marie Louise of Austria. A son was born one year later. Unfortunately for the conduct of the Spanish conflict, Napoleon became a "homebody" and remained in Paris. However, he continued to work to extend French control over more areas of Europe. And from the end of 1810, when Tsar Alexander of Russia withdrew support from the Continental System and broke his alliance with France, Napoleon began massive preparations for war. Russia's actions were indicative of widespread discontent in Europe, an increasingly prevalent anti-French sentiment.

Napoleon was determined to force Russian adherence to the Continental System. The campaign must be short and swift; if anything but a decisive victory, the emperor knew his allies would take advantage of his failure and desert him, or worse, rebel against French domination. Even the French might turn against him and threaten his regime.

In June 1812, Napoleon had 611,000 French and allied troops ready to invade Russia. As the Grande Armée approached the Russian frontier, the tsar's army withdrew into the vastness of their country, relying on a "scorched-earth policy" to weaken the advancing enemy. Finally at Borodino, the armies clashed in an indecisive battle. Napoleon entered Moscow on September 14, and that night the city was in flames. But the occupiers lacked food, forage, and shelter. Tsar Alexander refused to negotiate, and on October 17, Napoleon gave the order to retreat. Men and horses outfitted for a summer campaign suffered horribly as the Russian winter set in. When the ragged, freezing, starving men reached Vilna (in Poland), only 40,000 remained of the main army. Napoleon left his army and hurried to Paris. News of the Russian disaster spread rapidly, and he feared the reaction of the French who were growing war-weary.

Napoleon had made two serous errors in judgment: fighting a two-front war—in Spain and in Russia—and forcing Europe to abide by the Continental System. In Spain, the French were being worn down and driven toward their own frontier. Napoleon ordered his brother Joseph to concentrate on protecting the southern frontier of France. After the French defeat at Vitoria in June 1812, Joseph fled to France, and Wellington crossed into France in October 1813. The subject states of Europe were encouraged by these events;

Napoleon would have to fight to save his throne. In May 1813, the French smashed the Russians and Prussians at Lützen and Bautzen. The Austrians joined the allies after learning of the French defeat at Vitoria. Badly outnumbered, Napoleon was able to defeat the Austrians at Dresden but at Leipzig (October 1813), his fortunes failed. The seemingly invincible warrior had been beaten. As he led the French army across the Rhine, imperial control in the German states crumbled.

Emperor Abdicates, Is Exiled to Elba

The allies did not intend to destroy Napoleon personally or France as a great power. Austria, for one, feared that crushing France would allow the Russians to become the ascendant power in Europe. The allies offered France its "natural frontiers"—the Alps, the Pyrénées, and the Rhine: a larger France than in prerevolutionary days. Napoleon vacillated until it was too late. The allies formed the Grand Alliance with the goal of invading France and defeating Napoleon. Greatly outnumbered, Napoleon fought the most brilliant campaign of his career. Ever hopeful, and viewing each success as a good sign, Napoleon simply could not triumph over allied numbers and determination. His wife and son fled Paris before it capitulated; he would never see them again. Conceding defeat when his generals refused to fight any longer, the emperor abdicated on April 11, 1814, and was exiled to the island of Elba off the coast of Italy.

Louis XVIII was restored to the throne of his ancestors by the allies who convened a European Congress at Vienna in September 1814. While they labored to redraw the map of Europe and restore some semblance of legitimate authority in the various states, Napoleon risked making a bid to return to power. After landing in southern France, he made his way towards Paris, gathering support as he marched. This brief episode of bravado and unrealistic expectations ended in inglorious defeat at the hands of the allies in the battle of Waterloo (June 1815). Even now, the French government was willing to accept Napoleon's son as his successor, but the allies forced them to accept the colorless Louis XVIII again.

Napoleon surrendered to the English on July 15 and asked for asylum in England. His request denied, the deposed emperor was put aboard a British ship, the *Northumberland,* and three months later reached the island of St. Helena in the south Atlantic (about 1,300 miles from Africa, 2,400 miles from Brazil). The golden eagles, under which the Grande Armeé had conquered an empire, were gone, and Napoleon, a lonely "eagle in a cage," died six years later, on May 5, 1821, probably of stomach cancer. "If I had succeeded, I should have been the greatest man known to history," Napoleon reflected near the end of his life. In his will, he said he wished to be buried "on the banks of the Seine, among the French people whom I have loved so much." And in December 1840, his remains were returned to France and buried beneath the grand dome of Les Invalides in Paris. His name has become legendary, and his legacy lives on in France today.

SOURCES:

Dufraisse, Roger. *Napoleon.* Translated by Steven England. McGraw-Hill, 1992.

Fisher, H. A. L. *Napoleon.* Oxford University Press, 1962.

Lockhart, John Gibson. *The History of Napoleon Bonaparte.* Dutton, 1947.

Ludwig, Emil. *Napoleon.* Pocket Books, 1954.

Markham, Felix. *Napoleon.* New American Library, 1963.

FURTHER READING:

Connelly, Owen. *French Revolution/Napoleonic Era.* Holt, 1979.

Geyl, P. *Napoleon For and Against.* Yale University Press, 1963.

Herold, J. Christopher. *The Age of Napoleon.* American Heritage, 1963.

Holtman, Robert B. *The Napoleonic Revolution.* Lippincott, 1967.

Lefebvre, George. *Napoleon.* 2 vols. Columbia University Press, 1969.

Napoleon III

(1808–1873)

President of the Second French Republic, who, in a coup d'état, crowned himself emperor of France.

Name variations: Known as Louis Napoleon until he became emperor. Born Charles Louis Napoleon Bonaparte in Paris on April 20, 1808; died in London on January 9, 1873; son of Louis Bonaparte, king of Holland (and brother of Napoleon Bonaparte) and Hortense de Beauharnais (daughter of the Empress Josephine); married: Eugenie de Montijo, 1853; children: one son, Napoleon Louis, known during the Empire as the Prince Imperial. Predecessor: King Louis-Philippe. Successor: President Adolphe Thiers.

When Louis Napoleon was born in 1808, his parents' marriage was already estranged. Arranged by Emperor **Napoleon I,** the match of Louis Bonaparte and Hortense de Beauharnais, produced three sons, only two of whom reached adulthood. In 1809, Louis Bonaparte sought, but was not allowed, a divorce by his brother Napoleon and in the following year was driven by his domestic misery to abdicate the throne of Holland. Thus, Louis Napoleon did not grow up with both parents; his father spent the rest of his days in Germany and Italy. The fall from power of Napoleon I, following the defeat at Waterloo in 1815, further disrupted the young boy's life. Though Louis Napoleon was too young at the time to retain many distinct memories of his famous uncle and his exile to St. Helena, the nephew measured the rest of his life by Napoleon I's achievements.

With the Empire's end, Hortense and her two sons were issued passports to Switzerland. While journeying to a new life, an agent of Louis Bonaparte came to claim the elder son, Napoleon Louis, whose custody the father had won. And, in 1816, the Restoration government passed a law

"When I do wrong, I have only to think of this great man, and I seem to feel his shade in me telling me to be worthy of the name Napoleon."

LOUIS NAPOLEON

Contributed by Maureen P. O'Connor, Ph.D. candidate in History, Harvard University, Cambridge, Massachusetts

exiling all Bonapartes from France forever. Thus, Louis Napoleon's earliest years were marked by the departures of his father and brother, his uncle's fall from power, and his entire family's enforced banishment from France.

By 1817, Hortense and Louis had finally settled in Thurgau, Switzerland, where she had purchased the Château of Arenenberg. First tutored by the abbe Bertrand from 1817–19, Louis made little progress in academic or physical pursuits because the tutor proved insufficiently rigorous. This situation was corrected at the insistence of the boy's father. Phillipe Le Bas, the new teacher, enforced a discipline in the life of the exiled prince. Louis Napoleon's every waking hour adhered to a strict schedule. The formerly lazy pupil blossomed under the regime of Le Bas. In 1821, the boy was enrolled at the local Gymnasium in Augsburg in Bavaria, where his mother had taken a house and where, within a year, he ranked in the top tenth of the class. Louis Napoleon first went to Italy in 1823, a country which would be significant to him for the rest of his life. Not only were a great many members of his family settled there, but it was the region which first gave his uncle glory. For financial reasons, Le Bas was released in 1827 from his tutorship.

In 1830, Louis Napoleon completed an artillery course with the Swiss army at Thun and in the following year, he and his brother Napoleon Louis associated themselves with an antipapal rebellion in central Italy. When Napoleon Louis died from a fatal case of measles, Hortense traced Louis to a rebel base and transported him out of Italy in a move to protect her sole surviving son. After a brief, quasi-secret and completely illegal stop in France, the mother and son went to England for three months before they secured safe passage back to Switzerland.

Napoleon I's son, the duc de Reichstadt, died in July 1832, nine years after his father, leaving Louis Napoleon the logical heir to the emperor's legacy. This "pretender" to the Bonaparte legacy maintained a low profile from 1831 to 1836, writing a pamphlet and a book on artillery tactics, having joined the Swiss militia in 1834. At Strasbourg in October 1836, with a band of fellow conspirators, the young Louis Bonaparte unsuccessfully attempted a coup d'état. He received a lenient punishment; the French authorities placed him on a New York–bound ship, and he returned to Europe the following year to care for his ailing mother. After her death, when France felt Louis's presence in Switzerland too threatening, he moved voluntarily to England. In London, in 1839, he published a propagandistic pamphlet, *Des Idees Napoleoniennes*, where he set forth the political program that he

CHRONOLOGY

1810	Louis Bonaparte abdicated throne
1815	Napoleon Bonaparte exiled to St. Helena
1831	Louis Napoleon and brother, Napoleon Louis, involved in a minor rebellion in Italy; brother died
1832	Napoleon Bonaparte's son died; Louis Napoleon closest male heir to the deceased emperor
1836	Attempted coup at Strasbourg; Louis placed on New York–bound frigate by French authorities
1840	Second bungled coup attempt at Boulogne; Louis imprisoned for life
1846	Escaped prison and relocated to London
1848	Lifetime exile lifted; elected president of Second Republic
1851	Seized control of government
1852	Crowned emperor
1870	Outbreak of Franco-Prussian War; Napoleon III surrendered to Prussians at Sedan; imprisoned
1873	Died in England, following several gallbladder operations

believed the Bonapartist legacy to represent. Perhaps it was the success of this treatise which prompted him to attempt another coup in 1840, this time in Boulogne. Captured and sentenced to life imprisonment, Louis Napoleon took advantage of his captivity to continue his education and was able to escape six years later when his prison underwent repair, whereupon he returned to England.

Louis-Philippe, the king of France, was deposed in the February 1848 revolution which paved the way for the return of Louis Napoleon to France; the latter arrived the day after the king's February 24 abdication. Louis Napoleon withdrew to England within a week, however, at the provisional government's request, taking care not to spoil the great opportunity he saw unfolding for himself. He knew that the universal suffrage proclaimed by the Second Republic would work in his favor. In May, he was elected a delegate from four districts to the Constituent Assembly, but felt the time unpropitious to take his fairly won seat. In supplementary elections in September, five constituencies elected him to the assembly, and this time he left London for Paris where he took his seat on September 26.

On November 4, the new constitution was passed and the date for the presidential election set for December 10. Because the assembly had decided that members of former ruling houses were eligible for election to public office, Louis Napoleon was able to stand for the presidency and was elected decisively in December, winning nearly four times the votes of his closest rival. Because he had spent most of his life outside France, Louis Napoleon's appearance and personality were unfamiliar to the assembly and the nation its members represented. He lacked his uncle's bearing but not his ego. Though standing only five feet five, with legs short in proportion to his body, a relatively large nose, a moustache, and pale gray eyes, he was possessed of a zeal to restore the nation's lost glory. Aiming to act as a force of order both within and outside France, he sent troops to Rome in 1850 when republican forces threatened papal supremacy.

Louis Napoleon Seizes Power in Coup

Constitutionally limited to one four-year term as president, he began to plan for a coup d'état with an eye to reestablishing the French Empire. He chose as the coup's date the anniversary of Napoleon's Austerlitz victory: on December 2, 1851, he seized power, with relatively little loss of blood, but with 26,884 arrests nationwide. On the 21st of that month, a plebiscite (vote) was held to confirm the president's action and 7.5 out of the 8 million voters responded in the affirmative.

He ruled as president for most of 1852 until a November 20th vote affirmed the reestablishment of the Empire. Louis Napoleon became Emperor Napoleon III in a December 1 ceremony and made his official imperial entrance to the capital the next day. In January 1853, he married the Spanish Eugenie de Montijo, who three years later bore him a son. Napoleon III's reign is curious in that it started out authoritarian but grew more liberal over time. He subordinated the legislative and judicial branches of the government to the executive; by careful manipulation, he was voted to dictatorship. The press was heavily censored. But this was all done in an effort primarily to restore the country's once dominant position in Europe; he genuinely believed that the nation needed a benevolent despot, protesting with some disingenuousness:

> If I do not represent the French Revolution I represent nothing.... Mine is a representative government with a freely elected Chamber voting laws and taxes. I am a sovereign possessing a civil list and I do not dip into the public purse whenever I like. We possess the *Code Napoleon* assuring everybody's equality before the law; an indepen-

dent judiciary; the opening of all posts, an army composed of the elite of the nation and not of mercenaries; there is liberty to write, think, and believe within the limits of the law.

With his nearly unlimited power, he reduced the senate and assembly to bodies which rubber-stamped his initiatives.

The emperor's political economy closely followed the ideas of the early 19th-century thinker, Comte Henri de Saint-Simon. He believed that massive government commitment to public works which improved transportation and communications were fundamental to France's economic health. Thus he supported, to the bourgeoisie's approval, vast increases in the nation's railroad network, improvements to port facilities, and the development in Paris of large financial concerns which soon came to rival the large banks of the rest of Europe. More than any other person, Napoleon III was responsible for shaping the Paris known to the 20th century with its wide boulevards, public gardens, public transport facilities, and buildings like the Opera. Though he kept a tight rein on the nation's political affairs, in economic dealings he offered a great deal of latitude. A firm proponent of economic liberalization, he wanted to break down France's protectionist barriers, a move which undermined middle-class support of his regime, for reforms promised bad times before improvement.

Though Napoleon III, upon accession to the throne, claimed peaceful intentions, he concentrated all foreign policy and military powers in his own hands and involved France in a number of foreign lands, none of which returned to the country the glory it had enjoyed under his uncle, Napoleon I. A believer in national self-determination, he believed even more, however, in the promotion of French national interest. French troops took part in the Crimean War of 1854 to 1856, the Franco-Austrian War over Italian unification in 1859, the attempt from 1862 to 1867 to install a Catholic-Austrian prince as ruler of Mexico, and, of course, the Franco-Prussian War; the nation asserted its colonial interests in Algeria, French Guyana, Indochina, and Senegal, among other places. In the European conflicts, the emperor generally ended up compromising his principles and gaining slight compensation in return. The colonial adventures provided little immediate payback, while requiring the dispersal of French troops around the world, unavailable for use on the European continent.

Domestically, Napoleon III had to make concessions to liberalism because he faced increasing discontentment with his rule. Beginning in 1860, the legislative branch started to regain some of the influence on national policy it had held prior to the Second Empire. Press controls were loosened later in the decade. Pressures in 1869 impelled him to consent to the formation of a cabinet, which came into being on January 2 of the following year, headed by Emile Ollivier. No longer any sort of absolute ruler, the emperor did nonetheless appoint himself the minister both of War and Marine. This marked the beginning of what has been called the "liberal empire," an empire of short duration.

In the summer of 1870, Count **Otto von Bismarck** maneuvered France into attacking Prussia to avenge a perceived affront that emerged in the contest over the succession to the Spanish throne. Bismarck had the objective of drawing all of the German states together to accelerate their unification and, not incidentally, of reducing France's military power while Prussia's was strong. Unfortunately for Napoleon III, the French army was poorly prepared for the efficient Prussian war machine. The emperor had been dilatory in recognizing the growing Prussian menace and in remedying the situation; he did not press for major military reforms until after the Prussians' decisive victory over the Austrians at Sadowa in 1866. In this case, it was too little, too late.

France Declares War on Prussia

France officially declared war on Prussia on June 19, to avenge the latter's insult to national pride. Plagued as always by the memory of his uncle, this emperor insisted upon taking field command of his troops, despite his advanced age and his tremendous suffering from gallstones. The Germans overwhelmed the French. Quicker to mobilize and endowed with valuable experience gained in its wars of 1864 and 1866, the Prussians and allies managed to surround a French army of 80,000, including Napoleon III, at Sedan, where, on September 2, he surrendered to King Wilhelm of Prussia. The emperor was imprisoned in Germany for six months at which point he was allowed to rejoin his family in London, where Eugenie and the Prince Imperial had fled from the newly established Third Republic. There Napoleon III spent the last two years of his life until his death in January 1873, after a series of gallbladder operations.

Napoleon III's legacy to his country was mixed. He betrayed no hint of having inherited his uncle's martial skills, proving a bungler in military and foreign policy issues. He did make a lasting impression on France economically and physically, guiding it through the dislocating forces of the industrial revolution and preparing its infrastructure for a modern economy. And his 22-year rule was not thoroughly despotic. He was an important stabilizing force as France groped its way toward a true republican government; his quasi-liberal reign may have served a crucial role in curbing the excesses which might well have appeared after the 1848 collapse of the monarchical system in France.

SOURCES:

Bierman, John. *Napoleon III and His Carnival Empire*. St. Martin's Press, 1988.

Bury, J. P. T. *Napoleon III and the Second Empire*. English Universities Press, 1964.

Thompson, J. M. *Louis Napoleon and the Second Empire*. Columbia University Press, 1983.

FURTHER READING:

Brodsky, Alyn. *Imperial Charade*. Bobbs-Merrill, 1978.

Gooch, G. P. *The Second Empire*. Longman, 1960.

Horatio Nelson

(1758–1805)

British naval commander, whose victories over Revolutionary and Napoleonic France assured British naval supremacy for over 100 years.

Born on September 29, 1758, at Burnham Thorpe, Norfolk, England; died in Battle of Trafalgar on October 21, 1805; son of Reverend Edmund and Catherine (Suckling) Nelson; educated at William Paston's School, North Walsham; married: Frances Nisbet, 1787; became almost equally famous for his naval victories and his scandalous love affair with Lady Emma Hamilton. Descendants: Horatia Nelson-Ward (Nelson's only child by Emma Hamilton); the Nelson peerage passed on through the Admiral's brother, Reverend William Nelson, 1st Earl Nelson and 2nd Duke of Bronte.

Far above London's Trafalgar Square, on a column towering 145 feet above the pavement, stands the statue of Admiral Horatio Nelson, the most renowned captain of the Age of Sail. His naval victories over Britain's enemies not only ensured his nation's survival at the beginning of the 19th century, they also gave his country dominion of the seas until the 20th century. Fittingly, Nelson faces southward in the direction of his greatest triumph over a joint French and Spanish fleet at Cape Trafalgar in 1805.

He was born on September 29, 1758, in Burnham Thorpe, Norfolk, England. His father Edmund Nelson was a modest Anglican rector, but his mother Catherine Suckling Nelson had important relations in the national Church and in the Royal Navy. Indeed, it was the young Nelson's uncle, Captain Maurice Suckling, who secured the boy a post as midshipman in the fleet in November 1770. Although Nelson's grand career could not have been anticipated, the appointment was a welcome deliverance for a boy from a large family of eight surviving children and a widower father. For Horatio Nelson had sustained the first great loss of his life at the age of nine when his mother died. As

Contributed by C. David Rice, Professor of History, Central Missouri State University, Warrensburg, Missouri

"England expects every man will do his duty."

NELSON'S SIGNAL TO THE BRITISH FLEET ON THE EVE OF THE BATTLE OF TRAFALGAR author Leonard Cowie has noted, however, Edmund Nelson, despite his limited means, managed to send Nelson to three schools: the Royal Grammar School at Norwich, the Downham Market School, and Sir William Paston's School at North Walsham. While he displayed no important scholarly talent, young Nelson did learn to read and spell well enough and gained a measure of classical Latin and some Shakespeare. He knew the Bible rather well, too, as might be expected of a parson's son. In later years, he passed many of his long hours at sea in reading, and his letters exhibit a talent for expression not given to many others of his profession.

Little is known of his boyhood before his departure for the navy, but from the age of 12 onward, when he joined the warship *Raissonable* as a midshipman under his uncle's command, his youth was filled with adventure. He learned the basic nautical skills and made his first voyage on an expedition to the West Indies on board the *Triumph* in 1771. It was his first assignment away from his uncle's protection, but he performed well enough to be accepted for an important polar expedition on board the *Carcass* in 1773. By age 15, then, the boy had gained valuable experience in two major voyages. He had learned much, including the fact that, despite his chronic seasickness, he loved the naval life. He made up his mind to become an officer and carve out a career in His Majesty's service.

With help and encouragement from his Uncle Maurice, Nelson obtained new assignments and studied to take the examination that would bring him an officer's commission. A mission to the East Indies in 1775 brought him his first taste of combat, off the Indian coast, and the first of several bouts of malaria. Then, the outbreak of the American War for Independence, with the demand for experienced officers the war provided, gave him his opportunity. In April 1777, he passed the examination and received a commission as a second lieutenant.

The American war was a disaster for his country, particularly after France and Spain joined the conflict against Britain, but it provided Nelson with combat experience that served him well. He performed convoy duty in the Atlantic, took part in actions against American, French, and Spanish privateers, and seized every chance to impress his superiors. Eventually, he was given command of the sloop *Badger* and gained the rank of captain. An attempt by Nelson to capture Spanish San Juan in Nicaragua in early 1780 failed, but despite defeat and the ravages of malaria, Nelson had attracted notice. A man who obviously sought

CHRONOLOGY

1758	Born at Burnham Thorpe in Norfolk, England
1770	Entered the Royal Navy as midshipman
1777	Became a lieutenant
1778	Assumed first command over HMS *Badger*
1789	French Revolution erupted
1793	Appointed commander of the *Agamemnon;* France declared war on Great Britain
1794	Nelson lost sight in right eye during combat at Calvi on Corsica
1795	Captured French warship, the *Ca Ira*
1796	Spain declared war on Great Britain
1797	Nelson distinguished himself in naval victory over Spain at Cape St. Vincent; promoted rear admiral; lost his right arm at Santa Cruz
1798	Destroyed French fleet in the Battle of the Nile; fell in love with Lady Hamilton
1800	Entered House of Lords; scandalized England
1801	Left his wife; fathered daughter with Lady Hamilton; destroyed Danish fleet at Copenhagen
1803	Assumed command of HMS *Victory;* British declared war on France
1804	Promoted to vice admiral; Spain and Britain resumed war
1805	Pursued French fleet; Battle of Trafalgar; Nelson decimated French-Spanish fleet; died on board the *Victory*
1806	Buried in St. Paul's Cathedral

recognition and reveled in the dangers of combat was certain to have a future in a fighting navy. The fighting ended, however, in 1783, when the Peace of Paris confirmed the independence of the United States from Great Britain.

Without a war, the Royal Navy constricted, and Nelson was a casualty of the reduction. Placed on half-pay, he passed some time in France, failed to win the heart of an English cleric's daughter at St. Omer, and despaired for his future. Finally given command of the *Boreas* in 1784, he returned to the West Indies. It was there that he met the widow, Frances Nisbet, and eventually married her on March 12, 1787. Frances, known as Fanny, was a good and faithful wife but proved to be uninspiring and unappreciative of her mercurial husband. By the summer, she was back in England with

Nelson where he was beginning a difficult five-year period of extended leave, marked by idleness and frustration at Burnham Thorpe. For a man like Nelson, it was a "piping time of peace." He was born for war.

War did return to England in 1793. While Nelson stewed in Norfolk, the great French Revolution burst upon Europe. A series of frightening events led to the collapse of the French monarchy, the execution of the French king and queen, and the formation of an aggressive French Republic. Europe reacted, and by 1793 France was at war with most of Europe's monarchies, including Great Britain. It was time for men of Nelson's caliber again. In January 1793, he was recalled to the fleet and given command of the *Agamemnon*, a 64-gun ship of war. Shortly, he was on patrol in the Mediterranean, and in August visited the Kingdom of the Two Sicilies. In Naples, he first encountered Sir William Hamilton, the 63-year-old English ambassador to the Neapolitan court, and Lady Emma Hamilton, then aged 28. In time, Nelson was to become completely infatuated with Lady Hamilton, beginning a celebrated love affair.

Exploits Win Honors for Nelson

For the moment, however, the adventures of war called him to action. Sent to attack an enemy position at Calvi on the island of Corsica, Nelson suffered the permanent loss of vision in his right eye on July 12, 1794, when a shell exploded near him and drove gravel into the eye. Undeterred, he resumed his duties and gained much respect in the fleet by capturing the huge French man-of-war, the *Ca Ira* off Genoa on March 14, 1795. For veteran naval men, it was evident that Nelson was a sailor of exceptional ability and personal courage. If the French war continued, he would certainly do great things. He proved them correct at the important naval battle off Cape St. Vincent, Portugal, in 1797. The battle, precipitated by Spain's entry into the war on the side of France, provided Nelson a splendid, if dangerous, opportunity. Commanding the *Captain*, a 74-gun vessel, he prevented a critical Spanish maneuver from succeeding by holding off the mammoth *Santissima Trinidada,* bearing 130 guns, the largest ship in the world at the time. The action provided the margin for victory, and Nelson became an instant hero at home and throughout the fleet. He was promoted to Rear Admiral of the Blue, the color, along with Red and White, providing certain precedence and rank, and awarded the Knighthood of the Bath.

Fame could not protect him from the hazards of war, however, and in July 1797, while lead-ing a raid on the Spanish town of Santa Cruz, Nelson was hit by a bullet in his right elbow. The arm had to be amputated. Suffering enormously, the admiral returned to England to recover.

As Nelson recuperated with his wife in England, a brilliant and successful French general, **Napoleon Bonaparte,** was preparing a great expedition to seize Egypt and eventually to march on British India. In May 1798, Bonaparte's force left Toulon and, by July, Egypt was in his power. Nelson, having returned to the Mediterranean in March, was assigned to tracking the French and destroying them. Unaware of Bonaparte's destination, Nelson, with 14 warships, anxiously scoured the inland sea for weeks, worried but determined to find and annihilate his prey. At last the French were found, and on July 25, 1798, although night was coming on, Nelson boldly led his ships into Aboukir Bay against 13 French sail of the line. A fierce, bloody action followed, and Nelson himself suffered a severe scalp wound while brilliantly directing the attack. When morning dawned, all but two of the French vessels were destroyed or captured, including the formidable flagship, the *Orient.*

Admiral Falls in Love with Lady Hamilton

The Battle of the Nile ruined French ambitions in the East and, besides bestowing British control of the Mediterranean, made Nelson the most celebrated sailor of his day. Honors and promotions flowed in his direction, but he did not return home to acknowledge them. Instead, he sailed to Naples to evacuate Sir William and Lady Hamilton and the Neapolitan royal family to Sicily to escape a French army moving on the city. Named Baron Nelson of the Nile and recalled to England, the victor of Aboukir would not leave the Mediterranean. He lingered, intervening in Italian politics, watching the French, and becoming hopelessly entangled with Emma Hamilton.

The affair with Lady Hamilton was open and obvious to everyone. William Hamilton appears to have silently accepted the situation and made no public protest, even appearing with the two lovers on most occasions. Nelson, with one arm and one eye gone, his teeth beginning to come out, his hair altogether white, behaved like a moonstruck boy, anxious to please the irrepressible Emma. He even disobeyed direct orders to return home or to report to other stations. When he eventually did make his way to England in 1800, he brought the Hamiltons with him. In London and elsewhere, the affair was the topic of conversation and speculation on every side. Fanny Nelson could only endure the chagrin of the estranged wife and finally separated from her husband in 1801. Soon thereafter, Emma gave birth to a daughter, fathered by Nelson, whom she named Horatia.

Nelson had little time to enjoy his romance or his new daughter. French pressure had created a Baltic confederation against Britain, and Nelson, under the overall command of Sir Hyde Parker, was ordered to attack the northern forces. At Copenhagen on April 2, 1801, on board the *Elephant*, Nelson engaged the entire Danish fleet. It was a grueling contest, and after three hours of heavy Danish fire, Nelson received a signal from Parker to disengage. He refused, telling his subordinates that he could not see the signal as he had looked through the telescope with his blind eye. It was the character of the man that he would not relent, nor shun grave danger. At the height of the action, Nelson was peppered with splinters from a shot hitting the mainmast. He commented: "It is warm work, and this day may be the last to any of us at any moment, but mark you, I would not be elsewhere for thousands."

Daring and persistence purchased the day. The Danish fleet was destroyed, and Nelson had once again thwarted his country's enemies and added to his own repute. Through it all, his love for Emma Hamilton and his daughter sustained him. In a letter to Lady Hamilton in February 1801, he said: "In fair or foul weather, at sea or on shore, I am for ever yours." Yet, it could not have been easy for Nelson to leave his wife and embrace the illicit union. Tom Pocock, in his biography of the admiral, points out that Nelson was, at bottom, the poor rector's son, the boy who had lost his mother. He longed for, demanded, approval and fame. Ironically, Pocock notes, Nelson found solace for his predicament in religion. Believing himself in "a privileged communion" with God, "he was able to persuade himself that his liaison was, despite the legal and social obstacles, a spiritual marriage."

After Copenhagen, Nelson—though lionized throughout the realm—could not be spared from duty. He was assigned to guard the English Channel from a possible invasion attempt by Napoleon, who had brought a vast army to the coast. A year-long peace in 1802 between Britain and France, however, allowed him some time with Lady Hamilton and Horatia at Paradise Merton, a house he had purchased in Surrey. But the peace did not last. When war was resumed in 1803, he was sent again to the Mediterranean on board the *Victory*, a 100-gun ship of the line. For two years, he blockaded the French coast, but in early 1805 the French fleet, commanded by Admiral Villeneuve, put to sea, hoping perhaps to lure most British ships from European waters in order that Napoleon's army could embark for England. Nelson pursued Villeneuve to the West Indies, but sufficient British ships remained to discourage any descent on the English shore.

Nelson Serves at Battle of Trafalgar

In the summer of 1805, Villeneuve brought his fleet back to Europe and was joined by the Spanish navy at Cadiz. Nelson took up station off the coast to await the enemy's next move. At last, in October, Villeneuve came out with the combined naval forces of France and Spain. There were 33 warships on the allied side; Nelson prepared to strike them with 28. His plan was to sail forward in two columns and cut the enemy line into three parts, disposing of each in turn with superior British navigation and gunnery. Nelson, on the *Victory*, would lead the northern column, and Admiral Collingwood, on the *Royal Sovereign*, would head the other. The enemy was sighted on October 21. Nelson drafted an addition to his will at about 11 o'clock, asking that Lady Hamilton be recognized for her services to England. About noon, he sent out the most famous signal of naval history: "England expects that every man will do his duty." Clearly, he expected much of himself as well on that climactic day. To Captain Henry Blackwood he remarked as the battle began, "God bless you Blackwood, I shall never speak to you again."

At one o'clock the *Victory* drove into the French line, tangling lines immediately with the French *Redoubtable* while French musket fire sprayed over her deck. As Nelson paced the deck with Captain Hardy, a shot passed through his shoulder and lungs, breaking his backbone. Conscious and aware of the bleeding wound's severity, he told Hardy, "They've done for me at last." Taken below decks, he lived for three more hours, occasionally speaking as news came of one French or Spanish captain after another striking his colors. Understanding that he had won the day, he said his last at four-thirty: "Thank God, I have done my duty."

Nelson's body was brought home in a barrel of brandy, and a splendid, solemn funeral took place on January 9, 1806, in London. Statesmen, admirals, and the entire crew of the *Victory* marched in the hours-long procession. His final resting place was the crypt of St. Paul's Cathedral.

Trafalgar was the capstone of the extraordinary career of this complicated, vain, brilliant, and, finally, indispensable man. His victories are justly famous, and it is no exaggeration to say that he made Britain the mistress of the seas. With his military counterpart, the duke of Wellington, Nelson made possible the ultimate defeat of Napoleon's imperial France and, in so doing, helped to shape the modern world. He had found his glory, and, more important, he had done his duty.

SOURCES:

Cowie, Leonard W. *Lord Nelson 1758–1805: A Bibliography.* Mecklin.

Pocock, Tom. *Horatio Nelson.* Bodley Head, 1987.

Walder, David. *Nelson.* Dial Press, 1978.

FURTHER READING:

Howarth, D. *Trafalgar: The Nelson Touch.* Collins, 1969.

Oman, Carola. *Nelson.* Greenwood Press, 1946.

Pettigrew, Thomas James, ed. *Memoires of the Life of Vice-Admiral Lord Viscount Nelson, K. B.* 2 vols. T. and W. Boone, 1848.

Nero

(A.D. 37—68)

Dilettante and self-proclaimed artistic genius, who was the last emperor of the Julio-Claudian house, Rome's first imperial dynasty.

"A closer study of the Domitian family history would probably suggest [that] many of Nero's vices were inherited, although indeed, he made a ghastly caricature of his ancestor's virtues."

SUETONIUS

Nero's father, Gnaeus Domitius Ahenobarbus ("the bronze bearded") was a notorious monster who, among his outrages, murdered a dependent for not imbibing as much wine as ordered. Somewhat thin-skinned, at another time he gouged out the eyes of a political critic. A man who recognized vice when he saw it, Domitius is reported to have predicted Nero's depravity when he first saw his son. Although Nero's mother, the younger **Agrippina,** was not so discernibly vicious, she nevertheless ruthlessly pursued imperial power. A sister of **Caligula,** she officially associated with his rule until she and one of her lovers (Aemilius Lepidus) were implicated in a plot against her emperor/brother. Following a period of exile, she was recalled to Rome with her uncle Claudius's accession.

Despite their biological affinity, Agrippina married Claudius and, as the emperor's wife through his declining years, she sought to secure her son Nero's future over that of Claudius's natural son, Britannicus. In the year A.D. 50, she convinced her husband to adopt Nero. In addition, she assured the loyalty of Rome's only standing troops, the Praetorian Guard, by arranging for Afranius

Name variations: Nero Claudius Caesar. Born Lucius Domitius Ahenobarbus on December 15, A.D. 37; committed suicide on June 9, A.D. 68; son of Gnaeus Domitius Ahenobarbus and Agrippina the Younger (sister of Caligula of the Julio-Claudian house); married: Octavia (daughter of Claudius), A.D. 53; married: Poppaea Sabina, A.D. 63. Predecessor: Britannicus. Successor: Vespasian

Contributed by William Greenwalt, Associate Professor of Classical History, Santa Clara University, Santa Clara, California

CHRONOLOGY

A.D. 37	Nero born
A.D. 41	Accession of Claudius
A.D. 49	Claudius married Agrippina
A.D. 50	Claudius adopted Nero as his son
A.D. 53	Nero married Octavia, daughter of Claudius
A.D. 54	Claudius poisoned
A.D. 55	Britannicus died
A.D. 59	Agrippina murdered at Nero's command
A.D. 62	Burrus died; Seneca forced to retire; Octavia divorced and executed
A.D. 63	Nero married Poppaea Sabina
A.D. 64	Central Rome destroyed by fire; Christians persecuted locally as scapegoats
A.D. 65	Seneca executed along with many prominent Romans; Nero murdered the pregnant Poppaea Sabina
A.D. 66	Nero bestowed the crown of Armenia on Tiridates; Judaea revolted against Rome
A.D. 67	Nero artistically toured Greece; famine in Rome
A.D. 68	Frontier legions rebelled; Nero committed suicide

Burrus to be named as their prefect. Not convinced that these were enough to insure Nero's preference in terms of succession, Agrippina further arranged a marriage between Nero and Claudius's daughter, Octavia. Once connections between Claudius and Nero were reinforced, and in anticipation of reigning as the power behind Nero's throne, Agrippina would eventually poison a bowl of mushrooms—Claudius's favorite food.

But until then, young Nero's future was by no means certain. His mother's exile and his father's death, which occurred when the boy was three, had prompted Caligula to confiscate Nero's estate. As a result, the boy lived with Domitia Lepida, his father's sister (and, allegedly, also his lover), until Claudius's accession restored Nero's fortune. Still, Nero remained vulnerable, especially since Claudius's third wife Messalina considered Nero a threat to the eventual accession of Britannicus (which, of course, he proved to be).

Perhaps it was the insecurity of his youth which led Nero to seek escape in music and sport. By age seven, he proved so adept at singing and

playing the lyre that he began to perform publicly (initially, outside of Rome), despite the disapproval of most of Rome's nobility who considered such displays beneath the dignity of one so close to imperial power. Eventually, he also took to acting in the tragic theater—again to the chagrin of Rome's elite. Nero clearly relished the applause he inevitably received while performing, even if one could not always tell whether the acclaim thus offered was sincere. Later, as an adult, Nero's need for adulation would grow to the extent that when performing, he would do everything possible to assure the undivided attention of his audience—even ordering doors locked against premature exit. (Vespasian, the future emperor, once greatly offended Nero and endangered his life by falling asleep during one of Nero's recitals.) Whatever his talent, Nero took his art seriously and spent considerable effort composing songs and perfecting his delivery.

His second great passion was chariot racing—a sport he both supported and enthusiastically practiced. His combined love of artistic performance and racing would eventually lead him to introduce to Rome two Greek-style festivals (the Juvenalia and the Neronia, organized in A.D. 59 and 61 respectively), so that he could share his passions with the inhabitants of his native city (in this way contributing significantly to the age of "bread and circuses").

Prior to his death, Claudius fostered Nero's formal education by choosing **L. Annaeus Seneca,** the renowned orator, playwright, and philosopher, as the boy's tutor. Under Seneca's hand, Nero began his official career as a legal advocate with the customary rhetorical demonstrations. Consequently, when Claudius died in A.D. 54, Nero was politically more advanced than Britannicus and was hailed emperor. Thereafter, the teenaged Nero presided over Claudius's lavish funeral and official deification, all of which proceeded according to Agrippina's plan.

But it soon became clear that Nero would not act as his mother's puppet. Although initially prominent, Agrippina's assumption of imperial prerogatives annoyed Nero, and convinced him that her presence should be balanced by the surprisingly responsible Seneca and Burrus, commander of the Praetorian Guard. Nero cleverly played an ambitious mother against two experienced public figures, liberating himself from the control of any one perspective. Thus assured that no one faction could usurp his imperial status, he created a situation in which he could continue to devote much of his time to the pursuit of private pleasures. Irked by her son's "ingratitude" and irate at seemingly modest rebuffs, such as when Nero refused to break off an affair with a lowly freedwoman, Agrippina attempted to temper Nero's impertinence by cozying up to Britannicus. Far from bringing Nero to heel, however, this strategy merely led to the "mysterious" death of Britannicus and the fall of Agrippina's alleged lover Pallas, in A.D. 55.

Agrippina Is Murdered

Agrippina's belief that Nero was emperor solely due to her own stratagems gravely insulted her son. As a result, she fell from grace, despite attempts to regain Nero's favor (including one effort at incestuous seduction). Nevertheless, Nero remained unmoved and for four years heaped humiliations upon his mother, until he grew tired of the sport and devised an elaborate plot to murder her. Feigning reconciliation in A.D. 59, he gave Agrippina a surprise birthday yacht. Above the couch where she was expected to recline, a weight was built which would be released by the crew when the boat was at sea. To hide the intended crime, the crew would then see to the breakup of the vessel. As devious as the plan was, it failed, and a furious Agrippina swam to shore. When the horrified Seneca and Burrus learned of the botched attempt, they realized the necessity of completing the deed, for in their minds the only thing worse than attempted matricide was the certain broadcast of its unsuccessful attempt. Thus, upon their order, Agrippina was dispatched in a more conventional fashion, but only after she ordered the assassin to strike, symbolically, through her womb.

Until the death of his mother eliminated a potent psychological restraint, Nero had ruled credibly—largely relying on the sober advice of Seneca and Burrus to spite the ambitions of Agrippina. During his first five years as emperor, therefore, Nero played his role to traditional expectations: he held public office, being consul four times; refused extravagant honors; esteemed the senate and subsidized many of its financially strapped members; distributed largesse to Rome's poor; founded colonies; and generally lived up to the imperial ideal established by **Augustus**. Nevertheless, his more reckless side even then made itself manifest through extravagant expenditure. Even more disturbing was his attraction to nocturnal hooliganism. Not only did the emperor carouse with Rome's lowlifes into the wee hours of the morning, he also engaged in overt criminal activity, including burglary and assault. Nero once nearly paid the price for such titillating lawlessness, when a senator unknowingly almost killed him after an assault on the man's wife. This narrow

escape did little to turn Nero into an honest man. It did, however, make him more cautious. Thereafter, he always roamed with a band of armed bodyguards.

Notwithstanding these early indications of irresponsibility, the murder of Agrippina seemed to free Nero from any need to abide by the constraints of conventional morality. In addition, his growing disregard for propriety was fostered by an increasing need for money—required not for the legitimate concerns of state, but to feed an insatiable demand for the high life. Among other policies introduced to offset a rapidly increasing indigence, Nero came to expect all of the wealthy in Rome to include the emperor as a legal heir to a significant portion of their estates upon their deaths. If anyone failed to do so, Nero both confiscated the entire estate in question and heavily fined the lawyer who drafted the offending will. Not surprisingly, as a result of such tactics, his relations with most of Rome's elite deteriorated. As things worsened, conspiracies grew. By A.D. 62, the old bane of imperial rule—the treason trial, complete with the professional informer—was once again resurrected, with those convicted losing their property to the emperor.

Also in that year, Burrus died, probably of natural causes; Seneca was forced into retirement (only to be falsely accused of treason three years later and compelled to commit suicide); and Nero divorced, and almost immediately executed, Octavia. Henceforth, with Nero bound by none of the influences of his youth, those near to him (such as one of Burrus's successors, Tigellinus) received and maintained their posts not through competence or integrity, but through their capacity to entertain Nero or to provide him with money so that he could entertain himself. Throughout, he maintained his love of sport in combination with public spectacle. While touring Greece in A.D. 67, he personally drove a novelty chariot with ten instead of the usual four horses at the Olympic Games. Nero's extra horses made his chariot so unwieldy that he fell during the race, preventing him from finishing the course. Nevertheless, the race officials proclaimed him the race's victor, much to Nero's delight. Being emperor had its advantages.

As Nero's hedonism grew, so did his lechery. One affair of note was that with Poppaea Sabina, beginning in A.D. 58. Poppaea was not just another of Nero's playthings—she was of senatorial background and married to Marcus Salvius Otho, who would briefly reign as emperor after Nero's death. Beautiful and ambitious, Poppaea seduced Nero, who ordered her husband to Lusitania so as to

Nero at the burning of Rome.

facilitate their adultery. Shortly after Nero divorced Octavia, he married Poppaea. Although Nero seems to have cared for her as much as he ever cared for anyone, in A.D. 65 he killed her by kicking her in the stomach while she was pregnant with their child, after she complained about his spending too much time at the racetrack.

Nero Profits from the Great Fire

Exhibiting an increasingly tyrannical arrogance, Nero alienated Rome's ruling class and estranged the rest of the city's population by his response to the great fire of A.D. 64 which ravaged Rome's central districts. His initial reaction upon learning of the disaster (he was out of the city when the blaze struck) was appropriate: he rushed home and drafted a set of ordinances mandating wider streets and safer construction materials in an attempt to limit the damage of future fires. Subsequently, however, he acquired cheaply a large tract of prime fire-leveled real estate for the construction of an urban villa with extensive gardens. His profiteering generated resentment, and soon rumors circulated suggesting that Nero had arranged the inferno for his own benefit. Before long, sullen mobs threatened violence. Seeking desperately for some unpopular scapegoat on which to blame the fire, Nero lit upon the small Christian community in the city. The resulting, short-lived persecution of the local sect led to the death of Saints **Peter** and **Paul** and helped to estrange the relationship between the Empire and the Church. Although Nero thus diverted blame from himself, his "Golden House" remained an irritant to most Romans, and he never recaptured what popularity he had previously possessed.

Although Nero's problems at home mounted as the irresponsibility of his unchecked rule grew, his most serious challenge arose among the armies on the frontiers. The Empire faced three revolts during Nero's reign—in Britain, Judaea, and Armenia. The first two were stimulated largely by Roman greed, insensitivity, administrative incompetence, and an indictable lack of foresight from the emperor on down. In Britain, oppressive moneylenders, land confiscations, and the violation of religious spaces sparked "**Boudicca**'s Rebellion" and the massacre of whole Roman settlements before Suetonius Paulinus brutally crushed all resistance as far north of the Dee and Humber rivers in A.D. 60. In Judaea in A.D. 66, a riot in Caesarea between Jews and Gentiles exploded into a wider conflict during which the Jewish Zealots overran some Roman positions before the future emperor, Vespasian, relieved the incompetent officials on the spot. Slowly, Vespasian reduced Galilee and the Transjordan regions before besieging Jerusalem (A.D. 67—68), where he was still in command when Nero died.

Armenia constituted Nero's only foreign policy "success." This kingdom in eastern Anatolia had long been coveted for strategic reasons by Rome and its eastern neighbor, the Parthian Empire. Claimed by Rome as a dependent state, the Romans preferred to rule the distant region indirectly, through the agency of a client king. In spite of Roman claims, Tiridates, the brother of the ruling Parthian king, had established himself on Armenia's throne at the time of Nero's accession in A.D. 54. Six years later, in A.D. 60, Nero sent a claimant named Tigranes, with an army under Gnaeus Domitius Corbulo, to secure the realm for Rome. Initially, Corbulo met with success, but in A.D. 62 after his army withdrew, Tiridates successfully drove the Roman puppet from Armenia. Corbulo then reestablished Rome's military reputation but realized that Rome had no competent alternative to Tiridates. Consequently, Corbulo negotiated a compromise whereby Nero agreed to recognize Tiridates as Armenia's king, but only after he had ceremoniously accepted the yoke of Roman dominion. In A.D. 66, Tiridates made his way to Rome where, in a grand display of imperial theater, he publicly prostrated himself before Nero. Nero made the most of the moment to rivet every Roman eye upon his own superior majesty, in an effort to enhance an otherwise nonexistent "military" reputation. Nevertheless, whatever renown Nero might have gained was quickly squandered when he (fearing the growing reputation of Corbulo and the latter's potential as a military/political rival) ordered Corbulo to commit suicide, which in A.D. 66 the general dutifully did. The enforced demise of a competent commander angered Rome's military professionals, especially coming as it did after 12 years of imperial neglect.

Open revolt was delayed until A.D. 68, when Nero's grand tour of Greece as a musical performer in a series of artistic contests during which he was awarded 1,800 artistic and athletic prizes by his subservient Hellenic subjects so bankrupted the state that he could no longer afford to pay his troops (despite a devaluation of the coinage, c. A.D. 62) or provide subsidized grain for the people of Rome. Attempting to pay for his hedonistic megalomania, Nero simply had run out of money. Long-festering resentments then flared in several provinces. The first to rebel was C. Julius Vindex in Gaul, but soon many—led by Servius Sulpicius Galba, whom Vindex proposed should replace Nero—joined the uprising. Vindex died in the resulting chaos, but by the time of his death a general conflagration had erupted throughout the Empire, in the East as well as the West.

The widespread revolt paralyzed Nero—only recently returned to Rome from the thunderous applause of his "adoring" Greek subjects. More than anything else, this inability to react to a serious threat enticed the initially reluctant, and there followed a complete breakdown in loyalty. Still Nero did nothing. A full-scale civil war resulted which did not abate until Vespasian from Judaea superseded Otho from Lusitania, who replaced Galba from Spain, who supplanted Nero (A.D. 68—69). As the bubble burst, the Praetorian Guard, which had long abetted Nero, insofar as it was richly rewarded for protecting him, reasoned that its own well-being demanded Nero's assassination. The guard, however, did not reach Nero in time. Aided by a small group of loyal slaves, Nero escaped the palace to Rome's suburbs, where he committed suicide just before his hiding place was discovered by the Praetorians. The final scene was prolonged by Nero's cowardice, but eventually the courage was found. As he plunged a knife into his own neck, he uttered the immortal words: "Death! And so great an artist!"

SOURCES:

Dio Cassius. *Roman History.* Vol. 8. Harvard University Press, 1917.

Suetonius. "Nero," in *The Twelve Caesars.* Penguin Classics, 1957.

Tacitus. *The Annals of Imperial Rome.* Penguin Classics, 1956.

FURTHER READING:

Garzetti, A. *From Tiberius to the Antonines.* Methuen, 1974.

Grant, M. *Nero.* Scholar's Bookshelf, 1989.

Warmington, B. H. *Nero: Reality and Legend.* Norton, 1969.

Alexander Nevsky

(c. 1220–1263)

Prince of Novgorod and grand duke of Vladimir, whose policy of collaboration with the Mongols resulted in the unification of Russia and forever altered its history.

"It is true what you [my grandees] have told me—that there is none equal to this prince."

BATU, KHAN
OF THE GOLDEN HORDE
THE NIKONIAN CHRONICLE

One of the most significant of early Russian rulers, Alexander Nevsky became prince of Novgorod at a time of the gravest danger for Russia. When most its principalities had been overrun and destroyed by the Mongols, and the country was invaded by Lithuanians, Swedes, and German Knights, the very existence of the country was at stake. Had Russia not had a leader of his character and foresight, the country might have been permanently destroyed and the history not only of Eastern Europe but of the entire world would have been severely altered.

Alexander was born in 1219 or 1220, probably in the city of Vladimir in northern Russia where he was more than likely raised. At the age of 17, when his father went to Kiev to take over the reigns of government, Alexander was sent to Novgorod to be its prince. Thereafter, though he frequently quarrelled with the merchant elite of the city and more than once left it to live elsewhere, his fate would be linked to that of the merchant republic.

After the 11th century, the great Principality of Rus, centered at Kiev and extending from the Baltic to the Black Sea, and one of the most

Contributed by Robert H. Hewsen, Professor of History, Glassboro State College, Glassboro, New Jersey

Name variations: Nevski. Pronunciation: NEV-skee or NEF-skee. Born Aleksandr Yaroslavovich in c. 1220; died on November 14, 1263, at Gorodets on the Volga, near Nizhni-Novgorod; member of the dynasty of Rurik, the semi-legendary founder of the first Russian state in the ninth century; one of six sons of Yaroslav II, Grand Duke of Vladimir (1238–46) and Theodosia (daughter of Mystislav the Gallant, Prince of Novgorod, one of the greatest warriors of his day); his brothers were Constantine, Andrew, Michael, Yaroslav, Prince of Tver, and Basil; married: a Polovetsian (Cuman or Kipchak Turkish) princess in 1238; children: Basil, Dmitri, Andrew, and Daniel.

promising states of medieval Europe, broke up into a welter of warring Russian principalities each ruled by one or another branches of the House of Rurik. In 1174, the new grand prince, Vsevolod, called "Big Nest" because of his numerous children, asserted his authority over the other princes of Russia, enforcing peace between them and imposing upon the merchant republic of Novgorod such princes as he chose. When Vsevolod died, however, in 1212, a civil war broke out among the princes of his family, and the Russian state seemed likely to disintegrate again. Each prince asserted his independence in his own realm, which was then divided and subdivided among his heirs.

The success of the Grand Duchy of Vladimir-Suzdal was based, first of all, on the triumph of its princes over their *boyars* ("nobles"), supposedly in defense of its "little people." In place of rule by local nobles, each prince appointed trusted agents to run his realm and make periodic journeys throughout his lands to see at first hand the condition of his people. Other factors were the good soil of the region, the relatively mild climate (by Russian standards), and the location of Vladimir, Suzdal, and later Moscow at the center of the new trade routes established in the Mongol period and several river systems running in all directions. Moscow, for example, was located on a large tributary of the Oka, itself a tributary of the mighty Volga.

To the east of Vladimir lay the khanate of the Volga Bulgars, a Turkic state centered on the upper Volga. In southern Russia, the principalities were ravaged by continuous raids of the Kipchak Turks, a nomadic people of the steppes whom the Russians knew as the Polovetsians. To the west lay the Grand Duchy of Lithuania; to the northwest, the German Knights and the Danes on the Baltic coast lording it over the local Baltic and Finnish tribes; and beyond them, the kingdom of Sweden. The Germans had been active in the easternmost Baltic for close to a century, where they founded the town of Riga from where they dominated the local Latvian tribes (Letts). The Danes arrived later, founding the town of Reval in 1219 and dominating the local Estonians. Russia thus had, as yet, no outlet to the Baltic Sea and depended on the northwestern lake cities of Novgorod—a kind of Baltic Venice called "Lord Novgorod the Great" for its wealth and power—and Pskov, both of them trading republics characterized by weak princes dominated by strong municipal councils representing the merchant grandees. Located close to the Baltic and having strong ties with the other Germans, Danes, and Swedes and with the various Baltic trading cities, these republics were of the greatest economic importance to the rest of the north Russian principalities, especially Vladimir-Suzdal.

The chief difference between the republics and the other principalities of north Russia was the fact that in the republics, the *veche* ("town council") had maintained its traditional powers and even enhanced them at the expense of the local prince, whereas in the rest of the Russian principalities the *veches* had either disappeared or fallen completely under the increasingly authoritarian power of the prince. Novgorod, however, was a city beset by constant turmoil between the merchants and craftsmen, the rich and the poor, and the pro- and anti-Vladimir factions. The rich and influential classes became extremely astute in playing off one Rurikid prince against another in order to maximize their own autonomy; the poor tended to favor the rule of the princes of Vladimir. Riots and other disorders were common.

Early in the 13th century, the nomadic Mongol tribes, a people living to the north of China, were united under a ruler known to history as **Genghis Khan.** Under his dynamic leadership China was conquered in 1215 and then Turkestan (Central Asia), after which the Mongols passed north of the Caspian Sea into the Crimean Peninsula attacking the Polovetsians whose *khan* ("chief"), Kotyan, appealed for aid to the Russian princes. Although the prince of Vladimir-Suzdal declined to help the enemies of south Russia, other princes rode out to meet the Mongols (or Tatars as the Russians called them). After an initial victory, the princes were defeated on the River Kalka in 1223, after which the Mongols withdrew as suddenly as they had arrived.

Genghis died in 1227 and was succeeded by his son Ugeday, who launched a massive invasion of the neighboring lands in three different directions. His nephew Batu was sent to conquer the northwest. The invasion began in 1237 with a crushing defeat of the Volga Bulgars, leaving the Russian principalities wide open to the invaders. Divided and unprepared, the Russians were able to offer virtually no resistance. Ryazan was the first city to fall, then the army of Vladimir-Suzdal was destroyed, after which Vladimir itself was overwhelmed, and then the principality of Tver.

The Mongols conquered by commanding their enemies to surrender, thereby preserving their lives and property; if the enemies resisted, the Mongols destroyed cities and murdered every man, woman, and child they could lay their hands on. Their chief strength lay in their numbers and their method of attack. Traveling en masse with horses, camels, and wagons, the Mongols would surround a city and drive as many people as possible within the walls. Bringing up siege engines, including battering rams and enormous catapults, they would then build a palisade, or fence of stakes, around the exterior wall to prevent anyone from escaping. Secure in their numbers, the Mongols would send wave after wave of attackers, wearing down the exhausted defenders until the city fell. Seizing everything of value, they would then slaughter the entire population. Sparing neither age, rank, nor gender, they would carry their fury into the countryside destroying every village, monastery, and country retreat in their range, taking what sustenance they needed, burning the rest of the crops, and slaying the cattle. The survivors, who fled to forests and caves, frequently perished of hunger and exposure.

The Russian prince Yuri went out to meet the Mongols with a number of other princes but was slain in battle on the River Sit. Batu, having destroyed Vladimir and Moscow both, was marching on Novgorod when suddenly he turned south either because of the forests that impeded his advance or perhaps because of the spring thaw which turned much of the low-lying region into a vast swamp. Making his base at a vast encampment (Mongol: *orda*; Engl.: *horde*) called Sarai on the lower Volga north of its entry into the Caspian sea, Batu gathered his strength for a fresh campaign. In 1240, the Mongols were on the march again with a force said to have been 500,000 strong. Kiev was taken and sacked, after which they poured into Poland defeating a combined Polish and German force and moving toward Western Europe. Batu had conquered Hungary, and the Mongols were advancing near Vienna, when news of the death of his uncle Ugeday reached him. Immediately, he turned eastward with his army, hurrying to Mongolia to protect his inheritance. Batu received as his share of the Mongol Empire, Khazakhstan and Khorezm east of the Caspian Sea and all that he had conquered for himself to the west of it, with his capital at the encampment at Sarai. Batu's empire came to be known as the "Golden Horde," a tribute to its great wealth. His sons, however, retained only the northwestern sector of the original share, from the River Yaik (now the Ural) to the Danube.

With the first withdrawal of the Mongols, Yaroslav II succeeded to the Grand Ducal throne in 1238 in place of his brother Yuri who had been killed in battle on the River Sit. Turning his attention to the west, where Russia's enemies were gathering their strength, Yaroslav protected Smolensk from the Lithuanians, placing a prince of his own choice on its throne (1239). Thereafter, he placed the defense of the western frontiers of his realm under the command of his son, Alexander, who built a new town on the Shelon River, apparently as part of a new defensive system. Journeying to Batu's camp on the Volga, Yaroslav was confirmed as prince over Russia.

Mongol rule in Russia was based on the simplest of premises: the Mongols owned everything in the country and held the power of life and death over everyone from the Grand Prince downward. Taxes were imposed, a tenth of all crops and a tenth of all other gains, plus such manpower as the Horde chose to conscript for its armies wherever they were to be sent. The princely administration was left intact in the Russian principalities and the princely feuds were allowed to continue and even encouraged by the khans to their own benefit.

The Mongol invasion of Russia provided her western neighbors with an unexpected opportunity to expand eastward at Russian expense, using as their excuse the "heresy" of the Orthodox Church. Urged on by Pope Gregory IX, the Swedes—led by Jarl Birger—were the first to launch a serious attack, hoping to capture the Neva River and Lake Ladoga, and perhaps even having designs on Novgorod itself. They were met, however, by Alexander, who, though scarcely 16 years of age, was familiar with Western military techniques and strategies. Alexander defeated the enemy on the banks of the Neva with a very small force on July 15, 1236. In spite of his later perhaps more impressive and decisive victories, he was thereafter known to Russia and to world history as Alexander "of the Neva"—in Russian: Aleksandr Nevsky.

The Battle on the Ice

The German settlers in the Baltic, spearheaded by the military religious order, the Livonian Knights, and then by another, the German Teutonic Knights that had absorbed the Livonians in 1237, now took Izborsk and Pskov (1241) at which point the citizens of Novgorod called upon Alexander to take command of their troops. In the winter of 1242, Alexander, together with his brother Andrew and the forces of Novgorod, marched against the German invaders and their allies drawn from the local Baltic tribes. Occupying all the roads to Pskov, they liberated the city and then went out to meet a German force sent against them. The two armies joined in battle on the frozen surface of Lake Chudskoe (now Lake Peipus) on Saturday, April 5, 1242. The Germans and their Finnish allies the Chud, forming an "iron wedge," advanced, thrusting through the center of the Russian forces; the Russians, however, by prior plan, closed around them in a great double-flanking movement and attacked the enemy from the rear, driving them five miles across the frozen lake. Hundreds of Germans were killed in this famed "Battle on the Ice," while others perished by falling through the ice and drowning. Some 50 German commanders were captured and taken to Novgorod in chains. The Germans then sent envoys to Novgorod suing for peace and surrendering all their conquests in Russia. Two years later, Alexander drove off Lithuanian raiders from Torzhok, defeating them twice, again with only a small force.

The defense of Novgorod and the recovery of Pskov were not acts of altruism. Rather, they were part of the earlier policy of the Grand Dukes of Vladimir which was to strengthen their hold on the two republics, and we are told that Alexander left Novgorod only after he had "come to terms" with the city-state. Now totally dependent upon Vladimir for their safety, the merchant grandees sent to Yaroslav asking for another of his sons to replace the departed Alexander. Yaroslav sent them his son Andrew but, in short order, the Novgorodians, faced with renewed threats from the West and knowing the military prowess of Alexander, sent again to Yaroslav requesting that Nevsky be sent back to them to be their prince.

Alexander Rules Russia

Alexander's decision to accept Mongol overlordship in spite of their terrorism, bloodthirsty massacres, and ruthless destruction of property, may have been based on his belief that the Mongols were less of a threat to Russia than her more traditional enemies in the West. But it seems very likely that the willingness of the still pagan but highly superstitious Mongols to leave the Russian Church in peace and to grant it tax exemption in return for praying for the Khan and his family may have played a prominent role. Russia's most dangerous enemies, the Swedes and the German Knights, were determined to reestablish Catholicism in Russia and this of course boded ill for the Orthodox Church, which had a great influence on the devout Nevsky. While some nationalist historians in Russia have been embarrassed by Alexander's refusal to take up arms against the Mongols, George Vernadsky is convinced that he saved Russia from Roman Catholic aggression, noting that Alexander had saved the lives of his people by submitting his own pride to Mongol rule while other princes, too proud to submit, allowed their subjects to pay for their pride with their lives. Alexander Nevsky thus became the leading member of the pro-Mongol faction among the Russian princes, whereas Prince Daniel of Galicia in southern Poland became the most prominent of the anti-Mongol faction, which for a time included Alexander's brother Andrew, who had fled to Poland. Their father Yaroslav II died in 1246, a victim of poisoning at the rumored hand of Batu Khan's mother.

Alexander Nevsky ruled Russia as Grand Prince of Vladimir for 11 years. Khan Sartak, son of Batu, had by now been killed and his uncle Berke ruled in his place. Alexander and his brother Andrew, who craved a return from his exile, sent emissaries to Sarai to plead for Alexander's recognition as Grand Prince and for Andrew's pardon but, although these favors were granted, Alexander and Andrew had to go to Sarai in person for their confirmation. Ruling from Vladimir, Alexander now appointed his son Basil, a mere boy, as Prince of Novgorod, but in one of the typical Novgorod tumults Basil was driven out and Alexander's brother Yaroslav III called in to take his place. Nevsky now intervened and, as he approached the city, Yaroslav was driven out, Novgorod capitulated on Alexander's terms, and Basil was reinstated as prince. Thereupon, Nevsky was forced to go out once again to fight the Germans, Swedes, and Lithuanians, imposing a crushing defeat on the latter that forever after defined the Russian frontier with Finland.

Throughout his reign, Alexander used his influence at Sarai to protect his people. He obtained forgiveness for Yaroslav's rebellion against Basil, got the Russians an exemption from the conscription for an army to fight in North Caucasia, and struggled to get the heavy Mongol imposts reduced. In time, however, the Mongols announced a census to enable them to impose a head tax on their subjects. Unable to get Russia exempted, Alexander aided the Mongols in the two-year survey the census required, and when Novgorod resisted he captured the rebellious leaders and executed them in what was perhaps the only brutal act of his reign, thus bringing Novgorod within the Mongol fold.

In the year 1262, Alexander made his fourth and last visit to his Mongol overlords at Sarai, trying to avert the punishment due the recalcitrance of Novgorod and trying to get the Mongols to relent on certain additional imposts. There, coolly received, he was forced to spend several months, but on becoming ill, he was allowed to return home. On the way, he grew worse and died at the town of Gorodets on the Volga on November 14, 1263, while scarcely in the prime of his life. His body was taken to Vladimir where it was buried in the Monastery of the Mother of God. Alexander was succeeded by his brother Andrew, who died the following year, and then by another son, also named Yaroslav, Prince of Tver, who ruled as Grand Duke of Vladimir and Novgorod until 1272. Of his other sons, Daniel (Dantilo) "the Holy," scarcely two years old, was granted the town of Moscow as his domain. There he founded the line of the princes of Muscovy, who were eventually to unite all Russia, become its first tsars, and rule until 1598. Alexander was a brilliant and undefeated commander and, as ruler, made a profound impression on all who met him. In his private life, he was known for his wisdom, justice, humility, and sobriety and for his devotion to the Greek Orthodox faith.

The death of Alexander at so early an age—scarcely 42 or 43—has been called a national calamity. None of the princes was more devoted to Russia, and no other was so respected. Through his efforts he was the savior of Russia from her enemies on the east and west, and his humiliating but ultimately wise and farsighted policies preserved the Russian state until better times would come. In spite of his subservience to the Mongol invaders, the traditional Russian attitude towards Alexander Nevsky has been very positive, and he has become both a national hero and a saint of the Russian Orthodox Church. The subject of a hagiographical ("idealized") biography, his feast is celebrated on November 23.

When **Peter the Great** founded the city of St. Petersburg at the mouth of the Neva, he had the relics of Alexander Nevsky brought to the new capital and interred in the newly founded Monastery of St. Alexander Nevsky, where they remain to this day. The 600th anniversary of the Battle of the Neva was commemorated by the erection of a triumphal arch in St. Petersburg in 1836 and by the naming of the principal street in the city as the Alexander Nevsky Prospect, a name which it retained throughout the Soviet period. In 1937, with the threat of imminent war with Germany, the famed Soviet film director Sergei Eisenstein was given the task of making a film on the subject of Alexander, which was both blatantly anti-German and an obvious warning of what would happen if the Germans were to dare attack Russia again. The film, with a magnificent choral score by Prokofiev, was much esteemed by critics, especially those on the Left, before and immediately after the Second World War, but now seems embarrassingly unsubtle and somewhat less impressive than when it first appeared.

SOURCES:

Zenkovsky, S. A., ed. *The Nikonian Chronicle.* Vol. III. Translated by S. A. and B. J. Zenkovsky. Kingston Press, 1986.

FURTHER READING:

Curtin, Jeremiah. *The Mongols in Russia.* Little, Brown, 1908.

Halperin, Charles J. *Russia and the Golden Horde.* Indiana University Press, 1985.

Riasanovsky, Nicholas. *A History of Russia.* 3rd ed. New York, 1977.

Vernadsky, George. *The Mongols and Russia.* Yale University Press, 1953.

John Henry Newman

(1801–1890)

English theologian, key figure in the Oxford Movement, and one of the most celebrated churchmen of the 20th century.

Name variations: Cardinal Newman. Born in February 21, 1801, in London, England; died on August 11, 1890; son of a London banker who suffered financial losses; eldest of six children.

Born in London on February 21, 1801, John Henry Newman was a European in the classical sense, both by heritage and inclination. His father's people were Londoners; his mother was descended from French Huguenots (Protestants) who had fled France after the revocation of the Edict of Nantes in 1685. Newman took on aspects of both parents: his father's love of music and literature, and his mother's sober disposition, handed down from her Puritan forebears, that disdained worldly pleasures which took time away from devotion to God. With a home life patterned after his mother's strict evangelical Anglicanism, it was Newman's own love of music and reading that led him to appreciate the wider world.

At seven, he was sent away to a boys' school at Ealing where he earned the name "the flyer" for his speedy ascent through the school's curriculum. Newman was only 11 when he cofounded the school magazine *The Spy*, a juvenile imitation of Richard Addison's popular 18th-century magazine *The Spectator*. Uncomfortable with the one-sided opinions his schoolmates were getting through his paper, he secretly brought out another magazine, *The Anti-Spy*, to generate controversy.

"What St. Augustine was for the ancient world, that St. Thomas Aquinas was for the Middle Ages, and that Newman must be held to be in relation to the world today."

LOUIS BOUYER

Contributed by Alison F. Dacey, M.A. in History, Lakehead University, Thunder Bay, Ontario, Canada

At Ealing for eight years (1808–16), Newman had read many famous books and articles on religious thought by age 14. Nearly half a century later, in his great work *Apologia Pro Vita Sua,* he recalled:

> When I was fourteen I read Paine's Tract's against the Old Testament and found pleasure in thinking of the objections that were contained in them. Also, I read some of Hume's Essays; and perhaps that on Miracles.... Also I recollect copying out some French verses, perhaps Voltaire's in denial of the immortality of the should, and saying to myself something like, "How dreadful, but how plausible!"

Newman's search for a deeper understanding of religion had begun at an early age, and in 1816, the 16-year-old underwent a significant conversion experience, believing that he had been saved by Jesus Christ. For Newman, the Bible was a perfect vehicle for gaining spiritual knowledge because it presented human history—the Patriarchs, the Prophets, Kings and the Apostles, Saints and Sinners—as a panoramic sequence of lives and events intimately connected with a powerful and omnipresent God. As a result of this conversion, Newman believed that some great sacrifice was required of him if he were to live a spiritual life; he pictured himself as a missionary, living celibate and apart from the rest of the world.

In the latter part of 1816, he went up to Oxford at Trinity College where he was to remain for the next 30 years. The university's quiet existence within the sheltered walls, away from the roar of the Napoleonic Wars, the Hundred Days, and Waterloo, was marked by the excitement of internal struggles and philosophical battles. Newman's friends at Oxford were fond of saying that he "grew old early and remained old a long time." Evidently, his "old nature" caused his parents some concern. As Gaius Glenn Atkins writes in his *Life of Cardinal Newman:*

> [His] letters were too melancholy for a youth of twenty-one... they fear that he does not allow himself a proper quantity of wine, does not take enough exercise, does not get into company enough.

Ever conscious of his failings, or what he regarded as his imperfections, Newman worked hard, studying long into the night, to overcome this fear of not doing enough. He slept a mere four hours or so, in order that he might read all that

CHRONOLOGY

1801	Born in London
1816–20	Attended Oxford
1820	Took his degree at Oxford
1822	Elected fellow of Oriel College
1827	Appointed vicar of St. Mary's, Oxford
1841	Wrote famous *Tract XC*
1845	Converted to Roman Catholicism
1847	Ordained as a priest
1854	Tried, unsuccessfully, to establish a Catholic university in Dublin
1864	Wrote *Apologia*
1870	Wrote *Grammar of Assent*
1878	Elected honorary fellow of Oxford
1879	Made a cardinal by Pope Leo XIII
1890	Died at age 89

interested him. Winning a fellowship to Oriel College in 1822, he was accepted as a teaching professor. He decided to seek religious orders as well and, in 1824, was ordained a deacon.

Appointed curate to St. Clement's Church, Newman wrote to tell his father of his intention to begin door-to-door visitations so that he could get to know his parishioners better. "An Englishman's house," replied his father, is "his castle which, though it might be open to the elements, should be defended from uninvited clergymen." His father's advice failed to dissuade him.

The Oriel fellowship proved an important intellectual association for Newman, where he found men of every age and social position with whom he could carry on debates about the merits of one Christian affiliation (Anglicanism or Methodism) over another. From 1822 to 1825, he gradually replaced his Evangelical, Low Church habit of thought with a High Church tradition that was closely linked to the rituals and ceremonies of the Catholic Church.

Ordained an Anglican Priest

In 1825, Newman was ordained a priest of the Anglican Church. Not entirely content with his intellectual and spiritual development, he stated in his *Apologia*:

> The truth is, I was beginning to prefer intellectual excellence to moral: I was drifting in the direction of the Liberalism of the day, I was rudely awakened from my dream at the end of 1827 by two great blows—illness and bereavement.

Preparing for examinations, Newman suffered a serious breakdown and the death of his youngest sister Mary. His internal conversion during 1827 and 1828 was barely perceptible to the outside world. He depended increasingly on the works of the early Church fathers for spiritual guidance and intellectual satisfaction. The spirit of genuine Christian humanism as revealed through such diverse writers and poets as Aeschylus, Pindar, Horace, Virgil, Aristotle, and Cicero—as well as the Church fathers, St. Ambrose, St. Augustine, St. Athanasius, and St. Gregory the Great—moved Newman to new understandings. With a growing concern for truth, Newman's ability to analyze and discover the nature of revelation eventually led him to abandon Anglicanism altogether and enter into the Catholic community. This conversion, Newman's second, caused much concern among the members of his family. Some speculate that had it not been for the death of his father in 1824, Newman would have been unable to break with the legacy of the family's Anglicanism. This seems an unlikely assertion, however, because Newman's own philosophical position became increasingly sympathetic to the Catholic Church's ideal of an individual commitment within an established framework of ritual and doctrine.

Many philosophers and theologians have traced Newman's spiritual maturation by closely examining the intellectual growth cultivated by experience. The pressure from a historical perspective faced by both the Anglican and Catholic Churches in the mid-1800s is, however, rarely taken into account, and the possibility that Newman's conversion was a byproduct of his attempts to preserve the integrity, or even the existence, of the Church must also be taken into account.

The early part of the 19th century saw an increase in the number of people who were not supporters of any church, but belonged, rather, to an all-encompassing, somewhat vague, deism which provided for the acknowledgement of God in a manner unintrusive in their daily lives and unobservable to the general public. Consequently, established churches suffered a reduction in numbers, battling as well a liberal humanism which placed emphasis on constitutional and social reform (Reform Bill of 1832). The Anglican Church was, in many ways, justly viewed with the same distrust as the ruling aristocracy by such English reformers and the society at large.

The Oxford Movement Begins

Reacting to these innovations in a characteristic manner, Newman, along with fellow churchmen R.H. Froude and E.B. Pusey, began a movement for his own brand of church reform, one seeking a prestigious role for the Church based upon the traditional truths as revealed in the Bible and Church history. Their movement became known both as the Oxford Movement, because it was led by Oxford professors, and the Tractarian Movement, because they distributed letters (or tracts) to explain their point of view among the Anglican parishes. Well received by the clergy, these tracts generated much discussion, debate, and enthusiasm. One of the central themes Newman's group promoted was that respect be shown for the clergy as the true successors of the Apostles. In the early days of the Oxford Movement, a genuine notion of Christian Humanism produced a clergy more dedicated and a society more aware of Christian ideals, leading many to acknowledge that the movement breathed new life into the declining Christian churches.

Through the Oxford group, Newman initially tried to steer the Anglican Church along the *Via Media*, or middle way, between Methodism and Catholicism. It became increasingly clear, however, that he found the truths of Roman Catholicism more suited to his temperament. As vicar of St. Mary's, the official church of the Oxford community, Newman was able to attract much attention to the movement through his sermons; these were later published (around 1870 under Newman's own direction) and provide excellent insight into Newman's concerns over various questions of faith. In an 1822 sermon on the theme "Out Of Weakness were made Strong," Newman states:

> Whereas in him who is faithful to his own divinely implanted nature, the faint light of Truth dawns continually brighter; the shadows which at first troubled it, the unreal shapes created by its own twilight-state, vanish; what was as uncertain as mere feeling, and could not be distinguished from a fancy except by the commanding urgency of it voice, becomes fixed and definite, and strengthening into principle, it at the same time develops into habit.

The conversion he experienced internally in 1828 found interim relief in the 90 letters written between 1832 and 1842 for the Tractarian movement and full expression in 1845 with his outward acceptance of Roman Catholicism.

Newman Converts to Catholicism

Newman's so-called "journey to Rome" began as an intellectual discovery of the early Church fathers, which in turn led to an emotional recognition of the rational doctrine which supported the religious traditions of the Church, and ended with a spiritual acceptance of a new faith. Written during this period, his *Essay of Development* reflected his views on a rational religion. His conversion shocked Oxford, although his close friends were aware of his beliefs and many shared similar views. For his family, however, Newman's conversion had tragic implications. Having spiritually moved into the Low Church community and become a missionary, his brother Francis never forgave him for converting, and his sister Harriet never spoke to him again.

But with his embracement of Catholicism came a peace and contentment that Newman had never before experienced. Bouyer's *Newman: His Life and Spirituality* describes the conversion:

> The Church of England had lost for ever the man who had done more than any other to inspire her with new life, while the Catholic Church at last welcomed to her bosom one who had long venerated as a Mother, yet had taken so long to discern her true features beneath her unfamiliar veil.

On the material side, however, Newman did not reap great rewards. If the diminished state of England's Anglican Church in the last century may be attributed to rising secularism, the condition of the Catholic Church was much worse. From the 1640s, the Catholics in England had been looked upon as a conquered people. Up until the latter part of the 19th century, even elementary civil rights were denied to Catholics, whose clergy—debarred from entering universities—were subsequently poorly educated. Aware of the social disadvantages he faced, Newman was determined to provide some practical solutions to the problems faced by the Church.

He traveled to Rome, hoping to put his experience and learning under the pope's authority, that he might help improve the predicament of Catholics in England. But Newman and Pope **Pius IX** could not communicate well, with Newman speaking little Italian or French, and many of the higher-placed clergy at the Vatican were distrustful of Newman's recent conversion. Despite the difficulties, the pope approved of Newman's and his Oxford companions' decision to join the Roman Oratory, a religious community later transplanted, with Newman at its head, into England. For the Vatican, the Catholic Church in Protestant England was a missionary outpost, and the Oratory in Birmingham, England, became an additional center from which religious work could be undertaken.

Newman's work was marred by disappointment after disappointment. In 1851, he undertook a challenging, and ultimately thwarted, task: the creation of a Catholic university in Dublin. Despite the obvious need for such an institution, there were too many in powerful positions who opposed it. In a similar vein, his proposition for a new English version of the Bible was canceled when it became clear that Newman's interpretations were too unorthodox. Despite such failures, Newman continued to carry on his priestly duties in England.

Finally, in 1864, he undertook the writing which would ensure his reputation as a scholar and great religious thinker, the *Apologia*. This work was the result of a series of public debates with **Charles Kingsley,** an energetic, popular man who distrusted Newman and attacked him in the press for deserting the Anglican Church. Newman answered Kingsley eloquently, explaining his thoughts regarding faith and religious expression in the *Apologia*. Through this work, as well as his poetry, letters, diaries, and sermons (many of which were published before his death), religious and secular scholars alike have been able to trace the consequences of his conversion.

Although Newman was largely ignored by Pope Pius IX, one of the first acts of the new pope Leo XIII was to reward him in 1879 for his contributions to the Church by making Newman a cardinal. His reflective nature, education, and sensitivity made him a popular counsellor, and it is not surprising that his worldwide correspondence was enormous. Dynamic and vocal in matters of faith throughout his career, in the last years of his life Newman devoted more time to silence and meditation. He died on August 11, 1890, at 89 years of age, having chosen his own epitaph, *"ex umbris et imaginibus in veritatem,"* or "out of shadows and dreams into the truth."

SOURCES:

Atkins, Gaius Glenn. *Life of Cardinal Newman.* Harper, 1931.

Bouyer, Louis. *Newman His Life and Spirituality.* P.J. Kenedy, 1958.

Dessain, Charles Stephen and Thomas Gronall, S.J. eds. *The Letters and Diaries of John Henry Newman, Vol. XXXI: The Last Years January 1885 to August 1890.* Clarendon Press, 1977.

Newman, John Henry. *Fifteen Sermons Preached Before the University of Oxford.* Christian Classics, 1966.

Trevor, Meriol. *Newman Light In Winter.* Macmillan, 1962.

Weatherby, Harold L. *Cardinal Newman in His Age.* Vanderbilt University Press, 1973.

FURTHER READING:

Flanagan, Philip. *Newman Faith and the Believer.* Sands & Co., 1946.

Harrold, Charles Frederick. *John Henry Newman: An Expository and Critical Study of His Mind, Thought and Art.* Archon, 1966.

Ward, Wilfrid. *The Life of John Henry Cardinal Newman.* Greer and Co., 1912.

Nicholas II

(1868–1918)

Last Russian tsar, whose failures as a leader combined with the deep problems of his country to bring on revolution in 1917.

"Do you mean that I am to regain the confidence of my people, or that they are to regain my confidence?"

NICHOLAS II

Nicholas II, the last tsar of Russia, ruled the largest country in the world. He was an amiable individual, a devoted father and husband. But, almost from the start of his reign, he faced a Russian population increasingly hostile to the government, and popular anger soon centered on the Tsar and his family.

When Nicholas took the throne in 1894, Russia contained 130 million people, most of them peasant laborers living in rural villages, who had been freed from serfdom only in the 1860s. Serfdom had tied Russia's peasants to a given chunk of land and placed them under the control of a local nobleman or government official. But the terms of the decrees that freed the serfs continued to keep most peasants dissatisfied. They never received enough land to meet their needs, they remained under close government control, and they had to carry a heavy burden of state taxes. The population was also growing with explosive speed.

Life in the Russian Empire was disrupted as well by the government's policy of building up a system of modern industry. Although Russia had been the most powerful country in Europe in the first half of the 19th century, by the 1850s, the

Born on May 18, 1868; executed on July 17, 1918; eldest son of Tsar Alexander III and Princess Dagmar of Denmark; married: Princess Alix of Hesse-Darmstadt, 1894; children: (four daughters) Anastasia, Tatiana, Olga, Marie; (one son) Alexis. Predecessor: Alexander III. Successor: replaced first by Russian Provisional Government in March 1917, then by V. I. Lenin at the head of the Russian Communist Party in November 1917.

Contributed by Neil Heyman, Professor of History, San Diego State University, San Diego, California

CHRONOLOGY

1887	Commissioned a junior officer in imperial guards
1891	Trip around world; survived assassination attempt in Japan
1894	Became tsar of Russia
1904	Start of war with Japan; birth of son, Alexis
1905	Russian Revolution of 1905; Nicholas forced to grant constitutional government to people of Russian Empire
1908	Rasputin entered personal circle surrounding imperial family
1914	Start of World War I
1917	March Revolution forced Nicholas to abdicate
1918	Nicholas and his family executed in beginning months of Russian Civil War

country found itself humiliated in confrontations with advanced, industrialized countries of Western Europe like Britain. Russia's defeat in the Crimean War (1854–56) was only the first in a series of military and diplomatic catastrophes.

Thus, by the start of the 1890s, officials of the Russian government like Finance Minister **Sergei Witte** were putting the government's resources into a program of building railroads and steel mills. This meant more taxes for the peasants to pay for the industrial program. It also meant creating dangerous industrial slums populated by poor, angry factory workers in government centers like St. Petersburg and Moscow.

Two other elements made the situation still more dangerous. First, the Russian state was an empire. No one could be certain of the exact number, but there were probably 100 separate nationalities within the Empire. Many of these peoples deeply resented the control of a brutal central government led by ministers of Russian nationality. Second, ever since the 1870s, revolutionary leaders from the educated part of the population had been at work to push the peasants into open rebellion. By the start of the 1890s, Marxist revolutionaries joined in the effort to overthrow the system. They were political rebels who believed the factory workers were the key to revolutionary change.

In 1894, Tsar Alexander III died suddenly of kidney disease. Only 49 years old and seemingly in robust health, Alexander had been expected to rule for several more decades. Suddenly raised to the throne, the 26-year-old Nicholas, who was occupied in the preparations for his marriage, expressed

his fear and dismay. His future brother-in-law heard him blurt out: "I know nothing of the business of ruling."

The late Tsar had been strong enough to bend coins with his fingers. His son Nicholas was a slim, almost timid-looking individual whose boyhood had been marked by tragedy. At the age of 12, he had seen his grandfather, Tsar **Alexander II,** dying at the hands of an assassin's bomb. The boy was terrified and only calmed down when he saw his father, now Tsar Alexander III, riding off to take up his duties guarded by a cavalry regiment of fierce Cossacks.

Nicholas's tutors had taught him a number of foreign languages, including excellent English. His most influential tutor, former law professor Konstantin Pobedonostsev, filled his head with the conviction that the Romanov family ruled as the agents of God, and that no tsar could surrender any part of his unlimited powers without throwing away a precious part of Russia's traditions.

The young heir to the Russian throne spent the happiest years of his life as a junior officer in a fashionable cavalry regiment. Only one incident marred this period. In 1891, he had narrowly escaped being stabbed to death by a religious fanatic in Japan during a world tour. But, by 1894, he was doubly content. He was happy in the role of a young military commander in the imperial guards. He could look forward to years of enjoyable service, free of serious responsibilities and with lots of leisure for drinking with his fellow junior officers. That same year, the beautiful Princess Alix of the German state of Hesse-Darmstadt, a granddaughter of Britain's Queen **Victoria,** agreed to be his wife.

The young Tsar's reign was marked from the start by sadness and tragedy. He and Alix had planned a gala wedding. Instead the young couple married in haste only a week after his father's funeral. The new Empress had just converted from the Lutheran religion to the Russian Orthodox faith, taking the Russian name Alexandra. Struck by the gloomy atmosphere in St. Petersburg, she described the marriage ceremony as "a mere continuation of the masses for the dead."

The coronation festivities for Nicholas II led to a particular horror. Half a million Russians, many of them peasants from distant parts of the Empire, had come to Moscow at the Tsar's invitation to help celebrate the coronation. They gathered for a feast at Khodynka Field, five miles out of Moscow. There were too few police to control the crowd, and no one in authority had remembered that Khodynka Field was covered with ditches and trenches left over from military maneuvers. When the great horde of people rushed across the field to the food stalls awaiting them, at least 1,300 people were trampled to death.

Although Nicholas visited the injured in the hospital and established a generous fund to aid the families of the dead, his reputation among the Russian population was hurt by the memory of Khodynka Field. Why, people asked, had he attended a party at the residence of the French ambassador the night following the tragedy? How could he hold a giant military review at Khodynka Field little more than a week after so many of his unfortunate subjects had been killed there?

Among educated and liberal Russians, the Tsar's reputation fell during his first years on the throne. In 1895, a group of local government officials addressed the Tsar, asking him to allow the people's representatives some voice in influencing the policies of Russia's government. According to some sources, it was Pobedonostsev who wrote Nicholas's reply: the young Tsar declared harshly that he would maintain his powers intact. He insisted that those who hoped for political changes should abandon such "senseless dreams."

The Tsar's desire to cling to the past at all costs soon crashed into the reality of Russia's problems. By the first years of the 20th century, the country was struck by massive peasant revolts in rural areas as well as industrial strikes in many major cities. Nicholas dismissed such troubles as the work of evil-minded agitators. In his view, no loyal Russian would deliberately challenge the tsar's authority.

A crisis not even Nicholas could ignore came when Russia went to war against Japan in 1904. The two countries had been competing for years over territory and influence in the Korean peninsula and the Chinese province of Manchuria. One of the Tsar's advisers enthused that "a victorious little war" against Japan would help bring the Russian population together. Nicholas himself was bitter toward the Japanese ever since the encounter with a Japanese assassin in 1891. Like most Russians, he thought Russia's military might would quickly crush the "Japanese monkeys," as he called them.

The war was a disaster from the beginning. The Japanese fleet pinned down most of the Russian war vessels in the Far East by blockading the Tsar's naval base at Port Arthur. Japanese armies landed in Korea, defeated Russian forces sent to halt them, and then advanced to besiege Port Arthur. This crucial center of Russian power in the Pacific fell in early 1905. Later that year, the Russian Baltic Fleet arrived in the Far East after sailing halfway around the world, only to be defeated disastrously by the Japanese at the Straits of Tsushima between Japan and Korea.

At home, Nicholas found popular unrest rising. The economic strains of the war and the failure of the government to lead the nation effectively were having their effect. In January 1905, on "Bloody Sunday," crowds of Russians tried to petition the Tsar to help them. Hundreds were shot down in front of Nicholas's Winter Palace. The Tsar and his family isolated themselves at the Tsarskoe Seloe palace outside St. Petersburg. The country was shaken by strikes, peasant unrest, and a growing call for political change.

Nicholas answered by moving only inches away from the position Pobedonostsev had taught him. He considered setting up a *Duma* (a Russian parliament), but he insisted that it could only have the right to advise him, not to make laws. Opponents of the Tsar, ranging from Marxist revolutionaries to middle-class reformers, rejected such half measures. By the fall of 1905, the Empire was paralyzed by a general strike. Everyone from bakers to ballet dancers refused to work.

In October, Nicholas faced a choice. He called in Sergei Witte, who advised him to establish a genuine parliament accompanied by a constitution. Clinging to his instinctive desire to preserve his powers in full, Nicholas looked for a member of his government or someone in the imperial family who would take over as military dictator. But there was no one. Nicholas could not find a dictator to put down national unrest at the cost of a bloodbath.

The Tsar found himself compelled to issue the "October Manifesto," granting the two concessions he had always rejected: a *Duma* with the power to make laws, and a Constitution. The Revolution of 1905 had apparently overturned much of the old order, but Nicholas remained stubbornly committed to the old ways. Almost from the moment he issued the October Manifesto, Nicholas showed his distaste for the changes that had been forced upon him. Ridding himself of Witte—the architect and first prime minister under the new system—in early 1906, Nicholas insisted on keeping the title of "autocrat" (or unlimited monarch). He repeatedly restricted the power of the *Duma* and frequently spoke of eliminating it entirely.

As Russia remained torn by internal divisions after the Revolution of 1905, the Tsar's prestige continued to decline. Exerting an important influence on him, the Empress Alexandra strengthened Nicholas's own conservative inclina-

Rasputin

(1864?–1916)

A Siberian peasant and self-proclaimed holy man, Gregory Efimovich Rasputin entered the circle of personal acquaintances surrounding the Russian imperial family sometime after 1905. Tsar Nicholas and especially Empress Alexandra welcomed Rasputin because of the healing powers he supposedly possessed; he seemed to be able to treat the imperial couple's only son, Alexis, who suffered from hemophilia.

Rasputin's influence on Nicholas and Alexandra alarmed both members of the *Duma* and Russia's prime minister, Peter Stolypin, who tried unsuccessfully to exile the holy man from St. Petersburg. Nonetheless, Rasputin remained in the Russian capital: his claim to the loyalty of the imperial family made him immune to political defeat.

Rasputin's role in Russian life reached its peak when Nicholas left to take command of the Russian army in the fall of 1915. Alexandra now ruled with Rasputin at her side. Forcing a number of Rus-

tions, in particular his view that restrictions on his power violated Russia's political and religious heritage. She insisted to her "Nicky" that he play the role of a strong, unmovable monarch, a fitting descendant of Peter the Great in the 18th century.

The Influence of Rasputin

The popular image of the Tsar, badly damaged by horrors like Bloody Sunday, suffered from the presence of disreputable figures around the imperial court. Sometime after 1905, Alexandra came in contact with a strange holy man from the Russian provinces, **Rasputin.** Rasputin's influence, first on the Empress, and through her on Nicholas, grew over the next several years.

Leaders of the Russian government tried in vain to limit Rasputin's power and even to ban him from St. Petersburg, but they never succeeded for long. Rasputin seemed able to treat the physical ailments of Alexis, the only son of Nicholas and Alexandra and the heir to the Russian throne. The boy suffered from hemophilia, and the slightest injury put him in danger of bleeding to death.

In 1913, the public showed its distaste for the imperial family and its sleazy circle of hangers-on. The year brought the celebration of the Romanov dynasty's 300th anniversary. There was an ominous silence during the Tsar's public appearances instead of the cheers called for by the occasion.

The outbreak of World War I in 1914 put Nicholas and his family on the road to disaster. As in the war against Japan, Russia suffered one military calamity after another in fighting Germany. Military defeats, in turn, cut away at the prestige of the Tsar and his ministers. In the fall of 1915, urged on by Alexandra, Nicholas left St. Petersburg to take personal command of the defeated Russian armies at the fighting front. This left the Empress, increasingly influenced by Rasputin, to wield the powers of the tsar. A clear danger signal for the future of the monarchy was the growing rumor that

Alexandra, who had been born a German princess, was actively betraying the Russian cause in World War I. By the end of 1916, such accusations were even heard in speeches in the Duma.

Revolution Forces Abdication

By the start of 1917, the political and military situation was desperate. Many observers expected an upheaval, perhaps in the form of a military coup. The Tsar's answer to the British ambassador, who had urged Nicholas to consider further political reforms, showed the distance between the monarch and the situation facing the nation: "Do you mean that I am to regain the confidence of my people, or that they are to regain my confidence?"

In March, food riots and labor strikes in St. Petersburg grew to massive proportions. When the army garrison refused to put down the unrest, the power of the old government crumbled. Nicholas wandered by train trying to travel from his military headquarters back to his capital. Strikes on the railroads stranded him at the military center of Pskov.

When Nicholas found that not even his military commanders were willing to help him remain tsar, he searched for a member of his family to take the throne. His young son Alexis, still in fragile health, could not do it. Nicholas's brother Michael was unwilling to become tsar in the midst of a popular revolution. Thus, the monarchy ended with Nicholas's abdication.

The former Tsar and his family continued to be the victims of war and revolution. They might have escaped to Britain, but the government in London hesitated to accept them: Nicholas's presence there could jeopardize the continuing alliance between Britain and the post-revolutionary government in Russia.

As the revolution in Russia deepened, Nicholas, Alexandra, and their children were sent to Ekaterinburg in the Ural Mountains. Civil War broke out in the spring of 1918, and White armies,

sia's most capable cabinet ministers to resign, Rasputin replaced them with his incompetent cronies. Public opinion grew increasingly hostile to the imperial family and to their dubious adviser.

It was dangerous to be so influential at a time of military catastrophe. In December 1916, a group of conservative aristocrats laced Rasputin's wine with potassium cyanide at a soirée in the Yousoupov Palace. When the poison proved inadequate to Rasputin's tremendous strength, they shot him. When he lurched at his attackers, they shot him again. Then they bashed him and kicked him. Finally dead, his body was dumped into an icy river. They had murdered the man the Empress Alexandra referred to as "our friend." ■

containing supporters of the Tsar, approached the Urals. On the night of July 16, the Tsar, his wife, their five children, and several members of their household were ordered by **Lenin** to be executed. Rousing them in the night, a local commissar escorted them to the cellar with a firing squad. The 11 victims were buried in an abandoned mineshaft, then reburied in an open field.

SOURCES:

Charques, Richard. *The Twilight of Imperial Russia.* Oxford University Press, 1965.

Crankshaw, Edward. *The Shadow of the Winter Palace.* Viking, 1976.

Lincoln, W. Bruce. *The Romanovs: Autocrats of All the Russias.* Dial, 1981.

FURTHER READING:

Fuhrmann, Joseph T. *Rasputin: A Life.* Praeger, 1990.

Lincoln, W. Bruce. *In War's Dark Shadow: The Russians Before the Great War.* Dial, 1983.

————. *Passage Through Armageddon: The Russians in War and Revolution, 1914-1918.* Simon & Schuster, 1986.

Massie, Robert. *Nicholas and Alexandra.* Atheneum, 1967.

Pipes, Richard. *The Russian Revolution.* Knopf, 1990.

Radzinsky, Edvard. *The Last Tsar: The Life and Death of Nicholas II.* Doubleday, 1992.

Florence Nightingale

(1820–1910)

Founder of modern nursing, who worked to reform Britain's War Office, though, as a woman, she could hold no official position in it.

Born May 12, 1820, in Florence, Italy; died August 13, 1910, in Britain; daughter of William Edward and Fanny (Smith) Nightingale.

During the Crimean War, it was William Howard Russell, London *Times* correspondent, who revealed to the British public the terrible medical and sanitary conditions present in the army hospitals. Accommodations for more than a thousand men were available at the base hospital in Scutari, on the Asiatic side of the Bosphorus, if they could live through the experience of being hospitalized there. Vermin scampered across the floors as the odor of enormous subterranean sewers wafted through the rooms. Devoid of basins, soap, and towels, the hospital also suffered a deficiency of medical supplies including anesthesia, ordinary drugs, and bandages. Forty-two percent of those treated did not live to recount the horrors of a war in which more lives were claimed by disease than in engagements with the Russian enemy. On November 4, 1854, a 34-year-old society girl arrived at the hospital with an infantry of nurses. Though she couldn't visit each injured man in Scutari on any given day, the men were content to kiss her shadow as the "Lady with the Lamp" passed by. Florence Nightingale, literally, saved their lives.

The second child of William Edward and Fanny Nightingale, Florence Nightingale was

"'We are ducks,' [said Nightingale's mother] with tears in her eyes, 'who have hatched a wild swan.' But the poor lady was wrong; it was not a swan they had hatched; it was an eagle."

LYTTON STRACHEY

Contributed by Deborah Klezmer, Associate Editor, Historic World Leaders

born on May 12, 1820, and named after her birthplace in Italy. According to her later notes, she was only six when she began to feel a certain pointlessness to her life in a well-to-do family. The accoutrements of wealth painted her childhood and adolescence in England, from house parties to houses in the country and tours across Europe. She and her sister Parnethope were raised to marry, throw dinner parties, and become shining society women. Throughout her youth, Nightingale apparently established only one genuine bond with a family who often opposed her; she developed an intimate teacher/pupil relationship with her father, as he taught her the classics, philosophy, and modern languages. By 16, the tall girl with the gray eyes and long chestnut hair had heard her first calling: "God spoke to me," she wrote, "and called me to His service."

Throughout the family's 1838 trip abroad, she awaited God's further instructions; but none came. Thus, by the time of their return to England in 1839, she had resolved to resist the influences of societal life, hoping to make herself more worthy. Familial conflict ensued when she refused to marry. A cousin named Henry Nicholson fell in love with her, but, according to biographer Elizabeth Longford, Nightingale instead held a great fondness for his sister Marianne. Not content with the prospects presented by a life of embroidery and entertaining, with the help of her maternal Aunt Mai she persuaded her mother to allow the study of mathematics; she was, however, forced to discontinue her lessons after a year. But if learning was not encouraged, visiting the poor and sick was, and Nightingale often accompanied her mother into the rural slums where they dispensed soup and small silver.

By the age of 24, Nightingale had decided to serve as a nurse. Wrote Lytton Strachey in his *Eminent Victorians,* a nurse "meant then a coarse old woman, always ignorant, usually dirty, often brutal, a Mrs. Gamp, in bunched-up sordid garments, tippling at the brandy-bottle or indulging in worse irregularities." Announcing to her parents her plan to spend several months nursing at Salisbury Hospital, Nightingale also revealed a desire to one day found "something like a Protestant Sisterhood, without vows, for women of educated feelings." Her parents were duly alarmed. According to Longford, they managed to dismiss her aspirations because "so varied and effective were the obstacles that a Victorian family could devise against the woman of action."

Her dreams shattered, in December of 1845, Nightingale wrote: "God has something for me to do for Him—or He would have let me die some

time ago.... Oh for some great thing to sweep this loathsome life into the past."

Three years later, during a six-month stay in Rome, she met two figures who would prove extraordinary influences upon her life and character. The first was the handsome, gentle-natured Sidney Herbert, and the second was Madre Santa Colomba, whose teaching methods Nightingale would later emulate in her girls' school. She might have chosen a career teaching had training not been required:

> The first thought I can remember and the last was nursing work and in the absence of this, education work, but more the education of the bad than of the young.... Still education is not my genius.

Having studied the Blue Books on public health and the yearbook of the Kaiserswerth charitable hospital and training institution, there were personal matters yet to resolve if she were to pursue her "genius." Richard Monckton Milnes had proposed in 1849. Wrote Nightingale:

> I have an intellectual nature which requires satisfaction... and that would find it in him. I have a passional nature which requires satisfaction, and that would find it in him. I have a moral, an active nature which requires satisfaction, and that would not find it in his life. Sometimes I think that I will satisfy my passional nature at all events.

The moral, active nature won out. She refused him, refusing by association to abandon her ambitions. Though outwardly she continued to

Florence Nightingale helps an ailing man.

nesses as "Fancy," Nightingale showed them compassion. Six months after her appointment, the home was running efficiently. Still, this was a far cry from her image of "serving." Her abilities were more strenuously utilized to assist prostitutes in the Middlesex Hospital following an outbreak of cholera in one of London's red-light districts.

After she had worked a year on Harley Street, the Crimean War broke out on the north shore of the Black Sea. In a dispute over guardianship of Palestinian holy places, Russia was at odds with Turkey, England, France and Sardinia. Gradually, through the first war correspondents, the abominable condition of Britain's military hospitals became more and more public knowledge. Sidney Herbert was by then serving in the War Office and in the cabinet. Perhaps a sign of fate, the letter Nightingale penned to Herbert, offering her services, and the letter he penned to her, requesting them, crossed in the post. The appointment made, she set off with 38 nurses, the backing of the War Office, and the *Times* Crimea fund to work the impossible in Scutari.

Her mission there would be not only to comfort those in need, but to perform the duties of an administrator, disperse prejudices against nurses, and set a precedent in nursing. Remarked Longford, "To send a *woman* attended by *women* was revolutionary. It could not have caused a greater sensation if Queen Victoria herself had gone out." Before departing, she had asked officials whether it would be advisable to take supplies, and they assured her that everything needed would be found at Scutari—a response that typified the communications breakdown between officials at home and those in the hospitals. Deciding to rely on her instincts, Nightingale purchased numerous provisions at Marseilles. She had not been too cautious. On November 4, 1854, one day before the battle of Inkerman, she and her nurses arrived in Scutari harbor to see the swollen body of a dead horse—a sign of things to come.

She Fights Bureaucratic Nightmare at Scutari

Following the voyage across the Black Sea to Scutari—during which 74 of every thousand men died—the sick, the injured, and the dying arrived at the hospital's doors behind which, wrote Strachey, "Hell yawned." But Nightingale's greatest war would not be against the appalling, inhumane conditions at the hospital, but rather against the bureaucratic machinery that had allowed for the nightmare's inception. Terrified of losing their posts, no one dared take a stand against the plethora of regulations; no one, that is, save

fulfill societal obligations, Nightingale pored over medical commission reports and information from the sanitary authorities, while studying the history of hospitals. But it was not until 1850 that she managed to secure her first, hands-on experience at Kaiserswerth, where she worked as a nurse and laid the groundwork for future endeavors. After three months, her father grew ill; she returned to him and to her old life, where stagnation again took its toll: "In my thirty-first year," she wrote in her diary, "I see nothing desirable but death."

Appointed Superintendent of Nursing Home

Another three years passed, and at last her family began to realize that her passions were not idle fancies, that, at 34, their daughter had gained a degree of independence. In August of 1853, with the help of Sidney Herbert, she was appointed superintendent of a charitable nursing home on Harley Street. She called the place a "Sanitarium for Sick Governesses run by a Committee of Fine Ladies." But the sick governesses adored her, and though she regarded three-quarters of their ill-

Nightingale who, much to the dismay of many of her male co-workers, believed there was an efficient hospital lurking beneath the layers of leeches and stench and filth.

Fighting incompetence and red tape, she secured towels, soap, eating utensils, and toothbrushes for the men. Often stores arrived but could not be unpacked until approved by the proper authorities. Stores from England were found gathering dust in the Turkish Customs House while other hospital materials made the journey across the Black Sea several times over before reaching Scutari. Under Nightingale's command, the hospital kitchens and laundries were reorganized, while she secured dressing gowns for the wounded. "The fact is," she reported to Herbert, "I am now clothing the British Army." If the doctors in Scutari were initially disgusted by her presence, the men who were fighting for the British army could not have been more thankful. Whether seeing a patient through an amputation without anesthesia or performing administrative functions and penning exhaustive reports to Herbert, Nightingale forged order. By May, the death rate at Scutari had plummeted from 42% to 2.2%.

Her work, however, did not end within Scutari's doors. She began inspecting the hospitals in the Crimea, spending entire days on horseback or in a baggage cart. Eventually, her body reached its breaking point; she contracted "Crimean fever." After days of delirium and near death, Nightingale regained her strength and was to be sent back to England. She refused, however, to return and went instead back to Scutari, where she remained for four months after the Declaration of Peace was issued. Before the war's end, she saw the Medical Staff Corps established and, in 1855, the opening of the Nightingale Fund which was dedicated to the training of nurses.

In July of 1856, she returned to England and a public overwhelmed by her achievements. Queen **Victoria** honored the national heroine with a brooch bearing the inscription "Blessed are the Merciful," as well as with a private correspondence:

> You are, I know, well aware... of the high sense I entertain of the Christian devotion which you have displayed during this great and bloody war, and I need hardly repeat to you how warm my admiration is for your services, which are fully equal to those of my dear and brave soldiers, whose sufferings you have had the privilege of alleviating in so merciful a manner.... It will be a very great satisfaction to me to make the acquaintance of one who has set so bright an example of our sex.

So, Nightingale, near collapse upon her return, went to see the queen, though doctors had told her to rest. The year was 1856, and having just witnessed an enormous cover-up in the War Office she determined that there could be no respite until a Royal Commission was established to overhaul the conditions in the entire British army. Otherwise, she said, "you might as well take 1,100 men every year out upon Salisbury Plain and shoot them." Her visit to Queen Victoria and Prince Albert was a political one to secure their support. Royalty was notably impressed by the accounts of her experiences and proposals for reform. Remarked the queen: "I wish we had her in the War Office." But Nightingale would never hold a position at the War Office. She couldn't. Nor could any other woman.

Consequently, in order to see her Royal Sanitary Commission established, there were men through whom she would have to work. The first was Sidney Herbert, who became one of her closest companions and championed allies, and the second was the secretary of war, Lord Panmure, the Bison, so named according to Longford because of his massive head.

Strachey described Nightingale's friendship with Herbert as that of a man and woman brought together by their common devotion to public cause:

> But what made the connection still more remarkable was the way in which the parts that were played in it were divided between the two. The man who acts, decides, and achieves; the woman who encourages, applauds, and—from a distance—inspires... but Miss Nightingale was neither an Aspasia nor Egeria. In her case it is almost true to say that the *roles* were reversed; the qualities of pliancy and sympathy fell to the man, those of command and initiative to the woman.

Terrified that Nightingale would bear witness to the public, Lord Panmure was persuaded to bully his officials into setting up the commission, and in May of 1857 it was in place with Herbert as chairman. Much more remained to be done; she envisioned as well four subcommissions, all with Herbert at their head.

She Takes to Her Bed, Yet Accomplishes Much

The same year, after months of physical exhaustion following her return from the Crimea, Nightingale took to her bed, where she primarily remained for the rest of her life. All her following activities were performed from couch, bed, wheelchair, or invalid carriage. Yet, wrote Strachey, "her real life began at the very moment when, in the popular imagination, it had ended." Though regarded by history as the high point of her career, Nightingale regarded her experiences at Scutari as stepping-stones to a larger work, that of the War Office's complete reform. The doctors constantly advised her to rest, and in response, Nightingale constantly ignored them. No matter what her physical condition, she could always hold council in her bedroom. She did, however, require a group of assistants, upon whose physical energy she fed when hers wavered; among them were the poet Arthur Clough and the devoted Aunt Mai who had joined her at Scutari and who now helped her niece through the breathlessness, nausea, fainting, and palpitations that accompanied what was then called "neurasthenia." Whereas, at that time Nightingale was thought to be suffering from exhaustion resulting from her work in the Crimea, Longford has suggested that perhaps the anxiety and fear concerning the magnitude of her mission, and the stress associated with repeated interruptions by her mother and sister, brought on her symptoms.

Regardless of the nature of her affliction, she worked like a woman who did not have long to live. She authored the 1,000-page *Notes Affecting the Health, Efficiency, and Hospital Administration of the British Army, Notes on Nursing,* and *Notes on Hospitals,* while privately coaching Herbert, who became secretary of state for war. From 1859 to 1861, the reform systems for which they'd been struggling finally began to materialize, thanks to the Royal Commission. Barracks and hospitals were remodeled, new regulations were put forth, and an army medical school was established. Unanimously considered the expert on subjects of hospitals and nursing, in 1860 Nightingale opened the Nightingale Training School for Nurses at St. Thomas's Hospital. Meanwhile, the reforms were showing fast results: by 1861, the army's mortality rate had fallen off by half since the Crimean War. Soon, from her bed in England, she was working with the British Army in India, earning the title "Governess of the Governors of India."

With still much to be accomplished within the War Office, Herbert's health was failing. His doctors strictly counseled him to rest, but Nightingale urged him on: "One fight more, the last and the best." But during the month of June 1861, he retired, provoking Nightingale's consternation:

> Beaten! Can't you see that you've simply thrown away the game? And with all the winning cards in your hands! And so noble a game! Sidney Herbert

beaten!... It is a worse disgrace than the hospitals at Scutari.

She said little else, refusing to speak to him following his resignation until the time of his death, less than three months later. He reportedly died with her name upon his lips: "Poor Florence.... Our joint work... unfinished." For the rest of her life, she referred to him as "My Master." Just after his death, Arthur Clough died. Then Aunt Mai's return to her own family devastated Nightingale and prompted a 20-year silence between her and her aunt.

With Herbert's death, the dream of a reformed War Office ended, though, until 1872, Nightingale remained a prominent influence in the office's workings. After that time, she spent her later years engaged in the study of mysticism, philosophy, and theology. She developed a nurturing relationship with Benjamin Jowett, the master of Balliol College, Oxford, whom she assisted with his translation of Plato. "I am becoming quite a tamed beast," she wrote.

At 81, she lost her eyesight, and in her advanced years she drifted even further into solitude. In 1907, at the age of 87, she was the first woman ever to be offered the Order of Merit. Three years later, in her home on South Street where she had lived for 45 years, the founder of modern nursing died. She was 91.

"Her illness," wrote Strachey of the turmoil that had confined her to home for half a century, "whatever it may have been, was certainly not inconvenient." He continued:

> It involved seclusion; and an extraordinary, an unparalleled seclusion was, it might almost have been said, the mainspring of Miss Nightingale's life. Lying on her sofa in the little upper room in South Street, she combined the mysterious and romantic quality of a myth. She was a legend in her lifetime, and she knew it.

SOURCES:

Longford, Elizabeth. *Eminent Victorian Women.* Weidenfeld & Nicolson, 1981.

Strachey, Lytton. *Eminent Victorians.* Harcourt, 1918.

Uglow, Jennifer S., ed. *The International Dictionary of Women's Biography.* Continuum, 1982.

FURTHER READING:

Woodham-Smith, Cecil. *Florence Nightingale,* McGraw-Hill, 1951.

Daniel O'Connell

(1775–1847)

Irish member of Britain's Parliament known as the Liberator, who rallied his country in the cause of Catholic Emancipation and, in the process, turned Ireland into a modern democracy.

"O'Connell stands with Gandhi and Martin Luther King, Jr. as a political leader devoted to non-violence... [and] the constitutional method of grappling with a nation's problems. By invoking these principles and using these means he gave to the Irish Catholics... their first taste of victory."

MAURICE R. O'CONNELL

The O'Connell family of County Kerry could accurately be counted among the Irish gentry; Morgan O'Connell was a prosperous landowner and farmer and ran a general store. Born on August 6, 1775, Daniel O'Connell was not to enjoy the benefits of his father's prosperity for several years. Like most children of wealthy parents of the time, O'Connell was given to a local peasant family to be nursed and fostered. This practice both spared women of the gentry the trials of dealing with infants and was said to toughen the children as well. O'Connell's foster family, the Morans, were true Irish peasants, speaking no English and living primarily on potatoes, milk, and fish. The Morans dressed O'Connell in a *caulac*, a girl's dress, a tradition kept for fear of fairies, who were said to steal small boys away.

O'Connell thought of the Morans as his family when he was small; he was so ignorant of his true parentage that when he was finally returned home and his father asked him if he'd ever eaten meat before, he answered, "Whenever my father killed one of Morgan O'Connell's sheep." Being suddenly taken from the Morans and returned to his true home was disconcerting

Born in County Kerry, Ireland, on August 6, 1775; died May 17, 1847; eldest son of Morgan O'Connell (a landed Catholic); married: Mary O'Connell (his third cousin once removed), 1802; children: ten (seven of whom survived infancy).

Contributed by Colleen Carpenter Cullinan, Ph.D. candidate, University of Chicago Divinity School, Chicago, Illinois

CHRONOLOGY

1775	Born in County Kerry
1793	Fled the country due to anti-Catholic sentiment
1798	Irish rebellion led by Wolfe Tone
1801	Irish Parliament dissolved; Union of Ireland and Great Britain began
1803–15	Napoleonic wars in Europe
1823	Catholic Association reinstituted
1828	O'Connell elected to Parliament
1829	Catholic Emancipation Bill passed
1831	Great Reform Bill passed
1837	William IV of Britain died; Victoria crowned
1841	O'Connell elected Lord Mayor of Dublin
1843	Arrested for conspiracy against the government; convicted
1845	Potato crop failed in Ireland; Great Famine began
1847	O'Connell died

Ireland, his uncle decided to send O'Connell and his younger brother Maurice to France. There, at Dr. Stapleton's school in St. Omer, Maurice and Daniel O'Connell studied Latin, Greek, English, French, and geography; their nonacademic subjects included music, drawing, dancing, and fencing. O'Connell scored second in the school in his Latin, English, and Greek exams, and Dr. Stapleton proudly predicted that the outgoing boy was "destined to make a remarkable figure in society."

The boys moved on to a Catholic seminary school in August of 1792, which was not a particularly wise move, as the French Revolution had stirred up anti-Catholic hatred throughout France. When the revolutionaries beheaded the French king, **Louis XVI**, in January of 1793, Hunting Cap decided that France was a far too dangerous place for his nephews to remain. Daniel and Maurice fled the country, wearing the Revolution's colors of red, white, and blue as a small measure of protection. They made it to London with their skins intact, but with no luggage, no schoolbooks—nothing. And of course, there was the problem of what to do about their interrupted schooling and career preparation.

He Studies for the Bar

Luckily, the Irish Parliament, composed of Protestant landowners who were descendants of English settlers (despite their huge majority in the population, there were no Catholics in Irish government), had recently seen fit to pass two Catholic Relief Acts, which gave some Catholics the vote and permitted Catholics to become officers in the army and navy, as well as to attend Trinity College (Dublin), become justices of the peace or jurymen, and become lawyers. Maurice O'Connell joined the army; Daniel O'Connell began studying for the bar. Daniel O'Connell, it would appear, made the better decision: his brother was dead of yellow fever less than four years later, one of many European victims of the diseases of the West Indies.

To study law, Daniel O'Connell traveled to London, where he not only pored over required text, but avidly devoured book upon book for pleasure. Included in his extra reading—meant, he stated, to relax his mind—were authors such as Rousseau, Paine, Hume, Voltaire, and Mary Wollstonecraft. All these progressive Enlightenment thinkers surely shaped young O'Connell's thought.

But not all of O'Connell's time was spent with books. He was a member of a radical debating club known as the Society of Cogers and was reputed to be quite popular with the young ladies.

for young O'Connell, and on his first day at home, he quickly shed the new boy's suit his father had given him. Returning to the comfort of his *caulac*, he left the O'Connell house and was later discovered heading "home" to the Morans.

O'Connell's uncle, known affectionately as "Hunting Cap," was a rich and childless man who adopted O'Connell as his heir; thus, O'Connell began to divide his time between the O'Connell home in Kerry and Hunting Cap's estate in Derrynane. Hunting, fishing, and playing rough-and-tumble games occupied much of O'Connell's boyhood. Hunting Cap taught his nephew to hunt on the rocky crags and mountainsides of Derrynane, and O'Connell grew to love the thrill of the chase. Hunting with hounds in Derrynane was not the refined sport it was in England—no elegant outfits or hunters on horseback here; the land was far too rough to support riding. Rather, a hunter followed the hounds on foot, scrambling up steep hillsides and bounding crazily down again. The sport was dangerous and required great stamina and strength. O'Connell loved it.

O'Connell's early schooling was conducted by the local parish priest, and he later spent two years at a Catholic school in Cork. He excelled at all his schoolwork. Since Catholics could not enter the Protestant universities of either England or

This led to a few altercations with other students, and one instance almost came to a duel; fortunately, his opponent's father stepped in and called a constable. O'Connell enjoyed good wine, yet did not have the constitution to stand up to the hard-drinking traditions of his time. After one evening of overindulgence, he recorded in his journal the next morning:

> Many find a vicious pleasure in drinking, but punishment soon awaits them; stupidity, sickness and contempt are in the train of this gratification. How feelingly ought I to write on this subject—I, whose head aches, whose stomach is nauseated... let me forever retain the salutary hatred which I now feel against this odious vice!

In 1796, O'Connell was judged to have completed his studies in London, and he returned to Dublin to await being called to the bar. But in Dublin rumblings of rebellion were growing every day and, as England and France neared war, some hopeful Irish revolutionaries tried to enlist French support for their cause. Not inclined to unite with the French after having been chased from that country, O'Connell convinced his uncle to let him join the Lawyers' Artillery Corps of the Irish Volunteers. During the rebellion led by Wolfe Tone, O'Connell remained firmly on the side of law and order—that is, on the side of the British. Still, it wasn't that he enjoyed British rule, just that he was deeply convinced that "a revolution would not produce the happiness of the Irish people." It was during this period that he decided to enter politics. O'Connell was determined to enter the Irish Parliament, if and when that became possible for Catholics, and work within the system for reform and justice.

Finally called to the bar in May of 1798, O'Connell did not begin practicing law until the following year. His first year was rather a lean one—he earned only £27—but in 1800, he earned £205, a respectable income for a bachelor. Although he should have been able to live on that amount, O'Connell had always been imprudent with money and was soon in debt.

Since O'Connell was now 25, reputedly good-looking and respectably employed—in other words, decidedly marriageable—his uncle was determined to arrange a profitable marriage for his heir. But O'Connell had other plans. Within a few weeks of meeting Mary O'Connell, a distant cousin and impoverished orphan, O'Connell asked her to marry him. For two years, O'Connell kept his engagement a secret from his uncle, along with his July 1802 wedding. But when Mary became pregnant within a few months, O'Connell had no choice but to journey to Darrynane to confess his deed; his uncle was furious and disinherited O'Connell. This meant the loss of a fortune, but O'Connell was convinced that his uncle would relent eventually. Time proved him right.

On the political front, the Rebellion of 1798 had led many to believe that the Irish Parliament was incapable of governing the country. After much political wrangling and gamesmanship, the Parliament decided to dissolve itself and enter Ireland into a union with England, effective on January 1, 1801. This move reduced Ireland to the status of a province, rather than a country in its own right, and O'Connell and other Irish patriots were outraged. O'Connell wrote of being:

> maddened when I heard the bells of St. Patrick's ring out a joyful peal for Ireland's degradation, as if it were a glorious national festival. My blood boiled and I vowed, on that morning, that the foul dishonour should not last if ever I could put an end to it.

But family concerned him for now, rather than politics. O'Connell's family grew every year—a son was born in 1803, another in 1804, a daughter in 1805—and every year O'Connell's income as a lawyer also grew. Still, most of it was owed before it was earned, and many of O'Connell's letters to his wife are full of instructions for paying off parts of various bills while putting off other creditors. Mary O'Connell certainly had her hands full with the children (she eventually raised seven) and with attempts at managing her husband's reckless spending, but common sense and steadiness were two of her primary virtues, and she created a good home for the O'Connell clan.

For the first 20 years following his marriage, O'Connell occupied himself primarily with becoming one of the best-known, most successful, and most feared lawyers in Ireland. His quick wit, clever questioning, and extensive knowledge helped him win an unsurpassed reputation—not to mention the great majority of his cases—but he was becoming more and more interested in issues of Irish liberation from British rule. In 1823, he was one of the driving forces behind the renewed founding of the Catholic Association whose aims revolved around promoting the interests of Catholics. Funding itself through what was known as "Catholic Rent," members were asked for a farthing a week, a tiny sum that even the poorest could afford—yet a sum that amounted to over

£50,000 a year, given the huge, nationwide membership of the association.

O'Connell Runs for British Parliament

In 1828, O'Connell ran for a seat in British Parliament from County Clare. This was an unprecedented step for a Catholic, since even if he were elected, he could not take a seat. The oath required of all Members of Parliament (MPs) declared that the king, not the pope, was head of the Church, and that the Catholic mass was both impious and abominable. No Catholic could swear to such propositions. Nevertheless, O'Connell ran—and won—overwhelmingly. Moreover, before it came time for him to take his seat in Parliament, a Catholic Emancipation Bill was passed (its passage was due in large part to agitation by O'Connell's Catholic Association), and Catholics were no longer held to the same oath as Protestant MPs. Still, when O'Connell arrived in London in 1829 to take his seat in the House of Commons, he was presented with the old oath, the one that had been in force when his election occurred. He declined to swear against his faith and did not take his seat in Parliament until after the next election later that year, when he ran unopposed in County Clare.

O'Connell was a reformer in Parliament—indeed, a radical—and worked for many reforms other than simply the repeal of the Irish union with England. He was a force in getting the 1831 Great Reform Bill passed, and his informal title of "the Agitator" was well deserved. But by 1840, O'Connell's enemies came into power and all hope of repealing the union was lost. The Whigs had reluctantly supported O'Connell during the 1830s, though never enough to actually repeal the Union; now, in the 1840s, the ascending Tories hated him. After a decade of fighting, O'Connell concluded that the cause for repeal had lost ground, and he returned to Ireland almost in despair.

In November of 1841, O'Connell was elected Lord Mayor of Dublin and at first enjoyed the prestige and honor of the role. However, by the end of the year, he had found that being a mayor leads to nothing but boredom, great expense, and the inability to be truly involved in national politics. He is said to have rejoiced as his term neared its close, "In another fortnight, I'll have the privilege of knocking down anyone who calls me My Lord."

The Campaign for Repeal

In 1843, O'Connell embarked on a last great campaign for repeal. He traveled the country, giving speeches that drew up to 100,000 listeners. All of Ireland was coming alive, turning out to hear their Liberator speak, and roaring their enthusiasm for repeal. It almost seemed as if O'Connell, ever the proponent of legal reform, was leading his country directly to civil war. A huge assembly was being planned in Dublin for October 8; it was to be the culmination of a long summer of rallies and meetings. The day before the assembly, Parliament passed a proclamation declaring it to be illegal, which presented O'Connell with a dilemma. Either he defied the order and went ahead with the meeting, risking slaughter or civil war when British soldiers arrived to disperse the crowd, or else he canceled the meeting—thus canceling hope that popular agitation could effect reform. O'Connell did the prudent thing: he canceled the assembly—and lost face terribly. In addition, he and four others were arrested for conspiracy against the government. An old man of 69, O'Connell was fined £2,000 and sentenced to two years in prison.

It was about the time of O'Connell's release from prison that the potato crop failed in Ireland, and the horror that would come to be known as the Great Famine began. Beaten, weary and ill, O'Connell returned to his seat in Parliament and made an impassioned speech on behalf of his starving country:

> Ireland is in your hands.... [I]f you do not save her she can't save herself. And I solemnly call on you to recollect that I predict with the sincerest conviction that one quarter of her population will perish unless you come to her relief.

The House of Commons, never much fond of the Irish and certainly eager to disparage the old troublemaker, did not see this as a distressing prospect. To a man, they rose to their feet and cheered.

Utterly defeated, O'Connell finally heeded his doctor's advice and set out for the Mediterranean, where it was hoped the mild weather might enable him to recover his health. But on May 17, 1847, he died. The Liberator, the Great Dan, succumbed to illness before his life's task was complete: Ireland's independence was not yet won and, in fact, would not be won until the next century. Still, Daniel O'Connell can be credited with molding the Irish into a people, a nation, where before a dispirited rabble had existed. He was one of a powerful line of Irishmen who struggled to make their land into an independent nation, and Ireland today still honors his achievements and his leadership.

SOURCES:

O'Faolain, Sean. *King of the Beggars: A Life of Daniel O'Connell.* Dublin: Poolbeg Press, 1980 (first published, 1938).

Trench, Charles Chenevix. *The Great Dan: A Biography of Daniel O'Connell.* London: Jonathan Cape, 1984.

FURTHER READING:

Dudley Edwards, R. *O'Connell and His World.* London, 1975.

McCartney, Donal, ed. *The World of Daniel O'Connell.* Dublin, 1980.

MacIntyre, Angus. *The Liberator: Daniel O'Connell and the Irish Party, 1930–47.* London, 1965.

O'Ferral, Fergus. *Daniel O'Connell.* Dublin, 1981.

Reynolds, J. A. *The Catholic Emancipation Crisis in Ireland, 1823–29.* Yale University Press, 1954.

Olaf I Tryggvason

(968–1000)

Viking warrior, who acquired wealth and fame by his raids in Britain and strove to bring national leadership and Christianity to pagan, politically divided tenth-century Norway.

To appreciate King Olaf Tryggvason's role in Norwegian history, it is helpful to provide a brief picture of his time, place, and position. Prior to the tenth century, although most of Western Europe had been Christian for centuries, Norway remained a pagan bastion of politically divided small kingdoms. The warriors of the North, untouched by ecclesiastical and cultural influences, harassed continental Europe from the eighth century on and were considered a major threat to the well-being of their southern neighbors. The ultimate involvement of Norway in the Christian network was due largely to the efforts of an energetic young king, Olaf Tryggvason. His policy of political consolidation and Christianization in Norway—a process which occurred at roughly the same time in Denmark and Sweden—helped to bring about the waning of the viking ("pirate") problem that had plagued Europe for many years.

Harald Fairhair (c. 870–c. 930) is generally recognized as Norway's first true king. By conquering rival *jarls* (earls) and forcing them into subservient positions, he created the precedent of one ruler for the many districts of Norway. During

"Olaf was the handsomest of men, very stout and strong, and in all bodily exercises he excelled every Northman that ever was heard of."

SNORRI SRURLUSON

Contributed by Cathy Jorgensen Itnyre, Instructor, College of the Desert, Joshua Tree, California

the tenth century, belonging to the family of Harald Fairhair was a political bonus for aspiring kings; in fact, Olaf Tryggvason was Harald's great-grandson. When Harald died around 930, his kingdom passed to his unpopular son Eirik Blood-axe. But Eirik and his widely detested wife Gunnhild proved unable to retain the throne, and Eirik's younger brother Haakon the Good—who had been raised as a Christian in the court of King Aethelstan of England—overthrew his sibling in 934. Although Haakon was the first Norwegian king who espoused Christianity, he found it politically necessary to revert to pagan ways. When he died in 961, his nephews—the sons of Eirik and Gunnhild—seized power. Among the five sons, the most prominent and politically effective was Harald Greypelt (961–70). During his nine-year reign, he eliminated many of his enemies, including his cousin Tryggve, the father of Olaf.

From 970 until Olaf Tryggvason's rise to power in 995, Norway was ruled by a series of *jarls* who owed allegiance to either the king of Denmark or the king of Sweden. One *jarl* in particular dominated the Norwegian political field: Jarl Haakon, who ruled for King Harald Bluetooth of Denmark and later for the latter's son Svein Forkbeard. Jarl Haakon regarded himself as the sole power in Norway, but his arrogance, violence, and lechery led to his defeat in 995, allowing Olaf Tryggvason to claim the throne as the successor of Harald Fairhair.

Olaf Tryggvason was born in 968, during a critical period in Norwegian history, to the recently widowed noblewoman Astrid. Young Olaf's life was immediately at risk: Gunnhild's sons plotted to kill their newborn cousin. According to the great medieval Icelandic historian Snorri Sturluson, who wrote around 200 years after the event but is considered to have used reliable older sources, Astrid sought refuge in Sweden in 969. By 971, she believed that her son's safety could best be achieved by seeking the assistance of her brother Sigurd in Russia, who enjoyed success as an aide to Duke Valdemar of either Novgorod or Kiev. But during the Baltic crossing, Astrid's party was assaulted by Estonian Vikings, and mother and son were separated and carried off into slavery.

Purchased by a kindly Estonian couple, the three-year-old Olaf Tryggvason was treated well. Six years passed. In 977, Valdemar sent Sigurd to Estonia to collect revenues. Then, according to Snorri:

> In the market place he happened to observe a remarkably handsome boy; and as he could distinguish that he was a foreigner, he asked him his

CHRONOLOGY

968	Olaf Tryggvason born
971–86	Olaf Tryggvason in Russia
986–94	Engaged in Viking activities in Baltic, the Low Countries, and Britain
994	Converted to Christianity
995	Assumed power in Norway
1000	Defeated by alliance of Danish and Swedish kings and Norwegian *jarl* at Battle of Svold; drowned or disappeared.

name and family. He answered him, that his name was Olaf; that he was a son of Tryggve Olafsson and Astrid.... Then Sigurd knew that the boy was his sister's son.

Impressed by the nine-year-old's adventures and touched to find his nephew still alive, Sigurd took Olaf back to the court of Valdemar. When Olaf's royal background was revealed to the Duke and his queen, the boy was granted every courtesy; indeed, says Snorri, Valdemar "received Olaf into his court, and treated him nobly, and as a king's son."

Remaining in Russia for nine years, Olaf Tryggvason used this time to develop the martial skills so crucial to a Viking career. One of the many poets who praised Olaf claimed that when Olaf was 12 years old, he successfully commanded Russian warships. Generosity toward his men was an essential component of his popularity, but this acclaim proved detrimental to Olaf's security in Russia. Valdemar allowed himself to be persuaded by Olaf's jealous detractors; the young Viking had to leave Russia with the covert assistance of Valdemar's queen. By 986, the 18-year-old Olaf was embarked on a Viking career in the Baltic, obtaining local fame and considerable wealth.

One of Olaf Tryggvason's marauding expeditions took him to Wendland (an area of northern Germany occupied by a fierce Slavic people in the late tenth century). There the king, Burislaf, allowed his daughter Geyra to marry Olaf, but the union proved short, as Geyra died three years later. Olaf's response to her death was to initiate another round of plundering, this time concentrating on areas from Frisia to Flanders.

Several sources attest to Olaf's presence in England by the year 991, including the *Anglo-Saxon Chronicle*:

In this year came Anlaf with ninety-three ships to Folkestone, and harried outside, and sailed thence to Sandwich, and thence to Ipswich, overrunning all the countryside, and so on to Maldon. Ealdorman Byrhtnoth came to meet them with his levies and fought them, but they slew the ealdorman there and had possession of the place of slaughter.

Snorri Sturluson extends Olaf's British activities to include all of the period 991–94, noting battles waged in Northumberland, Scotland, the Hebrides, and the Isle of Man.

Olaf Converts to Christianity

Olaf Tryggvason's acceptance of Christianity most likely occurred in the year 994, during his British campaigns. Snorri attributes his conversion to a legendary hermit who correctly predicted Olaf's future and claimed to have acquired this ability from the Christian God. Olaf was so impressed with the accuracy of the predictions that he and his men were immediately baptized. According to Snorri, Olaf then left the hermit's home in the Scilly Islands and sailed to England, where he "proceeded in a friendly way; for England was Christian and he himself had become Christian." On the other hand, the *Anglo-Saxon Chronicle* attributes no such refined manners to Olaf, stating that in 994 the Christian Olaf was every bit as dangerous as the pagan Olaf had been:

> Anlaf and Svein came to London with ninety-four ships, and kept up an unceasing attack on the city, and they… set it on fire. But there, God be thanked, they came off worse than they ever thought possible; so they went away thence, doing as much harm as any host was capable of… wherever they went. Then the king and his councillors decided to offer him tribute: this was done and they accepted it.

To seal the efficacy of the bribe, the English king Ethelred the Unready stood as Olaf's sponsor in the sacrament of confirmation.

Having traveled widely, Olaf Tryggvason had firsthand knowledge of the splendor of Christian courts and the ecclesiastical ritual that permeated Christian kingdoms. It is very likely that such observations—combined with the opportunity to topple the unpopular, lecherous Jarl Haakon in Norway—led Olaf to begin his mission to both conquer and Christianize the native land he had scarcely lived in.

By 995, Norwegians were tired of the rule of Jarl Haakon who, apparently lacking in moderation in his libidinal appetites, was subjecting many noble girls to the indignity of becoming short-term concubines. When Olaf learned of the extensive discontent in Norway, he decided to leave England (financed in large part by the bribe paid by Ethelred), return to his native land, and restore the rule of Harald Fairhair's line. Shortly after Olaf Tryggvason's arrival in Norway, Jarl Haakon was treacherously beheaded by his own slave. The Jarl's son Eirik fled to Sweden and nursed his discontent with the sympathetic support of King Olaf of Sweden. Thus, a drawn-out conflict was unnecessary, and in 996 Olaf Tryggvason was proclaimed king of all Norway at a general meeting, called a *thing* in Scandinavia.

Tenth-century Scandinavian kings were constantly in motion: there was no fixed residence (such as a palace), and it was necessary to have the royal presence felt from district to district in order to prevent insurrections. Olaf Tryggvason, only 27 years old in 995, had the energy and charisma to leave his imprint on all of Norway. Perhaps his success may be attributed to his unyielding personality: as Snorri puts it, "He would… either bring it to this, that all Norway should be Christian, or die." Certainly Olaf did not hesitate to resort to extreme coercive measures to convert his new realm; Norwegians who refused Christianity were killed, banished, or mutilated. Various sources affirm Olaf's energetic approach to convert not just Norwegians, but Icelanders and Greenlanders as well. Twelfth-century Icelandic historian Ari the Wise mentions the arrival in Iceland of priests sent by Olaf Tryggvason. It is suggested by Snorri that the great Viking Leif Eriksson adopted Christianity at Olaf's insistence, and in this way Christianity was brought to Greenland.

Olaf Tryggvason spent his five years as king of Norway battling not only pagans, but political enemies as well. For example, the last son of Eirik Bloodaxe and Gunnhild was defeated by Olaf's forces in 999. Despite an earlier alliance with the Danish king Svein Forkbeard during his Viking days in Britain, the political opposition of Olaf's fellow Scandinavian kings remained a constant feature of his five-year reign. Snorri credits Olaf Tryggvason's successful kingship to his Christian zeal and no-nonsense domestic policy:

> King Olaf… was distinguished for cruelty when he was enraged, and tortured many of his enemies. Some he burnt in fire; some he had torn in pieces by mad dogs; some he mutilated, or cast down from high precipices. On this account his friends were attached to him warmly, and his enemies feared him greatly; and thus he made such a

fortunate advance in his undertakings, for some obeyed his will out of the friendliest zeal, and others out of dread.

During Olaf's brief reign, pagan temples were torn down and churches were erected throughout Norway. Legends tell of the attempts Olaf made to rid his country of pagan spirits, including witches. By demonstrating his superior power over evil spirits, Olaf accomplished two purposes: winning converts to Christianity, and expressing his fitness to rule.

While not all of the sources mention Olaf Tryggvason's four marriages, there seems to be general agreement regarding the major details of his last union. This wedding took place in 999, and the lady was Thyre, a sister of King Svein Forkbeard of Denmark and the ex-wife of Olaf's former father-in-law, King Burislaf. Thyre had fled from Wendland to Norway, appalled at the prospect of married life with an old, pagan king such as Burislaf. Olaf proposed and Thyre considered what "luck it was for her to marry so celebrated a man."

A Dowry Returned; A Kingdom Lost

Soon after the wedding, Thyre began to complain to Olaf of her relative poverty. She had left the dowry her brother Svein Forkbeard bestowed on her in Wendland; since Svein disapproved of her flight from old Burislaf, he refused to help her retrieve her dowry. Thyre begged Olaf Tryggvason to go to Burislaf to accomplish this task. Always keen for a foreign adventure, Olaf agreed to gather his warships for an expedition to Wendland. In the summer of 1000, he set out with a large number of warships and men. The reunion with his former father-in-law was a peaceful one, and Olaf was able to obtain Thyre's dowry.

But while Olaf spent the summer in Wendland, the rival Scandinavian kings plotted to ambush him on his way back to Norway. Svein Forkbeard formed an alliance with King Olaf of Sweden and the Norwegian Jarl Eirik, who had gone to Sweden in exile when Olaf Tryggvason came to power in 995. The three leaders met and waited for Olaf Tryggvason's return to Norway, planning to ambush him as he sailed near Svold, an island off of Denmark.

The Battle of Svold is given great attention in Snorri's account, which relates touching anecdotes about Olaf Tryggvason's last fight. Although it is nearly impossible to separate embellishment from fact, there can be no doubt that as a result of the battle, Olaf lost his kingdom. Svein Forkbeard and Olaf of Sweden were successfully repulsed by the Norwegian king, but Olaf Tryggvason was unable to withstand the attack of his fellow Norwegian Jarl Eirik. When the latter's men boarded Olaf's magnificent ship called the *Long Serpent*, Olaf Tryggvason and his few remaining supporters jumped overboard and drowned or disappeared.

Legends immediately sprang up after Svold, claiming that Olaf Tryggvason escaped; some held that he was rescued by one of Burislaf's ships and that he embarked on a long pilgrimage to the Holy Land to atone for his youthful Viking days. "But however this may have been," writes Snorri, "King Olaf Tryggvason never came back again to his kingdom of Norway."

King Olaf Tryggvason was not the first to unite all the districts of Norway, nor was he the first Norwegian ruler to espouse Christianity. His significance stems from the vibrant way he managed to combine both of these accomplishments, firmly turning Norway away from its isolated pagan past and focusing the nation's attention on becoming a settled member of the European Christian community.

SOURCES:

The Anglo-Saxon Chronicle. Translated by G. N. Garmonsway, J. M. Dent, 1953.

Sturluson, Snorri. *Heimskringla: The Olaf Sagas.* Vol. 1. Translated by Samuel Laing, J. M. Dent, 1914.

FURTHER READING:

Foote, P. G., and D. M. Wilson. *The Viking Achievement.* Praeger, 1970.

Jones, Gwyn. *A History of the Vikings.* Oxford University Press, 1973.

Larsen, Karen. *A History of Norway.* Princeton University Press, 1948.

Turville-Petre, G. *The Heroic Age of Scandinavia.* Greenwood Press, 1951.

Otto I, the Great

(912–973)

One of the dominant figures of early medieval Europe, who established a strong kingship in Germany, founded the Holy Roman Empire, and decisively defeated the Magyars, creating a climate favorable for the growth of Western European civilization.

Born in 912; died on May 7, 973, at Memleben; eldest son of Henry I, the Fowler, and Matilda; married: Edith (sister of King Athelstan of England; died 946); married: Adelaide (daughter of King Rudolf of Lorraine); children: (first marriage) Liudolf and Liutgard; (second marriage) Matilda and Otto II. Predecessor: Henry I, the Fowler (r. 919–936). Successor: Otto II (r. 973–983).

Otto I, king of Germany and Holy Roman Emperor, often called Otto the Great, was one of the dominant figures of early medieval Europe. He was responsible for establishing a strong kingship in Germany, for founding the medieval empire known as the Holy Roman Empire which endured in one form or another until the time of Napoleon, and for defeating the Magyars at the battle of the Lech in 955 which created a stable climate for the growth of Western European medieval civilization.

In order to understand Otto's achievement, it is necessary to understand the development of Europe following the death of **Charlemagne**. Scarcely a generation after his death in 814, his (Carolingian) Empire was partitioned into three kingdoms by the Treaty of Verdun in 843: (1) west Frankia, (2) the middle kingdom, and (3) east Frankia, with modern Germany falling within the bounds of the latter two. When the future Otto I was born in 912, Germany was still a wild land of forests, with some clearings and small settlements surrounded by their open fields, a few villages and towns, and, here and there, abbeys and minsters (churches). Within what is now Germany there

"At the very first glance Otto appears as a born ruler.... Open-handed, accessible, and friendly he attracted many hearts and yet was more feared than loved."

WIDUKIND OF CORVEY

Contributed by Russell Andrew McDonald, Ph.D., University of Guelph, Guelph, Ontario, Canada

were five great duchies: Franconia, Saxony, Thuringia, Swabia, and Bavaria, each ruled by a duke who was first and foremost a military leader. In the turmoil ensuing from the collapse of the Carolingian Empire, and after the death of the last of the Carolingians in 911, just a year before Otto's birth, these dukes had become as powerful as kings. When Otto's father, Henry I, was designated as king by Conrad I, his succession was recognized only within his own duchy of Saxony and Conrad's duchy of Franconia. Henry was forced to gain the support of the dukes of Swabia and Bavaria by making concessions to them, and although he had succeeded in gaining back the losses by the end of his reign, in the years of Otto's youth the German king was still very much first among equals with regard to the dukes. It was the achievement of Otto I to elevate the German monarchy to one of its highest peaks.

Like most medieval rulers, little is known of Otto's boyhood and early life because of a lack of documentation. Born in 912, he was the eldest son of Henry I and his wife Matilda, and was heir to the duchy of Saxony. When his father died, Otto was 24 years old, and his succession had been ensured by his father, who had obtained the assent of the magnates shortly before his death. As a young man, Otto would have received the normal training accorded to any early medieval noble: hunting, horsemanship, and the use of arms. Much of his time would therefore have been spent out-of-doors. Historian Widukind of Corvey left a detailed portrait of the king. "He hunted as often as he could," and he "loved to play chess and games of draught and sports which could be done on horseback." He was, however, like Charlemagne and most kings of this age, without a formal education, and also like Charlemagne he only learned to read in middle life. But if not a scholar, Otto took care to foster the arts and learning in the monasteries. Of languages he knew some Latin, Old French, and Slavonic, in addition to his native tongue. As king, he was faithful to the Church; he rose day after day to hear Mass. He married early, as was the usual practice, in 929 taking Edith, an Anglo-Saxon princess who was the sister of King Athelstan of England, to be his wife (the wedding had been arranged by Otto's father.) Their two children, Liudolf and Liutgard, were both born before he ascended the throne.

Otto Is Crowned at Aachen

Otto's coronation in 936 took place at Aachen, the favorite residence and capital of Charlemagne. There, all the dukes and nobles of the realm had

CHRONOLOGY

843	Treaty of Verdun partitioned Charlemagne's Empire
919	Henry I, the Fowler, Duke of Saxony, elected king of Germany
936	Henry I died; Otto I elected king
937–38	Magyars raided Germany; German dukes and members of royal family rebelled against Otto
938–40	Otto suppressed rebellions; only his brother Henry (Duke of Bavaria) held out
941	Henry swore loyalty to Otto and was pardoned
951	Otto led army to Italy
953–54	Otto in Germany; more revolts broke out
955	Magyars invaded Germany; Otto victorious at battle of the Lech
961	Crowned his son co-ruler; campaigned in Italy, taking title king of Italy
962–64	Crowned and anointed emperor by the pope; remained in Italy to suppress risings
965	Returned to Germany
972	Treaty with Byzantines; Otto's son married Byzantine princess
973	Returned to Germany; died at Memleben; Otto II succeeded his father

gathered together to promise their support to the new king, each putting their hands in his. Next, Archbishop Hildebrandt of Mainz presented Otto to the assembled crowd and then girded him with the sword and placed in his hands the orb and scepter. After being crowned and anointed, there followed a sumptuous feast. As Widukind recorded: "A marble table was set for Otto, royally decked out, and trestle tables beside, and the new King sat himself down with his nobles and all the folk to great eating and drinking."

But although the general prospects for the reign of the young king appeared bright, action was needed almost immediately. From outside his realm, Otto was threatened by enemies on the frontier: on the Elbe, the Slavonic peoples rose against the new king. While Otto was dealing with this threat, the Magyars seized the opportunity to raid into Germany. In Bohemia, a reaction against the German expansion undertaken in earlier years also threatened. While Otto was able to successfully deal with these crises, he was also faced with a serious challenge to his authority at home from three German dukes and from some members of his own family. In 938, Otto's jealous half-brother Thankmar joined the dissident dukes and rose in rebellion. Otto took immediate and vigorous action, leading an army against his brother who was eventually killed claiming sanctuary in a church, apparently without the king's knowledge. But by 939 more plotting against the king was taking place. A key conspirator this time was Otto's full brother Henry who, for two years, attempted to raise a faction against Otto. But on Christmas 941, Henry appeared clad as a penitent before his brother to swear loyalty in return for a pardon. After much pleading, Otto found he could not refuse and eventually, in 947, he made Henry the duke of Bavaria.

Thus, in the first three years of his reign, Otto had been faced with a series of threats from both within and without his kingdom. Although it must be considered fortunate that the crises did not present themselves simultaneously, Otto had proved himself in adversity and shown his ability to take decisions under difficult circumstances. Accordingly, Otto earned the respect of his contemporaries, and ensured a period of comparative peace in his kingdom for some 12 years.

Having proven his ability, Otto now turned to addressing the government of his realm, especially the problem of how to bind the duchies more closely to the crown. His solution was to give these important offices to members of his own family, but, since his children were not yet of age and his brother could not yet be fully trusted, it was not until about 947 that his plan could be put fully into effect. By then, Saxony and Franconia were in the king's own hands, and the other three dukes were his son, his son-in-law, and his brother. Otto had thus established his right to appoint dukes, and in so doing had broken down some of the power of these provincial officers. With the duchies now held by members of his family, Otto could feel satisfied that his German kingdom was securely organized. The one remaining rebellious duchy, Bohemia, was brought to heel in a campaign led by the king himself in 950.

Unlike his father, Otto was not content to rule Saxony alone and leave the power of the dukes unchecked. His ultimate objective was empire, and his model was that of Charlemagne. Once he had established his power at home, he could turn his attentions to his ultimate objective, Italy. And, indeed, an opportunity did present itself shortly after Otto had completed the consolidation of his own kingdom. A complex chain of events in Rome and Italy ultimately led to Otto's involvement

there. An appeal for help had come from Adelaide (Adelheid), whose husband, Lothar, co-king of Italy with his father, Hugh, had been checked in his bid for power in Italy by Berengar, count of Ivrea. Hugh had died in 947, Lothar in 950, and Berengar had shut Adelaide up in prison, where her friends worked hard to rescue her and eventually succeeded. When the cry for help had gone out to Otto, the invitation could not have been more welcome. Acting decisively, the king led a huge army out of Germany in 951. Berengar fled before his advance, and Otto, whose first wife had died in 946, now married Adelaide, only half his age. Taking for himself the title of King of Italy, he sent envoys to the pope Agapitus II praying for approval and suggesting that he move on to Rome to be crowned emperor. But Alberic II, the master of Rome, naturally opposed such a move, and pressured the pope, who helplessly had to refuse. In 952, Otto took his new wife back to Germany, while Berengar quickly became king of Italy again.

For the next two years, Otto was too preoccupied at home to give much thought to imperial ambitions. In 953, Otto's eldest son (Liudolf) by his first marriage to Edith burst into revolt over perceived snubs and threats to his position; he was quickly joined by Conrad, duke of Lotharingia, and Frederick, archbishop of Mainz. Weary of rebellion in his own family, Otto decided the time had come for strong measures. Conrad and Frederick were stripped of their positions; Otto's army met that of his son at Mainz. As Widukind recorded, "The son, in battle array, awaited his father. There a war began, more bitter than civil strife and all tragedy." But the battle was indecisive, and Otto was forced to abandon the siege of Mainz. Then, in June 954, Conrad and Frederick submitted to the king, leaving Liudolf alone in rebellion. Widukind seized the opportunity to place an appropriate speech in the mouth of Otto (a favorite tactic of ancient authors): "I would bear all," he has Otto say, "if the wrath of my son and of his fellows in intrigue hurt me alone and did not bring confusion upon all people of Christian name.... Here I sit, a man bereft, my son my most eager enemy." To make matters worse, while Otto was occupied with civil strife, the Hungarians had once again ravaged Germany territory. Widukind has Otto continue: "Now they have laid waste my kingdom, they have seized and killed my people. My towns lie in ruins, the temples burned, the priests slain, the very streets running red with blood." Finally, after having been besieged at Regensburg, Liudolf threw himself at his father's feet and begged a pardon, which was duly given, although the son was deprived of his duchy.

He Wins Significant Victory over the Magyars

But Otto had no time in which to rejoice at his victory, for the Hungarian invaders were again ravaging Bavaria and its duke was calling urgently for help. The king immediately gathered an army and went forward to meet the invading Magyars: "He would rather die," wrote the chronicler Theitmar, "than tolerate such evil." Finally, in early August of 955, the German army, led by Otto, confronted the Magyar force on a plain along the bank of the river Lech near Augsburg. In the early morning of August 10, the king and his army heard Mass, and Otto promised that if the victory was his he would found and endow a bishopric at Merseburg. Then, with the banner of Michael the Archangel carried before him and the Holy Lance in his hand, he gave the signal for the attack. Initially, the German army was thrown into disarray by an attack on its rear by a large force of Magyars. Once again Otto acted swiftly, decisively, and with great courage. Sending his son-in-law, only recently returned to the fold after his involvement in the civil war of a year earlier, to fend off the attack in the rear, the king at the head of his division rushed into the main host of the enemy. This determined charge broke the ranks of the Magyars, who turned their horses and fled. Otto's army pursued them over the countryside, and their leaders were hanged for all to see at Regensburg.

The victory was complete; not only had Otto freed Germany from further invasion but his dominance also allowed the inhabitants of France, Burgundy, and Italy to breathe easier as well. Modern historians regard the victory as significant because it created more stable conditions under which medieval Western civilization could flourish. Also from this victory dates Otto's title of "the Great," and even contemporaries recognized its significance: one chronicler wrote that "He freed the whole Occident from the Magyars." The successes of the year 955 were rounded off with further victories over the Slavs, and with the birth to Otto's wife Adelaide of a son, who was to be Otto II (r. 973–983).

Having restored the peace in Germany and eliminated the threat on his frontiers, Otto was now able to turn his attention to Italy and Rome again. Pope John XII (bastard son of Alberic II, who was a particularly depraved character and decried by contemporaries), joined many of his bishops as well as other secular nobles of Italy in their pleas to Otto to intervene in order to alleviate the tyranny of Berengar and Adalbert in Rome. After having his young son Otto recognized as king in union with him in May 961, Otto, Ade-laide, and a formidable army made their way into Italy, where the king displaced Berengar and promised to maintain papal security. Then, on February 2, 962, the ceremony of the imperial coronation was celebrated in St. Peter's at Rome where Otto and Adelaide were crowned emperor and empress. Otto had thus gained his ambition, but a story recorded by Theitmar tells us that as he entered Rome he whispered to his sword-bearer:

> While today I make my prayer at the sacred shrine of the apostles do thou cease not to hold the sword over my head. Well I know that the faith of the Roman people has very often been matter of doubt for our predecessors.

Otto's doubts were well founded, for the pope soon turned to fomenting rebellion against what he perceived to be Otto's oppressive rule. Otto then convoked a synod that deposed the pope, and from then on the emperor and his successors took it for granted that they could create popes in Rome.

In many respects the coronation of Otto in 962 marked the zenith of his reign. He had fulfilled his imperial ambition and, as the medieval historian Z.N. Brooke wrote, "Otto may be regarded as the creator of the Empire which was known to the Middle Ages." Certainly by now he was the most powerful ruler in the West; embassies from all over Western Europe and North Africa visited his court. Manuscript illustrations show him sitting upon his throne with the orb, the symbol of world rule, in his right hand, and with the scepter of authority in his left. His feet rest upon Terra, the Christian earth, and the protecting finger of God reaches down from Heaven to touch his forehead. Despite such symbolism, modern historians have been careful to point out the many differences between Otto's Empire and that of Charlemagne—the most important being that, while Charlemagne was in effect the ruler of almost all of Christian Europe, Otto's Empire was confined to Germany, Italy, and Burgundy. Nevertheless, in one form or another the Empire that he had created endured for nearly 900 years, until the time of Napoleon.

Otto's assumption of the imperial title and his deposition of the pope created problems in Italy, where, with the exception of the year 965, when he returned home to Germany, he spent much of the rest of life. His assumption of the imperial title was particularly upsetting to the Roman emperors of Constantinople, and after a series of indecisive campaigns in southern Italy,

Otto was finally able to negotiate a peace settlement by which his son married Byzantine princess Theophano in 972 (their son ruled as Otto III from 983–1002). His work was finally completed in Italy, and his fame had spread throughout the Western world.

The chronicler Widukind, who lived through the reign of Otto, has left a lively description of the king, recording that, "His body was strong and firm but not without a certain grace. Even in his later years he remained a rugged hunter and agile horsemen." His eyes, Widukind wrote, were lively, and sparse gray hair covered his head although his beard, "flowed long and mighty over his chest which was very hairy—like a lion's mane." Although Widukind praised Otto's open-handed nature, he also recorded that "his anger was hard to bear.... The old emperor could be severe unto harshness." "Otto had a will of iron, from youth to old age," the chronicler continued, and then went on to praise his virtues of "rocklike fidelity to his friends, magnanimity toward his humbled foes," and his "royal and imperial dignity."

By 972, Otto was longing for Germany, from which he had been absent for six years. Much had happened while he had been campaigning in Italy: his mother had died, as had his son William, and there were once again rumblings of rebellion as the king had been away too long. He celebrated Easter of 973 at his palace of Quedlinburg, surrounded by his friends, and then in early May he moved on to Memleben in the Harz mountains, where his father had died. His long and eventful reign ended there on May 7, 973. He rose early, as usual, to hear the services of nocturns and matins, then heard Mass, and gave alms to the poor before eating his spartan breakfast. At dinner, he was reported to have been cheerful, but during vespers his friends noticed that he was ill. A priest was called, and then, "with great tranquility and no lament he committed his soul into the care of the Creator of all." Dying just a few months after his 60th birthday, having ruled as king for 37 years and as emperor for 11, he was buried in his cathedral of Magdeburg in Saxony on the river Elbe.

SOURCES:

Barraclough, G. *The Origins of Modern Germany*. Norton, 1984.

Brooke, Z. N. *A History of Europe 911–1198*. Methuen, 1938.

Duckett, E. S. *Death and Life in the Tenth Century*. University of Michigan Press, 1971.

Erdoes, R. *A.D. 1000. Living on the Brink of Apocalypse*. Harper, 1988.

FURTHER READING:

Barraclough, G. *The Crucible of Europe: The Ninth and Tenth Centuries in European History*. University of California Press, 1976.

Ignace Jan Paderewski

(1860–1941)

Polish statesman, orator, pianist, and composer, who possessed a genius rarely observed in the course of human history.

"Beloved as a great personality, admired as a consummate pianist and composer, and deeply respected as statesman and patriot, [Paderewski] gained an ever-widening circle of friends who today speak of him with veneration."

FRANK NOWAK

With the Third Partition of Poland in 1795, Austria, Prussia, and Russia, finished a process that began in 1772. The result was the breakup of the Polish state. Poland would be under foreign rule for nearly the next 125 years. Throughout those years the ethnic Poles struggled against both Russian and German authority to maintain their language, traditions, and culture. Occasionally, citizens rebelled; the largest of these revolutions took place in 1830 and in 1863. Ignace Jan Paderewski grew up during a time when his ancestral Poland did not exist.

He was born in the country village of Kurylowka, in the province known as Podolia, which was in the southeastern part of the old Polish Republic. The region of Podolia was described as "one of the most beautiful places in existence." The country was filled with "picturesque" landscapes and some of the richest soil to ever grace the earth. Despite these many pleasantries, Paderewski also endured the hardships of a rural existence. His home was several hundred miles from the nearest railway station and even further from a major city. The Paderewski family traveled very little, and when they did travel it was by horse.

Contributed by Christopher Blackburn, Ph.D. candidate in history, Auburn University, Auburn, Alabama

Name variations: Ignacy. Pronunciation: EN-yas Yan Pad-e-REF-skee. Born on November 18, 1860, in the small village of Kurylowka, Podolia, in southeastern Poland; died on June 29, 1941; son of Jan and Polixena Paderewski; married: Antonina Korsak; married: Madame Gorska; children: Alfred.

CHRONOLOGY

1863	Polish Insurrection
1872	Paderewski entered the Warsaw Conservatory
1887	Made successful Vienna appearance
1889	Established himself as a world-class pianist with Paris debut
1891	Gave first American concert at Carnegie Hall
1914	Assassination of Archduke Ferdinand; World War I began
1917	Paderewski became Polish National Committee representative to United States.
1919	Accepted post of premier of Poland and secretary of foreign affairs; resigned both
1920	Polish forces destroyed Soviet army at gates of Warsaw, ending Russo-Polish War
1933	Hitler came to power in Germany
1939	Germany invaded Poland; Paderewski appointed president of exiled Free Polish Government
1941	Died in America while rallying support for Poland

Russians Jail His Father

Young Paderewski, called "Ignas" in his childhood, never knew his mother, who died when he was only a few months old. When the boy was three, his father was imprisoned by Russian authorities for more than a year. Like many belonging to the class of small nobility, his father had taken part, although not actively, in the Polish Insurrection of 1863. "He was always encouraging his friends to participate," wrote the great pianist, as he later recalled his father's arrest in *The Paderewski Memoirs:*

> I ran again to the tallest of the Cossacks, frightened as I was, and cried, "What is happening to my father?" But he never answered or even looked at me. But I insisted and I kept on asking, as a child will, what had happened—why were they taking my father away, and if he would soon be back again. And then, the tall Cossack laughed, threw back his head and again gave me several very heavy strokes with the knout.... It was very sad and very terrifying to us, and we cried bitterly together, my sister Antonina and I. We could not understand it when our father, who was so good, was taken away from us and we were left alone.

The oppressive nature of Russian-dominated Poland remained with Paderewski throughout his lifetime.

> This first contact with the Russian authorities affected me very deeply—it will always affect me. First of all it was very painful, it cut my flesh, but I also considered it a supreme insult—in the pride of boyhood, not quite four years old! It wounded my spirit.

These early unpleasant encounters with Russian authorities, coupled with his father's teachings, caused the boy to become a staunch Polish patriot and led him to later write: *"La patrie avant tout, l'art ensuite"* ("Fatherland before everything, art afterward").

During his third year, the boy had begun to display an interest in music, particularly the piano. By the age of four, he was using all ten fingers at the piano and attempting to create simple melodies. His father recognized his great musical talent and began to encourage "some education in that direction." His formal music instruction began at the age of four, while his father was in prison.

Thus, the first music teacher, the old violinist Runowski, conducted lessons while the children were staying at the home of their aunt in Nowosiolki, about 60 miles from Kurylowka. Paderewski acknowledged that because Runowski was "a violinist, naturally he knew nothing about the piano. But he was a nice and very conscientious old man... [and he] gave me my first rudiments of piano playing." When their aunt soon realized the futility of having a violinist give piano lessons, she sought out a reputable pianist of the region. The new teacher, Peter Sowinski, reportedly came from a family famous for its musicians and poets, therefore, Ignace thought "his entrance into my musical life certainly seemed a step forward." Sowinski proved no better than Runowski. "These lessons proved not very important after all, because he was not a real piano teacher, but just a poor musician who was giving lessons to the children of the nobility." Since neither of these early music teachers were well versed in piano technique, the boy's "only real musical enjoyment was to sit down to the piano and improvise."

Following his release from jail, the elder Paderewski moved the entire family to the small town of Sudylkow, which is in the old Polish province of Volhynia, and began managing a large estate. By age 12, the young Paderewski's talent began attracting the attention of music lovers throughout the region. He was quickly recognized as a promising musician by the wealthy Count Chodkiewicz. The Count soon insisted on exposing the young prodigy to the Kievan music scene for a few weeks. Until that point Paderewski "had never heard any concerts at that age, nor any music really. I had never heard an orchestra, a pianist, violinist, or even a singer. So this was a great adventure—my first."

Later that same year, accepted to the Warsaw Conservatory, he studied music theory and piano with some of the finest Polish pianists of the day. But Paderewski proved somewhat undisciplined and was ultimately expelled from the institute. Eventually readmitted before his 16th birthday, he began to give recitals of Chopin and Liszt throughout the towns and villages of northern Poland. In 1878, Paderewski received excellent marks on his final examinations at the conservatory and remained there to teach piano.

Less than two years later in 1880, Paderewski married a young student of the conservatory named Antonina Korsak. His marriage was one of both incredible happiness and pain, for within one year of his wedding he witnessed the birth of his son and the death of his wife. Paderewski later reflected:

I had a little home of my own at last and I was happy—but it was a short happiness.... I had lived through a brief—a beautiful—experience. Even at twenty, one can plumb the heights and depths and feel the pain and mystery of life.

After the death of his wife, a somber Paderewski placed his infant son in the care of his mother-in-law and then traveled to Berlin to study piano composition with Friedrich Kiel. He worked feverishly with Kiel for nearly seven months before he returned to teach music at the Warsaw Conservatory. By 1883, Paderewski had grown tired of the mundane life of a music teacher and returned to Berlin to study orchestration with Heinrich Urban.

He then took a short vacation in Poland's Tatra Mountains to "work on the native music of the peasants." It was there that he met the famous Polish actress Madame Helena Modrzejewska. Soon after their initial meeting, they performed together before a packed house in Krakow. The success of the concert allowed Paderewski to continue on to Vienna and study with "the greatest teacher of his generation," Theodor Leschetizky. His time was well spent: he learned both a proper work ethic and the proper use of the piano pedal.

Concerts Bring World Acclaim

With the recommendation of Leschetizky, Paderewski soon accepted a teaching position at the Strasbourg Conservatory, then traveled to Paris and held his first recital on March 3, 1888. His career advanced at an incredible pace. By the end of the month, he was hailed as the "Lion of Paris." Paderewski later recalled, "Here is perhaps the moment that I may say they hailed me as 'a great star.' My career as a pianist was then launched. There was solid ground under my feet at last." His reputation and his following quickly grew as he crisscrossed Europe for one engagement after another. In late 1891, Paderewski gave his first New York concert and within six months had added America to his list of adoring fans. Between the years 1891 and 1905, Paderewski successfully toured the world, from Russia to Australia and back to America. By late 1905, however, his health began faltering, and he only performed sporadically for the rest of his life.

With the outbreak of World War I in 1914, Paderewski put aside his musical career to work for the freedom of Poland from foreign domination. He actively supported the wartime Committee for Aid to Poles in the Homeland, and, in February 1915, he established the Polish Victims Relief Fund. Throughout the war, Paderewski traveled the globe using both speaking engagements and concerts to raise money for the Polish cause. With the American declaration of war in 1917, Paderewski immediately became the Polish spokesman in the United States. He then used his remarkable powers of persuasion and masterful oratory to help secure an independent postwar Polish state. His efforts were instrumental in convincing President **Woodrow Wilson** to include guarantees to Poland in his Fourteen Points. Wilson eventually gave in and added his 13th point, which guaranteed the existence of an independent postwar Polish state with access to the sea.

Represents Poland at Versailles Peace Conference

At the close of the war on December 25, 1918, Paderewski returned to his homeland and accepted the offices of prime minister and minister of foreign affairs for the newborn Polish Republic. He then traveled to Paris to represent Poland at the Versailles Peace Conference, and on June 28, 1919, he signed the peace treaty with Germany. In reference to Paderewski's work on behalf of Poland at the conference, the Big Four (Wilson, Clemenceau, Lloyd George, and Orlando) wrote:

Polish statesman Ignace Jan Paderewski was an accomplished pianist, who learned to play when he was three.

his failing health he accepted the post and moved to Paris. In November 1940, Paderewski once again crossed the Atlantic to raise support for Poland in America. His aged body, however, would not allow him a repeat performance of his World War I whirlwind tour. A few months after entering the United States, he contracted pneumonia and died on June 29, 1941. At Paderewski's funeral, Justice Harlan Fiske Stone eulogized: "It is hard to face again a divided world. We linger not only because Paderewski is the world's greatest pianist, but because he is perhaps the greatest living man."

By order of President **Franklin D. Roosevelt**, Ignace Jan Paderewski was laid to rest in a crypt at the Battleship *Maine* Memorial in Arlington National Cemetery in July 1941. But it was Paderewski's dying wish that his body be returned to his country when Poland recovered its independence. In June 1992, President George Bush regarded it as "one of the greatest honors of my presidency" to take part in reinterment ceremonies in a Poland that had "thrown off the yoke of Soviet communism." Paderewski's heart, however, would forever remain in his beloved America, where it had been transferred to Our Lady of Czestochowa Shrine in Doylestown, Pennsylvania, in June 1986.

SOURCES:

Kellogg, Charlotte. *Paderewski*. Viking, 1956.

Kmiec, Ronald. "Ignacy Jan Paderewski (1860–1941)," in *The Kosciuszko Foundation Newsletter*. Kosciuszko Foundation, March 1991.

Mizwa, Stephen, ed. *Great Men and Women of Poland*. Macmillan, 1941.

Paderewski, Ignace Jan, and Mary Lawton. *The Paderewski Memoirs*. Scribner, 1938.

Strakacz, Aniela. *Paderewski As I Knew Him*. Rutgers University Press, 1949.

Zamoyski, Adam. *Paderewski*. Atheneum, 1982.

FURTHER READING:

Duleba, Wladyslaw, and Zofia Sokolowska. *Paderewski*. Kosciuszko Foundation, 1979.

Landau, Rom. *Ignace Paderewski: Musician and Statesman*. Crowell, 1934.

Phillips, Charles. *Paderewski: The Story of a Modern Immortal*. Macmillan, 1934.

"No country could wish for a better advocate than he." Following the conference, the aging statesman/musician returned to Warsaw to try and form a united Polish government from the fragments of both the partitions and the First World War. Within a matter of months, he lost his patience with the many competing political factions and resigned his office on December 5, 1919.

Paderewski devoted his next 20 years to intermittent speaking engagements and recitals but remained far from the Polish political scene. He was, however, drawn back into Polish politics at the outbreak of World War II in September 1939. With the collapse of the Polish state, he was called to be president of the National Council, the legislative branch of the Free Polish government. Despite

Lord Palmerston

(1784–1865)

British politician, who championed liberalism and national aspiration abroad and preservation of England's parliamentary system at home.

"[A]s the Roman, in days of old, held himself free from indignity, when he could say Civis Romanus sum *[I am a Roman citizen]; so also a British subject, in whatever land he may be, shall feel confident that the watchful eye and the strong arm of England will protect him against injustice and wrong."*

LORD PALMERSTON
DON PACIFICO SPEECH (1850)

Henry John Temple, the 3d Viscount Palmerston, was born at his father's house on the south edge of London's St. James Park on the evening of October 20, 1784. He was the eldest of five children born to the 2d Viscount Palmerston and his youthful and aptly named wife, Mary Mee, daughter of a wealthy merchant who had nursed her future husband back to health following a fall from a horse. The Temples had been involved in public life and politics for generations, going back to the reign of James I. Palmerston's great-grandfather, Henry Temple, was created the 1st Viscount Palmerston in 1723 by George I, but as an Irish peerage did not entitle its holder to a seat in the English House of Lords, he represented several English borough constituencies as a member of the House of Commons in London; it was he who purchased the family estate at Broadlands in Hampshire. Palmerston's father, the 2d Viscount, also served as an English M.P. from the age of 22 until his death some 40 years later and was a consistent supporter of the government, holding offices at the Admiralty and Treasury boards. The Temples were Tory aristocrats, if minor Irish ones, in an age of oligarchy; they believed in the "mixed constitution" which had been established at the

Contributed by Richard Francis Spall, Jr, Associate Professor of History, Ohio Wesleyan University, Delaware, Ohio

Born Henry John Temple, 3rd Viscount Palmerston on October 20, 1784, at what is now 20 Queen Anne's Gate, Westminster, London, England; died October 18, 1865, at Brocket Hall, Hertfordshire, England; son of 2nd Viscount Palmerston and Mary Mee; married: Emily Lamb (widow of the Earl of Cowper and sister of Lord Melbourne), December 16, 1839; children: none. Predecessors: (as prime minister) Aberdeen 1855, Derby 1859. Successors: (as prime minister) Derby 1858, Russell 1865.

Chronology

1807	Entered Parliament
1809	Began 20 years at War Office in five Tory administrations
1828	Dismissed from Wellington's government with Canningites
1830	Appointed foreign secretary in Grey's Whig ministry
1835	Returned for Tiverton, borough he represented until death
1846	Returned to the Foreign Office in Russell's Whig cabinet
1851	Dismissed by Russell and Queen Victoria for expressing approval of Napoleon III's coup in France
1852	Appointed home secretary in Aberdeen coalition
1855	Became prime minister in midst of Crimean War
1858	Resigned after defeat on Conspiracy to Murder Bill
1859	Recalled to office as prime minister in Liberal ministry
1865	Died in office, at age 80, after winning general election

Glorious Revolution of 1688 in which government was posited on monarchy, leadership of the aristocracy, and representation of "interests" in the House of Commons.

The French Revolution was a formative experience for many of Palmerston's generation, but it was especially so for young "Harry" and his family as they witnessed firsthand the Revolution in France when they traveled abroad in 1789. Two years later, Palmerston's father was persuaded by his friend Charles James Fox to return to Paris on a mission to "moderates" in the Revolution. This succeeded only in confirming the family's opinion of the perils of revolutionary change; Lady Palmerston described to a correspondent how peasants had seized a gentleman, cut him to bits before his family, and then roasted the pieces before eating them. Still, in 1792 the Temples returned to France for yet another stay and arrived in Paris just two days after revolutionaries from Marseilles entered the capital singing the song that would become the national anthem of France. After being presented at court, a friend warned that royal guards would likely desert if the palace were stormed, so Lady Palmerston determined that the family should visit Paris another time "when liberty is not at such a height." To their horror, the departing family became separated at the gates of the city, when the carriage carrying Harry and his parents was allowed through while the other carriages with the younger children and servants were detained for questioning by revolutionaries. In less than a week, the Tuileries were stormed, and the French royal family imprisoned.

Palmerston's education began while he was abroad. A tutor, Signor Gaetano, was engaged while the family traveled in Switzerland and Italy, and Harry soon become quite fluent in Italian and later in French. The family returned to England in 1794, and at home an Italian refugee named Ravizzotti tutored Palmerston. In May of 1795, Palmerston went off to Harrow where he rose to become a monitor. Among his classmates was the future earl of Aberdeen with whom he engaged in a famous pillow fight, and Palmerston developed a reputation for sobriety and for taking on bullies.

In 1800, Palmerston went to board with Professor Dugald Stewart, a former colleague of Adam Smith, at the University of Edinburgh. Under Stewart, Palmerston was a diligent student and embraced the doctrines of political economy thoroughly. In April of 1802, at the age of 17, Harry was urgently summoned to London and arrived to discover that his father had died. Shattered by the news, Harry remained sullen for some weeks, but Lady Palmerston was determined that he should return to Edinburgh for a third year of studies. It was as Lord Palmerston that Harry Temple returned to Scotland. The following year, Palmerston entered St. John's College, Cambridge, where noblemen received all manner of special privileges including exemption from certain examinations. He applied himself under his tutor, Dr. Outram, and took an active part in social life. The premature death of Lady Palmerston in 1805 delayed his graduation until early the next year, and though he was required to take his M.A. *jure natalium* (by right of birth), the young lord was allowed to sit for his college examinations and won first-class honors for his studies.

In a by-election occasioned by the death of **William Pitt the Younger** in 1806, Palmerston stood unsuccessfully as a Tory candidate for M.P. at Cambridge; he also stood that same year as the Tory candidate for the borough of Horsham in a disputed election in which his initial victory was invalidated. When Palmerston's guardian, Lord Malmesbury, persuaded the duke of Portland in 1807 to appoint him a junior lord of the admiralty, it became essential to find him a seat in Parliament. Sir Leonard Holmes nominated Palmerston for his pocket borough of Newport on the Isle of Wight on condition that he never set foot in the borough, even at election times, so as not to diminish his patron's influence. Thus began a parliamentary career that lasted, with the exception of one six-month period, for 58 years.

Enters Parliament, Becomes War Secretary

Palmerston's maiden speech in 1808 was in support of George Canning's order to attack Copenhagen and seize the Danish fleet in order to prevent it from falling into **Napoleon**'s hands. Palmerston defended the controversial action as being "in conformity to the law of nature, which dictated and commanded self-preservation." The next year, Spencer Perceval offered Palmerston a place in the cabinet as chancellor of the exchequer, but Palmerston refused, so the prime minister offered him the post of secretary for war which he accepted while declining to enter the cabinet. Palmerston remained at the War Office for 20 years and was responsible for the financial and general administration of the army. Since the secretary for war and the colonies directed military policy and was responsible for strategic decisions in cabinet, Palmerston rarely spoke in the Commons on matters that did not touch upon his office. He earned a reputation as an able administrator while becoming expert in military affairs and instituting reforms dealing with procurement, economy of expenditure, and training.

Palmerston had grown to maturity during the Regency period, and his social character seems to have reflected thoroughly that era. He led a most active social life attending dinner parties and acquired the nickname "Lord Cupid" for his well-deserved reputation as a friend of the ladies. He became, for example, a member of the most exclusive club in London, Almack's, through his intimate relationships with several of the Lady Patronesses who ruled the club, including the Countess Cowper. Palmerston was once wounded by something other than Cupid's arrows, for in 1818 a retired army officer, Lieutenant Davies, attempted to assassinate him at the War Office but managed only to fire a pistol shot into Palmerston's posterior. Characteristically, Palmerston paid the legal expenses of his assailant, who was found to be insane and sent to Bedlam.

Palmerston's path to the Foreign Office was slow. In 1811, he was at last returned to House for Cambridge which he represented through six general elections until losing in 1831 for his support of parliamentary reform. In the Liverpool ministry, especially after 1822, he emerged as a Canningite, opposing the slave trade and supporting Catholic emancipation. Liverpool offered Palmerston numerous offices, but he steadfastly declined and remained at the War Office. When he became prime minister, Canning too offered Palmerston the office of chancellor of the exchequer, but the offer was withdrawn, as was that of Viscount Goderich when he succeeded Canning as prime minister later in the year, because of opposition from George IV who did not like Palmerston personally. Palmerston stayed at the War Office, but did at last enter the cabinet in 1827 and served briefly as acting commander in chief in the Wellington ministry. Palmerston and the Canningites resigned in 1828 over the government's refusal to give representation to large cities in the industrial north, but in opposition he found his parliamentary voice.

In 1829, Palmerston established himself as a major political figure with a stirring indictment of Wellington's foreign policy in which he accused "The Iron Duke" of having aligned Britain with the forces of absolutism in Europe instead of being the patron of constitutional liberty. He charged the ministry with standing idly by while a liberal government was overthrown and replaced by a police state in Portugal. He denounced too Wellington's support for a limited new Greek state which contained "neither Athens, nor Thebes, nor Marathon, nor Salamis, nor Palataea, nor Thermopylae, nor Missolonghi." Palmerston's popularity after his foreign policy speech, his prominence as a Canningite after William Huskisson's (president of the board of trade) untimely death in a railway accident, and the influence of some ladies with whom he was acquainted made him sought after by Earl Grey when he was asked to form a Whig ministry in 1830. At the age of 46, Palmerston embarked on a new career as foreign secretary without wide expectation of success in a Whig administration.

Palmerston Is Success in Foreign Office

It was at the Foreign Office that Palmerston left his greatest mark. With the tenacity of an English bulldog, he tried to advance what he perceived to be British interests and honor, to protect the rights of British citizens abroad, to oppose absolutist regimes, and to foster where possible liberal governments under constitutional monarchs. He was a natural diplomat and was called "Protocol Palmerston" by the clerks whom he worked mercilessly. His management style was clear, short, and direct, and he used "brinksmanship" in negotiation, being prepared to use force to intervene when necessary. Critics complained that his foreign policy was too often based on "gunboat diplomacy," but the 1830s witnessed a series of brilliant foreign policy successes. Despite a tendency to see constitutional states as the natural allies of Britain, Palmerston was willing to act in concert with the powers when it seemed advantageous. His combination of consultation between the powers and willingness to use the navy unilaterally was instrumental in preserving Belgian independence as a neutral state. He lent the weight of British diplomacy to the fledgling Greek state and aided them in their negotiations with the Turks for cession of ancient Greek territory. In the parallel succession crises of Portugal and Spain, royal daughters (who could not inherit under Salic law) were challenged by their illiberal uncles. Palmerston proposed an alliance system to preserve the reigns of Queen Donna Maria and Queen Isabella. When France balked and civil war erupted in Spain, a British naval blockade and landing of independent "volunteer" forces soon restored a liberal regime.

In the mid-1830s, the Turkish sultan faced a new rebellion from his opportunist vassal, Mohammad Ali, the pasha of the province of Egypt in the sultan's Ottoman Empire, who hoped to gain control of the eastern Mediterranean. Palmerston was anxious that the "Sick Man of Europe" (Ottoman Empire) not succumb and that Tsar Nicholas I's influence which was growing in Constantinople not turn Turkey into a Russian satellite. In 1840, after fighting between the Sultan and the Pasha had broken out again, Palmerston proposed that the powers jointly guarantee Turkish integrity on condition that the Dardanelles be closed to all warships in any conflict in which the Sultan was neutral. Russia, Austria, and Prussia agreed, but the French who were sympathetic to the Pasha balked until, at the brink of war with Britain, they accepted Palmerston's plan.

On December 16, 1839, Palmerston married Lady Cowper who had been widowed two years earlier. The new Lady Palmerston was 52, three years younger than her husband, and had been his mistress for some years. When **Robert Peel** and the Conservatives won the general election of 1841, Palmerston found himself in opposition for six years during which time he devoted more attention to his private affairs but still was active in public life. He criticized Aberdeen's foreign policy, endorsed adoption of a moderate fixed duty on imported grain, and supported Lord Ashley's (later **Shaftsbury**) effort to restrict labor of women and children in the Ten Hours Bill. Ashley later married Lady Palmerston's daughter, Minnie, whom some contemporaries believed might have been Palmerston's child as well.

Returned to the Foreign Office in Lord Russell's ministry after Peel split his party over the Corn Laws in 1846, Palmerston condemned Spanish misgovernment and opposed French intrigue in the Spanish royal marriages controversy. In the revolutions which swept Europe in 1848, he was sympathetic to the aspirations of oppressed nationalities but refrained from intervention. Protecting British subjects and their interests abroad was always a hallmark of Palmerston's conduct of foreign policy. It was on this basis and upon his abiding belief in free trade that he had aided British merchants and representatives when they were imprisoned by Chinese officials in 1839 in the so-called First Opium War by bombarding Canton, capturing Shanghai, and invading the Yangtse Valley until the Chinese came to terms.

Similarly, in 1850, Palmerston sent the navy to press the claims of Don Pacifico, a moneylender of Portuguese-Jewish descent who was entitled to British citizenship by virtue of having been born in Gibraltar. Don Pacifico's home had been pillaged by a mob in Athens, and when the Greek government refused compensation, Palmerston sent the fleet to blockade Greece until the government recognized the claims. France and other nations were furious with British interventionism, and opponents in Parliament demanded his resignation. But Palmerston rallied the House and the nation to his cause in his most famous and five-hour-long speech in which he defended his foreign policy since 1830 and rejected the notion that evil acts from a small state ought not be met with force. With dawn breaking, Palmerston declared that protection of Britons was the moral foundation of his policy and that British subjects could claim the protection of a Pax Britannica as ancient Roman citizens could proclaim, *"Civis Romanus sum."*

Queen **Victoria** did not much care for Palmerston and often complained that her foreign secretary sent off dispatches without consulting either the queen or his cabinet colleagues. When Palmerston expressed his private approval of **Napoleon III**'s coup d'état in 1851 to the French ambassador, the queen insisted that Russell dismiss her foreign secretary. Palmerston was offered an English peerage but refused it and withdrew to Broadlands. He three times declined invitations to join the earl of Derby's Conservative government, but did accept the Home Office in the coalition ministry of his old schoolmate, Lord Aberdeen. As home secretary, Palmerston extended factory legislation, implemented prison reforms, and instituted a ticket-of-leave (parole) system.

Queen Recalls Palmerston

The Aberdeen Coalition fell in 1855 over the Crimean War debacle and, after Derby was unable to form a government, the queen sent for "Old Pam" to form a ministry. He reorganized the military administration uniting the secretary for war and the secretary at war into one office, improved supply and sanitary conditions, and pressed on the diplomatic front to keep the Black Sea from becoming a Russian lake. A peace was concluded in March 1856, and Victoria conferred a knighthood upon Palmerston.

Free Trade Radicals, led by **Richard Cobden** and **John Bright,** brought down the Palmerston ministry in 1857 over the *Arrow* Incident in which British gunboats had been used to defend a Chinese pirate ship of lapsed British registry. In the general election which followed, Palmerston's critics in the "Manchester School" were obliterated, and he continued as prime minister. In the wake of the Indian Mutiny, Palmerston transferred control of India from the East India Company to the Crown in early 1858. Once, unable to persuade a suitable colleague to serve as colonial secretary, Palmerston told an aide, "Well, I'll take the office myself. Just come upstairs and show me on the map where these damned places are." After losing a vote on the Conspiracy to Murder Bill in February, put forward as a result of the Orsini Plot to assassinate Napoleon III, Palmerston resigned, and Derby and the Conservatives took over the government for a time. Palmerston met with the coalescing Liberal Party at Willis's Rooms in London in early June 1859 and within a week returned to 10 Downing Street as prime minister.

Lord Palmerston was gout-ridden but capable in his last ministry. His chancellor of the exchequer, **William Ewart Gladstone,** put forward brilliant budgets that allowed for repeal of the paper duties, reduction of the income tax, and refortification of the English coast. Palmerston was wary of Gladstone's High Church leanings and especially of his growing sympathy for suffrage extension, observing that should Gladstone become prime minister "we shall have strange doings." Believing as he did that the constitution had been brought into appropriate balance by the Reform Act of 1832 and fearful of unleashing revolutionary change all his life, Palmerston was unwilling to entertain any notion of further parliamentary reform. In the American Civil War, Palmerston maintained British neutrality, but he displayed sympathy for the South, especially when British interests or honor were at stake as in the "Cotton Famine" occasioned by the Northern blockade of Confederate ports which harmed Britain's textile industry or in the disputes over the *Trent* and the *Alabama.* Palmerston won the general election of 1865 but died at his wife's estate before the new Parliament assembled. Though he had wished to be buried at Romsey Abbey near Broadlands, the cabinet insisted upon a state funeral and burial in Westminster Abbey to which Lady Palmerston agreed upon condition, quickly acceded to, that she could be buried next to him. The man who entered politics as a Tory, emerged as a Canningite, served as a Whig foreign secretary, joined a coalition government headed by a Peelite, and led a Liberal ministry in which he himself opposed further political reform was laid to rest among the nation's great and good.

SOURCES:

Arnstein, Walter L. *Britain Yesterday and Today.* 5th ed. Heath, 1988.

Guedalla, Philip. *Palmerston.* Hodder & Stoughton, 1926.

Hansard's Parliamentary Debates

Ridley, Jasper. *Lord Palmerston.* Granada, 1972.

FURTHER READING:

Bell, Herbert C. F. *Lord Palmerston.* Longmans, 1936.

Schroeder, Paul. *Austria, Great Britain, and the Crimean War.* Cornell, 1972.

Webster, Charles. *The Foreign Policy of Palmerston.* Bell, 1951.

Emmeline Pankhurst

(1858–1928)

Leader of the suffrage movement in Great Britain, whose repeated imprisonment did little to deter her aggressive tactics to see voting rights granted to women.

Born in 1858 in Manchester, England; died in 1928; daughter of Robert Goulden and Sophia Jane (Craine) Goulden; married: Richard Marsden Pankhurst; children: (three daughters) Christabel, Estelle Sylvia, and Adela; (two sons) Henry Francis Robert and Harry. Descendants: Richard Keir Pethick Pankhurst (author and professor).

Emmeline Pankhurst, who would spend her adult life leading the fight for women's suffrage in Great Britain, was one of 11 children. Born in Manchester, England, on July 4, 1858, she was the third child and eldest daughter of calico printer Robert Goulden and his wife Sophia Jane Craine Goulden. That Pankhurst grew up to be a militant activist is not surprising; her parents were enthusiastic supporters of various causes, including the antislavery movement in the United States. When Reverend Henry Ward Beecher, the famous American opponent of slavery, visited Manchester, Robert Goulden was a member of the welcoming committee. As a child, Emmeline joined her mother in collecting money to aid African-Americans.

In 1867, when Emmeline was nine, two leaders of the Fenian Movement (a secret society whose members sought to make Ireland independent of England) were arrested in Manchester. When sympathizers tried to free them by firing a shot to break the lock on the van transporting them to prison, a policeman inside the van was killed. Following a trial, the three sympathizers were put to death, despite the fact that the murder

Contributed by Marilyn E. Weigold, Professor of History, Pace University, New York, New York

had not been premeditated. Like many in her hometown, young Emmeline believed the "Manchester Martyrs" had been unjustly executed.

A few years later, Emmeline became interested in another group she believed was not being treated fairly: women. Living in Manchester, where she attended boarding school, she grew up in a town alive with women's rights activity. Indeed, women were not the only members of the community who supported the struggle for suffrage; the mayor opened the town hall for meetings of the Suffrage Society and even served as moderator. At age 14, Emmeline accompanied her mother to a suffrage meeting, and from that time on she was involved with the women's movement.

Emmeline's enthusiasm for revolutionary causes was reinforced during her high school years at a private school in Paris. When her best friend Noemie, daughter of French radical Henri Rochefort, tried unsuccessfully to arrange a marriage for Emmeline, Emmeline's father was unwilling to provide the dowry his prospective son-in-law expected. But Emmeline did marry. In 1879, at age 21, she became the wife of Richard Marsden Pankhurst, an attorney nearly twice her age who was a prominent figure in the women's suffrage movement. By 1885, the couple had four children: Christabel (1880), Estelle Sylvia (1882), Henry Francis Robert (1884), and Adela Constantia Mary (1885).

Despite her family responsibilities, Emmeline Pankhurst became active in the suffrage movement. Initially a member of the Manchester Women's Suffrage Committee, she and Mrs. Jacob Bright formed their own committee to work for the cause. Pankhurst was also a supporter of the Married Women's Property Bill of 1882 which gave wives the right to control their own earnings. The bill had been drafted by her husband, who had also written Great Britain's first women's suffrage bill in the 1860s and the Married Women's Property Act of 1870. As time went on, both Pankhursts became less enthusiastic about the Liberal Party whose leader, **William E. Gladstone,** failed to include women's suffrage in a voting reform bill in 1884. After withdrawing from the Party, the Pankhursts joined the Fabian Society, an organization trying to create a democratic socialist state in Great Britain. Meetings of the Fabian Society and other organizations considered radical at the time were held at the Pankhurst home.

When not hosting these gatherings, Pankhurst was coordinating other activities aimed at improving conditions for women. Despite the death of her firstborn son and the birth of another boy, Harry, in 1890, she championed the cause of striking female workers and campaigned for passage of an 1894 law granting women the right to vote in local elections. For a time, she also ran a home-furnishings business.

CHRONOLOGY

1903	Founded the Women's Social and Political Union (W.S.P.U.)
1906	Organized a march on Parliament
1909	Called for the use of militant measures to secure suffrage
1912	W.S.P.U. offices raided; Pankhurst arrested; began hunger strike
1928	Women granted full and equal suffrage to men at age 21; Pankhurst died

Pankhurst and Daughter Organize New Group

Following her husband's death in 1898, Pankhurst held a minor governmental position as a registrar of births and deaths while working on behalf of several causes. Her efforts included calling attention to the inadequate treatment of the elderly in British poorhouses, the plight of undernourished school children, and the low wages of female teachers. But her work for women's suffrage remained a priority. As a member of the Independent Labour Party, she advocated votes for women. When fellow party members did not share her enthusiasm, she resigned; in 1903, with the help of her daughter Christabel, she established a new organization—the Women's Social and Political Union (W.S.P.U.).

Within two years of its founding, the W.S.P.U. made headlines at a Liberal Party election gathering in Manchester. Although Pankhurst had, by this time, overcome a youthful shyness and become a forceful spokesperson for the cause, it was her daughter Christabel who took the spotlight on this occasion. When Christabel and her friend Annie Kenney questioned Sir Edward Grey, a member of the House of Commons, about women's suffrage, no response was forthcoming. The question was asked a second time. At that point, the two young women were forced to leave the meeting. They were arrested in the midst of a protest gathering in the street. Every

Sylvia Pankhurst
(1882–1960)

The second child of Emmeline and Richard Marsden Pankhurst, Estelle Sylvia Pankhurst was born in Manchester, England, on May 5, 1882. After studying art in Manchester, Venice, and at the Royal College of Art in London, Sylvia joined her mother and elder sister Christabel in the fight for women's suffrage. In America, she made speeches for the cause in 1911 and 1912. In England, she organized the East London Federation of Suffragettes in a working-class neighborhood, thereby creating interest in the women's movement among the lower classes. As was true with her mother and sister, Sylvia's suffrage activities repeatedly led to imprisonment. Following one period in jail, she said:

I had been forcibly fed for five weeks, and only secured release by walking up and down my cell for twenty-eight hours, staggering, falling and fainting, a horrible ordeal I shudder even now to recall.

During World War I, her opposition to Great Britain's participation in the conflict led to an estrangement from her mother, who supported the war effort. A supporter of the Russian Revolution and of Ethiopian independence, Sylvia was active in the resistance movement organized in the 1930s following the Italian invasion of Ethiopia (or Abyssinia, as that country was then called). In later years, she was editor of the newspaper Ethiopia Observer and the author of numerous books, including *The Life of Emmeline Pankhurst* (1936); Sylvia Pankhurst was also a painter.

Equally wellknown as a champion of unmarried mothers, she contended that unmarried women should not be denied the joy of motherhood. At age 45, she gave birth to her son Richard Pankhurst without publicly identifying the father whom she described as eight years older than herself and a "dear friend." Her son Richard, author of *Sylvia Pankhurst, Artist and Crusader,* became a faculty member at University College, Addis Ababa, Ethiopia. His mother died in that city on September 27, 1960. ■

detail of the incident was reported in the newspapers. Now there would be no turning back.

Pankhurst would do whatever necessary to keep the cause before the public, even if it meant risking arrest. In February 1906, the W.S.P.U. organized a parade and rally to coincide with the opening of Parliament. Dubbed "Suffragettes" by the *London Mail* newspaper, female supporters of the cause turned out to hear Pankhurst, who was promptly arrested. Over the next few years, the W.S.P.U. would stage numerous protest rallies and the leaders of the organization would repeatedly be arrested. Among those sent to jail would be Pankhurst's daughters, including the youngest Adela who had given up a teaching career to devote herself to the suffrage movement. When Pankhurst was arrested again in February 1908, her daughter Sylvia described her ordeal:

After hours locked up in dark, cold reception cells, she and her companions were let out to strip and be searched in a great room thronged with wardresses and other prisoners. Against that indignity she revolted....She shuddered at the filthy bath, the shapeless clothing, patched and stained, and daubed with the broad arrow, the heavy old shoes, mismated. Then, staggering painfully down long corridors, she was conducted to her cell and locked in for the night.

Weakened in body but not in spirit, Pankhurst was released at the end of February—just in time to address a huge meeting at London's Albert Hall. She told the gathering:

No woman with any spark of womanliness in her will consent to allow this state of things to go on any longer. We want to have the power to make the world a better place for both men and women.... The old cry was "you will never rouse women." We have done what they thought, and what they hoped was impossible; we women are roused!

And so they were, for in 1909 the W.S.P.U. began resorting to violence to drive home their point. Window-breaking sprees and outright attacks on the gathering places of male politicians, who were unsympathetic to women's causes, became commonplace. Pankhurst refused to abandon such tactics. To cease, she said, would be "folly, weakness and wickedness." In response, the government strengthened its resolve to halt the violence in the streets. Thereafter, when women protesters were arrested, they would remain in jail, even if they resorted to hunger strikes. Rather than free female prisoners whose health deteriorated due to self-imposed starvation, the authorities would resort to the use of stomach tubes to forcibly feed the women.

Despite the depredations endured by her followers and the spinal inflammation that left her son Harry paralyzed, Pankhurst embarked upon a

Called Christabel by her father, who borrowed the name from a poem by Samuel Coleridge, the oldest child of Emmeline and Richard Marsden Pankhurst was born in Manchester, England, on September 22, 1888. In 1903, she helped her mother establish the Women's Social and Political Union (W.S.P.U.), which battled for women's right to vote. She emerged as a prominent member of the organization in 1905 when she interrupted a meeting of the Liberal Party by holding up a "Votes for Women" banner. Along with her friend and fellow W.S.P.U. member Annie Kenney, Christabel was forced to leave the meeting. When she then tried to make a speech outside the Free Trade Hall where the Liberal Party gathering was being held, she and Kenney were arrested. After her release from prison, Christabel was invited to speak inside the Free Trade Hall at a meeting of the Independent Labour Party. Another triumph followed when she obtained a law degree.

In 1907, she became organizing secretary of the W.S.P.U. Besides coordinating meetings and demonstrations, she was a powerful spokesperson. In June 1908, she delivered one of her most famous speeches at a rally attended by 500,000 people in London's Hyde Park. The following October, Christabel put her natural talent as a speaker to use cross-examining government officials in court, after she and her mother were arrested for encouraging suffragists to storm Parliament. This time, Christabel's words proved ineffective: she was sentenced to prison for two and a half months.

In 1912, when the W.S.P.U. resorted to more aggressive tactics, Christabel once again faced the threat of arrest—this time for conspiracy. She escaped to France, where she edited a newspaper called *The Suffragette*. Two years later, she was back in England.

Once English women had been granted the right to vote, in 1918 she ran unsuccessfully for a seat in Parliament. Following World War I and the disbanding of the W.S.P.U., Christabel became an evangelist, preaching in both Great Britain and the United States about the second coming of Christ. In 1936, she was honored by King George V who named her a Dame of the British Empire. Four years later, Christabel Pankhurst moved to the United States, where she died in Los Angeles, California on February 13, 1958. ■

journey to North America to raise money for the cause. Speaking before a crowd at New York City's Carnegie Hall, she delighted the audience by saying: "I am what you call a hooligan." Although her tour of the United States and Canada proved a great success, she returned home in December 1910 to discover that her son's condition had worsened. He died a short time later.

Following her son's death, Pankhurst temporarily halted the W.S.P.U.'s militant activities while she and her followers awaited the outcome of an attempt by a parliamentary committee to introduce a Women's Suffrage Bill. When the Liberals withdrew their support, the W.S.P.U. again resorted to violence. In 1911, Pankhurst returned to the United States to discover that the women's suffrage movement had intensified its efforts; inspired by the British suffragists, the Americans had established a Women's Political Union. Harriet Stanton Blatch, daughter of **Elizabeth Cady Stanton,** the famous women's rights advocate of the 1800s, was active in the American movement. Introducing Pankhurst to an American audience, Blatch described the British heroine of the women's rights movement as "the woman in all the world who is doing most for the suffrage." Following a successful foreign tour which raised money for the cause, Pankhurst returned home to resume the struggle.

Pankhurst Imprisoned, Begins Hunger Strike

Dissatisfied with the lack of progress, she urged her followers to employ aggressive tactics. In March 1912, Pankhurst broke a window in the prime minister's official residence, while her followers smashed shop windows throughout London. Two hundred women were arrested. The following day, the police raided the headquarters of the W.S.P.U. Pankhurst was arrested and charged with conspiracy. Sentenced to nine months in prison, she began a hunger strike. When her fellow prisoners followed suit, the government mandated forced feeding. But despite her weakened condition, when about to be fed, Pankhurst threatened to attack the prison doctors. She was released the following day. She then headed for Paris where she and her daughter Christabel planned for secret attacks on both private and public property.

In the months that followed, museums, railroad stations, the residence of the archbishop of Canterbury and other buildings were attacked and Pankhurst was again arrested. This time the hunger strike nearly killed her. According to her daughter Sylvia:

> Believing the Government intended not to release her, and that her end was near, she was exalted to a great happiness, convinced that her death would bring victory to her cause, and crown her life with fragrant memory in women's hearts.

But Pankhurst did not die. Instead, she was released from prison under a new law, known officially as the Temporary Discharge for Ill-Health Act and unofficially as the "Cat and Mouse Act"; it permitted the rearrest of hunger strikers once their physical condition had improved. She was in and out of jail a dozen times in the following year. While in, she refused both food and water, slept little, and insisted on walking back and forth in her cell until near collapse, resulting in shorter periods of imprisonment. While out, she continued her suffrage work.

During one period of freedom, she headed for the United States only to be detained on Ellis Island under charges of moral turpitude or perversion. Prevented from entering the U.S., she vowed to begin a hunger strike. President **Woodrow Wilson** ordered her release after receiving appeals from prominent American suffragists. Pankhurst was thus able to undertake a successful speaking tour. Upon her return to England, despite W.S.P.U. attempts to get her off the ocean liner *Majestic* before the authorities could board the boat, the police launch reached the liner before her supporters and Pankhurst was arrested.

The endless cycle of arrest, freedom, and rearrest finally ended with World War I. In England, and other countries, the women's movement was scaled down as citizens devoted their energies to war work. With her followers released from jail, Pankhurst too became involved in the war effort. She made speeches in England, America, and Russia supporting the war and coordinated a parade of munition workers in England.

In 1916, Pankhurst's lifelong goal was partially realized when Parliament enacted the Representation of the People Act which permitted women over 30 to vote. In the postwar years, she lectured on health issues and child welfare in Canada and worked for the Conservative Party in England, considering at one point a run for Parliament as a Conservative. She lived to see women granted full and equal suffrage when the second Representation of the People Act (1928) lowered the voting age for women to 21. Her life's struggle ended, she died on June 14 of the same year.

SOURCES:

Mitchell, David. *The Fighting Pankhursts.* Macmillan, 1967.

Pankhurst, E. Sylvia. *The Life of Emmeline Pankhurst.* Houghton Mifflin, 1936.

Pankhurst, Emmeline. *My Own Story.* Hearst's International Library, 1914.

FURTHER READING:

Kamm, Josephine. *The Story of Emmeline Pankhurst.* Meredith Press, 1961.

Charles Stewart Parnell

(1846–1891)

Irish Protestant landlord, who entered politics fighting for land reform and Irish Home Rule and became the beloved and respected leader of his predominantly Catholic country before being brought down by a divorce scandal and dying in disgrace.

"There is but one of two fates for an Irish patriot. Unlike most Irish patriots, Mr. Parnell did not sell his country and his colleagues, and the result was that his colleagues sold him."

AUGUSTUS MOORE

C harles Stewart Parnell was born on June 27, 1846, the seventh of eleven children. Like almost all of his brothers and sisters, he was born at Avondale, the Parnell family estate in County Wicklow, Ireland. His father John Henry Parnell was a typical country gentleman of the time with one notable exception: he had married a young American girl, Delia Tudor Stewart. It is said that Delia Parnell never really adjusted to life in the Irish countryside, and that her American love of independence influenced Charles's dedication to freeing Ireland from British rule. More than either of his parents, though, it was Charles's brothers and sisters who had a great effect on his intellectual formation and political convictions. Charles was closest to his older brother John and his younger sister Fanny, whose passionate love of Ireland was evident even when she was a child.

Delia Parnell was not a particularly attentive mother, and the children endured a long series of nurses and governesses. As a small boy, Charles was willful, jealous, and prone to fights—in short, spoiled. John, three years older and Charles's favorite sparring partner, described his brother as:

Born at Avondale, County Wicklow, Ireland, on June 27, 1846; died in October 1891; seventh child in an old Irish family known for its dedication to reform and Home Rule; son of John Henry Parnell and Delia Tudor Stewart (an American); married: Katherine O'Shea in June 1891 after her divorce from Captain O'Shea; children: two daughters.

Contributed by Colleen Carpenter Cullinan, Ph.D. candidate, University of Chicago Divinity School, Chicago, Illinois

CHRONOLOGY

1846	Born in County Wicklow
1861–65	American Civil War
1869	Left Cambridge University
1875	Elected member of Parliament for County Meath
1879	Irish National Land League founded; Parnell elected president of the League
1880	Gladstone and Liberals defeat Conservatives in general election; Parnell elected chair of Irish Parliamentary Party
1881	Parliament passed the Protection of Person and Property Act and the Land Law Act (Ireland); Parnell arrested; Land League suppressed
1882	Katherine O'Shea had her first child by Parnell; Phoenix Park murders in Dublin
1886	Gladstone introduced Government of Ireland Bill (Home Rule Bill); bill defeated
1889	Parnell cited as corespondent in a divorce
1890	O'Shea divorce came to court
1891	Married Katherine O'Shea; died in her arms three months later

a wiry little boy, very bright and playful, making fun of everybody and everything. He was fond of mechanics, like his eldest brother Hayes. He had dark brown hair, a pale complexion, very dark brown and very piercing eyes. His figure was slender and he was small for his age. He did not grow until late, and was nicknamed "Tom Thumb" at home.

Charles was sent off to boarding school at the relatively young age of seven, where his willfulness was greatly tamed. He became gravely ill with typhoid fever, however, and returned home after only a year away. Back at Avondale, he was taught by his sisters' tutors, who—not used to an unruly young boy—soon gave up on him. He was sent away to school again, but once more it lasted little over a year. By 1856, he was home to stay; he was taught by one tutor after another, none of whom he liked.

Charles became an excellent cricket player and enjoyed other typical pastimes of children of country gentry: riding horses, fishing, playing soldiers, building rafts, and visiting neighbors. While his education seems to have been haphazard and limited, most other aspects of his boyhood were

normal for a child in his social position. His father's sudden death in 1859, however, abruptly ended Charles's childhood. Charles was 13 at the time, and the only one of the Parnell children in Ireland. The others were at school in England or in Paris with their mother, and so Charles attended his father's funeral alone.

The death of John Henry Parnell completely changed the lives of his family. His financial affairs at the time of his death were nothing short of disastrous, and the family was forced to rent out Avondale and auction off most of the estate's livestock and farm equipment. They moved from the country to the suburb of Dalkey, and later to Dublin itself. Charles inherited Avondale but was not able to come into his inheritance until 1867, when he turned 21. The children and their respective inheritances were all under the watchful eyes of the Chancery Court. Delia Parnell, guardian of the children's persons but not of their property or financial affairs, had made them all wards of the court.

Throughout the 1860s, while the Parnell family was living in Dublin, the country was in the grip of rising nationalist fever. Controlled by England for centuries, Ireland began yet another episode of its long struggle for independence. Fanny wrote poetry for a *Fenian* newspaper (*Fenians* were Irish nationalists who fought British rule), and it was rumored that Delia Parnell hid *Fenian* fugitives from the police. At this point, Charles seemed uninterested in politics, at least in Irish politics. The American Civil War was a great topic of conversation in the Parnell household. Since Delia Parnell was American, Charles was greatly interested in all the details he could discover about the war.

But Parnell's entry into politics was still years off. In 1865, he traveled to England to enroll in Magdalene College at Cambridge University. Not noted at the time for being strong academically, Magdalene had very lenient entrance requirements. Considering Parnell's background, it was surprising that he made it to a university at all. He did not like Cambridge and was not successful there, either in his studies or in making friends. He was involved in several fights and was finally brought to court for assault in 1869. Magdalene College promptly suspended him, due to the court case, and—while it was understood that he could have returned had he wished—Parnell left Cambridge permanently, without graduating.

In 1871, Parnell journeyed to the United States to visit his brother John, who had a farm in Alabama. He also went, in part, to pursue a Miss

Woods, whom he had hoped to marry. But Miss Woods wasn't interested in marrying a country gentleman with no real occupation. After the breakup, Parnell spent several months touring the South, then convinced John to return home with him to Ireland. It was from this time on that Parnell seriously took up the life of managing Avondale and living as an active and respected figure in Wicklow County.

Parnell Advocates for Home Rule, Land Reform

In 1874, Charles Parnell made the decision to enter politics. "Home Rule" was the issue of the day; Ireland was seeking by political means what uprisings had failed to accomplish—the right to govern itself, free of Britain's coercive overlordship. While many theories have been advanced to account for Parnell's sudden interest in the Irish national political scene, it is not, perhaps, so surprising as some would make out. Parnell, like others of his class, had a paternalistic interest in the welfare of his tenants—and by extension, an interest in securing just treatment for all tenants throughout Ireland. And it was Catholic tenants who made up the great majority of the Irish; Protestant landowners, originally from England, were a decided minority. While not previously involved in *Fenianism* or Home Rule agitation, Parnell nevertheless came from a family that identified itself as decidedly Irish, not British or English. The Parnells had arrived in Ireland two and a half centuries previously; he could easily emphasize his deep roots in Ireland and his firm attachment to the country to attract voters. Further, Parnell's family had a history of public service, most notably in his grandfather, William Parnell. The Parnell name was well-known and respected, and when Charles announced that he was running for a seat in British Parliament out of Dublin, he was heartily endorsed by many local organizations. The Home Rule League and the County Dublin Tenant's Defence Association both stood for Parnell, and many expected that he would win easily. But things did not work out as planned. Parnell lost, and quite badly. Not one to be discouraged, he ran in County Meath the following April and won.

Parnell's politics were a unique mixture of agitation for both land reform and Home Rule. He was of the opinion that land reform, eliminating the conflict between Protestant landowners and their Catholic tenants, would lead to the landowners finally seeing themselves as truly Irish and not displaced English citizens. Once the "respectable" class joined the Home Rule movement, Parnell

believed, it was inevitable that Ireland would come to be ruled by those who actually lived in Ireland. "Deprive [the landlords] of their privileges, show them that they must cast themselves in with the rest of their countrymen… [and] the last knell of English power… in Ireland has sounded," Parnell stated in a speech at Liverpool in 1879. While it may seem odd that Parnell, a Protestant landlord himself, was interested in eliminating the privileges of his class, it should be noted that the Parnell family finances had not been on a solid footing since well before the death of his father. Parnell was deeply in debt and saw no reason to fight for the perpetuation of a landlord system that was obviously failing (at least in his case). Many other landlords, successful or not, disagreed with Parnell's ideas, sometimes violently. Still, his goal of uniting all the Irish—Protestant and Catholic—was a noble one, and one that has not yet been achieved, even today.

Parnell's career in British Parliament began quietly enough. He spent time listening and learning; more important, he gradually began to identify himself to his colleagues in Parliament and to the public as a man who sympathized with *Fenian* thought. In 1877, he joined with the other Irish M.P.'s (Members of Parliament) in a campaign of obstruction. While this tactic—making long irrelevant speeches to delay the progress of a bill—had been used before to try to prevent passage of bills relating to Ireland, this time the Irish M.P.'s attempted to obstruct all bills concerning the many countries that, like Ireland, were colonial possessions of the British Empire. Parnell's speechmaking grew more and more radical, and he became known as one of the more important Irish politicians in Britain.

In 1878, terrible weather and a crop failure in the west of Ireland led to growing unrest throughout the country. Those who remembered the Great Famine of 30 years before were determined that it should not be repeated. The worst aspect of that famine, in the minds of the Irish, was that the failure of a single crop (potatoes) meant starvation and eviction from their farms for countless peasants—while the landlords grew rich exporting wheat and other foodstuffs to England. There had been food in Ireland during the Great Famine—food that was escorted by armed British soldiers to the ports and from there overseas. A.M. Sullivan, an Irish M.P., warned Parliament that those who had survived the Great Famine and those who had grown up hearing horror stories about it all regarded it with a "deep, savage, mad feeling," and that action must be taken to avert another crisis.

While Parliament debated how to handle the problem, the Irish formed the National Land League. The league's more conservative members simply wanted a rent rebate during this time of poor crops; its more radical wing seemed to be pushing toward an armed peasant's revolt. Parnell saw the league as a platform for pushing his ideas about land reform leading to Home Rule, and became a spokesman and fundraiser for the league.

In 1880, a general election for Parliament was called, and Parnell hurried home from the United States where he had been gathering money and support for the Land League. Prime Minister **William Gladstone** and his Liberal Party won far more seats in Parliament than the opposition Conservative Party, and Parnell himself captured three seats, from counties Meath, Cork, and Mayo. It was also in 1880 that Parnell met Katherine O'Shea, who had been living apart from her husband, Captain William O'Shea, for almost five years. This liaison, a poorly kept secret from the start, eventually would destroy Parnell's career. Most political insiders knew of the affair, and Captain O'Shea—although claiming later that he had not known—almost certainly knew and expected to benefit from it politically. Parnell and Mrs. O'Shea's relationship was nothing if not domestic; Parnell established a study and lab for himself at her home in Kent by 1882, and he and Mrs. O'Shea were eventually to have two daughters, Clare and Katie.

Despite this newfound (and short-lived) domestic tranquility, Parnell's political life in the 1880s became quite tumultuous. The agitation by the Land League seriously unnerved the ruling British authorities. Parliament passed the Protection of Person and Property (Ireland) Act in early 1881 as a coercive measure and followed it quickly with the Land Law (Ireland) Act, which offered several concessions to the League. This large-stick-and-small-carrot policy did not go over well and unrest continued. Becoming desperate, the British government had Parnell and other leaders of the league arrested in October of 1881 on suspicion of treasonable activities. The Kilmainham Treaty, under whose terms Parnell and the others were released, was not agreed to until the following May.

The Murders in the Park

The Kilmainham Treaty was the beginning of an alliance between Prime Minister Gladstone and Parnell. This alliance could have resulted in good things for Ireland—Home Rule, in particular—but was soon put under great strain. On the 6th of May, 1882, Lord Frederick Cavendish, Gladstone's chief secretary for Irish Affairs, along with his under secretary, was stabbed to death while walking in Phoenix Park, Dublin. The public outrage in England over these murders—assassinations really—was immense, and Parliament promptly passed an extremely harsh crimes bill for Ireland.

As the decade wore on, the question of land reform and tenant rights became increasingly subordinated to the issue of Home Rule. Gladstone introduced a Home Rule bill in 1886, but it was defeated by 40 votes. Despite the fact that Home Rule was not yet a reality, Parnell's popularity soared in Ireland throughout this time. One interesting measure of how well he was beloved came through the public disclosure of Parnell's finances: once the people of Ireland realized how indebted their leader was, they promptly set up a subscription fund for him and raised over £37,000.

A hero in Ireland, Parnell was seen as a villain in England. In 1887, the London *Times* published a series of articles on "Parnellism and Crime," featuring several forged but damaging letters supposedly written by Parnell. The troubles caused by these articles did not abate for over two years—at which point, Captain O'Shea filed for divorce. O'Shea named Parnell as a corespondent in the suit and portrayed him as the most sordid of adulterers. The fact that Parnell considered himself, for all intents and purposes, married to the woman that Captain O'Shea had abandoned years ago was lost amid patently false stories of Parnell beating hasty retreats from the O'Shea home by slipping down fire escapes.

Divorce Creates Scandal

The divorce created an enormous scandal, but Parnell's countrymen did not immediately abandon him. The outcry in England, however, was so great that other Irish leaders were privately informed that they could expect no cooperation in Parliament—and no hope of Home Rule—as long as Parnell was one of them. Perhaps reluctantly—no one is sure—Parnell was condemned by the country that had once hailed him as its uncrowned king. In late 1890 and early 1891, candidates for Parliament supported by Parnell were defeated, and Parnell began to recede from the Irish political scene. He married Katherine O'Shea in June of 1891, and it was only a little over three months later that he died in her arms.

The reaction to the divorce was certainly what cost Parnell his political leadership, but it is to be remembered that there was deep-rooted opposition in England at the time to both Parnell and

Home Rule. It is quite possible to see the moral outrage directed at Parnell's personal life to be, for the most part, a convenient way to eliminate his political threat to the order of the British Empire. Nevertheless, his long-standing adulterous relationship with Katherine O'Shea was in direct contradiction to the morality of his day. His death so soon after the scandal makes his political fall appear particularly tragic; in his passing, Ireland lost one of its great leaders.

SOURCES:

Bew, Paul. *C. S. Parnell.* Gill and Macmillan, 1980.

Foster, R. F. *Charles Stewart Parnell: The Man and his Family.* Humanities Press, 1976.

FURTHER READING:

Larkin, Emmet. *The Roman Catholic Church and the Fall of Parnell.* Liverpool, 1979.

Lyons, F. S. L. *Charles Stewart Parnell.* London, 1977.

O'Brien, Conor Cruise. *Parnell and His Party, 1880–1890.* Oxford, 1957.

O'Shea, Katherine. *Charles Stewart Parnell: His Love Story and Political Life.* London, 1914.

Parnell, J. H. *Charles Stewart Parnell: A Memoir.* London, 1916.

Saint Patrick

(c. 396–459)

Patron saint of Ireland, who returned from his British home where he had been a slave and devoted his life to preaching Christianity in the face of widespread Irish opposition.

Born c. 396; died c. 459; son of Calpurnius, grandson of Potitus, (both priests in Roman Britain); one chronicler gives his mother's name as Concessa. Predecessors: Palladius, the first bishop of Ireland, appointed by Pope Celestine I in 431.

Remembered as the man who converted the Irish people to Christianity, Patrick is honored by Irish men and women throughout the world each year on March 17. But the events of his life, even its dates, are disputed by historians, and most knowledge about his life is probably lost forever in the mist of time. Our best sources of information about him are his own *Confessions* and one *Epistle*, which are the only Latin texts written beyond the boundaries of the Roman Empire to have survived from that era. The many chronicles and *Lives* of Patrick written later are full of wildly improbable miracle stories which even their authors admit are hard to believe. Many legends have gathered about his name, such as that he explained the Holy Trinity to an Irish king with the help of a clover leaf (hence his symbol), and that by his piety he drove all snakes out of Ireland. Historically, however, we must proceed with caution.

According to his *Confessions*, Patrick was born in England and was the son of Calpurnius, a minor Roman nobleman (*decurion*), and grandson of a priest Potitus (in those days the rule of clerical celibacy was not everywhere enforced). We cannot date his birth more closely than to say that it was in

"We have the names of scores of Britons who lived in the time of the Roman Empire.... But we do not know anything of significance about the personality of any one of them with the single exception of Patrick."

E.A. THOMPSON

Contributed by Patrick Allitt, Assistant Professor of History, Emory University, Atlanta, Georgia

the late fourth or early fifth century (most likely in the last days of the Roman Empire in Britain, whose collapse began in A.D. 409), nor do we know in which part of the country he lived, though it was probably near the west coast. After a frivolous youth, Patrick was captured by pirates at the age of 16 and carried across the Irish Sea to be sold into slavery. In Ireland, he was made a shepherd at "Voclut," which is probably in modern County Mayo.

Although his own family had been slave-owners, and now he was a slave in turn, there is no evidence that Patrick opposed slavery as a labor system, though he recognized that it was a terrible hardship for those who converted to Christianity. During the years of his enslavement, his religious life began in earnest and he devoted himself to prayer. "The love of God came to me more and more," he recalled, "and my faith was strengthened. My spirit was moved so that in a single day I would say as many as a hundred prayers, and almost as many in the night."

Patrick believed he and other slaves had been captured and humiliated "because we departed away from God and did not keep his commandments." It is a common theme in Christian literature to see one's outward circumstances as a test sent by God and to find exaltation through abasement. "This I know," he added, in an eloquent use of the idea, "that before I was humiliated I was like a stone lying in the deep mire. Then He that is mighty came and lifted me up, and raised me aloft, and placed me on the top of the wall. Therefore I ought to cry aloud and render thanks to the Lord for His great benefits here and in eternity."

After six years of slavery, he was prompted in a dream to escape and return home. According to the *Confessions* he had to cover "two hundred miles" to get to the coast, and then had to persuade a group of sailors to take him on board their ship. The ship sailed for three days, landed, and was abandoned by its crew, who then had to travel through deserted countryside for 28 more days before finding food. This is a puzzling passage of his *Confessions* since neither Gaul (France) nor Britain had any "wilderness" so extensive that a group of walking men could be lost in it for 28 days. Unfortunately Patrick was, as he himself admitted, a poor writer, and he failed to explain this and other mysteries, such as a cryptic reference to re-enslavement for another 60 days.

Dream Calls Him to Priesthood

Eventually, he returned home to the welcome of his family, who begged him never to leave, but

CHRONOLOGY

396	Possible birthdate of Patrick
409	Roman withdrawal from Britain
c. 418–30	Patrick probably studied for priesthood in Gaul (France)
431	Appointment of Palladius as Bishop of the Irish by Pope Celestine
432	Possible arrival of Patrick in Ireland
EARLY 440s	Possible date for *Confessions* and *Epistle*
459	Date given by later annalists as that of Patrick's death

once again dreams spurred him to action and insinuated the idea of a missionary life. The crucial dream, in which he was "visited by a man named Victoricus," held out to him the task of converting the Irish people to Christianity. There is no sign that he had grown to love Ireland or the Irish people during his enslavement there; he simply describes himself as a servant of God responding to this dream-borne imperative. To this end, he studied for the priesthood, possibly in Auxerre, France, under the tutelage of Saint Germain, if the later chronicler Muirchu is reliable on this point; he may even have gone as far as Rome.

Patrick's education was poor despite his noble birth: his writings are composed in a strange mix of classical and vulgar Latin and, like all inexperienced writers, he often finds it difficult to get his phrases straight. When he asked to be sent on a mission to Ireland, he was discouraged by monks who thought him too badly educated to attempt it. "Many tried to prevent this mission," he wrote later, "and talked among themselves behind my back and said: 'Why is this fellow walking into danger among enemies who do not know God?' Not that they were being malicious, but they did not like the idea.... [I]t was because of my lack of education." But eventually the mission was approved. Although he is the patron saint of Ireland, Patrick was not the first Christian to preach there. He had been preceded by Palladius, a bishop sent by Pope Celestine I in the year 431, but there were apparently many areas where Palladius had made no headway, so that Patrick himself was the first to attempt conversions in much of the country.

By his own account he was successful, converting and baptizing hundreds of Irish men and women. At that time Christianity in the Roman Empire was mainly an urban religion, to such a degree that the Latin word for countryside-dweller, *paganus* or pagan, was synonymous with non-Christian. But in the late third century, Martin of Tours in Gaul had begun to preach to poor farmers and rustics, and this approach Patrick seems to have shared, daringly taking it out beyond the perimeter of the Roman Empire. One of Martin's pupils, Victricius of Rouen (possibly the Victoricus who appeared in Patrick's dream) was the only European ecclesiastic known to have practiced missions to the heathen and to have had an important following in Britain in the time of Patrick's father. As a result of Patrick's efforts, many of the rural Irish "who till now always worshipped idols and abominations are now called the people of the Lord and the sons of God." This was a part of his work of which he obviously felt proud. He knew the costs of converting, especially for those in bondage. "It is the women kept in slavery who suffer especially; they even have to endure constant threats and terrorization; but the Lord has given grace to many of His handmaidens, for though they are forbidden to do so they resolutely follow His example."

Patrick was nevertheless also pleased to convert the high-born whose Christian influence on others would be greater. He notes of one such convert:

> And there was also a blessed lady of native Irish birth and high rank, very beautiful and grown up, whom I baptised; and a few days later she found some reason to come to us and indicated that she had received a message from an angel of God, and the angel had urged her too to become a virgin of Christ and to draw near to God.

The decision cannot have been an easy one because this convert had acted without parental consent and like many such converts "they endure persecution and their own parents' unfair reproaches." At times, he ran into danger in his efforts to convert local dignitaries. Encountering one group of "kings," he offered them gifts as a prelude to preaching the gospel but they were hostile: "They arrested me and my companions and that day were extremely eager to kill me, but my time had not yet come; they seized everything that they found on us and put me in irons." Two weeks later, however, Patrick and his companions were released and their property restored. Again he does not say why, attributing it simply to God and to "the close friends whom we had previously acquired."

The later chronicler Muirchu tells many stories of Patrick's conversions in Ireland and embroiders them with tales of miracles by which his preaching was reinforced. For example, when Patrick approached Tara, the "Babylon" of Ireland, he provoked the king, Loegaire, by lighting an Easter bonfire on the same night as a pagan festival when by tradition the king's fire must be the first one lit. The king, says Muirchu, "with wizards, enchanters, soothsayers and devisers and teachers of every art and deceit" went to see who had dared violate the rules in this way. One of the king's magicians, Lochru, who had foretold Patrick's coming, "was insolent to the saint's face and had the effrontery to disparage the Catholic faith in the most arrogant terms." In response, Patrick called down God's wrath upon him.

> At these words the wizard was carried up into the air and then dropped outside from above; he fell head-first and crashed his skull against a stone, was smashed to pieces and died before their eyes; and the heathen were afraid.

God then aided Patrick with earthquakes, sudden darkness, and general confusion, in which all but a handful of the king's men were killed. Finally, says Muirchu, the queen begged Patrick for mercy and the king pretended to convert. The next day Patrick and a surviving magician, Lucetmail, had a contest to see whose miraculous powers were the best. Lucetmail could bring a waist-deep snowfall over the whole area and plunge the land into darkness but, as this mythical Patrick observed, Lucetmail's miracles caused nothing but trouble whereas Patrick's own miracles, through God's intervention, were benign and productive. At last, the king was convinced to make a real conversion when the magician and one of Patrick's converts were shut up together in a house, which was set on fire. Patrick's assistant, Benignus, emerged unscathed while Lucetmail burned to death. This is one of dozens of delicious but completely implausible miracle tales attributed by Muirchu to Patrick; later chroniclers were even wilder with their reports of his deeds.

Patrick Seeks to Clear His Name

Patrick's *Confessions*, a much more reliable source, was written when he was an old man; from this document we have some knowledge of his life, but its purpose was not autobiography. Rather, a confession he had made more than 30 years before, even before his ordination to the priesthood, was being brought up against him by a friend in whom he had earlier confided, and he was writing a long response to clear his good name and vindicate his life's work. The sin, though he does not name it, had apparently been so grave that it cast doubt on his fitness as a priest and bishop. His accusers wanted Patrick to go to England, but he refused to do so, arguing that he had promised God to spend the rest of his life in Ireland.

It seems that Patrick was also accused of getting rich during his missionary work. We do not know the names of his accusers but we can tell from the aggrieved tone of voice which dominates the *Confessions* that the accusations hurt Patrick's feelings and that he wanted to refute them down to the last jot and tittle. Denying that he had become rich from his missions, he insisted that they had impoverished him. At times, he notes, "Christian brethren and virgins of Christ" and "pious women would give me unsolicited gifts and throw some of the jewelry on the altar" but, aware that they might impair his good name, he "would return it to them" even though "they would take offense at my doing so." He did this, "for the hope of eternity, to safeguard myself carefully in everything so that they would not catch me out... under some pretext of dishonesty and so that I would not give unbelievers opportunity for denigration or disparagement." He ended his confession by begging God for martyrdom as the final seal of his good intentions and his true faith: "I beg Him to grant that I may shed my blood for His name," even if it meant being "torn most pitiably limb from limb for dogs or savage beasts to share or the birds of the air devour."

Patrick's other surviving writing, the *Epistle*, is a letter written in protest against a British chieftain Coroticus, who in a raid on Ireland had killed some of Patrick's recent converts and captured others to be sold into slavery. In this letter Patrick excommunicates Coroticus (also a nominal Christian) and warns him of eternal punishment for his crime. Coroticus and his men are not his "fellow citizens," he says, "but fellow-citizens of the demons, because of their evil actions.... These bloodthirsty men are bloody with the blood of innocent Christians, whom I have begotten in God in countless numbers." Patrick was particularly scandalized that they, or captives from other raids, "have been carried far off and transported to distant lands, where sin is rife, openly, grievously and shamelessly; and there freeborn men have been sold, Christians reduced to slavery—and what is

more, as slaves of the utterly iniquitous, evil and apostate Picts" (inhabitants of what is now Scotland). Only if Coroticus and his men were willing to undertake "gruelling penance," he said, should they be readmitted into the Christian community.

The nature and date of Patrick's death are unknown except, once again, from later unreliable chronicles and hagiographies, one of which reports that he died at the place now known as Downpatrick. About 200 years after his death, the bishops of Armagh, claiming that theirs was the oldest and dominant bishopric in Ireland, began to argue that Patrick himself had been bishop of Armagh as a way of adding weight to their claim. The chief Armagh propagandist, Tirechan, declared that Patrick had consecrated 450 bishops, whereas the impression we get from Patrick's own work, and even from Muirchu, is that he was throughout his mission the *only* bishop in Ireland. None of the documentation from Patrick's own day mentions Armagh. The final irony about him is that, from his writings, Patrick seems to have been an austere, humorless, inflexible dogmatist. That he should have become associated with the jollity and celebrations which have long been traditional on St. Patrick's Day is an example of a simple history being transformed into a fanciful and colorful fiction. But, as historian John Morris aptly summarized: "The mass of rubbish that has been piled about the memory of Patrick in ancient and modern times has done little positive harm, for Patrick is his own truthful witness."

SOURCES:

Patrick, St. *Confession and Epistle.* Edited and translated by A. B. E. Hood (with an introduction by John Morris and including Muirchu's Life of St. Patrick.) Old Woking, Surrey: Phillimore Press, 1978.

Thompson, E. A. *Who Was Saint Patrick?* St. Martin's Press, 1985.

FURTHER READING:

Bieler, L. *Four Latin Lives of Saint Patrick.* Dublin: 1971.

Bury, J. B. *The Life of Saint Patrick and His Place in History.* London: 1905.

Carney, James. *The Problem of Saint Patrick.* Dublin Institute for Advanced Study, 1961.

Robert Peel

(1788–1850)

Leader of the Conservative Party and prime minister, who carried Catholic emancipation, established the London Metropolitan Police, put British finances on a firm footing, and ushered in an era of free trade with tariff reform and repeal of the Corn Laws.

Born in Bury, Lancashire, England, on February 5, 1788, and christened Robert in honor of both his grandfather and father, Peel was the eldest son, and the third child of 11, born to the first baronet and the former Ellen Yates. Peel's father represented the second generation of a Lancashire family which had risen to both wealth and prominence in the early Industrial Revolution as a result of success in the cotton manufacturing trade. As the mark of the family's new status as industrial magnates, the elder Peel purchased the old manor of Drayton Bassett near the borough of Tamworth for which he was elected M.P. (Member of Parliament) in 1790; a decade later his support of Pitt's ministry and organization of local militias during the revolution in France was recognized in the form of a baronetcy.

Young Peel was a good-natured, bright, and rather sensitive boy with the blue eyes, fair complexion, and reddish blond hair which was characteristic of his family. Much of his early education he received from his father who made him repeat the points of the sermons which he heard in the parish church in Bury each week. Peel read much on his own, and his father often asked him to ana-

"The most liberal of conservatives, the most conservative of liberals, and the most capable man of all in both parties."

FRENCH PREMIER
FRANÇOIS GUIZOT

Contributed by Richard Francis Spall, Jr, Associate Professor of History, Ohio Wesleyan University, Delaware, Ohio

lyze and recite from his readings. The Peel children were also tutored in their home by the local Anglican curate two hours each day. In 1798, however, the family took up residence in the refurbished house at Drayton Manor in southeast Staffordshire where Peel attended a small school for the sons of the gentry, kept by the vicar of Tamworth, extending his study of classics and distinguishing himself as a student.

At age 12, Peel entered Harrow, a well-known boarding school, where what were regarded as deficiencies in his Latin were addressed. His tutor Reverend Drury was much impressed with the diligence of his pupil and even kept some of his schoolwork as models for other students, telling them that "you boys will one day see Peel Prime Minister." Lord Byron, one of Peel's Harrovian schoolmates recollected, "I was always in scrapes, and he never; in school he always knew his lesson and I rarely."

In late 1804, Peel left Harrow and spent the next several months in London with his father. He attended a few lectures on natural science at the Royal Institution but was most attracted to the gallery of the House of Commons. These were heady days, and they left a considerable impression on Peel. **Pitt the Younger** had just returned to office, and Peel was able to witness first-hand the final bouts of parliamentary dueling between Charles James Fox and William Pitt which had dominated the House of Commons since the end of the American War of Independence.

At Michaelmas term in the autumn of 1805, Peel entered Christ Church College, Oxford. He first studied classics with Thomas Gaisford, and he developed an interest in mathematics (which focused mainly on geometry in those days at Oxford) under the tutelage of Charles Lloyd who became Peel's closest friend and later both Regius Professor of Divinity and bishop of Oxford. Under new more rigorous university regulations which had just come into force, Peel determined in 1808 to attempt degree examinations in two subjects, Literae Humaniores and the field of mathematics and physics. Always conscientious and often high-strung by nature, Peel became increasingly anxious as the exams approached, studying obsessively and at one point despairing of his future. Encouraged by his father, Peel regained his self-confidence so that schoolmates were astonished to find him playing tennis on the day before exams. Receiving the rare distinction of a "double first," Peel demonstrated such mastery that his examiners joined those in attendance in spontaneous applause at the conclusion of the questioning.

CHRONOLOGY

1809	Entered Parliament at age 21 for Cashel in Tipperary
1810	Became undersecretary for War and Colonies
1812	Began six years as chief secretary for Ireland and leading opponent of Catholic emancipation
1819	Headed commission on Bank of England which resulted in Peel's Act, putting currency on stable footing
1822	Appointed home secretary; began legal reforms to 1827
1828	Resumed office as Wellington's home secretary
1829	Introduced Catholic emancipation, angering his Party; established London Metropolitan Police ("Bobbies")
1834	Became prime minister for "The Hundred Days"
1839	Resigned commission to form a government for Queen Victoria in "The Bedchamber Crisis"
1841	Rejuvenated Conservative Party won general election; Peel formed second ministry; income tax adopted
1842	Introduced major tariff reforms moving toward free trade
1846	Repealed the Corn Laws to avert famine in Ireland; split his Party and fell from office

Young Peel Elected to Parliament

Peel stayed on at Oxford for an extra term's residence in the spring of 1809. In February, when he came of age, his father arranged for him to have his name put forward for a vacant seat in Parliament for the borough of Cashel in Tipperary. There were few electors in this small and easily corrupted Irish constituency, and Sir Robert had little difficulty in providing enough money to ensure that voters elected his son. Peel took his seat in April, as a Tory, on the government side of the aisle. During the parliamentary recess, he enrolled at Lincoln's Inn (a law school), but his interest in a parliamentary career apparently did not allow for continued study of law.

In 1810, despite a rustic Lancashire accent, Peel's maiden speech seconding the program of the duke of Portland's ministry was enormously successful and attracted the further notice of the leaders of his Party; in the cabinet reshuffle of 1809–10, when Lord Liverpool took over the Department of War and Colonies, he offered a position as undersecretary to Peel. In May of 1812, when Prime Minister Spencer Perceval was assassinated, Lord Liverpool succeeded him and asked his young assistant to take the important post of chief secretary for Ireland. In Britain, accepting office meant having to stand for election again, and rather than compromise his position by seeking re-election for his Irish seat, Peel offered himself and was elected to represent the borough of Chippenham.

As chief secretary for Ireland from 1812 to 1818, Peel was in charge of the Irish administration with its patronage and its responsibilities for maintaining law and order in the wake of Roman Catholic discontent stemming from the failure to adopt Catholic emancipation along with the Act of Union in 1801. Ireland was restive and presented opportunities for the French during the Napoleonic Wars, and insurrection persisted. Confronted with much agitation and considerable violence, Peel brought forward legislation in 1814 giving the government power to "proclaim" disturbed districts and establishing the first police force in the British Isles; the force came to be known as "Peelers" and later evolved into the Royal Irish Constabulary. From an Anglican family and with a profoundly Anglican education and outlook, the Irish chief secretary emerged as an outspoken opponent of George Canning's Catholic Emancipation Bill. Tories perceived "Orange Peel" as the champion of the Protestant cause, and with the support of his old college, Christ Church, Peel soon defeated Canning to become M.P. for Oxford in 1817.

With the General Elections of 1818, Peel announced his intention to step down as chief secretary for Ireland, and for the next four years he remained only a private member in the Commons. In 1820, he married Julia Floyd, the daughter of General John Floyd who had served in Ireland during Peel's tenure at Dublin Castle. Twice during this period Peel refused cabinet office, concentrating instead on domestic matters, particularly the refurbishment of a new town house in Whitehall Gardens in London and collecting paintings. Yet even out of office Peel made a significant contribution heading up a parliamentary committee on the Bank of England in 1819 and bringing forward what came to be known as Peel's Act, which allowed gradual return to the gold standard and settled the issue of a stable and convertible currency.

London Police Known by Founder's Name

In January of 1822, Peel returned to office as home secretary, and when Viscount Castlreagh took his own life in August was considered to succeed him as Leader of the House of Commons, an honor that went instead to Canning. At the Home Office,

Peel distinguished himself as a most able administrator and as a reformer of considerable skill and daring. He introduced measures to consolidate and simplify the criminal law, reducing significantly the number of capital offenses. He proposed reform of the gaols (jails), prisons, and houses of correction throughout the country and rationalized the penal system while bringing it under central direction. He put forward a program to improve the jury system, and scrutinized scores of statutes recommending mitigation of many penalties in accordance with the Benthamite principle that "the punishment should fit the crime." Of perhaps greatest significance was an innovation which was undoubtedly rooted in his successful Irish experience; Peel saw to the establishment in 1829 of the London Metropolitan Police whose officers became known for their founder as "Bobbies."

When Canning became prime minister in 1827 owing to the state of Liverpool's health, Peel resigned from office on the principle that his continuing opposition to Canning on the issue of Catholic emancipation made it inappropriate for him to serve in his cabinet. But within a few months Canning was dead, and Peel returned to the Home Office as well as assumed the leadership of the House of Commons in the new ministry of the **Duke of Wellington.** Catholic emancipation came to the fore again in 1828 when **Daniel O'Connell,** the leader of the Catholic Association in Ireland and himself a Roman Catholic, was elected M.P. for County Clare. All Ireland was in an uproar because O'Connell was ineligible to take his seat. Wellington's government faced the dilemma of revolution in Ireland or conceding the end of Catholic disabilities and in the process alienating the Protestant stalwarts in their own Tory Party. The Tories resigned but were shortly called back into office by King George IV when it was apparent that there was no alternative to their administration.

Though personally opposed to Catholic emancipation, Peel rightly perceived that civil unrest posed a greater danger to the country than did constitutional concession. "In the spirit of peace," he put forward the government's plan in 1829 to remove all civil and political disabilities for Roman Catholics while at the same time suppressing the Catholic Association and limiting the Irish franchise. Explaining his shift of policy after years of being associated with protection of the established Anglican Church, Peel told the House that as a minister of the Crown he believed that it was his duty to act in a fashion which promoted the interests of the nation regardless of opinions which he may have held in the past. Catholic emancipation, he said, was now necessary in order to preserve, "the safety, honour, and happiness of the King; the public wealth, peace, and tranquility of the realm." The measure passed with the aid of Whigs and Radicals, but Peel was denounced as a traitor to both his Party and his church by the Tory rank and file. On the strength of clerical voters, he was defeated at Oxford but was elected for Westbury shortly thereafter. With the Party divided and many of its supporters alienated, the Wellington government was defeated in the general election the following year.

Upon the death of his father in May 1830, Peel succeeded to the baronetcy and later that year became MP for Tamworth. It was as Sir Robert Peel that he entered the House of Commons and for the first time sat on the opposition benches when the new Parliament assembled in November. Peel vigorously opposed the parliamentary reforms proposed by Earl Grey's ministry of Whigs and Radicals and won back the allegiance of many members of his Party. Peel opposed the particulars of the Reform Bill but not the principle of reform saying he "was not prepared for so extravagant a measure." He believed that the country was more advanced in its constitutional views than was Parliament, but he hoped that a moderate reform instead might be adopted.

When the new House of Commons created under the Reform Act of 1832 assembled the following year, Peel found himself leader of a shattered Party. However, a chance at government came earlier than expected when William IV, in November 1834, dismissed Lord Melbourne, who had succeeded Grey, and called upon the Tories to form an administration. The Tory leader was in Rome, and it was several days before a courier informed Peel that he had been commissioned to form a ministry.

Peel Forms Ministry for "Hundred Days"

Peel's "Hundred Days" began with his hurried return to England. Taking office necessitated a by-election in his home constituency, and an address to electors was published which outlined the principles of Peel's administration and party. *The Tamworth Manifesto* committed Conservatives to acceptance of the 1832 Reform Act as "a final and irrevocable settlement of a great constitutional question" pledging the ministry to a review of the nation's institutions and to "correction of proved abuses and the redress of real grievances." Peel and his Party thus accepted the new political realities in Britain and committed themselves to progressive reform while conserving what was valuable.

Though Tories, now called Conservatives, increased their numbers in the general election, they did not achieve a majority and in April 1835 Peel resigned. Apart from reinvigorating his Party, the brief first Peel ministry also managed to establish the Ecclesiastical Commission to reform the Church of England and make it the instrument of its own regeneration.

In many respects, it was Peel who was the instrument of regeneration for the Conservative Party. With Wellington and **Lord Salisbury** he helped found the Carlton Club as a social and political center of Tory conservatism, and *The Tamworth Manifesto* hinted at something of a new philosophy. Peel's conservatism was expressed at a dinner on the occasion of his election as Lord Rector of the University of Glasgow when he said that there was much work for the machinery of government to do to promote progress but that political machinery could not operate unless it were free of constant meddling, tinkering, and redesign. In the elections occasioned by the accession of Queen **Victoria,** the Conservatives gained a good many seats in the House of Commons. At Merchant Taylors Hall in 1838, Peel began rebuilding his Party at the constituency level, urging Tories to exploit the registration clauses of the Reform Act to enlist every qualified Conservative elector. The Conservative Party was reviving, and Peel had a clear view of the constitutional duty of a loyal opposition to be available as the nation's alternative government.

While Conservative fortunes improved, the support for the government of Lord Melbourne and his Irish, Radical, Dissenter, and Whig supporters ebbed. When in May of 1839 they were nearly defeated on a measure to suspend the Jamaican constitution, the government resigned, and Queen Victoria summoned Peel to form a ministry. The youthful queen was sympathetic to the Whigs and to Lord Melbourne in particular. Peel knew his ministry would be in the minority and believed that he needed a clear sign of royal confidence if he were to succeed. He proposed that the queen dismiss several of her attendants (Ladies of the Bedchamber), most of whom were the relatives of the former Whig Cabinet, and replace them with the wives and daughters of the suggested new Tory ministers. Sensitive on the issue of the Queen's Household because of charges of impropriety at court which had appeared in the press and horrified at the prospect of losing Melbourne, the Whigs, and her closest friends, Victoria recalled Melbourne to office in a constitutional jumble that has become known as the Bedchamber Crisis. The Melbourne ministry limped along for two more years until the Conservatives won the general election of 1841, and Peel was again asked to form a government.

He Lowers Tariffs, Repeals Corn Laws

The second Peel Ministry was dominated by three deeply intertwined and closely related issues: trade policy, finance, and Ireland. Concerned with inadequate public revenues, Peel proposed reinstitution of a temporary income tax in 1841 which created a surplus, embraced the principle of direct taxation, and reduced the dependence of the government upon uncertain tariff revenues. Peel became convinced that tariff reduction could improve the state of industry and at the same time increase customs revenues by stimulating the volume of trade. In 1842, he introduced major tariff revisions cutting the duties on more than 700 commodities, particularly those which were raw materials for British industry, and moving the nation closer to a policy of free trade. By 1845, the wisdom of such reform was clear, and Peel announced his intention to keep the income tax and use its revenues to experiment with further tariff reductions. In 1844, Peel undertook further reform of the banking system. The Bank Charter Act made the Bank of England a central bank, separated its currency issue and banking functions, and laid down principles by which paper currency would be backed by a supply of bullion.

The following year, in hopes of improving education and mollifying Ireland, Peel proposed to increase the endowment to the Roman Catholic seminary at Maynooth and to make the grant permanent, but the old anti-Catholic sentiment in his Party and the nation was reawakened by the effort. In late 1845, it became clear that the potato crop in Ireland, which Peel knew from his experience was depended upon by millions for life itself, was in the process of being ruined by blight. The Anti-Corn Law Leaguers led by **Richard Cobden** and **John Bright** had been agitating for repeal of the laws which restricted the importation of cereal grains for several years, and Peel himself had been moving consistently towards free trade. Peel's Party was dominated, however, by landed interests that depended upon agricultural protection to keep rents high and tenants on the land. But Peel knew that unless the Corn Laws were removed and grain allowed into Ireland, mass starvation would result. As he had in 1829, Peel carried a measure which he believed the exigency of the moment demanded of a responsible minister of the crown; he repealed the Corn Laws and in the process divided his Party once again. The ministry collapsed, and Peel never held office again.

During the Lord John Russell ministry which succeeded his own, Peel remained prominent in Parliament, and a small group of former Tories known as "Peelites" continued to associate with him in support of free trade and thoughtful progressive reforms. In opposition, Peel was critical of "gunboat diplomacy," saying **Palmerston** misused British warships "to fester every wound, to provoke instead of soothing resentments," and Peel participated in the famous all-night debate over Palmerston's handling of the Don Pacifico episode of July 28–29, 1850. On the morning after that debate, Peel rode a newly purchased horse on his way to a meeting to plan the Great Exhibition and was mortally injured when the beast threw him and crushed his chest with its knees. Peel died July 2, 1850, at his London home where friends called and crowds gathered to keep watch. One week later, the nation still in mourning for a leader of great integrity and ability, his body was returned to Tamworth and buried in the parish church at Drayton Bassett.

SOURCES:

Gash, Norman. *Mr. Secretary Peel: The Life of Sir Robert Peel to 1830.* Harvard University Press, 1961.
———. *Sir Robert Peel: The Life of Sir Robert Peel After 1830.* Rowman and Littlefield, 1972.
Haly, W. T. *The Opinions of Sir Robert Peel.* Whittaker, 1893.
Hansard's Parliamentary Debates.
Peel, Sir Robert. *Memoirs by the Rt. Hon. Sir Robert Peel.* ed. by Earl Stanhope and Edward Cardwell. Murray, 1857.
———. *Sir Robert Peel from his Private Papers.* 3 vols. Edited by C. S. Parker. Murray, 1891.
Thursfield, James R. *Peel.* Books for Libraries Press, 1891.

FURTHER READING:

Clark, G. Kitson. *Peel and the Conservative Party.* 1929.
Gash, Norman. *Politics in the Age of Peel.* Norton, 1953.
Randell, K. H. *Politics and the People 1835–1850.* Collins, 1972.
Read, Donald. *Cobden and Bright: A Victorian Political Partnership.* Arnold, 1967.

Pericles

(c. 495–429 B.C.)

Greek general, politician, and statesman, who dominated the political and intellectual life of democratic Athens when that city-state was at the height of its imperial and cultural power.

"Pericles, because of his position, his intelligence, and his known integrity, could respect the liberty of the people and at the same time hold them in check. It was he who led them, rather than they who led him."

THUCYDIDES

Few have been born with rosier prospects than Pericles. Although little is known of his father's family, it was certainly noble, for Xanthippus not only married the aristocratic Agariste, he was also one of the most important public figures of his generation. Perhaps Xanthippus greatest claim to fame came in 479 B.C. when he led Athens to victory over the Persians at Mycale, a battle which virtually assured that Persia would never again invade European Greece. Pericles' mother Agariste was an Alcmeonid, an old and influential aristocratic family. The Alcmeonids were among the elite when Athens had been a true aristocracy and had intermarried with the houses of autocratic tyrants. Nevertheless, they had also been responsible for the overthrow of Athenian tyranny when Agariste's uncle, Clisthenes, inaugurated his democratic reforms in 507 B.C.

As a child, Pericles enjoyed a progressive education. From an early age he was exposed to the intellectual innovations fostered by the so-called Sophists ("Wisemen"), who were revolutionizing education by concentrating on "scientific" training and placing less emphasis upon the physical exercise, piety, and notions of morality traditionally

Born c. 495 B.C.; died a victim of the plague in 429 B.C.; son of Xanthippus and Agariste (both from prominent aristocratic families); divorced from first wife; although never legally married, entered into a long relationship with Aspasia; children: (first marriage) two sons; (with Aspasia) son Pericles.

Contributed by William S. Greenwalt, Associate Professor of Classical History, Santa Clara University, Santa Clara, California

CHRONOLOGY

490 B.C.	Athenian victory over Persians at Marathon
480 B.C.	Athenian naval victory over Persians at Salamis
477 B.C.	Delian defense league formed against Persia
460–70 B.C.	Athens transformed the Delian League into an Athenian Empire
463 B.C.	Pericles began political career by prosecuting the conservative, Cimon
461 B.C.	Ephialtes and Pericles stripped the Areopagus court of its judicial review; Ephialtes murdered
453 B.C.	Pericles elected general
449 B.C.	Peace arranged between Athens and Persia
447 B.C.	Pericles sponsored reconstruction of the Acropolis
443 B.C.	Maneuvered the ostracism of Thucydides
440 B.C.	Athens colonized Thurii in southern Italy
437 B.C.	Athens colonized Amphipolis in the northern Aegean; Pericles commanded a naval expedition into the Black Sea
431 B.C.	Peloponnesian War began
429 B.C.	Pericles died of plague
404 B.C.	Sparta won the Peloponnesian War

expected. The Sophists focused on logic as a vehicle for deductive analysis as they sought to comprehend the natural world. Among Pericles' teachers were the renowned Zeno of Elea and Anaxagoras of Clazomenae, who together introduced their charge to a rigorous study of natural philosophy, refutation, and rhetoric—the last being especially important for a rising politician. Under such influences Pericles came to disdain religious superstition and the belief that the gods played an active role in human affairs. Instead, he embraced logic and believed that humanity could master its own fate. As intellectually oriented as Pericles became, it is ironic that his head was oddly elongated and out of proportion. To compensate, Pericles habitually wore a Corinthian war helmet pushed back from his brow. This affectation became his trademark, especially after he became the foremost proponent of Athenian imperialism.

Although Pericles was heir to a fortune most in his city envied, it was neither great enough to afford the extravagant lifestyle expected by his wife and sons, nor large enough to permit Pericles to finance a political career out of his own pocket. As an adult, he kept a tight rein on his household finances, and his parsimony seems to have contributed to the eventual divorce from his unnamed wife and the subsequent alienation from his legitimate children.

Cimon Is Prosecuted

Pericles began his political career in 463 B.C. when he joined in the prosecution of the conservative Cimon, Athens's leading politician and the architect of the successful war against Persia. Cimon's vulnerability lay less in his military competence than in his support for close relations between Athens and its potential Greek rival, Sparta. With Athens's power on the rise as a consequence of its Persian war (a war from which the Spartans had withdrawn in 478 B.C. when it became clear that it would be fought in Asia, far from Sparta), friction with the traditionally powerful Sparta grew. Cimon, however, sought to defuse the mounting strain by inducing a spirit of cooperation between the two cities, reasoning that the Greek world was large enough for both—especially since Sparta's power was primarily land-based, while that of Athens was seaborne. Yet this policy overlooked the fact that a military elite enslaved the vast majority of the Spartan population. Many Athenians saw in Sparta the antithesis of democratic values and were extremely uncomfortable with embracing Sparta as a close ally. As Athens's power grew with the war against Persia prospering, many thought the time was ripe for the overthrow of Sparta and the exportation of democracy to cities where it had never flourished.

When a number of factors converged to sour Athenian/Spartan relations in 463 B.C., a liberal faction in Athens, led by one Ephialtes and ardently supported by the younger Pericles, obtained the ostracism ("temporary exile") of Cimon—a feat which disturbed many of Athens's wealthiest citizens. Their fears were well-founded, since it soon became clear that the liberals intended to "radicalize" Athenian society by making it practical for the poor to participate fully in the government. Although Athens had been a democracy since the reforms of Clisthenes, the traditional clout of the propertied classes had remained into the 460s B.C., since few officials were paid for public service, elections were expensive, and not many people could afford the education necessary to prepare a would-be politician for the rhetorical battles fought in the public arena. In order to open public positions to the poor (and in the process, to assure their political support), the liberals sought to provide salaries for public service—a modest move by modern standards but an unheard-of reform at the time.

The opening salvo in the assault upon privilege came against the *Areopagus* ("a kind of Supreme Court or court of judicial review"), the origins of which predated the Clisthenic reforms. The *Areopagus* was composed of ex-magistrates who entered the court for life as soon as they stood down from public office. Although after Clisthenes these *Areopagites* became eligible for judicial service by being democratically elected to a magistracy, by the 460s B.C. it had been discovered that their life tenancy inclined them to represent the interests of their privileged class rather than those of their one-time constituents. In 461 B.C., Ephialtes and Pericles stripped the *Areopagus* of most of its review powers and divided them among other constitutional bodies open to all Athenian citizens by way of several lotteries. An expanded series of courts was established, the juries of which were selected by lot from a pool composed of citizens willing to serve. This important reform stirred up considerable controversy and violence, which culminated in the assassination of Ephialtes.

Thus, Pericles was propelled to the political forefront. If, however, the conservatives hoped that he would promote a more restrained domestic policy than that of Ephialtes, they were mistaken. Rather, they discovered that the "Olympian" (as Pericles came to be nicknamed because his stentorian rhetoric conjured up images of rumbling thunder) was both ideologically motivated and extremely capable. After Ephialtes' death, Pericles embarked on a policy which integrated foreign and domestic affairs, which was as imperialistic as it was democratic, and which made him the most prominent politician in Athens. Although his foreign and domestic policies complemented each other, it is easier to consider them separately, after first considering Athens's standing in the Aegean area at the time.

Following Sparta's withdrawal from the Persian war, the Athenians formed a new Greek alliance to sustain the conflict. As a result, in 477 B.C. a new league was formed around the sanctuary of Apollo on the island of Delos. There, an assembly composed of all members met, and a treasury was established to pay the expenses associated with the war. (The treasury was later removed to Athens in 453 B.C. and put under the direct supervision of the Athenian assembly.) The members who voluntarily joined this *Delian* League agreed to an *eternal* alliance under Athenian leadership, presumably since they could not foresee a future without a Persian military threat. So that the financial burdens of war could be fairly distributed, the Delian assembly agreed that an Athenian commission should audit each member city's finances in order to discover what each could afford to pay at a sustained rate. The League's larger cities initially contributed men, ships, and the money to sustain both while campaigning, while the smaller members paid cash to the League's treasury. The League also agreed that Athens should annually provide the commander who would lead the united army/fleet against Persia. Among the commander's responsibilities was to draw funds from the League treasury in order to construct ships and hire additional men to complement the contingents donated by the larger cities. The Athenians appointed this commander from among the ten *strategoi* ("generals") annually elected in that city. The *strategos* ("general") thus appointed (usually Cimon until his ostracism) inevitably decided to reward his constituents by returning to Athens in order to hire Athenian shipwrights to build the League's ships, and Athenian sailors to sail them. Thus, Athens profited from the League and came to depend on a growing war industry.

The military force had had such stunning success by the 460s B.C. that the preservation of the League seemed unnecessary to many. Before the League reached a consensus about its future, however, some of its larger members decided to secede unilaterally. In response, a majority of the League's membership supported Athens by refusing to acknowledge the legitimacy of these secessions, arguing that the enemy could return if the League disbanded. This argument had a certain validity, but the truth of the matter was that by the 460s B.C., the Athenian economy depended on the League. When these rebellions were broken, Athens converted their contributions to tribute paid in cash to the League's treasury (thereafter to be spent in Athens, increasing the city's dependency on the League). The result was a subtle, but real, transmutation of the *Delian* alliance into an Athenian Empire.

The "Long Walls" Are Constructed

As this metamorphosis occurred, Athens extended its influence within the Greek world and beautified its own city. Pericles never questioned the ethics of supporting Athenian democracy by enforced contributions, but rather became Athens's most ardent imperialist ("advocating the expansion of his country's borders"). What most seemed to open up the floodgates of brazen Athenian aggression was the construction of the famous "Long Walls" (urged by Pericles), linking the city to its fortified harbor of Piraeus, five miles away. One consequence of this project was jobs, but a more important one was that Athens became impregnable to assault by land, and thereafter never feared starvation while its fleets controlled the sea. The sense of security these walls provided stirred Athens to flaunt its power.

Although Pericles opposed the short-lived and unsuccessful attempt to extend the Athenian Empire to the Greek mainland in the 450s B.C., he wholeheartedly supported the expansion of Athens's maritime power. As a *strategos*, Pericles humbled Sicyon (453 B.C.), restored the famous sanctuary of the Delphian Apollo to friendly hands (early 440s B.C.); crushed the rebellions against Athens on the islands of Euboea (445 B.C.) and Samos (439 B.C.); and led the Athenian fleet into the Black Sea (437 B.C.). Pericles also advocated the extension of Athenian economic influence through the establishment of colonies at Thurii in southern Italy (440 B.C.) and Amphipolis on the Thracian coast of the northern Aegean (437 B.C.). The latter, in particular, became a valuable asset as long as it remained in Athenian hands, since it lay close to the extensive forests which provided the wood, pitch, and other materials essential to an ancient naval power, and because it was not far from the productive silver mines of Mt. Pangaeus.

The Peloponnesian War Looms

Perhaps Pericles' greatest strategic influence, however, came in the 430s B.C. as the Peloponnesian War against Sparta loomed. At that time he advised his city to take a hard line against any encroachment on its imperial interests, even though such extremism put Athens on a collision course with Sparta. As a result of Pericles' recommendation, Athens strengthened its presence in the west through a defensive alliance with Corcyra, although that pact threatened the economic lifeline of Sparta's ally, Corinth. Shortly thereafter, Pericles also convinced the Athenians to close the harbors of their Empire to Megara, another Spartan ally, after a series of disputes erupted with that city. When Sparta learned (432 B.C.) of the consequent damage wrought upon the economies of its allies, it demanded immediate redress and a curtailment of Athenian international activities. Pericles, arguing that Sparta's demands amounted to extortion, convinced his fellow citizens to reject them and to pursue the city's advantage regardless of whether or not Sparta approved.

Hostilities ensued (431 B.C.), and Athens relied again on Pericles to devise its war strategy. Unwilling to meet Sparta's army head-on when it invaded Attica, Pericles ordered all Athenians within the city's walls. This meant the abandonment of much food and the destruction of many farms, but the sea would provide the besieged with sustenance at public expense. Then, to convince the Spartans that he could hurt them more than they could Athens, Pericles ordered the Athenian fleet to despoil the Peloponnesian coast and to encourage Sparta's *helots* ("state-owned slaves") to revolt, a specter the Spartans always feared. Had Athens stuck to this strategy—and avoided any more foreign entanglements until after a secure peace with Sparta was established—it probably would have won the war. However, Pericles died of the plague (429 B.C.) that flourished amid unsanitary conditions made intolerable by thousands of Athenians seeking shelter within a crowded city. With Pericles dead, no one kept his strategy alive. As a result, after a conflict which lasted over a generation and which brought Athens incalculable distress, Sparta defeated its rival and appropriated the Athenian Empire for itself (404 B.C.).

Turning now to Pericles' domestic policy: sometime before the Persian War officially ended (449 B.C.), Pericles foresaw an economic depression in peacetime Athens unless something was done to absorb the shock of unemployment in the city's maritime war industry. Consequently, Pericles legislated new ways for Athenians to take advantage of the imperial tribute, while simultaneously promoting the ideals of radical democracy. In 453 B.C., he sponsored a law which paid Athenian citizens for their service as jurors in the courts proliferating at the time. This growth of the Athenian judiciary was the result of a conscious decision to force most imperial business to be adjudicated in Athens where Athenians could insure that the Empire was being run in their interests. In addition, Pericles successfully sponsored a bill which guaranteed that citizens could attend the popular state-supported theater if they otherwise could not afford the price of admission. Again, the Empire was to foot the bill.

One consequence of such privileges was that Athenian citizenship became an increasingly valuable commodity which many non-Athenians coveted—much to the dismay of those who feared that an extension of citizenship through any means would dilute the benefits doled to citizens. There ensued a Periclean law (451 B.C.) which limited Athenian citizenship to those whose fathers and maternal grandfathers were both full citizens. Interestingly, this law was very popular among citizens with daughters. Since Athenians were becoming rich by Greek standards, many sought Athenian bachelors as husbands for their daughters. The popularity of Athenian grooms increased the dowries they traditionally could demand with marriage. By restricting citizenship, Pericles magnified the importance of Athenian women, for the children of non-Athenians were ineligible for the growing list of city welfare benefits. Of course, Athenian fathers were happy at the lower dowries they could expect to pay for a citizen son-in-law after this law was enacted. And, as Pericles fully understood, happy voters vote for those who make them happy.

His Vision of an Ideal City

In thanksgiving for the victorious peace treaty arranged with Persia (449 B.C.), Pericles proclaimed a one-year moratorium on the collection of the imperial tribute. The next year, however, saw its restitution. Along with the renewal of the tribute came an implicit Athenian claim of sovereignty over the onetime autonomous members of the *Delian* League. This clearly demonstrated Athens's financial dependency on its Empire, but it also provided Pericles with the financial wherewithal to engage in an experiment the likes of which the world had never seen. Henceforth Pericles spent much tribute to promote the interests of the imperial democracy, but he also dedicated significant amounts to a nobler cause: he meant to fashion an ideal city to inspire its inhabitant to levels of intellectual and cultural achievement which he believed were attainable only in a *democratic* society, but which having been attained, would become a model for others to copy. In short, Pericles drafted a vision for a society he dreamed would become, in his own words, "the school which educated all Greece."

The Acropolis became the symbolic crown of this utopia. Although its heights visually dominated the city, no building had stood on them since **Xerxes** had razed their original temples (480 B.C.) shortly before the Athenians expelled the Persians from the Greek mainland. For about a generation, the Athenians had employed their ruins as a visual incitement to war, but with peace, Pericles reckoned the time right to rededicate the site to the deities (especially Athena) most associated with the foundation, development, and prosperity of the Athenian state. This coupling of the gods and democracy was paramount in Pericles' mind, and both had their place in the Acropolis's reconstruction. The most majestic blend of piety and propaganda can still be seen in the Parthenon (built 447–432 B.C.)—a temple which simultaneously venerated Athena's virginal purity and exalted the uprightness of democracy as a way of life. Although the modern world often sees virtue

in the separation of church and state, the ancient Greeks did not.

Other temples followed, including especially the Erechtheum and that of Athena Nike ("the victorious"), but it was not Pericles' intent merely to beautify Athens physically. In addition, he promoted its intellectual and cultural development. It was no coincidence that the period of Pericles' ascendancy coincided with the most creative phase in the history of the Athenian theater, where tragic and comedic masterpieces were routinely produced for the entertainment and edification of the city's population. The careers of Sophocles, Euripides, and Aristophanes were all spawned when Pericles' influence was at its zenith. In addition, Pericles' interest in Sophism created such excitement about the latest scholarly controversies that the greatest thinkers of the age flocked to Athens. Consequently, historians like Herodotus and philosophers like Anaxagoras resided in Athens where they sparked locals like Thucydides and Socrates to pursue their calling.

Athens attracted many others as well, but perhaps the most remarkable of all was **Aspasia,** who came from Miletas about 445 B.C. in order to found a school of rhetoric. Her arrival in Athens created a stir because, traditionally, "respectable" women were expected to stay at home and acknowledge the intellectual superiority of their male counterparts. Aspasia, however, had few intellectual peers and no superiors, and soon won the admiration of the city's intelligentsia, even as her liberated ways scandalized those more conservatively inclined. She drew criticism from those envious of her talent or offended by her flaunting of tradition both on the stage—where comedic playwrights would occasionally lambast her "immorality," and in court—where she was once prosecuted for impiety (a charge stemming from her sophistic tendency to question everything, even the customary understanding of the gods).

Despite her detractors, her intellect, her wit, and her irrepressible desire to exploit her natural talents won her some impressive friends, among them Socrates (with whom she frequently conversed) and Pericles. Actually, Aspasia became much more than Pericles' friend. Drawn together by mutual intellectual interests, the two lived as husband and wife from shortly after her arrival to Athens until Pericles died. Although not a legal marriage, thanks to Pericles' own law debarring foreign wives, their union was emotionally far more egalitarian and loving than most in Athens. Together they produced a son, the younger Pericles, who, after his father's death, was given a special grant of citizenship to honor his parents. Tragically, the younger Pericles died amidst the hysteria which increasingly struck Athens as the Peloponnesian War wound down to defeat. In an illegal trial which sought to attach blame for the loss of some Athenians at sea, a jury found the fleet's *strategoi*, including the younger Pericles, guilty of a dereliction of duty. They were quickly executed over the vociferous protests of Socrates, although none was guilty (406 B.C.).

With this inhumanity, the direct line of Pericles came to an end, but his fame lived on. No politician in democratic Athens had as long or as illustrious a career, and though he always had some opposition, after the ostracism of Thucydides, Pericles enjoyed an unparalleled ascendancy within his city. During this period, his political opposition dared not confront him directly, but contented itself with sniping at him through his friends, including Aspasia, whose unorthodox thinking frequently clashed with traditional mores. Although occasionally characterized as aloof and

uncaring by those who would replace him in the people's hearts, Pericles' unceasing devotion to the political interests of the Athenian poor, his consistency of insight, the power of his oratory, the splendor of his social vision, his clearly discernible courage, and his fabled personal integrity—all combined to make him seem to the constituency he served like an Olympian among mere mortals.

SOURCES:

Moore, J. M. *Aristotle and Xenophon On Democracy and Oligarchy.* University of California Press, 1975.

Plutarch. *The Rise and Fall of Athens.* Penguin, 1960.

Thucydides. *The Peloponnesian War.* Penguin, 1954.

FURTHER READING:

Hignett, C. *A History of the Athenian Constitution.* Oxford University Press, 1952.

Meiggs, Russell. *The Athenian Empire.* Oxford University Press, 1972.

Michael, Nancy. *Pericles.* Garland, 1985.

Johann Pestalozzi

(1746–1827)

Educator and social reformer who promoted the education of children, regardless of their social background, and whose method resulted in the introduction of an elementary school system in Europe and overseas.

"The Alpha and Omega of my politics is Education."

JOHANN HEINRICH PESTALOZZI

Johann Heinrich Pestalozzi was born in Zurich, Switzerland, on January 12, 1746, the son of Susanne Hotz and surgeon Johann Baptiste Pestalozzi. His father died when Pestalozzi was only five, leaving him and his siblings to be raised by their mother and their faithful maidservant, Barbara Schmid "Babeli." The family was supported by the children's grandfather Andreas Pestalozzi, minister of nearby Hoengg, and, as their father had left little money, the widow Pestalozzi and Babeli became skilled economizers.

After visiting the "house school," an elementary school for Zurich citizens, in 1757 young Pestalozzi went to the Latin school at the Great Minster, where he was considered one of the best pupils. His marks, however, varied constantly, a problem he later attributed to carelessness. At the Collegium Carolinum, Pestalozzi took up philology and psychology. Among his favorite professors were Johann Jakob Breitinger and Johann Jakob Bodmer. Both emphasized questions and discussions rather than memorization; self-reliance in thinking was preferred to the mere repetition of traditions and dogmas. This attitude clearly reflected the spirit of the Enlightenment.

Contributed by Susanne Peter-Kubli, Historian, Wädenswil, Switzerland

Born Johann Heinrich Pestalozzi in Zurich, Switzerland, on January 12, 1746; died in Brugg on February 17, 1827; son of Johann Baptiste (a surgeon) and Susanne (Hotz) Pestalozzi; married: Anna Schulthess, 1769; children: one son, Johann Jakob ("Hans").

CHRONOLOGY

1746	Born in Zurich, Switzerland
1763–65	Studied philology and psychology at the Collegium Carolinum in Zurich
1769	Farmer in Muelligen
1781–83	Published *Leonhard and Gertrude*
1798–99	Supervisor of a poorhouse in Stans
1800–04	Teacher in Burgdorf
1801	Published *How Gertrude teaches her children*
1806	Institute founded in Yverdon
1825	Institute in Yverdon closed down
1827	Died in Brugg

Pestalozzi left the Collegium after he'd passed the exams, yet without attending the final courses.

In 1764, he joined the Helvetical Society as a student. This was a society comprised of liberal-minded scholars, graduates, students, and citizens who promoted literary discussions and social reforms according to French philosophers Jean Jacques Rousseau and Charles de Secondat Montesquieu. Pestalozzi was particularly impressed by Rousseau's *Émile*, a "visionary and highly speculative book" which he recommended to his fiancee Anna Schulthess.

Following his departure from the Collegium, Pestalozzi showed some interest in a political career, but his experiences at his grandfather's home in Hoengg soon changed his mind. In Hoengg, young Pestalozzi was confronted with the problems of a rural population suffering from the disadvantages which resulted from the policies of Zurich's Council. During the 18th century, the city of Zurich made it increasingly difficult for people from the countryside to acquire Zurich citizenship; thus, a large percent of the population of the state of Zurich was unable to hold public office or to be elected members of the council. Formerly, democratic procedures had been gradually substituted by oligarchical ones, a tendency that brought on the rural population's disaffection for Zurich's government. The conflict made a marked impression on Pestalozzi.

After two years of courtship and a regular, revealing correspondence, in 1769 he married Anna Schulthess, eight years his senior. The marriage was far from acknowledged by the bride's wealthy merchant family, who questioned Pestalozzi's ability to sustain a family of his own; nevertheless, the lovers persisted, and the parents finally gave in.

Impressed by Rousseau's vision of a life in peaceful harmony with Nature, Pestalozzi and several of his friends praised agriculture as the true source of self-fulfillment. They not only embraced the French philosopher's *retour a la Nature* but were determined to become farmers living on the countryside, purchasing land and livestock, and adopting the lifestyle of the peasants. After a few months' apprenticeship as a farmer, Pestalozzi bought land near the little town of Birr (in today's state Aargau) which he began to cultivate. But his fellow farmers never wholly trusted the gentleman farmer of Zurich. To make matters worse, the years 1771–72 brought bad harvests, attributing to the failure of his enterprise; those who had financed the undertaking wanted their money back.

No longer able to make a living farming, Pestalozzi transformed the farm *Neuhof* into a poorhouse for children. There the neighborhood children were provided with food, clothing and some elementary schooling. According to Pestalozzi's vision, this institution was thought to be self-sustaining with the children working part-time as weavers and spinners. Some children, however, complained of hard work and meager diet, and ran away as soon as they had earned decent clothing and acquired a knowledge of spinning or weaving. By 1780, due to a lack of finances, the poorhouse had to be closed.

Pestalozzi Begins His Novel

Encouraged by a close friend, Pestalozzi started to enlarge his meager income by writing. Following literary attempts about liberty, society, and the evolution of mankind, in 1781 he published the first part of the book *Leonhard and Gertrude*, a novel intended for the rural population.

As was the case with Pestalozzi's own childhood, it is the story's wife, Gertrude—not Leonhard, the head of the household—who exercises the bold initiative to save the family. In his later work, *How Gertrude teaches her children*, Pestalozzi repeatedly emphasized the role of the mother. His mother's maidservant Babeli, who'd promised his father that she would not desert the widow or her children, likely served as a model for Gertrude. Another maid, Elisabeth Naef, who kept the farm running after the failure of Pestalozzi's experiment, was also said to have influenced him. Pestalozzi believed the most fundamental values in human development to be love, gratitude, trust, and readiness to obey. These feelings, he asserted:

> have their chief source in the relation that exists between the baby and his mother. The mother is forced by the power of animal instinct to tend the child, feed him, protect and please him.... [Thus] the germ of love is developed in him.

Then, the baby learns to trust his mother. "When he hears her step, he is quiet, when he sees her, he stretches out his hands. When he is fed, he is satisfied and grateful." Where obedience was concerned, Pestalozzi differentiated between passive and active obedience:

> As want precedes love, nourishment precedes gratitude, and care trust, so passionate desire precedes obedience. The child screams before he waits, he is impatient before he obeys. Patience is developed before obedience, he only becomes obedient through patience.

Active obedience, in his view, is developed later, when the child realizes that "he himself is not in the world for his own sake only."

Leonhard and Gertrude revealed a belief that monarchy, in its enlightened and absolute form, is perhaps the best way to govern a country. The novel asserts that moral values, such as love, trust, gratitude, and obedience, are developed in the microcosm of the family and, from there, transferred to the macrocosm of the nation. In Pestalozzi's words: "a sense of fatherhood makes rulers, and one of brotherhood makes citizens; both of them work for order, in the home, and in the nation."

Nevertheless, he did approve of the changes that took place in neighboring France in 1789. Witnessing the French Revolution, he fully realized the injustices the French monarchs had committed against the people: the royal family and favorites lived in extravagant splendor while forcing much of the population to live in extreme poverty. Closely observing events across the French border, Pestalozzi fully sympathized with the suffering population; he would have preferred, however, a gradual change resulting from reforms, rather then a revolution. Surprisingly, in 1792, Pestalozzi was given the Honorary Citizenship of the French Republic. Although he certainly felt somewhat flattered by this honor, he was confronted with considerable suspicion at home. In 1795, in the town of Staefa, discontent on the part of Zurich's rural population turned into open resistance. The leaders demanded that their old rights be returned to them. Zurich, despite offered negotiation by some states of the Confederation, harshly put down the revolt. Zurich's reaction was no doubt influenced by events in France that had recently turned the neighboring country from an absolute monarchy into a republic. The French Revolution and its messages of *liberte, egalite,* and *fraternite* were embraced by the more liberal minded and just as strongly condemned by those guaranteed to lose power. Pestalozzi was partly held responsible for the outbreak of resistance in Staefa.

Only a few years later, in 1798, the Swiss Confederacy was invaded by French troops. First Consul **Napoleon Bonaparte** had included the neighboring country in his hegemonical plans to enlarge his empire, and the "Swiss Helvetian Republic," as it was to be called, was of some strategic value to his further military campaigns. The population of the so-called *Untertanengebiete* and parts of the upper classes who believed in the realization of liberty, equality, and brotherhood welcomed the arrival of the French "liberators." But those who had hitherto governed the states and adopted a lifestyle similar to the French aristocracy strongly opposed the invasion. Open resistance, however, was only halfhearted, and in March of 1798, Berne, the capital of the Swiss Confederation, was taken by the French army under General Brune. The Confederation was transformed into the Helvetian Republic. Though the states in central Switzerland—Uri, Schwyz, Unterwalden, Zug, and Glarus—continued their opposition against the newly inaugurated Republic and its constitution, in September French troops defeated the resistors and burned Stans, the center of the opposition, to the ground.

Meanwhile, Pestalozzi had been appointed adviser of General Affairs. Although appalled at the cruelties the French troops had inflicted upon the civilians of Stans, on the whole he justified the putting down of resistance. In order to assist the numerous orphans living on the brink of starvation, the Helvetic government appointed Pestalozzi supervisor of a poorhouse which was to be set up in a former monastery in Stans. Yet, Pestalozzi, a Protestant who represented the new and ill-liked "order," found it extremely difficult to win the hearts and support of the predominantly Catholic population. At times, he cared for 80 children, assisted only by a housekeeper. Under the increasing pressure of the French-Austrian war, the poorhouse closed down after seven months of immense struggle to make rooms available for billeting soldiers. Pestalozzi, on the verge of physical breakdown, was invited by a friend to spend some weeks in Gurnigelbad, a health resort near Berne.

He Promotes Better Education for Pupils, Teachers

Yet another of his attempts had failed. Though his latest enterprise had lasted only a couple of months, Pestalozzi's experience in Stans signified the turning point of his life. From then on, he would dedicate himself to the promotion of a sounder education for pupils as well as teachers. As quoted by William Kilpatrick, he was annoyed that "the children of the poorest were in effect excluded from education" and that in school a "superficial verbosity" characterized pupil recitation. He believed that students hardly knew the meaning of the words they recited and, accordingly, were set up to fail. "These children," he said, "were flogged unmercifully for failing even though the failure was not their fault."

Nor did Pestalozzi think highly of the qualifications of the teachers of his time. Indeed, there were then few places for teachers to acquire techniques of instruction. Thus, Pestalozzi concluded that "for children, teaching of the parents will always be the core." In regard to teachers, he remarked sarcastically, "and as for the schoolmaster, we can give thanks to God if he is able to put a decent shell about the core."

Over the following years, he developed a "method," according to which children should be taught. Contrary to his earlier conviction, at the turn of the century Pestalozzi completely abandoned Rousseau's thesis of leaving the evolution of Man to Nature. A child, so he was now convinced, needed firm guidance first by his parents and later by a teacher:

> Wherever you carelessly leave the earth to Nature, it bears weeds and thistles. Wherever you leave the education of our race to her, she goes no farther than a confused impression on the senses, that is not adapted to your power of comprehension, nor to that of your child, in the way that is needed for the best instruction.

Pestalozzi believed that primary instruction should be based on the teaching of sounds, the teaching of words, and finally the teaching of language. He introduced a spelling book to enable children to learn the alphabet and made them write down the letters and words on slates.

Teaching his method in Burgdorf near Berne, Pestalozzi had difficulties at the beginning convincing parents and fellow teachers of the benefits. In the summer of 1800, Hermann Kruesi, Johann Georg Tobler, and Johann Christoph Buss joined Pestalozzi's institute in the castle of Burgdorf. More protection and support were offered by Philipp Albert Stapfer, minister of the arts and sciences of the Helvetian Republic. In autumn, Pestalozzi informed his friends that he planned to open a seminary for teachers. His method then took the form of a series of 14 lectures, published in 1801 under the title *How Gertrude teaches her children*. The same year, his son Hans Jakob died at only 31 years of age.

The events that took place in the country during the following years forced Pestalozzi to give up the institute and seek a suitable location elsewhere. In 1802, the Helvetian Republic came close to bankruptcy, and the central government which had financed the institute was no longer able to do so. In 1803, the Act of Mediation, designed by Napoleon, brought Switzerland back to a prerevolutionary confederation of independent states. While the castle of Burgdorf was therefore claimed back by the state of Berne, Pestalozzi was offered two new locations: one in Muenchenbuchsee (Berne) and another in Yverdon (Vaud). He decided to accept them both. In addition, he won two new teachers, Joseph Schmid, a genius in mathematics, and Johannes Niederer, whose philosophical knowledge and writing skills made him a welcome collaborator for Pestalozzi.

Finally, Pestalozzi's efforts began to bear fruit. Leading personalities of Western Europe, especially in the German-speaking parts, showed interest in his method. Johann Gottlieb Fichte, the German philosopher, not only realized the advantages of Pestalozzi's new approach but succeeded in introducing the method in Prussia. Though others, such as Johann Wolfgang von Goethe, remained skeptical, the number of students who came to Yverdon to be instructed as teachers grew steadily and in autumn of 1809 amounted to 166—less than half of them were Swiss.

Switzerland, for its part, remained at all times distrustful of Pestalozzi. His public alignment with the French and his vote for a central government made him more enemies then friends. When a delegation of representatives from each state inspected the institute in 1809, its mostly negative report harmed Pestalozzi's reputation. Meanwhile, a conflict arose between Joseph Schmid, who was beginning to interpret Pestalozzi's method in his own way, and the other teachers; the report only widened the gap between opposing parties. Though Schmid, obviously the source of discontent, left the institute in 1810, several other teachers left as well, thus discrediting the institute in the eyes of the public. In addition, the military campaign of French Emperor Napoleon against Russian Tsar **Alexander I** in 1812–13 hindered many students from entering the institute.

Consequently, debts kept rising. Pestalozzi, as evident in his earlier experiments, seemed to lack administrative qualities which, again, would prove fateful. In 1815, he gladly accepted Schmid's offer to return to Yverdon, but—while the institute was gradually recovering—Pestalozzi suffered yet another blow, the sudden death of his wife in December of 1815. Soon after, new disputes arose between Schmid and the other teachers. This time Pestalozzi sided with Schmid, and the following year 16 teachers left the institute. Their departure, and another quarrel between Pestalozzi and Niederer which started soon after, marked the institute's decline. In 1825, it was closed down. Pestalozzi used up his remaining energy in writing justifications and defensive letters against Niederer's attacks and criticisms.

He died two years later, on February 17, 1827, and was buried in the cemetery in Birr, nearby to the beginnings of his first experiment, farming, 58 years before.

In 1846, a monument was erected on his grave, carrying the following inscription:

Here lies
Heinrich Pestalozzi
born in Zurich on 12th January 1746
died in Brugg on 17th February 1827.
Savious at the Poor in the Neuhof
Preacher of the People in "Leonhard and Gertrude,"
In Stans Father to Orphans,
In Burgdorf and Muenchenbuchsee
Founder of the new Elementary School
In Yverdon Educator of the Mankind
Man, Christian, Citizen
All for Others, Nothing for Himself
Blessed be his Name.

SOURCES:

Kilpatrick, William H., ed. *The Education of Man: Aphorisms.* Translated by Heinz and Ruth Norden. Philosophical Library, 1951.

Pestalozzi, Johann Henrich. *How Gertrude teaches her children: An attempt to help mothers to teach her own children and an account of the Method.* Translated by Lucy E. Holland and Francis C. Turner. Edited by Ebenezer Cooke. Remax House, 1966.

Silber, Kate. *Pestalozzi: The Man and His Work.* Routledge & Kegan Paul, 1960.

FURTHER READING:

Anderson, Lewis F. *Johann Heinrich Pestalozzi.* Greenwood Press, 1975.

Monroe, Will Seymour. *History of the Pestalozzian Movement in the United States.* Syracuse, 1907.

Pestalozzi, Johann Henrich. *Leonhard and Gertrude: A Book for the Poor.* Translated by Eliza Shepherd. 2 Vol. London, 1827.

———*Letters on early Education addressed to J.P. Greaves.* London, 1827.

Walch, Sister Mary Romana. *Pestalozzi and the Pestalozzian Theory of Education.* Washington, 1952.

Henri-Philippe Pétain

(1856–1951)

Leader of France's successful defense against the Germans at the battle of Verdun in World War I, who emerged as a hero, then headed the collaborationist Vichy government while France was occupied by German forces during World War II.

Name variations: Marshal Pétain. Pronunciation: PAY-tan. Born Henri-Philippe Benoni Omer Pétain in 1856 in Cauchy-à-la-Tour in the Artois region of northern France; son of Omer-Venant Pétain (a fanner) and Clotilde Legrande; married: Eugénie-Alphonsine Hardon Dehérain, 1920; children: one stepson. Predecessor: Paul Reynaud, Premier, Third Republic (in 1940). Successor: Charles de Gaulle, Head, Provisional Government (in 1944).

Had it not been for World War I, Philippe Pétain—a career military man who rose slowly through the ranks—would probably have retired in relative obscurity. With the war, however, he was promoted to general and became one of France's heroes by organizing the successful defense of Verdun against the Germans in 1916, then by quelling a mutiny in the French army in 1917. A believer in cautious defensive firepower as against risky offensive charges, Pétain acquired the reputation as the most humane of the French military leaders. After the war, he was named Marshal of France. At the age of 84 in the spring of 1940, he used his immense prestige to take over the leadership of the government during the disastrous battle of France during World War II, secured from Nazi Germany an armistice, and then led an authoritarian government based in Vichy that collaborated with the Nazi war machine until the liberation of France by the Allies in the summer of 1944. With the defeat of Germany in 1945, Pétain, who had been taken to Germany by the retreating Germans, returned to France where he was tried for collaboration with the enemy in wartime and sentenced to death. Because of his World War I record and his advanced age, his sen-

Contributed by Bertram M. Gordon, Professor of History, Mills College, Oakland, California

"It is with honor and in order to maintain French unity, a unity ten centuries old, in the framework of a constructive activity of a new European order that I have today entered the path of collaboration.... It is I alone who will be judged by history."

HENRI-PHILIPPE PÉTAIN (1940)

tence was commuted to life imprisonment. He died disgraced, at the age of 95, in 1951.

Henri-Philippe Benoni Omer Pétain was born in 1856 into a peasant family in Cauchy-à-la-Tour, a small village in the Artois region of northern France. He was the only boy in a family of five children. Philippe's mother died in childbirth when he was a year old, and his father remarried when Philippe was three; the new couple had three additional children. In later years, Pétain recalled having been more or less abandoned by his stepmother, but there are few records left regarding his early years. He attended a local primary school and in 1867 enrolled in the Collège Saint-Bertin at nearby Saint-Omer. Pétain's early education appears to have oriented him toward either a clerical or a military career. The shock of defeat in the 1870 war by the Prussians, followed by the Paris Commune uprising in 1871, may have pushed him in a conservative direction.

With no family farm or business to inherit, the military became a logical career choice. Pétain was admitted in 1876 to the French Military Academy at Saint-Cyr, from which he was graduated two years later as a second lieutenant. In the wake of the defeat by the Prussians, the curriculum of the Military Academy was being reorganized to reflect technical advances, and it is possible that during these years Pétain developed his strong views on the importance of firepower. His first assignment, in 1879, was at Villefranche-sur-Mer, on the Mediterranean coast, and his second, in 1883, in Besançon, near the foot of the Jura mountains. In 1888, he entered the War College in Paris, where evaluations of him praised his intelligence and military skills but also noted a "cold," though not unfriendly personality. The young officer, on horseback in his uniform, with blonde hair and blue eyes, must have cut a dashing figure to young women in the 1880s. Prospects for marriage to "good families," however, faded when they learned that he was virtually without financial resources or material prospects. Pétain would retain an inclination for liaisons with women through his 80s.

In 1895, now a captain, Pétain joined the staff of the military governor of Paris, in charge of the defense of the city in the event of war. His new assignment brought him to Paris at the height of the Dreyfus affair, which began in 1894 when Captain Alfred Dreyfus, the highest-ranking Jewish officer in the French army, was convicted of passing military secrets to the Germans. The "affair," as it came to be known in France, ended with the exoneration of Dreyfus, but not before France had almost come to civil war. Republicans, liberals, and socialists supported the secular

Republic and demanded the revision of the guilty verdict. Church leaders, Royalists, anti-Semites, and many high military officials, including some of Pétain's superiors, argued that reopening the case would weaken the French army in the face of a powerful and hostile German neighbor. Keeping his own counsel, Pétain left no written record of his views on the affair, which may have served him well in maintaining a clean political record for future promotions under the victorious Republic. While in Paris, he resumed relations with the Hardons, a family with whom he had become friendly while serving in Villefranche-sur-Mer. In 1901, he asked for Eugénie-Alphonsine Hardon's hand in marriage but was refused because there was a 20-year age difference. Not told of the proposal, Eugénie-Alphonsine married the artist François Dehérain, with whom she had a son.

Promotions came slowly to Pétain in the peacetime army, usually on the basis of seniority. In 1901, he was appointed to teach infantry tactics at the War College. At the time, French military leadership was divided between those who favored massive frontal assaults using large numbers of men and those who emphasized superior and more accurate firepower to conserve lives. Becoming known as a protagonist of firepower, Pétain in 1908 was promoted to lieutenant colonel and named professor of military tactics at the War College. At the end of 1911, he was made a full colonel and was sent to command the 33rd Infantry Regiment at Arras in northern France, where in the fall of 1912 he made the acquaintance of a young second lieutenant, with whose destiny he would be tied through the 20th century: **Charles de Gaulle.**

When the First World War broke out, Pétain was still a colonel, in command of a brigade in Saint-Omer, where he had gone to school; he had never commanded in wartime. Aged 58 and still a bachelor, he was anticipating an honorable and comfortable, if not luxurious, retirement. With the war, however, he was promoted to brigadier general and commanded the Fourth Infantry, which advanced into Belgium at the outset of hostilities, then was forced to withdraw in the face of a major German offensive in August 1914. The Germans were stopped in northern France, and through the remainder of the war Pétain battled repeatedly with his fellow generals, **Joseph Joffre,** Edmond de Castelnau, Charles Mangin, Robert Nivelle, and **Ferdinand Foch,** who called for massive offensive operations, for which Pétain rarely seemed to believe his forces were ready.

Pétain a Hero after Defense of Verdun

In February 1916, the Germans attacked the fortress city of Verdun on the eastern edge of the western front. Their strategy was to pierce the French lines or force the French into a battle of attrition that they would lose because of superior German resources. Joffre put Pétain in charge of the French defense. The Germans captured the Douaumont and Vaux fortresses, on the perimeter defenses of Verdun, but, in a battle that lasted through the end of the year, the French held. Pétain's slogan *"on les aura"* (we will win) became immortalized, and he became a national hero in France. Mangin and Nivelle led offensives that regained the territory around Verdun that had been lost to the Germans; as their reward, Nivelle replaced the retiring Joffre in command of the entire front in December. In 1916, Pétain also resumed his liaison with Eugénie-Alphonsine Hardon Dehérain, after her divorce.

Convinced of the wisdom of the defensive strategy he had successfully employed at Verdun, Pétain watched in dismay as Nivelle launched an offensive, which, amid thousands of French casualties in April 1917, failed to pierce the German lines. On May 15, Pétain succeeded Nivelle at the head of the front. Upon taking command, Pétain was faced by the most serious crisis of the entire war. Embittered by the failure of the Nivelle offensive and inflamed by pacifist and leftist literature infiltrating the military after the March 1917 collapse of tsarism in Russia, soldiers mutinied in perhaps as many as half of the French army divisions. With a minimum of bloodshed, Pétain suppressed them by improving food supplies to the troops, exhorting the French newspapers to paint a more encouraging picture of the war situation, and promising the troops, often in person, that they would be sent on no further risky offensives and that they would hold tight until the arrival in force of the Americans, who had entered the war in April. A German assault in May 1917 might have cut straight through to Paris, but the Germans did not learn of the mutinies until order had been restored. Pétain's successful suppression of the mutinies, together with his defense of Verdun the previous year, gave birth to the legend of "the man who had saved France." In 1918, however, Pétain was somewhat marginalized when Foch, who wanted more resources devoted to the front lines, as opposed to Pétain's strategy of defense in depth, was put in charge of the entire Allied effort on the western front. Foch supervised the offensives that finally broke through the German lines and won the war. Pétain was promoted to Marshal of France, a title he now shared with Joffre and Foch.

Pétain was now a hero of France. He aged well, continued to cut a handsome figure, and projected a calm commanding demeanor that was said to cover an innate peasant shrewdness. As the years went on, he seems to have become increasingly pessimistic about what he saw as a loss of martial spirit in the France of his day. He was also said to have grown increasingly vain. In 1920, he was appointed vice president of the Higher War Council and two years later was named Inspector General of the Armies, positions which he held through the 1920s and which gave him full power over French military planning. On September 14, 1920, at age 64 and contemplating retirement, Pétain married Eugénie-Alphonsine and acquired a small estate at Villeneuve-Loubet, on the Riviera, overlooking the Mediterranean. In 1925, Captain Charles de Gaulle joined his staff. The two men planned to collaborate on a book dealing with the history of the French army from before the Revolution through the First World War, but they differed on style and substance. Amid mutual recriminations, the project was never completed.

Maginot Line Is Built

Two years later, Pétain supervised the beginning of construction of a chain of fortifications connected by underground passages along the Franco-German border, which did not, however, extend to protect the French frontier with Belgium. Named after the war minister who pushed the plan through the French Parliament, it came to be known as the Maginot line. In 1931, Pétain was elected to the Académie Française, one of the highest honors in France, with only 40 posts available at any one time. Ironically, Pétain succeeded Foch, who had died in 1929. He also stepped down from his position of commander in chief and was made Inspector General of Air Defense, a pulpit from which he advocated greater resources for air power. In the early 1930s, however, his demands ran against three factors: (1) the economic realities created by the Great Depression; (2) the election of a Radical government, backed by the socialists in 1932 who supported deep cuts in the military budget; and (3) a mood that hoped for the success of the Geneva conference on international disarmament then in progress.

Events in 1934 elevated Pétain's public role still more. The depression, together with a series of scandals in the government that culminated with the accusation of Alexandre Stavisky of fraud in collusion with members of Parliament, led an angry mob, on February 6, 1934, to march across the Pont de la Concorde toward the Chamber of Deputies, threatening to throw the deputies into the Seine river. Some feared a fascist coup. The demonstration of February 6th was followed by leftist counterdemonstrations several days later. Premier Édouard Daladier resigned and the chamber called upon former President Gaston Doumergue to form a government of national unity. Pétain was asked to become minister of war. As a cabinet minister, he called again for increased resources for air power. He also argued that the Maginot line need cover only the Franco-German border and not the border with Belgium, for he anticipated that in a future war French forces would carry the fight into the Low Countries. With a nod to **Mussolini**'s Italy and **Hitler**'s Germany, Pétain also spoke of the need for a moral regeneration of the French that would emphasize authority and military preparedness. Austere as ever, a man of few words, Pétain gave to some the impression of great wisdom behind often simple statements. His reputation as the most humane of the World War I generals endeared him even to many socialists in the 1930s. His role in the unpreparedness of the French army for the onslaught of 1940 is still debated in France.

The Doumergue government fell late in 1934 without achieving significant political reform, but Pétain, who resigned with the government, emerged with enhanced popularity. Press campaigns depicted him as a possible Cincinnatus who could save France from the threefold problems of economic depression, the increasing threats from the fascist countries abroad, and parliamentary stagnation. The marshal made plain his distaste for any kind of coup against the constitution but also let his personal physician and close confident Dr. Bernard Ménétrel know that with the right men he might be ready to take power in France. Pétain wondered, however, whether there would be enough time. He was approaching 80. In 1938, the marshal made out his will in which he specified that he be buried at an ossuary at the Douaumont fort near Verdun, the site of his 1916 success. He was called again to service, however, in March 1939 as ambassador to Spain. Franco's forces were about to win the Civil War in progress there since 1936, and it was believed that the military prestige of Pétain might help wean **Francisco Franco** away from the Axis powers which had helped him win power.

The outbreak of World War II in September 1939 found Pétain in Spain, where he remained through the *drôle de guerre* or "phoney war," in which there was little fighting on the western front, until May 1940. On May 10, 1940, the Germans attacked through Belgium, outflanking the Maginot line. Within days, the French forces were in a state of collapse. Desperately trying to shore up his government and public morale, Premier Paul Reynaud named Pétain vice-premier on May 17. During what had become increasingly a rout, Pétain called for an armistice.

Although accounts of the 84-year-old marshal differ widely for this period, with some picturing him as deeply pessimistic, lethargic, even senile, and others seeing him as robust and alert, it appears that while his physical condition remained strong, his powers of intellectual concentration showed his years. In his biography, *Pétain, Hero or Traitor: The Untold Story*, Herbert R. Lottman notes that politicians gradually discovered Pétain's diminishing powers of concentration and made varying uses of this knowledge in succeeding years. The degree to which he was manipulated in the frenetic days of May and June 1940 by politicians, such as former Premier **Pierre Laval**, seeking their own advancement under the terms of an armistice, may never be precisely known.

Clearly, however, the old marshal was convinced that a continuation of the war would result in the physical ruin of France. An armistice, he believed, was urgently needed to keep the army intact as a force for order in the country—he worried about the possibility of revolutionary outbreak in Paris. Only a moral regeneration of France, turning toward her spiritual, agrarian, and martial roots, he argued, and away from the cosmopolitanism and materialism of the Republic, would save the country. He attributed the 1940 defeat to a failure of the French spirit and education in the interwar years. On June 17, Pétain was named premier. His maiden speech was essentially a request for an armistice. The next day, General de Gaulle, who refused to accept the finality of defeat, broadcast from London his first appeal calling for the French to defend their national honor and resist the German forces.

Vichy Government Aligns France with Germany

The armistice granted by the Germans left them in occupation of roughly the northern three-fifths of France, including Paris, and stipulated that France was to pay the costs of the war. It allowed, however, the maintenance of the French government, with theoretical control over domestic order in France, though in reality the Germans effectively ran the occupied zone. The French were allowed to keep their fleet, their one remaining major military asset, from falling into German hands. As the Germans consolidated their hold on northern France, Pétain's government moved to the spa resort of Vichy in the unoccupied zone. The government tried to reestablish itself in the south, as well as cope with the multiple problems of the military debacle, the severe economic dislocations, the German demands, and the flight of millions of refugees from the German invaders. Meanwhile, Laval and a group of political leaders at Vichy organized to restructure the government in an authoritarian manner that would enhance Pétain's powers and align France more closely with the victorious Axis powers. On July 10, the French Parliament (Senate and Chamber of Deputies combined) voted 569 to 80 to give full powers to Pétain to prepare the constitution for the French State. In what he called a "National Revolution," Pétain outlined the character of his new state: authoritarian, based on national *élites* rather than on either capitalist or socialist *internationals,* and oriented around the motto: "Work, Family, Fatherland."

From July 1940 through the liberation of France by Allied forces in the summer of 1944, Pétain remained in France as head of state. At the outset, he talked of four major themes: (1) a moral renovation; (2) a return to the soil, and a social order based on the peasantry; (3) a sort of corporate worker-employer social solidarity that would be neither capitalist nor socialist; and (4) the elimination of the "non-French" influences of Freemasons and Jews. A law of October 1940 barred Jews from public office, teaching, and the military command. Jews could not be officials of businesses receiving government funds. With limited exceptions, they were also barred from the press, film, theater, and the radio. After meeting with Hitler in the small town of Montoire in October 1940, Pétain ordered the French to follow him on the "path of collaboration." Politics during the four-year Vichy period were byzantine, which was ironic because Pétain had complained so much of the parliamentary intrigues of the Third Republic. Laval, who stood for close collaboration with the Germans, served as vice-premier until December 1940. Then, for reasons still debated today, he was fired by Pétain. Early in 1941, Admiral François Darlan succeeded to the vice-premiership, only to be replaced in April 1942, under German pressure, by Laval, who occupied the post through the end of the Vichy years. During Darlan's tenure, the Vichy cabinet included technocrats, who, despite the Pétainist "return to the soil" campaign, pushed industrial planning into the forefront of government discussion. Back in office in 1942, Laval used his new-found influence to write into the constitution that as head of the government he was responsible for all policy, subject only to the approval of Pétain.

In November 1942, the Allies landed in Algeria, then a French colony. Pétain ordered French forces to refrain from interfering with the Germans, who were deploying against the Allies in Tunisia, also a French colony at the time. Within six months, however, the Allies completed the conquest of the French Empire in North Africa. The Allied landings brought on the German occupation of the remainder of metropolitan France, and the French scuttled their fleet. Without the fleet and with the Germans now at Vichy, Pétain's government lost whatever independence it had previously possessed. Attached perhaps to the perquisites of power or the belief that he could still interpose himself between the French and the Germans and spare his fellow countrymen increased suffering under the occupation, or as a result of increasing senility at age 86, or a combination of all these factors, Pétain chose to stay on. The Vichy government encouraged, then forced, French laborers to go work in Germany, where the Nazis needed foreign labor for their war effort.

Pétain's humane reputation with respect to soldiers under his command had obvious limits as Vichy's police helped round up Resistants and thousands of French Jews for deportation to the German extermination camps. By 1944, his government was acting as a virtual proxy for the Germans. After the liberation of France, the Germans installed Pétain at the Sigmaringen castle on the Danube in Germany, but he refused to have anything to do with a French government in exile they set up there. With the final defeat of Germany in May 1945, he returned to France to face trial by a special High Court established by the new Provisional Government under General de Gaulle. In a highly charged courtroom atmosphere, Pétain defended his course of action from 1940 on, arguing that he had come to power legitimately, that he had interposed himself between the defeated French and their conquerors, and that his stance had fostered resistance against the Germans and the renaissance of France. Found guilty of collaboration with the enemy, however, he was sentenced to death. De Gaulle commuted the sentence to life imprisonment and had Pétain transferred to a military fortress at the Ile de Yeu, where he died at age 95 in 1951. Contrary to his wishes to be interred at Douaumont, he was buried, by government order, on the Ile de Yeu. Madame Pétain, who remained with her husband until his death, moved back to Paris where she died in 1962.

Since the end of the war, Pétain has been a symbol for former Vichy officials and their supporters, as well as an unreconstructed nostalgic political Right in France. In April 1950, Colonel Rémy, a leading Resistant and close supporter of de Gaulle, argued that de Gaulle himself had said privately that France in 1940 had needed two strings in her bow, represented by Pétain and de Gaulle. Others have argued that while de Gaulle carried the sword of France in 1940, Pétain was her shield, or that Laval, not Pétain, was the true collaborator. An association to defend the memory of Marshal Pétain and revise the High Court verdict has existed since his death. In 1973, supporters tried to remove Pétain's remains from the Ile de Yeu and transfer them to Douaumont, but they were caught and the coffin was reburied on the island.

Pétain's activities may have spared France an even worse fate during the occupation, but without him, the Vichy government, its collaboration, and its anti-Semitism would have been inconceivable. Hitler's policy during the occupation was to keep France pacified so that she could be exploited for the German war effort. Pétain lent his personal prestige to the effort. Many of those punished for collaboration after the war pointed to Pétain's lead after his meeting with Hitler at Montoire in October 1940. As Jean-Pierre Rioux notes, Pétain was a part of the "sinister rendezvous" of collaboration: the Montoire meetings with Hitler, the deportation of Jews, the fervent wishes for German victory, and the creation of the Militia, in 1943, as a governmental paramilitary organization to fight against the Resistance. To paraphrase General de Gaulle, had Marshal Pétain died in 1925, he would have been remembered as one of France's greatest heroes. His longevity soured his place in history.

SOURCES:

Ferro, Marc. *Pétain.* Fayard, 1987.

Gillouin, René. "Pétain," in André Bellesort, *et. al., France 1941, La Révolution Nationale Constructive, Un Bilan et un Programme.* Alsatia, 1941: pp. 63–83.

Jäckel, Eberhard. *Frankreich in Hitlers Europa: Die Deutsche Frankreichpolitik im zweiten Weltkrieg.* Deutsche Verlags-Anstalt, 1966.

Michel, Henri. *Pétain et le Régime de Vichy.* Presses Universitaires de France, 1978.

Noguères, Louis. *Le Véritable Procès du Maréchal Pétain.* Fayard, 1955.

Pétain, Philippe. *Discours aux Français, 17 juin 1940–20 aout 1944.* Edited by Jean-Claude Barbas. Albin Michel, 1989.

Rioux, Jean-Pierre. "Les duettistes de Vichy," in *Le Monde,* International Edition, May 2, 1987: p. 12.

FURTHER READING:

Gordon, Bertram M. *Collaborationism During the Second World War.* Cornell University Press, 1980.

Griffiths, Richard. *Pétain, A Biography of Marshal Philippe Pétain of Vichy.* Doubleday, 1972.

Lottman, Herbert R. *Pétain, Hero or Traitor: The Untold Story.* Morrow, 1985.

Marrus, Michael R., and Robert O. Paxton. *Vichy France and the Jews.* Basic Books, 1981.

Pédroncini, Guy. *Pétain, Général en Chef, 1917–1918.* Presses Universitaires de France, 1974.

Webster, Paul. *Pétain's Crime, The Full Story of French Collaboration in the Holocaust.* Macmillan, 1990.

Peter I, the Great

(1672–1725)

Tsar and emperor of Russia, who was the first ruler of a non-Western nation to appreciate the implications of the growing power of the West and who attempted to modernize his country to cope with it.

Name variations: (Russian) Piotr Alekseevich Romanov. Born in Moscow on May 30, 1672; died in St. Petersburg on January 28, 1725, the fifth ruler of the Romanov dynasty; son of Tsar Alexis Mikhailovich Romanov and Natalia Naryshkin; married: Eudoxia Lopukhin (a Russian princess), 1689 (marriage repudiated in 1703); married: Catherine Skavronsky (an illiterate Lithuanian peasant who had been his mistress for several years), 1712; children: (first marriage) two sons; (second marriage) 12; (only two daughters, Elizabeth and Anna, survived him).

Peter the Great and his sister Natalia were the children of Tsar Alexis Mikhailovich Romanov (1645–76) by his second marriage to Natalia Naryshkin. By his first wife, Maria Miloslavsky, however, Alexis still had four surviving children out of a total of 14: Theodore, John, Sophia, and Maria. Upon his death, the throne passed to Theodore, and the widowed Natalia moved to the nearby village of Preobrazhenskoye with her children. Theodore had no male heir, however, and when he died in 1682 the hostility between the families of Alexis's successive wives came to a head. The Miloslavskys wanted John, another son who suffered from poor health and bad eyesight and who appears to have been epileptic, to succeed his father; the Naryshkins, however, pressed for Peter, who, though only ten, was already a bright and promising youth. A massive revolt of the elite corps known as the *streltsy* (musketeers) led to the bloody slaughter of a number of Naryshkins and their supporters, an event that Peter witnessed and which could only have had a baleful effect on his character and development. The patriarch of the Russian Church then engineered an agreement that provided for John and Peter reigning jointly under the regency of Sophia.

"I have great bundles of grain but I have no mill and there is not enough water close by to build one. But there is water enough at a distance if only I shall have time to build a canal, but the length of my life is uncertain. Therefore, I build the mill first and have only given the order to build the canal, which will better force my successors to bring water [to put the mill to use].

PETER THE GREAT

Contributed by Robert H. Hewsen, Professor of History, Glassboro State College, Glassboro, New Jersey

As a result of her own intrigues, Sophia fell in 1689, however, and when John died in 1696, leaving his half-brother sole ruler, Peter's reign may be said to have begun.

It is often said that Peter's education was deliberately neglected by Sophia to dull his ability to rule. As a matter of fact, he received a good if traditional Orthodox upbringing. Heavily dominated by the Bible, it also included choir-singing, an activity that Peter enjoyed throughout his life. Playing at soldiering was his chief boyhood occupation at Preobrazhenskoye, where he built a fort and formed his own regiment from among his playmates, and where a chance discovery of an English boat nearby led to his lifelong preoccupation with the navy. About 1690, when he was still 18, Peter began to spend increasing amounts of time in the so-called "German" or foreign quarter, which he had to pass whenever he visited Moscow. This was a walled area adjoining the capital where lived the foreign specialists brought into Muscovy in increasing numbers all through the 17th century. Here, away from the stuffiness of the Muscovite court, Peter consorted freely with Western Europeans, learned Dutch and German, and was able to study technological advances; here also he could satisfy his tastes for mechanical contraptions, strong drink, and women, forging lasting links with technical experts, artisans and craftsmen which he clung to throughout his life.

He Embarks on Visits to the West

Peter began his reign by taking a direct part in the current Russian war against the Ottoman Turkish Empire, the goal of which was to secure a Russian port on the northern coast of the Black Sea. The war was a temporary success and for a time the Russians acquired Azov near modern Rostov-on-the-Don. Although victorious against the Turks, the war had made Peter aware of the deficiencies of the Russian army and this led him to embark upon a personal visit to the West in order to learn for himself whatever was necessary to bring Russia to the level that her size and potential might warrant. Despite the obvious dangers in leaving his own country, Peter set out incognito on his 250-man "Grand Embassy" that was to spend more than a year abroad. Forced to return at the outset to put down a revolt of the *streltsy* in which Sophia was deeply involved, Peter clapped his half-sister into a convent and, undaunted, set out once again. Traveling through various German states, he settled in Holland for four months mastering carpentry and shipbuilding. From Holland, he went to England, where he lived for several weeks at Dept-

ford, south of London, receiving a doctorate from Oxford University, visiting Windsor Castle and Hampton Court Palace, and seeing as much as he could of every novelty that the country had to offer. Upon his return to Russia, he brought with him hundreds of technicians and other specialists of every European nationality. Bullying his nobles into shaving their beards and adopting Western dress, he forced them to allow their women out of their traditional seclusion and otherwise Europeanized court life. Seriously outmatched at the Battle of Narva (1700) at the opening of his war against Sweden (then under the rule of the dynamic wunderkind Charles XII), wherein the largest nation in Europe was defeated by one of the smallest, Peter began his first reforms in earnest; in 1702, he extended an open invitation to Western technicians, soldiers, artisans, and craftsmen to

CHRONOLOGY

1672	Peter the Great born
1682	Became co-tsar with his half-brother John *(Ivan)* V
1696	John V died; Peter became sole ruler; Turks defeated at Azov
1699	Peter's reforms began
1700–21	Great Northern War with Sweden
1700	Russians defeated by Swedes at Battle of Narva
1703	St. Petersburg founded
1708	Swedes invaded Russia; Russia defeated Swedes at Battle of Lesnaia
1709	Swedes defeated by Russians at Battle of Poltava
1710–11	Second Turkish war; Russians defeated by Turks
1711	Senate and ten colleges established
1714	Russian navy defeated Swedes at Hangö
1715	First Naval Academy opened
1717	Government administrative "colleges" opened
1721	Peace of Nystadt ended Northern War; Peter abolished the patriarchate of the Russian Orthodox Church; took title "emperor" and "the Great"
1722	Peter's Persian war began; Table of Ranks established; new law of succession
1724	Peter crowned Catherine "empress"
1725	Peter the Great died

enter Russia at will and began sending talented sons of the Russian nobility to study abroad.

Peter's reforms were accomplished in a haphazard manner with no overall plan behind them. On the contrary, he had but one specific goal: to make his country a great power commensurate with its size and potential so that it might forever be safe from foreign invasion or domination. But to achieve this goal, Peter found that certain prerequisites were necessary. To make Russia a great power, Peter needed a modern army, but to create a modern army he needed vast sums of money; to get more money meant the reform of the system of taxation; to reform this system required an improved administrative system; a modern administration required educated administrators capable of managing public affairs in a modern way; to provide such people required a European educational system, and, since there were few teachers in Russia and no means of training any in the skills that needed to be taught, foreign teachers had to be brought in, which, naturally, meant further westernization. A better army also required an industrial base to make Russia independent of imports of foreign arms, while the development of industry, though generating additional taxes, required capital to get it started. Peter's problems were monumental, and it is to his everlasting credit that he was able to accomplish anywhere near as much as he did. Not the least of his problems were the incredible backwardness of the Muscovite state that he had inherited, the sheer weight of inertia that pervaded the country, the lack of qualified people who understood his vision, and the enormous opposition that met him at every turn.

When Peter came to the throne, the Russian army consisted of some 150,000 men badly trained, poorly equipped, and poorly disciplined. The core of the army was a medieval feudal cavalry, long in decay, and the *streltsy*, a Western-style elite corps very inferior to its Western counterparts. When he returned from his first trip abroad, Peter reorganized the army along Western lines, abolishing the *streltsy* and turning his boyhood regiment into the new elite "Preobrazhensky Guard" consisting of two battalions totaling 4,000 men. The bulk of the new army, however, consisted of a force of 200,000 commoners based on a periodic conscription that took one out of every 20 men in the country and from which only the clergy and merchants were excused (the latter paying 200 rubles for their exemption). Every conscript was required to serve from age 15 to disability, the older men being used to garrison the towns. In addition, Peter added a force of 100,000 irregular troops consisting of Cossacks and Mongol nomads. A particular passion of

Peter was the navy, which he personally created for the first time in Russian history. By the time of his death, Peter's Baltic Fleet consisted of 800 ships served by 20,000 men, though a decade later, as a result of neglect, only about 15 of the larger ships were still in service. All of these military undertakings cost money and lives. The former Peter had to deal with; the latter counted but little in Russia.

By 1701, the annual expenses of the army amounted to 2 million rubles out of an annual state income of 3 million; by 1724, 4 million was being spent annually on the army alone and another million on the navy. Between 1701 and 1708, expenses amounted to 80% of the annual budget. To pay for all of this, Peter abolished the earlier tax on each household and instituted a "soul" or head tax, levying additional taxes on inns, bath houses, mills, fishing operations, beehives, beards, coffins, stamps, and non-Christian marriages. An enormous bureaucracy encumbered with miles of "red tape" was established to supervise the administration of these taxes, a bureaucracy that grew without cease, survived the Revolution of 1917, and continued to grow thereafter. The government also established certain trade monopolies whose profits poured solely into the imperial coffers: salt, tobacco, tar, fats, fish oil, and caviar.

Major economic reforms were found to be necessary to increase the tax yield through increasing prosperity. The concept of mercantilism was very important to Peter, and he worked hard to get Russia into a position where she exported more than she took in. Entrepreneurs of every kind received encouragement. Armenians, for example, were granted religious freedom to encourage them to settle in southern Russia where they established both viticulture (the wine industry) and sericulture (the silk industry) in the tsar's domains. Horse-breeding, textiles, mining, and tobacco raising also were encouraged, as was the building of roads and canals. All such undertakings were hindered, however, by the lack of labor, the masses being tied to the land as serfs on the great estates of the Crown, the Church, and the nobility. Peter thus had to pry people from this frozen layer by allowing industrialists to own serfs without land. Such industrial serfs were quickly indistinguishable from common slaves and Peter solved this embarrassment by ordering the term for slave (*kholop*) stricken from the law books. By 1725, Russia was exporting 2.5 million rubles worth of goods and importing only 1.5 million—less than Peter had hoped for but a good beginning.

To manage these and other reforms, Peter soon realized that his government required a total overhauling of its administrative machinery.

Drawing upon Sweden as his model—while overlooking completely that Russia was not Sweden—Peter introduced the collegial system whereby the government machinery was made up of committees called "colleges" that answered collectively to the tsar. To supervise these colleges and to run Russia while he was away traveling or at war, Peter established an appointed senate. Although the colleges were abandoned a century later for the more modern system of ministries, the senate lasted until 1917 by which time its function had narrowed to that of a quasi-supreme court. Both the senate and the colleges were weakened in Peter's time by the ignorance, incompetence, and corruption of their members, but they were a considerable improvement over the chaotic Muscovite system of 40 departments with ill-defined and overlapping jurisdictions that had obtained before his reign.

Peter Restructures Russian Society

In Peter's time, Russian society consisted of (1) titled nobles, among whom the various levels and the various ethnic elements tended to become fused into one self-seeking, self-serving class: the Russian nobility; (2) non-noble, untitled landowners, the gentry, who swelled the government service; (3) the clergy; (4) merchants (chiefly foreigners); (5) serfs, and (6) slaves, the last two of which, as we have seen, fused into one downtrodden underclass. Upon this structure Peter now imposed his table of ranks, a system of three pyramids—the civil service, the military and the Church—consisting of 14 ranks each. All Russians were expected to serve in one of the ranks except the serfs, the clergy, the doctors, traders, bankers, artisans and craftsmen, and the merchant class. Through this system, which, with modifications, remained in force until 1917, the nobility and gentry were converted into a managerial class in which all were exposed to three years of compulsory education, all had to start at the bottom, and from all of whom 25 years of service were required. Anyone who reached the eighth rank could become a noble; at the attainment of rank six this nobiliary passed to one's heirs. Peter also introduced Western nobiliary titles and took the unprecedented step of actually creating new princes. Foreigners were given complete freedom to trade in the Empire and could serve the state if they wanted to, receiving higher pay than Russians. In return, they received freedom of worship and the right to special courts, a concession borrowed from Ottoman Turkey. As always, the peasantry bore the brunt of the new order. After 1700, the nobles began to abrogate the traditional rights of their serfs, and the government, needing the nobles' support, did nothing to stop this. Serfs were sold without the land, families were broken up in the process, and the status of the common people soon became no better than that of the contemporary African slaves in the colonial American south.

Ivan III (1462–1505) had warred to unify Russia and to break free of the Mongol yoke; **Ivan IV** (1533–84) had conquered the Mongols and warred unsuccessfully to acquire a warm water port. In the 17th century, Russia expanded westward at the expense of Poland, acquiring the Ukraine in the process, and then expanded to the Pacific and to the frontiers of China. Following upon all this, Peter's foreign policy may be reduced to three simple goals: (1) reaching the Baltic Sea; (2) reaching the Black Sea; and (3) expanding southward at the expense of Iran. Ultimately, only the first of these thrusts was successful, though it took the 21-year Swedish or Northern War to complete it. Much territory was then seized from Iran but at a horrible cost in human life, and Peter had to abandon these conquests almost as soon as they had been acquired. Azov, too, was lost to Turkey and a successful thrust to the Black Sea was left for **Catherine the Great** (1762–96) to achieve.

Ever in search of competent men to share his vision and execute his will, Peter displayed none of the traditional Muscovite bigotry towards foreigners and individuals not of the Orthodox Faith. He appointed a Jew, Kafirov, to be Russia's first foreign minister because of his skills in language, and welcomed such foreigners as the Swiss Lefort, the Scot Bruce, the Englishman Perry, the Armenian Israel Ori, who was Russia's first ambassador to Iran, and an Ethiopian who became the ancestor of the poet Pushkin. His chief collaborator, however, was the rascally Alexander Menshikov, a wily Russian adventurer of humble origin, who lined his pockets in Peter's service but who remained his confident and drinking partner, serving him faithfully to the end of Peter's life.

Peter's foreign policy also included an elaborate matchmaking program. In the past, Russian rulers had married only Russians and no European house was willing either to take a Russian bride or to send its daughters to marry a Romanov groom, the dynasty being considered upstart, the country barbarous, the climate appalling, and the language impossible. Above all, the Romanovs were Greek Orthodox, and Catholics and Protestant rulers alike were reluctant to agree to their daughters' changing their faith. Peter's astonishing exploits, however, made the Romanovs seem more respectable and the other problems in regard to matrimonial alliances less onerous.

Although Peter could never get the great houses of Europe to take a Romanov bride, failing miserably in his attempts to marry his daughter Elizabeth to Louis XV, he did succeed in marrying his niece, the future Empress Anne (1730–40), daughter of John V, to the Duke of Courland; her sister Catherine to the Duke of Mecklenburg, their infant grandson reigning briefly as John VI (1740–41), and his own daughter Anne to the Duke of Holstein, their son reigning briefly as Peter III (1761–62). Peter was equally unsuccessful in securing a brilliant match for his son, Alexis, having to be content with Charlotte, a princess of the German house of Brunswick-Wolfenbüttle, who died in childbirth.

He Crowns Catherine as Empress

As a youth of 21, Peter had dutifully married a boyar princess, Eudoxia Lopukhin, and duly sired two sons, but he rarely lived with his wife and took a number of mistresses. In time, he settled down with an illiterate Lithuanian peasant girl of dubious reputation who had previously been Menshikov's mistress and by whom Peter eventually had 12 children. Hard-drinking but good-natured, Catherine was reputed to have been the only one who could calm Peter during his ferocious and unpredictable rages, which could often be dangerous to those around him. In 1712, Peter scandalized his court and startled Europe by marrying Catherine. In 1721, he crowned her his empress, and after his death she was recognized as his heir. In time, their daughter would rule as Empress Elizabeth (1741–61).

Peter's original heir was Alexis, his elder son by Eudoxia. Typically, Peter ignored the boy, leaving him to be raised by his old-fashioned mother and her conservative cronies until he was old enough to be of use to him. By then, however, Alexis had become a weakling and, under Peter's direct tutelage, came to manifest all of his father's vices and none of his virtues. A drunkard and a wastrel, he became the locus where the old guard gathered and around whom the general opposition to Peter began to coalesce. Disgusted with Alexis and discovering him at the center of a plot, Peter subjected him to torture after which he shortly died. Peter then intended the throne to pass to Alexis's son, Peter, but his throne passed to his second wife and Peter II did not succeed him until 1730.

Reputed to have been 6' 7" in height, Peter the Great is believed to have suffered from a mild form of a glandular disorder known to cause gigantism. Highly intelligent and physically strong, but erratic, hot-tempered and given to drinking and debauchery, he was devoted to his duty as he saw it. Dynamic, ambitious, ruthless, brutal, hard driving, hard working, and concerned above all for the aggrandizement of his country, Peter brooked no opposition. He was free-thinking in religious matters, uncomfortable with ceremony and exceedingly down-to-earth. In keeping with his character, Peter died at 52 from the effects of having dived into icy waters to save a boatload of common sailors who were about to capsize.

Peter inherited the weak, backward, decaying, essentially Asiatic state of Muscovy on the fringes of Europe and left it the Russian Empire, one of the great European powers whose articulate upper classes were fully participating in Western civilization. For all this, however, his achievement was not quite as world-shaking as it is often made out. First of all, it is a misunderstanding to say that he wanted to "westernize" Russia. Had he sought westernization for its own sake, for example, he would surely have abandoned the Cyrillic alphabet and reformed the Russian Church. Had Ottoman Turkey or China been more advanced than Western Europe there is little doubt that Peter would have drawn his models from them. Second, a considerable amount of westernization of Russia had been going on throughout the 17th century. Some nobles were wearing Western dress long before Peter, and his half-sister Sophia was well educated for her time. Third, many of his reforms were only on paper and many died on the vine. Fourth, most of them were ad hoc reforms based not on any philosophy, conviction, or prior plan but simply introduced as the need arose.

Peter did nothing to alter the traditional role of the ruler of Russia. The tsar answered to God alone; his ministers, and indeed his entire administration, were simply incarnations of the tsar's will. Peter made and unmade laws as he saw fit; outside authority, apart from his delegation, simply did not exist. The Russian church was placed squarely under the tsar's thumb. Peter allowed the patriarchate to remain vacant after 1700 and, in 1721, abolished it, placing the church under the governance of a council of bishops called the "holy synod" headed by a layman of his own choosing. There was no cabinet, each minister or college answering directly to the tsar; no consultation of the people was ever undertaken, and there was not even the pretense of an advisory body let alone a parliament or legislature of any kind. Peter thus introduced the curious idea that one could establish a modern state on the order of England or France while continuing to rule it as if it were Turkey, China, or Iran, a naive notion that the tsars were unable to relinquish until the very end.

Nevertheless, it must be said that Peter the Great, with little support and considerable opposition, dragged Russia forcibly into the 18th century, and there has never been a time since his day that affairs in Europe could be conducted without the wishes and policies of Russia being taken into consideration. The true depth of the westernization and modernization of Russia, however, was only achieved after his death when, for a variety of reasons, one ruler, either Western (Peter III, Catherine the Great), pro-Western (Elizabeth), or Western-oriented (Anne) followed another until the old Muscovite state was left too far in the past to be remembered and there was no turning back from the road upon which Peter had set his homeland.

SOURCES:

Kliuchevskii, V. O. *Peter the Great.* Random House, 1963.

Schuyler, E. *Peter the Great: Emperor of Russia.* Scribner, 1884.

Vernadsky, G., et al., eds. *A Source Book for Russian History.* 3 vols. Yale University Press, 1972.

Waliszewski, Kazimierz. *Peter the Great.* D. Appleton, 1897.

FURTHER READING:

Anderson, M. S. *Peter the Great.* Thames & Hudson, 1978.

Massie, Robert. *Peter the Great: His Life and Work.* Knopf, 1980.

Sumner, B. H. *Peter the Great and the Emergence of Russia.* English Universities Press, 1950, Collier, 1962.

Troyat, H. *Peter the Great.* Dutton, 1987.

Philip II
(1527–1598)

King of Spain, who ruled one of the largest empires of all time, including England, Portugal, the Netherlands; and territories in the Caribbean, the Philippines, Italy, Germany, Africa, and South, Central and North America.

Name variation: Phillip the Prudent. Born May 21, 1527, in Valladolid, Spain; died September 13, 1598, at the Escorial in Spain; son of Charles V (Habsburg Holy Roman Emperor and king of Spain) and Isabella of Portugal; married: Maria of Portugal; married: Mary Tudor, queen of England; married: Elizabeth of Valois; married: Anne of Austria; children: (first marriage) Don Carlos; (third marriage) Isabella Clara Eugenia and Catherine Micaela; (fourth marriage) Philip III. Descendants: Louis XIV, king of France. Predecessor: Charles V. Successor: Philip III.

Few monarchs throughout recorded history have endured the slings and arrows of scholars as regularly as Philip II of Spain. Indeed few, if any, historical personages have been as maligned and misunderstood as the "Prudent King." Even today, Philip remains a figure shrouded in mystery, clothed in conjecture, his innermost thoughts and emotions wrapped in the utmost obscurity.

He was born in 1527, the son of one of the greatest monarchs in all of Western civilization, **Charles V.** Although Philip's reign extended for over 40 years, in many ways he never outlasted the enormous shadow of his father. If it can be argued—and it has—that Spain achieved her finest hours during the reign of the great emperor, it can also be said that Spain fell from its highest peak in 1588 during the reign of Philip the Prudent.

Yet far too much has been made of the loss of the Spanish Armada. Undeniably it was great and tragic. But in some ways it was a defeat that revealed the extent of Spain's power as much as her weakness. Philip attempted what no other 16th-century ruler was even capable of considering; according to many historians, he came excruciat-

"He is by any standards one of the most remarkable men ever to sit on a throne in Europe. He created a pattern of government not only in Spain and his European possessions, but also in Spanish America and the Philippines, a pattern that was to last for three hundred years after his death."

J. H. PLUMB

Contributed by Glenn Feldman, Ph.D. candidate in History, Auburn University, Auburn, Alabama

ingly close to realizing his goal. "If," as Geoffrey Parker notes, "on that Monday morning, 7 August 1588, the Army of Flanders had been marching toward London, everyone today would regard the Invincible Armada … as Philip II's masterpiece." But it was not to be. As a result, Philip's critical reign, and Spanish history in general, has been eclipsed by an event that has grown with each retelling. Instead we have been left with only a perverted portrait of the life and times of the Prudent King. Historians have "portrayed him," writes Parker:

> as a dedicated fanatic, sitting like a black spider in his bleak cell at the Escorial, working endlessly day and night to crush the Dutch, to reimpose Catholicism on England, to convert or destroy the Amerindians, and to monopolize all the riches—gold, silver, spices—of the known world. For these ends he was prepared to imprison his own children, to assassinate opponents, and to rack and torture all who thwarted him.

Somewhere between the extremes of the "Black Legend" and a sympathetic portrait of a kind and misunderstood introvert lies a man; intelligent, meticulous, industrious, yet still a man, susceptible to all the whims, desires, and shortcomings of even lesser men.

Philip grew up for the first eight years of his life in his mother's household. He enjoyed a relatively unencumbered lifestyle and still could not read or write by the age of seven—a development which concerned his father tremendously. From 1535 on, Philip resided in his own household, yet he was placed under the watchful eye of **Don Juan de Zuniga.** Although his mother died when he was 12, and his father was often absent for long stretches of time, the young Philip never wanted for company. His personal household numbered over 190 persons, including eight chaplains and 51 pages, the sons of the most illustrious noblemen in Spain. Later in life, Philip often complained of wanting to be left by himself; solitude was one of his greatest pleasures.

Critics have often charged that Philip was "too Spanish," and he was incontrovertibly "a Spaniard among Spaniards." Zuniga taught him to be proud, self-disciplined, and regal but unlike most of his countrymen, to hide his emotions. He learned to read and understand French, Italian, and Portuguese. Yet he seldom spoke any language but Spanish in public.

The young prince loved nature, books, music, and art. As he grew older, he developed an

CHRONOLOGY

1556	Inherited the kingdom of Spain and all of her vast territories
1557	Won a landmark victory over French forces at St. Quentin
1559	Peace of Cateau-Cambresis
1566	Dutch Revolt began; not to end until 1648
1567	Sent the Duke of Alva to crush the rebellion in the Netherlands
1571	Won an epic naval victory over the Ottoman Turks at Lepanto
1580	Defeated Portugal; annexed their empire for Spain; became the Portuguese monarch
1584	The Escorial completed after 20 years of construction
1585	Duke of Parma completed the pacification of the southern provinces of the Netherlands (modern Belgium)
1588	Lost the "Invincible" Spanish Armada
1589–98	Intervened openly in the French Wars of Religion

insatiable appetite for hunting. To prevent the depletion of the royal preserve of wolves, bears, deer, and rabbits, Charles V was forced to restrain Philip's crossbow-hunting to a weekly maximum. Philip also spent much time in prayer, tapestry weaving, and jousting.

His health was never particularly good. Throughout his lifetime, Philip remained pale and frail looking, yet still handsome. At the age of eight, he contracted salmonella poisoning and was incapacitated for two months. Later in life, he suffered chronically from asthma, arthritis, gallstones, malaria, and other assorted ailments.

Tutors schooled Philip in mathematics, history, geography, science, architecture, Latin, and Greek. He "received a wide and enlightened education," and developed an encyclopedic knowledge that was often betrayed by the copious notes he scribbled as king. He adored books and collected over 14,000 volumes, including those by such leading humanist scholars as Erasmus, Pico, Ficino, and Reuchlin. Charles V took great interest in his upbringing, and near the occasion of Philip's first wedding at 16 to **Maria of Portugal,** the emperor gave his son the following advice:

> Transact business with many, and do not bind yourself to or become dependent upon any indi-

vidual, because although it may save time, it does no good.... [N]ever trust anyone, never show your emotions, always have fixed hours to appear regularly in public, be devout and God-fearing at all times, be just in all things.

Philip was nothing if not dutiful. He took his illustrious father's advice to heart in a way that even the great "globe-trotting warrior" could never have foreseen.

From 1548 to 1551, Philip took a "Grand Tour" throughout his father's Spanish, Italian, Dutch, and German lands. By 1551, Charles had arranged for his 24-year-old son to learn how to rule by engaging often and actively in the affairs of state. To this end, he sought the prince's counsel on issues major and minor, and often the pair made decisions together. In January 1556, Charles abdicated most of his vast possessions to his son. The title of Holy Roman Emperor and the ancient Habsburg ancestral estates reverted to Philip's uncle, Ferdinand I. Two years later, as he died clutching a crucifix, Charles finally relinquished practical power to Philip.

Philip Reigns as King of Spain

Philip's reign began auspiciously. He concluded the fourth and last Habsburg-Valois War by decisively defeating the French at St. Quentin in 1557, and at Gravelines the following year. The 1559 Treaty of Cateau-Cambresis firmly cemented Spanish hegemony ("dominance") in Italy—an issue that had occupied the two dynasties for over half of a century.

Philip II's reign was characterized chiefly by three elements: its long duration; an intricate and at times ponderously slow administration; and Spain's absolute preponderance in Europe and the world. Global Spanish preeminence had begun in 1492 with the joining of the crowns of Aragon and Castile, and the epic voyage of Columbus to the New World. In spite of monumental victories, and equally spectacular defeats, Spain did not pass on the mantle of supremacy until 1659. From 1492, Spain's famed infantry gained an awesome reputation, never losing a pitched battle for 150 years.

The bureaucracy involved in administering an empire as vast as Spain's can only be described as overwhelming. To this already oppressive base was added the complication that Philip insisted that every decision, trivial or momentous, be made personally and privately by himself. Pathologically suspicious, meticulous to a fault, Philip slowed down an already laborious process to a crawl at times by this desire. One veteran bureaucrat complained that "decisions are taken so slowly that even a cripple could keep up with them." Still, Philip "was indefatigable: he could work at all times and in all places," and often did. He even took dispatches and a portable desk with him to the country, to his beloved gardens at the palaces of Aranjuez and Casa de Campo, and on board ships. The Prudent King absolutely detested being forced to make a decision "on the spur of the moment," or in front of people. He preferred to work alone, or with one trusted secretary, in the dark elegance of his monastery-palace on the slopes of the Sierra de Guadaramma, the Escorial. On one occasion, the king waded his way through an unheard of 400 documents in a single day—reading, signing, and making his customary notes in the margins.

For most of the first two decades of Philip's reign, the Ottoman Empire proved the most serious threat to Spanish world power. Yet the Spanish colossus never had the luxury of opposing only one of its foes at a time. Charles V had left Philip the legacy of a war begun in 1551 with the powerful Muslim Turks. In 1560, the Spanish attempted unsuccessfully to wrench Tripoli from the Turks. Still in 1563 and 1565, Philip's troops managed to heroically repulse Turkish attacks on Oran and Malta, the stronghold of the Knights of St. John. But all accounts were not settled until 1571, when Philip's ambitious, illegitimate, half-brother—**Don John of Austria**—led a combined Catholic Armada over the Turks in the epic naval battle of Lepanto. The Spaniards took 127 Ottoman ships and thousands of soldiers and seamen, and effectively scotched the Turkish threat to Spain's rich possessions in Italy and along the Mediterranean.

Duke of Alva Crushes Revolt

Meanwhile, simmering religious animosities and Philip's dislike of local privileges led to the Revolt of the Netherlands in 1566. Though the revolt did not end until 1648 with Dutch independence, it was marked primarily by Spanish military victories during Philip's reign. Following religious riots, which featured violence and the smashing of the statues of Catholic saints, Philip sent the duke of Alva to crush the revolt in 1567. Alva initiated a repressive regime seldom matched in the annals of history. He combined military genius and victories with a grotesque form of terrorism. After arresting the counts of Egmont and van Hoorne, and instituting the Council of Troubles, Alva had the pair of rebel leaders summarily executed along with perhaps 12,000 other rebels. Some notable leaders fled to sanctuary in Germany; one of the most important was **William of Orange,** the spiritual leader of the rebellion. Alva's repression continued unchecked though, and by 1573 Philip had seen enough. He recalled Alva and replaced him with Don Luis de Requesens, and in 1577 with Don John.

In 1568, at the height of his Dutch troubles, Philip experienced several other serious misfortunes. He lost his third, and most beloved wife, Elizabeth of Valois, as she was delivering a baby daughter. The Moriscos, converted Moors, revolted in Granada and had to be forcibly restrained. His only son Don Carlos clearly demonstrated a profound insanity and was locked away in a tower. It was Don Carlos who had thrown a page out the window who crossed him; it was Don Carlos who had attacked his father's ministers with a knife, even the duke of Alva; it was Don Carlos who had made a shoemaker eat a pair of boots because they were too tight. Don Carlos went on a series of hunger strikes and died later that year.

In 1578, the Dutch troubles worsened when Philip approved the assassination of Juan de Escobedo, Don John's dangerous and ambitious secretary. Two years later, Philip issued a royal proclamation condemning William of Orange as an outlaw and the main source of the unrest in the Netherlands. The king's announcement also put a price on Orange's head of 25,000 ducats. In "an equally vicious and groundless onslaught upon Philip," Orange answered with his infamous *Apologie.* Philip blamed "this wicked hipocrite... (who) by his sinister practices, devises and crafts... has bin the head, authour and promoter of these troubles." He branded Orange the "publick plague of Christendome," and pledged a reward of "good land or readie money" for the deliverance of Orange "unto us quicke or dead." Orange responded with "an elegant piece of propaganda" that accused Philip of incest, adultery, the murder of his son and Elizabeth of Valois, and with "mischiefs, calamities, murthers, slaughters, cruelties, barbarousnesse, rage and abhominable enterprises."

Philip was convinced, however, that God had granted him a special commission to defend the Catholic faith, and expected him to do just that. Indeed, it seemed to many Europeans that "God had turned into a Spaniard" by 1584. An assassin killed William of Orange in his home on the Delft, and the Netherlands' ineffectual French protector, the duke of Anjou, died within a month. In 1585, the talented **Alessandro Farnese,** the duke of Parma, eclipsed the military skill of even the bloody Alva when he captured the great walled town of Antwerp. The successful siege capped a five-year offensive which netted over 30 rebel Dutch towns, and effectively kept the southern provinces of the Netherlands Spanish and Catholic until 1714.

Meanwhile in 1580, Philip had laid claim to the throne of Portugal. Forced to fight for what he considered to be his hereditary rights, he had sent in the redoubtable Alva with 22,000 troops. The old and brutal duke was again successful, and the vast dominions of Portugal fell into Philip's hands. To cap matters, Philip's navy, under the talented Marquis de Santa Cruz, smashed a combined Anglo-French force off of the Azores in 1582 and 1583. In the New World, the Prudent King accomplished the "taming of America" by subduing various rival Native American groups—to some, his most impressive achievement.

Spanish Armada Goes Down to Defeat

On the verge of regaining the northern provinces of the Netherlands, Philip's attention was diverted by open war with England. Queen **Elizabeth I,** concerned with the inexorable Catholic advance in the Low Countries, joined hands with the Dutch rebels openly in 1585. This action led to the loss of the "Invincible" Armada, a story which has been told hundreds of times. The powerful armada, led by a brave and illustrious land general due to the untimely death of Santa Cruz, numbered 130 ships and 30,000 men. Yet it failed to make its appointed rendezvous with Parma's forces off the coast of Flanders in the summer of 1588. The English and Dutch cleverly employed fireships, long-range cannon-fire, and smaller, swifter ships to break the Spanish formation. Then a "Great Protestant Wind" appeared to scatter the once-proud fleet, and only about half of the ships finally limped home. Philip's public demeanor was philosophical, but in private he was "shocked that God had allowed such a thing."

Still Philip had come dangerously close to turning England into a Spanish province. In 1614, Sir **Walter Raleigh** wrote that the English were "of no such force to encounter an Armie like unto that wherewith it was intended that the prince of Parma should have landed in England." Philip revealed the incredible strength of the Spanish Empire by sending even larger armadas into the English Channel in 1596 and 1597, only to have them also scattered by storms. Noted historian Geoffrey Parker observed that:

> In spite of the defeat of the Armada, Philip II was, and appeared to be, the most powerful mor-

tal in Christendom, if not the world.... The lines written by Shakespeare... applied to the King of Spain. "Why man, he doth bestride the narrow world Like a Colossus, and we petty men Walk under his huge legs."

In 1588, France also presented a problem for Philip. Since the death of Henry III's younger brother, the duke of Anjour, in 1584, the Valois line had threatened to become extinct. Two rival Bourbon claimants for the throne, Henry of Navarre and Cardinal Charles of Bourbon, jockeyed for position. Navarre clearly had the stronger claim. But the Catholic League, led by Henry, duke of Guise, and his brother, openly opposed Navarre because he was a Protestant. By the Treaty of Joinville in December 1584, Philip II agreed to aid the Guise with 150,000 florins per month. So began the Spanish financial aid to France's Catholic League that reached the outlandish sum of 91 million florins. Events in France unfolded in rapid order. In 1585, the Guise were murdered. When Navarre arrested his uncle, Cardinal Charles, and forced the latter to swear allegiance to him, a Protestant-Catholic civil war erupted in France. And on August 11, 1589, a Catholic fanatic assassinated King Henry III.

Throughout the tumult in France, the Prudent King exhibited restraint. After two military victories by Navarre in 1589, Philip decided to hold his hand no longer. Accordingly in April 1590, he ordered Alessandro Farnese to invade France.

For two years, Farnese did the impossible: defeated the talented Navarre twice and held the line against the Dutch rebels despite his long absences. Aragon revolted in 1591. Late in 1592, Farnese breathed his last. And the following year, Navarre cleverly adopted the Catholic religion. Although Philip held on until 1598, France was no longer so divided. Navarre managed to consolidate his hold over the country and become King **Henry IV**. England too escaped the full wrath of imperial Spain. Although English intervention in the Dutch Revolt had proved a costly embarrassment, circumstances constantly prevented Philip from landing his matchless armies on English soil. While England was unable to inflict any serious damage on the Spanish giant, she elusively remained Protestant and free. Though England and France eventually escaped Philip II, he was able to die with the knowledge that he had preserved the bulk of his fantastic inheritance in the face of tremendous odds. On September 13, 1598, also clutching a crucifix, Philip II died at the Escorial.

SOURCES:

Parker, Geoffrey. *Philip II*. Little, Brown, 1978.
———. *Spain and The Netherlands, 1559–1659*. Enslow Publishers.
Wansink, H., ed. *The Apologie of Prince William of Orange Against The Proclamation of the King of Spaine*. E. J. Brill, 1969.

FURTHER READING:

Merriman, Roger B. *The Rise of the Spanish Empire in the Old World and the New: Volume IV, Philip the Prudent*. Macmillan, 1934.
Pierson, Peter. *Philip II of Spain*. Thames & Hudson, 1975.

Philip II Augustus

(1165–1223)

King of France and victor at the Battle of Bouvines, whose leadership in conquest, diplomacy, and administration significantly increased the power of the French monarchy.

"Not only did his celebrated conquests enrich the king with lands far more extensive than those possessed by any other baron in France, but his accompanying governmental innovations enabled the monarchy to exploit these resources and eventually to dominate both the kingdom and western Europe by the close of the thirteenth century."

JOHN W. BALDWIN

The first contribution that Philip II made to the French monarchy and the history of France was his birth. For six generations, from the accession of Hugh Capet in 987, the Capetian dynasty had asserted royal power in France largely because of the unbroken and undisputed succession of male heirs. After two wives and the birth of several daughters to King Louis VII, the male inheritance of Capetian kings seemed to be in doubt. The great rejoicing and celebration that accompanied Philip's birth by Louis VII's third wife, Adela of Champagne, in 1165, expressed the promise that the Capetian monarchs would continue to rule France.

Although it could not have been anticipated in 1165, Philip not only continued the Capetian dynasty but also became one of the most important kings in the development of the French monarchy. During his reign, he quadrupled the territory that the French kings controlled directly, mostly at the expense of the English rulers. His innovations in governmental administration effectively consolidated these territorial gains to enhance royal power. Thus by the end of Philip's reign, the geographical and political concept of a French nation

Name variations: Philip II, Philippe Auguste (French). Born August 21, 1165, at Paris; died July 14, 1223, at Mantes; son of Louis VII (king of France) and Adela of Champagne (his third wife); married: Isabella of Hainaut, 1180 (died 1189); married: Ingeborg of Denmark, 1193 (divorced 1193); married: Agnes of Meran, 1196 (died 1201); reinstated marriage: Ingeborg of Denmark, 1213 (died 1223); children: (by Isabella of Hainaut) Louis VIII; (by Agnes of Meran) Philip Hurepel, Marie; (illegitimate) Pierre Charlot. Descendants: the Capetian dynasty until the end of the lineage in 1328, including Louis VIII (1223–26); Louis IX (Saint Louis; 1226–70); Philip the Fair (1285–1314). Predecessor: Louis VII (1137–80). Successor: Louis VIII (1223–26).

Contributed by Karen Gould, Consultant in Medieval and Renaissance Manuscripts, Austin, Texas

had begun to emerge. The title "Augustus" which a contemporary chronicler bestowed on Philip was merited by both his August birthdate and, more important, his crucial role in augmenting the French realm.

As with most medieval figures, little specific information is known about Philip's childhood. He probably received some education from a cleric who taught him the liberal arts of reading and writing based on the Latin of the Bible and both Latin and vernacular histories relating the lineage and deeds of French kings. The development of his administration indicates that he also must have learned rudimentary mathematics, for he had some awareness of how to maximize the economic situation of the French crown and realm. The majority of his education, however, was probably devoted to training for medieval knighthood which required abilities in horsemanship, military prowess, and hunting.

Philip's formal education was cut short at 14 when his aging father Louis VII decided to have his son crowned and joined with him as ruler. Scheduled to take place in August 1179, the coronation ceremony had to be postponed, however, when Philip became seriously ill after a hunting mishap. Fearing for the life of his son, his father summoned the strength to make a pilgrimage to the shrine of **Thomas Becket** to plead for saintly intercession in his recovery. Philip did recover and was crowned at Reims—the national cathedral for royal French coronations—in November 1179, but by this time his father was too ill to attend. Indeed, Louis VII died in 1180, leaving the adolescent Philip as the sole ruler of France.

Philip II faced a difficult situation when he became king. Although he had the sanction of royal coronation to bolster his position, the actual royal domain of the French kings was small, consisting primarily of territory around Paris known as the Ile-de-France. To the north and east of these lands were the powerful counties of Flanders and Champagne and the duchy of Burgundy. To the north, west, and south stretched the imposing Plantagenet Empire controlled by the English king, Henry II. Henry was king of England in his own right; on the continent, he was duke of Normandy, Brittany, Anjou, and Touraine; through his wife **Eleanor** he held the large duchy of Aquitaine to the south. In theory, the French king was overlord of these larger and many smaller feudal territories on the continent; in reality, the military strength and feudal wealth of these lands could at any time threaten the French monarchy.

The main achievement that occupied most of Philip's reign was to reverse this situation and to build a large territorial base for the French realm at the expense of these neighboring feudal powers. However, in 1180, as a young and inexperienced 15-year-old king, he had few personal resources on which to draw. He was never imposing in stature, nor was he especially strong on the battlefield. However, he was shrewd and ultimately courageous, and his determined character helped him to achieve his goals.

During the first decade of his reign, Philip began to solidify his position by marriage alliances and by pitting various feudal factions against one another. In 1180, he married Isabella of Hainaut, one of the important Flemish feudal territories. Through her dowry, he gained the northern French county of Artois and claims to other cities and areas to the north such as Amiens. She also gave Philip a son and heir, the future Louis VIII.

Philip's principal concern, however, was with the Plantagenet lands. By 1188, he had temporarily allied with Henry II's son Richard to rise up against the old king in some of the Plantagenet's continental possessions. Philip made modest territorial gains around Berry and in the Auvergne from this effort. Shortly thereafter, in

1189, Henry II died leaving his kingdom to his son, **Richard the Lionheart.**

Philip and Richard Start on Crusade

Philip and Richard's alliance continued as they started on crusade in 1190 to fulfill a vow made in 1188. But before they reached the Holy Land, their tenuous association failed in Sicily when Richard married Berengeria of Navarre, instead of his long-time fiancée, Alix (Alice), Philip's sister. Although the two kings managed to capture Acre together in 1191, Philip abandoned the crusade soon thereafter and returned to France. His reasons included illness—a disease called *arnoldia* or the "sweating sickness" which caused a permanent exacerbation of a nervous condition—and concern about the situation of his realm and the young prince Louis, his heir.

His illness may partially explain one of the most puzzling aspects of his life. Because his first wife had died before he departed on crusade, he wished to remarry to ensure the continuation of the Capetian line in the event of Prince Louis's premature death. In 1193, he married a Danish princess Ingeborg, sister of King Knud VI of Denmark. The day after his marriage, he sent her to a monastery near Paris and immediately sought an annulment which a council of French bishops granted a few months later.

In 1196, Philip married Agnes of Meran who bore him a son, Philip Hurepel (literally "bristling hide," because his hair, like his father's, was always bristling), and a daughter, Marie. However, the pope never recognized the divorce or third marriage, and Ingeborg and her supporters continued to press her claims for the validity of her marriage and her royal position as queen of France. But just as the powerful Pope Innocent III was about to place France under interdict because of Philip's disputed marital status, Agnes died in 1201. Finally in 1213, Philip agreed to recognize Ingeborg as queen, but he never resumed marital relations with her. He probably had numerous alliances with women, at least one of which produced an illegitimate son, Pierre Charlot, whom he acknowledged.

Philip's primary concern during the next two decades was how to augment his territorial position by dismantling the Plantagenet holdings on the continent. In Richard the Lionheart, he faced a formidable adversary. During Richard's absence in the Holy Land and captivity by the German emperor until 1194, Philip took the opportunity to ally with Richard's brother **John** and annexed the Vexin, a disputed territory on the border of Normandy, and other strategic castles such as Gisors. After his release, Richard devoted his superior military abilities to reclaiming these possessions.

Upon Richard's death in 1199, John, the youngest son of Henry II and Eleanor of Aquitaine, became the English king. Because John lacked the military skill and political acumen of his two predecessors, Henry II and Richard the Lionheart, Philip was finally able to capitalize on this weakness. In 1200, John married Isabella of Angoulême who had been engaged to Hugh of Lusignan, one of Philip's vassals. When John failed to pay reparation and refused a summons to the court of Philip II, his continental overlord, the French king proceeded to consider John's territories in forfeiture and to seize them. Between 1203 and 1206, Philip gained control of Normandy, Brittany, Anjou, Maine, and Touraine. Only the southern territorial possessions of the Plantagenets, Poitou, and Aquitaine remained in the hands of the English king.

Although the balance of power had shifted significantly in favor of Philip, the important point was his ability to hold these territorial gains and integrate them into his kingdom. His new political strength aroused concern and opposition from many feudal lords, including some of the French barons and King John. In addition, the contested candidacy for the German imperial crown became the focus of shifting alliances involving Pope Innocent III, Philip II, John of England, and others. By 1212, John was allied with Otto of Brunswick, one of the imperial contenders, and the counts of Boulogne and Flanders whose domains were just northeast of the French realm. Philip sided with another imperial candidate, **Frederick II** Hohenstaufen.

Battle of Bouvines Expands French Kingdom

In 1214, John and Otto of Brunswick collaborated in a military plan against Philip. John would attack Philip's lands from the south while Otto, along with other members of the northern French and Flemish nobility, would engage Philip's forces in the north. The famous battle between these powers took place on July 27, 1214, at Bouvines near Tournai in Flanders. In this battle, Philip and his forces won a decisive victory. Even though Philip was at one point unhorsed, French knights saved him and, in the end, it was Otto who fled the battle scene. John's military venture to the south also collapsed.

In military terms, the battle of Bouvines consolidated Philip's position as one of the major European powers. He was now king of a much expanded French royal domain. His victory had simultaneously diminished the stature of King John of England and the German empire while enhancing his own prestige.

The enlarged French kingdom brought new challenges for Philip's government. The feudal domain he'd inherited had been small, and its administration had been accomplished primarily on a personal level by an itinerant court of "the tent, the wagon, and the packhorse," aided by some local officials known as *prevots.* Throughout Philip's reign, changes gradually occurred. Government became more centralized in Paris with a chancery to maintain records and a treasury at the tower of the Knights Templars. A new type of civil servant, the *baillis,* was sent out to supervise the king's financial and judicial business in various regions. This evolution of a more systematic bureaucracy not only gave Philip greater control and stability in his extended lands but also provided the foundation for future growth of power and resources for the French monarchy.

The final decade of Philip's life was relatively peaceful. He tacitly approved but did not openly support an aborted plan for Prince Louis to invade England. When this venture collapsed with the death of King John in 1216, Louis turned his attention to the Albigensian crusade against heretical religious sects that had flourished in southern France. Primarily, however, Philip worked, along with a few trusted councillors, to consolidate the administration of the enlarged royal domain.

Philip died on July 14, 1223, after a lengthy illness. He was buried with great ceremony at the royal abbey of Saint Denis. Philip II was a complex and calculating man, and his illness in the Holy Land left a legacy of a nervous, erratic temperament. During his long reign of 43 years, however, his accomplishments had transformed the French nation and its monarchy. By manipulating the inherent instability and rivalries of the feudal political situation and by capitalizing on his opportunities for military conquest, he made the French king one of the most powerful monarchs in Europe. His administrative innovations enhanced the efficiency and effectiveness of his ability to govern his expanded realm. Although he was only minimally literate and apparently disinterested in cultural matters, during his reign Paris was becoming a major political, economic, intellectual, and artistic capital of Europe. Philip II Augustus thus ranks as one of the most significant kings of France and in the medieval world.

SOURCES:

Baldwin, John W. *The Government of Philip Augustus.* University of California Press, 1986.

Duby, Georges. *The Legend of Bouvines.* University of California Press, 1990.

Hollister, C. Warren, and John W. Baldwin. "The Rise of Administrative Kingship: Henry I and Philip Augustus," in *American Historical Review.* 83 (1978).

Levron, Jacques. *Philippe Auguste.* Librarie Academique, 1979.

FURTHER READING:

Duby, Georges. *France in the Middle Ages, 987–1460.* Blackwell, 1991.

Fawtier, Robert. *The Capetian Kings of France.* Macmillan, 1960.

Hallam, Elizabeth M. *Capetian France, 987–1328.* Longmans, 1980.

Józef Pilsudski

(1867–1935)

Socialist revolutionary, military genius, father of the modern Polish state, who engineered the Polish victory over the Soviets in 1920.

"'The George Washington of Poland'… Jozef Pilsudski did more than any other single Pole… to achieve the independence of Poland after the first World War and to set up the national housekeeping."

STEPHEN P. MIZWA

B y the Third Partition of Poland in 1795, Russia, Prussia, and Austria completed the process begun in 1772 of dismembering the Polish state. With this event, Poland disappeared from the European map. The Poles would remain under the yoke of foreign masters for nearly 125 years, occasionally rebelling against the partitioning powers. Two of the largest revolutions took place in 1830 and 1863.

Józef Kiemens Ginet-Pilsudski—known to his family as "Ziuk"—grew up during this time of national nonexistence when the ethnic Poles were struggling to maintain their language and traditions. Actively encouraging the preservation of Polish culture, his family participated in the Polish Insurrection of 1863. Pilsudski's mother (as described by Alexandra Pilsudska in *Pilsudski: A Biography by his Wife*) was "an irreconcilable patriot" who taught him at an early age what it meant to be a Polish subject of the Russian Empire:

> In every Polish and Lithuanian home, patriotism could only flower in secret. In the evening… Maria Pilsudska would unlock a drawer in her cabinet and take out the forbidden books of Polish history and literature to read them to her children.

Contributed by Christopher Blackburn, Ph.D. candidate in history, Auburn University, Auburn, Alabama

Name variations: Jósef or Joseph, Marshal Pilsudski. Pronunciation: PILL-soot-SKEE. Born Józef Kiemens Ginet-Pilsudski on December 5, 1867, just north of Wilno, Lithuania; died in Warsaw on May 12, 1935; descended from Polish-Lithuanian nobility, with just a hint of Scottish blood from an ancestor of the ancient house of Butler; fourth of twelve children of Józef and Maria Pilsudski; married: Maria Juszkiewez; married: Alexandra Szczerbinska; children: (two daughters) Wanda and Jadwiga. Successor: General Edward Rydz-Smigly.

CHRONOLOGY

1887	Pilsudski arrested on charges of conspiring to assassinate Alexander III of Russia; sentenced to five years in Siberia
1892	Became a leader of the Polish Socialist Party (*Polska Partia Socjalistyczna*)
1894	Named editor in chief of party newspaper, *The Worker* (*Robotnik*)
1905	"Bloody Sunday" began a series of revolts throughout Russia
1914	Assassination of Archduke Ferdinand; Europe moved irrevocably toward World War I
1917	Russian Revolution; Lenin established a communist state
1918	Pilsudski entered Warsaw as a national hero; proclaimed an independent Polish state
1920	Polish forces destroyed Soviet army at gates of Warsaw; end of Russo-Polish War
1922	Pilsudski resigned as chief of state
1926	Led military coup that overthrew the government; installed a virtual dictatorship
1933	Hitler came to power in Germany
1934	Nazi *putsch* in Austria; assassination of Dollfuss
1935	Pilsudski died in Warsaw

During his formative years the young Pilsudski's entire being permeated with the belief: "When one is born a Pole, one must of necessity be born a patriot."

Pilsudski was born on December 5, 1867, at Zulow, in the district of Swienciany, some 37 miles north of Wilno, Lithuania. The Pilsudski country estate, both sizable and picturesque in appearance, included approximately 9,000 hectares (22,239 acres). Madame Pilsudska describes the Lithuanian residence:

> The Pilsudski property consisted of a rambling one-storied manor house built of larchwood and set on the banks of a stream. Flanking it were rows of tall chestnuts and fragrant limes; in front was a lawn where the children played and had their swings in summer. Behind it were the outbuildings, the barns and carpentering sheds, the vats and presses, for among the industries of the estate was a brewery.

In 1874, fire destroyed the great estate and the entire family was forced to move to nearby Wilno, where they lived in more modest accommodations. Wilno was the ancient capital of the Grand Duchy of Lithuania and served as an eastern focal point for the Russian suppression of all things Polish. The anti-Polish sentiments of the city only served to strengthen the young Pilsudski's resolve to see Poland resurrected and returned to the list of autonomous European nations. As he entered the Wilno *Gimnazjum* (the Russian Secondary School), which was housed in what was once the Polish University of Wilno, his unhappiness and bitterness toward Russia became obvious. In 1882, Józef Pilsudski and his older brother Bronislaw formed a Polish learning circle called *Spojnia* ("Union"). The group organized a secret library, imported Polish publications from Warsaw and Krakow, then read the illegal books and lent them to other interested individuals. In 1884, his mother died abruptly just as Pilsudski entered grade eight, his final year of high school. He later recounted his time at the Wilno *Gimnazjum* as a "sort of penal servitude":

> The masters there were Czarist schoolmasters, teachers and trainers of youth who brought all their political passions to school with them, and whose system was to crush as much as possible the independence and personal dignity of their pupils.... My hatred for the Czarist administration and the Muscovite oppression grew with every year. Helpless fury and shame that I could do nothing to hinder my enemies often stifled me; my cheeks burned, that I must suffer in silence while my pride was trampled upon, listening to lies and scornful words about Poland, Poles and their history.

After completing high school, Pilsudski ignored his father's advice to study at the Technological Institute or the Communication Institute of St. Petersburg; instead, he chose to study medicine at the distant University of Kharkov. His first year was satisfactory, but because of "some trifling formalities which were not in order," the authorities at Kharkov refused to accept Pilsudski for his second year. During his university days he was exposed to Russian socialism by a students' organization called *Narodna Wola* ("National Will"). Although this brand of socialism did not particularly impress Pilsudski, he did conclude that Poles must create such an organization in the Polish lands.

Returning to Wilno, Pilsudski formed a socialist group designed to help both Poles and Lithuanians. He later admitted that their "circle did not work out a programme, it only became clear that we all laid emphasis on the defense of the people from the brutal denationalization for which the government worked in Lithuania." At the beginning of 1887, Pilsudski and his older brother were arrested in connection with an assassination attempt on the life of Tsar Alexander III of Russia. Though accidently involved and innocent of attempted murder, Pilsudski was sentenced to five years in the Irkutsk prison in Siberia. After completing his sentence, he returned to Wilno in 1892.

Assuming the name "Comrade Victor," Pilsudski joined the newly formed *Polska Partia Socialistyczna* (Polish Socialist Party or PPS). He then traveled throughout the three partitions of Poland learning all he could about the underground networks of the Polish revolutionaries. By 1894, the PPS assigned Pilsudski the burdensome task of editing, publishing, and printing the unauthorized party news bulletin *Robotnik* (*The Worker*). Through his own admission, the six years spent as editor were some of the most turbulent of his life. Writes Madame Pilsudska:

> It was a hand-to-mouth existence for him in those days, for the party had scarcely any funds behind it and his political activities had estranged him from his family. He was constantly in flight from the Russian authorities; he could rarely remain in the same place longer than a few days. When he was in Wilno he slept out in the forest night after night because none of his acquaintances dared to take him into their houses for fear of a search by the secret police.

Eventually arrested by Russian authorities in 1900, he was placed in the Tenth Pavilion of the Citadel of Warsaw. Feigning insanity, he was transferred to the heavily guarded insane asylum at St. Petersburg and, with the help of a Polish doctor, soon escaped from the torturous institution. After a brief visit to London in the winter of 1901–02, Pilsudski settled in Krakow and began cultivating a loyal group of followers. Author Stephen Mizwa reports: "His influence among the masses grew rapidly and he was soon recognized as the acknowledged head of the whole Polish revolutionary or insurrectionist movement."

In 1904, Pilsudski and his supporters came into direct conflict with Roman Dmowski's *Endecja* (Polish National Democratic Party). The two political entities were at opposite ends of the spectrum. While Pilsudski's socialists advocated a military revolt and enjoyed the support of many ethnic minorities inhabiting the Polish lands, Dmowski's nationalists urged diplomacy and cooperation with Tsarist Russia to restore Poland. Also, the National Democrats were, as their name implies, rabidly nationalistic and wanted all non-Polish ethnic groups removed from Polish soil. Dmowski began losing political power soon after 1905, because he continued to support the Russians even after they had committed brutal atrocities against Polish citizens. In spite of his political decline, Dmowski remained Pilsudski's foremost political opponent until his death.

In 1905, Pilsudski organized the *Bojowka*, a militant guerilla brigade of the Polish Socialist Party. Madame Pilsudska comments that between the years 1905 and 1912:

> The Bojowka waged an incessant guerilla warfare against the Czarist Government.… Convoys were attacked to provide funds for the release of Polish political prisoners, the upkeep of the Military Training Schools and the purchase of arms and ammunition.

Forced by Austrian authorities in 1910 to reorganize his "private army" into the *Zwiazek Strzelecki* (The Union of Riflemen's Clubs) or disband it entirely, Pilsudski willingly reorganized and began openly training his small army of about 10,000 soldiers.

The outbreak of World War I in 1914 was a calamity for Poland. As Russia, Germany, and Austria conscripted thousands of Polish citizens into their respective armies, Poles were forced to fight one another on behalf of the partitioning powers, rather than unite in an attempt to regain Poland's independence. Theorizing that Russia was Poland's primary enemy, Pilsudski immediately offered his Polish legions to the Austrians. He was convinced that Germany would defeat Russia, the French and British armies would in turn defeat Germany, and then Poland would be free from both the Central Powers (Germany and its allies) and Russia.

By late 1916, the Central Powers proclaimed an independent Polish state and quickly formed a governing council, of which Pilsudski became a participant. He refused, however, to order his troops against British and French forces and was eventually imprisoned in the summer of 1917 in the ancient German fortress at Magdeburg. Once inside the prison walls, Pilsudski was surprisingly elevated to the military rank of general and treated with the respect due that rank. He describes his time in the Magdeburg prison in *Moje Pierwsze Boje* (*My First War Experience*):

> I lived very comfortably. I had the use of three cells on the first floor, a bedroom, a room that looked as if I was meant to receive people in it—

Józef Pilsudski (third from left) stands with his new cabinet following the May 1926 coup d'état in Poland.

which in my situation could only make me laugh—and a third which served as a dining-room. All three cells were open the whole day long, and led out on to a little garden containing some fruit trees and a few small bushes and plants.

Pilsudski Leads Independent Poland

As the war ground to a halt and revolution swept across Germany in 1918, Pilsudski was released from Magdeburg and escorted to Warsaw by German dignitaries. Arriving by train on November 10, 1918, he was instantly proclaimed a national hero, a leader of independent Poland, and given the title of Chief of State, General in Command of the Polish military, and Marshal of Poland. On the morning of November 11, 1918, the new Polish leader observed that the "hardest fight of his life was still in front of him.... The independent Polish state had been born, but it was so frail an infant that its survival seemed problematical."

Pilsudski was left with the enormous task of uniting the three distinctly different political systems of the partitioned lands under his single Warsaw-based government. In addition to the assignment of creating a unified Poland, Pilsudski was forced to supervise the disarming and removal of German and Austrian troops from Polish soil. Throughout this domestic crisis, Pilsudski had to argue continually over Polish boundaries and jus-

tify Polish territorial claims to the victorious Allied Powers at the Paris Peace Conference. The many Polish territorial claims quickly led to conflicts with the newly created Czechoslovakia, Lithuania, and the newborn Bolshevik government of the Soviet Union.

Basically, Marshal Pilsudski sought to establish a federation of eastern states. This federation was to be organized along the lines of the historic Polish-Lithuanian Commonwealth and would be made up of several independent states, including Poland, Lithuania, Byelorussia, and the Ukraine. He viewed the federation as the only way to maintain an independent Poland. He also insisted that this was the only way the peoples of Eastern Europe could resist the aggressive tendencies of both Russia and Germany. Russia and Poland were eventually propelled into war in 1919 because of the Polish pursuit of a large East European Federation and the Soviet quest for a weak communist-controlled Poland.

A Miraculous Victory Over Russia

Pilsudski's forces initially pushed far into the Ukraine and Lithuania but were soon driven back to Warsaw by the advancing Russian armies. By August 12, 1920, when the Russians reached the outskirts of Warsaw, all believed Poland would be destroyed. But one day later, Marshal Pilsudski launched a daring flank attack which cut through the Russian rear areas. The surprise offensive encircled the Red Army, forcing the Russians into a rapid retreat from Poland. Before the day was over, the Polish army had taken some 100,000 Soviet prisoners of war and had nearly destroyed the Russian army. Pilsudski's gamble worked; Poland's certain defeat was turned into Poland's great victory known as the *Cud Nad Wisla* (Miracle on the Vistula). An armistice was quickly signed and on March 18, 1921, the Treaty of Riga officially ended the war and established the Polish-Soviet border.

In December 1922, Pilsudski resigned his post as head of state and moved to his country home at Sulejowek, occupying himself with literary work. He continued, however, to wield a great deal of power in Polish politics. In May 1926, when the Polish economy was in shambles, the coalition government had collapsed, and the *Sejm* ("Parliament") had lost most of its power, Pilsudski felt compelled to return to the political arena. On the afternoon of May 12, the old Marshal advanced on Warsaw with a sizable military force and supporters from the political parties of the left. Although his troops occupied the northern half of the town with little bloodshed, the government refused to yield power to Pilsudski, resulting in two days of intense fighting in the streets of Warsaw. Renouncing their positions on May 15, the government was replaced by followers of Pilsudski. But the coup d'état of May 12–14 haunted Pilsudski throughout the remaining nine years of his life, because he had used military force to overthrow a democratic government.

Pilsudski was now the virtual dictator of Poland; he was the Polish minister of war and held the post of premier of Poland from 1926 to 1928 and again in 1930. Throughout those years the real power in Poland rested in his hands and did not pass from them until his death in Warsaw on May 12, 1935. "The whole nation mourned him," writes his wife:

> Reverent crowds lined the street as his body was borne with military honours from the Belvedere Palace to the Cathedral to lie in state for a week. Thousands, from the highest to the lowliest, filed past to look their last upon him.... He was laid to rest at the Wawel in Cracow with the kings and heroes of Poland, but his heart is buried, in fulfillment of his last wish, at the feet of his mother in Wilno, in the same cemetery where so many of his soldiers are laid.

SOURCES:

Dziewanowski, M. K. *Joseph Pilsudski: A European Federalist, 1918–1922.* Hoover Institute Press, 1969.

Gillie, D. R., trans. and ed. *Joseph Pilsudski: The Memories of a Polish Revolutionary and Soldier.* Faber & Faber, 1971.

Jedzejewicz, Waclaw. *Pilsudski: A Life for Poland.* Hippocrene Books, 1982.

Mizwa, Stephen, ed. *Great Men and Women of Poland.* Macmillan, 1941.

Pilsudska, Alexandra. *Pilsudski: A Biography by his Wife.* Dodd, 1941.

FURTHER READING:

Humphrey, Grace. *Pilsudski: Builder of Poland.* Scott and More, 1936.

Machray, Robert. *The Poland of Pilsudski.* Dutton, 1937.

Rothschild, Joseph. *Pilsudski's Coup D'Etat.* Columbia University Press, 1966.

William Pitt, Earl of Chatham

(1708–1778)

Brilliant orator, cabinet member, head of state, greatest wartime leader in British history and architect of the First British Empire, whose courage and patriotism brought his country to the zenith of its imperial power in the 18th century.

Name variations: Pitt, the Elder; 1st Earl of Chatham; the Great Commoner. Born in London on November 15, 1708; died on May 11, 1778; younger son of Robert Pitt (Tory member of Parliament) and Lady Harriet Villiers (daughter of Viscount Grandison of the Anglo-Irish nobility); married: Hester Grenville (youngest sister of the Earl of Temple and George Grenville), 1754; children: (sons) John (Second Earl of Chatham), William, and James Charles; (daughters) Hester (Lady Mahon) and Harriet. Descendants: William Pitt, the Younger (prime minister, 1783–1801, 1804–06).

From 1688 to 1815, Great Britain and France were locked in a tremendous struggle for commercial, colonial, economic, and political supremacy. Seven of the nine world wars of modern times were fought between these nations, largely motivated by this quest for world hegemony (dominance). At the end of the 17th century, France, under King **Louis XIV,** was the first and foremost power in the world. By 1815, Great Britain fully supplanted France as the world leader.

In 1763, England had defeated France in the fourth Anglo-Gallic war, the Seven Years' War. With the signing of the Treaty of Paris in 1763, England became the world's greatest commercial and colonial power. William Pitt was the architect of this first British Empire.

William Pitt (the elder) was born in London, on November 15, 1708, to a distinguished family: he was the younger son of Robert Pitt, a member of Parliament, and Lady Harriet Villiers, daughter of Viscount Grandison of the Anglo-Irish nobility. Pitt's paternal grandfather Thomas "Diamond" Pitt, a governor of the East India factory at Madras, amassed a fortune and obtained a large diamond, later purchased by Philippe II, duc

"I know that I can save this country and that no one else can."

WILLIAM PITT

Contributed by Donna T. McCaffrey, Assistant Professor, Providence College, Providence, Rhode Island

d'Orleans, the regent of France. From 1719–26, young William studied at Eton and then in 1727–28 at Oxford and Utrecht. Though frequent bouts of poor health prevented Pitt from taking an active role in hunting and field sports, his classical education provided a rich background in literature, history, and oratory. Two favorite authors, Virgil and Cicero, had a lasting influence.

The impecunious younger son, Pitt early developed a select circle of friends, including George Lyttleton, Charles Pratt (later chief justice of Common Pleas), and the Grenville brothers—Richard and George (future prime minister). In 1731, Lord Cobham, a wealthy and influential patron, paid for Pitt's "Grand Tour" to France and Switzerland and provided him with a cornetcy (commission) in his regiment. In 1735, when Pitt entered Parliament for the family borough of Old Sarum, he joined a small group known as "Cobham's Cubs" and the "boy patriots," who opposed chief minister Sir **Robert Walpole.** Walpole dismissed Pitt from his regiment in order "to muzzle this terrible young cornet of horse." Out of favor with the ruling Cabinet government from 1737–45, Pitt joined the court of George II's son, Frederick, the Prince of Wales, as Groom of the Bedchamber with a £400-a-year income. Robert Walpole was succeeded by Carteret, whom Pitt attacked as the "Hanover Troop Minister." When Carteret resigned in 1744, King George II refused at first to appoint Pitt to the new (Henry) Pelham government.

In May 1744, Pitt became seriously ill for the first time. This and frequent later illnesses have never been completely nor fully diagnosed. Head and stomach gout, bowel disorders, insomnia, high fevers, no appetite, "bouts of insanity," depression, and nervous agitation were repeated symptoms reported variously by contemporaries. Poor health plagued Pitt for the rest of his life.

Upon Pitt's return to public life in 1746, George II relented and reluctantly allowed Pitt to become a joint-vice-treasurer of Ireland, followed by paymaster general of the forces. To avoid criticism for "selling out" to the administration, Pitt ostentatiously refused to take any money above the official salary of £4,000 a year. A second bout of illness kept him largely out of public life from August 1751 to September 1753. Thereafter, Pitt changed his previous foreign policy by supporting the Pelham government's alliance with Prussia.

In the confused political scene following the 1754 death of Henry Pelham, Pitt attacked Pelham's replacement, the duke of Newcastle, and was dismissed from office in 1755. With no

CHRONOLOGY

1731	Took "Grand Tour" and secured a military commission
1735	Entered Parliament for Old Sarum
1740–48	War of the Austrian Succession
1741	Entered Parliament for Old Sarum
1746	Became vice-treasurer in the Pelham government; served as paymaster general until 1755
1747	Entered Parliament for Seaford, Sussex
1754–55	Entered Parliament for Aldborough, Yorks; attacked Newcastle; dismissed from office
1756–57	Entered Parliament for Okehampton, Devon; formed a government with Devonshire; entered Parliament for Bath, Somerset
1756–63	The Seven Years' War
1757–61	Pitt and Newcastle joined forces in coalition government; forced out of office; opposed Peace of Paris
1766	Supported repeal of Stamp Act; accepted peerage as Earl of Chatham; formed his Second Administration; health broke down; Charles Townshend seized leadership of Cabinet
1777	Returned to Parliament; defended American colonists in House of Lords
1778	Collapsed after his final speech of April 7; buried with full honors in Westminster Abbey

income, Pitt received financial assistance from Richard Grenville, whose sister Hester he had recently married in 1754. This love match produced three sons and two daughters, while providing Pitt with domestic happiness.

Pitt Leads Cabinet in Wartime

The Seven Years' War began on August 29, 1756, when Prussia, England's ally, invaded Saxony. No British Cabinet seemed able to prosecute the war until William Pitt accepted the leadership of the British Cabinet in July 1757, after an 11-week crisis which had brought the government to a standstill. Locked in the fourth Anglo-Gallic war, Britain's arms suffered major disasters in the opening phase. The unbroken succession of English reverses resulted in a national humiliation which caused a traumatic psychological shock. George II and the nation turned to Pitt, who had previously said to the duke of Devonshire in 1756, "I know that I can save this country and that no one else can."

The news from all fronts was devastating. In America, General Braddock and the British regular army were cut to pieces in 1755 by the French and Indians at Fort Duquesne. The lucrative fur trade, the valuable fisheries, and the American colonies were threatened by the French enemy who built a chain of forts from the Great Lakes to New Orleans. In the Mediterranean, the French had captured the strategic island of Minorca in 1756, valued more highly than Gibraltar. The news from India was equally discouraging. The British forces were greatly outnumbered by the army under the clever French general, François Dupleix. Nor was the news from Europe, Africa, or the Caribbean any better. In the overall picture, the population of France was more than double that of England. The French navy was formidable, while the army was reputed to be among the finest in the world. Diplomatically, England's only major ally was Prussia, while France was aligned with a powerful continental coalition that included Austria and Russia, as well as smaller European states. Britain and the Empire faced an extremely grave crisis for survival.

Pitt's leadership led the nation to new heights and gave to it five of the most glorious years (1757–61) in its long and illustrious history. As a wartime leader of courage and vision, Pitt eagerly accepted the challenge and assumed full responsibility. He inspired the nation with his confidence and with his conviction that victory was possible. He consolidated executive and political authority and united all factions and parties in a vigorous prosecution of the war effort. With his great popularity, he became in fact the war dictator.

Pitt was directly involved in the direction of military and naval planning. Suspending the traditional rule of seniority as the basis for promotion, he appointed and removed commanders as he saw fit. Talent, merit, and results were rewarded. Instructions for military and naval operations were drafted by Pitt and communicated directly to the commanders. He made a major contribution in coordinating the complex actions between the army and the navy. His determination and his energy inspired all who came in contact with him. Colonel Isaac Barre claimed that no man ever entered his office "who did not feel himself, if possible, braver at his return than when he went in." Canada and India were conquered. Under Pitt's charismatic leadership, victories from every corner of the globe kept the bells of England ringing out the glorious news. The year 1759 has been called the wonderful year (*annus mirabilis*) in contrast to 1756, which could be termed the calamitous year (*annus calamitosus*). Bringing Britain to its imperial apex by 1761, his vision was boundless, while others remained myopic. In October 1761, Pitt resigned as secretary of state over the issue of expanding the conflict. When the Cabinet and new king, George III, opposed Pitt's demand for an immediate declaration of war against Spain, Pitt was forced out of office. His successor Lord Bute settled for a peace in 1763, which was a bitter disappointment to Pitt.

With Pitt ousted from power, George III began to exercise his postwar goal to be a more effective ruler. He wanted to regain royal prerogatives lost in Cabinet evolution under the first two Georges. The king and his advisors were also determined to implement a new colonial program for regulating the vastly enlarged boundaries of the Empire won from the French, and to address the staggering national debt of £137,000,000 left by the Seven Years' War. Their plans called for enforcement of standing colonial legislation ignored in the period of salutary neglect, a military force of 10,000 soldiers for security in America, and an increased British naval presence to put an end to American smuggling. A revenue had to be found in new taxes for the colonies. In order to provide a fund to defray these new imperial expenses, Parliament passed the Stamp Act in 1765.

He Supports Repeal of Stamp Tax on Colonies

William Pitt was absent from Parliament because of illness when the Grenville administration enacted the Stamp Act to tax the Americans. The bitter resistance of the American colonists to the tax provoked a major imperial crisis. The new Rockingham administration was faced with the dilemma of enforcing, amending, or repealing the obnoxious measure. Recovered by January 1766 but having thrice refused the king's attempts to bring him back into office, Pitt nevertheless returned to the House of Commons. In one of the most eloquent and effective speeches ever given in Parliament, Pitt supported the repeal of the stamp tax in 1766. He argued in the House of Commons that it was unconstitutional to levy a direct tax on the colonies because they were not represented in Parliament. With respect to American shortcomings, Pitt urged Parliament: "Be to her faults a little blind, be to her virtues very kind." His espousal of their position made Pitt a hero in the 13 American colonies.

In July 1766, William Pitt accepted the peerage as the earl of Chatham and allowed the king to persuade him to take office and form a new government. This second administration was a most unfortunate arrangement, with the duke of Grafton as first lord of the treasury and Charles

Townshend as chancellor of the exchequer. When a March 1767 illness forced Pitt from active leadership of the cabinet, the brilliant but erratic Townshend became what Cornelius Forster termed the "Uncontrolled Chancellor."

In 1767, Parliament enacted the Townshend Duties, which levied import taxes on the Americans and thus reopened the dispute between England and the colonies. After the death of Townshend in 1767, the king appointed Lord North, who repealed the taxes except for the duty on tea. America's response was the Boston Tea Party, which led Parliament to enact the punitive measures which exacerbated the imperial controversy.

Pitt's return to Parliament in 1777 witnessed his final efforts to avoid civil war. As relations between America and the mother country worsened, Pitt appealed for moderation and a suspension of the punitive measures against Boston. He defended the Americans and proposed a compromise to recognize the Continental Congress while maintaining the integrity of the British Empire. With respect to military action, he warned that Britain could never conquer America. His final speech on April 7, 1778, was of no avail, and he collapsed in the House of Lords and died shortly afterwards on May 11, 1778.

Pitt personified British courage, patriotism, and imperialism. A comparison has been drawn between his contributions in the Seven Years' War and those of **Winston Churchill** in World War II as the two greatest wartime leaders in British history. Perhaps the accolade belongs first to William Pitt, earl of Chatham. Even today, over 30 locations, embracing cities, towns, counties, squares, rivers, lakes, mountains, and straits from England to the Galapagos Islands, from Alaska to New Zealand, and in the United States and Canada, have been named in honor of Pitt/Chatham.

SOURCES:

Almon, John. *Anecdotes of the Life of Right Honorable William Pitt, Earl of Chatham.* 3 vols. Longmans, 1810.

Ayling, Stanley. *The Elder Pitt, Earl of Chatham.* David McKay, 1976.

Forster, Cornelius P. *The Uncontrolled Chancellor, Charles Townshend and His American Policy.* R. I. Bicentennial Foundation, 1978.

Godwin, William. *The History of the Life of William Pitt, Earl of Chatham.* G. Kearsley, 1783.

Kimball, G. S. *Correspondence of William Pitt with the Colonial Governors.* 2 vols. Macmillan, 1900.

Macaulay, Thomas B. "William Pitt, Earl of Chatham," in *Edinburgh Review.* 58 (1834): 508–544.

Plumb, J. H. *Chatham.* Collins, 1953.

Rosebery, Lord, ed. *Chatham His Early Life and Connections.* Arthur L. Humphreys, 1910.

Sherrard, O. A. *Lord Chatham.* 3 vols. Bodley Head, 1952–58.

Taylor, W. S., and J.S. Pringle. *Correspondence of William Pitt, Earl of Chatham.* 4 vols. John Murray, 1838.

Thackeray, Francis. *A History of the Right Honorable William Pitt, Earl of Chatham.* 2 vols. C. and J. Rivington, 1827.

Tunstall, W. C. B. *William Pitt, Earl of Chatham.* Hodder & Stoughton, 1938.

Von Ruville, A. *William Pitt Earl of Chatham.* 3 vols. Heineman, 1907.

Williams, Basil. *The Life of William Pitt, Earl of Chatham.* 2 vols. Longman, Green, 1914.

FURTHER READING:

Corbett, Sir Julian. *England in the Seven Years' War: A Study in Combined Strategy.* 2 vols. Longmans, 1907.

Hotblack, Kate. *Chatham's Colonial Policy.* Routledge, 1917.

Middleton, Richard. *The Bells of Victory.* Cambridge University Press, 1985.

Namier, Lewis B. *The Structure of Politics at the Accession of George III.* Macmillan, 1929.

———. *England in the Age of the American Revolution.* Macmillan, 1930.

Winstanley, Denys A. *Lord Chatham and Whig Opposition.* Cambridge University Press, 1912.

William Pitt the Younger

(1759–1806)

Britain's youngest prime minister, who led his country through the French Revolution and early Napoleonic Wars, attempted to reorganize government finances, and sought a political union between Great Britain and Ireland.

Born May 28, 1759, at Hayes, near Bromley, Kent, England; died at Putney Heath in London, England, on January 23, 1806; fourth child and second son of William Pitt, first earl of Chatham, and Lady Hester Grenville; never married; no children. Predecessor: (as prime minister) William Henry Cavendish-Bentinck, 3rd Duke of Portland. Successor: (as prime minister) Henry Addington, 1st Viscount Sidmouth, in 1801; Lord William Wyndham Grenville, in 1806.

Britain in the late 18th and very early 19th centuries was riddled with "powerful currents of reaction and reform," which influenced the lives of many of Britain's political leaders. The effects of industrialization, warfare, and famine were evident in the parliamentary career of William Pitt the Younger who was forced to deal with such changes.

William Pitt the Younger was born to an established and respectable family at Hayes, in Kent, England. His father **William Pitt the Elder,** Member of Parliament for Bath, was at the zenith of his career when his second son was born. His great grandfather was "Diamond" Pitt, who had been in the service of the British East India Company as governor of Fort St. George. Pitt's mother Hester—intelligent and devoted to her family—was from the politically influential Grenville family.

Pallid and of delicate health, Pitt was a fragile child, but he was also alert and intelligent to the point of precociousness. Health problems, including frequent coughs, colds and fevers, played a significant role (along with his father's own childhood experiences at Eton) in the decision that Pitt would be educated at home by a tutor. The Rev-

Contributed by Donna Beaudin, Ph.D. candidate in History, University of Guelph, Guelph, Ontario, Canada

erend Edward Wilson, a graduate of Pembroke Hall, Cambridge University, was engaged as tutor in 1765. As a boy, Pitt learned to ride and to shoot, but he was always more interested in books. The education he received emphasized the classical tradition then followed by social elites, with its focus on Latin composition, poetry, and mathematics. Pitt's father took an interest in his education and encouraged his son's fascination with political intrigue.

Pitt was just 14 years old when he arrived at Pembroke Hall, Cambridge, to take up residence in October 1773; put under the care of George Pretyman Tomline, one of the hall's tutors, Pitt studied Latin and Greek, mathematics, English history, and political philosophy. Subjects like modern literature and theology held less interest for him, and the only modern language he had any knowledge of was French. Fellow students regarded Pitt as cheerful, witty, and generally excellent company. Among the friends he made at Cambridge was abolitionist William Wilberforce. When he was 17 and still a student, a doctor diagnosed Pitt with hereditary gout and prescribed the daily consumption of one bottle of port wine. Both gout and a liking for port stayed with Pitt for the rest of his life. In 1776, he took his master of arts degree by right, since peers and sons of peers did not have to take examinations to receive their degrees.

Following graduation, Pitt continued to reside at Cambridge. He had already developed a habit of attending parliamentary debates in Westminster and was, thus, in the House of Lords in April 1778 to help carry his father out of the chamber after the earl collapsed during what proved to be his last speech. Pitt's father died soon after, willing him an annual income of £300.

Young Pitt Enters Parliament

Pitt's parents had determined early that he was suited to a parliamentary career and, following the next logical step, he began to study law at Lincoln's Inn, one of the four Inns of Court that had the right to provide such education. In 1780, he was called to the bar and began his work on the western legal circuit. This was also an election year, and Pitt stood for Cambridge University in the election. Although he placed last in the polls, he was noticed by Sir James Lowther, who caused Pitt to be elected for the constituency of Appleby in Westmorland. In January 1781, when Pitt entered Parliament as a Whig, he sided with Lord Shelburne, placing himself in opposition to both Lord North's government and the American war. In only one month, Pitt had made his first speech,

CHRONOLOGY

1783	Peace of Versailles recognized independence of American colonies; Pitt formed ministry
1784	Pitt's East India Act
1788–89	George III ill; regency crisis in Britain
1789	French Revolution began
1793	Outbreak of war between Britain and France
1794	Habeas Corpus Act suspended in Britain (until 1804)
1798	Pitt introduced income tax in Britain
1801	Union of Great Britain and Ireland; first census taken in Britain
1802	Peace of Amiens between Britain and France
1803	War between Britain and France renewed
1805	Battle of Trafalgar
1806	C.J. Fox died; Napoleon victorious
1811	George, Prince of Wales, made prince regent

supporting **Edmund Burke**'s bill for economical reform. In June of the same year, the young politician spoke in support of Charles James Fox's motion for peace with the American colonies.

Pitt was first offered an appointed political office in 1782 by the new Rockingham administration. He was offered the vice-treasurership of Ireland (valued at £5,000 per year and once held by his father, but of only small political importance), but refused it, declaring in the House of Commons that he wanted only such positions that included a seat in the cabinet. His political wishes were met when, following the death of the marquess of Rockingham later in 1782, he became chancellor of the exchequer at the age of 23. Upon moving into 10 Downing Street in August 1782, as Robin Reilly asserts in *William Pitt the Younger*, Pitt was "in all but name, leader of the government in the House of Commons." While he continued to push for parliamentary reform and a conclusion to the war with America, Pitt was also chosen to approach C.J. Fox on the possibility of a coalition government with Lord Shelburne. After the two met in February 1783 and the suggestion was refused, Pitt and Fox never again spoke to each other in private.

While peace preliminaries to conclude the war with America were being debated in the House of Commons, Lord Shelburne resigned as first lord of the treasury and recommended to George III that the office be offered to the youthful but capable Pitt. According to Reilly:

> Pitt's situation was one of great delicacy. On the one hand there was the temptation to become his country's Prime Minister at the age of twenty-three; on the other the realization that he would be unlikely to succeed where Shelburne had failed.

This continued to be Pitt's dilemma through the short-lived Fox-North administration of 1783. In March, Pitt had resigned as chancellor of the exchequer, and in September and October spent six weeks vacationing in France with friends. This was the only period of Pitt's life spent away from England. In December 1783, he was asked by George III to form a government. While Pitt was, without doubt, loyal and able, he was not subservient, a characteristic that was repeatedly made evident to the king. Initial reaction in the House of Commons to Pitt's appointment was bitter and derisive. Since Pitt was the first commoner to form a government since 1766, and all the cabinet ministers save Pitt were peers, doubts were raised that the ministry would last much beyond Christmas; it was referred to as the "Mince Pie Administration."

Pitt's earliest legislative concerns included the reform of Parliament (which the House of Commons generally regarded as "dangerous innovation"), reorganization of government finances in order to reduce the national debt, and reorganization of the administration of British India. In February 1784, he was presented with the freedom of the City of London. Returning home from the banquet, his carriage was attacked by some of Fox's supporters. Pitt managed to escape without injury.

Following the 1784 election (Pitt would now represent Cambridge University for the rest of his life), he commenced financial reforms: duties were reduced to deter smuggling, a window tax was introduced, and a number of indirect taxes levied. A bill changing the role of the British East India Company in the governance of India, and which had the support of the company's directors, was introduced and passed both houses of Parliament easily. Pitt's brilliance as a speaker was evident. Lord Macaulay, in a small biography, notes:

> Even intricate questions of finance, when explained by him, seemed clear to the plainest man among his hearers. On the other hand, when he did not wish to be explicit—and no man who is at the head of affairs always wishes to be explicit—he had a marvelous power of saying nothing in language which left on his audience the impression that he had said a great deal.

Pitt's ideas regarding government finance, both revenues and expenditures, were not new (some had previously been articulated by Adam Smith and Richard Price), but the ways in which he combined these ideas were innovative. Thus, government administration should be handled by trained professionals, offices should be amalgamated wherever possible, profitable sinecures should be abolished, and trade with both Ireland and the United States should be expanded. Pitt even advocated reforming the Post Office in 1784; for this he was challenged to, and engaged in, a duel with Charles Grey. One of the most notable financial measures introduced by Pitt was, in 1784, a sinking fund to generate surplus revenue to be applied against the national debt.

He Faces Impeachment, Insanity Issues

Two problems beset William Pitt in 1788: the impeachment for corruption, and subsequent trial, of **Warren Hastings** (governor-general of British India), and the regency crisis occasioned by the temporary insanity of George III. Pitt remained detached throughout Hastings's seven-year trial, while Foxite opposition sought to expose government corruption, cruelty, and injustice. The decision to proceed with the impeachment process was "one of the most painful moral decisions of his career."

The king's insanity created a very immediate and personal problem for Pitt. If the king's son, George, Prince of Wales, became regent, Pitt perceived that his dismissal in favor of Fox and his party would be almost instantaneous. Pitt, therefore, investigated all constitutional means by which he could continue in government and deny complete sovereign power to the Prince of Wales. By the time a Regency Bill was ready to go to the House of Lords, in mid-February 1789, the king had recovered. Throughout this crisis, Pitt had been seen by many as the king's champion in the face of considerable antagonism. Conscious of the debt he owed to Pitt, George III offered him the Order of the Garter in December 1790. Pitt declined the offer with the suggestion that the honor be conferred upon his elder brother, Lord Chatham.

Pitt's interest in reform continued to be evident in colonial matters. Following the general election in late 1790, he sought to reform the government in the Canadian colonies. Two separate colonies, Upper Canada and Lower Canada, were created by the Constitution Act of 1791.

The outbreak of revolution in France, in July 1789, suggested that Pitt's "peaceable intentions" for economic stability in Britain were threatened. Although the immediate reaction was that Britain was secure against French revolutionary consequences, attitudes soon changed when the Revolution ceased to be a French domestic concern. In 1792, France declared war on Austria and Prussia, conquered Savoy and Nice, and began to move toward Holland (a country which England was bound to protect by a 1788 treaty). Although Pitt sought to preserve peace as long as possible, in February 1793 he was forced to respond to **Napoleon**'s declaration of war against Britain and Holland. Initially believing that French finances would not permit a lengthy war, Pitt was determined to meet war-related expenses through loans. By doing this, commercial development could continue, and increased levels of taxation would be avoided. With regard to the possibility of revolution in Britain, Pitt perceived the threat to be very real and encouraged by such organizations as the London Corresponding Society. This contributed to the decision to suspend habeas corpus (the need for a writ providing reasons for detention) in 1794. By quelling all sources of potential domestic dissension, Pitt could focus on the fighting of the war.

The outbreak of war strained Pitt's health, and in 1793–94, he suffered frequent and recurrent attacks of gout. In line with the prescribed advice of daily consumption of port, Pitt drank heavily, though only once was he visibly drunk in the House of Commons. But Pitt was now showing some signs of alcohol dependence, and his health began to deteriorate during periods of stress and disappointment.

Pitt Attempts to End War with France

In the early months of the conflict, Pitt was determined to handle French aggression by forming a European coalition against France. Though the plan was initially well received, by 1795 Austria and Sardinia were Britain's only active allies. At home, Pitt had to deal with the need to increase taxation, widespread food rioting throughout England, demonstrations in London against the war, and an attack on the king's coach by antiwar protesters at the opening of Parliament. In the last months of 1795, Pitt's government introduced what became known as the "Two Acts," which extended the law of treason and prohibited mass meetings of any kind unless approved by a magistrate. Though he was anxious for peace, Pitt's proposals laid before the French directory failed and attempts to obtain peace throughout 1796 proved

futile. As the war continued, Pitt had to find ways to finance Britain's participation: there were new loans, additions to already assessed taxes, and new duties imposed on horses and tobacco.

When he opened negotiations with France again in 1797, Portugal was Britain's only ally; Pitt had also to be concerned about government finances and the possibility of open rebellion in Ireland. War costs continued to increase. He proposed increases in assessed taxes and a scheme of graduated tax on annual incomes of £60 or greater at a rate of ten percent. "Income tax" was introduced in April 1799 as a temporary measure to generate revenue to pay for the war.

Not pleased with the progress of the war, Pitt had contemplated resigning his office, as early as autumn 1797, in favor of Henry Addington. He believed this might better their chances for negotiating peace with France. He also continued to worry about his health.

Tyrannical and corrupt practices continued in Ireland, and the Catholic question became an increasingly urgent problem. Favoring legislative union with Ireland, Pitt was determined to push legislation through the British Parliament; he renewed his efforts every session until he was successful in August 1800. A Parliamentary Union which admitted Irish representatives to the British Parliament established the United Kingdom on January 1, 1801. Still a reformer at heart, Pitt regarded an Anglo-Irish union without Catholic emancipation (full civil and political rights for Roman Catholics) as incomplete. Motions for this emancipation were blocked by George III, who made a clear distinction between toleration and equality on the grounds of religion. In poor health again, the independent and single-minded Pitt resigned his office in February 1801. Henry Addington was appointed first lord of the treasury and prime minister.

Before his resignation, Pitt had shown signs of stress and illness for several years. In 1796, he had had an attack of gout, as well as facial swelling and a yellowing complexion. The two latter conditions were directly related to Pitt's alcohol consumption. In general, his health now varied in relation both to seasons and situations.

Out of office in February 1801, Pitt's own, as well as George III's, health deteriorated. By early March, the king was in a coma, and Pitt held himself responsible. Further, Pitt had declined the king's offer to pay off Pitt's personal debts. He continued to sit as M.P. for Cambridge and was supportive of Addington's government concerning peace preliminaries with France, which resulted in the Peace of Amiens in March 1802. Later in the year, Pitt suffered an acute attack of gout, from which he slowly recovered. In April 1803, his mother died, and his grief contributed to a renewal of illness. When he returned to the House of Commons the next month, he still had a bad cough and a jaundiced appearance.

Pitt's "income tax" had been abolished by Addington in 1802 but had to be reintroduced as the war with France resumed in May 1803. Making what has since been reputed as his finest speech, Pitt warned that this struggle with France would be more severe than the last. By early 1804, as the probability of invasion by France increased, he was actively hostile toward the Addington administration. In late April, he twice spoke out against the government. Addington's resignation was imminent, and the king asked Pitt to prepare plans for a new government, which he effected in May 1804.

The theme of personal reconciliation figured prominently in Pitt's life in 1805. He was involved in negotiating relations between George III and George, Prince of Wales. This did not, however, swing political support to Pitt from any of the Prince's followers. Pitt secured Addington's elevation to the peerage and made promises of secondary offices in return for political support. From this small success, he moved on to coordinate the finances necessary to fight the war against France and Spain. At the close of the parliamentary session, Pitt's ill health was aggravated by the mixed news of a victory at Trafalgar at the cost of **Admiral Nelson**'s life. But the victory renewed Pitt's hopes for the outcome of the war.

"Prematurely aged by exhaustion and disease," Pitt went to Bath in December 1805 to partake of its curative waters. He stayed only a few days before returning to his house at Putney Heath in London, his body debilitated by disease. He was suffering from cirrhosis of the liver, and gout had crystallized in his kidneys; his jaundiced complexion, from 1801, was symptomatic of renal failure. On January 22, 1806, he dictated his will to his former tutor, George Pretyman Tomline, and died in the early hours of January 23 at the age of 46. It was the 25th anniversary of Pitt's first taking his seat in Parliament.

Within hours of his death, Pitt's friends sealed his papers and possessions in 10 Downing Street from creditors. On January 27, 1806, the House of Commons voted to pay Pitt's debts, to grant pensions to his three nieces, and to provide a public funeral, which was held February 22 after two days of lying in state in Westminster Hall. Toasted by some as the "savior of Europe," William Pitt was the subject of statues, painted portraits, drawings, and engravings. His achievements lay in peaceable concerns: the revival of national finances, the implementation of long-term administrative reforms, and the reorganization of British imperial commitments. A man of principle, the welfare of his country was William Pitt's first concern and in this his "dedication was absolute."

SOURCES:

Babington, Thomas, Lord Macaulay. *Life of William Pitt.* Delisser & Proctor, 1859.

Oliver, Robert T. *Four Who Spoke Out: Burke, Fox, Sheridan, Pitt.* Books for Libraries Press, 1979.

Reilly, Robin. *William Pitt the Younger.* Putnam, 1979.

FURTHER READING:

Barnes, Donald Gove. *George III and William Pitt, 1783–1806: A New Interpretation Based Upon a Study of Their Unpublished Correspondence.* Octagon Books, 1965.

Chatterton, E. Keble. *England's Greatest Statesman: A Life of William Pitt, 1759–1806.* 1st ed. c. 1930.

Cooper, R. "William Pitt, Taxation, and the Needs of War," in *Journal of British Studies.* 22(1), 1982.

Mackesy, P. *War Without Victory: The Downfall of Pitt the Younger, 1799–1802.* Clarendon Press, 1984.

Pius IX

(1792–1878)

Last pope to govern a worldly empire, first to enjoy infallibility in questions of faith and morals, and the first in modern times around whom a personal cult developed.

"Pius IX was an attractive person, sympathetic and charming, intelligent and witty. He once blessed some Anglican clergymen with the words taken from the blessing of incense during High Mass: 'May you be blessed by Him in whose honour you shall be burnt.'"

DEREK HOLMES

Giovanni Maria Mastai-Ferretti, who took the name Pius IX on his election in 1846, reigned longer than any pope in history, dying in 1878 at the age of 86. During his reign, he turned the Catholic Church decisively away from reconciliation with the modern world. When he resisted the unification of Italy, the political power of the Vatican collapsed; he tried to compensate by increasing its spiritual authority. The declaration of papal infallibility at the First Vatican Council (1870–71) was the decisive step in his elevation of papal authority above that of the world's Catholic prelates in council.

Mastai-Ferretti was born in 1792 in central Italy and grew up in the shadow of the Napoleonic Wars. He came from a reform-minded family of the lesser nobility in the Papal States and was guided towards the priesthood from early life. He admired Pope Pius VII, who was persecuted by **Napoleon,** and took his own pontifical name from this hero. During his training for the priesthood, he suffered from epilepsy but was able to be ordained in 1819, after which he rose rapidly through the Church hierarchy. All his work was close to Rome except for an expedition to Chile

Born Giovanni Maria Mastai-Ferretti in 1792 into a minor noble family in the Papal States of central Italy; died in 1878. Predecessor: Pope Gregory XVI. Successors: Following Leo XIII, three of the next four popes also took the name Pius, in honor of his memory.

Contributed by Patrick Allitt, Assistant Professor of History, Emory University, Atlanta, Georgia

and Peru as assistant to the apostolic delegate in 1823–25. By his early 40s, he was an archbishop, first of Spoleto (1827–32) and later of Imola (1840–46). In these years, sympathizing with the ideal of Italian unity and disliking the reactionary politics of Pope Gregory XVI, he was regarded as a reformer. At his election in 1846, the Catholic liberal Frederic Ozanam declared that Pius was "the envoy sent by God to conclude the great business of the nineteenth century, the alliance of religion and liberty."

Unlike most popes in recent centuries, Pius had had little diplomatic and political experience and his education had been scanty. Stubborn and inflexible in his official role, he was at the same time personally magnetizing and widely loved, as even his adversaries had to admit. He held garden parties at his palace and showed a warm interest in the spiritual and personal welfare of his subjects. The English convert **John Henry Newman,** who did not like his policies, nevertheless said of him:

> His personal presence was of a kind that no one could withstand.... The main cause of his popularity was the magic of his presence.... His uncompromising faith, his courage, the graceful mingling in him of the human and the divine, the humour, the wit, the playfulness with which he tempered his severity, his naturalness, and then his true eloquence.

Pius enjoyed social life, mingled freely with the population, and made himself available to visi-

tors seeking an audience. He was the first of the modern popes to develop a huge personal following of loyalists, some of whom took their love for him to almost idolatrous extremes. As his cult developed, European Catholic newspapers loyal to Pius denounced with brutal rhetoric anyone who dared to challenge the Holy Father in any way.

The pope loved company and, taking advantage of improved world communications, encouraged his bishops to visit frequently. He held a massive gathering in 1862 to celebrate the canonization of missionaries martyred in Japan, and another assembly in 1867 to celebrate the 1,800th anniversary of the martyrdom of Saint **Peter** and Saint **Paul.** He also established colleges at Rome for trainee priests from different nations (including Polish, French, American, and Irish colleges) as a way of strengthening Rome's influence in the Church's far-flung provinces. He lived for such a long time that by the end of his reign almost every Catholic bishop in the world had been appointed by him and felt a close sense of obligation to him.

When, soon after his election, he created a parliament for the Papal States, arranged for gas-fired street lights in Rome, and projected railroads, his "liberal" credentials seemed assured. Ever since the French Revolution 50 years before, the political landscape of Europe had been split between sympathizers with the Revolution and those who detested its memory. Republicans, liberals, democrats, and socialists generally favored it; monarchists opposed it. The papacy, as a wealthy and ancient monarchy, was usually well towards the conservative end of the political spectrum; most cardinals and bishops rejected the idea of freedom of religion, freedom of the press, and constitutional government. Within the Catholic Church, however, a minority of influential thinkers, notably the Frenchmen Lammenais, Montalembert, Lacordaire, and Dupanloup, the German theologian Dollinger, and the Englishman Lord Acton, believed that the "Barque of St. Peter" could be navigated in the uncharted waters of a new world order. Industrialization, modern science, modern biblical criticism, and philology all presented challenges which they regarded as opportunities as they hoped the new pope would realize. After an early period of turning a sympathetic ear to these and other liberal Catholics, Pius, like Gregory XVI, sided with their authoritarian enemies Louis Veuillot in France and Donoso Cortes in Spain, and condemned all forms of liberalism out of hand.

Several factors account for Pius IX's swerve away from liberalism. Ever since the era of Pope **Gregory I** (the Great) at the end of the sixth century, the Vatican had been a political presence in central Italy. Its empire, the Papal States, had waxed and waned with the fortunes of war, and recurrent scandals in Catholic life had been caused by the pope's political interests compromising his spiritual role as leader of Christendom. The leaders of the 16th-century Reformation had revolted against the political and commercial character of the papacy and split from Catholicism, partly in the name of a purer piety and a simpler Christianity. "Christendom" as a religiously united Europe was no more than a distant memory by Pius IX's day, three centuries after the Reformation, and the justification for the Papal States, which were anything but models of enlightened government, seemed to many Italians flimsy. In Pius's view, however, they were essential; he referred to his domains as "the robe of Jesus Christ." His predecessors had lost the States altogether during the Napoleonic wars but, as part of the pacification of Europe at the Congress of Vienna (1815), they had been restored.

Italian Soldiers Besiege Pope

In 1848, two years after Pius IX's ascension to St. Peter's throne, Europe experienced a period of revolutionary upheaval, in France, Germany, and Italy. **Giuseppe Mazzini,** the Italian republican leader, believed Pius would support him as he tried to overthrow Austrian influence in Italy and was dismayed when Pius refused to back an anti-Austrian crusade. Disillusioned Italian soldiers, returning from a defeat at Austrian hands, murdered Pius's prime minister Rossi and besieged the pope in the Quirinal Palace. Disguised as an ordinary priest, Pius was forced to make a humiliating retreat from Rome to Gaeta in southern Italy, where he could only find lodging in a cheap hotel. Mazzini declared Rome a republic.

This trauma stilled whatever liberal impulses Pius IX had once felt, and he became a stern opponent of Italian unification and republicanism. With the help of a French army, he reentered Rome in 1850 and expelled Mazzini. French help hardly came cheap, however. In return for their aid, the pope was required to leave "most" Church appointments within France in the civil government's hands, which rendered him little more than a figurehead to French Catholics. The memory of his humiliation and exile never left Pius, and his advisors often reminded him of it as a warning against concessions. "Henceforth," says historian Alec Vidler, "the pontificate of Pius IX was to be marked by the citadel mentality, which supposes that the only hope for the Church is to fortify itself against all new ideas and democratic reforms."

New threats to the Papal States emerged in the late 1850s and early 1860s. Count **Camillo Cavour,** the central figure in the politics of the north Italian state of Piedmont between 1852 and 1861, was unpopular with Pius because he had closed down many monasteries and taken education out of the hands of the Church; he aimed at building a modern, centralized secular state. Cavour now tried to unify Italy under the Piedmontese monarchy and guarded his rear by making an 1858 agreement with France, to be certain that it would not again intervene on the pope's behalf. After a period of diplomatic maneuver, Cavour's army marched on Rome in 1860, shattered a makeshift army of Catholic loyalists recruited from around Europe at the battle of Castelfidardo, and overran all but a narrow coastal strip of the Papal States.

A few remnants of the Papal States survived until 1870, but their political significance was ended. Eager to conciliate rather than antagonize his defeated rival, Cavour offered the pope full authority over the Church in Italy and a guarantee of all jeopardized Church property. Pius IX contemptuously turned his back on Cavour, described himself as "the prisoner of the Vatican," and forbade all loyal Catholics from participating in Italian politics. This standoff persisted until 1929 when Pope Pius XI finally made a treaty with **Benito Mussolini,** under terms quite similar to those offered by Cavour. This 70-year "prisoner" phase weakened the influence of the Church in Italy and increased the secular direction of the new nation's political life. "To realists who tried to persuade him that sooner or later he must negotiate," says historian R. Aubert, "Pius IX opposed a mystical confidence in divine providence, nourished by the conviction that the political convulsions in which he was implicated were only an episode in the great battle between God and Satan, in which Satan's defeat was inevitable."

In intellectual affairs as in politics, Pius IX refused to compromise with modernity. The vestiges of the French Revolution, along with the growing influence of the United States, which then appeared as a beacon of republican virtue and inspiration to the Old World, had made the ideas of political liberty and religious freedom attractive to many influential authors. The mid-19th century also saw the transformation of scientific thought with the rise of evolutionary theory, notably in the works of Charles Darwin and in a new physics based on the discovery of entropy. Bible scholars and archaeologists were meticulously unraveling the history of the ancient Middle East to enhance the understanding of Jesus' life and times.

Pope Publishes Syllabus of Errors

Pius IX cold-shouldered all these developments. When the liberal Catholic Montalembert made a speech equating Catholicism with modern civilization and progress during 1863, Pius responded by publishing his *Syllabus of Errors* (1864). In this decree, he summarized all the significant modern ideas and theories which Catholics were forbidden to hold, including freedom of speech, press, and religion. He had already declared against freedom of religion: "The Church will never admit it as a benefit and a principle that error and heresy should be preached to Catholic peoples." Now he added: "It is an error to say that it is no longer expedient that the Catholic religion should be established to the exclusion of all others." Another prohibited belief was the faith that "the Roman pontiff can and ought to reconcile himself to, and reach agreement with progress, liberalism, and modern civilization." No wonder that in progress-minded America, as elsewhere in the modernizing world, the Catholic Church was regarded by all but its sons and daughters as atavistic (a throwback to ancestors). Dupanloup, one of the French liberal Catholics, tried to soften the hammer blows of the *Syllabus of Errors* by arguing that it represented the ideal Catholic position on these questions, but that, in the realities of the contemporary world, the Church was not going to try fulfilling it step by step. The pope was so surprised by the outcry his *Syllabus* had provoked that he let Dupanloup's tactful formulas stand.

The perception of Pius as an aggressor against religious freedom was particularly keen in England, which had been severed from Rome since the days of **Henry VIII**, 300 years before. Catholics had suffered civil ostracism since then until the stirrings of British liberalism in the early 19th century led to "Catholic emancipation" in 1829. In 1850, the Catholic Church took advantage of emancipation by reestablishing a hierarchy of dioceses and bishops in England, first under Cardinal Nicholas Wiseman and later under Cardinal Henry Manning, both of whom were militant supporters of Pius IX and bombastic apostles of Catholic world supremacy. To the British prime minister, Lord John Russell, this unforseen reestablishment was "Papal aggression" without trying to prevent it, he labeled it "insolent and insidious." Pius IX was burnt in effigy by an anti-Catholic mob in London, but the new hierarchy managed to reestablish itself, and to prosper. Catholicism was also reestablished three years later in Holland, another Reformation stronghold.

Despite a rhetoric of unity, the world's Catholic people have always been at odds with one another; each country has had its distinctive forms of Catholic faith and tradition, and each, over the centuries, has won concessions from the Vatican. One measure of this variety could be seen in the United States during Pius IX's reign. The first big group of Catholic migrants came from Ireland in the 1840s, and they became the dominant ethnic group in American Catholicism. German and Italian Catholics, arriving in subsequent decades, found a Church they scarcely recognized, run by men unsympathetic to their own quite different traditions; they responded by appealing (unsuccessfully) for a permanent division of American Catholicism along ethnic lines.

Some Catholics were scandalized by the differences in the Church from place to place and the wide margin of local variations. They wanted a strong centralized papacy in Rome, governing and regulating the whole Church; they are remembered as the Ultramontanes. By contrast with the Ultramontanes, the defenders of Catholic pluralism were known as Gallicans. The long-lasting tension between Ultramontanes and Gallicans came to a head in Pius IX's reign; a passionate Ultramontanist, he compensated for his loss of political power by strengthening his spiritual powers, which seemed to him especially necessary in a world which was shrugging off Church leadership and pursuing materialist and secular ends. Some liberal Catholics also favored Ultramontanism. The early and mid-19th century was a period in which nation states were becoming far more powerful; having a counterweight in Rome seemed to some liberals, such as Lammenais, a good way of curtailing the danger of state tyranny. By the later days of Pius IX's reign, however, Ultramontanism was generally the faith of conservatives.

In 1854, he declared the new doctrine of the Immaculate Conception of the Blessed Virgin Mary. In other words, he said, Mary, like Jesus, was the product of a virgin birth to her mother, St. Anne, and was devoid of original sin. There was no biblical warrant for this doctrine (except the ambiguous greeting, "Hail Mary, full of grace," made by an angel at the Annunciation), though it had been a popular belief among some Catholics for several centuries. Pius himself was devoted to the Virgin and believed that she had cured him of epilepsy earlier in life. By making the declaration without first consulting the world's bishops and cardinals, Pius IX in effect served notice of his preeminence on questions of doctrinal definition. He also implied that of the two sources of Catholic authority, scripture and tradition, tradition should take the upper hand, even though in its name new as well as venerable doctrines could develop. To a critic, Pius once remarked: "Tradition? I am Tradition!" Meanwhile, the apparition of the Virgin to Bernadette Soubirous of Lourdes in 1858 confirmed, in many Catholics' eyes, his wisdom. Mary allegedly told Bernadette: "I am the Immaculate Conception," a declaration treasured by orthodox Catholics as confirmation of the pope's decree.

Papal Infallibility Declaration Approved

Pius moved to strengthen his authority further by summoning the world's bishops to a Vatican Council, which convened in St. Peter's Basilica, Rome, at the end of 1869. With the help of his secretary of state, Cardinal Antonelli, and the influential English convert Cardinal Manning, the *Curia* (Vatican civil service) had carefully orchestrated the event beforehand, and when the prelates assembled they were presented with a fait accompli: documents proclaiming papal infallibility which they were expected to endorse by acclamation. A minority of the world's bishops, the Gallicans, along with many theologians, were dismayed at this Ultramontane scheme, because they saw the declaration as a crucial shift in Catholic power relations, designed to strip them of their own authority and many time-honored privileges. Many of the bishops from the United States, led by Kenrick of St. Louis, Missouri, were opposed to the decree of infallibility because they realized that it would intensify Protestant hostility and make their task of spreading Catholicism in America harder then ever. But despite their superior intellectual skills, which they used to restrict the sweeping language of the declaration, limiting infallibility to declarations only on questions of faith and morals, the anti-infallibilists lacked the numbers to forestall the declaration. Rather than scandalize the council, 60 of the bishops who could not in conscience vote for infallibility left Rome on the day before the crucial vote, which was carried on July 18, 1870, with 533 for and only two against (one of the two was the bishop of Arkansas). When the constitution, *Pastor Aeternus*, was read out in St. Peter's, the two knelt at the pope's feet and pledged their full assent to the will of the majority.

Infallibility became the centerpiece of Catholic "triumphalism" for the next century. No sooner had the vote on infallibility been passed than war broke out in Europe, and as the French troops guarding Rome withdrew to serve **Napoleon III** in the Franco-Prussian War, an Italian army moved into Rome, forcing the bishops to disperse. It was, politically, the final humiliation of Pius IX, but it coincided almost exactly with his greatest spiritual exaltation. Not until the pontificate of **John XXIII** and the Second Vatican Council (1962–65) was the stern logic of Pius IX's Ultramontanism mitigated. His last act as a political ruler was to climb the *Scala Santa* on his knees (he was now nearly 80 and had long flowing white hair) to address his troops in the Lateran piazza, telling them to put up only a token resistance, to show that they were yielding to force. After a brief bombardment, they surrendered the next day, and Rome became the new capital of a united Italy. For the remaining seven years of his life, Pius never showed by either word or deed that he acknowledged the new king, **Victor Emmanuel II.**

Shortly before Victor Emmanuel's death in 1878, Pius almost admitted that he had blundered in his uncompromising attitude towards the rest of the world. "I hope," he said, "that my successor will be as much attached to the Church as I have been and will have as keen a desire to do good: beyond that, I can see that everything has changed; my system and my policies have had their day, but I am too old to change my course; that will be the task of my successor."

Bitterly disliked by many of the Roman population, a mob pelted his coffin during the funeral procession which brought his reign to an inglorious end. By then, as historian Carlton Hayes observes:

> the Catholic Church seemed to be feuding with the whole modern world, intellectually, politically, and morally. Its influence on the life and thought of the fashioners of public opinion—leading men of letters, journalists, educators, and scholars—was fast disappearing, and its hold was gone on a large fraction of the bourgeoisie and on the bulk of the urban proletariat. It appeared impotent to dike anywhere the flood tide of "science," liberalism, Marxism, anti-clericalism, and secularization. Its foes had mastered Italy and despoiled the Church of its age-old capital city and of a vast deal of popular prestige.

The task of Leo XXIII was to create a new place in the world for this jeopardized Church, and to restore its dignity as a purely spiritual organization.

SOURCES:

Aubert, R. "Pope Pius IX" in *New Catholic Encyclopedia*. Vol II. 1967.

Bokenkotter, Thomas. *A Concise History of the Catholic Church.* Doubleday, 1979.

Hales, E. E. Y. *The Catholic Church in the Modern World.* Hanover House, 1958.

Hayes, Carlton. *A Generation of Materialism.* Harper, 1941.

Homes, Derek. *The Triumph of the Holy See: A Short History of the Papacy in the Nineteenth Century*. Burns & Oates, 1978.

Vidler, Alec. *The Church in an Age of Revolution*. Pelican, 1971.

FURTHER READING:

Hales, E. E. Y. *Pio Nono*. Eyre & Spottiswoode, 1954.

Ward, Wilfrid. *William George Ward and the Catholic Revival*. Macmillan, 1893.

Francisco Pizarro

(c. 1475–1541)

Spanish conquistador, who conquered the fabled Inca Empire, winning unparalleled wealth for his monarch Charles V and for Spain.

Of all the Spanish conquerors, the name of Francisco Pizarro has been the most sorely maligned and misunderstood. Many have equated his name, somewhat simplistically, with greed, treachery, and dark acts of violence. Yet each of these critics has been forced to grant him his due for bravery. If Pizarro represented all of the basest qualities of the Spanish conquistadors, he also represented the best. In a breed renowned for its courage, Pizarro stands apart as the most audacious of all. If his name today recalls avarice, deceit, and blood, it is also synonymous with a fortitude and intrepidness rarely found.

Francisco Pizarro was born around 1475 in the rugged region of Estremadura in Old Castile. His father was a royal infantry captain and his mother a maid of humble origin. The couple never married and the young boy was raised in the household of his paternal grandparents. So abject was the poverty of his youth, legend has it, that he was suckled by a sow and turned early to a life of crime. Eventually the silent, gloomy but robust Pizarro turned to a career as a soldier, taking part in local manorial feuds and later serving the Spanish crown in Italy.

Born c. 1475 in Trujillo, Estremadura, in Castile; died on June 26, 1541, in Lima, Peru; son of Gonzalo Pizarro (royal infantry captain) and Francisca Gonzalez; never married; children: Francisco, Gonzalo, Juan and Francisca (all illegitimate). Descendants: Francisco de Ampuero of Peru. Successors: Gonzalo Pizarro (brother), governor of Peru.

Contributed by Glenn Feldman, Ph.D. candidate in History, Auburn University, Auburn, Alabama

1502	Journeyed to Hispaniola from Spain
1509	Accompanied Alonso de Ojeda on his exploration of Colombia
1513	Acted as chief lieutenant for Balboa on the exploration that discovered the Pacific Ocean
1519–23	Accumulated a fortune as mayor and magistrate of the town of Panama
1524–28	Made three initial voyages of discovery along the western coast of South America
1531	Began the conquest of Inca Peru
1532	Defeated and kidnapped Atahualpa at Cajamarca
1533	Seized and occupied the Inca capital of Cuzco
1535	Founded the city of Lima, Peru
1541	Assassinated at his palace in Lima

In 1502, the young man journeyed to Hispaniola where an uncle probably helped him become a settler. But restlessness was the most abiding Pizarro trait after courage, and he enlisted in Alonso de Ojeda's 1509 expedition to the Gulf of Urabá on the Caribbean coast of Colombia. Ojeda was then renowned as the bravest man of his day, and Pizarro gained valuable experience as well as a reputation for reliability and level-headedness.

Four years later, Pizarro served as Vasco Núñez de Balboa's chief lieutenant in the epoch-making exploration of Panama and discovery of the Pacific Ocean. Wading waist-deep into the waters of the Pacific, Balboa claimed the ocean and all of the territories it touched for the king of Spain. From 1519 to 1523, Francisco Pizarro built a small fortune as the mayor and magistrate of the fledgling town of Panama.

Hearing fantastic rumors of an advanced civilization to the south (Peru) that held inestimable wealth, Pizarro formed a partnership in Panama with three other men for the express purpose of southern exploration: Diego de Almagro raised men and supplies, Father Hernando de Luque gathered funds, and Judge Gaspar de Espinosa provided financing as a silent partner. Pizarro was assigned to lead the actual explorations. But the governor of Panama, Pedro Arias de Ávila (Pedrarias)—a shallow, embittered, jealous old man and treacherous executioner of the noble Balboa—was resentful of anyone else's good fortune, perceiving it as a threat to his own authority.

Accordingly, he forbade the partners from engaging in explorations to the south.

Pizarro Departs on First Voyage of Discovery

After tedious negotiations by the gifted Luque, Pizarro left Panama in November 1524 on the first of four voyages of discovery. The disheartened group returned the next year, minus 30 of its original number. They had been forced to endure severe privations, and at one point even ate seaweed to avoid starvation. In November 1526, Pizarro and Almagro set sail again, this time with two ships and more men. "Endless mangrove swamps, insects, starvation, disease, and the wounds inflicted by the poisoned arrows of the natives" soon diminished their number and drove them "to the verge of madness and despair."

The unhappy party divided at the San Juan River. After a near mutiny, Almagro returned to Panama with the malcontents to raise additional recruits, while Pizarro and his men remained behind, stranded on the Isle of Gallo. Ordering a raft built, Pizarro and the small party sailed to the somewhat more hospitable neighboring island of Gorgona and stayed there for the remainder of 1527. When Ávila sent a relief ship to fetch the stranded adventurers, Pizarro greeted news of his rescue with a dramatic act of willpower disguised as a gesture of defiance. Gathering his shivering, half-clad, starving men on the beach, the mercenary leader drew a line with his sword in the sand and dared all those "who were not fools and cowards to follow him" to wealth and glory. Only 13 men decided to stay; they subsequently became known throughout the New World as "the thirteen of fame."

Pizarro greeted a second rescue ship by commandeering it and steering it southward towards Peru. Making port at Túmbes in late 1527, the Spanish leader and his men were welcomed by a rich Inca noble and gained firsthand evidence of the vast wealth that would one day make the Inca Empire legendary. The encouraged party sailed back to Panama to regroup in early 1528.

Though the Panamanian governor officially forbade any new southern enterprises, it was too late. Pizarro's appetite had been whetted at Túmbes. Luque and Almagro agreed to send Pizarro to Spain in the spring to gain the consent of **Charles V** for their enterprise. The young Spanish monarch and his Council of the Indies eagerly accepted Pizarro's gifts of gold and silver. Making Pizarro governor of any new lands discovered, as well as captain-general for life, the council guaranteed his jurisdiction for 600 miles along the coast of South America and reinvoked the ancient coat of arms worn by his father. Meanwhile, Luque and Almagro were granted minor honors and placed in subaltern roles. It was a slight from which the proud Almagro never recovered.

Pizarro had trouble raising new men in Spain for the venture. Returning to his roots in Estremadura, he convinced four of his brothers and a cousin to throw in their lot. These men were "poor, proud and avaricious, qualities which led them to do and dare anything for the sake of sudden wealth." By January 1530, the Pizarro brothers had arrived in Panama and spent the remainder of the year raising soldiers and supplies for the imminent venture. In January 1531, while Almagro remained behind to follow with reinforcements, the expedition sailed with one ship, 180 men, 37 horses, and two light cannon.

Arriving in Peru, Pizarro immediately involved himself in local politics, allying with friendly native chieftains and winning a large battle at Puna. In early 1532, Hernando de Soto, a dashing cavalier, joined the expedition with a fine ship, 100 fresh men, and numerous horses. After founding San Miguel de Tangarara (Piura) and further enmeshing himself in local disputes, Pizarro pressed onward, leaving behind a token garrison in the new town.

With "sublime audacity," Pizarro and his handful of men penetrated the heart of the great Inca Empire. **Atahualpa,** the Inca emperor, recently weakened in a series of civil wars with his brother Huáscar, at first allowed the intrepid Spanish party to advance through his realm unmolested. But on November 15, 1532, Pizarro's men had their first real glimpse of the Inca's overwhelming forces: 40,000 troops encamped in bright tents outside of Cajamarca. The Spaniards were momentarily taken aback but "with that hardy courage which was their best characteristic, the Castilians smiled grimly at one another and went on with the game."

Francisco Pizarro sent 30 expert horsemen under de Soto and his most physically intimidating brother, Hernando, to request an interview from the proud Inca. A ferocious equestrian display by de Soto gained the desired effect of sufficiently cowing Atahualpa's courtiers. The Inca agreed to meet the Spanish leader on the following day.

Inca Emperor Meets the Spaniards

On November 16, when Atahualpa arrived in Cajamarca for the historic appointment, he was arrayed in a brilliant garment studded with gold, silver, and emeralds, and borne regally aloft on a golden litter. Perhaps overconfident, Atahualpa brought a retinue of only 4,000 armed men with him.

Pizarro's men presented the emperor to Father Vicente de Valverde who began a torrid excoriation of the natives, charging Atahualpa to accept Christianity as his religion and Charles V as his overlord. The Inca replied by expressing only scorn for the Spanish sovereign and his God, "who was three persons and one more, which makes four." In a final fit of disgust, Atahualpa flung de Valverde's Bible to the ground.

At this apparent sacrilege, Pizarro and his men leapt from hiding and began to attack the startled natives. The Incas, taken by surprise, were thoroughly discomfited by the Spaniards' horses, shining armor, steel weapons, and firearms. Though Pizarro had only two light artillery pieces and a few arquebuses, the foreign noise stunned the terrified Incas. Within a short time, the Spaniards had cut the Incas to pieces. Pizarro himself rushed forward and "rescued" Atahualpa, whose litter had been overturned, by placing him in personal custody.

After Cajamarca, Pizarro—much as **Hernán Cortés** had done in Mexico—held the Inca empire through the person of Atahualpa, stipulating that Atahualpa's release could be gained only by filling a large room with gold and silver. By June 1533, Atahualpa's ransom had been fulfilled, confirming the wildest dreams of the Spaniards, but Almagro's force arrived too late to share in the spoils. Pizarro cut short a feud between his brother Hernando and Almagro by sending Hernando to Madrid to present the Spanish king with the "royal fifth." Still, the simmering feud portended volumes for the future.

On August 29, 1533, despite fulfillment of the ransom, Pizarro ordered the execution of Atahualpa. Without a doubt, the act was a treacherous and cruel one, yet it has often been viewed out of context. It occurred in the midst of an age frequently distinguished by its treachery, deceit, and barbarity. Pizarro had initially objected to the murder of the Inca overlord but had been vehemently opposed by Almagro and the priest, de Valverde. To complicate matters, an Inca interpreter who had quarrelled with Atahualpa had aroused Spanish fears of conspiracy by deliberately misinterpreting between Pizarro and the Inca.

The assassins bided their time until Hernando de Soto, the Inca's protector, left Cajamarca on a reconnaissance. After a staged trial and a series of essentially baseless charges (except for Atahualpa's ordering of his brother Huáscar's

Gonzalo Pizarro
(1502–1548)

Gonzalo Pizarro, brother of Francisco Pizarro, was born in Trujillo, Spain, around 1502. Ably assisting his more famous brother in the conquest of Peru from 1531 to 1533, Gonzalo became a wealthy man in the process. In April 1538, he successfully helped another brother, Hernando, at the bloody Battle of Las Salinas against Deigo de Almagro, the sworn enemy of the Pizarro family.

Francisco Pizarro appointed Gonzalo to the governorship of Quito in 1539 and charged him with the exploration of the wilderness to the east of Ecuador, known only as the "Land of Cinnamon." On Christmas Day of that year, Gonzalo led an expedition of 200 Spaniards and 4,000 natives into the eastern wilds. During the expedition, Pizarro and his men were treacherously betrayed by his lieutenant Francisco de Orellana who, on the pretense of returning to Quito for supplies and fresh troops, instead sailed east until he inadvertently reached the Atlantic Ocean.

Two and a half years of "hideous tribulations" ensued for Pizarro's men, with the Spaniards being saved only by Gonzalo's "soldierly qualities." At one point, Pizarro and his men had to eat their dogs and horses to survive. In June 1542, a small remnant of the expedition staggered into Quito.

Upon his arrival Gonzalo learned of Francisco Pizarro's assassination at Lima and of the New Laws issued by Charles V. The laws reflected the influence of Father Bartolome de Las Casas, author of the legend of Spanish cruelty and greed. Las Casas, although he had never personally visited Peru, wrote of the Pizarros as "abominable demon[s] who laid waste [to] whole cities and countries." The New Laws called for drastic reductions in the amounts of land and natives the Spanish conquerors could own.

Appealing to Gonzalo for protection, the Spanish settlers began the first serious rebellion against royal authority in the New World. Gonzalo and his stout warlord, Francisco de Carvejal, known as "the demon of the Andes," soundly defeated a royal force at Anaquito in January 1546; but after crushing a strong army at Huarina in October of the following year, they were deserted by most of their troops and finally lost to Viceroy Pedro de la Gasca in the Valley of Xaquixaguana in April 1548. On April 10, 1548, Pizarro and Carvejal were captured and beheaded as rebels. ∎

assassination), the Spaniards condemned the Inca to death. At the last instant, Atahualpa avoided being burned at the stake by agreeing to accept a Christian baptism. Instead, he was strangled in the public square at Cajamarca. Upon his return, an enraged de Soto took his portion of the Inca fortune and departed for future glory in the southeastern section of North America.

Soon after the execution, Pizarro and his forces marched on Cuzco, the Inca capital. After surviving numerous skirmishes, they occupied the city in March 1533 without a serious struggle. Building a cathedral in Cuzco, Pizarro set up a broad administration and encouraged his soldiers to seek fortunes in nearby provinces. The wealth of Inca Peru shocked even the gold-crazed Spaniards and fueled Spain's expansionist foreign policy for the next 300 years. At one typical site, Pizarro's troops discovered 150 silver bars, 20 feet long and eight inches in width. Pizarro also wisely resurrected an Inca emperor in the person of Atahualpa's half-brother, Manco Capac. Through the young Inca, Pizarro ruled all of Peru.

In early 1534, Pizarro narrowly avoided a serious crisis when he was able to buy off a formidable rival. Pedro de Alvarado, Cortés's cruel Mexican lieutenant and the governor of Guatemala, marched into Ecuador at the head of a 500-man army. After a desperate race to Quito between Alvarado and two Pizarro lieutenants, the pair bought Alvarado's peaceful withdrawal for $200,000 in Inca gold. Alvarado left South America after a cordial dinner with Pizarro. He also left behind a large group of restless soldiers, many of them of higher social standing than Pizarro's own men.

Spanish Monarch Divides South America

When Hernando Pizarro sailed for Spain in September 1534 and presented Charles V with a fantastic cache of Peruvian treasure, the Spanish monarch formally divided South America between Francisco Pizarro and Diego de Almagro. To the former, he granted New Castile and to the latter New Toledo, the southern territory of Chile. Early in 1535, Governor Francisco Pizarro established a new capital at Lima.

At this point, he actually considered granting Almagro the ancient city of Cuzco to repay him for old slights. At a critical moment though, Pizarro learned that Almagro planned to take Cuzco for himself. "To make the graceful gesture," thought Pizarro, "was one thing; to let him keep it properly as his own was quite another." After a reversal of his Cuzco policy, the rival camps faced off for six months in armed vigilance over the city.

Pizarro eventually met with his old partner and convinced him to explore his territories in Chile. When Almagro set forth in July 1535 with 550 men, Cuzco was drained of over a thousand additional Spaniards as three other expeditions of discovery left the ancient city at about the same time.

Manco Capac, chafing under his bridle as a ruling puppet, chose this opportune moment to launch a massive revolt. Escaping to the Inca highlands, Manco organized a great siege of Cuzco, Lima, and other cities along the Peruvian coast in February 1536. Led by Hernando, the resistance of the Pizarro brothers in Cuzco was heroic. For over a full year, 700 Spanish soldiers held off 100,000 Inca besiegers. Francisco Pizarro, himself besieged in Lima, could not come to his brothers' rescue. One brother, Juan, was killed at the fighting in Cuzco, and even the redoubtable Hernando was temporarily cowed when he observed five Spanish heads impaled on Inca spears displayed by the side of a road.

In March 1537, unsuccessful in his Chilean treasure hunt, Almagro returned unexpectedly to Cuzco with a dispirited army. The Incas, frightened by the Spanish reinforcements, fled to Vilacampa where Manco maintained sporadic guerilla warfare until 1541. More bitter than ever, Almagro was bent on taking Cuzco for himself.

During the next year fighting between Almagro and the Pizarro brothers raged. Finally Hernando Pizarro, having been imprisoned by Almagro and recently released, met the enemy at Las Salinas (the Salt-pits) on April 6, 1538. Reinforced by yet another Pizarro brother, Gonzalo, Hernando crushed Almagro's forces in "a fratricidal carnage of the most ghastly description." In the aftermath of the battle, Hernando ordered Almagro's execution.

From 1538 until 1541, the Pizarros worked to subdue Manco Capac and other hostile natives in the area. Francisco appointed Gonzalo to the governorship of Quito and charged him to explore the eastern wilds. Hernando, on another treasure-bearing trip home, was imprisoned by Charles V for the Pizarro sins in Peru. Before leaving Peru, he had solemnly warned Francisco to "beware the men of Chile." In Spain, he was kept in captivity for 20 years at the Castle de La Mota but allowed to marry one of Francisco's daughters.

On June 26, 1541, 20 armed men led by the Almagro's *mestizo* (mixed blood) son burst into Francisco Pizarro's palace in Lima. The old man, near 70, was seated at dinner with several close friends and relatives. "Like a lion roused in his lair," Pizarro leapt up, tore a sword from the wall,

The assassination of Francisco Pizarro.

and killed three of his assailants before being stabbed mortally in the throat. Crying "Jesus!" the conqueror fell. Lying on the cold palace floor, Pizarro made the sign of the cross with his own blood and kissed it before he died.

Historian William Prescott wrote about the Spanish leader: "[T]hough neither a good man nor a great man… it is impossible not to regard him as a very extraordinary one."

SOURCES:

Hemming, John. *The Conquest of the Incas.* Harcourt, 1970.

Means, Philip Aimsworth. *Fall of the Inca Empire and the Spanish Rule in Peru: 1530–1780.* Guardian Press, 1964.

Prescott, William H. *History of the Conquest of Peru.* Vol. II. Boston, 1847, Funk & Wagnalls, 1905.

FURTHER READING:

Helps, Sir Arthur. *The Life of Pizarro.* George Bell and Sons, 1888.

Lockhart, James. *Spanish Peru, 1532–1560: A Colonial Society.* University of Wisconsin Press, 1968.

Monzans, H. J. *Along the Andes and Down the Amazon.* D. Appleton, 1923.

Pompey

(106–48 B.C.)

Roman general, who cleared the Mediterranean Sea of pirates, conquered many eastern lands, and became the most important rival of Julius Caesar, against whom he fought, and lost, a Roman Civil War.

Name variations: Pompey the Great; became Gnaeus Pompeius Magnus in 81 B.C. when the title Magnus ("Great") was given to him by Sulla. Born Gnaeus Pompeius Strabo on September 29, 106 B.C., at Alba, Italy; murdered on September 28, 48 B.C., at Pelusium, Egypt; son of Gnaeus Pompeius Strabo and Lucilia (daughter of C. Lucilius Hirrus); married: Antistia, 86 B.C. (daughter of Publius Antistius); married: Aemilia, 82 B.C. (stepdaughter of Sulla); married: Mucia, 80 B.C. (related to the Mucii Scaevolae and the Caecilii Metelli); married: Julia, 59 B.C. (daughter of Julius Caesar); married: Cornelia, 52 B.C. (daughter of Metellus Scipio); children—third marriage: (sons) Gnaeus Pompeius Magnus Junior and Sextus Pompeius Magnus Pius; (daughter) Pompeia. Predecessor: (as "First Man in Rome") Sulla. Successor: Julius Caesar.

Pompey was born into a family of military and political importance in Rome. His father, Gnaeus Pompeius Strabo, served as *quaestor* (treasurer) in 104 B.C., *praetor* (second highest magistrate) in 92 B.C., and consul (chief magistrate) in 89. But it was in warfare, rather than civil administration, that both father and son would achieve their greatest recognition. Pompey's mother Lucilia, daughter of Gaius Lucilius Hirrus, was niece of the poet Gaius Lucilius. Pompey, however, never attained any distinction in literature.

As he grew into a handsome young man, it was said that Pompey bore a physical resemblance to **Alexander the Great,** a coincidence that foreshadowed his later travels in the Macedonian conqueror's footsteps at least partway through the East, earning him recognition as the "Roman Alexander." Also like his famous predecessor, Pompey became a warrior as a young man. At 17, he joined his father Strabo on the battlefield, having just put on the *toga virilis*, the garment that symbolized Roman manhood.

When the Italian allies rebelled, forming a league that waged the Social War against Rome's

"No Roman was ever held in such affection by the people as Pompey."

PLUTARCH

Contributed by J. Donald Hughes, Professor of History, University of Denver, Denver, Colorado

hegemony (dominance) with initial success, Pompey's father raised an army and led it into the hostile territory of the Marsi, the most prominent members of the anti-Roman coalition. Breaking through their forces, Strabo besieged the city of Asculum, eventually defeating the rebel leader Vidacilius and capturing the town. Pompey accompanied him throughout the campaign and fought at his side. In 89 B.C., the year of his consulate, Strabo was granted the privilege of a triumph, the Roman custom of a parade by a victorious general through the streets of Rome. When he died suddenly two years later, reportedly as the result of lightning that struck his tent, Pompey inherited the family estates in Picenum, a district on the Adriatic coast of Italy. He also inherited the military and political support his father had enjoyed there, unpopular though Strabo may have been with most Romans in the capital city.

None of Rome's leading politicians expected much of the dour general's precocious son. Pompey had been most noticed for his dalliance with a courtesan named Flora, who had become remarkably devoted to him. The months after his father's death were difficult: the bodyguard of Cinna, a leader of the popular party, ransacked his house, and Pompey was put on trial for keeping some of the money recovered in the capture of Asculum that rightfully belonged in the public treasury. Though he won a verdict of innocent, rumor said that it was because Pompey had made friends with the judge, Publius Antistius, whose daughter Antistia he married soon after the verdict.

In 83 B.C., Pompey entered the violent political arena on the side of Lucius Cornelius Sulla Felix, the conservative champion of the *optimates,* the party of the rich senatorial class. Sulla had invaded Italy after a campaign in the East and was engaged in a bitter struggle with the *populares* (popular) party, formerly led by Marius and Cinna. Pompey raised troops in Picenum, defeated three military units of the *populares,* and was rewarded by Sulla with *imperium,* or high-ranking command. In the following year, he defeated Sulla's rivals in Sicily and North Africa for which Sulla allowed him to celebrate a triumph. Sulla also granted him the title *Magnus* (the Great), which he attached to his name and would later pass on to his sons.

To cement his alliance with the great conservative leader, Pompey married Sulla's stepdaughter, Aemilia, a union for which he'd had to divorce Antistia. (In those days, marriages were the means of cementing political alliances.) But when his new wife Aemilia died soon afterwards, Pompey married Mucia, a relative of Sulla's most prominent supporters. Though the marriage was to be marked

by ill feeling and infidelity and eventually terminated by divorce, it lasted 17 years, during which time Mucia became the mother of Pompey's three surviving children: Pompey Junior, Sextus, and Pompeia.

In 79 B.C., Sulla retired due to illness and died the following year. Thus the way was open for Pompey to maneuver for the position of most powerful man in Rome. He first defeated Marcus Aemilius Lepidus, who wanted to repeal the antidemocratic constitution that Sulla had imposed on Rome, and drove him out of Italy. Then Pompey reluctantly became embroiled in a long, ultimately successful war in Spain in which he saved Sulla's old ally Metellus Pius from destruction by the popular general, Sertorius. On his return from Spain, Pompey helped Marcus Licinius Crassus mop up the last remnants of a slave uprising headed by Spartacus, the Thracian gladiator, and contrived to share the glory of that victory. At the end of 71 B.C., Pompey was granted his second triumph and served as consul with Crassus as his colleague the following year.

It was not long before it became clear that Pompey was not, after all, a doctrinaire follower of Sulla's conservative program, but an opportunist looking for the most expedient route to power. With new allies from the popular side, he worked to dismantle the Sullan constitution and reestablish the traditional ancestral constitution of the Roman Republic, with elements including the tribunes (officers whose duty it was to protect the rights of common citizens). Though such actions caused a rift with Crassus, a well-to-do citizen named Gaius Aurelius is said to have reconciled the two by telling them that "Jupiter had appeared to him in a dream and had instructed him to tell the consuls that they must not lay down their office until they had made friends with each other." This, at least for a time, they did.

Pompey Wins Stunning Military Victories

Pompey's most stunning series of military victories began in 67 B.C. with the extraordinary command granted to him against the pirates. He was given the power to requisition all of Rome's naval power, and all the resources of the coastlands, to rid the sea of them. So confident were the Romans of his success that the price of grain fell the moment he was appointed, as the pirates had been interfering with food shipments from Egypt and elsewhere; now the sea-lanes were to be opened. It took him only three months to sweep the Mediterranean free of the troublesome raiders. The crucial battle was fought off the shores of Cilicia (southern Turkey), where Pompey won at sea and pursued the pirates on land, capturing 90 warships and taking more than 20,000 prisoners.

At the time, the Roman general Lucius Lucinius Lucullus was facing defeat by the charismatic King Mithridates VI of Pontus, who managed to pose as a defender both of Greek and Iranian culture as he threatened the Romans over a wide area of the Near East. Lucullus' own troops were at the point of mutiny when Pompey was sent to replace him. The Roman army in the East was soon in good shape, and Pompey won brilliant victories in Asia Minor, Armenia, and the Caucasus region. Mithridates fled to the north side of the Black Sea, but Pompey captured his palace at Caenum and many secret documents, including love letters and a book in which the king had recorded his own dreams.

Pompey's explorations added to Roman botanical, geographical, and medical knowledge. After Tigranes I of Armenia became a Roman vassal, Pompey turned his attention southward, marching all the way from the Black Sea to Antioch in Syria, which he reached in 64 B.C. This area, the remnant of the kingdom of the Seleucids (the successors of Alexander the Great), he turned into a new Roman province of Syria. The next year, he annexed Palestine. Jerusalem resisted him, but Pompey captured the city after a three-month siege and replaced Aristobulus II, the high priest and Maccabean king of Judaea, with his brother John Hyrcanus II. Having heard about the unusual God worshipped by the Jews, Pompey marched into the Holy of Holies in the Temple, only to discover to his astonishment that it was an empty room containing no image. This was a terrible offense to Jewish religious sensibilities. Leaving Jerusalem, Pompey led his army toward another hostile center, the Nabataean citadel of Petra, but was interrupted by the welcome news that Mithridates had died. Settling matters in the East, he prepared to return to Rome.

The third triumph of Pompey, celebrating his eastern victories, was held on his 45th birthday in 61 B.C. It lasted more than two days and proved to be the most memorable in Rome's history. He had by then captured 1,000 fortified places and established 39 new cities—more even than Alexander the Great. With the plunder from the conquered lands carried on floats in the great parade, it would seem that Pompey's popularity should have reached its zenith. It did not. Scandal had surfaced in his absence, and he had to divorce his wife Mucia. This made enemies of her family, the powerful Metelli. Even Rome's common citizens seemed to turn against him, and he had to look for allies.

In 60 B.C., Pompey found the power he sought in a new coalition, the famous First Triumvirate, with Crassus and **Julius Caesar.** Caesar was elected consul for the following year and then went to Gaul as governor and conqueror, but in the division of responsibility between the three men, Pompey had authority over most of the Empire. To cement the bond between the leading men, Pompey married Caesar's daughter, Julia. But Pompey wanted to mend his fences in Rome while Caesar was out of the city, so he sought reconciliation with the senate and its influential member, Marcus Tullius **Cicero.** The senate granted him supervision of Rome's grain supply, and once again the markets were filled with inexpensive wheat and barley.

In April 56 B.C., the three strong men met again, this time at Luca, and renewed the triumvirate. In the year 55 B.C., Caesar was to return to Gaul, and Crassus would receive Pompey's old command in the East. Pompey was allotted Spain, but he never returned there, preferring to send legates to administer the provinces on his behalf while he stayed at Rome and attempted to expand his power base. During this period, his great building project came to fruition. The Theater of Pompey was inaugurated with elaborate displays of sports, musical contests, and wild-animal fights including the slaughter of lions and elephants. The latter, however, was a debacle if Pompey had expected his shows to add to his popularity. The elephants gained the crowd's sympathy when, wounded by javelins, they defended themselves by snatching the shields of their attackers and trumpeting piteously.

Events moved toward an inevitable break between Pompey and Caesar. Julia died in 54 B.C., dissolving the marriage bond between them, and Pompey would refuse to negotiate a new one. Crassus was killed on his eastern campaign in the next year, which brought the triumvirate to an end. Increasingly, Pompey made common cause with the extreme senatorial *optimates,* and in 52 B.C., they arranged to make him sole consul (though constitutionally there were always two) and prolonged his military command for a period of five years. Pompey married Cornelia, daughter of Metellus Scipio, thus mending his fences with the faction that had supported Sulla. At the end of 50 B.C., Pompey accepted from the senate the appointment as commander in chief of the Republic's forces in Italy. This forced Caesar's hand; if he wished to save any vestige of his power, he would have to fight Pompey.

Caesar Crosses the Rubicon, Defeats Pompey

The border between Caesar's legal province of Gaul and Italy proper, which was in Pompey's domain, was the small river called the Rubicon. When Caesar crossed it in 49 B.C., he placed himself outside Roman law and challenged both Pompey and the senate. Civil war had been declared. Instead of confronting Caesar in Italy, however, Pompey took his army across the Adriatic Sea to Macedonia. Many senators followed. Caesar swiftly occupied Rome and took the opportunity to capture those of Pompey's troops that were still in Spain. In the first clash of the two commanders, Pompey repelled Caesar at Dyrrhachium on the Adriatic coast. But Caesar was far from giving up. On August 9, 48 B.C., the armies met again at Pharsalus, on the edge of the plain of Thessaly in Greece. The night before, Pompey had dreamed that he was adorning the Temple of Venus in Rome—an inauspicious vision because Venus was Caesar's mythological ancestor. Although his forces outnumbered Caesar's almost two to one, Pompey adopted defensive tactics in the battle; Caesar's men seized the initiative, winning a decisive victory. As it turned out, Caesar had won the war as well as the battle.

Pompey fled to the Aegean shore and took ship for Egypt, stopping on the way at Mytilene to pick up his wife Cornelia and son Gnaeus. Though he had hoped to find support in Egypt, civil war was raging there too between the young queen Cleopatra and her even younger brother, the boy-king Ptolemy XIII. Arriving off the coast near one of the mouths of the Nile, at Pelusium, Pompey was ferried ashore in a small boat. He was then stabbed without warning by Septimius, a centurion who had once served under him, another officer named Salvius, and Achillas, one of the regents of Egypt for Ptolemy XIII.

Had the murderers hoped to gain favor with Caesar by killing Pompey, they were certainly disappointed. They gave his head to Caesar, who was horrified and put Achillas and his colleague Pothinus to death. Caesar treated the head of his adversary with the greatest honor and gave it a proper Roman cremation with incense, spices, and prayers. After Caesar's death, the ashes of Pompey were taken to Cornelia for burial.

SOURCES:

Appianus of Alexandria. *Roman History.* Translated by Horace White, Harvard University Press (Loeb Classical Library), 1958–1962.

Caesar, Julius. *The Civil War.* Translated by Jane F. Mitchell, Penguin, 1967.

Cocceianus, Dio Cassius. *Roman History.* Translated by Earnest Cary, Harvard University Press (Loeb Classical Library), 1955–1961.

Lucanus, Marcus Annaeus. *Civil War (Pharsalia).* Translated by P.F. Widdows, Indiana University Press, 1988.

Plutarch. *Fall of the Roman Republic: Six Lives by Plutarch.* Translated by Rex Warner, Penguin, 1972.

FURTHER READING:

Greenhalgh, Peter. *Pompey: The Roman Alexander.* University of Missouri Press, 1981.

———. *Pompey: The Republican Prince.* University of Missouri Press, 1982.

Holliday, Vivian L. *Pompey in Cicero's Correspondence and Lucan's Civil War.* Mouton, 1969.

Leach, John. *Pompey the Great.* Croom Helm, 1978.

Rawson, Beryl. *The Politics of Friendship: Pompey and Cicero.* Sydney University Press, 1978.

Seager, Robin. *Pompey: A Political Biography.* University of California Press, 1979.

Post-Stalin Soviet Leaders

Georgi Malenkov, Nikolai Bulganin, Alexei Kosygin, Leonid Brezhnev, Yuri Andropov, Konstantin Chernenko, Viacheslav Molotov

The death of **Joseph Stalin** on March 5, 1953, left the Soviet Union in a state of crisis. In international affairs, the Cold War with the United States had created a powerful enemy along Stalin's western border in Europe. In Asia, the Korean War dragged on. Begun in 1950 when the Soviet satellite state of North Korea attacked South Korea, it now involved Communist China on the North Korean side, while United Nations forces led by the United States helped to defend South Korea.

Within the Soviet Union the harshness of Stalin's dictatorship during his last years paralyzed political and economic initiative. The standard of living remained low as most of the country's resources were poured into the development of heavy industry and military power. Moreover, by the time of Stalin's death, many Soviet citizens expected a repetition of the bloody purges of the 1930s to break out. The earlier purges had eliminated political and economic leaders at all levels of society, and they had gone on to place millions of ordinary Russians under long prison terms.

Thus, the deadening effect of dictatorship at home combined with opposition abroad to create a

Contributed by Neil Heyman, Professor of History, San Diego State University, San Diego, California

highly dangerous situation. Stalin's death, however, opened possibilities for change in Soviet life and in the Soviet role in international affairs.

Each of the men listed above competed for power during the years following 1953, and each had a role to play in shaping the history of the Soviet Union in the post-Stalinist era. All of them came from a single generation. The oldest, **Viacheslav Molotov,** was born in 1890; the youngest, **Yuri Andropov,** was born in 1914. The first to die was **Nikolai Bulganin** in 1975; the last to die was **Georgi Malenkov** in 1988.

Several of these future national leaders participated in the November 1917 Revolution by which the Communists had come to power, or the Civil War from 1918 to 1921 in which the new government successfully imposed its control on the country. Each played a leading role in the Soviet Communist Party, and each rose to positions of power and influence under Stalin in the 1930s or 1940s. Together with **Nikita Khrushchev,** they dominated Soviet leadership from 1953 through the middle of the 1980s and the rise of **Mikhail Gorbachev.**

Just as the careers of these individuals were an important part of Soviet history, so also was the way in which each ended his life. Many Soviet leaders like Nikolai Bukharin or Grigory Zinoviev, who had been Stalin's contemporaries and his rivals, were murdered by the dictator. After the deaths of Stalin and **Lavrenti Beria** in 1953, the system became less harsh. Three of these individuals (Brezhnev, Andropov, and Chernenko) rose to power, became weakened by illness, but still ruled the Soviet Union to their death. Four (Malenkov, Bulganin, Kosygin, and Molotov) lost the struggle for power, but they were permitted to retire peacefully.

Georgi Malenkov
(1902–1988)

Georgi Malenkov was the first of these individuals to rise to prominence after the death of the great dictator in the spring of 1953. When Stalin's funeral was held in early March, Malenkov was the chief pallbearer and mourner at the gathering. His role on this occasion matched both his past and his apparent future. He was Stalin's man, an individual who had never directed a major regional Party organization, a figure who had always run the Party from the center under Stalin's eye. Unlike many of the leading figures in the history of the Soviet Union, Malenkov had made his career

entirely within the Secretariat, the central body in Moscow that ran the Soviet Communist Party. He seemed to be Stalin's chosen successor.

Malenkov's appearance gave no hint of his power and his ruthlessness. He was a short, plump, ordinary-looking man, someone who would have melted into the crowd on a Moscow street corner. In the end, he disappeared into that kind of obscurity.

Born in Orenburg on January 13, 1902, Malenkov was just old enough to serve in the Civil War as a military commissar. Military commissars were Communist Party members assigned to accompany combat officers who were often drawn from the prerevolutionary officer corps. The job of the commissar was to make sure that the officer remained loyal to the Communist government while carrying out his military duties. Thus, Malenkov apparently joined the Communist Party while he was still a teenager.

Malenkov became a member of the staff of the Soviet Central Committee, the official governing body of the Party, in 1925. The Communist Party was supposed to meet periodically in national congresses, and one of the duties of each congress was to choose the Central Committee who then chose the Politburo, the Party's chief policy-making body. In fact, Party congresses were held less and less frequently from the mid-1920s onward. Power was concentrated in the Politburo. By the end of the 1920s, Joseph Stalin had won control of the Politburo, the Central Committee, and thus the entire Party.

Picked by Stalin for high responsibility, Malenkov rose rapidly in the Central Committee bureaucracy. In 1934, barely 32 years old, he was put in charge of the Central Committee's personnel bureau and participated in the brutal purges that wiped out many of the Party's leaders between 1935 and 1939.

In 1939, Malenkov was made a member of the Central Committee. Since a majority of its members had been purged over the last several years, loyal Stalinists were now lifted up to take their places. In 1941, he became a candidate member of the Politburo. A candidate member was a junior member who did not yet have the power to vote. Malenkov became a full member in 1946.

If Malenkov distinguished himself in helping to carry out the purges, his second significant role was in helping to direct the Soviet defense effort in World War II. As a member of the State Defense Committee, a small group of Communist Party leaders that functioned as a war cabinet, he

Nikolai Bulganin (left) meets with U.S. president Dwight D. Eisenhower in February 1958 shortly before he was ousted as Soviet premier.

and 1955, both offered the Party and the Soviet public reform programs. Malenkov concentrated on changes in industry designed to produce more consumer goods; Khrushchev took the lead in agricultural reform. Malenkov's resignation from the post of premier in early 1955 was a signal of Khrushchev's victory.

In a more dangerous second stage, Malenkov joined with other opponents of Khrushchev like Molotov and Lazar Kaganovich in an attempt to force Khrushchev from power in June 1957. Khrushchev rallied support in the Central Committee, and Malenkov's "anti-Party group" was defeated.

In Stalin's time, Malenkov and the others would have been executed. It was a sign of important changes in the Soviet political system when Malenkov was sent off to manage a power station in Kazakhstan. Retiring a few years later, Malenkov, who had once been at the top of the Soviet political system, lived out the final decades of his life in obscurity. He died in Moscow sometime in late January 1988.

Nikolai Bulganin

(1895–1975)

When Nikita Khrushchev removed Malenkov from the position of premier in 1955, he carefully chose an individual who was well-known but also unlikely to become a serious rival. That figure was Nikolai Bulganin. Bulganin had a brief period of fame from 1955 to 1958 as the man who ran the Soviet government for Khrushchev. He was also Khrushchev's traveling companion and drinking partner as the Soviet Communist Party leader began to tour the world.

Nikolai Bulganin was born on June 11, 1895, in Nizhni Novgorod, the son of an accountant. Joining the Bolshevik Party in the middle of 1917, he began a career that spanned service in the army, the secret police, the Soviet industrial establishment, and the government.

After a brief period in the Red Army during the Civil War, Bulganin was recruited for several years by the *Cheka*, the newly established Bolshevik secret police. In the 1920s, he made a name for himself as a factory manager in Moscow. His reputation as an industrial leader soared when he went on to direct an important factory in the years from 1927 to 1931. Bulganin was thus a model for others during Stalin's First Five Year Plan to expand Soviet industry.

played a key role in maintaining military industrial production.

Although Stalin promoted Malenkov as a possible successor, the Soviet dictator never permitted any of his lieutenants to rest unchallenged. In the years after World War II, Stalin brought several regional Party leaders back to high posts in Moscow to compete against Malenkov. Thus Andrei Zhdanov was called in from Leningrad in 1945. When Zhdanov died in 1948, Stalin then turned to Nikita Khrushchev from the Ukraine. But Malenkov played a prominent role at the 19th Party Congress in the fall of 1952, the last one Stalin attended, giving the most important report to the gathering. When Stalin died the next spring and Soviet leaders divided his offices, Malenkov was made both premier of the Soviet government and head of the Communist Party.

In short order, however, he lost the top post in the Communist Party to Nikita Khrushchev. Malenkov's colleagues were unwilling to let him control too many powerful offices at one time. The rivalry between Malenkov and Khrushchev that followed went through two stages. Between 1953

In 1931, Bulganin switched over to the government as head of the city administration in Moscow. Here he began a long partnership with Nikita Khrushchev, a rising leader in the Moscow Communist Party organization. The two of them carried out highly publicized industrial projects of the Five Year Plan like the construction of the Moscow subway system. These years marked Bulganin as a favored Stalinist official. He not only survived the purges of the 1930s but took over posts vacated by its victims: in 1939, for example, Bulganin was made a member of the Communist Party Central Committee.

During World War II, Bulganin served in the army as a high-ranking commissar, a political representative of the Party empowered to oversee the work of the fighting commanders. Two honors after the war showed his success: in 1947, he received the elevated military rank of Marshal of the Soviet Union; the next year, he was named a member of the Politburo.

In the division of power following Stalin's death, Bulganin supported Khrushchev. When Khrushchev defeated his rival Malenkov and forced him to resign as premier in early 1955, Bulganin took the vacated post of head of the government. Together Khrushchev and Bulganin embarked on a series of foreign travels ranging from China to Britain between 1955 and 1957. The trips were notable as a signal that Soviet leaders were interested in improved ties with the outside world. Many observers thought Bulganin, with his neatly trimmed beard and white hair, looked the part of a national leader—in contrast to the crude and pudgy Khrushchev. Nonetheless, both men became infamous for their alcohol consumption in public during these foreign trips.

Bulganin's time at the top ended within three years. Identified with the "anti-Party group" that tried unsuccessfully to overthrow Khrushchev in June 1957, he was ousted less than a year later, and Khrushchev himself took the post of premier.

Like Malenkov, Bulganin received a minor post in a locale far removed from Moscow—the Caucasus. Retiring in 1960, the former head of the Soviet government lived obscurely on his pension until his death in Moscow on February 24, 1975.

Alexei Kosygin
(1904–1980)

The departure of Khrushchev from office in 1964 brought to power a very different kind of Soviet leader, men like Alexei Kosygin and **Leonid Brezhnev.** Khrushchev's fall also brought a novel development in Soviet government: the Soviet Union came under the prolonged rule of several leaders acting jointly. Kosygin was Brezhnev's coequal for years. This was a different situation from the state of affairs under Lenin, Stalin, and Khrushchev. Even though Kosygin was eventually overshadowed by Brezhnev, the mild-looking prime minister continued to play a visible role in Soviet life for nearly a decade until his death.

Alexei Kosygin was born on February 21, 1904, the son of a factory worker in St. Petersburg. Both his family background and his birthplace set the tone for much of his career: Kosygin became the leading industrial administrator of the Stalin and post-Stalin years, and many of his achievements centered around the city of St. Petersburg (renamed Leningrad until 1991).

While still a teenager, Kosygin fought with the Red Army in the Civil War. Trained as an engineer, he built a reputation as an industrial manager in Leningrad, starting in 1934. Like Bulganin, his success in carrying the Five Year Plans in a key city led to an important political post: head of Leningrad's city government in 1938. The following year, he was put in charge of the entire textile industry of the Soviet Union. Young industrial managers like Kosygin often rose quickly in the late 1930s as Stalin's purges wiped out the older generation of leaders.

World War II added to Kosygin's reputation as an individual who got things done. He directed the evacuation of Leningrad in 1942 when hundreds of thousands of people were pulled out of the city in the face of a German siege. He then turned to the job of rebuilding industries and cities wrecked during the war. In the middle of the war in 1943, he was appointed prime minister of the Russian Republic, the largest political unit within the Soviet Union. Elected a candidate member of the Politburo in 1946, Kosygin's career as a key government official in charge of industrial production continued following World War II. It was the same role that he filled after Stalin's death in 1953.

Alexei Kosygin was one of several top Party and government leaders who conspired to remove Nikita Khrushchev from power in 1964. Although he had defended Khrushchev against an earlier threat in 1957, he turned against the older leader in the 1960s as Khrushchev's economic and political reforms became increasingly hasty and poorly planned.

When the country's most important offices were redistributed following Khrushchev's fall,

Kosygin was made the premier and Leonid Brezhnev took charge of the Party. The new leaders pursued a policy that scholar Robert McNeal dubbed "dekhrushchevization," that is, ending the erratic moves for change pursued under Khrushchev and adopting a quiet, undramatic style of leadership.

It seemed likely that Brezhnev would soon overshadow Kosygin; leadership of the Communist Party had always had more weight in the Soviet system than any government office. Moreover, Kosygin seemed to have a quiet, retiring personality in contrast to the more forceful figure of Brezhnev.

Surprisingly, Kosygin's influence balanced Brezhnev's for several years. Kosygin, not Brezhnev, served as the country's chief negotiator with foreign countries. In 1966, for example, Kosygin worked out a peace settlement between India and Pakistan at the Tashkent Conference. The following year, Kosygin met with U.S. president **Lyndon Johnson** in a summit conference at Glassboro, New Jersey.

Kosygin had less success in trying to promote economic reforms based on giving more authority to individual factory managers. Decentralizing the economic system meant challenging the authority of numerous powerful figures in both the Communist Party and the government. They were able to stall, then stop any serious change.

By the early 1970s, Kosygin was less visible as a Soviet leader, and there were rumors he would be replaced by one of Brezhnev's lieutenants. Brezhnev did become the nation's political leader and replaced Kosygin in important diplomatic encounters. Nonetheless, Kosygin's talents as an economic manager remained needed. Kosygin retired as head of the Soviet government in October 1980 after holding that position longer than any other individual. He died two months later in Moscow on December 18, 1980.

Leonid Brezhnev

(1906–1982)

In contrast to Kosygin, Leonid Brezhnev became the commanding figure in the two decades separating Nikita Khrushchev and Mikhail Gorbachev. In the end, the Brezhnev era lasted 18 years, from 1964 to his death in 1982. It was a period of gradual change, hesitant reform, and sometimes dramatic moments in which Brezhnev turned the clock backward toward the days of Stalin. The crackdown on Soviet dissident writers like Alexander Solzhenitsyn and the invasions of Czechoslovakia in 1968 and Afghanistan in 1979 showed the darkest side of Brezhnev's leadership. Far more important over the long run was the decline of the Soviet economy in the Brezhnev years, the growing gap between the Soviet standard of living and that in the West. By the time an exhausted and corpse-like Brezhnev died in 1982, his country's internal condition was pointed toward disaster.

Born December 19, 1906, in the Ukrainian city of Dneprodzerzhinsk, the son of a steelworker of Russian nationality, Leonid Brezhnev began his Communist Party career in the *Komsomol,* the Communist youth organization, at the age of 17. Educated as a land surveyor and then an engineer, he devoted his energies to work as a Communist Party official. He became a Party member in 1931.

Brezhnev rose to national importance under the sponsorship of Nikita Khrushchev, the leader he helped to overthrow in 1964. The two first came into contact in the late 1930s when Khrushchev was the Communist Party leader in the Ukraine and Brezhnev was a rising young Party official there. During World War II, Brezhnev served as a military commissar in the Ukraine, ending the war with the rank of major general. During his years of power, Brezhnev's supporters produced highly colored accounts of his military exploits during the war.

Brezhnev received a crucial opportunity to make his mark as a Party leader in 1950. He was appointed to lead the Party in the Moldavian Soviet Socialist Republic, a region taken from Rumania at the close of World War II. Following the fall of Stalin, he was put into an even more important post: head of the Communist Party in Kazakhstan. This was the region in which Nikita Khrushchev's plan to expand the cultivated territory of the Soviet Union—the "Virgin Lands Scheme"—was carried out. Brezhnev successfully produced good harvests in 1955 and 1956, and his reputation rose.

The young Party leader had another opportunity to render service to Khrushchev in 1957. He took the older leader's side when Khrushchev was challenged by the "anti-Party group." By the early 1960s, Brezhnev had been elected to the Party Politburo (now called the *Presidium),* and he had accumulated a number of other key offices. He seemed to be Khrushchev's chosen successor.

Brezhnev did not wait, however, for Khrushchev to pass from the scene. In October 1964, he participated in the plot that ousted his longtime protector from office. First in partnership with Alexei Kosygin, then after the early 1970s in a more singular role, Brezhnev held the reins of Soviet power.

The Brezhnev years saw a mixture of contradictory elements. In domestic affairs, Brezhnev and his colleagues seemed determined to halt Khrushchev's liberalization. Just before the meeting of the 23rd Communist Party Congress in March 1966, for example, it seemed likely that they would formally rehabilitate Stalin. That did not occur, but the crackdown on literary dissent and the privileges and renewed security given to established Party officials marked an important change from the Khrushchev era. Nonetheless, there was no mass terror. During the first decade after 1964, the standard of living rose as the amount of economic resources devoted to consumer goods increased.

In foreign affairs, there was also a mixed picture. Conflict between the Soviet Union and the People's Republic of China, building during the Khrushchev years, erupted into large-scale warfare in 1969. Soviet control in Eastern Europe was maintained by armed invasion in Czechoslovakia in 1968. In 1981, the possibility that Poland would throw off Soviet control was blocked by a coup carried out by the Polish army. In 1979, the Soviet army invaded Afghanistan, beginning a war that lasted beyond the Brezhnev era.

Nonetheless, the Brezhnev years also brought periods of close cooperation with the United States. Brezhnev and American president **Richard Nixon** exchanged visits. In response to American pressure, Jews were allowed to leave the Soviet Union in large numbers. The two countries cooperated in a joint space venture in 1975. The Soviet Union purchased huge quantities of American wheat.

By the closing years of the Brezhnev era, however, numerous problems were combining to create a crisis for the system. The invasion of Afghanistan and the resulting crackdown on dissidents like **Andrei Sakharov** created deep concern in foreign countries toward the Soviet Union. The Soviet economy had ceased to grow by the mid-1970s. Political awareness among the non-Russian peoples of the Soviet Union was growing. Most serious of all, Brezhnev himself was crippled for years by serious illnesses before his death in Moscow on November 10, 1982. As the difficulties mounted, the country seemed adrift, without effective leadership.

Yuri Andropov

(1914–1984)

The Andropov era in the history of the Soviet Union was brief, but Andropov brought novel elements into the picture.

Yuri Andropov.

invasion force. When Andropov returned to Moscow in 1957, he continued to work in foreign affairs, now as a Central Committee official dealing with Eastern Europe. He was elected as a member of the Central Committee in 1961.

In 1967, Andropov was appointed head of the KGB, and placed in the Politburo at the same time. It was a time of significant domestic dissent: many intellectuals protested the Soviet invasion of Czechoslovakia in 1968, and writers like Solzhenitsyn and Sakharov criticized both the Stalinist past and present-day Soviet policies. Andropov's KGB combatted such dissent effectively but without resorting to the mass terror of the Stalinist era. Many dissidents were confined in mental institutions, for example. Solzhenitsyn was exiled abroad in 1974; Sakharov was expelled from Moscow to the provincial city of Gorky in 1980.

With Brezhnev's health failing, Andropov prepared for the coming succession struggle by leaving his KGB post in the spring of 1982. No KGB leader had ever won a succession struggle, and Beria had paid with his life for trying. Andropov broadened his political base by becoming a Secretary (that is, a leading official) of the Central Committee. Combined with his post in the Politburo, this allowed him to successfully take power as head of the Communist Party when Brezhnev died in December 1982.

At that time, Andropov was the oldest individual to serve as head of the Communist Party. He soon became seriously ill, and during his brief period in power he was mainly hidden from public view. His significance came to be found in two decisions: (1) he began to face up to the economic stagnation that had become a pressing problem for his country during the Brezhnev years and to institute reforms; and (2) he promoted the career of a young Communist Party leader from the Southern provinces, Mikhail Gorbachev. In all, Andropov had only 15 months to lead the Soviet Union. He died of kidney disease on February 9, 1984.

With the death of Andropov, the leadership of the Soviet Union found itself faced with a dramatic choice. It might choose an energetic young leader like Mikhail Gorbachev, committed to continuing and expanding the reforming ideas sketched out by Andropov. The second possibility was to choose a safe figure from an older generation of Soviet leaders, someone who would keep the status quo rather than thrust into the unknown. Chernenko was the elder leader chosen to head off—or at least to delay—dramatic change.

The new Soviet leader was a former leader of the KGB, the Soviet secret police, an organization that penetrated and supervised most areas of national life. The first Soviet leader with this background to reach the peak of power, he was no sooner installed than rumors spread outside the Soviet Union that he was a secret admirer of Western culture. Unlikely as it seemed, Andropov was pictured in foreign newspapers as fluent in English, fond of American whiskey, and an enthusiastic fan of James Bond novels.

Yuri Andropov was born on June 15, 1914, in Nagutskoe, a village in the Caucasus. Coming of age in the 1930s in the midst of Stalin's Five Year Plans, he began his political work as an official in the *Komsomol* in 1936. Andropov became a Communist Party official in Karelia, a region taken from Finland in the Russo-Finnish War of 1939–40. Like many rising young Communist Party officials, his career was promoted by a more senior leader. Andropov's mentor was Otto Kuusinen.

In 1951, Andropov began to serve as an official of the Central Committee administration. His career took its first unusual turn for a future Soviet leader in 1954: he was appointed ambassador to Hungary. This meant that he spent several years outside Russia, something no leader since **Lenin** had done. It also meant that he was at the center of events in 1956 when Hungary tried to break away from Soviet control, and Nikita Khrushchev crushed Hungarian independence with a massive

Konstantin Chernenko

(1911–1985)

Konstantin Chernenko.

Son of a peasant, Konstantin Chernenko was born on September 24, 1911, in a small village in the Krasnoiarsk region in southern Siberia. Chernenko was too young to play a part in the Bolshevik Revolution or the Civil War, but, after military service in the early 1930s, he joined the Communist Party and began to work his way up its organizational ladder in his home region in Siberia.

During World War II, he did not see military service; instead, Chernenko attended a school providing advanced training to Communist Party leaders. In 1948, his career took a decisive turn; he was assigned to the Party organization in the Soviet Moldavian Republic near the border with Rumania. There he began his association with Leonid Brezhnev.

For the next 34 years, Chernenko served as a loyal assistant to Brezhnev. This meant that Brezhnev's success in replacing Khrushchev in 1964 put Chernenko near the top of the Soviet system. He directed the administration of the Central Committee for Brezhnev, and he slowly acquired the posts that marked a Soviet leader of the first rank. In 1971, he was elected a member of the Central Committee. Seven years later, he became a full member of the Politburo.

As Brezhnev's health deteriorated in the late 1970s, he depended increasingly on Chernenko. Chernenko was his traveling companion and a spokesman for the ideology of the Communist Party. But Brezhnev's death in late 1982 did not bring Chernenko to power as many expected. Instead, he was defeated for the key post of head of the Communist Party by Yuri Andropov. Although he remained a member of the Party's top policy-making body, Chernenko did not play a large role in the year or so Andropov led the country.

Konstantin Chernenko's turn came in February 1984 after Andropov's death. Since Andropov's brief era had been marked by movement toward reform, Chernenko appeared to be the candidate of Soviet leaders who wanted to prevent sweeping change. He was 72 years old, the oldest leader the Soviet Union had ever had. In contrast, Lenin had taken power at the age of 48, Stalin at 49, and even Khrushchev had been in his early 60s. Besides, Chernenko seemed an unlikely individual to challenge the existing order. As MacKenzie and Curran's text on Soviet history put it, "During a 50-year party career, Chernenko had never initiated projects nor enunciated original ideas."

Chernenko's period in power turned out to be even shorter than that of Andropov. He suffered badly from emphysema, and observers were reminded in one way of the Andropov period when Chernenko failed to appear in public even for important occasions.

The major policy shift under Chernenko was the resumption of arms control talks with the United States. Soviet negotiators had stopped attending these meetings at Geneva in 1983 when Andropov was in power. Another important development was the growing presence of Mikhail Gorbachev among the small number of men at the top of the Soviet system.

It is likely that Chernenko was chosen Party leader in 1985 as a result of a compromise between advocates and opponents of reform. The agreement placed Gorbachev in line to succeed him. Thus, even while Chernenko was still hanging on to power, Gorbachev exercised sweeping authority and began the groundwork for his era of change.

Viacheslav Molotov

(1890–1986)

Like the other figures discussed here, Viacheslav Molotov played a significant role in the post-Stalin era. But the scope of his career as a revolutionary and then as a Soviet leader

Viacheslav Molotov signs the Russo-German pact in August 1939. Josef Stalin is second from right.

far exceeds that of the others. In his early political life, he was a significant Bolshevik leader before the November Revolution of 1917, and he was a colleague of both Lenin and Stalin. His career lasted until 1961 when he lost his last political post, and his life stretched to the age of 96. To some Muscovites who encountered Molotov in his last years, he seemed like a ghost from an ancient and awful time.

Viacheslav Molotov was born on March 9, 1890, in the village of Kukarka in Viatka Province. The boy's real name was Viacheslav Scriabin; Molotov was a revolutionary pseudonym (meaning "hammer") that he took early in his career. His father was probably a small businessman, and their family was related to the famous composer Alexander Scriabin.

Drawn into Marxist political circles at school, Molotov joined the Bolshevik Party after the Revolution of 1905. Like many young revolutionaries before 1917, he was caught by the police and exiled for a time in Siberia. But Molotov played an important role in 1917 as editor of the Bolshevik Party newspaper *Pravda,* and his association with Stalin began during the year of the November Revolution. A fervent supporter of Stalin throughout the 1920s, he moved into top Party positions under Stalin's sponsorship. In 1926, for example, Molotov was named a full member of the Politburo.

The decade of the 1930s, when Andropov was still a teenager and Chernenko was only a minor Party official in Siberia, saw Molotov become head of the Soviet government (from 1930 to 1941) and Soviet foreign minister (from 1939 to 1949). From 1939 until the end of his active political life, he was mainly concerned with Soviet foreign relations. With his eyeglasses and his black moustache, Molotov appeared to some observers as a "high school mathematics teacher," but he soon acquired a reputation as a skilled, stubborn, and tireless diplomat.

Under Molotov, the Soviet Union signed a nonaggression pact with **Adolf Hitler** in August 1939, setting the stage for World War II. In November 1940, Molotov made an important visit to Berlin to deal with the growing difficulties in the Soviet-German alliance. When the meetings failed to bring an agreement, Hitler ordered his generals to begin preparations for the 1941 invasion of the Soviet Union. It was Molotov who received the declaration of war from the German ambassador in June 1941.

As a member of the small State Defense Committee set up by Stalin to run the war effort, Molotov's main task was to deal with the Soviet Union's allies. When the wartime alliance broke down after 1945, Molotov became a symbol in the United States of Soviet stubbornness. He was the spokesman articulating the Soviet position on the two issues that promoted the most friction: Soviet control over Eastern Europe and the Soviet rejection of cooperation with the Western powers over the future of Germany.

In the last years of Stalin's life, Molotov's position at the top of the Soviet system grew shaky. Stalin's growing anti-Semitism struck at Molotov's wife, who came from a Ukrainian Jewish family. She was arrested and imprisoned in 1949. That same year Molotov lost his position as foreign minister. If Stalin had lived to conduct a final purge, Molotov was likely to be one of its star victims.

But Stalin's death in 1953 restored Molotov to a vital role in Soviet life. Once again he took over as foreign minister, participating in the maneuvering of the succession struggle. At first he threw his support to Khrushchev; but, as a long-standing loyal lieutenant to Stalin, he refused to support Khrushchev's policy of de-Stalinization and joined in the covert alliance of Party leaders to oust Khrushchev in the spring of 1957. When the plot failed, Molotov was punished by a form of foreign exile; twice foreign minister of the Soviet Union, he was now made Soviet ambassador to the Mongolian People's Republic. He was soon reduced to an even less important post in a Soviet delegation to a United Nations body in Vienna.

Molotov continued his criticism of Khrushchev in the early 1960s. This led to his expulsion from the Communist Party in 1962 after a membership of more than 50 years. Living out his remaining years on a pension in Moscow, Molotov died there on November 8, 1986.

SOURCES:

Dornberg, John. *Brezhnev: The Masks of Power.* Basic Book, 1974.

Ebon, Martin. *Malenkov: Stalin's Successor.* McGraw-Hill, 1953.

MacKenzie, David, and Michael W. Curran. *A History of the Soviet Union.* 2nd ed. Wadsworth, 1991.

Medvedev, Roy. *All Stalin's Men: Six Who Carried out the Bloody Policies.* Doubleday, 1983.

Medvedev, Zhores A. *Andropov.* Norton, 1983.

Shipler, David. *Broken Idols, Solemn Dreams.* Rev. ed. Times Books, 1989.

Talbott, Strobe, ed. and trans. *Khrushchev Remembers.* Little, Brown, 1970.

FURTHER READING:

Bialer, Seweryn. *Stalin's Successors: Leadership, Stability, and Change in the Soviet Union.* Cambridge University Press, 1980.

Doder, Dusko. *Shadows and Whispers: Power Politics Inside the Kremlin from Brezhnev to Gorbachev.* Random House, 1986.

Linden, Carl A. *Khrushchev and the Soviet Leadership.* Updated ed. Johns Hopkins Press, 1990.

McNeal, Robert. *The Bolshevik Tradition.* 2nd ed. Prentice-Hall, 1975.

Tatu, Michel. *Power in the Kremlin: From Khrushchev to Kosygin.* Viking, 1969.

Grigori Potemkin

(1739–1791)

Military commander, statesman, and courtier, who survived his term as Catherine the Great's lover to serve as her most influential advisor.

Grigori Potemkin's career and especially his rise to power at the court of **Catherine the Great** must be seen against the background of the Empress's personality and the characteristics of her reign. Sensual and self-indulgent but well-educated and highly intelligent, Catherine was initially drawn to Potemkin for physical reasons, but it was his own keen intelligence that enabled him to survive at court as her chief advisor long after he had ceased to be her paramour. On the other hand, her desire for glory on the battlefield, her designs against the Ottoman Empire, her grandiose ambitions for the restoration of the Byzantine Empire under Russian auspices, and her dreams of expansion in Asia all created an atmosphere in which a "doer" such as Potemkin could flourish. By no means a great general or a valiant warrior, he supported Catherine in all of her undertakings, mixing flattery with genuine confidence in her abilities and enthusiasm for her schemes, and he was more than willing to serve her personally in battle if circumstances dictated.

Potemkin was born at Chizheva near Smolensk in western Russia, attended the University of Moscow and in 1755, at the age of 16,

"His rarest quality was a physical, intellectual and moral courage that set him absolutely apart from the rest of mankind, and because of this we understood each other perfectly."

CATHERINE THE GREAT

Contributed by Robert H. Hewsen, Professor of History, Glassboro State College, Glassboro, New Jersey

entered the Horse Guards during the reign of the empress Elizabeth (1740–61), daughter of **Peter the Great.** Childless, Elizabeth had called in her Prussian nephew Peter of Holstein to be her heir and had arranged his marriage with a German princess, Sophia-Augusta of Anhalt-Zerbst, who upon her marriage and conversion to Greek Orthodoxy was rechristened Catherine. Elizabeth died in January 1761 and was duly succeeded by Peter (III) as planned, but the new Tsar was not only incompetent and unpopular, he was positively deranged. When it became known that he intended to put Catherine aside and marry his mistress, Catherine's lovers and other supporters rallied to overthrow Peter and put her on the throne in his place (July 28, 1762). As a member of his regiment, Potemkin, now 23, participated in the coup, in the course of which he met Catherine for the first time. Given the conflicting accounts of the episode, his exact role remains something of a mystery. Like the others who aided her at the critical moment, he was rewarded with 10,000 rubles, 400 serfs, and the gift of a small estate. Soon made a Kamer-Junker at court, he was promoted to the rank of junior lieutenant shortly after Catherine's accession, but the details of his early career are obscure. On poor terms with the Orlov brothers, consecutive lovers of Catherine and chief architects of her coup, the story that the loss of his eye in 1763 occurred in a duel with one of them is a myth; his blinding was the result of a medical mishandling of a local infection.

Returning to court at Catherine's urging, Potemkin was given his first command with the Izmailovsky Horse Guards in 1766 and the following year was sent to Moscow where he served in connection with the sessions of the Legislative Commission appointed by Catherine to devise a new law code for Russia. Transferred from military to court service, he worked as guardian of the delegations to the Commission sent by various Asiatic tribesmen; during this time he developed his lifelong interest in the Asian inhabitants of the Empire. A Gentleman of the Household as early as 1768, Potemkin was still relatively unknown at court when he left for the first Russo-Turkish War (1768–74), and it was only after two years at the front (1771–73) that he would become romantically involved with the Empress or, perhaps better, that she would become romantically involved with him.

Potemkin's first post as he resumed his military career was an assignment to the staff, first of Field Marshal Dmitry Golitsyn and then to that of his replacement General Nikolai Rumiantsev. Because of his court connections, Rumiantsev

made Potemkin his aide-de-camp, which guaranteed Potemkin both safety and easy promotion. Potemkin, however, desired a chance to demonstrate himself as a soldier and appealed directly to the Empress for a post at the front. There, as cavalry commander, he distinguished himself in battles in what is now eastern Rumania, and participated in the brilliant victories that earned Rumiantsev the rank of field marshal. Though still a junior commander, Potemkin's role in routing a Turkish army earned him a promotion to lieutenant-general and the award of the coveted Orders of St. Anne and St. George. By this time, he was recognized as one of the best cavalry commanders in Russia and had once again come to the attention of Catherine, who had recently ended her long affair with Grigori Orlov. Late in 1774, when the Empress had Potemkin reassigned to her personal service, he returned to St. Petersburg.

He Becomes Catherine's Lover

When Grigori Potemkin assumed the role of lover of Catherine II, she was 44; he was ten years her junior. In the permissive moral climate of the 18th century and the even more permissive atmosphere of the Russian court, Potemkin's relationship with the Empress was anything but a secret, and he served openly as her escort and consort in all public affairs. Once installed in the Imperial Palace in the suite below hers, the new favorite rose rapidly through the ranks, being appointed, in short order, a Count of the Russian Empire, a member of Catherine's Secret Council, vice-president of the Council of War, and Knight of the Order of St.

Andrew, and was granted the Order of Alexander Nevsky. **Frederick II (the Great)** awarded Potemkin the Black Eagle of Prussia, while a host of other medals and awards were soon forthcoming from Poland, Denmark, Sweden, and especially Austria, where the Emperor **Joseph II** made Potemkin a prince of the Holy Roman Empire. Only France and England withheld their highest honors.

A man of mercurial temperament, religious but dissolute, Potemkin was a spendthrift, a gambler, a hearty eater, and a heavy drinker, as well as a seducer of women, including his five nieces. Full of good humor, but rough, moody, vain, jealous, and temperamental, Catherine saw him as courageous, devoted, intelligent, and judicious. Fascinated by his coarse masculinity, in her moments of chagrin she called him her Cossack, Muscovite, Tatar, imbecile, or infidel.

That Catherine was truly in love with Potemkin there can be no doubt, as demonstrated by her 23 surviving—and priceless—letters, written to him either in French or Russian. Besides her devotion, the Empress bestowed upon her beloved enormous benefices in lands, estates, serfs, clothing, orders of distinction, medals, jewels, and cash. The true nature of Potemkin's own feelings for Catherine may never be known although there seems to be no doubt that he genuinely admired her intellect and her talents as a ruler. There is some reason to believe that Catherine and Potemkin were secretly married, or at least married in each other's eyes, for Catherine refers to him as her husband and spouse in her love letters and to herself as his wife. In any case, their romantic relationship, passionate and feverish as it certainly was on the Empress's part, lasted but two years. The end of their affair and of Potemkin's role as Catherine's lover did nothing to terminate their mutual admiration or their intellectual and political association. In order to retain his hold on Catherine, Potemkin shrewdly undertook to replace himself in her bed with lovers of his choosing. Knowing that he could continue to fill her needs outside the bedchamber, Potemkin cheerfully selected a series of good-looking nonentities.

Although Catherine's affair with Potemkin had run its course by 1775, he remained thereafter a major figure at the court and was its virtual director. As far as Catherine was concerned, her confidence in Potemkin's abilities never flagged, and she was ever mindful of the proper way in which she might reward him for his friendship, devotion, and good counsel. She conceived of a new state to be erected in the Balkans from a Russian conquest of the Rumanian principalities of Moldavia, Wallachia, and Bessarabia; the new entity, with proper attention to classical antecedents, was to be called the "Kingdom of Dacia" and to have Potemkin as its king. Catherine also had intentions in the regions south of the Caucasus Mountains where, bemused again by her readings in antiquity, she contemplated a revival of the Kingdom of Armenia under Russian auspices—again with Potemkin as its sovereign. He was especially enthusiastic and supportive of her dream of reviving the Byzantine Empire as a vassal of Russia—her so-called "Greek Project"—with one of her two grandsons to be placed on its throne, ruling either from Constantinople or Athens.

By 1776, Potemkin's position at court was sufficiently strong for him to assume appointments at a considerable distance from the capital. Accepting the position of governor of New Russia, Azov, and Astrakhan, as well as that of the governorship of Saratov founded in 1781, he took charge of the new lines of fortifications being constructed along the Dnieper River. He devoted considerable energy to the settlement of the newly acquired southern lands with peoples drawn especially from among the Greek Orthodox Slavs and Rumanians of the Balkans eager to escape Turkish rule. He also founded a number of settlements, some of which—Kherson, Sevastopol, Ekaterinoslav and, above all, the port of Odessa completed shortly before Catherine's death—grew to become important cities. The grateful Empress rewarded him with the Anichkov Palace in St. Petersburg (later the residence of the Dowager Empress of Russia, mother of the last tsar) and obtained the rank of Prince of the Holy Roman Empire from her colleague and crony on the Austrian throne, Joseph II. Appointed commander of all of the light cavalry and the other irregular troops in the army, Potemkin devoted himself to military organization, redesigning the uniforms to facilitate fighting, limiting corporal punishment, and setting inspectors to supervise health and sanitation.

Presides Over Annexation of Crimea

The successful conclusion of the Russo-Turkish War by the Treaty of Kuchuk Kainarji in 1774 left the Khanate of the Crimea, the last remnant of the Mongol Empire in Europe, a virtual vassal of Russia; now Potemkin, with Catherine's authorization, began formulating his plans for its outright annexation. Potemkin was put in command of the army sent to occupy the territory. Proceeding with little serious opposition, Potemkin successfully occupied the peninsula and on July 26, 1783, its formal annexation was announced.

The annexation of the Crimea began the greatest period of Potemkin's career. In St. Petersburg, Catherine had built for him the magnificent Taurida Palace, which from 1906 to 1917 would be used to house the Russian Imperial *Duma* (Parliament); she also gave him a magnificent estate on the Crimean Peninsula, with gardens designed by an English architect that were the talk of Europe. Potemkin was allowed to play a major role in the development of the new provinces acquired in the south. It was he who presided over the transfer of the Greek and Armenian population of the territory and the establishment of new colonies for them in the Ukraine: the Greeks were settled at Mariupol on the Sea of Azov; the Gregorian Armenians were settled at Grigoriopol and New Nakhichevan near Rostov-on-the-Don; and the Catholic Armenians were settled at another new town called Ekaterinoslavl.

By 1784, Potemkin had attained the highest military rank possible, that of field marshal. President of the War College (ministry), he was then placed in charge of the organization of the Black Sea Fleet, all the while advising Catherine on economic and other affairs and negotiating treaties. Devoted to the glory of Russia, which he saw incarnated in the person of its Empress, never for a moment did Potemkin flag in his devotion to his former lover, nor she in her faith in his devotion to Russia or to her personal cause. Of the 92 million rubles Catherine is said to have spent on her favorites, no less than 50 million are estimated to have been lavished on Potemkin.

The "Potemkin Villages" Are Erected

In 1787, Potemkin supervised the famous "progress" of Catherine II, down the Dnieper River in the company of Joseph II. It was on this route that Potemkin is said to have erected the dummy hamlets—derisively referred to in the West as the "Potemkin villages"—filled with happy peasants in holiday garb singing and dancing to vodka supplied for the occasion. The same year saw the outbreak of the second Russo-Turkish War (1787–91) and, though Potemkin's reformed army did less well than expected, the war reached a victorious conclusion, and Catherine heaped additional cash, orders, and estates on her hero. All the while Potemkin made continual use of his St. Petersburg residence, the Taurida Palace, which he had surrounded by a park with its own lake, and which he had filled with gardens, pavilions, and statuary. However, in 1791, his health impaired by a number of fevers experienced in the south, Potemkin died suddenly on October 16. He was buried in the church of St. Catherine in Kherson, in the Crimea, where his niece Alexandra erected a mausoleum to hold his remains. On learning the news, a disconsolate Catherine collapsed.

Grigori Aleksandrovich Potemkin was perhaps the most significant of the individuals who formulated the "tsarist system" without actually sitting upon the Russian throne, the system that made Russia a great nation from the reign of Peter the Great until the end of that of **Nicholas I** (1825–55). Whether as courtier, soldier, governor, statesman, administrator, or planner, Potemkin conducted himself in an exemplary manner, and no ruler could have asked for a more trusted advisor, loyal patriot, or devoted subject. In an Empire officially ruled by the sovereign, Potemkin was certainly the greatest of the de facto prime ministers in Russian history. One can only speculate, for example, on the manner in which he would have dealt with Napoleon had he lived to be 70 instead of dying at 52.

Careless of his appearance, socially inept, and by no means a military hero on the order of **Alexander Suvorov** or **Mikhail Kutuzov,** Potemkin made innumerable enemies but never lost the favor of his sovereign. He fought battles, increased the territory of the Russian Empire by a third, reorganized the army, founded cities, and moved entire populations, yet his greatest achievement was his ability to retain the favor of Catherine the Great long after their liaison had come to an end. Given Catherine's intelligence and practical approach to affairs of state, this says more about the nature of Potemkin's undoubted genius than anything else, and it has been said that the Empress never fully recovered from his death.

SOURCES:

Potemkin, Grigori. *Collected Papers, 1744–1793* (in Russian). St. Petersburg, 1893–1895.

FURTHER READING:

Alexander, John T. *Catherine the Great: Life and Legend.* Oxford University Press, 1989.

Soloveytchik, George. *Potemkin; Soldier, Statesman, Lover and Consort of Catherine of Russia.* New York, 1947.

Troyat, Henri. *Catherine the Great.* Dutton, 1980.

Vidkun Quisling

(1887–1945)

Norwegian military officer and infamous political leader, who served during Hitler's occupation as minister president of Norway.

Born July 18, 1887, in Fyresdal, a small village in southern Norway in the region of Telemark; executed on October 24, 1945, near Oslo, Norway; son of Jon L. and Anna (Bang) Quisling; married: Maria Vasilievna Pasek.

Vidkun Quisling was the eldest son of a Norwegian Lutheran pastor who never rose above small rural appointments. From his father—a book collector who wrote extensively on Norse history, legend, theology, and ethics—the boy inherited his romantic nationalism. From his mother—a woman who had distant but real connections with some of the most important social and intellectual families of Scandinavia (Norway, Sweden, and Denmark)—he inherited his tremendous drive and intellectual arrogance.

Always at the head of his class, Quisling's pursuit of a military career, rather than university work in theology or the sciences, surprised both family and teachers. After graduating from the Royal Norwegian Military Academy, he began work with Norway's newly formed General Staff. Because staff officers had to become specialists on a particular country and master its language, Quisling chose Russia and went there to serve in the Norwegian embassy.

Arriving in early 1918, after a successful coup by **V.I. Lenin** and **Leon Trotsky** had overthrown Tsar **Nicholas II** and put the Bolshevik Party in power, Quisling saw the first year of the

"It is ironic that Major Quisling, like Judge Lynch and Captain Boycott before him, should have been immortalized by giving his name to a word in the English language, for in many respects he was not the archetypical traitor."

PAUL M. HAYES

Contributed by Homer H. Blass, Associate Professor of History and Government, Liberty University, Lynchburg, Virginia

Russian Civil War from the center of Communist power. An attitude of mutual admiration and trust developed between the young Norwegian officer-diplomat and the Russian Communist Party leaders. He then moved, in 1919, to the new Norwegian embassy in Finland, which had been part of the Russian tsar's lands since 1809. Finnish nationalists and anti-Communists, under the leadership of the Finnish military officer, Field Marshal **Karl Mannerheim,** had set up an independent non-Communist Finnish state. Mannerheim had secured its independence by cooperating with anti-Communist leaders in the Russian Civil War and by cooperating with German troops stranded along the Russian frontiers at World War I's end.

By 1921, when Quisling returned to Norway to assume full-time military duties, a new opportunity appeared. Although the Russian Civil War had ended with Lenin and the Communist Party victorious, the Russian state and its borderlands were in chaos. Since 1914, the four horsemen of the apocalypse—famine, war, disease, and death—had been at work, and Russia needed massive aid to prevent further catastrophic loss of life; but the Communist leaders did not trust the League of Nations nor the main Western democracies. The United States, Britain, France, and other League of Nations' members had put an aid package together, but only the small neutral state of Norway was allowed to administer it, and **Fridtjof Nansen**—a world-famous Norwegian polar explorer and colleague of **Herbert Hoover** in the famine-relief programs of World War I—was appointed director. Nansen, however, did not speak Russian or know the Communist Party leaders, so he took Quisling on as the project's official secretary, administrative assistant, and Russian linguist.

From 1922 to 1927, Quisling served as troubleshooter and administrative assistant in a series of programs in European Russia and her neareast borderlands, meeting his wife Maria Vasilievna Pasek while administrating famine relief in the Ukraine. For the next two years, he was posted once more at the Norwegian embassy in Moscow. Having broken off diplomatic relations with the Soviet Union, Britain asked Norway to look after British interests and nationals. Quisling directed that project, remaining in Moscow until British-Soviet relations had normalized. The British government made Quisling a member of the Order of the British Empire (OBE) for his good offices, while he was winding down other, uncompleted League relief projects. By 1929, the emergence of **Joseph Stalin**'s police state made all foreigners unwelcome, and Quisling lost whatever enthusi-

CHRONOLOGY

1905   Norway became independent monarchy

1917   Russian Revolution

1919   World War I ended; League of Nations born

1922–29   Quisling served as secretary and Russian linguist for League of Nations' relief and refugee programs

1931–33   Served as Norwegian defense minister

1933   Hitler became dictator of Germany

1933–45   Quisling founded and led the NS Party of Norway

1939   World War II began

1940   Hitler invaded Norway; Quisling served as self-proclaimed Norwegian head of state

1942–45   Returned as minister president

1945   Germany surrendered; Quisling arrested and executed

asm and optimism he once had for the Russian Revolution and its communist ideals.

Shortly after returning to Norway in 1930, Quisling retired from active duty with the army at the rank of major. He then entered politics, serving as minister of defense from 1931–33. Along with other free-market countries, the great depression of the 1930s hurt Norway and polarized politics between socialists and conservatives. The coalition cabinet in which Quisling served as defense minister represented a last attempt to keep a popular-front coalition of the Norwegian Socialist Party and the Norwegian Communist Party from running the nation. For reasons not totally clear, Quisling became the whipping boy for all opponents of the government. Opponents accused him of using the army to shoot strikers, asking for excessive military funding, being a "redbaiter," and even of being mentally unbalanced.

Returning their attacks with equal vigor and rationality, Quisling named names, called certain Socialist Party and Communist Party leaders Stalin's paid stooges, and tried to drum any active Communist Party members out of the Norwegian military. Finally, Quisling felt that his own Party's head, who was the interim prime minister of the coalition, had become too compromising. Quisling's attempt to replace the leader with himself as Party head and prime minister led to his forced resignation. Shortly thereafter, a popular-front government assumed power, governing Norway until April 9, 1940. The Socialist-Communist coalition assumed power legally and constitutionally in 1935 but remained in power after 1938 by using the Crown to suspend the constitution and delay required elections, first from 1938 to 1939, then from 1939 to 1940.

After 1933, Quisling sought new political, social, and economic solutions for Norway's problems. Drawing from **Adolph Hitler** in Germany, **Benito Mussolini** in Italy, and **Franklin D. Roosevelt**'s New Deal, he called for forced cooperation between business and government; elimination of the political power of traditional vested interest groups; a return to the basic values of God, the family, and patriotism; and the establishment of a sense of community among all the people, while dressing up these ideas in the language and imagery of romantic Norse nationalism and legend inherited from his father.

The results of such a synthesis can be illustrated by the following: *Volk* is interchangeable with "community," "Aryan race" is interchangeable with "Norse race," and the Christian church must resist atheistic Marxism and the spirit of Judaism. Quisling became the leader of his national unification movement, but the Norse word for leader is *forer*, and the abbreviation of the Norse words for national unification, *Nasjonal Samling*, is NS. To most observers, Quisling and his NS Party appeared to be another parochial Nazi spinoff group. The Party continued to shrink from 1933 to 1939 and was only saved from possible extinction by German subsidy money given after the outbreak of war. In December 1939, Quisling paid his first documented visit to Berlin and received a sympathetic hearing from some German leaders, who felt he could be useful, and from Hitler, who appeared to feel sorry for him.

To the mutual benefit of Germany and themselves, the Scandinavian nations had remained neutral throughout World War I. Germany, Norway, Sweden, and Denmark began World War II intending to repeat the same policy and relationship. But England and France, Germany's enemies, had other ideas. Germany received about half of the iron ore used in weapons production from Swedish mines, because the ore could reach German factories by avoiding the English naval blockade, following sea routes that remained inside Norwegian territorial waters. England considered plans to deny Germany the ore, even if it meant violating Norwegian neutrality. Meanwhile, certain German leaders, especially Admiral Erich Raeder of the navy, also considered a military occupation of Norway; German naval bases in Norway would greatly simplify the process of getting German submarines and surface raiders out to sea, thus threatening British trade routes.

By the spring of 1940, another factor turned the heads of the national leaders toward Norway. A factory in Norway was the world's only source of heavy water, a substance considered an absolute necessity in building an atomic reactor or atomic bomb. The German government wanted all the Norwegian production, while Britain and France wanted to cripple any German atomic research before it could get started. When English and French plans to occupy Norway reached Hitler's ears, he authorized the German navy to carry out a preemptive invasion. Whether or not Quisling was consulted, assisted in, encouraged, or knew in advance of the invasion has never been adequately determined. In a history of Norway written shortly after the war, Karen Larsen maintained that Vidkun Quisling visited Hitler and told him that:

> western powers were planning… to occupy bases of operation in Norway. He was very insistent and persuaded the Führer that to prevent this it was advisable to occupy Norway which, he claimed, was a point of vital importance in the war.

Germans Invade; Quisling Names Himself Head of State

The German invasion occurred on April 9, 1940. By daybreak, German troops were ashore in most of the key ports, while King Haakon VII and the Norwegian government fled toward the Swedish frontier. German plans called for a team of political administrators to take over the abandoned reins of government, providing a quick, smooth transition; all the team, however, and most German senior officers were stranded in Oslo Harbor after their flagship *Blücher* was sunk by Norwegian fire. Norwegian destruction of the *Blücher* represented nearly the only serious Norwegian resistance of the first day. Meanwhile, a political vacuum occurred in Oslo: the Norwegian government was gone, and no German of sufficient rank was present to take over. In early evening, Quisling marched into the national radio station and declared himself the new head of state, taking upon himself the responsibility for protecting Norway from its invaders. His broadcast had two effects: (1) it made him appear to be a German puppet brought out for the occasion, and (2) it united most German and Norwegian leaders behind the scenes in a joint effort to get the government away from Quisling.

By April 15, Josef Terboven, a senior German Nazi Party official, took power as *Reichscom-*

missar of Norway, a post he held until May 8, 1945. Terboven set up a Norwegian shadow government drawn from those members of the royal government who remained in the country. Faced with almost universal opposition to Quisling, Hitler ordered Terboven to protect Quisling's dignity—even if that meant his exclusion from any scheme of occupation. For the next two years, Quisling remained in retirement, while Terboven sought to gain Norwegian participation or legitimacy.

An Epithet of Treason

Actually, Quisling had the worst of both worlds. After the April 9 broadcast, he appeared to the world as the most effective and dangerous foreign Nazi sympathizer, a view actively promoted by the Norwegian and English governments who needed a scapegoat to explain their disastrous handling of the German invasion. What chance did England and Norway have when a former defense minister, and his Party members in the upper circles of the government, had given away all the military secrets and subverted the resistance of true patriots? Also, since Quisling was the first open Nazi sympathizer in a conquered country, and because his name in English sounds rather unpleasant, *Quisling* became the epithet of treason—the equivalent of *Judas*—from 1940 to 1945. An English cartoonist of the time expressed the situation with a foreign leader in a Nazi-style uniform saluting Hitler and saying, "I am Quisling." To which Hitler replies, "What is your name?" But if Quisling was the center of world and Norwegian attention, he was totally without power or influence. No German official would work with him, and Terboven attempted to encourage recently joined leaders of the NS Party to purge Quisling and seize control of the organization.

In 1942, after all other attempts of governing without Quisling had failed, Terboven finally turned to the Norwegian and appointed him minister president, a post Quisling held until the end of the war. While Quisling and the NS Party served as a facade and lightning rod in regard to German occupation policies in Norway, his was not always a passive relationship. He actively pro-moted such controversial policies as the arrest and deportation of Norwegian Jews to German death camps and attempted to put the Norwegian state church, and the Norwegian teachers, under leaders active in the NS. When defied by the teachers, Quisling ordered the arrest of several hundred leaders and deported them to forced labor camps above the Arctic Circle. By the end of the war, he was more hated than the Germans by the Norwegian people. King Haakon promised to "hang him three times." On the first two occasions, the King explained, the rope would "accidently break," and Quisling would be returned to his cell only to be brought out on another day for another hanging.

Actually, many Norwegians thought the best way to dispose of Quisling at the end of the war would be for the Norwegian resistance to kill him on the last day before liberation. He was arrested instead and stood trial for treason and murder in the summer of 1945. While guilty of many of the charges, he had little opportunity to defend himself; the Norwegian government turned his trial into a show trial of the type associated with Stalinist Russia. In fact several months later, when a leading Norwegian author who belonged to the NS underwent a similar trial, Stalin's foreign minister remarked to his Norwegian counterpart that the Norwegians were being excessive in their desire for revenge and humiliation. The Norwegian diplomat replied to the Stalinist official, "You are too soft." Quisling was found guilty and died by firing squad on October 24, 1945.

SOURCES:

Hayes, Paul M. *Quisling: The Career and Political Ideas of Vidkun Quisling 1887–1945*. Indiana University Press, 1972.

Hewins, Ralph. *Quisling: Prophet Without Honour*. John Day, 1966.

Larsen, Karen. *A History of Norway*. Princeton University Press, 1948.

FURTHER READING:

Petrow, Richard. *The Bitter Years: The Invasion and Occupation of Denmark and Norway, April 1940 to May 1945*. Morrow, 1974.

Rich, Norman. *Hitler's War Aims*. 2 vols. Norton, 1973–1974.

Sir Walter Raleigh

(1554–1618)

Elizabethan statesman, explorer, and man of letters, who became the protégé of Elizabeth I.

Name variations: Ralegh. Born Walter Raleigh in 1554 at Budleigh Saltonton, South Devonshire; executed on October 29, 1618, at London; son of Walter (country gentleman) and Katherine (Champernoun) Raleigh; married: Elizabeth Throngmorton, c. 1592; children: Walter, Carew.

In many ways, Sir Walter Raleigh symbolizes the energy, indeed even the hubris, of the Elizabethans. He was by turns poet, historian, philosopher, scientist, soldier, sailor, courtier, legislator, explorer, entrepreneur, and colonial administrator. As one of the best known figures in England, he gathered enemies as quickly as friends, and on both sides one found monarchs, ecclesiastics, eminent attorneys, and people of great wealth.

Raleigh's formative years, however, are obscure. He was probably born in 1554 in a thatched house called "Hayes" at Budleigh Saltonton, two and a half miles from the Devon coast. He was the youngest son of a country squire who was neither particularly important nor particularly wealthy. Yet his old Devon family was practically part of a fighting border clan: uncle Sir Arthur Champernoune was vice-admiral of the West, commanding at Plymouth; Sir **Francis Drake** was a cousin of his father's first wife; Sir Richard Grenville, who died commanding the *Revenge* in the Armada, was his cousin; the famous English navigator, Sir Humphrey Gilbert, was his half-brother, being the product of his mother's first marriage.

"We have not such another head to be cut off."

BYSTANDER AT
RALEIGH'S EXECUTION

Contributed by Justus D. Doenecke, Professor of History, New College of the University of South Florida, Sarasota, Florida

In 1568, Raleigh entered Oriel College, Oxford, where he studied intermittently for several years but received no degree. In 1569, joining the hundred Devon Volunteers fighting alongside the Huguenots in the French wars of religion, he witnessed the battles of Jarnac and Montcontour and hunted Roman Catholics in the caves of Lanquedoc. In 1575, he enrolled at the Middle Temple in the Inns of Court. Although a member of the squirearchy needed some knowledge of the law, he undoubtedly saw the Inns of Court as the best kind of London club. He soon became a hanger-on in the court of Queen **Elizabeth I,** published verses of decent quality, and gained a reputation for dueling and general boisterousness.

In September 1578, Raleigh joined Sir Humphrey Gilbert on an expedition originally headed for North America. Gilbert, 15 years Raleigh's senior, had received permission from the Privy Council to annex unoccupied territory on its coast. Yet his modest fleet of 11 ships soon met with failure: it was first driven back into Plymouth by storms; then in November, defeated by Spaniards who attacked off Cape Verde. A desperate struggle took place in which Raleigh's crew suffered many casualties, and he himself was lucky to escape with life. Returning in disgrace, Raleigh engaged in several brawls and was imprisoned twice within six months for disturbing the peace. For a gentleman, prison was something like a third-class hotel: one could receive visitors and occasionally leave the premises.

In August 1580, through the influence of Elizabeth's chief favorite the earl of Leicester, Raleigh landed in Ireland as captain of a band of 100 foot soldiers. His task: to suppress a rebellion created by Elizabeth's effort to force Protestantism on a Roman Catholic people. Raleigh was responsible for the massacre of 600 people at the Spanish-Italian garrison at Smerwick, which included about 100 women and children, Irish and foreigners alike. By a clever ruse, he captured Lord Roche of Bally, an Anglo-Irish nobleman who lived some 20 miles from Cork, in the man's own castle. As a temporary administrator of Munster, he made no secret of his scorn for the British commander, Earl Grey of Wilton, whom he found too weak in crushing rebellion but also inept in winning over the smaller Irish chieftains.

By now, as biographer Hugh Ross Williamson notes, Raleigh was:

Six feet tall, with a swarthy complexion, long, melancholy face, pointed beard and heavily-lidded eyes, he outdistanced every fashion. His jew-

CHRONOLOGY

1558	Reign of Elizabeth I began
1581	Raleigh became a favorite of the Queen
1584	Knighted; received royal charter giving permission to establish settlement in New World; sent out preliminary expedition
1585	Sat in Parliament; sent out expedition under Grenville, which settled on Roanoke island
1587	Sent relief expedition to Roanoke
1588	Defeat of Spanish Armada
1592	Raleigh sent briefly to the Tower of London
1595	Led voyage of exploration to northern coast of South America
1596	Battle of Cádiz
1600	Appointed governor of Jersey
1604	Reign of James I began; Raleigh arrested for treason; sent to the Tower for 13 years
1614	*History of the World* appeared
1616	Raleigh released from Tower; began second voyage to South America the following year
1618	Returned to Britain sick; arrested; executed

elled shoes were said to be worth more than 6,600 gold pieces, his hatband of pearls, his ear-rings, the silks and damasks he wore and the ornaments with which he bedecked himself were worth a king's ransom. And he had the pride of the peacock he appeared.

Returning to Britain in December 1581, Raleigh became "the Queen's dear minion." Elizabeth was undoubtedly impressed by this obscure soldier from Ireland with handsome dark countenance, sumptuous dress, and spirited conversation. According to the account of Thomas Fuller, a 17th-century antiquarian, when the queen met up with a muddy patch and was considering whether or not to go on:

Raleigh cast and spread his new plush coat on the ground, whereon the Queen trod gently, rewarding him afterwards with many suits, for his so free and seasonable tender of so fair a footcloth.

Although it is debatable whether Raleigh spread his costly cloak for her to walk upon, he did write love poems to the queen. She in turn, as one contemporary noted, "took him for a kind of oracle." The couple was so intimate that when, in February 1582, he went on a diplomatic mission to the Low Countries, she asked him to write her every day as if she were his wife. Moreover, Raleigh was the recipient of many royal favors; during the period 1583–84, he received the splendid Durham house in London, a monopoly on the right to retail wine, and a license to export woolen broadcloth. Knighted by the queen, he became Member of Parliament for Devonshire in 1584, and in the following year, he was appointed lord warden of the Stanniers (the tin-mines), lord lieutenant of Cornwall, and vice admiral of the West (Devon and Cornwall). In 1586, he received vast estates in five Midland counties, not to mention over 40,000 acres in Ireland. The year 1587 brought the most coveted honor of all, captain of the queen's guard, the highest office at court and one which gave him access to the queen at all times. At age 35, Walter Raleigh had become one of the richest people in England but also, according to a contemporary account, "the best hated man of the world, in Court, city and country."

All this time, Raleigh was involved in overseas ventures. In December 1582, an impoverished Sir Humphrey Gilbert organized a company to settle English Catholics in the New World. Though the jealous Elizabeth refused to let Raleigh accompany his half-brother, he nonetheless invested money and a ship of his own in the venture. (The *Bark Raleigh*, which composed half the total tonnage of the voyage, was forced back the second day after a fierce thunderstorm.) With his four ships, Gilbert reached Newfoundland, annexed it, left colonists there, and then continued in a search for the legendary Northwest Passage.

Raleigh Names Colony in Queen's Honor

When, in September 1583, Gilbert died as the result of a tempest off the Azores, Raleigh was given a charter to "occupy and enjoy" the new lands. In April 1584, Raleigh's expedition of two ships set sail (without its founder) under the command of Philip Amadas, a Plymouth seaman, and Arthur Barlow, who had been with Raleigh in Ireland. Arriving at the Carolina coast on July 13, the men took possession of the island of Wokoken in the queen's name. Wrote Barlow, "We found the people most gentle, loving, and faithful, void of all guile and treason." Seeking to win Elizabeth's support for more extensive involvements, Raleigh named the colony Virginia in her honor. (She was known as the "Virgin Queen.") He also brought to her attention the pri-

matial treatise of geographer Richard Hakluyt, *Discourses Concerning Western Discoveries,* a work Raleigh had personally commissioned.

Though Elizabeth failed to give wholehearted support, she did contribute a ship and some funds towards another expedition. Sent out in April 1585, the party—consisting of ten ships—was headed by Raleigh's cousin Sir Richard Grenville and by Ralph Lane, a professional soldier. After reconnoitering Spain's Caribbean defenses, the expedition entered what is now Albemarle Sound on the coast of North Carolina. Landing first in July at Wokoken, then at Roanoke Island, Grenville returned to England in mid-September, leaving Governor Lane behind with 107 settlers. Indian resistance and tension with the Spaniards caused most settlers to return home in June 1586, when Sir Francis Drake, stopping by after a raid on the Spanish West Indies, offered them passage. The group brought back potatoes and tobacco, which Raleigh popularized in Britain. Grenville, who appeared at the settlement a fortnight after Drake had departed, left 15 men at Roanoke who disappeared without a trace.

Another Raleigh expedition, this one led by cartographer and painter John White, arrived on the island in July 1587 with 100 settlers. White in turn left a group of colonists at Roanoke while sailing home to obtain needed supplies. Delayed in his return until 1590 by the events surrounding the Spanish Armada, he found no survivors, only the word CROATOAN carved on a doorpost. In March 1602, Raleigh dispatched an expedition to search for the survivors of the "lost colony," but the effort was futile. Raleigh had lost a fortune in this abortive effort to found an empire.

When, in November 1587, Elizabeth expected the inevitable Spanish attack, Raleigh served on a special council of war, where he was responsible for many improvements in coastal fortifications. When, a year later, the Spanish Armada struck, he organized the Devon militia but did not participate in the naval conflict. He faced a rival for the queen's favor in the young Robert Devereux, earl of Essex, and in December 1588, the Privy Council had to break up an incipient duel between them. Yet Raleigh was by no means estranged from the monarch, as she conferred upon him the lease of Sherborne Castle, a West Country estate he had long desired. During the last six months of 1589, he returned to Ireland, where having received 42,000 acres in Munster, he sought to populate his tracts with English settlers. Here he built Lismore Castle, drained bogs, conducted experiments in mining, planted trees, studied vegetation, and probably introduced what

would be Ireland's chief crop, the potato. Returning to court in 1590, he introduced his newfound friend and neighbor in Ireland, the poet Edmund Spenser, whose *Faerie Queen* celebrated Elizabeth's glories and for whom Raleigh wrote the introduction. Spenser in turn praised Raleigh as "The Shepherd of the Ocean."

Jealous Queen Imprisons Raleigh

When the queen authorized raids on Spain's West Indian fleet, Raleigh hoped to command an expedition. But Elizabeth, jealous as ever, chose his cousin Grenville in his place. When in September 1591, Grenville's famous ship, the *Revenge,* was ambushed and its captain killed, Raleigh immediately wrote a eulogy of his cousin, *Report of the Truth of the Fight about the Azores,* and outfitted subsequent minor though successful expeditions.

In May 1592, several months after he had received Sherborne, he invested in an expedition to capture the Spanish fleet and sack Panama. Although he had originally been slated for command, Elizabeth could not bear his departure and ordered him to return after the ships had sailed 60 leagues. Once he returned to Plymouth, he was immediately interned, by royal orders, at the Tower.

To the queen, Raleigh had committed the unpardonable act. He had secretly married one of her maids of honor, Elizabeth Throgmorton, a woman aged 27 and hence at least a decade younger. Her father, a soldier, had been Elizabeth's ambassador to France. The couple spent their honeymoon in prison. It was only when Raleigh was needed for the queen's service that he was released. His last expedition had captured an immensely valuable Portuguese treasure ship, the

Sir Walter Raleigh's conquest of the city of St. Joseph on the Isle of Trinidade in March 1595.

Madre de Dios, the largest ship that had ever entered an English port and one laden with spices and jewels. It was feared that the rebellious British crew might seize the treasure. As Raleigh appeared the only person who could maintain discipline, he was released from prison in mid-September 1592 and sent to the port of Dartmouth. Raleigh kept order and Elizabeth pocketed half the booty.

That fall, Raleigh gained his freedom. While at Sherborne, his wife gave birth to their first son Walter. As a member of the House of Commons, Raleigh opposed the death penalty for Separatists (or, as they were then called, "Brownists"). He joined dramatists Ben Jonson and William Shakespeare at London's famous Mermaid Tavern and was a confident of playwright Christopher Marlowe and mathematician and astronomer Thomas Hariot.

By February 1595, Raleigh was sufficiently in the queen's favor to be sent on a new expedition, this one to Guinea (now Venezuela). His task: to search for the fabled highland city of El Dorado, which the British called Manoa or the Golden City. He undoubtedly had several motives: personal wealth, rehabilitation by Elizabeth, the sheer desire for adventure. In March, he landed at Trinidad, where he captured the Spanish fort St. Joseph and held the governor captive. He proceeded up the Orinoco River, where he met with hospitable natives and gathered samples of gold ore as well as the earliest specimens of mahogany Europe had ever seen. Upon his return home in August, he wrote a bestseller, *The Discovery of the Large, Rich and Beautiful Empire of Guinea.* In his effort to refute claims that his narrations were fictional, he wrote of a veritable Eden:

> I never saw a more beautiful country, nor more lively prospects;... the deer crossing in every path; the birds towards evening singing in every tree with a thousand different tunes; cranes and herons of white, crimson and carnation perching in the river's side; the air fresh, with a gentle easterly wind; and every stone we stopped to take up promised to be either gold or silver by its complexion.

Though he conceded that he was often reporting only what he had been told, such tales made many doubt his credibility.

In 1596, England experienced financial crisis. For two years, rain had spoiled harvests and food prices reached famine heights. With frequent rioting and people dying in the streets, the desperate queen sanctioned a raid on Cádiz, hopefully to capture Spain's entire treasure fleet. Raleigh, seen as the last of the great seamen, was ordered to cooperate in the attack with Essex; Charles Howard, earl of Nottingham; and Lord Thomas Howard, earl of Suffolk. In the subsequent battle, which took place on June 21, Raleigh received a thigh wound from which he never recovered while Essex received credit for the victory. Yet it was Raleigh's strategy that resulted in the burning and looting of the Spanish fort. Though the Cádiz victory has been called "Elizabeth's Trafalgar" and ensured England's supremacy at sea, the queen was furious when British forces failed to seize the expected hoard.

A subsequent attack in June 1597 on the Azores island of Fayal put Raleigh back in the queen's good graces, even though the booty was only three captured ships so small that they barely covered expenses. Raleigh was readmitted to court and received more naval commands. In 1600, he became governor of the island of Jersey, whose trade with Newfoundland he did much to foster.

When **James I** assumed the English throne in 1603, however, Raleigh's days were numbered. James had heard that Raleigh had supported a rival claimant to the throne, the Infanta of Spain. Immediately, Raleigh was dismissed as captain of the guard, stripped of his monopolies, evicted from his royal residence, and compelled to resign the governorship of Jersey. On July 17 of that year, Raleigh was arrested and again sent to the Tower. This time the charge was high treason. He was accused of plotting with Henry Brooke, Lord Cobham to approach the Spanish, dethrone James, and place the king's English cousin, Arabella Stuart, on the throne. In reality the charges were trumped up by James's adviser, Sir Robert Cecil, a gray-haired dwarf and hunchback skilled in political infighting who opposed Raleigh's desire for continued cold war with Spain. Cobham made and retracted eight separate charges.

Within a few days after internment, Raleigh stabbed himself. The table knife he used, however, was stopped by a rib, and the resulting gash healed quickly. Taken to Winchester for trial, he ably conducted his own defense but was soon found guilty. Both Cecil and Henry Howard, earl of Northampton, Raleigh's bitterest enemy, were among the judges. The prosecutor was Attorney General Sir Edward Coke, who in this case did not show the respect for the law that later won him fame.

Raleigh Writes World History

Thinking death imminent, Raleigh wrote his wife: "My love I send you, that you may keep it when I am dead; and my counsel, that you may remember it when I am no more." Yet on December 10, Raleigh experienced a reprieve, followed by 13-year internment in the Tower. He lived far better than most prisoners, dwelling in a large apartment and being attended by three live-in servants and cared for by a physician and clergyman. Each day his wife and son visited him, and in 1605 Bess gave birth to a second son, Carew. James's wife, Queen Anne of Denmark, had Raleigh tutor her 13-year-old son, Prince Henry. During his imprisonment, he completed volume one of his *History of the World* (1614), which began at the Creation and took events down to Rome's second war with Macedonia. Though it stressed God's movement through history, James had the book suppressed, finding it "too saucy in censuring princes." Still in all, within the century, many editions appeared.

Aware of James's need for money, Raleigh posed another expedition to the Orinoco. Count Condomar, the Spanish ambassador to London, got James's promise that if Raleigh harmed either Spanish subjects or property, he would be sent to Madrid for punishment. Released from prison on March 19, 1616, the 62-year-old Raleigh—by now gray, lame, and ridden with malaria—invested most of his remaining funds in the venture and, by the end of the following year, arrived at the river's mouth. Falling ill with fever, he turned leadership over to his pilot and old comrade-in-arms Lawrence Keymis. Acting contrary to King James's instructions, Keymis blundered into a Spanish fort of San Thome. A conflict ensued in which young Walter Raleigh was killed. Furthermore, Keymis could not find the valuable gold mine that was the object of the entire voyage. Berated mercilessly by Raleigh, he stabbed himself in the heart.

In June 1618, Raleigh returned to Britain discredited. The Spaniards had demanded his life, and James—seeking to avoid war—concurred. Sir Walter was arrested as he was about to board a ship headed for France. He was able to write his *Apology for the Voyage in Guinea* before October 29, 1618, when he was beheaded at the Tower.

SOURCES:

Robert Lacey, *Sir Raleigh, Walter.* Atheneum, 1974.

Wallace, Willard M. *Sir Walter Raleigh.* Princeton University Press, 1959.

Williams, Norman Lloyd. *Sir Walter Raleigh.* Eyre & Spottiswoode, 1962.

Williamson, Hugh Ross. *Sir Walter Raleigh.* Faber & Faber, 1951.

FURTHER READING:

Greenblatt, Stephen J. *Sir Walter Ralegh: The Renaissance Man and His Roles.* Yale University Press, 1973.

Rowse, A. L. *Sir Walter Raleigh, His Family and Private Life.* Harper, 1962.

Richard I, the Lionheart

(1157–1199)

Second of the Angevin kings and lifelong warrior, who led the Christian forces in the spectacular failure of the Third Crusade, neglected his English kingdom almost completely, and died in a trivial squabble at only 41 years of age.

Name variations: Richard the Lionhearted; Richard I, Coeur de Lion; Duke of Aquitaine. Born 1157; son of King Henry II and Eleanor of Aquitaine; married: Berengeria of Navarre, 1191; no legitimate children. Predecessor: King Henry II. Successor: brother John.

In Kingsley Amis's comic novel *Lucky Jim* (1954), his antihero—a history professor specializing in the Middle Ages—asks himself: "Had people ever been as nasty, as self-indulgent, as dull, as miserable, as cocksure, as bad at art, as dismally ludicrous, or as wrong as they had been in the Middle Ages?" Amis might well have had the reign of Richard I, the Lionheart in mind. To English historian William Stubbs, Richard was "a man of blood" and to the more recent American historian James Brundage, he was "a peerlessly efficient killing machine." Although his reputation in chivalric lore and among the early chroniclers is high, Richard must rank among the worst kings of England in terms of the benefits of his rule for his subjects. During his ten-year reign as king, he spent less than six months in England. For the rest, he was fighting either on crusade in the Holy Land or in his large French possessions of which Aquitaine, his mother's duchy, was always his first concern.

Born 1157, one of four argumentative and bad-tempered brothers, the young Richard became involved in several family fights over the question of inheriting his father **Henry II**'s estates. Richard, as duke of Aquitaine, hired a group of Dutch mercenaries to keep order in his duchy, letting them

"Once we look a little more closely at some of the stories about Richard it soon becomes obvious that the coat of legendary paint which conceals him is a very thick coat indeed."

John Gillingham

Contributed by Patrick Allitt, Assistant Professor of History, Emory University, Atlanta, Georgia

loot monasteries in lieu of payment at the end of their campaigns. The death of his older brothers Henry and Geoffrey left his way clear to the throne, an event which Richard tried to hasten by allying with **Philip Augustus,** the king of France, and making war against his own father. Richard was, by age 20, famed as a doughty warrior, brave, impetuous, and tactically gifted. Hounding his father across northern France in 1189, Richard finally forced him to surrender at the castle of Gisors; he then made Henry formally appoint him heir. A few weeks later, he witnessed his father's death with no apparent remorse.

The previous year, the Saracen leader Saladin had won a major victory over the crusaders' outpost at Hittin and had captured one of the crusaders' prized relics, a fragment of the true cross. Upon hearing the news, Richard had at once resolved to restore Christian fortunes in the Holy Land kingdom of Outremer and asked the archbishop of Tours to bless him as a crusader. One of his motives for warring against his father had in fact been to earn recognition as Henry II's heir before he set out for the East. Accordingly, as soon as he had been crowned king, Richard prepared to set off on crusade, leaving England prey to rival factions in the regency. Aware that Richard might well die on his hazardous crusade, his brother Prince **John** hoped to make sure of his own succession by setting up a rival court and attracting all those who had quarreled with Richard's official regent, Longchamp, a venal and widely hated man.

Part of Richard's preparation for crusade consisted of raising money from every available source, including the sale of lands, offices, towns, and castles. He joked: "I would sell London itself if I could find a buyer." One wealthy and vulnerable source of money was the Jewish community of England, whom the Angevin kings intermittently protected in return for their financial aid. The only ethnic and religious minority in the kingdom, the Jews were, however, objects of recurrent suspicion in the eyes of the Christian population, who accused them of satanic practices. Richard's coronation on September 3, 1189, was accompanied by anti-Jewish riots in London, and worse pogroms followed in the next few months throughout the English provinces. On March 16, 1190, the riots reached an ugly climax during the Jewish festival of Shabbat ha-Gadol, when 150 Jews in York castle were attacked—some massacred, others driven to preemptive suicide.

Richard and King Philip Set Off on Crusade

Though Richard and the French king Philip each faced formidable domestic problems, they left such

CHRONOLOGY

1157	Richard born
1189	Victorious over his father Henry II; Henry died; Richard crowned
1190	Crusade expedition began
1191	Married Berengeria in Cyprus; Acre fell under leadership of Richard
1192	Battle of Joppa
1192–93	Richard captured en route to England by Leopold of Austria
1194	Ransomed by Henry VI, Holy Roman Emperor, for 100,000 marks
1199	Died at Chalus

difficulties behind and set off together on crusade. Despite several formal vows of friendship made between the two kings, they remained uneasy partners—fully aware of each other's territorial ambitions—and were frequently falling out over the conduct of the crusade. Indeed, riven with mutual rivalries and suspicions of treachery among the leaders, as a whole this Third Crusade was poorly coordinated. When **Frederick Barbarossa,** leader of a German contingent to the crusade, drowned en route to the Holy Land during a river crossing, the surviving German troops were led by Duke Leopold of Austria. The French and English kings traveled separately, Richard mainly by sea, pausing en route first to befriend the king of Sicily, then later to marry Berengeria, daughter of the king of Navarre. Both of these actions were provocative: the Sicilian connection because it angered the Holy Roman Emperor Henry VI, and the Navarrese marriage because it contradicted Richard's long-standing pledge to marry a French princess and was clearly aimed at strengthening Richard's position in southwestern France against the interests of his crusading partner Philip.

Besieging the Saracen stronghold in the city of Acre, Philip was annoyed that Richard had stopped along the way, annoyed too that he had become involved in a war on the island of Cyprus rather than attending to the business of regaining Jerusalem for Christendom. Richard finally arrived in the Holy Land after sinking a Saracen supply ship, but had no sooner landed than he contracted malaria and was unable to fight. Philip made four attempts to storm Acre, all of which failed, before he too came down with a disease which the chroniclers called Arnaldia, possibly malaria, scurvy, or a form of trenchmouth, which caused his hair and fingernails to fall out. While sick, Richard was carried to the siege on a litter; he then recovered long enough to lead a successful assault on the city, which fell to the crusaders on July 12, 1191. The attackers were forced to admire the two-year defense of the city made by the determined Saracens. Gillingham cites on attacker as saying:

> Never were there braver soldiers than these, the honour of their nation. If only they had been of the true faith it would not have been possible, anywhere in the world, to find men to surpass them.

Delight in victory was impaired when Richard discovered that Philip, having had enough of crusading, was returning to France pleading ill-health. Richard had reason to be dismayed; back in France, Philip began scheming with Prince John to seize the English throne, while spreading scandalous rumors that Richard was living a luxurious and indolent life on crusade. At Acre, Richard rashly fell out with another of the Christian leaders, Leopold of Austria, by flinging Leopold's standard into the mud, rather than letting it stand beside his own and Philip's in the moment of victory—an act that was to later have resounding consequences.

Philip's absence at least gave Richard uninterrupted command, and he showed his skill, daring, and ruthlessness in successive battles against Saladin, notably in a victory at Arsuf, despite being outnumbered three to one. Although rudimentary rules of war had been worked out among Christian princes in the preceding centuries, none of them applied to the "infidel" Muslims, and Richard showed his mercilessness by massacring the Saracen prisoners taken during the battle of Acre. The fighting in the Holy Land was punctuated by periodic negotiations, but the crusaders' demand for the entire Holy Land was far more than Saladin was willing to yield. At one point, Richard even suggested that in return for Jerusalem he would arrange for a marriage between his widowed sister and Saladin's brother Saphadin; the plan was scotched, however, when she indignantly refused, unless Saphadin would convert to Christianity (which, of course, he would not).

Army Is Too Ill to Attack Jerusalem

As his plans for an attack on Jerusalem—the goal of all crusaders—matured, Richard learned from messengers that his brother John and Philip of France were conspiring against him, and that he must return home. But before he could set out, his intended successor as crusade-leader, Conrad of Montferrat, was murdered by assassins of Rashid ad-Din Sinan, the "Old Man of the Mountain." Richard's rivals suspected that he had ordered the killing himself since he and Conrad had been on bad terms throughout the crusade. Richard rescued his reputation by organizing a daring defense of the crusader garrison in the city of Joppa, again in the face of superior Saracen numbers, but was forced to recognize that his army was so weakened by illness that they could not prevail in an attack on Jerusalem.

For northern European soldiers, an expedition to the Holy Land meant an introduction to a wide array of killer diseases against which they had few immunities. Armies have always carried epidemics with them, acting as breeding grounds for disease, and the deadliness of the situation has tended to increase when the armies have operated in climatically and biologically unfamiliar territory. Environmental historian Alfred Crosby remarks:

> Richard led his army along the coastal plain, an especially malarial region, and then inland toward Jerusalem. This first advance stumbled during the heavy rains of November, often the worst month for malaria in Palestine, and halted in January as sickness and want weakened many to such a degree that they could scarcely bear up.

The best that can be said for the Third Crusade is that it prevented the extinction of the Crusaders' Kingdom; in fact, it clung to the Mediterranean shore for another century before ultimately succumbing to its political and biological enemies. Acre was held until 1291 by the Knights Hospitaller, one of the crusading orders of the Church. Richard, meanwhile, had made so many enemies among his ostensible allies during the crusade that he had to plan a secret route back to his kingdom, with the aid of Rumanian pirates. Despite artful maneuvering, they were shipwrecked in the Adriatic. His disguise uncovered, Richard was pursued and ultimately captured in Vienna by soldiers of Duke Leopold of Austria, whom Richard had earlier offended in the Holy Land. Leopold handed Richard over to the Holy Roman Emperor Henry VI who imprisoned him first at Durnstein, later at Trifels, leaving England to face the question of ransoming this most valuable of hostages at the staggeringly high cost of 100,000 marks and 200 lesser hostages—the equivalent of which in contemporary currency is, according to Elizabeth Hallam, in the region of 100 billion dollars. Richard, however, maintained a high opinion of his own value. He told the emperor: "I am born of a rank which recognizes no superior but God," and waited confidently for the money to arrive.

Prince John used the occasion of Richard's capture to raise rebellion against Richard and make himself king instead, but their mother **Eleanor of Aquitaine** rallied enough force against John to prevent him from succeeding. Despite his status as a captive, Richard, meanwhile, held his own court within prison and became cordial friends with the emperor. Wanting Richard to become his own vassal and to help him in subsequent wars against the king of France, Henry VI refused to aid John. When the first installment of the ransom was paid, Richard was released and became—as Emperor Henry had hoped—an untiring enemy of France, passing the remaining six years of his life in constant anti-French warfare.

Another legend of Richard's reign tells of Robin Hood, an English knight wrongly outlawed by Prince John during Richard's absence. According to the tale, Robin Hood resisted the arbitrary exactions of Prince John and the Sheriff of Nottingham, stealing from the rich and giving to the poor in the expectation that Richard, on his return, would exonerate him and his forest outlaws and bring the villains to justice. There is, however, no historical evidence to support this lovely old story, and it is ironic that anyone should have looked to Richard for financial relief, since his unquenchable thirst for money to conduct his campaigns (quite apart from the cost of his ransom) made his reign burdensome to taxpayers to an unprecedented degree.

His domains were so extensive, covering all of England and half of today's France, that Richard had to build lines of castles to defend them. At the same time, he tried to keep a standing army at his disposal to fight back against French raids. It was expensive and unpopular among the lords who had to provide fully equipped knights. But by extortion and threats against his vassals, Richard was able to keep his army in existence and ensure its ferocity. When knights from England proved reluctant to fight in France, they were supplemented by mercenaries, who could be used anywhere without argument. Historian W.L. Warren describes the mercenaries thus:

> Right at the bottom were the disorderly *routiers*, the ruffians recruited into companies of foot and hawked for sale by enterprising captains.... [They] were often known as "Flemings" or "Brabantines," but the outcasts and criminals of every nation were to be found among them. They plun-

dered without much regard to friend or foe, and were feared and hated as much by the people of the rulers who hired them as by their opponents in war.

Whereas most feudal wars took place only in the summer months, followed by a long truce from harvest time until Christmas, Richard kept campaigning straight through winter, often surprising his enemies and forcing them to fight much sooner than they had anticipated, when they were ill prepared.

Warfare Leads to Economic Problems

Despite his many victories and the glamour attached to them by minstrels and chroniclers, his warfare led to severe economic difficulties throughout Richard's realm. His efforts to raise money became increasingly frantic and reckless; he threatened to outlaw barons who would not pay large fines, and in 1198 he even declared that the Great Seal—with which all charters were confirmed—had been replaced with a new one, so that anyone wanting to assure his rights had to pay again for use of the new seal. At a time when the entire annual income of the British Crown was normally about £30,000, he spent £49,000 in a single year on castles in Normandy—much of it on the complex fortifications of Château Gaillard on the River Seine which was later lost by his brother and successor King John. Hallam cites one of his contemporaries remarking on Richard's fierce pride in this castle:

> If an angel had descended from heaven and told him to abandon it, that angel would have been met by a volley of curses and the work would have gone on regardless.

Providing he won victory after victory against Philip of France, Richard could get away with his extortions. But by weakening the economic condition of England, he sowed the seeds of disaster and left them for his brother to reap.

The successive wars of Richard's last five years were anticlimactic by comparison with his crusading campaigns, and their net consequence for European history was negligible. He met his end when he went to assert his right to part of a treasure trove uncovered in the territory of Limousin. There, at the fortress of Chalus, he neglected to wear his armor during a reconnaissance and was hit in the shoulder by a crossbow bolt. Ignoring it, he carried on his attack. But later, when part of his shoulder had to be cut away by a surgeon seeking to remove the bolt, Richard developed gangrene and realized that he was dying. Despite his military genius, he had won no victory of lasting significance and had, in fact, laid the groundwork for King John's loss of the French territories that his family had owned since the Norman Conquest.

Richard's legend is extraordinary. It is understandable that English chroniclers, for patriotic reasons, should have celebrated his victories, but more surprising is that French chroniclers—servants of his enemies—should have taken the same line. Even the Saracen historian Beha ed-Din praised Richard the Lionheart as fulsomely as he praised Saladin himself. Although recent historians have stripped away many of the legendary accretions surrounding Richard's name, new ones regularly appear.

SOURCES:

Broughton, Bradford. *The Legends of King Richard I, Coeur de Lion.* Mouton and Co., 1966.

Brundage, James. *Richard Lionheart.* 1973.

Gillingham, John. *Richard the Lionheart.* Times Books, 1978.

Hallam, Elizabeth, ed. *The Plantagenet Chronicle.* Weidenfeld & Nicolson, 1986.

Warren, W. L. *King John.* University of California Press, 1978.

Richard III

(1452–1485)

Last of the Plantagenet kings of England and the subject of five centuries of controversy for his usurpation of the throne and his role in the death of his nephew, King Edward V.

"At [Richard's] nativity Scorpio was in the ascendant.... And like a scorpion he combined a smooth front with a stinging tail. He received his lord king Edward V blandly, with embraces and kisses, and within about three months or a little more he killed him together with his brother."

KEITH DOCKRAY,
AN EARLY TUDOR HISTORIAN

Minutes before his death in 1485, when King Richard III was surrounded by foes at the Battle of Bosworth Field, Shakespeare had him crying: "A horse, a horse, my kingdom for a horse." But Shakespeare never worried about getting the historical details right when he could heighten the drama, and the King Richard he drew, a hideously cruel hunchbacked villain, is mainly dramatic invention—designed more to please Tudor audiences than to advance historical knowledge.

Richard III was no saint, to be sure; he almost certainly killed his nephew, the boy-king Edward V, and died in just the kind of fight by which he had lived. But his bad press started early, and a reputation for villainy has stuck with him ever since, except in cases where his over-compensating champions have tried to make him an exemplary king, absolving him of all sins.

Being the 11th child of a noble family, Richard did not at first seem a likely candidate for the throne. But the depredations of the Wars of the Roses soon catapulted him to prominence. In 1459, when he was only seven, his father, the duke of York, suffered a catastrophic defeat at Ludlow

Name variations: Duke of Gloucester. Born the 11th son of 12 children in 1452; killed at the Battle of Bosworth Field; son of Richard Duke of York and Cecily Neville; married: Anne Neville (a cousin); children: one son, Edward. Predecessors: King Edward IV (Richard's older brother), King Edward V (Edward IV's son and Richard's nephew). Successor: Henry VII.

Contributed by Patrick Allitt, Assistant Professor of History, Emory University, Atlanta, Georgia

1452	Richard born
1459	His father Duke of York defeated at Ludlow
1460	His brother Edward victorious at Battle of Northampton
1461	Duke of York defeated and killed at Battle of Wakefield
1461	Brother Edward won battle of Towton; Richard returned from exile in Burgundy
1465	Studied in the household of Richard Neville, Earl of Warwick ("Warwick the Kingmaker")
1470	Fled to Europe with brother, Edward IV, to escape rebellion of brother George, Duke of Clarence, and Earl of Warwick
1471	Edward IV and Richard won Battles of Barnet and Tewkesbury; Henry VI died
1475	Richard on campaign to France with Edward IV
1482	Richard victorious over the Scots
1483	Edward IV died; regency of Richard for Edward V, followed by Richard's usurpation of throne; Princes vanished
1483	First invasion of Henry Tudor; Buckingham rebelled
1484	Richard's son Edward, Prince of Wales, died
1485	Henry Tudor landed in Wales, marched to Bosworth, and defeated Richard, killing him

on the Welsh border and had to flee abroad to save his life. The next year, family fortunes revived dramatically when Richard's older brother Edward and the earl of Warwick won the battle of Northampton, seizing effective control of the Lancastrian king, Henry VI.

But holding power was as difficult as gaining it for the Yorkists; months later, Richard lost his father and his brother Edmund at the battle of Wakefield. In 1461, his brother Edward avenged their father's death with an overwhelming victory at the battle of Towton, and became King Edward IV. Still not ten years old and already familiar with the brutalities of his world, Richard was now made duke of Gloucester and admiral of England. During much of his teens he lived in the household of Richard Neville, the earl of Warwick, the most powerful nobleman in England, and almost certainly met his cousin there, the earl's daughter Anne Neville, whom he was later to marry.

Warwick and his family resented the influence of the lowly Woodville family into which

Edward IV married in 1464, because a large crowd of Woodville relatives had flocked to court seeking offices and estates. In alliance with another of Richard's brothers, George, the duke of Clarence, Warwick rebelled against Edward IV in 1470, forced him into temporary exile in France, and restored Henry VI to the throne (hence his nickname "Warwick the Kingmaker").

Richard Helps Capture Henry VI

In 1471, Edward IV and Richard (who had refused to join Warwick and Clarence in rebellion), reequipped by the duke of Burgundy, marched from their Yorkshire landfall to London, captured Henry VI, and defeated the earl of Warwick at the battle of Barnet, just north of London, on Easter Day. The Kingmaker died in the battle. Richard, still aged only 19, then led his brother's army on a forced march westward to intercept another hostile army at Tewkesbury, where he won again. Edward now decided to do away with his Lancastrian rival and, using Richard as his messenger, ordered the death of Henry VI in the Tower of London. As one of the chroniclers put it at the time:

> I would pass over in silence the fact that at this period King Henry was found dead in the Tower of London; may God spare and grant time for repentance to the person, whoever he was, who thus dared to lay sacrilegious hands upon the Lord's anointed.

Edward IV, whom the same chronicler praised mightily, was obviously the culprit, but the pretense of mystery about Henry VI's death was officially maintained.

To cement his authority, Edward IV now attempted to have all the powerful noblemen of England sign an oath of allegiance, recognizing his son Edward (later Edward V) as heir to the throne. Richard, who was almost certainly responsible for later killing this child, was the second layman to sign after each of the bishops had taken his turn. Grateful for his brother's proven loyalty, Edward IV granted Richard large estates, making him one of the richest noblemen in England. Unfortunately, Edward IV forgave his rebellious brother Clarence and enriched him also.

Greedily the king's two brothers fought for more, especially the extensive estates of Warwick the Kingmaker. Richard was determined to marry Warwick's younger daughter Anne Neville, for dynastic and financial rather than romantic reasons, but to get her he would have to kidnap her from Clarence, who, according to legend, disguised her as a London cook while himself wedding Anne's sister Isobel. On the verge of coming to blows over who would get the lion's share of the Neville sisters' estates, Richard and Clarence were finally brought to arbitration by the king, in a disputation where each of the three brothers showed great rhetorical and legal skills in making the case for his own claims. "In fact," wrote an admiring contemporary, "these three brothers, the king and the two dukes, were possessed of such surpassing talents that, if they had been able to live without dissensions, such a threefold cord could never have been broken without the utmost difficulty."

Clarence, one of the most turbulent men in a chaotic era of English history, was impossible to mollify for long. When Isobel died in childbirth and his next series of matrimonial adventures backfired, he again plotted against his brother King Edward IV—trying among other things to procure his death through sorcery. The king finally had him convicted of treason and thrown into the Tower where Clarence died in 1478. A colorful tradition has it that he was "drowned in a butt of Malmsey wine." Richard later got blamed for this—as for so many other deaths in the Tower—but, at the time, the responsibility for fratricide lay squarely on Edward IV's shoulders.

Throughout much of English history, the people of the northern and southern counties have mistrusted one another: customs, manners, beliefs, and convictions north of the River Trent have often been the antithesis of those south of it. Richard III's career illustrates the point. He was granted large estates in the northern county of Yorkshire as part of the settlement with his brothers, spent most of the 1470s there, in Middleham Castle, and probably knew the northern counties more intimately than any other king in English history, being accepted into the clannish circle of the major landowners there. The north remained his power base after he seized the throne, whereas he was widely disliked and mistrusted by southerners and Londoners.

Richard Declares He Is Legitimate King

Unlike Clarence, Richard was throughout the 1470s and early 1480s loyal to his brother Edward IV, accompanying him on a campaign to France in 1475 and leading a successful invasion of Scotland in 1482, where he continued to enhance his military reputation. But in 1483, when Edward IV died unexpectedly at the age of 40 and his son Edward V appeared to be the new king, Richard hastened southward. Imprisoning Edward V's Woodville relatives—whom he saw as rivals for the regency—Richard declared himself Lord Protector (Regent) for his young nephew. His first act was to delay the new king's coronation; then he declared that he, Richard, was the legitimate king because Edward IV had in fact been illegitimate. Not content with traducing his mother's reputation (she was enraged at the slur on her honor), he also argued that Edward IV's marriage to Elizabeth Woodville had been bigamous because of an earlier secret marriage to Eleanor Butler which had never been dissolved (as Butler was already dead, she could not disprove it). Therefore, Richard concluded, Edward V was also a bastard, and added him along with his brothers (then aged 13 and 11) to the growing roster in the Tower of London.

These stories were, to say the least, far-fetched, but Parliament held its nose and accepted them in the face of Richard's coup d'état, when it confirmed his claim to the throne the following year. "It was at the time rumored that this address had been got up in the north, whence such vast numbers were flocking to London," wrote the antinorthern author of the *Croyland Chronicle,* "although, at the same time, there was not a person but what very well knew who was the sole mover at London of such seditious and disgraceful proceedings." A large contingent of Yorkshire soldiers encamped outside London and witnessed Richard's coronation on July 6, 1483. He then had all the Woodville prisoners killed.

Richard was king of England for only 26 months, and reigned for too short a time to have much impact on the development of English government for good or ill. Following his coronation, he went on a "Royal progress," a visit to the various parts of his kingdom, to greet (and, he hoped, exact promises of loyalty from) his subjects. While he was back in the north, he learned that his ally in usurpation, Henry Duke of Buckingham, had raised rebellion against him. At first Buckingham's uprising claimed the intention of restoring Edward V to the throne, but rumors were already circulating that Edward and his brother, the "Princes in the Tower," had been murdered, after which the rebels looked instead to Henry Tudor, earl of Richmond (later **Henry VII**), the Lancastrian-Tudor claimant to the throne. Richard marched to meet the rebels, as resolute in military actions as ever, and found it a simple matter to capture Buckingham, whose forces had been trapped by floods in the southwest of England. Buckingham paid for his temerity by having his head chopped off in the market place of Salisbury "notwithstanding the fact that it was the Lord's day," while Henry Tudor scuttled back to his sanctuary in Brittany to await a second and more propitious opportunity to attack Richard.

In 1484, still insecure on his throne, Richard suffered the death of his only son, another Edward, Prince of Wales, which for a king in the troubled 15th century was not only a personal calamity but a sure catalyst for further scheming among rivals. When his wife Anne also died in the following year, many of Richard's subjects suspected that he had poisoned her so that he could marry Elizabeth of York (who in the end was to marry Richard's successor and enemy Henry VII). The rumors about poisoning were so widespread that Richard had to call a council to refute them publicly and deny that he was intending to marry Elizabeth of York.

Who Killed the Princes in the Tower?

Defenders of Richard's reputation in the centuries since these events have denied that Richard also killed the princes in the Tower. They point out, for example, that the Act of Attainder passed by Henry VII listed all manner of crimes against Richard but did not mention the death of the princes. Murder of a beloved brother's children, a particularly heinous form of regicide, would surely have been the first charge to throw at Richard after his death by those seeking to discredit and disgrace his memory. Henry VII's omission of this charge has led to the claim that Henry, going to the Tower, found the princes still alive and killed them himself. While not absolutely impossible, the story is highly unlikely. In early 1483, many people had seen the princes playing in the Tower gardens, but after that they were never seen again.

The important issue from an historical point of view is that many influential English people believed that Richard had killed them, just as they believed that he had poisoned his wife. Indeed, knowledge of his own life's experiences makes it easy to believe that he thought the death of the princes imperative, and difficult to believe that he would have taken the risk of letting them live. He had witnessed the killing of Henry VI and of his own brother George, duke of Clarence, as well as dozens of other nobles' deaths in the wake of his battles. Closeness of blood-relationship was no protection against execution in the Wars of the Roses, and Richard knew perfectly well that Edward V, if he lived, was certain to be the focus of future rebellions. As the historian Charles Ross summarizes:

> Why should it be supposed that Richard, as king, would depart from this established pattern of rai-

son d'être, especially given that his position was more insecure than that of his predecessors, and the legality of his claim seems to have been generally disbelieved.... Reasonable inferences from the behavior of those closely concerned add a further element of support to this argument. We may begin with the Queen mother, Elizabeth Woodville. She was clearly implicated in the plan of autumn 1483 to place Henry Tudor on the throne, on condition that he married her eldest daughter, Elizabeth of York. It totally passes belief that she would have been willing to support a plan which would automatically disinherit her sons by Edward IV unless she had excellent reasons to believe them already dead.

In the face of a rebellion on behalf of Henry Tudor, Richard would have had cause to produce the princes, if they were still alive, to explode the hopes of a pretender whose claim on the throne was dynastically weak. That Richard did not do so points to the probability that they were already dead.

Richard, then, was a ruthless man who saw his chance of supreme power and trampled over all rivals and all decencies to get it. Despite the colorful Shakespearean language by which he is best remembered, there is no good contemporary evidence that he was hunchbacked or deformed in any way. Shakespeare's Queen Margaret denounces him with a memorable blast of curses: "Thou elvish-marked, abortive and rooting hog.... Thou rag of honour!" But the real Queen Margaret was dead by the time Richard seized his crown. The portraits and descriptions we have of him do not add up to a picture of a physical monstrosity, and X-ray photographs have proved that some paintings were changed after the fact to give the impression of a deformity.

Richard's downfall came quickly. Disillusioned Yorkists as well as Lancastrian remnants were united in their detestation of Richard, and looked with hope to Henry Tudor across the English Channel. When he landed at Milford Haven and advanced to meet Richard at Bosworth, Henry Tudor had far less battle experience than the king and a considerably smaller army. Nevertheless, Richard's treachery was catching up with him. Many of those in his own army were untrustworthy, and the opening shots of the battle were watched by William Stanley's army from a nearby hill, waiting to see who would prevail. Richard and the powerful Stanley family were nominal friends, but Richard was sufficiently unsure of Lord Stanley's devotion that he had taken his son as a hostage. Richard's suspicions proved to be justified at the crucial moment of the battle. Stanley's response to a plea for help from Henry settled the issue and brought Richard's reign to an abrupt and violent end, though even his critics admitted that Richard fought bravely. Refusing the chance to escape, says the "Ballad of Bosworth Field," Richard resolved to stake all on the battle:

> He said "Give me my battle-axe in my hand,
> Set the crown of England on my head so high,
> for by Him that shaped both sea and land,
> King of England this day will I die!"

The Latin chronicler Polydore Vergil added: "Alone he was killed fighting manfully in the press of his enemies." At his death, Richard III was only 32 years old.

Controversy over Richard's qualities and conduct persists. In the 1930s, the American "Friends of Richard III, Incorporated" enjoyed the support of James Thurber, Salvador Dali, and Tallulah Bankhead. The Richard III society in England still does all it can to improve the king's reputation and publishes its own journal, *The Ricardian*. In 1951, Richard's reputation got a boost from an ingenious detective novel, *Daughter of Time* by Josephine Tey, whose detective-hero Inspector Grant, temporarily immobilized in hospital, tries to solve the "murder mystery" of the princes in the tower and finds the king not guilty.

The continuing controversies surrounding Richard III are fueled by the relative lack of trustworthy contemporary sources; there is enough material to get at many of the basic facts, but enough lacunae (missing parts) to give scope to a host of conspiracy theories. Anyone living in the aftermath of the Kennedy assassination, another controversial political killing, should have no difficulty understanding the fascination and the uncertainty which surrounds the demise of the young princes.

SOURCES:

Chrimes, S. B. *Henry VI*. University of California Press, 1972.

Dockray, Keith. *Richard III: A Reader in History*. Alan Sutton, 1988.

Hammond, P. W., and Anne F. Sutton. *Richard III: The Road to Bosworth Field*. Constable, 1985.

Ross, Charles. *Richard III*. University of California Press, 1981.

———. *The Wars of the Roses*. University of California Press, 1976.

Cardinal Richelieu

(1585–1642)

First minister of France, who increased the authority of his monarch, King Louis XIII, at home and abroad.

Name variation: Armand Jean du Plessis is known commonly in history by his title the Cardinal-Duke of Richelieu, rather than his personal name (nobles were known by the title of the landed estate owned by their family and managed by the eldest male member). Name pronunciation: Rish-eh-loo. Born Armand Jean du Plessis on September 9, 1585, in the province of Poitou; died on December 4, 1642; son of François and Suzanne (de la Porte) du Plessis.

A rmand Jean du Plessis, Cardinal Richelieu, was born on September 9, 1585, the fourth child of François du Plessis (d. 1590), a nobleman of ancient lineage from the province of Poitou, and Suzanne de la Porte, the daughter of a lawyer in the Parlement of Paris (France's high court of appeals). Sickly as a boy, he would continue throughout his life to be laid low by recurring illnesses. Nonetheless, he fulfilled his family's desire for him to serve the crown. On the day of his baptism, his father, like many royal servants, offered a spectacular procession with roses and triumphal arches to entertain the king. When the brocaded crib reached the church, King Henry III (d. 1589) could read a streamer above the infant with the words "Armand for the King."

Before he was nine, as was then typical, Richelieu's career was selected so that he could best serve the family interests at the royal court. He was to be an officer and a gentleman in the king's army. As a student at the fashionable College of Navarre, he mastered Latin, rhetoric, and philosophy. At 17, he was the epitome of a traditional nobleman, trained in arms and able to distinguish himself from commoners by means of dress,

Contributed by Abel A. Alves, Ph.D., Ball State University, Muncie, Indiana

"Christians must forget offenses dealt them privately. But magistrates are obliged not to forget those which concern the public."

CARDINAL RICHELIEU

speech, and manner. Then his brother Alphonse, who originally had been chosen by the family to assume the local bishopric of Luçon, decided to become an unpropertied monk. Alphonse was jeopardizing an opportunity to increase the family prestige and fortune (since bishops often used their church estates for personal profit), so Richelieu wrote his mother that he would take his brother's place in the clergy to promote "the good of the Church and the glory of our house."

Richelieu returned to the College of Navarre to study theology, and in 1606, through family influence, he was nominated bishop of Luçon, going to Rome to be ordained a priest and consecrated a bishop by Pope Paul V. Upon returning to France, he was accepted as a Fellow of the Sorbonne. Then, in December 1608, he made his formal entry into his diocese of Luçon, where he gained experience at local administration and the problem of imposing order on chaos.

The province of Poitou, where both Luçon and the family estate of Richelieu were to be found, had been badly affected by the 16th-century Wars of Religion. These wars pitted France's Catholic majority against a substantial minority of Protestant Calvinists known as the Huguenots. In 1598, a compromise was reached when King **Henry IV** (d. 1610) issued the Edict of Nantes, permitting Huguenots to worship freely in specified places as long as they remained loyal to the king in political matters. Yet in Poitou, chaos was still endemic, as family feuds merged with religious hatreds. Though a bishop of the Roman Catholic Church, Richelieu's solution was to follow the Edict of Nantes, and not to raise the sword against Protestant heretics. While he believed that Protestants were courting eternal damnation and trying to have others follow them in that path, Richelieu proposed that Catholic prayer, persuasion, and example be the only weapons used against the Huguenots. For the sake of peace and order, he was willing to tolerate two religions, though some others still could be found vehemently arguing for the maintenance of "one true Catholic faith" at all costs.

Bishop Armand was so successful at promoting peace and order in Luçon that he came to the attention of the Queen Mother, Marie de Medici, who was the head of a regency council ruling on behalf of her young son Louis XIII. In 1617, Richelieu briefly became one of the king's ministers—an office he owed to the Queen Mother's favorite, an Italian adventurer named Concini. Then, on April 24, 1617, Richelieu's position was lost when Concini was shot dead as he entered the royal palace of the Louvre. There, atop a billiard table, 16-year-old Louis XIII proclaimed, "I am

CHRONOLOGY

1622	Made a cardinal of the Catholic Church
1624	Became first minister of France
1627–28	Successfully besieged La Rochelle
1630	Louis XIII confirmed his trust in Richelieu on the Day of the Dupes
1631	Richelieu arranged the Treaty of Bärwalde with Sweden
1639	Revolt of the Nu-Pieds in Normandy
1640	Richelieu provided funds to rebels within the Spanish monarchy
1642	Died on December 4
1643	Richelieu's foreign policy came to fruition with the defeat of Spanish Habsburg forces at the Battle of Rocroi

King now; I am your King." The Queen Mother was made a prisoner in her own apartments, and all the old favorites of Marie and Concini were left to fend for themselves. Richelieu, in an effort to ingratiate himself, made an appearance to applaud the king's billiard table speech, and then fled Paris in a coach.

Despite his demonstration of support for the king, Armand Jean du Plessis was disgraced and temporarily exiled to Avignon. This difficult period was saddened further when, in 1619, his eldest brother Henri died in a duel. The correspondence between Henri and Richelieu attests to close collaboration and real affection. His brother's title of Marquis of Richelieu now descended to Armand, but there was no joy in this. He later wrote of this loss as an affliction greater to him than his own death. To compound matters, much time was spent convincing Henri du Plessis's anxious creditors that he died solvent, and a charge actually was raised that Richelieu invented false debts so that his brother's true creditors were kept waiting longer than necessary for payment. This accusation led to a case before the Parlement of Paris, and on September 6, 1622, the high court of appeals vindicated Armand, the new marquis of Richelieu.

Politics seldom grind to a halt before the onslaught of personal tragedy, and Richelieu still had to try to restore his political fortunes. In 1620, Marie de Medici and her supporters failed in an attempted rebellion. Rather than siding fully with Marie, Richelieu watched and waited, a position which allowed him to serve as a go-between, reconciling mother and son in August 1620 by means of a series of agreements signed at Angoulême. As a reward, the king applied to the pope to have Richelieu made a cardinal in 1622. That same year, however, when Marie de Medici tried to secure his appointment to the Royal Council, Louis XIII adamantly refused, saying he hated Richelieu like the devil.

Louis XIII Makes Cardinal Richelieu a Minister

On April 29, 1624, Louis XIII capitulated to Cardinal Richelieu and made him a minister, or adviser, in the Royal Council. There were several interrelated reasons for this. Louis was a devout Catholic who was impressed by a cardinal's trappings, and, more specifically, by the praises lauded Richelieu by Father Joseph, a Capuchin monk with a reputation for saintliness. Joseph was impressed by Richelieu's personal religious discipline, and the cardinal would later employ this ragged holy man on several diplomatic missions as a reward. In addition, Marie de Medici had never ceased to request a ministerial post for her favorite, who, gradually, through diplomacy, was helping her to regain favor in her son's eyes. In late April, Richelieu was a minister, and by August he became first minister. In the brief time intervening between his appointment to the council and his preeminence in it, Richelieu had boldly claimed that he should have precedence on the council as a prince of the Church. No doubt he had gained the king's attention by means of his daring.

Once given the opportunity to be first minister of France, Richelieu did not waste it, immediately engaging in a number of reforms. He promoted trading companies to secure a French position in a newly developing global economy built on the spice trade and the colonization of the Americas, and he engaged in the construction of the very first French navy to protect trade routes and ports. Domestically, he usurped the powers of independent provincial governors by sending out *intendants* with special commissions to collect specific taxes and settle legal disputes. Then in 1625, at a council held at Fontainebleau, Richelieu proposed the abolition of the *paulette*, a tax on the sale and inheritance of bureaucratic offices, which permitted wealthy commoners to buy their way into the nobility by serving in an aristocratic office. Richelieu felt that the *paulette* unduly rewarded wealth in place of the honor of one's ancestry, and he fervently believed that a common birth seldom produced the faculties necessary of a magistrate. Facing massive opposition from a number of officials who were paying the *paulette,* the cardinal

bowed to their will rather than risk all out civil war or the loss of his office.

In his *Testament politique,* dictated to and edited by his secretaries, Richelieu defended the expediency of his political behavior by arguing that the monarchy's servants must always promote the state's survival and prosperity, while preventing internal disorder. These "reasons of state" often demanded that a king and his ministers abandon their personal sense of morality and propriety on behalf of the common good. It was this position which worried many in Richelieu's France and greater Europe, and it was this perspective which made Richelieu the complex villain of Alexandre Dumas' 19th-century novel, *The Three Musketeers.* Above all else, Richelieu's *Testament politique* stresses that all Frenchmen must be loyal to the king, the embodiment of the state and the chief provider of law and order. To this end, any noble or Huguenot disobedient to the king would have to be crushed.

Fearing that a Catholic cardinal, surrounded by devout men like Father Joseph, might revoke the Edict of Nantes, the Huguenots twice tested the monarchy's strength between 1625 and 1628. In 1625, they rose up in rebellion under the leadership of two high-ranking Huguenot noblemen, the dukes of Rohan and Soubise. Richelieu put a quick end to this, reaffirming the Edict of Nantes in the Peace of Paris, signed with the Huguenot leadership in February 1626. Then, for 14 months, from 1627 to 1628, the Huguenots of the important port city of La Rochelle rose in revolt. Throughout the siege of the walled city, a siege personally supervised by the cardinal in an armored cuirass, the Huguenots pathetically awaited relief from the Protestant English, but a quickly constructed dike and Richelieu's new navy successfully blockaded the city. The port surrendered on October 28, 1628, and Richelieu's terms were constructed to strengthen the central monarchy. He eliminated La Rochelle's privileges of locally appointed government, fortifications, and militia maintenance, and he forced the city to accept Catholics in what had been a virtually independent and exclusively Protestant town, but he did not forbid the Huguenots to worship as they chose. The Cardinal had eliminated the Huguenots as a political threat, but he enforced religious toleration to assure their political loyalty in a de facto instance of separation of church and state. From this point on, the Huguenots remained loyal.

While preoccupied with the Huguenots, Richelieu did not forget his eldest brother's death in a duel. In a desperate attempt to tame the nobility, he banned dueling. To the nobility, dueling was a means of defending one's name and honor against insufferable insults. Richelieu respected noble honor but dueling wasted valuable aristocratic lives in the cardinal's eyes. The state alone was to exercise the power over life and death. The young nobles of France, however, thought the cardinal was joking, and one of their number, Montmorency-Bouteville, who had already killed 22 men in duels, chose to duel under Richelieu's own window in broad daylight. Richelieu promptly had the young man arrested and sentenced to death in accordance with the new law. On June 22, 1627, the shocked Montmorency-Bouteville was executed in Paris, an example to all.

The King, the Cardinal, and the Day of the Dupes

By 1630, feeling that she had lost a great deal of power to her former protégé and detesting his leniency to Protestants, Marie de Medici turned against Richelieu. In November, during one of the king's protracted illnesses, the Queen Mother took advantage of his weakness, pampering Louis and trying to get him to dismiss Richelieu as first minister. The cardinal himself thought that he was losing the king's support when, on November 30, he was summoned to Versailles. There, he knelt speechless before the king, awaiting his doom. To his surprise, Louis raised him in a gesture of acceptance. By all accounts, the king and the cardinal were overcome with emotion. This day became known as the Day of the Dupes. It was the occasion when Louis XIII publicly avowed his trust for the man he had once despised. Truly, as had been prophesied on the day of his baptism, the Cardinal was "Armand for the King," and in 1631 the Cardinal-Marquis was duly rewarded by being made a duke.

Secure in his position, Richelieu concentrated his energies fully on the enemies of his beloved monarchy abroad. France was surrounded on all sides by the domains of the Austrian Habsburg family. One branch of this aristocratic family controlled much of southern Germany and Austria, while most of the Americas, present-day Belgium, portions of Italy, and Spain and Portugal were ruled by another branch of the family represented by Philip IV of Spain. The two branches of the Habsburg family ultimately claimed to have but one crusading purpose to their wars and policies: the elimination of Protestantism and the reunification of western Christendom under Catholic Habsburg authority. This immediately raised the question as to whether Catholic France should subordinate its autonomy and interests to those of Spain and Austria. While some answered in the affirmative, Cardinal Richelieu believed that the French monarchy should be subordinate to no other earthly force. He even patronized political pamphleteers to prove his case in a series of propaganda pieces. In short, the last 11 years of Richelieu's life saw him engaged in an ongoing struggle to crush Habsburg ambitions in Europe.

By means of secret negotiations between the trusted Father Joseph and the Italian duke of Savoy in 1631, France was able to gain the fortress of Pinerolo in Italy—a position in close proximity to the route Spanish reinforcements took to join Habsburg troops already battling Protestants in Germany. By the end of 1631, French forces invaded Lorraine, a territory traversed by this route called the "Spanish Road." Gradually, Richelieu was chipping away at Habsburg mobility around France.

That very same year, Cardinal Richelieu engaged proxies to fight the Spanish and Austrians for him. The Treaty of Bärwalde provided Lutheran King **Gustavus Adolphus** of Sweden with six French monthly payments to maintain an army of 36,000 men in defense of Protestant Germany. In return for Richelieu's financial aid, Sweden's king promised not to molest any prince friendly to France and to permit Catholics freedom of worship in any territories he controlled. For reasons of state (namely to weaken Habsburg might), a Catholic cardinal was aiding the Protestant cause in a war which, after the fact, came to be called the Thirty Years' War (1618–48). This treaty pointed the way to purely secular arrangements between states based upon mutually beneficial goals, though Richelieu would probably have insisted on his defense of Catholic worship as a religious motivation.

France Enters the Thirty Years' War

At first the alliance worked for France, when in September 1631 the king of Sweden decimated Habsburg armies at the battle of Breitenfeld. However, in the spring of 1632, he broke his word to Richelieu by marching into Bavaria, a Catholic duchy which Richelieu had been wooing for some time. France protested, until, on November 16, 1632, fortune favored the cardinal, and King Gustavus Adolphus fell dead at the battle of Lützen. The Swedish king's own first minister, the chancellor Axel Oxenstierna, proved more amenable to Richelieu's interests but less capable on the battlefield. At the battle of Nördlingen in September 1634, regrouped Spanish and Austrian forces won a decisive victory over the Swedes. Oxenstierna traveled to Paris with one emphatic demand: that France openly declare war and send men to his aid. Richelieu complied on May 21, 1635. The proxy war was over. France officially entered the Thirty Years' War.

Open French aggression did not work well at first, and French forces met defeat, until Richelieu learned to manipulate Spain's soft underbelly. In 1640, two maritime trading centers of the Spanish Empire revolted: namely Portugal and Catalonia, lands with their own customs, traditions, and variations of the Spanish language. Prompt to respond, Cardinal Richelieu almost immediately provided aid to the Catalans; though there is some doubt, Portuguese conspirators probably also received French funds before their coup on December 1, 1640. Though he died before his efforts would ultimately bear fruit, Richelieu's use of proxies to wear down the Habsburgs was a factor when his last military appointment, the young commander Enghien, decisively shattered Spanish might once and for all at the battle of Rocroi in 1643.

At home, Cardinal Richelieu's own war policies contributed to the increment of the monarchy's debt, and of taxation. The possibility of royal bankruptcy was never very far away in France throughout the 1630s, and as Richelieu tried to increase taxation to foster his war efforts, revolts did occur. In 1639, a mostly peasant band known as the Nu-Pieds revolted in Normandy when the cardinal tried to extend the *gabelle* (salt tax) to a previously exempt territory. Richelieu responded with some flexibility, revoking the royal tax order, but he followed the revocation with a series of harsh exemplary punishments and executions. The cardinal realized that the common folk could not be overburdened, but he thought that they should serve the state to their utmost since the state provided them law and order. In the *Testament politique*, it is stated that the common people are like mules. Their burdens should be consistent with their strength but they should never be lightened, since mules grow lazy and impertinent if they are not consistently worked. The common people of France could expect as many taxes as the cardinal thought they could bear.

Richelieu Profits from Power

Richelieu, himself, used his political power to economic advantage. When he died on December 4, 1642, he left behind approximately 22.4 million livres in assets and only 6.5 million livres in debts.

The total value of his political offices alone was 2.6 million livres. Though he had denounced the *paulette*, he was the first to benefit from tax-farming, a system of collecting royal taxes whereby private collectors could legally turn a profit by overcharging. He may have left the monarchy 1.5 million livres in his will, but the crown owed him, in turn, 1,037,000 in loans. Thus, he personally participated in the increasing indebtedness of the French monarchy as one of its creditors.

With Cardinal Richelieu's death, devout Catholics speculated as to whether he could find eternal peace in heaven after all his political machinations. Using the cunning of a fox, he had sought out means best suited to achieving his two premier goals: the survival and empowerment of the French state. Though rebellions, and even duelling, persisted for some time, the cardinal-duke had taken decisive steps to eliminating enough internal chaos to make France the preeminent power on the European continent. Richelieu's contribution to French history was a notion of the state as so supreme on earth that it did not depend on anything but its own might for its survival. It could decree toleration, even if that made popes and other Catholics uneasy. Though he would not have recognized it, and though it would have made him supremely uneasy, Cardinal Richelieu, in his pursuit of domestic order, and in his foreign policy, foreshadowed the separation of church and state. In the *Testament politique*, it is written that good Christians must forgive offenses done them as private individuals, but the servants of the state, as promoters of the public welfare, must never forgive and forget. On his deathbed, when his confessor requested that he forgive his enemies, Richelieu responded: "I have never had enemies other than those of the State."

SOURCES:

Bergin, Joseph. *Cardinal Richelieu: Power and the Pursuit of Wealth.* Yale University Press, 1985.

Brown, W. E. *The First Bourbon Century in France.* University of London Press, 1971.

Church, William F. *Richelieu and Reason of State.* Princeton University Press, 1972.

Elliott, J. H. *Richelieu and Olivares.* Cambridge University Press, 1984.

Mavrick, Elizabeth Wirth. *The Young Richelieu: A Psychoanalytic Approach to Leadership.* University of Chicago Press, 1983.

Plessis, Armand Jean du, Cardinal de Richelieu. *Testament politique.* Edited by Louis Andre. Robert Laffont, 1947.

Wedgwood, C. V. *Richelieu and the French Monarchy.* Collier, 1962.

Miguel Primo de Rivera

(1870–1930)

Spanish general and second Marquis of Estella, who ruled as dictator from 1923–1930 and whose fall led to the Second Republic and the Spanish Civil War.

Born on January 8, 1870, in Jerez de la Frontera; died in Paris on March 16, 1930; sixth of eleven children born to Miguel Primo de Rivera y Ortiz de Pinedo and Inés de Orbaneja; married: Casilda Sáenz de Heredia, July 16, 1902 (died June 9, 1908); children: José Antonio, Miguel, Carmen, Pilar, Angela, and Fernando. Descendants: José Antonio Primo de Rivera, founder of Spanish Falange party; grandson Miguel, fifth Marquis of Estella and third Duke of Primo de Rivera. Predecessor: father Miguel, colonel; Fernando (uncle), Minister of War and first Marquis of Estella. Successor: General Dámaso Berenguer.

"Spaniards: For us has arrived the moment more feared than awaited… to gather the anxieties, to attend to the clamorous demand of so many who love the Fatherland but see for it no other salvation than to free it from the professional politicians, from those that for one reason or another offer us the scene of misfortunes and immoralities that began in 1898 and threaten Spain with a proximate tragic and dishonorable end.

MANIFESTO OF
MIGUEL PRIMO DE RIVERA (1923)

Miguel Primo de Rivera was born into a landowning and military family in the sherry-producing city of Jerez de la Frontera. His father was a retired colonel, and his uncle Fernando—as captain general in Madrid and soon-to-be first marquis of Estella—assisted the plot to restore the constitutional monarchy in 1875, ending the tumultuous First Republic. So the young Miguel grew up as part of what Gerald Brenan called "a hard-drinking, whoring, horse-loving aristocracy" that ruled "over the most starved and down-trodden race of agricultural labourers in Europe." Yet the boy developed more sympathy for the workers than was common within his class. Studying history and engineering before deciding upon a military career, he won admission to the newly created General Academy in Toledo, perhaps with his uncle Fernando's help, and was graduated in 1884.

Duty stationed him in posts within Spain and overseas. He showed courage and initiative in battles against the Berbers of Morocco, and promotions and decorations came steadily. Primo de Rivera became convinced that Spain probably could not hold on to its North African colony. For

---

Contributed by Kendall W. Brown, Professor of History, Brigham Young University, Provo, Utah

1155

couraged with the fortunes of his country. Having returned to Morocco, he was raised to brigadier general in 1911, the first graduate of the General Academy to receive such a promotion. Yet social revolution had flared briefly in Barcelona, during the "Tragic Week" of 1909. After the army had called up conscripts for service in Morocco, radical republicans and anarchists in Catalonia had proclaimed a general strike. Violence had erupted when the government declared martial law. Anticlerical rioters had burned churches and convents, and tensions grew as socialists and anarchists pressed for radical changes in Spain. Even so, the government proved unable to reform itself or the nation. Frustration mounted.

After 1918, post–World War I economic difficulties heightened social unrest in Spain. The Cortes (parliament) under the constitutional monarchy seemed to have no solution to Spain's unemployment, labor strikes, and poverty. In 1921, the Spanish army suffered a stunning defeat in Morocco, which discredited the military's North African policies. By 1923, deputies of the Cortes called for an investigation into the responsibility of King Alfonso XIII and the armed forces for the debacle. Rumors of corruption in the army were rampant.

Military Establishes Dictatorship

On September 23, 1923, the indignant military, headed by Captain General Miguel Primo de Rivera in Barcelona, overthrew the parliamentary government and established Primo de Rivera as dictator. In his typically florid prose, he issued a Manifesto explaining the coup to the people. Resentful of the parliamentarians' attacks against him, King Alfonso tried to give Primo de Rivera legitimacy by naming him prime minister. In justifying his coup d'état, Primo de Rivera announced: "Our aim is to open a brief parenthesis in the constitutional life of Spain and to re-establish it as soon as the country offers us men uncontaminated with the vices of political organization." In other words, he believed that the old class of politicians had ruined Spain, that they sought only their own interests rather than patriotism and nationalism.

Although many leftists opposed the dictatorship, the public supported Primo de Rivera. Spaniards were tired of the turmoil and economic problems and hoped a strong leader, backed by the military, could put their country on the right track. As he traveled through Spain, his emotional speeches left no doubt that he was a Spanish patriot. He proposed to keep the dictatorship in place long enough to sweep away the mess created

many years, the government had tried without success to crush the Muslim rebels, wasting lives and money. He concluded Spain must withdraw from Morocco if it could not dominate the colony. Posted to Cuba and the Philippines, he witnessed their loss to the United States in 1898, bringing a close to his nation's once-great empire. That loss frustrated many Spaniards, Primo de Rivera included. They criticized the politicians and the parliamentary system which could not maintain order or foster economic development at home, nor preserve the vestiges of Spain's imperial glory.

Tall and thin, filled with energy, talkative and charismatic, Primo de Rivera went to Madrid to serve in the Ministry of War with his uncle. Renowned for his amorous conquests, he reverted to the carefree days of his youth in Jerez. Then in 1902, he married a young Hispano-Cuban, Casilda Sáenz de Heredia. Although his wife could never escape jealous suspicions about her husband's womanizing, their marriage was happy, and Casilda bore six children before her death in 1908, following the birth of Fernando. Perhaps to ease his sorrow, his superiors sent him on a military mission to France, Switzerland, and Italy in 1909. The ladies of France and the joys of Paris restored his optimism and cheer.

Between 1909 and 1923, Primo de Rivera's career blossomed, but he became increasingly disby the politicians. In the meantime, he would use the state to modernize the economy and alleviate the problems of the working class.

Primo de Rivera began by appointing a supreme Directory of eight military men, with himself as president. He then decreed martial law and fired civilian politicians in the provinces, replacing them with middle-ranking officers. When members of the Cortes complained to the king, Alfonso dismissed them, and Primo de Rivera suspended the constitution and dissolved the legislative body. He also moved to repress separatists, who wanted to make the Basque provinces and Catalonia independent from Spain. Despite some reservations, the great Spanish philosopher and intellectual, José Ortega y Gasset, wrote:

> The alpha and omega of the task that the military Directory has imposed is to make an end of the old politics. The purpose is so excellent, that there is no room for objections. The old politics must be ended.

Nevertheless, other intellectuals such as Miguel de Unamuno and Vicente Blasco Ibáñez criticized the regime and were exiled.

The dictator enjoyed several successes in the early years of his regime. Chief among them was Morocco, which had been festering since the turn of the century. Primo de Rivera talked of abandoning the colony altogether, unless sufficient resources were available to defeat the rebellion, and began withdrawing Spanish forces. But when the Moroccans attacked the French sector, they drove the French and Spanish to unite to crush the defiance in 1925. Primo de Rivera himself went to Africa to help lead the troops, and 1927 brought victory to the Franco-Spanish forces. Grateful Spaniards rejoiced to think that decades of North African bloodletting and recriminations were over.

Regime Promotes Economic Growth

He also worked to build infrastructure for his economically backward country. Spain had few cars when he came to power; by 1930, it possessed Europe's best network of automobile roads. His economic planners built dams to harness the hydroelectric power of rivers, especially the Duero and the Ebro, and to provide water for irrigation. For the first time, electricity reached some of Spain's rural regions. The regime upgraded Spain's railroads, and this helped the Spanish iron and steel industry prosper. Between 1923 and 1927, foreign trade increased 300%. Overall, his government intervened to protect national producers from foreign competition. Such economic nationalism was largely the brainchild of Primo de Rivera's finance minister, José Calvo Sotelo. While Spain benefited from the European post–World War I boom, its economic growth also came from Primo de Rivera's policies and the order his regime gave the country.

That tranquility existed, in part, because the dictatorship found ways to accommodate the interests of Spanish workers. Imitating the example of **Benito Mussolini** in Italy, Primo de Rivera forced management and labor to cooperate by organizing 27 corporations representing different industries and professions. Within each corporation, government arbitrators mediated disputes over wages, hours, and working conditions. This gave Spanish labor more influence than ever before. Individual workers also benefited because the regime undertook massive public works. The government financed such projects with huge public loans, which Calvo Sotelo argued would be repaid by the increased taxes resulting from economic expansion. Unemployment largely disappeared.

But Primo de Rivera brought order to Spain with a price: his regime was a dictatorship, albeit a mild one. He censored the press. When intellectuals criticized the government, he closed El Ateneo, the country's most famous political and literary club. To suppress the separatist fever in Barcelona, the regime tried to expunge Catalan culture. It was illegal to speak Catalan publicly or to dance the *sardana*.

Yet despite his paternalistic conservatism, Primo de Rivera was enough of a reformer and his policies were radical enough to threaten the interests of the traditional power elite. According to Gerald Brenan, one of modern Spain's most insightful students, "Spain needed radical reforms and he could only govern by the permission of the two most reactionary forces in the country—the Army and the Church." Primo de Rivera dared not tackle what was seen as Spain's most pressing problem, agrarian reform, because it would have provoked the great landholding elite. Writes historian Richard Herr, "Primo was not one to waken sleeping dogs, especially if they were big."

Primo de Rivera chiefly failed because he did not create a viable, legitimate political system to preserve and continue his reforms. He seems to have sincerely wanted the dictatorship to be as brief as possible and initially hoped that Spain could live with the Constitution of 1876 and a new group of politicians. The problem was to find new civilian leadership to take the place of the military.

In 1923, he began to create a new "apolitical" party, the Patriotic Union (UP), which was formally organized the following year. Primo de Rivera liked to claim that members of the UP were above the squabbling and corruption of petty politics, that they placed the nation's interests above their own. He thought it would bring ideal democracy to Spain by representing true public opinion. But the UP quite obviously was a political party, despite the dictator's naive protestations. Furthermore, it failed to attract enthusiastic support or even many members.

On December 3, 1925, he moved to restore legitimate government by dismissing the military Directory and replacing it with civilians. Still, the constitution remained suspended, and criticisms of the regime grew. By summer 1926, former politicians, led by conservative José Sánchez Guerra, pressed the king to remove Primo de Rivera and restore constitutional government. To demonstrate his public support, Primo de Rivera ordered the UP to conduct a plebescite in September. Voters could endorse the regime or abstain. About a third of the eligible voters defied the dictatorship by refusing to go to the polls.

New Political System Created

Nevertheless, buoyed by his victory, Primo de Rivera decided to create an entirely new political system. On October 10, 1927, with the king in attendance, he opened a National Assembly. Although they met in the Cortes chamber, members of the regime-appointed assembly could only advise Primo de Rivera. They had no legislative power. In 1929, following guidance from the dictator, the assembly finally produced a new constitution. Among its provisions, it gave women the vote because Primo de Rivera believed their political views less susceptible to political radicalism. He intended to have the nation accept the new constitution in another plebiscite, to be held in 1930.

As Spaniards tired of the dictatorship, the economic boom ended. The value of the peseta fell against foreign currencies, 1929 brought a bad harvest, and Spain's imports far outstripped the worth of its exports. Conservative critics blamed rising inflation on the government's spending for public works projects. Although no one recognized it at the time, the final months of the year brought the international economic slump which turned into the great Depression of the 1930s.

When Primo de Rivera lost the support of the king and the armed forces, his dictatorship was doomed. The Spanish military had never unanimously backed his seizure of power, although it had tolerated his rule. But when Primo de Rivera began to inject politics into promotions for the artillery corps, it provoked hostility and opposition. Troubled by the regime's failure to legitimize itself or to solve the country's woes, the king also began to draw away. Alfonso, who had sponsored establishment of Madrid's University City, watched with dismay as the country's students took to the streets to protest the dictatorship and the king's support for it. A clandestine pamphlet portrayed Alfonso as Primo de Rivera's dancing partner. Yet the king did not have to remove Primo de Rivera. On January 26, 1930, the dictator asked the military leaders if he still had their support. Their lukewarm responses, and his recognition that the king no longer backed him, persuaded him to resign two days later. Primo de Rivera retired to Paris, where he died from fever and diabetes on March 26, 1930.

Back in Spain his beloved country degenerated into a decade of chaos and civil violence. Alfonso XIII appointed General Dámaso Berenguer, one of Primo de Rivera's opponents, to govern. But the monarch had discredited himself by siding with the dictatorship. Social revolution fermented in Catalonia. In April 1931, General José Sanjurjo informed the king that he could not count on the loyalty of the armed forces. Alfonso abdicated on April 14, ushering in the Second Republic. Two years later Primo de Rivera's eldest son, José Antonio, founded the Falange, a Spanish Fascist party. Both José Antonio and his brother Fernando were arrested by republican forces once the Spanish Civil War began in July 1936 and were executed in prison by leftist gunmen. Led by **Francisco Franco,** the Nationalists won the Civil War and established a new, vengeful dictatorship. By that time, many Spaniards regarded Primo de Rivera's relatively mild regime and its economic optimism with greater fondness.

SOURCES:

Brenan, Gerald. *The Spanish Labyrinth: An Account of the Social and Political Background of the Spanish Civil War.* Cambridge University Press, 1943.

Carr, Ramond. *Spain, 1808–1975.* Oxford University Press, 1982.

Díaz-Plaja, Fernando. *La España política del siglo XX en fotografías y documentos.* vol. 2. Plaza & Janes, S. A., 1972.

Herr, Richard. *An Historical Essay on Modern Spain.* University of California, 1971.

Ruano, Cesar Gonzalez. *Miguel Primo de Rivera; la vida heróica y romántica de un general español.* Ediciones Nuestra Raza, 1935.

Sagrera, Ana de. *Miguel Primo de Rivera: el hombre, el soldado y el político.* Ayuntamiento de Jerez de la Frontera, 1973.

FURTHER READING:

Rial, James H. *Revolution from Above: The Primo de Rivera Dictatorship in Spain, 1923–1930.* George Mason University Press, 1986.

Shlomo, Ben-Ami. *Fascism from Above: the Dictatorship of Primo de Rivera in Spain, 1923–1930.* Clarendon Press, 1983.

Maximilien Robespierre

(1758–1794)

French lawyer, statesman, and popular leader, who rose to great—if not supreme—power in the National Convention, the Jacobin Club, and the Committee of Public Safety during the Reign of Terror in the French Revolution.

Pronunciation: Rôbz-pyâr. Born Maximilien-François-Isidore de Robespierre at Arras, France, near the Pas-de-Calais, on May 6, 1758; guillotined on July 28, 1794; son of François and Jacqueline-Marguerite (Carraut) Robespierre; education: college of the Oratorians at Arras and the college Louis-le-Grand in Paris; received law degree from University of Paris in 1780.

Charles Dickens called it the best of times and the worst of times; the French Revolution was a time of remarkably high idealism and predictably low selfishness. For ten years, France inspired the world with its call for the liberation of mankind and terrified the world with its relentless war and terror on all opponents of its crusade for liberty, equality, and fraternity.

No individual of the French Revolutionary era, with the exception of **Napoleon Bonaparte,** has excited more passion in his time or in later generations than the small, sincere, and dedicated provincial lawyer, Maximilien Robespierre. Removed with brutal suddenness from leadership of the Revolution in 1794, after forging the weapons of victory over the Revolution's enemies, he was reviled as the Drinker of Blood, as the Seagreen Monster, as the principal cause of a ghastly Terror. Those who hated the Revolution could find in him a simplistic explanation for revolutionary extremism and violence; those who grieved for a Revolution undone could fasten upon him the blame for a lost cause. Only in the latter days of the 19th century, and in our own time, have the currents of revolutionary activity brought defenders of

"Europe cannot conceive of life without kings and nobles; and we cannot conceive of it with them. Europe is lavishing her blood to preserve her chains, whereas we are lavishing ours to destroy them."

MAXIMILIEN ROBESPIERRE

Contributed by C. David Rice, Professor of History, Central Missouri State University, Warrensburg, Missouri

Robespierre to the surface. He has become, by the late 20th century, an ambiguous figure. Part heroic democrat, part immovable ideologue, and part pathological terrorist, he haunts the pages of modern revolutionary history.

Born on May 6, 1758, in Arras, in northern France, Robespierre was the son of a lawyer in a family of lawyers, and never appears to have considered any other vocation. His mother, Marguerite, was a brewer's daughter who died giving birth in 1765 to a child who died as well. By the time Robespierre was ten, his father had deserted him and his brother and two sisters. Virtually an orphan, Maximilien, as the oldest, had to lead the family as it moved in with relatives then he had to struggle to find a position in life to sustain his siblings. As his biographer, George Rude, has noted, Robespierre was one of the few leaders of the Revolution who knew what it meant to be poor. If he grew up a grave young man, it was because he had no choice.

With local financial assistance, the young Robespierre attended the Arras Oratorian college for four years and then went, on a scholarship, to the Collège of Louis-le-Grand at the University of Paris. An outstanding scholar, he was presented a degree in law by the University of Paris in 1780. At the time, he was not unlike many young gentlemen of the Old Regime and called himself de Robespierre.

Robespierre Is Influenced by Rousseau

Back in Arras, Robespierre did not prosper in the law, possibly because he accepted cases involving the poor and the disadvantaged against persons of wealth and privilege. Instead, he focused on the Enlightenment, the primary intellectual movement of his century, and became devoted to the works of Jean Jacques Rousseau. Particularly appealing to him was Rousseau's arguments on behalf of *virtue*, a word with a richer meaning then than now. Robespierre understood *virtue* to mean a willingness to subordinate personal desires and vanity and a dedication to an upright life and to service for the community. In later years, when he saw his *patrie*, or nation, in danger, he had no patience for—or even understanding of—men who did not exhibit the *virtue* that so dominated his own life and personality.

In the last decade before the eruption of the Revolution in France, Robespierre lived the quiet life of a small town lawyer, writer, and social critic. In 1789, the royal government, ill led and nearing bankruptcy, summoned an assembly called the Estates General to Versailles. The king, **Louis**

CHRONOLOGY

1781	Robespierre took up law practice in Arras
1786	Became director of Academy of Arras
1788	Published *Appel a la nation artésienne*
1789	King called Estates General; Robespierre elected deputy for the Third Estate of Artois; Bastille stormed; Robespierre called for liberty of the press, demanded civil rights for Jews, actors, and Protestants
1790	Called for limitations on royal power; defended revolutionary activities; National Assembly abolished all titles
1791	Robespierre opposed extra qualifications for the national legislature and death penalty; Louis XVI failed in attempt to escape
1792	King overthrown; Robespierre elected deputy to National Convention
1793	Louis XVI executed; Robespierre condemned Girondist faction; appointed to Committee of Public Safety; the Terror began
1794	Robespierre led attack on Hébertist faction; quarrelled with Jacobins; arrested and guillotined

XVI, hoped only to solve his financial problems, but reformers meant to restructure the nation entirely.

Robespierre, and others like him, believed that the ordinary people of France should have a greater role in their government. In a publication he called *Appel a la nation artésienne,* he argued that henceforth the poor should not be excluded from public life and that they had rights as valid as those of any privileged order. Standing as a candidate for the Third Estate—or common order of Frenchman—he was elected in March 1789 to represent the poorest occupational guild in Arras at the Estates General.

When the Estates General gathered at Versailles in May, a crisis ensued when the Third Estate refused to be dominated by the other two estates, the nobility and the clergy. Robespierre took part when the Third Estate seized the initiative by declaring itself a National Assembly and took an oath to draft a modern constitution for France. On June 6, he gained attention by denouncing the wealth of the higher clergy and calling for much of the Church's riches to be distributed among the poor.

Most of the delegates desired a peaceful, legislative reform of their country, seeking constitutional government and leadership by the wealthier, better educated elements of the Third Estate. But Robespierre understood that the millions of French peasants and urban workers expected far more from the Revolution than he and his middle-class associates in the assembly had launched. Rural violence and the storming of the Bastille by the people of Paris on July 14 dramatically confirmed his views.

He Becomes Central Figure in Revolution

Great struggles to modernize France dominated the years 1789 to 1791. Robespierre, a central figure, spoke fervently for universal suffrage, abolition of all privileges, an end to religious discrimination, and personal rights for Jews, actors, and black slaves. Always demanding the rights of the people, he gained a reputation as the most honest man of the Revolution. By 1790, he was very popular, particularly in Paris, and was already known as the Incorruptible; **Count Mirabeau,** the lion of the early Revolution, wisely noted that Robespierre would go far for "he believes everything he says."

Joining other "Patriots," the most progressive faction in the National Assembly, Robespierre also spoke often in the Jacobin Club, a political association that influenced the assembly. The club established satellite organizations all over France as the Revolution progressed, and Robespierre—selected president of the Jacobins in April 1790—made effective use of their support.

By early summer of 1791, a constitution was ready for the king's acceptance. On June 20, however, the royal family tried and failed to flee the country, and the nation was thrown into turmoil. Some deputies, including Robespierre, were disgusted by the king's duplicity and demanded his removal and trial. But most could think of nothing better to do than implement the new constitution and trust the king to adhere to it, as he said he would. For his part, Robespierre proposed a self-denying ordnance by which the members of the National Assembly would be ineligible for election to the new constitutional Legislative Assembly. The Legislative Assembly, lacking experience and denied the talents of the leaders of the National Assembly, drifted into factionalism and strident demands for an armed liberation of Europe from the tyranny of kings. Louis XVI and his queen, **Marie Antoinette,** urged the leadership on to war in the vain hope that a lost war would restore them to their former powers. Robespierre, noting that Europe would not welcome liberation at the point of French bayonets, worried that war would deflect the Revolution and perhaps make a popular general a military dictator. When war did come in the spring of 1792, however, the armies of France suffered defeats at the hands of Prussia and Austria, and the nation and Revolution were in genuine danger.

By late summer, Paris was gripped by fear and suspicion. Defeat and a belief in royal treachery, combined with discontent with the Girondists, the ruling faction, produced a great popular rising in Paris on August 10, 1792. The Jacobins were involved in the insurrection led by the city government, the Commune, and the popular clubs in the sections of Paris. Initially aloof, Robespierre soon joined the Insurrectional Commune. The rising was bloody and decisive: Louis XVI was deposed and arrested and many deputies in the Legislative Assembly either fled or were jailed. In early September, with the foreign enemy nearing Paris, thousands of suspects were murdered in the city's jails. While the Commune orchestrated these September Massacres, Robespierre was not directly involved. His rising popularity in the frightened city, however, was his reward for not denouncing the judicial murders.

Robespierre Denounces Girondists

With the king deposed, France required a new government to fight the war, save the Revolution, and draft a new constitution. Elected a deputy from the city of Paris to the new National Convention, Robespierre denounced the Girondists, who tried to prevent the king's trial and execution, and took the lead in the Jacobin faction known as the Mountain. When reviled by the Girondists, Robespierre retorted with a powerful address on December 3 which routed his opponents and virtually assured the king's death.

The war, which had proceeded well for a period after September 1792, took a disastrous turn in the spring of 1793 when powerful states such as Great Britain and Holland joined the European crusade against what was regarded as a bloody, atheistic, and aggressive Revolution. The convention, riven by factional struggles between Girondists and Jacobins, struggled to produce a new constitution, prevent uncontrolled popular violence and terror, and prosecute a war against a formidable coalition. To these burdens was added a series of revolts within France against the convention. Allying himself and the Jacobins with the Parisian sections, controlled by the radical *sans culottes,* the working men and small proprietors of the city, Robespierre struck against the Girondists in early June, demanding a government of "a single will." By late June, an advanced democratic constitution was finished, but the convention decided to set it aside until the emergency had passed.

The desperate situation seemed to demand desperate solutions in 1793. The convention had formed a Committee of Public Safety to assume executive authority in April 1793; now it moved to give the committee extraordinary authority. On July 27, Robespierre was named to the committee, and he and his colleagues rapidly recommended and obtained a host of measures, including price and wage controls, a virtual universal draft of citizens for the war effort, unrelenting pressure and terror against all enemies of the Republic, and the crushing of the internal rebellions. Representatives of the committee and convention were sent to the rebellious regions where they combined force, terror, and vicious repression to enforce the Republic's will. Although hardly the author of all these measures, as his opponents would later say, and, in fact, shocked by the barbarity of many actions of the representatives on mission, Robespierre nevertheless gave his consent to the committee's general policies. A bachelor, aloof and distant by nature, Robespierre had few friends, if many admirers. His only passion was for the Revolution, and he would stop at nothing to save it from those he thought its enemies.

The Terror Expands

The committee's drastic policies were rewarded with success. By the spring of 1794, the Republic had suppressed the rebellions and gained the initiative in the war. But Robespierre believed it would be folly to relax the committee's vigilance. At the same time, it would be counterproductive to allow more radical elements, such as the Parisian leaders associated with Jacques Hébert, to discredit the Revolution with their violent attacks on Christianity. In March, Robespierre persuaded the committee to proscribe the Hébertists, and in April, engineered the arrest and execution of **Jacques Danton** and Camille Desmoulins, both personal friends of Robespierre, and major popular leaders who had called for an end to the Terror. If Danton, often regarded as the savior of the Republic in 1792, could go to the blade, who was safe?

It would be a mistake to think Robespierre alone was responsible for the mounting Terror, a Terror that seemed no longer necessary to moderates. Eleven other members of the committee must share responsibility. Yet to some in the convention and to all of his enemies, it seemed Robespierre was establishing a dictatorship based on the blood of his critics. Many feared that he would condemn them next: zealous representatives on mission,

speculators, those who hated the power of the Commune, and, of course, all counterrevolutionaries concluded that Robespierre might read their names in the convention any day. Meanwhile, the Terror expanded. On June 8, Robespierre led a Festival of the Supreme Being in an attempt to replace the discredited Catholic Church with a civic religion of virtue. To some he seemed a priggish, intolerant pope of a new sect. Then, on June 10, the committee pushed through a law depriving suspects of the most basic means of judicial defense. A dread hung over Paris and the country as in no other crisis of the Revolution.

Was Robespierre truly seeking a dictatorship of himself and his friends as some have claimed? Probably not. But he does appear to have become convinced that the national safety could never be assured so long as the war persisted and treason abounded. To relax the Terror would be to consent to selfishness and the abandonment of civic virtue. In normal times, he said:

> [T]he mainspring of popular government is virtue, so it is both virtue and terror in revolutionary times; virtue without which terror is disastrous, terror without which virtue is helpless.... Mercy for the scoundrels! No! Mercy for innocence, for mankind!

He knew his enemies meant to destroy him. For a month, he absented himself from the committee, but in late July 1794, he returned and promised to provide a new list of traitors. On July 27, or 9 Thermidor in the Revolutionary calendar, he rose to speak in the convention. He was interrupted by shouting and charges of dictatorship by a number of his desperate enemies who had formed a conspiracy to denounce him in the Convention. His voice drowned out in the din of accusations, he knew his hour had come. Demanding his own death, he was indicted by the convention and arrested. Yet the final act of the drama remained. Shaken by the news of their leader's fall, officials of the Paris Commune delivered Robespierre from confinement and frantically urged him to rouse the city and the army to overturn the convention. Unwilling or unable to turn on the legislature that he had meant to use to regenerate the nation, he did nothing. By evening, having pulled together its courage, the convention declared Robespierre an outlaw and sent forces to arrest him. When armed men broke into the city hall where Robespierre and his associates were assembled, he either shot himself in the jaw or was shot by one of the attackers. Resistance collapsed, and Robespierre was taken back to the convention, bleeding, in pain, and scarcely conscious. On the following day, the first 22 "Robespierrists" were executed in the Place de la Revolution. Maximilien Robespierre, his jaw shattered and bleeding, was the 21st to die on the guillotine to which he had sent so many before him.

Robespierre stood for democracy and the common man. He was defeated by men of property who feared his ideas and men of guilt and ambition who feared his righteousness and his vengeance. A man of virtue, he could not condone those who were not and so was doomed to be their victim. He was, wrote his best biographer, J.M. Thompson, a man for opposition, not for governance. Yet in him were witnessed courage and vision and the best hopes of a great revolution. His failing was his conviction that men could be forced to be good, and for all his merit, and despite the volumes written to exonerate him, the blood cannot be purged from his hands. With him, the forward thrust of the Revolution ended, and the way was prepared for the coming of the military tyrant he had predicted.

SOURCES:

Furet, Francois, and Mona Ozouf, eds. "Robespierre," by Patrice Gueniffey in *A Critical Dictionary of the French Revolution.* Translated by Arthur Goldhammer. Harvard University Press, 1989.

Robespierre, Maximilien. "Relation of Religion and Morality to Republican Principles," May 7, 1794.

Rudé, George. *Robespierre: Portrait of a Revolutionary Democrat.* Viking, 1976.

Scott, Samuel F., and Barry Rothaus, eds. *Historical Dictionary of the French Revolution 1789-1799.* Greenwood Press, 1985.

Thompson, J. M. *Robespierre and the French Revolution.* Collier, 1962.

FURTHER READING:

Mathiez, Albert. *The Fall of Robespierre.* Williams and Norgate, 1927.

Palmer, R. R. *Twelve Who Ruled: The Year of Terror in the French Revolution.* Princeton University Press, 1941.

Madame Roland

(1754–1793)

French writer and political figure, who presided over a salon and was influential in her husband's career during the early years of the French Revolution until she was arrested and executed for treason.

"Oh Liberty, what crimes are committed in thy name."

MADAME ROLAND, ADDRESSING THE STATUE OF LIBERTY AS SHE APPROACHED THE GUILLOTINE

Marie-Jeanne "Manon" Philipon, better known as Madame Roland, was born in Paris sometime in 1754. The only surviving child of a master engraver, she was born into an age of reason and wit, the France of the *philosophes*. After spending the first two years of her life with a wet-nurse, Manon returned to her parents' middle-class household where she watched her father and his apprentices make decorated snuffboxes, jewel and watch cases, elaborate buttons, and picture frames. Taught to read at an early age, her intellectual curiosity was insatiable. She devoured books on virtually every subject including history, philosophy, poetry, mathematics, and religious works. From her mother, she learned the domestic duties of cooking and sewing. It was reading, however, that remained her greatest joy, and she spent the majority of her waking hours engaged in study. As she herself noted: "I need study as I need food." At the age of nine, Manon discovered Plutarch's *Lives* which made an indelible impression upon her. It was Plutarch, she later admitted, who made her a firm believer in the republican form of government.

Religion held a strong hold on the young girl who, at age 11, expressed an earnest desire to

Name variations: Marie-Jeanne Philipon; family nickname "Manon," better known as Madame Roland. Born in 1754 in Paris; executed for crimes against the state during the French Revolution on November 8, 1793; only surviving daughter of Gatien Philipon (a master engraver) and Marie-Marguerite Bimont; married: Jean-Marie Roland de la Platière, February 4, 1780; children: one daughter, Marie-Thérèse Eudora.

Contributed by Margaret H. McIntyre, Ph.D. candidate in History, University of Guelph, Guelph, Ontario, Canada

less, she concluded that orthodox Christianity was useful and necessary for poor people in order to give them hope. Historian Gita May has concluded that "from her study of the *philosophes*, Manon came away a resolute optimist and a firm upholder of the dignity of the individual."

Her Reading Leads Her to Rousseau

Her optimism was temporarily shattered by the death of her mother in June 1775. Estranged from her father, whose heavy financial speculations began to destroy his business, Manon kept to herself, spending more and more time alone. In 1776, at the age of 22, she resolved to remain a spinster for the rest of her life. Rejecting the young suitors her father suggested, she preferred the company of older men, with whom she could enjoy intellectual and social companionship without the burden of physical attraction. It was during this period that she first read Rousseau. Gita May asserts that "Rousseau... shaped her whole moral being and... determined her every important act both in her private and political life." In her *Memoirs*, Madame Roland discussed the philosopher's impact:

> Rousseau... made the same impression on me as had Plutarch when I was nine.... Plutarch had predisposed me to become a republican; he had inspired in me the true enthusiasm for public virtues and liberty. Rousseau showed me the domestic happiness to which I had a right to aspire and the ineffable delights I was capable of tasting.

Of all her elderly companions, Manon had not yet chosen a suitor whom she could consider marrying until January 1776 when she was introduced to Jean-Marie Roland de la Platière, an inspector of Commerce and Manufactures at Amiens. Twenty years her senior, M. Roland was a thin, slightly stoop-shouldered man who dressed like a Quaker and whose angular, sharp features gave him a somewhat striking appearance. Roland appeared more respectable than seductive, and Manon appreciated his broad range of interests and gravity of mind.

Their courtship was lengthy and often stormy. Roland spent long periods without visiting or corresponding with her. In addition, Manon's father disliked him intensely while Roland's family were wary of allowing their son to marry a dowerless bourgeoisie. In spite of these objections, they became engaged in April 1779 and, after Roland's procrastination, were finally married on February 4, 1780. As a couple the Rolands made an interest-

become a nun. Her parents agreed to a one-year trial and on May 7, 1765, she entered the Convent of the Ladies of the Congregation, in the Faubourg Saint-Marcel. Here, she met the Cannet sisters, Henriette and Sophie, who became her lifelong friends.

Convinced that the monastic life was not for her, Manon left the convent in the spring of 1776 to live for a year with her grandmother Philipon on the Ile Saint-Louis. It was during one of their infrequent social outings that Manon was introduced to Madame de Boismorel, a wealthy noblewoman who left an unfavorable impression on the young bourgeoisie. Madame Boismorel exhibited all of the pretentiousness and arrogance of the *ancien regime* aristocracy, and Manon maintained a critical and hostile attitude towards them for the rest of her life.

Upon her return home, Manon continued her extensive reading by making use of circulating libraries. Mastering Italian and with a good knowledge of English, she delighted in reading the works of English novelists and poets such as Fielding, Richardson, Pope, and Shakespeare. Voltaire became one of her favorite authors and, from the age of 14, she began to have serious doubts about her religion. She eventually chose to reject the staunch Catholicism of her childhood and instead relied on a sentimental form of deism. Nonethe-

ing sight. He looked more like her father than her husband while she, with her dark hair and pale complexion, radiated youth and vigor.

For the first six months of their marriage they lived in Paris even though Roland's office was in Amiens. During this time, he came to rely more and more upon his wife's literary and intellectual talents. Madame Roland helped him edit his writings, becoming not only his secretary, but also his copyist, editor, researcher, proofreader, and, finally, coauthor. In Paris, she became acquainted with men of letters and scientists with whom she was to maintain lifelong friendships. Louis Bosc, a botanist, and François Lanthenas, a businessman, quickly became enamored of her lively wit and charming personality. It was with some regret that she left Paris for Amiens in the autumn of 1780. One year later, on October 4, 1781, she gave birth to the couple's only child Marie-Thérèse Eudora.

For the next four years, Manon's life remained uneventful. She continued to work along side her husband, providing him with invaluable assistance. In spite of her intellectual abilities and obvious talents, Madame Roland was no feminist. In a letter addressed to her friend Bosc she confessed:

I believe… in the superiority of your sex in every respect. In the first place, you have strength, and everything that goes with it results from it: courage, perseverance, wide horizons and great talents…. But without us you would not be virtuous, loving, loved, or happy. Keep therefore all your glory and authority. As for us, we have and wish no other supremacy than that over your morals, no other rule than that over your hearts…. It often angers me to see women disputing privileges which ill befit them…. [Women] should never show their learning or talents in public.

Her quiet life in Amiens was interrupted when she embarked on a trip to Paris in March 1784 in order to obtain a patent of nobility for Roland. They both believed that his long service of duty entitled him to recognition and respect. Unfortunately, her charm, intelligence, and perseverance did not win over the hostile attitudes which the officials held about her husband, although she did manage to obtain for him a transfer from Amiens to Lyon and a promotion to general inspector. After a brief trip to England in July 1784, the Rolands moved to his family home at Villefranche-sur-Saone. Much of their time, however, was spent at their country retreat, Le Clos, which Manon greatly admired and enjoyed. In spite of the abject poverty she encountered, she was content and serene.

This was not the situation in the rest of the country. The French monarchy had become increasingly unpopular from the mid-18th century, and revolutionary language was circulating in France after the revolt of the American colonies. By 1787, the royal treasury was bankrupt from the wars with Great Britain, and a disastrous harvest in 1788 caused food shortages and subsequent bread and grain riots. **Louis XVI,** in order to alleviate the crown's financial difficulties, summoned a meeting of the Estates General which had not met since 1614. The Third Estate, made up of mostly lawyers, doctors, engineers, and merchants, demanded double representation which the king and his finance officer, Jacques Necker, granted. It was a fatal move. The delegates, who had drawn up a number of grievances, or *cahiers,* were disappointed when the Estates General met on May 4, 1789, and the king failed to address their concerns. More important, he chose to ignore the question of whether the assembly would vote by order, which usually ensured the dominance of the privileged estates, or by head, which would give the Third Estate control. Disappointed by the king's reluctance to decide upon this issue, the Third Estate took a momentous step and proclaimed itself the National Assembly on June 17. The king finally intervened by locking the delegates out of their meeting hall but, defying his will, they met in a nearby tennis court and bound themselves by a solemn oath not to separate until they had drafted a constitution for France. The French Revolution had begun.

The Rolands Support the Insurgents

Madame Roland's complacent and quiet life in the country was disrupted when news of the events taking place in Paris reached her. From the outset of the Revolution, she and her husband supported the goals of the insurgents. Convinced that the revolutionary movement would only be successful if it abolished the monarchy, she continued to suspect the King of plotting with counterrevolutionaries which turned out to be true. Remaining in Lyon, Manon and her husband became correspondents for a revolutionary newspaper, the *Patriote français* published by Jacques-Pierre Brissot, a lawyer whom they had met in 1787 and who was currently an active leader of the revolutionaries. In November 1790, sympathizers of the Revolution dominated the municipal council of Lyon, and Roland was subsequently appointed an officer.

The city was in the midst of an economic crisis due to its exorbitant debt, and Roland was appointed to negotiate for a loan from the National Assembly. Accompanying her husband to Paris in February 1791, Madame Roland opened her first political salon at the Hôtel Britannique in the rue Guénégaud. Many of the leading revolutionary figures attended, including Brissot, Petion, **Robespierre,** Buzot and **Thomas Paine.** Unlike other hostesses, she did not choose to be the center of attention, refraining from speaking until the meetings were finished.

By August 1791, with her husband's mission nearing its end, they decided to return to Le Clos. Their residence was short-lived. On September 27, the Inspectorate of Manufactures was abolished and Roland was consequently deprived of his profession. Having served for nearly 40 years, he felt that he deserved a pension and, as a result, the Rolands returned to Paris in December 1791 where they immediately became embroiled once again in revolutionary politics.

Louis XVI had signed the constitution on September 14, 1791, and from the first meeting of the Legislative Assembly on October 1, the question of war dominated its mood and work. The strongest advocates for war came from a group later known as the Girondists, whose unofficial leader was Roland's friend and fellow journalist Brissot. In speeches to the assembly and to the radical Jacobin Club, the Girondists advocated war with Austria as a means of rallying popular support for the Revolution, testing the loyalty of the king, and suppressing counterrevolutionaries. In March 1792, Louis XVI appointed a new cabinet which included Roland as minister of the interior. One month later, on April 20, war against Austria was finally declared.

Madame Roland, who had already proved a worthy partner to her husband, was now virtually indispensable. She was often present when colleagues and friends brought up matters of state with her husband at home. Enjoying his fullest confidence, she wrote much of his correspondence and provided advice and support for his policies. With the reopening of her salon, Madame Roland found herself at the social and political center of the new government.

King Is Criticized for His Veto

In spite of his earlier cooperation, Louis XVI became increasingly intractable by consistently refusing to endorse Girondist legislation. Military losses contributed to growing accusations that the king was secretly encouraging the Austrians. Distrust between the king and the government reached a climax in May 1792 when he vetoed three Girondist decrees. On June 10, Roland addressed a letter to the king, actually written by his wife, reprimanding him for his veto and encouraging him to become more patriotic. Madame Roland's dislike for the monarchy was clear: "I know that the stern language of truth is rarely welcomed by the throne, I know too that it is because truth is almost never heard there that revolutions become necessary."

Louis not only ignored the letter but dismissed all of the Girondist ministers including Roland. His action led to an armed uprising of the Paris populace on June 20 and heightened anxiety throughout the country. Political excitement continued to increase until August 10 when a crowd of armed Parisians marched on the palace at the Tuileries, forcing the royal family to flee for protection to the National Assembly. The crowd, however, was in control, and the assembly had no choice but to suspend Louis XVI from his functions. As the monarchical constitution was clearly dead, they ordered elections for a new body, the National Convention. Roland and his colleagues were reappointed, and **Danton** was named minister of justice.

Madame Roland was once again in a position of influence as helpmate to her husband, although she fell increasingly under attack from Robespierre and his Jacobin allies. The Girondists were rapidly losing support in the French capital, and when the convention held its first meeting on September 21, 1792, the divisions were clear. On one side were the Girondists; on the other sat the Jacobin deputation from Paris which became known as the Mountain (*Montagne*) from the high seats it took at the back of the assembly. The rest of the deputies formed the Plain (*Plaine*) and were uncommitted to either faction.

The fate of the king led to a struggle for control of the convention itself. Roland became a favorite target of the opposition who accused him of royalist sympathies and secret correspondence. The slander directed against the Roland ministry included his wife who was summoned before the bar of the convention on December 7, 1792. After a dramatic defense of her politics, she was not only cleared of the charges brought against her but was voted honors of the session. Her husband was less successful. The convention voted in favor of the king's execution by a majority of one vote, and Louis XVI was guillotined on January 21, 1793. Roland handed in his resignation the following day.

Historians have debated upon the real reasons for Roland's decision to resign at this particular time and, until recently, were unaware of the personal crisis he and his wife were undergoing. Sometime before her husband's resignation, Madame Roland confessed to him her romantic attraction to the Girondist deputy from Evreux, François Leonard Buzot. Faced with a painful dilemma but realizing his dependence on her, Manon chose to remain with Roland. Thus, they continued to live and work together although their relationship was strained not only for personal reasons but by the uncertainty and growing danger of their political position.

In spite of repeated requests and petitions, they were prohibited from leaving Paris. Manon's sense of doom was realized when 21 Girondist deputies were expelled from the convention and arrested on May 31, 1793. Engineering her husband's escape, she did not elude the authorities. For the next five months, she spent her time in prison writing her *Memoirs* and her autobiography entitled *An Appeal to Impartial Posterity*. Throughout her imprisonment, she maintained a calm composure. After visiting Madame Roland in prison, an Englishwoman noted that:

> She conversed with the same animated cheerfulness in her little cell as she used to do in the hotel of the minister.... She told me she expected to die; and the look of placid resignation with which she spoke of it, convinced me that she was prepared to meet death with a firmness worthy of her exalted character.

During her imprisonment she refused to agree to several plans for her escape; her fate was sealed when the Girondists, after a seven-day trial, were found guilty of counterrevolutionary activities and were executed on October 31, 1793. Madame Roland's trial before the Revolutionary Tribunal was set for November 8. Dressed in a gown of white muslin, she listened to witnesses against her but was forbidden to speak in her own defense. Pronounced guilty of a "horrible conspiracy against the unity and indivisibility of the Republic, and the liberty and safety of the French people," she was ordered to be executed that very afternoon. On a bleak, wintry November day, Madame Roland traveled in a cart to the foot of the guillotine in the Place de la Revolution. Mounting the platform, her eyes fastened on the artist David's statue of Liberty as she exclaimed, "Oh Liberty, what crimes are committed in thy name."

Her death produced a grievous sense of loss in the two men who loved her. Two days after hearing the news of his wife's execution, Roland left his sanctuary at Rouen and was later found impaled upon his sword cane. Buzot, also heartbroken, met a similar fate when his body was found on June 25, 1794, half-devoured by wolves.

SOURCES:

Clemenceau-Jacquemaire, Madeleine. *The Life of Madame Roland.* Longmans, Green, 1930.

May, Gita. *Madame Roland and the Age of Revolution.* Columbia University Press, 1970.

Erwin Rommel

(1891–1944)

German general, known as the "Desert Fox," who helped quickly defeat France in 1940, nearly drove the British from North Africa, tried to defend France from Allied invasion in 1944, and collaborated in a plot against Hitler.

Born Erwin Johannes Eugen Rommel on November 15, 1891, in Heidenheim, Württemberg, Germany; died on October 14, 1944, in Herrlingen, Württemberg, Germany; son of Erwin Rommel (a schoolmaster) and Helena von Luz Rommel (daughter of a regional government president); married: Lucie Maria Mollin (daughter of a landowner), 1916; children: Manfred (longtime mayor of Stuttgart).

I n 1891, in the southwest German state of Württemberg, far from Germany's political and military center, Prussia, Erwin Rommel was born. Neither his native region nor his family had a strong military tradition, yet by dint of his almost reckless bravery under fire and his willingness to innovate, Rommel would rise to become one of the most respected military tacticians his country or the world has ever produced. One of five children in a Protestant family, Rommel had a quiet childhood; his schoolwork was average, his conduct unobjectionable. Only as an adolescent did he show signs of awakening to his potential, and even then it was less as a military strategist than as an engineer. In 1910, for example, he wrote that his favorite subjects were science and mathematics. Bearing this out, he and a friend had tried their hands at building a glider, and Rommel thought about working for the great Zeppelin dirigible firm not far from his home.

Despite growing up the son of a stern schoolmaster, Rommel did not have the knack for further studies at the exclusive German universities of the day. Instead, his father persuaded him to join the Württemberg army (Germany's military

"It is not only the merits of the victor that decide the issue, but also mistakes on the part of the vanquished."

ERWIN ROMMEL

Contributed by Daniel Emmett Rogers, Assistant Professor of History, University of South Alabama, Mobile, Alabama

was organized on a state basis until after the First World War). After the artillery and the engineers rejected him, Rommel was accepted by the infantry as an officer candidate. Completing basic training and a stint in the lowest ranks, he was sent to officer school at Danzig, far away in Germany's northeast. While there, he met his future wife, Lucie Maria Mollin, the descendant of Italians and the daughter of a local large landholder. Rommel passed his officer's exams with above average marks but without distinction. He was sent back to the small but charming Württemberg town of Weingarten to serve with his infantry unit as a recruit trainer. Once again, he did little to make himself stand out from his fellow officers.

Early in War, He Wins Iron Cross

War changed Rommel's life in 1914. Along with his regiment, the reserved young lieutenant was quickly shipped to France. In his first action on August 22, 1914, he showed how he would react repeatedly in combat throughout his life: even when outnumbered, he made sure his forces got off the first shots, since the shock and surprise that accompanied opening fire most often led to victory. In January 1915, he won the Iron Cross, First Class, for leading his platoon on a daring raid behind French lines and capturing their positions. Rommel was twice wounded in the first months of fighting, was withdrawn from service in France, and was sent to train with a Württemberg mountain fighting battalion. Thereafter, he was assigned to the Rumanian front in Eastern Europe.

Rommel's exploits in the mountains of Eastern and Southern Europe earned him still more recognition for his courage and leadership in taking small groups of his men behind enemy lines. For his efforts in Italy, to whose mountainous front he was dispatched in 1917, he was awarded the highest of combat medals, the *Pour le Mérite;* since when worn it was a visible sign of his military prowess, it would stand him in good stead throughout his later career. Much to his disgust, however, the reward for his combat valor came in a planning staff appointment, where he was serving as a captain when the war ended in 1918.

Germany's defeat in 1918 politicized many officers of Rommel's generation. Distraught over their country's surrender and its transformation from the familiar, traditional monarchy into the turmoil of a republic, the officers were seldom reluctant to make known their hostility to the turn of events. Not so Rommel. Unlike many of his young comrades, he was allowed to serve in the much-reduced army of the Weimar Republic, so

CHRONOLOGY	
1871	Germany united by Prussia under Otto von Bismarck
1910	Rommel joined the Württemberg infantry
1914	WWI began; Rommel served in France
1915	Awarded Iron Cross; posted to mountain fighting unit in Rumania
1917	Awarded the *Pour le Mérite,* Germany's highest medal for bravery; promoted to captain
1919	Weimar Republic established
1929	Great Depression; Rommel instructor at infantry school in Dresden
1935	Germany began open rearmament; Rommel assigned to the War Academy
1939	Germany invaded Poland
1940	Rommel led 7th Panzer Division across France
1941	Named to lead *Afrika Korps*
1942	German forces under Rommel charged across North Africa; repelled by the British
1943	Rommel withdrawn from Africa; sent to Italy, then France, to prepare for Allied invasion
1944	Conspiracy against Hitler; Rommel severely wounded; forced to commit suicide on Hitler's orders

named for the city in which its constitution was drafted. Thus, while the others were tempted into joining paramilitary outfits like the right-wing Free Corps or into conservative politics, Rommel remained aloof from almost all political considerations. He was frozen in rank as a captain until 1933 but did not seem to mind the endless drill and sterile exercises of the peacetime army, which he most often served in his native southwest. He lived for his work, had no other intellectual interests, drank little, and did not smoke. His true diversions were his wife Lucie, whom he had married in 1916, and his sole child, son Manfred, who was born in 1928. His only two hobbies were photography and mechanical tinkering.

In 1929, the year the Golden Twenties died in Germany and gave way to the rigors of the Great Depression, Rommel was sent to the city of Dresden to act as an infantry instructor. He would later gather his lectures there into a book, *Infantry Attacks* (1937). He paid little attention to the growing popularity of the National Socialist Party of **Adolf Hitler.** After Hitler was named chancel-

lor in 1933 and quickly transformed the Weimar Republic into a totalitarian state, Rommel was fooled like most Germans by Hitler's outward allure; Hitler seemed to be the man who would save Germany from communism and make Germany—and especially its army—great again. In 1933, Rommel was promoted to major and given command of a mountain fighting unit in Goslar in northwest Germany. There he met Hitler for the first time when the führer paid a visit in 1935. That same year, Rommel was promoted yet again and sent to the War Academy at Potsdam; although he was close to Berlin and the center of power, he socialized neither with the Nazi nor the military elite. The Nazis did try to use him to instill stronger discipline in the Hitler Youth organization, but it was only a temporary distraction. In 1938, now a full colonel, he taught at the War Academy near Vienna (Austria was now part of Germany) and from there was called back by Hitler himself to command the army troops providing his personal security. Hitler was aware of the prestige of the author of *Infantry Attacks* and apparently wanted him close by.

When Hitler launched the Second World War by attacking Poland in September 1939, Rommel had the most unpleasant of duties for a soldier: a post in the rear area. A handful of top German officers quietly opposed the attack on Poland; Rommel did not. Like most Germans he thought it justified. But he got his chance for a major command only in February 1940, when despite years of service as an infantry officer, he was given charge of Germany's 7th Panzer Division. A Panzer division had as its centerpiece hundreds of tanks, and the tactics it used differed substantially from those of foot soldiers. Nonetheless, in the German invasion of France of May and June 1940, Rommel's division performed with distinction. It led the way in cutting off British and French forces in the north of France from the rest of the country, and then it moved to the south and west to finish off resistance. France sued for peace on June 17, in no small measure due to the work of Rommel in penetrating enemy lines, moving to the rear, firing first, and causing chaos. These were his old infantry tactics applied to highly mobile warfare.

Hitler Assigns Rommel to North Africa

Unlike many of the other heroes of the French campaign, Rommel did not obtain a command in the upcoming German struggles against the Soviet Union. He owes his posthumous reputation to this fact, since his room for maneuver was far greater in the remote theater to which Hitler did assign him. This was North Africa, and it was in those barren stretches of sand that he earned the respect of friend and foe alike as the "Desert Fox." In 1941, Hitler was forced against all his plans to send a small German contingent under Rommel to North Africa to shore up the quickly deteriorating situation of Germany's ally, Italy. The Italian dictator **Benito Mussolini** had sent his forces in Libya into combat against British troops based in Egypt, and the result had been humiliation for the Italians. To prevent the British from taking all of North Africa and using it as a base to threaten his southern flank during operations in Russia, Hitler sent Rommel with a small force to restrain British advances. But Rommel was not one to know how to treat war as a purely defensive challenge.

Rommel's—and therefore Germany's—fortunes in North Africa waxed and waned between February 1941, when he arrived, and October 1942. Rommel's greatest successes came when he defied his superiors' orders (and his enemies' expectations) that he stay on the defensive; his forces rolled eastward towards Cairo and the Suez Canal, threatening both in mid-1942, as the Germans and Italians pulled to within 60 miles of the mouth of the Nile River at Alexandria. Paying too little attention to Germany's supply shortages, Rommel was enchanted with the prospect of capturing Egypt and Palestine and proceeding to the oil fields of Iraq and Iran. When his supply situation improved somewhat in early 1942, and when the Germans were able to neutralize the threat to their supplies from the stubborn British base on the island of Malta, Rommel made his most spectacular advance. But the new British commander, **Bernard Montgomery,** himself now properly supplied and in possession of the Germans' secret codes, rallied British and Commonwealth forces into an offensive at El Alamein in October 1942. Beginning a drive in combination with forces under the American general **Dwight Eisenhower** that were moving eastward from Morocco, Montgomery would surround the last of the German troops in Tunisia in May 1943.

Rommel had been gone from Africa for two months by then. Hitler had ordered him out of Africa in March, and after two months in a hospital for nervous exhaustion, he exchanged his role as field commander for that of part planner and part policeman. That is, he led German efforts to take direct control of Italy after Mussolini was overthrown in mid-1943 and the Italians withdrew from the war. Not until the autumn of 1943 did Rommel receive another important assignment, although once again it was not in direct combat. Rather, he was to prepare the German-occupied Atlantic coast for the coming Anglo-American invasion. The "defenses" were shockingly inadequate from the German point of view, although German propaganda about an "Atlantic Wall" had

chastened the Americans and British into a long, slow buildup to invasion. Rommel's energy and his willingness to innovate shone through again, as he personally supervised the installation of newly-developed mines on the coast, the erection of other water obstacles, and glider barriers to hinder the first Allied assaults. But Rommel worried that such tinkering with the landscape would amount to little if the Allied forces could not be held on the beach in the first hours of the invasion, and then repelled into the sea. He disagreed sternly with superiors who, ignorant of the exact locale for the Allied landings, wished to allow the Allies to land in force and only then to counterattack with massive reserves. Rommel had learned from his days in the desert that Allied air superiority would render such movements of reserve units almost impossible. Nobody really won the dispute, and the divided command and defensive plans led directly to the German inability to throw the invaders back into the sea.

The Allies Invade at Normandy

When the expected Allied invasion came on June 6, 1944, in Normandy, so thorough was the surprise that Rommel was at home in Württemberg celebrating that most German of holidays, the significant birthday of a near relative. His wife Lucie was turning 50, and his trip by car to his home in Württemberg displayed the same steadfast devotion Rommel had exhibited in his frequent, if short letters to her throughout even the most hectic parts of the war. After June 6, his rapid return to France made little difference, since Allied air superiority meant that their tenuous beachheads could be guarded against the massive movements of German reserves. Rommel's pleas for Hitler to come to the front and talk with the field commanders were only partially fulfilled when Hitler visited France on June 17. The führer's movements were so secret that Rommel only learned of the visit several hours in advance, and he had to hurry by car to meet Hitler. Their encounter was as stormy as it was brief. Rommel pleaded for Hitler to come closer to the front to see that what he had been telling his commander was true; Hitler left France in a hurry without informing Rommel of his departure or agreeing to speak to the officers in the field.

We are still not exactly sure what motivated Rommel in 1944 to begin considering opposing Hitler actively, or of the precise extent of his participation. Smart conspirators, in any case, leave no written record of their plans. But since his days in Africa, Rommel had harbored little respect for Hitler's military abilities; now in light of the Allied successes in France, Rommel was certain the war was lost in the West. He seems to have approved of the idea of pushing Hitler out of power but without killing him, and he did not know beforehand of the attempt on Hitler's life that nearly succeeded in killing the führer on July 20, 1944. In fact, Rommel lay in the hospital on that date, his staff car having been strafed by British fighters on July 17. Rommel suffered severe head injuries, and his right eyelid stayed closed for the remaining three months of his life.

While he was recuperating at home, the German secret police, the Gestapo, swept Germany high and low for anyone remotely involved with plans to oppose Hitler and Rommel's name came up during some of the interrogations. On October 14, 1944, he was visited by two army generals who offered him a choice dictated by Hitler: Rommel could either take a poison that very day which would kill him almost instantly, or he would be tried publicly along with his family. Rommel calmly chose to spare himself and his family the gruesome show trial and execution, rode off with the generals after informing his wife and son of his decision, and was never seen alive again. Half an hour later, a call came to his residence notifying his family of his death. Instead of a trial and painful execution, Rommel had done the Nazi party and its leader one last service: his casket was the centerpiece of a bombastic funeral that made excellent grist for the Nazi propaganda mill. His "treason" concealed, he was now portrayed as a fallen Nazi hero. The "Desert Fox," who had earned glory for himself, his troops, and his nation while trying to remain aloof from politics, had paid the ultimate price for trying to separate military efficiency and national duty from moral considerations. He had served Hitler loyally and willingly when the war went Germany's way; only when defeat loomed did he realize that soldiers have a moral duty to ensure that the force they direct is being used in a just cause.

SOURCES:

Irving, David. *The Trail of the Fox*. Dutton, 1977.

Rommel, Erwin. *The Rommel Papers*. Harcourt, 1953.

Young, Desmond. *Rommel, The Desert Fox*. Harper, 1950.

FURTHER READING:

Erwin Rommel *Attacks*. Athena Press, 1979 (first published as *Infantry Attacks* in German in 1937).

Speidel, Hans. *Rommel and the Normandy Campaign*. Regnery, 1950.

Rudolf I, of Habsburg

(1218–1291)

Holy Roman Emperor and first of the Habsburg line to achieve kingship, who established a political power base in Austria where his family ruled for nearly seven centuries until 1918.

"Bishop Heinrich... exclaimed, 'Sit tight, Lord God in Heaven, or this Rudolf will usurp your place!'"

ADAM WANDRUSZKA

The first of his line to achieve kingship and the imperial title, Rudolf of Habsburg was chosen as the lesser of several possible evils by the prince electors of the Empire, from his positions as count in Swabia and several holdings in Alsace and present-day Switzerland. Already 55 years of age, he had been involved in a number of minor wars and skirmishes with neighboring princes and bishops, a career that had begun with his father's death in 1240 and had continued up to the moment of his selection as emperor. At the time, he was attacking the bishop of Basel, Heinrich von Neuenburg, when the representative of the electors found Rudolf in his tent in front of the besieged city. After convincing Rudolf of the validity of the news, the emperor-elect suspended the siege and brought hostilities to an end. Bishop Heinrich uttered the well-reported phrase, warning God to "sit tight... or this Rudolf will usurp your place!" He may have been premature.

Rudolf's selection by the imperial electors to be king of the Germans and Holy Roman Emperor was intended to bring to an end the 19-year "Great Interregnum" that had followed the 1254 death of Conrad IV, Hohenstaufen. Even though Richard

Name variations: Rudolph I. Born in Aargau Canton, just west of Zurich, Switzerland, in 1218; died in 1291; took family name from castle Habichts-burg in Aargau. Predecessor: Conrad IV, House of Hohenstaufen. Successor: (as emperor) Adolf of Nassau; (as duke of Austria) son Albert (whose harsh rule gave rise to the legend of William Tell).

Contributed by H.L. Oerter, Professor of History, Emeritus, Miami University, Oxford, Ohio

CHRONOLOGY

1218	Rudolf born in Aargau
1240–73	Engaged in local feuds with petty rulers, independent bishops
1254	Conrad IV, Hohenstaufen, died; interregnum began
1273	Rudolf elected king of Germans by imperial electors; Ottokar II of Bohemia refused to recognize Rudolf's election
1274	Diet of Regensburg voided Ottokar's possessions
1275	Rudolf renounced imperial claims in Italy; confirmed papal rights
1278	Battle of Marchfeld (Durnkraut); Ottokar slain
1291	Rudolf died; Swiss Forest Cantons revolted and formed Confederation; Adolf of Nassau succeeded as emperor

of Cornwall (related to the Hohenstaufens by marriage) and **Alfonso X** of Castile had been elected in 1257, the resulting squabbles between the papacy and the House of Hohenstaufens kept the two foreigners from ascending the throne.

The Habsburgs, who traced their beginnings from the castle of Habichts-burg (freely translated as "Hawk's Castle") in Aargau Canton, just west of Zurich, Switzerland, were petty German princes with no great pretensions. Despite his nearly constant warfare, Rudolf had a reputation as a reasonable man with a sense of humor and a touch of compassion.

Chosen because the electors hoped that he would not become too powerful, Rudolf, in keeping with their wishes, renounced imperial claims in the southern part of Italy, allowing the French Angevins to retain their conquests, and confirmed papal rights in central Italy. This kept the electors in a contented state and enabled Rudolf to concentrate on acquisitions in the eastern part of the empire.

The Bohemian king Ottokar II (Premyslid) disputed Rudolf's succession to imperial rank, claiming that he had the inherited rank of elector and had not taken part in the election. Withholding his assent, Ottokar refused to render homage. The other electors retaliated and in 1274, through the Imperial Diet convening in Regensburg, stripped Ottokar of all his possessions, while the papacy placed the ban of excommunication on him.

The need for action now lay with Rudolf who was more than equal to the task of coping with Ottokar. Through skilled negotiation and clever diplomacy, he gained dependable allies, including Austrian and Styrian nobility who had previously been considered allies of Ottokar. Faced with this fait accompli, Ottokar surrendered his claims to Upper and Lower Austria, Carinthia and Carniola, as well as Styria and three other minor sites. Coincidentally, Rudolf and Ottokar exchanged offspring—in a manner of speaking—as Rudolf gave a daughter in marriage to a son of Ottokar and the Bohemian king gave one of his daughters to be married to one of Rudolf's sons. All of this was accomplished without a single battle since Ottokar, faced with overwhelming superiority of potential enemies, dared not risk warfare.

Later, however, when it began to appear that Rudolf might not be as powerful as Ottokar had thought, hostilities broke out between the German King/Emperor and the Bohemian ruler. Despite his lack of an imperial army, Rudolf mobilized Hungarian support in the person of King Ladislas IV, and the nobility of Hungary—with their well-mounted and armed troops—gathered in other supporters and set up a sound defense of Vienna, where Rudolf had begun to establish a base of operations.

In the meantime, Ottokar dissipated his chances of victory by besieging towns in Lower Austria, while Rudolf united his forces and led them across the March River, which lay between Austria and Bohemia. Near the town of Durnkraut, on August 26, 1278, Rudolf's forces decisively defeated the Bohemians, killing King Ottokar, the last of the Premyslid line.

With his principal opponent out of the way, Rudolf immediately set about acquiring lands in the Danube Valley of Austria, gaining those lands renounced by Ottokar and including the provinces of Carniola and Carinthia. Secured in the names of his sons, Albrecht and Rudolf, and confirmed by the Diet of Augsburg as late as 1282, these lands—Upper and Lower Austria, together with the province of Styria, acquired later—were to remain the nucleus of the Habsburg dynasty's inheritance until 1918, when the last ruling Habsburg was deposed.

Although the bluff, feudatory soldier may not have disappeared when Rudolf took the crown of Charlemagne, his earlier self was carefully concealed in the pious and earnest actions and statements of the new king and emperor. On the day of his coronation, he reportedly vowed to forgive offenses by all who had harmed him and ordered the release of all he had imprisoned. His reputation for piety dates from this period and persists throughout the rest of his life.

Another Habsburg tactic first appeared during the reign of Rudolf. He skillfully arranged for the marriage of his offspring to other royal houses, thereby solidifying the Habsburg claim to preeminence in European affairs. Later generations would coin the phrase that best described the House: "Oh fortunate Austria! You gain by marriage what others must get by war."

The Start of the Swiss Confederacy

Historian Adam Wandruszka describes Rudolf as tall, long-legged, pale, with the characteristic hawklike Habsburg nose. No mention is made of the pendulous lower lip, which would mark many of the later Habsburgs, and his tendency to baldness is reported diplomatically. The same author, citing a contemporary chronicler, says that he was valiant all of his life, powerful, and intelligent. Other sources verify that he was energetic and direct with—perhaps—"a certain amount of harshness." This harshness was more noticeable in his subordinates and in his son Albert (Albrecht). His lieutenants were single-minded in collecting taxes and exercised their offices diligently, so much so that at Rudolf's death in 1291, three of the Swiss cantons (provinces) united in rebellion against their Austrian overlords, forming a confederacy they labelled "Eternal." It was the beginning of the Swiss Confederacy which still exists.

The same kind of harshness probably gave rise to the apocryphal tale of William Tell who, legend says, led the rebellion against the unnamed Habsburgs after the unverified incident of the apple being shot from the head of his son. There is no confirming documentation for the tale, even though it reflects popular unrest in 13th-century Switzerland, parts of which were then ruled by the Habsburgs.

A contradiction, Rudolf appears as a rough and domineering military commander in the early part of his life, utterly convinced of his invincibility and "rightness." On the other hand, he also had a self-deprecating sense of humor, as evidenced by an anecdote reported by Dorothy McGuigan,

involving an encounter on a narrow trail with another horseman coming in his direction. Looking pointedly at Rudolf's undoubtedly large nose, the other horseman demanded to know how he could get around *that* on a narrow trail. Rudolf placed a finger aside his nose, pushed it to the right and said: *"Nicht wahr, nun geht's?"* ("How's that? Will that take care of it?")

The heroic and near-saintly Rudolf has been celebrated in folklore, balladry, and formal poetry in the centuries since his time. The Austrian poet Grillparzer, in the 19th century, dedicated a typically Teutonic piece of Romantic stagecraft to the good Emperor, calling it "King Ottokar's Good Fortune and Death," and devoting a major part of the verse to the virtues of the first great Habsburg.

Despite his sustained and dedicated efforts to be crowned Holy Roman Empire in the Eternal City, Rudolf never managed to get to Rome for the coronation. This fact effectively negated the inheritance of the post by son Albert, allowing the rest of the German princes, alarmed by the rapid rise of the Habsburgs, to breathe more easily and choose the least offensive of their number, Adolf of Nassau, to succeed Rudolf. But when Adolf, who ruled from 1292–98, also showed imperialistic tendencies, he was deposed by the prince electors who then reverted to Rudolf's son, Albert, thereby giving the House of Habsburg another leg up on the Holy Roman inheritance.

More than any other royal figure of the Middle Ages, Rudolf imprinted his character and policies on the imperial institutions. Essentially Germanic, the Holy Roman Empire—as Voltaire remarked a few centuries later—was not Roman, nor was it imperial, nor was it ever Holy. It did, however, dominate the minds and politics of the High Middle Ages and persisted for nearly seven centuries until **Napoleon Bonaparte** dissolved it by fiat in the early 19th century.

SOURCES:

McGuigan, Dorothy Gies. *The Habsburgs.* Doubleday, 1966.

Previté-Orton, C. W. *The Shorter Cambridge Medieval History. Vol. II: The Twelfth Century to the Renaissance.* Cambridge University Press.

Wandruszka, Adam. *The House of Habsburg: Six Hundred Years of a European Dynasty.* Translated by Cathleen and Hans Epstein. Doubleday, 1964.

Andrei Sakharov

(1921–1989)

Russian scientist, who played a crucial role in the development of the Soviet Union's hydrogen bomb and emerged as a leading dissident whose status in Soviet society symbolized the political currents of his time.

Born in Moscow on May 21, 1921; died in Moscow on December 14, 1989; married: Klavdia Vikhierva (died 1969); married: Elena Bonner, 1971; children: (first marriage) one son, two daughters.

When Andrei Sakharov was born in Moscow on May 21, 1921, the Communist government, established in 1917, had just won a three-year Civil War against its opponents. While his first years were passed in the comparatively relaxed political atmosphere of the 1920s, following 1929 he lived in the harsh dictatorship of **Joseph Stalin.** The 1930s brought brutal political purges to the country; Stalin not only murdered his rivals inside the Communist Party but arrested and imprisoned millions of Soviet citizens from all walks of life. Sakharov's family was touched by these events when his uncle Ivan, after several arrests, died in prison.

As the son of a distinguished physics teacher—his father wrote the physics text used by most Russian high school children—Sakharov was educated largely at home, tutored by his father, his father's scientific colleagues, and his grandmother, who taught him to appreciate the classics of Russian literature. In 1942, he graduated from Moscow State University after compiling a brilliant record as a physics student. Due to the German invasion the year before, the university moved to Ashkhabad, near the border with Iran, where young Sakharov

"To keep one's self-respect one must... act in accordance with the general human longing for peace, for true detente, for genuine disarmament."

ANDREI SAKHAROV

Contributed by Neil Heyman, Professor of History, San Diego State University, San Diego, California

finished studying for his degree. During the remaining war years, he worked as an engineer in an armaments factory.

Quickly making a name for himself as one of the country's leading young physicists following World War II, Sakharov received his candidate's degree in physics (the equivalent of an American Ph.D.) in 1948. The American development of nuclear weapons at the close of the war, and the breakdown of the wartime alliance between the United States and the Soviet Union, led to a frantic Soviet effort to build such weapons. As a prominent young scientist, Sakharov became a part of the arms race, entering his country's program to develop nuclear weapons. His supervisor was his former teacher, Igor Tamm, who would receive the Nobel Prize for physics in 1958.

Soviets Explode Their First Atomic Bomb

The Soviet research team had its first spectacular success in 1949 with the testing of an atomic bomb; four years later, a second success followed with the creation of a thermonuclear (or hydrogen) bomb. Sakharov later recalled his willing participation in these efforts: "I had no doubts as to the vital importance of creating a Soviet super-weapon for our country and for the balance of power throughout the world." Although the details of such weapons research are still secret, Sakharov is widely considered to have been the Soviet Union's "father of the hydrogen bomb." His scientific reputation received a spectacular confirmation in 1953. Elected to the Soviet Academy of Sciences at the age of 32, he became the youngest member in its history.

During the second half of the 1950s, Sakharov's interests turned in a new direction. He continued as a research scientist participating in the development of weapons; at the same time, he began expressing his opinions on government policy. When Sakharov first criticized the actions of the Soviet government publicly in 1958, his comments took a mild form and dealt with a relatively uncontroversial issue. In an attempt to solve the country's labor shortage, Soviet leader **Nikita Khrushchev** wanted to require students to use one third of their last year of high school for work in farms or factories. Objecting to the plan, Sakharov wrote in the Communist Party newspaper *Pravda* that such a policy would seriously harm the training of scientists and mathematicians. But he also quietly called for changes in much more sensitive areas as he became increasingly alarmed at the effects of nuclear weapons on the environment. Between 1958 and 1962, he objected repeatedly to Soviet

CHRONOLOGY

1948	Began work in Soviet nuclear weapons program
1949	First explosion of Soviet atomic bomb
1953	First explosion of Soviet hydrogen bomb; Sakharov elected to Soviet Academy of Sciences
1958	Protested Soviet educational policies
1961	Attempted to prevent Soviet nuclear testing
1963	Attacked Lysenko movement in Soviet science
1966	Protested rehabilitation of Stalin prior to 23rd Soviet Communist Party Congress
1968	Published *Progress, Coexistence, and Intellectual Freedom;* lost security clearance
1975	Awarded Nobel Peace Prize
1979	Condemned Soviet invasion of Afghanistan
1980	Sent to internal exile in city of Gorky
1985	Mikhail Gorbachev chosen leader of Soviet Communist Party
1986	Released from exile by Gorbachev
1989	Elected to Congress of People's Deputies

atomic testing by writing letters to the government and making personal appeals to Khrushchev.

Sakharov later recalled that he was especially shocked by the test carried out in September 1962. Khrushchev seemed to take his protests seriously, leading Sakharov to believe the tests would be put off. Sakharov then learned that Khrushchev had lied to him: the explosions had in fact already taken place.

As a scientist Sakharov was also shocked by the way in which government policy corrupted scientific values. Since the 1930s, the Soviet government had endorsed the ideas of Trofim Lysenko on genetics. Lysenko presented the view that an organism could acquire new biological characteristics and pass them on to its offspring. This was the kind of science that Stalin's government favored; it seemed to confirm the idea that communism could create a new kind of society, with a new kind of citizen, and pass the changes to succeeding generations. Accordingly, as the careers of Lysenko and his followers flourished, opponents of his ideas—including some of Russia's best geneticists—suffered in the purges. Leading an attack within the Academy of Sciences on the Lysenko movement in

1963, Sakharov helped block the membership of one of Lysenko's followers.

Following his years of criticizing government policy in a private way, Sakharov entered public debate. Khrushchev was removed from power in late 1964 by a group of Communist Party figures led by **Leonid Brezhnev** and **Alexei Kosygin**. In some ways, Khrushchev had been a reforming figure in Soviet life, and the symbol of his willingness to make change had been his attacks on the memory of Joseph Stalin. With his removal, Sakharov and other Soviet intellectuals soon became alarmed that the new leadership might try to restore Stalin's reputation, reestablishing many features of Stalin's harsh dictatorship, including perhaps a purge of the entire Soviet population like that of the 1930s.

Prior to the 23rd Communist Party Congress in the spring of 1966, Sakharov and other noted scientists, along with Soviet writers, addressed an open letter of protest to the country's political leaders, warning against the dangers of a return to Stalinist ways. They specifically objected to rumors that Stalin's memory might be rehabilitated at the coming Party Congress. The letter seemed to have an effect, since Stalin's reputation was not revived for approval at the Congress.

Sakharov's Essays Call for Freedom of Thought

The great dividing line in Sakharov's life came in 1968, a critical year for the Soviet Union. A reform movement in the Communist Party of Czechoslovakia was radically transforming that important Soviet satellite. After months of delay and uncertainty, Brezhnev's government crushed the Czechs with a massive invasion by Soviet troops along with the forces of several other satellite states. In the middle of the crisis, Sakharov published a long essay, *Progress, Coexistence, and Intellectual Freedom*, calling for freedom of thought and discussion. Smuggled to the West, it first appeared as an article in the *New York Times*. The Soviet Union, he urged, must wipe out the remaining influence on Stalin's followers in its political life. His bold statement ended his career as an honored Soviet scientist.

Sakharov was an ordinary looking man. Hedrick Smith of the *New York Times* described him as being "as plain as an off duty night-watchman"—an unlikely figure perhaps to stand at the center of political dissent in the Soviet Union. In 1970, he organized a Human Rights Movement intended to ensure that Soviet citizens really enjoyed the rights provided by the Soviet Constitution. The next year he married Elena Bonner,

another political activist. But Sakharov paid for his role as a dissenter. His three children from his first marriage cut their ties with him, and when awarded the Nobel Prize for Peace in 1975, he was not allowed to leave the country to accept it; his wife Elena went in his place.

Condemns Afghanistan Invasion; Is Exiled

The final crisis in his career as a dissident came with his criticism of the Soviet invasion of Afghanistan. Brezhnev claimed that the Soviet Union needed to aid a friendly Socialist government in this neighboring state, and Soviet troops began pouring into Afghanistan at the close of 1979. Sakharov condemned the invasion. As a penalty, he was seized by the police and sent off to Gorky. Located 250 miles east of Moscow, Gorky was off-limits to foreigners.

There Sakharov remained—a symbol perhaps of the Soviet government's harshness toward those who disagreed with it. He did his best not to be forgotten. Word reached the West of his poor health due to heart disease and his protests against captivity by way of hunger strikes. Finally, on December 20, 1986—after being confined in Gorky for nearly seven years—Sakharov was freed by Communist Party chairman **Mikhail Gorbachev.** The news came a few days after the 11th anniversary of the award of the Nobel Prize. Sakharov was advised that a special telephone line was being installed in his apartment. Within a few hours, he received a personal phone call from Gorbachev, informing the exiled dissident that his years of captivity were at an end. When Sakharov went home to Moscow a few days later, his first statement at the railroad station called for the release of other dissidents as well.

Finally free to travel outside the Soviet Union in the last years of his life, Sakharov was received by American president Ronald Reagan during a visit to Washington in 1988. During that trip, Sakharov was made an honorary member of the American Academy of Science. The following year he visited Italy and was honored by a private audience with Pope John Paul II.

At home, Sakharov again took up his political activities. By now many of the changes he had called for as an isolated rebel in the 1970s had begun to take place. A popularly elected Congress of People's Deputies was chosen in March 1989. The Congress selected the members of the Supreme Soviet, the lawmaking body for the Soviet Union, and it provided a forum for discussing important national issues. Elected a member of the Congress, Sakharov joined Boris Yeltsin and other reformers in July 1989 in forming a formal opposition group to the Communist Party within the Congress. He also spoke out against Gorbachev's plans to expand the powers of the president of the Soviet Union. Sakharov rejected the idea that any individual, even the man responsible for his release, should be allowed to have such extensive powers.

Only a few days before his death in December 1989, Sakharov attacked the part of the Soviet Union's constitution that guaranteed the leading role of the Communist Party in Soviet life. Three months later, in February 1990, Gorbachev himself adopted Sakharov's position and established a multiparty political system in the country—22 years after Sakharov had first set this goal in *Progress, Coexistence, and Intellectual Freedom.*

SOURCES:

Bailey, George. *Galileo's Children: Science, Sakharov, and the Power of the State.* Little, Brown, 1988.

Kaiser, Robert G. *Why Gorbachev Happened: His Triumphs and His Failure.* Simon & Schuster, 1990.

Smith, Hedrick. *The Russians.* Quadrangle, 1976.

"Special Issue: Andrei Sakharov," in *Physics Today.* Part 1. August 1990.

FURTHER READING:

Babyonshev, Alexander, ed. *On Sakharov.* Knopf, 1982.

Bonner, Elena. *Alone Together.* Knopf, 1986.

Sakharov, Andrei. *Moscow and Beyond.* Knopf, 1991.

———. *Progress, Coexistence, and Intellectual Freedom.* Norton, 1968.

Tokes, Rudolph L. *Dissent in the USSR: Politics, Ideology, and People.* Johns Hopkins Press, 1975.

António Salazar

(1889–1970)

Portuguese dictator admired by some and hated by others, who created the corporatist "New State" in 1933 which continued under his successor until the Portuguese Revolution of 1974 restored democracy.

Pronunciation: Sal-eh-zär. Born António de Oliveira Salazar on April 28, 1889, in the village of Vimieiro near the small town of Santa Comba Dão, Beira Alta province, Portugal; died in Lisbon on July 27, 1970; son of António Oliveira and Maria do Resgate Salazar (Portuguese tradition would have been to adopt father's last name rather than mother's); bachelor; children: (two adopted girls) Micas and Maria Antónia. Predecessor: General Domingos Oliveira. Successor: Marcelo Caetano.

People's perceptions of António Salazar vary radically. Some admire him as one of the greatest and most devoted leaders Portugal ever had. Others consider him to be just another ruthless, Fascist dictator who led the nation for far too long. As French journalist Christine Garnier notes, "Some people considered him a saint who would, soon after his death, be beatified. Others saw in him a heartless, inhuman leader." Hugh Kay, a British journalist, argues that people often judge Salazar without regard to the problems which existed under the First Republic (1910–26), but perhaps the cost in freedom which they were forced to pay during the dictatorship was too high. Kay points out that when Salazar came to power:

> Portugal was a bad joke in the European chancellories, her currency worthless, her army an obsolete remnant, the nation fragmented and beggared. Within a few years, Salazar had balanced the budget, restored the currency, started to build a modern army, constructed thousands of homes.... The other side of the coin is the story of political repression... with particular stress on police activity, censorship and allegedly rigged elections.

"[T]here is no record of the classical trappings of dictatorship, the chanting crowds, the demagogic threats and utterances, parades or displays."

HUGH KAY

Contributed by Carlos A. Cunha, Assistant Professor of Political Science, Dowling College, Oakdale, New York

A glimpse of Salazar's childhood provides insight to his character later in life. He was born on April 28, 1889, to Maria do Resgate Salazar, who was 43 at the time, and António Oliveira, who was 50. Antonio de Figueiredo, a journalist, postulates, "This unusual gap of two generations between parents and son obviously left its mark upon Salazar, who always remained suspicious of youth and modernity." He was the fifth child and only boy in the family. From his sisters' perspective he was the mother's favorite. Maria do Resgate, a devout Catholic, greatly influenced her son until her death in 1926. Some argue that if she had not died, he would not have become prime minister because she was "very troubled and needed his support."

Salazar's native village, Vimieiro, was situated near the town of Santa Comba Dao approximately halfway between the university city of Coimbra and the district capital of Viseu. The region was a relatively poor one, with small, subsistence peasant farms (*minifundio*) dominating. This mountainous, but very picturesque, wine-producing region of Portugal meant a hard life for most peasants. While from an economic standpoint the peasants would have belonged to the proletarian (worker) class, the region was politically conservative because many were small property owners. In addition to working his own small plot, his father, who died in 1932, was an estate manager for one of the few large landholders of the district. As was the case for most of northern Portugal, the Catholic Church was very influential in the region.

These environmental variables had a profound impact on the young Salazar—a shy, sweet, pensive child who preferred long, solitary walks with his dog Dao to playing with other children. Despising sports, he preferred to read and was considered a kind and patient adolescent who attended private school because he did not learn well in public school. Discipline was a sacred matter to him, and he questioned all the rules, even though he followed them most rigorously.

At the age of 11, Salazar did what many other poor children hungry for a free education did: he entered the seminary in Viseu. He studied there for eight years, taking minor orders in 1908 and later abandoning the priesthood, like many other seminarians. "I shall be of more purpose to the church and Portugal by remaining on the layman's side," he is said to have stated. His years at the seminary profoundly influenced him. Although he later made governing his own priesthood, he insisted on keeping church and state separate. He felt that religion provided a spirit of charity and justice but it did not supply the rules or

CHRONOLOGY

1910	Revolution ended monarchy and created First Republic; Salazar enrolled at University of Coimbra
1916	Portugal entered First World War
1921	Salazar attended Parliament as elected representative; walked out after one day
1926	Military revolt ended First Republic; replaced with a military dictatorship; Salazar appointed minister of finance; resigned after several days
1928	Salazar appointed minister of finance
1932	Became prime minister
1933	Corporatist Constitution adopted
1936	Spanish Civil War began
1939	Portugal announced neutrality in impending Second World War
1961	National Liberation war began in Angola; Indian army invaded Goa
1963	National Liberation war began in Portuguese Guinea
1964	National Liberation war began in Mozambique
1968	Salazar collapsed from blood clot in the brain; Marcelo Caetano named prime minister
1970	Salazar died in Lisbon
1974	Military coup ushered in Portuguese Revolution which ended the 48-year dictatorship and restored democracy

concrete solutions required to resolve the problems of world affairs, national behavior, or education.

Salazar Becomes Teacher and Writer

He taught arithmetic, literature, and history at the Via Sacra School in Viseu until 1910 when he left to study at the University of Coimbra, Portugal's Oxford. Salazar lived in Coimbra for about 18 years. As a law student he passed his exams with flying colors, studying economics and public administration as well. Again he continued to prefer solitude to conviviality, taking long solitary walks in the Botanical Gardens rather than meeting at cafés for intellectual discussions with fellow students. He shared living arrangements for about 15 years with Manuel Gonçalves Cereijeira who later became Cardinal Patriarch of Lisbon. In many ways, the mold which he shaped in Coimbra set his boundaries for the future. The quiet, simple life which he led there continued to his dying days. Although he remained remote, he made enduring friendships.

While a student he was an active member of the Academic Center for Christian Democracy (CADC) whose motto was "piety, study, and action." The emergence of Portugal's First Republic and the overthrow of the monarchy (1910) in many ways repressed conservative traditional values. Salazar and the CADC were committed to reviving these values, so he gave speeches and wrote articles for the organizations's newspaper, *Impartial*, under the pen name Alves da Silva. He continued to champion traditional values, with emphasis on the family, throughout his career.

By this stage both religion and nationalism were also important aspects of Salazar's life. Catholic nationalists had lofty views of Portugal's "distant golden past and 'civilizing mission.'" Whether we look at disgruntled traditionalist monarchs or the victorious progressive republicans, both were interested in reviving the nation from the decadence into which it had fallen. According to Figueiredo:

> the traditionalists blamed the libertarian period of the constitutional monarchy, freedom of the press, and all those other features of parliamentary government which "carried the seeds of subversion of established social and religious values."

In 1916, Salazar became a lecturer at the University of Coimbra in political economy and finance, receiving his doctor of philosophy degree (Ph.D.) two years later. He was a distant and reserved instructor whose lectures often reflected accounting more than they did economics. His political views were most influenced by St. Thomas Aquinas, Pope Leo XIII, Charles Maurras's Action Française, Pope Pius XI, and António Sardinhas's Integralism. His articles on Portuguese economics contributed to his reputation as a brilliant scholar in some circles.

Salazar was elected to Parliament in 1921 as the Catholic Center Party's representative of Guimaraes. When the "tall, thin figure with big ears and bushy hair" arrived in Lisbon to take up his seat, he was immediately disgusted with the chaos he saw in the chambers and resigned after only one day in office.

In 1926, the military staged a coup which ended the First Republic. After agreeing to become minister of finance, Salazar held the post for several days but then resigned and returned to his teaching post in Coimbra. He did not like to take on responsibilities unless his rules were obeyed, and he felt the prevailing political situation did not allow him to do a worthwhile job. Although he turned down several subsequent offers to hold that post, the economic incompetence of Portugal's military leaders would eventually compel him to return to this position in 1928 at age 39. This time the military gave him the leeway he requested, and he balanced the budget with miraculous speed. But historian Tom Gallagher points out that the politically shrewd Salazar often exempted the military from the economic cuts despite their overgrown bureaucracy.

He Makes His Mark as Finance Minister

As finance minister, Salazar left his mark on practically every aspect of government. He dominated his colleagues, controlled spending, was a man of ideas, and generally had great influence beyond the scope of his portfolio. The strict conditions that he set down in order to accept the ministerial position in 1928 are an insight into his probable political ambitions. Subsequent events demonstrate that he may not have been the apolitical idealist that many of his supporters would like us to believe. Upon assuming the finance position, he made a very abrasive speech closing with:

> I know quite well what I want and where I am going, but let it not be insisted that I shall reach the goal in a few months. For the rest, let the country study, let it suggest, let it object, and let it discuss but when the time comes for me to give orders I shall expect it to obey.

The military leaders put up with this type of arrogance because they needed his services, and Salazar quickly adjusted his language to avoid alienating them. Gallagher traces the beginning of his political hegemony (dominance) to July 1929, when President Oscar Fragoso de Carmona made it clear he would not accept a government that did not include Salazar.

Salazar was able to balance the budget within one year. By 1932, the military's short-term goals—economic stability and law and order—were in place. Two years earlier, Salazar had begun laying out a long-term vision for Portugal. He offered a new system based on strong authoritarianism which would maintain order rather than revert to the chaos of the 1910 to 1926 republican period. He felt that Portuguese political culture required a "National Revolution" creating a more ordered political system dominated by corporatist (also known as corporativist) ideology. In what came to be called the "New State," political parties and trade unions would be abolished, censorship applied, political power focused on the executive branch, and the values of God, country, and family implanted in society.

By these later years, a real dichotomy began to form among observers who followed Salazar's development. Some, such as Kay, emphasize that he did not like and was ill at ease with the responsibilities that power bestowed on him. Gallagher, however, demonstrates that humility was not one of the dictator's strong points. The American political scientist, Howard Wiarda, argues that Salazar was fascinated with power and did not want to share it:

> [But he] was not particularly interested in the perquisites that usually go with power: money, mansions, opportunities for private self-enrichment. Power for its own sake—hoarded, monopolized, held absolutely—plus the stature, prestige, authority, and dominance that its exercise gave him, these seem to be the ends and purposes of Salazar's drives.

By 1932, the military regime had transferred power to a civilian government with Salazar as prime minister. He set about framing the constitution for the "New State," ratified in a 1933 referendum, which declared Portugal to be a corporatist and unitary (rather than pluralist) republic.

Salazar saw corporatism to be a rival ideology to liberalism, socialism, and communism. He once said:

> We are anti-parliamentarian, anti-democrats, anti-liberals, and we are determined to establish a corporative state. Such statements may shock those nations which are used to adjusting the deficiencies of their own political systems by virtue of improved social conditions, and which are unable to appreciate the harm that may result from the application of similar methods in countries differently constituted.

Briefly, corporatism emphasizes that while social classes have different interests, they can be harnessed to work for the good of the entire society. Each class or interest group is represented by its own corporate body. The state mediates the varied interests so the society can become harmonious. Divisions between workers and employers can be eradicated by ending capitalist exploitation.

The public benefits through increased production and the end of class conflict. Salazar's view of corporatism replaced the government's National Union, a civic association, for what he considered the divisiveness of political parties which merely created chaos.

While many have labeled Salazar a Fascist, he did not accurately fit the label. He did not, for example, allow a government party to exist. He also did not believe in mass mobilization. Although a secret police existed, it was relatively small. Gallagher argues that perhaps Salazar did have fascistic tendencies and looked to corporatism so he would not be labeled as just another Fascist. Corporatism may have been a propaganda exercise even if his views were more traditional and restrained than Fascists such as Mussolini and Hitler. As Gallagher notes:

> he was able to make use of the social justice aspects of corporativism to cloak anti-working-class economic measures in idealistic garb.... He was depicted as a compassionate if authoritarian idealist and not a mere seeker after power.

While corporatism may have sounded good in theory, in reality Salazar preferred to maximize his personal power rather than mediate. He also sided with business interests over the workers' interests.

Salazar was of the opinion that Portugal had to steer a middle course between looking to the past or focusing on the future. He attacked what he saw as the endemic Iberian trait of pursuing elaborate expensive development schemes before attending to the nation's essential need, infrastructure development. By 1937, he could point to considerable achievements such as a drastic reorganization of administrative services, infrastructure improvements, a strengthened military, and improvements in education and housing.

During the Spanish Civil War of 1936, Salazar supported General **Francisco Franco** and the nationalists for geostrategic reasons and because of his staunch anticommunism. Salazar did not have much aid to give to Franco but allowed German aid to flow through Portugal to the nationalists. The war led Portugal further toward authoritarianism with intensified secret police activity, censorship, and repression of the left (especially the communist party). As a result, resistance increased throughout the decade in reaction to Salazar's human rights and economic policies. A bombing attempt in July of 1937 came close to killing him.

Portugal Maintains Neutrality in World War II

Salazar maintained Portuguese neutrality, and was influential in maintaining Spanish neutrality, throughout World War II. Though he did not like the Nazis, he did appreciate their defense against communist insurgency. For six years, he walked a tightrope between neutrality and alliance, managing to maintain the former. Kay describes Salazar's policies as neither pro-German nor pro-British but pro-Portuguese. One of his major concerns was with German desire for territory in Africa and the fear that the United Kingdom would negotiate away Portuguese colonies in exchange for peace in Europe. While maintaining its neutrality, Portugal profited handsomely by selling goods, especially the strategic mineral wolfram, to both sides.

After World War II, the major foreign policy issues which Salazar dealt with were primarily related to the Portuguese overseas colonies. The issue blocked Portuguese membership to the United Nations until 1956. His policies made industrial and economic development in the African colonies peripheral to the needs of the mother country. By the 1960s, wars of national liberation had begun throughout its African colonies, and Portugal also lost control of its Indian colonies.

Portugal was ready for economic growth because of infrastructure developments and substantial foreign currency reserves, but Salazar refused to allow such expansion. He feared that modernization, which would accompany development, would imperil his attempt to preserve Portugal's traditional values. Economic stagnation led to waves of foreign emigration, legally and illegally, to the African colonies, Brazil, the United States, the rest of Europe, and virtually the entire world. In the end, Salazar sacrificed growth and welfare for stability. By 1965, he felt compelled to move in a different direction as he began allowing foreign investment.

Salazar disliked public appearances. People often complained that he was seldom heard and little known. His response to Garnier was: "But how can I find time for such outings when the public office that I hold keeps me snowed under with work…. The state does not pay me to lead a social life; it pays me to spend my time solving its vital problems." He believed in the virtues of hard work, thrift, and self-control. "His working day was unremitting," writes Kay:

He breakfasted at eight, read the papers, worked until two. Then lunch and visitors. From four to six a rest, and a walk in the garden; then back to the desk until ten. A light supper, and back to work until midnight. The routine rarely changed.

As prime minister, Salazar made short, dispassionate speeches and did not exhibit public display of emotion or enthusiasm. It appears that he purposefully kept a distance because he was afraid public opinion would pressure him to make promises he could not keep. Salazar told Garnier, "One can throw one's heart into politics but to govern one must only use one's head…. I'd rather be respected than loved." He rarely went to friends' houses in Lisbon or accepted dinner invitations because, "I must feel free from any sentimental attachment. I do not want to have to fear that some new decree, for instance, might either favor or hurt a person with whom I had had a friendly meeting the day before." He argued that his way of governing required solitude and a minimal amount of public exposure. Solitude was important to achieve great feats because one needed to draw from inner strength to avoid disappointment when setbacks occurred.

The image that Salazar portrayed, therefore, is of a cold, hard person. He had a wooden, unsmiling face, an apparent disregard for greetings from passers-by, and a lack of reaction to cheers on public occasions. He was quite a different person when dealing with individuals on a one-to-one basis. His voice was warm and appealing then.

By his mid-60s, after being in power for approximately 23 years, Salazar had an earnest appearance. According to Garnier, he had dark, intense, but sharp eyes; a flat, willful chin; lipless mouth; and a melodious low voice with soft inflections. He was taller than the average Portuguese man and had shiny gray hair. He had aged rapidly, gained weight, and had been ailing since the 1940s but refused to delegate authority or develop a system of more collective decision-making.

Salazar had also developed a reputation for stinginess. Garnier recounts how some restaurants offered "Codfish Salazar," a plate with hardly any codfish and only four or five boiled potatoes. But he also refused to allow the state to pay many expenses which could have been legitimately charged to it such as heating bills and maid service at his residence. He was not a typical dictator who used the powers of office to increase his own wealth.

Salazar led an almost monastic life and was distant from the daily lives of the people he governed. A punctual man of action and a philosopher influenced by the French masters, he wrote in a powerful and pure style of logic and clarity of exposition. Sarcasm and irony were foreign to his nature. He was very subtle and reserved and expected people to understand the spirit of his views rather than the actual words he expressed. All his life Salazar allegedly lived in solitude, a virtual hermit. He had loved one woman when he was young, but her upper-class status prevented a courtship. As she had in his student days in Coimbra, his maid and lifelong companion, Doña Maria de Jesus Caetano, continued to care for him until his death.

On June 9, 1968, Salazar fell off of a deck chair while at his seaside residence near Estoril and developed a blood clot in the brain which eventually led to a cerebral stroke that incapacitated him. Until his death on July 27, 1970, he continued to believe he was in power, even though Marcelo Caetano (not related to his maid) had replaced him as prime minister.

Despite his low visibility, Salazar left his mark internationally as a result of his policies during World War II and because of his response to other foreign events. The controversy continues on whether Salazar was a good or bad leader. As Kay suggests, one must consider the sad state Portugal was in when he came to power. On the other hand, as the *London Observer* stated in 1954: "The father of his people has dedicated his life to their welfare, but refuses to give them the opportunities to grow up." And Figueiredo concludes, "The cruel fact is that, if Salazar inherited a poor nation, when he handed it to Caetano forty years later it was still the most backward and the poorest nation in Western Europe." Perhaps the true Salazar lies between the extremes. The National Library in Lisbon is scheduled to provide public access to the sealed Salazar/Caetano archives in 1995 which may shed additional light on his character.

SOURCES:

Figueiredo, Antonio de. *Portugal: Fifty Years of Dictatorship.* Homes & Meier, 1976.

Gallagher, Tom. *Portugal: A Twentieth Century Interpretation.* Manchester University Press, 1983.

Garnier, Christine. *Salazar: An Intimate Portrait.* Farrar, Straus, 1954.

Kay, Hugh. *Salazar and Modern Portugal.* Hawthorn, 1970.

Wiarda, Howard J. *Corporatism and Development: The Portuguese Experience.* University of Massachusetts, 1977.

FURTHER READING:

Clarence-Smith, Gervase. *The Third Portuguese Empire, 1825–1975: A Study in Economic Imperialism.* Manchester University Press, 1985.

Derrick, Michael. *The Portugal of Salazar.* Campion Books, 1939.

Ferro, Antonio. *Salazar: Portugal and Her Leader.* Translated by H. de Barros Gomes and John Gibbons. Faber and Faber, 1939.

Fryer, Peter, and Patricia McGowan Pinheiro. *Oldest Ally: A Portrait of Salazar's Portugal.* D. Dobson, 1961.

Girolamo Savonarola

(1452–1498)

Italian Dominican monk, who preached concern for moral reform and social welfare in a period of decadence and violence, and freed the Florentine Republic from the control of the Medici family.

Born Girolamo Maria Francesco Matteo dalla Savonarola on September 21, 1452; martyred on May 3, 1498; third son of Niccolo di Michele dalla Savonarola and Elena Bonacossi; grandson of a famous Renaissance physician.

Born the grandson of Michele dalla Savonarola, the famous Renaissance physician, Girolamo Savonarola grew up and received his education in the shadow of wealth at the courts of the dukes of Ferrara. His father Niccolo, who had originally planned to send his third son to a medical school, hoped to recoup the family's fortunes through this son. A diligent student, Savonarola learned Latin, art, and music from his grandfather, along with the elder's 14th-century ideas. Strongly influenced by these attitudes, the young boy found himself constantly aware of the difference between the Roman Catholic Church's teaching about social welfare and priestly vows, and its failure to practice these ideals. When his grandfather died, Savonarola left the humanistic studies to acquire a university degree in philosophy. Ultimately, he received his master's degree and went on to pursue the medical degree as originally planned. But his search for absolute truth led him away from science to theology.

On April 26, 1475, Savonarola received the habit of a Dominican monk from the prior of San Domenico in Bologna and continued his search for truth as a novice in peaceful contemplation. Once

"His message struck a deep vein of moral sensibility in Florence.... His career shows both the intensity and shallowness of the concern among Italian laymen for significant moral reform."

DONALD WILCOX

Contributed by E. Lanier Clark, Assistant Professor of History, Albany State College, Albany, Georgia

1188

he took his vows, however, the spiritual idyll ceased. He was ordered to teach the novices, lecture on philosophy, and study further in preparation for a pulpit. From 1476 to 1479, the young monk studied with a number of lecturers, concentrating on theology. In May 1482, he began his monastic career as a lecturer in the convent of San Marco in Florence.

A city of wealth, power, and splendor, Florence contained the beauty of the Renaissance which it had birthed. Yet the city was in the last years of its greatness. Within a decade or two, Rome would become the center of artistic and intellectual endeavor in Renaissance Italy. Overseeing this display stood the great thinker and political leader, **Lorenzo de' Medici.** The web of power in Florence depended upon the approval of Lorenzo "the Magnificent," a calculating, ambitious man who could be both generous and cruel. Lorenzo would not allow intrusion into that web, a fact which dictated his reaction to the growing influence of Girolamo Savonarola after 1491.

In the convent of San Marco, Savonarola's primary duty was to explain Scripture. As reflected in his teachings which he used as exhortations on moral behavior, he was strict in his religious observances, nearly to excess. Between 1482 and 1484, he preached in the surrounding countryside until he received the pulpit of the cathedral of San Lorenzo. 1484 proved to be a momentous year: Innocent VIII was elected pope; and Savonarola reported his first vision about the "Scourge of the Church" which would come to correct the evil materialism of the Church. Continuing this vein of prophetic sermons, the visionary monk preached in the church of San Gimignano in early 1485 and again during Lent (the 40 days preceding Easter) of 1486. From the surviving manuscripts of these early sermons come the first references to Savonarola's ideas about reform in the Church and the chastisement of Italy for its sins. The corruption so evident in the behavior of the higher clergy, even the pope, angered Savonarola. Calling for stricter adherence to the expected spiritual standards of the Church and for greater social awareness of the poor, he earned the title of the "Preacher of the Despairing."

By 1487, his reputation for learning led to his appointment as master of the college for the University of San Domenico in Bologna. Between 1487 and 1490, this itinerant preacher/scholar was in Ferrara, Genoa, Brescia, and several other cities. With his return to Florence in 1490, Savonarola came to his spiritual home to be lecturer again in San Marco. The following year, he began preaching in his convent, but the crowds were too great for the small chapel to accommodate them.

CHRONOLOGY

1453	Constantinople fell to Turks; Hundred Years' War ended
1474	First book printed in English by William Caxton
1475	Savonarola became a Dominican monk
1492	Lorenzo de' Medici died
1494	Charles VIII invaded Italy
1491	Elected Prior of San Marco
1497	Florence witnessed the first "Bonfire of the Vanities"
1498	Savonarola tried and executed for heresy

Savonarola's Sermons Outrage Lorenzo

By request, Savonarola, now recognized as an exciting preacher with a different style of sermons, went to preach the Lenten sermons in the Florentine cathedral of Santa Maria del Fiore. In these sermons, he became more strident—criticizing the worldly materialism of the people and their leaders. This criticism, and the prophecies contained therein, outraged Lorenzo de' Medici. The Florentine leader threatened to banish Savonarola for his covert attacks on the policies of the government, policies that Lorenzo had helped institute. Savonarola replied that he was not afraid; he also predicted that Lorenzo would depart this life before him. In the end, Lorenzo did not banish Savonarola, though this was probably due to the influence of Count Giovanni Pico della Mirandola rather than fear of the prophecy. In addition to the prophesied death of Lorenzo, the monk predicted the death of Innocent VIII. Both would die the following year.

Before the end of 1491, Savonarola assumed the duties of prior of San Marco. His sermons reached their first peak during Advent (the 40 days preceding Christmas) of 1492 when he prophesied the coming of the "Scourge of Italy" for the first time. This vision may have been prompted by the election of Pope Alexander VI (formerly Cardinal Rodrigo Borgia), after the death of Innocent VIII. The behavior of the new pope, taking mistresses, advancing members of his own family (including his son Cesare) to prominent Church positions, and squandering money on clothes and horses, became outrageous even in a time known for its corruption and decadence.

During the first year of Savonarola's priorate, San Marco experienced spiritual vigor and growth. This growth mirrored the renewed spiritual purpose which Savonarola infused in his plans to reform the Florentine branches of the Church. Calling to mind the laxness of Church discipline in Tuscany (the region where Florence was located), Savronola led his convent to break from the ruling organization of monasteries, the Congregation of Lombardy, to which it belonged. In seeking to form a new, stricter organization (or Congregation), Savonarola received the support of Lorenzo's son, Piero de' Medici, the king of Naples, and Cardinal Oliviero Caraffa. Though Savonarola was opposed by Cardinal Ascanio Sforza and his brother Duke Lodovico Sforza of Mantua, Cardinal Caraffa was able to swing the pope to Savonarola's side, and the separation was accomplished on May 22, 1493.

Savonarola saw the separation as the beginning of the reform of the Roman Catholic Church. Expanding his movement, he worked for the separation of other convents, ultimately with their attachment to his own organization. In his own monastery, he demanded that his monks give up all possessions, which were then sold to raise money for the poor. The following year, Savonarola used San Marco as a base to build the Congregation of San Marco, adding the convent of Santa Caterina in Pisa.

The year 1494 saw the fulfillment of another prophecy, the coming of the "Scourge of Italy." Though he called Charles VIII of France the "great servant of Divine Justice," Savonarola was quick to criticize the French king when he did not act in a fashion acceptable to him. Traditionally Francophones, the Florentine citizens were becoming upset at Piero de' Medici's anti-French policies, fearing that the French king might lay siege. Support for the French was partly political necessity, since Florence had to balance the power of the pope and the emperor to prevent the loss of her freedom. When Charles VIII saw an opportunity to increase his own prestige and power, he invaded Italy in late October of 1494. Fleeing Florence, Piero de' Medici threw himself upon the mercy of the French king. The following month, the leading political body of Florence, the *Signoria*, elected Savonarola to approach Charles to insure Florence's security and safety.

Savonarola then turned to the problem of a new government without the Medicis. In his sermons, he suggested new policies and constantly pointed to universal peace coupled with wise reform of the government. Ultimately, the prior of San Marco was seeking a way to bring peace between the factions of the city and to ensure a just state. All of his suggestions became law, even some which were not popular. In the end, the Signoria asked Savonarola to give his final approval of the new republican government. But Savonarola was not without opposition. It was primarily centered upon a group known as the *Arrabbiati*, composed of men who did not share power under the Medicis or the new government. Such opposition did not stop the new government from being instituted on December 24, 1494.

During the spring of 1495, Savonarola called for further reform in Florentine social policies. He demanded an increase in jobs for the lower classes and relief for the poor, urged the churches to melt down their gold and silver ornaments to buy bread for the hungry, and called for modesty in social customs and ornamentation of the body.

That same spring, new opposition emerged in a group called the *Tiepidi* (the lukewarm), a name collectively applied to priests, nuns, and monks opposed to strict observance of vows of poverty and obedience. The *Tiepidi* found support from Pope Alexander, Lodovico Sforza, and the emperor **Maximilian,** who had formed an armed League to oppose Charles VIII. The League had a great success when it inflicted a defeat on Charles VIII's army on July 6 at Fornovo, Italy, while Charles VIII's navy suffered great losses in a battle near Rapallo. But in order to bring Florence to its side, the League would have to decrease the influence and power of the pro-French Savonarola.

The Pope Orders Him to Rome

Over the summer of 1495, Girolamo Savonarola developed dysentery and a high fever. After only ten days of rest, though his doctors forbid him to preach, Savonarola returned to the pulpit to castigate his opponents, especially the *Tiepidi*. While he was ill and Charles VIII's influence was in decline, Lodovico Sforza tried to woo the Florentine leaders away from the preacher. Joining Sforza, Pope Alexander sent a papal brief in July stating that certain people had accused Savonarola of heresy, false prophecy, and troubling the peace of the Church. Though he praised Savonarola's work, Alexander insisted that he come to Rome to defend himself.

The great reformer understood the implications in this brief, that once he was in Rome, he might never leave. Pleading grave illness and the instability of the new municipal reforms, Savonarola instead remained in Florence. Fortunately, the pope did not dissent and merely ordered him to stop preaching until the accusations could be repudiated.

Over the course of the fall, the pope became more hostile and ordered a trial judged by Fra Sebastiano Maggi, vicar general of the Congregation of Lombardy. The pope also ordered Savonarola to recognize the authority of Maggi and reattached San Marco to that congregation. Such actions destroyed Savonarola's ability to act independent of normal ecclesiastical channels. The defense raised by Savonarola and the Florentine Signoria, coupled with the positive findings of Maggi, forced the pope to beat a diplomatic retreat in mid-October. After praising Savonarola as a respectful son of the Church, Alexander ordered the monk not to preach until he could present himself in Rome.

Fortunately, the Florentine people obtained permission from the pope to allow Savonarola to preach the Lenten sermons of 1496. As these sermons progressed, Savonarola changed his tone from moderate to strident, from conciliatory to savage. The abuses of the Church, he said, had gone beyond all bounds; no longer did the Church observe its own rules. He called the people to repentance as well, but here he met his first defeat. He demanded that the government pass more stringent laws governing the dress and ornamentation of the Florentine women. By refusing to pass such a statute, the city leaders took their first step away from Savonarola's reform platform.

In Florence, support of France had brought mounting financial problems. Such problems gave fuel to Savonarola's enemies, especially when the French king demanded large sums of money to pay debts incurred from the Italian war. In November, the armed papal League headed by Sforza and Maximilian suffered a major defeat at Leghorn, an event which Savonarola had prophesied. The setback forced Sforza to make renewed overtures to Savonarola to bring Florence over to the League. At the same time, Alexander created a Tuscan-Roman Congregation and ordered the monasteries under Savonarola to join it.

New governmental elections in December brought greater trouble for the monk. Francesco Valori received the highest elected office and consequently opened the government councils to younger men who were predominantly part of the *Arrabbiati*. In addition, Valori's arrogance and swaggering attitude alienated many moderates, even when Valori pushed the reforms of Savonarola.

Savonarola's Supporters Light Bonfire

On February 7, 1497, Florence witnessed the first "Bonfire of the Vanities." Young supporters of Savonarola gathered donations from the citizens of the city for a great fire of repentance. With huge fanfare, the supporters carried these items to the central piazza where the bonfire consumed them. But Savonarola's health and support continued to decline, and his illness forced him to cut many sermons short. At the same time, Charles VIII concluded a truce with the papal League and left Savonarola and Florence without French backing. Knowing that Charles had abandoned Florence, Piero de' Medici attempted unsuccessfully to return in late April. New members of the Signoria who supported the papal League began passing statutes limiting the preaching of Savonarola.

On May 4, a group of rowdies known as the *Compagnacci* started a riot during a Savonarolan sermon, evidently hoping to kill the monk. Though loyal monks saved Savonarola, the Florentine leaders identified him as the chief source of discontent, and many demanded his exile. Swiftly upon the heels of the riot, Alexander sent two briefs which excommunicated Savonarola (and anyone who would listen to him) for heresy. This event brought a greater split among the Florentine factions. On July 19, the pope and his cardinals decided Savonarola must come to Rome (and become a permanent prisoner) or join the new congregation (and abandon his reforms and prophecies.)

The final showdown between Savonarola and the pope began on February 11, 1498. At this point, however, the ecclesiastical situation had changed. No longer did the reformer have a vacillating pope who had given consent for his preaching. Alexander VI was fighting to prove the validity of his own decisions concerning Savonarola, especially in regard to the excommunication. Brandishing the threat of an interdict, Alexander ordered the Signoria to silence the disobedient monk. By March 18, the Signoria bowed to the political and economic pressure which the pope brought to bear and ordered Savonarola to cease preaching. The duke of Ferrara, a longtime supporter, also abandoned the monk.

The Florentine officials conducted two trials, one from April 9–12, the other from April 21–24. In both, they tortured and questioned Savonarola for evidence with which to condemn him and two companions, Fra Domenico da Pescia and Fra Silvestro Maruffi. Though Savonarola signed a confession on April 19, lack of sufficient evidence led to the second trial. With the verdict predetermined, an ecclesiastical trial then ran from May 21 to 22. That court passed a death sentence for all three clergyman.

On May 23, 1498, Fra Girolamo Savonarola and his two companions were hung and their bodies cremated. Government officials scattered the ashes in the Arno River to prevent the veneration of the remains. The attempt to reform the Church had failed. But such spiritual inspiration would reappear 19 years later when another young monk, full of fire for a renewal of spiritual purpose, would split the Roman Catholic Church forever. That man was **Martin Luther.**

SOURCES:

Ridolfi, Robert. *The Life of Girolamo Savonarola.* Knopf, 1959 (reprinted by Greenwood Press, 1976).

Van Paasen, Pierre. *A Crown of Fire: The Life and Times of Girolamo Savonarola.* Hutchinson, 1960.

FURTHER READING:

Oliphant, Mrs. *The Making of Florence: Dante, Giotto, Savonarola, and Their City.* Macmillan, 1914.

Roeder, Ralph. *The Man of the Renaissance; Four Lawgivers: Savonarola, Machiavelli, Castiglione, Aretino.* Doubleday, 1983.

Villari, Pasquale. *Life and Times of Girolamo Savonarola.* Scribner, 1888.

Rosika Schwimmer

(1877–1948)

Hungarian feminist and international peace activist during the First World War.

"Known as the comedienne of the European women's movement who provoked 'shouts of laughter' from female audiences for her pungent attacks on the male sex, she was much in demand as a speaker and could make men laugh their way into agreeing with women's suffrage...."

ANNE WILTSHER

A spirited speechmaker and polemicist, Rosika Schwimmer was one of the first international feminists. First in her native Hungary, then throughout Europe, Britain, and the United States, she argued for women's rights and the dignity of working women. The outbreak of World War I diverted her energy into the cause of peace, but two years of intense work yielded few results. The war dragged on, her health and her spirit broke, and she lived a long, disappointing later life as an exile in America.

Born to a wealthy Jewish family in Budapest, Schwimmer was the daughter of an agricultural scientist. But when her father's efforts to develop grain hybrids were unsuccessful, the family fell on hard times. To help support them she went to work as a bookkeeper at the age of 18, and after two years, in 1897, volunteered to work with a trade union, the National Association of Women Office Workers. Before long she was its crusading president. In 1903, she founded the Hungarian Association of Working Women, then traveled to Germany as its delegate in the following year to attend the first meeting of the International Woman Suffrage Alliance (IWSA). Forming yet

Born in Budapest in 1877; died in New York in 1948; daughter of an agricultural scientist; married: Paul Bedy (a journalist), 1911 (divorced 1913); no children.

Contributed by Patrick Allitt, Assistant Professor of History, Emory University, Atlanta, Georgia

CHRONOLOGY

1877	Born in Budapest
1905	Organized Hungarian suffrage organization
1913	Organized International Woman Suffrage Congress, Budapest
1914	Outbreak of World War I
1915	Hague Conference and Ford Peace Ship
1918	Schwimmer appointed Hungarian ambassador to Switzerland under Károlyi
1920	Escaped from Horthy fascist regime
1929	Supreme Court verdict denied citizenship to pacifist Schwimmer
1937	Schwimmer and Lola Maverick Lloyd created the Campaign for World Government
1948	Died in New York

pince nez.... [S]he referred to herself as a "very, very radical feminist."

The climax of Schwimmer's early work for women's rights came in 1913 when she hosted the IWSA annual conference in Budapest, with its record number of 3,000 participants. At the end of the conference, Catt, who was then president of IWSA, wrote her a warm letter of thanks, adding a memento of their first meeting:

> When I remember the young girl who could understand no English and who knew so little about the movement for the enfranchisement of women only nine years ago, and then see the wonders of your own development and growth, and the great work you have accomplished in Hungary, I am filled with amazement, gratitude, and pride.

In 1914, the year the First World War began, Schwimmer was at work in London as the press secretary to the IWSA and as a well-paid journalist for several European newspapers. This was a crucial moment in the history of the British women's suffrage campaign. Many prominent suffragists, led by **Emmeline** and **Christabel Pankhurst,** had undertaken the tactic of direct action in the last few years, smashing windows, sabotaging the mail, and defacing public monuments to publicize their cause. One feminist, Emily Davison, had dramatically rushed onto the Derby race course, snatched the bridle of the King's horse, and been trampled to death, becoming a martyr to the cause of suffrage. But as soon as the war began, many British feminists put the issue to one side and became fervent supporters of war against Germany and Austria. Others, with Schwimmer's support, believed that rights for women and world peace were inseparable issues and pledged themselves to advance their work despite the war.

By this time, Schwimmer had mastered nine languages, which was the ideal preparation for her international peace work in the following years. She was well-informed about Eastern European affairs from her extensive travels and had a huge circle of friends and acquaintances from her work in the IWSA. In 1909, she had been the first foreign woman to address the House of Commons Foreign Affairs Committee and was by now a familiar figure in Parliament. (She even had breakfast with Chancellor of the Exchequer **David Lloyd George** and pointed out that the assassination of the Austrian Archduke augured a world war. He admitted after the fighting began that she alone among his friends and advisors had had the prescience to grasp the consequences of the killing.)

another association for Hungarian feminists on her return, this time helped by Budapest friend and teacher, Vilma Glucklich, Schwimmer inaugurated a campaign for women's votes which ultimately gained its objective in 1920 at the end of the First World War.

These early experiences led her to favor expanded job opportunities for women, dress reform, and improved legal rights. She shared with her American contemporary **Charlotte Perkins Gilman** the conviction that housework should be done by efficient women's collectives rather than separately in every household, freeing women for more interesting and rewarding pursuits. She translated into Hungarian Gilman's book *Women and Economics* in which these ideas were advanced and justified. In 1908 and then again in 1912 and 1913, she toured Eastern Europe with the American women's rights champion Carrie Chapman Catt, the two of them making brilliant speeches in support of women's suffrage and law reform. All who met Schwimmer were impressed by her dynamism and energy. Historian Caroline Moorehead writes:

> She was eloquent, tough, and indefatigable, producing opinions and pamphlets on everything from state child care to home economics and marriage in both Hungarian and German, writing short stories and a novel and delivering innumerable lectures. She wore brightly colored, loose fitting dresses and no corset, as was only proper for a follower of the dress-reform movement, and a

Rosika Schwimmer was a writer of pamphlets, speeches, short stories, and a novel.

Pacifism and the Women's Movement

Pacifism ran deep in Schwimmer's family. One of her uncles, Leopold Katscher, had founded the Hungarian Peace Society, while another uncle, Edler von Lederer, even though an army officer, also spoke out against militarism. When a family friend, Baroness Bertha von Suttner, had tried to organize a pan-European peace movement, Schwimmer appealed to the U.S. government to use its influence to prevent bloodshed. Just after the war began, she sailed for America to promote this scheme, believing that President **Woodrow Wilson** could convene a conference of neutral powers to preside over negotiations. Her repute was sufficient to win her an audience with Secretary of State **William Jennings Bryan,** himself very eager to keep out of the war, then with the President, who at this stage was also ardently opposed to intervention but made no promises. But when she spoke to the press afterwards, she angered Wilson by misrepresenting his remarks,

and he refused to see any peace workers for several months. Undeterred, Schwimmer toured the country, making speeches against war to women's groups, again being helped by her friend from the IWSA, Carrie Catt. The two women were slightly at odds. With her country already at war, peace had become the overriding issue to Schwimmer, whereas women's suffrage remained uppermost in Catt's mind and she wanted to direct Schwimmer's marvelous oratory in support of it. During the tour, Schwimmer met **Jane Addams,** founder of the Hull House social settlement, in Chicago. A British feminist and peace worker, Emmeline Pethick-Lawrence, was also touring America on behalf of a negotiated peace, and the two women joined forces.

Although they were technically enemies with their countries at war, Schwimmer and Pethick-Lawrence, speaking dramatically side by side, were the first to suggest a specifically women's peace movement. But given their situation they needed the help of renowned indigenous American women, such as Addams, who had already written *Newer Ideals of Peace* (1907) and who had a national reputation. The stirring lectures given by the two Europeans led to the creation of emergency peace committees in several cities, including Boston, Nashville, St. Paul, and Chicago. Addams agreed to call a peace meeting in Washington, D.C., in January 1915, with a view to forming a Women's Peace Party (WPP), but Schwimmer, afraid that the meeting had been hijacked by divisively militant suffragists, at first declined to take part except as a journalist. Reassured by the irenic ("conciliatory") tone of the meeting, Schwimmer changed her mind and spoke in praise of the American women's action. She added that peacemaking and women's votes went hand in hand because at present the women in her audience were "voiceless to prevent some incident" that might "bring for your children what has happened to our children."

Three months later, Schwimmer sailed back to Europe and spoke at the International Congress of Women, convened by the talented Dutch feminist Dr. Aletta Jacobs. Although the Congress was to have met in Berlin, the German faction—realizing that women from enemy nations would be excluded—settled for The Hague instead. As it was, most of the British women who had hoped to attend were denied passports by the British government, which also declared Schwimmer an enemy alien, so that she could not return. The conference participants passed resolutions urging an end to the fighting, immediate peace talks, the right of all peoples to self-government, and equal rights for women—some of which would show up again in 1918 among Woodrow Wilson's "Fourteen Points." Schwimmer wanted members of the conference to take the resolution personally to heads of government in the belligerent and neutral nations, and made a passionate floor speech to promote the idea of personal missions: "When our sons are killed by millions, let us, mothers, only try to do good by going to the kings and emperors, without any other danger than a refusal!" Though many had misgivings about the value of these excursions, the delegates voted in favor, and Schwimmer was asked to lead a group of representatives to Denmark, Norway, Sweden, Russia, and the Netherlands. The government officials they met were polite but noncommittal, and the women's actions generated a disappointingly small amount of discussion and publicity.

Henry Ford and the Peace Ship

Back in America in mid-1915, Schwimmer, always eager for prompt and dramatic action, learned that the automobile magnate, Henry Ford, was devoting himself to peacemaking. An American woman named Rebecca Shelly, who was convinced that God was directing her to make peace, arranged a massive antiwar demonstration in Detroit to draw Ford's attention when he refused to meet her in person. Schwimmer spoke to the meeting and won an audience with Ford on November 18, explaining to him her plan for a mediated peace. Louis Lochner, head of the National Peace Federation, joined them the next day, and together they persuaded Ford of the plan's viability. Ford in turn approached President Wilson and asked him to establish an official neutral commission which he, Ford, would finance. Wilson politely declined.

The Women's Peace Party tried to increase the pressure on Wilson by holding a large demonstration in Washington, D.C., on November 26 with Schwimmer as keynote speaker. Unfortunately, when Henry Ford followed her to the podium after another of her rousing speeches, he claimed that he would find a way to "get the boys out of the trenches by Christmas," then only a month away. This assertion was bound to be refuted by the facts and helped undermine rather than strengthen the movement. Ford also financed a ship, the *Oscar II*, to take peace delegates to a second European conference the following week. Schwimmer, now marked by the press as Ford's "expert assistant," was making a poor impression on many of the leading American pacifists, who considered her hotheaded and thoughtless. Her calls for immediate peace negotiations seemed not to be backed by consideration of the political complexities of the issue, and some WPP women, concluding that she was hurting rather than helping their cause, declined to join the peace ship.

The voyage of the *Oscar II* received much adverse publicity, and many of the journalists traveling on it (there were almost as many newspapermen as delegates) treated the whole venture as a joke. Fear of being torpedoed by a German submarine, overcrowding, and a rough winter sea led to constant animosities among the passengers. Schwimmer, whose behavior historian Barbara Steinson describes as "secretive and authoritarian," asserted that she had a bagful of documents proving that the warring powers were ready to negotiate, but when she showed them to eager passengers they turned out to be no more than the vague promises her earlier mission had elicited. She declared that Ford had promised the International Committee $200,000, but no money was forthcoming.

Tiring of the venture in Christiana, Sweden, when it yielded no quick results, Ford soon slipped away, while Schwimmer and Lochner carried on with the project, setting up a Neutral Conference for Continuous Mediation in Stockholm. Finally the two of them fell out and Schwimmer resigned in protest from the Conference, pursued by malicious rumors that she was actually an agent being paid by the Central Powers (for which Hungary was fighting) to bring the peace process into disrepute. Almost at once she collapsed with a serious heart condition and had to take an unaccustomed three-month break from work. She spent the rest of the war in Stockholm, depressed at the mounting casualties and the seeming futility of all the peace efforts to date, but returned to Hungary in November 1918.

Schwimmer Named First Hungarian Woman Ambassador

At the end of the war the Austro-Hungarian Empire collapsed. Count Michael Károlyi, one of Schwimmer's friends, overthrew Emperor Charles I in a bloodless coup and invited Schwimmer to become a member of his National Council of Fifteen. The liberal-minded Károlyi then invited Schwimmer to become ambassador to Switzerland, making her the first woman ambassador in Hungarian history. While there, she worked on another women's peace conference but had hardly started her official duties when she was recalled to Budapest, partly because she had equipped herself as ambassador by using state funds for a fur coat, an expensive apartment in Berne, and a chauffeured limousine. At a time when people all over Europe, including Hungary, were starving to death, these seemed like outrageously provocative purchases, even if they were designed to bolster her dignity as ambassador. The next month, Károlyi was overthrown by the Communist coup d'état of Béla Kun. Denied a passport, Schwimmer was unable to attend the fourth Women's International Congress at Zurich. Delegates sent her letters of encouragement (though some were secretly relieved by her absence), and then constituted themselves as the Women's International League for Peace and Freedom (WILPF).

The Communists treated Schwimmer as a bourgeois ("middle class") enemy for her work in the Károly regime and denied her the right to work, but worse was to follow. The fascist regime of Admiral Nicolas Horthy, which soon overthrew the Hungarian Communists, began to purge the Jews and singled out Schwimmer for extermination. Loyal friends, Quakers, and American peace workers managed to smuggle her out of Hungary on a Danube steamer and into Vienna in 1920, and

from there she was able to make her way to the United States. But America was then undergoing a "Red scare" of its own, a panicky reaction to the Russian Revolution abroad and labor militancy at home. In the worst violation of civil rights since slavery, the Attorney General, A. Mitchell Palmer, was summarily deporting, without trial, hundreds of foreign-born citizens suspected of radical sympathies. Not surprisingly in this atmosphere, the old accusation that Schwimmer was a spy came up again, along with the allegation that her peace work between 1914 and 1917 had been aimed at neutralizing America for the benefit of the Central Powers. Other critics suggested, ludicrously enough, that she might be the source of Henry Ford's growing anti-Semitism.

Supreme Court Denies U.S. Citizenship

Her sister Franciska, a New York pianist, and her friend Lola Maverick Lloyd, a wealthy woman whom she had first met in 1914, supported Schwimmer when she was at first denied the right to work. By now she was suffering from a severe case of diabetes and found it more difficult than previously to lead an active life. Hoping nevertheless to resume her work as a journalist and lecturer, Schwimmer applied for citizenship, but the oath taken by new citizens required candidates to swear that they would bear arms in defense of America if necessary. As a pacifist she refused to take the oath, but sued for citizenship nevertheless, declaring that as a point of conscience she would be unable to take up arms for any country or any cause. The case went all the way to the Supreme Court which ruled, in 1929, that she should not be granted citizenship. Justices Oliver Wendell Holmes and Louis Brandeis dissented from the majority opinion, claiming that her case should be considered as a First Amendment freedom of thought issue. Holmes wrote: "The applicant seems to be a woman of superior character and intelligence, obviously more than ordinarily desirable as a citizen of the United States." Superior character and intelligence did not make her likable, however, and even her supporters were finding her dogmatic and high-handed ways hard to endure.

Permitted to stay in America as a stateless person, she remained intensely devoted to the peace cause. In 1925, she attended the first Conference on the Cause and Cure of War, in Washington, D.C., but found it too halfhearted in its approach. The second conference, the following year, seemed even worse to her, especially as all 30 of the lecturers were men, and Schwimmer rebuked the organizer—her old friend Carrie

Catt—for this gender imbalance. Catt was not the only one she annoyed. Gradually, as she aged, she became increasingly abrasive, launching a succession of libel suits against journalists who had handled the peace ship scheme roughly; she also began a prolonged correspondence with Henry Ford and his associates, who she believed had wronged her and damaged her reputation.

Despite her deteriorating health, Schwimmer kept busy in America. She and Lola Maverick Lloyd founded the Campaign for World Government in 1937, in the years when another world war seemed imminent and the hopeless failure of the League of Nations was apparent to all. At first the organization was a small antiwar group dedicated to world government, but its ranks swelled during the Second World War, especially after the Hiroshima and Nagasaki nuclear bombings of 1945. She started, but never finished, an autobiography and began to work at creating a world center for women's archives, but once again her personal tactlessness alienated many of the people whose help and cooperation she needed. Schwimmer died in 1948 of bronchial pneumonia after living largely on her sister's and Lloyd's charity for 27 years. It was a disappointing end for the woman who had seemed incandescent to her associates before, and in the early days of, the First World War.

SOURCES:

Hershey, Burnet. *The Odyssey of Henry Ford and the Great Peace Ship.* Taplinger. 1967.

Kraft, Barbara S. *The Peace Ship: Henry Ford's Pacifist Adventure in the First World War.* Macmillan, 1978.

Moorehead, Caroline. *Troublesome People: Enemies of War, 1916–1986.* London: Hamish Hamilton, 1987.

Steinson, Barbara J. *American Women's Activism in World War I.* Garland, 1982.

Wiltsher, Anne. *Most Dangerous Women: Feminist Peace Campaigners of the Great War.* London: Pandora, 1985.

Seneca

(c. 4 B.C.–A.D. 65)

Stoic philosopher and Roman literary figure, who tutored Nero and later served as his trusted advisor and minister.

"Overcoming the limitations of my birth and measuring myself not by my lot but by my soul, I stood equal to the most important men."

SENECA

Lucius Annaeus Seneca, a man of great fame and influence during the reign of **Nero,** rose to prominence more by his wit and wisdom than by the greatness of his family. He was born c. 4 B.C. in Corduba (Cordova), a Roman colony in the province of Baetica (southern Spain) which had been stabilized and "Romanized" almost two centuries before. Seneca's family was wealthy and influential only within its own province. His father Seneca the Elder is known to have often traveled to Rome, avidly observing political and literary life there. Though he remained personally uninvolved in Roman politics and never rose to senatorial status, he demonstrated his superior intelligence and memory by recording, years after the fact, trial arguments which he had witnessed.

Seneca's mother Helvia managed the family land and interests. She bore three sons: Annaeus Novatus, who by a later adoption took the name L. Junius Gallio Annaeanus, and whose fame was assured by his mention in the New Testament (Acts 18: 12–17); Lucius Annaeus Seneca, our present concern; and M. Annaeus Mela, father of Lucan the poet who wrote the epic *The Civil War.*

Full name: Lucius Annaeus Seneca. Born at Corduba (Cordova, Spain) sometime between 4 B.C. and 1 B.C.; died of forced suicide by the orders of Emperor Nero, A.D. 65; son of Seneca the Elder and Helvia; brother of Annaeus Novatus (Iunius Gallus), the unconcerned "Gallio" mentioned in the New Testament; brother of Annaeus Mela, father of the poet, Lucan; married: (first wife) name unknown; (second wife) Pompeia Paulina; children: one son who died in childhood (41 B.C.).

Contributed by Sylvia Gray Kaplan, Adjunct Faculty, Humanities, Marylhurst College, Marylhurst, Oregon

As a youth Seneca was drawn to philosophic studies, and philosophy remained a primary interest throughout his life. He admired the teaching the ancient Pythagoras (of both numerical and philosophic fame), and he sat under the Pythagorean teaching of a certain Sotion. This philosopher prescribed a strict vegetarian diet, and for at least a year Seneca observed the recommended practices. However, when under the emperor **Tiberius** abstinence from certain meats was considered a mark of adherence to a questionable cult, Seneca's father, who viewed philosophy unsympathetically anyway, asked Seneca to discontinue the diet. Seneca acquiesced. Eventually he embraced Stoicism, a Hellenistic philosophy (espousing an indifference to pleasure or pain) which had gained a Roman following; Seneca became one of its prominent Roman proponents. Many of his extant works, particularly his *Moral Essays* and *Moral Epistles*, contain explanations of Stoic thought and practical advice for implementing Stoic principles into daily life.

He did not spend his entire childhood in the backwaters of Baetica. Helvia's stepsister was married to a prominent equestrian (one step below the senatorial class), and since they resided at Rome, Seneca went to live with them for the sake of his studies. After his uncle was appointed prefect (chief delegated ruler) of Egypt, his aunt took Seneca there to live with her for a time. As he suffered from tuberculosis, his hope for a cure may have provided the motive for the trip, for Egypt's climate was considered salutary. This illness had hindered any plans Seneca may have had to pursue a political career. At one point, he was so ill that he even considered suicide (a respectable manner of death for a Stoic)—but claimed later that love for his father and the company of friends had kept him from taking this drastic step. Whether or not his stay in Egypt effected the cure, Seneca gradually began to recover.

Seneca Achieves Political Office

After he returned to Rome in A.D. 31, his aunt combed the city for connections and sought favors from all her acquaintances, so that at a rather late age Seneca finally achieved senatorial status and his first political office: quaestor. But Seneca did not gain his fame or power as a direct result of his political office. Power in Rome emanated from the imperial court; in Seneca's case, his talent as an orator and author gained him fame and perhaps the friendship of Emperor **Caligula**'s three sisters.

What may have at first appeared fortuitous for Seneca soon worked to his disadvantage. Because Seneca's gift for oratory seems to have aroused the emperor's jealousy rather than admiration, Caligula did not extend any favor to him. Caligula called Seneca "a mere text-book orator," and his oratory "sand without lime." This was dangerous criticism, coming from the emperor. Dio Cassius, a historian of the early third century A.D., records that Seneca escaped execution only because it was pointed out to Caligula that Seneca would soon die from his illness anyway. Any benefit the orator might have derived from his friendship with members of the royal family vanished when all three women were sent into exile for an alleged plot against the emperor.

Claudius succeeded Caligula as emperor when the latter was murdered in A.D. 41 by members of the Praetorian Guard (elite troops whose main task was to guard the emperor). Claudius immediately recalled from exile Caligula's two surviving sisters, Julia Livilla and **Agrippina the Younger.** Messalina, Claudius's wife, saw both of these women as threats to her own power, however, and soon contrived charges against Julia Livilla involving Seneca, asserting that they were having an affair. The ancient sources generally present this as a trumped-up allegation, but Claudius did perceive their association as a serious political threat to his own life and power. He sent Julia Livilla again into exile where she soon died; the senate formally tried Seneca and sentenced him to death, but Claudius mitigated his sentence to merely exile. From A.D. 41 to 49, Seneca lived in the barren, rugged, uncivilized, and primitive (at least by his description) island of Corsica.

Most of Seneca's writings from this period of his life contain traces of bitterness. One letter, written near the beginning of his exile, is addressed to his mother Helvia and has the expressed intent of offering consolation to her. In this letter, Seneca holds that exile is merely "a change of place," but adds, "I will admit that this changing of place is attended by disadvantages—by poverty, disgrace, and scorn." Still, he claims that his mind is "free from all other engrossment, has leisure for its own tasks, and now finds joy in lighter studies, now, being eager for the truth, mounts to the consideration of its own nature and the nature of the universe."

Later in his exile, this high-mindedness seems to have dissolved completely. In a letter of consolation to Polybius, a prominent freedman serving the emperor Claudius, Seneca includes not only stock exhortations for Stoic acceptance of death, but also sycophantic praise of Claudius and a plea for his own restoration to Roman life. He ends the letter:

> I have put these things together, as best I could, with a mind now weakened and dulled by long rusting. If they shall seem to you to be ill suited to your intelligence, or to ill supply the heating of your sorrow, reflect how he who is held fast in the grip of his own misfortunes is not at leisure to comfort others, and how Latin words do not suggest themselves readily to one in whose ears the uncouth jargon of barbarians is ever ringing, distressing even to the more civilized barbarians.

The letters made no impact. Seneca remained in Corsica for eight long years until his fortunes finally rose with a shift of power in the imperial court. Claudius had discovered that Messalina was party to a plot against his life and throne, and along with many others, she was executed. Claudius then settled on another wife from the formerly out-of-favor faction—Agrippina, sister of the former emperor Caligula and mother of young Nero. One of the first results was Seneca's recall to Rome in A.D. 49.

Tacitus, a historian of the early second century, suggests Agrippina's motives for arranging Seneca's return:

> She judged that owing to his literary eminence this would be popular. She also had designs on him as a distinguished tutor for her young son Lucius Domitius Ahenobarbus (the future Nero). Seneca's advice could serve their plans for

supremacy; and he was believed to be devoted to her—in gratitude for her favours—but hostile to Claudius whose unfairness he resented.

Agrippina arranged for Seneca's appointment to a praetership, the next respectable political office on the path to formal prominence, but his most important assignment was tutoring Nero. Although Agrippina warned Seneca against teaching philosophy, which she believed was antithetical to political life, Seneca polished Nero's Greek and Latin and taught him the humanities, eloquence, and extemporaneous speaking. During his five years as Seneca's pupil, Nero seems to have developed a genuine trust in and respect for his teacher.

Claudius died in A.D. 54, generally believed to be a victim of poisoned mushrooms fed to him by his wife Agrippina. The ancient sources agree that Agrippina's goal had always been to place her own son Nero on the throne of the Empire. Although he had been well tutored, and although his claim to the emperorship was upheld by the senate, at Claudius's death Nero was only 16 and not adequately prepared to rule an empire. Agrippina had planned ahead by arranging for two able counselors. One, of course, was Seneca; the other was the prefect of the Praetorian Guard, Burrus, who had also achieved his authority through Agrippina's influence. In the informal but extremely powerful role of *"amicus principis,"* or "friend of the emperor," together these men guided the first years of Nero's rule. Tacitus assesses their functions in this manner:

> These two men, with a unanimity rare among partners in power, were, by different methods, equally influential. Burrus' strength lay in soldierly efficiency and seriousness of character, Seneca's in amiable high principles and his tuition of Nero in public speaking. They collaborated in controlling the emperor's perilous adolescence; their policy was to direct his deviations from virtue into licensed channels of indulgence.

Seneca's influence on the Empire as *amicus principis* cannot be measured in terms of legislation he enacted or battles he won. His influence was more subtle, though widely acknowledged and sometimes resented by other Roman citizens.

Seneca clearly continued his role as Nero's advisor on moral, court, and state issues, often appointing men of his choosing to prominent offices, thus assuring their loyalty to him and to the Emperor. One incident recorded in several sources illustrates his sense of protocol, his role as general advisor, and Nero's early dependence on him. As Nero sat on the tribunal with Seneca at his side, ready to meet a foreign emissary, his mother Agrippina came to meet him with the intent of ascending the tribunal. Seneca quickly grasped the situation and instructed Nero to descend and meet his mother before she reached the steps, thus preserving Roman decorum. Nero did as he was told.

He Writes Treatise on Role of Emperor

One of Seneca's major tasks was to provide an explicit ideology for the principate under Nero. His presentation of the rationale for rule is contained in a treatise, *De Clementia* (On Mercy), in which he describes the proper role of an emperor. His central thesis is that an emperor, given his powerful position, needs good character more than anything in order to rule well. Seneca advocates mercy as the most important attribute of a ruler. Seneca is known to have written speeches for Nero, often containing explanations for imperial actions or intents. He began this activity immediately, for he composed Claudius's funeral oration, which Nero delivered, as well as Nero's accession speech to the senate. This aspect of Seneca's job, easy at first, grew more difficult with time. As Nero began to assert himself and follow his own whims, Seneca was still expected to offer an explanation to the public for Nero's untempered actions.

In spite of the good Seneca may have accomplished as advisor to the emperor, he could not escape criticism. He was, for instance, disparaged for his wealth. As favored advisor, he received many gifts of land and money from the emperor, and he became a very wealthy man; in the popular eye, this was interpreted as inconsistent with his pretenses as a philosopher. And it is true that though he did not consider riches an evil per se, Seneca's own treatises often downplayed the importance of wealth. He was criticized for using flattery, though he considered flattery a psychological strategy to be used wisely for achieving desirable ends. He was criticized for political involvement, whereas his Stoic philosophy actually advocated that "the wise man will engage in public affairs, unless something prevents him;" even in some of his own writings the detached, meditative life was considered a higher good.

Dio Cassius encapsulates much of the criticism to which Seneca was prey:

> Nor was this the only instance in which his conduct was seen to be diametrically opposed to the teachings of his philosophy. For while denouncing tyranny, he was making himself the teacher of a tyrant; while inveighing against the associates of the powerful, he did not hold aloof from the palace himself; and though he had nothing good to say of flatterers, he himself had constantly fawned upon Messalina and the freedmen of Claudius.... Though finding fault with the rich, he himself acquired a fortune of 300,000,000 sesterces.

There was a kernel of truth in these accusations, and Seneca seems to have felt obliged to answer them. In one of his moral essays, he parried them in this manner:

> Later I shall outdo your reproaches and bestow on myself more blame than you think of; for the moment I shall make this reply: "I am not a 'wise man,' nor—to feed your malevolence!—shall I ever be." And so require not from me that I should be equal to the best, but that I should be better than the wicked. It is enough for me if every day, I reduce the number of my vices; and blame my mistakes.

In short, Seneca did not claim perfection and admitted that he made mistakes. Technically, therefore, he does not merit the label "hypocrite" which is sometimes applied to him even today. Still, as the privileged advisor to the immoderate Nero, Seneca found himself placed more and more in a compromising position. This was despite his good intentions, and despite the degree to which he kept matters from degenerating into an even worse state.

The difficulty of Seneca's position is perhaps most aptly demonstrated by Nero's unsuccessful attempt to murder his own mother Agrippina. Upon receiving news of the botched attempt, Nero frantically called both Burrus and Seneca in the middle of the night, seeking their advice. Neither of them approved Nero's action. Tacitus speculates that these ministers may have felt the moment for choice between loyalty to the son or the mother had arrived. After waiting some minutes in silence, Seneca "ventured so far as to turn to Burrus and ask if the troops should be ordered to kill her." As Seneca knew he would, Burrus asserted that the Praetorian Guard was loyal to the memory of Agrippina's father and would do no harm to his offspring. Ultimately, however, both Seneca and Burrus were indirectly involved in her death, for Burrus found a freedman who gladly carried out the murder, and Seneca as "press secretary" composed Nero's speech to the senate, attempting to obscure and excuse the murder. Even so, the fact that neither of them participated wholeheartedly caused Nero to depend upon them less.

Seneca's Influence on Nero Wanes

Burrus died soon after, probably of natural causes; from this point Seneca's influence on the emperor began to diminish. According to Tacitus, Nero began listening to Seneca's critics. They argued, "How long must merit at Rome be conferred by Seneca's certificate alone? Surely Nero is a boy no longer!" They went so far as to criticize the poetry Seneca wrote, asserting that he composed it only to retain his favored position, since Nero had recently begun to appreciate poetry.

As Nero indulged more and more in his cruelty, Seneca observed his moderating influence slipping away. He therefore requested an audience with Nero where, claiming age and weakness, he expressed his desire to return much of his wealth to the emperor and to retire from public life. Although Nero did not formally concede his retirement, in A.D. 62 Seneca began to curtail his active public lifestyle, claiming that "ill-health or philosophic studies kept him at home."

During this period Seneca wrote many of his letters of moral exhortation addressed to a friend, Lucilius. One of them states:

> I have withdrawn not only from men, but from affairs, especially from my own affairs; I am working for later generations writing down some ideas that may be of assistance to them. There are certain wholesome counsels, which may be compared to prescriptions of useful drugs; these I am putting into writing; for I have found them helpful in ministering to my own sores, which, if not wholly cured, have at any rate ceased to spread.

Seneca argued that he was doing good for future generations, accomplishing more by recording moral truths than by involving himself in political life. However, it seems certain that despite his genuine love of philosophy, he had pulled away from his active public life with some regret. In another letter to Lucilius, he wrote:

> Although people may often have thought that I sought seclusion because I was disgusted with politics and regretted my hapless and thankless position, yet, in the retreat to which apprehension and weariness have driven me, my ambition sometimes develops afresh. For it is not because my ambition was rooted out that it has abated, but because it was wearied or perhaps even put out of temper by the failure of its plans.

After the disastrous burning of Rome, Seneca once again asked for formal permission to retire, and he gave much of his acquired wealth back to Nero in order to help restore the city. Once again, permission to retire was not officially granted, but Seneca now claimed a muscular complaint and kept to his room, reverting to a diet of fruit and water. Soon afterwards he was accused of participating in a conspiracy against Nero. Although Dio Cassius believes Seneca was guilty, Tacitus states that Nero had no proof of his complicity. Seneca was staying at a villa a few miles from Rome when he received the order from Nero to commit suicide. In Seneca's last hours of life, he called on his philosophy for comfort, as well as to console his grieving friends.

> Where had their philosophy gone, he asked, and that resolution against impending misfortunes which they had devised over so many years? "Surely nobody was unaware that Nero was cruel!" he added. "After murdering his mother and brother, it only remained for him to kill his teacher and tutor."

Tacitus describes Seneca's death scene in vivid detail, and some have noted the resemblance, contrived or not, between his death and that of Socrates, the famous Greek philosopher. Seneca cut his veins, but his "aged body, lean from austere living, released the blood too slowly." Still, "even in his last moments his eloquence remained. Summoning secretaries, he dictated a dissertation"—no doubt a philosophical one.

Meanwhile Seneca drank poison to hasten his death. When the poison proved ineffective, he was placed in a vapor bath where he finally suffocated. When Nero heard that Paulina, Seneca's wife, had loyally cut her veins along with her husband, he sent orders to prevent her death. Seneca, however, was cremated without a major ceremony in accordance with a wish he had expressed.

Many of Seneca's writings have survived to the present. His *Moral Essays* and *Epistles to Lucilius,* while sometimes considered insincerely moralistic, are an important source for our knowledge of both Stoic beliefs and competing Epicurean beliefs. His plays, written in dramatic "Silver Latin," influenced many later playwrights, particularly the Elizabethans, and they are sources for our knowledge of ancient mythology. His "scientific" writings, *Natural Questions,* give us a glimpse into the mind and world view of educated Romans living in the early Roman Empire.

Seneca sought throughout his life to balance two impulses: one toward an active political life, and the other toward philosophy. He saw no inherent conflict between the two interests, but others interpreted his life as inconsistent and hypocritical. Regardless, any fair assessment of Seneca's life must give proper weight to his moderating influence for eight years on the excessive Nero. Tacitus's description of Seneca as a man of "amiable high principles" may come closest to the truth.

SOURCES:

Dio Cassius. *Dio's Roman History.* Translated by Earnest Cary. 9 vols. Harvard University Press, 1968.

Griffin, Miriam. "Imago Vitae Suae," *Seneca.* Edited by Charles Desmond Nuttall Costa. Routledge & Kegan Paul, 1974.

Moral Epistles (*Epistulae Morales*). Translated by Richard M. Gummere. 3 vols. Harvard University Press, 1970.

Seneca, Lucius Annaeus. *Moral Essays.* Translated by John Basore. 3 vols. Harvard University Press, 1958.

Seneca: A Philosopher in Politics. Clarendon Press, 1976.

Tacitus. *The Annals of Imperial Rome.* Translated by Michael Grant. Viking Penguin, 1987.

FURTHER READING:

Sorensen, Villy. *Seneca, the Humanist at the Court of Nero.* Translated by W. Glyn Jones. University of Chicago Press, 1984.

Sullivan, J. P. *Literature and Politics in the Age of Nero.* Cornell, 1985.

Wladyslaw Sikorski

(1881–1943)

Son of a provincial Polish farmer, who was miraculously
transformed into one of the greatest soldier-statesmen
in the history of modern Europe.

"From the first dark days of the Polish catastrophe and the brutal triumph of the German war machine until the moment of his death... [Sikorski] was the symbol and the embodiment of that spirit which has borne the Polish nation through centuries of sorrow and is unquenchable by agony."

WINSTON CHURCHILL

As the 18th century came to an end so did the independence of Poland in 1795. Following the heroic Kosciuszko Uprising of 1794, Russia, Prussia, and Austria wasted little time before completing the process begun in 1772 of dismembering the Polish state, an event that removed Poland from the European map. The Polish populace endured foreign rule for nearly 125 years. Throughout the ensuing years, the Poles managed to preserve their distinctive national heritage and on occasion revolted against the partitioning powers; the largest of these revolutions took place in 1830 and in 1863.

Wladyslaw Eugeniusz Sikorski, like all Poles of the 19th century, was born into a world without a Poland. He and his countrymen were confronted with an intense Russification program in the eastern Polish lands and an equally relentless attempt by Germany to cultivate Germanic culture in the western Polish territories. It was a demanding struggle through the dismal years of partition for the Poles to preserve their native language, traditions, and culture.

Sikorski was born in the small town of Tuszow, near Sandomierz, in the southern Polish

Pronunciation: LAD-i-slaw SEE-kor-skee. Born Wladyslaw Eugeniusz Sikorski on May 20, 1881, in the small Polish town of Tuszow, near Sandomierz, in the eastern quarter of Galicia; died in a plane crash shortly after taking off from Gibraltar in 1943; son of a gentleman farmer who died when Sikorski was a child; married: Helena Zubczewska; children: (one daughter) Zofia. Predecessor: General Edward Smigly-Rydz. Successor: Stanislaw Mikolajczyk.

Contributed by Christopher Blackburn, Ph.D. candidate in history, Auburn University, Auburn, Alabama

CHRONOLOGY

1881	Tsar Alexander II of Russia assassinated
1905	"Bloody Sunday" began a series of revolts throughout Russia
1907	Sikorski employed as an engineer
1908	Organized a military youth group
1914	Assassination of Archduke Ferdinand; Europe moved irrevocably toward World War I
1917	Russian Revolution established a Communist state
1918	Józef Pilsudski entered Warsaw as a national hero; independent Polish state proclaimed
1919	Russo-Polish War began; Sikorski commanded the Polish Fifth Army
1920	Polish forces miraculously destroyed the Soviet army at the gates of Warsaw
1920	Sikorski took command of the Polish Third Army, which was instrumental in the liberation of Eastern Poland from Soviet Forces
1922	Became prime minister of Poland
1924	Named Polish minister of war
1934	Nazi *putsch* in Austria
1938	Hitler effected *Anschluss* with Austria; Munich Agreement ceded Czechoslovakian Sudetenland to Germany
1939	Germany invaded Poland; Sikorski named prime minister and commander in chief in exile
1943	Mass grave of Polish officers discovered in Katyn Forest; Sikorski killed in a plane crash

region known as Galicia. His father, a typical gentleman farmer of the region, died during Wladyslaw's childhood. His premature death forced the young Sikorski to mature quickly, and he began working to help support his family at an early age. During his teenage years he taught classes and tutored to help pay for his education.

While continuing to support himself, Sikorski moved to Krakow and began his university career. He later transferred to the Polytechnic University in Lwow, where he completed his studies and received a degree in civil engineering, and then moved on to Brussels to receive more advanced technical training. Despite his humble origins, Sikorski proved himself a very able student of the sciences. The *Times* of London later attested: "He was a brilliant student, and the scientific training he received was to stand him in good stead." As 1907 came to a close, Sikorski returned to his homeland to take a job with the Galician Waterways Association.

Sikorski soon began to display the characteristics of a young patriot. Totally devoted to the restoration of Poland, he began actively participating in the clandestine Polish organizations of the day. By 1908, he had formed his own nationalistic "Youth Circle of a military character," which developed into the League for Active Struggle. Within a relatively short time, Sikorski made many friends and gained enough popularity to become the first president of the Lwow Riflemen's Association. Soon after, he began editing a clandestine political journal and was named to the post of general secretary of the Temporary Commission of the Independent Parties.

Despite his active lifestyle, Sikorski managed to find time to renew his friendship with the director of the Lwow University. That relationship proved very beneficial as Sikorski began vigorously pursuing the director's daughter, Helena Zubczewska. Following a proper courtship and the prerequisite engagement, they were married in 1912.

Sikorski's marital bliss was short-lived. The beginning of the First World War forced him into the military service of his country. The war, however, did bring the many clandestine groups of Galicia out of hiding and united them in the Polish Legion of Marshal **Józef Pilsudski.** The Polish Legion wasted little time in joining the Austrian military and beginning the fight against the Russians in the east. Marshal Pilsudski and his Polish Legionaries did not fight for the Central Powers because of an affinity for Germans and Austrians, but rather, they believed the defeat of Russia would bring about the resurrection of Poland.

The nationalistic groups that formed the Legions and their leadership were known as the "Chief National Committee." Sikorski was soon appointed head of the Chief National Committee's war department and given the rank of lieutenant-colonel. By 1917, he was stationed in Warsaw as the chief recruiter for the Polish army. Following this stint, he took command of the Polish Auxiliary Corps in Przemysl and later in Bolechow. Despite their brilliant military record and service to the Central Powers, the Poles were once again betrayed at Brest-Litovsk. The Treaty of Brest-Litovsk, which ended the war between Russia and the Central Powers, ceded Russian-Poland to Germany, not to its Polish inhabitants. Sikorski and his fellow patriots adamantly believed that the

Polish people deserved an independent Polish state for their assistance in the war against Russia. Confronting the Austrian administration, they vehemently opposed yet another partition of their homeland. Sikorski's outburst and rebellion gained nothing for Poland, but it did get him roughly one year in an Austrian internment camp.

With his release in 1918, Sikorski immediately began reorganizing his secret groups and took command of the Polish forces that were operating in eastern Poland against the Ukrainians. By late 1918, the war was over in the West and the Germans and Austrians were in full retreat from the Polish lands. The Poles were then left to create their own state and fill the power vacuum created by the withdrawal of the partitioning powers. The limited Polish forces under Marshal Pilsudski had to establish and defend the Polish borders against Lithuanian, Byelorussian, Ukrainian, Czech, Slovak, Russian, German, and Austrian incursions. This ring of opportunistic neighbors continually tried to bite off chunks of Polish territory. Miraculously, the small Polish army not only held but, by 1919, actually advanced into Lithuania and seized the ancient capital of Wilno. In order to capture Wilno, the Polish army defeated elements of the advancing Soviet army and forced them to retreat from western Lithuania. Major-General Sikorski commanded the Polish Ninth Infantry Division during the engagement and "played a distinguished part in forcing a Russian retirement."

Sikorski Commands Armies in Russo–Polish War

Russia and Poland were eventually propelled into full-scale conflict in 1919, because of the Polish pursuit of a large East European Federation and the Soviet quest for a weak communist-controlled Poland. It was the Russo-Polish War that provided Sikorski with his first opportunity to command large military formations, such as an army, and it was during this campaign that he began to realize his "outstanding military talents." Pilsudski's Polish forces, with Sikorski in command of the Polish Fifth Army, initially pushed far into the Ukraine and Lithuania, but they were soon driven back to the gates of Warsaw by the advancing Soviet army.

By August 12, 1920, the Russians had reached the outskirts of Warsaw and all believed Poland would be destroyed. Sikorski's Fifth Army was deployed just north of Warsaw, in order to defend the city's exposed flank. In an unforeseen turn of events, the Fifth Army faced the bulk of the Russian assault and held out against overwhelming odds. As Sikorski held the Russian Fourth Army,

Marshal Pilsudski launched a daring flank attack on August 13 which cut through the Russian rear areas. After successfully repelling the Russian onslaught, Sikorski's forces shifted to the offensive and won key battles along the Wkra and Vistula Rivers, thus assuring the rout of the Soviet army.

Pilsudski's surprise offensive had encircled the Red Army, forcing the Russians into a rapid retreat from Poland. Before the day was over, the Polish army had taken some 100,000 Soviet prisoners of war and nearly destroyed the entire Russian army. After the initial rout along the Vistula, Sikorski was given command of the Polish Third Army, which successfully cleared out all Russian troops remaining in eastern Poland. Pilsudski's gamble worked for several reasons, but the two most prominent were the sheer brilliance of the Marshal's plan and the herculean efforts of General Sikorski. Because of these courageous men certain defeat was turned into the great Polish victory known as the *Cud Nad Wisla* (Miracle on the Vistula). The London *Times* later confirmed the bravery of Sikorski and his men: "Their stubborn stand and later successful attack must be largely attributed to the leadership and personal inspiration of their commander."

Becomes Prime Minister, Institutes Reforms

In reward for his outstanding service in the Russo-Polish War and as recognition of his military abilities, Sikorski was appointed chief of the Polish General Staff in 1921. By 1922, Poland was threatened by political chaos following the assassination of President Gabriel Narutowicz. When Sikorski's supporters encouraged him to step forward and form a new cabinet, he became prime minister of Poland in late 1922. Promptly taking firm control of the country, he restored a democratic system of order. Prime Minister Sikorski then launched an intensive program of sweeping internal and external reforms, including land reform. To secure Polish access to the Baltic Sea, he built the foundation for a new Polish port at Gdynia and soon the traditionally small fishing village was transformed into one of the largest and most modern Baltic ports of the day. After much labor, he also gained international acceptance of the Polish-Soviet border, as drawn by the Treaty of Riga. Perhaps Sikorski's most notable accomplishment was his extensive military reform package, which enabled Poland to assemble a large well-trained army, supported by an unprecedented military industrial base.

In 1924, Sikorski stepped down as prime minister, but he remained active in Polish politics as the minister of war and continued to reorganize and improve the Polish military machine. His term as head of the military was short lived, however; by the time of Marshal Pilsudski's coup d'état in 1926, Sikorski was back in the ranks of the regular army. Throughout the successful revolt, Sikorski remained neutral, although during the ensuing months he grew increasingly hostile to the virtual dictatorship of Pilsudski. By 1928, completely disillusioned with the Pilsudski regime and the conservative slant of Polish politics, Sikorski retired from active service and left the Polish political scene.

After abandoning Warsaw, he moved to Paris and began an active writing career. During his ten-year, self-imposed exile, Sikorski devoted himself to the study of military tactics and produced three reputable volumes on the art of war. His first book, *The Polish-Russian Campaign* (1928), simply analyzed the events of the 1919–20 Polish victory. Only three years later, he produced an analysis of the peace treaties of World War I in *The Problems of the Peace* (1931). In 1935, Sikorski released his final volume, *Modern Warfare,* before returning to his native Poland and making his home at both a country estate near Poznan and his flat in Warsaw.

Sikorski soon realized the growing threat Nazi Germany posed for Poland and all of Europe. As early as November 1937, he recorded his thoughts on the rise of German power and the unfortunate state of Polish affairs:

> Even Hungary is alive to the dangers of German hegemony in Europe. She is doing what she can to avert this prospect and spoil Berlin's game. Can it be that the Poles are the only ones who are blind to all this?

Following the completion of the Nazi occupation of Czechoslovakia in March 1939, the General wrote in his diary of the ill-fated policies of the Polish government:

> The Soviets are also suspicious of the present government. They have been asking London and Paris who will give them a guarantee that a Poland militarily reinforced with their material help will not one day join up with Germany in a march against Russia. Here the warped policy we have followed toward Russia is coming home to roost. Meanwhile [Poland's foreign minister] Beck wants to hedge his bets and believes he can still come to terms with Hitler.

Although Sikorski rightly proclaimed the threat of German expansionism, the Polish leaders ignored his suggestions and his prophesies of German imperialism.

As the Germans invaded Poland in September 1939, Sikorski offered his considerable military talents to Marshal Edward Smigly-Rydz; the Polish commander in chief, however, conveniently found no position in the Polish army for Sikorski. After being refused a command, Sikorski left Poland in an attempt to raise a Polish army abroad. He quickly gathered a volunteer detachment of Polish workers and miners in Paris, France. As Poland collapsed under the German advance, Sikorski was nominated premier of the Polish provisional government and formed a cabinet on September 30, 1939. A few weeks later, he was appointed commander in chief of all Polish forces.

Sikorski continued his enlistment drive. By the spring of 1940, he had built an army of 100,000 Poles in France. His troops fought magnificently against the German assault on France, but following the French surrender, they were forced to join the British and flee the continent for England. Only 24,000 Polish troops were successfully evacuated. By June 25, 1940, General Sikorski had established his new headquarters in London.

While in London, Sikorski established good relations with the Allied leaders and began organizing Polish forces around the world. In the summer of 1941, as the Soviet Union was being decimated by the German blitzkrieg, Sikorski took the opportunity to offer Polish assistance in return for a Polish-Soviet alliance and recognition of pre-1939 Polish borders. He also secured the release of all living Polish soldiers captured in the Russian advance of 1939. The relationship between Sikorski and **Joseph Stalin** slowly deteriorated, and in 1943, Soviet-Polish relations were destroyed by the Polish demand for a Red Cross investigation of Soviet atrocities against some 4,000 Polish officers at Katyn Forest.

Soon after the discovery of the mass graves in the Katyn Forest, General Sikorski went to the Middle East to inspect the large concentration of Polish troops training in the area. Just before leaving Cairo, he told his troops that he would be in command "of the first troops to enter Poland." Within a few days, however, on July 4, 1943, Sikorski died in a plane crash off the coast of Gibraltar as he returned from his tour of the Middle East. The *Times* of London promptly paid tribute to the fallen leader:

Unswervingly since 1939—through all difficulties and sorrows of his position—he sought to serve Poland by serving the cause of allied unity. In his mind the two causes were one, indissoluble; without allied unity there could be no allied victory, and without allied victory Poland could not rise again.

SOURCES:

Kleczkowski, Stefan. *Poland's First 100,000: The story of the rebirth of the Polish Army, Navy and Air Force after the September campaign, together with a biographical note about its creator General Sikorski.* Hutchinson & Company, 1943.

Sikorski, Wladyslaw. "General Sikorski's 1936–9 Diary (extracts)," translated by Edward Rothert. *Polish Perspectives,* May 1970: 26–42.

Terry, Sarah Meiklejohn. *Poland's Place in Europe: General Sikorski and the Origin of the Oder-Neisse Line, 1939–1943.* Princeton University Press, 1983.

Times. London, July 5, 1943–July 10, 1943.

Wapinski, Roman. *Wladyslaw Sikorski.* Wiedza Powszechna, 1978.

FURTHER READING:

Huddleston, Sisley. *Those Europeans: Studies of Foreign Faces.* Putnam, 1924.

Irving, David. *Accident: The Death of General Sikorski.* William Kimber, 1967.

Sikorski, Wladyslaw. *Modern Warfare: Its Character, Its Problems.* Hutchinson & Company, 1942.

Strumph-Wojtkiewicz, Stanislaw. *Gwiazda Wladyslawa Sikorskiego.* Czytelnik, 1946.

Solon

(638 B.C.–558 B.C.)

Acclaimed lawgiver of ancient Athens, who outlawed slavery for native citizens, guaranteed equal treatment in the courts of law, and set the standards for the world's first great democracy.

Name variations: Solon, son of Execestides (sometimes incorrectly called son of Euphorion). Born about 638 B.C., perhaps on the island of Salamis; died about 558 B.C., possibly on the island of Cyprus; son of the Athenian noble Execestides (a descendant of Codrus, last king of Athens); his mother's name is unknown; married: unknown; children: unknown. Predecessor: The position of archon was filled annually by election, and his immediate predecessor is unknown. Successor: After Solon, there was a chaotic period; within the next nine years, the archonship was twice left vacant, and one archon, Damasias, held onto the office illegally for two years and two months.

The future Athenian lawgiver Solon was born into a noble but impoverished family called the Medontids who claimed descent from Codrus, the last king of Athens. According to legend, Codrus had sacrificed himself to save the city from Dorian invaders some 500 years before. Solon's mother, whose name has been lost to history, was a cousin of the mother of the future tyrant, Pisistratus. His father Execestides had reportedly lost the family fortune as a result of his generosity to friends. But Solon became a successful merchant, living comfortably on his own income. By the time he came to a position of prominence in government, Solon could understand and sympathize with all levels of the Athenian citizenry.

Also admired as a poet, Solon left the best profile of himself in his poetry, some of which was quoted at length by later authors. The verses that are extant are political in nature, but it was said that in his younger days he wrote less didactic works, such as love poetry, as well.

During Solon's childhood, Athens experienced severe political turmoil as the Athenian nobleman Cylon seized the Acropolis in an

"Savior of his country and the ideal lawgiver."

ARISTOTLE

Contributed by J. Donald Hughes, Professor of History, University of Denver, Denver, Colorado

attempt to make himself tyrant of Athens. Having married the daughter of Theagenes, tyrant of the neighboring city of Megara, Cylon had Megarian help in this unsuccessful coup. Although Cylon managed to escape from the city, his followers were not so fortunate and were executed despite a promise to spare them. This incident of civic violence was only symptomatic of a deeper conflict between the Eupatrids, a group of aristocratic families who controlled the government, and the rest of Athens's citizens.

The dissatisfaction of the middle class with the self-serving administration of justice by the Eupatrids led to the appointment of Draco (Dracon) as a special legislator with the duty of writing a new law code for the city. His laws were very strict—even minor crimes such as stealing cabbage were punishable by death—leading the later orator Demades to remark that Draco's laws "were written not in ink, but in blood."

When the Megarians captured the Athenian island of Salamis (which is closer to Megara than to Athens) around 600 B.C., Solon used his poetry to urge fellow citizens to "go to Salamis and fight... and wipe away our shame." Heeding his own advice, he served as general in the war that recovered Salamis. It was said that his kinsman Pisistratus served with him in the campaign; if that is true, the future tyrant was then very young. Tradition also connects Solon with the Athenian participation in the First Sacred War, fought in defense of free travel to the oracle of Apollo at Delphi.

The beginning of the sixth century B.C. saw the land of Attica, the home territory of Athens, in both economic and political distress. The aristocratic government had failed to meet the needs of the people in a time of economic, military, and social change, leading to conflict between poor and rich. Many poorer citizens had been reduced to a form of serfdom as tenant farmers called *hektemoroi*, who had to give their landowners one sixth of their produce each year. Many of the common people fell deeply into debt. Since their persons were security for loans from their patrons, they were sold into slavery to pay off a portion of their indebtedness. Before that happened, some of them first sold their children into slavery. Thus divided into hostile camps, the city was on the brink of revolution.

Solon Begins Year of Sweeping Reforms

This was the landscape into which Solon stepped as *Nomothetes*, or lawgiver. As Plutarch wrote, "The most level-headed of the Athenians began to look toward Solon," who was asked to adjudicate

between the two bitterly divided sides. Since the end of the monarchy, nine *archons* ("leaders")—elected annually and ineligible to succeed themselves—were part of Athens's government. The most important of these was the *Eponymous Archon,* the civil executive head of government, after whom the year was named; this was the post to which Solon was elected in 594 B.C. The other *archons* included the *Archon Basileus,* or "king," whose functions were mostly religious and who had no royal power; the *Polemarch,* or war leader, a military commander; and six *Thesmothetae,* or law keepers, who served as judicial officials. While Solon's task of reorganizing the city and drafting a new law code was unique and not part of the ordinary duties of the *Eponymous Archon,* he avoided tyranny. Plutarch tells us, "He was concerned above all with applying morals to politics."

Solon's reforms were sweeping, affecting most areas of the city's life, but they may be divided into three classes: economic measures, political reforms, and miscellaneous enactments. Among his economic measures was a debt cancellation called the *seisachtheia,* or the "shaking off of burdens." This measure applied to loans made with land as security and provided that small farmers would no longer lose their land to rich creditors. The inscribed stones called *horoi,* previously placed on the land to indicate that the land was mortgaged, were uprooted as a sign of this new freedom. One of Solon's poems celebrated that act:

> I call to witness at the judgment seat of time one
> who is noblest, mother of Olympian divinities,

and greatest of them all, Black Earth. I took away the mortgage stones stuck in her breast, and she, who went a slave before, is now set free.

In addition, Solon outlawed debts with persons as security, effectively abolishing debt slavery. He also sent out agents to recover Athenians who had been sold into slavery elsewhere, asserting, "Into this sacred land, our Athens, I brought back a throng of those who had been sold, some by due law, though others wrongly;... These I set free."

Solon encouraged and regulated trade and production. He standardized the measures of weight and volume. Athenian coinage was revalued from a mina worth 70 drachmas to one worth 100 drachmas. This meant a change from the coinage standard of the Dorian island of Aegina, a rival of Athens, to the standard of Euboea, an Ionian ally and trade partner. Particularly important was a law mandating that only olive oil, and no other agricultural crops, could be exported. This measure was intended to keep valuable food grains at home and to encourage trade in Attica's most plentiful agricultural surplus product. Solon encouraged manufacturing, including the pottery industry that produced the ceramic ware in which the olive oil was shipped. To protect domestic animals, bounties were set on predators: for example, five drachmas were paid for a wolf (other sources indicate that a wolf-killer had to provide for the honorable burial of the animal). To expand irrigation and horticulture, he regulated the digging of wells and urged the planting of trees, especially olive trees. Evidently, the results of these measures were positive, as Athens would grow and prosper in the century after Solon.

Realizing "how many evils a city suffers from Bad Government and how Good Government displays all neatness and order," Solon enacted many political reforms as well. His legislation repealed the capital punishment set by the Draconian laws, except in cases of murder. The old family-based tribes (called Hoplites, Ergadeis, Gelontes, and Aigikoreis), whose structure had supported the previous aristocratic government of the Eupatrids, were supplemented by four classes based on wealth, thus allowing greater participation in government by the affluent middle class and, to a certain extent, making social mobility possible. The new classes were: the *Pentacosiomedimni*, or "Five-Hundred-Bushel Men," composed of citizens with an annual income equivalent to at least 500 measures of grain; the *Hippeis*, or "Knights," with an income worth between 300 and 500 bushels, who could presumably afford to keep horses; the *Zeugitai*, or "Teamsters," with income between 200 and

300 bushels, who could afford a yoke of oxen; and finally the laboring class called *Thetes*, with income under 200 bushels, which included those with no property at all. This reorganization opened governmental positions to wealthy citizens, rather than just the Eupatrids. The *thetes* were given the privileges of attending the *Ecclesia* ("Assembly") and sitting on juries but were not otherwise permitted to hold office.

The constitutional structure of government was altered. Solon created a Council of Four Hundred which took over some of the functions of an older aristocratic council called the *Areopagus*. The new council was composed of 100 members from each of the four tribes and had the duty of preparing the agenda for discussion in the *Ecclesia*. *Archons* and other magistrates were to be chosen by lot ("a chance drawing of names") from candidates selected by the four tribes. While using a lottery to select public officials may seem strange today, it was then considered democratic, since it gave each candidate an equal chance to serve; election with voting by name, on the other hand, was believed to favor the rich. Another provision that might appear odd by today's standards required every citizen to take sides in a time of civil strife. The ancient Athenians did not believe that citizens who tried to be non-political were "minding their own business," but were avoiding their public responsibilities. Solon also allowed naturalization of foreigners who came to Athens to live and to carry on a trade, a provision that would encourage the economic growth of Athens as well as broaden the political base.

Finally, Solon's miscellaneous enactments included laws regulating marriages and wills and prohibiting the abuse of the dead or the living. There were also sumptuary laws ("laws forbidding excessive public display of wealth"); these applied especially to women, limiting their adornments, what they could carry, and where they could go.

All of Solon's laws were set up in the *Agora* ("marketplace") of Athens, inscribed on *axones*, or *kurbeis*, boards that could be revolved for the reading of both sides. Every year, according to Aristotle, "the nine Archons... regularly affirmed by an oath... that they would dedicate a golden statue if they ever should be found to have transgressed one of the laws."

Moves Athens Toward Democracy

Aristotle also emphasized the most democratic of Solon's reforms: (1) the abolishment of debt slavery; (2) a provision enabling any citizen to undertake action in court for someone who has been wronged; and (3) the right of appeal to a jury court. Solon certainly moved the constitution of Athens in a democratic direction. He did not, however, create a full democracy. Rather, as his writings attest, he achieved a mixed government that balanced the interests of rich and poor:

> I gave the people as much privilege as they have a right to: I neither degraded them from rank nor gave them a free hand; and for those who already held the power and were envied for money, I worked it out that they also should have no cause for complaint. I stood there holding my sturdy shield over both the parties; I would not let either side win a victory that was wrong. Thus would the people be best off, with the leaders they follow: neither given excessive freedom nor put to restraint.... Acting where issues are great, it is hard to please all.

After receiving a promise from the people of Athens that they would obey his laws for at least ten years, Solon left the city to travel abroad, perhaps wishing to avoid constant requests to amend his decrees. He went to Egypt, where, according to Plato, he heard the tale of the lost continent of Atlantis. On Cyprus, he is said to have been honored by having a city (Soli) named after him. Herodotus credited him with a visit to Lydia and a conversation with King Croesus that appears impossible on chronological grounds, as Croesus's reign began in 560 B.C. According to Herodotus, Croesus—the richest man in the world—asked Solon to name the happiest man he had ever met or heard of, expecting Solon to choose Croesus himself. Instead, Solon recalled an Athenian citizen who had died in battle, and two Argives who received death as a gift after pulling the chariot of their mother, a priestess of Hera, to a festival. Solon's point—that the happiness of a human life may not be judged until it is over—did not escape Croesus's anger.

Returning to Athens, Solon discovered that while his reforms had satisfied some citizens, there were many yet unsatisfied. The citizens had splintered into three parties based on economic interests and family loyalty. The first group of moderates was called the Party of the Shore; the second group of reactionaries, including most of the Eupatrids, was the Party of the Plain; and the third group of radicals was the Party of the Hill. Pisistratus, as champion of the common people, became the head of the Party of the Hill, and in 561 B.C., he seized power. Solon, seeing his life's work apparently being swept away, broke with his kinsman and former good friend, whose tyranny he then opposed. Some authors record that Solon left Athens to live in Cyprus for the last months or years of his life. After his death in approximately 558 B.C., his bones were returned to Salamis, the island he had recovered for Athens and which may have been his native land.

Pisistratus kept Solon's laws nominally in effect through much of the sixth century, although he ran the state as a benevolent despot. From 508 to 507 B.C., Cleisthenes modified the constitution so as to make Athens a true democracy, at least insofar as the citizens were concerned. Solon was remembered in Athens in the fifth and fourth centuries B.C. as having been the greatest of lawgivers. Both liberals and conservatives appealed to his authority for their own programs. With so great a reputation, the story of his life rapidly took on the quality of political myth, so that accounts written of him in ancient times offer an indistinguishable line between history and legend.

SOURCES:

Aristotle. *Aristotle's Constitution of Athens and Related Texts.* Translated by Kurt von Fritz and Ernst Kapp. Hafner, 1964.

Herodotus. *The Histories.* Translated by Aubrey de Selincourt. Revised by A. R. Burn. Penguin, 1972.

Plutarch. "Life of Solon," in *The Rise and Fall of Athens: Nine Greek Lives.* Translated by Ian Scott-Kilvert. Penguin, 1960.

Solon of Athens. "Poems," in *Greek Lyrics.* 2nd edition. Translated by Richmond Lattimore. University of Chicago, 1960.

FURTHER READING:

Forrest, W. G. *The Emergence of Greek Democracy.* McGraw-Hill, 1970.

Freeman, Kathleen. *The Work and Life of Solon: With a Translation of his Poems.* University of Wales, 1926.

Linforth, Ivan M. *Solon the Athenian.* University of California, 1919.

Woodhouse, William John. *Solon the Liberator.* Octagon, 1965.

Madame de Staël

(1766–1817)

French activist, whose portrayal of Napoleon Bonaparte as an opportunistic and emotionally cold ruler who threatened to banish liberty from the continent made her the most politically influential woman of her time.

Name variation: Madame de Staël-Holstein; Germaine. Pronunciation: Duh-STAHL. Born Anne-Louise-Germaine Necker in Paris, France, on April 22, 1766; died in 1817; only child of Jacques Necker (a Genevan banker who served as finance minister to the French monarch Louis XVI, whose reign was ended by the French Revolution of 1789) and Suzanne Curchod (daughter of a Swiss-French Calvinist minister); married: Baron Erik de Staël-Holstein, January 14, 1786 (marriage ended by formal separation agreement in 1797); children: August, Albert, and Albertine (allegedly fathered by a lover, Benjamin Constant); after her death, it was announced that she was secretly married on October 10, 1816, to Albert de Rocca, a Swiss army officer; a son, named Louis-Alphonse, had been born in 1812.

It has been said that Madame de Staël was an intellect in the service of a passion, but the passion was not love; it was the preservation of liberty and free speech. From 1800 to 1815, as the French armies of Emperor **Napoleon Bonaparte** swept across Europe, no individual was as influential in shaping European public opinion as was Madame de Staël. Intelligent, articulate, and energetic, she traveled throughout the courts of Europe, portraying Napoleon as a tyrant who had suppressed freedom of speech in France and who threatened all of Europe with dictatorship. Her free-ranging lifestyle and assertive personality were rare for a woman of her time. Fiercely independent, she allowed her parents to arrange her first marriage—to the Swedish ambassador to France—but for the rest of her life, she charted her own courageous course.

Born into a Swiss Calvinist family, de Staël was intimidated by her stern mother but adored her doting father, a respected banker who eventually became finance minister of France. She came to share her father's interest in politics; when she was 12 years old, France intervened in the American war of independence against Britain, helping

Contributed by Niles Holt, Professor of History, Illinois State University, Normal-Bloomington, Illinois

"Madame," the general informed the lady in question, "I do not want women mixed up in politics."

"You are perfectly right," came the reply, "but in a country where their heads are cut off, it is only natural for them to want to know why."

EXCHANGE BETWEEN
NAPOLEON BONAPARTE AND
MADAME DE STAËL

the Americans end their status as a British colony. De Staël followed the events of the American Revolution with an intense interest; she memorized terms such as "constitution" and "liberty" while imagining the English government as a tyrannical power, holding captive an American nation determined to be liberated. At age 14, she wrote an article on a major political book of the time, Baron Charles de Montesquieu's *Spirit of Laws*.

After her father was named finance minister of French king **Louis XVI** in 1776, de Staël was a witness to many of the elaborate ceremonies of the royal government, particularly the 1789 opening of the Estates General, the representative body called into session to help solve problems in government finances. She shared her father's belief that France needed tax reforms which would require the nobility to pay a higher share of government expenses.

Her father's ideas were not popular with the queen, **Marie-Antoinette,** and the queen was also not impressed with his daughter, whom she described as stumbling and undignified. Necker was fired in 1781. (He was rehired in 1788 when financial troubles worsened.) In 1784, Necker purchased a château distant from Paris, at Coppet, Switzerland; it would be a retreat for his daughter during the rest of her life, a protective cocoon when she was periodically banned or declared unwelcome in Paris.

De Staël Weds Swedish Ambassador

In an era when arranged marriages were considered an important parental duty, de Staël's parents struggled to find her a suitable husband. Eligible men were interested: contemporaries observed that she was not beautiful but "she talks well, and her talk has so much charm that she makes you believe she is beautiful." As Calvinists in Catholic France, the Neckers sought a suitable Protestant for their independently minded daughter, who—not easily pleased—tended to intimidate potential husbands.

The eventual marriage—to Baron Erik de Staël-Holstein, Swedish ambassador to Paris—was no love match, but her new husband's occupation opened doors to the highest diplomatic circles of Europe; in turn, she advanced her husband's career by establishing one of the most famous literary and political salons in Paris. One major problem strained the marriage: de Staël was wealthier than her husband, who frequently was heavily in debt. The marriage ended with a formal separation in 1797.

De Staël would later become the mistress of Louis de Narbonne, a minister of King Louis XVI,

CHRONOLOGY

1776	Necker named finance minister to Louis XVI; favored increased taxes on nobility
1788	Necker reappointed royal finance minister; Louis XVI called Estates General into session
1789	French Revolution began; Paris mob stormed the Bastille; nobility began to flee; Third Estate took charge of the Estates General
1793	Execution of Louis XVI ordered by the National Assembly; de Staël in Coppet
1794–95	Reign of Terror
1802–10	De Staël published works to rally opposition to Napoleon
1804	Napoleon crowned emperor of France
1813	First defeat of Napoleon's armies by a European coalition
1815	Second defeat of Napoleon's armies, near Waterloo, Belgium; Napoleon abdicated
1817	De Staël died

and still later the mistress of the French writer and politician Benjamin Constant, who was apparently the father of her third child. When Constant challenged Narbonne to a duel, she intervened to prevent it. In 1816, at the age of 44, she would marry Albert de Rocca, a Swiss army officer who was 21 years her junior. The couple would nickname Louis-Alphonse, the child born to them before the marriage, *Petit Nous* ("Little Us"), though the marriage would not be officially announced until de Staël's will was read after her death.

When the French Revolution of 1789 began, she at first acquired a reputation for favoring Jacobinism (an "extreme" political movement which sought to abolish the monarchy), but she eventually accepted the more moderate view of retaining a limited monarchy. She attended regular sessions of the National Assembly, the French legislative body established during the Revolution which eventually approved the execution of King Louis XVI. De Staël proved to be a perceptive commentator on the political scene: the king of Sweden commented that he preferred her reports on the proceedings to those of anyone else.

The violence of the Revolution alarmed her, particularly what she believed to be the persecution of the nobility. She agreed with American diplomat Gouverneur Morris, who told her that "the French have moved beyond liberty." During massacres, she courageously appeared on the streets of

Paris, attempting to save members of the nobility from mob violence. She even spoke of buying land near the seaport city of Dieppe, hoping to save victims of the Revolution from execution by guillotine. She planned to transport them to safety there, two or three at a time, in the guise of being her traveling companions and relatives.

Unfortunately, her actions, taken in the name of humanity, made her suspect to all parties in the French Revolution. Despite her insistence that she hoped for "a republic as the sole form of government which will not dishonor France," she was denounced as a Swiss meddler in French affairs "who should be sent back to where she came from without delay."

When she admitted that she had met with aristocrats who were banished from France, she was denounced in the Paris press for her activities. The Committee of Public Safety, which ruled during the most violent period of the Revolution, the so-called "Reign of Terror," threatened to banish her. Her first husband (de Staël-Holstein) intervened, protecting her with diplomatic immunity, and she retreated for a brief time to Sweden. During 1793 and 1794, she went to Coppet, where she drew visits from many of the leading intellectuals and diplomats of Europe, including Romantic writer Vicomte François Chateaubriand.

The rise to power of Napoleon Bonaparte, who was declared emperor in 1804, brought her back to France. Alternately fascinated and repelled by Napoleon, de Staël recognized him as a new type of monarch. Napoleon, a contemporary observed, expected enemies and knew how to deal with them, but he did not know how to deal with a political woman. When Napoleon and de Staël met, they frequently sparred verbally. De Staël noted that Napoleon often enjoyed directing rude comments to females; "therefore, before I [was to meet] him, I would write a series of tart and sharp answers in advance."

She did not like what she saw: "Far from being reassured, the more I saw of Napoleon Bonaparte, the more alarmed I became…. [H]e is a man without emotions," and also, "a calculating chess player" for whom people were either "facts or objects." "Every time I listened to him I was impressed by his intelligence," she observed. She added that whenever Napoleon realized that anyone was staring at him, "he extinguished the last sign of life in his eyes…. At such times there would be no expression on his face but a vague smile, confusing anyone who hoped to read his mind." Even when she was banished to Coppet, as frequently happened, Napoleon recognized her as a troublesome adversary. "They say," he observed, "that she does not speak of politics or me; but how does it happen that all who speak to her come to like me less?"

Between 1802 and 1810, de Staël published books which were, in some way, designed to shake the basis of Napoleon's dictatorship. Two of the books—*Delphine* (1802) and *Corinne* (1807)— were novels that established her as one of the early Romantics in France. The former displeased Napoleon for its praise of England and Protestantism; it also discussed the subject of divorce at a time when Napoleon was considering divorcing his first wife Josephine and would have preferred that the topic not enter public discussion.

Napoleon's Government Bans Her Book

The book which brought the strongest reaction from the emperor, however, was her *De l'Allemagne (On Germany),* published in 1810. Though it contained no direct criticisms of Napoleon, the emperor condemned the work as anti-French because Germans were portrayed in sympathetic terms. Napoleon understood that the praise of Germany was, at least in part, a ploy to arouse German nationalism against his rule: the implication of the book was that the spirit of resistance against him would be found everywhere and that any attempt at a European dictatorship was futile. When Napoleon's government banned the book in France, de Staël attacked his "slavery of the press," observing that the action amounted to banning it on the entire continent, since other governments would hesitate to anger the French emperor. "Everything is controlled by one man," she noted, "and no person can take a step, or form a wish, without him. Not only liberty but free will seems banished from the earth."

Beginning in 1803, de Staël journeyed throughout Europe. She used her travels to encourage resistance to the French emperor, whose armies were beginning a triumphant march across much of Europe. She visited Germany in 1803 and 1804, cultivating a friendship with the German translator and critic August Wilhelm von Schlegel, who became a frequent companion after 1804.

A tour in 1813 of Austria, Russia, Finland, Sweden, and England gave her the opportunity to argue, before royal courts all over Europe, that it was important for nations to rise up against the dictatorship in France, "the very country which has introduced the spirit of liberty to the world." In Russia, she met Tsar **Alexander I,** whom

Napoleon had ridiculed, and called him a well-informed man of real intellect; she wept when school girls recited passages from her writings, and she was outraged when she heard that a Russian audience had booed the presentation of a classic French play.

In England, she dined with the **Duke of Wellington,** and the poet Lord Byron, but she was ultimately disappointed that the English were not inclined to move quickly against Napoleon. The English in turn were offended by her spirited defense of the former American colonies and her criticisms of the British army for burning the White House in the War of 1812. She told her hosts that "old and free England should be inspired with admiration by the progress of America."

The final defeat of Napoleon, in 1815 at the battle of Waterloo, brought her back to Paris. She returned slowly, saying she did not want to seem to "follow in the tracks of conquerors." Her role in helping defeat Napoleon was widely recognized. "There are," a contemporary insisted, "only three powers left in Europe—Russia, England, and Madame de Staël." She praised foreigners for "having broken the yoke" of Napoleonic rule but was sad to return to a France dominated by foreign armies. The sight of Russian Cossack troops on the streets of Paris proved depressing.

Despite her humanitarian work during the French Revolution, she was treated coldly by the nobility who had returned to France, as well as by the new monarch, Louis XVIII. They remembered that she had supported the Revolution, even if she had condemned its violence. She lived only two years following Napoleon's defeat. By coincidence, de Staël died in Paris on July 14, 1817—Bastille Day—the day commemorating one of the first events of the French Revolution.

SOURCES:

Andrews, Wayne. *Germaine: A Portrait of Madame de Staël.* Atheneum, 1963.

Herold, J. C. *Mistress to an Age: A Life of Madame de Staël.* Bobbs-Merrill, 1958.

de Staël-Holstein, Baroness Germaine. *Ten Years' Exile.* Centaur Press, 1968.

Stevens, Abel. *Madame de Staël: A Study of Her life and Times.* Harper and Brothers, 1881.

FURTHER READING:

Forsberg, Roberta. *Madame de Staël and the English.* Astra Books, 1967.

de Pange, Victor, ed. *The Unpublished Correspondence of Madame de Staël and the Duke of Wellington.* Translated by Harold Kurtz. The Humanities Press, 1966.

West, Anthony. *Mortal Wounds.* McGraw-Hill, 1973.

Joseph Stalin

(1879–1953)

One of the most ruthless dictators in modern history, who built the Soviet Union into an industrialized nation and a dominant world power, but whose brutal regime sacrificed millions of human lives.

Name variations: Josef; as a revolutionary, Stalin used 37 aliases and cover names; he first used "Stalin"—meaning "man of steel"—in 1913. Born Iossif Vissarionovich Djugashvili on December 9, 1879 (this date corresponds to the Julian calendar, used in Russia until 1917; by the Gregorian calendar, his birthdate is December 21) in Georgia, a small country between the Black and Caspian seas, incorporated into the Russian Empire in 1801; died March 5, 1953, in his country home near Moscow; son of Vissarion Ivanovich (a cobbler) and Ekaterina Geladzea (a peasant woman born a serf); married: Ekaterina (Keke) Svanidze (died, 1907); married: Nadezhda Allilueva (committed suicide on November 8, 1932); children: (first marriage) one son, Yasha or Yakov; (second marriage) one son, Vasily, and one daughter, Svetlana Alilueva, who has written several books about life with her father. Predecessor: Vladimer Ilych Ulyanov, or Lenin. Successor: Nikita Khrushchev.

Stalin was born in a two-room hut in the small Georgian village of Gori. The Djugashvili family was poor, and Joseph—or "Soso"—was the only child of four to survive. His father, a shoemaker, drank excessively and died in a bar-room brawl when "Soso" was only 11 years old. His mother was a pious, hard-working woman who wanted her son to be educated and eventually enter the priesthood. Through her efforts, he attended the elementary school run by the Orthodox Church, where he was a top student; he loved to read, especially tales of legendary Georgian heroes. According to a childhood friend, Stalin's favorite was the story of a mountain bandit and rebel named "Koba"; the young boy "wanted to become another Koba, a fighter and hero as famous as he." Later, as a young revolutionary, he took Koba as his first secret name.

In 1894, Stalin received a scholarship to enter the Orthodox theological seminary in Tbilisi, the major city in Georgia, but he was not happy there. He later told a journalist that he became a rebel in reaction to its "humiliating regime." With other students, he joined secret study groups opposed to the Russian tsarist government. They

---

Contributed by Elaine McClarnand, Ph.D. candidate in history, Emory University, Atlanta, Georgia

"The triumph of one man turned into the tragedy of an entire nation."

DMITRI VOLKOGONOV

discussed the radical ideas of the German writer **Karl Marx,** who depicted history as a struggle between classes. Marx forecast a future revolution led by workers which would result in a more just society organized along communal principles. By his fourth year, Stalin had joined the first Marxist group in Georgia, the "Mesame Dasi." Expelled in 1899, he left the seminary totally devoted to the revolution and to Marxism, with, as historian Robert Tucker explains, "a grim and bitter hatred against the school administration, the bourgeoisie [middle class], and all that... represented tsarism."

For the next 18 years, Stalin was a "professional revolutionary" living and working in the underground. Always on the move, from 1899 to 1917 he had only one fixed address besides jail or Siberia. He wrote articles for Marxist newspapers, organized strikes, and worked as a propagandist among industrial workers in Transcaucasia (Armenia, Georgia, Azerbaijan). Stalin excelled at conspiratorial tasks and reportedly organized a number of notorious bank robberies, known as "expropriations," designed to raise funds and destabilize the tsarist regime.

By 1901, Stalin was a member of the illegal Russian Social Democratic Party. Two years later, when the Party split into two factions, Stalin supported the more radical Bolsheviks, led by V.I. **Lenin.** He liked Lenin's militancy and his conception of the Party as a tightly organized core of trained revolutionaries. Unlike most Georgian Marxists, Stalin steadfastly promoted the Bolshevik line. By 1912, he caught the attention of Lenin, who was now trying to establish his faction as an independent party. Meeting with supporters in Prague, Lenin formed a new executive organ, known as the Central Committee, and co-opted Stalin into it. Stalin's career as a revolutionary, however, was disrupted eight times by arrest. Six times he managed to escape. Finally, in February 1913, he was sent to a remote area of northcentral Siberia where escape was impossible; he spent the next four years north of the Arctic Circle, quietly fishing and hunting.

During his exile, Russia experienced a revolution. Weakened by four long years of war, the tsarist regime collapsed in February 1917. Having lost all support, Tsar **Nicholas II** abdicated the throne. Parliamentary leaders established a Provisional Government to maintain control until a new constitution could be written.

For Stalin, as for Russia, the events of 1917 were a turning point. He began the year as a convicted prisoner, but by its end he was a government minister with an office in the Kremlin, the former

CHRONOLOGY

1903	Lenin formed Bolshevik faction of the Russian Social-Democratic Party
1914–18	World War I; Stalin exiled in Siberia
1917	February Revolution in St. Petersburg; Nicholas abdicated; moderate Provisional Government formed; October Revolution; Bolshevik Party overthrew the Provisional Government; Stalin appointed commissar of Nationality Affairs
1918–21	Civil War in Russia
1922	Stalin elected general secretary of the Communist Party
1924	Death of Lenin
1929	Stalin triumphant in leadership struggle; launched "Revolution from Above"
1934–39	"The Great Terror"
1939	Germany invaded Poland; WWII
1941	Germany launched surprise attack against the Soviet Union; Stalin led Soviet armed forces
1945	Allied powers (U.S., Great Britain, France, and the Soviet Union) defeated Germany; conferences held at Yalta and Potsdam
1945–49	Communist governments arose in Eastern and Central Europe
1953	Stalin died of a brain hemorrhage

fortress of the tsars. In March 1917, freed by an amnesty, Stalin hastened back to Petrograd (formerly St. Petersburg), the capital city. He took over as chief editor of the main Bolshevik newspaper *Pravda* and recaptured a place in the Party's Central Committee.

Stalin's role in 1917 was important, though not heroic. One observer even referred to him as a "gray blur, looming up now and then dimly and not leaving any trace." He did not go out into the streets, man barricades, or rally workers, peasants, and soldiers. He was not a popular or charismatic leader who stirred crowds with his oratory, as fellow revolutionary **Leon Trotsky** did. Stalin preferred to work within Party committees and became special assistant to Lenin for "delicate assignments" where he utilized his astuteness, reliability, and conspiratorial skills. In October, when the Bolsheviks, led by Trotsky, seized power in the name of the *soviets* (popular governing councils formed in 1917), Stalin's part was minor or nonexistent. But he did receive a post in the new government as commissar of Nationality Affairs (the Bolsheviks preferred the term *commissar* rather than *minister,* which they considered too bourgeois. Over the next five years, his main task was to help design the federal structure of the Soviet Union.

By 1918, Russia was embroiled in a brutal Civil War that lasted until 1921. For Stalin, the period marked his first involvement in military affairs. Though he never commanded troops, he traveled to many fronts as a military advisor and administrative troubleshooter. His participation left a deep impression on him; for the rest of his life, his customary dress was a military tunic and breeches stuffed into high-topped black boots.

The Bolshevik regime survived the Civil War, but it faced almost total economic collapse and extreme unrest, particularly among the peasants. Lenin had been forced in 1918 to institute harsh controls over agriculture and industry. To help rebuild the economy and quell revolt, in 1921 Lenin instituted the "New Economic Policy" (*NEP*), which legalized private enterprise in agriculture, trade, and light industry. But Lenin refused to allow other political parties, which he accused of being anti-socialist and thus "counter-revolutionary." The Soviet Union became a one-party state in which the real governing force was the Bolshevik Party, which changed its name to the Communist Party in 1918. Important decisions were made in Party committees, not in the *soviets.*

Emerges as New Leader of Communist Party

Lenin's death in 1924 set off a bitter struggle for succession. It was Stalin who emerged five years later as the new leader of the Communist Party. He had triumphed over four rivals, skillfully outmaneuvering them with acute political instincts and a driving ambition to be the "new Lenin." To reach the top, Stalin had turned the largely routine post of Party general secretary into the most powerful office in the Soviet Union. He had built a personal empire for himself through his control over committee appointments at all levels. Most importantly, he had expanded the leading Party organs with his supporters, who then voted against his rivals.

Throughout his life, Stalin had shown a tendency to be authoritarian, sullen, and harsh to colleagues, though this had not hurt his standing in the Party. But before he died, Lenin had clashed with Stalin on a number of issues. Growing uneasy over his personal characteristics, Lenin had written a letter to the Party advising that Stalin be transferred to another post:

After taking over the position of General Secretary, Comrade Stalin has accumulated in his hands immeasurable power and I am not certain whether he will always be able to use this power with the required care.... Stalin is excessively rude.

The Central Committee chose not to heed his warning. Many felt that Stalin's strong qualities outweighed the negative, and that the Party needed his determined will and tough, practical approach to the tasks of building socialism in the Soviet Union.

In his defeat of rivals Trotsky, G. Zinoviev, and Lev Kamenev, Stalin loudly condemned their call for rapid development of heavy industry and large-scale, *collectivized* or communal agriculture. But, in 1928, he adopted this strategy as his own. Nikolai Bukharin, who had allied with Stalin against the other rivals, now opposed him, arguing instead for the continuation of the New Economic Policy and a more gradual approach to industrialization. Stalin, however, correctly sensed that many in the Party were dissatisfied with the progress being made toward socialism. With their support, he ousted Bukharin and all other opponents from their posts.

Having won the leadership struggle, Stalin then proceeded to launch what some scholars term a "Revolution from Above." He pushed through policies which were much more extreme than most of his supporters expected. In agriculture, the Party sought control over grain supplies as a source of capital for industrialization. Stalin insisted that prosperous peasants (*kulaks*) be "liquidated," meaning executed or deported, and that all of the rest enter into state-controlled communal farms. Collectivization turned into a civil war as peasants resisted, often killing their livestock and burning their grain rather than surrendering their crops to the state. Stalin pursued the campaign relentlessly, despite a terrible famine in 1932–33. By 1936, 89.6% of the peasantry were collectivized, but at the cost of at least ten million lives.

Stalin abolished the *NEP* and nationalized all industry and trade. He instituted central planning, designed to rationalize production, but demanded growth rates that were impossibly high. As justification, he proclaimed that Russia had only a limited time to prepare itself for outside attack:

One feature of the history of old Russia was the continual beatings she suffered because of her backwardness.... We are fifty or one hundred

years behind the advanced countries.... We must make good this distance in ten years. Either we do it, or we shall go under.

The country joined in a frenzied but enthusiastic campaign to build new factories, cities, canals, and mines. Stalin exhorted them to produce more and more raw materials and engage in "socialist competition" to raise output. Those who took part, particularly young people, genuinely believed that they were building a new world. As a result, the Soviet Union did achieve industrialization within a remarkably short period. But Stalin's methods put an enormous strain upon the country and its resources.

To carry out these goals, Stalin expanded the Soviet state into an enormous bureaucratic structure, which regulated every aspect of economic, cultural, and social life. At the same time, Stalin's personal authority grew increasingly more powerful. He intervened in every sphere from the economy to linguistics. His pronouncements became the single authoritative guide in art, history, literature, philosophy, science, even architecture. Beginning in 1929, Stalin permitted the development of a "cult," a worshipful public adulation on a scale truly unmatched by any other leader in modern times. Books, poetry, movies, and newspapers compared him to the sun, moon, and stars. He was the "Lenin of today" and the "Genius of all mankind," who "didst give birth to man... who didst make fertile the earth."

Millions Caught in Reign of Terror

Behind Stalin's power lay a monstrous policy of terror. It reached its height between 1934 and 1939, when Stalin and his secret police carried out mass arrests, executions, and deportations. Stalin claimed that throughout the country traitors were masking as loyal citizens and Party cadres. Countless millions of innocent people perished or spent long years in forced labor camps. Victims included top Party and government elites, army officers, artists, writers, scientists, ordinary citizens, even children. From the Party's Central Committee, elected in 1934, 98 out of 139 members were shot. Of the 1,966 delegates to the 17th Party Congress in 1934, 1,108 were arrested.

Stalin played a direct and commanding role in the "Great Terror." There is strong evidence that in 1934 Stalin arranged the murder of Sergei Kirov, the Party chief in Leningrad (formerly Petrograd), which he then used as the pretext for the first wave of mass arrests. Stalin himself ordered or approved many of the arrests, particularly those of higher level Party and state officials. On just one day, December 12, 1938, a Soviet historian has revealed that "Stalin and Molotov signed about 30

British Prime Minister Winston Churchill, U.S. President Franklin D. Roosevelt, and Soviet leader Josef Stalin meet at the Yalta Conference in 1945.

lists whose overall content was 3,182 people condemned to death."

In 1939, arrests and executions began declining in number. Terror did not end, but it did subside. Stalin was now absolute dictator of the Soviet Union. Below him lay a subdued population and a docile party-state apparatus manned by a new generation who owed their positions to Stalin and his "blood purge."

The dictator's obsession with internal enemies did not keep him from attending to foreign affairs. He became increasingly concerned in the 1930s about Hitler's rise to power in Germany. Stalin did not trust Western "capitalist" nations and feared that Britain, France, and Germany would unite against the Soviet regime. After negotiations with Britain and France failed, he signed a nonaggression treaty with Hitler in 1939.

But on June 22, 1941, Hitler turned on his ally and invaded the Soviet Union. Initial Soviet losses were devastating, for Stalin ignored all warnings that an attack was pending. For nearly two weeks, Stalin secluded himself, apparently suffering a nervous breakdown. He reemerged, however, on July 3 to take personal command of the war effort, and in October 1941, with German troops at the gates of Moscow, he refused to leave the city, reportedly walking out among the people to restore confidence. Despite costly mistakes during the first two years of the war, Stalin matured into an effective strategist. He kept in touch with all fronts and made many day-to-day decisions.

In 1945, when Soviet armies reached Berlin, Stalin stood at the height of his power and fully shared in the glory of the victory. His generals awarded him the title *Generalissimus,* meaning "the very best general." During the war, he had insisted on conducting diplomacy himself. At the wartime conferences (Tehran, Yalta, and Potsdam), he won the respect of the Allied leaders **Roosevelt** and **C**hurchill and secured the status of the Soviet Union as a major world power.

Stalin lived for seven more years. Contrary to the hopes of many, peace did not bring any softening of his harsh dictatorship. In many ways, he ruled even more arbitrarily; he rarely convened Party organs, usually delegating tasks to one or two of his confederates. Several waves of repressions took place. Stalin sent returning prisoners of war directly into forced labor camps, calling them traitors for having surrendered. Whole nationalities, which he accused of treason, were deported and their national republics eliminated. Those arrested between 1945 and 1953 included the wives of two of his closest associates and his own sisters-in-law.

In January 1953, he announced discovery of a "plot" involving seven Kremlin doctors, including his personal physician who had taken care of him for years. He came to suspect that his own inner circle was plotting against him. Before his death, Stalin seems to have been planning to execute them and purge a substantial proportion of the Party. **Nikita Khrushchev,** his successor as general secretary, wrote in his memoirs that Stalin told him in 1951, "I'm finished. I do not trust anyone, not even myself."

The Cold War Begins

World affairs occupied much of his attention during this period. The postwar climate was tense and saw the beginning of an undeclared Cold War between the Soviet Union and United States. Stalin grew increasingly suspicious of the motives of his former Western allies. He saw the Soviet system as continuously imperiled by the capitalist states and reportedly told his lieutenants, "You'll see, when I'm gone the imperialist powers will wring your necks like chickens." To strengthen national security, Stalin extended Soviet control into Eastern and Central Europe. He supported the rise of Communist regimes in Poland, Bulgaria, Albania, Rumania, Yugoslavia, Hungary, and Czechoslovakia, then bound them economically, politically, and militarily to the Soviet Union. Relations with the West deteriorated as Stalin opposed Allied policies in Germany and in 1948 tried unsuccessfully to blockade the Western occupied zones in Berlin.

On the night of March 1, 1953, Stalin unexpectedly suffered a stroke and died three days later. The nation was stunned, and all over the country people wept. At his funeral, the press of mourners was so great that some were crushed to death. Many were unsure that the country could survive without him at the head.

But in time, the Soviet Union had to confront the reality of Stalin's brutal regime and its impact. In Adam Ulam's words:

> Even in his death Stalin hovers over contemporary Soviet reality. His memory is both a burden and a challenge to his successors and to the people over whom he reigned for more than a generation.

In 1956, at the 20th Party Congress, Nikita Khrushchev denounced Stalin as a "capricious and despotic" murderer who had committed crimes against the Party and people. His speech spurred a period of reform in which the Party altered many of the worst aspects of the Stalinist system. But after **Leonid Brezhnev** became Party leader in 1964, "de-Stalinization" came to end. Many people felt that criticism of Stalin was denigrating the achievements of the Soviet Union, which had become a world power under his rule. In 1985, the Soviet Union renewed the effort to confront Stalin and his tragic legacy, subjecting every aspect of his regime to public exposure and criticism.

Stalin was a complex figure. He had qualities that carried him to the heights of power and, once there, made him one of history's worst tyrants. He was cruel, malicious, and perhaps insane. The death toll from his regime may be as high as 30 or 40 million. But he was not simply a power-mad despot. He was an intelligent and pragmatic leader who mastered the art of domestic as well as international politics. Deeply committed to Marxism, he seemed to feel that the goals of the revolution could only be secured by terror and force. According to Khrushchev, Stalin believed he was acting "in the interest of the party, of the working masses.... In this lies the whole tragedy." Milovan Djilas, a former Yugoslavian Communist who met with Stalin, wrote that Stalin "was convinced that he was carrying out the will of history." Always conscious of Russian tradition, Stalin may have seen himself as the means necessary to lead a backward, illiterate nation surrounded by hostile capitalist powers to socialism and industrialization. He once praised the tsarist despot **Ivan the Terrible** as a "great and wise ruler who protected the country from the infiltration of foreign influence," which

Robert McNeal feels was a self-conscious appraisal of himself. In Robert Tucker's view, Stalin's actions arose from a deep psychological need to be seen as a revolutionary hero equal to Lenin.

Such analyses of Stalin and his motivations cannot be definitive. Many questions remain unanswered. But his significance is unquestionable and the attempt to make sense of his tragic life and legacy will continue.

SOURCES:

Cohen, Stephen. "The Stalin Question Since Stalin," in *Rethinking the Soviet Experience.* Oxford University Press, 1985.

Khrushchev, Nikita. *The Crimes of the Stalin Era.* The New Leader, 1962.

Laquer, Walter. *Stalin: The Glasnost Revelations.* Scribner, 1990.

Lewis, Jonathon, and Phillip Whitehead. *Stalin: A Time for Judgment.* Pantheon, 1990.

McNeal, Robert. *Stalin: Man and Ruler.* Macmillan, 1988.

Medvedev, Roy. *Let History Judge.* Columbia University Press, 1989.

Tucker, Robert. *Stalin as Revolutionary.* Norton, 1973.

Ulam, Adam. *Stalin, the Man and His Era.* Expanded ed. Beacon Press, 1989.

FURTHER READING:

Conquest, Robert. *The Great Terror: A Reassessment.* Oxford University Press, 1990.

Deutscher, Isaac. *Stalin, a Political Biography.* 2nd ed. Oxford University Press, 1966.

Urban, G. *Stalinism.* St. Martin's Press, 1982.

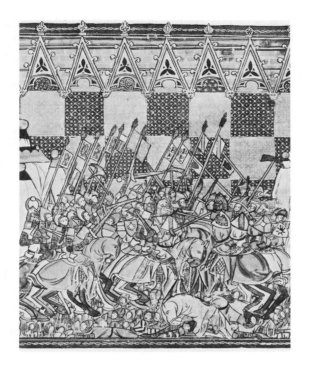

Stephen of Cloyes

(fl. 1212)

French shepherd boy of the early 13th century and semilegendary leader of the Children's Crusade, who thought Jesus had commanded him to go on crusade for the salvation of the Holy Land.

In the year 1212, Stephen of Cloyes was the leader of the "Children's Crusade," one of the most bizarre incidents in medieval history. Very few details are known about his life, and, like his English contemporary Robin Hood, he stands on the brink of legend rather than history. The earliest chroniclers of the Children's Crusade say the least about him; most do not mention him at all. Later, as chroniclers wove the event into their fabric of inspirational tales (and into poems and songs of Christian romance), his story was elaborated with miraculous claims which would make all but the most credulous historian doubtful. Stephen probably existed, one of the hundreds of self-appointed messengers of God who dot the landscape of Christian history, and a large movement of children across Europe in 1212 certainly happened, but, beyond these bald statements, not much about him is certain.

The Crusades, launched by Pope **Urban II** in 1095, were the first of many expansionist movements undertaken by Europeans, forerunners of the occupation of the Americas, and of the Great Powers' empires in the 19th century. The ostensible target of the crusades was the Holy Land

"Stephen, as befitted the leader, insisted on having a gaily decorated cart for himself, with a canopy to shade him from the sun. At his side rode boys of noble birth, each rich enough to possess a horse. No-one resented the inspired prophet travelling in comfort. On the contrary he was treated as a saint, and locks of his hair and pieces of his garments were collected as precious relics."

STEVEN RUNCIMAN

Contributed by Patrick Allitt, Assistant Professor of History, Emory University, Atlanta, Georgia

(today's Israel), and especially the Holy City of Jerusalem, which was held by Islamic "Saracens." In practice, however, crusaders were easily diverted by the opportunity for plunder and conquest elsewhere. In 1204, for example, the Fourth Crusade had spent its energy in attacks on other Christians, culminating in the plundering of the predominantly Christian city of Constantinople.

Crusaders were often members of the surplus population of Europe, which by the 12th and 13th centuries was greater than the land could easily support. Some of them hoped for a new life in the East, and for a time crusader kingdoms lived a precarious existence beyond the old boundaries of Christendom. Meanwhile, fervent crusade-preachers in Europe roused periodic fits of enthusiasm for "taking the cross" in the name of rescuing the Holy Land. After 1200, war against the Albigensian heretics in southern France, or against the Muslims of southern Spain, also came to be regarded as crusading missions closer to home.

The Children's Crusade was never a crusade in the official sense because it was never approved or blessed by the pope; because its members never received the dispensations, holy relics, and legal protections given to men who had "taken the cross"; and because it never left Western Europe. Some historians see it as an outbreak of mass hysteria, one of the recurrent surges of popular madness which were channeled into religiously acceptable forms but which threatened to become social revolts. It occurred just when preachers were raising recruits for the Albigensian Crusade, and the children who joined it may have been inspired by the words of these preachers; many believed that the crusades were God's way of rewarding the poor with glory.

In May 1212, the king of France, **Philip Augustus,** in his court at Saint Denis, was visited by Stephen, a shepherd boy aged about 12 from the town of Cloyes near Orleans, in the company of other local shepherds. Stephen told the king that Jesus, disguised as a poor pilgrim, had miraculously visited him while he was watching his sheep, and that Stephen had offered bread to this pilgrim who in return had handed him a letter for the king, urging him to go on crusade. The king was not impressed by this story, but the boy soon showed that he had magnetic abilities as a preacher. He began to tour the countryside urging other children to join him.

One chronicler, from Laon, reported:

The bands, composed of boys and girls with some youths and older persons, marched in procession

CHRONOLOGY

1204 Fourth Crusade captured Constantinople; failed to advance to Jerusalem

1211–12 Preaching of the Albigensian Crusade against heretics in Southern France

1212 Stephen's first appearance at French court to preach Children's Crusade; simultaneous appearance of Nicholas in Germany; Stephen's march over the Alps to Genoa; child crusaders dispersed in Marseilles and Italy

through the cities, castles, towns, and villages, carrying banners, candles, and crosses, and swinging censers [incense fires], singing in the vernacular, "Lord God, exalt Christianity! Lord God restore to us the true cross."

The chronicler of Andres adds that when their parents asked the children where they wanted to go, "they replied, as if they had been moved by one spirit, 'To God!'" According to legend, Stephen had soon raised 30,000 children aged 12 and under, whom he instructed to rally at the town of Vendome before setting out on the journey to the Holy Land. Pope **Innocent III,** an ardent advocate of crusading, is supposed to have said: "These children put us to shame, because while we sleep they rush to recover the Holy Land."

It is difficult to imagine that so many parents would willingly let their children loose for such a quixotic adventure, and the numbers are almost certainly exaggerated. But such was the feverish enthusiasm for the honor of crusading that Stephen's oratory seems to have struck a responsive chord among hundreds of children, both peasants and nobles. As the chroniclers tell it, the majority of this crowd of children, both boys and girls, began to walk toward the French south coast. Stephen himself, says one, was given a decorated cart with a sun shade and was regarded by the other children as a living saint, whose hair, and the threads of whose clothes, had miraculous healing powers. It is possible, however, that these chroniclers' tales are sheer embroidery on a more prosaic truth. Historian D. C. Munro, examining the evidence early this century, was skeptical, and concluded that there was no crusade, only local enthusiasm, and he had some telling evidence. "Not one chronicle," he wrote, "mentions the band of children at any place between Paris and Marseilles. And not a single chronicle written south of the Loire mentions the movement at all. It is very clear that the contemporaries were right and that the children returned home, after marching around and singing in processions for a time." The more recent historian Norman Zacour, on the other hand, takes the view that fairly detailed chroniclers' accounts of the children in Marseilles make it likely that at least some of them appeared there.

Marching through France in the early 13th century at the height of summer cannot have been easy or pleasant. The only provisions would have come from the communities through which the children passed, none of which could have managed to feed several thousand newcomers, however admiring they may have been of the children's courage. Arriving in Marseilles at last, say several versions of the story, those children who had not already dropped out or starved camped in the streets. They then gathered at the Mediterranean waterfront, preparing to see the waters of the sea part, as they had for Moses during the escape of the Children of Israel from Egypt. Stephen had been told in a dream that the waters would part again so that his crusade could walk to the Holy Land, but for some reason the miracle did not take place. Some of the children denounced Stephen as a false prophet, but others waited, expecting that God would soon fulfill his promise and enable the march across the water to Jerusalem to continue.

Merchants Betray the Crusaders

Meanwhile, two local merchants, named Iron Hugo and William the Pig, offered to pay for ships to take the children on the next stage of their journey. Stephen, apparently making a prosaic concession to the lack of miracles, accepted the offer, and the children piled aboard the seven ships offered. Due to the treachery of these two merchants, however, their destination was the slave markets of North Africa rather than the Holy Land. Two of the ships foundered in a storm and sank with all souls lost, while the other five were soon in enemy hands at Bougie, Algeria. Most of the children were then sold into slavery, and for nearly two decades no further word was heard of them. Pope Gregory IX later built the Church of the New Innocents on the island of Recluse where the two ships had foundered, and the bodies of the children who had been washed ashore were preserved there. Another chronicler reported that the bodies remained uncorrupted, a sure sign of their sanctity.

Eighteen years later, a priest appeared in France with the news that he, as one of the few adults to accompany the crusade, had been enslaved like all the others and had enjoyed a lenient captivity at the hands of a scholarly caliph who had learned about Western ways from him and his fellow priests. The priest also reported, however, that another 700 captives had been tortured into becoming Muslims and had been set to work on plantations in Egypt belonging to the governor of Alexandria, where they were now fully grown men and women. Eighteen more, said the priest, had been taken to Baghdad where, refusing to recant their Christianity, they were slain. Of Stephen's own fate, however, nothing is known, and, at this point, after his moment in the sun, he vanishes from the historical record completely.

At the time of the Children's Crusade in France, several chroniclers attributed Stephen's inspiration to divine intervention and accepted at face value his declaration of Jesus' mission to him. In later years, in view of the crackpot nature of the venture and its disastrous outcome, chroniclers were more inclined to look back on it as an episode of deviltry. Thomas Fuller, for example, writing 400 years later, said, "it was done by the instinct of the devil who, as it were, desired a cordial of children's blood to comfort his weak stomach long cloyed with murdering of men." In general, the chroniclers were priests who looked askance at a mass movement of the laity. Typical was the Annales Marbacenses which said that the Children's Crusade was "a useless expedition" of children and "stupid adults."

German Children Led by Nicholas

Whatever its provenance, divine or demonic, the French Children's Crusade was emulated by a group of German children, and they had a "Stephen of Cloyes" of their own, a boy named **Nicholas.** He too preached and gathered to himself a following of boys and girls in the Rhine Valley who "left their ploughs, carts, and herds" and hurried to join the growing band of children that marched south across the Alps to Genoa on the Italian coast. Like their French counterparts, they at first declared "with one heart and one voice that they would pass through the seas on dry land and would recover the Holy Land and Jerusalem." Another version of the story says that they believed they could walk on the tops of the waves without getting their feet wet, as Jesus had done on the Sea of Galilee. Whatever the version, there seemed to be a special point to divinely assisted sea crossings. The German children's rhetoric emphasized converting the infidels to Christianity rather than overwhelming them by force of arms.

Historian Steven Runciman describes their arrival at Genoa:

The Genoese authorities were ready at first to welcome the pilgrims, but on second thoughts they suspected a German plot. They would allow them to stay for one night only; but any who wished to settle permanently in Genoa were invited to do so. The children expecting the sea to divide before them next morning, were content.

Once again the miracle was lacking, and the group began to break up, some going east to Venice, some west to Marseilles, and some south to Brindisi. Those few who ever got aboard a ship went not to the Holy Land but, like the French children, to a life of slavery. A few, including Nicholas, journeyed to Rome to see Pope Innocent III—some perhaps hoping he would release them from their crusading vows, though most were too young in the first place to have ever made such a binding vow. Innocent "was moved by their piety but embarrassed by their folly," says Runciman. "With kindly firmness he told them that they must now go home." Innocent either dissolved the vows or postponed them, and "it is recorded that Nicholas afterwards fought bravely at Acre [in a later crusade] and in the siege of Damiette, and returned unharmed."

In the case of this slightly better documented German Children's Crusade, as with the French one, the breakup of the united force caused it to disappear from the chroniclers' view, though one mentions that "the people who had so generously supplied their wants on their triumphant progress now turned a deaf ear to their entreaties and pointed in derision at the maidens who had gone forth as virgins and now returned in shame." Another says that the parents of children who had died in the expedition were so angry with Nicholas's father, whose "vainglory" had set it in motion, that they arrested and hanged him.

The Children's Crusade was not the last episode of its kind. In 1237, more than a thousand children were seized with what appears to have been a form of St. Vitus's Dance and to have danced their way from Erfurt to Arnstadt in Germany. In 1251, another group of shepherds, who like Stephen of Cloyes claimed to have a letter from Jesus, set out to rescue their captive king, **Louis IX,** from the Holy Land. Most famous of all, in June 1284 a handsome young man with a silver flute is said to have appeared in the German city of Hamlin and, by his playing, spirited away 130 boys who were never seen again. The "pied piper" story, in its earliest form, makes no mention of rats, but offers a fascinating point of comparison with the Children's Crusade 70 years before.

SOURCES:

Munro, D. C. "The Children's Crusade." *American Historical Review*. Vol. 19. 1913–14: pp. 516–524.

Runciman, Steven. *A History of the Crusades*. Vol. III. Cambridge University Press, 1954.

Setton, Kenneth, ed. "The Children's Crusade" by Norman Zacour in *A History of the Crusades*. University of Wisconsin Press, 1969: pp. 325–342.

Stephen I of Hungary

(c. 973/77–1038)

Hungarian king, who went from pagan tribal leader to Christian leader of a powerful nation in the space of one generation and left a remarkable imprint on the history of Europe and the world.

Name variations: St. Stephen, Steven, Istvàn, Vajk. Possibly born around 973–77; died in 1038, with no direct heir; son of Duke Géza (died 997); grandson of Taksony (died 972); married: Gisela, Princess of Bavaria. Successors: During the "Interregnum" 1038–46, Pietro Orseolo (nephew of Stephen; Doge of Venice); Andrew I, Béla, Solomon.

The Hungarian kingdom was established by descendants of Arpad, a Magyar nomad from the steppes of Asia whose horsemen had terrorized central Europe in the first half of the 10th century. After a decisive defeat by the Germans at Lechfeld, just south of Augsburg, Bavaria, in 955, the Magyars, under Arpad's great grandson Taksony, settled down in what is now Hungary.

Taksony's son, the duke Géza, established a semblance of order and initiated moves to Christianize the Magyar/Hungarians by appealing to the Holy Roman Emperor Otto I for Christian missionaries. His move has been termed the "Quedlinburg Mission." Fortunately, for the Hungarians, Otto did not take the request seriously. Although a number of German Benedictine missionaries came to the Hungarian lands and began the process of Christianization, their methods were so crude that they caused many problems and delayed progress.

When Géza died in 997, his son Stephen took a more direct action some three years later by appealing to Pope Sylvester II, asking that he be baptized and crowned Christian king of Hungary.

"The coronation of Saint [Stephen] with the Crown sent by Pope Sylvester II in the year 1000 A.D. was an epochal event which the British historian Christopher Dawson called 'the birthyear of Christian Europe.'"

STEPHEN SISA

Contributed by H.L. Oerter, Professor of History, Emeritus, Miami University, Oxford, Ohio

This move reduced the possibility that the Holy Roman Emperor might assume the role of feudal lord over Hungary, making the Hungarian ruler his vassal.

Acting quickly, Sylvester II sent a bishop and a group of clergy; he also sent a crown which was slightly damaged en route. When the coronation took place on Christmas Day in the year 1000, that same crown with its bent cross was set on Stephen's head; the defect remains to this day, symbolizing the origin and function of the crown and its wearer.

Stephen was faced with great problems from all sides as he began the task of organizing, defending, Christianizing, and bringing his nation into the European fold. One of these problems was the revolt of a cousin who ruled in Transylvania. Koppàny claimed not only the throne, but the hand of Stephen's widowed mother. Immediately moving against him, Stephen finally defeated Koppàny, executing him in 1003. Then another Magyar—known only by the title Gyula—claimed the rule in Transylvania and usurped it. He too was disposed of by the new king, who was actively supported by German knights in the service of his wife/queen, Gisela, a Bavarian princess.

Stephen established the seat of his kingdom at Esztergom, site of an old Roman settlement called Strigonium, allegedly where the Roman Emperor Marcus Aurelius wrote his *Meditations.* He lost no time in setting up a number of bishoprics and instituting a vigorous program of Christianization of his people. Some have reported that this was accomplished through forceful means—in much the same manner as the Frankish king **Clovis** Christianized his pagan tribesmen in the sixth century, and the Emperor **Constantine** his Roman subjects in the fourth century.

Successfully Christianizes Magyars

Stephen I ruled for four decades. Considering that his father Géza, who began the first attempts to Christianize the Magyars, had been anything but successful, Stephen achieved nearly miraculous results, leaving a clear majority of his subjects following the new religion at his death in 1038. In addition to establishing dioceses for the propagation of the faith, Stephen established schools and churches and encouraged his nobility to endow monasteries. He also invited Jewish and Muslim traders into the kingdom to build up the economy, ordering a strict toleration of their religious practices in order to profit from their trading activities.

970	Géza became duke on death of Taksony
973	Géza asked Holy Roman Emperor to send missionaries to Hungary (Quedlinburg Mission); possible birth of Stephen
997	Death of Géza; accession of Stephen
1000	Stephen asked Pope Sylvester II to baptize and crown him as king of Hungary
1001	Revolt of Koppàny of Transylvania
1003	Defeat and execution of Koppàny by Stephen
1018	Stephen & Basil II (Byzantium) defeated Bulgars, opening way for pilgrims to Jerusalem
1030	Conrad II attacked western Hungary; Germans driven from Hungarian territory
1038	Stephen died; Pietro Orseolo claimed throne, but opposed by Council of Nobles
1038–46	Interregnum; struggles between claimants to throne continued; "bloodbath" of 1046 saw Andrew I succeed

He sponsored the drafting and enactment of law codes for his new nation, in what appears—retroactively—to be a close adaptation of what other European monarchs of the period were accomplishing. One element that makes Stephen's legal pronouncements different from the others is that he sought, with some degree of success, to prevent Hungary from becoming a theocratic protectorate. The laws were Christianized versions of Magyar customs and traditions; they reflected the need of his people as much as the requirement for order.

He allied himself with the Byzantine emperor, **Basil II,** in his battle with the Bulgarian ruler John Vladislav in 1018, the results of which action saw the establishment of pilgrimage routes to Jerusalem through Constantinople. In later years, Stephen's treatment of Bulgarian prisoners was humane and considerate and led to a satisfying relaxation of tensions between the two kingdoms. This was especially fruitful when the German emperor Conrad II launched attacks against the western parts of Hungary in 1030. Since he didn't have to worry about his eastern and southern flanks, Stephen was able to concentrate his forces and defeat the Germans in the west, forcing their withdrawal.

Stephen's personal life included a series of tragedies. His only son Imre (Emeric), who enjoyed a reputation for virtue and valor, died in what has been reported as a hunting accident (killed by a "wild boar"). But Stephen Sisa, in his book *The Spirit of Hungary,* alleges that the death was a successful assassination attempt by the *Thonuzoba* family, who were resisting conversion to Christianity. Sisa points out that the term, thonuzoba, means "wild boar" in the language of the Petcheneg (a pre-Christian steppe-dwelling people, some of whom settled in Transylvania). Because he had led an exemplary life and was well-loved by the Hungarian peoples who had accepted Christianity, Imre was canonized in the late 11th century, at about the same time as his father.

The successful implantation of a substantial group of non-Slavs in Eastern Europe in the midst of what was becoming a Slavic empire is one of the minor mysteries of European history. To the north, the Poles held sway, but the Hungarians successfully intermarried with Polish aristocracy, and it is a verified fact that Stephen sent to Poland two young men who might become eligible for his throne when their lives appeared to be in danger. They subsequently returned after Stephen's death and each of them later ruled for brief periods. To the east, Bulgars could have posed threats to the peace of the kingdom, yet Stephen, through careful diplomacy, managed to keep the Bulgarian rulers either pacified or immobilized. To the northeast the Bohemians (Czechs) represented a highly developed culture that acted as a buffer for their Slavic brothers to the east, while they did not pose any kind of a threat to the Magyar kingdom. Other minor groupings of Slavs—including Slovenes, Slovaks, Croats, Ruthenians, White Russians, Ukrainians, Serbians, Vlachs (Rumanians)—formed a demographic ring around the Carpathian Basin. Yet the Magyars/Hungarians survived and prospered. Their history and their historians assert that the chief architect of this was Stephen—Saint Stephen—whose vision and energy made the beginnings possible.

SOURCES:

Kosztolnyik, Z. J. *Five Eleventh Century Hungarian Kings: Their Policies and Their Relations with Rome.* East European Monographs, distributed by Columbia University Press, 1981.

Sisa, Stephen. *The Spirit of Hungary: A Panorama of Hungarian History and Culture.* Ontario, Canada, 1983 (2nd edition published in U.S., 1990).

Sugar, Peter A., ed. *A History of Hungary.* Indiana University Press, 1990.

FURTHER READING:

Dragomir, Sylvius. *The Ethnical Minorities in Transylvania.* Sonor Printing, 1927.

Ignotus, Paul. *Hungary: Nations of the Modern World.* Praeger, 1972.

Konnyu, Leslie. *A Condensed Geography of Hungary.* American-Hungarian Review, 1971.

Gustav Stresemann

(1878–1929)

Foreign minister of Germany during the 1920s, who restored Germany to diplomatic respectability, stabilized its first democratic government, and won the Nobel Peace Prize.

"He (could have been) Winston Churchill's brother. The same silhouette—almost the same coloration. Brilliant, daring, and bold. In both, more than a dash of recklessness."

LORD EDGAR D'ABERNON

Even today, Gustav Stresemann, Germany's foreign minister from 1923 through 1929, remains an enigma. For some historians, he was the "Good European," the German leader who tried to restore Germany to a position of international respectability after World War I. For others, he was a "realistic and opportunistic conservative" who foresaw that Germany's plight after the war might be improved only if his nation demonstrated peaceful intentions. For still others, he was a shrewd German nationalist who used pledges of international cooperation and peaceful intentions to divert attention from illegal German rearmament activities.

Stresemann was born only eight years after Germany was unified under a single government and grew to adulthood at a time when Germany was emerging as a world military and industrial power. With its geographic position in the center of Europe, and with its large army—which had made possible the unification of the nation with its victory over France in 1870—the new nation quickly achieved the status of a Great Power. By the end of the 19th century, its steel production

Pronunciation: GOO-stahf STRAY-seh-man. Born in Berlin on May 10, 1878; died in Berlin on October 3, 1929; son of Ernst Stresemann (a Berlin beer distributor); married: Käthe Kleefeld (daughter of Berlin industrialist, Adolf Kleefeld), October 20, 1903; children: (two sons) Wolfgang and Joachim.

Contributed by Niles Holt, Professor of History, Illinois State University, Normal-Bloomington, Illinois

CHRONOLOGY

1914	World War I began
1918	WWI ends; Germany promised a negotiated treaty
1918	Revolution in Germany topples Wilhelm II
1919–20	Constituent Assembly created new German government, termed the "Weimar Republic"
1919	Germany signed Treaty of Versailles, imposed by the victorious Allies
1920	Kapp Putsch failed to bring down Weimar Republic
1923	French army occupied Ruhr section of western Germany
1923	Munich Beer Hall Putsch failed to bring down Weimar government
1933	Hitler appointed chancellor of the Weimar Republic

exceeded that of Great Britain and was second only to that of the United States.

The son of a beer distributor, Stresemann benefited from the new German prosperity as he grew up in the capital city of Berlin. Although he was described as a melancholy child who preferred solitude to social gatherings, he became the only member of his family who attended both high school and German universities. Interested in history as a young boy, he changed his major in college to economics, apparently because he anticipated a career in business. Earning his doctorate after study at the universities of Berlin and Leipzig, his dissertation topic was—appropriately—the growth of the bottled beer industry in Berlin.

A successful businessman while still very young, Stresemann worked as an administrator for the German Chocolate Makers' Association from 1901 through 1904. At age 25, he became the legal representative for the Manufacturers' Association of Saxony and was soon promoted to a major position with the Association of Industrialists, which represented German light industry. Financially secure (and able to support a wife and family), he married the daughter of a Berlin industrialist in 1903.

His rise in political ranks was equally meteoric. His capacity for work led an associate to describe him as a "possessed person." His "short, corpulent body, thick neck, round balding head, and nondescript mustache" became a common sight in Berlin restaurants. The man who loved solitude as a child became a gregarious companion at many din-

ner tables, using table conversations to expand his knowledge of people and politics. He became a member of the city council of Dresden in 1906. As editor of the magazine *Saxon Industry*, he frequently wrote editorials on German politics. Some four years later, with major financial backing from German businesses, he was elected to the lower house of the German parliament, the Reichstag, as a deputy for the National Liberal Party. At age 28, he was the youngest deputy in the Reichstag.

Stresemann had joined the right wing of German liberalism, the National Liberals. With financial support mainly from German industrialists, the National Liberals were strongly nationalistic, favoring measures to expand German military and economic power. Favoring the goals of the highly nationalistic Pan Germanic League, Stresemann supported the attempts of Admiral **Alfred von Tirpitz** (1849–1930) to construct a German navy large enough and modern enough to rival British naval power. More interested in social reform than most National Liberals, however, Stresemann had become interested, as a young man, in the social reform theories of Friedrich Naumann, who favored reforms to aid the working class in Germany.

The young politician drew the attention of the Party leader, Ernst Bassermann, who became a mentor for Stresemann, teaching him many of the intricacies of German politics; Stresemann became known as "Bassermann's crown prince." When Stresemann lost his bid for reelection in 1912, Bassermann helped him win a special election two years later. Upon Bassermann's death in 1917, Stresemann succeeded him as leader of the Party's Reichstag delegation.

The years of World War I, from 1914 to 1918, drove Stresemann politically to the right. While he believed that the war was purely a defensive struggle for Germany, he also came to accept the view, common in wartime Germany, that the country should annex parts of Belgium, to its east, and parts of Russian land to its west. His pro-annexationist stance placed him at odds with the German chancellor, Theobald von Bethmann-Hollweg, who attempted to steer a moderate course during the war.

Stresemann Supports General von Ludendorff

Stresemann gave his support, instead, to the Supreme Military Command, particularly to its most assertive general, **Erich von Ludendorff.** Ludendorff, whose wartime powers made him the virtual military dictator of the country, attempted to use German submarines to force one of the enemy countries, Great Britain, to withdraw from the war. Under a policy called "unrestricted submarine warfare," German submarines were ordered to torpedo any ship in waters off the coast of Britain, whether the ship was clearly war-related or not. The policy backfired, eventually causing the United States to enter the war.

With his deep veneration of the German past, and his deepseated conviction in German moral and cultural superiority, Stresemann refused to criticize Ludendorff. "I know that people are looking for a scapegoat and hope to find it in Ludendorff," he declared. "But I shall not be a party to it." So vociferous were his defenses that he came to be regarded as Ludendorff's "young man," a virtual mouthpiece for the military.

Like most Germans, Stresemann believed, until the war's final days, that there would be a German victory. He was shocked when Ludendorff told Emperor **Wilhelm II** in October of 1918 that Germany would have to ask for a cease-fire. Even more jarring was the German Revolution of the following month, when the Reichstag took control of the government and the emperor, after abdicating, fled to Holland. Declaring that the Revolution was the "day of the death of Germany's greatness in the world," Stresemann blamed the revolutionaries for bringing humiliation and collapse to Germany. He accepted the "stab-in-the-back theory," which argued that German military leaders would have won the war if cowardly civilian politicians had not asked for peace prematurely.

Still loyal to the principle of monarchy, Stresemann nevertheless won a seat in the Constituent Assembly which met in the city of Weimar in 1919 and 1920 and created Germany's first democracy, popularly known as the "Weimar Republic." Modeled after the British political system, it included a powerful Reichstag, elected by all adult males; the chancellor, elected by a majority of the Reichstag, was the major national leader.

Most Germans were unenthusiastic about the new Republic, and Stresemann was no exception. The long, involved debates in the new Reichstag seemed to some Germans to be a sign of national division and weakness. For many, the Republic was an "expediency" created in order to win easier peace terms from the victorious democracies of Britain, France, and the United States. The Republic was further damaged in terms of public opinion when the Treaty of Versailles imposed harsh peace terms on Germany—awarding parts of German land to Poland, restricting the size and activities of the Germany military, and

requiring Germany to pay an unspecified amount of reparations. Not only was the Republic unable to block such a treaty, but the leaders of the Republic were forced to sign the document.

Bitter over the results of the war, Stresemann did not oppose the right-wing Kapp Putsch of 1920, when veterans of the war, in paramilitary units, attempted to take control of the government. When the putsch failed, Stresemann grudgingly accepted the new Republic.

He Founds German People's Party

Stresemann's brand of liberalism—nationalistic but concerned for social reforms—made it difficult for him to find a new party to join in the early months of the Republic. The National Liberal Party had been fatally weakened by its support of the war, and by 1917 held only 45 seats out of nearly 400 in the Reichstag. When the Party collapsed, Stresemann considered joining the new Democratic Party founded by Naumann and the famed sociologist Max Weber. Denied a position in that Party's leadership councils because of his wartime hawkishness, Stresemann finally chose to found his own party—the German People's Party—and remained its leader until his death.

In 1923, Stresemann became chancellor of Germany for 100 significant days. During his brief term as chancellor, financial reforms were initiated which eventually brought under control Germany's high rate of inflation during the early 1920s; at one point, several million German marks were required to buy one American dollar. Two events weakened his control over the government. First, the French government, complaining that Germany was in arrears in reparations payments (a charge the Germans contested), occupied the highly industrialized western section of Germany (the Ruhr), intent on using the profits from the factories to repay reparations.

Second, Ludendorff and a new political figure, **Adolf Hitler,** attempted to topple the Weimar Republic with the Munich or "Beer Hall" Putsch of 1923. Although unsuccessful, the putsch threatened Germany with civil war and stunned Stresemann, who was embittered that Ludendorff had played a prominent role and that another World War I military hero, **Paul von Hindenburg,** had not spoken out against the putsch.

Ousted as chancellor, Stresemann accepted the position of foreign minister in a newly formed government, a post he held for six crucial years until his death in 1929. His financial reforms as chancellor, plus his success as foreign minister in restoring Germany to diplomatic respectability, stabilized the Weimar Republic and made it secure. There would be no more "putsches."

As foreign minister, his main policy aim was to secure revisions in the detested Treaty of Versailles. He wanted to restore to Germany territory given to Poland at the end of the war, such as the Polish Corridor, the port city of Danzig, and the Upper Silesia area, which was rich in natural resources. He also wanted to annex Austria. He hoped to achieve all such goals by negotiation, by demonstrating that the new Germany was peaceful and trustworthy, and by exploiting diplomatic splits between Germany's former wartime enemies.

The second year of his foreign ministry, he agreed to the Dawes Plan, a United States–sponsored scheme to ease Germany's reparations payment schedule. In 1926, he committed Germany to the Locarno agreements, a series of nonaggression pacts among European nations; by doing so, he angered members of his own Party, because the pact was a de facto recognition of the border between Germany and France. Many Germans still hoped to regain Alsace-Lorraine, a border area taken by Germany after the Franco-Prussian War of 1870 but returned to France after World War I. The pacts also committed European nations, including Germany, to resolve disputes by arbitration rather than war.

Stresemann Awarded Nobel Peace Prize

For all these conciliatory gestures, Germany was rewarded with membership admittance to the League of Nations, and Stresemann was awarded the Nobel Peace Prize of 1926 (along with French foreign minister Aristide Briand). Two years later, Germany was also a signatory to the Kellogg-Briand Pacts of 1928, which outlawed war. One result of such diplomacy was that some French troops were withdrawn from parts of western Germany.

It is sometimes claimed that Stresemann's work for peace diverted international attention from secret rearmament activities in Germany during the Weimar years. The Treaty of Versailles limited the German army to 100,000 troops. In order to evade this provision, the German army reduced the training period to four months, shuttling 400,000 troops through the army each year. In order to evade the Versailles Treaty's ban on training with tanks and airplanes in Germany, secret arrangements were made for German troops to train with such weapons in Russia.

Stresemann had some knowledge of these activities, although the extent of his knowledge is not clear. He did not have a close relationship with the military leaders of the Weimar Republic—the army was so suspicious of his "diplomacy of reconciliation" that his telephone was tapped. There is no convincing evidence that he was consciously trying to provide "cover" for the illegal rearmament activities of the German army. In fact, leading generals opposed Stresemann's diplomatic policies, fearing that the result would be reduced military budgets. They also believed that Stresemann devoted too much attention to Western Europe and not enough to Eastern Europe. It is true that Stresemann made some militaristic statements, but most of them were probably for domestic political consumption—such as his promise to the crown prince that Germany would someday regain Alsace-Lorraine.

When Adolf Hitler came to power in Germany in 1933, his initial foreign policy aims seemed to have more than a slight resemblance to Stresemann's. First, renouncing the Treaty of Versailles, Hitler annexed Austria to Germany. Then he started World War II by invading Poland, ostensibly to regain "German" land. The main difference, however, was that Stresemann rejected military action and worked to achieve such things peacefully—by diplomacy and arbitration. Stresemann, whose family had suffered from anti-Semitic rumors that his wife was a member of a prominent Berlin Jewish family, held an unfavorable opinion of Hitler, whom he believed was partly responsible for his ouster as chancellor in 1923.

It is all too easy to speculate about history, to play "what might have been." But if Stresemann had been able to achieve his aims in his own way, there is at least the possibility that some of the disasters that followed in Europe, including World War II itself, might have been avoided.

SOURCES:

Gatzke, Hans W. *Stresemann and the Rearmament of Germany.* Johns Hopkins Press, 1954.

Grathwol, Robert P. *Stresemann and the DNVP: Reconciliation or Revenge in German Foreign Policy, 1924–1928.* Regents Press of Kansas, 1980.

Sutton, Eric, ed. *Gustav Stresemann: His Diaries and Letters.* 3 vols. Macmillan, 1935–40.

Turner, Henry Ashby, Jr. *Stresemann and the Politics of the Weimar Republic.* Princeton University Press, 1963.

FURTHER READING:

Bretton, Henry L. *Stresemann and the Revision of Versailles.* Stanford University Press, 1966.

Halperin, Samuel. *Germany Tried Democracy*. Crowell, 1946.

Holborn, Hajo. *The Political Collapse of Europe*. Knopf, 1951.

Jacobson, Jon. *Locarno Diplomacy: Germany and the West, 1925–1929*. Princeton University Press, 1972.

Warren, Donald, Jr. *The Red Kingdom of Saxony: Lobbying Ground for Gustav Stresemann, 1901–1909*. Nijhoff, 1964.

Alexander Suvorov

(1729–1800)

One of the greatest generals in history and probably the greatest Russian military commander prior to the Second World War.

Name variations: Souvoroff. Born Aleksandr Vasil'evich Suvorov in Moscow on November 24, 1729; died in St. Petersburg on May 18, 1800; son of Basil Suvorov (a military man who had a brilliant career under Peter the Great and Catherine II) and the daughter of an Armenian merchant; married; children: (son) Arkadin (1783–1811; a general who fell in battle); grandchildren: Alexander (1804–82; also a general).

A great general and military strategist, Alexander Suvorov devoted a considerable amount of time and energy to developing a theory of military training. Living as he did in the 18th century, he might almost be called the philosopher of the subject. A simple man, he understood to its depths the character of the Russian soldier, and his training methods and military leadership were based on that knowledge. A ruthless pursuer of his military goals, Suvorov drove both himself and his men to their limits and was, as all too often in Russian history, quite cavalier in regard to human life. But it has been said that in an age when the art of war had given way to that of diplomacy, he restored international conflict to an act of force.

Like so many prominent men of his generation, Alexander Suvorov was the son of a father who had already begun a brilliant career of his own in the time of **Peter the Great.** A military man, Basil Suvorov guided his son's first steps in the study of artillery science. In 1742, Alexander entered the Semenovsky Guards Regiment serving until 1754, when, at the age of 25, he was promoted to the rank of lieutenant and transferred to

"Suvorov was a lunatic, but he was a pragmatic general: there is no telling what he might have won if he had been able to march against Bonaparte."

GINA KAUS

Contributed by Robert H. Hewsen, Professor of History, Glassboro State College, Glassboro, New Jersey

the Ingermanland Infantry Regiment. In the Seven Years' War (1756–63), Suvorov fought the Swedes in Finland, acquiring experience in a number of capacities in army life, including quartermastering and organizing reinforcement groups. Thereafter, he was promoted to the rank of lieutenant colonel and assigned to the staff of General V.V. Fermor (1760–61), commander in chief of the Russian army. In the latter half of 1761, Suvorov was attached to the light corps of Lieutenant General G.G. Berg, seeing battle against the Prussians in Poland.

Theories of Military Training and Tactics

In 1763, Suvorov was promoted to the rank of full colonel and made commander of the Suzdal Infantry Regiment at Novaia Ladoga, a position which he held until 1769. These six years were important for Suvorov; they were also important for Russia and for the fields of military science. During this time, he gradually developed the basis for his system of military training and the organization of an army for battle. This was codified in his book *Regimental Principles* (*Polkovoe Uchrezhdenie*), a manual for the training of soldiers, the preparation of armies and the organization of guard service. In his training procedures, Suvorov stressed the necessity of sound preparation and had no use for the common practice of throwing raw troops into the front as "cannon fodder." He not only saw to it that his men were well-trained in the principles of combat but also took a great interest in their morale, instilling in them lofty sentiments of devotion to duty, national pride, and a sense of their own worth. He knew the great love that the common Russian soldier felt for his village, and more abstractly for his native soil, and was able to transmute this into a love of country that became manifest on the battlefield. As a result, Suvorov had the devotion and trust of his men and this proved invaluable to him in campaign after campaign.

In tactics, Suvorov attached great importance to bold and swift advances with forceful river crossings and night marches, and he trained his troops extensively in these maneuvers. He was also a great advocate of the use of the bayonet, which reduced the use of expensive ammunition though it required intense hand-to-hand combat, and he saw to it that his soldiers had intensive training in the use of this brutal but effective weapon. In battle, Suvorov preferred the concentration of his troops rather than their deployment over broad expanses, and rejected feints, devious approaches, and the sending of dummy units to make diversionary assaults while the main army prepared to

CHRONOLOGY

1729	Born in Moscow
1760	Promoted to lieutenant colonel
1769–72	Fought against the Confederation of the Bar
1770	Promoted to major-general
1773	Sent to the front in the Russo-Turkish war of 1768–74
1774	Battle of Koluja (Kodludzha)
1776	Chief of infantry of the Crimean Corps
1778–79	Commander of the Kuban and Crimean Corps
1780–84	Served in the Kuban region
1785–87	Commander of the St. Petersburg division
1789	Created Count of Rymnik
1791	Commander of the tsarist forces in Finland
1794	Captured Warsaw from Polish rebels; promoted to rank of field marshal
1797	Discharged from the army; retired to his estate at Konchanskoe
1798	Called back to serve against the French in Italy
1799	Named prince of Italy
1800	Died at St. Petersburg

attack elsewhere. As far as Suvorov was concerned, the most effective and economical way to defeat the enemy was to find his weak spot and to attack it boldly, directly, and decisively. He also attached great importance to the pursuit of the enemy army after its defeat, so as to leave it no opportunity to regroup and counterattack. Suvorov had no patience with the simple defeat of the enemy; he wanted him routed and decisively crushed so that there might be no ambiguity as to who had won the battle. Suvorov's techniques were used effectively by his pupils Field Marshal **Mikhail Kutuzov** and Peter Bagration in the Napoleonic War, less so in the Russo-Japanese War, and had a considerable influence on the training of the Red Army in its early years.

Somewhat of an eccentric, Suvorov was very devout, not only prostrating himself before the holy icons of the Orthodox Church but also before **Catherine the Great** who expressed her indignation at such an affront to religion. His sense of humor could be crude and his barbs and gibes made him many enemies as did his open contempt—natural for a man of action—for courtiers, favorites, and other idlers. Unlike his great pupil Field Marshal Kutuzov, Suvorov totally rejected luxury in the field, eating the same rations as the common soldier and sleeping on the same bed of straw. He was, however, politically conservative and never questioned the autocracy, serfdom, or privileged nobility that characterized the Russia of his day.

In 1768, when the Russians became involved with a war against the Polish armies of the Confederation of the Bar, Suvorov was sent to Smolensk with his regiment to take part in the hostilities under the command of General I.I. Veimarn. Using his own tactics, Suvorov inflicted several defeats on the forces of the Confederation and in 1770 was promoted to the rank of major-general.

Transferred to take part in the final stages of the first Russo-Turkish War (1768–74), Suvorov arrived at the front in 1773. Serving under the command of Field Marshal Nikolai Rumiantsev, he quickly showed the brilliance of his leadership, attacking Turkish detachments and launching a number of daring raids, one of which crossed the Danube and captured an entire Turkish fleet. His greatest victory, however, was against the Turks at the Battle of Koluja (Kodludzha), where he defeated a Turkish army of approximately 40,000 troops with a force less than half that size. It was on this campaign that Suvorov first came into contact with **Grigori Potemkin,** favorite of Catherine the Great. Along with such experienced generals as Rumiantsev, Suvorov resented having to take orders from a man whom he considered his junior.

Suvorov's victory at Koluja, coupled with that of Rumiantsev at Shumla, forced the Turks to surrender, after which Suvorov was transferred east to the area of the Ural Mountains to take part in the closing operations in the suppression of the great Pugachev revolt. This insurrection of peasants and Cossacks in northeastern Russia had been suppressed with great difficulty. Although Pugachev had been captured by the time he arrived, Suvorov was given full command to clear out surviving pockets of resistance. Thereafter, he was placed in charge of the Crimean Corps and then of the Kuban Crimean Corps, working with Potemkin on the military aspects of the annexation of the Khansdate of the Crimea. In the years 1780–82, Suvorov was sent to the North Caucasian steppe country, where he was involved in preparations for a war with Persia and, in 1782–84, with the building of the Kuban lines, taking part in the annexation of the Kuban River basin. The Russians were now inching their way toward the Caucasus Mountains, the traditional frontier between Europe and the Middle East; the lines being a chain of fortifications stretching across the isthmus between the Black and Caspian seas comprised of fortresses, forts, and military outposts that were progressively moved forward as Russian strength and local opportunities permitted.

The Hero of the Second Russo-Turkish War

In the second Russo-Turkish War (1787–91), Suvorov was given the supreme command of the Russian forces operating in what is now Rumania, winning an important victory at Fort Kinburn, where he crushed a Turkish amphibious attack at the cost of serious enemy losses (October 1, 1787). This was a major feat. Had the fortress fallen, it would have been impossible for the Russians to have held Kherson in the Crimea. Then, at Rymnik, he destroyed a Turkish force of 90,000 men (September 11, 1789) in a brilliant offensive for which he was granted the title "Count Suvorov-Rymniksky" by a grateful Catherine the Great. The following year, Suvorov, with the assistance of the Austrian general Laudon, won a decisive victory over the Turks at Fochani in Rumania. Able to get more out of his men than any previous Russian commander, including Rumiantsev and Potemkin, whom he now completely overshadowed, Suvorov was the real hero of the Second Russo-Turkish War, the courage of his forces and the skill of their bayonet charges carrying all before them. Completely overwhelmed, the Turks were forced to sue for peace, signing the disastrous Treaty of Kuchuk Kainarji (July 10, 1774), that left the Ottoman Empire virtually at the mercy of Russia for the rest of its history, subject only to the restraints of the British and the French, who feared Russian expansionism in the Balkans and the Middle East.

After the war with Turkey ended, Suvorov was sent to Finland where he oversaw the construction of various military installations and canals, after which he was transferred to the Ukraine. Shortly thereafter, the second partition of Poland between Russia, Austria, and Prussia in 1793 was followed by a Polish rebellion. Sent to participate in this conflict, Suvorov defeated the Poles at the battles of Brest, Krupchitsky, and Kobylka; stormed Praha, a suburb of Warsaw on October 24, 1794; and then made a triumphal entry into the Polish capital. There, Suvorov forced a complete capitulation to Russia for which Catherine awarded him the rank of field marshal and a gift of 6,900 serfs. Back in St. Petersburg, Suvorov lobbied for a war against revolutionary France and continuously begged the Empress to allow him to march against **Napoleon.** Although Catherine was planning on sending him on an expedition against the French, she died in 1796, and her heir Paul I (1796–1801) had his own military ideas. Like his presumed father **Peter III,** Paul was devoted to Prussian militarism and began the introduction of Prussian military techniques into the Russian army. Suvorov's attempts to resist the plans of the Tsar only resulted in removal from his post and forced retirement from the army, after which he was banished to his estate at Konchanskoe.

In 1798, Russia joined the coalition against revolutionary France and, at the request of the British, presented through the Austrian government, Suvorov was placed at the head of the Russian armies sent against the French forces campaigning in northern Italy. Everywhere, Suvorov was victorious, capturing the city of Turin and driving the French from almost the whole of the Po valley and defeating them at Naples far to the south. After his victories at Cassano, Trebbia, and Novi, Suvorov was awarded the title "Prince Italisky" by Tsar Paul. Suvorov then drew universal admiration by leading his army into Switzerland via the St. Gottard Pass to join the second army under General Alexander Rimsky-Korsakov, but after the latter's defeat by Massena at Zurich, Suvorov was forced to retreat through the Grisons and the Vorarlberg to the upper Rhine. By October 12, 1799, the Russian participation in the victorious war was completed, and Suvorov and his troops returned to Russia. Granted the extraordinary title, *generalissimus,* he nevertheless soon fell out of favor with the erratic Paul and was banished from the court. Falling ill, Suvorov died soon after on May 18, 1800, and was buried in the Alexander Nevsky cathedral in St. Petersburg.

His Influence on History

Alexander Suvorov was one of the most remarkable military commanders in world history and certainly the greatest in the history of Russia. Undefeated throughout his career, he demonstrated, by his own successes in the field, the validity of his military theories, and his writings on the art of war not only served as manuals for the training of military men in Russia but attracted great interest in the outside world as well. The most important professional influence upon Field Marshal Kutuzov, Suvorov exercised through his worthy pupil a decisive influence upon the Russian victory against Napoleon and thus influenced the course of Russian and European history even after his death.

As the foremost military commander in Russian history, Field Marshal Suvorov has attracted great attention in the two centuries since his death, especially during the First and Second World Wars when his example was held up for emulation in a time of supreme military threat. His letters, papers, and other writings were collected and edited in tsarist Russia and republished in the Soviet period, and he has been the subject of several biographies, including the three-volume work by Petrushevsky. On July 29, 1942, in the midst of the Second World War, the Soviet Union instituted the Order of Suvorov as one of the country's highest military decorations and, shortly thereafter, by a decree of August 21, 1943, the specialized intermediate military schools in the Soviet Union were renamed the Suvorov Military Institutions.

SOURCES:

Suvorov, A. V. *Sbornik dokumentov.* Moscow, 1952.
————. *Sbornik dokumentov materialov.* Moscow, 1947.

FURTHER READING:

Longworth, Philip. *The Art of Victory: The Life and Achievements of Field-Marshall Suvorov, 1729–1800.* New York, 1965.

Teresa of Avila

(1515–1582)

Mystic and Spanish nun of the 16th century, who reformed the Carmelite order, bringing it back to the strictness its founders had intended and rejecting the worldly values of Spanish society.

Name variations: Teresa Jesus. Born Teresa de Cepeda Ahumada in Avila, Castile, Spain, in 1515; died in Alba de Tormes in 1582; daughter of Don Alonso de Cepeda and Doña Beatriz de Ahumada. Successor: Nicolas Doria.

The Protestant Reformation of the early and mid-16th century provoked a crisis for those Christians who remained loyal to the Catholic Church. Aware that it was in many ways corrupt and that spiritual life had become diluted by secular concerns, Catholic reformers tried to recover the integrity of primitive Christianity without violating Catholic tradition and the religious authorities. The effort at an internal Catholic reformation was particularly intense in Spain, where Saint **Ignatius Loyola,** Saint John of the Cross, and an influential group of Christian humanists created new religious orders and a new form of spirituality. None of these Catholic reformers was more successful than Saint Teresa of Avila, creator of the Discalced Carmelites and an influential spiritual writer.

Spain in the 16th century was an aristocratic society obsessed by the idea of blood purity (*limpieza de sangre*) which in our eyes seems no better than a form of fanatical racism. Recently reunited by the "Catholic Kings"—**Ferdinand and Isabella**—after a long era of fragmentation and partial Muslim occupation, Spain had a large population of Moors and Jews who had converted to

"Where it was a question of obeying what she believed to be the divine guidance, Teresa showed all the ruthlessness, as well as the fortitude and patience, of a saint."

STEPHEN CLISSOLD

Contributed by Patrick Allitt, Assistant Professor of History, Emory University, Atlanta, Georgia

Christianity under threat of expulsion or death. The Spanish Inquisition, doubting the sincerity of some of these conversions, launched periodic investigations of *conversos;* among them, in 1485, was Juan Sanchez, a rich textile trader of Jewish descent and Teresa's grandfather. After a hearing where he confessed to "many grave crimes and offences against our Holy Catholic Faith," he was publicly humiliated in the Inquisition's *auto de fe,* a procession of backsliders bearing extinguished candles in the streets of Toledo (to show that the light of salvation had gone out in their souls). Despite his confession, his "crimes" cannot have been very grave or he would have been put to death.

Surviving the ordeal and working to expunge its memory by dynastic alliances with older Catholic families, Juan Sanchez moved to the nearby city of Avila in Castile; there, his son Alonso, a taxgatherer and financier, lived an ostentatious life, fathering Teresa de Ahumada by his second wife. Teresa grew up in the protected environment of an honor-conscious society and faced the prospect of either marriage or taking the veil; no other alternatives presented themselves to highborn women of her age. As a child, she enjoyed romantic fiction, of the kind which Cervantes later lampooned in *Don Quixote,* and she seems to have had a brief flirtation with a young man connected with her family. They responded by placing her in a nunnery, where—after an early shock at this comparatively Spartan life—she came to believe that she had a lifetime's vocation.

The convent of the Incarnation in Avila was centrally placed in the city and, although the nuns were supposed to be cloistered, there was in fact a good deal of contact between the nuns and the other citizens of the town. The Carmelite nuns had for two centuries deviated from the austere ideals of their founders, and within the convent, social distinctions from the outside were still observed. Wealthier nuns, such as Teresa herself, had to bring a "dowry" to the convent, just as they would have had to take one to a husband; by this means, and by promises of payment from novices' parents, the convent was sure of a steady income. The more privileged and high-born nuns had private rooms rather than sleeping in the dormitory shared by poor nuns; they had their own servants (even slaves in a few cases); and they continued to enjoy the honorific name "Doña" inside the convent just as they had outside.

A custom had also developed that if a woman in one of the major families in Avila needed a female companion in times of bereavement or stress she could summon one from the convent to spend time with her; on several occa-

sions, Teresa was thus called away from the Incarnation for periods of months at a time. Thus, she spent two years with Doña Guiomar de Ulloa, an influential widow who became one of Teresa's principal benefactors in her later experiments in reforming the Carmelite order. In the same way, she would return to her family in times of sickness. During one such sickness, when she was in her early 20s, Teresa was so near death that her family had dropped wax onto her eyes, a local custom with the dead, before she surprised them by reviving. The episodic nature of convent life, along with the free access of outsiders to the residents, made the Carmelite existence a relatively relaxed affair in Teresa's youth.

Teresa Experiences Revelations, Visions

Without ever complaining about the convent life, she began to draw attention to herself by an exceptional form of spirituality. Sometimes while praying, she would receive messages from Christ, usually in the form of sudden convictions sown in her mind as she meditated. As her life continued, they became more intense and insistent, giving her at times the radiant assurance that she was in direct contact with God. Fearing nevertheless that she might somehow be under the influence of the devil, like some recently denounced spiritual charlatans, she treated her own revelations guardedly and consulted a succession of confessors about how to proceed. Most of them, similarly afraid of a demonic visitation, and responding to the defensive Spanish religious mood of the times which regarded any novelty as a possible sign of "Lutheranism," discouraged her. But then a meeting at Doña Guiomar de Ulloa's house with Peter of Alcantara, a reformer who believed in reviving the early Christian life of heroic austerity, led her to recover confidence. Peter of Alcantara assured her that her visions came from God and that she should heed them. One vision gave her a premonition of Hell, a claustrophobic inferno; although it terrified her, it led her to believe that she was being shown the need to trust in the divine messages which also came to her. On another occasion when a frivolous nun was gossiping, she saw a vision of a huge and repulsive toad standing next to the gossip and took it as another of God's warnings. She told one doubting confessor, in a nicely down-to-earth metaphor, that the certainty she felt of God's presence in these visions was comparable to the feeling she would have if after being very hungry, she suddenly felt well fed.

Her religious development continued through her 20s and 30s and became progressively more intense; at times, she would enter a trancelike state, which local people sought to oversee out of fascination. Particularly embarrassing to her were episodes of involuntary levitation during prayer, which had induced weightlessness, widely reported and seemingly well authenticated at the time. She tried to prevent herself from being carried into the air by asking other nuns to stand on the hem of her robe. Perhaps the best-remembered of her visions, and one which was later immortalized in stone by the baroque sculptor Bernini, was that in which an angel repeatedly plunged a spear into her heart causing her an almost unbearably pleasurable sensation. Not surprisingly these miraculous happenings, which some Catholic historians take as proof of Teresa's sanctity, have been a source of concern to secular historians who tend to doubt all reports of miracles but who also value eyewitness accounts of any event. Freudians, of course, have their own theory.

Whatever our judgment of Teresa's reports of divine visitation it is certain that she was a woman of courage, integrity, and resolve. In response to one confessor's request, she wrote her life history, which now constitutes our best source of information about her experiences; written in a form influenced by Saint Augustine's *Confessions*, which she had read and admired, it speaks of her as a dreadful sinner and attributes all her merits to God.

She Works to Reform Convent

As she advanced into middle age at the Incarnation convent, her sense of dissatisfaction with life there, coupled with the promoting of her visions, led her to attempt a reform of the convent; in this project several of her relatives, also young nuns, were eager to cooperate. Hoping to revive the old simplicity of Carmelite life, she arranged to acquire a house in another part of Avila and to live there with a handful of like-minded disciples. It seemed to her that the only way she as a woman could help to prevent the spread of heresy throughout Europe was to pray more fervently and to live a more devout life, and in its way she saw her reform as a missionary activity, even though it did not require leaving home ground.

The experiment faced many obstacles. First, Teresa wanted to live without the financial security which was enjoyed by the other monastic houses of Avila, but to trust entirely to alms, like Jesus. She would accept "dowries" if they were offered but would not make them a condition of admission; a novice's character alone would be decisive. She would make no distinction between the rich and poor, noble and plebeian, within the house; all titles would be dropped and the nuns would call one another "sister." It may be that as the descendant of *conversos*, even rich ones, she remained sensitive to the disadvantages of those without the coveted degrees of blood purity. In her book *The Way of Perfection*, Teresa explained that this dramatic contrast with the outside world was a way of reminding the sisters that "it is the Lord who provides for all in common" and that they were freed from trying to please their relatives outside the walls.

The city authorities, the local bishop, and many noble families protested against the plan, on the grounds that it would disrupt a convenient way of life (in which convent and city interacted to the convenience of the city) and that it would deny their daughters the honors and dignity they had previously preserved as nuns. Besides, with the way things stood, the twice-yearly payments the families made to a convent guaranteed its continued association with, even dependence on, *them*, a dependence which was now threatened. They also feared that a convent without regular means of support could easily become a burden on the finances of the city. As the gilt was already peeling off the facade of Spain's "golden age," in the form of bad harvests, inflation, and urban discontent, these were grave matters.

Teresa had sufficient supporters among the clergy and lay nobility, however, that she was able to persist, and she was steadied by a vision of Peter of Alcantara, recently deceased, who urged her not to falter. On the day that her convent opened, it was surrounded by a chanting mob of angry townsmen who tried to break down the door. Teresa's diplomatic gifts, and her capacity to win over once-intractable opponents, ultimately secured for her the right of the Convent of St. Joseph to exist in Avila and a law suit against it was resolved. The small but well-educated and influential religious reform party in Avila was pleased to see this example of discipline and religious humility in the heart of the city as a form of living sermon to the other residents. For Teresa, the simple life of this new convent was much superior to the luxuries of the old; most of her supporters, many of them cousins, agreed, but a few were unable to endure it and returned to the Incarnation with her consent. Sleeping on straw mattresses, without servants, wearing harsh sackcloth robes, the sisters at St. Joseph were soon afflicted by a plague of lice in their clothes and hair, but after intercessory prayers by Teresa she reported that the lice departed once and for all.

She called her reformed sisterhood the "Discalced Carmelites." *Discalced* means that they did not wear shoes but went barefoot, again in tribute to Jesus' simplicity and suffering. Some historians have seen their harsh way of life as a form of repression of women, the antithesis of feminist goals. In one sense it was, but historian Jodi Bilinkoff has pointed out that the issue can be seen in a different and more positive light:

> For Teresa voluntarily chosen enclosure had a potentially liberating effect. Her years of experience at la Encarnacion convinced her that the communication of nuns with secular society inevitably brought "worldliness" and temptations of various sorts.... Nuns who remained cloistered were, paradoxically, more "free" than those who interacted with, and thereby became entangled in the demands of, the world.

When St. Joseph's was established, Teresa, again prompted by divine visitation, moved to establish another convent, at the market town of Medina del Campo. This and her other houses were usually in market centers (including Toledo, Segovia, and Seville) because urban centers alone seemed likely to be able to provide the money in occasional benefactions which her new rule specified. Later, when rural houses were established, some kind of regular financing became imperative or they would have foundered quickly. The cities also possessed large *converso* populations, and the merchants and professionals who sympathized with the new spirituality of Catholic reform, rather than the older legalistic form of faith, looked more favorably on Teresa's reforms.

Teresa Establishes More Convents

Despite recurrent illnesses, Teresa lived into her late 60s, the last year being the most active, as she moved from place to place in Spain establishing new convents of the Discalced Carmelites—a total of 17 in her last 20 years. Inspired by her example, Carmelite friars as well as nuns began to organize reforms, the most distinguished of whom was Friar (ultimately Saint) John of the Cross, who for a time was Teresa's confessor. He was many years her junior and admired her greatly but could still rebuke her when necessary. "When you make your confession, Mother," he told her on one occasion, "you have a way of finding the prettiest excuses." Around him gathered many stories of supernatural events and stern dealings with demonic interventions; one of the nuns of St. Joseph's was "lifted bodily from her feet and left suspended upside down in the air until ordered back to her stall by St. John of the Cross" while another was "glued so firmly to the ground that no one could make her budge until she was released by a mere glance from the friar."

As the Discalced Carmelites established themselves, however, the older "Calced" branch became increasingly suspicious and resentful; they used their influence with the authorities to prevent new houses—even when guaranteed an income by wealthy enthusiasts—from being established, so that some of Teresa's long and difficult journeys across Spain were made in vain. They also arranged for the imprisonment of John of the Cross in Toledo where he was flogged and ordered to abandon the Reformers; although he steadfastly refused. Teresa was anxious about his fate, writing to one friend:

> I am fearfully distressed about Friar John and afraid they might bring some fresh charge against him. God treats his friends in a terrible way, though they really have no reason to complain, for that is how he treated his own Son.... For a good nine months they kept [the Friar] in a prison-cell so tiny that, small as he is, it would hardly hold him.

John of the Cross's sufferings ended after eight months when he managed to escape, but he was so sick that Teresa thought he would die in any case.

A papal nuncio to whom Teresa appealed that the Calced and Discalced Carmelites might be officially divided into two separate congregations (the only way she could see to end the conflict) was not at first disposed to listen sympathetically. Teresa, he declared, was "a restless, disobedient and contumacious gadabout who, under the guise of devotion, has invented false doctrines and broken her enclosure against the orders of the Council of Trent and her own superiors, teaching as if she were a Master, in disregard of what St. Paul said about women not being allowed to teach." This attack in turn, however, aroused Teresa's growing body of friends and supporters within Spain who sent reassuring messages to Rome about her good qualities (and those of John of the Cross). Finally, in June 1580, she managed to get a brief from the Pope officially dividing the Carmelites into two distinct provinces and settling most of the points of conflict between the branches.

Teresa traveled extensively right up to the end of her life and endured a long coach ride during her final illness. Neither did death bring an end to her peregrinations. The nuns who attended her in her final illness reported that her sickroom was filled with a delicious aroma, and those who laid her to rest discovered that her body was immune to decay, another sign, in their view, of her exceptional sanctity. Far from decomposing, her body emitted a sweet aroma ("the odor of sanctity") not only at first but for years thereafter as it was repeatedly dug up and examined. Not only was it inspected; the body was also moved from place to place as rival convents and cities vied to get their hands on what was now a holy relic. And with each exhumation parts of the miraculously preserved body were hacked off to be used as relics: first a finger, next an arm, later the heart (which was said to bear signs of the angels piercing spear) until by the next century the incorruptible body was scarcely more than a fragment. "The cult of relics was still as fervent in sixteenth century Spain as ever it had been in the Middle Ages" said one biographer, and "Teresa, as a true daughter of the Church, would never have dreamed of questioning it" but she could hardly have anticipated "that her own remains would be added to the sacred stock, to be avidly fought over, ghoulishly examined, discussed, subdivided, and ultimately distributed throughout Christendom." Forty years after her death, in 1622, Teresa of Jesus was named a saint while the order she had founded continued to endure, though it had been forced early to accept permanent endowments as the only viable way of surviving the economic austerities of a Spain which was now entering a long period of decline and senescence.

SOURCES:

Bilinkoff, Jodi. *The Avila of Saint Teresa: Religious Reform in a Sixteenth Century City*. Cornell University Press, 1989.

Clissold, Stephen. *St. Teresa of Avila*. Seabury, 1982.

FURTHER READING:

Cohen, J. M. *The Life of St. Teresa*. Penguin, 1957.

Elliott, J. H. *Imperial Spain*. New American Library, 1966.

Peers, E. Allison. *Studies in the Spanish Mystics*. Sheldon, 1927.

Margaret Thatcher

(1925–)

First woman prime minister of any major Western nation and first British prime minister since the 1820s to win three consecutive elections.

"Once a woman is made equal to a man she becomes his superior."

MARGARET THATCHER
QUOTING SOPHOCLES (1968)

In the 1950s, Margaret Thatcher did not emphasize her humble background; later, she felt it was a political asset. As the eldest of seven children, her father Alfred had to quit school at 12 or 13 to help support his family. He later moved to the small railroad equipment manufacturing and market town of Grantham, where he met Beatrice, his wife to be, in the Methodist Church. Hard workers and careful savers after they married, Thatcher's parents bought a three-story brick building equipped with a grocery shop on the ground floor and family quarters above. There was an outhouse, no running water, and no garden. Not until Thatcher was ten did the family acquire a radio.

Beatrice—a quiet woman who wore her hair in a bun—kept house, sewed, baked, and helped in the store, while Alfred—six feet two or three, good looking, blond—ran the store, cofounded the Grantham Rotary Club, became president of the town Grocers' Association, local head of the National Savings Movement, and a member of the boards of both the boys' and girls' schools in Grantham. Joining the Borough Council in 1927 as an Independent, he served for 25 years, becom-

Born Margaret Hilda Roberts on October 13, 1925, in Grantham, England; daughter of Alfred (a grocery store owner and community leader) and Beatrice Ethel (Stephenson) Roberts (a dressmaker); married: Denis Thatcher, December 13, 1951; children: (twins) Mark and Carol.

Contributed by Corinne L. Gilb, Professor of History, Wayne State University, Detroit, Michigan

1245

1943–47	Studied chemistry at Somerville College, Oxford
1946–47	President of Oxford University Conservative Association
1947–51	Worked as chemical researcher
1950–51	Conservative candidate for Parliament, representing Dartford, North Kent
1951–54	Studied to become a barrister
1959	Elected to represent Finchley; youngest of 25 women in the House of Commons
1961	Joint parliamentary secretary, Ministry of Pensions and National Insurance, under Harold Macmillan
1970–74	Secretary of state for education and science under Ted Heath
1974	Second in command at Centre for Policy Studies
1975	Elected leader of Conservative Opposition in the House of Commons
1979	Elected prime minister
1990	Withdrew as prime minister; replaced by John Major

ing chairman of its finance committee. For nine years, he was a town alderman and became mayor in 1943 as well as a justice of the peace at quarter sessions. He was also a Methodist lay preacher.

Margaret Thatcher was never close to her sister Muriel, a quiet girl born in 1921. Family life revolved around the grocery store, which was open six days a week, 10-to-12 hours a day. While the girls helped weigh and measure bulk goods into paper sacks, their parents vacationed separately so as not to leave the store unattended. The family's social life revolved around the Methodist church, attended three times on Sunday and at various times during the week. Thatcher's parents were teetotalers and stern moralists who donated to charities, said grace before every meal, and observed the sabbath strictly; emphasis was on thrift, citizenship, and self-improvement. Attending weekly extension lectures and monthly music club recitals, the family frequently discussed current affairs and read extensively. From age five to fifteen, Thatcher took piano lessons and sang in the church choir.

Perhaps projecting his own thwarted ambitions onto his daughter, Alfred saw to it that Thatcher went to the best council school, about a mile from home. At ten, she passed the scholar-

ship examination to attend Kesteven and Grantham Girls' School, a grammar school where she eventually concentrated on chemistry, biology, and mathematics. A diligent student, she was nearly always at the top of her class, though not very popular among peers. Going with her father to watch his court in action and to both hear and meet nationally important politicians, she also did routine work in the 1935 and 1942 elections. At 13 or 14, she declared that she wanted to be an MP (Member of Parliament). Her parents, originally Liberals, voted Conservative in the interwar period. Since Grantham was the site of munitions factories in World War II, it was heavily bombed.

During the war, Thatcher studied to prepare for a scholarship examination with the hope of entering Oxford University. In October 1943, she was admitted to Somerville College to study chemistry at Oxford but not on full scholarship. Teaching at Grantham's Central School for Boys during the summer of her second year, she earned money for a bicycle. At the university, she sang in the Bach Choir and joined the Scientific Society but donated most of her spare time to the Oxford University Conservative Association, of which she became president in her third and fourth years. **Winston Churchill** was her hero, and in 1945 she was deeply impressed by Friedrich A. Hayek's antisocialist book *The Road to Serfdom*.

After winning a second-class degree, Thatcher went to work as a research chemist. In 1948, she attended the annual Conservative Party Conference as a representative of the Oxford Graduates Association. By this time, under Prime Minister Clement Attlee, the salaries of MPs had been raised, allowing her to think in earnest about running for Parliament.

In 1950 and 1951, the 24-year-old studied to become a barrister and ran as the Conservative candidate in industrial Dartford in North Kent. In the process, she met Denis Thatcher, a man ten years her senior and managing director of his family's company in Erith in North Kent, whose brief wartime marriage had ended in divorce. A Methodist—despite his drinking, smoking, and cursing—he was even more of a Conservative than Thatcher. Married on December 13, 1951, they became the parents of twins Mark and Carol in August 1953, and baptized their children in the Church of England. Following the advice she'd put forth in a February 17, 1952, article entitled, "Wake Up, Women," which asserted that a woman could have a family and a career, Thatcher pursued her legal studies to completion, emphasizing tax law, and enjoyed her husband's strong support.

After applying unsuccessfully a number of times to be a Conservative candidate for MP between 1955 and 1958, she was finally selected in 1958 to campaign for the safe seat in Finchley, a district of middle-aged to elderly homeowners; nearly one-fourth of the voters were Jewish.

Thatcher Is Youngest of Women in House of Commons

In 1959, Thatcher became the youngest of 25 women in the House of Commons. Though treated as an outsider, she worked very hard (a life-long trait), mastered detail (another lifelong trait), and did the necessary political homework. Her speeches in Commons commanded attention, and beginning in 1961 she was rewarded with a series of posts, first in the **Harold Macmillan** government, then in the Conservative shadow cabinet, and finally as Prime Minister Ted Heath's secretary of state for education and science. In this post, she stuck to her guns through repeated bitter controversies over charging for milk at school and over the demand for comprehensive schools which would be more egalitarian. In 1971, *The Sun* called her, "The Most Unpopular Woman in Britain." She did believe in spending on education, especially at the primary level. She said she was for quality, standards, and choice in education, and for equality of opportunity, while in favor of tying universities closer to industry.

Second in command at the Centre for Policy Studies, founded in 1974 by Conservative Keith Joseph, Thatcher worked with Joseph to promote the kind of monetarism advocated by the American, Milton Friedman, as opposed to Keynesian economic policies supported by the Labour Party and by many Conservatives; they also sponsored the kind of social market policies that had been introduced into West Germany by Ludwig Erhard.

By early 1975, many Conservatives in Commons were disaffected with Ted Heath as their leader. When most of the other Conservative leaders would not run against him, Thatcher stepped forward. Regarding her as a stalking horse against Heath, many did not expect her to win. With her campaign managed by Airey Neave, who was later killed by an I.R.A. bomb, others helped her as well, and Thatcher won on the second ballot with 146 votes.

Meanwhile, Thatcher's private life was thriving. In 1965, her husband's company had been acquired by Burmah Oil of which he became a director. Thatcher's daughter Carol studied law at London University and passed her law examina-

tions, but never practiced, traveling instead to Australia where she worked for five years. Their son Mark failed to pass the examinations which would have made him a chartered accountant; often seen at the Queen's Tennis Club, he is strongly interested in motor racing. Retiring from Burmah Oil in 1975, Denis Thatcher remains on the board of two companies. He is an ardent golfer and rugby referee.

Labour prime ministers gave Thatcher a hard time as Opposition leader in Commons, but she held her own. Her speech in 1976 which stated that the U.S.S.R. wanted to dominate the world prompted the Soviets to label her, "The Iron Lady." With little knowledge of foreign affairs, she embarked on foreign travel and attracted controversy again in 1978 by saying that immigration from Commonwealth countries had made the British afraid of being swamped by people of a different culture.

She Becomes Prime Minister

The winter of 1978–79 was one of discontent in Britain. When the Conservatives won the majority of seats in the 1979 general elections, Thatcher became prime minister. She did not make a radical break with the Conservative elite because she needed the backing of various Heath supporters' constituencies in Commons; of the 22 members of her first cabinet, 18 had been in the Heath government. Yet, she did believe in a free market system and—in this year of economic depression—her first budget cut government spending drastically. Saying she wanted to set people free from socialism, she stood firm despite a torrent of criticism as the economy worsened. To deal with the major problem of controlling her cabinet, she reshifted its members in September 1981 and began to work through an informal group of her close followers, mostly self-made men. (Thatcher was no friend of the feminist movement.) By 1989, the cabinet was mostly Thatcherized. Her style with her ministers was domineering, which did not sit well with understated Tory gentlemen who had been taught to be courteous or patronizing to women.

Adept at handling the press, Thatcher at first nurtured her following among the backbenchers in Commons. Her popularity leapt forward in 1982 when she led a counterattack against Argentina's invasion of the Falkland Islands. She annoyed European Economic Community (EEC) leaders by fighting vigorously to get revisions of the British contribution to the EEC budget, which was slanted in favor of France and Germany. She also refused to join the European Monetary Sys-

tem, and in general worked to preserve British sovereignty. Her close rapport with American President Ronald Reagan and the U.S.S.R.'s new leader, **Mikhail Gorbachev,** brought her international power. A nationalist in foreign affairs, she backed Reagan whenever feasible. Gorbachev sought to use her influence with Reagan and, consequently, she played a significant role in the transformation of East-West relations. Becoming an international political star, she displayed remarkable energy and stamina. Her relationship with Queen Elizabeth remained professional, although Thatcher sometimes seemed to seek a queenly role and disagreed with the queen's belief in sanctions against South Africa.

In domestic affairs, she preached the Radical Right doctrines to which the label "Thatcherism" became attached; in practice, she was often pragmatic and cautious. Her policies have been described as a break with the consensus politics both of establishment Conservatives and of the Left. She did not agree with traditional Tory paternalism but instead preached self-reliance. The Conservatives sought to curtail the power of local councils, which were largely Labour-dominated, including a policy of selling council-owned houses to their occupants and tax measures designed to reduce the role of local councils as deliverers of social services. British "privatization" became a model for many other countries.

Thatcher's primary concern was that Britain's economic strength, pride, and power be restored by denationalizing industry; encouraging entrepreneurial enterprise, hard work, and strong family life; increasing opportunities for social mobility; and building a strong national defense. She thought that welfare should be a private responsibility, not a public concern. While national pride did improve, many of her other goals were not achieved. Direct taxes were reduced, but the total tax bill for individuals rose. Public expenditure continued to rise in real terms, helped by windfall assets from North Sea oil and privatization.

Never one to mince words, she made enemies, not only in the Labour Party, but also among more traditional Conservatives, in the Church of England, the Foreign Office, the British Broadcasting Corporation, among civil servants, and especially among intellectuals. Some said her personal values were more American than British, and some scorned her as a *petit bourgeois* (lower middle class). One critic called her "Attila the Hen"; others simply called her Victorian. But her personal staff was deeply devoted to her. Thatcher's political downfall came because of popular discontent about the poll tax instituted by her government and because of discontent within her cabinet.

When Thatcherite John Major became prime minister, many feared Thatcher would continue to dominate public policy. She became a grandmother in 1989, after Mark had married the daughter of a Dallas, Texas, automobile dealer, but did not retire to private life. Still a member of the House of Commons, she has spoken against European federalism. With visits to foreign countries, lecture tours, and the writing of her autobiography, she has remained in the public eye.

SOURCES:

Abse, Leo. *Margaret, Daughter of Beatrice, A Politician's Psychobiography of Margaret Thatcher.* Jonathan Cape, 1989.

Brown, Gordon. *Where There is Greed—Margaret Thatcher and the Betrayal of Britain's Future.* Mainstream Publishing, 1989.

Bruce-Gardyne, Jock. *Mrs. Thatcher's First Administration.* Macmillan, 1984.

Butcher, Hugh, Ian G. Law, Robert Leach, and Maurice Mullard. *Local Government and Thatcherism.* Routledge, 1990.

Byrd, Peter, ed. *British Foreign Policy under Thatcher.* Philip Allan, 1988.

Filo della Torre, Paolo. *Viva Britannia, Mrs. Thatcher's Britain.* Sidgewick & Jackson, 1985.

Gaffney, John. *The Language of Political Leadership in Contemporary Britain.* St. Martin's Press, 1991.

Gardiner, George, M.P. *Margaret Thatcher: From Childhood to Leadership.* William Kimber, 1975.

Haseler, Stephen. *The Battle for Britain: Thatcher and the New Liberals.* I. B. Tauris, 1989.

Jessop, Bob, et al. *Thatcherism—A Tale of Two Nations.* Polity Press, 1988.

Junor, Penny. *Margaret Thatcher: Wife, Mother, Politician.* Sidgewick & Jackson, 1983.

Lewis, Russell. *Margaret Thatcher: A Personal and Political Biography.* Routledge & Kegan Paul, 1984.

Mayer, Allan J. *Madam Prime Minister: Margaret Thatcher and Her Rise to Power.* Newsweek Books, 1979.

Ogden, Chris. *Maggie, An Intimate Portrait of a Woman in Power.* Simon & Schuster, 1990.

Prior, Jim. *A Balance of Power.* Hamish Hamilton, 1986.

Raban, Jonathan. *God, Man and Mrs. Thatcher.* Chatto & Windus, 1989.

Riddell, Peter. *The Thatcher Decade, How Britain Has Changed During the 1980s.* Basil Blackwell, 1989.

———. *The Thatcher Government.* Basil Blackwell, 1985.

Skidelsky, Robert, ed. *Thatcherism.* Chatto & Windus, 1988.

Smith, Geoffrey. *Reagan and Thatcher.* Norton, 1991.

Thatcher, Margaret. *The Revival of Britain, Speeches on Home and University Affairs, 1975–1988.* Compiled by Alistair B. Cooke. Aurum Press, 1989.

Webster, Wendy. *Not a Man to Match Her.* Women's Press, 1990.

Tiberius

(42 B.C.–A.D. 37)

Stepson of Caesar Augustus and an outstanding military leader, who served as the second emperor of the Roman Empire.

Pronunciation: Tie-BEER-ee-us. Born Tiberius Claudius Nero Caesar (some ancients refer to him as Nero [not to be confused with the fifth Roman emperor known more commonly by that name]) on November 16, 42 B.C., either at Fundi (a city to the south of Rome) or more likely in Rome; died on March 16, A.D. 37, at Misenum, just north of Neapolis (modern Naples); son of Tiberius Claudius Nero (an aristocrat) and Livia; married: Vipsania Agrippina (later forced to divorce her and marry Julia, daughter of Augustus); children: (first marriage) Drusus the Younger (poisoned by Sejanus in A.D. 23). Predecessor: Augustus. Successor: Gaius (Caligula).

In 509 B.C., Rome abolished the rule of kings with the creation of the Roman Republic. Several hundred years later, the Republic was threatened by several dictators who assumed absolute control. The last of these great dictators, **Julius Caesar,** set the stage for the establishment of the Roman Empire. It is ironic that Tiberius became the second emperor of Rome because his ancestors were loyal to the Republic. He was named after his father, Tiberius Claudius Nero, an aristocrat aligned with the principles of the Republic. His mother **Livia** was also from an aristocratic family.

The 44 B.C. assassination of Julius Caesar, which divided the people of Rome, also divided the family of Tiberius. Though Octavian, Mark Antony, and Lepidus who had formed the Second Triumvirate joined forces to eliminate those who had plotted against Caesar, they soon began to struggle for power with one another. Tiberius's father, a loyal follower of Mark Antony, conspired against Octavian, and with tensions growing between Octavian (the future Augustus) and Mark Antony, Tiberius's family fled Italy. Escaping first to the island of Sicily, they later traveled to the

"Goodbye my dear Tiberius, and the best of luck go with you in your battles on my behalf.... Goodbye, dearest and bravest of men and the most conscientious general alive! If anything goes wrong with you I shall never smile again!"

CAESAR AUGUSTUS

Contributed by John D. Wineland, Ph.D. in Ancient History, Miami University, Oxford, Ohio

eastern region of the Roman world. Roman historian **Suetonius** wrote that Tiberius's childhood and youth were "beset with hardships and difficulties, because Nero [Tiberius's father] and Livia took him wherever they went in their flight from Augustus." According to Suetonius, as the family fled, the infant Tiberius "nearly betrayed them twice by crying."

In 39 B.C., an agreement was signed allowing the family to return to Rome. But shortly after their arrival, Octavian developed a passion for Tiberius's mother Livia. Thus, when Tiberius was two years old, his father agreed to divorce Livia, who was six months pregnant with Tiberius's brother Drusus, and Octavia and Livia were married on January 17, 38 B.C. This marriage linked Tiberius to the most powerful man in Rome and ultimately resulted in his own rule as emperor.

As Tiberius grew, he was carefully educated, studying with the finest tutors available in the Empire. He learned rhetoric under the tutelage of Theodore of Gadara; he also studied philosophy as well as Greek and Roman literature. Tiberius became a *philhelene,* a lover of Greek culture, language, and philosophy. Certainly, such early training was to make a profound impact on his life as a Roman ruler.

The public life of Tiberius began (in 33 or 32 B.C.) at the age of nine when he delivered his father's funeral eulogy. Octavian developed closer ties with his stepsons, Tiberius and Drusus, after the death of their father. In 20 B.C., the 22-year-old Tiberius accompanied his stepfather to the East to recover the Roman standards lost 33 years earlier in a war with the Parthians. (Octavian, who was now known as **Caesar Augustus,** had become emperor in 27 B.C.) This journey began an outstanding military career for Tiberius, whose personal life was also happy at the time. He married Vipsania Agrippina, daughter of Augustus's powerful lieutenant, Marcus Vipsanius Agrippa. In 13 B.C., Vipsania bore Tiberius's only son Drusus the Younger.

But the following year, Tiberius's situation became more difficult as Augustus forced Tiberius to divorce the mother of his child and marry the emperor's own recently widowed daughter Julia. In love with Vipsania, Tiberius was very unhappy with the marriage to Julia, who had a scandalous reputation. Suetonius remarked: "One day, [Tiberius] accidently caught sight of Vipsania and followed her with tears in his eyes and intense unhappiness written on his face." Henceforth, safeguards were taken to ensure that he would never see her again.

CHRONOLOGY

50 B.C.	Tiberius's father named consul of Rome
49 B.C.	Julius Caesar crossed the Rubicon
44 B.C.	Julius Caesar murdered
42 B.C.	Anthony and Octavian defeated Brutus and Cassius at the Battle of Philippi; Tiberius born
29 B.C.	*Pax Romana,* or Peace of Rome, established by Octavian
12 B.C.	Tiberius forced by Augustus (Octavian) to divorce Vipsania and marry Julia
A.D. 4	Tiberius adopted by Augustus
14	Augustus died; Tiberius began reign
26	Moved to the island of Capri
31	Sejanus executed
33	Jesus of Nazareth executed
37	Tiberius died (probably of natural causes)

Tiberius Leads Successful Military Campaigns

Despite the pain in his personal life, Tiberius's military campaigns were successful. From 12–9 B.C., he led the conquest to the north in the region called Pannonia (part of Yugoslavia, Austria, and Hungary), which was added to the Empire. Another personal loss followed in 9 B.C., when his younger and highly favored brother Drusus fell from a horse to his death during campaigns to subdue the Germany territories. Tiberius continued to fight against the stubborn German forces until 7 B.C., when suddenly, at the height of his successful military career, he retired to the Aegean island of Rhodes.

Many have speculated about the motivation for his abrupt departure. Indeed, several factors may have led to his self-imposed retreat from public life, among them his unhappy marriage to Julia, who was finally exiled by her father Augustus in 2 B.C. for sexual promiscuity. Another underlying reason for his withdrawal was the problem of succession. Augustus's lack of a male heir to the throne—with only one daughter by his first wife Scribona—had in part led to his marriage with Tiberius's mother Livia, who provided him with two stepsons and a hopeful chance for bearing a male heir to become emperor. Livia, however, did not fulfill Augustus's dream of having a son of his own. Therefore, Augustus turned his favor toward

Drusus while ignoring the elder stepson Tiberius. Following Drusus's unexpected death, Augustus passed over Tiberius again and made clear his intention that his grandsons Gaius and Lucius, Julia's sons by her marriage to Agrippa, would become his heirs apparent. Tiberius's decision to move to the island of Rhodes came on the heels of this announcement. But by A.D. 2, both grandsons had died, Tiberius had returned to Rome, and Augustus had somewhat reluctantly recognized him as his heir. Two years later, in A.D. 4, Augustus adopted Tiberius as his son. Tiberius was then ordered to adopt his nephew Germanicus as his son, revealing Augustus's desire that Germanicus become the emperor upon the death of Tiberius, rather than Tiberius's natural son, Drusus the Younger.

During the next decade, however, power and control slowly shifted from Augustus to Tiberius, who returned to Germany from A.D. 4 to 6 and put down new rebellions. From A.D. 6 to 9, he fought to maintain Roman authority once again in Pannonia and in Illyricum (Yugoslavia and Albania). By A.D. 13, Tiberius was granted powers equal to that of Augustus.

Augustus died on August 19, A.D. 14. He was soon deified by the senate, which shortly thereafter recognized Tiberius as emperor of Rome—though he seemed somewhat reluctant to accept this honor. When news of Augustus's death spread to the legions, rebellions broke out in Pannonia near the Danube River and in lower Germany along the Rhine River. Tiberius sent his son Drusus the Younger and his adopted son Germanicus to put down these insurrections.

While Germanicus was very popular in Rome and among the troops, he always remained loyal to his adoptive father. Regardless, while stationed in Antioch, Syria, in A.D. 19, his unexpected death eliminated him as a possible rival to Tiberius and his son Drusus. The convenience of Germanicus's death did not escape Roman historian, Tacitus, who retold rumors that Tiberius had arranged for the popular Germanicus to be poisoned. Now clearly, Drusus the Younger was the logical heir to Tiberius's throne, but he died in A.D. 23. Rumors surrounding his death pointed to Sejanus as his murderer.

Sejanus Persuades Emperor to Retreat to Capri

Sejanus's father was the leader of the emperor's personal army, known as the Praetorian Guard. As far back as A.D. 15, a close relationship had developed between Sejanus and Tiberius, when the ambitious Sejanus was named to succeed his father. Tiberius's reign was soon marred by a succession of trials for treason and executions, and Tiberius grew vulnerable to suspicion and treachery. In A.D. 26, he was finally persuaded by Sejanus to retreat to the island of Capri, located near Italy in the Mediterranean Sea. This afforded Sejanus the opportunity to seize even more power, and he virtually became emperor by default.

For ten years, Tiberius retired to his magnificent villas on Capri and did not return to Rome for the remainder of his reign. He came accompanied by his favorite astrologers who were to help guide him in his self-imposed isolation. Suetonius reiterates rumors of his day that charged Tiberius with indulging in many violent sexual encounters and orgies while at Capri. It seems likely that he stayed away to avoid the crowded cities and his domineering mother Livia. He was also aware that he lacked popularity, especially with the senators who did not agree with many of his policies. Fearing he was in danger, Tiberius found in Capri a secure, secluded island stronghold.

While Tiberius attempted to govern the Empire from his island villas, Sejanus easily intercepted his written decrees. As Sejanus's power grew in Rome and with the senate, he systematically plotted to eliminate any possible rivals to his control of succession to the throne; he used charges of treason, quick trials, and assassinations to achieve his goals. In A.D. 31, Sejanus finally obtained Tiberius's permission to marry Livilla, the widow of Drusus the Younger. But soon Tiberius received information revealing Sejanus's plot to kill Gaius, the late Drusus's teenaged son. In order to eliminate Sejanus, Tiberius secretly removed him from power and placed his trusted friend Macro in charge of the Praetorian Guard. Sejanus was then arrested during a meeting of the senate which immediately ordered him executed. As several other arrests and executions were soon carried out, it became clear that Gaius was to be Tiberius's heir to the throne. In March of A.D. 37 in Misenum, Tiberius died, passing power to his grandson Gaius, who had acquired the name of **Caligula,** in a succession that historian David Stockton called Tiberius's "blackest of all indictments."

Tiberius was a reluctant emperor who inherited the difficult task of following the Empire's founder. During his rule, he continued many of the policies of his predecessor Augustus and attempted to maintain the empire as he had received it; his decision to abandon Rome and leave Sejanus in charge was certainly his greatest mistake. Even with his faults, it seemed Tiberius was both more effective and content as a general than as an emperor. In his time, the new religion Christianity was born, which would later dominate the empire that attempted to crush it. **Jesus of Nazareth** carried out his ministry in Palestine and was executed while Tiberius was emperor. When the Pharisees questioned Christ about paying taxes, showing him a coin, he responded: "Give unto Caesar what is Caesar's and unto God what is God's." That coin undoubtedly bore the portrait of Tiberius.

SOURCES:

Dio Cassius. *Roman History.* Translated by Earnest Cary. Loeb Classical Library, Harvard University Press, 1961.

Grant, Michael. *The Roman Emperors.* Scribner, 1985.

Levick, Barbara. *Tiberius the Politician.* London: Thames & Hudson, 1976.

Stockton, David. "The Founding of the Empire," in *The Oxford History of the Classical World.* John Broadman, et. al. eds. Oxford: Oxford University Press, 1986.

Suetonius. *The Twelve Caesars.* Translated by Robert Graves. Penguin Books, 1985.

Tacitus. *The Annuals.* Translated by Alfred John Church and William Jackson Brodribb. Random House, 1942.

FURTHER READING:

Hoehner, Harold. *Herod Antipas.* Cambridge: Cambridge University Press, 1972.

Maranon, Gregorio. *Tiberius: The Resentful Caesar.* Duell, Sloan, and Pearce, 1956.

Marsh, Frank. *The Reign of Tiberius.* London: Oxford University Press, 1931.

Seager, Robin. *Tiberius.* University of California Press, 1972.

Tarver, J. C. *Tiberius the Tyrant.* Dutton, 1902.

Alfred von Tirpitz

(1894–1930)

Professional sailor and amateur politician, who founded and built the imperial German navy with such intensity that it quickly surpassed the fleets possessed by France and Russia and became second only to Britain's royal navy.

Pronunciation: Teer-PEETZ. Born Alfred von Tirpitz in Küstrin in 1849; died in Munich in 1930; son of a lawyer.

Like many other officers in the imperial German navy, Alfred Tirpitz was born into a middle-class family, the son of a lawyer. At the age of 16, he persuaded his somewhat reluctant parents to permit him to pursue a naval career, one in which he was remarkably successful. Regarded early as a leader of the future, as a young lieutenant, he quickly made his mark and was frequently called the "master." In 1877, Tirpitz became the head of the torpedo division of the navy, a branch that had hitherto received little attention. Tirpitz labored with considerable technical virtuosity to improve the accuracy and range of his weaponry, although he curiously did not recognize the future potential of submarines as a powerful ingredient of naval power.

In 1896, Tirpitz was posted to Asia and given the command of the German flotilla stationed on the Chinese coast. At that time, Germany possessed no naval station in China, where Queen **Victoria**'s Royal Navy presided over not only the Chinese shoreline but many of the declining Celestial Empire's internal affairs as well. Tirpitz resented the secondary position that Germany was forced to occupy, and his observations of

Contributed by Lamar Cecil, William R. Kenan, Jr. Professor of History, Washington and Lee University, Lexington, Virginia

British predominance in China reinforced his already well-developed Anglophobia, one which soon became a mania. Tirpitz argued persuasively that Kaiser **Wilhelm II** should force the Chinese emperor to grant Germany a concessionary port in northern China; this occurred in 1896 with the acquisition of Kiaochow.

Wilhelm II had his eye on Tirpitz as a figure suitable for assuming the command of the entire German navy, a body created after the formation of the Empire in 1871. It was a very divided force, with operations, personnel, procurement, and other tasks parceled out among various naval authorities. The egomaniacal kaiser, fascinated by the sea from childhood and, like Tirpitz, jealous of his English grandmother's (Victoria's) vast navy, wanted his fleet to be increased. Wilhelm II had no clear idea of what sort of navy he should have nor what it should do when and if it came into being, but it was clear to him that the leadership of the German navy as it existed was incapable of persuading either the German people or the Parliament that financial sacrifices should be made to obtain a German armada. Tirpitz, the kaiser was convinced, could bring order to the navy and convince his subjects to approve its expansion, and in 1896 he appointed him state secretary of the Imperial Naval Office.

Tirpitz, who would inhabit this position for almost two decades, did not disappoint his imperial master. Dictatorial by nature, he moved swiftly to make his position in naval affairs supreme and only the kaiser could stand in his way. This in fact sometimes proved to be the case; for Wilhelm II was as hard-headed as Tirpitz and did not like the admiral's insistence on having his way. This "extraordinarily autocratic personality," as the kaiser described Tirpitz, was suspiciously like the former Iron Chancellor, **Otto von Bismarck,** whom Wilhelm had dismissed from office in 1890 because of insubordination. Tirpitz, for his part, had no great opinion of the kaiser's intelligence, but he recognized that Wilhelm II's enthusiasm for ships was a very useful asset. For all his Caesarian temperament, the admiral was a person of considerable social grace, and he managed to hold his position far longer than any other of the kaiser's governmental officials.

Tirpitz Lobbies for Greater Navy

On taking office as state secretary, Tirpitz was determined to proceed at once with a major increase in Germany's naval strength. This would require extensive funding from the Reichstag (Parliament), a body which in the past had been hostile

to naval expenditures. Tirpitz recognized that he would have to persuade the deputies to grant the requisite funds, which would be more forthcoming if a clearly reasoned naval budget were presented. The Reichstag, the creature of the electorate, would also respond to public appeals for a navy, and to encourage such an enthusiasm Tirpitz in 1898 created the Naval League. The league, which was the most successful lobbying force in the history of imperial Germany, was tireless in advancing the claims for a great navy in a variety of publications, by entertaining members of the Reichstag on warships, and by arranging for inspection tours of ships and port facilities by ordinary Germans, especially those who lived far from the sea.

In propagandizing the navy, Tirpitz was able to draw upon the increasing conviction felt in Germany, and indeed everywhere in Europe, that a navy was a prerequisite for national survival. Without battleships and cruisers in abundance, Germany would be unable to protect her trade abroad, to ensure the importation of food in the event of war, and in general to play a role in world affairs commensurate with her economic and military strength. In 1898, Tirpitz prepared a masterful outline of the navy he wished to have, stressing the economies that would derive if the Reichstag were to authorize naval expenditures for an extended period, rather than the traditional policy of requiring the state secretary of the Imperial Naval Office to appear hat in hand every year. What Tirpitz did not tell the deputies was that in granting money for a six- or seven-year period, he was thereby free from their interference. This Tirpitz valued, not only because the Reichstag was in his opinion a body of landlubbers ignorant of naval affairs but, in the framework of his conservative political notions, an unpalatable nuisance in what should properly be a monarchical-bureaucratic state. The Reichstag agreed to Tirpitz's demands, and in 1898 the so-called First Naval Law was passed, authorizing a sizable increase in the size of the imperial navy.

But Tirpitz was not satisfied. In 1900, he returned to the Reichstag and succeeded in obtaining a Second Naval Law, providing for still more ships to be built in the remainder of the decade. By this time, he had developed his "risk theory," the basis for every subsequent act in his career. According to the admiral's conception, Great Britain, intensely jealous of Germany's rising economic might, was determined to destroy the kaiser's empire. Only if Germany possessed a navy could this be avoided, and Tirpitz was persuaded that if he had enough ships to get through what he called the "danger zone," the Fatherland would be safe. What was required was maintaining a 2:3 ratio of British/German ships of the line. This, Tirpitz argued, would have two important effects. If Britain elected to attack Germany, Tirpitz's fleet could inflict such substantial damage that Russia and France, whom he believed to be as opposed to England as he was, would then deliver the coup de grace to Britain's wounded Royal Navy. England might be prudent enough to realize this, in which case the German navy would be the force that would cause London to make a diplomatic accommodation with Berlin, one by which the two great naval powers would divide the world. Since Britain was the prospective enemy, Tirpitz insisted that the major force in his navy be powerfully armed, short-range battleships and heavy cruisers, vessels that would have a narrow sailing range across the Channel and up into the North Sea but no real utility elsewhere unless they could be furnished with coal and other supplies at friendly ports. His navy had therefore to be strong enough to force its way out into the Atlantic, but to do so it would have to penetrate waters that for centuries had been commanded by the Royal Navy.

Nothing worked out as Tirpitz hoped. His expectation that France and Russia would always be Britain's enemies—ready to fall upon her—proved erroneous; in 1904, the French, thoroughly alarmed by the kaiser's army, signed a treaty of friendship with their old enemy England, and a few years later the British also reached an accommodation with Russia. The cementing force in all these diplomatic alignments was the common fear of Germany, with its massive army, its impetuous kaiser, and its vast navy. Tirpitz soon found that he could not maintain the necessary 2:3 ratio because the British, alarmed by the sudden appearance of a formidable rival, did not flinch from building more and more ships. London was of course not blind to the fact that Tirpitz's goliath battleships could, by their very design, be directed only against Britain. In 1905, a new "Dreadnought" class of battleships began to join the Royal Navy, vessels that were fearsome in destructive power and unprecedentedly costly to build. Unfortunately for Tirpitz, more and more Germans, including some in the government, were convinced that the armament race in which Tirpitz had involved the Fatherland was financially ruinous and likely to lead to war with England. The only way out was to negotiate a reduction in ships and personnel, the solution proposed by Theobald von Bethmann Hollweg, chancellor from 1909 on. Tirpitz would have none of such compromises, and his recalcitrance succeeded in destroying all the numerous attempts at arms reductions attempted in the last years before the war between London and Berlin.

British Navy Thwarts German Fleet

When the war opened in 1914, Tirpitz's great battlefleet was at once bottled up by the Royal Navy, which patrolled the English Channel and which was also drawn up behind vast mine fields in the North Sea. Although Tirpitz was prepared to risk the fleet, the kaiser would not agree until 1916, when Tirpitz was allowed to send out his armada against the British. The resulting battle of Jutland, in which the enemies sank approximately an equal number of one another's ships, was in fact a British victory, for Tirpitz's much vaunted navy had failed to pierce the protective cordon maintained by the Royal Navy. Germany, denied its victory, remained cut off from its trade, while the British continued to be able to supply France and to be reinforced from the United States.

Tirpitz had been tardy in recognizing the value of submarines, but with his battlefleet useless he turned now to the U-boat (*Unterseeboot*) as the means of Germany's deliverance. He argued that a ruthless policy of unrestricted submarine warfare should be introduced, with almost indiscriminate sinking of all enemy vessels or other ships suspected of carrying contraband. Tirpitz was convinced that England could thus be "brought to her knees," before the United States—which would resent this violation of its commerce and probably enter the war—could render effective aid to the Allies. Chancellor Bethmann Hollweg would not endorse Tirpitz's scheme, and the kaiser, disenchanted with the failure of his battlefleet to defeat England, dismissed Tirpitz in 1916.

Out of office, Tirpitz worked vindictively against Bethmann, using his influence to help topple him from office in July 1917. Two months later, Tirpitz was one of the founders of the Fatherland Party, a political body dedicated to rejecting any peace that did not give Germany enormous portions of France, Belgium, and Russia. Although the party attracted over a million members, its aims became increasingly utopian. Not only could the German navy not defeat the British, the army, bogged down in trench warfare in the West, was equally unable to succeed. With the entry of the United States into the conflict in April 1917, the war went steadily against Germany in spite of the gains she maintained in Russia. Meanwhile, the deeply dissatisfied German people had clearly had enough of such a bitter war. In November 1918, aware that the conflict could not be won and the nation now torn by violent revolution, the kaiser abdicated and two days later, on November 11, 1918, the new socialist government agreed to an armistice, which was renewed periodically until the signing of the punitive peace treaty at Versailles in June 1919.

Tirpitz followed all these developments with bitterness, incapable of realizing that his naval mania had been largely responsible for Britain's enmity toward Germany or that his "risk theory" had been a worthless jumble of ideals. Instead, Tirpitz declared it was not he who had been the architect of the Fatherland's defeat, but rather the parliamentarians who had quibbled about naval appropriations, or the socialist traitors who had chosen peace rather than victory, or the incompetent bureaucrats, or the fickle kaiser. He refused to support the Weimar Republic established in 1919, calling instead for a restoration of the Hohenzollern monarchy, publishing three volumes of memoirs containing vitriolic condemnations of all of his enemies. He served as a Reichstag deputy from 1924 to 1928 as a member of the conservative German-National party, constantly attacking the initiatives of Gustav Stresemann, the foreign minister during that period, to fulfill the terms of the Versailles treaty and to get on with the work of rebuilding a shattered Germany. Tirpitz died in 1930 just a few days short of his 81st birthday, unrepentant of his past and full of hope that some day Germany might once again become a great power.

SOURCES:

Von Tirpitz, Alfred. *Erinnerungen.* Leipzig, 1919.

————. *Politische Dokumente.* 2 vols. Hamburg and Berlin, 1924–26.

FURTHER READING:

Berghahn, Volker R. *Der Tirpitz-Plan.* Düsseldorf, 1971.

Lambi, Ivo N. *The Navy and German Power Politics, 1862–1914.* Boston, 1984.

Steinberg, Jonathan. *Yesterday's Deterrent: Tirpitz and the Birth of the German Battle Fleet.* London, 1965.

Marshal Tito

(1892–1980)

Yugoslavian who, after rising to prominence as a leader of his country's victory over the Fascists during World War II, established Yugoslavia's Communist government following the war, and headed it until his death in 1980.

Name variations: Josip Broz (since East European governments had outlawed Communists, many revolutionaries, such as Lenin, Stalin, and Trotsky, chose pseudonyms, which they retained after the Communist Party seized power; after trying several pseudonyms, in 1937, Broz settled on "Tito," a common Croatian name, which he first used in 1934). Pronunciation: TEE-toe. Born Josip Broz on May 7, 1892 (birthday officially celebrated on May 25), near the Slovenian border, in the small Croatian village of Kumrovec; died in 1980; son of Franjo (a Croat) and Marija (Javersek; a Slovene) Broz; married: Pelagia Belousova (or Belousnova), January 1920; married: Herta Hass, 1937; married: Jovanka Budisavljević, 1952; children: three by his first wife and one by his second, but only two sons, Zarko and Aleksandar, survived. Predecessor: Milan Gorkič. Successor: None.

As the 19th century neared its end, national unrest was increasing among the Balkan peninsula's South Slavs. The Slovenes and Croats in the northwestern corner of the Balkan peninsula were subjects of the Austro-Hungarian Empire. Centuries of German and Hungarian domination had oriented their cultures towards Western Europe. The most visible sign of this influence was their Roman Catholic faith. Although the Slovenes and Croats had much in common, linguistic differences plus the Slovenes' closer association with German culture had raised barriers between them. These differences were much less than those separating them from the other South Slavs who had converted to Orthodoxy and fallen under Byzantine influence before living in the Muslim Ottoman Empire for around 400 years. The Serbs were the largest segment of this group, which, in addition to them, had splintered into Bosnians, Montenegrans, and Macedonians after the Turkish 14th-century conquest of the Balkans. First the Montenegrans in the 15th century and then the Serbs in the 19th century had freed themselves from the Turks. By the end of the 19th century, Serbia was leading an increasingly

Contributed by Robert Frank Forrest, Assistant Professor of History, McNeese State University, Lake Charles, Louisiana

"Tito stands as one of the most complete, one of the most complex and enigmatic, of politicians."

MILOVAN DJILAS

popular movement to unite the South Slavs into a single state.

Such was the Balkan political situation when, near the Slovenian border, in the small Croatian village of Kumrovec, Marija Javersek Broz gave birth on May 7, 1892, to a son. Marija, a Slovene, and the boy's father Franjo, a Croat, named the baby Josip. He was the seventh of their 15 children, eight of whom died in infancy. Large families were common among the peasants of this region. Josip's mother was the eldest of 14 children, for example. Tito's parents, although they owned some land and the family house, were poor and decided to place Josip with his maternal grandfather in order to save money. Until around 1900, Tito remained mostly under his grandfather's care. During these years, he learned the Slovene language and developed a love for hunting and fishing, which he retained throughout his life. When Tito turned seven, he started working on the Broz family farm and attending Kumrovec's elementary school, which had opened in 1899. Tito's academic career ended in 1904, but not before he became literate. Most Croatian peasants felt that school prevented children from doing something productive, thus Tito's family sent him to work for an uncle. This proved to be a very unpleasant experience for the boy, and he returned home.

Tito's life as a peasant ended in 1907 when he obtained his father's permission to join his cousin, a staff sergeant in the Austro-Hungarian army, at Sisak, a town about 50 miles from Croatia's capital Zagreb. After working briefly in a restaurant, Tito spent the next three years as a locksmith's apprentice while receiving his introduction to Marxism and trade unionism from two other apprentices. In 1910, he moved to Zagreb to ply his trade, found a job, and joined the Metal Workers' Union, which also made him a member of the Marxist Social Democratic Party of Croatia. An unstable job market prevented Tito from finding a secure job, so he held several jobs in Croatia and Slovenia as a metal worker and bicycle repairman. His search for steady work led him to Bohemia and finally to Vienna where he worked in the Daimler automobile plant during most of 1912. While in Vienna, he learned fashionable dancing, fencing, and German, which Milovan Djilas maintains he knew better than Russian. Throughout these years, Tito also maintained his union membership but was not involved in politics.

In 1913, when Austro-Hungarian law obliged the 21-year-old Tito to serve two years in the imperial army, he was assigned to the 25th Regiment at Zagreb. Before World War I began, he had become the regimental fencing champion and

CHRONOLOGY

1910	Joined the Metal Workers' Union
1914	World War I began
1915	Captured by Russians
1917	Russian Revolution
1918	World War I ended; Yugoslav kingdom established
1920	Tito returned from Russia
1928	Received five-year prison sentence
1940	Became leader of the Yugoslav Communists
1943	Became head of the Yugoslav government
1948	Stalin expelled Yugoslavia from the Cominform
1963	Tito became Yugoslavia's president for life

the youngest noncommissioned officer in the regiment. When the Austrians ordered his regiment to the Serbian front at the beginning of World War I, Tito was arrested, probably by mistake, for antiwar activities and held in prison until January 1915. Following his release, Tito served with distinction on the Serbian and the Carpathian fronts, specializing in reconnaissance missions and capturing prisoners. While serving in Bukovina, the Russians attacked on Easter Sunday, March 25, 1915, and after a Cossack stabbed Tito with his lance, the Russians captured him.

Tito spent the next 13 months in a very poor Russian hospital in Kazan near the Volga River. Not until the summer of 1916 did he recover sufficiently for the Russians to transfer him to Ardatov in the adjoining province of Kuibischev. He remained there for a few months, working as a mechanic, before the Russians transferred him to Kungar, a village near Perm in the Ural foothills. Tsar **Nicholas II**'s abdication on March 17, 1917, turned Russia into a republic, which created enough confusion at Kungar that Tito, assisted by a Polish Bolshevik friend, escaped. He traveled to Petrograd (formerly St. Petersburg) and participated in the Bolsheviks' unsuccessful attempt to seize power during July 1917. Agents of Russia's Provisional Government caught him trying to reach Finland and put him on a train bound for Kungar, but Tito left the train shortly before it reached its destination. Subsequently, he joined the Bolshevik Red Guards, with whom he remained until 1920. While a member of the Red

Guards, he met Pelagia Belousova (or Belous-nova), whom he would marry in January 1920.

Josip Broz and his bride traveled to Kum-rovec during September 1920. His native village had changed greatly. On December 1, 1918, the Kingdom of Serbs, Croats, and Slovenes (Yugoslavia) had replaced the Austro-Hungarian Empire. Shortly after Yugoslavia's creation, Tito's mother had died, and his father had sold the family property and moved to a nearby village. Tito devoted the next three years to his wife, who bore him three children, only one of whom, a boy named Zarko, lived. These were difficult years for them because an economic depression prevented Tito from finding a steady job. He remained an active trade unionist, but, despite having been a Communist in Russia, he ignored the Communist Party of Yugoslavia (CPY), which had been banned since the end of 1920.

He Gets Involved with Yugoslav Communists

In 1923, Tito became involved with the Communists after being elected to a trade union committee. The CPY also recruited him to distribute Communist leaflets, an illegal activity that landed him in jail for eight days. Through 1924–25, he selected jobs for political rather than economic considerations, which led to more problems with the police. While an employee of a Kraljevica shipyard, Tito belonged to a secret Communist cell ("unit") that organized strikes. This time he received five months in prison. Rather than go to jail, Tito and his family fled to Zagreb where he became the secretary of the Metal Workers' Union of Zagreb and a member of the Zagreb Committee of the CPY. Henceforth, Tito's vocation was politics. His political activities in Zagreb led to another arrest on August 4, 1928. During the trial, he denied the court's right to try him and his comrades, but the court still gave him five years in prison, plus the five months he had failed to serve earlier.

While Tito was in prison, his wife returned to the Soviet Union with Zarko and eventually married someone else. Tito divorced her in 1935, and she died in 1938. Not long after Tito began his sentence, on January 6, 1929, Yugoslavia's king Alexander established a royal dictatorship and proceeded to purge all his political opposition, including the CPY. Some members of the Central Committee fled to Vienna, where Tito joined them in October 1934. Upon arriving in Vienna, Milan Gorkič, the general secretary of the CPY, persuaded Tito to shift his attention from trade unionism to CPY political activities. Having made that decision, Tito was quickly elected to the CPY's Central Committee and then to its Politburo. For his first major assignment, the Party sent him to Moscow in February 1935 to work at the Comintern's Balkan Department. He returned to Vienna in October 1936 and became the CPY's organizational secretary charged with enforcing Party discipline in Yugoslavia and finding recruits for the Republican Army in the Spanish Civil War. This mission required frequent trips to Yugoslavia, rendering it dangerous as well as difficult.

Tito preferred to rebuild the decimated CPY with youth. In 1937, while Tito was reorganizing the CPY, **Joseph Stalin** began a purge of Yugoslav Communists living in Moscow, which ultimately reached beyond the U.S.S.R. and claimed Gorkič. For unknown reasons, Stalin spared Tito, whom the Comintern's Executive Council appointed general secretary of the CPY late in 1937. Tito immediately started holding meetings of the CPY's Central Committee and elevated some his young recruits into the leadership. The Fifth Party Congress held in Zagreb between October 17–19, 1940, confirmed Tito as the CPY's leader. While reorganizing the CPY in 1937, Tito meet his second wife, Herta Hass. She bore him a son in 1941 shortly before he left her for Davorjanka Paunovič, who remained his unofficial wife until her death in 1946. Herta remarried after the war and lived in Belgrade.

When German armed forces attacked Yugoslavia on April 6, 1941, and Russia on June 22, Tito publicly called for a general unified resistance to the Nazi invaders and began to organize National Liberation Partisan Detachments, popularly known as the Partisans. But the formation of two rival groups dashed Tito's hopes for national unity. Colonel Ivan Mihailov commanded the Army of the Fatherland (*Chetniks*), which represented the exiled king Peter II and enjoyed Allied recognition. Ante Pavelič commanded the pro-Fascist Ustasi, composed mostly of Croats whose goal was to drive Serbs and Muslims from Croatia and Bosnia. Despite the civil war that erupted among them and the absence of any foreign help, the resistance movement had freed nearly half the country by the end of September 1941. German counterattacks regained some of this liberated territory but failed to crush the resistance, which regained what the Germans had and more until they drove the Fascists from Yugoslavia. Throughout the war, and although Stalin disapproved, Tito organized People's Committees for the parts of Yugoslavia the Partisans controlled.

Due to the Partisans' ability to meet the people's housing, food, and health needs better than the inactive *Chetniks,* the ranks of the Partisans

swelled to more than 250,000 by 1943, when the Allies shifted their support from Mihajlovič to Tito. In 1942, Tito had created an Anti-Fascist Council of the National Liberation Committee of Yugoslavia. Convening in November 1943 without informing any of the Allies, the Council proclaimed itself Yugoslavia's government and elected Tito its president and field marshal. Despite all of Tito's military honors, Djilas maintains that Tito, while a master politician, was not an excellent military commander. Immediately thereafter, the Allies accepted the Council's decisions at their Teheran Conference.

In the fall of 1945, the CPY emerged victorious from a general election in which the CPY provided all the candidates. Tito then declared, on November 29, 1945, that the Federal Republic of Yugoslavia had replaced the monarchy and proceeded to create a Communist regime for Yugoslavia modeled on the U.S.S.R. Assisted by a secret police, he crushed all his political opposition. Although he announced a Soviet-style five-year plan to industrialize Yugoslavia, Tito delayed collectivizing agriculture because he feared the peasants would revolt and mass starvation would ensue. With the CPY and himself as its leader firmly in power, in 1946 he promulgated a constitution that established the federal state promised by the Anti-Fascist Council in 1943. It consisted of six republics (Serbia, Croatia, Slovenia, Mon-

tenegro, Bosnia-Herzegovina, and Macedonia) and two autonomous regions (Kosovo and Vojvodina). Tito also pursued an anti-Western foreign policy, but angered Stalin when he openly aided Greek communists trying to overthrow the Greek government.

Stalin Threatens Tito's Regime

Since Yugoslavia was the only Eastern European country that had liberated itself from Fascism, Tito felt that it deserved second ranking to the U.S.S.R. in the Communist world. Stalin, on the other hand, considered Tito too independent and unorthodox for the good of the international Communist movement and expelled Yugoslavia from the Soviet-dominated international association of Communist Parties (Cominform) on June 28, 1948. Tito tried to regain Stalin's favor by collectivizing agriculture and curtailing his expansionist foreign policy, but to no avail. Stalin proclaimed a Cominform economic boycott of Yugoslavia, sent agents to assassinate Tito, and massed Soviet troops on Yugoslavia's borders. The Yugoslav people, the CPY, and the West rallied to the embattled Tito, who began decentralizing the economy and the government. He stopped collectivizing agriculture and created workers' councils, which theoretically allowed elected representatives of factory workers to participate in all management

Marshal Tito of Yugoslavia dances with residents of the town of Kola just prior to the 1950 election.

decisions concerning their factories. In practice, the CPY continued to control all aspects of economic activity. Politically, the federated republic became more of a reality as Tito allowed some local autonomy under the watchful eye of the still dominant CPY. He also started arresting fewer people for political reasons. These reforms coupled with large amounts of Western aid rescued Yugoslavia's economy and defeated Stalin's threat to Tito's regime.

Later, beginning with **Nikita Khrushchev** in 1955, Soviet leaders achieved a reconciliation with Tito, which always remained partial because Tito would never sacrifice Yugoslavia's independence for better relations with the Soviet Union. He also refused to ally Yugoslavia with the West. In 1954–55, along with India and Egypt, he organized other uncommitted countries into a bloc of nonaligned states. Traveling about the world in support of this ideal, Tito also hosted a conference of the nonaligned states in Belgrade in 1961.

Victory over Stalin only enhanced Tito's enormous personal prestige, and thus on January 13, 1953, Yugoslavia's national hero became its president. Ten years later he was confirmed in that position for life. In 1952, still handsome and energetic, he had married his last wife, a Serb 32 years his junior named Jovanka Budisavljevič. Tito and his wife enjoyed a peaceful life of regal luxury that permitted him to indulge in his taste for fine clothes and automobiles. Although Tito had numerous villas built for himself during these years, several of which he never visited, he preferred his lavish Brioni island estate on the north Adriatic. Here he entertained an endless procession of foreign leaders, film stars, and athletes. Domestically, Yugoslavia remained decentralized during these years, but Tito never renounced his personal power, which he continued to exercise with the same energy, decisiveness, and attention to detail until he died on May 4, 1980. For over 30 years he achieved his goal of keeping Yugoslavia unified, prosperous, and stable.

SOURCES:

Auty, Phyllis. *Tito: A Biography.* McGraw-Hill, 1970.

Djilas, Milovan. *Tito: The Story from the Inside.* Translated by Vasilije Kojic and Richard Hayes. Harcourt Brace Jovanovich, 1980.

Moorthy, K. Krishna. *After Tito What?* Humanities Press, 1980.

FURTHER READING:

Christman, Henry M., ed. *The Essential Tito.* Newton Abbot: David & Charles, 1970.

Dedijer, Vladimir. *Tito.* Simon and Schuster, 1953.

Schiffman, Ruth. *Josip Broz Tito.* Chelsea House, 1987.

Singleton, Fred. *Twentieth-Century Yugoslavia.* Columbia University Press, 1976.

Wilson, Duncan. *Tito's Yugoslavia.* Cambridge University Press, 1979.

Trajan

(c. A.D. 53–117)

A brilliant general and second of the "five good Emperors," whose conquests in the Balkans and the Middle East brought the Empire to the peak of its territorial expansion.

"In the time of Trajan the empire's life seems to have brought to a conclusion... one of the great epochs in the civilization of the ancient world."

ALBINO GARZETTI

Name variations: Marcus Ulpius Traianus. Born in c. A.D. 53; died at Selinus in Cilicia on August 8, 117; member of a ranking provincial family Italica in Spain; married: Pompeia Plotina (a Roman of Nemausus [Nimes] in Gaul): children: none, eventually adopted Publius Aelius Hadrianus (Hadrian) as his heir.

One of the greatest Roman emperors, Trajan was born to a family descended from Italian colonists settled in southern Spain in the first century B.C. A distinguished soldier with a broad background as an administrator both in Rome and in the provinces, Trajan enjoyed the favor of the bachelor emperor Nerva, who chose him as his son and heir. Liberal and moderate in his rule, Trajan was popular with the people and the army and had the confidence of the senate, which, while ever an autocrat, he treated with respect. Noted for his generalship, he conquered the kingdom of Dacia, comprising much of the present Rumania, and extended Roman rule in Asia to the Persian Gulf and the Caspian Sea.

Trajan lived after the time of the great Roman historians (Tacitus, Suetonius, etc.) so that, despite his importance, the sources for his reign are sparse; Dio Cassius and Pliny the Younger being the most important. We know, however, that Trajan's rise was facilitated by the career of his father, a member of a good family descended from Italian settlers in Spain, who, beginning as a magistrate in his native Italica, near Hispalis (Seville), distinguished himself under Emperor Vespasian, becom-

Contributed by Robert H. Hewsen, Professor of History, Glassboro State College, Glassboro, New Jersey

ing Roman consul, governor of Syria, and proconsul of Asia. Trajan himself was prepared for the throne by his own career under Emperor **Domitián** (A.D. 81–96), serving as *tribunus militum* (A.D. 71–81), *praetor* (c. A.D. 87), legionary commander (A.D. 89), consul (A.D. 91), and finally, as governor of Lower Germany. Trajan ascended the throne upon the death of Nerva in A.D. 98 and was to rule as emperor of Rome for 19 years.

When Trajan became emperor, the northeastern frontier (*limes*) of the Roman Empire in Europe had long been established along the right (southern) bank of the Danube River. Beyond the river, to the north of the Roman provinces of Dalmatia (Yugoslavia), Pannonia (Hungary), Upper and Lower Moesia (western Bulgaria), and Thrace (eastern Bulgaria and European Turkey), extending as far as the Transylvanian Alps and the Carpathian Mountains, lay the kingdom of the Dacians, a tribal people of north Thracian stock with some Scythian and German admixture. Rich in flocks and metal ores, including gold, and practitioners of human sacrifice, the Dacians had frequently raided the lands of the Empire. Expeditions sent by Emperor Domitián to curb their incursions—during which the heavily armored Dacian cavalry, partly influenced by Roman fighting techniques, had shown itself to be a formidable opponent—had failed miserably, and Trajan took it as his first responsibility to reestablish respect for Roman authority in Dacian eyes.

Relying on Roman unfamiliarity with his hilly and heavily forested realm, replete with numerous fortified strongpoints, the Dacian king Decabalus was willing to take on the might of Rome and the war was shortly joined. The two Dacian Wars (A.D. 101–02; 105–06) are considered models of military expertise and still excite the admiration of military historians. After carefully studying the logistic and supply problems involved in a major campaign, Trajan threw two barge-bridges across the Danube, and then had a 12-mile stretch of road cut into the rock face of a Danube gorge to ensure his communications. Then, led by the emperor himself, 13 of the 29 existing Roman legions took part in the wars to which Trajan added a new one: the *XXX Ulpia.* These legions were accompanied by auxiliary forces drawn from all over the Empire and had the support of the Roman Adriatic fleet stationed at Ravenna, chiefly used in transporting troops and supplies along the Danube. The Dacians were eventually defeated, their country reduced to a Roman province and colonized with Roman settlers, and their capital, Sarmizegetusa, renamed *Ulpia Traiana.* Decabalus committed suicide. The name "Rumania" and the romance language spoken by its present inhabitants are living testimony to Trajan's achievement in extending Roman arms and civilization north of the Danube.

The years A.D. 106 to 113 were spent at Rome where, in his domestic policies, Trajan acquitted himself with wisdom and restraint, pursuing a policy of public order and sound finances and soliciting the cooperation of the senate while firmly retaining all real power in his own hands. While respecting the senatorial and equestrian classes, the two most significant elements in Roman society, Trajan opened both orders to provincial grandees, thereby ending their domination by Italians. This policy was carried on by Trajan's successors, so much so that by the end of the second century, the senate was more fully representative of the population of the Empire as a whole than it had ever been before, and it was under the "Five Good Emperors" that the upper classes in the Roman provinces appear to have finally accepted the permanence of Roman rule. Adored by the soldiers, Trajan had no need to bribe or cajole their loyalty, and he was able to reduce the traditional donations paid to the *Praetorians* (palace guards) upon his accession and to curb the earlier unhealthy power of freedmen (ex-slaves) in the palace. Although he extended the grants of free grain to the people of Rome, spent much on special donatives of wine and oil to them, and is said to have made a special grant of corn for the needs of indigent children, Trajan was essentially a frugal ruler, who stood for sound financial policies and who left the treasury full. Modest in his demeanor, benevolent and tactful, ungiven to ceremony and always easily accessible, Trajan was frugal in his tastes and virile in his private amusements, which appear to have been mainly hunting and swimming. Tall and well built, his statues and portrait busts show him to have had a stern but curiously weak face.

Trajan Considered Patron of the Cities

In dealing with the Empire at large, Trajan is notable for his increased interference with provincial affairs, emphasizing law and order and fighting the corruption of provincial governors. Although he respected the autonomy of the self-governing "free cities," he attempted to supervise their finances to prevent extravagance, waste, and corruption, particularly those in Greece and Asia Minor; to these ends, he sent an imperial *corrector* (legate) to Greece and another styled *curator* to Bithynia, the latter post being held (A.D. 111–13) by the famed Pliny the Younger, son of the great naturalist. Provincial governors were now allowed to send supervisors to these cities, whose powers superseded those of the local officials, and attempts were made to settle the feuds between such cities as Nicaea and Nicomedia in Bithynia, Smyrna and Ephesus, Prusa and Apameia, and Tarsus and the other cities of Cilicia. Efforts were also made to deal with the class, factional, and social conflicts within the individual cities themselves. In spite of this, or perhaps because of it, Trajan was regarded as a patron of the cities, heaping benefices on them to the extent that many of them (Apameia, Aphrodisias, Apollonia, Ephesus, Magnesia, etc.) reciprocated by erecting temples, statues, and inscriptions in his honor; instituting commemorative athletic games; and heaping him with such extravagant titles as "Savior of the World" at Chios and "Lord of Land and Sea" at Pergamum. Trajan founded two cities in Asia Minor bearing his name, a Traianopolis in Lydia and another in Cilicia. He is also noteworthy for the large number of Roman colonies that he founded, especially in Thrace, and it would not be an exaggeration to say that in the second century the level of urbanization in the Roman Empire reached its height.

In his own domestic life, Trajan maintained the same order that he professed in his public and military affairs. His strong-willed but loyal and virtuous wife Pompeia Plotina was devoted to religion and philosophical pursuits, especially epicurianism, and was highly respected in Rome, as were his sister Ulpia Marciana and her daughter Matidia, mother-in-law of the future emperor Hadrian, both of whom were very close to the emperor. The senate voted the title *augusta* to Plotina and Marciana in A.D. 105, and in A.D. 112 gave both of them the right to issue coinage. After Trajan's death, Plotina, Marciana, and Matidia would all be deified; a temple would be erected to Plotina, who, in the first two centuries of the Empire, was the only empress who might be compared to **Livia,** the consort of Augustus.

Trajan is notable for the restraint of his constructions at Rome, and the forum and basilica (court house) erected by him on the edge of the Quirinal hill had originally been planned by Domitián as had, perhaps, Trajan's baths. With the aid of the Syrian architect Apollodorus, these structures were nevertheless built with great splendor, the new forum including two fine libraries, one for Greek books and one for Latin; an equestrian statue of the emperor; and a large basilica, which, centuries later, served as a model for Renaissance churches. Adjoining the forum there was added a large new market building. Trajan also extended the aqueducts of Rome in an effort to improve the city's water supply and even built a completely new one, the *aqua Traiana*. The original Roman forum he endowed with a new rostrum.

Great Column Commemorates Dacian Wars

The best preserved of Trajan's monuments is the great column erected by him in his new forum to commemorate his achievements in the Dacian Wars. Built of 17 marble drums, totaling 100 feet in height, the column rests upon a cubical structure 17-feet square which, whatever its original purpose, was destined to hold the remains of the emperor and his consort. The outer surface of the column consists of a wide spiral band of 400 slabs on which is depicted in bas relief a chronological exposition of the events of the campaigns in 155 scenes with 2,500 figures; inside, a narrow staircase lit by 43 small windows enables one to reach a square balcony surrounding the top of the column upon which once stood a gilded bronze statue of the emperor—long ago supplanted with one of St. **Peter.**

Besides adorning Rome and extending its amenities, Trajan was also active in provincial construction, building or repairing roads and improving harbors; the arch at Benevento, the repaving of the Appian Way, and the construction of a new harbor at Ostia, the port of Rome, are the best known of his works in Italy outside of the capital. Of particular value was his construction of the harbor at the ancient Greek colony of Trapezus (Trebizond, now Trabzon), to facilitate the supplying of the Roman army bases and other defenses along the Euphrates River. Formerly an insignificant place, Trajan's harbor launched the town on its career as a Black Sea port. Apart from Trajan's own constructions, many others were erected at various places by a grateful citizenry, in particular, the magnificent temple dedicated to Zeus and Trajan at Pergamum in Asia and the commemorative arches at Leptis Magna, Mactaris, and Thamugadi in Africa.

Along the eastern frontiers of the Empire, the Romans faced the ramshackle and relatively weak Parthian Empire, which nevertheless could be troublesome, the chief bone of contention between the two empires being the domination of the strategic Armenian Plateau and, to a lesser extent, Mesopotamia. Flushed with his triumphant success with the Dacian problem, Trajan attempted a similar solution to the Eastern Question by attempting to push the Roman frontier from the Euphrates River eastward to the Tigris and even beyond. Preparations for this campaign were extensive and included the annexation of the Nabataean kingdom of Arabia Petraea and the breakup of the large province of Cappadocia into two smaller ones, Cappadocia and Galatia, the first of which became a military province to which was added Armenia Minor, Pontus, and certain other territories that made it an effective bastion of the existing Euphrates frontier.

The immediate cause of the Parthian War was the appointment of Parthamasiris as king of Armenia by his uncle, the Parthian Great King Chosroes, in place of the former's brother, Axidares, whose accession to the Armenian throne had been approved by Rome. The removal of Axidares in this arbitrary manner was a clear violation of the Treaty of Rhandeia of A.D. 63, which had stipulated that the king of Armenia was to be a member of the Parthian Arsacid royal house but must be approved by Rome and serve as her vassal. Marching from Rome to Brindisium in October A.D. 113, Trajan, now about 60 but eager to take to the field, sailed to Greece with his wife and niece and, after rejecting pleas from Parthian negotiators who met him at Athens, sailed on to Ephesus in Asia Minor and from there marched to Syria reaching Antioch in early January A.D. 114. Realizing that a war was unavoidable, the Parthians had launched an initial campaign that had captured Antioch, but the great Syrian capital, third city of the Empire, was immediately liberated by the arrival of the emperor. At Antioch, Trajan gathered his forces, the legions in Syria and those called from Egypt, Judaea, Arabia and Egypt, as well as those congregated in Cappadocia, and there joined to them units brought from the now pacified Danube.

Our sources for Trajan's Parthian War are particularly fragmented but, although the details are uncertain, the broad outline of the campaigns is known. The first began in the spring of A.D. 114. Trajan headed directly into Armenia where, at Elegeia (Ilica, near modern Erzurum), he was met by Parthamasiris, making a last desperate attempt to gain Roman recognition of his kingship over Armenia. Trajan, however, not only refused to recognize the Parthian candidate as king of Armenia, but rejected the Roman candidate, Axidares, as well, announcing that henceforward Armenia was to be a Roman province à la Dacia. Delegations now arrived from all over Caucasia, seeking Roman friendship. Trajan assigned or approved kings over the Apsilians (Abkhazians) and Caucasian Albanians; set up client principalities over the Iberians (East Georgians), Colchians (West Georgians), Heniochians, and Machelonians; and established a string of coastal stations and fortifications along the Black Sea coast from Trapezus to Diocourias (Sukhumi).

A remarkable monument to Trajan's policy in Armenia was uncovered during the excavations of the ancient Armenian capital Artaxata (Artashat), after World War II: an enormous Latin inscription in which the name and titles of the emperor Trajan were given in exceptionally fine and scarcely worn lettering. The inscription had obviously fallen face down from a large public building not many decades after it was erected, and it probably graced the palace of the first (and last) Roman governor, Lucius Catilius Serverus, an indication that, at least in Trajan's view, the Romans had come to Armenia to stay.

He Leads Military Conquests

After dispatching exploratory and punitive campaigns in different directions, Trajan led his army to Mesopotamia that autumn of A.D. 114, probably leaving Armenia via the Bitlis Pass. Here our sources become extremely vague, and it is difficult to account for the entire year that Trajan now spent in the plains between the Eurphrates and the Tigris rivers as contrasted with his virtual lightning campaigns in Armenia. We know that he captured the city of Nisibis from its Arab ruler, whereupon the kingdom of Osrhoene submitted, and Trajan spent the winter of A.D. 114–15 as the guest of its king, Abgar, at his capital Edessa (Urfa). Meanwhile, Trajan's lieutenant, Lusius Quietus, seized the caravan city of Singara. East of the Tigris, the kingdom of Gordyene and the Marcomedian tribe of Media Atropatene (northwestern Iran) were subjected, the former apparently added to the territory of Armenia within which the Gordyaians were living when **Ptolemy** wrote his *Geography* a generation and a half later. South of Gordyene lay the kingdom of Adiabene which was conquered the following year (A.D. 116) being reduced, like Armenia, to a Roman province under its archaic name **Assyria.** Then, marching in two columns from Nisibis, the Romans invaded Babylonia (southern Iraq). Capturing the old Hellenistic city of Seleucia on the Tigris and the newer Parthian capital Ctesiphon lying across the river from it, Trajan sent the Parthian Great King Chosroes fleeing to the East. The emperor now marched directly to the Persian Gulf, where he assigned new kings to the Parthian vassal states of Mesene and Characene, lamenting that his age prevented him from continuing on to India itself.

When news of these conquests reached Rome, the senate and the public were delirious with enthusiasm. At this point, however, major revolt ensued in the East brought about by a Parthian reaction to the loss of Ctesiphon, and soon the whole of Mesopotamia had risen including Abgar of Osrhoene. Here, once again, Trajan showed his mastery of military and diplomatic skills. The rebellions were put down, a Parthian army invading from Media was crushed by Lusius Quietus, Nisibis and Singara were destroyed, and Trajan gave a new king, Parthamaspates, to Parthia. The following year (A.D. 117) was clouded by serious riots in Egypt as well as by massive revolts among the Jews of Judaea, Cyrenaica, and Cyprus and by the recalcitrance of Hatrene, an Arab polity in central Mesopotamia which refused to submit, and whose capital, the oasis city of Hatra, Trajan declined to besiege for very long. Though retaining most of his conquests, there is evidence that Trajan made certain territorial concessions in Armenia to secure immediate peace, and the ultimate settlement of the Eastern Question was left to Hadrian whom Trajan had made governor of Syria. Upon his return to Antioch, Trajan found the city still suffering the effects of the earthquake of December A.D. 116 in which members of his own staff had been killed.

Trajan did not live to return from his Parthian campaign. In failing health, probably brought about by the rigors of two years of campaigning in the field, he suffered what appears to have been a stroke while still in Syria. Although he recovered sufficiently to appear in public, Plotina insisted upon their immediate return to Italy. The emperor and his entourage left Syria by ship but were forced to put in at the port of Selinus in Cilicia, where Trajan died on August 8 or 9, A.D. 117. Although it seems clear that the moody but popular Hadrian was his choice for successor, for some reason Trajan delayed in adopting him until he was on his deathbed, thereby giving rise to rumors that it was Plotina who engineered Hadrian's succession while Trajan was dying and perhaps even made the decision after his demise. Trajan's ashes were buried in a golden urn and placed in the base of his famed column at Rome; Plotina's were placed beside them when she died a few years later in A.D. 120 or 121. After his death, a temple dedicated to Trajan's cult was erected in his forum, and Selinus was for a time officially renamed Traianopolis. So impressed with Trajan's column was one medieval pope that he is said to have "prayed" Trajan out of purgatory. Despite his Italian ancestry, the Spaniards have made Trajan their own and the name *Trajano* is still in common use among them.

Marcus Ulpius Trajan is considered to have been the second of the five good emperors beginning with Nerva and ending with **Marcus Aurelius.** There is no doubt that the title is justified. An excellent general, energetic and able, he extended the frontiers of the Roman Empire to their greatest extent while maintaining the favor of the people and the good will of the senate.

Nevertheless, many of his accomplishments proved to be short-lived; his successor, Hadrian, abandoned all of his conquests beyond the Euphrates River and, in effect, reverted to the policy of Augustus in making the Euphrates once again the frontier of the Empire. Although Trajan was an excellent administrator, autocratic yet wielding his vast power with discretion, and enriched the treasury of Rome with the wealth of the Dacia, there is no doubt that under his rule the senate, the provincial governors, and the free cities became less independent, so much so that Trajan's reign may be seen as another step in the decline of traditional Roman republican institutions that culminated in the totally dictatorial regime established by Diocletian 170 years after his death.

SOURCES:

Cassius Dio Cocceianus. *Historiae Romanae.* Edited by V. P. Boissevain. Berlin, 1955.

Pliny the Younger. *Letters.* (Many editions.)

FURTHER READING:

Garzetti, Albino. *From Tiberius to the Antonines: A History of the Roman Empire A.D. 14–192.* London: Methuen, 1974.

Magie, David. *Roman Rule in Asia Minor.* Princeton University Press, 1950.

Rossi, Lino. *Trajan's Column and the Dacian Wars.* Cornell University Press, 1971.

Leon Trotsky

(1879–1940)

Russian socialist, who led the Petersburg Soviet of Workers' Deputies in the 1905 revolution, joined Lenin to lead the Bolshevik revolution in 1917, and founded the global opposition to Stalin's regime.

Born Lev Davidovich Bronstein in 1879 in Yanovka, the Ukraine; killed in Mexico City, August 21, 1940; son of Russian Jewish peasants; married: Alexandra Sokolovskaya, 1900; married: Natalia Sedova, 1903; children: (first marriage; two daughters) Tina and Zina; (second marriage; two sons) Leon and Sergei.

Lev Davidovich Bronstein was born in 1879 near the Black Sea to Jewish farmers who lived modestly, though better than most peasants. When nine, he was sent to school in Odessa, a port city. His father hoped the bright child would return as an engineer, but as the young Bronstein grew exposed to European culture his interests expanded.

At 17, when sent to Nikolayev to complete his education, he grew attracted to socialism. He joined a study group and advocated the Narodnik idea of peasant revolution. Alexandra Sokolovskaya, a Marxist, also attended the sessions, arguing instead that only a workers' revolution could liberate Russia. She soon won him over, both politically and romantically.

The couple founded the South Russia Workers' Union and distributed leaflets condemning terrible factory conditions. In 1898, the police closed in. Bronstein spent over a year in an Odessa prison and was sentenced to four years in Siberia. Since he and Alexandra married in jail, they were sent together beyond the Arctic Circle. Siberia seemed hopelessly remote, so Bronstein risked escape with a fake passport, assuming the identity

Contributed by Christopher Phelps, Graduate Teaching Fellow, University of Oregon, Eugene, Oregon

of "Trotsky," the name of one of his Odessa jailers. In late 1902, he reached London where—since the brutal conditions of tsarist Russia forbid any sort of political activity—many socialist leaders lived. The young, energetic Trotsky was soon embroiled in their disputes.

Trotsky's first duty was a fundraising trip for the newspaper *Iskra* to emigré colonies around Europe. In Paris, he met Natalia Sedov, who became his second wife and lifelong companion. In 1903, he participated in the Second Congress of the Russian Social Democratic Workers' Party in London, where a split emerged between the *Bolsheviks* (the Majority) led by **V.I. Lenin** and the *Mensheviks* (the Minority) led by Julius Martov. While agreeing mostly with Lenin, Trotsky sided with Martov on the issue of how to organize. Martov wanted the party open to anyone who agreed with its program. Lenin contended that a disciplined, secretive body was necessary to survive the severe tsarist repression. Trotsky believed Lenin's intransigence caused the split to harden and warned that hierarchical discipline would lead to tyranny. "Lenin's methods," Trotsky wrote soon afterward, "lead to this: the party organization substitutes itself for the party as a whole; then the Central Committee substitutes itself for the organization; and finally a single 'dictator' substitutes himself for the Central Committee."

But Trotsky was no Menshevik. After the Congress, he remained aloof from both factions. If his attacks on Lenin were fierce, he also scorned the Mensheviks. Trotsky agreed with them that the first task was to overthrow the aristocracy and create democracy. But he believed that workers, not the liberal bourgeoisie ("middle class"), would lead the revolution.

In 1905, the dispute lost the character of a debate in exile and acquired great importance. Russia was afflicted by economic crisis and a disastrous war with Japan. In late 1904, oil workers won a major strike in Baku. In January 1905, a strike broke out at a St. Petersburg arms factory and spread. Though troops killed 1,000 demonstrators outside the Tsar's palace, the strikes only grew. Returning in February to Russia, Trotsky wrote for both Bolshevik and Menshevik presses until, hounded by the police, he retreated to Finland; he returned again in October to join the Petersburg Soviet of Workers' Deputies. The *soviet* (council) was a new type of democracy, representing trade unions, socialist parties, and other groups. Trotsky—only 26 but widely admired—became chairman of this embryonic government. In one electrifying speech, he defiantly tore up a sheet of the Tsar's promises, calling it "paper freedom."

CHRONOLOGY

1897	Became a Marxist
1902	Escaped from prison; joined Lenin in London
1905	Led Petersburg Soviet in failed uprising
1917	Joined Bolsheviks; led October Revolution
1918	Led Red Army in Civil War
1923	Stalin became general secretary
1927	Trotsky expelled from Communist Party
1929	Deported from the Soviet Union
1936	Moscow Trials began
1940	Assassinated in Mexico City

In December, after only 50 days, the Petersburg Soviet was defeated. Troops arrested its executive, and Trotsky and the other leaders were brought to trial in 1906 after being locked in the Peter-Paul Fortress for nearly a year. Unrepentant, they railed against the Tsar for his pogroms and were sentenced to life. In early 1907, en route to Siberia, Trotsky escaped again, reaching Finland before the authorities even realized he had fled.

His Theory of "Permanent Revolution"

In exile, he developed his theory of "permanent revolution," first elaborated in his 1906 book *Results and Prospects*. Most Marxists of Trotsky's day, especially Mensheviks, assumed that historical development would take place in "stages"; Russia would rise from a semi-feudal peasant society to capitalism, and after protracted industrial development, to socialism. Trotsky argued instead that unlike the bourgeoisies of Western Europe, which defeated feudal absolutism, the Russian bourgeoisie was timid, tied to the Tsarist state. In Russia, bourgeois aims—removing the Tsar, abolishing feudalism, winning liberal rights—would be made *in spite of* and *against* the bourgeoisie. Who would carry it out? Not the peasantry, which was too dispersed and enamored of small property. Only the urban working class was sufficiently cohesive and combative. But after taking power, the proletariat ("lower class") would inevitably enter battle with the bourgeoisie. Thus the "democratic revolution," wrote Trotsky, "grows over immediately into the socialist, and thereby becomes a *permanent*"—continual and complete, not endless—"revolution." Backwardness, he concluded, made Russian socialism dependent on successful revolutions elsewhere.

The Mensheviks considered Trotsky's theory absurd: only the bourgeoisie could lead a bourgeois revolution. The Bolsheviks agreed with Trotsky, but insisted that the proletariat was too weak numerically to lead the vast peasantry. They advocated joint revolution, with unspecified relations between workers and peasants. Trotsky stood almost alone in 1914 when war pushed him closer to Bolshevism. As Social Democrats all over Europe capitulated to nationalism, most Mensheviks followed suit, and Trotsky broke off relations with them. The Mensheviks' position on bourgeois revolution, he concluded, had led them to accommodate imperialism. In 1915, he joined an international group of war opponents, including Lenin, in Zimmerwald, Switzerland, and drafted the group's manifesto. Subsequently, he was deported from France and arrested in Spain. Frustrated, Trotsky quit Europe for the United States, living briefly in New York.

Though the Bolsheviks had yet to accept permanent revolution, events soon confirmed it. The war devastated Russia, causing rampant inflation and food shortages. Workers and peasants hated the war and the government. In February 1917, women textile workers in Petrograd (formerly St. Petersburg) struck, calling metalworkers out with them. Within days, hundreds of thousands were demonstrating. Trotsky and others hurried back to Russia. As troops defected to the revolution, the Tsar was deposed. Mensheviks, Bolsheviks, and other leftists formed the Petrograd Soviet of Workers' and Soldiers' Deputies. The Soviet ruled, but the Mensheviks' belief that Russia had to pass through capitalism led them to back a shaky, liberal Provisional Government under **Alexander Kerensky.**

Trotsky arrived in Petrograd in early May, heading straight to the Tauride Palace, where the Soviet was in session. "Remember three commands," he told the assembly. "Distrust the bourgeoisie; control your own leaders; and rely on your revolutionary strength!" The Mensheviks and others criticized Trotsky, endorsing the bourgeois coalition. But Lenin had arrived at the Finland Station in April 1917 and astounded his audience by espousing permanent revolution. The bourgeois stage of revolution, he argued, was over, and the time had come for socialist revolution against the Provisional Government. With little left between himself and Lenin, Trotsky declared his error on the issue of organization and joined the Bolsheviks.

In July, workers rose in armed demonstration. The Bolsheviks had cautioned against the premature action, but the Provisional Government saw a chance to attack and arrested Trotsky. Simultaneously, it moved toward a restoration of aristocratic rule. General Lavr Kornilov, the Cossacks commander, conspired with Prime Minister Kerensky to overthrow the Soviets. When Kerensky backed down, Kornilov did not. The attack caused the bourgeois government to fall apart as workers, sailors, and soldiers, who primarily backed the Bolsheviks, fended off Kornilov's army and the counterrevolution collapsed.

The governing liberals, Mensheviks, and others were discredited and in disarray. The Bolsheviks raised the slogan: "All Power to the Soviets!" In late September, the Petrograd Soviet elected Trotsky, now freed, as president. Army and naval units continued to defect to the Soviets, and a Soviet Military Revolutionary Committee led by Trotsky began to plan for insurrection. On October 24, the Bolshevik-led Soviet revolution took place.

The new government's first task was to pull Russia out of the war. As People's Commissar for Foreign Affairs, Trotsky opened negotiations with Germany. There was considerable debate among Bolsheviks over what course to take in the talks. Three main positions emerged, and Lenin, despite his prestige, was in the minority. The debate, which showed Bolshevik adherence to democracy, concluded with a March 1918 peace treaty.

Russia's Civil War Begins

Another threat loomed: civil war. Tsarist ("White") generals had regrouped, joined by 50,000 Allied soldiers—including U.S. troops. Trotsky, assigned to organize the military, in two years built a Red Army of five million and turned back a number of White offensives. To oversee the campaign, he equipped an armor-plated train as his mobile headquarters and lived on it, rushing from front to front, restoring morale and directing troops.

While Civil War confirmed Trotsky's belief that socialism would fail without successful revolutions elsewhere, the revolution demonstrated that the strategy against imperialism—proposed earlier in Zimmerwald, Switzerland—was viable. In 1919, delegates came to Moscow to create a Third International (or *Comintern,* for "Communist International") to supplant the Second International, discredited in the war. Trotsky arrived from the front to deliver the founding manifests. Despite high hopes, however, defeats came soon afterward in Bavaria and Hungary. Russia was forced to hold out alone.

The Civil War was savage. Though defeated in 1921, the Whites did their job of wrecking socialism. Many committed socialists who had volunteered for duty died. Blockade and conflict ruined Russia's already impoverished economy, and nine million died between 1919–20 from cold, famine, and disease. The Bolsheviks, who initially practiced democracy, banned all parties but their own in a "temporary" move supposedly necessitated by the Civil War.

Trotsky had ruthlessly favored the strict "war communism," but in 1920 he realized that the regime, by confiscating grain from the hard-pressed peasantry, was alienating the masses. He decided positive incentives were needed instead of coercion, but his approach was rejected by the Bolshevik leadership. Peasant rebellions swept the country, and in 1921 sailors at the Kronstadt naval base rebelled, demanding legalization of all socialist parties and new elections. The Red Army suppressed the rebellions, but the Bolsheviks saw the need for change. At the 1921 10th Party Congress, Lenin proposed a New Economic Policy (*NEP*) to end grain requisitions and permit a partial free market. However, the 10th Congress not only refused elections but even banned factions—again, "temporarily." Soviet democracy was all but extinguished. Trotsky's record, though complicitous, was mixed; in 1923, he published *Literature and Revolution*, which refuted suggestions that the revolution should dictate to art by edict.

After the Civil War, Trotsky again turned to world events. The global revolution had crested, but leaders like Grigori Zinoviev and Nikolai Bukharin refused to acknowledge it. Against their revolutionary posturing, Trotsky proposed a "united front." Communists would work in coalition with all worker organizations. Only through solidarity, he argued, would communists win over the workers to revolutionary ideas. Lenin agreed, and the Comintern adopted the united front.

The Rise of Stalin and Fall of Trotsky

Meanwhile, another figure had methodically risen within the party: **Joseph Stalin.** Stalin sought to dominate, and Trotsky was his greatest hurdle. In 1921–22, Trotsky became convinced that NEP should be abandoned for a national plan, and that growth was being choked by a monstrous bureaucracy, epitomized by an agency headed by Stalin. Stalin, however, had used his position to build his power, and the 1922 11th Party Congress elected him general secretary. Lenin, who soon afterward suffered an immobilizing stroke, became increasingly alarmed. In a series of notes meant for publi-

cation after his death, Lenin recommended that Stalin be removed as general secretary. In early 1923, Lenin lost the power of speech; he would die a year later.

Had Trotsky acted decisively by releasing Lenin's political testament at the 1923 12th Party Congress, Stalin might have been ruined. However, Trotsky avoided a challenge, perhaps since Lenin might still recover. Stalin, meanwhile, appointed amenable officials to key positions. When Lenin died in 1924, his widow demanded that the party be told of his testament, but the Central Committee, deciding Lenin's fears about Stalin were exaggerated, did not release it.

Stalin began full-scale war against Trotsky, dredging up the latter's old disputes with Lenin to make him appear a Menshevik. Stalin even boasted that he had led the October revolution himself, that "Trotsky did not and could not play any leading part." Meanwhile, Stalin proclaimed "socialism in one country," contending socialism could be built within the Soviet Union alone and that to claim otherwise was defeatist. The argument contradicted all Marxist theory, including permanent revolution. The campaign against Trotsky descended to anti-Semitic whisper campaigns and the accusation that Trotsky sought to be military dictator. Grotesque though they were, the charges stuck. In January 1925, the Central Committee stripped Trotsky from the Commissariat of War and warned him that if he stirred further controversy he would risk expulsion from the Central Committee.

For a year, Trotsky refrained from opposition, but the silence only gave Stalin time to consolidate his rule. In 1926, Trotsky joined Zinoviev and Lev Davidovich Kamenev after Stalin turned on his erstwhile allies. Criticizing Stalin's blunders in China and Britain, where revolutionary movements had met disaster, they demanded party democracy, improved wages and an industrialization plan. In November 1927, Trotsky and Zinoviev were expelled from the party, leading Zinoviev and Kamenev to recant and submit to Stalin. In 1928, Trotsky was banished to Central Asia; in 1929, he was deported.

Again in exile, Trotsky became the most perceptive critic of the Stalin regime. Conditions were unfavorable to his work. His old comrades—including his daughters, sons, and former wife—suffered imprisonment or death at Stalin's hands. Trotsky lived in constant danger of assassination. He would find an oasis—Turkey, France, Norway, Mexico—only to have his expulsion demanded by fascists and pro-Stalin Communists.

Writing masterfully, Trotsky produced the autobiographical *My Life* (1930) and a massive *History of the Russian Revolution* (1933). He also strove to unite dissident Marxists who had been ejected from Communist parties around the world. By the late 1920s, he had begun to compare the increasing bureaucracy of the Soviet state under Stalin to *Thermidoreans* in the French revolution. In 1794, *Thermidor* (July) had brought the overthrow of France's **Robespierre,** bringing the revolution's radical period to a close without reversing its basic conquests: monarchy's destruction and capitalism's establishment. Similarly, argued Trotsky, the Soviet revolution's leaders were defeated, but the foundation of a worker's state—state property—remained. The Soviet Union was a "deformed" workers' state needing reform.

Trotsky grew even more critical in exile. After vanquishing Trotsky in 1928, Stalin had veered leftward, forcibly collectivizing peasant land and demanding enormous worker output. Trotsky had advocated industrialization, but what he wanted achieved voluntarily through increased wages, Stalin achieved through terror and heavy exploitation. Abroad, Stalin abandoned failed collaborations with liberalism, only to insist on revolution's imminence and Communist righteousness. Trotsky criticized this sectarianism, which in Germany led Communists to refuse cooperation with Social Democrats, and proposed another "united front"—all workers against the Nazis. When **Hitler** seized power in 1933, it was the last straw for Trotsky. Stalinism, he knew, could not be reformed. It was a dangerous cancer that had to be removed.

Trotsky called for a Fourth International to oppose both the reformism of the Second and the Stalinism of the Third. In 1936, he completed *The Revolution Betrayed,* a resounding refutation of Stalin's claim that socialism had "completely triumphed" in the Soviet Union. After demonstrating the anti-socialist character of Soviet life—deteriorating economy, income inequalities and artistic clampdowns—Trotsky called for a second revolution, political rather than social, to overthrow the bureaucracy and establish socialism.

As *The Revolution Betrayed* went to press, Zinoviev, Kamenev, Bukharin, and other old Bolsheviks were brought to trial for allegedly plotting with Trotsky and the Nazis to overthrow socialism. The defendants "confessed" to incredible acts and were executed. Trotsky strained to refute the lies. To return to the Soviet Union and defend himself would be suicide, so Trotsky offered to sit before an independent hearing. In 1937, a group of prominent intellectuals led by the American philosopher John Dewey met in Mexico City, held extensive hearings, and found Trotsky "not guilty."

Though innocent, Trotsky was vulnerable. He helped establish and guide the Fourth International, but on August 20, 1940, Stalin silenced him forever when a Soviet agent buried an ice axe in Trotsky's skull. The following day, Leon Trotsky died.

SOURCES:

Callinicos, Alex. *Trotskyism.* University of Minnesota, 1990.

Howe, Irving. *Leon Trotsky.* Viking, 1978.

King, David, Tamara Deutscher, and James Ryan. *Trotsky.* Basil Blackwell, 1986.

FURTHER READING:

Ali, Tariq, and Phil Evans. *Trotsky for Beginners.* Pantheon, 1980.

Deutscher, Isaac. *The Prophet Armed.* Oxford University Press, 1954.

———. *The Prophet Outcast.* Oxford University Press, 1963.

———. *The Prophet Unarmed.* Oxford University Press, 1959.

Trotsky, Leon. *The Permanent Revolution.* Pioneer, 1965.

———. *The Revolution Betrayed.* Doubleday, 1937.

———. *The Russian Revolution.* Doubleday, 1959.

Walter Ulbricht

(1893–1973)

and the Creation of East Germany

German Communist leader, who became the most prominent Marxist politician of the Soviet Occupation Zone of Germany, and from 1949 to 1971 was the unchallenged leader of the German Democratic Republic (East Germany).

"It is quite clear—it must look democratic but we must have everything in our control."

WALTER ULBRICHT (1945)

Walter Ulbricht, who ruled East Germany for more than two decades, and was arguably the most important German Marxist since **Karl Marx,** played a major role in the public life of his country for half a century. Born into a poor, militantly socialist, working-class family in Leipzig, by 1914 he had become a committed Marxist who viewed life and political action entirely from a perspective of class struggles between the dominant bourgeois ("middle class") capitalist ruling elite and an oppressed proletariat ("lower class"). His experiences in World War I only strengthened Ulbricht's convictions that the capitalist system was founded on a program of inequality and economic exploitation, and that because it needed to seek overseas markets and fostered imperialistic rivalries, capitalism made ever bloodier international conflicts inevitable. By 1918, when he was twice arrested for desertion from the German army, Ulbricht had become a revolutionary socialist who looked to the recent revolution in Russia as the best model for radical change in Germany.

The World War I defeat of Germany in November 1918 unleashed revolutionary forces

Name variations: Walther. Born on June 30, 1893, in Leipzig, Germany; died in Berlin on August 1, 1973; son of Ernst (a tailor) and Pauline (Rothe) Ulbricht (both militant Social Democrats); married: Martha Schmellinsky; married: Lotte Kühn; children: (daughter) Dorle. Predecessors: Ernst Thälmann and Wilhelm Pieck. Successor: Erich Honecker.

Contributed by John Haag, Associate Professor of History, University of Georgia, Athens, Georgia

throughout the country, and among those radical Marxists was the young Walter Ulbricht. After the founding of the German Communist Party (KPD) in December 1918, a premature bid for power in January 1919 was bloodily suppressed, resulting in the murder of KPD leaders Karl Liebknecht and **Rosa Luxemburg.** In his native Leipzig, Ulbricht was actively building up the organization of the local KPD while at the same time serving on a short-lived Workers' and Soldiers' Council, a German version of a Russian Soviet. For the next half-century, he would display remarkable energy and organizational talent, working up to 16 hours a day to place the right people in the right slots in the Communist power apparatus. His talents were recognized early, so that by 1922 he was chosen to attend the Fourth Congress of the Communist International, held in Moscow and Petrograd. It was at one of these sessions that he was able to meet the Russian dictator and leader of the world communist movement, **V.I. Lenin.** In the post-Stalinist years after 1953, Ulbricht, as the sole survivor of this heroic period of the Bolshevik revolution still in power, would point out his personal ties to Lenin to argue a point.

By the late 1920s, the KPD had become a political party, loyal to the wishes of Lenin's ruthless successor **Joseph Stalin.** Ulbricht played a major role in this Stalinization; through his efforts, cells ("small units") became the fundamental basis of KPD organization throughout Germany; because of his successes, he became known within the German Communist leadership as "Comrade Cell." Along with the older Wilhelm Pieck, the indefatigable Ulbricht was able to eliminate all opposition and turn the most important Communist party outside the Soviet Union into a pliant tool of the Soviet Communist Party (CPSU) Politburo and the Executive Committee of the Communist International, both of which were firmly under Stalin's personal control by 1929.

The onset of the Great Depression in 1929 plunged German society into a severe political as well as economic crisis. Massive unemployment led to a rapid growth in political radicalism as voters were attracted by either Communist or Nazi slogans demanding change. By 1932, German democracy was as good as dead when Communists and Nazis fought one another in bloody street clashes and exchanged insults in a deadlocked *Reichstag* ("House of Representatives"). Ulbricht, who since 1928 had been a KPD *Reichstag* deputy, stubbornly defended the Stalinist position that the other political party of the German working class, the Social Democrats (SPD), "objectively" aided the cause of Hitler and the Nazis and that any anti-Nazi collaboration with the SPD was impossible because the SPD was a "Social Fascist" organization. The orthodox KPD line was that the destruction of German bourgeois democracy would create a chaotic situation which would quickly lead to a triumph of Communism. Accordingly, Ulbricht encouraged activities that would hasten the end of the tottering Weimar Republic. One such event was the disruptive strike of the Berlin public transport workers in November 1932. Trade unions refused to sanction the strike, but for political reasons both the Nazis and Communists backed the strikers, and a fund was created to prolong the strike for almost a week. An unholy Nazi-Communist alliance hastened the end of German democracy, with catastrophic results for not only the German people but the entire world.

The triumph of Nazism in early 1933 resulted in a wave of bloody terror against not only Communists but Social Democrats, Catholics, liberals, and others deemed "un-German" by the Nazis. Despite its boasts of having organized a superb underground organization, the KPD was rapidly destroyed by the Nazis, who killed and tortured thousands of political opponents. The capture of the KPD leader Ernst Thälmann in March 1933 effectively decapitated the leadership of the German Communist movement. Walter Ulbricht was able to survive undetected until October, when the Comintern ordered him to go to Paris. In Paris, Ulbricht at first continued to condemn Social Democrats and other anti-Nazi exiles as insufficiently militant in their opposition to Hitler. Only with the switch in Soviet policy in 1935 from narrowly sectarian Marxist anti-Fascism to a policy of supporting a united front would Ulbricht work to forge a broad coalition of exiles to fight the Nazi foe. Recalling his earlier uncritical work to advance the Stalinist cause in Germany, many of the non-Communist exiles continued to view Ulbricht's motives with skepticism.

In the increasing struggle with Nazism, Ulbricht's partisan defense of the Stalin regime meant that preservation of Stalinist domination of the KPD was at times more important than tolerance of political deviations. On one occasion, he demanded that Hans Kippenberger, head of the KPD's secret military intelligence network, denounce anti-Stalinist Communists to the Gestapo, the German secret police; Kippenberger refused and was shot after a secret trial. To preserve absolute loyalty to Stalin, Ulbricht was sent to Spain several times starting in December 1936. Here he worked with the GPU (Soviet Secret Police) to ferret out and eliminate German, Austrian, and Swiss members of the International Brigades who were suspected of being "Trotskyites."

After settling permanently in Moscow in 1938, Ulbricht was able to survive purges that decimated the German Communist exile community. Unlike Wilhelm Pieck, who attempted on occasion to intervene with Stalin to save the lives of imprisoned German Communists, Ulbricht accepted the bloody purges as a fact of life and concentrated on his own survival. When Stalin signed his notorious nonaggression pact with Nazi Germany in August 1939, making Hitler's attack on Poland inevitable, Ulbricht penned a vigorous defense of the abrupt turn in Soviet foreign policy, asserting that those who refused to accept the new German-Soviet "friendship" should be regarded as "enemies of the German people." Ulbricht did not protest when many German Communists during the years 1939–41 were handed over to the Gestapo by Soviet authorities; virtually all of these individuals died in Nazi concentration camps.

With the Nazi attack on the Soviet Union in June 1941, Ulbricht could once again publicly appeal to his German countrymen to overthrow the Hitler regime. He made radio broadcasts to both German soldiers and the German civilian population, calling on them to desert or engage in sabotage. To the end of the war, he insisted that Hitler's regime and the German people were separate entities and that an overthrow of the Nazi dictatorship by a national uprising would spare the nation immense suffering. When it became increasingly apparent that these hopes of a revolt would not bear fruit, Ulbricht worked as a propagandist among Russia's German prisoners of war, organizing them into anti-Nazi, but not Communist, groups which eventually took form as the National Committee for a Free Germany and the League of German Officers. The existence of these organizations made clear a major theme in Soviet policy for postwar Germany: the need to draw on conservative and nationalistic sentiments in the process of reconstruction, given the fact that the majority of Germans were not sympathetic to Marxism or radical Socialist ideals.

By the last months of the war, Ulbricht had proven his potential importance for the new, post-Nazi Germany to the Soviet leadership. Along with nine other exiles, he was flown into occupied Germany on April 30, 1945. On June 11, the KPD was officially reborn as the first post-Nazi political party. Ulbricht, following the new Soviet policy for occupied Germany, helped write a platform that called for the creation of a democratic antiauthoritarian social and political order that was by no means radical; indeed, the names of Marx and Engels were not even mentioned. By April 1946, Ulbricht, Pieck, and other German Communists were able to bring about a fusion of the Communist and Social Democratic parties in the Soviet Occupation Zone (SBZ). The new party that resulted from this shotgun marriage, the Socialist Unity Party (SED), continued to insist that it desired democracy for Germany rather than the imposition of a totalitarian Marxist regime. From the very outset, however, it took advantage of the presence of Soviet troops in the SBZ to apply ever-increasing pressure to dissident Social Democrats and others unwilling to accept the veiled dictatorship of the renamed Communist Party.

Some of the changes that took place in the SBZ after 1945 were genuinely popular and were essential for the creation of a viable democratic system in Germany. These included a program of land reform that confiscated 13,700 estates of *Junker* landowners (Prussian aristocrats), turning the farmland over to formerly landless peasants. Other reforms opened up educational opportunities to workers and farmers, while a realistic and rapidly executed program of de-Nazification made it possible for most ex-Nazis to once again enter the public arena. But whatever chances there were for democratic evolution in the SBZ were dashed by the onset of Cold War tensions. Soviet policy in Germany vacillated between a desire to hold onto the SBZ and exploit it economically as reparations for the immense destruction caused by the Nazi attack on the Soviet Union and the hope that a neutralized united German state might yet be created that would be on friendly terms with its eastern neighbors. These contradictory goals were never resolved, and by 1949 it was clear that Germany would be divided into two states with vastly different political, social, and economic systems. Once Soviet policy was resigned to the creation of a separate eastern German state, the talents of Walter Ulbricht and other German Communists were very much in demand.

Germany Is Divided Into Two Republics

The proclamation of the German Democratic Republic (GDR or East Germany) on October 7, 1949, marked the start of four decades of a Marxist experiment on German soil. (The Federal Republic of Germany [or West Germany] had been created a few weeks earlier.) The conditions for East German success were extremely limited at this juncture, and not only because of the unpopularity of the Soviet occupation regime. With a territory roughly equal in size to that of Tennessee, the

GDR lacked fuels and raw materials, and much of its industrial plant lay in ruins. Furthermore, it suffered from a brain-drain for the first dozen years of its existence because many of its youngest and most ambitious citizens fled to West Berlin and then went to a booming Western Germany that had been granted generous American aid as a result of the Marshall Plan.

Firmly in charge of the GDR political system starting in July 1950 (his position as general secretary of the SED Central Committee of 151 members corresponded closely to that of Stalin in the U.S.S.R.), Walter Ulbricht responded to these challenges by imposing a harsh political and economic regime modeled after the Stalinist society he had lived in from 1938 to 1945. The results were predictable: a massive eruption of worker discontent on June 17, 1953, in East Berlin and other GDR cities brought the regime to the point of collapse. Only the intervention of Soviet troops saved the SED dictatorship from its angry citizens. Ulbricht himself was able to hold onto his position because of the disappearance in the Soviet Union of his greatest foe, Secret Police chief **Lavrenti Beria,** who wanted a foreign policy success and was willing to sacrifice the GDR hardliners as part of a deal leading to detente with the West over the German issue.

After purging his opponents within the SED, Ulbricht concentrated on building up the weak GDR economy. This was a difficult task because the terms of Soviet-GDR trade agreements favored the Soviet Union, and because his struggling state almost completely lacked natural resources, being obliged to import more than 95% of its raw materials and more than a third of its grain supply. The harshly repressive nature of life in the GDR and the growing prosperity of West Germany led to a massive exodus of people, a permanent crisis that was only solved with a drastic measure.

A Wall Is Built Around Berlin

Ulbricht assured journalists on June 15, 1961, that "nobody intends to build a wall" between East and West Berlin; on August 13, GDR armed forces began to erect a wall in and around Berlin, cutting off the flow of refugees from the GDR to West Berlin. Eventually the wall divided the whole of East Germany from West Germany and encircled all of West Berlin. (From 1949 to mid-1961 more than 2,600,000 people would flee the GDR and East Berlin; as many as 400 people would die trying to cross the Berlin Wall and other parts of the frontier.)

Paradoxically, it was the hated Berlin Wall that enabled Ulbricht's German Democratic Republic to become a stable and prosperous albeit authoritarian society. As younger and skilled workers could no longer flee to the West, their labor could be effectively harnessed to economic plans that had up to that time remained largely theoretical. By 1969, when the state celebrated its 20th anniversary, its industrial output had increased five times, and the national income had increased more than four times that of 1949. As the second most important industrial power in the Communist world after the Soviet Union, the GDR standard of living was much higher than that of the U.S.S.R. and matched that of a number of Western societies, including Great Britain.

With economic prosperity came a distinct sense of national identity. Increasingly accepting the fact that they could not flee to the West, many GDR citizens displayed a spirit of defiant pride. A new class of technocratic managers, pragmatic rather than ideological in their approach to economic problems, sometimes pointed out to Western visitors that the real economic miracle in postwar Germany had taken place in the GDR rather than in the long-prosperous Federal Republic. With economic achievements came other signs of national self-assertiveness. Although he had been a hard-line Marxist revolutionary since his 20s, in his own way Ulbricht was also a German nationalist. While he officially endorsed the Oder-Neisse boundary between the GDR and Poland which resulted from the loss of large areas of historically German-inhabited territories, his personal notion of the territorial definition of a future Communist Germany was emotionally based on the 1914 boundaries of the German Reich. As a fellow exile later recounted the story, Ulbricht screamed in outrage at the decision reached at the February 1945 Yalta Conference to place Silesia under Polish sovereignty. Thus it was not surprising to see in the GDR certain traditions taken from the old, pre-1914 authoritarian Germany, including the use of the Prussian goose-step in the National People's Army (NVA). Indeed, by the 1960s some astute observers of the new national culture of the GDR believed they detected in it a distinct spirit of "Red Prussianism."

Culture and Sports in East Germany

Internationally, the GDR under the Ulbricht regime became known for certain aspects of its culture, including superb performances of the music of Johann Sebastian Bach in Leipzig and of George Frederick Handel in Halle an der Saale; the world-class symphony orchestras of Berlin, Leipzig (*Gewandhaus*), and Dresden (*Staatskapelle*); and the first-class opera performances presented at the German Opera House in East Berlin. In theater, the glory of the GDR was without a doubt the Berliner Ensemble, which performed the controversial plays of Bertolt Brecht in authentic style at the Theater am Schiffbauerdamm. Internationally, by the late 1960s Ulbricht's regimented but in some ways dynamic and successful society was best known for its successes in the area of sports. Starting in 1968, when separate East and West German teams were permitted to participate in the Olympic Games, an extraordinary number of medals were won by a state that, after all, was an essentially artificial creation with fewer than 17 million citizens. Only after the collapse of the GDR in 1989 did the full story of athletic drugging come to light, revealing a massive system of control that made a mockery of claims that East German athletes had been amateurs whose talents had unfolded naturally in an advanced socialist society.

Although the GDR regime never unleashed bloody purges like the ones that resulted in death sentences for high officials in Czechoslovakia, Hungary, and Bulgaria during the years 1949–52, the SED would be periodically "cleansed" of those members deemed to be ideologically unsound. Along with political regimentation in the 1950s came cultural controls that pressured writers to conform to the Soviet propagandist notion of "Socialist Realism." By the time of the Polish reforms and the Hungarian revolution, both of which took place in 1956, a few courageous GDR intellectuals had begun to speak out for fundamental freedoms in the arts and humanities. But Ulbricht, ever the defender of hard-line orthodoxy, saw such moderate requests as dangerously subversive. Thus the talented Marxist scholar, Professor Wolfgang Harich, who taught at East Berlin's Humboldt University, was sentenced in 1957 to ten years' hard labor for his advocacy of greater intellectual freedom. (In 1975 another dissident Marxist, the noted physicist Robert Havemann, was punished only with house arrest.)

The results of such repression were predictable: many eminent scholars, including the philosopher Ernst Bloch and the literary critic Hans Mayer, who had originally settled in the SBZ in the hope that an open form of socialism might somehow evolve, fled the GDR. By the late 1960s, despite its considerable achievements, the Ulbricht system of social control had created not the desired activist nation of committed Marxist militants, but rather a passive citizenry largely interested in private pursuits such as building their own summer bungalows. Doubtless Ulbricht and the SED leadership found it relatively easy to impose their rule on such people, but there were no doubt also many men and women who could only be kept in line with the Wall and a secret police (*Stasi*) apparatus that penetrated into every nook and cranny of daily life.

Walter Ulbricht was in many ways a remarkable political personality, having held power in his part of Germany for a period of time longer than Bismarck was Chancellor of the German Reich or Hitler was Führer of the Third Reich. Ulbricht's personal power lasted for well over two decades, roughly equal to the period of time Joseph Stalin was unchallenged dictator of the Soviet Union. Ulbricht was able to transform a war-ravaged part of occupied Germany into a stable and relatively prosperous society that by the early 1970s had achieved world recognition for its achievements in industry, culture, and sports. Yet even his great power and prestige began to wane in the late 1960s when, as a result of his advancing years, a new group of SED insiders led by Erich Honecker appeared ready to assume the mantle of leadership. Ulbricht's last great moment of power came in 1968, when he took the lead in the Soviet bloc by aggressively opposing the humanistic version of socialism that appeared in Czechoslovakia under the leadership of **Alexander Dubcek.**

Honecker and his allies seized the opportunity to remove an aging Ulbricht in 1971 when the GDR economy began to falter, and more importantly, when the Soviet leadership wished to present a new, more flexible face to the West in order to more effectively pursue a policy of detente in Central Europe. The opportunities created by *Ostpolitik*, the new Eastern policy of Chancellor **Willy Brandt** meant that a relic of the Stalin period, a veteran Cold Warrior like Walter Ulbricht, needed to be eased out of power. This was done effectively in early May 1971 when Ulbricht stepped down "voluntarily" and, unlike most previously deposed Communist rulers, continued to enjoy the symbols, if not the substance, of political power. Even while he was still alive, Ulbricht was obliquely but sharply criticized by Honecker. At the Eighth Congress of the SED held in June 1971 Honecker vowed to undo the damage done to GDR political leadership by "abuse of the collective," noting that Ulbricht had been retained in the SED Politburo in order to teach him, in his last years, "the importance of the Party collective."

After Ulbricht's state funeral in August 1973, public mention of his name became rare; Walter Ulbricht Stadium in East Berlin was renamed only two months after his passing. By

1975, the GDR writer Stefan Heym could note that Ulbricht had become "the nearest thing to an unperson that we have."

Walter Ulbricht learned to speak excellent Russian during his many years in the Soviet Union, and clearly enjoyed the physical resemblance he bore to the Bolshevik demigod Vladimir Lenin. Ulbricht may well have thought of himself as a "little Lenin" by growing a Leninist goatee and imitating the Russian revolutionary to the extent of holding his left shoulder higher than his right and chopping the air with his hands while orating. But Ulbricht was not a Russian revolutionary but a German Communist, a man with a croaky Saxon accent and astonishingly simple personal tastes who attempted to create a socialist society among fellow Germans who were hostile to the Soviet occupation forces and to radical Marxism as represented by the KPD. To bring about the triumph of socialism in Germany Ulbricht engaged in a political career of extraordinary complexity.

The human price he paid for his considerable political success is difficult to assess, but most contemporary observers noted that this man of many talents was unfeeling in his private life. In the final decades of his career he felt no need to contact his first wife Martha in Leipzig, his brother Erich in New York, his sister Hildegard in Hamburg, or his only child, his daughter Dorle, who also lived in West Germany. Unlike Honecker and the others who succeeded him, Ulbricht had little interest in luxuries imported from the West. The exercise of power and the belief that he was executing the will of the inexorable forces of the dialectic of history apparently was a sufficient reward for the aging revolutionary. Walter Ulbricht, while not achieving the stature of a Vladimir Lenin, nevertheless was able to earn a place in the history of 20th-century Europe, and by virtue of his longevity and political skill effectively ended his career as "the last Bolshevik."

SOURCES:

Hangen, Welles. "East Germany: The Prosperous Prisoner," *The Reporter*. Vol. 35, no. 2, August 11, 1966: pp. 30–33.

Leonhard, Wolfgang. *Child of the Revolution*. Regnery, 1958.

McCauley, Martin. *The German Democratic Republic since 1945*. St. Martin's Press, 1983.

Stern, Carola. *Ulbricht: A Political Biography*. Praeger, 1965.

Wilhelm, Bernhard. "Walter Ulbricht: Moscow's Man in East Germany," in Rodger Swearingen, ed., *Leaders of the Communist World*. The Free Press, 1971: pp. 295–316.

FURTHER READING:

Baras, Victor. "Beria's Fall and Ulbricht's Survival," in *Soviet Studies*. Vol. 27, no. 3, July, 1975: pp. 381–395.

Fischer, Ruth. *Stalin and German Communism: A Study in the Origins of the State Party*. Harvard University Press, 1948.

Hoberman, John M. *Sport and Political Ideology*. University of Texas Press, 1984.

Smith, Jean Edward. "The Red Prussianism of the German Democratic Republic," in *Political Science Quarterly*. Vol. 82, no. 3, September, 1967: pp. 368–385.

Urban II

(c. 1042–1099)

Shrewd and politically dexterous pope, who repaired the damage done to the 11th century papacy by his larger-than-life predecessor Gregory VII, and launched the First Crusade.

"Barred for most of his pontificate from the Roman headquarters of the Curia, always on the move and working in difficult conditions, Urban II adapted himself to circumstances with such skill that he completely regained the leadership in Europe which Gregory [his predecessor] had disputed with the Emperor."

NICHOLAS CHEETHAM

U rban II, a French pope, ascended the Throne of Peter in the aftermath of one of its most bitter and costly conflicts with the secular power of the Holy Roman Empire. A skillful diplomat, he carried on his predecessors' reform works within the Church, restored the papacy's credit among the warring princes of Europe, and persuaded many of them to settle their differences by uniting in Holy War against the Muslim enemies of Christianity. His sermon of 1095 at Clermont, which launched the First Crusade, is the event for which he is best remembered, but it was only one element in a complex and exacting papal reign.

In the 1070s and early 1080s, the Catholic Church went through a momentous period of reform under the leadership of Pope **Gregory VII** (1073–85), the stormiest of all medieval pontiffs and probably the most important in his effect on the Church since Gregory I (500 years earlier). Gregory VII, the son of Tuscan farmers, attempted to improve the personal and moral conduct of worldly clerics and to strengthen the claims of Rome over all other bishoprics. More startling, he also tried to subordinate the most powerful sec-

Born Odo of Chatillon-Sur-Marne, c. 1042, in northeastern France; died in 1099. Predecessors: Gregory VII, Victor III. Successor: Paschal II.

Contributed by Patrick Allitt, Assistant Professor of History, Emory University, Atlanta, Georgia

ular ruler in Europe, the Holy Roman Emperor Henry IV, by denying him the right to appoint bishops within his territories. Gregory insisted that secular power had its origins in the Church and that he, as pope, was God's political as well as religious agent on Earth. Inevitably, that kind of novel challenge to the secular powers entangled him in fierce political controversy.

Henry surrendered to the pope's demands in 1077 in the face of temporary political reversals (according to tradition he had to stand in the snow for three days, wearing penitential garb, at the mountain fortress of Canossa). He changed his mind in 1080, however, and, with the help of a large party of cardinals who disliked Gregory's reforms, supervised the election of an antipope, Wibert, archbishop of Ravenna, who took the papal name of Clement III. Recurrent fighting in and around Rome during the early 1080s saw the emperor's army with its antipope pitched against a Norman army under Robert Guiscard, defending Gregory's papacy. Just when Gregory saw victory at hand, his advantage turned literally to ashes: the Normans and their unruly mercenaries sacked and burned most of Rome and forced Gregory, despairing, into exile. Throughout the reigns of his successors (including Urban II) and all through the early 12th century, this most important of European cities was hardly more than a scorched ruin, what one historian has called "a fire-scarred no-man's land," and scene of a continuous "desultory guerrilla war."

The job of pope now seemed so unappealing that the reforming cardinals who had remained loyal to Gregory found it difficult to find a new candidate capable of maintaining Gregory's program in the face of its enemies. The abbot Desiderius of Monte Cassino, whom they elected as Pope Victor III, was so reluctant to take up the office that on three different occasions he abandoned the papal insignia and tried to run away from war-torn Rome, back to his monastery.

French Nobleman Odo Becomes Pope Urban II

When the unsatisfactory Victor died in 1087, the reformers turned their eyes instead to the tough-minded Cardinal of Ostia, a French nobleman named Odo of Chatillon-Sur-Marne, who had grown up surrounded by the fervent piety of the Cluniac monastic reform movement. Where Gregory had been low-born, Odo—who took the papal name of Urban II—was a nobleman, privileged from birth, well educated, already skilled in diplomacy, and familiar with administrative affairs from his years as a monastic prior, from work in his diocese, and from service under Gregory VII, whose aims he shared. Urban realized that under the circumstances there was no value in trying to make Rome his headquarters, and he lived there only occasionally during his 11-year reign. Instead, he traveled widely and found welcome in various French cities. By making tactful concessions to powerful French figures, of the kind Gregory had never managed, Urban was able to recover much of the lost prestige of the papacy, though throughout his reign he had to accept the coexistence of antipope Clement III, in a schism which was to persist for several more decades.

Urban's first act as pope was to reconfirm the excommunication of this antipope and his patron, the emperor Henry IV. While shrewder and more conciliatory than his predecessor, Urban II was not going to compromise on so basic a question as the sole legitimacy of his position as pope. War against Henry therefore continued. Urban's strongest supporters were the countess **Matilda of Tuscany,** around whom "warrior-queen" legends have gathered, and Count Welf of Bavaria. Urban arranged a marriage between these two papal loyalists, though Welf was only 18 and Matilda 43. Their lands, straddling the Alps, made imperial armies' access to northern Italy much more difficult. Unfortunately, when Welf discovered that Matilda's inheritance was destined for the Church rather than himself, he contemptuously abandoned her, providing Henry's army an opportunity to move south once more and reestablish its antipope in Rome. What Urban II had lost with the defection of Welf, however, he soon more than gained with the adherence of the emperor's son Conrad, who left his treacherous father in disgust and became a figurehead for the orthodox papalists. Soon afterwards, the emperor's second wife Praxedes also deserted Henry and entertained the Council of Constance (1094) with tales of her husband's perversions. These defections put quite a dent in the emperor's prestige.

Urban II found the Church's administration in ruins. Always narrow and autocratic, it had been weakened further by the warfare around Rome in his predecessors' reigns, and the schism between pope and antipope. Urban tried to model his government on that of the French court and for the first time, under his direction, it gained the structure of a European monarchy and took on the name and character of a court, or *curia,* which it retains to the present. The cardinals became his equivalent of a king's council, taking care of papal business in the various administrative departments which he laid out and meeting periodically to discuss vital issues and advise the pope. Urban II also remodeled the papal financial system, basing it on the one he had developed at Cluny, and substituted priests for laymen in all secretarial and lower administrative posts of the Church. His secretary, the priest John of Gaeta, appointed in 1089, held the job for 30 years and himself became pope 30 years later as Gelasius II.

As his administration improved, so did Urban II's ability to win powerful political adherents. His reign coincided with the expansion of Norman power in Europe. In one of the best remembered events of the 11th century, **William the Conqueror,** duke of Normandy, had seized England in 1066. The Normans also conquered Sicily and forcibly converted it and southern Italy from eastern Orthodoxy to Catholic Christianity, tasks in which they gained Urban II's active support. Many of the Norman leaders sympathized with the Gregorian reform party and became strong supporters of Urban.

Urban also won the loyalty of Spanish rulers and clerics who were struggling to recover central Spain from the Moors. The king of Aragon and the count of Barcelona were among the Spanish leaders who declared their allegiance to the pope. The best-remembered figure of this period of Spanish Christian reconquest was "El Cid," **Rodrigo Diaz de Vivar,** "the personification of the heroism of medieval Spain." As the legends of El Cid suggest, the reconquest of Spain took on the characteristics of a Holy War, although the Church's attitude to warfare was at that time still ambiguous. From the earliest days of Christianity, it had condemned war and imposed penances on

warriors. Yet, by the mid-11th century, expeditions like William the Conqueror's and the Spanish campaigns against Islam were receiving papal blessings and banners. Earlier in the century, the popes had tried to restrict the depredations of warring Christians by introducing the "Peace of God" (which exempted monks, clergy, women, merchants, and the poor from war) and the "Truce of God" (which prohibited campaigning in several seasons of the Church calendar and, ideally, between Wednesday evening and Monday morning each week). Urban carried through another decisive shift by officially sanctioning Holy War against infidels for the first time and by launching a great papal adventure in the Holy Land, the First Crusade.

The First Crusade Gets Under Way

The Roman Empire, which had decayed in the West centuries before, remained intact in the Middle East, centered in Constantinople (today's Istanbul). Its Byzantine emperors and the Western popes and kings were periodically in contact and trade with one another, though the chronic wars of the Middle Ages often broke down communications. In the late 11th century, the old Empire faced the attacks of the militant Seljuq Turks, which it was ill equipped to repulse, and Emperor Alexius I Comnenus sent messengers to the pope's synod at Piacenza in 1095, begging for aid from the Western Christians.

Piacenza was one of two major church gatherings in 1095, at which the idea of the crusade appears to have matured in Urban II's mind: in an armed pilgrimage, the emperor could be aided and the holy places of Jesus' life and death recovered from the Muslims at the same time. Urban waited until a series of internal Church affairs had been settled (including condemnation of the French king for bigamy) before ending the second of these meetings, the Council of Clermont, with the passionate speech which sparked the First Crusade. Dismayed by warfare among Christians, Urban said that he relished the prospect of war against the infidels:

> O race of the Franks, we learn that in some of your provinces no one can venture on the road by day or by night without injury or attack by highwaymen, and no one is secure even at home. Let us then re-enact the law of our ancestors known as the Truce of God. And now that you have promised to maintain the peace among yourselves you are obligated to succour your brethren in the East, menaced by an accursed race, utterly alien-

ated from God.... Start upon the road to the Holy Sepulchre to wrest that land from the wicked race and subject it to yourselves.

After this stirring speech, say the chroniclers, the thousands of onlookers threw themselves to the ground, shouting "Deus Vult," or "God wills it," and began to "take the cross" (pledge to go on crusade) in large numbers. Emperor Henry IV suffered further affronts by being excluded from the crusade in the months of preparation which followed. Urban II appointed Adhemar, the bishop of LePuy, as papal legate to the venture, and Adhemar became one of the crusade's most effective leaders, though neither he nor Urban was ever able to discipline the lawless and bloody crusaders' trek across Europe and Asia with which the expedition began.

Until then, any form of fighting by priests and monks, though it often took place, had been regarded as an abuse of Holy Orders. Now, for the first time, the Church treated it as a high duty for clerics to fight in the circumstances of a crusade; crusaders marked their dress with a large cross cut from cloth and worn across the breast. A holy man named Peter the Hermit led one large band on the long journey east, starting from Cologne. Many of Peter's followers were poor men and women, however, aroused by the wave of religious enthusiasm sweeping through Europe but totally lacking in military training or discipline. As a result of indiscipline and a constant search for food, they became involved in a succession of brawls and minor battles among the unwelcoming people of the Balkans whose farms they raided. They had no sooner arrived in Constantinople, the crusaders' rendezvous, than they began to plunder the city, prompting the Byzantine Emperor Alexius to ship them hastily across to the Asian side of the Bosphorous. Shortly afterwards, they were all but massacred by the Turkish sultan; Peter the Hermit, temporarily absent in Constantinople, was one of the few survivors.

Other bands of crusaders were even more chaotic; one band raised in western Germany first showed its zeal for Christ not by marching off toward the Holy Land, but by massacring the Jews of the Rhine and Moselle valleys, even those who had fled to the local Catholic bishops for protection. Other atrocities followed as they marched eastward. More effective and slightly more pious leaders were William the Conqueror's son Robert of Normandy, **Godfrey of Bouillon,** and his brothers Eustace and Baldwin of Boulogne, whose knights fought with a fair degree of discipline and skill.

The journey, whether by land or sea, was extraordinarily difficult, especially for armies tens of thousands strong whose proper provisioning was almost impossible. They inevitably preyed on the people whose lands they crossed en route. Crusaders had to overcome not only problems of distance and supply, and determined military enemies, but also fearsome medical challenges. Historian Alfred Crosby explains:

> In September and October of 1098, thousands of members of the First Crusade died of some sort of pestilence. It seems to have been infectious: an army of 21,500 Germans, freshly arrived, suffered rapid annihilation, which suggests infection rather than malnutrition, although the latter could certainly have contributed to the rapid rate at which they died.

Despite the innumerable horrors of their campaign, the crusaders slogged across Asia Minor between 1096 and 1099, and in a series of battles and sieges captured the cities of Nicea, Antioch, and ultimately Jerusalem itself. This crowning achievement, accomplished in 1099, led to the scene which chronicler Raymond of Agiles in his *Historia Francorum* described rapturously:

> Some of our men (and this was more merciful) cut off the heads of their enemies; others shot them with arrows, so that they fell from the towers; others tortured them longer by casting them into the flames. Piles of heads, hands, and feet were to be seen in the streets of the city.

Meanwhile, he added, at the Temple of Solomon, "men rode in blood up to their knees and the bridle reins. Indeed it was a just and splendid judgment of God, that this place should be filled with the blood of unbelievers, when it had suffered so long from their blasphemies." The chronicler concluded that "on this day the Lord revealed Himself to His people and blessed them."

No other crusade in the following centuries would get so far as to seize Jerusalem itself, after its recapture by **Saladin** in 1187. The crusaders on this, as on subsequent ventures, were plagued by mutual antipathies, were easily turned aside by the temptation to plunder or to set up petty empires of their own, and were enfeebled because of their continuing vulnerability to deadly illnesses and their reluctance to stay in large numbers after the great campaigns.

Ironically, Pope Urban II died two weeks before news of the capture of Jerusalem reached

Rome; in his eyes, it would have been a full vindication of his hopes. By the time he died, he had recovered the papacy from the chaos in which he had found it and paved the way for several centuries of enhanced papal influence. By contrast, his great rival Henry IV died in 1106 discredited, his throne challenged by his son, and as much wounded in prestige by his exclusion from the crusade as Urban II was enhanced by it.

SOURCES:

Bainton, Roland H. *The Medieval Church*. Van Nostrand, 1962.

Baldwin, Marshall. *The Medieval Papacy in Action*. Macmillan, 1940.

Barraclough, Geoffrey. *The Medieval Papacy*. Harcourt, 1968.

Cheetham, Nicholas. *Keepers of the Keys*. Scribner, 1982.

Cowdrey, H. E. J. *Popes, Monks and Crusaders*. Hambledon Press, 1984.

Crosby, Alfred. *Ecological Imperialism*. Cambridge University Press, 1986.

Mourret, Fernand S.S. *A History of the Catholic Church*. Vol. 4. Translated by Newton Thompson. B. Herder, 1941.

Eleutherios Venizelos

(1864–1936)

Prime minister, who played a crucial role directing Greece's foreign affairs, brought his country major territorial gains at the expense of Turkey in the First Balkan War, and led Greece into World War I as an ally of France, Britain, and the United States.

Pronunciation: Elef-THEY-rios Veni-ZAY-los. Born in Mournies, Crete, on August 23, 1864; died in Paris on March 18, 1936; married: twice; children: one son.

Eleutherios Venizelos dominated Greek political affairs during the first decades of the 20th century. Beginning as a Greek leader on the island of Crete while it was still under Turkish control, Venizelos was called to Greece as that country's political problems threatened to become unmanageable in 1909. The Cretan leader made Greece a newly powerful force in Balkan affairs through his domestic reforms and his aggressive foreign policy. But his strong and decisive leadership led to a rivalry with Greece's monarch, Constantine I, that brought Greece to the edge of civil war. By the closing days of World War I, Greece was divided into pro-Venizelos and anti-Venizelos factions. Judgments about the value of Venizelos's achievements continue to differ down to the present time.

Greece at the start of the 20th century was a small European country whose independence dated from the 1820s. Under Turkish control since the 15th century, Greece rebelled against its Muslim rulers in 1821, winning its independence in 1832. Throughout the remainder of the century, the new country was burdened with severe difficulties. Independent Greece contained only a fraction

"Venizelos was the dominant figure of southeast Europe… a genius in diplomacy, a humane and far-seeing statesmen, and an unchallenged leader of his fellow-countrymen."

C.M. WOODHOUSE

"Of principles, however, he was totally devoid. If he appeared to have any… it was because they all provided useful means which he was always clever enough to disguise as ends."

DOUGLAS DAKIN

Contributed by Neil Heyman, Professor of History, San Diego State University, San Diego, California

of the Greeks of southeastern Europe and Asia Minor. Greeks were clearly aware that many areas inhabited by their ethnic brothers were still under Turkish control. These areas included the large island of Crete and regions north of the Greek border of 1832 like Thessaly and Epirus. When Greeks in places like Crete rebelled against their Turkish governors—as happened in the 1860s and 1890s—the Greek government in Athens faced the problem of whether to go to war with Turkey in order to help them.

Conflict with Turkey brought other international complications. The powers of Western Europe, notably Great Britain, were committed to propping up Turkey, since they saw that country as a necessary barrier against Russian expansion toward the Mediterranean. Thus, Greeks on the mainland found themselves threatened with the powerful British fleet whenever they sought to oppose Turkey. Greeks on Crete faced British intervention when they tried to rebel against their Turkish rulers.

Moreover, Greece was one of the poorest countries in Europe. Dependent on exporting a few crops like olives and currants, the Greek economy was severely hurt when the world price for such goods dropped. Poverty and overpopulation forced large numbers of Greeks to emigrate, many of them going to the United States. The country was ruled by a succession of monarchs brought in from other parts of Europe. Conflict between the Greek population and such rulers combined with poverty and international tensions to create an unstable political situation.

Eleutherios Venizelos was born in Mournies, a village near the Cretan city of Canae, on August 23, 1864. His merchant father was an ethnic Greek who was expelled from Crete in 1866 for his part in a rebellion against Turkey. The elder Venizelos lived for a time in Athens, where he acquired Greek citizenship, then was subsequently allowed to return to Crete. This period of residence in Greece made his son Eleutherios a Greek citizen as well.

The young man grew restless at the prospect of becoming a merchant like his father. Despite his family's objections, he went to Athens to study law. Accounts of his student days mention how he clashed with a prestigious professor over the interpretation of a point of law.

Back in Crete in 1887, Venizelos participated in the Cretan rebellion of 1896–97 against the Turks. As the British navy intervened to support the Turks, Venizelos began to seriously study English so that he could negotiate with British

CHRONOLOGY

1832	Greece became independent; Prince Otto of Bavaria became king
1866–1905	Anti-Turkish revolts in Crete
1908	Venizelos became prime minister of Crete; declaration of union of Greece and Crete
1909	Military revolt in Athens
1910	Venizelos became prime minister; domestic reforms began
1912	First Balkan War
1913	Constantine I became king; Second Balkan War; Crete annexed by Greece
1914	Start of World War I
1915	French and British landings in Greece; Venizelos resigned
1916	Established Provisional Government
1917	Abdication of Constantine; Venizelos became prime minister for second time; Greece entered World War I
1919	Greek forces landed at Smyrna in Asia Minor
1920	Venizelos defeated in national elections; restoration of Constantine
1922	Greeks defeated by Kemal Ataturk; second abdication by Constantine
1924	Venizelos prime minister for third time
1928–32	Prime minister for fourth time
1933	Prime minister for fifth and final time

military commanders. Over 20 years later at the Versailles Conference in 1919, Venizelos would remind British diplomats, now his allies, how he came to know their language.

Even during his years on his small Mediterranean island birthplace, Venizelos struck European politicians, such as Joseph Chamberlain, as a future Greek leader. He made a particularly deep impression on **Georges Clemenceau,** the future premier of France. Following a visit to Crete, Clemenceau wrote of this remarkable young leader that "the whole of Europe will be speaking of him in a few years."

The Cretan rebellion of the 1890s led directly to Venizelos's political career on the mainland. First, it discredited the existing order in Greece. The government in Athens went to war with Turkey in 1897. When the Turks faced only a single Balkan opponent in war, they usually won easily, and this conflict followed the established pattern. The sting of defeat discredited the Greek monarchy and led to massive discontent among the officers of the Greek army.

Second, the rebellion led to the collapse of Turkish control over Crete and the emergence of Venizelos as the island's leader. In 1908, under Venizelos's leadership, the Cretan assembly declared the island united with Greece. In Athens, however, the government was unwilling to run the risk of formally adding Crete to its territories. This further undercut the government's popularity.

Becomes Prime Minister, Launches Reforms

In 1909, rebel officers launched a coup against the weak and discredited Greek government. Early the following year, Venizelos moved to Greece at the invitation of military rebels. By the close of the year, he had arranged a reform of the constitution and, in September 1910, he became Greece's prime minister. As one historian put it, his "career on his native island prepared him admirably for the larger political stage on the mainland, where he played the leading role for many years."

Venizelos quickly launched Greece into a program of domestic reform. There were sweeping changes, for example, in the civil service and education. But Venizelos's most important reforms came in rebuilding and modernizing Greece's armed forces. Greece was never again, he hoped, to be a second-rate military power compared to Turkey.

Venizelos's policy brought spectacular results in the two Balkans wars that took place in 1912–13. In the first war, Greece fought alongside Serbia and Bulgaria and administered a spectacular defeat to the Turks. In the second war, Greece, Serbia, and Rumania fought Bulgaria. In the end, Venizelos won enough territory to almost double the size of Greece. His homeland of Crete now formally joined the kingdom of Greece, along with large areas that extended Greek territory northward and eastward.

The Involvement of Greece in World War I

During World War I, the rival policies of Venizelos and King Constantine I nearly led Greece into civil war. Venizelos assumed that the Entente, led by Britain and France, would win the war. Thus, Greece would benefit by becoming their ally. With traditional Greek enemies like Ottoman Turkey and Bulgaria fighting alongside Germany and Aus-

tria, Greece could hope to expand its territory and influence by joining Britain and France. In particular, Venizelos hoped to put Constantinople under some kind of Greek control and to win a foothold on Asia Minor around the city of Smyrna. The region around Smyrna, although a part of Turkey, contained a substantial Greek population.

Constantine saw the trends of the war differently. As the brother-in-law of Emperor **Wilhelm II** (William), he had close personal ties to Germany, and some historians see his policies as determined by his pro-German views. Others consider him genuinely neutral, but they believe his policies were shaped by his expectation that the Entente would lose the war. As he put it, if he led Greece to war against the Central Powers (Germany and its allies), no one would come to his aid. If he joined the Central Powers, Greece would be even more helpless in facing the deadly seapower of Britain and France.

Although Venizelos offered Greece's help to London and Paris in 1914, Entente leaders refused it. They did not want the war, then being fought in Western and Eastern Europe, to spread to the Balkans.

By 1915, Turkey had joined Germany and Austria-Hungary. In the spring, Allied naval forces, soon augmented by army units, attacked the Dardanelles, the Turkish Straits connecting the Mediterranean and the Black seas. In the fall, Germany and Austria, now joined by Bulgaria, combined to crush Serbia. In October, a hurried and confused set of events took place. Venizelos allowed French and British troops to land in Greece in order to move northward to aid the Serbs. In the midst of the landings, however, he was forced from power by King Constantine.

The following year, Venizelos formed his own Greek Provisional Government, opposed to Constantine. In 1917, Constantine was forced to resign and Venizelos led his country into the war as a formal member of the Entente. Large numbers of Greek soldiers fought against Bulgaria in the last year of the war. In particular, they participated in the final allied offensive in the Balkans in September and October 1918. In this effort, the Allies broke out of their bridgehead at Salonika and advanced northward into occupied Serbia and eastward into Bulgaria.

Thus, when Venizelos went to the Versailles Peace Conference wearing the laurels of an important member of the winning side, his claims on Turkish territory were successful. Since other countries like Italy and Britain were also slicing territory away from Turkey, there seemed no danger in asking that Greece receive Smyrna and a large region surrounding that city.

In the midst of his diplomatic successes, Venizelos suddenly found himself thrown from power. The election of 1920 was decided on domestic issues, and the heavy taxes his government had placed on the Greek people to support his ambitious foreign policy contributed to his defeat.

In a tragic series of events, the Greek foothold Venizelos had won was destroyed in bloody fashion. Turkish power revived under the dynamic leader of **Mustafa Kemal Atatürk,** a leading Turkish general during World War I. In fact, Turkish anger at the loss of territory to the Greeks and others helped Kemal gain widespread support. Other countries gave up most of their ambitions, leaving the Greeks isolated in their effort to keep their hold on part of Asia Minor.

Greek leaders, including King Constantine, who had returned to the throne in 1920, pursued Venizelos's aims only to see the Greek army forced to evacuate Smyrna in 1922. Most of the Greek population, which had lived there for thousands of years, was wiped out or expelled.

The divisions of the World War I years and the bitter legacy of defeat in 1922—including the absorption of more than a million refugees—prevented renewed political stability in the next several decades. The Greek scene featured ineffective republican governments as well as military dictatorships. In this atmosphere, Venizelos was forced into exile but was also able to return to power in the 1920s and again in the 1930s. In 1935, however, he had to go into a final exile in France; he died in Paris the following year. His body was returned to the island of Crete, and there, as one biographer put it, "they buried the creator of modern Hellas."

SOURCES:

Alastos, Doros. *Venizelos: Patriot, Statesman, Revolutionary.* P. Lund, 1942.

Dakin, Douglas. *The Unification of Greece, 1770–1923.* St. Martin's Press, 1972.

Stavrianos, Leften. *Balkans since 1453.* Holt, 1958.

Woodhouse, C. M. *Modern Greece: A Short History.* Rev. Faber and Faber, 1991.

FURTHER READING:

Clogg, Richard. *A Short History of Modern Greece.* Cambridge University Press, 1979.

Helmreich, Ernest Christian. *The Diplomacy of the Balkan Wars, 1912–1913.* Harvard University Press, 1938.

Helmreich, Paul C. *From Paris to Sevres: The Partition of the Ottoman Empire at the Peace Conference of 1919–1920.* Ohio State University Press, 1974.

Leon, George B. *Greece and the Great Powers.* Institute for Balkan Studies, 1974.

Palmer, Alan. *The Gardeners of Salonika.* Simon & Schuster, 1965.

Victor Emmanuel II

(1820–1878)

First king of united Italy, who owed his good fortune to an exceptional prime minister, passionate patriots, and favorable historic events.

Born Prince of Savoy-Carignano in Turin, capital of Piedmont in 1820; died in 1878; son of Charles Albert, King of Sardinia, Duke of Savoy and Duke of Piedmont; married: his first cousin, Princess Maria Adelaide (daughter of Austrian Archduke Ranieri). Successor: His son, Humbert.

In the early 19th century, Austrian Prime Minister **Metternich** once dismissed Italy by saying that it was "only a geographical expression." In a very real sense this was true, despite over 3,000 years of history. Not until 1860 was there a viable nation named "Italy" on that boot-shaped land, and its first king was Victor Emmanuel II, of the House of Savoy, a dynasty that was more French than Italian. Having been governed by his forbears for several centuries, the duchy of Savoy occupied a mountainous area just south and west of present-day Switzerland. This gave the House of Savoy control of access to the Alps, that formidable barrier between Western Europe and Italy, where Rome—the center of Christianity—lay. Thus, these *Savoyards* were very important people, especially between the 12th and 18th century. Their sons and daughters married into the greatest royal houses of Europe; some served as generals in armies of the Holy Roman Empire, some served as popes, others held other high ecclesiastical offices, and some of the daughters were queens in the West. But, by the early 19th century, the House of Savoy had fallen on hard times. It ruled over Savoy, the duchy of Piedmont in northern Italy, and the island Kingdom of

Contributed by H.L. Oerter, Professor of History, Emeritus, Miami University, Oxford, Ohio

"No one ever thought (Victor Emmanuel) a clever person, nor at any stage of his life did he read any books.... Legend made him out to be a strong character with a capacity for firm decision. The legend was wrong.

DENIS MACK SMITH

Sardinia—this last as a kind of consolation prize for having lost greater honors elsewhere.

The Italian peninsula, in keeping with a tradition that reached back to the period after the fall of the Roman Empire in the West, was composed of a number of autonomous, semi-autonomous or dependent duchies, "Republics" and kingdoms over which the dying institution of the Holy Roman Empire in the shape of the grand duchy of Austria held sway, either directly or through client rulers.

The Kingdom of the Two Sicilies included the island of Sicily and the southern portion of the peninsula centering around Naples. The Spanish Bourbon line of kings who ruled here were subservient to the Habsburgs of Austria. The Papal States, centered on Rome, included the regions of the Marches, Latium, Umbria, and, at varying times, Emilia and the Romagna. These were governed by the papacy through precedents that stretched back to the time of Pepin the Short, father of **Charlemagne.** The remainder of the peninsula included the grand duchy of Tuscany, which was ruled by a member of the Habsburg family, while the states of Modena, Parma, Lombardy, and Venetia existed under Austrian rule of one kind or another. While the Austrians could not justly be accused of misrule, the fact remained that they were not Italians and for this reason Italian scholars, literati, and patriots for the past two centuries had been studying ways by which they might be expelled from Italy.

This setting provided the historical time, place, and climate for the cultural and political upsurge that has been labelled *Il Risorgimento* (The Resurgence), which brought about the "unification" of an Italy that had never before existed—not even in the most powerful era of the Roman Empire. Metternich, an exceptionally capable and well-read cynic, knew whereof he spoke.

He did not, however, appreciate the power of the press, the poets, composers, and novelists. All they needed was a figure who could symbolize a United Italy. The figure chosen by accident of birth was that of Victor Emmanuel, born as Prince of Savoy-Carignano on March 14, 1820, in the family palace in Turin, capital of Piedmont. His father Charles Albert was to become king of Sardinia, a rather empty title; he was also to be hereditary duke of Savoy and duke of Piedmont, the latter of which would be the principal source of his economic power and such military power as could be summoned from a relatively small population base. The court language of Piedmont-Savoy was mostly French. Italian was a foreign language.

CHRONOLOGY

1820	Victor Emmanuel born in Turin
1848	Rising of Milan; Lombard revolt against Austria; Victor Emmanuel commanded some troops
1849	Defeat at Novara; Charles Albert abdicated; Victor Emmanuel ascended the throne
1852	Cavour became prime minister
1855	Piedmont/Sardinia entered Crimean War allied with England and France
1858	Agreement at Plombières between France and Piedmont/Sardinia
1859	War against Austria; France entered on side of Piedmont/Sardinia; war ended by Treaty of Villafranca, by French withdrawal
1860	Kingdom of Italy established; Victor Emmanuel II; crowned first king; capital in Florence
1861	Cavour died
1866	War against Austria; Italy allied with Prussia
1870	Franco-Prussian War; French troops withdrawn from Rome; Italy took Rome
1878	Victor Emmanuel II died

The young heir-presumptive to the Savoy-Piedmont-Sardinian throne was raised in Florence, capital of the grand duchy of Tuscany. He had a brother Ferdinand, two years younger, whose title was duke of Genoa. Biographer Rupert Sargent Holland, writing effusively in the early 20th century, stated that Victor and Ferdinand were inseparable as boys, although "widely different in temperament." Victor is described as "enthusiastic, impulsive, overflowing with animal spirits," while Ferdinand was "more prudent, calm and thoughtful, strongly resembling his father," Charles Albert.

The young men were intensely educated and trained in the military arts, as were all high-born males of that period. When Victor was 11, his father succeeded to the throne and the family moved back to Turin. Holland enthuses about Victor's appearance at the age of 21, "He was of middle height, powerfully built, with features strong rather than handsome." Pictures of the period show that Victor Emmanuel was, indeed, short and slightly stout, sporting an enormous moustache and presenting features that could be described most kindly as "plain."

By the time he was 22, he had met and fallen in love with a first cousin, the princess Maria Adelaide, daughter of Austrian Archduke Ranieri. For commoners, first cousin would have been a bar to marriage, but royalty did not conform to these norms. Her only defect was that she was Austrian, an unfortunate fact that could be overlooked by an indulgent court and a populace that promptly fell in love with the princess. They were married in 1842.

Victor Emmanuel Leads Counterattacks

In 1848, the people of Milan rose in patriotic fervor against their Austrian overlords and attempted to expel them. The "Rising of Milan" was supported by the House of Savoy, which brought its forces into the field, some of them led by Prince Victor Emmanuel. The troops of Piedmont-Savoy were ignominiously defeated by the Austrians in a succession of battles, in two of which Victor Emmanuel distinguished himself by leading counterattacks which did not affect the outcome of the battles but which *did* establish his reputation as a brave—if somewhat less than brilliant—leader of men. After a year of fruitless campaigning, Charles Albert of Savoy surrendered to the Austrian commander, Marshal Radetzky, and abdicated in favor of his elder son, in order to make peace more possible.

Victor Emmanuel, the second of that name in the House of Savoy, assumed the mantle of leadership at a difficult moment. Facing the indomitable Radetzky, he assumed a belligerent pose, but eventually concluded an armistice that required him to disband all military units composed of foreign volunteers (including Poles, Lombards, and Hungarians, among others), to pay a heavy war indemnity, to permit Austrian occupation of part of Piedmontese territory and to dismantle some of his military fortifications.

It was anything but a promising start for a new king, but he and the queen faced their problems and called on their subjects to support them. Victor Emmanuel confirmed the constitution that had been granted by his father. It was a modern document that gave a lot of lip service to then fashionable political ideals; it was also carefully constructed to prevent any usurpation of royal power by the new force called "republicanism." This document, called *Lo Statuto,* would be the governing force of the future Italian kingdom.

The new king faced many obstacles, among which was the obstinate opposition of the papacy. Ruling over several small Italian states, the Church of Rome was determined that the House of Savoy would not acquire any of its lands to adorn the Savoyard crown. Other obstacles included an economy in need of revitalization, continued antagonism between Turin and Vienna, and a crying need for talented political leaders. Those were found in the persons of Massimo D'Azeglio, a marquis, and **Camillo di Benso di Cavour,** a count. Cavour became the power and genius who helped to solve most of the problems and to create the new Kingdom of Italy.

England and France were engaged in a war against Russia in the Crimean Peninsula, at the north end of the Black Sea. Cavour and Victor Emmanuel saw this as a means of gaining approval from the larger European states. Siding with France and England, they fielded a "Sardinian" army in the Crimea which performed creditably. The aftermath of this effort was recognition from British statesmen and an increased awareness of the problems of the Sardinian-Piedmontese-Savoyard government.

Cavour managed to meet with the Emperor **Napoleon III** at the French town of Plombières in July of 1858. Napoleon agreed that if Austria attacked Piedmont, France would come militarily to its aid. With this agreement in hand, Cavour set about to harass the Austrians into attacking his kingdom. It was easily done, thanks to the vociferous news media of the Italian peninsula—even where under Austrian control—and to the prevailing mind-set.

Slogan Links Composer and Patriots

Popular literature, plays, and the most typical Italian contribution to the theatrical arts, grand opera, played on Italian pride and glorified past events in scarcely concealed librettos that ridiculed Austrians (or anyone resembling them) and limitlessly praised *Patria,* the notion of country. The most popular composer of the day was Giuseppe Verdi. By chance, his name became the watchword for Italian patriots who sought to unify the peninsula. "VIVA VERDI" was written on walls, streets, anywhere that could be seen. It actually stood for *Viva* (long live) *Victor Emmanuel, Re* (King) *D'* (of) *Italia* (Italy). The frustrated Austrians could not acknowledge the play on words, and Verdi—a truly great composer—was swept into further heights of popularity. He obliged by including patriotic motifs in nearly every one of his operas, all of which performed to sold-out audiences all over the peninsula, even under the forbidding eyes of Austrian censors.

In 1859, when Victor Emmanuel opened Parliament's annual session, his speech from the throne included what would today be called a "sound bite." He said: "While we respect treaties, we are not insensible to the cry of anguish that comes up to us from many parts of Italy." The phrase was picked up and repeated all over Europe, but especially in the Italian states. When it was heard in Vienna, it resulted in an Austrian ultimatum being delivered to Turin, demanding that the kingdom disarm its forces.

This constituted "an attack" on Piedmont-Sardinia, and Cavour activated the provisions of the agreement between his country and France. Napoleon's troops came to the rescue, landing at Genoa on May 13, 1859, following which they—and the Piedmont-Sardinian army—fought a series of battles at Montebello, Palestro, and Magenta. Lombard volunteers flocked to the commands of Victor Emmanuel and Napoleon III. In early July, Victor Emmanuel and the French emperor entered Milan at the head of their armies. The French (at Malegnano and later at Solferino), the Piedmontese (at San Martino), and the Alpine volunteer "Irregulars" under the command of **Giuseppe Garibaldi,** a professional revolutionary who had offered his services to Victor Emmanuel, administered crushing defeats to the Austrian forces.

But the victories were Pyrrhic (won at excessive cost) as far as Napoleon was concerned. Any more such "victories" and he might have no more army. Accordingly, he sued for peace, withdrew his troops from battle, and signed an accord with the Austrians at Villafranca, on the southern coast, on July 12, 1859. Then—although his withdrawal was regarded as a betrayal by Cavour and Victor Emmanuel—Napoleon exacted a price for his support by ceding to France the duchy of Savoy and the city and province of Nice. The loss of Savoy was a source of deep sorrow to Victor Emmanuel, but the transfer of Nice was regarded by Giuseppe Garibaldi as a treacherous betrayal. His home was in Nice, and he fought with the firm belief that his home would become part of the new Italian kingdom. Cavour was literally prostrated with grief and anger, but eventually withdrew his resignation and returned to the service of the House of Savoy. It was Cavour who had engineered the successful war, and it was Garibaldi who had brought other Italians into it in his volunteer forces.

Lombardy became a part of the new kingdom, and the states of Modena, Parma, Bologna, Ferrara, Umbria, Perugia, and the Marches signified their intention of petitioning the crown for admission to the kingdom. The Tuscans evicted their grand duke, enthusiastically applauding as his carriage drove out of the city for the last time. Then Baron Ricasoli of Tuscany, together with Farini of Modena, called for an assembly of all these states to resolve that they become subjects of the House of Savoy as the Kingdom of Italy.

The northern and central parts of Italy were now united under King Victor Emmanuel II, but Rome and the Kingdom of the Two Sicilies still remained outside his control. Napoleon III had stationed French troops in Rome to "protect and preserve" the independence of the papacy, even though the rest of its dominions had sought the more preferable position as subjects of the Kingdom of Italy. Venetia, too, remained under the control of the Austrian monarchy.

England, under the leadership of Lord John Russell and **Gladstone,** strongly supported Italian independence, while Napoleon was mollified with the gain of Savoy and Nice. Sicily and Naples remained to be added and their accession was accomplished by Garibaldi and his immortal Thousand Red Shirts, who stormed into southwestern Sicily, swept across the island, gaining volunteer adherents from all parts, then onto the mainland, despite "official" instructions from Victor Emmanuel to halt at Messina—and "unofficial" instructions that told him to go ahead. He took over the city and the Kingdom of Naples.

Naples and Sicily Join Kingdom of Italy

Victor Emmanuel and Cavour, fearing that Garibaldi would continue on to Rome, interposed the new Italian army between the forces of Garibaldi and the city of Rome. In the process Victor Emmanuel's army gained some more territory. Garibaldi and the king finally met, shook hands, and Garibaldi turned over his conquests to "his" king. The Garibaldian gains of Naples and Sicily were confirmed in the form of a plebiscite (vote) which overwhelmingly agreed to the annexation to Italy. There were some questions as to its validity, but this 19th century form of chicanery was usually successful and nothing further came of it. As of early October 1860, Naples and Sicily joined the Kingdom of Italy.

At this juncture Cavour died, unable to see the completion of his labors. Although he had nearly succeeded in getting Napoleon to withdraw his support from Rome, his death terminated that arrangement. Rome remained a prime objective of Victor Emmanuel's government. The rigid resistance of Pope **Pius IX,** who utterly refused to negotiate with anyone on the subject, made things more difficult. Baron Ricasoli, who had succeeded Cavour, died in office and his successor Rattazzi hinted to Garibaldi that he might avail himself of the prevailing will, attacking Rome with more of his "Volunteers."

In 1862, when Garibaldi moved against Rome from Sicily with a small force, Rattazzi became frightened at the prospect and ordered the Italian army to stop him. The result: Garibaldi, one of Italy's greatest heroes, suffered the only wound he ever received—from an Italian weapon. His plight forced Rattazzi out of office.

In 1865, the Italian monarchy moved its capital to Florence as a signal to Napoleon that the objective of Rome was thereby abandoned. But only for the moment. One year later, the Kingdom of Prussia, with the able direction of Otto von Bismarck, turned its forces against Austria. By prior arrangement, the Kingdom of Italy also declared war on Austria, with the acquisition of Venetia as its promised reward. Despite appalling losses on both land and sea, Italy gained the territory it sought, inasmuch as Prussia rolled over Austria as though there were no resistance. The venerable Republic of Venice and all its lands on the mainland were joined to the Italian Kingdom.

One of the consequences of the Austro-Prussian War was the Franco-Prussian War in which the burgeoning power of the Prussian military machine was employed against Napoleon III, commander of what was supposedly Europe's greatest armed forces. Faced with this war, Napoleon finally withdrew his protecting cover of French troops from Rome, whereupon the Italian army moved to the city, assaulted one of the gates and marched into Rome, stopping only at the confines of Vatican City, a tiny spot near the banks of the Tiber River.

The papacy considered itself "imprisoned" in the Vatican. As it had already excommunicated Victor Emmanuel and members of his court, there was not much else it could do, except to make every attempt to block conciliation from that point forward and to forbid devout Catholics from taking part in the Italian government. This last stricture was observed mostly in the breach until 1929, when it was finally abrogated by the Lateran Treaty. The seat of the government of Italy was moved to Rome from Florence, and the Italian Kingdom finally had shaped itself within its "natural" borders.

Thereafter, all events in 19th-century Italy seem to have been anticlimactic. Pius IX, the unyielding enemy of modernism, and Victor Emmanuel II, the symbol of Italian unity, died in the same year, 1878.

Victor Emmanuel II has been granted the mantle of leadership largely because of having existed at the right time and the right place. He was not insignificant, nor was he one of the towering figures of history. His "greatness" stems from the accident of time and place and rests on the unquestioned talents of many devoted Italian patriots, such as Cavour, Garibaldi, D'Azeglio—and even **Giuseppe Mazzini.** The king happened to command great men. It is the irony of history that sometimes inferior players on its stages bask in the reflected glow of greater stars who receive lesser billing. Such was the case with Victor Emmanuel II.

SOURCES:

Holland, Rupert Sargent. *Builders of United Italy.* Henry Holt, 1908.

Smith, Denis Mack. *Victor Emmanuel, Cavour and the Risorgimento.* London: Oxford University Press, 1971.

Trevelyan, Janet Penrose. *A Short History of the Italian People.* Revised ed. London: Allen & Unwin, 1956.

FURTHER READING:

Fitz-Hardinge, George, and J. Berkeley. *Italy in the Making.* 3 vols. Cambridge: The University Press, 1968.

Forester, C. S. *Victor Emmanuel II and the Union of Italy.* Dodd, Mead, 1927.

King, Bolton. *A History of Italian Unity: Being a Political History of Italy from 1814 to 1871.* 2 vols. London: Nisbet, 1934.

Smith, Denis Mack. *Italy: A Modern History.* University of Michigan Press, 1969.

Victoria

(1819–1901)

Britain's longest lived and longest ruling monarch, who presided over her country's rise to world economic and imperial domination, saw the gradual democratization of its political institutions, and gave her name to an historical era.

Born on May 24, 1819, at Kensington Palace, London; died at Osborne House, Isle of Wight, on January 22, 1901; daughter of Edward, Duke of Kent (fourth son of George III) and Victoria of Saxe-Coburg and Saalfeld, Princess of Leiningen; married: Albert of Saxe-Coburg and Gotha, 1840 (died December 14, 1861); children— four sons and five daughters: Albert Edward (Prince of Wales and King Edward VII), Alfred (Duke of Edinburgh and Duke of Saxe-Coburg and Gotha), Arthur (Duke of Connaught), Leopold (Duke of Albany), Victoria (Princess Royal and Empress of Germany), Alice (Grand Duchess of Hesse-Darmstadt), Helena (Princess of Schleswig-Holstein), Louise (Duchess of Argyle), and Beatrice (Princess of Battenberg). Descendants: H. M. Queen Elizabeth II and the House of Mountbatten-Windsor; Wilhelm II of Hohenzollern, last German emperor; kings Carl XVI Gustaf of Sweden and Juan Carlos I of Spain, and Queen Margrethe II of Denmark; the former kings of Greece, Rumania, and Yugoslavia; the head of the former Russian imperial house of Romanov.

Queen Victoria's eventful life can be divided into three broad periods: from her birth in 1819 until her marriage to Prince Albert in 1840; her married life of 21 years, from 1840 to 1861; and her widowhood of almost 40 years.

Victoria was conceived because it looked as if the House of Hanover was heading toward extinction. Although the aging King George III had sired 15 children, his daughters were either spinsters or childless, only three of his seven living sons were validly married, and only one son, George the Prince Regent (later King George IV), had a child, Princess Charlotte. When Charlotte died in childbirth in 1817, the Crown lost its only heir in the third generation.

The pillars of the British Establishment— Parliament, the Privy Council, the bishops— pressed publicly for the unmarried princes to marry and for the married ones to try harder to produce an heir, and offered to increase the allowances of those who did. The old king's fourth son, Edward, duke of Kent, put away his mistress of 20 years' standing, married the German princess Victoria of Saxe-Coburg and Saalfeld, and fathered the future Queen Victoria. Then the fifth son, Ernest, Duke

Contributed by D. G. Paz, Professor of History, Clemson University, Clemson, South Carolina

CHRONOLOGY

1837	Death of William IV; Victoria succeeded to throne
1841	Sir Robert Peel became prime minister
1845–49	Irish Potato Famine
1846	Repeal of the Corn Laws
1847	Lord John Russell became prime minister
1848	Continental revolutions throughout Europe; in Britain, the Chartist Movement
1853–56	Crimean War
1855	Lord Palmerston became prime minister
1857	Indian Mutiny threatened British control of subcontinent
1867	Second Reform Act passed
1868	Gladstone became prime minister
1870–71	Franco-Prussian War
1874	Disraeli became prime minister
1884	Third Reform Act enfranchised farm laborers
1886	Lord Salisbury became prime minister
1897	Victoria celebrated her Diamond Jubilee
1899–1902	South African War
1901	Victoria died at age 81, having reigned 63 years

of Cumberland, already married, fathered a son, as did the seventh son, Adolphus, Duke of Cambridge. Because British law did not exclude females from the succession, Victoria outranked her uncles Ernest and Adolphus and her two cousins.

When Victoria was only eight months old, both her grandfather King George III and her father died, leaving only two childless uncles between her and the throne. From the beginning, her mother and her mother's majordomo, Sir John Conroy, raised her as the heiress presumptive to the throne. Determined that Princess Victoria would be their puppet, they devised a regimen called the "Kensington System" to attain their ends. Victoria was made to keep a diary, which the duchess and Conroy inspected every evening to monitor her thoughts. She slept in her mother's room every night. She could not receive visitors unless her mother or Conroy was present. She was not allowed to walk downstairs unaided. Her guardians planned that when she became queen, her mother

would be her regent and Conroy her private secretary; between them, they would rule the land.

Supported only by her governess, Baroness Lehzen, and her faraway uncle Leopold I, king of the Belgians, Victoria managed to cultivate a distinct personality, despite the machinations of her guardians. After 1830, when she stood to succeed her childless uncle William IV, he also encouraged her to become independent of her mother. Then, in 1836, when Victoria was 17, her uncle Leopold arranged for her to meet her first cousin, Prince Albert of Saxe-Coburg and Gotha, hoping that they would marry. King William encouraged Victoria to meet other suitable candidates for her hand but left the final choice to her.

The king was more concerned that he might die before Victoria turned 18 and became a legal adult. Publicly, he expressed his concern that Victoria's mother was "surrounded by evil advisers"; privately, he offered Victoria an income sufficient to maintain her independence. Nothing, however, had been resolved when King William died on June 20, 1837, a month after Victoria had celebrated her 18th birthday.

Young Victoria Takes Control

From the moment that she was awakened at 6 A.M. to learn that she was queen, Victoria jettisoned the Kensington System and took control of her life. Insisting on receiving the messengers alone, she then demanded a bedroom of her own and dismissed Sir John Conroy from her household. Eager for something useful to do, the new young queen welcomed the duties of a reigning queen. She relied heavily upon her Whig prime minister, Lord Melbourne, seeing him almost every day. She kept up the round of reviews, state openings, and other ceremonial activities that went with the position of monarch. She read, understood, and made written comments on the reports and papers that came to her each day from the government departments. "It is to me the greatest pleasure to do my duty for my country and my people," she told her Uncle Leopold, "and no fatigue, however great, will be burdensome to me if it is for the welfare of the nation."

Life was not all work. She loved parties and balls and delighted in staying up till dawn dancing. She was not keen on hunting but liked to ride and kept dogs. So hard did she play that some of her ministers began to fear that she was exhibiting the Hanoverian love of sensual pleasure that had led her uncles into sexual escapades and debt.

Her prime minister Melbourne took an important role in her development during these years, teaching her about her family's and country's histories and showing her how a constitutional monarch should behave. He thought that monarchs should support their ministers and should avoid taking an independent line. Victoria accepted these ideas but interpreted them in such a way as to allow herself considerable freedom of action. She never hesitated to question her ministers, to demand time to think things over, to express her own opinions frankly, and to criticize her ministers if they adhered to policies she disapproved of, or if their policies failed.

Melbourne and Victoria enjoyed a close relationship. The queen looked to him as the father she had never known; the prime minister, deeply saddened by an unhappy marriage and a retarded son who had died young, found in the young queen an outlet for his paternal love. But Victoria became too dependent upon the Whig Melbourne, at least in Tory eyes. Melbourne recognized this and tried to convince Victoria that she should put away her unreasonable dislike for Sir **Robert Peel,** the Tory (Conservative) Party leader, for he knew that the time would come when governments would change. Victoria, however, proclaimed her loyalty to Melbourne; in the Bedchamber Crisis of 1839, she refused to remove her Whig ladies-in-waiting to make way for Tory ladies, and Peel felt unable to form a government.

Victoria was rescued from her Whig associations by her marriage to her first cousin, the younger son of her mother's brother, Prince Albert of Saxe-Coburg and Gotha in 1840. Since their meeting in 1836, they had corresponded, visited, and fallen in love. Smitten with his face and figure, Victoria proposed in October 1839, and the two were married on February 10, 1840. "When day dawned (for we did not sleep much) and I beheld that beautiful angelic face by my side, it was more than I can express!," Victoria wrote in her journal the morning after the wedding. As her marriage to Albert closed the first portion of her life, Victoria began a new life of marriage, motherhood, and nonpolitical monarchy.

The Queen and Albert Raise a Family

The 21 years of married life saw the creation of that quintessentially middle-class image of Victoria and Albert and their family. They had nine children in 17 years (1840–57); all the children married, and all save one had children of their own. So began the great intermarriage of the British royal family with those of the Continent. Not for nothing did Victoria become known as the Grandmother of Europe.

The most significant of the children's marriages, from a diplomatic perspective, was that of Victoria's namesake, the Princess Royal (1840–1901), to Crown Prince Frederick of Prussia (1831–88). The two were Victoria's favorites, which contributed to Britain's pro-Prussian foreign policy in the 1860s. The marriage cultivated Frederick's liberal, constitutional politics, and those who wanted to see Germany develop into an English-style parliamentary monarchy pinned their hopes on his succession. But this was not to be. Frederick had throat cancer when he became German kaiser in 1888 and died before the year was out. He was succeeded by his son, the authoritarian kaiser **Wilhelm II;** although a dutiful grandson who would hold Queen Victoria in his arms as she died, he had no love for English institutions, and his jealousy of British might contributed to the coming of the First World War.

From a psychological perspective, the marriage of Victoria and Albert produced the model Victorian relationship between husband and wife. Their marriage was a change from the marriage styles of the French Revolutionary and Regency periods, in which adultery and promiscuity were tolerated, and in which conspicuous consumption by the rich went hand in hand with contempt or indifference towards the poor.

Albert's own political influence on the queen was important. When it had become evident that he was likely to marry Victoria, his uncle, King Leopold, and Baron Frederick Stockmar, confidential advisor to the Coburg family, began to educate him in British political and constitutional history. Thus Albert, an intelligent man to begin with, was well prepared for his role as Prince Consort (a title granted him in 1857) and in effect Queen Victoria's private secretary. Albert continued where Lord Melbourne had left off, helping the queen accept the fall of the Whigs and the coming to power of Sir Robert Peel and the Tories in 1841. That the queen accepted the loss of her most favored minister was important, for it showed that the monarch was becoming "above party" and would work with whichever faction commanded a majority in the House of Commons.

In his role as unofficial private secretary, Albert encouraged Victoria to support progressive projects such as the Crystal Palace Exhibition of 1851 and the creation of a science center in South Kensington. He became a fixture on committees to promote the sciences and mathematics. He also promoted the fine arts by encouraging Victoria, who had artistic interests of her own, to direct the royal patronage to young, up-and-coming painters. The Victoria and Albert Museum and

the Royal Albert Hall are fitting monuments to the cultural patronage of the royal couple.

As unofficial private secretary to the queen, Albert worked closely with the prime ministers of the day—the Conservatives Peel and Derby and the Whigs Lord John Russell and **Lord Palmerston.** The queen shared more and more of her official business with her husband and depended upon him for advice. The best example of his role came at the end of his life, when he worked behind the scenes to diffuse the Trent Affair, a quarrel over American violations of the freedom of the seas that threatened to drag Britain into the American Civil War.

Yet Victoria never forgot that she was queen, and thus bore final responsibility for her acts. She and Albert became estranged for a few years in the mid-1850s, when he seemed to be going beyond his proper role, but they had been reconciled by the time that he died in 1861. The queen always insisted that no diplomatic correspondence be sent out without her prior approval, and on several occasions she reprimanded Russell and Palmerston, who chafed under the necessity of showing her their dispatches first. Her personal diplomacy was significant in healing the traditional suspicion between Britain and France. She got along well with Emperor **Napoleon III** and Empress Eugenie, and on several state visits to France she charmed her Gallic audiences.

She Presides Over a Moderate Government

In domestic affairs, the queen presided over a moderate government that was slowly modernizing the British constitution. During the 1840s and 1850s, the state became increasingly involved in the provision of education, and in the 1847 Factory Act reduced the working day in textile mills to ten hours. Dissenters from the religious establishment received greater equality, being admitted to Oxford and Cambridge universities. The Chartist Movement, which petitioned Parliament for universal manhood suffrage in 1839, 1842, and 1848, frightened the landed and middle classes, especially in the last year, which coincided with a wave of European revolutions. But this working-class movement, committed as it was to parliamentary ends, made no attempts to overthrow the government. Britain was thus spared violent revolution in 1848.

The two violent convulsions of the 1850s were the Crimean War and the Indian Mutiny. Russia's desire to control the eastern Mediterranean as the Turkish Empire decayed led to the outbreak of war in 1853, which Britain, France, and Sardinia joined in the following year. The war was not an immediate success, and indeed revealed serious inefficiency in the way the troops were supplied while encamped and led into battle. Although Victoria and Albert became convinced that the administration of the War Office was incompetent, they remained loyal to the ministry until it was ousted by Lord Palmerston, who became prime minister in 1855 and brought the war to a satisfactory conclusion.

Hard on the heels of war came the Indian Mutiny, a rebellion led by indigenous Indian rulers who resented the loss of their power. Victoria took as direct an interest in the suppression of this revolt as she had in the conduct of the Crimean War. In both cases, she gave Palmerston unsolicited advice and pressed the cabinet to prosecute vigorously a military solution. Yet she also opposed harsh reprisals against the Indians, and supported the governor-general of India whose conciliatory policies had led to calls for his dismissal.

This portion of Victoria's life was brought to an abrupt and unexpected end by the death of the prince consort on December 14, 1861. The year had opened with the death of Victoria's mother. Although Victoria had not been close to her mother since the days of the Kensington System, she had come to realize that her mother loved her and was depressed by the missed opportunities to return the affection. Throughout the year, Prince Albert's health worsened, and at some point in late November, he contracted typhoid. At this juncture, two crises, one public and the other personal, worsened the situation.

The aforementioned Trent Affair gave Victoria and Albert an anxious time, as it looked as if Britain and the United States were moving toward war. In what proved to be his last memorandum, the prince consort redrafted the ministry's protest to allow the Americans to retreat with honor. At the same time, the royal couple's eldest son, future king and Prince of Wales, was caught in bed with an actress, and Albert left his sickbed to sort out his son's affair and redeem him from this moral failing. After his return, Albert sank into his bed as to his grave. Victoria poured out her grief in her diary:

Two or three long but perfectly gentle breaths were drawn, the hand clasping mine, & (oh! it turns me sick to write it) all all was over.... I stood up, kissing his dear heavenly forehead & called out in a bitter agonising cry: "Oh! my dear Darling!" & then dropped on my knees in mute, distracted despair, unable to utter a word or shed a tear!

During the third, and last, part of Queen Victoria's life, from her widowhood in 1861 to her death in 1901, the two-party system of parliamentary democracy solidified, the British Empire spread into Asia and Africa, and the queen aged into the matriarchal symbol of the age.

In politics, the period saw the expansion of political institutions to include the working classes. The Second Reform Act of 1867 and the Third Reform Act of 1884 gave the vote to most adult working men, and the Ballot Act of 1872 allowed them to cast their votes in secret. In response to the expanded electorate, the Liberal and the Conservative parties (which had evolved out of the old Whigs and Tories) adjusted their campaign tactics, paying more attention to matters of working-class concern such as labor law, public housing, and education. The Labour Party was created in 1893, signaling the new politics of the 20th century.

Disraeli Brings the Queen Back to Public Life

The queen, bereft of Prince Albert's advice, went into seclusion during most of the 1860s and early 1870s, until her most-favored politician, **Benjamin Disraeli,** charmed her back into public life. Although the queen formally supported Disraeli's archrival, four-time prime minister **William Ewart Gladstone,** she did so in such an obviously grudging way as to leave no doubt of whom she approved.

Liberal Gladstone's political slogan was "Peace, Retrenchment, and Reform." He opposed imperial expansion, and only reluctantly took control of Egypt in 1882 (to protect the Suez Canal, which Disraeli had bought in 1875). He declined to retain control of Egypt's province of the Sudan and delayed the extrication of **General Gordon** from the siege of Khartoum until it was too late. Victoria, who had persuaded Disraeli to make her empress of India in 1876, disliked Gladstone's reluctant imperialism. Instead, she fully supported **Lord Salisbury**'s more aggressive policies, which resulted in the partition of Africa and the expansion of British influence in Iran, Afghanistan, and China. When she celebrated her 50th year on the throne, the Golden Jubilee of 1887, she added Indians to her retinue of servants and included Indian princes in the jubilee parade.

At the very end of her life, the queen maintained her imperial interests by fully supporting government policy during the South African War, 1899–1902. As usual, she bombarded her ministers with advice and pressed them to prosecute the war with greater vigor. One of the last acts of her life was to receive Field Marshal Lord Roberts to learn at first hand of the war's course.

The last great issue of the day was the relationship of Ireland to Britain. Separated from the British by religion, exploited by absentee landlords, and stimulated by the nationalistic spirit of the age, the Irish grew increasingly restive in the United Kingdom. The Conservative and Liberal governments of the 1860s and 1870s attempted to satisfy Irish grievances with laws designed to give peasants greater rights over the land, but Irish nationalism was not appeased. The queen visited Ireland four times, in 1849, 1853, 1861, and 1900. Each time she was welcomed with enthusiasm, even in 1900, after 40 years of hostility. Despite these welcomes, Irish nationalists wanted nothing less than self-government, and Gladstone tried to give them that in the two Irish Home Rule Bills of 1886 and 1893. The queen hated Home Rule and rejoiced at his failure.

Queen Victoria's last years were made unhappy by family problems. She blamed the Prince of Wales's sexual misconduct for having contributed to Prince Albert's death, and never fully trusted him. "I never can see B[ertie]—without a shudder!" she confided to the Princess Royal. "Oh! That bitterness! Oh! That cross!" She kept the official correspondence from her son until the last few years before her death, and he spent his adult life in a useless pursuit of pleasure. (It should be noted, however, that he proved to be a competent ruler when he came to the throne as **Edward VII** in 1901.)

Having enjoyed robust health until the autumn of 1900, she began to complain of aches and pains, loss of appetite, insomnia, and depression. After her seasonal move from Windsor Castle to Osborne House on the Isle of Wight in December, she grew weaker and weaker, her children were sent for, and the kaiser rushed from Berlin. Queen Victoria died quietly at 6:30 P.M. on January 22, 1901.

SOURCES:

Hibbert, Christopher. *Queen Victoria in Her Letters and Journals.* John Murray, 1984.

Kidd, Charles, and David Williamson, eds. *Debrett's Peerage and Baronetage.* St. Martin's Press, 1990.

Longford, Elizabeth. *Queen Victoria, Born to Succeed.* Harper, 1964.

FURTHER READING:

Arnstein, Walter L. "Queen Victoria and Religion," in Gail Malmgreen, ed. *Religion in the Lives of English Women, 1760–1930.* Indiana University Press, 1986.

James, Robert Rhodes. *Albert, Prince Consort: A Biography.* Hamish Hamilton, 1983.

Lant, Jeffrey L. *Insubstantial Pageant: Ceremony and Confusion at Queen Victoria's Court.* Taplinger, 1979.

Thompson, Dorothy. *Queen Victoria: Gender and Power.* Virago, 1990.

Weintraub, Stanley. *Victoria, An Intimate Biography.* Dutton, 1987.

Woodham-Smith, Cecil. *Queen Victoria, From Her Birth to the Death of the Prince Consort.* Knopf, 1972.

Vladimir I

(c. 950-1015)

Grand prince of Kiev and first Christian ruler in Russia, whose reign consolidated the Eastern Slavs and Finnish-Baltic tribes into a single Russian state.

Although information concerning Vladimir's youth is scarce, it is known that he was the youngest son of Grand Prince Sviatoslav Igorevich of Kiev and Maluska (Malfried), a servant girl who was possibly the daughter of the ruler of Liubeck Malk. Vladimir was born in Kiev sometime after the year 950, but the recorder of the Chronicle of Bygone Years (Primary Chronicle), the main contemporary source, does not give his birth date. His father was of Norman-Russian descent in the Rurik lineage and a brave warrior who had fought against the Volga Bulgars, the Khazars, the Bulgarians, and the Byzantine Empire. Despite his grandmother grand princess Olga's influential conversion to Christianity, Vladimir was reared in a pagan tradition; his father remained adamantly opposed to Christianity during his lifetime.

In 969, Sviatoslav, then constantly involved with warfare and administration in his newly conquered lands on the Danube, entrusted the administration of certain Russian regions to three of his 12 sons. The eldest son Yaropolk was appointed to rule Kiev, the second son Oleg was installed in the territory of the Drevliane, and the young Vladimir,

Name variations: St. Vladimir; Prince of Kiev. Born c. 950 in Kiev in the modern Ukraine; died at Berestova, near Kiev, on July 15, 1015; son of Sviatoslav Igorevich, Grand Prince of Kiev, and Maluska (Malfried; possibly the daughter of a courtesan of Liubeck Malk); married: nine times (most important was Anna, daughter of Basil II of Byzantium); children: 12 sons from various wives, including Yaroslav, Mstislav, and Iziaslav by Rogneda; Sviatopolk by his former sister-in-law; Sviatoslav by a Czech wife; Boris and Gleb by Anna or a Bulgarian wife. Predecessor: Grand Prince Sviatoslav Igorevich (962–72) of Kiev. Successor: Sviatopolk the Accursed (1015–19), who succeeded his father at his death in a fratricidal civil war.

Contributed by Phillip E. Koerper, Professor of History, Jacksonville State University, Jacksonville, Alabama

with an older relative as his advisor, was established in Novgorod. Sviatoslav's territorial divisions among his sons did not imply a permanent partition of his empire but was simply a temporary method of maintaining his authority in these independent regions. But Sviatoslav's death at the hands of the Pechenegs (a Mongol tribe), while returning from a disastrous military campaign in 972, resulted in a fratricidal civil war. Vladimir and his brothers fought over the succession for the next five years.

Yaropolk, who may have initiated the struggle in an effort to unite all the family lands under a single Kievan prince, killed Oleg in battle and conquered his lands. Vladimir, whose army was vastly inferior, was forced to flee to Scandinavia. Two years later, with the help of his Varangian relatives, Vladimir raised an army of mercenaries and adventurers and returned to Russia. After liberating Novgorod from Yaropolk's governor, Vladimir's army opened a campaign to seize the land of the East Slavs. He then proposed a marriage alliance with Rogvolod, Prince of Polotsk. When Rogvolod refused the hand of his daughter Rogneda, Vladimir ruthlessly attacked Polotsk, torched the city, executed Rogvolod and his two sons, and married Rogneda. Within a year, Rogneda—now given the Slavic name Gorislava—gave birth to Iziaslav, a legitimate Russian prince.

Vladimir marched southward against Yaropolk and Kiev. Receiving traitorous advice from a general named Blud, Yaropolk believed the people of Kiev favored his younger brother and planned to surrender the city and negotiate with Vladimir. But Yaropolk was treacherously murdered in 977 by the Varangian mercenaries. Vladimir, utilizing his various armies of Novgorodians, Varangians, Slovenians, Krivichians, and loyal Kievans, forged a new commercial union of Kiev and Novgorod by 980.

The civil war had considerably weakened the domination that Kiev had held over the borderlands. Vladimir had to secure those borders, particularly the eastern and southern frontiers where nomadic tribes posed a constant threat to his Kievan empire. In 981–82, he defeated the Viatichians in two campaigns and forced them to accept the hegemony ("leadership") of Kiev. Vladimir's victory over the Radimichi in 984 completed the unification of all the eastern Slavic peoples. His next objectives were the Volga Bulgars, descendants of the Huns, and the powerful Khazar tribes. In 985, Vladimir initiated a series of campaigns that resulted in victory over the Volga Bulgars, but he was still forced to send expeditions in 994 and 997 to reassert his control. Sometime prior to 989, he had subdued the Khazars and then constructed a series of forts along the southeastern border to prevent the warlike Pechenegs from attacking his empire. As another means of providing security, loyalty, and unity, he had replaced independent and rebellious local tribal chieftains with his own relatives and loyal officers.

Vladimir even employed religion as a unifying factor by accepting the deities of the various local tribes. He also tried to establish a pagan cult center in Kiev that would have produced a religious bond between the prince and his people. In time, Vladimir may have realized that the pagan polytheism of his empire would remain isolated from the mainstream of the monotheistic civilizations surrounding Russia. The single God of Christianity would also better support the concept of an absolutist ruler in his personal realm. According to the famous story recorded in the *Primary Chronicle*, he sent emissaries to investigate various religions in order to help him arrive at a conclusion. Vladimir would eventually choose the "heavenly beauty" of the Greek Orthodox rites over those of Islam, Judaism, and Latin Christianity. His retainers probably added the argument that his grandmother Olga had, in her great wisdom, adopted the Greek faith. In truth, it is most likely that the economic and political ties to Constantinople offered by a marriage proposal involving the Byzantine emperor's sister swayed the mind of the pragmatic Kievan prince.

Years earlier, when Vladimir had wrested the Black Sea port of Tmutoraken from the Khazars, he had brought his realm into contact with the powerful Byzantine Empire. With rebellions threatening Byzantium, Emperor **Basil II** (976–1025) had sought military assistance from Vladimir. During the insurrection of Bardas Phocus in 987–88, Vladimir had sent a Kievan-Varangian force of 6,000 warriors to help the Emperor. As an inducement, Basil had proposed that Vladimir could marry his sister Anna if Vladimir were to accept Christianity.

The Russians proved to be decisive against Bardas Phocus at the Battle of Abydos, and Vladimir was baptized and given the Christian name of Basil in honor of the Emperor in February 989. But the Emperor, sensing that the danger had passed, was less inclined to send Anna to the prince of Kiev. An angry Vladimir returned to the battlefield and conquered the Crimea in 989. His victories gave him control of several Orthodox episcopal centers, and his attack on the Byzantine port of Chersonesus (modern Korsun) was purposely carried out to eliminate Basil's reluctance. When Vladimir informed Basil that it would be the same with his city as with Chersonesus, the Emperor finally dispatched Anna to marry Vladimir and recognized the presence of the Kievan state on the Black Sea.

Christianity Replaces Paganism

Obtaining church books, vestments, and priests from the Crimean bishops, Vladimir returned to Kiev in the summer of 990 along with his bride, priests, icons, and sacred relics. He ordered that the statues of pagan gods be destroyed and pagan sanctuaries were replaced by Orthodox Christian churches. Then the population of Kiev was forced to march to the Dnieper River where they were baptized by the Crimean priests. Couriers were dispatched to the other cities of Vladimir's kingdom with instructions for the destruction of paganism and the mass baptisms of the populace. He inaugurated a massive program for the construction of churches, cathedrals, monasteries, libraries, and schools. The children of the upper class were ordered to attend the church schools whose basic purpose was to train future clergymen. Vladimir ignored the Patriarch of Constantinople and there was very little religious contact between Constantinople and Kiev until long after his reign. The authorities at Constantinople were so skeptical about Vladimir's faith that they used a Crimean

bishop to head the Russian Church and did not appoint a patriarch to Kiev until 1037.

Vladimir's foreign policy with established states was nonaggressive, and he lived in harmony with King **Stephen of Hungary,** Prince Boleslav of Poland, and Prince Uldarick of Bohemia. While he did not wage war on his Christian neighbors following his conversion, he did protect the Kievan borders along the Black Sea from the nomadic and warlike Pechenegs from 992–97. Because he could not guarantee the safety of his citizens from these invaders, Vladimir constructed a chain of fortifications along the northern banks of the steppe Rivers Oster, Desna, Trubezh, Sula, and Stugna. Colonists were sent from the northern tribes—Novgorodians, Slavians, Krivichians, Chudians, and Viatichians—to augment the local defenders against the Pechenegs.

Following the example of his father, Vladimir used his sons to rule the vast regions of his empire. Yaroslav was governor of Novgorod; Boris of Rostov; Sviatopolk of Turov; Gleb of Murom; Iziaslav of Polotsk; Sviatoslav of Drevlians; and Mstislav of Tmutoraken. He also utilized the upper-class sons educated in the church schools to create a new bureaucracy. Cleverly abolishing the old tribal boundaries, Vladimir established new administrative centers in the regions governed by his sons and other administrators.

In domestic policy, Vladimir made a few innovative changes. In addition to suppressing tribal autonomy, he integrated the officers of the old tribal system of military organization into a princely class of administrators, revenue collectors, and military officials. They were treated lavishly which insured Vladimir's popularity and loyalty from this new class.

The administration of justice was also reformed by Vladimir. His legal innovations preceded the *Russkaia Pravda* (Russian Law Code) of his son Yaroslav in the 1030s. He introduced a principle of fixed fines in the justice system to replace the traditional dependence upon vengeance and blood feuds. The principal purpose was to replace tribal justice with a princely justice of centralized administration based on legal codifications of fines and punishments. His legal reforms were not influenced by the Church, which had to convince the well-intentioned Vladimir that it was not improper to execute bandits after due process of law.

In religion, Vladimir often consulted with the bishops on issues of state and church. There is a Church tradition that Vladimir initiated the collection of the tithe ("tax"), a Western church custom, from the princely courts, custom duties, estates, herds, and crops of his realm. Many churches, including the cathedral of the Dormation of the Holy Virgin in Kiev, were known as tithe churches because they were built with the tax. He issued the Church Statute of 996 which decreed the tithe and also established the foundation for Church courts. Vladimir's decision to accept the Greek Church also influenced the culture of Russia: Byzantine architecture, icon art, eastern thought, and monasticism were adopted by the Russian people.

In 1014, Yaroslav, reflecting the dissatisfaction of his subjects, refused to send the annual two-thirds of the tribute money collected in Novgorod to Vladimir's treasury. Vladimir responded by preparing for a military campaign, but he died in 1015 before he could march against his son and the succession was left in question. The news of his death was kept secret because his unscrupulous and ambitious son Sviatopolk wanted an undivided inheritance. In his later years, Vladimir had given signs that he might bequeath his entire kingdom to Boris, probably one of the sons born of Anna. Unfortunately, Vladimir's death resulted in a bloody conflict which culminated in the murder of Boris and Gleb and the brief reign of Sviatopolk the Accursed (1015–19).

Vladimir had brought a new civilization to Russia by his acceptance of Orthodox Christianity. He had unified the vast Russian lands and given the people a feeling of nationalism. In addition to being remembered as a powerful and successful prince, Vladimir was canonized in the 13th century as the baptizer of the Russians, "equal to the apostles."

SOURCES:

Cross, Samuel Hazzard, and Olgerd P. Sherbowitz-Wetsor. *The Russian Primary Chronicle.* Medieval Academy of America, 1953.

Vernadsky, George. *Kievan Russia.* Yale University Press, 1948.

Volkoff, Vladimir. *Vladimir: The Russian Viking.* Overlook Press, 1985.

FURTHER READING:

de Grunwald, Constantine. *Saints of Russia.* Macmillan, 1960.

Grekov, Boris D. *Kiev Rus.* Foreign Languages Publishing House, 1959.

Albrecht von Wallenstein

(1583–1634)

General who led the armies of the Holy Roman Empire during the first half of the Thirty Years' War (1625–1634) and attempted to establish direct Habsburg and Catholic control over Germany.

"War must nourish war."

ALBRECHT VON WALLENSTEIN

One of the most controversial and enigmatic figures in German history, Prince Albrecht von Wallenstein's career and achievements have been alternately condemned and glorified by the politicians and historians of Central Europe. Raised to the command of all the armies carrying the Habsburg Counter-Reformation into Protestant Germany, he died accused of treason by the Habsburg emperor he served. He has been hailed as the first to attempt the nationalist unification of Germany, a statesman of peace, seeking to unite Central Europe under a revived German Empire. He has been called a greedy mercenary, a coward, a traitor, and a cruel pillager whose armies laid waste to Germany. Schiller's dramatic trilogy *Wallenstein* portrays his rise and fall as the life of a great and tragic Romantic hero. Wallenstein was truly a man of his era, a time of bitter and fratricidal conflict which saw the violent end of the medieval world, the confirmation of the Reformation, and the birth of what would become modern Europe. The Thirty Years' War was the last great religious war, and by its end had become the first great war of political and economic rivalries. Medieval Europe was dead, yet the shape of modern Europe was not yet defined.

Contributed by Kevin Cramer, Ph.D. candidate in history, Harvard University, Cambridge, Massachusetts

Name variations: Albert of Wallenstein. Pronunciation: WALL-en-stine. Born Albrecht Eusebius Wenzeslaus von Waldstein on September 24, 1583 (in an age of casual spelling conventions, Wallenstein, became the popular German form somewhat later); murdered at Eger in Bohemia on February 24, 1634; son of Wilhelm von Waldstein and Margarethe Smiricky (minor Bohemian nobility); educated at the Latin School at Goldberg and Nuremberg Academy at Altdorf; married: Lucretia von Wishkow, 1609 (died, 1614); married: Isabella von Harrach, 1623; children: Maria Elisabeth, Albrecht Karl. Successor: Maximilian von Waldstein (brother-in-law; cousin).

CHRONOLOGY

1615	Wallenstein made chamberlain of Archduke Ferdinand of Styria
1618	"Defenestration of Prague"
1619	Ferdinand elected emperor; Wallenstein victorious at Tein
1622	Granted hereditary fief of Friedland-Reichenberg in northern Bohemia
1623	Made commander of all imperial infantry
1625–26	Invaded central Germany; defeated Danes and Protestants; Gustavus invaded northern Germany; Tilly defeated Danes at Lutter; Peace of Bratislava
1627	Baltic coast conquered by imperial forces; princes protest Wallenstein's growing power
1628	Danes defeated at Wolgast; Wallenstein's removal demanded
1629	"Edict of Restitution"; peace with Denmark
1631	Imperial forces under Tilly defeated at Breitenfeld
1632	Wallenstein defeated Swedes at Nuremberg and Saxons in Bohemia; victory over Swedes at Lutzen, Gustavus killed
1633	Wallenstein negotiated with Saxony for peace in northern Germany; Protestants invaded Bavaria
1634	Removed from command, accused of treason; murdered by imperial envoys

Wallenstein was born on September 24, 1583, in the Waldstein family castle at Hermanitz in Bohemia. His father Wilhelm von Waldstein was a petty Bohemian nobleman; his mother Margarethe von Smiricky came from a wealthy and influential family of Slavonic nobility.

As a child, Wallenstein was raised and educated as a Protestant, as befitted the son of the Bohemian gentry. Orphaned at 12, he was sent by a Catholic uncle to Latin schools. Around 1602, after he completed university, the ambitious Wallenstein converted to Catholicism, the faith of the Habsburgs.

His military career in their service began shortly thereafter, and he saw action in Transylvania, Slovakia, and Italy. In 1606, he was made a colonel in command of a regiment of Moravian militia, while at the same time entering the service of Archduke Matthias, the eldest son of Emperor **Rudolf II,** and his likely successor. Wallenstein's ambitions were furthered when he married Lucretia von Wishkow in 1609. His new wife had inher-

ited considerable Moravian lands from her late husband, thus providing Wallenstein with a handsome income and political and military base. Matthias had meantime gained the crown of Bohemia, vital to Habsburg power, and when Rudolf died in 1612, Matthias became Holy Roman Emperor. It seemed Wallenstein had hitched himself to a rising star.

Life at court did not meet his expectations, however, and he became restless. He returned to military service in 1615, serving as colonel and chamberlain to his cousin, and future emperor, Archduke Ferdinand of Styria (**Ferdinand II**). Unlike Matthias, Ferdinand was an ardent Catholic and militant supporter of the Counter-Reformation. During an imperial campaign against Venice in 1617 led by Ferdinand, Wallenstein came to the Archduke's attention when Wallenstein's cavalry dramatically broke the Venetian siege of the imperial fortress of Gradisca. Ferdinand would not forget this service.

Religious Conflicts Explode, Lead to Thirty Years' War

Wallenstein was made a count and given a high command in the Moravian militia. When, in September of 1617, Matthias secured the kingdom of Bohemia and Hungary for his cousin Ferdinand, Wallenstein was once again on the path to power. The religious conflicts in the Empire exploded into violence and revolt in Bohemia. The Protestant nobility were fearful for their power, lands, and religious freedom. If Ferdinand became emperor, they expected an intensification and expansion of the Counter-Reformation throughout the Empire.

On May 23, 1618, Count Thurn led the Protestant nobles (*Ultraquists*) to confront the imperial councilors in Prague; they carried a list of grievances addressed to Emperor Matthias, who had earlier given them no reply. The scene that followed saw two of the Emperor's representatives flung from the windows of Karlstein Castle to fall 50 feet into a dry moat filled with rubbish. Although they miraculously survived the "Defenestration of Prague," the news of the revolt soon reached Vienna. The fuse that ignited the Thirty Years' War (a conflict between Catholic and Protestant Europe) had been lit.

In September, Vienna was threatened by a Bohemian invasion under Count Thurn. Wallenstein allied himself to the imperial cause, and at the Battle of Rablat helped turn away the invasion. Wallenstein's abandonment of the Bohemian cause has been denounced by Czech historian Josef Pekar as the act of a "cowardly and megalomaniac traitor." Yet an Austrian, Heinrich von Srbik, sees Wallenstein as pursuing the unity, preservation, and revival of a powerful and modern German empire ruled from Vienna.

In March 1619, Matthias died, and Ferdinand was elected Holy Roman Emperor; the Protestant ruler of the Palatinate (a district in Germany), **Frederick V,** was elected king of Bohemia by her rebellious Estates; and Wallenstein was made a colonel. In the meantime, the Hungarian Bethlen Gabor was advancing on Vienna. Wallenstein won a victory at Tein in southern Bohemia and successfully defended the Danube bridges to Vienna against the Hungarian attacks.

In the spring of 1620, imperial forces under the command of Duke Maximilian of Bavaria and Count Tilly advanced on Prague, winning a crushing victory over the Bohemians in the Battle of White Mountain outside Prague on November 7. Though he was not present, the troops Wallenstein raised played a significant role the battle, which ended the Bohemian revolt.

Bavaria's subsequent annexation of the Palatinate on the Rhine, as a reward for Maximilian's support of the Emperor, turned the war into a more general European conflict. France, Holland, Britain, Denmark, and Sweden feared this extension of Catholic power, and the German princes feared the usurpation of the sovereignty and rights of their states within the Empire.

Wallenstein also received his reward, being granted extensive tracts of confiscated Bohemian lands. He was thus able to raise and equip even more soldiers, and he marched to put down risings in Moravia and counter yet another Hungarian advance on Vienna and Bohemia.

In the summer of 1622, Ferdinand granted Wallenstein the hereditary fief of Friedland-Reichenberg in northern Bohemia. A year later, in 1623, Wallenstein—widowed in 1614—married Isabella von Harrach, the daughter of a highly placed advisor to the Emperor. Already an imperial count and palsgrave, Wallenstein was made "Duke of Friedland" and "general of all infantry." He had risen far, but a faction at the imperial court, led primarily by adherents of the Duke of Bavaria, was gathering to block his further advance.

After a short campaign in Moravia in October 1623, Wallenstein negotiated an armistice with Bethlen Gabor. Most of that year, however, was spent in consolidating and organizing his new estates and equipping a new army. In March 1624,

Friedland was declared a principality by the Emperor. Wallenstein was now ruler of a formidable base of supply and manpower, situated in a strategic position in Central Europe. The imperial position in 1624 was strong, but storm clouds loomed on the horizon. The Protestant kingdoms of Denmark and Sweden, as well as the Dutch Republic, were combining against the Habsburgs and the Counter-Reformation. They were to find allies in the Protestant German princes, who feared for their independence within the Empire.

Accordingly, Ferdinand ordered Wallenstein to raise a new army of 50,000 men. A force this size was unheard before the advent of modern transport and supply systems. Soldiers then lived off the land, ravaging entire districts and leaving the populace to starve. But Wallenstein had previously demonstrated unique ability to raise and equip large numbers of soldiers and move them quickly and efficiently.

On June 13, 1625, the Emperor made Wallenstein "Chief over all imperial troops in the Holy Roman Empire." Wallenstein's newly assembled army moved from Bohemia into central Germany in July. Tilly's Catholic League forces joined Wallenstein in October, though the alliance was uneasy, as the two generals constantly and jealously disputed over the demarcation of authority. The two armies marched northward, seeking to enforce the imperial will by intimidation and occupation, not open battle. Wallenstein wanted to secure a base for the coming battle with the Danes and Swedes for control of the Baltic and northern Germany.

After successfully attacking and compelling the Danes and their king **Christian IV** to retreat, Wallenstein was forced to abandon his offensive and turn south to counter a Protestant invasion of Saxony and Silesia led by General Ernst Mansfeld. At Dessau on the Elbe, on April 25, 1626, Wallenstein gained a decisive victory, although Mansfeld was able to retreat in good order. But Wallenstein had achieved his aim of intimidating the princes of northern Germany, if only temporarily. He was looking ahead to what he saw as the inevitable and decisive clash with Sweden. "In the Swedes," he said, "we find a worse enemy than the Turks."

Wallenstein was forced to confront a renewed invasion of Silesia by Mansfeld, marching his army 300 miles in three weeks to meet the invaders at Gran in Moravia. In the meantime, Tilly defeated the Danes at Lutter-am-Barenberg, and **Gustavus Adolphus** of Sweden had invaded northern Germany. Recognizing that his soldiers had been seriously weakened by their long march and inconclusive skirmishing, Wallenstein negotiated the Peace of Bratislava in December, pacifying for the moment the Empire's eastern frontiers so he could meet the much more serious Swedish threat in the north.

Wallenstein's strategy against Sweden had three main components: (1) to keep the war as far as possible from the Bohemian and Austrian possessions of the Habsburgs; (2) to negotiate a "just and profitable peace" from a position of strength; and (3) to keep a powerful army intact until the other side was disarmed. First, Wallenstein had to defeat Denmark and Sweden, occupy northern Germany, and take control of the Baltic ports. Ferdinand approved this plan, over the opposition of the anti-Wallenstein faction at court.

Launching his campaign in June 1627, Wallenstein marched through Silesia and Brandenburg to join with Tilly's forces in Brunswick in August. After offering harsh peace terms to the Danes on the assumption that they would be rejected, the march north began. Outnumbered and without allies, Denmark was overrun by October, and the imperial forces were advancing eastward along the Baltic coast, past the Hanseatic city of Lübeck toward Stralsund in Swedish-dominated Pomerania. Wallenstein could now turn his attention to the Swedes.

Sweden renewed her alliance with Denmark and moved troops into Pomerania. Wallenstein, now duke of conquered Mecklenburg, moved to capture Stralsund in the summer of 1628, but he was forced to break off the siege in order to deal with a renewed Danish threat in the west. Although he defeated the Danes at Wolgast in September, he had been severely hampered by Swedish and Danish naval control of the coast and a lack of reinforcements from Tilly. Also, the princes of the Catholic League were again demanding Wallenstein's removal, and the princes of northern Germany chafed under the rapacious occupation of his soldiers.

Ferdinand Announces "Edict of Restitution"

In the spring of 1629, Wallenstein made peace with Denmark, freeing him to face Sweden. But now other factors began to make themselves felt. In March, Ferdinand announced the "Edict of Restitution," which attempted to secure the restoration of Catholicism and Catholic property within the German states of the Empire. The effect was to solidify Protestant opposition to Ferdinand and the Counter-Reformation. The Catholic League princes, for their part, wanted peace negotiations and a restriction of Wallenstein's power, if not his outright dismissal. Most ominously, France had now entered the fray, offering financial support to Sweden for an invasion of Germany. A great coalition of forces was gathering against Wallenstein and the Empire.

In July 1630, the princes met at the Diet of Ratisbon to air their grievances against Wallenstein to the Emperor. Despite Sweden's renewed invasion of Germany, Ferdinand demanded Wallenstein's resignation, in hopes of gaining the princes' support for his son's succession. Wallenstein gave up his command in August and retired to Friedland. Tilly took over his army.

Wallenstein's retirement was short. In April 1631, the Swedish army moved deep into Germany, tacitly supported by the north German princes and French money and also aided by Bavarian neutrality. After defeating Tilly at Frankfurt-am-Oder, Gustavus continued his advance through northern Germany. The Swedish King won another decisive victory over Tilly at Breitenfeld and the imperial army was scattered. Central Germany now lay open to the victorious Swedish army, the sword of the Protestant cause. With an Empire devoid of allies and disrupted by peasant revolts in the hinterland, by December 1631, the Emperor and the princes again turned to Wallenstein.

Resuming command in April 1632, Wallenstein raised a new army and moved cautiously to meet Gustavus. While Wallenstein was gathering his forces, Tilly had beaten the Swedes at Bamberg in the Upper Palatinate, though the old Catholic League campaigner was fatally wounded. Gustavus pressed on, however, and took Munich in May 1632.

Pushing the Saxon invaders out of Bohemia and advancing slowly into Germany and Bavaria, Wallenstein beat back the Swedish attacks on Nuremberg and pursued them into Saxony. At the bloody battle of Lützen in November, Gustavus Adolphus was killed, but his Swedes gained the victory, forcing Wallenstein to retreat into Bohemia.

By 1633, Wallenstein had raised new forces and expelled the Swedes from Silesia by his victory at Steinau in October. It was to be his last triumph. Sweden had united with the Protestant German princes in the Heilbronn League, and France renewed her subsidies to the Swedish forces. Bavaria remained partially occupied by Protestant troops under the Duke of Weimar.

Wallenstein, recognizing his perilous situation, attempted to negotiate with Saxony and Sweden and try to gain a general peace in northern

Germany, buying time to secure the borders of Bohemia and the Habsburg dynastic lands.

In January 1634, the anti-Wallenstein party at the imperial court brought charges of treason against him before the Emperor, citing his parleys with the Swedes and Saxons, though Wallenstein may well have believed he had a legitimate right to negotiate, given the mandate of his command as granted in 1632. The charges were inflated to accuse him of attempting to detach Bohemia from the Empire and create a new, unified German state. In January 1634, Wallenstein was stripped of his command. In February, a patent of treason was issued by Ferdinand, and Wallenstein was declared an outlaw.

Attempting to flee to the protection of the Duke of Weimar, Wallenstein was apprehended by the imperial envoys at the Bohemian border fortress of Eger on February 24, 1634. As he prepared for bed, his guards were overwhelmed, and he was caught in his nightshirt, unarmed, ill, and alone. As the soldier's cry of "Quarter!" escaped his lips, he was brought down with a single pike thrust.

Wallenstein's fall was as sudden as his rise. His motives remain shadowy, but he served his Emperor well in his quest to make the Holy Roman Empire a German imperium. Unifier, destroyer, traitor, general, statesman, prince, he was all of these and none. As the British historian Liddell Hart has eulogized: "Obscured by factions, hatred, and applause," Wallenstein's character "still floats, unfixed and stationless in history."

SOURCES:

Benecke, Gerhard, ed. *Germany in the Thirty Years' War*. St. Martin's Press, 1979.

Gindely, Anton. *History of the Thirty Years' War, Vols. I and II* [1885]. Books for Libraries Press, 1972.

Hart, B. H. Liddell. *Great Captains Unveiled* [1928]. Books for Libraries Press, 1967.

Parker, Geoffrey. *The Thirty Years' War*. Military Heritage Press, 1987.

Rabb, Theodore K., ed. *The Thirty Years' War*. D.C. Heath, 1964, 1972.

Watson, Francis. *Wallenstein: Soldier Under Saturn*. D. Appleton-Century, 1938.

FURTHER READING:

Mann, Golo. *Wallenstein*. Translated by Charles Kessler. Holt, 1976.

Polisensky, J. V. *The Thirty Years' War*. Translated by Robert Evans. University of California Press, 1971.

Roberts, Michael. *Gustavus Adolphus: A History of Sweden, 1611–1632*. Longmans, Green, 1953, 1958.

Wedgwood, C. V. *The Thirty Years' War*. Jonathan Cape, 1938.

Robert Walpole

(1676–1745)

British statesman and Whig parliamentary leader, often identified as the first British prime minister, who supported the Hanoverian Succession and sought to promote trade, decrease tariffs, and keep Britain out of continental European wars.

Born on August 26, 1676, at Houghton, Norfolk, England; died in London, England, on March 18, 1745; first surviving son of Robert Walpole (a member of Parliament) and Mary Burwell; married: Catherine Shorter; married: Maria Skerrett; children: (first marriage) three sons and a daughter; (second marriage) two daughters born before the marriage. Descendants: Robert, Lord Walpole of Walpole, succeeded his father as second Earl of Orford. Successor: Earl of Wilmington, as prime minister, 1742.

In 17th- and 18th-century England, child mortality was high, affecting all social classes, and the family of Sir Robert Walpole was no exception. The Walpoles lived in Houghton, Norfolk, and both the boy's father and grandfather were elected representatives in the House of Commons. Robert was the third son and fifth child, born August 26, 1676, to militia colonel Robert Walpole and Mary Burwell, heiress of Sir Geoffrey Burwell of Rougham, Suffolk. Ultimately, they had 19 children, most of whom did not survive childhood.

Events which occurred during Walpole's childhood and adolescent years were clearly incorporated in a parliamentary career that lasted 41 years. At the age of six, he was boarded at the Reverend Ransome's private school in Great Dunham, where he stayed for six years. While he was there, two things occurred which would have a lasting impact: the Exclusion Bills of 1678–81 and the Glorious Revolution of 1688–89. The Exclusion Bills were attempts by the Whig political party to prevent the then Prince of Wales, James, from succeeding his brother **Charles II** as the next king of England on the grounds of James's Catholic faith.

"All those men have their price."

ROBERT WALPOLE,
ON THE DECLARATION
OF WAR WITH SPAIN

Contributed by Donna Beaudin, Ph.D. candidate in History, University of Guelph, Guelph, Ontario, Canada

Although these efforts depicted the Tories as being supporters of James, by 1688 parliamentary members of both political parties believed that James, now king, was ruling England in a subversive, dangerous, and unconstitutional manner. A politically-mixed group of seven statesmen managed to bring about the removal of James II from the throne and, in turn, invited his daughter Mary and her Protestant husband **William III of Orange** to become joint sovereigns of England on the condition that they accept the Hanoverian succession advocated by Parliament.

Shortly after these developments, Walpole was admitted to Eton as a King's scholar, where he boarded for another six years; he was then elected to King's College, Cambridge, in 1696. Since the third son of a family of landed wealth traditionally studied for a career in the Church of England, he most likely undertook theological studies. His younger brothers, Horatio and Galfridus, were directed to parliamentary and naval careers. But Walpole was forced to leave Cambridge after only two years to return to the estate at Houghton. Edward, family heir and Walpole's eldest brother, had died in early manhood, and Burwelf, the next eldest son had died in 1692 in a naval battle. Walpole was now heir to the family holdings and had to learn to manage the estate and to prepare himself for a seat in the House of Commons.

The elder Walpole deemed that a wife and heirs were now appropriate for his son, primarily for dynastic and economic reasons. In July 1700, young Robert married Catherine Shorter, from a London merchant family, whose dowry would go a considerable way toward paying some of the Walpole family debts. Further alliances were made through the marriages of two of Walpole's sisters, Mary to Sir Charles Turner, a wine merchant, in 1689, and Dorothy to Charles, viscount Townshend, in 1713. These alliances, a normal part of marital considerations among the upper classes, strengthened Walpole's political and social position.

Walpole began his parliamentary career in 1701 as a Whig in the House of Commons in a period that was characterized by "the rage of party." But the 25-year-old was to represent the family borough of Castle Rising, Norfolk, only briefly. In the following year, Walpole was returned to the House of Commons for King's Lynn, Norfolk, and he was to retain this seat, except for a six-month period, for the balance of his Commons career. This membership in Parliament did not signify the fulfillment of Walpole's ambitions; rather, it represented an avenue to power, money, and social mobility beyond the Norfolk squirearchy.

CHRONOLOGY

1688-89	"Glorious Revolution"
1694	Bank of England created
1701	Walpole elected to House of Commons as a Whig
1712	Convicted of corruption and expelled from House of Commons
1713	First Peace of Utrecht signed; Britain obtained Asiento contract
1714	Queen Anne died; George I crowned; Jacobite rising in Scotland
1720	Banks collapsed, investors financially ruined
1721	Walpole appointed first lord of the treasury; formed his first government
1727	George I died; George II crowned
1729	Treaty of Vienna signed, concluding the War of the Polish Succession
1739	War of Jenkins' Ear against Spain
1741	Parliamentary motion for Walpole's dismissal defeated
1742	Walpole resigned political offices; raised to peerage as first Earl of Orford
1745	Died of combined effects of exhaustion, gout and kidney stones; second Jacobite rising

The earliest years of Walpole's political career coincided with the period of constitutional uncertainty which followed the Glorious Revolution. Government ministries during the reign of Queen **Anne** were still composed of members of Parliament from both political parties, as they had been under William III, though a marked preference for the Tories was in evidence. In the face of increased constitutional limitations placed on the Crown by the parliamentary Declaration of Rights (1689), these so-called "mixed ministries" were an attempt by both William III and Anne to exert the full force of the executive branch of the government. Henry St. John (later Viscount Bolingbroke), a Tory M.P. (member of Parliament), was not yet, but would become, Walpole's greatest lifelong political opponent.

He Becomes a Leader in the Whig Party

Walpole quickly assumed a position of leadership within the Whig Party. Although his was not a dominant voice in the matter of English parliamentary union with Scotland, which was accomplished in 1707, he strengthened his position with his appointment as war secretary (1708–10) and then as treasurer of the navy (1710–11). His early political power also provided access to sources of official income and to the patronage system. Like most politicians of his day, Walpole benefited by this system, which granted income-generating government positions and permitted him to extend those benefits to family members and political friends. These successes were short-lived as Tory enemies charged Walpole with corruption in 1712. Expelled from his seat in the House of Commons, he was also imprisoned, by the Tories, in the Tower of London for six months.

Upon his release, Walpole was re-elected to the House of Commons as the Whigs, along with some dissident Tories, defeated the Tory government on the question of the Protestant Succession. The defeat of the Tory government and the death of Queen Anne created an opportunity for the Whig administration to secure the support of the new Protestant monarch, George I, who had been brought from Germany. Like his predecessors, George I did not want to be at the mercy of an overpowerful minister. The Whigs gradually removed Tory politicians from positions of power and their consequent sources of income.

This purge was compounded by other developments, such as the suppression of the Jacobite rising of 1715–16 (conducted with the support of James Francis Stuart, claimant to the British throne and son of James II), and passage of the Septennial Act in 1716. This legislation altered the frequency of national elections, from every three years to every seven years, and passed in the House of Commons while Walpole was absent due to illness. Potential M.P.'s spent less money prevailing upon the electorate, and government had longer control of important patronage appointments. Walpole held such an appointment, first lord of the treasury, for two years (1715–17) before resigning from the government. He also attempted to put a "sinking fund" plan into operation. Under this plan a portion of government revenue was applied to the national debt to reduce its size, and the plan was successful for nearly ten years. Less frequent elections, the development of the first sinking fund, and the reduced power and impeachments of Tory politicians gave Walpole his first serious taste of power and political management, but while the Whig majority grew, the Party's unity decreased and Walpole spent a few years out of power, in opposition to a Whig government.

By 1720, Walpole was back in political office as paymaster general. Following the collapse of the South Sea Company which made an attempt to assume and decrease the national debt, he was perceived as the financial savior of the nation. Legislation was enacted to restrict the formation of such joint-stock companies. The following April, Walpole was again appointed first lord of the treasury, a position he held for the next 20 years, and one which effectively made him first, or *prime*, minister and head of the government. During these years, Walpole carefully managed to limit the political effectiveness of the Tories by labeling Tories as Jacobites, or supporters of James Stuart and his family. The trial for treason, and subsequent exile, of Francis Atterbury, the Tory bishop of Rochester, was utilized by Walpole to assert this interpretation. In his biography of Walpole, John Morley concluded that:

> when men got in his way, he thrust them aside, without misgiving or remorse, just as a commander in the field would remove a meddling, wrongheaded, or incompetent general of a division without remorse. But to be remorseless is a very different thing from being unscrupulous.

Significant political rivals of Walpole also resigned during this period, including Lord Carteret in 1724 and Viscount Townshend in 1730. It was not that Walpole went unchallenged in his position, however. When George II came to the throne in 1727, he attempted to replace Walpole with the earl of Wilmington. With the support of Queen Caroline, Walpole continued as first lord of the treasury and head of the government. Aside from the queen's support, Walpole enjoyed some measure of personal and political success during the mid-1720s. The marriage alliances made by the Walpole family were generally reaping benefits. In May 1725, he was made a knight of the Order of Bath but left it for the Order of the Garter, an important, nonpolitical patronage position, within a month. Since Walpole was the first commoner promoted to the Order of the Garter since 1660, he also secured the jealousy of some of the nobility.

Walpole Government Faces Domestic Problems

As leader of the Whig government, Walpole sought domestic harmony while he kept Britain out of European conflicts. To meet this objective, his foreign policy favored France but was not fully supported in Parliament or in the nation. The discord Walpole engendered over his foreign policy was only one aspect of the increasing hostility he faced in the 1730s. His use of patronage was seen, by some as early as 1726, as tyrannical, and his efforts to impose an excise tax, a tax on commodities like tobacco and wine (while decreasing the rate of the land tax) also served to increase his political unpopularity. His efforts on behalf of this tax initiated what was subsequently called the Excise Crisis and provided a focus for Walpole's political opponents, most notably Tories and former Whig colleagues. Walpole's government was strong but it was vulnerable on popular issues, particularly when addressed in the popular press.

His policy of noninvolvement kept Britain out of the War of the Polish Succession in 1733; he similarly resisted, as long as he could, entering into war with Spain over illegal seizures of British ships and rough treatment of sailors (including the loss of an ear on a seaman named Jenkins), and he remarked in a House of Commons speech in November 1739 that:

> I have lived long enough in the world to see the effects of war on this nation; I have seen how destructive the effects, even of a successful war, have been; and shall I... advise [the King] to enter upon a war while peace may be had? No, Sir, I am proud to own it, that I have always been, and always shall be, an advocate for peace.

Walpole continued to propose a nonaggressive foreign policy, even though Britain's war with Spain had begun a month earlier with the War of Jenkins' Ear. Although she was initially successful, Britain began to suffer military losses and faced tax increases to cover the costs of war, which contributed to Walpole's unpopularity among political critics. By the end of the decade, he had also suffered personal losses and political setbacks: his chief court ally, Queen Caroline, had died in 1737, as had his estranged first wife, and his second wife Maria died in childbirth in the summer of 1738. Maria's death left Walpole depressed for the rest of his life, and his political activities served as a diversion but not as a consolation.

In 1741, Walpole was accused of being *prime minister* (an office not officially recognized until 1905). His contemporaries believed him to have monopolized the king's favor and confidence, suggesting that he acted as an ally of the king. According to Betty Kemp's study, *Sir Robert Walpole*, he:

> became Prime Minister firstly because of his ascendancy in the commons, and only secondly because of the King's favour. This was the other way round from William Cecil, Elizabeth I's great

minister, to whom Walpole's contemporaries sometimes compared him. His position would have been less remarkable, and his task easier, if he had repeated Cecil's role, that of a Prime Minister sent by the monarch to manage the Commons.

Walpole was criticized by both Tories and Whigs for not sharing the responsibilities of governing with his colleagues. By early 1742, Tories were ready to move against him after their earlier unwillingness to effect his removal through a censure motion. Walpole withstood the first vote that was taken in the House of Commons but resigned his offices on February 2, 1742, the date of the second vote in the lower house. The campaign against him was built on the reversals of Britain's fortunes in the war with Spain. One week later, George II raised him to the peerage as first earl of Orford, which entitled him to a seat in the upper parliamentary chamber, the House of Lords.

The Secret Committee Investigates Walpole

Once out of political office, Walpole was offered a pension, which he declined, though he did apply for it in 1744. He was also the focus of a parliamentary Secret Committee, comprised of 20 members, that was assembled to determine what punishments he should receive for his conduct. Only one Secret Committee member was not a political opponent of Walpole. The inquiry investigated the distribution of secret service money but was unable to gather sufficient evidence to form a case against him. Undertaking a second investigation in the summer of 1742, the Secret Committee presented three charges against Walpole: distribution of secret service money, exercising undue influence on elections, and granting fraudulent contracts. The inquiry again failed to arrive at a suitable punishment. For the next two years, 1743–44, Walpole remained in political correspondence with Henry Pelham and advised George II. In autumn 1744, Walpole returned to London from his Norfolk estate, at the king's suggestion. He was ill throughout the trip, suffering from gout and kidney stones, and although he eventually reached London, he died on March 18, 1745, at the age of 68. His son Robert, Lord Walpole of Walpole, succeeded him as second earl of Orford, while his collection of paintings was sold to Empress Catherine II (the Great) of Russia, and his home at 10 Downing Street was bequeathed to the nation. The earl of Wilmington was finally appointed first lord of the treasury.

Sir Robert Walpole was a sociable, generally popular minister though a coarse conversationalist for the times. Even during the 1742 investigations, the Tories opposed him on political, not personal, grounds. He has been called Britain's first modern prime minister and, though he ultimately relied more on the Crown's support than did any of his successors, he played a major part in developing the role and functions of the office of prime minister. He dominated foreign affairs (over the efforts of the secretary of state), controlled finances and political patronage, skillfully managed both houses of Parliament, and increased ministerial autonomy in the face of the emergence of a new style of Cabinet. He was an M.P. for over 40 years who improved Britain's balance of trade largely through his tariff policies; his policy of avoiding military conflict because it would damage trade and other domestic concerns confirms that Sir Robert Walpole, a Norfolk squire who became a statesman, was a man of outstanding personal and political ability.

SOURCES:

Hill, Brian W. *Sir Robert Walpole: "Sole and Prime Minister."* Hamish Hamilton, 1989.

Kemp, Betty. *Sir Robert Walpole.* Weidenfeld & Nicolson, 1976.

Morley, John. *Walpole.* Macmillan, 1909.

FURTHER READING:

Dickinson, H. T. *Walpole and the Whig Supremacy.* English Universities Press, 1973.

Langford, Paul. *Walpole and the Robinocracy.* Chadwych-Healey, 1986.

Plumb, J. H. *Sir Robert Walpole.* 2 vols. Cresset Press, 1956–60.

Arthur Wellesley, 1st Duke of Wellington

(1769–1852)

British General, who fought the French during the Peninsular War and defeated Napoleon at the Battle of Waterloo, later becoming prime minister.

"It may be conceded that the schemes of the French emperor were more comprehensive, his genius more dazzling, and his imagination more vivid than Wellington's. On the other hand, the latter excelled in that coolness of judgement which Napoleon himself described 'as the foremost quality in a general.'"

LORD ROBERTS

Arthur Wellesley was born on May 1, 1769, probably at Merrion Square, Dublin, Ireland. He was the sixth child of Lady Anne, wife of Garrett Wesley, the first earl and second baron Mornington. Lord Mornington had inherited estates in County Meath, and a mansion not far from Dublin. Renowned for his extravagant parties and "kindness and hospitality," Mornington managed to fritter away most of the family fortune. In 1774, he moved his family to London, where he was hotly pursued by his creditors, and took to buying lottery tickets in an attempt to clear his debts. At his death in May 1781 at the age of 45, he left his widow and children in what was described as "straitened" circumstances. Though lacking wealth, the family retained its aristocratic values and family connections.

Arthur Wellesley has been described as a "lonely, awkward boy, often in bad health." He studied at "Mr. Brown's academy at Chelsea," an inexpensive but mediocre school, and from there was sent to Eton. He was a poor student, especially weak at Latin and Greek, and remained at the bottom of his class. Apparently making no friends, he

Born Arthur Wesley (but later reverted to older form of family name, Wellesley) in Ireland in 1769; died in England in 1852; fourth son of Garrett Wesley, First Earl of Mornington, and Anne Hill-Trevor; brother of Richard Colley Wellesley, Earl of Mornington and 1st Marquis Wellesley; married: Catherine Sarah Dorothea, 1806 (died 1831); children: (two sons) Arthur Richard (second duke of Wellington) and Charles Wellesley (who became a general).

Contributed by John A. Hall, Assistant Professor of History, Albion College, Albion, Michigan

1787	Joined the British army
1789	French Revolution began
1793	Britain joined a coalition of nations determined to overthrow the republican government in France; war in Europe
1794	British campaign failed in the Netherlands
1796–1805	Wellesley put on active service in India
1801	Napoleon became First Consul for Life, later emperor of France
1808	Wellesley appointed commander of a British army sent to Portugal; Battles of Rolica and Vimeiro; Wellesley returned to England
1809–14	Peninsular War; Wellesley commanded British armies fighting in Spain and Portugal; Napoleon's forces retreated to France
1814	Napoleon abdicated; exiled on the Isle of Elba; French monarchy restored; Wellesley made Duke of Wellington
1815	Napoleon escaped Elba; returned to France and raised a new army; Battle of Waterloo; Napoleon abdicated again; exiled on St. Helena
1828–30	Wellington served as prime minister

preferred swimming or walking to the team sports of cricket and rowing.

By age 15, the family had to find a suitable profession for the decidedly unpromising Arthur. He had expressed an interest in becoming a financier, but his family had insufficient capital to entertain this idea. Since he had not learned enough Latin to enter the Church, the family settled on a career in the army. His mother was convinced that he would be more attractive to a future regiment if he studied at one of the French military academies, which were held in high regard. Arthur, however, had learned no French, so he moved with his mother to Bruxelles in Belgium to study the language. When Lady Mornington sent her son to the French military academy at Angers in 1785, she announced despairingly that he was "food for powder and nothing more."

A year later, he returned to London, where his eldest brother **Richard, the earl of Mornington,** resided. Considered a disappointment to his family, various attempts were made to find Arthur a regiment willing to allow him to purchase a commission as a junior officer. The selling of commis-

sions was common practice at this time. When someone left a regiment, he could sell his commission to the highest bidder. Some commissions in more prestigious regiments could cost thousands of pounds and were seen as investments much like stocks and bonds. Obviously a corrupt system, it allowed wealthy men to purchase promotion even if they were militarily incompetent and made it difficult for impoverished men of talent to be promoted. Nevertheless, there was considerable opposition to making the system more equitable, particularly from those officers who had large sums of money "invested" in their commissions. Arthur's family was not in a position to buy an expensive commission, especially since they had little confidence in Arthur's military future. Brother Richard wrote on Arthur's behalf: "There is a younger brother of mine.... He is here at this moment, and perfectly idle. It is a matter of indifference to me what he gets, provided he gets it soon." Finally, on March 7, 1787, Arthur Wellesley was able to purchase a commission as ensign in the Seventy-Third Foot, a Scottish regiment about to embark for India. So began the most remarkable military career in British history.

Wellesley showed immediate interest in and dedication to his new career. Impressed with this newfound enthusiasm, his family used their influence to advance his career. In 1788, he was appointed aide-de-camp to a family friend, the marquis of Buckingham, Lord-Lieutenant of Ireland, and shortly thereafter was promoted lieutenant in the Seventy-Sixth Foot. His mother was delighted, "Never did I see such a change for the better in anybody." The Seventy-Sixth, like the Seventy-Third, was under orders to sail to India. To avoid that distant and unhealthy posting, Lady Mornington used her influence to have her son transferred once again, this time to the Forty-First. Upon arrival in Dublin, the marquis of Buckingham had him formally transferred to the Twelfth Light Dragoons. Cavalry regiments were less likely to be posted to such unhealthy places as India.

Wellesley Gains Experience in Army and Politics

Though he retained his army career, Wellesley was elected as a member of the Irish Parliament, even though he was under age and technically elected illegally. The dual responsibility of soldier and politician taught him the need for hard work, time management, and long hours. In 1791, he was promoted captain in the Fifty-Eighth Foot, and then moved once again, to the Eighteenth Light Dragoons. By the age of 23, he had gained valuable experience not only in two branches of the army, but also in politics.

In 1793, war broke out between France and Britain. The French had overthrown and executed their king, and established a republic somewhat similar, though more radical, to that of the United States. Horrified by this "outbreak of republicanism" in the heart of Europe, a number of monarchies, including Britain, were determined to crush what they feared would otherwise become an "infection of revolution." Hoping to win fame leading a regiment in battle, Wellesley convinced his brother to sell the family home in Ireland in order to raise the money necessary for him to purchase the rank of lieutenant colonel in the 33rd Regiment of Foot.

In June 1794, his regiment was sent as part of an ill-fated campaign against the French in Holland. Plagued by corrupt and incompetent leadership, vastly outnumbered, and suffering under terrible conditions, barely 6,000 men out of the original 25,000 were still alive when they were withdrawn back to England in March 1795. As Wellesley commented later: "It has always been a marvel to me how any one of us escaped." Though he had led his regiment brilliantly, having fought a number of fierce rearguard actions to cover the army's withdrawal, this failed campaign had not brought him the recognition he had hoped for. When the remnants of the expedition returned home, they were ridiculed and abused, and the public and politicians did everything they could to quickly forget the fiasco. This was a bitter blow for Wellesley, who became so disenchanted with the army—in particular the corrupt system of promotion—that he seriously considered resigning his commission. He searched in vain, however, for a suitable post in the government. The "Dutch episode" was not without some merit for the young officer, however: "I learned more by seeing our faults and defects of our system in the campaign in Holland than anywhere else."

In 1796, Wellesley sailed for India, arriving with his regiment at Calcutta in February 1797. India was largely controlled by the British at this time, and Britain kept troops stationed there in order to "protect her interests," which included keeping the French, Dutch, and Portuguese at bay, and periodically subduing hostile Indian princes. In March 1799, Wellesley led one wing of a large British army which invaded the province of Mysore and overthrew the hostile sultan, Tippoo. During the campaign, Wellesley led an unsuccessful night attack on the fortress at Seringapatam. Following the death of Tippoo, Wellesley was appointed governor of Mysore and took command of all British troops in the area. In 1800, he led his forces against Dhoondiah Waugh, who had invaded Mysore with 40,000 men in an attempt to drive the British out. In a brilliantly organized campaign, Wellesley's troops killed Dhoondiah and scattered his army.

In April 1802, Wellesley was promoted to major general and led another highly successful campaign, this time against the rebellious Mahrattas. So successful was his leadership in India that he received the formal thanks of Parliament. Having established his reputation as a skilled military tactician and leader, Wellesley decided to return to England, where he felt his chances of further promotion would be better. In March 1805 he set sail, no longer the obscure and inexperienced junior officer who had left England eight years previously. Upon his arrival, he was given command of a brigade of troops, and in 1806 was elected to Parliament.

Wellesley found England totally preoccupied with the war with France. Under the leadership of **Napoleon,** French influence was extending throughout Europe, and many in England feared a French invasion. In May 1808, the Spaniards openly rebelled against their French occupiers, and Wellesley urged that British troops be sent to assist them. A small British army in Spain or Portugal would, he argued, "distress the French," and cause them to divert large numbers of troops away from other areas of Europe. It was preferable, he concluded, to fight the French in Spain rather than wait for them to invade England. On June 14, he was given temporary command of an army of about 9,000 men, with the general instructions to "assist the Spaniards or the Portuguese." Wellesley decided to land in Oporto in Portugal, which was a bold move as the French had over 30,000 men in the surrounding countryside. Wanting to secure a quick victory before more senior officers arrived to take overall command, Wellesley attacked a French army at Rolica. The French were driven off, but at heavy cost to the British. Wellesley then pulled back to Vimeiro to cover the landing of British reinforcements, and successfully repulsed a French attack. He was frustrated, however, by the arrival on the scene of Sir Harry Burrard, who took over command, and refused to give Wellesley permission to pursue the French. Wellesley could barely contain his anger.

When an armistice was negotiated with the French in Portugal, Wellesley was instructed to sign it. Angered by the way that his suggestions were ignored, he declared it "quite impossible for me to continue any longer in this army." Leaving Portugal, he arrived back in England in October

1808, where he found that he was being unjustly blamed for failing to destroy the French army when the opportunity had presented itself, and for having negotiated the armistice. It was only at a court of inquiry that he was able to prove that he was blameless. Not only was he vindicated, but he was formally thanked for his actions at Rolica and Vimeiro.

To counter a small British army under Sir John Moore, Napoleon sent over 300,000 troops to Spain. The British were ignominiously driven from the country and Moore was killed. In response, the number of British troops in Portugal was raised to 25,000, and Wellesley was appointed to command. Received warmly by the Portuguese when he landed in Lisbon on April 22, 1809, Wellesley immediately ordered his army to advance. So began one of the most remarkable campaigns in military history, which was to result over four years later in the remnants of the huge French army being driven back into France, and which was to be a contributing factor to the downfall of Napoleon.

He Triumphs in the Peninsular War

The "Peninsular War," as it came to be called, captivated popular attention in England, and turned Wellesley into a national hero. Enormously outnumbered, he maneuvered his forces brilliantly, retreating in the face of overwhelming odds, carrying out a scorched earth policy, fighting a series of successful defensive battles, and then attacking when he felt he had gained the advantage. The French were forced to fight a drawn-out campaign where their supplies had to be brought from France, where they were constantly harassed by brutal Spanish partisans, and where they had to fight a British opponent who seemed to "appear and then disappear, as if by magic." Even when the campaign was not going well, Wellesley never despaired, being totally convinced of his superiority to any of the French generals he faced, and sure that the entire Bonapartist "dictatorship" would ultimately collapse.

Wellesley won the respect and admiration of the French, who dubbed him "the hideous leopard"; he also won the respect of his soldiers. Though he had a rather cold, aloof personality, he did not throw away their lives as did many generals of that period, and his men came to have absolute faith in him. This high morale was, undoubtedly, one of the significant factors in the ultimate British victory. Napoleon, who in 1812 invaded Russia, referred to the lengthy war in Spain as his "Spanish ulcer." Just as Wellesley had predicted in

1808, the presence of the British in Spain and Portugal caused the French "distress" and forced Napoleon to squander men and matériel that were needed elsewhere.

The war in Spain and Portugal brought Wellesley the recognition that he had hoped for. In 1812, he was given £100,000 by Parliament and was created Marquis of Wellington. Wellington, as he was now called, finally drove the surviving French out of Spain, over the mountains of the Pyrenees back into France in 1814. He continued to pursue them, reaching Toulouse in April 1814 before news arrived that Napoleon had abdicated. The war was over.

Arriving back in England, Wellington's journey from Dover became a triumphal procession, with the eager crowds frequently pulling his carriage. New honors were offered by a grateful country: an additional £400,000—an astronomical sum—and the formal title of the Duke of Wellington.

In March 1815, Wellington was in Vienna when news arrived that Napoleon had returned to France, having escaped exile on the island of Elba, and was rallying an army with the intention of reclaiming power. Wellington hurried back to Bruxelles in Belgium, and there received his commission as commander of the British forces on the continent. By June, his army numbered over 100,000 men, of whom one-third were British and the remainder Dutch and Hanovarians. Few of the troops he had commanded in Spain were available to him, as these veterans had been sent to America where Britain was in another war. Wellington also found that few of his most trusted officers were available. Instead, he lamented, he found himself "overloaded with people I have never seen before."

In May 1815, Wellington met Blücher, commander of the Prussian army, and together they agreed on a tentative plan to counter Napoleon. They knew that he would probably attack, hoping to defeat them before the huge Austrian and Russian armies were able to arrive later in the summer. What was uncertain, however, was where Napoleon would attack and what his plan would be. Would he attack Bruxelles? Would he defend Paris? On June 15, Napoleon moved against Prussian outposts. His plan involved splitting the British and Prussian armies, each of which was slightly smaller than his own, threatening the British supply lines which would force them to withdraw towards the sea, and then turning on the Prussians and crushing them. If the British and the Prussians were able to converge on him, he knew he would be vastly outnumbered. When news arrived of

Napoleon's move, Wellington immediately ordered his army to begin moving to join the Prussians; he then went to the duchess of Richmond's ball.

On the morning of the 16th of June, the British encountered one wing of the French army under Marshal Ney at Quatre Bras, south of Bruxelles, while at the same time the Prussians encountered the main body of the French at Ligny, a few miles away. The Prussians were soundly defeated, losing about 12,000 men, and began a swift retreat towards Wavre. Wellington's men managed to fight off the French at Quatre Bras, though they had over 5,000 casualties. Finding his flank now dangerously exposed by the precipitate retreat of the Prussians, Wellington withdrew his army to positions at Mont St. Jean, near the town of Waterloo, an area he had previously noted would be suitable for defense. He then sent a note to Blücher, saying that he expected to receive the attack of the French main army on the 18th, and requesting that the Prussians join him there. Napoleon was convinced that victory was soon to be his: after having been beaten so decisively at Wavre, "and being pursued by a substantial body of troops, it is impossible for the Prussians to join the English in less than two days," he concluded. In addition, "We should be delighted that the English are standing their ground. The coming battle will save France and be renowned in history." The battle of Waterloo is, indeed, remembered as one of the most significant battles in history, and one that determined the course of Europe's future, though not in the way Napoleon had envisaged.

The Duke Defeats Napoleon at Waterloo

On the morning of the 18th of June, the French and British armies faced each other across a long sloping valley. Napoleon, still convinced that the Prussians were in full retreat, was delighted that the British had not slipped away: "There is no longer time for them to retreat. Wellington has gambled and lost. He has made defeat certain." Napoleon had reason to be happy, for not only did he have a numerical advantage over Wellington, but also many of Wellington's forces were either inexperienced or totally unreliable. The French army of over 65,000 men and 266 cannons made a spectacular sight that none of the survivors of that day were to forget. One British cavalryman recalled:

> I could see the French army drawn up in heavy masses opposite me. They were only a mile from where I stood.... There were great columns of infantry, and squadron after squadron of cuirassiers, red dragoons, brown hussars and green lancers with little swallow-tail flags at the ends of their lances. The grandest sight was a regiment of cuirassiers dashing at full-gallop over the brow of the hill opposite me, with the sun shining on their steel breastplates.

The battle opened at 11:20 A.M., with a French bombardment of the British line, and soon each side was firing on the other. As one Frenchman remembered:

> Eighty guns fired together, blotting out every other sound. The whole valley was filled with smoke.... We could scarcely see our comrades.... We could hear the whistle of their cannon-balls in the air, the dull thud as they struck the ground and that other noise when muskets were smashed to matchwood and men hurled twenty paces to the rear, every bone crushed, or when they fell with a limb gone.

Wellington fought a classic defensive battle at Waterloo, with his men maintaining their positions against repeated and determined French assaults. His men suffered heavy casualties but repulsed each new French attack. Since early that morning, he had known that the Prussians were marching fast and expected to join him on the battlefield at Waterloo by late afternoon. "The Duke sat unmoved," noted one observer.

> I recollect his asking Colonel Stanhope what o'clock it was, upon which Stanhope took out his watch and said it was twenty minutes past four. The Duke replied, "The battle is mine; and if the Prussians arrive soon, there will be an end of the war."

When Napoleon heard that the Prussians were threatening his flank and were not in full retreat as he had thought, he knew that time was running out and launched a number of even more desperate assaults on the British positions, sending into the attack the elite regiments of the Imperial Guard. For the first time in their history, the Imperial Guard were defeated and forced to retreat. At that moment the Prussian army appeared on the French flank, and the entire French army began to pull back in retreat. Wellington, who had bided his time for so long, now ordered his own men to advance, and suddenly the French retreat became a rout.

The victory at Waterloo was absolute. Napoleon escaped capture, but his army was destroyed, and he himself was soon forced to sur-

render to the British. He was thereafter exiled to the distant island of St. Helena in the Atlantic, from which he was never to return. But the cost of this victory was terrible. "In traversing the field," noted one artilleryman, "it was barely possible to clear with the guns the bodies of both armies which strewed the ground." More than 50,000 men had been killed or wounded that day, including over 15,000 British. That evening, when he read through the casualty lists, Wellington burst into tears. Writing to his brother, William, he confided:

> I never took so much trouble about any Battle, & never was so near being beat. Our loss is immense particularly in that best of all Instruments, British Infantry. I never saw the Infantry behave so well.

His victory at Waterloo secured Wellington's reputation as the greatest British general of his era and made him a national hero. Upon his return to Britain, he became involved in politics once again, being given a cabinet appointment in the government in 1817. He remained involved in national politics until his death over 30 years later, and it was in this arena that his aristocratic and elitist views became particularly apparent. He distrusted democracy, believed that an elite should rule, spoke out against the "ignorance and presumption and licentiousness" of a free press, and opposed reforms aimed at making elections more equitable. His conservative views reflected his aristocratic background and privileged position, and like many he felt threatened by the rise of liberalism in England which, he feared, would result in social disintegration. He was always a stout defender of his values and beliefs, even when this made him deeply unpopular. In 1831, for example, he had to add iron shutters to his house after angry mobs repeatedly smashed the windows and various threats were made on his life. Wellington openly despised politicians who tried to secure what he termed "low, vulgar popularity." In 1828, King George IV asked him to form a cabinet, which he did somewhat reluctantly. Until the government collapsed in 1830, he ran the country with little regard for public opinion. By 1831, his opposition to electoral reform had made him, temporarily, the most widely hated man in Britain. "Trust nothing to the enthusiasm of the people," he urged. "Give them a strong, and just, and if possible, a good government." His tenure as prime minister was not entirely without significant change, however, for he introduced, in an attempt to avoid rebellion in Ireland, an act which permitted Catholics to become members of Parliament.

Wellington saw his political life in the same terms as he had viewed his military career: requiring him to sacrifice everything in order to carry out his duty to his monarch and his nation. When he died in 1852, the "Grand Old Man" of British public life, even his political critics mourned the loss. The "Victor of Waterloo," the man who had defeated Napoleon, the greatest British general of his age, had lived a remarkable life. Yet despite his enormous fame, Wellington maintained throughout his life a modest view of himself and did not enjoy the hero-worship he so often encountered. As he said in 1836:

> Perhaps there is no man now existing who would like to meet me on a field of battle; in that I am superior. But when the war is over and the troops disbanded what is your great general more than anybody else?... I cannot saw and plane like a carpenter, or make shoes like a shoemaker, or understand cultivation like a farmer. Each of these, on his own ground, meets me on terms of superiority. I feel I am but a man.

SOURCES:

Aldington, Richard. *The Duke, Being an Account of the Life and Achievements of Arthur Wellesley, 1st Duke of Wellington.* Viking, 1943.

Cotton, Sargeant-Major Edward. *A Voice From Waterloo.* Kiessling, 1895.

Haythornthwaite, Philip J. *The Napoleonic Source Book.* Arms and Armour, 1990.

Longford, Elizabeth. *Wellington: Pillar of State.* Harper, 1972.

———. *Wellington: the Years of the Sword.* Harper, 1969.

Napier, Sir William. *History of the War in the Peninsula and the South of France From 1807 to 1814.* A. C. Armstrong, 1882.

FURTHER READING:

Chalfont, Lord, ed. *Waterloo: Battle of Three Armies.* Knopf, 1980.

Sutherland, John. *Men of Waterloo.* Prentice-Hall, 1966.

Wenceslas

(907–929)

Christian prince and tenth century King of Bohemia (Czech Republic), who tried to convert his people by his saintly example but was overthrown by his brother.

Name variations: Wenceslaus; St. Wenceslas, patron saint of Bohemia. Born at Stochov in 907 (dates are approximate); assassinated at Stara Boleslav on September 28, 929; one of seven children and son of Duke Vratislav of Bohemia and Drahomira; married and had one child. Predecessor: his father Vratislav. Successor: his brother Boleslav (who assassinated Wenceslas).

Good King Wenceslas lived more than a thousand years ago, at a time when written records were sparse. As a saint he became the focus of legends and miracle tales, many of which should not be taken literally, but do give some idea of the events his life and of the veneration in which he was held within a generation after his death.

Christianity first came to the Bohemian region of Central Europe in the ninth century, through the work of two Byzantine Greeks, Saints Cyril and Methodius. The Przemyslide family, gathered near the city of Prague, ruled Bohemia, and its patriarch, Duke Borijov, was converted by Methodius. At first the Bohemian Christians practiced the Slavonic rite, but the duchy later made links with Rome and converted to the Latin rite. Not all its people converted, however, and the duchy bore witness to a long period of conflict between pagan and Christian factions during the next generation.

Wenceslas, grandson of Borijov and son of Duke Vratislav, was born in about 907 and at first was cared for by his grandmother Ludmilla, Borijov's widow. Eager that he carry on the faith to

"Whereas Boleslav [his brother] was ambitious, domineering, and worldly, Wenceslaus was retiring, humble, and ascetic."

MARVIN KANTOR

Contributed by Patrick Allitt, Assistant Professor of History, Emory University, Atlanta, Georgia

which she had converted, Ludmilla arranged for him to study with her chaplain Paul and later to attend a primitive college at Budec where he learned Latin from a priest named Ucen. All the chroniclers agree that Wenceslas was a studious and conscientious man, but not all agree on his proficiency in the military arts as he prepared for his seniority. When his father Vratislav died in about 920, while at war with the Magyars who threatened his duchy from the east, his mother Drahomira became regent. Daughter of a Slavic prince, she was only a nominal Christian and resented the pious education Ludmilla had given Wenceslas. She decreed that all Christian education must stop, dismissed all magistrates who had converted to Christianity, prohibited priests from approaching her son, and finally had Ludmilla strangled by two of her nobles in 921 at the castle of Tetin. Her measures did not destroy Wenceslas's faith, however, and he continued to meet his Christian friends in secret and to be visited by priests at night.

After five years of Drahomira's regency, Wenceslas took control of the duchy in 925 when he was about 18, with the help of his father's old friends. He tried to reconcile the Christian and non-Christian groups by uniting them against an invader, Arnulf, Duke of Bavaria, but it seems that Wenceslas lacked the power to repel Arnulf until a greater challenger appeared as counterweight. He at first sent his mother away from court as a way of controlling the intrigues of her faction. Once they had been chastened, he invited her back, and there is no further record of conflict between them.

Wenceslas Seeks Peace with German Emperor

An approach by overpoweringly superior German forces in 929 led Wenceslas to sue for peace with their leader, Emperor Henry I, rather than see his duchy devastated; it was the first of many occasions on which Bohemians temporized with German power rather than oppose it. The empire of the East Franks, later to be known as the Holy Roman Empire, was one of the vestigial fragments of **Charlemagne**'s Empire, which had briefly united France, Germany, the Low Countries, and Italy. An elective monarchy since 911, the first emperors were preoccupied with protecting their eastern flank against Magyar (Hungarian) tribal invasions. Because of his easterly position, Wenceslas was more immediately threatened by the Magyars than Emperor Henry I. Taking the view that overlordship from the comparatively remote Emperor was preferable to that of Bavaria, which was all too close, Wenceslas surrendered his

duchy to Henry and received it back as a fief. From then on he paid an annual tribute to Henry of 600 silver marks and 120 head of cattle.

According to tradition Wenceslas, deep in prayer, kept the Emperor waiting most of the day when they agreed to meet, but Henry's initial anger at this perceived insult melted away when he met Wenceslas, because he saw an angel beside the saintly Duke and a shining cross on his forehead. Asked by the Emperor what gift or favor he would like, Wenceslas answered that he wanted a precious relic, the arm of St. Vitus, which he then used as the central object of veneration in the foundation of his cathedral at Prague (built 926–929). Vitus was at that time patron saint of Saxony, and since Henry I was also king of Saxony, this was a tactful way for Wenceslas to acknowledge his new master. One chronicler, Christian of Slavnic, who wrote at the end of the tenth century, adds that Wenceslas and Henry became close friends.

Wenceslas's biographers dwelt more on his piety than his statecraft, about which much is permanently lost. Hagiographical (idealized) accounts of his deeds stressed his humility. Christian of Slavnic, the earliest biographer, wrote:

> During Lent, and even in winter it was his custom to go barefoot over the steep and icy paths from castle to castle in order to visit the churches of Christ, and people saw the bloodstained footprints that he left behind him. In order to preserve the chastity which he had vowed he wore a hair-cloth which has been preserved to our days in honor of him. Beneath the magnificent robes of royalty he wore a woollen garment like a simple monk, thus shining equally before God and man.

The claim of perpetual chastity is probably wrong, since even the most devout of medieval rulers were obsessed by the need for strong male heirs. Another chronicle says that Wenceslas married, had a son, and then agreed to live with his wife as though they were brother and sister.

The story of Wenceslas helping the poor by bringing them stacks of firewood—basis for the sentimental Victorian Christmas carol by John Mason Neale—comes from a much later pious biography written at the end of the 13th century. Another legend says that Wenceslas bought pagan slaves in the markets in order to convert them to Christianity. We know from an Arabic historian of the era that Prague was then a center of the slave trade (the words *Slav* and *slave* have the same origin), so the tale may have some basis in fact.

Even when the biographies describe political affairs, they are presented with strong religious and didactic overtones. For example, Christian of Slavnic says that soon after his accession Wenceslas was obliged to go to war against the neighboring Zlicane tribe when they tried to overrun his duchy. To avoid the mass slaughter of a pitched battle, says the chronicle, Wenceslas proposed a single combat between himself and the Zlicane leader, Duke of Kourim. They advanced to meet each other, but then Kourim saw a vision of the Holy Ghost on the breast of Wenceslas and at once surrendered, after which the two men lived in peace. This tale lacks independent historical verification. The most recent English-speaking student of early Bohemian Christianity, Marvin Kantor, says:

> What emerges from the *Lives* [early chronicles] is the picture of a man under the thumb of priests, retiring, neglectful of and perhaps even insensible to the affairs of government. Christianity had not eliminated the necessity for a strong leader. Wenceslas appears to have lacked this important dimension. Left to his own devices he would have preferred to become a monk and withdraw to a monastery.

His brother Boleslav expected to succeed Wenceslas, but the birth of a son to the Duke denied him his chance. It seems likely that Wenceslas became the focus of the anti-Christian party at court which deplored the growing influence of the clergy over him. Boleslav apparently also disliked Wenceslas's decision to surrender to the Emperor and later rebelled against Henry's successor. Besides, as Christian of Slavnic expressed it: "The arrows of the Demon had touched him from every side, and he was tormented by the lust to rule." Boleslav first invited Wenceslas to a banquet at Stara Boleslav, ostensibly to celebrate the dedication of a new church. Despite a premonition of coming disaster, Wenceslas accepted the invitation and proposed a toast in honor of St. Michael to the assembled guests. The next morning Boleslav waylaid Wenceslas on his way to the new church to celebrate the feast of its patron saints, Cosmas and Damian; they began to quarrel, then to struggle. Several of Boleslav's cronies ran to the scene and stabbed Wenceslas to death.

Declared Christian Martyr; Adopted as Patron Saint of Bohemia

Almost at once miracles were attributed to Wenceslas. Terrified at the prospect of divine disfavor, the usurping Boleslav soon had his brother's body moved to Prague, where by popular acclaim Wenceslas was declared a Christian martyr. Like his grandmother Ludmilla, Wenceslas was found to have a body which did not decay after death, further evidence, in medieval eyes, of his preternatural sanctity. In the tenth century, the practice of reserving canonization to the pope alone was not yet accepted. Books about Wenceslas's life and death were written in Slavonic and Latin, and one consequence of their spread was the dawning of a sense of Czech identity around his memory. He was soon adopted as the patron saint of Bohemia and his shrine became a focus for pilgrimages. His feast day in the Catholic Church is September 28, the anniversary of his death.

Eventually, Boleslav seems to have converted to Christianity and gone on to conduct a long reign. In 936, at the death of Henry I, Boleslav revolted against the new emperor Otto I and refused to pay tribute. Although he kept his revolt alive for 14 years, Boleslav was obliged in 950, after years of destructive warfare, to declare allegiance once more to the Empire, by which time its position as the major power in Central Europe was unassailable.

SOURCES:

Dvornik, Francis. *The Life of Saint Wenceslas.* Prague Archdiocese, 1929.

———. *The Making of Eastern and Central Europe.* London: Polish Research Center, 1949.

Holmes, George, ed. *The Oxford History of Medieval Europe.* Oxford University Press, 1988.

Kantor, Marvin. *The Origins of Christianity in Bohemia.* Northwestern University Press, 1990.

John Wesley

(1703–1791)

English evangelist and founder of Methodism, who popularized open-air preaching and traveled Britain for more than 50 years to communicate the Methodist message.

"I look upon all the world as my parish."

JOHN WESLEY

In an era noted more for wars, political maneuvering, and economic changes than for religious beliefs, John Wesley made significant contributions to 18th-century British society through his evangelical work. Though his effect was felt in areas such as social reform and health, as well as in spiritual matters, not all people welcomed the changes that he and his activities initiated.

John Wesley was born the 15th child and second surviving son of Samuel Wesley and Susanna Annesley on June 17, 1703. His father, a rector of the parish of Epworth in Lincolnshire, was greatly concerned with matters of duty and individual piety. He was also impetuous and obstinate, two traits evident in his son's personality. Wesley's strong-willed mother Susanna was the daughter of a dissenting (that is, Protestant but not Church of England) minister, though she later converted to Anglicanism.

Wesley was not permitted to mix with the children of the neighborhood farmers or gentry. Most of his early years were spent in the company of his sisters and mother, who taught him the alphabet, prayers and the Bible, and "the virtue of

Name variations: John Westley. Born June 17, 1703, at Epworth Rectory, Lincolnshire, England; died in City Road chapel-house, London, England, on March 2, 1791; 15th child and second surviving son of Samuel Wesley and Susanna Annesley; married: Mary Vazeille (a widow); no children. Successor: John Fletcher.

Contributed by Donna Beaudin, Ph.D. candidate in History, University of Guelph, Guelph, Ontario, Canada

1701	Act of Settlement passed, securing Protestant Succession to thrones of England and Ireland
1725	Wesley ordained deacon in Church of England
1728	Ordained priest
1729	Charles and John Wesley organized Oxford Methodists
1732	Charter for colony of Georgia granted
1739	Wesley began open-air preaching
1760	George II died; George III crowned
1778	Wesley began publishing *Arminian Magazine*

obedience." When he was six, he was rescued from a fire in the rectory that had been set by an arsonist. He would later interpret this event as as affirmation that he had been chosen to do the Lord's work.

On the nomination of his father's patron, the duke of Buckingham, the 11-year-old Wesley was sent to Charterhouse school in London as a foundation scholar. It was his first time away from home. He matriculated from Charterhouse in July 1720, having been elected a scholar of Christ Church College, Oxford, a month earlier. Just prior to leaving for Oxford, young Wesley met Henry Sacheverell, a popular Anglican preacher who had once been suspended from preaching for three years for speaking against the ideals of the Glorious Revolution of 1688–89.

The years spent at Oxford were crucial to Wesley's development. A diligent student, he read in a variety of subjects, including contemporary theology, Latin composition, and the Greek New Testament. Due to an almost constant lack of money, Wesley learned to economize; he even wore his auburn hair long to save the cost of a wig and barbers. Despite his financial situation and rigorous scholarly pursuits, he was a sociable undergraduate who enjoyed rowing, tennis, playing cards, and visiting the coffeehouse for long conversations. He graduated in 1724 and received his bachelor of arts degree.

From an early age, John Wesley had been raised to expect a ministry in the established Church of England. Following graduation, his father urged him to take religious orders, though Wesley took time to consider this decision. Concerned with his moral as well as his physical well-being, he determined to follow an orderly and temperate lifestyle, amending such habits as boasting, lying, greed for praise, and excessive emotion in arguing. In late February 1725, he notified his parents of his decision to take Anglican orders and began to prepare for his career.

John Wesley's clerical career began modestly enough. On September 19, 1725, he was ordained a deacon by John Potter, Bishop of Oxford. Wesley preached his first sermon at South Leigh, Oxfordshire, on the Sunday following his ordination. In expectation of a college fellowship, he remained at Oxford. With the influence of John Morley, rector of Lincoln College, he secured election as a fellow of Lincoln College on March 17, 1726. As long as he held the fellowship, he was required to remain single. In return, he was assured of financial security and independence while pursuing the life of a scholar.

As a Lincoln fellow, Wesley was chosen to be a lecturer in Greek and a moderator in classes. He also continued with his own scholarly study, receiving his master of arts degree from Oxford in February 1727. Although he returned to Epworth as his father's curate, Wesley still made occasional visits to Oxford. On September 22, 1728, after his second ordination, John Wesley became a priest of the Church of England, and returned to his Lincoln College residence the following year to resume tutoring undergraduates.

While at Oxford in the late 1720s and early 1730s, Wesley's theological views were challenged by his "spiritual disquiet." Biographer V.H.H. Green writes that he was "concerned with practical Christianity, with the adaptation of theology to the realities of daily life." This coincided with Wesley's association with the Oxford Methodists, as they were already called in 1729, comprised of his younger brother Charles, William Morgan, and Robert Kirkham. Others called the group the Holy Club, though in reality the society was nameless. Initially, the society's members met for pious study and weekly communion, but the tenor and function of the society soon became evangelical and philanthropic. Wesley honed his daily schedule into precise allotments of time for sleep, prayer, charitable works, and so on. Thus, he usually rose at four o'clock in the morning; one product of his diligence was the 1733 publication of a small collection of daily prayers. Oscar Sherwin, in a biography of John Wesley, concluded that:

> Wesley's passion for order led him to become a great organizer. The societies were almost semi-military; the whole Methodist organization was benevolently autocratic. But no great religious leader was less of a doctrinaire, less of a dictator.

The mid-1730s were an anxious time for John Wesley. His correspondence with Mary Pendarves (which was opposed by his brother Charles) did not come to a fruitful conclusion. In early 1735, he applied for the position of Epworth parish, but his efforts were thwarted by the bishop of London. Further, his father died in late April of the same year. In the wake of these developments, Wesley declared himself ready to assume missionary work in the new American colony of Georgia.

Wesley Travels to North America

His trip to North America started out slowly, leaving England eight weeks after the original departure date. He shared the Atlantic crossing with his brother Charles, two other Englishmen, and 26 members of the German Moravian Brethren. Not one for wasting an opportunity, Wesley learned German and also learned about the apostolic nature of Moravian belief. Indeed, he seems to have had a gift for learning languages: he spoke French; he and Charles could converse in Latin; and he would soon learn Spanish in order to communicate with the Jews in Georgia. After a three-month trip, the ship reach Savannah.

Wesley was naive and inexperienced in missionary work, but he was young, tireless, and enthusiastic. Some colonists perceived his preaching, with its emphasis on grace and justification by faith, as papist. Though he based himself in Savannah, he considered all of Georgia to be his parish. But the Georgia mission lasted less than two years and ended on an unfortunate note. Wesley fell in love with Sophia Hopkey, the daughter of a Savannah magistrate. In the end, she married another colonist, but not before Wesley withheld communion from her and was arrested for defaming her character. The case never came to trial, and he fled the colony on December 2, 1737, in defiance of a magisterial order, arriving back in England in early February 1738. He viewed the Georgia mission and the state of his own faith with disappointment.

After returning to England, he preached tirelessly in parish churches. He also imbibed the doctrine of saving faith from Peter Bohler of Germany. While attending a society meeting in Aldergate Street on May 24, 1738, Wesley had a spiritual conversion. Imbued with new confidence, he spent the summer months in Europe, visiting Count Zinzendorf and the Moravian center. He returned to Oxford by October and resumed preaching—outdoors. Open-air preaching had initially offended his sense of what was orderly and decent, but he gradually adopted this technique. Due to his small stature—5'6", 120 pounds—he often had to modify his preaching technique to include standing on a box or chair to achieve the desired effect.

Wesley began to distance himself from the Moravians after his 1740 exclusion from the Fetter Lane society. He also moved away from Calvinist teachings with the delivery of a free grace sermon delivered in Bristol. This move initiated a split within the Methodist societies and resulted in the founding of groups like the Welsh Calvinistic Methodists; it also made him the target of Calvinist hostility. V.H.H. Green concludes:

> What, however, the Calvinists lacked in charity they made up in virulence. They attacked Wesley as a papalist [sic], as a heretic, as worse than an atheist. They accused him of dishonesty and ambition; they muddied his character as far as they were able.

More purposeful than ambitious, Wesley continued to develop the Methodist societies. In 1739, he had purchased the Foundery, an old government building in London, to serve as the headquarters of the Methodist societies which had been formed in the previous decade. He stressed the need to preach the gospel to the poor of Great Britain, and emphasized the fact that his societies and lay preachers were still followers of the Church of England.

He Is Affirmed as Head of Methodists

In the 1740s, he began to preach outside of Oxford more and more. In June 1742, after being excluded from the church at Epworth, he preached a sermon while standing on his father's tombstone. He was also involved with the opening of more chapels, two in London in 1744. Wesley's iron will dominated these Methodist chapels: for instance, men and women were forced to sit apart. His opinions on preaching and the sacraments were evident at the Methodist conferences of the mid-1740s. At the 1744 conference, England was divided into "circuits," and the following year Wesley was affirmed as the head of all Methodist congregations. With these parameters, he began his missionary work through central and northeast England, expanding to Ireland in 1749. His emphasis on northern England was not accidental. As this region became industrial and the population of the towns increased, he recognized an audience in need of his services. By the close of the decade, Methodism was virtually a church within the established church.

As a circuit preacher, Wesley required both mental stamina and physical endurance. For decades, he traveled Great Britain, especially England, first on horseback and later by chaise. Since he endeavored to make good use of his time, he frequently read, particularly history, poetry, and philosophy, as he traveled from town to town. Over the next half century, his habits of personal austerity and thrift would serve him well. Wesley stressed cleanliness and somber clothing of good quality. From time to time, however, his health broke down (he suffered from hereditary gout and much later from diabetes), and he was forced to stop preaching to speed his recuperation. Wesley fell ill in Newcastle-on-Tyne in August 1748 and was nursed by Grace Murray. He fell in love with her and proposed, but she went on to marry one of his preachers instead.

Disappointed in love for the third time, he consoled himself by writing verse and devoting himself to his work, but a friend persuaded him to marry. Convinced that this was the proper course of action, and despite his brother's disapproval, John Wesley finally married on February 18, 1751. His bride was Mary Vazeille, widow of a merchant and the mother of four children. Perhaps the most significant consequence of Wesley's marriage was that it meant the resignation of his Oxford fellowship and its income. The early years of the marriage were modestly happy, with Mrs. Wesley accompanying her husband on his circuit, including his trip to Scotland in 1753. The marriage began to deteriorate, however, because of her violent temper and jealousy and because of his trying ways and familiar style of correspondence with female Methodist helpers. Though a serious breach occurred in September 1755, Mary Wesley did not desert her husband until 1776.

Once married, Wesley continued to write and publish pamphlets and books, which were now his chief source of income. His earlier publications included a hymn book (1737), *Thoughts on Marriage and Celibacy* (1743), *Primitive Physic* (1747), and the 50-volume *Christian Library* (1749–55). These works and others provided him with more income than expected, and he continued to write until his death. The most significant project of his later years, the *Arminian Magazine,* was established in 1778.

Wesley continued his itinerant preaching, though by 1763 he seemed to be one of the few preachers who still traveled a regular circuit. While carrying out his evangelical work, he was beset by vicious physical attacks, rumors of scandal, and the duty of providing clerical leadership for the Methodist societies. But to Wesley, it was more important to communicate to others a belief in justification by faith (though he did not disparage good works), while he firmly opposed the doctrine of predestination. His brother Charles feared that Wesley was leading Methodism toward a complete separation from the Church of England, but John maintained until his death that Methodism was a movement within the Church of England and that the idea of separation was abhorrent.

As a dynamic preacher, he continued to attract large congregations well into his advanced years. In his late 70s, Wesley founded a magazine which enabled him to voice his opinions in the Methodist-Calvinist controversy. For 30 years, he had presided over the annual conferences at which preachers were selected, based on their academic learning, voice and delivery, and common sense.

By 1784, he became concerned with the prospects of the Methodist chapels after his demise. The result, after advice from Thomas Coke, was the "deed of declaration," the effective charter of Wesleyan Methodism. The issue of the chapels and the formation of a decision-making body were settled and a council of 100 preachers selected. Wesley also began to personally "ordain" ministers for work in America.

A forthright man of conservative political views, Wesley spoke out, readily and ably, on the issues of the day. From 1775, his disapproval of the American colonists increased his popularity. Likewise, he joined the protest against the slave trade and was the first leading religious figure to take such a position. He also took a stand on the matter of toleration for Roman Catholics and asserted that the Irish penal laws against Roman Catholics were foolish.

As an elderly man, even into his 80s, Wesley continued to travel and to preach and to publish the *Arminian Magazine.* In 1790, he visited Ireland for the last time, and he preached his last sermon on February 23, 1791, at the age of 87. He died on March 2, in the City Road chapel-house in London; friends and crowds of admirers came to pay their respect.

John Wesley was an administrative genius who was quick to adopt and adapt the ideas of others to his own ends. He dedicated five decades of his life to taking the gospel of Christ throughout the British Isles. In this work, he was a practical man who lived by the principles that he espoused to others, but he did not anticipate that Methodism would become a widespread phenomenon.

SOURCES:

Dreyer, Frederick. "A 'Religious Society under Heaven': John Wesley and the Identity of Methodism," in *Journal of British Studies*. January 25, 1986.

Green, V. H. H. *John Wesley*. Nelson, 1964.

Sherwin, Oscar. *John Wesley: Friend of the People*. Twayne, 1961.

FURTHER READING:

Edwards, M. L. *John Wesley and the Eighteenth Century: a Study of his Social and Political Influence*. Epworth Press, 1955.

McConnell, Francis J. *John Wesley*. Abingdon Press, 1939.

Wilhelm II

(1859–1941)

German emperor and king of Prussia from 1888 to 1918, who led his subjects to defeat, and his crown to extinction, in the First World War.

Name variations: William II; Kaiser Wilhelm. Pronunciation: VIL-helm. Born in 1859; died in exile in 1941; son of Friedrich Wilhelm (the crown prince of Prussia) and Victoria. Predecessor: Wilhelm I.

Wilhelm, born in 1859, was the descendant of many of the proudest royal houses in Europe. On his mother's side, he was the grandson of Queen Victoria, who ruled Great Britain and its Empire from 1837 until her death in 1901. On his father's side, he could trace his descent not only through the great Hohenzollern dynasty that had produced **Frederick the Great** in the 18th century, but also to Frederick's enemy, the Russian empress, **Catherine the Great,** who died in 1796, ten years after Frederick the Great's death.

Wilhelm's mother, a daughter and namesake of Queen Victoria, was a strong-willed, ambitious woman who dominated her husband, Friedrich Wilhelm, the crown prince of Prussia. She never liked Prussia because it was an absolute monarchy rather than a constitutional regime such as England. She never hesitated to draw unfavorable comparisons between her native England and Berlin, to which she had moved as a young bride. Wilhelm was her first child, and she was deeply disappointed that he was born with a defective left arm. The baby's crippled condition led his parents to try many medical and gymnastic cures, to no

Contributed by Lamar Cecil, William R. Kenan, Jr. Professor of History, Washington and Lee University, Lexington, Virginia

"God knows everything, but the Emperor knows it even better."

LEO VON CAPRIVI,
GERMAN CHANCELLOR

avail. Wilhelm's arm proved to be permanently paralyzed, and as a mature man it was withered and about four inches shorter than his powerful right arm.

Wilhelm accepted his deformity with aplomb, learning to ride, to be a celebrated marksman in the hunting field, and even to play billiards. It seems, however, that he was resentful that his mother frequently expressed her bitterness at his condition, declaring that she regretted that he did not resemble his contemporaries in England, "the land of healthy children and rosy cheeks." His mother's obvious disappointment in his body stung Wilhelm and contributed to his eventual alienation from her, a development on which Sigmund Freud once commented. He also resented the fact that his mother dominated his father, encouraging his father to reject his Prussian heritage in favor of English ideas. The result was that Wilhelm fell out with both his mother and father, having little to do with them once he went to the University at Bonn at the age of 18 and rejecting the liberal English political ideas which they tried in vain to teach him.

Wilhelm proved to be an ordinary student, and after two years he abandoned the University to enter the Prussian army; shortly thereafter, he married a German princess by whom he had six sons and a daughter. His family life was minimal, however, for the army always came first. Wilhelm became an ardent officer, enthusiastic about every aspect of military life and describing the army as the place "I found my family, my friends, my interests—everything that I had in my youth been deprived of." One of the effects of Wilhelm's attachment to the Prussian army was his increasing hostility to England, which as a liberal nation was much disliked in the highly conservative Prussian aristocracy from which most officers were drawn.

Wilhelm's fellow officers, who saw an advantage in having their future sovereign be a military man, fawned over him and encouraged him to believe that he was a person of uncommon distinction and ability. Wilhelm was, in fact, intellectually quite ordinary and even in military affairs, where his interests were greatest, of limited talent. The result was that he became a martinet, fanatically insistent on having his own way. He was insensitive to other people, peremptory, rude, and full of gestures that he thought appropriately martial. He impressed himself and some of the figures in his retinue, but to many people Wilhelm seemed dangerously unstable and difficult.

As a young army officer, he was second in line to the German throne, which was occupied by his grandfather Wilhelm I, the German emperor

or kaiser. Kaiser Wilhelm I lived to be very old, dying early in March 1888, just a few days short of his 91st birthday. Young Wilhelm's father succeeded as Kaiser Friedrich III but unfortunately died of throat cancer, after a reign of only 99 days. Wilhelm blamed his mother for this tragedy. She had insisted on entrusting her husband's health to an English doctor, who, contrary to German medical opinion, had mistakenly diagnosed Friedrich's condition as one that was harmless and that could be cured by rest.

He Becomes King of Prussia and German Emperor

Thus it was that Wilhelm II became king of Prussia and German emperor at the age of 29, far earlier than anyone had expected and without much experience. The German Empire had been founded in 1871 by the military victories of the Kingdom of Prussia against Denmark, France, Austria, and other German states. The constitution of the Empire declared that the king of Prussia would always simultaneously serve as German emperor. Since the king of Prussia enjoyed almost dictatorial power, he was also granted wide authority as emperor. Like the Russian tsars, the Prusso-German king-emperor was a supreme autocrat, and Wilhelm II by nature intended to make maximum use of his prerogatives. He soon found that exercising this authority brought him into conflict with Prince **Otto von Bismarck,** the so-called "Iron Chancellor."

Bismarck was a diplomatic genius who had engineered the wars that had resulted in 1871 in the creation of the German Empire under the king of Prussia, and it was he who had written the constitution that gave to the emperor his vast powers. Bismarck, however, was a person of great arrogance and determination, and he had intimidated

Wilhelm's father and grandfather so much that they had essentially let him govern Germany. Wilhelm II, who was over 40 years younger than Bismarck, had too much pride and vanity to allow himself to be ordered about. Although Bismarck realized how imperious Wilhelm was, he believed that he could also intimidate the young emperor by threatening to resign if he could not have his way. Wilhelm acknowledged Bismarck's heroic role in the creation of the German Empire, but he was determined to rule himself. Therefore, to Bismarck's great astonishment, Wilhelm accepted the resignation the chancellor submitted in March 1890 in the course of one of their quarrels, declaring that he would now rule Germany himself. "Full steam ahead," Wilhelm proudly declared.

Unfortunately, Kaiser Wilhelm II was intellectually and temperamentally unsuited to his high office. He had little interest in hard work, greatly preferring military parades, hunts, and trips to visit his "colleagues," as he called his fellow sovereigns. Wilhelm liked or disliked people according to their willingness to fulfill his wishes, and his entourage therefore was composed largely of mediocre men who toadied to him. Bismarck's successors as chancellor stayed only as long as they were prepared to do the kaiser's bidding, and when they became too opinionated, they were dismissed in favor of more pliable men. Wilhelm's interests lay primarily in diplomatic and military affairs; the rest he left to his underlings. It was thus that the kaiser's contribution to the development of imperial Germany was for the most part in relations with other powers and in building up the Fatherland's armed forces. In both areas, Wilhelm II's influence was disastrous.

As a diplomat, the last kaiser was particularly anxious to win favor with the British and the Russians, but neither in London nor in St. Petersburg did he have any success. The British royal family thoroughly disapproved of their German kinsman because they resented Wilhelm's dislike of his English mother, to whom Queen **Victoria** and the future king Edward VII were closely related and much attached. On visits to England, Wilhelm was often ill behaved, claiming that neither his relatives nor statesmen in London appreciated his talents or his desire to improve Anglo-German relations. As the kaiser often admitted, he could not bear to be taken lightly or to be treated condescendingly, and what he saw as England's unappreciative behavior greatly annoyed him. In Russia, the same unfortunate situation occurred. Tsar **Alexander III,** who ruled from 1881 to 1894, thought that Wilhelm was mentally unbalanced, an opinion shared by the tsar's son **Nicholas II,** the last Russian monarch, who was murdered in

1918. The effect of Wilhelm II's maladroit diplomacy was not only to alienate both of these powers from Germany but to lead them to overcome their many differences.

In Wilhelm II's opinion, Germany, as the wealthiest nation on the European continent, had a right to play a decisive part in world affairs. He was convinced that Great Britain resented this ambition and for that reason had rejected his overtures of friendship. His resentment was great, although it never occurred to him that his own personality was largely responsible for British suspicion of Germany. Great Britain therefore had to be forced to pay attention to Wilhelm II and to Germany, and the only means through which this could be accomplished was military power. Germany had the most powerful professional army in all Europe, but that alone could not challenge Britain, whose power was built upon a worldwide empire. What the Fatherland lacked was a fleet, and the kaiser was certain that with a great German navy the British would be forced to pay him, and his country, the respect that was their due.

Germany and Britain Compete in Arms Race

It was thus from a highly personal motive that Wilhelm II embarked on the construction of a German navy. This he inaugurated in 1898, and by 1914 his armada had become second only to that of Great Britain. From the British perspective, the construction of a Germany navy, especially one composed of heavy battleships with limited cruising range, was aimed against England. The response in London was to build still more warships, with the result that after the turn of the century Germany and Great Britain became locked in an armament race of such vast proportions that the financial structure of both countries became endangered. In spite of numerous attempts to arrive at a reduction in arms, no agreement could be reached because the kaiser would not give up his naval construction schemes. As a result, the British, thoroughly alarmed by Germany's might both on land and on water, turned to the French and the Russians, forming diplomatic arrangements with both powers.

By the end of the first decade of the 20th century, Wilhelm II and the statesmen he had appointed to office found themselves in a difficult position, one for which the kaiser himself was in part responsible. Russia and England had been alienated and had become diplomatically aligned with France; the result was that Germany was "encircled" by enemies. The only power on whom the kaiser could depend was Austria-Hungary, with whom Wilhelm II's grandfather, Wilhelm I, had made a defensive alliance in 1879. The maintenance of the Austro-Hungarian alliance, given Germany's "encirclement," was therefore imperative. It was also very troubling, for the Empire ruled from Vienna by the aged emperor **Francis Joseph I** was very fragile, economically backward, and militarily incompetent. Moreover, the Austro-Hungarian Empire was itself encircled by enemies, who were resentful of the fact that Francis Joseph, like Wilhelm II a German, presided over an empire that consisted for the most part of non-Germans. There were Italians who wanted to be united with Italy, there were Hungarians who wanted more authority within the Empire, and there were millions of Slavs who wanted to form their own ethnic states. This last group was especially troubling since they had the support of the Kingdom of Serbia, an independent Slav monarchy on Austria-Hungary's southern border, and of Russia, who claimed to be the mother of all Slavic peoples. Both the Serbs and the Russians supported Francis Joseph's Slavic subjects in their desire for independence. If realized, this would mean the breakup of the Empire, and Germany would be left without allies. The existence of Austria-Hungary had to be maintained at all costs, even if it meant war.

By 1912, the situation had become perilous. Slavic agitation from Serbia, supported by Russia, seemed likely to undermine and destroy the existence of the Austro-Hungarian Empire, while in Western Europe the Anglo-French entente, also supported by Russia, was poised against Germany. Meanwhile, within Germany itself the socialist movement, which called for the democratization of the Fatherland and thus an end to Wilhelm II's dictatorial power, had won increasing numbers of voters in spite of Wilhelm II's attempts to deal forcibly with this rising danger. To the kaiser, as well as to many of his military and civilian advisors, Germany stood at the crossroads, at home and abroad. War might be necessary to preserve the monarchy and to secure Germany's place in the world. With that in mind, in December 1912 Wilhelm II ordered his generals and admirals to commence whatever planning was necessary for a war that might break out in the near future.

Archduke's Assassination Provokes War

The crisis that did in fact provoke war was the assassination on June 28, 1914, of the heir-apparent to the Austro-Hungarian throne, the archduke Franz Ferdinand. The assassins were arrested and found to have recently been in Serbia; there officials had allowed them to pass over the border and had failed to warn the Austrians that there was likely to be an attempt on the archduke's life. The Austrians were now determined to use this outrage to settle their score with the Serbs, but since to declare war might bring Russia into the conflict, the Austrians had to secure Germany's aid. A week after the assassination, Wilhelm and his government gave Vienna a "blank check" to deal with the Serbs; armed with that, the Austrians issued an ultimatum to Serbia that, if accepted, would have robbed the kingdom of its autonomy. The Serbs, who were in no position to fight, agreed to most but not all of the terms, whereupon the Austrians declared the response unacceptable and declared war.

Kaiser Wilhelm II, confronted with the reality that war was now at hand, became alarmed. His martial gestures in fact masked a personality that was very reluctant to engage in conflict. The kaiser therefore quickly attempted to limit the war to one between Austria and Serbia. Unfortunately, Russia had meanwhile mobilized her army on the German and Austrian frontiers. Wilhelm II demanded that the mobilization be retracted; when it was not, he declared war on Russia. An alliance of 1894 that the French had entered into with Russia required that they respond to this hostile act by entering the war. Germany was now confronted, to Wilhelm II's horror, with the specter of a war on two fronts: in the West against France, in the East against Russia.

The strategic plan for such a war, made in the 1890s, called for the swift elimination of France at the outset so that the Germans could then deal with the Russian army, the largest in Europe. Speed was therefore essential in crushing the French. That meant that it would be necessary for the German army to march through Belgium, which was relatively flat in comparison to the mountainous terrain on the Franco-German frontier. Belgium, however, was protected by an international treaty signed in 1831 that proclaimed that it would forever be neutral and that no foreign army would ever put foot on its soil. Germany proposed now to violate this treaty, which it did on August 1, 1914, in sending its army into Belgium en route to France. Great Britain, a signatory of the 1831 treaty, now declared war on Germany for having violated international law. The World War had begun.

Kaiser Wilhelm II's role in the conflict was of limited importance. Although he insisted on being consulted, Wilhelm left most decisions to his generals. From the beginning, the war did not go well for Germany. Her great battle fleet, bottled in port by Britain's Royal Navy, proved useless. The attempt to deliver a swift blow to the French failed, and hostilities in the West degenerated into a costly trench warfare that had neither victor nor vanquished. In the East, German troops pressed deep into Russia but never succeeded in forcing Tsar Nicholas II to make peace.

It was only in March 1918, after Nicholas had been removed from the throne and a socialist government established under **Lenin,** that peace with Russia, now the Union of Socialist Soviet Republics, was made. By then it was too late. At home, the German people had become thoroughly dismayed by a war that apparently could not be won and that had exposed them to terrible loss and hardship, a war which they blamed on the incompetence of Wilhelm II and his advisors. More and more demands for a renovation of the Empire into a constitutional monarchy were heard. Then in April 1917, the United States, angered by the sinking of its ships by German submarines, entered the war and began sending troops to reinforce the French and the British. In March 1918, the Germans began one last mighty attempt to break through the Allied defenses in the West. In spite of initial success it ended in failure. The chief of the General Staff, Field Marshal **Paul von Hindenburg,** in September 1918 advised Wilhelm II that the war could not be won and that Germany would have to accept whatever terms the Allied powers were prepared to grant.

By this time, the Allies, certain that victory would be theirs, refused to deal with a German government headed by Wilhelm II. The only path to peace lay in his abdication, but this the kaiser refused to do. He remained in his military headquarters at Spa in Belgium as the situation deteriorated around him. Meanwhile, at the beginning of November 1918, a revolution calling for the establishment of a republic broke out in Germany, and on November 9, 1918, Wilhelm II's government surrendered its powers to a group of socialists, who proclaimed the establishment of a republic. The kaiser, finally aware that all was lost, abdicated and implored his friend, Queen **Wilhelmina** of the Netherlands, to grant him exile in Holland. This she did, and Wilhelm never returned to Germany.

Although the kaiser lived for another 20-odd years, he was a pathetic, inconsequential figure, ignored by Germans and Europeans and revealed in the publication of memoirs and official documents as a ruler of extraordinary ineptitude. Wilhelm himself was unforgiving, accusing his former subjects of ingratitude and attributing the fall of his empire to anyone other than himself. It was Jews, or Bolsheviks, or his English relatives who had hounded him to defeat. Insulated by his unreasoning confidence in his own ability, Wilhelm II, the ex-kaiser, lived on for years in remarkable serenity for a man who had lost his throne and led a once great nation into ruin. He finally died, aged 82, in the summer of 1941, pleased that **Adolf Hitler** had the summer before won the great victory over France that he himself had failed to accomplish in 1914.

SOURCES:

Cecil, Lamar. *Wilhelm II, Prince and Kaiser, 1888–1918.* University of North Carolina Press, 1989.

Hull, Isabel G. *The Entourage of Kaiser Wilhelm II, 1888–1918.* Cambridge University Press, 1982.

Röhl, John C. G., and Nicolaus Sombart, eds. *Kaiser Wilhelm II, New Interpretations: the Corfu Papers.* Cambridge University Press, 1982.

FURTHER READING:

Balfour, Michael. *The Kaiser and his Times.* Cresset Press, 1964.

Lerman, Katherine Anne. *The Chancellor as Courtier.* Cambridge University Press, 1990.

Wilhelmina

(1880–1962)

Fiercely patriotic and devoutly religious monarch who became the living symbol of her country in the first half of the 20th century, especially in epitomizing Dutch resistance to German occupation during World War II.

"Queen Wilhelmina... has, as I see it, two important achievements to her name. In 1940, she saved the [Netherlands'] reputation; and if now,... the monarch is still seen as a healthy and stabilizing element in society, no one made a greater contribution to that view than Queen Wilhelmina."

LOUIS DE JONG

Born into the calm and regal world of European royalty in the second half of the 19th century, Wilhelmina of the Netherlands came to symbolize both her country's hopes for peace and her countrymen's fierce love of freedom, during the turbulent and savage years of the first half of the 20th century.

Throughout two world wars, a German occupation of her country, and the decline and fall of her country's colonial empire, this deeply religious woman insisted that decency and commonsense morality should govern diplomacy between nations. She was one of the first world leaders to condemn Nazi treatment of European Jews, arguing that "this inhuman treatment is something being done to us personally."

Born on August 31, 1880, Wilhelmina's earliest memories concerned horses. She declared that she had a "very vivid recollection of my wild joy and excitement at the prospect of having my own Shetland ponies." Her father William III, king of the Netherlands, died when she was 18, and his funeral left her with another vivid memory: she had to walk with her father's coffin in the funeral procession, face covered with a veil. The task left

Contributed by Niles Holt, Professor of History, Illinois State University, Normal-Bloomington, Illinois

Pronunciation: Will-hell-MEE-nah. Born Wilhelmina Helene Pauline Maria on August 31, 1880, at The Hague, the Netherlands; died on November 28, 1962, at Het Loo, the Netherlands; daughter of William III (king of the Netherlands and Grand Duke of Luxembourg) and Emma of Waldeck; married: Duke Hendrik van Mecklenburg, February 7, 1901; children: (daughter) Juliana. Predecessor: William III. Successor: Juliana.

her with a headache and "nervous stomach." Her mother Emma of Waldeck, a widow at age 40, became regent until Wilhelmina assumed the full powers of the throne, at age 18.

The new queen was pleased when a congress of European feminists, meeting at The Hague, honored her accession to the throne. But her own early life followed traditional rules: she saw her husband only a few times before they were wed, and the marriage was arranged by her family, particularly her grandmother.

Wilhelmina proved to be a serious and demanding monarch, much in the mold of Queen **Victoria** of England. She loved to catch her ministers in mistakes, and they were warned that "she never attaches her signature onto documents until she reads every word and knows every point involved." When a worker in a mill corrected her when she said that the mill produced wool cloth (instead of cotton), the worker was later berated by Wilhelmina's aides; the queen's word, he was told, was not to be challenged.

During the late 19th and early 20th centuries, The Hague was the site of two conferences seeking world peace and universal disarmament. Wilhelmina favored pacifism for religious reasons; she once expressed a desire to participate in missionary work, which, she said, "much more closely relates to my own spiritual experience." Although she supported the peace conferences, she later admitted that she "had not imagined the extent to which these agreements would be ignored in the future."

Although she was a monarch in name, Wilhelmina was not, in her view, a monarch in fact. Her family, the House of Orange, had fought heroically three centuries before to free the Netherlands from Spanish rule. Since that time, members of the House of Orange had held the office of *Stadtholder,* which commanded the armed forces. In 1815, when a diplomatic conference (the Congress of Vienna) combined Belgium and the Netherlands, the House of Orange was made the royal family over this joint realm (although Belgium gained its independence in 1830). The monarchy became a symbol of Dutch national unity; as a republican monarchy, its kings and queens were *inaugurated* but not crowned.

Wilhelmina Takes Oath as Constitutional Monarch

At her *inauguration,* Wilhelmina had taken an oath to be a constitutional monarch—to function in a way that would preserve the "precious rights and liberties of the Dutch people." She took the oath very seriously. As monarch, Wilhelmina could speak—she could attempt to persuade—but she was required to sign documents presented to her by the national parliament, the States-General. When socialists attacked her as a useless symbol, she was deeply offended. She generally found politicians timid and all too calculating; the sole politician with whom she maintained a good relationship was the prime minister during World War I, a former college professor who valued her opinion and consulted her often.

When Holland declared itself neutral during World War I, Wilhelmina had no role in that decision, but she agreed with it and supported it. She insisted that neutralism was not an easy path. "One should try," she wrote, "to imagine how difficult it is to maintain this attitude for more than 40 years!" Together with the United States, the Netherlands claimed the right, as neutrals, to conduct trade with both sides. At the same time, the Netherlands also established camps to aid refugees from Belgium, a neutral country which had been invaded by the German army on its way into France in 1914.

Neutrality involved the Dutch in constant bickering with both Germany, which on several occasions claimed the right to march its armies across Dutch land, and Britain, which claimed the right to search Dutch ships for any war materials bound for Germany. When rumors circulated that her country would be drawn into the war, Wilhelmina took a very public walk from her palace to her mother's home, some distance away. The public "correctly concluded from this that I had absolutely nothing to do and that the rumors were completely unfounded."

Although the entry of the United States into World War I hurt Dutch interests by removing a major neutral power from the world scene, Wilhelmina took an optimistic tone, noting that the "completely fresh and excellently equipped Americans" might save lives by shortening the war.

She was no admirer of **Wilhelm II,** the emperor of Germany; she remembered the sight of Belgian refugees fleeing the German invasion of their country. When, at the end of the war, the emperor sought asylum in her country, she believed that her country could not refuse. "I was called one November morning with the news that the Kaiser had crossed our frontier," she wrote. "I was astonished."

Disappointed that it was not a humanitarian gesture (done with the idea of saving soldiers' lives by abruptly ending the war), she also knew that her country would be criticized for giving sanctuary to him. She argued that the Allies did not really want to capture him—and have to deal with the sticky question of a war crimes trial—and that the Dutch solution was the best for all concerned. Of the emperor, who spent much of his time gardening and growing tulips in the Netherlands until his death more than 20 years later, she noted, "Can any man have devised a punishment more humiliating than that which befell Wilhelm of Hohenzollern?"

Wilhelmina watched the approach of World War II with undisguised impatience. She regarded **Adolf Hitler** as a brutal upstart, and she stood by uneasily as the Dutch cabinet debated the possibility of reaching an understanding with him. Referring to *Mein Kampf,* she warned her subjects that neutrality might not last forever, since "Hitler has written a book, and the contents might be of some consequence."

When German troops crossed the Dutch frontier in May 1940, Wilhelmina was 60 years old. In an attempt to capture her and the leaders of Holland's cabinet, German paratroopers landed near The Hague. But Wilhelmina evaded them by changing her residence, then boarding a British destroyer. She hoped that the British would be able to transport her to southwestern Belgium, where the Belgian royal family had hidden during World War I. Informed that the destroyer could not reach the desired area, she accepted advice to seek refuge in Great Britain. And then she wept.

She sent her daughter Juliana and her granddaughters to Canada—an allied country—so that "in the case of my death [Juliana] would be able to exercise the power of her throne." Wilhelmina remained behind in Britain throughout the war, regularly speaking to her occupied country by radio. Her cabinet had belatedly made its way to Britain as well. But she was convinced that she embodied the spirit of the Netherlands better than her cabinet. When her prime minister again mentioned trying to reach an understanding with Hitler, she successfully maneuvered to have him replaced.

She Symbolizes Dutch Resistance to Occupation

The next five years were difficult ones. She had been raised in an atmosphere of royal isolation, and now she had become a very public figure, the very symbol of Dutch resistance to German occupation. "My conviction that it was necessary to keep my head cool under all circumstances," she wrote, "led me to maintain a calm and unmoved exterior." During 1940, when it appeared the German military might launch an invasion of the British Isles, she ordered her secretary to shoot her if it ever appeared that she might be captured. She remained calm even when her cottage was bombed by German planes—whether by a coincidence, or deliberately, she could not tell—and two of her guards were killed. She not only survived, but led the search for others in the building.

Her response was defiant. "For the moment," she said in a radio broadcast, "all of our work and thoughts are fused in that single all-embracing effort towards one single goal: to win the struggle that will set us free again." Her "subjects" responded. She became a symbol for the Dutch underground resistance to Nazi rule. Many citizens in the Netherlands began placing the German occupiers' postage stamps in the upper left-hand corner of the envelope, arguing that the upper right-hand corner was reserved for stamps bearing the likeness of Wilhelmina. When German authorities declared in 1940 that Jews would no longer be admitted to the civil service, one half of the country's professors signed a letter of protest. More than 80% of university students refused to sign a statement of loyalty to the Nazi regime.

Wilhelmina fretted that she could not learn enough details about what was happening in her country, although Dutch citizens who escaped to Britain were amazed at how much she knew. Impatient to return to the Netherlands, she lamented that "my life is dominated by endless waiting." She was unhappy that she was "not told any military secrets and could follow developments only from a distance." She was certain, however, that Hitler, by failing to launch a naval invasion of the United Kingdom, was going to lose the war.

By 1942, reports of German atrocities in the Netherlands had reached her. "We could clearly discern," she said, "the intention of the occupying power to destroy our national traditions and institutions by... imprisonments and concentration camps." In her October 1942 radio broadcast, she declared to her people:

> I share wholeheartedly in your indignation at the fate of the our Jewish countrymen and with my whole people, I feel that this inhuman treatment, this systematic extermination of these countrymen who have lived for centuries in our blessed fatherland, is something done to us personally.

In November 1942, she used the radio to tell her country that:

> Liberation means that law and justice will return to our native soil and to all our lives, in short it means the revival of all the liberties with which we were brought up and which are dearer to us than ever before.

By 1943, boarding an airplane for the first time, she began traveling outside Britain. She visited her grandchildren in Canada, as well as President **Franklin Delano Roosevelt** in the United States. Roosevelt became godfather to one of her grandchildren.

When British, Canadian, Free French, and American forces landed in France in June 1944, Wilhelmina made the free Dutch forces and the Dutch resistance part of the allied forces. When the liberation of her country took longer than she had planned, she constantly pressed her advisors for information as to when she might be able to return to the Continent. Overjoyed when that time came, she walked, slowly and proudly, across the border between Belgium and the Netherlands on May 14, 1945. On her face was the sly smile of someone who has triumphed over great challenges.

Although Wilhelmina hoped that, in the postwar era, the monarchy would become the main institution leading the country, her hopes were not fulfilled. She had hoped that the resistance fighters would become her fervent supporters. As much as she was admired, however, the resistance had splintered into too many factions to be able to help her. The age of strong monarchies was over; hers was one of the last monarchies, of any kind, to remain in Europe.

When the specter of a Third World War was raised in 1948—because of tensions over Berlin and a Communist takeover of Czechoslovakia—Wilhelmina decided the time had come to abdicate. On May 12, 1948, she formally turned royal authority over to her daughter Juliana. Wilhelmina later reflected that her 50-year career as queen of the Netherlands had been centered around protecting everything that was admirable and special about her country. "My love for my fatherland," she wrote, "was like a consuming fire, and not only in me; it reflected itself in fires around me.... Anyone who threatened to damage these interests was my personal enemy."

SOURCES:

Barnouw, A. J. *Holland Under Queen Wilhelmina.* Scribner, 1923.

Jong, Louis de. *The Netherlands and Nazi Germany.* Harvard University Press, 1990.

Two Queens: Wilhelmina-Juliana, 1898–1948. New York: Netherlands Information Bureau, 1948.

Wilhelmina of the Netherlands, H. R. H. Princess. *Lonely But Not Alone.* McGraw-Hill, 1960.

FURTHER READING:

Paneth, Philip. *Queen Wilhelmina: Mother of the Netherlands.* London: Alliance Press, 1943.

William the Conqueror

(1027/8–1087)

Illegitimate duke of Normandy, who successfully restored order to his duchy and went on to achieve the 1066 military conquest of Anglo-Saxon England.

"1066: In this year came William and conquered England."

PARKER CHRONICLE

In 1066, the Norman duke William the Bastard became King William the Conqueror by his successful military venture against Anglo-Saxon England. To understand the career of one of the 11th century's leading men, it will be helpful to consult a portrait of his times. William's Normandy was the product of 10th-century Vikings who raided and obtained what is now northern France. By the 11th century, intermarriage with native French had produced a thoroughly blended Norse-French society. Normans—meaning "Northmen" and thereby recalling their Norse origin—were the military strongmen of 11th-century Europe who achieved successful exploits in Sicily, France, and, ultimately, Anglo-Saxon England.

Anglo-Saxon England was, in the 11th century, a dynamic, well-organized society that was nevertheless in the throes of an identity crisis, struggling to decide whether to be part of a northern Scandinavian realm or turn southward and share in the Christian civilization of the Continent. Early in the century, Danish King Canute conquered England. The throne later went to Edward, known as "the Confessor," whose child-

Contributed by Cathy Jorgensen Itnyre, Instructor, College of the Desert, Joshua Tree, California

Name variations: William the Bastard; William, Duke of Normandy; William, King of England. Born 1027 or 1028; died on September 9, 1087; illegitimate son of Duke Robert I of Normandy and Herleve (daughter of a prominent tanner of Falais); became duke of Normandy in 1035; married: Matilda of Flanders, c. 1052; children: (four sons) Robert Curthose, Richard, William Rufus, and Henry; (five or six daughters) Agatha, Constance, Adela, Cecilia, Adeliza(?), and Matilda(?). Predecessor: Duke Robert I of Normandy; King Harold Godwineson of England. Successor: Robert Curthose as duke of Normandy; William Rufus as king of England.

lessness was a significant factor in determining events of the 11th century.

Who was to be Edward's successor? His Norman background and pro-Norman policies made it conceivable that he intended the duke of Normandy to ascend the English throne upon his death; this is the tenor of the Norman contemporary sources. On the other hand, a powerful, native Anglo-Saxon family with strong Norse affiliations, the Godwinesons, considered themselves to be the rightful successors and challenged the Norman claim to the English throne. Thus, tension between Anglo-Scandinavian and Anglo-Norman parties characterized the entire first half of the 11th century, setting the stage for William's decisive moment in 1066.

William the Bastard was born in 1027 or 1028, the illegitimate son of Duke Robert I of Normandy and Herleve, daughter of a prominent tanner of Falais. Though Robert and Herleve never married, they produced a daughter, Adelaide, in addition to William. As Frank Barlow, one of William's prominent biographers, has pointed out: although such illicit relationships were common in the 11th century, William was not accepted by the social hierarchy without reprobation. His father Duke Robert married off his lover Herleve to a powerful vicomte, Herlwis of Conteville, and their marriage produced two half-brothers for William, Odo and Robert—both of whom would play important roles in William's later life. Duke Robert married the Danish King Canute's sister, but this marriage failed to produce any heirs; thus, when Robert decided to go on pilgrimage to Jerusalem in 1035, he convinced his nobles to accept the illegitimate William as his successor. To strengthen William's case, Robert obtained the support of his feudal overlord, King Henry I of France.

At 15, William Is Knighted

Robert died on the return journey from Jerusalem. His son William was then a boy of only seven or eight, and the political reality of rule by a minor was harsh: the Norman nobles expected, and got, a period of anarchy that lasted for at least the next nine years. The two guardians appointed over William both died violent deaths, and the duchy was subjected to ceaseless violence. But William's knighting in 1042 marked a turning point in favor of a strong ducal power; the 15-year-old William determined to play a more prominent role in Norman affairs.

At the time of his knighting, William was typical of the feudal leaders of his day: he was illiterate and trained almost exclusively in warfare. Yet he also understood the necessity of securing strong allies, and this awareness served him well throughout his early manhood. In 1046, he survived a strong rebellion by appealing to his feudal overlord King Henry I of France for assistance, and the two cooperated again in the 1051 venture against the powerful count of Anjou, Geoffrey Martel, against whom William's bravery and skill in battle were amply attested. (It is interesting to note that relations between William and his feudal overlord Henry I soured as William's power grew throughout the 1050s.) Though the Norman town of Alencon had supported Geoffrey Martel, he was forced to flee the city because of William's siege. During the siege, the townspeople had taunted William, hanging hides from the town walls inscribed with the insult "Hides for the tanner!" To avenge the slur on his mother's family, William savaged Alencon and mutilated many of its prominent citizens. Thus, he built a reputation for bravery and tenacity and was clearly a ruler to be feared.

William's talent for courting assistance from strong allies was exhibited in his 1049 marriage negotiations. He sought Matilda, daughter of the influential count Baldwin V of Flanders, who was also a great ally of King Henry I. But Pope Leo IX forbade the marriage on the grounds that the pair were too closely related. It is likely, however, that other considerations lay behind the papal ban: for Pope Leo IX was the supporter of the Holy Roman Emperor Henry III, who was at odds with Baldwin and Henry I of France. Despite the ban, the marriage between William and the tiny Matilda—who apparently stood only four feet tall—took place in 1052 or 1053.

They produced many children: four sons and at least five or six daughters. Interestingly, there is no evidence that William had children outside the marriage; perhaps he was too sensitive to his own precarious position as "the Bastard." The Norman sources are unanimous in deeming this a happy marriage, although the Scandinavian *King Harald's Saga* implies that William ultimately kicked Matilda to death. Indeed, William's physical stature stood in great contrast to Matilda's. According to a monk of Caen who wrote soon after William's death in 1087: "He was great in body and strong, tall in stature but not ungainly."

Having fought campaigns to bring the rebellious Norman nobles under control, and strengthened by marriage to the Count of Flanders's daughter, by the early 1060s William had established himself in Western Europe as a power with which to be reckoned. Other factors, too, enhanced his position, such as the deaths of important opponents. For example, in 1060, King Henry I of France died, and William profited from the anarchy that accompanied the accession of the minor Philip I. William's enemy Geoffrey Martel, the count of Anjou, also died in 1060, allowing William to take advantage of the weakness of the new Angevin count by conquering Maine.

In addition, William's generally favorable relationship with the Church strengthened his position. He sought and received ecclesiastical support by way of his donations and by the appointment of his own family members to important ecclesiastical sees. For example, his half-brother Odo, still in his teens, was made bishop of Bayeux in 1049. Indeed, William's close ties to the Church paid off: in 1066, during the crisis initiated by the death of King Edward the Confessor, William received papal support for his invasion of England.

When Edward the Confessor died in early January of 1066, Earl Harold Godwineson was elected king by the English *witan,* or council. Writing after the event, Norman chroniclers strongly upheld William's claim to the English throne, based on his distant family ties (William was Edward's mother's great-nephew) and on a promise that Edward supposedly made to William back in 1051. In fact, one version of the *Anglo-Saxon Chronicle* has William visiting Edward in England that year: "Then soon came duke William from beyond the sea with a great retinue of Frenchmen, and the king received him... and let him go again."

Harold Godwineson would not enjoy England's throne for long. He spent the summer preparing for the anticipated confrontation with William, but, when William's attack had not materialized by September, Harold felt free to send his army home. Learning that the colorful king of Norway, **Harald Hardraade,** had landed in the north, the English Harold hastily reassembled an army and moved north to engage. Though the English Harold defeated the Norwegian Harald at the battle of Stamford Bridge in Yorkshire, he received word shortly thereafter that the Norman landings in England had begun. Harold pushed his already exhausted army southward to meet the new threat.

William Conquers English at Hastings

On September 28, 1066, William landed an army of perhaps 7,000 men at Pevensey in southern England and occupied Hastings the next day. True, by the time Harold reached the Norman force his troops probably numbered slightly more than 7,000, but they were worn out by the recent battle at Stamford Bridge and the subsequent movement south. When the battle at Hastings commenced on October 14, William defeated the English by effectively employing archers and cavalry against the English infantry. During the battle, which is vividly portrayed in the famous Bayeux Tapestry (probably produced for Bishop Odo), Harold was killed. One version of the *Anglo-Saxon Chronicle* describes the battle as follows:

> As soon as his [William's] men were fit for service, they constructed a castle at Hastings. When King Harold was informed of this, he gathered together a great host, and came to oppose him at the grey apple tree, and William came upon him unexpectedly before his army was set in order. Nevertheless the King fought against him most resolutely with those men who wished to stand by him, and there was great slaughter on both sides. King Harold was slain... and many good men. The French had possession of the place of slaughter, as God granted them because of the nation's sins.

Again according to the *Anglo-Saxon Chronicle,* several of the earls and bishops of England "submitted from force of circumstances... they gave him hostages and swore oaths of fealty, and he promised to be a gracious lord to them." On Christmas day, 1066, William was crowned king of the English by Archbishop Ealdred of Canterbury. But disturbances continued throughout the realm, and William's power was far from secure.

Although the most serious challenges to his power occurred between 1066 and 1071, the years 1075, 1078, and 1083 all witnessed revolts against William. The 1078 rebellion is noteworthy because its leading figure was Robert Curthose—William's eldest son. (Robert was reconciled to his father in 1079 but attempted another rebellion in

1083, and the two were never in accord after that.) William's brother Odo quarreled with the king in 1082, resulting in Odo's imprisonment until after William's death.

These persistent rebellions illustrate a significant feature of William's rule as duke of Normandy and king of England. His possessions in England and continental Europe were never secure from attack. For instance, King Philip I of France, who wished to separate Normandy from England, encouraged Robert Curthose in his 1078 revolt. While William fought his son in France in 1079, King Malcolm of Scotland raided northern England. In addition, the loyalty of Maine, conquered by William in 1063, remained a constant problem for him in the post-Conquest years. Thus, threats to William's continental possessions often necessitated the king's absence from England, and the kingdom's wealth was used to finance expeditions in defense of Normandy and other French possessions.

Such turmoil provided the context for several measures that characterized William's style of rule. First, he used earls— enfeoffed with land to support their military obligations—to maintain security at his borders. Next, he insisted that such armies support the king's interests alone, rather than the private interests of the local leaders. We can see from the *Domesday Book,* commissioned in 1085 and carried out in 1086, the extent to which William altered the landholding patterns of England's nobility. William is listed, of course, as the major landholder of England, followed by his brother Odo. The *Domesday* survey was initiated to determine the taxable potentiality of England. According to the *Anglo-Saxon Chronicle*:

> [William] sent his men all over England... to ascertain how many hundreds of "hides" of land there were in each shire, and how much land and live-stock the king himself owned in the country, and what the annual dues were lawfully his from each shire. He also had it recorded how much land his archbishops had, and his diocesan bishops, his abbots and his earls, and... what or how much each man who was a landholder here in England had in land or in live-stock.... So very thoroughly did he have the inquiry carried out that there was not a single "hide"... not even one ox, nor one cow, nor one pig which escaped notice in his survey.

England's nobility was altered by William's placement of military obligations on land grants to vassals and by his elevation of Norman families to high positions in England. Private armies were forbidden; castle building became a royal prerogative: such measures underscored William's ultimate feudal control over his kingdom. Indeed, William would remain an active military figure until his death.

Norman chroniclers record that in his later years William became obese. Specifically, he developed a large belly. The chronicler William of Malmesbury stated that King Philip I of France compared William to a pregnant woman about to give birth. During one of William's campaigns in the summer of 1087, he injured his abdomen on the pommel of his saddle, and, either through this injury or by some concurrent illness, became mortally ill.

The 60-year-old king lingered in great pain for over a month. The events of his death are given in two Norman chronicles. From the anonymous monk of Caen, we learn of the bequests that William made to the Church and to the poor, and of his plans for his sons to succeed him. Robert Curthose was acknowledged as duke of Normandy; William Rufus was to be heir to the English throne; and the youngest surviving son, Henry, was to receive 5,000 pounds of silver. According to Orderic Vitalis, who wrote half a century after William's death, the king sent William Rufus to England to lessen the likelihood of anarchy following his death; Henry immediately went off to supervise the collection of his inheritance; and Robert Curthose—estranged from his father since Matilda's death and his own revolt in 1083—was not present at William's deathbed. On September 9, 1087, William the Conqueror died alone.

Immediately following his death, Norman nobles fled to their estates, fearing that violence would threaten their holdings. According to the Norman chroniclers, preparations were made to transport the body to Saint Stephen's monastery in Caen for burial, but when the funeral mass was held, William's swollen corpse was too large for the tomb. In the struggle to fit the body into the stone sarcophagus, the pallbearers broke the corpse, and the entire church was filled with the odor of decomposition. As Orderic Vitalis poignantly implied, such was a sad final chapter in the life of such a strong, shrewd, and effective leader.

SOURCES:

The Anglo-Saxon Chronicle. Translated by G.N. Garmonsway. J. M. Dent, 1953.

English Historical Documents, Volume II (1042–1189). Edited by D.C. Douglas and G.W. Greenaway. London, 1953.

FURTHER READING:

Barlow, Frank. *William I and the Norman Conquest.* Collier Books, 1965.

Douglas, David C. *William the Conqueror.* University of California Press, 1967.

Finn, R. Welldon. *An Introduction to Domesday Book.* Longmans, 1963.

William the Silent

(1533–1584)

Prince of Orange, count of Nassau, who was the spiritual, diplomatic, and military leader of the Dutch people in their revolt against Habsburg rule and Spain.

Name variations: William of Orange, Prince of Orange, Count of Nassau. Born on April 24, 1533, in Dillenburg, Nassau; died on July 10, 1584, at the Delft in Holland; son of Count William of Nassau-Dillenburg and Countess Juliana of Stolberg-Wernigrode; married: Countess Anne of Egmont; married: Anne of Saxony; married: Charlotte of Bourbon-Montpensier; married: Louise de Coligny; children: (first marriage) Philip William; (illegitimate after first marriage) Marie and Justin of Nassau; (second marriage) Emilie and Maurice of Nassau; (third marriage) Louise Juliana, Elizabeth, Catherine Belgica, Brabantina, Flanderina and Antwerpina; (fourth marriage) Frederick Henry. Descendants: William III of Orange, King of England. Predecessors: Henry and Rene de Chalon, Princes of Orange, and Count William of Nassau. Successor: Maurice of Nassau.

William the Silent was the very embodiment of the Dutch Revolt against Spanish rule in the 16th century. A tolerant man, born to a high station, William at first advised compromise but later actively led the rebellion. While not a military leader of the first rank, the prince of Orange was blessed with a charisma rarely found and was loved by the diverse population of the Netherlands. It was William alone who was able to gain succor from the Great Powers for the Dutch cause, and thus to sustain it in its darkest moments.

William was born at Dillenburg in the German principality of Nassau on April 24, 1533; his father was Count William of Nassau; his mother was the Countess of Stolberg. William was originally raised as a Lutheran and inherited the territories of Orange and Nassau at the age of 11 when Rene de Chalon, Seigneur of Orange, was killed in 1544. Because of the importance of the inheritance, **Charles V,** the Habsburg Holy Roman Emperor and king of Spain, then insisted that young William of Nassau—now prince of Orange—be raised as a Catholic.

"It was a strange, almost unique thing, to be the idol of a nation and remain uncorrupted, to be oneself the guardian of the people's rights sometimes against the emotional impulse of the people themselves."

C.V. WEDGEWOOD

Contributed by Glenn Feldman, Ph.D. candidate in History, Auburn University, Auburn, Alabama

Moving to Breda and then Brussels, William was raised at the court of Mary of Hungary, the regent of the Low Countries. A German by birth, he was taught French and Dutch and readily adopted the customs of the Dutch people. The teachings of the Christian humanist, Erasmus of Rotterdam, held particular significance for the young heir and later played a large part in the religious toleration for which William was renowned.

At the age of 18, William married Countess Anne of Egmont, gaining several additional territories in the Netherlands. As one of the most powerful magnates in Europe, he enjoyed considerable favor at the court of Charles V in Brussels. Upon Charles's abdication in 1556, William continued to enjoy prestige under the Habsburg's son and successor, **Philip II.**

In 1559, when the fourth and final Habsburg-Valois War was concluded between Spain and France, and the Treaty of Cateau-Cambrésis ended over 60 years of internecine strife over Italy by firmly cementing Spanish hegemony (dominance), Philip appointed the prince of Orange, the violent duke of Alva, and Bishop Granville of Arras as his deputies to the historic treaty negotiations.

Other honors soon followed. The Spanish sovereign named William to his prestigious Council of State and the Order of the Golden Fleece; the king also agreed to become the godfather of Orange's first son, fittingly named Philip William. In 1561, Philip made Orange his *stadholder* (governor and captain-general) in the important provinces of Holland, Zeeland, Utrecht, and Franche-Comté.

Soon after this appointment serious dissension arose in the Netherlands over Philip's rule. Two issues were of paramount importance: religion and the king's rigid absolutism. The Spanish monarch's rule contrasted sharply with the relative independence allowed the Dutch nobles under Charles V. Philip, confronted by both discontent among the magnates and the clash between Catholicism and Calvinism, remained rigidly uncompromising on both issues. Opposition soon crystallized around the person of Granville, now a cardinal. It was generally believed that Granville held an inordinate amount of influence at the court of the Dutch regent, Margaret of Parma. William himself bordered on open defiance during an impassioned address in the Council of State, in which he challenged the right of any ruler to control the religious conscience of his subjects.

By 1565, leadership of the Dutch opposition had been assumed by a cadre of lesser nobles, called the *Gueux* or Beggars. This group, unlike the great

CHRONOLOGY

1544	Inherited the territories of Nassau and Orange
1559	Appointed a Spanish deputy by Philip II at the Treaty of Cateau-Cambrésis
1561	Named as a stadholder in the Netherlands
1566	Revolt of the Netherlands began
1567	Retired to his estates at Dillenburg and earned the nickname "the Silent"
1568	Began first campaigns against the Spanish crown; lost battles to the Duke of Alva
1573	Converted to the Calvinist faith
1576	Wrote and passed the Pacification of Ghent
1578–84	Unsuccessfully opposed the Duke of Parma
1579	Organized the northern territories as the United Provinces
1581	Persuaded the States to accept the Duke of Anjou (Alencon) as the protector of the Dutch
1584	Assassinated at his home on the Delft

nobles, was less settled, more Calvinist and more inclined toward violence as a possible solution for their grievances. While most of the greater lords quickly divorced themselves from the more radical *Gueux,* William retained his ties to them. His brother, Count Louis of Nassau, was a prominent personality among them. Though openly connected to the *Gueux,* the Prince of Orange counselled religious toleration and non-violence:

> I am no Calvinist but it seems to me neither right, nor worthy of a Christian to seek, for the sake of [religious] differences... to have this land swarming with troops and inundated with blood.... [T]here must be a compromise.... A very large part of our people have embraced the new [religious] views, and rather than forsake them they will give up their lives and homes.

Despite William's pleas for temperance, open revolt against Spain erupted in August 1566. The first stage of the rebellion featured iconoclastic violence on a large scale. Frenzied Calvinist mobs sacked Catholic churches throughout the provinces, smashing religious idols and vandalizing church property. King Philip responded by summoning the duke of Alva to crush the revolt. William himself quelled a Calvinist riot in

Antwerp, Europe's richest city. He then closed the city's gates and denied access to both the rebels and the royalist forces. In 1567, William withdrew to his family's estates at Dillenburg, and there gained his famous sobriquet "the Silent" for his guarded neutrality.

Alva's reign was marked by military victories but also by a repression of epic proportions. The Spanish general instituted a Council of Troubles, aptly dubbed the "Council of Blood," to arrest, try, and execute religious "heretics." The executions of rebel leaders—the counts of Egmont and van Hoorne—did little to quash the revolt but went far toward fomenting a more rigid defiance of Philip. These executions, along with perhaps 12,000 others, effectively etched the duke of Alva's name in blood in the annals of European history.

William Defends His Conduct

William responded to Alva's summons to appear before the Council of Troubles with an emotional defense of his conduct entitled the *Justification*. Despite his nickname, William was anything but silent and timorous. Alva responded by confiscating the Dutch lord's possessions and deporting one of William's sons to Spain. This harsh treatment pushed the prince of Orange irrevocably to life as a rebel, and forever altered the complexion of the Revolt of the Netherlands.

William, through his family's name and connections, raised an army and marched on the Low Countries in the spring of 1568. Alva, a far superior general, met and crushed William's forces at the Ems River and forced his Brabant campaign to be aborted. The prince of Orange then fled to sanctuary in a Huguenot region of France. Though he despised the excesses and rigidity of Calvinist fanaticism, William gradually came to realize that Calvanism afforded the only possible route to French, German, and English aid, and the only chance of actually winning the revolt. In 1572, he succeeded in convincing Queen **Elizabeth** of England to send troops and money to help the Dutch Protestant rebels.

The period was an especially dark one for William. His son was being held in Spain, a brother had been killed in the fighting, and Alva appeared to be invincible. To make matters worse, William's second wife Anne of Saxony was causing him constant distress through her "poor, deranged, deluded and unhappy" behavior. Defying him publicly, denying him access to his children, Anne tormented the Dutch lord. She eventually had an affair with an older German lawyer in the Rhineland. When it was discovered, Anne confessed her part and pleaded that William kill both her and her lover; the lawyer asked only that he be beheaded like a gentleman. But Orange was "notoriously compassionate" in an age that was often barbaric. "Fugitives had an odd way of evading his grasp, he rarely inflicted capital sentences and was sickened by torture." It was a "strange contradiction," one of his biographers has written, that "his softer qualities" pushed him "inevitably towards the lonely, hard and dangerous part of a national saviour." William quietly divorced Anne and pardoned the lawyer.

April 1572 brought a reprieve from his private agony. News arrived of an independent, surprise attack by the Beggars on Breille that had been successful. Calvinist Holland and Zeeland immediately declared their part in the rebellion and called for the prince of Orange to lead them. In accepting leadership, William insisted upon equal protection for both the Catholic and the Calvinist faiths.

Louis of Nassau invaded the southeastern provinces at Mons and Alva rushed to confront him. William meanwhile marched virtually uncontested into the Brabant and captured several strategic towns. But, by the fall of 1572, Alva had overcome both brothers at Mons. The prince of Orange, "utterly crushed... even now would not give way to despair." Instead, he moved to the northern provinces to reorganize his forces.

Philip, repelled by Alva's brutality and threatened by his success, recalled him in 1573. William formally became a Calvinist, though he objected to the rigidity of the Calvinist provinces in declaring Catholicism illegal. At Nijmegen in 1574, Alva's successor inflicted a humiliating defeat on the Dutch rebels.

Pacification of Ghent Is Accepted

In 1576, the death of Spain's governor-general in the Netherlands granted a brief respite to the embattled rebels. William leapt into the temporary power vacuum, took control of the States-General, and, on November 8, 1576, arranged to have the Pacification of Ghent, calling for a union of the 17 disparate provinces of the Netherlands and for religious moderation, accepted.

Philip installed his half-brother—the hero of Lepanto, Don **John of Austria**—as the new ruler in the Low Countries. Preoccupied by grandiose visions of an English invasion and marriage to Catholic Mary Stuart, Don John was not overly concerned with suppressing the revolt. Nevertheless, he did enjoy military success at William's expense until his efforts bogged down due to inadequate military and financial support. Upon Don John's death in 1578, **Alessandro Farnese,** the duke of Parma, stepped into the problematic role of governor-general of the provinces.

While the Spanish offensive to 1578 had been tactically successful, it had the unforeseen effect of helping William to consolidate his diverse bases of support. In Farnese, William finally found a match for his own considerable political skill. The duke of Parma was every bit as gifted a diplomat as William and the best soldier in Europe.

Farnese spent 1578 subduing the French-speaking southern provinces. In May 1579, he outmaneuvered William to conclude the Treaty of Arras, which united the southern provinces under Spanish rule and Catholicism in return for some royal concessions. In late June, Farnese inflicted a severe blow to William's military prestige by completing the siege of the powerful town of Maastricht.

The prince of Orange countered by agreeing to the Union of Utrecht and creating the United Provinces based on the Calvinist faith. The move, although a unification of sorts, finally acknowledged William's failure to unite all of the Dutch provinces. In growing desperation, he turned to Alencon, the duke of Anjou, Henry III's brother and the last Valois heir to the French throne.

In 1580, Farnese embarked on a brilliant offensive that resulted in the capture of over 30 rebel towns and the successful siege of Antwerp, and brought Holland and Zeeland to the brink of defeat. On March 15, Philip issued a royal proclamation condemning the prince of Orange as an outlaw and the primary source of trouble in the Netherlands. In biting language the Spanish king blamed "this wicked hipocrite... [who] by his sinister practices, devises and crafts... has bin the head, author and promoter of these troubles." Philip also branded William as "the publick plague of Christendome" and pledged a reward of "good land or readie money [25,000 ducats]" for the deliverance of Orange "unto us quicke or dead."

In a caustic but "elegant piece of propaganda," William responded by accusing Philip of incest, adultery, and the murder of his son and third wife Elizabeth of Valois. Orange also blasted the "mischiefs and calamities... murthers and slaughters... crueltie and barbarousnesse... rage [and] abomnable enterprises" of these "bloodie people, vermin... [and] miserable wretches." William's *Apologie* burned him indelibly into the collective consciousness of the Dutch people as the very personification of their struggle.

Yet only adversity awaited William the Silent. Alencon's Catholic troops were "both unsuccessful and unpopular" as Farnese consistently outfought them. To make matters worse, in July 1583, Alencon attempted to seize Antwerp in a coup d'état. The Dutch rose to crush this "French Fury" by killing 2,000 Frenchmen and taking 1,500 prisoner. In desperation, William contracted his fourth marriage, to Louise of the powerful Huguenot family of Coligny.

But even this alliance could not rescue the Dutch in the face of the inexorable advance of Parma. William narrowly avoided an assassination attempt, and in June 1584, was greeted with news that Alencon, the duke of Anjou, had died. Then, on July 10, a fanatical Catholic assassin shot and killed the prince of Orange in his home on the Delft.

Though the revolt continued for another 64 years, and eventually ended in success, no one embodied the struggle like William of Orange. A model of moderation and tolerance in a vortex of religious and political chaos, no ruler has ever been loved more by his people.

While there have certainly been better generals, and arguably better diplomats, there has never been a better leader of men. No one ever adopted the cause of a nation more willingly, with more wisdom and more selflessness, than William. He persisted in the face of adversity, he persevered in spite of great odds, and he lent his name, his energy, and ultimately his person to his chosen cause. Historian C.V. Wedgewood remarked:

> Few statesmen in any period... cared so deeply for the ordinary comfort and trivial happiness of the thousands of individuals who are "the people." He neither idealized nor overestimated them... [b]ut he respected in all men what he wished to have respected in himself, the right to an opinion.... [S]ome men have a quality of greatness which gives their lives universal significance. Such men... exist to shame the cynic, and to renew the faith of humanity in itself. Of this number was William of Nassau, Prince of Orange, called the Silent.

SOURCES:

Harrison, Frederick. *William the Silent.* Kennikat Press, 1970.

Parker, Geoffrey. *The Army of Flanders and the Spanish Road, 1567–1659.* Cambridge University Press, 1912.

———. *The Dutch Revolt.* Cornell University Press, 1977.

Thompson, S. Harrison. *Europe in Renaissance and Reformation.* Harcourt, 1963.

Wansink, H., ed. *The Apologie of Prince William of Orange Against The Proclamation of the King of Spaine.* E. J. Brill, 1969.

Wedgewood, C. V. *William the Silent.* Yale University Press, 1944.

FURTHER READING:

Geyl, Pieter. *The Revolt of the Netherlands, 1555–1609.* Williams and Norgate, 1945.

Putnam, Ruth. *William the Silent, Prince of Orange: The Moderate Man of the Sixteenth Century.* Putnam, 1895.

William III of Orange

(1650–1702)

Stadholder of the United Provinces of the Netherlands, who assisted in the overthrow of King James II, thus becoming, along with his wife Mary, England's first constitutional monarch.

"No office ennobles its possessors."

WILLIAM III OF ORANGE

The second half of Europe's 17th century was dominated by struggles over religious differences and territorial assertions by various heads of state; it was also the "Golden Age" of Dutch culture. These elements were reflected in the life of William III, prince of Orange, stadholder (governor) of the United Provinces of the Netherlands, and king of England, Scotland, and Ireland.

While biographers have tended to consider his childhood and his adult years as separate, loosely-related periods, the connections between the two are as significant as were his family ties with European royalty. Born November 14, 1650 (or, November 4 according to the calendar then in use in England) in The Hague in the United Provinces of the Netherlands, he was the only child of William II, prince of Orange, and Mary Stuart of England. Eight days before his son was born, William II had died of smallpox—the scourge of 17th-century Europe. The infant's paternal grandfather, **William the Silent,** Prince of Orange, had led a Dutch rebellion against Spanish rule and was the founder of the University of Leiden. The infant's mother Mary Stuart was the daughter of Charles I of England and the niece of Elizabeth of Bohemia, the "Winter Queen."

Contributed by Donna Beaudin, Ph.D. candidate in History, University of Guelph, Guelph, Ontario, Canada

Born on November 14, 1650, in The Hague in Holland of the United Provinces of the Netherlands; died at Kensington House palace, London, England, on March 8, 1702; only son and only child of William II, Prince of Orange, and Mary (daughter of Charles I of England); married: Mary Stuart (his cousin; daughter of James II of England); no children. Predecessor: (as elective stadholder of the United Provinces of the Netherlands) William II; (as sovereign of England, Scotland, and Ireland) James II. Successor: (as stadholder) William IV; (as sovereign of Great Britain and Ireland) Anne.

him as petulant, irritable, and often impatient. The standard of his early education and the state of his health remained under constant public scrutiny; as early as age six, he received religious instruction on a daily basis and lessons on secular subjects from his tutor and his governess. Regular church attendance, scripture and psalm reading, and composition of personal prayers were meant to instill rigid self-control and develop an awareness of virtues and vices. By eight, he was preparing for the University of Leiden; his studies included languages (Latin, French, and Dutch), music, writing, history, military strategy, and current politics. This rigorous program was balanced by a requisite amount of fresh air, a simple diet, and exercise—particularly ball games, fencing, hunting, and riding.

William's Mother Dies

The 1660 Restoration of the English monarchy was to have a drastic effect on William's life. The relationship between England and the principality of Orange changed, with the latter becoming more important for diplomatic and dynastic reasons. Foreign diplomats now visited William when they were in The Hague, though he was only ten years old. That same year, William was presented to the city of Amsterdam, and it was agreed that he would be prepared for the offices of stadholder and captain- and admiral-general of the United Provinces. Following this decision, William's mother Mary chose to return to England. When the news reached William in early January of 1661 that his mother—ill with smallpox—had died on Christmas Eve, he was devastated. His health deteriorated and he had to wear a brace to support his back. The death of his mother—the only parent he had known and the prominent figure in his group of guardians—raised the question of guardianship for the second time and was still being debated four years later when William was an independent, withdrawn, headstrong adolescent.

Soon after coming of age, William paid his first visit to England in the winter of 1670–71. This trip lasted nearly four months, during which time he received honorary degrees from two English universities and experienced English court life. But neither the country itself, nor court life at Whitehall, impressed him. The years following his visit to England were busy ones, prompting historian Nesca Robb to record:

> [In the next two years] he was swept suddenly from powerlessness to power, from obscurity to fame. The pattern of his future activities was determined; the public personality that was to

Due to the untimely death of his father, the matter of William's guardianship was seriously debated. It was eventually decided that his mother would be the dominant figure, along with his paternal grandmother and his uncle Friedrich Wilhelm, elector of Brandenburg. William's early years were spent with his mother at the Binnenhof, the family palace of the princes of Orange. While leading a quiet life, partly because the States-General would not increase the amount of Mary's pension, they received frequent visits from William's great-aunt Elizabeth of Bohemia. Within a few years of his birth, calls were heard that William should be made stadholder, or chief magistrate, of the United Provinces. Though he lived in the traditional residence of the stadholders, Binnenhof Palace, the stadholdership was not a hereditary position in the mid-17th century.

William's adult personality emerged early. While in public he was seen as moderate and reserved, those who knew him privately described

hold the eyes of Europe for a generation appeared with all its salient characteristics.

In February 1672, William was made captain- and admiral-general and, in June, he accepted the office of stadholder. These two positions gave him control of the Dutch armed forces and diplomatic direction of the state. Hans Willem Bentinck, once William's page, became his inseparable friend and aide. William's position of leadership and authority was further strengthened in 1673 when the provinces of Holland and Zeeland made him hereditary stadholder. During the Third Dutch War with England and in a separate war with France, both of which had begun in 1672, he was in Robb's words "the incarnate symbol of hope and deliverance" for the Dutch. This assessment was borne out by his conduct on the battlefield where he was severe and displayed considerable personal courage. Henri and Barbara van der Zee write of an August 1674 encounter with the French army in which William:

> discovered something within himself that stamped him for the rest of his life: a passion for battle that was even greater than his love for hunting, and many times stronger than his interest in politics.

This period of intense activity was abruptly checked in April 1675 when he was diagnosed with smallpox. Unlike his parents, he survived the disease after a three-week illness.

Following the 1674 Treaty of Westminster which ended the Third Dutch War, **Charles II** looked to improve relations between England and the United Provinces, but at his own pace. William, meanwhile, began to press his suit to marry his cousin, the king's niece Mary—a proposed union that had been a subject for speculation since 1672. The couple were eventually married in a private ceremony at St. James Palace on November 4, 1677, by the bishop of London. At the ceremony the cousins presented quite a contrast: William had an asthmatic cough, slightly stooped posture, and was only five feet, six and a half inches tall; Mary Stuart, at 16, was 11 years younger than he, was considered darkly attractive by her contemporaries, and at five feet eleven inches was distinctly taller than her husband. In December, they arrived in The Hague to a reception in honor of their marriage and to some criticism that their marriage was a symbol of William's personal ambitions.

While William and Mary's early years together were generally happy ones, they were clouded by Mary's frequent ill health, often psy-chological in origin, and their continuing failure to produce an heir. Coinciding with this phase in William's personal life was the larger issue of the order of succession to the British throne. Throughout the Exclusion Crisis of 1678–81 against James, duke of York, politicians and other advisors tried to persuade William to travel to England and discuss the English succession with King Charles II; by marrying his English cousin, William had improved his position in the line of succession. He went to see Charles in the summer of 1680, but this meeting was unsatisfying to William and relations with Charles cooled.

In 1685, circumstances became more difficult for William. Charles II had died and was succeeded by his brother, the duke of York, as **James II** of England and VII of Scotland. James was not only William's uncle, but he was also Mary's father. Relations between James and William were mistrustful at best; James prorogued (suspended) Parliament indefinitely, and considered his Protestant son-in-law to be an enemy of England. William, meanwhile, believed that England, without Parliament in session, could not be an ally of the United Provinces and was possibly receiving financial support from his long-time enemy, France's Louis XIV. William's personal life was equally unsettled; in autumn 1685, it was revealed that he was having an affair with Elizabeth Villiers. (The affair eventually received court acceptance and lasted more than 15 years.)

As a continental champion of Protestant liberties, William was considered to be a potentially more desirable sovereign than James II. Before the end of June 1688, William was invited to England by a group of dissatisfied politicians who wished him to assist in the maintenance of England's laws and her subjects' religious freedoms. Though ready to accept this invitation, William also realized that he stood a greater chance of becoming king if he physically led the action against James. By assuming the throne of England while retaining the stadholdership of the United Provinces, William reasoned that he could safeguard Dutch diplomatic and commercial interests against English maneuverings. His decision to take an active role in English politics was bolstered by the territorial aggression of Louis XIV. William's role, as it was explained to the Dutch provinces, was to help with the restoration of the reformed religion, but not necessarily to dethrone James II.

William and Mary Reign Together

Personally leading his troops, William arrived in England in the autumn of 1688. As a commander he was famous for maintaining discipline within the Dutch army, an achievement also evident in civilian concerns. His military movements in England were eased by the voluntary departure of James II and his family for France. In late December 1688, William agreed to assume the leadership of the provisional government and to assemble a convention the following month. The subject of discussion at the convention Parliament in January 1689 was to determine who should wear the crown of England. Most Tory politicians and Anglican clergy advocated a combination of James II with a Regency Council, while a smaller group of Tories argued that Mary should be queen since her father had abdicated the throne. Whig politicians, who were dominant in the Convention Parliament proposed William and Mary, singly or jointly, as the new monarchs. The decision eventually reached by the Convention was to offer the crown to them jointly, with administrative authority to be vested in William for the duration of his life. The couple were crowned in April 1689 and promised to govern according to the laws of Parliament and to uphold the Protestant religion. In his *History of England,* Lord Macaulay concluded with respect to the Glorious Revolution:

> For the authority of law, for the security of property, for the peace of his streets, for the happiness of our homes, our gratitude is due, under Him who raises and pulls downs nations at his pleasure, to the Long Parliament, to the Convention, and to William of Orange.

Limitations on the powers of the Crown were introduced by Parliament in the form of the Declaration of Rights. In keeping with his personal religious beliefs, William refused to perform some of the traditional coronation ceremonies which he regarded as "mere superstition."

Only a month after their coronation, William declared England at war with France, a move for which he received considerable criticism in England; he was accused of paying too much heed to Dutch interests. Meanwhile, his Dutch subjects complained that he was defending English interests at the expense of his own countrymen. William was further censured for preferring Dutch company over that of English people, for showing favor to his good friend Bentinck, and for distributing government positions equally between his English and Dutch supporters.

Coincidental with these international developments, William also faced serious domestic challenges. Jacobites (supporters of James II) collided unsuccessfully with William's troops at Killiecrankie (July 1689) and the battle of the Boyne (July 1690). For the most part, William found domestic political affairs less comprehensible and interesting than those on the Continent.

The first years in England were trying for William: his health continued to be poor, he suffered from severe homesickness, and he was frustrated by English politics which he believed sought to limit his authority. Further, relations between William and his old friend Bentinck, now duke of Portland, were in decline. With hopes of repairing his health, William and Mary moved away from Whitehall to Hampton Court, and eventually to Kensington House. In these palaces, they were able to relax while William's personal popularity reached a high point in the autumn of 1690. General anti-Dutch feeling, however, was spreading through the court, London, and the rest of the country.

In 1694, Louis XIV tried to make the English succession an issue in the ongoing war between France and the alliance of European states. Financing the war effort through credit ceased to be a worry with the creation of the Bank of England, but even this development did not ease political tensions concerning the succession. William's health declined again in November, and Mary was diagnosed with smallpox; she died on December 28, 1694, ending joint sovereignty. For months, William appeared inconsolable and his health continued to suffer. The relationship with Elizabeth Villiers was terminated, and William paid tribute to his wife's memory by ordering the completion of her planned conversion of the palace at Greenwich to a naval hospital.

After Mary's death, William became the focus of dynastic and constitutional discussions and actions. A Jacobite plot against him was discovered and dismantled, while a parliamentary bill affirmed and recognized him as king of England. The suggestion was put to William that he should remarry to beget an heir, but the idea failed to appeal. The succession seemed secure with the presence of Mary's sister **Anne** and her son, the duke of Gloucester. Instead, William kept increasingly to himself, and a new favorite, Joost van Keppel (later, earl of Albemarle), became his most frequent companion. While some of his contemporaries tried to accuse William, without success, of homosexuality, Henri and Barbara van der Zees noted "throughout his life William never troubled to justify even his most criticized actions in public."

French King Recognizes William as King of England

Louis XIV finally recognized William as king of England in 1696, which suggested that the War of the Grand Alliance was nearing conclusion. Within four months, warfare on the battlefield had ended and William returned to London for a glorious welcome. Then in 1698, the succession to the Spanish throne appeared to be a volatile situation; William returned to the Continent without conferring with his English political ministers, as was his habit in the arena of foreign affairs. Anti-Dutch feeling was inflamed by such conduct, and he faced severe restrictions from the recently elected members of Parliament, including a reduction in the size of England's army. He interpreted these actions as ingratitude, and only William's strong sense of duty stopped him from abdicating and returning to the United Provinces. In less than ten years, his popularity had plummeted; politicians considered him out of step with the desires of the English people.

In the face of this political hostility, William's health worsened, though he tried to continue with his duties as king and stadholder. He made trips to the Continent, including one undertaken with **John Churchill,** first duke of Marlborough, to familiarize Marlborough with European affairs. Constitutionally, the matter of the succession was in jeopardy again with the July 1700 death of William's nephew, the duke of Gloucester. New arrangements were made by Parliament in the Act of Settlement of 1701, placing the succession after Anne to the Protestant ruling family of Hanover. The issue was complicated by Louis XIV's new support of the pretender Prince of Wales after the death of James II in September 1701.

William's own death on March 8, 1702, was the result of a riding accident, not of a military engagement. Falling from his horse, he broke his collarbone, and the fracture failed to heal properly. He died at Kensington House, one of his favorite English residences; the next day, Anne was proclaimed queen of England. Usually seen as a cold, dour, reserved man, he had been loyal to his close friends, had placed a strong emphasis on moral behavior and home life, and had deeply loved his English bride who had died years before him. Neither an intellectual nor a superior strategist, William was a soldier-king, and one of the last European monarchs to personally lead his troops in battle. His funeral was conducted in accordance with his manner of living, without ostentation. While mourning was more widespread in the United Provinces than in England, the English gradually came to realize that Protestant Europe had looked to William for leadership. As a foreigner, William was never loved or admired by the English people; when Anne was crowned in April 1702, it was proclaimed that England had, at last, a real English monarch.

SOURCES:

Macaulay, Lord. *The History of England.* Abridged. Penguin, 1968 (originally published 1848–61).

Robb, Nesca. *William of Orange.* 2 vols. Heinemann, 1966.

van der Zee, Henri, and Barbara van der Zee. *William and Mary.* London: Macmillan, 1973.

FURTHER READING:

Baxter, Stephen B. *William III and the Defence of European Liberty 1650–1702.* Harcourt, 1966.

Ogg, David. *England in the Reigns of James II and William III.* Clarendon Press, 1963.

Pinkham, Lucile. *William III and the Respectable Revolution.* Archon, 1969.

Harold Wilson

(1916–)

Four-time British prime minister who, as leader of the Labour Party, was one of the most successful politicians of the 20th century.

Name variations: Baron Wilson of Rievaulx. Born James Harold Wilson on March 11, 1916, in Huddersfield, Yorkshire, England; son of James Herbert (an industrial chemist) and Ethel (Seddon) Wilson (a teacher); married: Gladys Mary Baldwin, 1940; children: two sons. Predecessors: Sir Alec Douglas-Home and Edward Heath. Successors: Edward Heath and James Callaghan.

James Harold Wilson was born in Huddersfield, Yorkshire, England, on March 11, 1916. His father James Herbert Wilson was an industrial chemist and his mother Ethel Seddon Wilson had been a school teacher prior to marriage. The Wilsons were Baptists who regularly attended chapel, and young Harold (the James was never used) went to Sunday School and was later active in the Boy Scouts. He attended the Milnsbridge Council School and the Royds Hall Grammar School until his father took another job in Cheshire. Wilson then completed his secondary education at Wirral Grammar School in Bebington, where he played cricket, captained the rugby team, and starred as a long-distance runner. An excellent student, he won an open exhibition scholarship in history to Oxford University.

As an undergraduate at Jesus College, Oxford, Wilson won the Webb-Medley Economic Scholarship, the Gladstone Memorial Prize, and two university essay awards. Disliking the communist influence in the Labour Club, he served on the governing committee of the Liberal Club until his views changed, prompting him to join the Labour Party in 1935. Wilson was a dili-

"There is no more dangerous illusion than the comfortable doctrine that the world owes us a living.... From now on Britain will have just as much influence in the world as we can earn, as we can deserve. We have no accumulated reserves on which to live."

HAROLD WILSON

Contributed by Phillip E. Koerper, Professor of History, Jacksonville State University, Jacksonville, Alabama

gent student whose only relaxation was cross-country running; he graduated in 1937 with first-class honors in economics, philosophy, and politics—the highest academic award available. The same year, at 21, he became a lecturer in economics at New College, Oxford, an extraordinary accomplishment for his age. At New College, Wilson became a research assistant for Lord Beveridge, master of University College and the leading proponent of the British welfare state. In 1938, he became a fellow of University College, where Beveridge described him as the best research student he ever had.

When World War II broke out in 1939, Wilson volunteered for the army but was instead drafted into the civil service. After briefly holding clerical appointments at the Ministry of Supply, the economic section of the Cabinet Secretariat, and as chief of the statistical department of the Mines department, he became director of economics and statistics in the newly created Ministry of Fuel and Power. His experience in the latter position led to his first book, *New Deal for Coal* (1945), which presented his first public argument for industrial nationalization on both practical and theoretical grounds.

In 1940, Wilson married Gladys Mary Baldwin, daughter of a Congregationalist minister, whom he had met six years earlier. With the war over, he had returned to lecturing in economics at University College but had a political career in mind. Selected as a prospective Labour Party candidate in 1944, he was adopted as a contestant for the Ormskirk district in Lancashire. In the 1945 general election, the anti-Labour vote split in Ormskirk, and Wilson easily won the seat by a majority of more than 7,000 votes over the Conservative candidate.

Wilson Takes Seat in House of Commons

Although only 29 years old, Wilson was appointed parliamentary secretary to the Ministry of Works by Labour Prime Minister Clement Attlee. Wilson took his seat in the House of Commons in August 1945; on October 9, he made his maiden speech concerning the terrible conditions in the workplace. Because of his effectiveness in parliamentary procedure and debate, in March 1947 Attlee elevated him to secretary for Overseas Trade. Six months later, at 31, Wilson became the youngest cabinet member in over a century when Attlee promoted him to president of the Board of Trade and also admitted him to membership in the Privy Council.

CHRONOLOGY

1916	Born Huddersfield, Yorkshire, England
1940–43	Economic assistant to the War Cabinet Secretariat
1943–44	Director of economics and statistics at Ministry of Fuel and Power
1945	Elected to Parliament as a Labour candidate for Ormskirk, Lancashire
1945–47	Parliamentary secretary, Ministry of Works
1947	Appointed president of the Board of Trade
1954	Member of parliamentary committee of the Labour Party
1959–63	Chairman, Public Accounts committee of the House of Commons
1963	Leader of Parliamentary Labour Party
1964	Elected prime minister
1970	Resigned as prime minister following the defeat of his Labour Party
1974	Returned as prime minister
1976	Resigned as Party leader and prime minister
1983	Created Life Peer as Baron Wilson of Rievaulx

Wilson's four-year tenure at the Board of Trade coincided with the depressing and dreary postwar years when virtually every product or consumer item was in short supply. His most successful accomplishment was the removal of many controls restricting British production which had been favored by his predecessor, the austere and unpopular Stafford Cripps. Wilson worked hard to increase British exports and proved a tough negotiator with world trade delegations. But because he would not remove wartime rations from many products, he was accused of being a fanatical nationalizer who kept the unpopular controls longer than necessary. In 1949, when he ended many of the economic controls, his popularity improved dramatically. Because of electoral redistricting in the general election of 1950, Wilson stood for election in the newly formed Lancashire working-class constituency of Huyton instead of in the reorganized middle-class district of Ormskirk. This proved a fortunate move as the winds of political change against Labour resulted in a Conservative Party victory at Ormskirk and a close victory of less than 1,000 votes for Wilson in Huyton. He would represent Huyton for more than 30 years before retiring from politics.

The Labour Party retained power but with a reduced majority. Although Attlee made several changes in his cabinet, he retained Wilson at the Board of Trade. Wilson became entangled in the Labour Party struggle between Hugh Gaitskell, the right-wing chancellor of the exchequer, and Aneurin Bevan, the left-wing minister of health. Also leftist in his political philosophy, Wilson supported Bevan's opposition to Gaitskell's 1951 budget which called for rearmament, support for the Korean War, and some nominal charges in the previously free National Health Services. And in April 1951, Bevan and Wilson resigned from the cabinet. While Bevan's resignation was dictated solely by dogmatic philosophy, Wilson's was also guided by a sensitivity to the efficiency and service in future socialist governments.

Though generally thought potentially fatal to his political future, Wilson's resignation did him relatively little harm. Shortly thereafter, the Labour Party was swept from power by **Winston Churchill** and his Conservative Party in the 1951 general election. Wilson—whose explanation for resigning had been accepted by his constituents—slightly improved his margin of victory in Huyton. He sat on the Opposition front bench when the new Parliament met and was a forceful critic of the Conservatives. Although associated with the radical left-wing in his Party, he gradually defined his own political agenda and struck out on his own course. When Bevan in anger resigned from the Shadow Cabinet in April 1954, Wilson did not emulate him. Next in line for membership on the parliamentary committee, in the name of Party unity he accepted the seat previously held by Bevan.

While in 1955 the Labour Party suffered a greater setback than in the previous general election, Wilson doubled his majority at Huyton. He was selected to chair a committee examining the election disaster and the Labour Party's organization. The report—deeply disappointing but accepted by the Party leadership—emphasized that nine members of the Shadow Cabinet were over 65, and that stagnation was hurting the Party. When the more conservative Hugh Gaitskell replaced Attlee as leader of the Labour Party in late 1955, he moved to unify the Party by appointing Wilson as shadow chancellor of the exchequer and Bevan as foreign secretary.

Known for his witty style and phenomenal memory of facts and statistics, Wilson improved his reputation in the House of Commons and throughout the British nation as a forceful debater. When the Labour Party suffered another crushing defeat by the Conservatives in the general election of October 1959, the uneasy alliance between the Party's conservative and liberal factions collapsed into disarray. Wilson, who had been one of the Party's leading spokesmen, was singled out as one of the scapegoats, but he could proudly point to his 6,000-vote majority at Huyton.

In the summer of 1960, Bevan died and Wilson became the leader of the Labour Party's left wing, a position he had held in practice for many years, though carefully remaining to the right of center. In an effort to move the Party to the left, in November 1960 he challenged Gaitskell for the leadership of the Labour Party. Wilson was soundly defeated, 166 votes to 81. In November 1962, he ran against George Brown for the deputy leadership of the Party to be defeated by a smaller margin: 133 to 103. When Gaitskell died on January 18, 1963, Wilson again challenged Brown—this time for the Party leadership. The first ballot eliminated a third candidate, James Callaghan, but did not result in the election of a leader. Then on February 14, 1963, Wilson defeated Brown on the second ballot by 143 to 103 votes and became the Labour Party leader.

He Becomes Prime Minister

As leader of the Opposition, Wilson proved a vigorous and skillful leader who carefully consolidated Party unity by including the Bevanites and the Gaitskellites in policy decisions. He cleverly followed a policy of blurring ideological views to ensure Party unity. In the general election of October 1964, Wilson led the Labour Party to victory by campaigning against the uninterrupted 13 years of Conservative rule. His positive message emphasized science, technology, and efficiency rather than socialism. Promising to inaugurate a second industrial revolution, he proposed the transformation of Britain by "the white heat of technological change." The election results produced an overall majority for Labour of only four seats over the combined Conservative and Liberal Parties in the House of Commons. Harold Wilson became prime minister on October 16, 1964.

For nearly 18 months, he cautiously proved his ability to govern with only a single-digit majority. His new government, however, faced a critical balance-of-payments deficit, inflation, and weak industrial production. Rather than devalue the currency to fight the balance-of-payments problem, he chose to keep international confidence in Britain by utilizing import taxes, budget cuts, and increases in interest rates. Although these measures and a "National Plan" (1965) for economic growth did not produce strong positive results, they did encourage enough response in public sentiment to warrant a general election. Needing to increase his operating margin in the House of Commons, and capitalizing on the electorate's belief that his policies should have time to work, Wilson called for an election on March 31, 1966, and led the Labour Party to a 96-seat majority over the combined opposition parties.

But the British economy did not respond to Wilson's economic policies, and by the fall of 1966 a continuing trade deficit was creating monetary problems. All new measures implemented by Wilson failed and in 1967 he reluctantly devalued the pound sterling by nearly 15%. He was also hurt in November 1967 when the president of France, **Charles de Gaulle,** vetoed Britain's entry into the European Economic Community (Common Market); this was also a divisive issue in the Labour Party because Wilson had deviated from his left-wing friends who violently opposed the membership. In addition, Wilson—whose Party depended on the Trade Union Congress for providing union support—looked weak when he withdrew a tough union reform bill in favor of a weaker bill to placate the unions.

Worse yet, his foreign policy was less productive than his domestic program. He was ineffective in his effort to moderate the racial policies of white-ruled Rhodesia, was reluctantly dragged into supporting the United States in the Vietnam War, was forced to withdraw British military forces east of the Suez Canal because of economic problems, and caused strained relations with many African nations by imposing immigration restrictions in an effort to ease British racial tensions at home.

Conservatives Upset Labour in Election

But by June 1970, Wilson was encouraged enough by an improvement in the balance of payments, and favorable public opinion polls, to call for an election. The Conservatives, led by Edward Heath, attacked Labour's economic and foreign policy record. Surprisingly placed on the defensive, Wilson was unable to explain the rising unemployment, high rate of inflation, increasing numbers of strikes, and the failure of his foreign policy. In one of Britain's greatest political upsets, the Conservatives won a majority of 30 seats over the combined opposition.

As leader of the Opposition, Wilson fought Prime Minister Heath's policies to prepare Britain for entry into the European Economic Community. Wilson opposed entry because of a major opinion change among his Labour Party supporters, but he also disagreed with Heath's efforts to

A campaign poster in 1964 touting the Labour Party's soon-to-be-elected Harold Wilson.

promote industrial investment by accepting higher living costs and food prices to slow consumption. By 1974, inflation was worse and the industrial expansion had faltered. Crippled by a miners' strike, Heath called a general election for February 28, 1974. Neither of the two parties won an overall majority, but as leader of the larger Party, Wilson once more was invited to form a government.

Briefly leading a minority government, he increased it to a small majority by calling a second election on October 10, 1974. Wilson gave the striking miners their pay increase and introduced a program of food price subsidies. As the economy continued to decline, he reluctantly raised taxes on upper-level personal and corporate incomes, acquired foreign loans to help the overseas trade deficit, and negotiated some economic concessions from the European Economic Community. During 1975, the rate of inflation continued to soar. Then on March 16, 1976—apparently weary from the intractable social and economic problems facing him—Wilson unexpectedly resigned his position as prime minister. He was succeeded by James Callaghan who continued his policies.

Following retirement from the cabinet, Wilson continued to represent Huyton in Parliament until 1983. On April 22, 1976, Queen Elizabeth II named him a Knight of the Garter. Wilson wrote several books after 1976, including: *The Governance of Britain* (1976); *A Prime Minister on Prime Ministers* (1977); *The Chariot of Israel* (1981); and *Harold Wilson: Memoirs 1916–1964* (1986). In 1983, he was elevated to a lifetime peerage as Baron Wilson of Rievaulx and took his seat in the House of Lords.

SOURCES:

Pike, E. Royston. *Britain's Prime Ministers From Walpole to Wilson.* Odhams Books, 1968.

Smith, Leslie. *Harold Wilson: The Authentic Portrait.* Scribner, 1964.

Wilson, J. Harold. *Final Term: The Labour Government 1974–1976.* Weidenfeld & Nicolson, 1979.

———. *A Personal Record: The Labour Government 1964–1970.* Little, Brown, 1971.

———. *The Relevance of British Socialism.* Pergamon Press, 1964.

FURTHER READING:

Crossman, R. H. S.. *Diaries of a Cabinet Minister.* 3 vols. Holt, 1975–1977.

Foot, Paul. *The Politics of Harold Wilson.* Penguin, 1968.

Roth, Andrew. *Sir Harold Wilson: Yorkshire Walter Mitty.* MacDonald & James, 1977.

Smith, Dudley. *Harold Wilson: A Critical Biography.* Hale, 1964.

Williams, Marcia. *Inside Number 10.* Coward, 1972.

Sergei Witte

(1849–1915)

Russian Minister of Finance who directed one of the fastest periods of economic growth in Russian history.

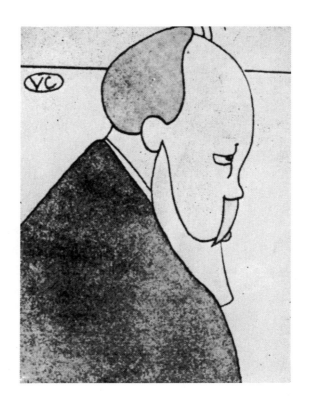

Sergei Witte often expressed sympathy for the many non-Russians in his country. Jews, Poles, and other peoples who were not Russian or Orthodox Christian frequently faced discriminatory laws in the businesses, education, and government of the Russian Empire. But there were basic contradictions in Witte's political career. On the one hand, he held very progressive views and stood for abolishing laws that discriminated on the basis of ethnic origins. Such laws, he felt, hindered the growth of Russia's productivity. Yet this modern outlook contrasted with his admiration for the old traditions of the Russian monarchy, whose absolute powers were often the source of discriminatory laws in the first place. When the Russian emperor Alexander II was assassinated by terrorists in 1881, Witte briefly joined a secret society dedicated to seeking out and destroying terrorists.

Witte spent his youth in the town of his birth, the Georgian city of Tbilisi, where his father worked as an official of the Russian government. As a young adult, he left to attend the Novorossiisk University in Odessa, Ukraine. His education centered on science, where he wrote a thesis on pure mathematics to complete his degree. But

Name variations: Count Witte. Born Sergei Yulevich Witte on July 17, 1849 (all dates follow the Julian calendar), in the city of Tbilisi in the country of Georgia, which was then part of the Russian Empire; died on February 28, 1915, in St. Petersburg; son of a Baltic German father and a mother who was a descendent of the Dolgorukys, an ancient princely family of Russia; married: N.A. (Ivanenko) Spiridonova, who had a daughter from a previous marriage, Sonya; married: Matilda Ivanova, 1892, who also had a daughter from a previous marriage, Vera.

Contributed by David Katz, Harvard University, Cambridge, Massachusetts

1849	Born in Tbilisi
1889	Became director of railroad affairs
1892	Became minister of finance
1903	Resigned as minister of finance
1905	Traveled to United States to conclude peace treaty with Japan; became prime minister after the Revolution of 1905
1906	Resigned as prime minister; left Russia
1907–12	Wrote memoirs
1914	Returned to Russia upon outbreak of World War I
1915	Died in Russia

early attempts for a career in mathematics did not pan out, and Witte secured a position as a railway administrator for the government. Later he took a job as director of a private railway company in southern Russia, where he won renown as the principal author of a charter that guided the operation of Russian railroads. When Russian emperor Alexander III offered to double Witte's salary to attract him back into government service in 1889, Witte became the director of a newly created department for railroad affairs in the Ministry of Finance.

It was in the early 1880s when Witte incurred social disapproval by marrying his first wife, a divorcée with a daughter from a previous marriage. A few years later, his wife died of a heart attack. Society again raised a furor in 1892 when he married another divorcée, also with a daughter from a previous marriage.

Witte was a proud man, quick to take personal credit for many of the successes under his term as finance minister. He became best known for his efforts to modernize and increase Russian industry, viewing industrial development as necessary to the continued prosperity of Russia:

> Industry gives birth to capital; capital gives rise to enterprise and love of learning; and knowledge, enterprise and capital combined create new industries. Such is the eternal cycle of economic life.

Under the patronage of the minister of finance Ivan A. Vyshnegradsky, Witte climbed rapidly in government service. An ambitious man, willing to compromise values, Witte conspired against Vyshnegradsky in late 1892 and managed to get himself appointed to the same position. Witte's vigor in pursuing his policies is sometimes referred to as the "Witte system." Some historians, however, downplay the originality of his plans and maintain that his policies merely continued the work of previous finance ministers.

Witte's policies had four basic aspects: tariffs and taxation, stability of money backed by gold, encouragement of foreign investment, and government supervision of heavy industries such as metal production and railroad construction. The motive behind the emphasis on industrial development was mainly political. If Russia was to remain a great power, she would have to match the economic might of other European powers. Critics of Witte's system charge that his plans caused long-term harm that offset any short-term gains. He raised revenue for the government by a heavy sales tax. In 1894, he established a state monopoly on liquor, the sale of which was extremely profitable. On the downside, Witte's high taxes took from Russian farmers money which could have been invested in new technologies to improve their agricultural productivity. High tariffs on imported goods like tea and salt meant higher prices that diminished the buying power of each peasant family.

The decade following Witte's activity as finance minister brought a slight slowdown to the growth of Russian industry. Government aid to businesses involved in heavy industry continued but on a lesser scale. This slowdown, however, also brought relief from the tax pressure Witte's policies put on the masses. Growth slowed, but prices also relaxed.

Thus, to build up industry in Russia, Witte put Russia through a period of austerity. The object was to buy up as much gold as possible with the sale of foodstuffs on foreign markets so as to increase Russia's gold reserves. In 1897, he accumulated enough gold to put Russia on the international gold standard, whereby each ruble (the unit of Russian currency) would be backed by gold. The arrival of the gold standard brought Russia recognition abroad and attracted foreigners to invest in Russian industry. One estimate values the amount of foreign investment at 200 million rubles in 1890, rising to 900 million rubles by 1900. The influx of foreign capital was so rapid that some Russians feared their country would be owned and controlled by foreigners.

In the area of foreign relations, Witte often exerted an important influence. In the 1890s, while diplomats tried to extend Russian influence in Asia, Witte established a Russo-Persian and

Russo-Chinese Bank to facilitate trade with Iran and China. Opposed to the efforts of the Russian military to acquire more funding for the manufacture of armaments, Witte preferred to spend the money building up the economy. For this reason, he persuaded Emperor **Nicholas II** to support worldwide disarmament by calling together an international peace conference at The Hague, Netherlands, in 1899.

Railroads Emphasized; Trans-Siberian Route Completed

Russia was primarily an agricultural nation. In an effort to earn the support of the people who viewed his industrial development with suspicion, Witte also made training in business education more readily available, establishing between 150 and 200 schools of commerce. Railroads held a pivotal role in Witte's plans because they acted as the primary means to ship the needed material to market for sale and to transport the raw materials to factories for manufacturing. During Witte's tenure, the miles of railroad tracks in Russia almost doubled. As a champion of government control, he advocated buying back existing railroads from private companies. By 1900, 60% of Russian railroads were owned by the government. Witte believed that railroads like the famous Trans-Siberian would serve two purposes: economically, they would strengthen Russian industry and provide access to new land for farmers who needed it; culturally, they would enrich Russian civilization.

The majority of the Trans-Siberian railroad was completed during Witte's term as minister of finance. This achievement, crossing the Eurasian landmass from Moscow to the Pacific, was of the same magnitude as that of the Union Pacific or Canadian Pacific railway crossing of the North American continent.

Russia at this time was headed by an autocratic ruler who in theory had absolute power over every sphere of government. Even after Russia received its first constitution in 1905, the Emperor and his circle of advisors exercised ultimate control; any of his edicts had the force of law and superseded all other laws. Often civil liberties were violated; the police could arrest anyone who voiced too loud an opposition.

Repeated agitation by socialist parties and strikes among Russia's urban proletariat of factory workers influenced Witte and others to enact labor legislation. He made it mandatory for factory owners to provide their employees on-the-job accident insurance. He also set limitations on the length of the work day and allowed workers to elect their own representatives.

Though Witte's ministry could be sympathetic to the conditions of Russian workers, it did not always act in their best interest. Early attempts to improve the conditions of the working class were made through the creation of labor unions under the close supervision of Sergei V. Zubatov, a police agent of the Ministry of the Interior. Factory owners opposed the intercession of government officials on behalf of workers. Witte, who did not want to jeopardize Russia's appeal to big business, voiced his objection to such beneficial measures. But the Ministry of the Interior proved to be one of Witte's main opponents. It was directed by people who were far more conservative than Witte and weary of the discontent and changes among the working class, which they linked to Witte's policies of rapid industrial growth.

While many of his programs for industrial development were known for their liberal or progressive nature, Witte, nevertheless, opposed any step toward democratic reform and diminution of the Emperor's absolute powers. Witte's distrust of democracy stemmed from the fear that the masses would not be able to elect competent representatives capable of working for the best interests of Russia. His ideal was a government administered by competent civil servants with a strong and decisive emperor as leader. Witte had almost worshipped Alexander III, who had died in 1894:

> If [Alexander] were not certain of what he thought or would do, he would hold his tongue, but if he said something, one could have complete confidence in his word.... Had Emperor Alexander III lived on... we would have enjoyed peace, peace that would have permitted us to move along the road of gradual liberalization, toward a life in which the state exists for the good of the people.

A beneficent autocracy, claimed Witte, should consult representatives of the people about their wants, but never subject itself to them.

True to his belief that the government must act in the interests of the people, Witte had initiated efforts by the Russian bureaucracy to respond to their needs. After a wave of assassinations and rural violence toward government officials swept Russia, Witte created a special commission in 1902 composed of civil servants and non-government representatives to study the sources of dissatisfaction in the countryside. Unfortunately, Witte's dismissal as finance minister the following year and the hesitancy of Tsar Nicholas II prevented the enactment of the recommendations of the commission.

Like Witte, Nicholas also stood firmly against any diminution of an emperor's absolute powers. Despite this common view, Witte and Nicholas never fully liked or trusted each other. Their relationship had started well when Witte appointed Nicholas to chair the committee in charge of building the Trans-Siberian railroad. To Witte's surprise, however, Nicholas was not a figurehead and voiced his own informed opinions on the progress of the railroad. This tension between the two men only grew with time. Yet Witte's insight was handicapped by his pretentious or sarcastic manner which did not charm his government colleagues. Later, he reluctantly admitted, "I should have been more restrained in speaking to him."

To complete the Trans-Siberian Railroad, tracks had to pass through the Chinese province of Manchuria. Witte at first insisted that Russia's relations with China be based upon the mutual economic benefit of each side. However, when Russian armies began to move south of Manchuria and into the Yalu River of Korea, Witte expressed his disapproval of further Russian expansion in the Orient. His dissent caused a scandal which forced him to resign as finance minister in 1903. Afterwards, Nicholas appointed Witte to the largely ceremonial post of chair of the Committee of Ministers, which coordinated the work of the various ministries of the Russian government.

But there was rivalry between China, Japan, and Russia for control of Korea, and Russia and Japan were moving toward a crisis. Witte warned that peace must be kept in the Far East because of Russia's unreadiness for war. As the only railroad to Russia's Pacific coast, the Trans-Siberian line remained unfinished and could not transport troops and supplies to the theater of battle with Japan. While the Russians stalled the negotiations, the Japanese launched a surprise attack in February 1904 which crippled the Russian navy anchored at the city of Port Arthur on the Chinese mainland.

Troops Massacre Workers on "Bloody Sunday"

Further misfortune befell the government when on Sunday, January 9, 1905, an incident took place that was later to become known as "Bloody Sunday"; government troops massacred hundreds of innocent Russian workers as they marched in demonstration of their grievances. Upon Witte's suggestion, the government formed the Shidlovsky Commission to study the causes of the tragedy. Once again, the hesitancy of Tsar Nicholas pre-

vented the government from taking firm action to make amends. The tragedy shocked the nation and set the tone for the rest of the year as unrest among workers and peasant crescendoed after the unnecessary violence.

By the summer of 1905, the war was going very badly for Russia, and Japan had sunk the rest of the Russian navy in the famous battle of Tsushima Straits. But despite its successes, Japan could not continue to finance its war and asked U.S. president **Theodore Roosevelt** to arrange a peace conference. Chosen to lead the Russian delegation at the conference held in Portsmouth, New Hampshire, in August 1905, Witte obtained a favorable settlement for Russia. Both parties agreed to withdraw their armies from Chinese Manchuria. Russia had to cede Port Arthur and part of the Sakhalin Island; it also had to recognize Japanese dominance over Korea. But Russia did not have to pay reparations for war damages to the victorious Japanese. Peace came none too soon, for Russia was rapidly being engulfed by domestic turmoil and massive waves of strikes protesting the unresponsiveness of the Russian autocracy to the needs of the people. Upon Witte's return to Russia, Nicholas granted him the title of count, in recognition of his efforts to secure a favorable peace. Witte, who was very status conscious, felt this to be a great honor.

Unfortunately the bureaucrats could not provide the responsible guidance that the autocratic regime desperately needed. The memory of bureaucratic mismanagement in handling the famine of 1891–92—compounded by the recent debacle with Japan—left the impression that the government bureaucrats were inept and insensitive.

During September and October of 1905, discontent in Russia had reached its peak. With nationwide strikes paralyzing the country and violent uprisings of peasants demanding more land, the government edged toward collapse. Witte advised Nicholas that unless some definitive action was taken, the wave of strikes would topple the remaining vestiges of autocratic power. He recommended an "all or none" strategy: either the government suppress all discontent with strict martial law or grant the public meaningful concessions. Since the majority of the army was still in the Far East because of the recent hostilities, it was not possible to stop the strikes with military force. Witte spoke candidly to Nicholas:

The inconsistent and clumsy actions... the administration resorted to in the past, and which continue to this day, have produced fatal results; it has nurtured a hatred for the government which grows from day to day.... The roots of this unrest unquestionably lie deeper. They lie in the disturbed equilibrium between the ideological aspirations of the thinking elements of Russian society and the external forms of their life [i.e. the government]. Russia has outgrown the existing regime and aspires to a rule of law based on civil liberty.

Witte concluded that acceptance of reform was the only "way to save the state."

The October Manifesto Is Issued; Witte Named Prime Minister

It took the Revolution of 1905 for the government to concede the need for political and economic reforms. The success of the Revolution culminated in the October Manifesto. On October 17, 1905, Nicholas issued this famous declaration which guaranteed civil rights and promised the rapid formation of an elected legislature or parliament (*duma*). Witte was appointed the first prime minister of the new Russian government. Though he preferred an autocratic state, he recognized the constitutional regime as the only way to make peace between government and society.

Witte's acceptance of democratic reforms surprised those who thought him to be an ardent supporter of autocratic government. Nicholas thought Witte too insistent on diminishing autocratic rule and too insistent on violent methods to restore order in Russia. He used the word "chameleon" to describe Witte's vacillation between liberal and conservative measures. Ironically, Witte's opinion of Nicholas echoed the Tsar's criticism; each viewed the other as inconsistent. Although Nicholas had a "good heart," Witte recalled, his "weak" leadership, which could be easily swayed into competing directions, was to a large degree to blame for the crisis that had faced the Russian government in 1905.

As prime minister, Witte's strategy was simple: to win the support of enough voters so that his government could function effectively with the backing of the *Duma*. He focused on the largest block of voters, the peasant farmers who made up approximately 80% of the Russian population. But the electoral laws did not allow for the elementary principle of "one person, one vote." The votes of the nobility counted many times more than the votes of the peasant farmers or factory workers. The peasants would control only 40% of the seats in the *Duma*. To ensure a favorable reception of peasant voters toward the government, Witte announced his intentions to introduce legislation into the new parliament to give peasant farmers desperately needed land—at the expense of the landlords. Since most of the Russian nobility were landlords, they spoke out against this measure; though the nobility only made up a small percentage of the population, their opposition carried weight within the imperial court of Nicholas II.

Witte experienced difficulties collecting support from other circles too. Instead of appointing government bureaucrats as ministers in his government, he had invited members of the liberal parties to join his cabinet. But his efforts to win support from non-government parties failed, and the liberals refused to serve, claiming that Witte's recent appointment of several arch-conservatives would stand in the way of effective cooperation. To complicate matters, his efforts to secure an alliance with conservatives also failed. When the Tsar saw the election results based on Witte's electoral law, he and other conservatives feared that the new *Duma* would be too liberal; indeed, the peasant bloc turned out to be hostile and distrustful toward the government, which was viewed as being too slow in addressing the need for more land. Nicholas had Witte dismissed and replaced him in March 1906 with a more conservative and pliable prime minister, Ivan L. Goremykin.

Meanwhile, the Russian government itself was teetering on collapse, not just from its inabilities to accept the *Duma* but from impending bankruptcy: the Russian treasury had critically exhausted its monetary reserves during the war with Japan. Although the government could turn to its *Duma* to raise new taxes, any dependence on the liberal-minded parliament repulsed Nicholas and his conservative advisors. Witte's last important act as prime minister was the successful negotiation of a 1906 loan from France—the "loan that saved Russia" as he liked to remember it—which supplied Nicholas with the financial strength to act independently of a liberal *Duma*.

Though visibly tired of being the center of complaints, Witte wanted to stay on as prime minister and enact his legislative policy for Russia. Part of Witte's program was designed to allow the peasant farmers to leave the communes (land collectively owned by the peasants) on a gradual and voluntary basis. Witte had come to believe that the peasant commune was inefficient and unproductive, preventing many peasants from consolidating their holdings. Later Peter A. Stolypin, an important prime minister who followed Witte, effectively abolished the communes, but not at the gradual pace which Witte recommended.

Witte's disapproval of Stolypin's methods exemplifies the basic contradictions in his thinking.

On the one hand, he remained a firm supporter of the Tsar's supreme powers; on the other hand, he objected when Stolypin used the Tsar's powers to override the *Duma*. In defiance of the Russian constitution, Nicholas—upon Stolypin's urging—abolished the electoral laws designed by Witte and decreed a new set of laws, insuring the Russian nobility of a majority in the *Duma*.

After his dismissal as prime minister, Witte traveled abroad in Europe and never again entered public service. He remained bitter with Nicholas for not fully supporting his programs and frustrated with himself and the government: "All sensible measures come too late." His death in 1915 went largely unrecognized, partly because of remaining resentment from the imperial court. Nicholas was to remark that Witte's passing left him in a calm and not unpleasant mood.

SOURCES:

Charques, Richard. *The Twilight of Imperial Russia.* London: Oxford University Press, 1958.

Falkus, M. E. *The Industrialisation of Russia 1700–1914.* London: Macmillan, 1986.

Marks, Steven G. *Road to Power: The Trans-Siberian Railroad and the Colonization of Asian Russia 1850–1917.* Cornell University Press, 1991.

Mehlinger, Howard D., and John M. Thompson. *Count Witte and the Tsarist Government in the 1905 Revolution.* Indiana University Press, 1972.

Modern Encyclopedia of Russian and Soviet History. Edited by J. L. Wieczynski. Academic International Press, 1976.

Riasanovsky, Nicholas V. *A History of Russia.* 4th ed. Oxford University Press, 1984.

Rogger, Hans. *Russia in the Age of Modernisation and Revolution 1881–1917.* London: Longman, 1990.

Von Laue, Theodore H. *Sergei Witte and the Industrialization of Russia.* New York, 1963.

Thomas Wolsey

(1471–1530)

Vain, ostentatious, but brilliantly gifted archbishop, who ruled England until he proved unable to arrange Henry VIII's divorce from Catherine of Aragon.

"For fifteen years he impressed England and Europe with his grandeur, his hard work, his skill and intelligence.... [E]ven if subsequent events showed his aims to have been mistaken and his solutions to have been patchwork... his age would have been very different without him."

GEOFFREY ELTON

The only way for a man of humble birth to achieve power in late 15th-century Britain was through the Church. Thomas Wolsey, son of an Ipswich butcher and innkeeper, rose through the ranks of the clergy by hard work, ruthless self-interest, and skillful manipulation of patrons and kings. But he had the misfortune of living on into the age of the Reformation and of serving the unscrupulous King **Henry VIII,** who repaid Wolsey's devoted services with accusations of treason. Only death from dysentery in 1530 spared Wolsey from the Tower of London headsman's axe.

Gaining a bachelor's degree from Magdalen College Oxford at the age of 15, Thomas Wolsey was made a fellow of the college, then its bursar. He was dismissed, however, for exceeding his authority when he ordered elaborate and costly building work on the Magdalen College tower—the first of his many grand architectural projects. Granted the parish priest's position—or "living"—of Limington in Somerset, Wolsey had no interest in burying himself in a country parish. He was more interested in the income which came with it and followed his first noble patron, the marquis of

Contributed by Patrick Allitt, Assistant Professor of History, Emory University, Atlanta, Georgia

Name variations: Cardinal Wolsey. Born in an Ipswich butcher shop in 1471; died en route to the Tower of London in 1530; son of a butcher and innkeeper in Ipswich; children: one son and one daughter, both illegitimate by his concubine, "Mistress Lark." Predecessor (as chancellor): Archbishop Warham of Canterbury. Successor: Sir Thomas More.

1471	Wolsey born
1486	Graduated from Magdalen College, Oxford
1498	Ordained to priesthood
1500	Made rector of Limington
1508	Made dean of Lincoln Cathedral
1509	Henry VII died; ascension of Henry VIII
1511	Wolsey made privy councillor
1514	Became bishop of Lincoln
1515	Named archbishop of York and cardinal; became lord chancellor and chief minister
1520	Francis I and Henry VIII met at Field of the Cloth of Gold
1529	Legatine court failed to secure divorce for Henry VIII; Wolsey accused and dismissed
1530	Arrested at York; died en route to the Tower of London

Dorset, to King **Henry VII**'s court in London. In 1501, he contrived to get a papal dispensation permitting him to hold more than one "living" simultaneously—thus, to Limington he added Redgrave in Suffolk, Lydd in Kent, and Great Torrington in Devon.

Wolsey then rose step by step at court by finding the right patron at the right moment and carrying out his tasks with speed and precision; a string of missions to foreign courts accustomed him to European diplomatic practices and developed his skills as a manipulator of the powerful. A conventional churchman of his day, he said mass regularly and took pleasure in religious conversation, but was never introspective on theological matters. He was hardly the ideal priest. In addition to his gathering of multiple parishes, from which he was an absentee, he had the common failing among renaissance clergy of keeping a concubine, "Mistress Lark," by whom he had a son and a daughter. As he rose in eminence, he pensioned off his mistress by paying her a dowry to marry, but he continued to supervise the education of his "niece" and "nephew" and arranged for the boy's own preferment in the Church.

Wolsey Climbs to Power

When Henry VII died in 1509, and his 19-year-old son became King Henry VIII, Wolsey, now nearly 40, skillfully wove his way into the new king's trust and esteem, being appointed a privy councillor in 1511. George Cavendish, one of Wolsey's household servants, whose *The Life of Cardinal Wolsey* is one of the first biographies written in England, put it this way: "His sentences and witty persuasions in the council chamber were always so pithy" that the other councillors, "as occasion moved them, assigned him, for his filed tongue and ornate eloquence, to be their expositor unto the king's majesty in all their proceedings." He finally won the bishopric of Lincoln in 1514, and then the archbishopric of York, plus a cardinal's hat, in 1515. Another papal decree of 1524 granted Wolsey primacy in England for life, over the normally preeminent archbishop of Canterbury, making him the chief minister in England of both king and pope.

Wolsey's climb to the top was stubborn and persistent, rather than meteoric; at every stage, he had mastered the necessary political skills and proved himself capable and trustworthy. Although he harbored grudges against those who impeded him and repaid old scores, he was withal rather likable. Historian Geoffrey Elton describes him thus:

> He was a eupeptic man, full of simple cheer, ready wit, and charm.... But the chief defects in his character were an uncomplicated greed and a passion for pomp. He enjoyed life recklessly—eating, building, fornicating—and in consequence needed more and more money.... Thus he gave a handle to his enemies, which mattered because he had only one friend—the King, whose trust formed the sole basis of his power.

In the long run, this lack of a party among Henry's courtiers would undo him.

Supreme among the king's ministers by 1515, Wolsey tried to centralize as much of the nation's administration in his hands as he could manage. Although he had no legal training, he ran the Court of Star Chamber as a board of arbitration, believing that it could be the place where poor men might get simple justice without the danger of facing bribed juries. In his legal and administrative affairs, he showed flashes of magnanimity; on one occasion, for example, he settled a 30-year-old dispute between the Cathedral and citizens of Norwich by personally paying for the draining and hedging of a disputed common (community land), when neither party was willing to do so.

Wolsey's zeal to defend the poor and dispense justice, which at first seems to have been from genuine motives, often took the form of attacking the rich, especially those who had crossed him. Elton comments: "The cardinal's cheerful and ruthless temperament rejoiced in cutting down the mighty and devising humiliations for them; and his rejoicing was too manifest." One by one, Wolsey alienated everyone who could have helped him when his position was threatened. The aristocracy, the city of London, his fellow bishops, even historians and poets, all came to detest Wolsey for his arrogance, tyrannical methods, personal vindictiveness, and ostentatious flaunting of new wealth.

Nevertheless for 15 years, he was Henry VIII's chief advisor. Wolsey had terrific powers of concentration. He was also a masterful organizer of the king's civil and military expeditions and arranged for the celebration of 1520 when Henry met King **Francis I** of France at "The Field of the Cloth of Gold" in Calais, England's remaining continental toehold. The two kings wrestled, entertained one another, but did little substantive business—that too was left to Wolsey, who maintained a grueling diplomatic schedule.

By relying, in his conduct of foreign policy, on close contacts with the Vatican, Wolsey tied English politics more closely to Rome than they had been for several hundred years. A shrewd move in 1518 when it enabled him to supervise a general European pacification at the Treaty of London, it sowed the seeds of later troubles. As the events of the late 1520s would show, Rome listened more closely to the Holy Roman Emperor than to the king of England. Henry VIII, Francis I, and the new Holy Roman Emperor, **Charles V,** were all young, ambitious, vainglorious men in 1518. Along with their territories, they had inherited ancient political rivalries, many of which were then intensified by the onset of the German Reformation; the three kings' reigns were to witness horrific and sustained dynastic and religious wars. The next general pacification of Europe came only in 1559, long after Wolsey's death, and it bore witness to a transformed and newly riven continent.

By piling up offices and patronage appointments, Wolsey made himself a prince of the Church in financial as well as ecclesial terms, and began to build monuments to his own glory. Christchurch, the Oxford College which he founded as "Cardinal College," is now regarded in Britain as a national treasure and one of the great monuments of Tudor architecture. Another monument is Hampton Court Palace, which Wolsey commissioned in 1515 and finished in five years. He had what was then regarded as extremely good taste and his discernment has withstood the test of time. The uses to which he put his ill-gotten gains have proved to be lasting sources of enjoyment to

the British people and, more recently, to countless thousands of tourists from around the world. To furnish Hampton with its almost 1,000 rooms, Wolsey brought treasures from all over Europe. Despite its incredible opulence, he decided to give Hampton to the king in 1525 in exchange for Richmond Palace, and it became a principal residence for the Tudors, though Wolsey remained free to use it at least until 1529. The cardinal's personal retinue as well as his palaces were designed to inspire awe in the onlooker. He took 250 personal servants with him to the Field of the Cloth of Gold, and by the mid-1520s had an entourage closer to 500. The best surviving portrait shows Wolsey dressed in the splendid red gown and hat of a cardinal, sending forth a clear message of power, wealth, and regality.

Reformation Targets Abuses

The Reformation took aim against men like Wolsey. When the ideas of **Martin Luther,** the German Augustinian friar whose theses of 1517 protested Church abuses, began to enter England in 1520, Wolsey led the counterattack, burning Luther's writings in public and searching out heretics in every diocese. A man whom he had advanced to the position of speaker of the House of Commons and then to the king's secretariat, **Thomas More,** was the author of *Utopia* and one of the great geniuses in all of English history. Unlike his humanist friend Erasmus, Thomas More believed that an intellectual should put his gifts at the service of his king, and with Wolsey's help was granted the opportunity. In the 1520s, More wrote mercilessly polemical counterattacks against the Lutheran position. Even Henry VIII, who fancied his own intellectual powers, wrote a *Defense of the Seven Sacraments* as a counterblast to Luther's new theology. The king, who within a decade would desert Rome, spent much of the 1520s scourging heresy, whereas his servant More would never abandon Catholicism, and ultimately paid for it with his life in 1535.

The English Church was full of abuses, high and low, and Wolsey was merely, for the moment, the most conspicuous abuser. Although indignation at these abuses was never Henry VIII's motive for engineering the English Reformation, the rotten structure of the English Church made it that much easier to knock it over with one good push when the time came. Criminal conduct and debauchery were common among the clergy, who were often figures of hatred or ridicule. The bishop of London told Wolsey in 1515, "that any jury of twelve men in London would convict any clergyman whatsoever, 'though he were as innocent as Abel.'" But juries rarely got this opportunity because anyone attached to the Church, even if not ordained, could claim "benefit of clergy" by which he would be tried in Church, rather than civil, courts and (usually) escape serious punishment. Benefit of clergy had become a shelter for some men who were no better than professional criminals.

There was already in England a history of protest against corrupt Church practices, and a history of popular spirituality dating back at least to **John Wycliffe,** who in the late 14th century had urged Church reform and the translation of the Bible into English. Wycliffe's followers, the Lollards, had maintained a small but devoted community in England ever since, in the face of recurrent persecution. More important from a political point of view, there was a powerful tradition of monarchical control over religious appointments. Historian Paul Johnson remarks:

> One of the reasons why the Reformation was successful in England was that there was absolutely nothing new about it. All its elements—anti-clericalism, anti-papalism, the exaltation of the Crown in spiritual matters, the envy of clerical property, even the yearning for doctrinal reform—were deeply rooted in the English past.

It was not Church reform which sparked the English Reformation, however, but two aspects of Henry VIII's personal life which led him to seek a divorce from his queen, Catherine of Aragon.

His primary motive for seeking the divorce was his desire—one shared by all kings of the age—to have a male heir for the sake of dynastic security. There were dozens of precedents in European history for such divorces being granted by the Vatican, but this time the pope, Clement VII, could not afford to decree it lest he antagonize Emperor Charles V, who was Catherine of Aragon's nephew. Henry, however, had convinced himself that his marriage to Catherine, despite a papal dispensation allowing it, had been illegal because she was his brother Arthur's widow. In effect, said Henry, with Wolsey's support, the marriage had never existed; Catherine should therefore go to a nunnery, Henry should marry and sire an heir, and all would be well. Pope Clement underestimated the gravity of the situation; it apparently never occurred to him that England might break cleanly from Rome, as some of the Lutheran princes of Germany had begun to do, and he told his ambassadors to equivocate when they went to England to discuss the matter.

Henry's second motive for seeking a divorce, which added urgency and personal animus to the dispute with Rome, was his lustful intoxication with Anne Boleyn, daughter of one of his courtiers. Henry had had a succession of beautiful mistresses, one of whom was Anne's sister, and he planned at first to make Anne the next in this line of royal favorites. Though she surprised him by refusing his advances on these terms, Anne was most certainly willing to be his queen. Her resistance to his amorous designs increased his desire, and lent urgency to his pursuit of a divorce. Trying at first to keep his reasons secret, Henry appointed Wolsey to work out a divorce agreement with the pope. But that year, 1527, a mutinous imperial army sacked Rome and imprisoned the pope, thereby cementing Charles V's control over Vatican policy, and Wolsey found he could gain no concessions.

Wolsey Fails to Obtain Divorce Agreement from Pope

Wolsey was unaccustomed to failure; he now felt his secure domestic leadership beginning to slip because Anne Boleyn, who disliked him, was becoming the focus of an opposition group at court. To save his position, however, Wolsey saw that he must succeed in arranging for Anne to become queen. He therefore urged his negotiators at Rome to sing the praises of Anne Boleyn as a paragon of virtue, and he exhorted them to underline to Clement how serious the matter had become to Anglo-Vatican relations. But the case dragged on unresolved. It was only when news of the pope's death arrived in England early in 1529 that a solution to the issue seemed to appear. If Wolsey could get himself elected as the next pope, he could smooth away the king's difficulties. His seniority in the Church made his election to the Throne of Peter at least conceivable, if never likely.

Unfortunately for Wolsey the news of Clement's death was premature—more letters arrived in London to say that he had recovered from a severe illness. When the pope did permit a hearing to take place in London, May 1529, in the presence of Wolsey and his own ambassador Campeggio, most of the witnesses agreed with Henry's interpretation of the marriage to Catherine of Aragon—that it had never been legitimate in the first place. But the fearless bishop of Rochester, John Fisher, who had been counseling Catherine and sustaining her in standing up for her rights, denied these assertions and declared the inviolable sanctity of the marriage. Before a verdict could be delivered, the papal ambassador Campeggio, who had again been told to stretch things out and prevent a decision, placed the court in recess until October 1529 and added that the case, when resumed, must be taken up at Rome.

Henry, who had reposed almost complete faith in Wolsey for 15 years, was horrified to discover that his chancellor was unable to prevail. He now cut his ties with Wolsey, removed him from his chancellorship, and had him indicted for abuse of his authority as papal legate. Courtiers who resented Wolsey's power had conspired with Anne Boleyn's father, Thomas, viscount Rochford, to allege treason against Wolsey in his negotiations with Francis I of France during the preceding years. Although the king apparently knew these charges to be groundless, it suited his interests to accept them, at least for the moment. Not only did Wolsey lose his office, he had to hand over all his property to the king and throw himself on Henry's mercy. Henry apparently did not wish to eliminate Wolsey altogether; rather, by humbling a papal legate in this way, he wanted to show the pope just how grave his divorce crisis had become.

For the remaining year of his life, Wolsey lived on the king's sufferance and charity, though he had little to worry about materially. Allowed the massive sum of £4,000 per year, he was still free to move about. For the first time since he had gained it in 1515, Wolsey actually went to live in his archdiocese of York. In late 1530, however, the king ordered him arrested for conspiracy and treason and brought him back to London. Exactly why Henry made this arrest has remained uncertain; Wolsey's death en route obviated the need for a trial or further clarification of the king's motives. As he died, Wolsey declared sadly that throughout his life he had served his king better than he had served God, and this appears to have been an accurate judgment.

Wolsey died largely unlamented and was sorely used by generations of English historians. He represented to many of them all that was wicked and corrupt about the pre-Reformation Church. To those who admired constitutional government, likewise, Wolsey appeared to have been an arbitrary despot urging the king to tyrannical acts, neglecting Parliament, and profiting from unrestrained central control. More recent historians, especially Peter Gwyn, whose 650-page book *The King's Cardinal* is the longest ever written about Wolsey, are beginning to repair his reputation, emphasizing what virtues he had and demonstrating at length his phenomenal political skills. Whatever the final verdict, there can be no doubt that Wolsey's failure to secure the king's divorce set off one of the greatest transformations in British history and made Wolsey, in retrospect, the valedictorian of Catholic England.

SOURCES:

Elton, Geoffrey. *Reform and Reformation: England 1509–1558.* Harvard University Press, 1977.

———. *Studies in Tudor and Stuart Politics and Government.* Vol. I. Cambridge University Press, 1974.

Gwyn, Peter. *The King's Cardinal: The Rise and Fall of Thomas Wolsey.* Barrie & Jenkins, 1990.

Harvey, Nancy L. *Thomas Cardinal Wolsey.* Macmillan, 1980.

Johnson, Paul. *A History of the English People.* Harper, 1985.

Roulstone, Michael. *The Royal House of Tudor.* Balfour, 1974.

Scarisbrick, J. J. *Henry VIII.* London, 1968.

John Wycliffe

(c. 1320–1384)

English religious reformer, who stood for political and religious liberty and instigated the first complete translation of the Bible into English, making it available to the common people of England.

Name variations: Wyclif, Wycliff, Wickliff. Pronunciation: Wick-lif. Born c. 1320 in Hipswell, Yorkshire; died on December 31, 1384, in Lutterworth, Leicester; a son of the lower gentry; never married.

One of the most important religious reformers prior to the Protestant Reformation, John Wycliffe was born about 1320 in Yorkshire, England. As a student at Oxford University, he excelled in philosophy and theology, earning a bachelor of arts degree, and later a doctorate. For most of his life, he lived at Oxford and served as rector at several nearby churches.

While establishing a reputation as an academic teacher, Wycliffe also became involved in Church politics. In 1366, he began to promote the interests of the English Crown against the demands of the papacy, at that time based in Avignon, France. Among the English delegates to a peace congress in France where the financial demands of the Avignon papacy were discussed, Wycliffe soon saw the need for reform within the Catholic Church. Theorizing that God owns all property and grants use of that property on the condition that the user render faithful service, Wycliffe believed that when the service is not faithful, the use of the property is forfeited. In light of such theories, he was later accused of heresy by the Catholic Church.

"I believe that in the end the truth will conquer."

JOHN WYCLIFFE

Contributed by Eric Jacobson, Ph.D., University of North Texas, Farmers Branch, Texas

In 1377, Pope Gregory XI issued a list of 18 charges against Wycliffe, calling for his arrest and examination by Church leaders; attempts to produce a condemnation of Wycliffe in England failed, however, due to the protection of powerful friends. Another attempt was made in 1382 at a council of Church leaders held in London named the Earthquake Council (so named after a May 21st earthquake disrupted proceedings). The participants threatened to break up the assembly until the archbishop of Canterbury declared the tremor a sign from God to purge England of erroneous doctrine. Though 24 of Wycliffe's conclusions were condemned as heresies or errors, he was permitted to continue teaching and writing.

Wycliffe Criticizes Administration of Sacraments

As long as Wycliffe only attacked the abuses of the Catholic Church, he could expect support from the English aristocracy and the local clergy (friars); but in 1380, he moved to a more radical position, criticizing the doctrine of transubstantiation. The Church taught that when a priest consecrated the bread and wine during the sacrament of communion, they were transformed into the body and blood of Jesus Christ. Wycliffe argued that "the substance of bread and wine remains after the consecration, and that Christ is not in the sacrament of the altar identically, truly, and really in his bodily person." What angered him was the notion that a priest could somehow change the bread and wine into the body of Christ, thereby assuming the transcendent power which God alone possessed. For the remainder of his life, Wycliffe wrote and preached on the topic, which eventually led to opposition within the University of Oxford.

Wycliffe maintained similar positions on other sacraments, not necessarily by opposing them outright, but by attacking the priesthood's power to administer them. Confession, he argued, was introduced in the 13th century for the sake of gain, replacing individual confession directly to God. For Wycliffe, the assertion that a priest could somehow absolve someone of sin represented an encroachment upon God's divine power. Penance, the act of showing regret for sin, was unnecessary, because the relationship between penance and sin could be determined only by God, not by a priest. Pronouncing all teachings and traditions not derived directly from the Bible invalid, Wycliffe similarly opposed the consecration of priests, believing that no priesthood could mediate between God and man, and no qualification for office required ordination by a bishop.

CHRONOLOGY

1309	Seat of papacy moved from Rome to Avignon after agents of the king of France captured the pope
1374	Wycliffe appointed Rector at Lutterworth
1376	Expounded theory that all church and state authority is derived from God and forfeited when its possessor falls into mortal sin
1377	Accused of heresy by Pope Gregory XI
1378	The Great Schism created two popes—one in Avignon, the other in Rome; Wycliffe denied power of priests to enforce confession; rejected paying priests for penances and indulgences
1380	Opposed doctrine of transubstantiation
1382	Twenty-four of Wycliffe's conclusions condemned by the Earthquake Council; Wycliffe initiated first complete translation of the Bible into English
1384	Died from paralytic stroke
1415	Condemned by the Council of Constance
1417	Council of Frequens reunited Church with one pope in Rome
1428	Wycliffe's body disinterred, burned, and thrown into the River Swift

Though he was not directly involved in either event, Wycliffe's reputation was further affected by the Great Schism of 1378 and the Peasant Revolt of 1381. Although a second pope remained in France until 1417, the Great Schism strengthened England's ties by returning the papacy to Rome. This led to a series of wars and crusades between Avignon and Rome, prompting Wycliffe's belief that as an institution the papacy was hopelessly corrupt.

Then, in 1381, an uprising of peasants occurred in England over the issues of high taxes, government mistakes, and repeated crop failures—all of which the peasants blamed on the English feudal system. Under feudalism, peasants toiled for the owner of a large country estate or manor. Half of England's peasants were chattel slaves, living in dreary conditions and barely surviving by tilling a few strips of ground; whatever meager wealth they did manage to accumulate was demanded by the village priest and the feudal lord. The priest would receive tithes and special fees at births, marriages, and deaths. The feudal lord received fines or fees if the peasant's son attended school, or if a daughter married. These conditions led to the 1381 revolt that was put down with great cruelty. In the meantime, the frightened aristocracy linked Wycliffe's ideas with the revolting peasants.

He Directs Translation of Bible into English

Wycliffe's greatest achievement is generally thought to have been his role in the translation of the Bible from the 14th-century Vulgate to English. Maintaining that unlettered men should study the Bible in order to appreciate the Scriptures as God's supreme authority, he knew that to make the Bible available to the common person would require the development of a simple, readable translation. He undertook the task of directing such a translation while his opponents ridiculed this work, lamenting, "the jewel of the clergy has become the toy of the laity."

To give wide currency to the Gospel as he understood it, Wycliffe sent out his followers—often referred to as "Bible Men"—as traveling preachers or "poor priests." Garbed in simple red robes and carrying only staffs, they preached the sovereignty of God while living in poverty, taking no formal vows, and seeking no consecration by the Church. Wycliffe hoped that his Lollards, as the Bible Men came to be called, would eventually replace the existing Church hierarchy.

As the Lollards attracted an increasing following, speaking out against the corruptions of the Church and clergy, a response became inevitable. The bishops feared a widespread movement led by unordained priests spreading discontent throughout the English countryside; in addition, Wycliffe's attacks on the Church doctrine of transubstantiation alienated orthodox believers. Consequently, in 1381, the English Church hierarchy persuaded the chancellor of the University of Oxford to openly accuse the theologian of heresy. Confronted in an auditorium on the Oxford campus, Wycliffe responded by declaring that "neither the chancellor or any other person could change

his convictions." He then appealed—not to higher clergy or the pope—but to the English king. The appeal only served to enhance his growing national reputation. "Every second man that you meet," wrote a contemporary, "is a Lollard."

In 1382, King Richard II issued a decree forbidding the distribution of heretical ideas on Catholic sacraments, clergy, and institutions by Wycliffe and his followers. Several of his more prominent helpers were forced to recant. Although a paralytic stroke left him frail and gaunt, Wycliffe himself was summoned to a synod at Oxford on November 18, 1382. Weak in body though not in spirit, he refused to recant. He was, however, not excommunicated or deprived of his Church income. After returning to his parish at Lutterworth, he spent the next two years writing and preaching, producing two works of significance: the *Trialogus* and *Opus Evangelicum.*

While hearing Mass on December 28, 1384, Wycliffe suffered a second stroke and died on the last day of the year. But even in his grave, he would be accused of heresy. In 1415, the Council of Constance decreed that Wycliffe's books be burned and his body exhumed. Though his works were destroyed immediately, 13 years passed before the theologian's body was disinterred, burned to ashes, and cast into the River Swift.

SOURCES:

Latourette, Kenneth Scott. *A History of Christianity.* 2 vols. Harper, 1975.

The New Schaff-Herzog Encyclopedia of Religious Knowledge. 16 vols. Baker Books, 1955.

Winn, Herbert W., ed. *John Wyclif: Select English Writings.* Oxford University Press, 1929.

FURTHER READING:

Dictionary of the Middle Ages. 12 vols. Scribner, 1989.

Lambert, Malcolm. *Medieval Heresy.* Holmes & Meir, 1976.

Wakefield, Walter L. *Heresies of the High Middle Ages.* Columbia University Press, 1969.

Francis Xavier

(1506–1552)

Jesuit missionary, sometimes called the "Apostle of the Indies," who attempted to introduce Christianity to India, Indonesia, and Japan.

"He was no mystic, contemplative or even 'proficient' in the ways of devotion. He performed the stock methods of devotion, exercises, prayer routines and taking the discipline exactly. He retained a strong rustic and Basque belief in signs, wonders, miracles, and devils."

J. C. H. AVELING

An order of priests dedicated to serving the pope in absolute obedience, the Jesuits became a spearhead of the Counter-Reformation in the second half of the 16th century. Founded by **Ignatius Loyola,** a Spanish soldier who turned to a life of ardent Christianity after being severely wounded, the Jesuit's most famous original member was Francis Xavier. The two men, both Basques, were friends in life and became saints together in 1622. While Loyola passed his life in Europe, Francis Xavier traveled to the Portuguese colonies in Asia to begin Jesuit missions there and to convert the "heathen" peoples of those lands. He tried to convert Indian pearl-fishermen, Malayan farmers, and Japanese warlords, and died of tropical diseases after 12 years in the Far East while on an almost suicidal mission to the forbidden kingdom of China.

Born and raised on the family estate at Xavier, in Navarre, Francis's native tongue was Basque. His father was a royal councillor and the boy, youngest son of a large family, was, says Jesuit biographer James Brodrick, "bred in an atmosphere of austere Catholic piety." When Francis was ten and his father had already passed away,

Born on the family estate at Xavier, in Navarre, Spain, in 1506; died on Sancian Island, en route to China, in 1552; son of Don Juan de Jassu y Atondo (a royal councillor) and Doña Maria de Azpilcueta y Aznarez de Sada; unmarried with no children.

Contributed by Patrick Allitt, Assistant Professor of History, Emory University, Atlanta, Georgia

Navarre revolted unsuccessfully against the rule of **Ferdinand II of Aragon.** As a result most of Xavier Castle, including all its fortifications, was demolished, and only a small house was left to shelter Francis's mother and siblings. A few years later in 1519, Francis's older brothers took part in another revolt against Ferdinand's successor King Charles I. They took part in the attack on Pamplona at which Ignatius Loyola, one of the defenders, received the wounds which changed his life. This dramatic event, a foundational moment for the Jesuits, saw the Loyolas and the Xaviers on opposing sides in the European wars. Soon they would be united as priests in the service of Rome.

Francis Xavier went to the college of Saint Barbara in Paris in 1525 and stayed there without interruption until 1536. Although he was less dissolute than many of his contemporaries, Francis was not yet a model of piety and seems to have enjoyed athletics and other games. His roommate was Pierre Favre from Savoy, and both men were swept up in the ascetic movement which transformed their college life with the arrival of Ignatius Loyola in 1528. At first Xavier seemed one of the least promising of Loyola's Paris Companions. Resentful of study, he led a busy social life, and still apparently looked forward to acquiring a well-paying parish in his Basque home or patents of nobility from the king. He took longer to persuade than Favre but at last was convinced of his divine mission, after which he apparently never wavered in his faith to the Jesuits or to Loyola himself. Loyola said that Xavier was "the lumpiest dough he had ever

kneaded." The seven companions made their vows at Montmartre in 1534, though Xavier, like Loyola, was not ordained a priest until 1537, in Rome.

Companions Walk to Rendezvous with Loyola

After graduation at Paris, Xavier got a job lecturing in classical philosophy at the College of Dormans-Beauvais, but the demands of the Jesuit Companions took up most of his time. When he undertook the arduous "spiritual exercises" which Loyola had worked out, he excelled in self-mortification by binding up his limbs so tightly that they swelled around the ropes, cut into his flesh, and made his friends fear that at least one arm would have to be amputated. But the cord broke and his arm healed in what seemed to the others a miraculous way. When in 1537 they all *walked* from Paris to Venice, to a prearranged rendezvous with Loyola (who was coming from Spain), Francis again bound up his legs with ropes, tightly enough almost to cripple him. The Companions had planned to go on pilgrimage to Jerusalem, but war with the Turks in the Mediterranean made it impossible for the pilgrim ships to set sail. Instead, the Companions made for Rome, living in evangelical poverty and helping the sick along the way. On arrival, they continued their good works in heroic poverty while Loyola resolved to ask for papal blessing on their official constitution as the Society of Jesus.

Soon Loyola and Xavier would be forced to bade one another farewell for the last time. King John III of Portugal had taken an interest in the Society of Jesus, becoming in effect its patron and not always a welcome one. In 1539, he asked Pope Paul III to send some of the new Jesuits on a mission to his Far East colonies. Loyola, still waiting for papal approval of his request to constitute the Society as an order in its own right, was obliged to comply. Reluctant to send Xavier, his secretary and right-hand man, he tried to send two others of the Companions instead, Nicolas Bobadilla and Simon Rodriguez. But Bobadilla had no wish to go and was gravely sick. When Xavier and Rodriguez arrived in Portugal on their way to the East Indies, they found King John III eager to keep them there. Thus, for a year they worked in hospitals with the sick and heard confessions at court. Rodriguez accepted the king's offer to stay permanently, but Xavier resolved to carry on to the Indies, having once begun. Though he obtained a letter from the pope making him *nuncio* in the East, his real mission seems not to have been properly worked out before he left. Once he arrived, his ambiguous status often provoked conflict with other Catholic missions and civil authorities in the Far East.

With a few exceptions, "the Jesuit missionaries went overseas very ignorant of the geography of the areas they traversed and settled in, and totally ignorant of their culture and history," notes historian J. C. H. Aveling. "What passed for geography in university and Jesuit College courses before the mid seventeenth century was a farrago of ancient speculation and a very little modern hearsay." Xavier was no exception. Although as a saint his legend has been greatly enlarged, he did not seem particularly imposing to many of his contemporaries; some found him decidedly ignorant. As historian Aveling concludes:

> He had all the astonishing courage, endurance, forthrightness and gambling instincts of his contemporaries, the Portugese and Spanish conquerors and, like them, no taste for the arts of diplomacy.... As with the conquerors, ignorance positively encouraged him in making crazy decisions and taking tremendous risks.

Despite the legend that he had the gift of tongues and could speak in the native languages of Asians everywhere, Xavier actually found it very difficult to learn languages. Though he spent much time and effort to improve his fluency, he never mastered more than a few phrases of Tamil, Malay, and Japanese. Nearly all his Asian work was done through interpreters.

Due to a long wait for favorable winds in Mozambique, an outbreak of scurvy, and other hardships, his ship set sail in 1541 but took over a year to reach Goa, the Portugese colony on the southeast coast of India. Xavier and his two companions, one of whom, says Brodrick, was "a well-meaning dunce who could not learn enough Latin to say Mass or Office and so remained forlornly unordained," were not made particularly welcome by the governor, especially when Xavier suggested making war against the Indian Muslims, with whom the colony traded, and when he began to denounce the many Portugese traders at Goa who kept private harems.

Xavier Undertakes "Automatic Conversion"

The governor put the Jesuits to work converting the pearl fishermen of Cape Cormorin, the Paravas, by teaching catechism to their children. The work was done by rote, as the missionaries managed to learn the Tamil phrases to fit the Ten Commandments and the catechism. At times, Xavier even settled for "automatic conversion," that is, baptizing people with whom he had no common language and who had not had even the

fundamental rudiments of Christianity properly explained to them. In a much-quoted letter home, he said that at times he had baptized so many that he could scarcely move his arms. His nominal success with the Paravas was not matched when he tried to proselytize among the high caste Brahmins, and he admitted that a year's preaching had converted only one Brahmin.

For the first time while working at Goa, Xavier recognized the need to adopt native dress when he saw that a man dressed like a guru was always honored. This adaptation led to claims from his 18th-century admirers that he was ahead of his time in making shrewd concessions to native cultures when proselytizing. But Xavier had no great sensitivity to indigenous cultures. He ordered all his converts to smash their idols and desecrate their shrines, sometimes leading gangs of boys to the attack, and treated the lack of Christian faith and morality, even in those who had never known of them, as a disgrace. Even Brodrick, his sympathetic biographer, has to admit that "St. Francis Xavier's knowledge of Hinduism was, if possible, even less adequate than his few biased notions of Mohammedanism." His lack of knowledge and imagination fed his singlemindedness, however, and enabled him to endure the otherwise intolerable hardships of his Asian wanderings.

Like Loyola, he understood the advantage of educating children to Christianity even if he could not attract their parents. In one letter to his simple-minded assistant Francisco Mansilhas, when they were working in pearl-fishers' villages a few miles apart, he wrote:

> I earnestly recommend to you the teaching of the children, and be very diligent about the baptism of newly born babies. Since the grown-ups have no hankering for Paradise, whether to escape the evils of life or to attain their happiness, at least let the little ones go there by baptizing them before they die.

During his second stay among the Paravas, Xavier became embroiled in a local chieftains' war and was dismayed to discover the unscrupulousness of many Portugese traders, who tried to turn local conflicts to their advantage. Their methods included selling horses and weapons to the enemies of Indian Christian converts and trying to prevent Xavier from arranging truces for fear that their profitable trade would slacken. At the same time, some Indian leaders realized that there were tactical benefits to converting, if being a Christian meant that the Portugese governor might intervene on their behalf with ships and troops against a traditional enemy. Francis Xavier was something of an innocent among these European and Asian Machiavellians.

When reinforcements arrived from Portugal in 1544, he left Goa and tried to establish Jesuit missions elsewhere. His new assistant priests were far from ideal. Several had died from tropical diseases on the grueling journey out, while others were mentally unstable or too dishonest to be useful; he also dismissed several members from the society outright. Despite these problems, Xavier moved on to establish a mission at Malacca, an important port in the spice trade on the Malay peninsula which the Portugese had founded in 1511. There he befriended Mendes Pinto, a capable Portuguese merchant who filled him in on Far Eastern geopolitics. As at Goa, Xavier annoyed many of the Europeans by denouncing their immoral conduct in the bluntest terms but won the sympathetic admiration of others, who helped him visit many of the islands in what is today Indonesia. He also met Anjiro, a Japanese exile, and after long conversations decided to visit Japan and attempt its conversion. Setting off in 1549 after another stop in Goa, he and his party, including Anjiro, who had been baptized and taken the name "Paul of the Holy Faith," landed at Kagoshima in southern Japan.

He Works To Convert Japanese

At first Xavier's appearance as an Indian guru led to ridicule. He modified his approach, dressed as a *bonze* (monk) and presented himself as an agent of the Portugese king. This posture, and his seeming imperturbability, led to an introduction to several of the Japanese warlords, whom he believed he could convert as a prelude to the conversion of their people. He also visited Buddhist monasteries to debate with the senior monks questions of immortality, the destiny of the soul, and the virtue of austerity and self-mortification. He formed a strong friendship with Ninjitsu, a monk of Kagoshima, but could not convert him. Language remained a severe problem. Although his convert Paul acted as interpreter, Paul was not a highly literate man, and Xavier feared that his translations were loose, especially as the Japanese language lacked the vocabulary for such key Christian concepts as incarnation, resurrection, and the Trinity. Xavier and his two European companions struggled hard through the first winter to master Japanese, but without either an aptitude or a good teacher Xavier found it hard going. His younger Jesuit companion Father Fernandez did slightly better and took to preaching at crossroads in a loud and strangely accented voice, denouncing the local men for homosexuality and the women for practicing female infanticide.

Francis Xavier met the local strongman Shimazu, the *daimyo* (feudal baron) of Satsuma, who was a Soto Zen Buddhist. Delighting him with the gift of a holy picture showing the Madonna and Child, Xavier won from him permission to preach and convert in his duchy. But after a year the *Daimyo*, who had overestimated Xavier's importance and had wrongly anticipated the arrival of European ships bringing wealth, began to sour on the Jesuit and encouraged him to leave Kagoshima in a small boat. Despite an exhausting winter journey to Kyoto, Xavier was unable to get an audience with the mikado (emperor)—who was accessible only after payment of a huge bribe—and gradually came to see that in this war-torn country the emperor was a nominal rather than genuine national leader. A surviving letter he wrote from Japan to the Jesuits in Goa suggests the difficulties he faced and the militant, unyielding faith with which he met adversity:

> The worst hardships you have hitherto endured are trifling compared with what awaits you when you come to Japan.... I do not say this as though to give you the impression that the service of God is hard. Indeed no; it is light and easy on condition that a man seeks God by the conquest of his own inclinations. But if he is not resolute in the time of trial, he will never know the infinite bounty of God, nor have the peace in this weary life, which to live without the intimate realization of God is not life at all but protracted death.

He added that he was freezing cold and that all future Jesuit visitors to Japan should bring plenty of Portuguese woolen clothes. Leaving Japan when there were just a few hundred converts, rather than the thousands he had boldly anticipated, he entrusted the mission to Cosmas de Torres, another Portuguese Jesuit, and returned to Goa. One of his Japanese converts, whom he baptized as Bernard, went to Europe, met Loyola in Rome, and became a member of the Jesuits but died young in Spain after making a good impression for his piety and learning.

Conflict between the Jesuits and the other orders at Goa, and between them and the governor, prompted Xavier to appoint a Flemish Jesuit, Gaspar Berze, as his vice provincial before setting out on an even more arduous mission to China. He also felt obliged to dismiss Father Antony Gomez, rector of his college at Goa, who had refused to teach native converts and wanted to preserve the college solely for the sons of Portuguese families. Gomez also had tried to build a monumental Catholic church in Goa, and his high-handed methods had attracted the animosity of both civil and religious authorities, undermining the respect which Xavier had won for the Jesuits.

China was the greatest Asian power, whose conversion would, Xavier anticipated, echo throughout the East. But foreigners were forbidden to set foot on Chinese soil on pain of execution. Undeterred, Xavier set sail, going first to Malacca, and planning to take his friend Diogo Pereira with him as Portugese ambassador to the Chinese court. The governor of Malacca, Don Alvaro d'Ataide, had a grudge against Pereira and refused to let him leave, but Xavier carried on regardless, though he now lacked even the minimal diplomatic protection an ambassador might have provided. He had been in the Far East for 11 years, and the cumulative effects of several tropical diseases contracted on his journeys, without proper treatment, finally caught up with him. Only 46, he was prematurely aged, with sparse white hair, and now increasingly frail and sick. He died on the offshore island of Sancian in December of 1552, without ever setting foot on the Chinese mainland.

Francis Xavier had had a magnetic personality, and even though the number of his converts was not great, devotees of other religions regarded him as a holy man with magical powers. His exhumed body, uncorrupted after two months in the grave in a coffin filled with quicklime, occasioned an outburst of veneration from Malacca sailors who had earlier mistreated him. It was moved first back to Malacca, where his tomb became a pilgrimage for Buddhists and Muslims as well as Christians, and then taken to Goa, where it remained as a shrine to Jesuit missionaries in the East. The Jesuit general Claudio Acquaviva ordered that the right arm be cut from the corpse and brought back to Rome for burial in the church of the Gesu.

Xavier was canonized at the same time as his leader Ignatius Loyola, in 1622, and Catholics celebrate his feast on the anniversary of his death, December 3. In the early 20th century, Pope (Saint) Pius X paid him the further compliment of naming him patron saint of all foreign missions. Francis Xavier was also one of few post-Reformation Catholic saints to enjoy the high esteem of Protestants and agnostics, who praised him for his patience and his willingness to adapt to local customs. The British novelist Sir Walter Scott, for example, said that:

> the most rigid Protestant, and the most indifferent philosopher, cannot deny to him the courage and patience of a martyr, with the good sense, resolution, ready wit, and address of the best negotiator that ever went upon a temporal embassy.

And, despite its makeshift character, his work in Asia did have lasting consequences. His successors in Japan succeeded in creating a thriving Christian community which flourished for a hundred years before succumbing to severe persecution in the late 17th century. His example, moreover, inspired hundreds of Jesuits and other priests to pledge themselves to Asian missionary work in the decades following his death.

SOURCES:

Aveling, J. C. H. *The Jesuits.* London: Blond and Briggs, 1981.

Boxer, C. R. *The Christian Century in Japan.* University of California Press, 1967.

Brodrick, James, S.J. *Saint Francis Xavier, 1506–1552.* Wicklow Press, 1952.

Butler, Alban. *The Lives of the Saints.* London: Burns, Oates & Washbourne, 1938.

Schurhammer, Georg, S.J. *Francis Xavier: His Life, His Times.* 4 vols. Rome: Jesuit Historical Institute, 1973.

Huldrych Zwingli

(1484–1531)

Swiss reformer who, by referring to the Bible as the only authority, condemned papacy and its practices and laid the foundation for the Swiss Protestant Church.

Born Ulrich Zwingli (he preferred Huldrych, "the gracious one") on January 1, 1484, in Wildhaus, Switzerland; died on October 11, 1531, in the Second Kappel War; son of Ulrich Zwingli (a free peasant and local magistrate in Wildhaus); married: Anna Reinhart (a widow); children: two daughters, one son. Successor: Henry Bullinger.

In 1484, Huldrych Zwingli was born on New Year's Day in Wildhaus, a small village in the Toggenburg valley. His father Ulrich, a magistrate and free peasant, was actively involved in local politics. At six, Zwingli was taken in by his uncle Bartholomew Zwingli, incumbent of the deanery in Weesen on Wallen Lake. At ten, in 1494, he was sent to Basel, later to Berne, to obtain his secondary education and was taught Greek and Latin by famous humanist teachers. For unknown reasons, Zwingli left Berne prematurely, without having completed his Latin studies. Henry Bullinger, who was to continue Zwingli's reformational work in Zurich, and Johannes Stumpf, a contemporary chronicler, suggested that the Dominicans' eagerness to see him join their order was to blame for Zwingli's early departure. The Dominicans were greatly impressed by his beautiful singing voice. In his later years, though having banished "noisy hymns" from the Church, Zwingli would privately maintain his passion for songs and instruments.

During the following years, 1498–1506, Zwingli took up liberal arts study at the universities of Vienna and Basle, ending his studies in Basle by receiving the magister of arts degree. He

Contributed by Susanne Peter-Kubli, Historian, Wädenswil, Switzerland

then assigned himself to the studies of theology. In Basle, he met Konrad Pellikan and fellow-student Leo Jud who were to become his closest friends, and who would later help to publish Zwingli's reformational pamphlets.

From 1506 to 1516, Zwingli was the parish priest in the small town of Glarus. The town's inhabitants seemed pleased with their new priest, who took a special interest in their children's education. Around 1510, he founded a school in which the town's youth had their first go at Latin. His spare time was devoted entirely to classical studies.

While preparing his Sunday services, Zwingli came to feel that too much attention was being paid to "externals" and to Bible commentaries, rather than to the Bible's actual text. Consequently, he turned to the original text, which, by 1515, was published by the great 16th-century scholar Erasmus of Rotterdam. In order to grasp the full meaning of the New Testament, Zwingli spent so much time in studying and copying out that he committed most of the Epistles of St. Paul to memory.

In Zwingli's day, the Swiss Confederation was a working—but relatively loose—alliance of communities, each of which was autocratic in internal affairs and simultaneously forced into cooperation with each other when extended market or commonly governed areas (the so-called *Untertanengebiete*) were at stake. Though as far back as 1291 the people of Uri, Schwyz, and Unterwalden had established what is now celebrated as the founding of Switzerland, it was not until 1499 that the Swiss Confederates had openly declared themselves independent of the Holy Roman Empire led by **Maximilian I.**

The people inhabiting the small towns, villages, and hamlets of the Swiss valleys lived primarily on a rarely changing diet of milk, gruel, dried fruit, and cheese. When cattle breeding proved less profitable than agriculture, many young men wanted to sign up as mercenaries for foreign kings, dukes, or the pope—provided that payment was good and prospects for plundering defeated cities were bright.

During the years which Zwingli spent in Glarus, the kings of France and Habsburg were engaged in a bitter war over the dukedom of Milan. Swiss troops, among them a detachment from Glarus with Zwingli as their chaplain, defended papal interests as well as their own. Back in Glarus, Zwingli recorded his impressions of the campaign. He wrote a fable called *The Ox,* in which he emphasized that—for the safety of the Swiss Confederation—it was essential not to sell out to for-

CHRONOLOGY

1484	Born in Wildhaus in the Toggenburg valley, Switzerland
1506-16	Parish priest in Glarus
1517	Martin Luther published his "95 Theses"
1519	Zwingli appointed foundation preacher at the Great Minster in Zurich
1523	First Zurich Disputation; presented Auslegungen und Gruende der Schlussreden
1525	*Commentary on True and False Religion*
1526	Disputation in Baden
1528	Disputation in Berne; Zwinglian reforms of the Church accepted and carried through in the state of Berne
1529	Debate with Martin Luther in Marburg; first Kappel War against Catholic Confederates
1531	Second Kappel War; Zwingli died in battle

eign warlords, but rather to stay altogether removed from the power-play of the European monarchs.

In 1515, the Swiss troops suffered their most bitter defeat against the French in Marignano. The following year, however, they signed a treaty with the French king **Francis I** in which they agreed to sign up as French mercenaries in exchange for economic benefits. When Zwingli's opposition to the treaty became public, he had to leave Glarus.

Zwingli Goes to Great Minster in Zurich

He then spent three years as a stipendiary priest in Einsiedeln's famous Benedictine abbey. There, in addition to taking care of the spiritual needs of the small community, he preached to hundreds of pilgrims who had come to do penance and receive absolutions for money. During his stay at the abbey, Zwingli continued to improve his knowledge of the Scripture by studying and imitating the works of Erasmus. By 1518, his preaching skills had been noticed at the Great Minster in Zurich, where he was soon appointed foundation preacher with parochial responsibilities.

To better enable his audience to understand the word of God, in January of 1519 Zwingli began a series of discourses on the Gospel according to St. Matthew, which used simple terms and incorporated references to events in every day life. Despite some opposition among the more traditional priests, his unusual method was soon to be followed by his fellow priests of the Great Minster. In Wittenberg, the Augustine monk **Martin Luther** had earlier experienced doubts similar to Zwingli's concerning the policy of the Roman Catholic Church. In 1517, Luther had published his "95 Theses" hoping to make clergy, as well as princes and dukes, focus their attention on the present state of the Church, in which canon law ruled over divine law, and corruption and illiteracy among the clergy was as common as among laics. Neither the bishops nor the pope were ready to discuss the matter. They answered Luther's appeal with his excommunication.

Luther, however, continued and doubled his efforts at guiding the Church back to its roots. In 1522, the first edition of his German translation of the New Testament was printed in Basle. Eagerly, it was purchased and studied by Zwingli and his friends in Zurich. Having miraculously survived the plague which broke out in Zurich in 1519, Zwingli by now saw himself as a man with a mission to reform the Roman Catholic Church. He would do so by making the Scripture—*sola scriptura*—the only authority. He wanted as well to prove to the world that each individual could enter into a direct relationship with God through **Jesus Christ.** On March 5, 1522, in the house of the printer Christopher Froschauer, some friends and early Zwingli supporters broke the rule of fasting during Lent by eating sausages. Zwingli turned this event into a public issue in his sermon, which he followed with the pamphlet *Vom Erkiesen und Freiheit der Speisen* which not only condoned the action but claimed that it was the right of every individual to choose freely what to eat.

This question of fasting triggered many other issues, including clerical celibacy. Though priesthood and marriage were considered incompatible by canon law, many clergymen of northern Switzerland were, indeed, married. And Zwingli was among them. Secretly, he'd married Anna Reinhart and had fathered several children. Together with ten other priests he sent a petition to the bishop of Constance asking for recognition by pointing out that the "bishops" of the early Church had also been married men.

Another issue on which Zwingli took a different stand was that concerning the practice of praying to the saints, asking them for help and earthly favors. In his view, the saints were thus used as a means of intermediating between man and God. Whereas, Zwingli thought it proper to learn humility, faith, and hope from the saints, he believed that prayer should be directed to God alone; the only medium accepted was Jesus Christ.

Intimately connected with the adoration of the saints was the belief that they worked miracles. Having witnessed crowds of pilgrims flocking to shrines asking for miracles, Zwingli realized that most people were left in ignorance and superstition, while the Church constantly enriched itself and claimed to be the judge of sin. Moreover, the pictures and images of the saints which, in Zwingli's eyes, offered only distraction—and even encouraged idolatry—had best be taken down. This measure was taken literally by some young enthusiasts, and from 1523 to 1525 all the churches of Zurich were stripped of decorations, statues, and pictures. The violence with which this "cleansing" was performed caused great disturbances among those states (cantons) which refused to adopt Zwingli's new method.

He Outlines Program of Religious Reform

In the 16th century, the so-called disputations (public debates) were the generally accepted means for settling matters of conflict. In January of 1523, Zwingli invited the leading clergy of various states of the Swiss Confederation, including the bishop of Constance, to Zurich's town hall to discuss these religious matters. Most of his opponents, however, refused to accept the invitation, with the bishop sending his personal adviser, Johannes Fabri, as an observer. Because of the strong support Zwingli could count on in Zurich—and because most of the disagreeing party either had not shown up or refused to enter into discussion—the outcome was a clear victory for Zwingli. *The Auslegungen und Gruende der Schlussreden* which Zwingli had written for this disputation would become a rudimentary outline of the program for religious reform in Switzerland. The two most vital issues decided were (1) that Zwingli had the consent of the Council of Zurich to continue his way of preaching; and (2) that it was the duty of the government to control public worship and religious observances—a measure which thus transferred the authority of the pope and the bishops to the state. Among those practices no longer acceptable to Christian believers were pilgrimages, processions, incense, noisy hymns, hired masses, and the purchase of prayers and indulgences. Along with these, Zwingli advised his audience not to give in to gambling, bad language, and costly garments, but rather to use their money to feed the poor and support widows and orphans.

A second disputation held in autumn dealt with radical members within Zwingli's circle who expressed such violence and fanaticism that they had to be brought before the council. Further steps that marked the reformation in Zurich included the closing of monasteries—most of the members having left voluntarily—and the confiscation of their land and fortunes in order to support the poor; the suppression of the Mass; and the introduction of the Eucharist. Bread and wine, according to the reformers, were not literally transubstantiated into the flesh and blood of Jesus Christ, but they were used as a remembrance of his sacrifice.

During the years to come, Zwingli turned Zurich into an evangelical city. Those who disagreed with him were forced by mandate to comply; those who did not comply, such as the Anabaptists, were made to leave. As early as 1524, disagreements surfaced among some of Zwingli's friends and disciples as to the meaning of the Last Supper and baptism. To them, the alterations proposed by Zwingli were too conservative, and they soon formed a separatist movement, known as the Swiss brethren, which was seen as a threat to the Zwinglians. Unlike Zwingli and Luther (who considered free will out of the question in Christian faith), the Anabaptists believed that "even the atheist had a right to his unbelief as long as he obeyed Civil Law." They also strictly separated the state from the Church. The main sources of dispute between Zwinglians and Anabaptists were Christian discipleship, baptism and the Lord's Supper. Yet, it was the recently inaugurated Believer's Baptism (as opposed to child's baptism) that in 1525 led to the suppression of the Anabaptist movement in Zurich and later to the banishment of its members. They were prosecuted, and in 1527 one of their leaders, Felix Mantz, was among those executed. This harsh policy, practiced by the council and supported by Zwingli, contributed to some loss of his popularity and was regarded as a sign of increasing mental inflexibility.

What had begun as a religious dispute rapidly developed into a force dividing the confederation. In 1524, the five central states formed a special alliance. Zurich, in turn, sought possible allies and defenders of its cause. In 1526, a Catholic-dominated conference held in Baden (Zwingli, though invited, did not take part for reasons of his personal safety) condemned Zwinglian reforms. Johannes Eck, a brilliant scholar from Ingoldstadt well known for his verbal attacks on Luther, and Johannes Fabri presided over the meeting, leaving no chance to close the gap that had opened between the states following the Zwinglian reforms which were condemned as the works of the "Antichrist of the Great Minster." The conference's outcome was a blow to the reformers in Zurich. Zwingli's absence, in the eyes of his opponents, was considered an act of cowardice.

On January 6, 1528, a public religious debate was allowed to take place in Berne, the largest state of the confederation and a state hitherto relatively indifferent to the reforms taking place in Zurich. All Bernese clergy were invited and so were the four bishops of Lausanne, Sion, Basle, and Constance. Zwingli and Johannes Oekolampadius of Basle, who had spoken on Zwingli's behalf in Baden, were to attend the debate. Similar to the first disputation held in Zurich, the pro-Catholic participants again refused to attend. The Catholics present tried to justify papacy on the grounds of an announcement made by Jesus that, through the apostle Peter, the authority of the pope and the hierarchy of bishops, priests, and laics were to be institutionalized. The reformers could not accept this reasoning because, as far as they were concerned, the Church was the body of Christ and Christ, therefore, its only head.

The debate lasted until the end of January, leaving no doubt that the reformation of the Church, as Zwingli had demanded in Zurich, was soon to be carried through in the state of Berne. In addition to the changes concerning preaching and religious observances, there was also a general agreement as to the prohibition of pensions and mercenary services. One region, the Berner Oberland, tried to resist the introduction of the reforms, asking the neighboring states of Valais, Uri, and Unterwalden for spiritual and, eventually, military support. To reprimand the rebellious subjects, Berne sent in troops. The peasants of the Berner Oberland soon gave up their resistance and acknowledged the innovations imposed by the capital.

Zwingli had reached the summit of his power and influence. Those states willing to conform to Zurich standards were looking to him for guidance and advice. Realizing that his dream of a Protestant Swiss Confederation could only come true with the help of foreign allies, he encouraged the council to form stronger ties with the cities of Muelhausen and Strassburg. Although they were part of the German Empire, the *zugewandte Orte*, as they were called, had for some time been on friendly terms with the Swiss Confederation.

Zwingli and Luther, both determined to reform the Catholic Church, held different views on the subjects of the Last Supper and the Eucharist. Both rejected the idea of transubstantiation. Yet, for Zwingli, according to John 6:63, this was to be taken primarily symbolically, because the body of Christ had already ascended into Heaven. Luther, on the other hand, drew his conclusions from the literal translation of the Last Supper. Luther claimed that, since Christ was everywhere and in all things, to deny his presence in the elements (bread and wine) was to deny the plain meaning of the words of Christ as well as his ubiquity.

Zwingli and Luther Debate at Marburg

The divergence of these opinions was enhanced by personal resentments. Because of the achievements they'd made so far, both men had no doubts that their way of interpreting the Scripture was the correct way. Luther was a regular priest who was said to have had a haughty way about him when speaking to Zwingli (whom he considered a coarse fanatic trying to show off his Greek and Latin because his German was so bad). When they finally met at a conference in Marburg in the fall of 1529, on the first day they were said to have parted without shaking hands. Thanks to the intervention and pleading of Philipp of Hesse, Luther's patron and host of the meeting, the participants drew up 15 articles constituting the Protestant faith.

The Marburg meeting took place between the two Kappel Wars. In 1528, immediately after Zwingli's successful appearance in Berne, Zurich had extended its influence to the territories of St. Gall, Thurgau and to the Lake of Constance. Furthermore, Protestant villages in the commonly governed areas were supported by Zurich. Accordingly, the Catholic states of Lucerne and Schwyz prohibited Zwinglian preaching within their borders. Jacob Kaiser, who did so preach, was sentenced to death by burning at the stake. On July 8, 1529, Zurich declared war on the Catholic Confederates, and the two armies met near the village Kappel. The Protestant troops far outnumbered the Catholics. Only a few moments before the actual fighting, the leaders of the opposite sides were called in for peace negotiations. Zwingli was disgusted. He warned the council against giving in to the pleading of the Catholics, because he was convinced that only a foul peace could be won that way. Nevertheless, a truce was drawn up and signed by both parties. Yet neither side seemed completely satisfied: the Catholics felt defeated by heretics, and Zurich's ambition was far from stilled.

When Zwingli returned home after the Marburg meeting, at first events seemed to develop quite to his approval. Evidently, his word had become absolute and, as a contemporary Catholic historian admitted, "Zwingli was Zurich's mayor, Town Clerk and Council all in one." But soon thereafter open resistance from the Catholic states of Switzerland was combined with opponents in his own ranks. Zwingli proposed a quick military campaign to put down opposition once and for all. Yet, the Bernese allies interfered, suggesting an economic blockade instead. This blockade proved very hard on the Catholic Confederates whose well-being largely depended on Zurich markets. Within Zurich, Zwingli's popularity began to shrink as merchants, millers, bakers, and other artisans complained of the damaging effect the blockade had on their trade. Constantly losing ground, Zwingli asked the council to relieve him from his post. Though he was begged to stay, his position remained undermined.

Filled with foreboding, Zwingli reportedly went out for a walk one evening, and a comet appeared in the sky. His companion inquired as to the comet's meaning, and Zwingli is said to have replied: "My dear George, it will cost my life and those of many men of honour, and the Truth and the Church will suffer much distress; but Christ will not desert us."

Some days later, news reached Zurich that the army of the Catholic Confederates had gathered near Zug. Hastily, Zurich's troops hurried in from all sides, but in a matter of only one day it was impossible to form orderly units. No time remained to ask the Protestant allies for support. Facing the well-prepared Catholic troops near Kappel in October of 1531, the Protestant army of about 1,500 fought bravely, but without a chance. After only a few days, the Protestant alliance was defeated. Zurich lost about 500 men in battle, among them its spiritual leader, Huldrych Zwingli.

The truce that had been drawn up in November was much to the disadvantage of the Protestants. It did, however, save the Swiss Confederation from disintegration. In Zurich, it was the young priest from Bremgarten, Henry Bullinger, who would succeed Zwingli at the Great Minster and fully establish Protestantism in the Swiss Confederation.

SOURCES:

Estep, William R. *Renaissance and Reformation.* Eerdmanns, 1986.

Farner, Oskar. *Zwingli the Reformer: His Life and Work.* Translated by D. G. Sear. New York, 1952.

Jackson, Samuel Macauley, and Clarence Nevine Heller, eds. *Huldrych Zwingli's Commentary on True and False Religion.* Labyrinth Press, 1981.

Potter, G. R. *Zwingli.* Cambridge University Press, 1976.

Zuck, Lowell Herbert, ed. *Christianity and Revolution, Radical Christian Testimonies 1520-1650.* Philadelphia, 1975.

FURTHER READING:

Chaunu, Pierre. *The Reformation.* Sutton, 1990.

Gaebler, Ulrich. *Huldrych Zwingli, his Life and Work.* Translated by Ruth C.L. Gritsch. Fortress Press, 1986.

Rilliet, Jean. *Zwingli: Third Man of the Reformation.* Translated by Harold Knight. Lutterworth, 1964.

Zygmunt II Augustus

(1520–1572)

Polish king and the last of the Jagiellonians, who is distinguished in the annals of Polish history because of his role as Renaissance king, benefactor of Protestantism, and creator of the Union of Lublin.

"Despite his regal manner and cosmopolitan education, Sigismund II entirely lacked the assertiveness of the typical Renaissance prince. His temper was mild, and in his later years distinctly melancholy. He was nobody's 'wise fool,' but he administered the realm with a grace and ease that bordered on the nonchalant."

NORMAN DAVIES

In a time of continuity and contradiction, 16th-century Poland realized her *Zloty Wiek* (Golden Age) under the leadership of the Renaissance kings, Zygmunt I Stary and Zygmunt II Augustus. Under the Zygmunts, political freedom flourished and Poland enjoyed a golden age of arts and sciences. But this time of prosperity came to an abrupt end when King Zygmunt II died without leaving an heir for the Polish throne. It also brought an end to Poland's stable, successful, and culturally progressive Jagiellonian dynasty which was soon replaced by a disjointed system of elective monarchy. During the Jagiellonian period, the Polish nobility had greatly increased their political leverage and, with the death of Zygmunt II, they secured the power necessary to elect their future sovereigns. This system, coupled with other factors, ultimately led to the decline and fall of the Polish state in the 18th century.

Born on August 1, 1520, in the Polish capital of Krakow, Zygmunt Augustus was a prince of the Polish-Lithuanian royalty and the only son of Zygmunt I Stary and Bona Sforza. His father is often considered an innovator and the father of the

Name variations: Sigismund II. Born on August 1, 1520, in what was then Poland's capital, the city Krakow; died in Knyszyn in 1572; descended from Jagiellonian royalty; only child of King Zygmunt I and Queen Bona Sforza; married: Elizabeth of Habsburg (died 1545); married: Barbara Radziwill (died 1551); married: Katherine of Habsburg; children: none. Predecessor: Zygmunt I Stary (Sigismund I the Old). Successor: Henryk III Walezy (Henri Valois).

Contributed by Christopher Blackburn, Ph.D. candidate in history, Auburn University, Auburn, Alabama

1522	Zygmunt Augustus proclaimed future Grand Duke of Lithuania
1528	Monetary union of Poland, Lithuania and Prussia
1529	Incorporation of Mazovia into Poland
1530	Ivan IV (the Terrible) named Tsar of Russia; Zygmunt elected "king apparent" of Poland
1548	Ascended the thrones of both Poland and Lithuania
1555	Peace of Augsburg signed
1561	Union of Wilno; Polish entered into Livonian Wars
1562	French wars of religion began
1563	Schism among Polish Calvinists
1564	Arrival of Jesuits in Poland
1568	Revolt of the Netherlands
1569	Union of Lublin signed; Poland acquired Ukraine
1572	St. Bartholomew's Day Massacre in France; Zygmunt died in Knyszyn

by the finest Polish and Italian humanist scholars, he quickly learned to appreciate art, literature and architecture.

Wasting little time, his ambitious mother "resorted to the most desperate tactics of a Renaissance harpy" to secure his inheritance. By the age of two, her son was elected the future Grand Duke of Lithuania. By the age of nine, in 1529, he was officially recognized as the future king of Poland. Following his election, Zygmunt moved to Wilno and began his reign as the Grand Duke of Lithuania. Thus, for nearly two decades there were two King Zygmunts—the father, Zygmunt I Stary, in Krakow and the son, Zygmunt II Augustus, in Wilno. This dual kingship remained in place to insure that Zygmunt Augustus would face no opposition from the Polish magnates (Great Nobility) of the *Sejm* (Parliament), and to assure his ascension to both the Polish and Lithuanian thrones. With the death of King Zygmunt I in 1548, Bona Sforza's labors bore fruit as her son simply stepped in and took control of both states.

The Untimely Deaths of the Daughters-in-Law

Bona Sforza's manipulations took other forms. On her urging before his father's death, Zygmunt had married Princess Elizabeth of Habsburg (1543), the daughter of Emperor Ferdinand I. Within one year, the marriage had fallen apart, Elizabeth had failed to produce an heir, and Bona was dissatisfied with her new daughter-in-law. In the second year of the marriage, Zygmunt and Elizabeth separated but did not divorce. His mother soon remedied the situation; she put an end to the marriage by poisoning the young princess in 1545.

Two years later, Zygmunt secretly eloped with Barbara Radziwill, the widowed daughter of a Lithuanian *Hetman* ("general"). This second marriage came as quite a shock to both Zygmunt's mother and the Polish *Sejm*. Fearing that Zygmunt's Lithuanian in-laws might influence his decisions in Polish matters, the *Sejm* immediately demanded an annulment. Zygmunt refused. But when the marriage failed to produce an heir over the next four years, the marriage's end had a similar ring: the untimely death of Barbara Radziwill. Although the Lithuanian princess's death was shrouded in mystery and intrigue, most observers concluded that Queen Bona had poisoned yet another daughter-in-law. The death of his second wife devastated Zygmunt, and he never forgave his subjects' intrusion into his love "for the beautiful Barbara."

After a year of mourning, Zygmunt once again catered to the dynasty's need for an heir. For

Polish Renaissance. Kenneth Lewalski's writings attest to the greatness of Zygmunt I:

> [Zygmunt]'s contemporaries at home and abroad lauded him for his political acumen and achievements. The Polish chroniclers of the Renaissance recounted the events of his reign with great reverence, frequently criticizing the nobility and often Bona for opposing his policies. His campaigns against the Turks evoked the admiration of Erasmus. Paolo Giovio included [Zygmunt] in his catalogue of illustrious men, eulogizing him for his military prowess as well as for his Christian piety.

While not being known for her "Christian piety," Zygmunt Augustus's mother remains a major figure in Poland's Renaissance history. Bona Sforza was from the great Sforza family of Italy, and her marriage to Zygmunt II's father in 1518 "is perhaps the most familiar event in Polish Renaissance history."

> Bona's journey to Cracow with a retinue of 287 persons, followed by that of her adviser Prosper Colonna with an added company of fifty-eight Italians, suggests something on the order of an Italian invasion of the Polish court.

It was in this Renaissance atmosphere that the young Zygmunt Augustus grew up. Tutored

several months, the young ruler and his advisors contemplated a possible marriage to **Mary Tudor.** In 1553, however, Zygmunt married his first wife's unattractive sister, Princess Katherine of Habsburg. The marriage was a catastrophe from the start. Soon after the ceremony, when a frightened Zygmunt learned firsthand that Katherine was subject to epileptic episodes, he walked away from any intimacy in disgust. But his mother was not to be of much help. In 1556, Queen Bona retired from Polish political life. Feeling a bit unpopular, she simply appropriated some "430,000 ducats in cash and jewels from the royal treasury" and fled to her native Italian lands. Thus, Zygmunt's new wife did not follow her predecessors into a premature grave. Since Zygmunt could not take another wife, his refusal to return to his tormented queen ensured that no Jagiellonian heir would be born to fill the Polish throne.

Upon Zygmunt's ascension to the throne, the *szlachta* (gentry) expected the Renaissance king to quickly enact several much needed political and social reforms. To their disappointment, the reforms were not realized until late in Zygmunt's reign.

Union of Lublin Joins Poland and Lithuania

Despite Zygmunt's numerous marital failures and countless conflicts with the nobles of both Poland and Lithuania, he ultimately secured his place in history with the Union of Lublin. Signed near the end of his reign on July 1, 1569, in the Polish town of Lublin, the act constitutionally bound all Polish and Lithuanian lands together, thus forming the republic known as the Polish-Lithuanian Commonwealth. The Union of Lublin not only joined the two states physically, but also provided for their governing apparatus. Following 1569, the king of Poland also held the office of Grand Duke of Lithuania and governed both states as one united entity. The king would rule from the new Polish capital of Warsaw and be elected by a joint Polish-Lithuanian *Sejm*. The Diet of Lublin mandated:

That the Kingdom of Poland and the Grand Duchy of Lithuania are now a body one and indivisible, a Republic one and indivisible consisting of two states and Nations, who joined to form one people.

This grand union secured the Polish-Lithuanian state's place as a major European power, which it remained until its final demise in the partitions of the 18th century.

Hence, the reign of Zygmunt Augustus drew to a close and with his death also came the end of the prosperous Jagiellonian dynasty. From his deathbed Zygmunt tried to further strengthen the Polish-Lithuanian bond; his last wish is recounted by Norman Davies in *God's Playground: A History of Poland:*

We give and bequeath to our two realms, to the Polish Crown and to the Grand Duchy of Lithuania, that love, harmony, and unity. . . which our forbearers cemented for eternity by strong agreements....Whosoever shall profess ingratitude and follow the paths of separation, may they quake before the wrath of God, who in the words of the prophet, hates and curses them who sow dissension between brother and brother.

King Zygmunt II Augustus came to power as the ruler of the kingdom of Poland and the Grand Duchy of Lithuania; he died as ruler of the massive Polish-Lithuanian Commonwealth. This accomplishment alone merits a place among the elite of world history; nevertheless, it should also be remembered that he maintained and developed the Renaissance institutions of his father. Despite his many territorial, political, and social achievements, Zygmunt II is often unfairly remembered as simply the Polish king that could not produce an heir or the last Jagiellonian.

SOURCES:

Davies, Norman. *God's Playground: A History of Poland.* Columbia University Press, 1982.

Garlicki, Andrzej, ed. *Poczet krolow i ksiazat polskich.* Czytelnik, 1980.

Gierowski, Jozef Andrzej. *Historia Polski: 1505–1764.* Panstwowe Wydawnictwo Naukowe, 1982.

Kieniewicz, Stefan. *History of Poland.* Polish Scientific Publishers, 1968.

La Renaissance et la Reformation en Pologne et en Hongrie (1450–1650). Akademiai Kiado, 1963.

Lewalski, K. F. "Sigismund I of Poland: Renaissance King and Patron," in *Studies in the Renaissance.* 14: 49–72.

Reddaway, W. F., ed. *The Cambridge History of Poland.* Cambridge University Press, 1941.

Zamoyski, Adam. *The Polish Way.* Franklin Watts, 1988.

FURTHER READINGS:

Jasienica, Pawel. *Jagiellonian Poland.* American Institute of Polish Culture, 1978.

Samsonowicz, Henryk. "Polish Politics and Society Under the Jagiellonian Monarchy," in *A Republic of Nobles: Studies in Polish History to 1864.* Cambridge University Press, 1982.

Appendix A:

Political and Royal Leader Chronologies

AUSTRIA

HOUSE OF BABENBERG

Margraves

976–94	Leopold I
994–1018	Henry I
1018–55	Adalbert
1055–75	Ernst
1075–96	Leopold II
1096–1136	Leopold III, the Pious
1136–41	Leopold IV
1141–56	Henry II

Dukes

1156–77	Henry II
1177–94	Leopold V
1194–98	Frederick I
1198–1230	Leopold VI, the Glorious
1230–46	Frederick II
1248–50	Hermann von Baden
1250–53	Several claimants
1253–78	King Ottokar II of Bohemia

HABSBURG DYNASTY

1278–91	Duke **Rudolf I**
1291–1308	Duke Albert I
1308–30	Duke Frederick III
1308–26	Co-regent: Leopold I
1330–58	Duke Albert II
1330–39	Co-regent: Otto
1358–65	Rudolf
1358–97	Co-regent: Albert III
1365–79	Co-regent: Leopold III
1379	Austria divided between Albert III and Leopold III

Line of Albert

1379–95	Duke Albert III
1397–1404	Albert IV
1404–39	Albert V
1440–57	Ladislaus

Line of Leopold

1379–86	Leopold III
1386–1406	William
1386–1411	Leopold IV
1406–24	Ernst
1457–63	Duke Albert VI

Holy Roman emperors

1457–93	Archduke Frederick V
1493–1519	**Maximilian I**
1519–22	**Charles V**
1519–64	Ferdinand I
1564–76	Maximilian II
1576–1612	Rudolf II
1612–19	Matthias
1619–37	**Ferdinand II**
1637–58	Ferdinand III
1658–1705	Leopold I
1705–11	Joseph I
1711–40	Charles VI
1740–80	**Maria Theresa**
1780–90	**Joseph II**
1790–92	Leopold II
1804–35	Francis I
1835–48	Ferdinand I, Der Gutige
1848–1916	**Francis Joseph**
1916–18	Charles I

FIRST REPUBLIC

1918	Austria became a republic
1920–28	President: Michael Hainisch
1928–38	President: Wilhelm Miklas
1938	Annexed by Germany
1938–39	German governor-general: Arthur Jon Seyss-Inquart

SECOND REPUBLIC

Presidents

1945–50	Karl Renner
1951–57	Theodor Korner
1957–65	Adolf Scharf
1965–74	Franz Jonas
1974–86	Rudolf Kirchschlaeger
1986–92	Kurt Waldheim
1992–	Thomas Klestil

Chancellors

1753–92	Wenzel Anton von Kaunitz
1821–48	**Klemens von Metternich**
1868–70	Eduard von Taaffe (prime minister)
1879–93	Eduard von Taaffe (prime minister)
1919–20	Karl Renner
1932–34	Engelbert Dollfuss
1934–38	Kurt Edler von Schuschnigg
1945–53	Leopold Figl
1953–61	Julius Raab
1961–64	Alfons Gorbach
1964–70	Josef Klaus
1970–83	Bruno Kreisky
1983–86	Fred Sinowatz
1986–	Franz Vranitzky

BELGIUM

862–78	Count of Flanders Baldwin I (Bras-de-fer)
878–918	Count of Flanders Baldwin II
918–50	Count of Flanders Arnulf I
950–61	Count of Flanders Baldwin III
961–64	Count of Flanders Arnulf I
964–89	Arnulf II
989–1035	Baldwin IV
1036–67	Count of Flanders Baldwin V
1067–70	Count of Flanders Baldwin VI
1070–71	Arnulf III
1071–93	Robert I
1093–1111	Robert II
1111–19	Baldwin VII, son of Robert II
1119–27	Charles the Good
1127–28	William Clito
1128–57	Didrik of Alsace
1157–91	Philip
1171–95	Baldwin VIII
1191	Countess Margareta
1195–1206	Count Baldwin IX (Emperor of Constantinople)
1206–44	Countess Johanna
1212–33	Co-regent: Ferdinand of Portugal
1244–80	Countess Margaret
1280–1305	Count Guy de Dampierre
1305–22	Robert III of Bethune
1322–37	Count of Flanders Louis I de Nevers
1336–45	Governor: Jacob van Artevelde
1346–84	Count Louis II de Male
1384–1405	Countess Margaret
1384–1477	Belgium under Burgundy
1477–1795	Under the Habsburgs
1795–1814	United with France
1815–30	United with Holland
1830	Independent kingdom

HOUSE OF SAXE-COBURG

1831–65	King Leopold I
1865–1909	**Leopold II**
1909–34	**Albert I**
1934–51	Leopold III
1951–	Baudouin I

Prime ministers

1944–45	Hubert Pierlot
1945–46	Achille Van Acker
1946	Paul-Henri Spaak
1946	Achille Van Acker
1946–47	Camille Huysmans
1947–49	Paul-Henri Spaak
1949–50	Gaston Eyskens
1950	Jean Duvieusart
1950–52	Joseph Pholien
1952–54	Jean Van Houtte
1954–58	Achille Van Acker
1958–61	Gaston Eyskens
1961–65	Theodore Lefevre
1965–66	Pierre Harmel
1966–68	Paul Vanden Boeynants
1968–73	Gaston Eyskens
1973–74	Edmond Leburton
1974–78	Leo Tindemans
1978	Paul Vanden Boeynants
1979–81	Wilfried Martens
1981	Marc Eyskens
1981–92	Wilfried Martens
1992–	Jean-Luc Dehaene

CZECHOSLOVAKIA

BOHEMIA

PREMYSLID DYNASTY

871–94	Count Borivoj I
894–95	Spithnjew I
895–912	Duke Spithnjew I
912–20	Vratislav I
926–25	Regent: Drahomire von Stoder
928–29	**Wenceslas**
929–67	Boleslav I
967–99	Boleslav II
999–1003	Boleslav III
1003–35	Vladivoj of Poland
1035–55	Bretislav I
1055–61	Spithnjew II
1061–92	Vratislav II
1092–1100	Bretislav II
1100–07	Borivoj II
1107–09	Swartopluk
1100–40	Internal conflicts
1109–25	Ladislas I
1125–40	Sobjislaw
1140–58	Ladislas II
1158–73	Ladislas II
1173–97	Internal conflicts
1197–1230	Ottokar I
1230–53	Wenceslas I
1253–78	Ottokar II
1278–1305	Wenceslas II
1305–06	Wenceslas III
1306–07	Rudolph
1307–10	Henry, Duke of Carinthia

LUXEMBURG DYNASTY

1310–46	John the Blind
1346–78	Charles
1378–1419	Wenceslas IV (Holy Roman Emperor)

1419–36	Hussite Wars
1419–37	Sigismund of Hungary

HABSBURG (AND OTHER) DYNASTIES

1437–39	Albert of Austria
1440–57	Ladislas Posthumus
1458–71	George of Podebrad
1469	Rival king: Matthias of Hungary
1471–1516	King Ladislas II (Vladislav)
1516–26	Louis
1526–64	Ferdinand I of Austria
1619–20	Frederick V of the Palatinate

REPUBLIC (FOUNDED IN 1918)

Presidents

1918–35	**Thomas Garrigue Masaryk**
1935–38	Eduard Beneš
1938	Jan Syrovy
1938–39	Emil Hácha
1939	Annexed by Germany
1939–45	(In London): Eduard Beneš
1945–48	Eduard Beneš
1948	Communist regime established
1948–53	**Klement Gottwald**
1953–57	Antonín Zapotocky
1957–68	Antonín Novotny
1968–74	Ludvik Svoboda
1975–89	Gustav Husak
1989–	Vaclav Havel

Premiers

1918–19	Karel Kramár
1919–20	Vlastimil Tusar
1920–21	Jan Cerny
1921–22	Eduard Beneš
1922–25	Antonín Svehla

1925–26	Antonín Svehla
1926	Jan Cerny
1926–29	Antonín Svehla
1929–32	Frantisek Udrzal
1932–35	Jan Malypetr
1935–38	Milan Hodza
1938	Jan Syrovy
1938–39	Rudolf Beran
1940–45	In exile: Jan Srámek
1945–46	Zdenek Fierlinger
1946–48	**Klement Gottwald**
1948–53	Antonín Zápotocky
1953–63	Viliam Siroky
1963–68	Jozef Lenárt
1968–69	Oldrich Cernik

COMMUNIST PARTY

First secretaries

1968–69	**Alexander Dubcek**
1975–89	Gustav Husak (retained this post after becoming president in 1975)

SLOVAKIA

1939–45	President Josef Tiso

DENMARK

Kings and queens

c. 810	Gudfred died
c. 940	Gorm the Old died
c. 935–85	Harald Bluetooth
c. 985–1014	Sweyn I Forkbeard
1014–18	Harald
1018–35	Canute the Great
1035–42	Hardicanute
1042–47	Magnus the Good
1047–74	Sweyn Estridson
1074–80	Harald Hén
1080–86	Canute the Holy
1086–95	Olaf Hunger
1095–1103	Eric Egode
1104–34	Niels
1134–37	Eric Emune
1137–46	Eric Lamb
1146–57	Sweyn Grathe, Canute, Valdemar I
1157–82	Valdemar the Great
1182–1202	Canute VI
1202–41	Valdemar the Victorious
1241–50	Erik IV Ploughpenny
1250–52	Abel
1252–59	Christopher I
1259–86	Eric V Clipping
1286–1319	Eric VI Menved
1320–26	Christopher II
1330–32	Christopher II
1340–75	Valdemar IV Atterdag
1375–87	Olaf II
1387–97	**Margaret**
1397–1438	Eric of Pomerania
1439–48	Christopher of Bavaria

HOUSE OF OLDENBURG

Kings

1448–81	Christian I
1481–1513	Hans
1513–23	Christian II
1523–33	Frederick I
1535–59	Christian III
1559–88	Frederick II
1588–1648	**Christian IV**
1648–70	Frederick III
1670–99	Christian V
1699–1730	Frederick IV
1730–46	Christian VI
1746–66	Frederick V
1766–1808	Christian VII
1808–39	Frederick VI
1839–48	Christian VIII
1848–63	Frederick VII

HOUSE OF GLÜCKSBURG

Kings and queens

1863–1906	Christian IX
1906–12	Frederick VIII
1912–47	Christian X
1947–72	Frederick IX
1972–	Margrethe II

EAST GERMANY
(GERMAN DEMOCRATIC REPUBLIC)

Established in 1955.

Chairmen, Council of State

1949–60	Wilhelm Pieck
1960–73	**Walter Ulbricht**
1973–76	Willi Stoph
1976–89	Erich Honeker
1989	Egon Krenz
1989	Manfred Gerlach
1989–90	Gregor Gysi

Prime ministers

1960–64	Otto Grotewohl
1964–73	Willi Stoph
1973–76	Horst Sindermann
1976–90	Lothar de Maiziere

ENGLAND

SAXONS

827–39	Egbert
839–58	Ethelwulf
858–60	Ethelbald
860–65	Ethelbert
865–71	Ethelred I
871–99	**Alfred the Great**
899–924	Edward the Elder
924–39	Athelstan
939–46	Edmund
946–55	Edred
955–59	Edwy
959–75	Edgar
975–78	Edward the Martyr
978–1016	Ethelred II the Unready
1016	Edmund Ironside

DANES

1016–35	**Canute**
1035–40	Harold I Harefoot
1040–42	Hardicanute

SAXONS

1042–66	Edward the Confessor
1066	Harold II

HOUSE OF NORMANDY

1066–87	**William I the Conqueror**
1087–1100	William II
1100–35	Henry I
1135–54	Stephen

HOUSE OF PLANTAGENET

1154–89	**Henry II**
1189–99	**Richard I**
1199–1216	**John**

1216–72	Henry III
1272–1307	**Edward I**
1307–27	Edward II
1327–77	**Edward III**
1377–99	Richard II

HOUSE OF LANCASTER

1399–1413	Henry IV
1413–22	**Henry V**
1422–61	Henry VI

HOUSE OF YORK

1461–83	Edward IV
1483	Edward V
1483–85	**Richard III**

HOUSE OF TUDOR

1485–1509	**Henry VII**
1509–47	**Henry VIII**
1547–53	Edward VI
1553–58	**Mary I**
1558–1603	**Elizabeth I**

HOUSE OF STUART

1603–25	**James I (James VI of Scotland)**
1625–49	Charles I

COMMONWEALTH

1649–60	**Oliver Cromwell**

HOUSE OF STUART (RESTORED)

1660–85	**Charles II**
1685–88	James II
1689–1702	**William III** jointly

1689–94	Mary II
1702–14	**Anne**

HOUSE OF HANOVER

1714–27	George I
1727–60	George II
1760–1820	George III
1820–30	George IV
1830–37	William IV
1837–1901	**Victoria**

HOUSE OF SAXE-COBURG

1901–10	**Edward VII**

HOUSE OF WINDSOR

1910–36	George V
1936	Edward VIII
1936–52	George VI
1952–	Elizabeth II

Statesmen

1216–19	Regent: William Marshall, Earl of Pembroke
1377–1408	Earl Marshal: Henry Percy, Earl of Northumberland
1454–60	Protector: Richard Plantagenet, Duke of York
1515–29	Lord Chancellor: **Thomas Cardinal Wolsey**
1529–32	Lord Chancellor: **Sir Thomas More**
1533–53	Archbishop of Canterbury: Thomas Cranmer
1533–40	Chief Minister: Thomas Cromwell, Earl of Essex
1547–50	Protector: Edward Seymour, Duke of Somerset
1572–98	Lord High Treasurer: William Cecil, Baron Burghley
1623–28	Chief Minister: George Villiers, Duke of Buckingham
1628–40	Chief Adviser: Thomas Wentworth, Earl of Strafford
1702–10	Lord High Treasurer: Sidney Godolphin, Earl of Godolphin
1710–14	Head of ministry: Robert Harley, Earl of Oxford
1714	Lord High Treasurer: Charles Talbot, Duke of Shrewsbury
1714–15	Prime Minister: Charles Montagu, Earl of Halifax
1715	First Lord of Treasury: Charles Howard, Earl of Carlisle
1715–17	Prime Minister: **Robert Walpole, Earl of Orford**
1717–18	First Lord of Treasury: James Stanhope, Earl Stanhope
1718–21	Charles Spencer, Earl of Sunderland
1721–42	Prime Minister: **Robert Walpole, Earl of Orford (Whig)**
1742–43	First Lord of Treasury: Spencer Compton, Earl of Wilmington (Whig)
1743–54	Prime Minister: Henry Pelham (Whig)
1754–56	Prime Minister: Thomas Pelham-Holles, Duke of Newcastle
1756–57	Prime Minister: William Cavendish, Duke of Devonshire (Whig)
1757–62	Thomas Pelham-Holles, Duke of Newcastle (Whig)
1762–63	John Stuart, Earl of Bute (Tory)
1763–65	George Grenville (Whig)

1765–66	Charles Watson-Wentworth, Marquess of Rockingham (Coalition)
1766–68	Privy Seal: **William Pitt,** Earl of Chatham (Whig)
1768–70	First Minister: Augustus Henry Fitzroy, Duke of Grafton (Whig)
1770–82	Prime Minister: Frederick North, Earl of Guildford (Tory)
1782	Prime Minister: Charles Watson-Wentworth, Marquess of Rockingham (Whig)
1782–83	William Petty, Earl of Shelburne (Whig)
1783	William Henry Cavendish Bentinck, Duke of Portland (Coalition)
1783–1801	**William Pitt the Younger** (Tory)
1801–04	Prime Minister: Henry Addington, Viscount Sidmouth (Tory)
1804–06	**William Pitt** (Tory)
1806–07	William Wyndham Grenville, Lord Grenville
1827	George Canning (Tory)
1827–28	Prime Minister: Frederick John Robinson, Viscount Goderich (Tory)
1828–30	**Arthur Wellesley,** Duke of Wellington (Tory)
1830–34	Charles Grey, Earl Grey (Whig)
1834	Prime Minister: William Lamb, Viscount Melbourne (Whig)
1834–35	**Sir Robert Peel** (Tory)
1835–41	Prime Minister: William Lamb, Viscount Melbourne (Whig)
1841–46	**Sir Robert Peel** (Tory)
1846–52	John Russell, Earl Russell (Whig)
1852	Edward George Geoffrey Smith Stanley, Earl of Derby (Tory)
1852–55	George Hamilton Gordon, Earl of Aberdeen (Peelite)
1855–58	**Henry John Temple, Viscount Palmerston** (Liberal)
1858	Prime Minister: Edward Stanley, Earl of Derby (Conservative)
1858–65	**Henry John Temple, Viscount Palmerston** (Liberal)
1865–66	John Russell, Earl Russell (Liberal)
1866–68	Prime Minister: Edward Stanley, Earl of Derby (Conservative)
1868	**Benjamin Disraeli,** Earl of Beaconsfield
1868–74	Prime Minister: **William Ewart Gladstone** (Liberal)
1874–80	**Benjamin Disraeli** (Conservative)
1880–85	**William Ewart Gladstone** (Liberal)
1885–66	**Robert Arthur Talbot Gascoyne-Cecil, Marquess of Salisbury** (Conservative)
1886	**William Ewart Gladstone** (Liberal)
1886–92	**Robert Arthur Talbot Gascoyne-Cecil, Marquess of Salisbury** (Conservative)
1892–94	**William Ewart Gladstone** (Liberal)
1894–95	Archibald Philip Primrose, Earl of Rosebery (Liberal)
1895–1902	**Robert Arthur Talbot Gascoyne–Cecil, Marquess of Salisbury** (Conservative)
1895–1903	Colonial Secretary: Joseph Chamberlain
1902–05	Prime Minister: Arthur James Balfour (Conservative)
1905–08	Sir Henry Campbell-Bannerman (Liberal)
1908–15	Herbert Henry Asquith, Earl of Oxford and Asquith (Liberal)
1915–16	Herbert Henry Asquith (Coalition)
1916–22	Prime Minister: **David Lloyd George,** Earl of Dwyfor (Coalition)
1922–23	Prime Minister: Andrew Bonar Law (Conservative)

1923–24	Prime Minister: **Stanley Baldwin, Earl Baldwin of Bewdley** (Conservative)
1924	**James Ramsay MacDonald** (Labour)
1924–29	Prime Minister: **Stanley Baldwin** (Conservative)
1929–31	**James Ramsay MacDonald** (Labour)
1931–35	**James Ramsay MacDonald** (Coalition)
1935–37	**Stanley Baldwin** (Coalition)
1937–40	**Arthur Neville Chamberlain** (Coalition)
1940–45	Prime Minister: **Winston Leonard Spencer Churchill** (Coalition) (Conservative)
1945–51	Clement Richard Attlee (Labour)
1951–55	**Sir Winston Churchill** (Conservative)
1955–57	Prime Minister: **Anthony Eden, Earl of Avon** (Conservative)
1957–63	Prime Minister: **Harold Macmillan** (Conservative)
1963–64	Sir Alec Douglas-Home (Conservative)
1964–70	**Harold Wilson** (Labour)
1970–74	Edward Heath (Conservative)
1974–76	**Harold Wilson** (Labour)
1976–79	James Callaghan (Labour)
1979–90	**Margaret Thatcher** (Conservative)
1990–	John Major (Conservative)

FINLAND

Ruled by Sweden until 1808.

Dukes

1284–91	Bengt
1302–18	Waldemar Magnusson
1322–26	Matts Kettilmundsson
1340–48	Dan Niklinsson
1353–57	Bengt Algotsson
1357–59	Erik Magnusson (Erik XII of Sweden)

Lagmen

1371–86	Bo Jonsson Grip
1440–48	Karl Knutsson Bonde (in Finland)
1465–67	Karl Knutsson Bonde
1457–81	Erik Ax elsson Tott (in Viborg)
1495–96	Knut Posse (in Viborg)
1497–1501	Sten Sture the Elder
1499–1511	Erik Turesson Bielke (in Viborg)
1520–22	Junker: Thomas Wolf
1556–63	Duke Johan

Governors

1561–66	Gustav Fincke
1566–68	Ivar Mansson Stiernkors
1568–71	Hans Larsson Björnram
1571–76	Henrik Klasson Horn
1576–87	Klas Akesson Tott
1587–90	Axel Stensson Leijonhufvud
1591–97	Eriksson Fleming
1597–99	Arvid Stålarm

Governor-generals

1623–31	Nils Bielke
1613–33	Gabriel Bengtsson Oxenstierna
1637–40	Per Brahe
1648–54	Per Brahe
1657–59	Gustav Evertsson Horn
1664–69	Herman Fleming
1710–12	Karl Nieroth

During the 18th century, Finland was partially annexed by Russia; in 1808, the country became an autonomous Grand Duchy united with Russia.

1808–09	Goran Magnus Sprengtporten
1809–10	Mikael Barclay de Tolly
1810–23	Fabian Steinheil
1823–31	Arsenii Zakrevski
1831–55	Prince Alexander Menshikov
1833–47	Alexander A. Thesleff
1848–54	Platon Rokassovski
1854–61	Fredrik Wilhelm Berg
1861–66	Platon Rokassovski
1866–81	Nikolai Adlerberg
1881–97	Feodor Heiden
1897–98	Stepan Gontscharov
1898–1904	Nikolaj Bobrikoff
1904–05	Ivan M. Obolenski
1905–08	Nikolai N. Gerard
1908–09	Vladimir K. Boeckmann
1909–17	Frans A. Seyn
1917	Mikael Stahovich
1917	Nikolai Nekrasov

Minister secretaries

1811–41	Robert Rehbinder
1841–42	Alexander Armfelt
1876–81	Karl Knut Emil Stiernwall-Wallen
1881–88	Theodor Bruun
1888–91	Johan Casimir Ehrnrooth
1891–98	Waldemar Karl von Daehn
1898–99	Victor Procope
1899–1904	Vyacheslav von Pleve
1904–05	Constantin Linder
1906–13	Karl Fredrik August Langhoff

1913–17	Vladimir Markov
1917	Carl Enckell

Prime ministers

1822–26	Carl Erik Mannerheim
1826–28	Samuel Fredrik von Born
1828–33	Anders Henrik Falck
1833–41	Gustaf Hjarne
1841–58	Lars Gabriel von Haartman
1858–82	Johan Mauritz Nordenstam
1882–85	Edvard af Forselles
1885–91	Werner von Troil
1891–1900	Sten Carl Tudeer
1900–05	Constantin Linder
1905	Emil Streng
1905–08	Leo Mechelin
1908–09	Edvard Hjelt
1909	August Hjelt
1909	Andrej Virenius
1909–13	Vladimir Markov
1913–17	Michael Borovitinov
1917	Andrej Virenius
1917	Oskari Tokoi
1917	Emil Nestor Setala
1918	Juho Kusti Paasikivi
1918–19	Lauri Johannes Ingman
1919	Kaarlo Castren
1919–20	Juho Heikki Vennola
1920–21	Rafeal Erich
1921–22	Juho Heikki Vennola
1922	Aimo Kaarlo Cajander
1922–24	Kyosti Kallio
1924	Aimo Kaarlo Cajander
1924–25	Lauri Johannes Ingman
1925	Antti Agaton Tulenheimo
1925–26	Kyosti Kallio
1926–27	Vaino Alfred Tanner
1927–28	Juho Emil Sunila
1928–29	Oskari Mantere
1929–30	Kyosti Kallio
1930–31	Pehr Evind Svinhufvud
1931–32	Juho Emil Sunila
1932–36	Toivo Mikael Kivimaki
1936–37	Kyosti Kallio
1937–39	Aimo Kaarlo Cajander
1939–40	Risto Heikki Ryti
1941–43	Johan Wilhelm Rangell
1943–44	Edwin Linkomies
1944	Antti Hackzell
1944	Urho Castren

1944–46	Juho Kusti Paasikivi
1946–48	Mauno Pekkala
1948–50	Karl-August Fagerholm
1950–53	Urho Kaleva Kekkonen
1953–54	Sakari Tuomioja
1954	Ralf Törngren
1954–56	Urho Kaleva Kekkonen
1956–57	K.-A. Fagerholm
1957	V. J. Sukselainen
1957–58	Rainer von Fieandt
1958	Reino Kuuskoski
1958–59	K.-A. Fagerholm
1959–61	V. J. Sukselainen
1961–62	Martti Miettunen
1962–63	Ahti Karjalainen
1963–64	Reino Lehto
1964–66	Johannes Virolainen
1966–68	Rafael Paasio
1968–70	Mauno Koivisto
1970	Teuvo Aura
1970–71	Ahti Karjalainen
1971–72	Teuvo Aura
1972	Rafael Paasio
1972–75	Kalevi Sorsa
1975	Keijo Liinamaa
1975–77	Martti Miettunen
1977–79	Kalevi Sorsa
1979–82	Mauna Koivisto
1982–87	Kalevi Sorsa
1987–91	Harri Holkeri
1991–	Esko Aho

Leaders of Independent Republic

1918	Regent: Pehr Evind Svinhufvud
1918	Head of Red Government: Kullervo Manner
1918	King Frederick Charles of Hesse (monarchy not established)
1918–1919	Regent: **Carl Gustaf Emil von Mannerheim**

Presidents

1919–25	Kaarlo Juho Ståhlberg
1925–31	Lauri Kristian Relander
1931–37	Pehr Evind Svinhufvud
1937–40	Kyosti Kallio
1940–44	Risto Heikki Ryti
1944–46	Carl Gustaf Emil von Mannerheim
1946–56	Juho Kusti Paasikivi
1956–81	Urho Kaleva Kekkonen
1982–	Mauno Koivisto

FRANCE

GAUL

(Roman province from 2nd century B.C. to A.D. 476)

462–86   Independent Roman governor Syagrius

MEROVINGIAN DYNASTY

(First Frankish Dynasty; no authentic information is available for the period before the Merovingians)

Kings

420–28	Pharamond
428–48	Clodio or Clodion
448–58	Merovech or Mérovée
458–81	Childeric I
481–511	**Clovis I**
511–34	Thierry I of Austrasia
511–24	Clodomir of Neustria
511–58	Co-regent: Childebert I of Neustria
511–58	King of Soissons: Clothaire I of Neustria
534–48	Theodebert of Austrasia
548–55	Theobald of Austrasia
558–61	Clothaire I
561–67	Charibert, son of Clothaire I
561–93	Gontram of Burgundy
561–75	Sigebert I of Austrasia
561–84	Chilperic I of Neustria
575–96	Childebert II of Austrasia
575–96	Regent: Brunhilde
584–628	Clothaire II of Neustria
584–97	Regent: **Fredegund**
596–612	Theodebert II of Austrasia
596–613	Thierry II of Burgundy
613	Sigebert II of Burgundy
613–28	King (whole kingdom): Clothaire II of Austrasia and Burgundy
628–39	King (whole kingdom): Dagobert I
639–56	Sigebert III of Austrasia
638–57	Clovis II of Neustria and Burgundy
657–71	Clothaire III of Neustria and Burgundy
663–73	Childeric II of Austrasia
673–78	Dagobert II of Austrasia
673–91?	Thierry III of Neustria and Burgundy
678–91	Thierry III of Austrasia
691–95	Clovis III of Neustria
695–711	Childebert III
711–15	Dagobert III of Neustria
715–20	Chilperic II
717–19	Clothaire IV of Neustria
720–37	Thierry IV
737–42	Interregnum
742–51	Childeric III

CAROLINGIAN DYNASTY

(Second Frankish Dynasty)

Mayors of the palace

628–39	Pepin I the Elder
687–714	Pepin II
741	**Charles Martel**
741–47	Carloman of Austrasia
741–51	Pepin the Short

Kings

751–68	Pepin the Short (Pepin III)
768–71	Carloman
768–814	Joint ruler: **Charlemagne** (Holy Roman Emperor, 800–14)
814–40	Louis I the Pious
838–40	Civil War
840–43	Joint rulers: Lothair, Louis and Charles the Bald, sons of Louis I
843–77	Charles I the Bald
877–79	Louis II
879–82	Louis III

879–84	Co-regent: Carloman
885–87	Charles II the Fat
888–98	Odo, Count of Paris
893–922	Charles III the Simple
922–23	Rival king: Robert, brother of Odo, Count of Paris
923–36	Rudolf
936–54	Louis IV
954–86	Lothair
986–87	Louis V

Frankish dukes of the House of Capet

861–66	Robert the Strong
866–86	Hugh the Abbot
866–86	Odo, Count of Paris
889–923	Robert II, brother of Odo, Count of Paris
923–36	Rudolf
923–56	Hugh the Great
956–87	Hugh Capet

(Duchy of Francia united with France)

KINGDOM OF FRANCE: HOUSE OF CAPET

987–96	Hugh Capet
996–1031	Robert II, the Pious
1031–60	Henry I
1060–1108	Philip I
1108–37	Louis VI, the Fat
1137–80	Louis VII, the Young
1180–1223	Philip II Augustus
1223–26	Louis VIII
1226–70	**Louis IX (Saint Louis)**
1270–85	Philip III, the Bold
1285–1314	Philip IV, the Fair
1314–16	Louis X
1316	John I
1316–22	Philip V
1322–28	Charles IV
1328–50	Philip VI
1350–64	John II
1364–80	Charles V
1380–1422	Charles VI
1422–61	**Charles VII**
1461–83	Louis XI
1483–98	Charles VIII
1498–1515	Louis XII
1515–47	François I
1547–59	Henry III
1559–60	François II
1560–74	Charles IX
1574–89	Henry III
1589–1610	**Henry IV**
1610–43	Louis XIII
1643–1715	**Louis XIV**
1715–74	Louis XV
1774–92	**Louis XVI**

THE FIRST REPUBLIC (1792–1804)

1804–14	**Napoleon I** (Emperor)
1814–24	Louis XVIII
1824–30	Charles X
1830–48	Louis Philippe

THE SECOND REPUBLIC (1848–52)

1852–70	**Napoleon III** (Emperor)

THE THIRD REPUBLIC (1871–1940)

Presidents

1871–73	Louis Adolphe Thiers
1873–79	Marie Edme Patrice Maurice de MacMahon
1879–87	François Paul Jules Grévy
1887–94	Marie-François Sadi-Carnot
1894–95	Jean Paul Pierre Casimir-Périer
1895–99	François Félix Faure
1899–1906	Émile Loubet
1906–13	Clément Armand Fallières
1913–20	Raymond Poincaré
1920	Paul Deschanel
1920–24	Alexandre Millerand
1924–31	Gaston Doumergue
1931–32	Paul Doumer
1932–40	Albert Lebrun

VICHY GOVERNMENT

1940–44	Chief of State: **Henri Philippe Pétain**
1942–44	Premier: **Pierre Laval**

PROVISIONAL GOVERNMENT

1944–46	Head of State: **Charles de Gaulle**
1946	President: Felix Gouin
1946	President (provisional): Georges Augustin Bidault
1946	President (provisional): **Léon Blum**

THE FOURTH REPUBLIC (1947–59)

1947–54	President: Vincent Auriol
1954–59	President: René Coty

THE FIFTH REPUBLIC (1959–)

1959–69	President: **Charles de Gaulle**
1969–74	President: Georges Pompidou
1974–81	Valéry Giscard d'Estaing
1981–	François Mitterrand

STATESMEN

1624–42	First Minister: **Richelieu, Duc de (Armand Jean du Plessis)**
1643–61	First Minister: **Jules Mazarin**
1666–91	Minister of War: François Michel Le Tellier, Marquis de Louvois
1726–43	First Minister: André Hercule de Fleury
1758–61	Foreign Secretary: Étienne François de Choiseul
1766–70	Minister of War: Étienne François de Choiseul
1774–76	Minister of Finance: Anne Robert Jacques Turgot
1776–81	Minister of Finance: Jacques Necker
1783–87	Minister of Finance: Charles Alexandre de Calonne
1788–90	Minister of Finance: Jacques Necker
1793–94	Dictator: **Maximilien Robespierre**
1797–1807	Foreign Secretary: Charles Maurice de Talleyrand-Périgord
1814–15	Prime Minister: Charles Maurice de Talleyrand-Périgord
1830–34	Minister of War: Nicolas Jean de Dieu Soult

Premiers

1840–48	François Pierre Guillaume Guizot
1880–81	Jules Ferry
1881–82	Léon Gambetta
1883–85	Jules Ferry
1906–09	**Georges Clemenceau**
1909–11	Aristide Briand
1912–13	Raymond Poincaré
1913–	Aristide Briand

1915–17	Coalition head: Aristide Briand		1951	Henri Queuille (3 days)
1917–20	**Georges Clemenceau**		1951–52	René Pleven
1921–22	Coalition head: Aristide Briand		1952	Edgar Faure
1922–24	Raymond Poincaré		1952–53	Antoine Pinay
1924–25	Edouard Herriot		1953	René Joël Simon Mayer
1925–26	Aristide Briand		1953–54	Joseph Laniel
1926–29	Raymond Poincaré		1954–55	Pierre Mendès-France
1929	Aristide Briand		1955–56	Edgar Faure
1930	Camille Chautemps		1956–57	Guy Mollet
1931–32	**Pierre Laval**		1957	Maurice Jean-Marie Bourgès-Maunoury
1932	Aristide Briand		1957–58	Félix Gaillard
1932	Edouard Herriot		1958	Pierre Pflimlin
1933	Edouard Daladier		1958–59	**Charles de Gaulle**
1933–34	Camille Chautemps		1959–62	Michel Jean-Pierre Debré
1934	Edouard Daladier (11 days)		1962–68	Georges Jean Raymond Pompidou
1936–37	**Léon Blum**		1968–69	Maurice Couve de Murville
1937–38	Camille Chautemps		1969–72	Jacques Chaban-Delmas
1938–40	Edouard Daladier		1972–74	Pierre Messmer
1940	Paul Reynaud		1974–76	Jacques Chirac
1946–47	**Léon Blum**		1976–81	Raymond Barre
1947	Paul Ramadier		1981–84	Pierre Mauroy
1947–48	Robert Schuman		1984–86	Laurent Fabius
1948	André Désiré Paul Marie		1986–88	Jacques Chirac
1948	Robert Schuman		1988–91	Paul Rocard
1948–49	Henri Queuille		1991–92	Edith Cresson
1949–50	Georges Augustin Bidault		1992–93	Pierre Bérégovoy
1950	Henri Queuille		1993–	Edouard Balladur
1950–51	René Pleven			

GERMANY

HOHENZOLLERN DYNASTY

Emperors

1871–88	Wilhelm I (of Prussia)
1888	Frederick III
1888–1918	**Wilhelm II**

REPUBLIC

Presidents

1919–25	Friedrich Ebert
1925–33	**Paul von Hindenburg**

NATIONAL SOCIALIST REGIME

1934	President: **Paul von Hindenburg**
1933–45	Leader: **Adolf Hitler**
1945–49	Allied occupation
1945	**Karl Dönitz** (8 days)

GERMAN FEDERAL REPUBLIC

Presidents

1949–59	Theodor Heuss
1959–69	Heinrich Lübke
1969–74	Dr. Gustav Heinemann
1974–79	Walter Scheel
1979–84	Karl Carstens
1984–	Richard von Weizsacker

Federal chancellors

1949–63	**Konrad Adenauer**
1963–66	Ludwig Erhard
1966–69	Kurt G. Kiesinger
1969–74	**Willy Brandt**
1974–82	Helmut Schmidt
1982–90	Helmut Kohl

FEDERAL REPUBLIC OF GERMANY
(established October 1990)

1990–92	Chancellor: Helmut Kohl
1992–	President: Richard von Weizsacker

STATESMEN

1807–08	First Minister: Karl von Stein
1813–15	(Prussia) Karl von Stein
1862–71	Prime Minister: **Otto von Bismarck**
1871–90	Chancellor: **Otto von Bismarck**
1894–1900	Prince Chlodwig Karl Viktor Hohenlohe-Schillingsfürst
1900–09	Prince Bernhard von Bülow
1909–17	Theobald von Bethmann-Hollweg
1917	Georg Michaelis
1917–18	Count Georg von Hertling
1918	Maximilian (Prince Max of Baden)
1918–19	Friedrich Ebert
1919	Prime Minister: Philipp Scheide
1919–20	Prime Minister: Gustav Adolf Bauer
1920	Hermaan Müller
1920–21	Konstantin Fehrenbach
1921–22	Karl Joseph Wirth
1922–23	Wilhelm Cuno
1923	**Gustav Stresemann**
1923–25	Wilhelm Marx
1925–26	Hans Luther
1926–28	Wilhelm Marx
1928–30	Hermann Müller
1930–32	Heinrich Brüning
1932	Franz von Papen
1932–33	Kurt von Schleicher
1933–45	**Adolf Hitler**
1945	**Karl Dönitz**

BAVARIA

Dukes

912–37	Arnulf the Bad
938–47	Berchtold
947–55	Henry I
955–78	Henry II
982–85	Henry III
985–95	Henry II
995–1002	Henry IV
1002–26	Henry V of Lützelburg (Luxemburg)
1026–42	Henry VI (Emperor Henry III)
1042–47	Henry VII
1049–53	Konrad I
1053–56	Henry VIII (Emperor Henry IV)
1056	Konrad II
1056–61	Duchess Agnes
1061–70	Otto of Nordheim
1070–1101	Guelph I
1101–20	Guelph II
1120–26	Henry IX
1126–39	Henry X the Proud
1139–41	Leopold IV of Austria
1143–56	Henry XI
1156–80	Henry XII the Lion
1180–83	Otto I
1183–1231	Ludwig I
1231–53	Otto II the Illustrious
1253–94	Ludwig II the Stern
1294–1317	Rudolph
1314–47	Co-ruler: Emperor Ludwig III
1329	Country divided into Bavaria and the Palatinate; Bavaria divided after 1347 into several parts)
1375–97	John of Munich
1397–1438	Ernst
1438–60	Albert III the Pious
1460–67	Sigismund
1460–1508	Albert IV
1508–50	William IV
1550–79	Albert V
1579–97	William V the Pious
1597–1623	Maximilian I
1623	The Duchy became an Electorate

Electors

1623–51	Maximilian I, the Great
1651–79	Ferdinand Maria
1679–1706	Maximilian II Emanuel (deposed after Blenheim, reinstated by Treaty of Utrecht)
1714–26	Maximilian II Emanuel
1726–45	Charles Albert (Holy Roman Emperor, 1742–45)
1745–77	Maximilian III Joseph
1777–99	Charles Theodore of the Palatinate
1799–1805	Maximilian IV Joseph

Kings

1806–25	Maximilian I Joseph
1825–48	Ludwig I
1848–64	Maximilian II Joseph
1864–86	Ludwig II
1886–1913	Otto
1886–1912	Luitpold
1912–13	Ludwig III
1913–18	Ludwig III

BRANDENBURG

Margraves

1134–70	Albert I the Bear
1170–84	Otto I
1184–1205	Otto II
1205–20	Albert II
1220–66	John I
1220–67	Otto III (ruled jointly with John I)
1266–1309	Otto IV
1309–19	Waldemar the Great
1319–30	Henry the Child
1322–51	Louis V
1351–65	Elector: Louis the Roman
1365–73	Elector: Otto
1373–78	Emperor: Charles IV
1378–1417	Emperor: Sigismund of Hungary

Electors

1417–40	Frederick of Nuremberg
1440–70	Frederick II
1470–86	Albert III
1486–99	John Cicero
1499–1535	Joachim I
1535–71	Joachim II
1571–98	John George
1598–1608	Joachim Frederick
1608–19	John Sigismund
1619–40	George William
1640–88	Frederick William, the "Great Elector"
1688–1701	Frederick III
1742–99	Charles Theodore

PRUSSIA (HOHENZOLLERN DYNASTY)

Kings

1701–13	Frederick I (Frederick III of Brandenburg)
1713–40	Frederick William I
1740–86	**Frederick II the Great**
1786–97	Frederick William II
1797–1840	Frederick William III
1840–61	Frederick William IV
1861–71	William I

SAXONY

1381–1423	Duke: Frederick I the Warlike
1423–28	Elector: Frederick I the Warlike
1428–64	Elector: Frederick II the Gentle
1464–86	Elector: Ernest
1464–1500	Joint ruler: Albert III
1485	Ernest and Albert divided Saxony
1486–1525	Elector: Frederick III the Wise
1525–32	Elector: John the Constant
1532–47	John Frederick the Magnanimous
1500–39	George the Bearded
1539–41	Henry the Pious
1541–47	Maurice
1547–53	Elector: Maurice
1553–86	Augustus I
1586–91	Christian I
1591–1611	Christian II
1611–56	John George I
1656–80	John George II
1680–91	John George III
1691–94	John George IV
1694–1733	Frederick Augustus I
1733–63	Frederick Augustus II
1763	Frederick Christian
1763–1806	Frederick Augustus III

1806–27	King: Frederick Augustus I the Just
1827–36	Anthony
1836–54	Frederick Augustus II
1854–73	John
1873–1902	Albert
1902–04	George
1904–18	Frederick Augustus III

SWABIA

916–26	Burchard I
926–48	Hermann I
948–57	Ludolf
957–73	Burchard II
973–82	**Otto I**
982–97	Conrad I
997–1004	Hermann II
1004–12	Hermann III
1012–15	Ernst I

1015–30	Ernst II
1030–39	Hermann IV
1039–45	Otto II
1045–47	Otto III
1047–57	Rudolf
1080–1105	Frederick I
1105–47	Frederick II
1147–52	**Frederick III** (assumed the throne of Germany in 1152, crowned emperor in 1155; known as Frederick I Barbarossa)
1152–67	Frederick IV
1167–91	Frederick V
1191–96	Conrad III
1196–1208	Philipp
1208–19	Frederick VI
1219–35	Heinrich II
1235–54	Conrad IV
1254–68	Conrad V

GREECE

Greece was ruled by Rome from 146 B.C. to A.D. 395; became part of the Eastern Roman or Byzantine Empire and was conquered by the Ottoman Turks in 1460; and achieved independence from the Ottoman Empire, 1821–1827.

Athenian leaders

c. 621 B.C.	**Draco**
c. 594–	
70 B.C.	**Solon**
560–27	Pisistratus
527–11	Hippias
527–14	Hipparchus
509–06	Founder of Cleisthenes democracy
493–c. 470	Themistocles
c. 470	Miltiades
489–88	Aristeides the Just
480–79	Strategos Aristeides the Just
470–60	Cimon
c. 460–29	**Pericles**
431–04	Peloponnesian War
411–10	Government of Four Hundred
404	Oligarchy of "Thirty Tyrants"
404	Theramenes
404–03	Critias
403	Thrasybulus
338	War with Philip of Macedon
334–23	Regent: Antipater
317–07	Demetrius Phalereus
306–00	King Demetrius I Poliorcetes
295	Lachares
295–88	Demetrius I Poliorcetes

Spartan leaders

(Sparta's constitution provided for two kings)

9th cent. B.C.	Lycurgus and Aristodemus
	Eurysthenes and Procles
	Agis and Sous

9th cent. B.C.	Echestratus and Eurypon
	Labotas and Prytanis
	Doryssus and [Eunomus]
	Agesilaus and Polydectes
	Archelaus and Charilaus
	Teleclus and Nicander
	Alcamenes and Theopompus
	King Polydorus
	Eurycrates and Zeuxidamus
	Anaxander and Anaxidamus
	Eurycratides and Archidamus I
	Leon and Agesicles
	Anaxandrides and Ariston
c. 519–491	Cleomenes I and Demaratus
505	War with Athens
490?–80	King **Leonidas I** and Leotychides
480	Pleistarchus
458	Pleistoanax and Archidamus II
431–22	Brasidas
431–04	Peloponnesian War
c. 426–399	King Pausanias and Agis II
c. 400–360	Agesipolis I and Agesilaus II
380–71	Cleombrotus I
371	Agesipolis II
370–09	Cleomenes II and Archidamus III
344	Defeated by Philip of Macedon
338–31	Agis III
330	Eudamidas I
309	Areus I and Archidamus IV
265	Acrotatus and Eudamidas II
264	Areus II
244–241?	Agis IV
285–36	Leonidas II and Eurydamidas
242–40	Cleombrotus II
235–19	Cleomenes III and Archidamus V
219	Agesipolis III and Lycurgus
210	Machanidas
207–192	Nabis
146	Conquered by Rome

MODERN GREECE

Leaders

1828–31	President: Ioannis Capodistrias
1831–32	President: Agostino Capodistrias
1832–62	King Otto I
1862–63	Interregnum
1863–1913	King George I
1913–17	King Constantine I
1917–20	King Alexander
1920–22	King Constantine I
1922–24	King George II
1924–35	Greece became a republic
1924–26	President: Pavlos Konduriotis
1926	President: Theodoros Pangalos
1926–29	President (provisional): Pavlos Konduriotis
1929–35	President (provisional): Alexandros Zaimis
1935	Regent: George Kondylis
1935–41	King George II
1941–44	German occupation
1946–47	King George II
1944–46	Administrator: Archbishop Damaskinos
1947–64	King Paul I
1964–67	King Constantine II
1967–73	Regent: George Zoetakis
1973	President: George Papadopoulos
1973–74	President: Phaedon Gyzikis
1974–80	President: Constantine Tsatsos
1980–85	President: Constantine Karamanlis
1985–90	President: Christos Sartzetakis
1990–	President: Constantine Karamanlis

Prime ministers

1910–15	Eleutherios Venizelos
1917–20	Eleutherios Venizelos
1924	Eleutherios Venizelos
1928–32	Eleutherios Venizelos
1933	Eleutherios Venizelos
1936–41	Ioannis Metaxas
1944–45	George Papandreou
1945	Nicolas Plastiras
1945	Petros Voulgaris
1945	Archbishop Damaskinos
1945	Panayotis Kanellopoulos
1945–46	Themistoclis Sophoulis
1946	Panayiotis Poulitsas
1946–47	Constantine Tsaldaris
1947	Demetrios Maximos
1947	Constantine Tsaldaris
1947–49	Themistocles Sophoulis
1949–50	Alexander Diomides
1950	John Theotokis
1950	Sophocles Venizelos
1950	Nicolas Plastiras
1950–51	Sophocles Venizelos
1951–52	Nicolas Plastiras
1952	Demetrios Kioussopoulos
1952–55	Alexander Papagos
1955–58	Constantine Karamanlis
1958	Constantine Georgacopoulos
1958–61	Constantine Karamanlis
1961	Constantine Dovas
1961–63	Constantine Karamanlis
1963	Panayiotis Pipinelis
1963	Stylianos Mavromihalis
1963	George Papandreou
1963–64	John Paraskevopoulos
1964–65	George Papandreou
1965	George Athanassiadis-Novas
1965	Elias Tsirimokos
1965–66	Stephanos Stephanopoulos
1966–67	Ioannis Paraskevopoulos
1967	Panayotis Kanellopoulos
1967	Constantine Kollias
1967–73	George Papadopoulos
1973–74	Adamantios Androutsopoulos
1974–80	Constantine Karamanlis
1980–81	George Rallis
1981–89	Andreas Papandreou
1989–90	Ioannis Grivas; Xenofon Zolotas
1990–93	Constantine Mitsotakis
1993–	Andreas Papandreou

HOLY ROMAN EMPERORS

Frankish kings and emperors (Carolingian)

800–14	**Charlemagne**
814–40	Louis I, the Pious
840–55	Lothair I
855–75	Louis II
875–77	Charles II, the Bald
877–81	Throne vacant
881–87	Charles III, the Fat
887–91	Throne vacant
891–94	Guido of Spoleto
892–98	Lambert of Spoleto (co-emperor)
896–901	Arnulf (rival)
901–05	Louis III of Provence
905–24	Berengar
911–18	Conrad I of Franconia (rival)

Saxon kings and emperors

918–36	Henry I, the Fowler
936–73	**Otto I, the Great**
973–83	Otto II
983–1002	Otto III
1002–24	Henry II, the Saint

Franconian emperors (Salian)

1024–39	Conrad II, the Salian
1039–56	Henry III, the Black
1056–1106	Henry IV
1077–80	Rudolf of Swabia (rival)
1081–93	Hermann of Luxemburg (rival)
1093–1101	Conrad of Franconia (rival)
1106–25	Henry V
1125–37	Lothair II

Hohenstaufen kings and emperors

1138–52	Conrad III
1152–90	**Frederick I Barbarossa**
1190–97	Henry VI

1198–1215	Otto IV
1198–1208	Philip of Swabia (rival)
1215–50	Frederick II
1246–47	Henry Raspe (rival)
1247–56	William of Holland (rival)
1250–54	Conrad IV
1254–73	The Great Interregnum

Rulers from different houses

1257–72	Richard of Cornwall (rival)
1257–73	Alfonso X of Castile (rival)
1273–91	**Rudolf I, Habsburg**
1292–98	Adolf I of Nassau
1298–1308	Albert I, Habsburg
1308–13	Henry VII, Luxemburg
1314–47	Louis IV of Bavaria
1314–25	Frederick of Habsburg (co-regent)
1347–78	Charles IV, Luxemburg
1378–1400	**Wenceslas of Bohemia**
1400	Frederick III of Brunswick
1400–10	Rupert of the Palatinate
1410–37	Sigismund, Luxemburg

Habsburg emperors

1438–39	Albert II
1440–93	Frederick III
1493–1519	**Maximilian I**
1519–58	**Charles V**
1558–64	Ferdinand I
1564–76	Maximilian II
1576–1612	Rudolf II
1612–19	Matthias
1619–37	Ferdinand II
1637–57	Ferdinand III
1658–1705	Leopold I
1705–11	Joseph I
1711–40	Charles VI
1742–45	Charles VII of Bavaria

Habsburg-Lorraine emperors

1745–65	Francis I of Lorraine
1765–90	Joseph II
1790–92	Leopold II
1792–1806	Francis II

HUNGARY

875–907	Arpád: Arpád dynasty ruled Hungary until 1301
972–97	Duke Geza
997–1038	**King Stephen I (St. Stephen)**
1038–41	King Peter Orseolo
1041–44	Aba Samuel
1044–46	Peter Orseolo
1046–60	Andrew I
1060–63	Bela I
1063–74	Salomon
1074–77	Geza I
1077–95	Ladislaus I (St. Laszlo)
1095–1116	Salomon
1116–31	Stephen II
1131–41	Bela II
1141–61	Geza II
1161–62	Stephen III
1162–63	Ladislaus II
1163–65	Stephen IV
1165–72	Stephen III
1173–96	Bela III
1196–1204	Emeric
1204–05	Ladislaus III
1205–35	Andrew II
1235–70	Bela IV
1270–72	Stephen V
1272–90	Ladislaus IV
1290–1301	Andrew III (end of Arpád Dynasty)
1301–05	Wenceslaus of Bohemia
1305–07	Otho of Bavaria
1308–42	Charles I
1342–82	Louis the Great
1382–87	Mary
1387–1437	Sigismund
1437–39	Albert
1439–40	Elizabeth
1440–44	Ladislaus of Poland
1444–57	Ladislaus V
1458–90	Matthias Corvinus

1490–1516	Ladislaus of Bohemia
1516–26	Louis II

(Hungary was divided after 1526 between Turkey and Austria)

VOIVODES OF TRANSYLVANIA

1526–40	Prince (governor) John Zapolya
1540–71	John Sigismund
1571–72	Gaspar Bekesy
1571–76	Stephen Bathory (King of Poland)
1576–81	Christopher
1581–98	Sigismund
1599–1600	Andrew
1600–01	Michael the Brave
1602–03	Moyses Szekely
1602–05	Rudolph II (Emperor)
1605–06	Stephen Bocskai
1607–08	Prince Sigismund Rakoczi
1608–13	Gabriel Bathory
1613–29	Gabriel Bethlen
1630	Stephen Bethlen
1630–48	George Rakoczi
1648–60	George II
1658–60	Achatius Bocskai
1661–62	Johann Kemeny
1682–99	Emerich Tokoli
1662–90	Governor (Turkish) Michael Apafi
1690–99	Michael II Apafi
1704–11	Prince Francis Rakoczi

(Hungary under Austria 1711–1918)

1919	Republic proclaimed
1919	President Mihaly Karolyi
1919	Head of Bolshevik government: Bela Kun
1919	Kingless monarchy established
1919	Regent: Joseph of Austria
1920–44	Regent: Admiral Miklos von Horthy of Nagybanya

1944–45	Regent: Ferenc Szalasi	1913–17	Istvan Tisza
1944–45	Regent (opposition government) Bela Miklos	1917–18	Alexander Wekerle
		1918–19	Mihaly Karolyi
1946	Republic proclaimed	1919–20	Karoly Huszar
1946–48	President: Zoltan Tildy	1920–21	Pal Teleki
1948–50	Arpad Szakasits	1921–31	Count Istvan Bethlen
1949	Communist regime established	1932–36	Gyula Gombos
		1936–38	Kalman Daranyi

Presidents

1950–52	Sandoe Ronai	1938–39	Bela Imredy
1952–67	Istvan Dobi	1939–41	Pal Teleki
1967–88	Pal Losonczy	1942–44	Miklos Kallay
1988–89	Bruno Ferenc Straub	1945–46	Zoltan Tildy
1989	Imré Pozgay	1946–47	Ferenc Nagy
1989–90	Matyas Szuros	1948–52	Istvan Dobi
1990–	Arpád Göncz	1952–53	Matyas Rakosi
		1953–55	**Imre Nagy**

Prime ministers

1848–49	**Lajos Kossuth** (governor)	1956–58	**Janos Kadar** (council president)
1867–71	Count Gyula Andrassy	1958–61	Ferenc Munnich
1875–90	Koloman Tisza	1961–65	Janos Kadar
1892–94	Alexander Wekerle	1965–67	Gyula Kallai
1903–05	Istvan Tisza	1967–75	Jeno Fock
1906–10	Alexander Wekerle	1975–88	Gyorgy Lazar
		1988–89	Karoly Grosz
		1989–90	Miklos Nemeth
		1990–	Jozsef Antall

IRELAND

200	Conn Céd-cathach founded the Middle Kingdom (Meath) and began the High Kingship of Tara
377–405	High King: Néill of the Nine Hostages
?–432	Loeguire
432	Possible arrival of **St. Patrick**
795–1014	Norse invasions
900–08	King of Cashel: Cormac MacCullenan
?–919	High King: Néill Glundubh
?–1002	King: Malachy II
1002–14	**Brian Boru**
1022–72	Interregnum
1014–72	King of Munster: Donnchad macBrian
1072–88	Tairrdelbach (Turloch) Ua Briain (O'Brien)
1088–1119	Muirchertach Ua Briain (Before the Anglo–Norman invasions, Ireland was loosely governed by four or five kings, under an elective overlord)
1119–53	High King: Turloch More O'Connor
1134–71	King of Leinster: Dermot MacMurrough
1153–66	King: Muirchertach MacLochlainn
1166–75	High King: Roderic or Rory O'Connor (Roderic was the last native king of Ireland before the Pope granted Ireland to King Henry II of England in 1172)
1177	Dominus Hiberniae: John
1235	Ruler of Connaught: Richard de Burgo
1376–1417	King of Leinster: Art MacMurrough
1477–1513	Gerald Fitzgerald, Earl of Kildare
1487	King: Edward VI (Lambert Simnel)
1513–34	Deputy Governor: Gerald Fitzgerald, Earl of Kildare
1541	King of Ireland: **Henry VIII of England**
1547–53	Edward VI
1594–1603	Tyrone War
1608–10	Foundation of British Colony in Ulster
1599	Lord Lieutenant: Robert Devereux, 2nd Earl of Essex of Ireland
1632–38	Lord Deputy: Sir Thomas Wentworth, Earl of Strafford
1640	Lord Lieutenant: Sir Thomas Wentworth, Earl of Strafford
1644–49	Lord Lieutenant: James Butler, Earl, Marquis and Duke of Ormonde
1649–50	Lord Lieutenant: **Oliver Cromwell**
1653–58	Lord Protector: **Oliver Cromwell**
1660–85	King: **Charles II**
1661–69	Lord Lieutenant: James Butler, Earl, Marquis and Duke of Ormonde
1670–72	John Berkeley, Baron Berkeley
1672–77	Arthur Capel, Earl of Essex
1677–85	James Butler, Earl, Marquis and Duke of Ormonde
1687–91	Lord Deputy: Richard Talbot, Earl of Tyrconnell
1703–05	Lord Lieutenant: James Butler, Earl, Marquis and Duke of Ormonde
1710–11	James Butler, Earl, Marquis and Duke of Ormonde
1713	Charles Talbot, Earl and Duke of Shrewsbury
1722–30	John Carteret, Earl Granville
1767–74	George Townshend, Viscount and Marquis Townshend
1795	William Wentworth, Earl Fitzwilliam
1795–98	Sir John Jeffreys Pratt, Earl and Marquis of Camden
1798–1801	**Charles Cornwallis, Marquis Cornwallis**
1798	Rebellion
1801	United with England

Lord lieutenants

1801–06	Earl of Hardwicke
1806–07	Duke of Bedford
1807–13	Duke of Richmond
1813–17	Earl Whitworth
1817–21	Earl Talbot
1821–28	**Marquis of Wellesley**
1828–29	Marquis of Anglesey

1829–30	Duke of Northumberland
1830–33	Marquis of Anglesey
1833–34	**Marquis of Wellesley**
1834–35	Earl of Haddington
1835–39	Marquis of Normanby
1839–41	Viscount Ebrington (afterwards Earl Fortescue)
1841–44	Earl de Grey
1844–46	Lord Heytesbury
1846–47	Earl of Bessborough
1847–52	Earl of Clarendon
1852–53	Earl of Eglinton
1853–55	Earl of St. Germans
1855–58	Earl of Carlisle
1858–59	Earl of Eglinton
1859–64	Earl of Carlisle
1864–66	Lord Wodehouse (afterwards Earl of Kimberley)
1866–68	Marquis of Abercorn
1868–74	Earl Spencer
1874–76	Duke of Abercorn
1876–80	Duke of Marlborough
1880–82	Earl Cowper
1882–85	Earl Spencer
1885–86	Earl of Carnarvon
1886	Earl of Aberdeen
1886–89	Marquis of Londonderry
1889–92	Earl of Zetland
1892–95	Lord Houghton
1895–1902	Earl Cadogan
1902–05	Earl of Dudley
1905–15	Earl of Aberdeen
1915–18	Baron Wimborne
1918–21	Viscount French
1921–22	Viscount Fitzallen of Derwent
1875–91	Nationalist leader: **Charles Stewart Parnell**
1916–21	**Eamon de Valera**

IRISH FREE STATE

1922	President: Arthur Griffith
1922	Head of Provisional Government: **Michael Collins**
1922–32	President of Executive Council: William Thomas Cosgrave
1932–37	**Eamon de Valera**
1921–27	Governor-General: Timothy Michael Healy of Free State
1928–32	James McNeill
1932–37	Donal Buckley

REPUBLIC OF IRELAND

Presidents

| 1938–45 | Douglas Hyde |
| 1945–59 | Seán Thomas O'Kelly (O Ceallaigh) |

1959–73	**Eamon de Valera**
1973–74	Erskine Childers
1974	Thomas O'Higgins (acting)
1974–76	Cearbhall O'Dalaigh
1976	Thomas O'Higgins (acting)
1976–90	Patrick Hillery
1990–91	Charles J. Haughey
1991–	Albert Reynolds

Prime ministers

1937–48	**Eamon de Valera**
1948–51	John Aloysius Costello
1957–59	**Eamon de Valera**
1959–66	Seán F. Lemass
1966–73	John Lynch
1973–77	Liam Cosgrave
1977–79	John M. Lynch
1979–81	Charles J. Haughey
1981–82	Garret Fitzgerald
1982	Charles J. Haughey
1982–87	Garret Fitzgerald
1987–90	Charles J. Haughey
1990–	Mary Robinson

NORTHERN IRELAND

1920	Separate government established in 1920
1922–45	Governor: James Albert Edward Hamilton, Duke of Abercorn
1945–52	William Spencer Leveson Gower, Earl Granville
1952–64	John De Vere Loder, Baron Wakehurst
1964–	Lord Erskine of Rerrick
1921–40	Prime Minister: James Craig, Viscount Craigavon
1940–43	John Miller Andrews
1943–63	Basil Stanlake Brooke, Viscount Brookeborough
1963–69	Terence Marne O'Neill
1969–71	J. D. Chichester-Clark
1971–72	A. B. D. Faulkner
1972–73	Secretary of State for Northern Ireland: William S. I. Whitelaw (the government of Northern Ireland was ruled by Great Britain through the Secretary of State)
1973–74	Francis Pym
1974	Chief Executive: A. B. D. Faulkner

Secretaries of state

1974–76	Merlyn Rees
1976–79	Roy Mason
1979–81	Humphrey Atkins
1981–83	James Prior
1984–85	Douglas Hurd
1985–89	Tom King
1989–92	Peter Brooke
1992–	Patrick Mayhew

ITALY

Prime ministers

1860–61	**Camillo di Cavour**
1861–62	Bettino Ricasoli
1862–62	Urbano Rattazzi
1862–63	Luigi Carlo Farini
1863–64	Marco Minghetti
1864–66	Alfonso Lamarmora
1866–67	Bettino Ricasoli
1867–67	Urbano Rattazzi
1867–69	Luigi Federico Menabrea
1869–73	Giovanni Lanza
1873–76	Marco Minghetti
1876–78	Agostino Depretis
1878–78	Benedetto Cairoli
1878–79	Agostino Depretis
1879–81	Benedetto Cairoli
1881–87	Agostino Depretis
1887–91	Francesco Crispi
1891–92	Antonio di Rudini
1892–93	Giovanni Giolitti
1893–96	Francesco Crispi
1896–98	Antonio di Rudini
1898–1900	Luigi Pelloux
1900–01	Giuseppe Saracco
1901–03	Giuseppe Zanardelli
1903–05	Giovanni Giolitti
1905–06	Alessandro Fortis
1906–06	Sidney Sonnino
1906–09	Giovanni Giolitti
1909–10	Sidney Sonnino
1910–11	Luigi Luzzatti
1911–14	Giovanni Giolitti
1914–16	Antonio Salandra
1916–17	Paolo Boselli
1917–19	Vittorio Emanuele Orlando
1919–20	Francesco Nitti
1920–21	Giovanni Giolitti
1921–22	Ivanoe Bonomi
1922–22	Luigi Facta
1922–43	**Benito Mussolini**
1943–44	Pietro Badoglio
1944–45	Ivanoe Bonomi
1945–45	Ferrucio Parri
1945–53	Alcide de Gasperi
1953–54	Giuseppe Pella
1954–54	Amintore Fanfani
1954–55	Mario Scelba
1955–57	Antonio Segni
1957–58	Adone Zoli
1958–59	Amintore Fanfani
1959–60	Antonio Segni
1960	Fernando Tambroni
1960–63	Amintore Fanfani
1963	Giovanni Leone
1963–68	Aldo Moro
1968	Giovanni Leone
1968–70	Mariano Rumor
1970–72	Emilio Colombo
1972–73	Giulio Andreotti
1973–74	Mariano Rumor
1974–76	Aldo Moro
1976–79	Giulio Andreotti
1979–80	Francesco Cossiga
1980–81	Arnaldo Forlani
1981–83	Giovanni Spadolini
1983–87	Bettino Craxi
1987–	Giovanni Goria

Heads of state

1861–78	**Victor Emmanuel II**
1878–1900	Umberto I
1900–46	Victor Emmanuel III
1946	Umberto II

Presidents

1946–48	Enrico de Nicola
1948–55	Luigi Einaudi

1955–62	Giovanni Gronchi
1962–64	Antonio Segni
1964–71	Giuseppe Saragat
1971–78	Giovanni Leone
1978–85	Alessandro Pertini
1985–	Francesco Cossiga

MACEDONIA

729 B.C.	King Perdiccas I
700	Philip I
500	Amyntas I
498–54	Alexander I
454–13	Perdiccas II
413–399	Archelaus
394–70	Amyntas II
369–68	Alexander II
368–60	Perdiccas III
360–59	Amyntas III
359–35	Philip II
336–23	**Alexander III the Great**
323	King Philip III (Aridaeus)
323–10	Alexander IV

316–297	Cassander
306–01	Antigonus I
297–94	King Alexander V
294–83	Demetrius I Poliorcetes
283–73	Antigonus II Gonatas
273	Pyrrhus of Epirus
272–39	Antigonus II Gonatus
239–32	Demetrius II
232	Philip
229–21	Antigonus III Doson
220–179	Philip V
179–68	Perseus
168–	Became a Roman province

THE NETHERLANDS (HOLLAND)

In early times, the country was inhabited by the Batavi, Frisii and Saxons; then, after A.D. 843, it split into small, independent states. When it attached itself to Burgundy in the 15th century, it was ruled by the Habsburgs.

1482–1506	Count Philip the Handsome
1506–56	**Charles V** (Holy Roman Emperor)
1556–81	**Philip II** of Spain
1572–1609	Revolt against Spain

Governors

1507–30	Margaret of Savoy
1531–55	Mary of Hungary
1555–59	Emmanuel Philibert of Savoy
1559–67	Margaret of Parma
1567–73	Fernando Alvarez de Toledo, Duke of Alba
1573–76	Luis de Zuñiga y Requeséns
1576–78	**(Don) John of Austria**
1578–92	**Alessandro Farnese**

DUTCH REPUBLIC

1579–84	Stadholder: **William I, the Silent, Prince of Orange**
1584–1625	Stadholder: Maurice
1621–48	War with Spain
1625–47	Frederick Henry
1650	William II
1650–72	Stadholdership suspended
1672–1702	**William III of Orange** (succeeded to the English throne, 1688)
1702–47	Republic
1747–51	Hereditary stadholder of all provinces: William IV Friso
1751–95	Stadholder: William V

BONAPARTES

1795–1806	Batavian Republic established by France
1806–10	King: Louis Bonaparte
1810–13	Holland incorporated in France

KINGDOM OF THE NETHERLANDS

1815	Belgium annexed to Netherlands
1815–40	King: William I
1830	Belgian provinces seceded
1840–49	William II
1849–90	William III
1890–1948	Queen: **Wilhelmina**
1948–80	Juliana
1980–	Beatrix
1940–45	German High Commissioner: Artur von Seyss-Inquart

STATESMEN

Grand pensionaries

1572–85	Paulus Buys
1586–1619	Johan van Olden Barnevelt
1621–29	Anthonis Duyck
1631–36	Adriaan Pauw
1636–51	Jacob Cats
1651–53	Adriaan Pauw
1653–72	Johan de Witt
1672–89	Gaspar Fagel

Prime ministers

1689–1720	Anthonie Heinsius
1720–27	Isaac van Hoornbeek
1727–36	Simon van Slingelandt
1736–46	Anthony van der Heim
1746–49	Jacob Gilles
1749–72	Pieter Steyn
1772–87	Pieter van Bleiswijk
1787–95	Laurens Pieter van de Spiegel

1945	Pieter Sjoerd Gerbrandy	1965–67	Joseph Maria Laurens Theo Cals
1945–46	Willem Schermerhorn	1967–71	Pieter de Jong
1946–48	Louis Joseph Maria Beel	1971–73	B. W. Biesheuvel
1948–58	Willem Drees	1973–77	Joop M. Den Uyl
1958–59	Louis Joseph Maria Beel	1977–82	Andreas van Agt
1959–63	Jan Eduard de Quay	1982–	Ruud Lubbers
1963–65	Victor Gerard Marie Marijnen		

NORWAY

Rulers

872–30	Harald I Fairhair
930–34	Eirik Blood-Axe
934–61	Haakon I the Good
961–70	Harald II Graypelt
970–95	Jarl Haakon of Lade
995–1000	**Olaf I Tryggvason**
1000–16	Jarls Eirik and Svein
1015–30	Saint Olaf II
1028–35	**Canute the Great** and Sweyn
1035–47	Magnus I the Good
1042–66	**Harald III Hardraade**
1066–69	Magnus II
1066–93	Olaf III Kyrri (the Peaceful)
1093–1103	Magnus III Bareleg
1103–16	Olaf IV
1103–22	Eystein I
1103–30	Sigurd I Jerusalemfarer
1130–35	Magnus IV the Blind
1130–36	Harald IV Gilchrist
1136–39	Sigurd II Slembe
1136–61	Ingi Hunchback
1136–55	Sigurd III Mouth
1142–57	Eystein II
1157–62	Haakon II the Broad-Shouldered
1162–84	Magnus V Erlingsson
1177–1202	Sverri
1202–04	Haakon II
1204–17	Ingi Baardsson
1217–63	Haakon IV the Old
1263–80	Magnus VI Lawmender
1280–99	Eirik II Priesthater
1299–1319	Haakon V
1319–50	Magnus VII
1350–80	Haakon VI
1380–87	Olaf V
1388–1405	**Margaret of Denmark**
1389–1442	Erik of Pomerania
1442–48	Christopher of Bavaria
1448–50	Interregnum with Karl Knutsson and Christian of Oldenburg as rival claimants
1450–81	Christian I
1481–83	Interregnum
1483–1513	Hans
1513–24	Christian II
1524–33	Frederik I
1533–36	Interregnum
1536–59	Christian III
1559–88	Frederik II
1588–1648	**Christian IV**
1648–70	Frederik III
1670–99	Christian V
1699–1730	Frederik IV
1730–46	Christian VI
1746–66	Frederik V
1766–1808	Christian VII
1808–14	Frederik VI
1814	Christian Frederik
1814–18	Karl XIII
1818–44	Karl XIV Johan
1844–59	Oscar I
1859–72	Karl XV
1872–1905	Oscar II
1905–57	Haakon VII
1957–91	Olav V
1991–	Harald

Prime ministers

1861–80	Frederik Stang
1880–84	Chr. Aug. Selmer
1884	Chr. Schweigaard
1884–89	Johan Sverdrup
1889–91	Emil Stang
1891–93	Johannes Steen
1893–95	Emil Stang
1895–98	Georg Francis Hagerup
1898–1902	Johannes Steen
1902–03	Otto Blehr

1903–05	Georg Francis Hagerup	1931–32	Peder Kolstad
1905–07	Christian Michelsen	1932–33	Jens Hundseid
1907–08	J. Lövland	1933–35	Johan Ludwig Mowinckel
1908–10	Gunnar Knudsen	1935–45	Johan Nygaardsvold
1910–12	Wollert Konow	1945–51	Einar Gerhardsen
1912–13	Jens Bratlie	1951–55	Oscar Torp
1913–20	Gunnar Knudsen	1955–63	Einar Gerhardsen
1920–21	Otto B. Halvorsen	1963	John Lyng
1921–23	Otto Blehr	1963–65	Einar Gerhardsen
1923	Otto B. Halvorsen	1965–71	Per Borten
1923–24	Abraham Berge	1971–72	Trygve Bratteli
1924–26	Johan Ludwig Mowinckel	1972–73	Lars Korvald
1926–28	Ivar Lykke	1973–76	Trygve Bratteli
1928	Christopher Hornsrud	1976–81	Odvar Nordli
1928–31	Johan Ludwig Mowinckel	1981–	Gro Harlem Brundtland

POLAND

PIAST DYNASTY

c. 962	Mieszko I
992–1025	Boleslaus I
1025–34	Mieszko II
1034–58	Casimir I
1058–79	Boleslaus II
1079–1102	Ladislaus I
1102–07	Tbigniew and Boleslaus III the Wrymouth
1107–38	Boleslaus III the Wrymouth
1138–46	Ladislaus II
1146–73	Boleslaus IV the Curly
1173–77	Mieszko III
1177–94	Casimir II
1194–1202	Mieszko III
1202	Ladislaus Spindleshanks
1202–10	Leszek the White
1210–11	Mieszko the Stumbling
1211–27	Leszek the White
1227–29	Ladislaus Spindleshanks
1229–32	Conrad of Mazovia
1232–38	Henry I
1238–41	Henry II
1241–43	Konrad I
1241–79	Boleslaus V, the Chaste
1279–88	Leszek the Black
1288–90	Henry IV Probus
1295–96	Przemyslav II
1300–05	Wenceslas II of Bohemia
1305–06	Wenceslas III of Bohemia
1306–33	Ladislaus I
1333–70	Casimir III
1370–82	Louis of Hungary
1382–84	Civil wars

HOUSE OF JAGIELLO

1384–99	Jadwiga
1386–1434	Ladislaus II Jagiello
1434–44	Ladislaus III
1447–92	Casimir IV
1492–1501	John I
1501–06	Alexander
1506–48	Zygmunt I
1548–72	**Zygmunt II Augustus**

ELECTIVE KINGS

1573–74	Henry III of Anjou
1576–86	Stephen Batory
1587–1632	Zygmunt III Vasa
1632–48	Ladislaus IV Vasa
1648–68	John II Casimir Vasa
1669–73	Michael Wisniowiecki
1674–96	**Jan III Sobieski**
1697–1706	Augustus II of Saxony
1704–09	Stanislaus Leszczynski
1709–33	Augustus II of Saxony
1733–63	Augustus III
1764–95	Stanislaus Augustus Poniatowski

Poland partitioned by Russia, Austria and Prussia in 1772, 1793, and 1795. Central Poland became Grand Duchy of Warsaw by order of Napoleon with Frederick Augustus I of Saxony as ruler 1807–1814; regained independence 1918.

REPUBLIC

1918–22	Head of State: **Józef Pilsudski**
1922	President: Gabriel Narutowicz
1922–26	President: Stanislaw Wojciechowski
1926–39	President: Ignacy Móscicki
1923–25	Premier: Wladyslaw Grabski
1935–39	Vice-Premier: Eugeniusz Kwiatkowski
1932–39	Foreign Secretary: Józef Beck
1939–45	German occupation
1939–45	In London: Wladyslaw Raczkiewicz

1939–43	Premier and commander in chief: Wladyslaw Sikorski		1956–70	**Wladyslaw Gomulka**
			1970–80	Edward Gierek
1944–47	Chairman of the National Home Council: Boleslaw Bierut		1980–81	Stanislaw Kania
			1981–89	Wojciech Jaruzelski
1947	Communist regime established		1989–90	President: Wojciech Jaruzelski
			1990	Polish Communist Party collapsed

POLISH PEOPLE'S REPUBLIC

1947–52   President: Boleslaw Bierut

PRESIDENT

1990–   Lech Walesa

CENTRAL COMMITTEE POLISH UNITED WORKER'S PARTY

First secretaries

1954–56   Boleslaw Bierut
1956   Edward Ochab

THE POPES

d. c. 64	Peter (saint and apostle)
c. 66–78	Linus (saint)
c. 79–91	Anacletus (saint)
c. 91–101	Clement I (saint)
c. 100–109	Evaristus (saint)
c. 109–116	Alexander I (saint)
c. 116–125	Sixtus I (saint)
c. 125–136	Telesphorus (saint)
c. 138–142	Hyginus (saint)
c. 142–155	Pius I (saint)
c. 155–166	Anicetus (saint)
c. 166–174	Soter (saint)
c. 174–89	Eleutherius, or Eleutherus (saint)
189–98	Victor I (saint)
198/9–217	Zephyrinus (saint)
217–22	Callistus I (Calixtus) (saint)
217–35	Hippolytus (saint and antipope)
222–30	Urban I (saint)
230–35	Pontian (saint)
235–36	Anterus (saint)
236–50	Fabian (saint)
251–53	Cornelius (saint)
251–58	Novatian (antipope)
253–54	Lucius I (saint)
254–57	Stephen I (saint)
257–58	Sixtus II (saint)
260–68	Dionysius (saint)
269–74	Felix I (saint)
275–83	Eutychian (saint)
283–96	Gaius or Caius (saint)
296–d. 304	Marcellinus (saint)
306–08	Marcellus I (saint)
310	Eusebius (saint)
311–14	Miltiades, or Melchiades (saint)
314–35	Silvester I (saint)
336	Mark (saint)
337–52	Julius I (saint)
352–66	Liberius
355–65	Felix II (saint and antipope)
366–84	Damasus I (saint)
366–67	Ursinus (antipope)
384–99	Siricius (saint)
399–401	Anastasius I (saint)
401–17	Innocent I (saint)
417–18	Zosimus (saint)
418–19	Eulalius (antipope)
418–22	Boniface I (saint)
422–32	Celestine I (saint)
432–40	Sixtus, or Xystus, III (saint)
440–61	Leo I (saint)
461–68	Hilarus (saint)
468–83	Simplicius (saint)
483–92	Felix III (II) (saint)
492–96	Gelasius (saint)
496–98	Anastasius II
498–514	Symmachus (saint)
498–99	Lawrence (antipope)
501–06	Lawrence (antipope)
507/08	Lawrence (antipope)
514–23	Hormisdas (saint)
523–26	John I (saint)
526–30	Felix IV (III) (saint)
530	Dioscorus (antipope)
530–32	Boniface II
533–35	John II
535–36	Agapitus I (saint)
536–37	Silverius (saint)
537–55	Vigilius
556–61	Pelagius I
561–74	John III
575–79	Benedict I
579–90	Pelagius II
590–604	Gregory I (saint)
604–06	Sabinian
607	Boniface III
608–15	Boniface IV (saint)
615–18	Deusdedit (later Adeodatus I) (saint)
619–25	Boniface V

625–38	Honorius I
640	Severinus
640–42	John IV
642–49	Theodore I
649–53	Martin I (saint)
654–57	Eugene I (saint)
657–72	Vitalian (saint)
672–76	Adeodatus II
676–78	Donus
678–81	Agatho (saint)
682–83	Leo II (saint)
684–85	Benedict II (saint)
685–86	John V
686–87	Conon
687	Theodore (antipope)
687	Paschal (antipope)
687–701	Sergius I (saint)
701–05	John VI
705–07	John VII
708	Sisinnius
708–15	Constantine
715–31	Gregory II (saint)
731–41	Gregory III (saint)
741–52	Zacharias (saint)
752	Stephen (II)
752–57	Stephen II (III)
757–67	Paul I (saint)
767–68	Constantine (antipope)
768	Philip (antipope)
768–72	Stephen III (IV)
772–95	Hadrian I
795–816	Leo III (saint)
816–17	Stephen IV (V)
817–24	Paschal I (saint)
824–27	Eugene II
827	Valentine
827–44	Gregory IV
844	John (antipope)
844–47	Sergius II
847–55	Leo IV (saint)
855–58	Benedict III
855	Anastasius bibliothecarius (antipope)
858–67	Nicholas I (saint)
867–72	Hadrian II
872–82	John VIII
882–84	Marinus I
884–85	Hadrian III (saint)
885–91	Stephen V (VI)
891–96	Formosus
896	Boniface VI
896–97	Stephen VI (VII)
897	Romanus
897	Theodore II
898–900	John IX
900–03	Benedict IV
903–04	Leo V
903–04	Christopher (antipope)
904–11	Sergius III
911–13	Anastasius III
913–14	Lando
914–28	John X
928	Leo VI
928–31	Stephen VII (VIII)
931–35/36	John XI
936–39	Leo VII
939–42	Stephen VIII (IX)
942–46	Marinus II
946–55	Agapitus II
955–64	John XII
963–65	Leo VIII
964–66	Benedict V
965–72	John XIII

973–74	Benedict VI
974	Boniface VII (antipope)
974–83	Benedict VII
983–84	John XIV
984–85	Boniface VII (antipope)
985–96	John XV
996–99	Gregory V
997–98	John XVI (antipope)
999–1003	Silvester II
1003	John XVII
1003–09	John XVIII
1009–12	Sergius IV
1012–24	Benedict VIII
1012	Gregory (VI) (antipope)
1024–32	John XIX
1032–45	Benedict IX
1045	Silvester III
1045–46	Gregory VI
1046–47	Clement II
1047–48	Benedict IX
1048	Damasus II
1049–54	Leo IX (saint)
1055–57	Victor II
1057–58	Stephen IX (X)
1058–59	Benedict X (antipope)
1058–61	Nicholas II
1061–73	Alexander II
1061–64	Honorius (II) (antipope)
1073–85	Gregory VII (saint)
1080	Clement III (antipope)
1084–1100	Clement III (antipope)
1086–87	Victor III, bl.
1088–99	Urban II, bl.
1099–1118	Paschal II
1100–01	Theodoric (antipope)
1101	Albert or Adalbert (antipope)
1105–11	Silvester IV (antipope)
1118–19	Gelasius II
1118–21	Gregory (VIII) (antipope)
1119–24	Callistus II
1124–30	Honorius II
1124–25/6	Celestine (II)
1130–43	Innocent II
1130–38	Anacletus II (antipope)
1138	Victor IV (antipope)
1143–44	Celestine II
1144–45	Lucius II
1145–53	Eugene III, bl.
1153–54	Anastasius IV
1154–59	Hadrian IV
1159–81	Alexander III
1159–64	Victor IV (antipope)
1164–68	Paschal III (antipope)
1168–78	Callistus (III) (antipope)
1179–80	Innocent (III) (antipope)
1181–85	Lucius III
1185–87	Urban III
1187	Gregory VIII
1187–91	Clement III
1191–98	Celestine III
1198–1216	Innocent III
1216–27	Honorius III
1227–41	Gregory IX
1241	Celestine IV
1243–54	Innocent IV
1254–61	Alexander IV
1261–64	Urban IV
1265–68	Clement IV
1271–76	Gregory X, bl.
1276	Innocent V, bl.
1276	Hadrian V
1276–77	John XXI

1277–80	Nicholas III		1555–59	Paul IV
1281–85	Martin IV		1559–65	PIus IV
1285–87	Honorius IV		1566–72	Pius V (saint)
1288–92	Nicholas IV		1572–85	Gregory XIII
1294–96	Celestine V (St. Peter)		1585–90	Sixtus
1294–1303	Boniface VIII		1590	Urban VII
1303–04	Benedict XI, bl.		1590–91	Gregory XIV
1305–14	Clement V		1591	Innocent IX
1316–34	John XXII		1592–1605	Clement VIII
1328–30	Nicholas (V) (antipope)		1605	Leo XI
1334–42	Benedict XII		1605–21	Paul V
1342–52	Clement VI		1621–23	Gregory XV
1352–62	Innocent VI		1623–44	Urban VIII
1362–70	Urban V, bl.		1644–55	Innocent X
1370–78	Gregory XI		1655–67	Alexander VII
1378–89	Urban VI		1667–69	Clement IX
1378–94	Clement (VII) (antipope)		1670–76	Clement X
1389–1404	Boniface IX		1676–89	Innocent XI, bl.
1394–1417	Benedict XIII (antipope)		1689–91	Alexander VIII
1404–06	Innocent VII		1691–1700	Innocent XII
1406–15	Gregory XII		1700–21	Clement XI
1409–10	Alexander V (antipope)		1721–24	Innocent XIII
1410–15	John XXIII (antipope)		1730–40	Clement XII
1417–31	Martin V		1740–58	Benedict XIV
1423–29	Clement (VIII) (antipope)		1758–69	Clement XIII
1425–?	Benedict (XIV) (antipope)		1769–74	Clement XIV
1431–47	Eugene IV		1775–99	Pius VI
1439–49	Felix V (antipope)		1800–23	Pius VII
1447–55	Nicholas V		1823–29	Leo XII
1455–58	Callistus III		1829–30	Pius VIII
1458–64	Pius II		1831–46	Gregory XVI
1464–71	Paul II		1846–78	Pius IX
1471–84	Sixtus IV		1878–1903	Leo XIII
1484–92	Innocent VIII		1903–14	Pius X (saint)
1492–1503	Alexander VI		1914–22	Benedict XV
1503	PIus III		1922–39	Pius XI
1503–13	Julius II		1939–58	Pius XII
1513–21	Leo X		1958–63	John XXIII
1522–23	Hadrian VI		1963–78	Paul VI
1523–34	Clement VII		1978	John Paul I
1534–49	Paul III		1978–	John Paul II
1550–55	Julius III		9th, 10th,	
1555	Marcellus II		or 11th c.	Pope Joan

PORTUGAL

Originally Lusitania, Portugal was under Roman and Moorish rule before becoming an independent state.

HOUSE OF BURGUNDY

1094–1112	Count: Henry of Burgundy
1112–28	Regent: Teresa of Castile
1128–40	Count: Alfonso I
1140–85	Alfonso I declared an independent monarchy in 1140
1185–1211	Sancho I
1211–23	Alfonso II (the Fat)
1223–45	Sancho II
1245–79	Alfonso III
1279–1325	Diniz
1325–57	Alfonso IV
1357–67	Pedro I
1367–83	Ferdinand I
1383–85	Internal conflicts

HOUSE OF AVIZ

1385–1433	John I
1433–38	Edward I
1438–81	Alfonso V (Africano)
1481–95	John II
1495–1521	Emanuel I
1521–57	John III
1557–78	Sebastian
1578–80	Henry
1580	Antonio
1580–1640	Ruled by Spain

HOUSE OF BRAGANZA

1640–56	John IV
1656–67	Alfonso VI
1667–83	Regent: Pedro II
1683–1706	Pedro II
1706–50	John V
1750–77	Joseph Emanuel
1777–1816	Maria I
1777–86	Joint ruler: Pedro III
1799–1816	Regent: John
1816–26	John VI
1826	Pedro IV
1826–28	Maria II
1828–34	Usurper: Miguel
1834–53	Maria II
1853–61	Pedro
1861–89	Louis I
1889–1908	Carlos I
1908–10	Emanuel II
1910	Republic proclaimed

REPUBLIC

Presidents

1910–11	Provisional: Teófilo Braga
1911–15	Manoel José de Arriaga
1915	Teófilo Braga
1915–17	Bernardino Luiz Machado Guimaraes
1917–18	Sidônio Bernadino Cardoso de Silva Paes
1918–19	Provisional: João de Canto e Castro Silva Antunes
1919–23	António José de Almeida
1923–25	Manoel Teixeira Gomes
1925–26	Bernardino Luiz Machado Guimaraes
1926–51	Antonio Oscar de Fragoso Carmona
1951–58	Francisco Higino Craveiro Lopes
1958–74	Américo Deus Rodrigues Tomás
1974	Antonio Sebastiao Ribeiro de Spinola
1974–76	Francisco da Costa Gomes
1976–	Antonio Ramalho Eanes

Statesmen

1505–09	Viceroy: Francisco de Almeida

1506–15	Afonso de Albuquerque
1756–77	Prime Minister: Sebastião José de Carvalho e Mello, Marquês de Pombal
1932–68	Premier: **António de Oliveira Salazar**
1968–74	Prime Minister: Marcelo Caetano
1974	Prof. Dr. Adelino da Palma Carlos
1974–75	Vasco dos Santos Goncalves
1975–76	José Baptista Pinheiro de Azevedo
1976–	Mario Soares

ROMAN EMPERORS

27 B.C.–A.D. 14	**Augustus (Octavian)**
14–37	**Tiberius**
37–41	**Caligula (Gaius)**
41–54	**Claudius**
54–68	**Nero**
68–69	Galba
69	Otho
69	Vitellius
69–79	Vespasian
79–81	Titus
81–96	**Domitián**
96–98	Nerva
98–117	**Trajan**
117–38	**Hadrian**
138–61	Antoninus Pius
161–80	**Marcus Aurelius**
161–69	Lucius Aurelius Verus
180–92	Commodus
193	Pertinax
193	Didius Julian
193–211	Septimius Severus
211–17	Caracalla
217–18	Macrinus
218–22	Elagabalus
222–35	Alexander Severus
235–38	Maximinus
238	Gordian I
238	Gordian II
238	Pupienus
238	Balbinus
238–44	Gordian III
244–49	Philip "the Arab"
249–51	Decius
251–53	Gallus
253	Aemilian
253–59	Valerian
259–68	Gallienus
268–70	Claudius II
270–75	Aurelian
275–76	Tacitus
276	Florian
276–82	Probus
282–83	Carus
283–84	Numerian
283–85	Carinus
284–305	**Diocletian**
286–305	Maximilian
305–06	Constantius I
305–11	Galerius
311–37	**Constantine I, the Great**
337–40	Constantine II
337–61	Constantius II
337–50	Constans
361–63	Julian, the Apostate
363–64	Jovian
364–75	Valentinian I (in the West)
364–78	Valens (in the East)
375–83	Gratian (in the West)
375–92	Valentinian II (in the West)
379–95	Theodosius, the Great (in the East, and after 394, in the West)
383–88	Maximus (in the West)
392–94	Engenius (in the West)
395–408	Arcadius (in the East)
395–423	Honorius (in the West)
421	Constantius III (co-emperor in the West)
408–50	Theodosius II (in the East)
425–55	Valentinian III (in the West)
450–57	Marcian (in the East)
455	Petronius (in the West)
455–56	Avitus (in the West)
457–61	Majorian (in the West)
457–74	Leo I (in the East)
461–65	Severus (in the West)
467–72	Anthemius (in the West)
472	Olybrius (in the West)
473	Glycerius (in the West)

RUSSIA

Some English historians anglicize Russian names: Ivan becomes John, Vasilii becomes Basil, Fedor becomes Theodore, Dmitri becomes Dimitry, Marfa becomes Martha, Mikhail becomes Michael, Grigori becomes Gregory. The Russian letter "Ts" is rendered as "Tz" or "Cz" which explains the variations in the spelling of "Tsar."

862–79	Rurik

Dukes of Kiev

879–912	Oleg
912–45	Igor
945–57	Olga
957–72	Svyatoslav
972–80	Yaropolk
980–1015	**Vladimir**
1015–19	Svyatopolk
1019–54	Yaroslav
1054–79	Isaslav
1078–93	Vsevold
1093–1113	Svyatopolk II
1113–25	Vladimir II (Monomach)
1125–32	Mstislav
1132–39	Yaropolk II
1139–46	Vsevold II
1146–54	Isaslov II
1154–57	Yury (Longarm)

Grand dukes of Vladimir

1157–75	Andrew I (Bogolubsky)
1169–75	Gleb (in Kiev)
1175–76	Michael I
1176–1212	Vsevold III
1212–16	Yury II
1216–19	Constantine
1219–38	Yury II

Grand princes

1238–46	Yaroslav II
1246–63	**Alexander (Nevsky)**
1263–72	Yaroslav III
1272–76	Basil Kostroma
1276–94	Dmitry I
1294–1304	Andrew III
1304–19	Michael I
1319–26	Yury III
1326–28	Alexander II

Grand dukes of Moscow

1328–40	Ivan I (Kolita)
1340–53	Simeon
1353–59	Ivan II
1359–63	Dmitry
1363–84	Dmitry (Donskoi)
1384–1425	Basil I
1425–62	Basil II (the Sightless)

Tsars of Muscovy

1462–1505	**Ivan III (the Great)**
1505–33	Basil III
1533–84	**Ivan IV (the Terrible)**
1584–98	Fedor I
1598–1605	**Boris Godunov**
1605–06	Demetrius (the "False"), the 1st Pretender
1606–10	Basil IV (Ivanovic Shuisky)
1613–45	Michael (Fedorovi Romanoff)
1645–76	Alexis I
1676–82	Fedor III, son of Alexis
1682–1725	Peter (the Great) and Ivan V
1725–27	Catherine I (Skavronsky)
1727–30	Peter II
1730–40	Anne (of Courland)
1740–41	Ivan VI
1741–62	Elizabeth
1762	Peter III

1762–96	**Catherine II, the Great**
1796–1801	Paul I
1801–25	**Alexander I**
1825–55	Nicholas I
1855–81	**Alexander II**
1881–94	Alexander III
1894–1917	**Nicholas II**
1917	Provisional Government (March 16 to Nov. 7, 1917); headed by Prince Lvov and later **Alexander Kerensky**
1917	Bolshevik Government formed the Union of Soviet Socialist Republics

Soviet premiers

| 1917–23 | **V. I. Lenin** |
| 1923–56 | **Joseph Stalin** |

1953–55	Georgi Malenkov
1955–58	Nikolai Bulganin
1958–64	Nikita Khrushchev
1964–80	Alexei Kosygin
1980–82	Leonid Brezhnev
1982–84	Yuri Andropov
1984–85	Konstantin Chernenko
1985–86	Viacheslav Molotov
1986–91	Mikhail Gorbachev

PRESIDENT OF THE RUSSIAN REPUBLIC

| 1991– | Boris Yeltsin |

SCOTLAND

No authenticated information is available for the period before Kenneth MacAlpine united Picts and Scots.

Kings

846–58?	Kenneth I MacAlpine
943–54	Malcolm I MacDonald
971–95	Kenneth II
997–1005	Kenneth III
1005–34	Malcolm II Mackenneth
1034–40	Duncan I
1034	Scots, Picts, Angles and Britons united in Kingdom of Scotland
1040–57	**Macbeth**
1057–93	Malcolm III MacDuncan
1093–94	Duncan II
1094–97	Donald Bane
1097–1107	Edgar
1107–24	Alexander I
1124–53	David I
1153–65	Malcolm IV the Maiden
1165–1214	William the Lion
1214–49	Alexander II
1249–86	Alexander III
1286–90	Queen Margaret ("The Maid of Norway")
1290–92	Interregnum
1292–96	John de Baliol (Balliol)
1296–1306	Scotland a dependency of England
1306–29	**Robert I the Bruce**
1329–71	David II

House of Stuart

1371–90	Robert II
1390–1406	Robert III
1406–37	James I
1437–60	James II
1460–88	James III
1488–1513	James IV
1513–42	James V
1542–67	**Mary Stuart**
1554–60	Regent: Mary of Guise
1567–1625	**James VI**
1603	Scottish Crown united with the Crown of England

SPAIN

Spain was under Roman rule until conquered by the Visigoths.

VISIGOTHIC SPAIN

Kings

412–15	Ataulfo (Ataulphus)
419–51	Teodoredo (Theodoric)
466–65	Eurico (Euric)
484–507	Alarico (Alaric)
507–31	Amalarico (Amalaric)
554–67	Atanagildo (Athanagild)
572–86	Leovigildo (Leovigild)
586–601	Recaredo (Reccared)
612–21	Sisebuto (Sisebut)
621–31	Suintila (Swintilla)
642–49	Chindavinto (Chindaswinth)
649–72	Recesvinto (Recceswinth)
672–80	Wamba
680–87	Ervigio (Euric)
709–11	Don Rodrigo (Roderic)

FIRST MOORISH EMIRATE

Emirs

711–14	Tarik and Muza
714–17	Abdelaziz
718–19	Alhor
730–32	Abderraman el Gafeki

SECOND MOORISH EMIRATE

756–88	Abd-al-Rahman I
788–96	Hisham (Hixen) I
796–822	Hakam (Alhaken) I
822–52	Abd-al-Rahman II
852–86	Mohammed

886–88	Mundhir
888–912	Abd Allah
912–29	**Abd-al-Rahman III**

OMAYAD CALIPHATE OF CORDOVA

Caliphs

929–61	**Abd-al-Rahman III**
961–76	Al Hakam (Alhaken) II
976–1009	Hisham (Hixen) II
1010–16	Hisham II
1009–27	Internal conflicts and division
1027–31	Hisham (Hixen) III
1031–1492	Moorish Spain was divided into numerous kingdoms, known as *Taifas,* which included Cordova, Toledo, Seville, Granada, Jaen, Murcia, Valencia, and Zaragoza

KINGDOM OF ASTURIAS

Kings

718–737	Pelayo
739–57	Alfonso I "the Catholic"
757–91	"Lazy Kings of Austurias": Fruela I, Aurelio, Silo, Mauregato, and Bermudo I "the Deacon"
842–50	Ramiro I
850–66	Ordoño I
866–909	Alfonso III "the Great"

KINGDOM OF LEON

Kings

914–24	Ordoño II
931–51	Ramiro II
951–56	Ordoño III

956–66	Sancho I "the Fat"
966–82	Ramiro III and Bermudo II
999–1027	Alfonso V "the Noble"
1027–37	Bermudo III

COUNTY (CONDADO) OF CASTILE

Counts

860?	Rodrigo, Diego Rodriguez, and the judges Nuño Rasura and Lain Calvo
?923–?970	Fernan Gonzalez
?970–95	Garci Fernández
995–1021	Sancho García
1021–28	García Sánchez

KINGDOMS OF LEON AND CASTILE UNITED

Kings and queens

1035–65	Fernando I
1065–72	Sancho II
1072–1109	Alfonso VI
1109–26	Doña Urraca
1126–57	Alfonso VII "the Emperor"

KINGDOM OF CASTILE

1157–58	Sancho III
1158–1214	Alfonso VIII
1214–17	Enrique I

KINGDOM OF LEON

1157–88	Fernando II
1188–1230	Alfonso IX

KINGDOMS OF CASTILE AND LEON UNITED

1217–52	Fernando III "the Saint"
1252–84	**Alfonso X "the Wise"**
1284–95	Sancho IV
1295–1312	Fernando IV
1312–50	Alfonso XI
1350–69	Pedro I "the Cruel"
1369–79	Enrique II
1379–90	Juan I
1390–1406	Enrique III
1406–54	Juan II
1454–74	Enrique IV
1474–1504	**Isabel I**
1504–06	Philip I (last separate sovereign of Castile)

KINGDOM OF NAVARRE

840–850?	Iñigo Arista
905–925	Sancho Garcés
925–970	García Sánchez
1000–35	Sancho "the Great"
1035–54	García I
1054–76	Sancho IV

KINGDOM OF ARAGON

1035–63	Ramiro I
1063–94	Sancho Ramírez

KINGDOMS OF NAVARRE AND ARAGON UNITED

1076–94	Sancho Ramírez

1094–1104	Pedro I
1104–34	Alfonso I "the Fighter"

KINGDOM OF NAVARRE

1134–50	García Ramírez
1150–94	Sancho VI "the Wise"
1194–1234	Sancho VII "the Strong"
1234–53	Teobaldo I
1253–70	Teobaldo II
1270–74	Enrique I
1274–1307	Juana (Joan) I
1284–1328	Navarre belonged to France
1328–49	Juana II
1349–87	Charles II "the Bad"
1387–1425	Charles III "the Noble"
1425–41	Doña Blanca
1441–46	Don Carlos de Viana
1461–79	Juan II of Aragon
1479–81	Francisco Febo
1481–1512	Catalina de Albret
1512	Navarre joined to Castile and Aragon

KINGDOM OF ARAGON

1134–37	Ramiro II "the Monk"

MAJORCA

1276	Detached from Aragon in 1276; established as a separate kingdom
1276–1311	Jaime I
1311–24	Sancho
1324–43	Jaime II
1343	Majorca reunited with Aragon

COUNTY (CONDADO) OF CATALONIA

Counts

874–898	Wifredo "the Hairy"
1035–76	Ramón Berenguer I
1096–1131	Ramón Berenguer III
1131–62	Ramón Berenguer IV

KINGDOM OF ARAGON UNITED TO CATALONIA

Kings

1162–96	Alfonso II
1196–1213	Pedro II
1213–76	Jaime I "the Conqueror"
1276–85	Pedro III "the Great"
1285–91	Alfonso III
1291–1327	Jaime II
1327–36	Alfonso IV
1336–87	Pedro IV "the Ceremonious"
1387–95	Juan I
1395–1410	Martin I "the Humane"
1410–12	Throne vacant
1412–16	Fernando I
1416–58	Alfonso V "the Magnanimous"
1479–1516	**Fernando II "the Catholic"** (whose marriage to Isabel of Castile united the Kingdoms of Aragon and Castile)

KINGDOM OF SPAIN

1479–1504	**Monarchs: Isabel I and Fernando V** (II of Aragon)
1505–06	Regent: Fernando V

1506	Regent: Philip "the Handsome"
1507–16	Regent: Fernando V
1516–17	Regent: Cardinal Cisneros
1516–56	**King: Charles I (or V of Holy Roman Empire)**
1556–98	**Philip II**
1598–1621	Philip III
1621–65	Philip IV
1665–1700	Charles II
1700–24	Philip V of Bourbon
1724	Louis I
1724–46	Philip V
1746–59	Fernando VI
1759–88	**Charles III**
1788–1808	Charles IV
1808–13	Joseph Bonaparte (imposed by Napoleon)
1808–33	Fernando VII
1833–40	Regent: Maria Cristina
1840–43	Regent: Don Baldomero Espartero
1833–68	Queen: Isabel II
1868–70	Regent: Francisco Serrano
1870–73	King: Amadeo of Savoy

FIRST REPUBLIC (HAD FOUR PRESIDENTS)

1873–74	Estanislao Figueras, José Pi y Margall, Nicolas Salmerón and Emilio Castelar
1874	Head of provisional government: Francisco Serrano
1874–85	King: Alfonso XII
1885–1902	Regent: Maria Cristina
1886–1931	King: Alfonso XIII

SECOND REPUBLIC

1931–36	President: Niceto Alcalá Zamora

1936	Manuel Azaña
1936–39	Civil War
1936–47	Chief of State: **Francisco Franco**

KINGDOM OF SPAIN

Chiefs of state

1947–75	**Francisco Franco**
1975–	King: Juan Carlos I

Vice-premiers

1962–67	Agustin Muñoz Grandes
1967–73	Louis Carrero Blanco

Premiers

1973	Louis Carrero Blanco
1973–74	Torcuato Fernandez Miranda
1974–76	Carlos Arias Navarro
1976–81	Adolfo Súarez Gonzalez
1981–82	Leopoldo Calvo-Sotelo y Bustelo
1982–	Felipe González Márquez

STATESMEN

1621–43	First Minister: Gaspar de Guzman, Count of Olivares
1715–19	Giulio Alberoni
1765–73	Pedro Pablo Abarca y Bolea
1777–92	José Moñino y Redondo, Count of Floridablanca
1792–1808	Manuel de Godoy
1844–68	Ramón María Narváez, Duke of Valencia
1923–30	Dictator: **Miguel Primo de Rivera**

SWEDEN

500	King Egil, Ottar, and Adils
600	Osten, Ingvar, Anund, and Ingjald Illråde
800	Sigurd Ring, Ragnar Lodbrok, and Bjorn Ironside
850–82	Eric VI, Bjorn, Olof, Emund Eriksson, and Eric VII (the Swedish Kingdom was established by Eric VII)
994–1022	Olof Sköttkonung
1022–50	Anund Jakob
1050–60	Emund the Old
1060–66	Steinkel
1066–80	Internal wars
1080–1110	King Halstan
1080–1112	Co-regent: Inge
1112–18	King Philip
1112–25	Co-regent: Inge

SVERKER AND ERIC DYNASTIES

1133–56	Sverker
1150–60	Rival: Eric IX (St. Eric)
1160–61	Magnus Henriksson
1161–67	Charles VII
1167–95	Knut Eriksson
1195–1208	Sverker Karlsson
1208–16	Eric X
1216–22	John I Sverkersson
1222–50	Eric XI, son of Eric X
1229–34	Rival: Knut Lange
1248–66	Regent: Earl Birger I

FOLKUNG DYNASTY

1250–75	Waldemar I
1275–90	**Magnus I Ladulås**
1290–1318	Birger II
1319	Union of Kalmar between Sweden and Norway
1319–65	Magnus Eriksson II
1356–59	Co-regent: Eric XII

1365–89	Albert of Mecklenburg
1389–1412	Regent: **Margaret**
1396–1439	Eric XIII of Pomerania (Eric VII of Denmark)
1397	Union of Kalmar between Sweden, Norway and Denmark
1435–36	Regent: Engelbrekt Engelbrektsson
1438–40	Karl Knutsson
1440–48	Christopher of Bavaria
1448–57	Charles VIII (Karl Knutsson)
1457–64	Christian I of Denmark
1464–65	Charles VIII (Karl Knutsson)
1465–66	Regent: Jons Bengtsson Oxenstierna
1466–67	Regent: Erik Axelsson Tott
1467–70	Charles VIII (Karl Knutsson)
1470–97	Regent: Sten Sture the Elder
1497–1501	John (Hans) II of Denmark
1501–03	Regent: Sten Sture
1503–12	Svante Nilsson Sture
1512–20	Sten Sture the Younger
1520–21	Christian II

HOUSE OF VASA

1521–23	Regent: Gustavus Eriksson Vasa
1523–60	**Gustavus I**
1560–68	Eric XIV
1568–92	John III
1592–99	Sigismund
1599–1604	Regent: Charles IX
1604–11	Charles IX
1611–32	**Gustavus II Adolphus**
1632–54	**Christina**

PALATINATE DYNASTY

1654–60	Charles X Gustavus
1660–97	Charles XI
1697–1718	Charles XII
1718–20	Ulrica Eleonora
1720–51	Frederick I of Hesse

HOLSTEIN-GOTTORP DYNASTY

1751–71	Adolphus Frederick
1771–92	Gustavus III
1792–1809	Gustavus IV Adolphus
1792–96	Regent: Charles
1809–18	Charles XIII
1814–1905	Sweden united with Norway

BERNADOTTE DYNASTY

1818–44	Charles XIV John (Bernadotte)
1844–59	Oscar I
1859–72	Charles XV
1872–1907	Oscar II
1907–50	Gustav V
1950–73	Gustav VI Adolf
1973–	Carl XVI Gustaf

YUGOSLAVIA

Established in 1918.

1919–21	King Peter I
1918–21	Regent: Alexander
1921–34	Alexander I, King of the Serbs, Croats, and Slovenes
1934–41	Regent: Paul
1934–45	Peter II
1945	Communist regime established

Presidents of the Collective Presidency

1945–53	Ivan Ribar
1953–80	**Marshal Tito**
1980	Lazar Kolisevski
1980–81	Crijetin Mijatovic
1981–82	Sergej Krajgen
1982–83	Petar Stambolic
1983–84	Mika Spiljak
1984–85	Veselin Djuranovic
1985–86	Radoran Vlajkovic
1986–87	Sinan Hasani
1987–88	Lazar Mojsov
1988–89	Raij Dizdarevic
1989–90	Janez Drnovsek
1990–91	Borisav Jovic
1991–92	Stepan Mesic May
1992	Milan Panic
1993	Dobrica Cosic

Presidents of the Central Committee Presidium, League of Communists

1987–88	Milenko Renovica
1988–89	Bosko Krvnic
1989	Stipe Suvar
1989–90	Milan Pancevski

Prime ministers

1977–82	Veselin Djuranovic
1982–86	Milka Planinc
1986–89	Branko Mikulic
1989–92	Ante Markovic
1992	Milan Panic
1992	Radoje Kontic
1992–	Milan Panic

Appendix B:
Maps

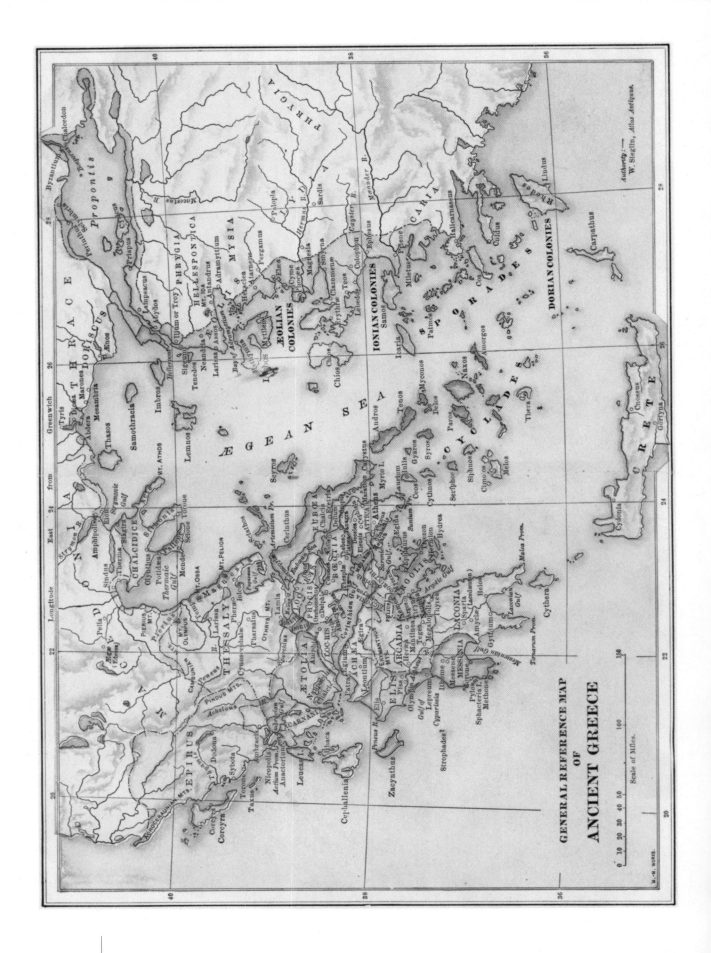

GENERAL REFERENCE MAP
OF
ANCIENT GREECE

Scale of Miles.

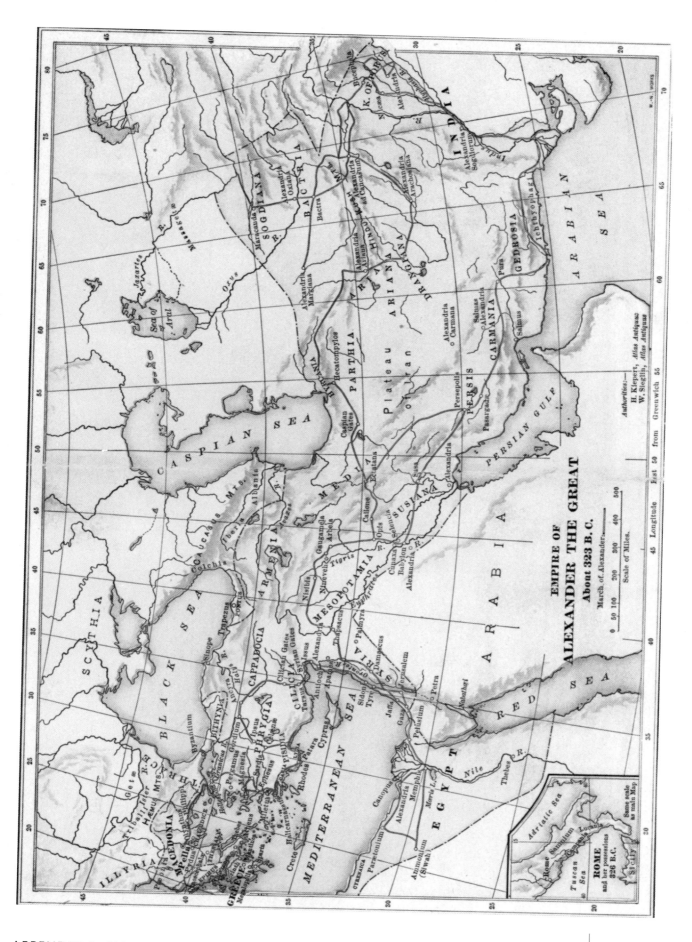

EMPIRE OF
ALEXANDER THE GREAT
About 323 B.C.

March of Alexander.

Scale of Miles.

0 50 100 200 300 400 500

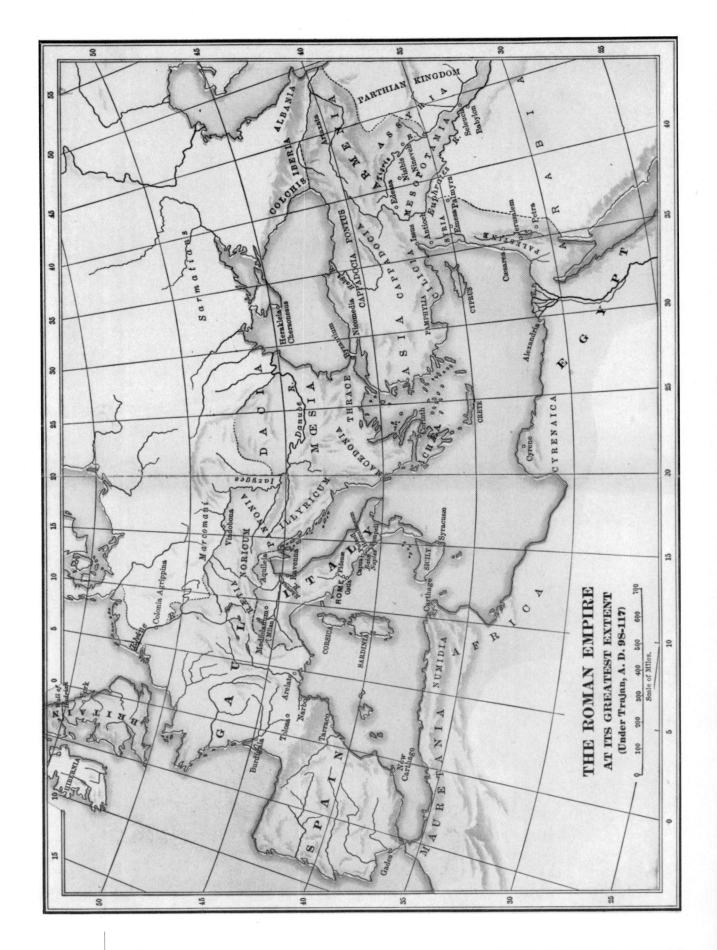

THE ROMAN EMPIRE
AT ITS GREATEST EXTENT
(Under Trajan, A.D. 98–117)

Scale of Miles.

0   100   200   300   400   500   600   700

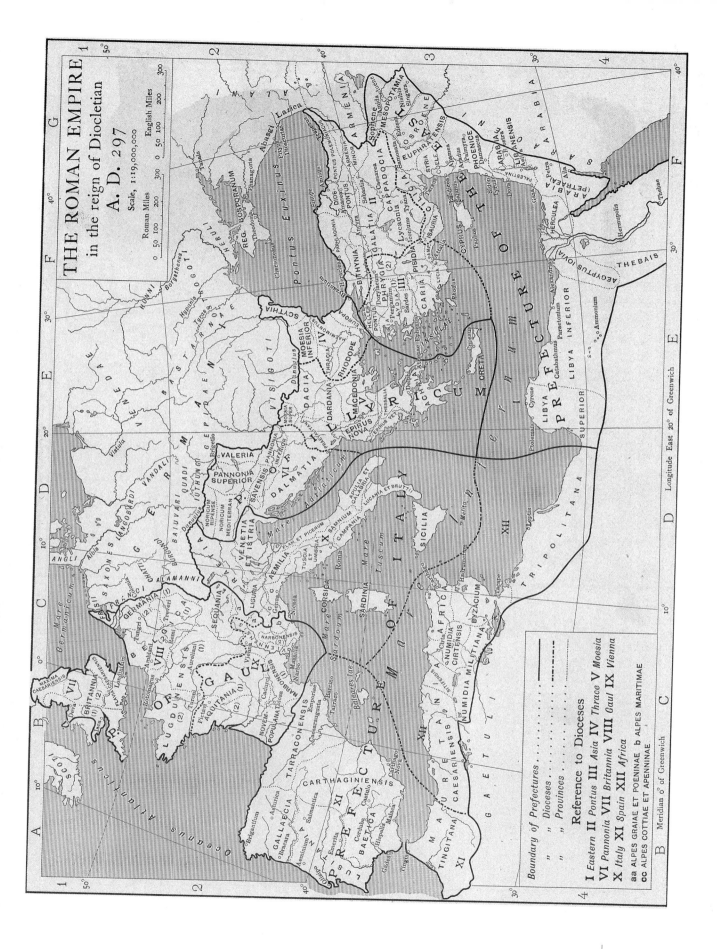

THE ROMAN EMPIRE
in the reign of Diocletian
A.D. 297

Scale, 1:19,000,000

Roman Miles
0 50 100 200 300

English Miles
0 50 100 200 300

Reference to Dioceses
I Eastern II Pontus III Asia IV Thrace V Moesia
VI Pannonia VII Britannia VIII Gaul IX Vienna
X Italy XI Spain XII Africa
aa ALPES GRAIAE ET POENINAE   b ALPES MARITIMAE
cc ALPES COTTIAE ET APENNINAE

Boundary of Prefectures . . . .
   "   "   Dioceses . . . .
   "   "   Provinces . . . .

Meridian 0° of Greenwich   Longitude East 20° of Greenwich

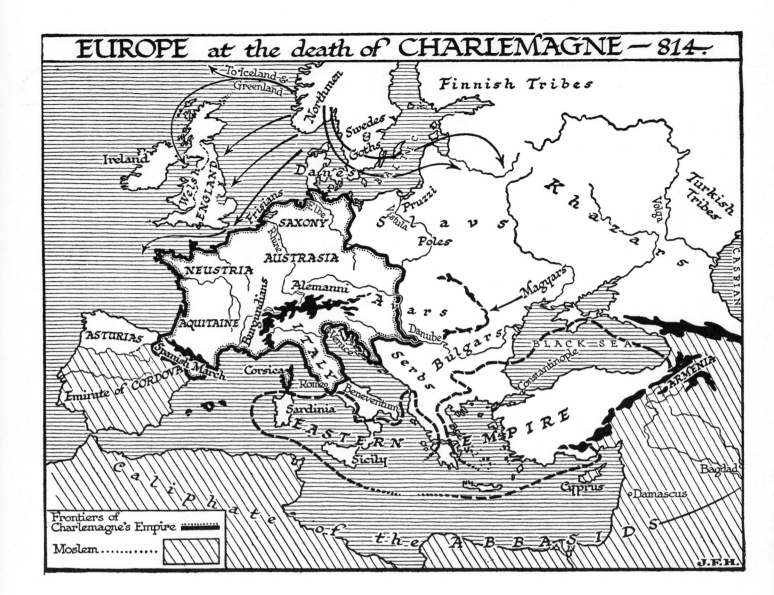

EUROPE *at the death of* CHARLEMAGNE — 814.

To Iceland & Greenland

Northmen

Finnish Tribes

Swedes & Goths

Ireland

Welsh

ENGLAND

Frisians

Danes

Elbe

SAXONY

Rhine

AUSTRASIA

NEUSTRIA

Alemanni

Burgundians

AQUITAINE

ASTURIAS

Spanish March

Emirate of CORDOVA

Corsica

ITALY

Rome

Venice

Beneventum

Sardinia

EASTERN

Sicily

Caliphate

of the ABBASIDS

Pruzzi

Vistula

S l a v s

Poles

A v a r s

Danube

Serbs

Bulgars

Magyars

Khazars

Volga

Turkish Tribes

CASPIAN

BLACK SEA

Constantinople

EMPIRE

Cyprus

Damascus

ARMENIA

Bagdad

Frontiers of
Charlemagne's Empire ••••••••••

Moslem ••••••••••

J.F.H.

Area more or less under FRANKISH dominion in the time of CHARLES MARTEL

c. early 8th century

Slavs

ENGLAND

Britons

Saxons

Frisians

Elbe

Britons

Meuse

Cologne

Rhine

Thuringians

AUSTRASIA

Soissons

Seine

Paris

Strasburg

Danube

Bavarians

NEUSTRIA

Loire

Tours

Poitiers

BURGUNDY

ALPS

Serbs

AQUITAINE

Rhone

LOMBARDS

Po

Venice

Ravenna
[to the
Eastern
Empire]

WEST GOTHS

J.F.H

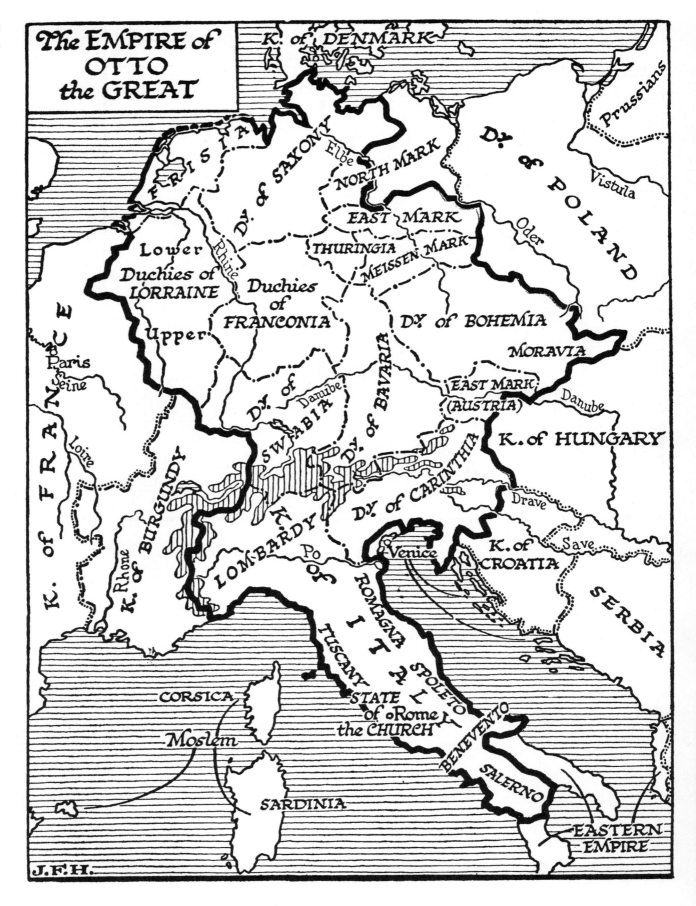

The EMPIRE of OTTO the GREAT

K. of DENMARK

FRISIA

Dy. of SAXONY

Elbe

NORTH MARK

EAST MARK

THURINGIA

MEISSEN MARK

Lower

Duchies of LORRAINE

Rhine

Duchies of FRANCONIA

Upper

Paris

Seine

Dy. of SWABIA

Danube?

Dy. of BAVARIA

Loire

K. of BURGUNDY

Rhone

Dy. of CARINTHIA

LOMBARDY

Po

K. of

Dy. of POLAND

Prussians

Vistula

Oder

Dy. of BOHEMIA

MORAVIA

EAST MARK (AUSTRIA)

Danube

K. of HUNGARY

Drave

Venice

Save

K. of CROATIA

SERBIA

ROMAGNA

TUSCANY

CORSICA

Moslem

SARDINIA

ITALY

SPOLETO

STATE of Rome the CHURCH

BENEVENTO

SALERNO

EASTERN EMPIRE

J.F.H.

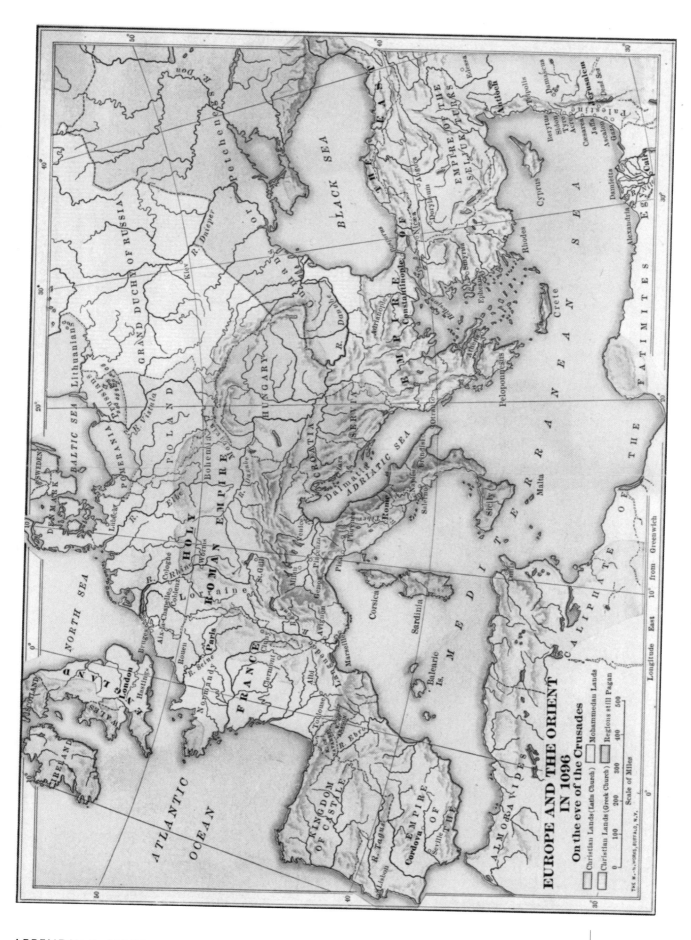

EUROPE AND THE ORIENT
IN 1096
On the eve of the Crusades

Christian Lands (Latin Church)   Mohammedan Lands
Christian Lands (Greek Church)   Regions still Pagan

Scale of Miles
0   100   200   300   400   500

THE M—N WORKS, BUFFALO, N.Y.

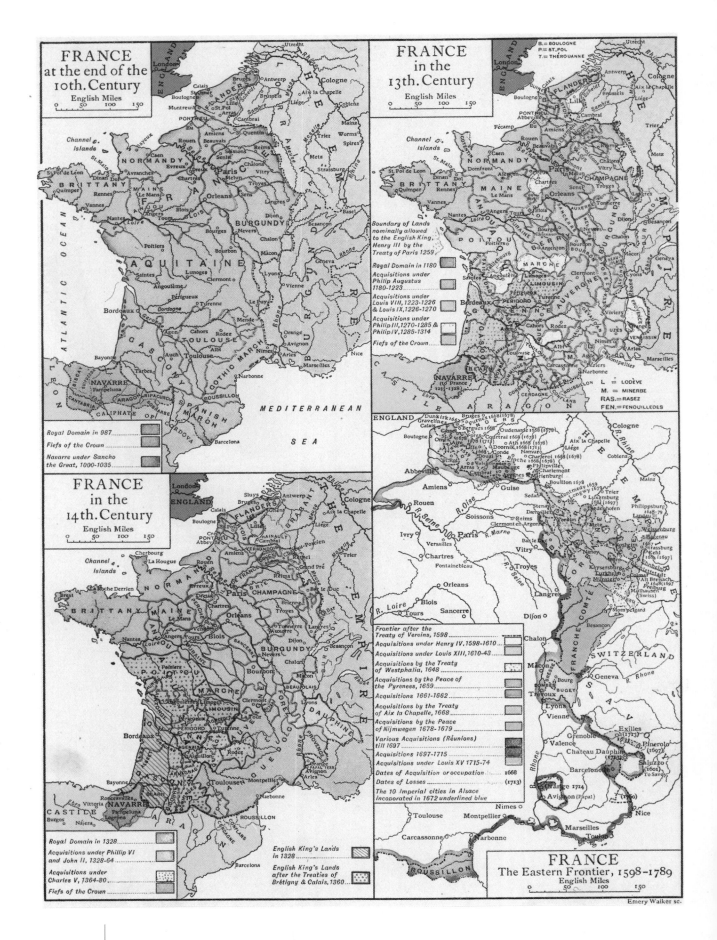

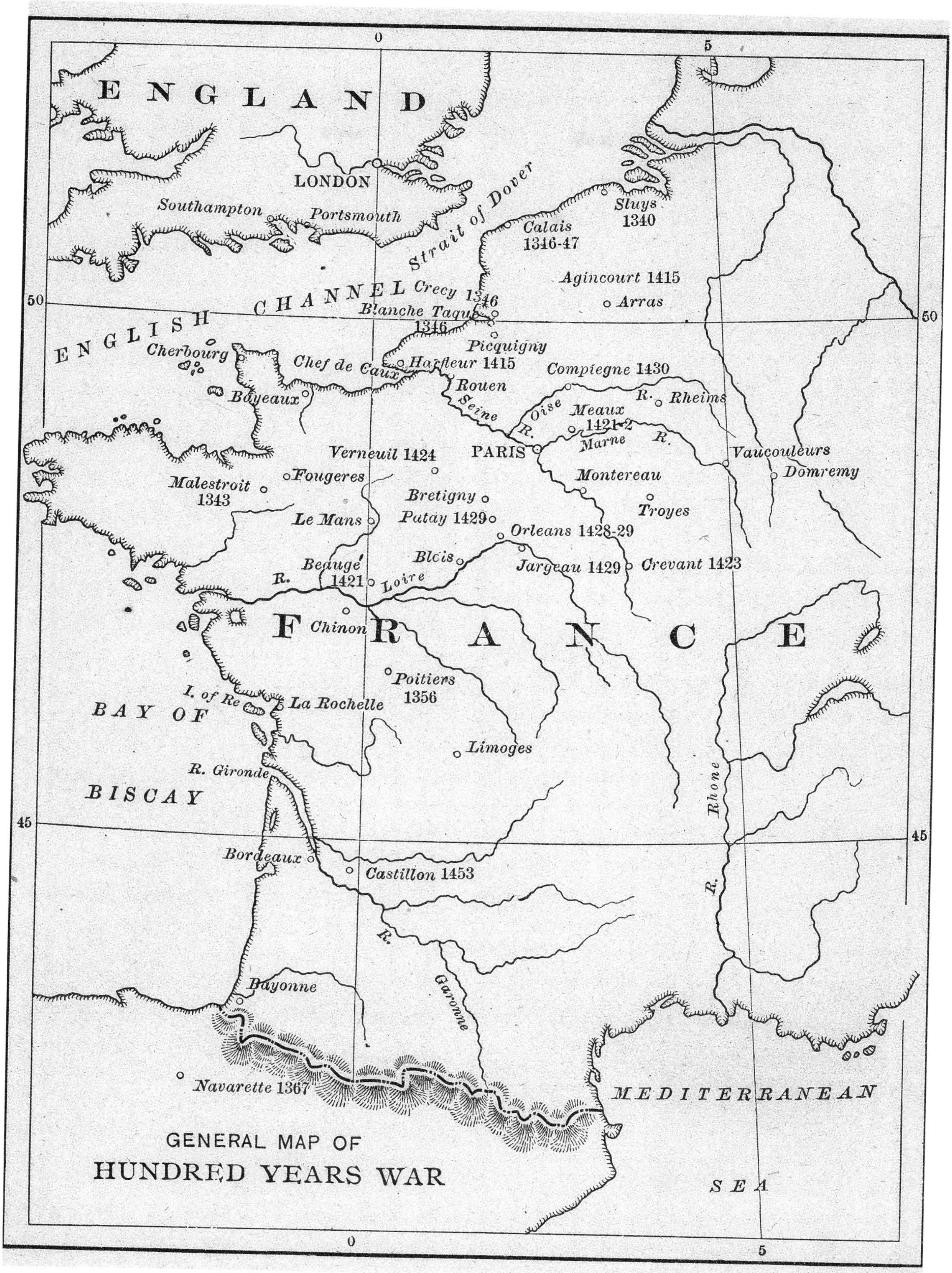

ENGLAND

LONDON

Southampton   Portsmouth

Strait of Dover

Calais
1346-47

Sluys
1340

Agincourt 1415

Arras

ENGLISH   CHANNEL   Crecy 1346

Blanche Taque
1346

50

Cherbourg

Chef de Caux   Harfleur 1415

Picquigny

Compiegne 1430

Rouen
Seine

Oise R.

R.   Rheims

Meaux
1421-2

Marne

R.

Bayeaux

R.

Verneuil 1424

PARIS

Vaucouleurs

Domremy

Montereau

Troyes

Malestroit
1343

Fougeres

Bretigny

Putay 1429

Orleans 1428-29

Crevant 1423

Le Mans

Blois

Jargeau 1429

Beaugé
R.   1421   Loire

F R A N C E

Chinon

Poitiers
1356

I. of Re   La Rochelle

BAY OF

Limoges

R. Gironde

BISCAY

R. Rhone

45   45

Bordeaux

Castillon 1453

R.

Bayonne

Garonne

Navarette 1367

MEDITERRANEAN

GENERAL MAP OF
HUNDRED YEARS WAR

SEA

0   5

14th and 15th centuries

SCOTLAND

Edinburgh   Berwick

Bambrough Cas.   Dunstanbrough
Cas.
Alnwick

Hexham

I. of Man

IRISH

SEA

Towton
1461   York

Wakefield   Pontefract   Ravenspur
1460

Blore heath
1459   Stamford
(Lose Coat Field)   Norwich
Shrewsbury   1470
Bosworth 1485
Aberystwith   Ludlow   Coventry   Northampton   Bury
Mortimer's Cross   1460   St. Edmunds
1461   Edgecote 1469

WALES   Tewkesbury
1471   St. Albans   Barnet 1471
Radcot   1455 and 1461
Bristol   LONDON   R. Thames
Blackheath   Sevenoaks
Bristol Channel   Dartford
Southampton   Portsmouth   Hastings
Exeter   I. of Wight

ENGLISH CHANNEL

FRANCE

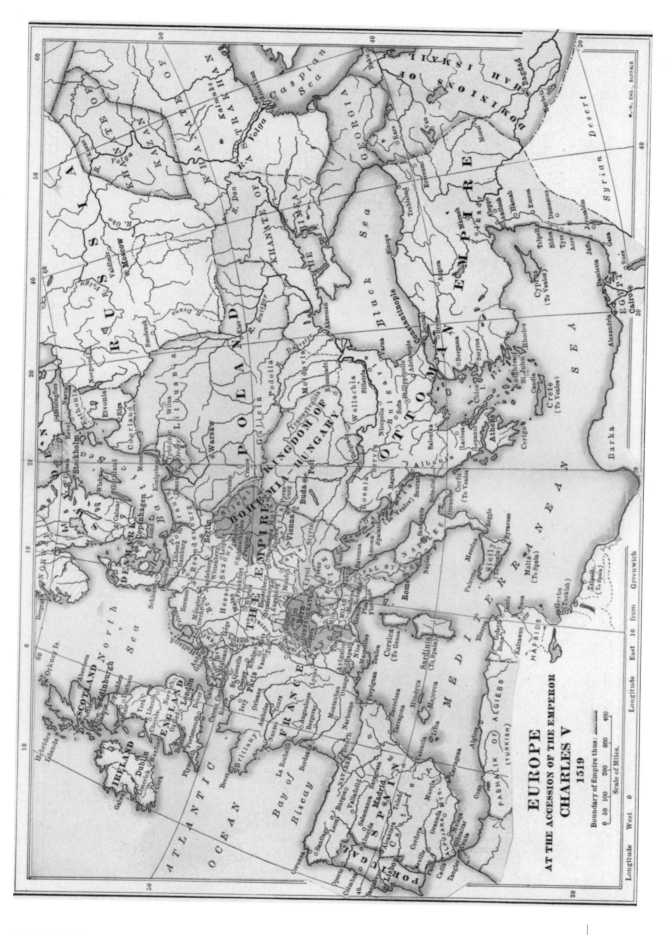

EUROPE
AT THE ACCESSION OF THE EMPEROR
CHARLES V
1519

Boundary of Empire thus: ▬▬▬
0 50 100   200   300   400
Scale of Miles.

Longitude   West 0   East 10   from Greenwich

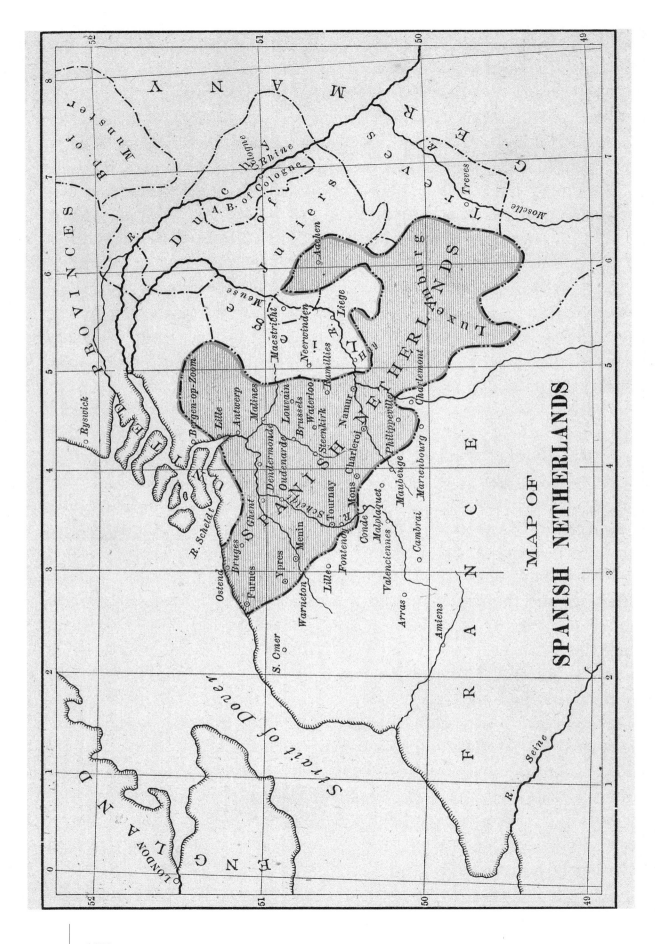

'MAP OF
SPANISH NETHERLANDS

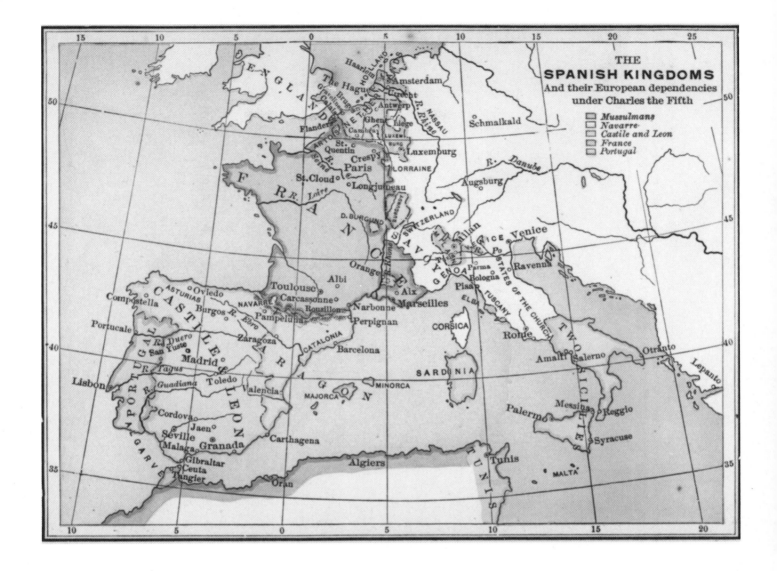

Early to mid–1500s

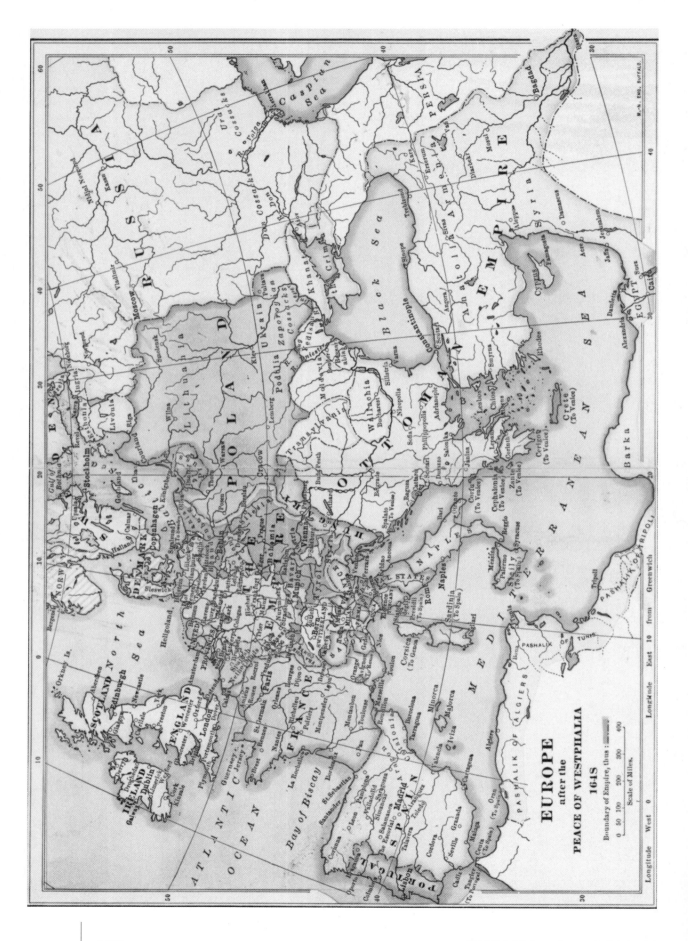

EUROPE
after the
PEACE OF WESTPHALIA
1648

Boundary of Empire, thus:

0 50 100 200 300 400
Scale of Miles.

Longitude West 0 Longitude East 10 from Greenwich 20

Central EUROPE after the Peace of Westphalia, 1648.

Boundary of the Empire

Free Towns, thus: •Cologne

Swedish territory ....
French   "   ....
Austrian Habsburgs ..

Spanish Habsburgs
Brandenburg
(Prussia)....

J.F.H.

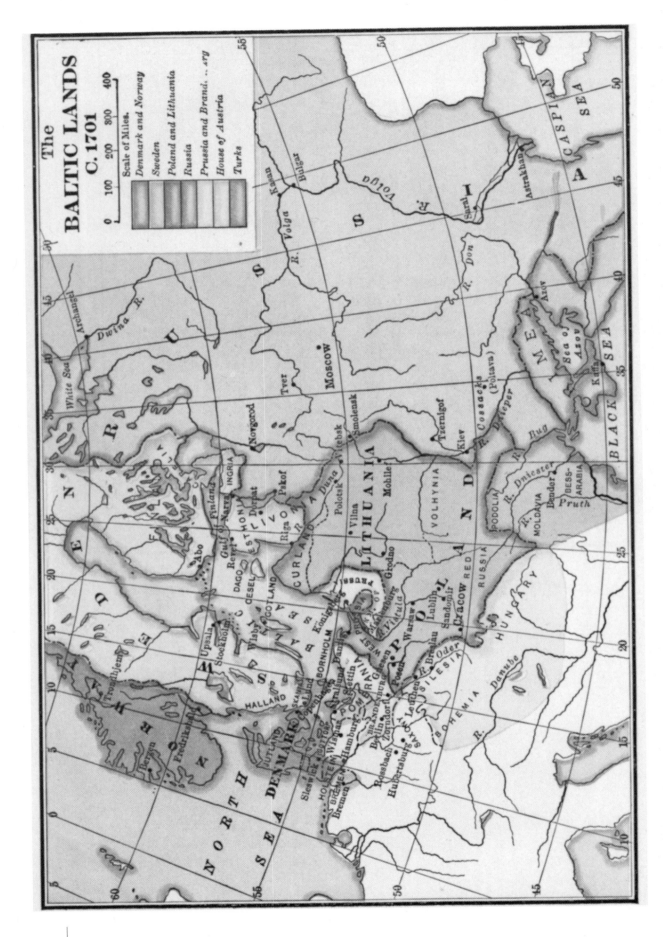

The
BALTIC LANDS
C. 1701

Scale of Miles.
0   100   200   300   400

Denmark and Norway.
Sweden
Poland and Lithuania
Russia
Prussia and Brandenburg
House of Austria
Turks

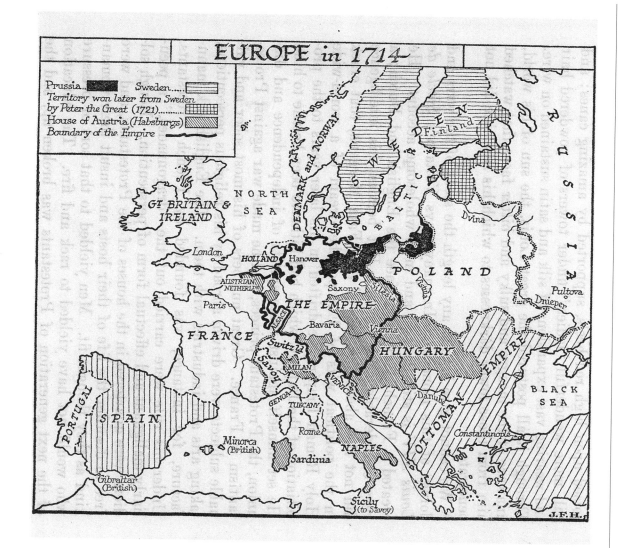

EUROPE in 1714

Prussia............
Sweden.............
Territory won later from Sweden by Peter the Great (1721)............
House of Austria (Habsburgs)............
Boundary of the Empire............

GT BRITAIN & IRELAND

NORTH SEA

DENMARK and NORWAY

S W E D E N

Finland

BALTIC

R U S S I A

Dvina

London

HOLLAND Hanover

AUSTRIAN NETHERL?S

Paris

THE EMPIRE

Saxony Silesia

Vistula

POLAND

Pultova

Dnieper

FRANCE

Alsace

Bavaria

Vienna

Switz?

Savoy

MILAN

Savoy

GENOA

TUSCANY

VENICE

HUNGARY

Danube

OTTOMAN EMPIRE

BLACK SEA

PORTUGAL

SPAIN

Minorca (British)

Rome

Sardinia

NAPLES

Constantinople

Gibraltar (British)

Sicily (to Savoy)

J.F.H.

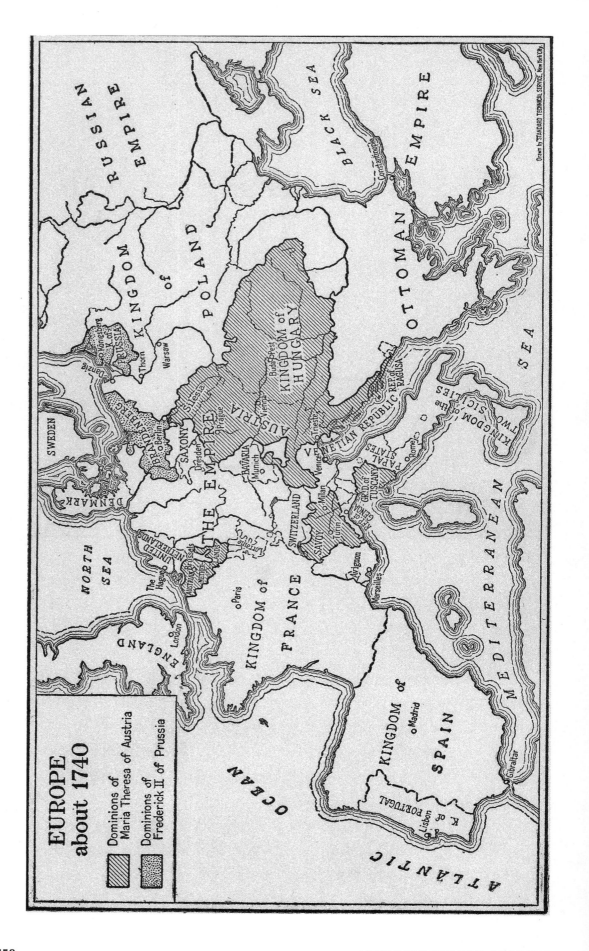

EUROPE
about 1740

Dominions of
Maria Theresa of Austria

Dominions of
Frederick II of Prussia

The PARTITIONS of POLAND

POLAND before 1772

after 1772

after 1793

after 1795

J.F.H.

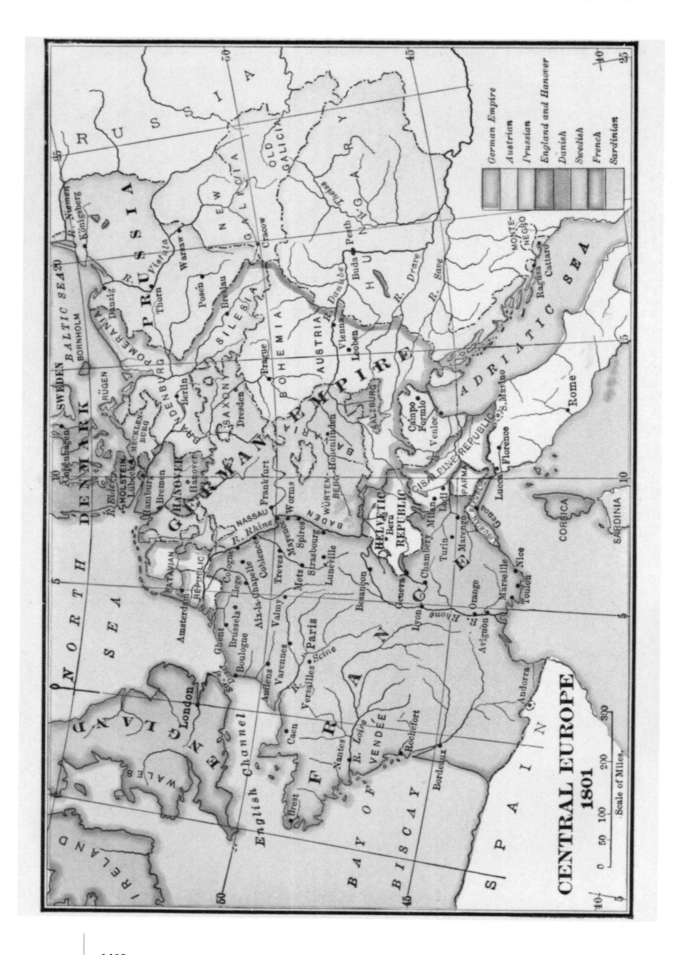

CENTRAL EUROPE
1801

Scale of Miles.

0   50 100   200   300

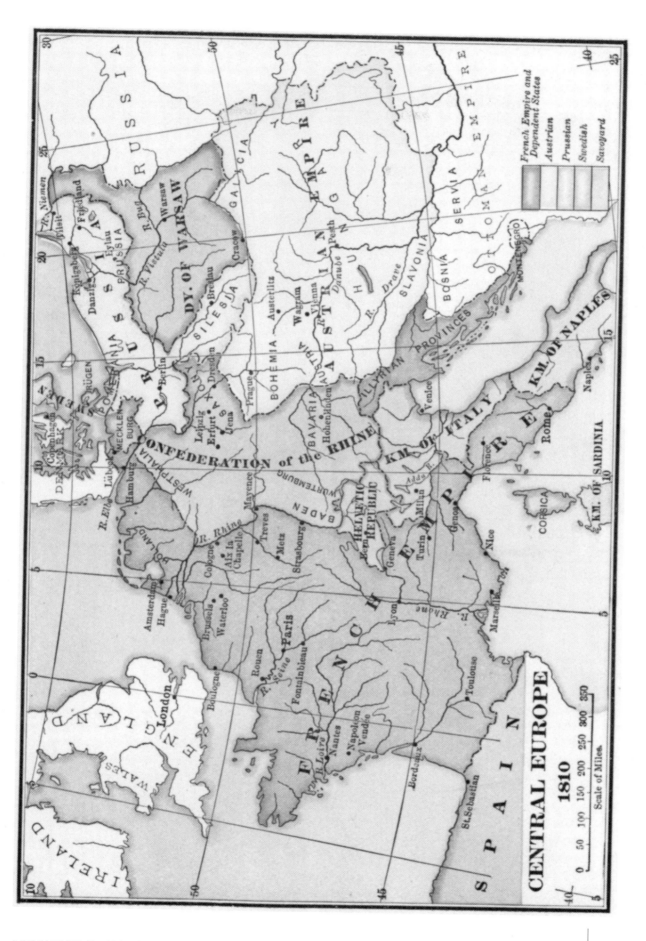

CENTRAL EUROPE 1810

French Empire and
Dependent States

Austrian

Prussian

Swedish

Savoyard

Scale of Miles.

0 50 100 150 200 250 300 350

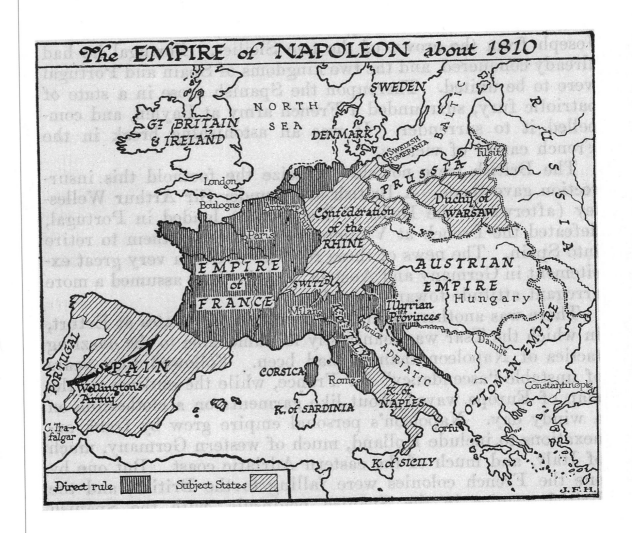

The EMPIRE of NAPOLEON about 1810

GT BRITAIN & IRELAND

NORTH SEA

SWEDEN

DENMARK

SWEDISH POMERANIA

BALTIC

PRUSSIA

Tilsit

RUSSIA

London

Boulogne

Antwerp

Paris

EMPIRE of FRANCE

Confederation of the RHINE

Duchy of WARSAW

SWITZ.

AUSTRIAN EMPIRE

Hungary

Milan

Illyrian Provinces

Venice

ADRIATIC

Danube

OTTOMAN EMPIRE

Constantinople

PORTUGAL

SPAIN

Wellington's Army

CORSICA

Rome

K. of SARDINIA

K. of NAPLES

Corfu

C. Trafalgar

K. of SICILY

Direct rule   Subject States

J.F.H.

EUROPE after the Congress of Vienna

Gt BRITAIN

DENMARK

Holstein

Hanover

K. of Netherlands

Luxembg

Paris

FRANCE

SPAIN

SWITZ⁰

Piedmont

K. of SARDINIA

CORSICA
(French)

Rhine

Baden

Hesse

Saxony

Bavaria

Bohemia

Lombardy

Parma

Modena

Tuscany

Papal States

K. of the
TWO SICILIES

RUSSIA

Poland

Galicia

Vienna

AUSTRIA

Hungary

Bosnia

Serbia

Dalmatia

Montenegro

OTTOMAN

EMPIRE

Greece

Ionian Is.
(British)

Boundary of the German
Confederation ━━━━━━

J.E.H.

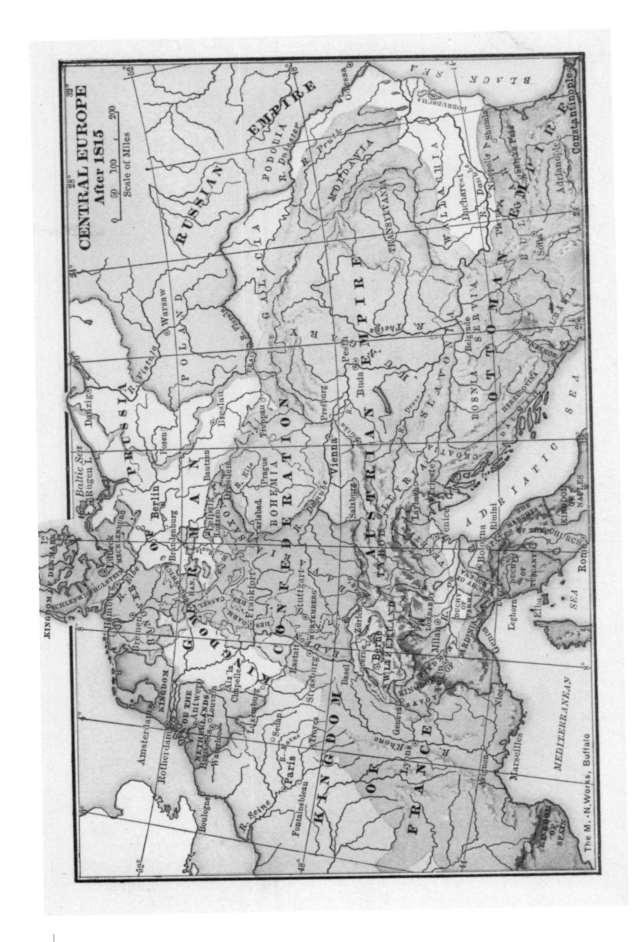

CENTRAL EUROPE
After 1815

Scale of Miles
0   50   100   200

The M.·N. Works, Buffalo

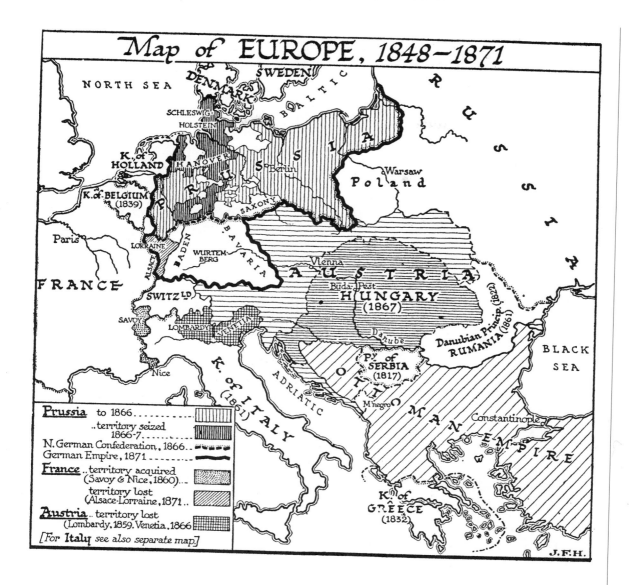

Map of EUROPE, 1848–1871

Prussia to 1866
.. territory seized 1866-7
N. German Confederation, 1866
German Empire, 1871
France .. territory acquired (Savoy & Nice, 1860)
territory lost (Alsace-Lorraine, 1871)
Austria .. territory lost (Lombardy, 1859, Venetia, 1866)

[For **Italy** see also separate map]

J.F.H.

The KINGDOM of ITALY, 1861.

SWITZERLAND

AUSTRIA

SAVOY
(to
France
1860

LOMBARDY
Milan
Turin
Po.
PIEDMONT
PARMA
MODENA
VENETIA
1866
Trieste
Venice

OTTOMAN
EMPIRE

(to France
1860)
Nice

LUCCA
Florence
TUSCANY

Km of

ELBA

CORSICA
(French)

STATES of the CHURCH

Rome
1870

ADRIATIC
SEA

SARDINIA

Naples

Cagliari

THE TWO

SICILIES

Palermo

Messina

Tunis

AFRICA

J.F.H.

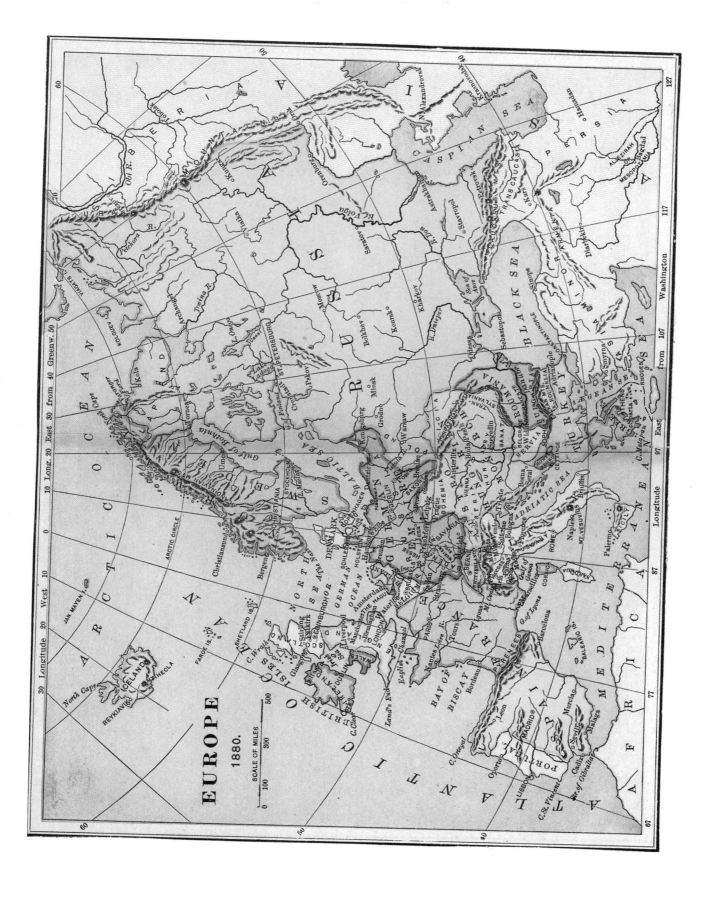

EUROPE
1880.

SCALE OF MILES
0   100   300   500

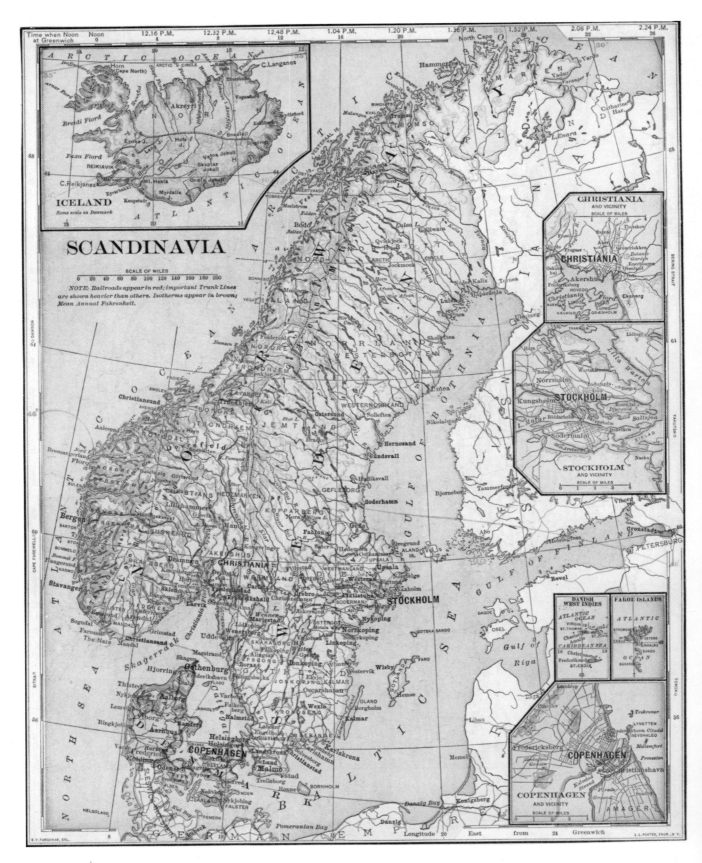

SCANDINAVIA

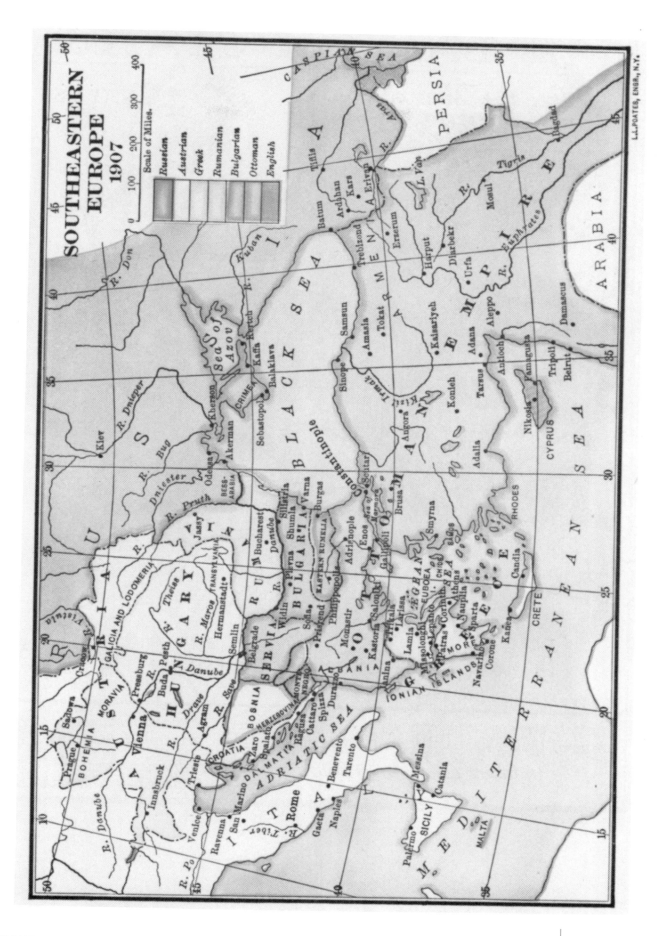

The BALKAN STATES
after the Wars of 1912-13

Legend:
Turkish territory acquired by Serbia
by Greece
by Montenegro
by Bulgaria
New autonomous princip.y of Albania...
Bulgarian territory acquired by Rumania

J.F.H.

The break-up of
Austria-Hungary, 1918

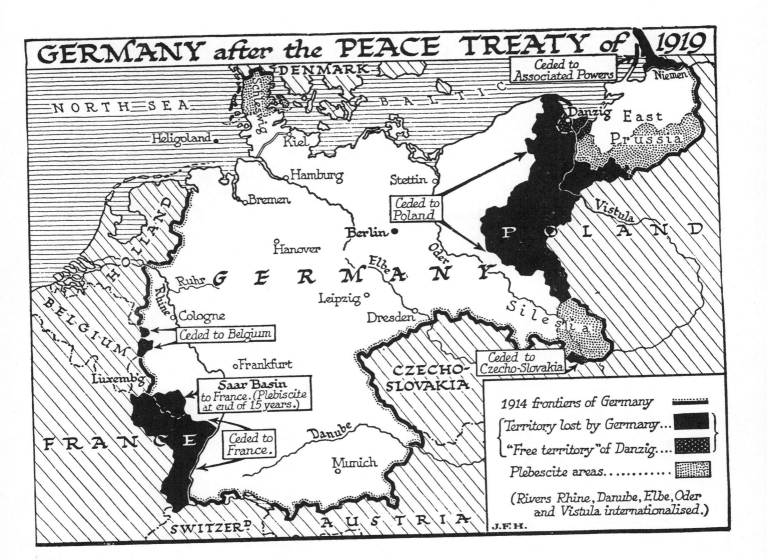

GERMANY after the PEACE TREATY of 1919

DENMARK

NORTH SEA

BALTIC

Ceded to Associated Powers

Niemen

Heligoland.

Schleswig

Kiel

Danzig

East Prussia

Hamburg

Stettin

Ceded to Poland

Bremen

Vistula

HOLLAND

Hanover

Berlin

POLAND

Ruhr

GERMANY

Elbe

Oder

Rhine

Leipzig

Silesia

BELGIUM

Cologne

Ceded to Belgium

Dresden

Ceded to Czecho-Slovakia

Luxemb'g

Frankfurt

CZECHO-SLOVAKIA

Saar Basin to France. (Plebiscite at end of 15 years.)

FRANCE

Ceded to France.

Danube

Munich

1914 frontiers of Germany ....

Territory lost by Germany...

"Free territory" of Danzig....

Plebescite areas...........

(Rivers Rhine, Danube, Elbe, Oder and Vistula internationalised.)

SWITZER.D

AUSTRIA

J.F.H.

INDEX

A

Aachen, 455, 1023
   Capitula of, 97
   Charlemagne at, 205
Abbas, Shah, of Persia, 500
Abbasids, 2, 3
Abd-al-Rahman, 872
Abd-al-Rahman I, 2
Abd-al-Rahman II, 2
Abd-al-Rahman III, *1*, **1–5**
   becomes caliph, 2
   chronology, 2
   moves court to Medina Azahara, 4
Abd Allah al-Zahid (son of Abd-al-Rahman
   III), 5
Abd Allah (grandfather of Abd-al-Rahman
   III), 2
Abélard, Peter, 105
Abenz, Otto, 763
Aberystwyth, 610
Abolition of slavery, 489
Aboukir, battle of, 973
Absolutism, 314–15, 1033
Abu Yusuf, Emir of Morocco, 37, 38
Abwehr (German military intelligence), Bon-
   hoeffer in, 769
Abydos, battle of, 1301
Abyssinia. *See* Ethiopia
Academie Française, 1069
Acatziri (Forest People), 61
The Accumulation of Capital (1918) (Luxem-
   burg), 830
Acerbo Law of 1923, 905
Acilius Altianus, 559
Acquaviva, Claudio, 1375
Acre, 370, 1141, 1142
Acropolis, 1059
Act in Restraint of Appeals, 622

Act of Attainer, 1148
Act of Mediation (1803), 1064
Act of Settlement, 51
Act of Settlement of 1701, 1351
Act of Succession, 887, 888
Act of Supremacy, 622, 887, 888
Act of the Thirty-Nine Articles, 393
Act of Uniformity of 1662, 424
Act of Union (1801), 320, 532
Actium, battle of, 65
Acton, Lord, 1102
Ad-Din-Barbarossa, Khair, 433
Ad-Din Sinan, Rashid, 1142
Adaloald, 537
Adam of Bremen, 574, 576
Adams, Charles, 323, 325
Adashev, Alexei, 665
Addams, Jane, 1195
Addington, Henry, 1099, 1100
Addis Ababa, 959
Adela of Champagne, 1083
Adelaide (wife of Lothar and Otto the
   Great), 1024
Adenauer, Konrad, *6*, **6–10**, 132
   chronology, 7
   elected mayor in Cologne, 8
   as West German chancellor, 9, 10
Adhemar, bishop of LePuy, 1282
The Admiral of Castile, 653
Adolf of Nassau, 1177
Adolphus, Gustavus, 1305
Adrianople, battle of, 62
Aeneid (Virgil), 67
Aetius, and Attila, 61
Affair of the Poisons, 807
Afghanistan, 24, 512
   Soviet invasion of, 1180
Afonso III of Portugal, 36

Afonso V, king of Portugal, 603, 654
Africa
   British colonization, 480
   during Cold War, 573
   Congo under Leopold II, 783
   exploration of, 603
   West, explored by Portugal, 602–3
African Atlantic, islands of, explored by Por-
   tugal, 602–3
African independence, 846
Afrika Korps, 949–50, *1172*
Agadir crisis (1911), 797
Against the Jews (Chrysostom), 241
Agapitus II, Pope, 1024
"Age of Greatness" (Swedish), 553
"Age of Metternich," 933
Agilulf, 537
Agincourt, battle of, 609, 610, 611, 675
"The Agitator." *See* O'Connell, Daniel
"Agitators," 307
Agnes of Meran, 1085
Agnes (sister of St. Clare), 429
Agora, 1212
Agricola (Tacitus), 127
Agriculture, and collective farming, 717
Agrippa (aid to Octavian), 791, 792
Agrippa Postumus (grandson of Augustus),
   793
Agrippina, Vipsania, 1251
Agrippina the Elder, 12, **14–15**, 161
Agrippina the Younger, *11*, **11–15**, 163,
   266, 987, 1200. *See also* Agrippina the
   Elder; Caligula; Claudius; Nero; Seneca
   chronology, 12
   murder of, 989
   Nero plots to kill, 15
Ahenobarbus, Gnaeus Domitius, 12, 987
Ahenobarbus, Lucius Domitius, 1201
Ahmad, Khan, 661

Seven Weeks' War, 437, 626–27
World War I, 1286
Austria-Hungary Empire, ethnic groups in, 435–36
Austrian Nazi Party, 587
Austrian People's Party, 586
Austrian Succession, War of, 862
Austrian Treaty, 845
Austro-Hungarian Empire, 896–97
and Balkans, 1258
World War I, 1259
Austro-Prussian (Seven Weeks') War, 437, 470, 626–27, 1292
Auto de fe, 816, 1241
Avanti (Mussolini, editor), 957
Aveling, J. C. H., 1371
Averroes, 457
Avignon, 873
antipope at, 701
Philip moves papal court to, 644
seige of, 873
Aviz (Avis) dynasty, 601
The Awakening of India (MacDonald), 839
Axelrod, Pavel, 772
Axidares, king of Armenia, 1266
Axis armies. *See* World War II
Ayrshire Miner's Union, 592
Azerbaijanis, Moslem, 513
Azores, exploration of, 603
Azpeitia, 817
Aztecs, 299–303
conquered by Cortés, 300–302
Moctezuma II, 300

B

"Babeli" (Barbara Schmid), 1061, 1062
Babington, Anthony, 885
Babington Plot, 394–95
Babushka, 139
"Babylonian Captivity," 644
Baden, prince Max von, 627
Bahamonde, Francisco Franco. *See* Franco, Francisco
Baibars, Sultan, 370
Baillis, 1086
Bailly, Jean-Sylvain, 939
Bakunin, Mikhail, 879
Balance of power, vs. noninterference, 479
Baldwin, Alfred, 70
Baldwin, Gladys Mary, 1353
Baldwin, John W., 1083
Baldwin, Louisa, 70
Baldwin, Marshall, 103
Baldwin, Stanley, *69,* **69–75,** *71,* 196, 253, 365, 841, 842, 844, 845
chronology, 70
encourages Edward VIII to abdicate, 74
named prime minister, 71, 72
Baldwin V of Flanders, 1338
Balfour, A. J., 480
Balia, 928
Balkan Question, 897
Balkan Wars (1912–1913), 1285–86
Balkans, 975
annexed by Austria-Hungary, 437
Slavs in, 1258
"Ballad of Bosworth Field," 1149
Balliol, Edward, 375
Balliol, John, king of Scotland, 371
Ballot Act of 1872, 1297

Balsdon, J. P. V. D., 709
Baltic. *See also* Hanseatic League
Gustavas Adolphus in, 555
Baltic and Sweden, 553
Baltic conquests, Vasa, Gustavus I, 555
Baltic Empire of Sweden, 226
Baltic tribes, 994
Bancroft, George, 741
Bank Charter Act (1844), 1054
Bank of England, 841–42, 1054
Bank of France, 974
Bannockburn, battle of, 373, 375
Baptism, 1379
Baranovskya, Olga, 721, 723
Barbarossa, Frederick, Holy Roman emperor, 458, 598
Barbarossa, Khair ad-Din-, 433
Barbarossa (pirate), 817
Barcelona, Treaty of, 432–33
Barlow, Arthur, 1136
Baronial Charters (1166), 597
Baroque era, 397, 401
Barr, Stringfellow, 917
Barre, Isaac, Colonel, 1094
Barthou, Louis, 762
Bärwalde, Treaty of, 1153
Basel, battle of, 910
Basil II, 1229, 1301
Basil II, Grand Duke, 658, 659
Basil III, 662
Basil V, 501
Basil, son of Alexander Nevsky, 996
Bassermann, Ernst, 1232
Bastille, storming of, 316, 758, 811, 939
Báthory, Stephen, king of Poland, 667, 696
Batthyany, Count Louis, 745–46, 747
Batthyany, Elenora, Countess, 400
Battle of Lutzen (Gustavus's death), 557
The Battle of the Marne, 418
"Battle on the Ice," 996
Batu, Khan of the Golden Horde, 993, 995
Baudricourt, Sir Robert de, 675
Bauer, Bruno, 876, 877
Bauge, battle of, 612
Baum, Herbert, **76–85**
group destroys Goebbels exhibit, 80–81
leads Berlin Jews, 79
trial of, 80–81
Baum, Marianne, *76,* 80
Bautzen, battle of, 976
Bavaria, 862, 1023
invaded by Magyars, 1025
wars with Palatinate, 910, 1305
Bavarian Succession, War of, 864
Bayazit, Turkish Sultan, 661
Bayeux Tapestry, 1339
Bea, Cardinal Augustine, 701
Bean na hEirean (Daughters of Ireland), 866
Beard, Hadrian's, 560
Beaton, Cardinal, 730
Beatrice of Lorraine, 899, 900
Beaufort, John, duke of Somerset, 86
Beaufort, Margaret, *86,* **86–89**
chronology, 87
promotes scholarship, 617
Beauharnais, Eugène de, 972, 975
Beauharnais, Hortense de (wife of Louis Bonaparte), 975, 978
Beauharnais, Josephine de, 972
Beazley, C. Raymond, 604
Bebel, August, 829
Beck, Ludwig, 770–71

Becker, Lydia, 408
Becket, Thomas, *90,* **90–93,** 382, 598, 649, 693, 1084
chronology, 91
murder of, 599
protests Constitutions of Clarendon, 598–99
Bedchamber Crisis, 1053–54, 1295
Bede's Ecclesiastical History of the English Nation, 43
Beecher, Rev. Henry Ward, 1036
Beeching, Jack, 687, 689
"Beer Hall Putsch," 638, 639, 641
Beggars, 1343
Bekbulatovich, Simeon, 667
Belgian Congo, 17, 573
Belgian Socialist Party, 17
Belgium, 782–84
Albert I, king of, **16–19**
and Congo, 573
Leopold II, 781–84
Montgomery liberates, 950
World War I, 17–18, 1331. *See also* Albert I
Belgrade, battle of, 400
Believer's Baptism, 1379
Bell, Christopher, 603
Belousova, Pelagia, 1260
Belvedere, 400
Belzec, 81
Bem, Josef, 746
Ben-Gurion, David, 572
Bender, battle of, 752
Benedict IX, Pope, 540
Benedict XIII, Pope, 646
Benedict of Nursia, Saint, *94,* **94–98,** 428
chronology, 95
Benes, Eduard, 893
Benes, Edvard, 516,
approves Communist government, 520
Benevento, arch at, 1265
Benevolent loans, 617
Benignus (assistant of St. Patrick), 1048
Bentham, Jeremy, 465
Bentinck, Hans Willem, 1349
Bentley's Quarterly Review (political magazine), 478
Berbers, Muslim in al-Andalus, 1, 2
Berchan's Prophecy (Berchan), 835
Berengar, count of Ivrea, 1024, 1025
Berengeria of Navarre, 1085
Berenguer, Dámaso. *See* Great Depression
Berg, grand duchy of, 975
Bergen, Norway, sack of, 859
Berhardt, Sarah, 385
Beria, Lavrenti, *99,* **99–102,** 1117
chronology, 100
cruelty of, 101
Berke, Khan, 996
Berlin, blockade of (1948), 788
Berlin, University of, 876
Berlin Conference of the Great Powers (1884–1885), 783
Berlin Decree (Napoleon I Bonaparte), 975
Berlin Wall, 701, 728, 1276
Berliner Ensemble, 1277
Bernadette, Saint, 1105
Bernadotte, Count Folke, 788
Bernard of Clairvaux, *103,* **103–7,** 388
chronology, 104
conflict with Abélard, 105
preaches Second Crusade, 105–6

Bernard of Quintavelle, 428
Bernardone, Giovanni. *See* Francis of Assisi
Berne, 1063
Bernstein, Eduard, 829
Berthold of Henneberg, 910
Berton, Pierre (Historian of the Arctic explorers), 968
Bertram, bishop of Bordeaux, 448
Berze, Gaspar, 1374
Besant, Annie, *108*, **108–11**
    champions radical reform, 109
    chronology, 109
    heads Theosophical Society, 110
    in India, 110–11
Bess of Hardwick, 885
Bethell, Nicholas, 503
Bethlehem Chapel (Prague), 645
Bethmann-Hollweg, Theobald von, 822, 1232, 1256, 1257
Bevan, Aneurin, 1354
Beza, Theodore, 923
Bialystok ghetto, 82
Bible, Vernacular
    English, 672
    German, 827
    Swedish, 550
The Bibliotheca, 43
Bibliothèque Nationale, 974
Bienvenue, Louise-Ursule-Julie, 417
Biétrix de Roziéres, Jacques, 526
"Big Nest" (Vsevolod), 994
Bigod, Roger, earl of Norfolk, 372
Bigotry, in Austria, 580, 582, 584
Bilganin, Nikolai, 1117
Bilinkoff, Jodi, 1243
Birger, Jarl, king of Sweden, 858, 995
Birgitta of Sweden, Saint 858
Birkenau, 81–83
Biron, Marshal, 608
Birrell, Augustine, 867
Bismarck, Otto von, 7, *112*, **112–17**, 344, 437, 981, 1255, 1329
    chronology, 113
    creates modern Germany, 115
    develops social welfare programs, 116–17
    quarrels with Moltke, 943
    Wilhelm II appoints as chief minister, 114
"Black and Tans," 869
Black Death, 376
Black Musketeers, 756
"Black Rubric," 731
Blackshirts, 631, 958
Blackwell, Elizabeth, 473
Blake, Robert, 341
Blanca of Namur, 858
Blanche of Castile, 800, 801, **802–3**
Blanche of France, 38
Blanco, Carrero, 443
Blanqui, Jerome, 878
Blatch, Harriet Stanton, 1039
Bleda, brother of Attila, 60
Bloc National, 761
Bloch, Ernst, 1277
Blomberg, Barbara, 685
"The Blond Beast," *See* Heydrich, Reinhard
Blondel, Robert, 612
Bloodaxe, Eirik, 1019
"Bloodbath of Stockholm," 549
Bloody Mary. *See* Mary I, Tudor
"Bloody Sunday," 867, 1005, 1360

Blücher (German flagship), 1132, 1316
Blue Max, 638
Blum, Leon, *118*, **118–21**, 763
    chronology, 119
    heads Popular Front government, 119
    helps defend Dreyfus, 119
    during World War II, 120–21
Bobadilla, Nicolas, 1372
Bobastro, 2, 3
Bock, Ernst, 907
Bodmer, Johann Jakob, 1061
Boer War, 481
    Haig in, 566
Bohemia, 411, 412, 862, 898. *See also* Czechoslovakia
    nationalism in, 644
    Wenceslas, 1320–22
Bohemia, king of, 380
Bohemians, 1230
Bohler, Peter, 1325
Bojowka, 1089
Bokenkotter, Thomas, 534, 650
Boleslav, prince of Poland, 1301, 1322
Boleyn, Anne, 393, *621*, 623, 887, 954, 1366–67
Bolingbroke, Henry, 609
Bologna, University of, 452
Bolshevik Party
    founded by Lenin, 774
    Kollontai joins, 735
    Tito joins, 1259
Bolshevik Revolution, 720, 721
    Kerensky, Alexander, 720–23
    Lenin, V. I., 772–75
Bolsheviks, 839, 1269, 1270. *See also* Bolshevik Party; Bolshevik Revolution; Communism; Red Army
Bona Dea (goddess of chastity and fertility), 158
Bonaparte, Eliza (grand duchess of Tuscany), 971
Bonaparte, Jerome, 971
Bonaparte, Joseph, 971, 975, 976
Bonaparte, Louis, 971, 975, 978
Bonaparte, Lucien, 971, 973
Bonaparte, Napoleon. *See* Napoleon I, Bonaparte
Bonar Law, Andrew, 70, 71, 797, 798
    becomes prime minister, 71
Bonaventure, St., 426
Bonhoeffer, Dietrich, 766, 768–69
Boniface, 872
Boniface II of Canossa, 899–900
Boniface VIII, Pope, 644
Bonn, University of, 876
Bonneval, Arnauld de, 388
Bonnier, Colonel Eugéne, 681
Book of Common Prayer, 424, 672, 731
Book of Common Prayer (Cranmer), 888
Book of Discipline (Knox), 732
Book of the History of the Franks (Charles Martel), 870
Bora, Katherine von, 827
Borghese, Pauline Bonaparte, 971–72
Borgia, Lucrezia, *122*, **122–25**
    chronology, 123
Boris, prince of Tver, 659
Borodino, battle of, 753, 976
Boru, Brian. *See* Brian Boru
Bose, Louis, 1167
Bosnia, 399
    annexed by Austria-Hungary, 437

Bosnia-Herzegovina, annexed by Austria, 897
Bosnians, 1258
Boston Tea Party, 1095
Bosworth, A. B., 20
Bosworth Field, battle of, 1145, 1148–49
Bothwell, earl of (James Hepburn). *See* Hepburn, James, earl of Bothwell
Bottomley, Horatio, 839
Boudicca, *126*, **126–29**, 991
    chronology, 127
Bourbons, 808, 809
    Henry IV, king of France, 605–8
    Louis XVI, 809–13
Bouvines, battle of, 693, 800, 1085–86
Bouyer, Louis, 998
Bowes, Elizabeth, 731
Bowes, Marjory, 731
Boyar Duma, 666
Boyars, 498, 994
    and Ivan the Terrible, 664, 665
Boyne, battle of the, 1350
Bräankyrka, battle of, 549
Braddock, General, 1094
Brandeis, Louis, 1197
Brandenburg-Prussia, Frederick II, the Great, 459–62
Brandi, Karl, 217
Brandt, Willy, *130*, **130–35**, *134*, 1277
    awarded Nobel Peace Prize, 134
    becomes chancellor, 133, *134*
    chronology, 131
    exile during World War II, 131
    named mayor of Berlin, 132
Brash, Hans, bishop of Linköping, 550
Bratislava, Peace of, 1306
Braun, Eva, 634
Brazil, Garibaldi in, 468
"Bread and circuses," 66
Bread riots
    before French Revolution, 811
    in Petrograd, 774
Breitenfeld, battle of, 414, 556–57, 1306
Breitinger, Johann Jakob, 1061
Brenan, Gerald, 1157
Breshkovsky, Catherine, *136*, **136–40**
    chronology, 137
    condemned to hard labor, 138
    following 1917 Revolution, 139
    torn between motherhood and the revolution, 138
Breslau, Treaty of, 461, 862
Brest-Litovsk, Treaty of, 627, 736, 774
Brétigny, Treaty of, 377
Brezhnev, Leonid, 134, 356, 503, 512, 1119–21, *1120*, 1180, 1223
    and Nixon, 1121
Brian Boru, *141*, **141–45**, *144*
    at battle of Clontarf, 144–45
    becomes high king, 143–44
    chronology, 142
Briand, Aristide, 761
Brietenfeld, battle of, 414
Bright, John, 57, *277*, **277–80**, 479, 1035, 1054
    elected to House of Commons, 278–79
    joins Anti-Corn Law League, 278
Bright, Mrs. Jacob, 1037
"Brinksmanship," 1033
Brissot, Jacques-Pierre, 1167, 1168
Britain. *See also* British Empire; England; Great Britain

Boudicca, 126–29
　　Hadrian's wall, 561
　　under Roman rule, 991
　　Viking raids on, 1019–20
　　World War I, 1038
Britannicus, 13–14, 266, 987, 989
British East Africa Company, 480
British Egyptian Expeditionary Force
　　(EEF), 47
British Empire, 1092
　　Disraeli, Benjamin, 341–45
　　Lord Salisbury (formerly Robert Cecil)
　　　and, 479–81
British Guiana, 481
British Labour Party, Keir Hardie, 594
British Legion, 568
British Medical Association, 476
British South Africa Company, 480
Britons
　　Boudicca, 126–29
　　conversion to Christianity, 537
　　Roman massacre of, 129
Broderick, James, 1371, 1373
Bromsbero, Peace of, 233
Bronstein, Lev Davidovich, 1268. *See also*
　　Trotsky, Leon
Brooke, Christopher, 169, 596
Brooke, Henry, 1138
Brooke, Z. N., 1025
Browder, Robert P., 723
Broz, Josip. *See* Tito, Marshal
Bruce, Robert, *146,* **146–50,** 371, 375, 670
　　chronology, 147
　　Comyn murdered in church at Dum-
　　　fries, 148
　　signs truce with Edward II, 149
Brumaire, coup of, 973
Brunhild, wife of Sigibert, 447, 538
Bruno, bishop of Toul (later Pope Leo IX),
　　540
Brunswick, duke of, 975
Brussels, 18, 404
Brutus, 64–65
Bruun, Geoffrey, 212
Bryan, William Jennings, 1195
Bucharest, Peace of, 753
Buchenwald, 82–83
Buckingham, duke of (George Villiers). *See*
　　Villiers, George, duke of Buckingham
Buda, 747
"Budapest Spring," 718
Budisavljeviacuc, Jovanka, 1262
Bukharin, Nikolai, 1117, 1220, 1271
Bukovina, acquired from Turkey, 863
Bulganin, Nikolai, 367, *726,* 727, *1118,*
　　1118–19
Bulgaria, Balkan Wars, 1285–86
*The Bulgarian Horrors and the Question of the
　　East* (Gladstone), 491
Bulgars, 1230
Bulgars, Volga, 994, 995
Bulge, battle of the, 951
Bullinger, Heinrich, 731
Bullinger, Henry, 1376, 1380
Bullock, David L., 45
Bulstrode, Sir Richard, 206
Bureaucracy, of vast Spanish Empire, 1080
Burgundian Wars, 908–9
Burgundy, 871
Burgundy, Duke John "the Fearless," 612
Burislaf, king of Wendland, 1019, 1021
Burke, Edmund, *151,* **151–55,** 310, 531, 1097

chronology, 152
　　publishes *Reflections on the French Revo-
　　　lution,* 154
　　and taxation of American colonies,
　　　153–54
Burrard, Sir Harry, 1315
Burrus, Afranius, 13, 987, 988–89
Burschenschaften (Austrian student fraterni-
　　ties), 582, 934
Buss, Johann Christoph, 1064
"Butcher of Berlin," 947. *See also* Wilhelm
　　II, Kaiser
Bute, Lord, 1094
Butler, George, 55
Butler, Richard Austin, 195, 845
Buzot, François Leonard, 1169
Byng, Admiral George, 52
Byron, Lord, 1051, 1217
Byzantine court, contacts with Abd-al-Rah-
　　man III, 3
Byzantine Empire, 452, 1301
　　Harald III Hardraade in, 575–76

C

CABAL, 54
Cabale des Importants, 914
Cacafuego, 352
Cacciatori delle Alpe (the Alpine Hunters),
　　469
Cadalus of Parma (antipope Honorius II),
　　541
Cadamosto, Alvise de, 604
Cádiz, raid on, 1138
Caesar, Julius. *See* Julius Caesar
Caetano, Marcelo, 1187
Cahiers, 938
Caillaux, Joseph, 761
Caithness, 832
Caius Octavianus (Octavian). *See* Augustus
Caladus of Parma. *See* Honorius II
Calais
　　capture of, 377, 380
　　English march to, 611
Caligula, *161,* **161–65,** 792, 987, 1252
　　becomes emperor, 162–63
　　chronology, 162
　　"invades" Britain, 164
Caliph, 2
Calixtus III, Pope, 678
Callaghan, James, 1354
Calvin, John, 106, *166,* **166–68,** 546, 605,
　　731, 922
　　chronology, 167
Calvinism, 688
　　vs. Catholicism, 1343
　　in Netherlands, 545–46
Calvinists, 166–68. *See also* Dutch Armini-
　　ans
　　French (Huguenots), 605, 924–25
　　in Scotland, 729–33
　　and Thirty Years' War, 412
Cambrai, Treaty of, 433
Campanella, Friar Tommaso, 696
Campbell, J. R. (editor), 840
Campbell-Bannerman, Sir Henry, 797
Campeador, 333
Campeggio (papal ambassador), 1366
Campo Formio, Treaty of, 973
Canadian colonies, 1098
Canary Islands, 602–3, 604

Cane, Catherine Anne, 45
Canning, George, 55, 1033
Canon law, 540, 650
Canossa, 901
　　Henry IV meets Pope Gregory VIII at,
　　　542
Canterbury, archbishop of, 537, 649
　　and Becket, Thomas, 90–93
The Canterbury Tales, 93
Cántigas de Santa María (Alfonso X)
Cantoni il volontario (Cantini, the Volun-
　　teer), 470
Canute I, king of Denmark, "the Great,"
　　169, **169–73,** 857, 1337
　　calls meeting of nobles, 172
　　chronology, 170
　　gains control of England, 171
Cape Bojador, 603
Cape Verde Islands, 604
Capet, Hugh, 1083
Capetians, 803
Capital (Marx), 879
Capitalism, and Roman Catholic Church,
　　701
"Capitula of Aachen," 97
Capitularies, 203
Capitulations, 433
Cappadocia, 1266
Capri, Tiberius at, 1252
Caprivi, Leo von, 1328
Caraffa, Cardinal Oliviero, 1190
Carbibari, 919
Carbonari ("charcoal burners"), 186
Cardinal-Infante, 414
Cardinals, College of, 541
The Caribbean, 862
Carlists. *See* Franco, Francisco
Carloman, 873
Carlos, Don (son of Philip II), 686
Carlsbad Decrees of 1819, 934
Carlton Club, 1053
Carmelites, 1241
　　divided into two congregations, 1243
　　Teresa of Avila, 1240–44. *See also* Dis-
　　　calced Carmelites
Carnet B, 761
Caroline, queen of England, 1310
Carolingian dynasty, 870
Carolingian era, 450
Carolus Magnus, 201
Carson, Sir Edward, 797
Cartel des Gauches, 761
Carter, Jimmy, *1248*
Carteret, Lord, 1310
Carthusians, 953
Carvejal, Francisco de, 1110
Carver, Betty, 947
Casement, Roger, *174,* **174–78,** 286, 783
　　chronology, 175
　　as Foreign Office consul, 176
　　as Irish nationalist, 177
Casimir, prince of Lithuania, 660, 661
Casket Letters, 884
Cassius, 64
Cassius, Avidius, 855
Castel del Monte (Sicily), 457
Castel Sant'Angelo, 562
Castelfidardo, battle of, 1103
Castile, 3, 653
　　Alfonso X, 35–39
　　de Vivar, Rodrigo Díaz, 332–35
　　gains control of Granada, 655

Chet-Murza, 498
Chetniks, 1260
Chevalier de Bayard, 430
Chiang Kai-Shek, 570, 788
Chichester, bishop of, 769
Childebert, King, 448, 449
Childebrand, Count, 870, 873
Chilperic, king of the Soissons, 445–48
Chilperic II, 871
Chiltern Hundreds, 57
China. *See* People's Republic of China
Chivalry, Renaissance, 430–31
Chlothar, son of Fredegund, 448, 449
  becomes king of Francia, 449
Chodkiewicz, Count, 1029
Cholula, 301
Choquard, Abbè, 937
Chosen Council, of Ivan the Terrible, 665
Chotek, Sophie, 437
Chou En-Lai, 572
Chrimes, S. B., 614
Christ Church, 1365
Christian II (Oldenburg) of Denmark, 548,
  549, 550, 551
Christian IV, king of Denmark, *230*,
  230–33, 413, 555, 556, 1305
  chronology, 231
  declares war on Sweden, 231–32
  defeated by Catholic forces, 232–33
  makes peace at Lübeck, 413
Christian Democratic Union (CDU), 9
Christian Humanism, 1000
Christian kingdoms, contacts with Abd-al-
  Rahman III, 3
"Christian Library" (Wesley), 1326
Christian socialism, Keir Hardie, 590–95
Christian Socials (Austrian), 583
Christianity. *See also* Protestantism; Roman
  Catholic Church
  in Bohemia, 1320
  conversion to
    Clovis I, 275
    Olaf I Tryggvason, 1020
    as required by Ferdinand and
      Isabella, 656
  in Hungary, 1228–30
  in Ireland, 1046–49
  in Norway, 1018, 1020–21
  in Russia, 1300–2
Christians, persecuted by Nero, 991
Christina, queen of Sweden, *234*, **234–38**,
  546, 554
  chronology, 235
  converts to Catholicism, 236
  murder of marquis of Monaldesco, 237
Christopher, 351
Chronicle, Parker, 1337
Chronicle (Fredegar), 872
Chronicle of Bygone Years, 1299
Chronicle of the Cordeliers, 676
The Chronicle of Fredegar (Charles Martel),
  870
Chrysostom, John, *239*, **239–44**
  chronology, 240
  consecrated bishop of Constantinople,
    242
Chud, 996
Chudskow, Lake, battle of, 996
Church, vs. state, 598
Church of England, 305, 479, 672, 887,
  1053. *See also* Anglican Church
    Act of Uniformity of 1662, 424

under Anne, 52
  Ecclesiastical Commission, 1053
  Evangelical (low church), 56–57
  Henry VIII as head of, 622, 954
  reform, in Germany, 542
  targeted during Reformation, 1365–66
Church of Ireland, 312
Church of Scotland, General Assembly of,
  733
Church reform, in Germany, 542
Churchill, John, 1st duke of Marlborough,
  52, *245*, **245–50**, 397, 400, 1351
  battle of Blenheim, 52
  charged with treason, 247–48
  chronology, 246
  march to Battle of Blenheim, 248
Churchill, Sarah Jennings (later Duchess of
  Marlborough), 50, 51, 52
Churchill, Winston, 69, 72, 197, 250, *251*,
  251–56, *253*, *254*, 355, 366, 485, 513, 634,
  786, 795, 797, 798, 799, 844, 849, 950,
  1095, 1205, *1221*, 1222, 1246, 1354
  becomes prime minister, *253*, 254
  chronology, 252
  elected to House of Commons, 252
  warns of Cold War, 255
  World War II, 254–55
Cicero, Marcus Tullius, 64, *257*, **257–61**,
  854, 1114
  attacks Mark Antony, 261
  begins political career, 258–59
  chronology, 258
  opposes Catiline, 259
  rivalry with Publius Clodius, 259
Cilicia, battle of, 23, 1114
Cimon, 1056
Cissians, 778
Cistercians, 93, 97
  Bernard of Clairvaux, Saint, 103–7
Citeaux. *See* Cistercians
The Citizen, 527
Civil Constitution of the Clergy (1789), 939
Civil War
  English, 304, 306–8
  Russian, 725, 736, 774–75, 1006–7,
    1220, 1270–71
  United States, 1035, 1042
The Civil War, 1199
Clare, Saint, 428–29
Clarence, Duke George, 1146–47
Clarendon, Constitutions of, 92, 598
Clark, Tom, 867
The Class Struggles in France (Marx), 878
Claudius, 13, 162, *262*, **262–66**, 562, 793
  and Agrippina the Younger, 13–15
  becomes emperor, 264
  chronology, 263
  popular with Roman people, 265
Clausewitz, Carl von, 941, 943
Claussat, Eugenie, 761
Clauswitz, Karl von, 418
Claviere, Étienne, 938
Cleisthenes, 1213
Clelia, o il governo del monaco (Clelia, or the
  Government of the Clergy), 470
Clemenceau, Georges, *267*, **267–72**, 269,
  269, 418, 761, 849, 1285
  chronology, 268
  involved in Dreyfus Affair, 270
  leadership during World War I, 271
Clément, Jacques, 607
Clement II, 540

Clement III, Antipope, 1280
Clement III, Pope, 452, 649
Clement VII, Pope, 432, 433, 921, 922, 954,
  1366
  and Henry VIII, 622, 887
Clement VIII, Pope, 412
Cleombrotus, 776
Cleomenes, 776
Cleopatra, queen of Egypt, 65, 159, 262,
  1115
Clergy, benefit of, 92, 1365
Clerical marriage, 540, 541, 542
Clermont, Council of, 1281
Clisthenes, 1055
Clontarf, battle of, *144*, 144–45
Clothar IV, 871
Clough, Arthur, 1012
Clovis, son of Fredegund, 447
Clovis I, 201, *273*, **273–76**, 1229
  chronology, 274
  converts to Orthodox Christianity, 275
  promulgates the Salic Law, 275
Club Breton, 939
Cluniac order, 97
Cluny, 104
Cnut, king of England, 834
Coal mining
  in Great Britain, 591–93
Cobden, Richard, 57, *277*, **277–80**, 479,
  1035, 1054
  elected to House of Commons, 278–79
  joins Anti-Corn Law League, 278
Cobden and Bright
  political partnership of, 278–79
  support for noninterference, 279
Coburg dynasty (Belgium), 16
Codes of law, Alfonso X, 39
"Coeur de Lion." *See* Richard I the Lion-
  heart
Cogers, Society of, 1014
Colbert, Jean-Baptiste, *281*, **281–84**, 807
  chronology, 282
  in ministry of Louis XIV, 282
  reforms tax system, 283–84
  treasury drained by war with Dutch, 284
Cold War, 519, 569, 785, 788–89, 846,
  1222, 1275
  Africa during, 573
  Gorbachev ends, 513
  Great Britain and, 367–68
  Trygve Lie, 785–89
Colet, John, 617
Coligny, Admiral Gaspard de, 394, 923–24
Collectives, agricultural, 512
Collectivization, 1220
  in Hungary, 717
College of Cardinals, 541
College of the Salii, 853
Collins, Michael, *285*, **285–88**, *287*, 869
  chronology, 286
Cologne, after World War II, 8
Colonia, 127
Colonialism, of Belgium, 782–83
Colonies, European, independence move-
  ments, 570
Colum, Padraic, 866
Columbanus, Saint, 96
Columbus, Bartholomew, 299
Columbus, Christopher, *289*, **289–93**, *291*,
  292
  backed by Ferdinand and Isabella, 656
  chronology, 290

England, 1296–97
medical conditions during, 1008,
1010–11
Sardinians in, 1290
Crimes Act (1881), 491
Crimes Act (1887), 480
Criminal Law (English), 1052
Crinan, abbot of Dunkeld, 834
Cripps, Stafford, 1353
Crispus, Gaius Sallustius Passienus, 13
Croats, 745, 746, 1258
Cromwell, Oliver, 199, 207, *304*, **304–8,**
306, 423
backs government reform, 306
chronology, 305
installed as Lord Protector, 308
Cromwell, Thomas, 621, 622, 623, 954
Crónica general de España (Alfonso X), 39
Crosby, Alfred, 1282
Crowe, Sibyl, Historian, 840
Crozier, Brian, 439, 442
Crusade(s)
First, 495–96, 1279, 1281–83
Second, 105–6, 389–90, 452
Third, 452, 691, 1141–43
illness of European army, 1142
Fourth, 651
Innocent III, Pope, 648–52
Seventh, 802
Eighth, 370, 802
anti-Semitism during, 580–81
Children's, 651, 1224–27
German, 1226–27
Crystal Palace Exhibition, 1295
Cuauhtémoc, 302
Cuba, 299
Cuban Missile Crisis, 701, 728, 846
Cud Nad Wisla, 1091, 1207
Cuitláhuac, 302
Cullen, Paul, *309*, **309–13**
becomes archbishop, 311–12
chronology, 310
delivers dissertation at Vatican, 310
influence in Vatican increases, 310
reforms Irish religious practices, 312,
313
"Cult of Gloriana," 396
Culture, in East Germany, 1276–77
Cumnock News (Liberal Party newspaper),
592
Curthose, Robert, 1339, 1340
Curule Aedile, 158
Curzon, George, 71, 72
Cuzco, 1110
"Cyclops." *See* Kutuzov, General Mikhail
"Czech Legion," 898
Czechoslovak National Committee, 893
Czechoslovak Republic, 898
Czecho-Slovak Republic, Masaryk, Thomas
G., 895–98
Czechoslovak-Soviet Treaty of Friendship,
Mutual Assistance and Post-War Cooper-
ation, 517
Czechoslovakia. *See also* Bohemia
annexed by Hitler, 634
Communist control of, 520–21
Dubcek and Prague Spring (1968), 354,
356–57
German invasion of Sudetenland,
197–98, 893
Gottwald refuses Marshall Plan aid, 519
Masaryk, Jan, 891–94

Ministry of National Security, 521
vs. Poland, 1090
post-World War II government, 517
rise of Communism in, 515–23
Russian invasion of 1968, 1120
short history of, 515–16
Soviet invasion of, 1180
as Soviet satellite, 519–520, 894
Soviet troops sent to, 506
World War II, 516–17, 893
Czechoslovakian Communist Party, 516–22
Czechs
prisoners of war form "Czech Legion,"
897–98
in World War I, 897
Czernin, Ottocar, 437

D

Da Pescia, Fra Domenico, 1191
Dachau, 78
Dache, Nils, 551–52
Dacia. *See also* Rumania
Hadrian conquers, 560
Dacian Wars, 1264
Dail Eireann, 288, 321, 869
Daily Graphic (London newspaper), 252
Daily Mail (right-wing publication), 841
Daimyo, 1374
Dakin, Douglas, 1284
Daladier, Édouard, 763, 1069
D'Albret, Jeanne, 605
Damascus, sultan of, 457
Danedeld ("tax"), 171
Danelaw, 43
Danes, Canute I, 169–73
Daniel, Metropolitan of Moscow, 663
Daniel (Dantilo) ("the Holy"), son of
Alexander Nevsky, 997
Daniel of Galicia, prince, 996
Danish raids, 41
Danish Vikings, Alfred the Great, 40–44
Danish War, 385
D'Annunzio, Gabriele, 959
Danton, Georges-Jacques, *314*, **314–18,**
1163, 1168
accusations against, 318
chronology, 315
Danube, 855
Danubian lands, conquered by Rome, 67
Danubian Monarchy. *See* Eugene of Savoy
Danzig (Gdansk), 462
Dardanelles, 1034
Darius, Persian king, 777
Darius III, 23–24
Darlan, Admiral Jean-François, 764
Darnley, Robert, 394
D'Arquien, Marie Casimere (Marysienka),
697
Darwin, Charles, 1103
Darwinism, 701
D'Ataide, Don Alvaro, 1375
Daubeney, Lord, 617
Daughter of Time (Tey), 1149
"Daughters of Ireland," 866
Dauphin, 431
David II, king of Scotland, 376
Davies, Emily, 472
Davies, Norman, 1381
Davison, Emily, 1194
Dawes Plan, 840, 1234

Day of the Barricades, 395, 607
Day of the Dupes, 1153
Day of the Jackal (Forsyte), 486
Days of the Barricades, 914
D'Azeglio, Massimo, 1290
De Abarca y Bolea, Pedro Pablo (count of
Aranda), 214–15
De Ahumada, Teresa, 1241
De Almagro, Diego, 1110
De Carmona, President Oscar Fragoso,
1184
De Castelnau, Edmond, 1068
De Clementia, 1202
De Consideratione ad Eugenium Papam
(Paganelli), 105
De Escobedo, Juan, 1081
De Figueiredo, Anhtonio, 1183
De Gaulle, Charles, 255, 366, **482–87,** 764,
786, 845, 846, 1068, 1355
chronology, 483
and Nazi resistance, 485
and Pétain, 1068, 1070, 1071
president of Fifth Republic, 486
during World War I, 484–85
De Gobineau, Arthur Joseph, 582
De Gray, John, 693
De Gregorio, Leopoldo, marquis of
Squilacci ("Equilache"), 214
De Jesus Caetano, Doña Maria, 1187
De Jong, Louis, 1333
*De jure belli et pacis (Concerning the Law of
War and Peace)* (Grotius), 546
De l'Allemagne (On Germany), 1216
De Montfort, Simon, earl of Leicester, 370
De Re Militari, 246
De Requesens, Don Luis, 1081
De Rivera, Miguel Primo, 440, 441, *1155,*
1155–59
chronology, 1156
creates new political system, 1158
establishes dictatorship, 1156–57
promotes economic growth, 1157
De Rocca, Albert, 1215
De Rosas, Juan Manuel, 468
De Sexe, 809
De Soto, Hernando, 1109
De Staël, Madame, *1214,* **1214–17**
chronology, 1215
De Staël-Holstein, Baron Erik, 1215
De Ulloa, Doña Magdalena, 686
De Valera, Eamon, 287, *319,* **319–22,** 509,
869
chronology, 320
De Valverde, Father Vincente, 1109
De Zuniga, Don Juan, 1079
Death camps. *See also* Hitler's Generals
World War II, 81–83
Decembrists, 29
*Déclaration des droits de la femme et de la
citoyenne* (Declaration of the Rights of
Woman and the Female Citizen) (de
Gouges), 525, 527
Declaration of Indulgence, 51
"Declaration of Irish Rights" (Grattan), 531
Declaration of Peace (Crimean War), 1011
Declaration of Pillnitz, 758
Declaration of Rights (English), 1350
Declaration of the Rights of Man and Citizen
(Lafayette), 316, 527, 758, 939
*Declaration of the Rights of Woman and the
Female Citizen* (de Gouges), 525, 527
Declaratory Act, repeal of, 530, 531

Eastern Church, John Chrysostom, 239–44
Eastern Europe. *See also* under individual
   country (e.g., Czechoslovakia)
    invaded by Attila, 61
    Ostpolitik of Willy Brandt, 133
    Soviet control of. *See* Poland
"Eastern Question," 490
Ebert, Friedrich, 628, 830
Ecceliastical Ordinances (Calvin), 168
Ecclesia, 1212
Eck, Johann, 826, 1379
École Supérieure, 418
Economic League of European Cooperation,
   845
Economic reform, British, Edmund Burke,
   153
Economic reforms
   Diocletian, 339
   Domitián, 347
Ed-Din, Beha, 1144
Eden, Anthony, 255, *364*, **364–68**, *366*, 798
   chronology, 365
Edgehill, skirmish at, 306
Edict of Milan, 296
Edict of Nantes, 806–7
   reaffirmed in Peace of Paris, 1152
Edict of Restitution, 232, 413, 1306
Edinburgh, 732
   Treaty of, 882
Edith, wife of Otto I, the Great, 1023
Edmund of Langley, earl of Cambridge, 377
Education
   Ashley-Cooper, Anthony, 7th earl of
    Shaftsbury, 54–58
   Besant, Annie, 108–11
   first English court schools, 43–44
   French system, 974
   Jesuits and, 818
   Johann Pestalozzi, 1061–65
   Prussian, 626
   Ragged Schools, 57
Education Act of 1870, 490
Education Act of 1902 (British), 797
The Education of Laura (Mirabeau), 937
Edward I, king of England, 37, 147, *369*,
   369–73, 374
   chronology, 370
   treatment of English Jews, 372
Edward I, king of Portugal, 603
Edward II, king of England, 373, 374
Edward III, king of England, 221, *374*,
   374–78, 379, 614
   chronology, 375
Edward IV, king of England, 87, 603
Edward V, king of England, 87, 1146, 1147,
   1148
Edward VI, king of England, 393, 623
   and Knox, 731
Edward VII, king of England, *383*, **383–87**,
   386, 566, 1298
   children of, 386
   chronology, 384
   liaison with Nellie Clifden, 384
   marriage of, 385
   relationship with prime minister, 387
   social attitudes, 387
   succeeds queen Victoria, 385
Edward VIII, king of England, abdicates, 74
Edward of Woodstock. *See* Edward, the
   Black Prince
Edward, the Black prince (prince of Wales;
   son of Richard III), 374, *379*, **379–82**, 1148

at battle of Poitiers, 381
chronology, 380
defies Charles V, 381
sack of Limoges, 381
Edward the Confessor, king of England,
   369, 834, 835, 1337–38
"Edwardian Age," 385
EEC. *See* European Economic Community
Egbert, king of Wessex, 40–41
Egmont, count of, 1080, 1344
Egypt, 480, 491
   Alexander the Great, 23
   Napoleon I Bonaparte in, 973
   Seventh Crusade to, 802
Egyptology, 973
Ehrlich, Paul (noted Jewish scientist), 587
Eichmann, Adolf, **636–37**
The Eighteenth Brumaire of Louis Napoleon
   (Marx), 878
86 Sermons on the Song of Songs (Bernard of
   Clairvaux), 104
Eisenhower, Dwight D., 420, 442, 845, 846,
   950, *1118*, 1173
Eisenstadter, Alfred, 81
El Alamein, battle of, 949–50
El Gran Capitan (de Cordoba), 219
El-Kamil, Sultan of Egypt, 456
Elba, Napoleon I Bonaparte exiled to, 976
Elderly, in war, 546
Eleanor of Aquitaine, 91, 370, **383–91**, *388*,
   597, 599–600, 690, 800, 1084
   besieged at Mirabeau, 692
   chronology, 389
   imprisoned by Henry, 390–91
   leaves Louis for Henry of Anjou, 390
   oversees the ransom of Richard the
    Lionheart, 391
   and son John, 691
Elena, mother of Dimitri, co-ruler with Ivan
   III, 661–62
Elizabeth I, queen of England, 236, 351,
   392, **392–96**, *394*, 405, 477, 499, 666, 669,
   671, 688, 882, 885, 888, 923, 925, 1081,
   1135, 1344
   and Boris Godunov, 499, 500–501
   chronology, 393
   and Ivan the Terrible, 666, 667
   Sir Walter Raleigh, 1134–39
Elizabeth II, queen of England, 1356
Elizabeth Christina, wife of Frederick II, the
   Great, 460
Elizabeth, Empress of Russia, 751, 862
Elizabeth Garrett Anderson Hospital, 475
Elizabeth of Bavaria, princess (wife of Albert
   I), 17–18
Elizabeth of Habsburg, 1382
Elizabeth of Valois, 1081
Elizabeth of York, 88, 621, 1148
Elizabeth (ship), 351
Elizabethan Period, 392
"Elizabeth's Trafalgar," 1138
Elliott-Binns, L., 649, 651, 652
Ellisif (daughter of king Yaroslav)
Elsinore Castle, 231
Elstob, Eric, 234
Elton, Geoffrey, 1363
Emancipation Act (Russia, 1861), 33
Émile, 1062
Eminent Victorians, 1009
Emir, 2
Emma of Waldeck, 1334
Emmanuel II, Victor, 1105

becomes king of Italy, 1291
leads troops, 1290
Emperor, as envisioned by Augustus, 66
Ems dispatch, 943
Enabling Act, 633
Enchiridion (Alfred), 43
Encomienda, 299, 302
Endecja (Dmowski), 1089
Engels, Friedrich, 749, 877
Enghien (commander at battle of Rocroi),
   1154
England, 1296–97. *See also* Great Britain
   and American Revolution, 755–57
   Anglo-Saxon, 577, 1337–38
    Harald III Hardraade wars against,
     574–78
   animosity toward France, 692
   Bank of, 1054
   barons present Magna Carta to John,
    693–94
   Civil War, 306–8
   commercial ties with Russia, 28
   constitutional guarantees, 304
   conversion of the Anglo-Saxons, 537
   Crimean War, 1296–97
   in Diplomatic Revolution, 461–62
   England, William the Conqueror,
    1337–41
   government under Cromwell, 308
   historic leaders
    Alfred the Great, 40–44
    Anne, Queen, 49–53
    Ashley-Cooper, Anthony, 7th earl of
     Shaftsbury, 54–58
    Baldwin, Stanley, 69–75
    Besant, Annie, 108–11
    Canute I, 169–73
    Chamberlain, Neville, 195–200
    Charles II, 206–11
    Drake, 351–52
    Edward I, 369–73
    Edward III, 369–73
    Edward VII, 383–87
    Eleanor of Aquitaine, 390–91
    Elizabeth I, 392–96
    Fox, George, 421–25
    Henry II, 596–600
    Henry V, 609–13
    Henry VII, 614–18
    Henry VIII, 619–24
    James I, 669–73
    John, king, 690–94
    Lloyd George, David, 795–99
    Mary, queen of Scots, 881–85
    Mary I, Tudor (Bloody Mary),
     886–90
    Nelson, Horatio, 982–86
    Newman, John Henry, 998–1002
    Palmerston, Lord, 1031–35
    Peel, Robert, 1050–54
    Raleigh, Sir Walter, 1134–39
    Richard I, the Lionheart, 1140–44
    Richard III, 1145–49
    Thatcher, Margaret, 1245–49
    Thomas Becket, 90–93
    Thomas More, 952–55
    Victoria, 1293–98
    Walpole, Robert, 1308–12
    Wellesley, Arthur, duke of Welling-
     ton, 1313–19
    Wolsey, Thomas, 1363–67
    Wycliffe, John, 1368–70

public health under, 457
Frederick II, (Hohenstaufen), 649
Frederick II, Holy Roman Emperor, 454
    crowned by new pope, 455
    excommunicated, 456
Frederick II, king of Prussia, 861, 938
Frederick II, the Great, *459*, **459–62**, 1128
    chronology, 460
    as Enlightened Despot, 460
    invades Saxony, 462
Frederick II (Hohenstaufen), 1085
Frederick II of Sicily, 38
Frederick III, Holy Roman Emperor,
    826–27, 907, 909
Frederick V, 232
Frederick V, Elector Palatine, king of
    Bohemia, 412–13, 1305
Frederick, archbishop of Mainz, 1024
Frederick, Cardinal, 540
Frederick the Great, 112, 180, 397, 705,
    757, 941, 1328
Frederick William I, 460
Frederick William II, of Prussia, threatened
    by French Revolution, 758
Free Education Act (1891), 480
Free French, 765
Free Polish government, 1030
"Free State," 869
Free trade, 842, 1054
    British, 1034
    in England, 277–79
    Peel's support of, 1054
Freeman, Edward, 450
French and Indian War, 1094
French Calvinists, 605–8
French exploration, 807
French Protestants, 922–23, 924–25. *See also*
    Huguenots
French Republic
    First, 316–18
    Second, 980–81
French Resistance, during World War II,
    482, 485–86
French Resistance Movement, 84
French Revolution, 315–18, 758–59,
    811–13, 938–39, 984, 1014
    Burke, Edmund on, 154
    Committee of Public Safety, 318
    Constituent Assembly, 316
    Danton, George-Jacques, 316–18
    de Gouges, Marie-Olympe, 524–28
    Legislative Assembly, 316, 812
    Louis XVI guillotined, 317
    Mirabeau, Count, 935–40
    mob marches on Versailles, 316, 811
    Napoleon during, 972
    National Assembly,, 316, 317, 811
    National Convention, 317, 813
    Reign of Terror begins, 318
    Roland, Madame, 1167–69
    royal family confined to the Tuileries,
        316, 811, 812
    September Massacres, 317
    storming of the Bastille, 316, 811
    witnessed by Palmerston, 1032
    witnessed by Pestalozzi, 1063
French Revolution of 1789, Metternich on,
    931
French Revolution of 1830, 759
French Wars of Religion, 921
Freud, Sigmund, 437
Freydal (Maximilian I), 910

Friars, mendicant, 652
Friedland, battle of, 975
Friedman, Milton, 1247
Friedrich III, Kaiser, 944
Friedrich Wilhelm, elector of Brandenburg,
    1348
Friedrich Wilhelm I, king of Prussia, 942
Friend of Mankind or Treatise on Population
    (Riqueti), 936
"The Friends of Blacks," 938
"Friends of Richard III, Incorporated," 1149
Frisia (later the Netherlands), 871–73
Frobisher, Martin, 395
Froissart, J., 377, 378
Fronde rebellions, 235, 805, 914–15
Frondeurs, 805
Fronto, Marcus Cornelius, 853, 854
Froschauer, Christopher, 1378
Froude, R.H., 1000
Fruits of Philosophy (Knowlton), 109
Fry, Elizabeth, **463–66**
    chronology, 464
Fry, Joseph, 464, 465
Fueros, 37
Fugger family, 909
Fulk of Neuilly, 651
Full Circle (Eden), 368
Fuller, Thomas, 1135, 1226
Furet, François, 935

G

Gabelle (salt tax), 1154
Gabor, Bethlen, 1305
Gaelic, suppression of, 509
Gaelic League, 320
Gaetano, Signor, 1032
Gaiseric, king of the Vandals, 61
Gaisford, Thomas, 1051
Gaitskell, Hugh, 1354
Gaius (grandson of Augustus), 792, 1252.
    See also under Caligula
Galatia, 1266
Galba, Servius Sulpicius, 13, 991
Galen, flees plague, 855
Galicia, 583, 653, 863
Galla Placidia, 61
Gallagher, Tom (historian), 1184, 1185
Gallicans, 431, 1104
    in Ireland, 311
    vs. Ultramontanes, 430
Galliéni, General Joseph, 680, 681
Galswinth, wife of Chilperic, 446
Gandhi, Mohandas, 110
Gans, Eduard, 876
Garcés, Sancho, 3
Garibaldi, Giuseppe, 186, **467–71**, 917, 919,
    1291
    chronology, 468
    and French Republic, 470
    Red Shirts at Calatafimi, 469
Garibaldi, Ricciotti, **470–71**
Garnier, Christine, 1182, 1186
Garrett Anderson, Elizabeth, 408, **472–76**
    becomes mayor of Aldeburgh, 476
    chronology, 473
    establishes medical college for women,
        475–76
    opens women's hospital, 474–75
Garrigue, Charlotte, 892, 896
Garzetti, Albino, 1263

Gascoyne-Cecil, Robert, Third marquess of
    Salisbury, **477–81**
    chronology, 478
    at Congress of Berlin, 479
    faces international crises, 480–81
    writes political essays, 478–79
Gaskell, James Milnes, 488
Gates, General Horatio, 740–41
Gaugamela, battle of, 24
Gaul, Roman, 274–75
Gauleiter (Nazi "district leader"), 638
Gaunt, John of, 614
Gaveston, Piers, 375
Gdansk (Danzig), 462
GDR. *See* German Democratic Republic
    (East Germany)
Gebhard, bishop of Eichstatt (later Pope
    Stephen IX), 540
Gelasius II, Pope, 535
Gelliner, Christian, 544
Genbloux, battle of, 689
General Military Academy (Spanish), 441
General Post Office (GPO) (Dublin), 868
General Strike of 1926 (British), 72, 844
    Stanley Baldwin 72
Generalissimus, 1239
Geneva, Calvin in, 167, 168
Geneva Disarmament Conference (1932),
    842
Geneva Protocol, 840
Genghis Khan, 994
Genoa, Christopher Columbus, 289
"Gentleman Mac." *See* MacDonald, Ramsay
Geoffrey, count of Anjou, 596
George I, king of England, 1310
George II, king of England, Elector of
    Hanover, in Diplomatic Revolution,
    461–62
George III, king of England, 671, 1094,
    1098, 1099, 1293
    and Catholic Emancipation, 532
George IV, king of England, 383, 1318
George V, king, 841
George V, king of England, 71, 840, 841
George V (British), 18
George, David Lloyd. *See* Lloyd George,
    David
George, duke of Clarence, 1146–47
George Ludwig (George I, king of Eng-
    land), 53
George of Denmark, 50–51
George, prince of Wales, 1100
Gerard, bishop of Florence (later Nicholas
    II), 541
Gerechtigkeit (Harand) (Justice), 587
Germain, Saint, 1047
German Catholics, in America, 1104
German Communist Party (KPD), 77–78,
    1274
German Democratic Republic, **1273–78**
German Democratic Republic (East Ger-
    many), 9
    culture and sports in, 1276
    Ulbricht, Walter, 1273–78
German Empire, 1329
    Moltke, Helmuth von, 941–44
German-French Yearbook (Marx), 877
"The German Ideology" (Marx), 877
German-Jewish Youth Community (DJJG),
    79
German military intelligence (*Abwehr*), Bon-
    hoeffer in, 769

German National Party, 1257
German Reich
    deports Polish Jews, 79
    Jews under, 78–85
German Social Democratic Party, Brandt,
    Willy, 132–34
German tribes
    cross into Pannonia, 856
    invade northern Italy, 855
German (Weimar) Republic, Hindenburg,
    Paul von, 625
German Workers' Party, Hitler recruits for,
    631
Germanicus,(great-grandson of Augustus)
    11, 12, 792–93, 1252
Germany. *See also* Holy Roman Empire
    after World War I, 1231, 1233–34
    annexes Austria and Czechoslovakia, 634
    vs. Austria (1866), 943
    vs. Denmark (1864), 943
    divided into two republics, 1275–76
    duchies of, 1022–23
    early, 450
    East. *See* German Democratic Republic
    vs. France (1870; Franco-Prussian War),
        943
    Frederick I (Barbarossa), 450–53
    geographic vulnerability, 944
    Great Depression, 1274
    Imperial
        Bismarck, Otto von, 112–17
        navy of, 1330
        under Wilhelm II, 1328–32
    invades Belgium (World War I), 18
    Jewish population, 77
    Laval collaborates with, 763–65
    led by Hitler in World War II, 634–35
    Maximilian I, 910
    and Metternich, Klemens von, 933
    National Liberal Party, 1232, 1233
    National Socialist (Nazi). *See* Göring,
        Hermann; Hitler, Adolf
    occupies France (World War II), 765
    Otto I, the Great, 1022–26
    pre-World War I relations with Britain,
        481
    rearmament of, 842
    Thirty Years' War (Vasa, Gustavus I),
        555, 1303–7
    Tirpitz, Alfred von leads navy, 1254–57
    united by Bismarck, 115
    wars with Sweden in Thirty Years' War,
        556–58
    Weimar Republic, 8, 1233
    West. *See* Germany, Federal Republic of
        (West Germany)
    World War I, 627, 821–23, 1171,
        1232–33, 1256, 1257, 1273, 1286,
        1331–32
    World War II, 893, 948–51, 1172–74,
        1234, 1274
        Casement calls for Irish support
        Dutch resistance to, 1335–36
        neutrality of Belgium, 17–18
Germany, Federal Republic of (West Ger-
    many)
    Adenauer, Konrad, 6–10
    after World War II, 6, 9
    Willy Brandt, 130, 132–34
Germany, National Socialist (Nazi). 631. *See
    also* National Socialist German Workers'
    Party (NSDAP)

censorship in, 638
    Hitler, Adolf, 628
    Neville Chamberlain appeases, 195–200
Gerö, Enrö, 964
Gestapo, 633, 767
Gewilib of Mainz, Bishop, 872
Géza, duke, 1228
Ghent, Pacification of, 1344
Ghettoes, Jewish, 76
Gibbon, Edward, 336, 852
Gilbert, Sir Humphrey, 1134, 1135, 1136
Gillacomgain (nephew of Findlaech), 833
Gillingham, John, 1140
Gilman, Charlotte Perkins, 1194
Ginet-Pilsudski, Józef Kiemens. *See* Pilsud-
    ski, Józef
Girei, Kazy, 500
Girondins, 317, 527
Gjerset, K., 857
Gladstone, 57
Gladstone, Margaret Ethel, 838
Gladstone, William Ewart, 57, 280, 312,
    343–44, 385, 409, 479, **488–92,** 593, 796,
    1035, 1037, 1044, 1297
    chronology, 489
    and the Irish question, 490, 491
    serves as prime minister, 490
    supports Irish Home Rule, 480–81
    and tax reform, 489–90
    and United States, 490
Glasnost, 358
Glendower, Owen, 610
Glinskaia, Anna, 663
Glinskaia, Helena, 663
Glinski, Mikhail, 663
Gloriana. *See* Elizabeth I, queen of England
Glorious Revolution, 51, 304, 1032, 1309,
    1324, 1350
Glynn, Catherine (wife of Gladstone), 489
Goa, 1373
    Francis Xavier at, 1373, 1374
Goderich, Viscount, 1033
Godfrey, duke of Upper Lorraine, 900
Godfrey of Bouillon, **493–96**
    chronology, 494
    in First Crusade, 495–96
    motives for First Crusade, 495
Godfrey the Hunchback, duke of Upper
    Lorraine, 900
Godolphin, Sydney, 52
Godoy (Spanish minister), 975
God's Playground: A History of Poland:
    (Davies), 1383
Godunov, Boris, **497–502**
    becomes sole ruler, 499
    becomes tsar, 500
    chronology, 498
    declares "Third Rome," 500
    fights Tatars, 500
Godwineson, earl Harold, 577, 1339
Godwinesons, 1338
Goebbels, Joseph, 632, **637–38,** *640*
    exhibit destroyed by Jewish resistance
        group, 80–81, 587
Goethe, Johann Wolfgang von, 1064
Gold standard, 72, 841–42
Golden Age of Rome, 63
The Golden Ass (Apuleius), 711
"Golden Decade" of Hungary, 717
The Golden Hind, 351
"Golden Horde," 661, 995
Golitsyn, Field Marshal Dmitry, 1127

Golytsin, prince Alexander N., 28
Gomez, Diego, 604
Gomez, Father Antony, 1374
Gomulka, Wladyslaw, 357, **503–6,** 964
    chronology, 504
    heads Polish Communist Party, 504
    reaches agreement with Khrushchev, 505
    supports Soviet invasion of Czechoslova-
        kia, 503, 506
Gonne, Maud, **507–10,** 866
    chronology, 508
    involved in Irish politics, 508–9
    mother of Sean MacBride, 510
    works for Irish political prisoners, 509
González, Count Fernán of Castile, 4
"Good Parliament," 377
Good Templars, 591
Good works, vs. faith, 825–26
Gorbachev, Mikhail, 358, **511–14,** 965,
    1117, 1122, 1180–81, 1248
    captured in coup, 513
    chronology, 512
    launches radical reform program, 512–13
Gorchakov, General Alexander, 32
Gördeler, Karl, 770–71
Gordon, Charles, 491
Gordon, "Chinese," general, 480, 1297
Gordon, General, 1297
Goremykin, Ivan L., 1361
Görgey, Arthur, 746
Göring, Dr. Heinrich, 638
Göring, Hermann, 8, **638,** *639, 640*
Gorkiacuc, Milan, 1260
Goshen, George Joachim, 480
Goths, 534–35
Gottwald, Klement, **515–23,** 893
    adopts Soviet Five Year Plan, 521
    allows purge of Slansky, 521–22
    appointed prime minister, 518
    becomes president, 520
    negative legacy, 522
Gouges, Marie-Olympe de, **524–28**
    angers Robespierre, 527
    authors declaration of woman's rights,
        527
    chronology, 525
    and French Revolution, 526–27
    as writer, 526
The Government of India (MacDonald), 839
Government of India Act (1935), 842
GPO. *See* General Post Office (Dublin)
GPU. *See* Soviet Secret Police
Graeculus ("The Little Greek") (Hadrian),
    559
Grafton, duke of, 1094
Granada, 653
    Ferdinand and Isabella retake, 655
Grand Alliance, 249, 398, 400, 808
    against Napoleon I Bonaparte, 976
Grand Alliance, War of the, 1351
Grand Assize, 598
Grand Cross of the Order of the British
    Empire, 409
Grand École, 974
"Grand Remonstrance," 306
Grande Armée, 753–54, 975. *See also*
    Napoleon I, Bonaparte
Grande e general estoria (Alfonso X)
Grandes, 298
Grandeur and Misery of Victory, 272
Grandmaison, François Loyzeau de, 418
Granicus River, battle at, 22–23

Il Risorgimento (The Resurgence), 1289
Ildico, 62
Ilgam, Khan, 661
The Iliad (Mirabeau), 937
Illness, and armies, 1142
Illyes, Gyula, 718
Illyrian Provinces, 975
ILP. *See* Independent Labour Party (ILP)
Imayyad dynasty, 1
Immaculate Conception, 1104
Immortals, 777, 778
Impartial, 1184
Imperial Diet at Worms, 218
Imperial University (France), 974
Imperialism, British, 1297
Imperium, 1113
Imre (Emeric), son of Stephen I of Hungary, 1229
In the Cause of Peace (Lie), 785
In the Evening of My Thought, 271
Incarnation, convent of the, 1241
Incas, 1109–11
Income tax, 1099
Independence Day (French), 939. *See also* Bastille
Independent Corps of Dublin Volunteers, 531
Independent Labour Party (ILP), 592, 593, 838, 1037
    Hardie, Keir, 592
    MacDonald, Ramsay, 838, 839
Independents, vs. Presbyterians during English Civil War, 307
Index, papal, 701
India, 73, 594, 862
    Alexander the Great, 24
    Besant, Annie, 108–11
    Montgomery in, 946
    practice of *Suttee,* 56
Indian Mutiny, England, 1035, 1296–97
Indian Round Table Conference, 841
Indochina, 486
Indonesia, 788
Indulgences, 826
    sale of, 646
Industrial Revolution
    in England, 463
    and Russia, 735
Industry, Soviet emphasis on, 521
Ingeborg (mother of Magnus Eriksson), 858
Ingeborg, princess of Denmark, 1085
Inigo of Loyola. *See* Loyola, Ignatius
Inner emigration, 768
Inner Light, 422–23
Innocent II, Pope, 105, 388
Innocent III, Pope, 427, 428, 455, *648,* **648–52,** 693, 1085, 1225
    chronology, 649
    excommunicates King John, 693
    fosters canon law, 650
    initiates the Inquisition, 651–52
Innocent IV, Pope, 370, 456
Innocent VIII, Pope, 615, 1189
Innocents, in war, 546
Innsbruck (Austria), 909
Innviertel, 864
Inquisition, 651–52, 816
Inside the Third Reich (Speer), 642
Institutes of the Christian Religion (Calvin), 167
Instruction (Catherine II, the Great), 181
"Instrument of Government," 308
Intercursus Magnus, 617

Interdepartmental Commission for the Struggle Against Prostitution (Russia), 736
Interdict, 649
    on England, 693
    England under, 650
    France under, 650
    of Prague, 646
    of Thomas Becket, 599
International Brigades, 79
International Conference of Communist Women (1920), 736
International law, 490, 544, 545
    basic principle of, 546
    Grotius, Hugo, 544–47
    and United Nations, 572–73
International Miners' Congress (1890), 593
International Russian Relief, 969
International Trades Congress (1888), 593
International Underground Committee, 82
International Working Men's Association, 879
Investiture, lay. *See* Lay investiture
Investiture Controversy, 494–95, 900–1
Iorwerth, Llewelyn, 693
IRB. *See* Irish Republican Brotherhood (IRB)
Ireland, 207. *See also* Easter Rising of 1916; Northern Ireland
    Catholic Emancipation, 1052–53
    Catholics fight for rights, 531–32
    crop failure of 1878, 1043
    Easter Rising of 1916, 868
    education in, 311
    Gaelic suppressed, 509
    and Gladstone, 491
    and Great Britain, 1297–98
    Great Famine, 1016
    historic leaders
        Brian Boru, 141–45
        Burke, Edmund, 151–55
        Casement, Roger, 174–78
        Collins, Michael, 285–88
        de Valera, Eamon, 319–22
        Gonne, Maud, 507–10
        Grattan, Henry, 529–33
        Markievicz, Constance, 865–69
        O'Connell, Daniel, 1013–17
        Parnell, Charles Stewart, 1041–45
        Patrick, Saint, 1046–49
    King John and, 691
    land reform legislation, 1043–44
    Montgomery in, 947
    Rebellion of 1798, 1014
    and Roman Catholic Church, 309–13
    tithe system in, 532
    trade restrictions lightened, 531
    Tyrone's Rebellion. *See* Elizabeth I, queen of England
    union with Great Britain, 1099
    World War I, 867
Irish Brigade, 312
Irish Catholics *See also* Roman Catholic Church
    in America, 1104
    Burke, Edmund, 154
    Cullen, Paul, 309–13
Irish Church, 490
Irish Citizen Army, 867
Irish College (Rome), 311
Irish Declaration of Independence, 868
Irish Free State, 321, 510, 798
Irish Home Rule, 408, 491, 1043–44, 1298

Hardie supports, 594
Salisbury against, 480, 491
Irish Joan of Arc. *See* Gonne, Maud
Irish nationalism
    Gonne, Maud, 507–10
    Roger Casement, 174–78
Irish nationalist, 865
Irish Parliament, 509–10, 530–32
Irish Party, 867
Irish Rebellion (1798), 532
Irish Rebellion (1916–1922), 865
Irish Republican Brotherhood (IRB), 320, 509, 867
Irish Volunteers, 320, 531, 867, 1014
Iron Duke. *See* Wellington, duke of
Iron Hugo, 1226
Ironsides, 306
Isaac, Heinrich, 910
Isaacs, Rufus, Lord Reading, 841
Isabella, (grandmother of Charles V), 685
Isabella, queen of England, 374, 375
Isabella I, queen of Castile, 215, 290, *653,* **653–57,** 909
    chronology, 655
    death of, 292, 656
Isabella II, queen of Spain, 1034
Isabella of Angoulême, 1085. *See also* John, king of England
Isabella of Hainaut, 1084
Isabelle of Gloucester, 691
Isaeus, 323
Islam, 687
    Portuguese war against, 602
Ismail, battle of, 752
Israel
    and Palestine, 788
    Suez Canal Crisis, 572
Issus, battle of, 23
Italian Catholics, in America, 1104
Italian Social Republic, 961
Italian Socialist Party (PSU), 903–5, 957
Italian Wars, 910, 921–22
Italy, 862
    after World War I, 903–5
    historic leaders
        Borgia, Lucrezia, 122–25
        Cavour, Camillo di, 185–89
        Francis of Assisi, 426–29
        Frederick I (Barbarossa), 450–53
        Garibaldi, Giuseppe, 467–71
        Mazzini, Giuseppe, 917–20, 1103
        Mussolini, Benito, 956–61
        Victor Emmanuel II, 1288–92
    insurrection in, 919
    kingdoms of, 1289
    and Metternich, Klemens von, 933
    Napoleonic Wars, 973
    unification of, 1101, 1291–92. *See also* Cavour, Camillio di; Garibaldi, Giuseppe; Mazzini, Giuseppe; Pius IX
    World War I, 904, 957
    World War II, 961
Ivan III, the Great, 497, *658,* **658–62,** 663, 1075
    chronology, 659
    defeats Novgorod, 660
    disputed succession, 661
    religious tolerance, 661
    takes name of Tsar, 661
Ivan IV, 497–98
    kills son, 498–99
    marriages of, 498

Ivan IV, the Terrible, 497, 552, *663*, **663–68**, 1075, 1223
    chronology, 664
    kills son, 667
    succumbs to paranoia, 666
Ivan Ivanowich (son of Ivan the Terrible), 665, 667
Ivry, battle of, 607
Izborsk, 996

J

Jackson, Frederick, 968
Jacobin Club, 758, 939, 1162
Jacobins, 316, 318
Jacobite uprising, 1310, 1350
Jacobs, Dr. Aletta, 1196
Jadamowitz, Hildegard, 80
Jagiello, Louis, king of Hungary and Bohemia, 910
Jagiello, Vladislav, king of Bohemia, 909
Jagiellonians, 695, 1381
James, duke of York (later James II), 49
James, Edward, 273
James Edward (the Pretender), 51, 52, 53
James I, king of England, 51, 305, 477, *669*, **669–73**, 1138
    chronology, 670
    serves as James VI, king of Scotland, 733, 884
James II, king of England, 50–51, 1349
James IV, king of Scotland, 88
James V, king of Scotland, 881
James VI, king of Scotland. *See* James I, king of England
Jameson Raid of 1895, 481
Jan Hus (Masaryk), 897
Jancso, Miklos, 718
Jansenists, 314
Japan
    attacks Pearl Harbor, 634
    Christianity and, 1373
    Francis Xavier visits, 1374
    vs. Russia, 46, 1005, 1360
Jaramillo, Juan, 302
Jarls (earls), 1018, 1019
Jeanne D'Arc. *See* Joan of Arc
Jefferson, Thomas, 27, 546
Jellacic, Joseph, 746
Jena, battle of, 975
Jena, University of, 877
Jeremiah, Patriarch of Constantinople, 499
Jerónimo. *See* John of Austria
Jerusalem, 496
    captured by Allenby, 48
    crusades to, 651
    first crusaders reach, 1282
    illness prevents crusader's attack, 1142
Jesuits, 816–18. *See also* Society of Jesus
    Francis Xavier as missionary, 1371–75
Jesus of Nazareth, 339, 535, 1253, 1378
Jewish Anti-Nazi Resistance Leaders, trial of Baum's group, **76–85**, 80–81
Jewish Brigade Group, 84
Jewish Councils (Judenräte), 81
Jewish Emigration Office, 637
Jewish Fighting Organization (ZOB), 83
The Jewish Question as a Race, Morals and Cultural Question (Duhring), 582
Jews

in al-Andalus, 2
in Austria, 581–89
Blum, Léon, 118–19, 121
under Caligula, 164
Christian hostility to, 580
discriminated against in Europe, 77
in England, 372, 692
English
    Edward I expels, 372
    Edward VII flouts anti-Semitism, 386
French, 764, 1070–71
German, 770
in Italy, 961
Nazi extermination of, 81–82
in Spain, 655–56, 816
during World War II, 76–85
Jingoism, 594
Joachim, Heinz, 80
Joachim, Marianne, 76, 81
Joan, countess of Kent, 381
Joan (*la loca*: "the Mad"), queen of Castile, 656
Joan of Arc, 223, 613, *674*, **674–78**
    battles English, 675–76
    captured in battle, 676
    Charles VII and, 223–24
    chronology, 675
    tried for heresy, 677–78
Joffre, Joseph, 418, *679*, **679–84**, *683*, 1068
    at Battle of the Marne, 418–19
    chronology, 680
    Plan 17 (offensive war plan), 681–82
Jogiches, Leo (Polish socialist), 829, 830
John, king of England, 370, 376, 599, 648, *690*, **690–94**, 801, 1085
    assumes throne, 693
    chronology, 691
    founds Royal Navy, 692
    and Innocent III, 649–50
    loses French holdings, 692–93
    Magna Carta, 693
John, prince of England, 1141
    rebels during Richard's ransom, 1143
John, son of Berengenia, 391
John Balliol, king of Scotland, 371
John George, Lutheran Elector of Saxony, 413
John II Casimir (Jan Kazimierz), 696
John III, king of Portugal, 1372
John III Sobieski, king of Poland
    defeats Turks at Vienna, 697–98
    elected king, 697
John (Juan) II, king of Aragon, 654
John of Austria, 220, 403, *685*, **685–89**, 1080, 1344–45
    chronology, 686
    commands Holy League, 687
    as governor-general of the Netherlands, 688–89
John of Aviz, 601
John of Gaeta, 1281
John of Gaunt
    duke of Lancaster, 86
    earl of Lancaster, 377
John of Luxembourg, 676
John of the Cross, Saint, 1240, 1243
John Paul II, Pope, 1180
John the Good, king of France, 377, 381
John William, Elector of Saxony, 557
John XII, Pope, 1025
John XXIII, Pope, 646, *699*, **699–703**, 1105

    announces Second Vatican Council, 701
    chooses controversial name, 701
    chronology, 700
    publishes encyclicals, 702
Johnson, Lyndon, 322, 1120
Johnson, Paul, 97, 618, 678, 692, 814, 818, 1366
Johnson, Samuel, 671
Joinville, Treaty of, 1082
Jonson, Ben, 1138
Joseph, Father, 1152
Joseph, Keith, 1247
Joseph II, Habsburg emperor, 183, 215, 400, 581, *704*, **704–8**, 810, 864, 934
    chronology, 705
Journey from St. Petersburg to Moscow (Radishchev), 184
Jowett, Benjamin, 1012
Joyce, James, 866
Joyce, James Avery, 785
Juan Carlos, king of Spain, 443
Juana (daughter of Henry IV, king of Castile), 654
Juarez, Benito, 956
Juba II, king of Mauritania (Morocco), 65
Jud, Leo, 1377
Juda I (celebrated rabbi), 856
Judaizers, 241
Judea
    Kingdom of, 67
    under Roman rule, 991
Judicature Ordinances (Swedish), 555
Judicial system
    under Augustus, 67
    first, 43
Judt, Tony, 765
Julia (Caesar's daughter, wife of Pompey), 1114
Julia (daughter of Augustus), 67
Julia (daughter of Julia), 67
Julia Domna, **709–13**
    chronology, 710
Julia Maesa, **709–13**
    chronology, 710
Julia Mammaea, **709–13**
    chronology, 710
Julia Soaemias, **709–13**
    chronology, 710
Juliana, queen of the Netherlands, 1335–36
Julias of Rome, *709*, **709–13**
    chronology, 710
Julio-Claudians, 262
Julius Caesar, 64, *156*, **156–60**, 164, 259, 264, 274, 756, 791, 854, 1114, 1250
    chronology, 157
    crosses the Rubicon, 159
    death of, 160
    forms First Triumvirate, 158
    and Pompey, 1114–15
Julius II, Pope, 910
July Days, 722, 774
Junker, as basis for Prussian military, 460
Junkers, 112, 460, 626
Junto, Whig, 52
Jurand, Jules, *683*
Justification (William the Silent), 1344
Justinian, Emperor, 96, 562
Jutes, 40
Jutland, battle of, 1256
Juvenalia, 988

Meaux, siege of, 612
Medes, 778
Medical College for Women (London), 475–76
Medical Staff Corps (British), 1011
Medici, Catherine de, 605, *921*, **921–25**
    chronology, 922
Medici, Lorenzo de', *926*, **926–30**, 1189
    chronology, 927
Medici, Maria de (mother of Louis XIII), 608, 1151, 1152
    Day of the Dupes, 1153
Medici, Piero de, 1191
Medici family, 921, 1189–92
Medina Azahara, 4
    Abd-Al-Rahman II, 1–5
Medina-Sidonia, duke of, 395
Meditation, 104
The Meditations (Aurelius), 852–53
Meetings, of Quakers, 424
Megara, allies with Sparta, 1058
Mein Kampf (My Struggle) (Hitler), 588, 632, 1335
Mela, M. Annaeus, 1199
Melanchthon, Philipp, 827
Melanius, Bishop, 448
Melbourne, Lord, 1053, 1294
Melfi, Constitutions of, 457
Mellon, Andrew, 71
Mellowes, Liam, 867
Memnon, 22
Memoir of the Life of Elizabeth Fry with Extracts from Her Journal and Letters, 465
Memoire de Mne Valmont (de Gouges), 525
Mendelssohn, Moses, 938
Mendicant friars, 652
Ménétrel, Bernard, 1069
Mensheviks, 735, 1269, 1270
Menshikov, Alexander, 1075
Mercantilism, 283, 1074
Mercia, 40
Mercure de France, 526
Mercy-Argenteau, 939
Merder, Captain Karl Karlovich, 31
Merovingian dynasty, 445
Merovingians, 274, 871
Merriman, Roger Bigelow, 35
Mers-el-Kabir, French fleet shelled at, 763
Merton, Thomas, 104
Messalina (wife of Claudius), 988
    plots against Claudius, 13
Mestizo, 1111
Metal Workers' Union of Zagreb, 1260
Metford, J. C., 538
Methodism, 1325–26
Methodists, at Oxford, 1324
Métier du ro, 805
Metternich, Klemens von, 112, 185, 435, 581, 745, 918, *931*, **931–34**, 1288
    appointed ambassador to France, 932
    becomes symbol of repression, 934
    chronology, 932
    effect of French Revolution on, 932
Metternich regime, 745
Mexico, 980
    Cortés, Hernán, 299–303
Mexico City, 302
Meyer, Gerhard, 80
Micia (wife of Pompey), 1113
Middle Ages
    Charlemagne, 201–5
    European Jews in, 580

Middle East, overshadows Hungarian uprising, 965
Middle Way, The (Macmillian), 844
"A Mighty Fortress is Our God" (Luther), 827
Mihailov, Colonel Ivan, 1260
Mikolajczyk, Stanislaw, 504
Mikoyan, Anastas, 964
Milan, 910
Milihacc, John, of Kromhacehacríhacz, 645
Militia, first, 42
Mill, John Stuart, 408
Millán Astray, José, 440
Millet, General, 418
Millevoye, Lucien, 508
Millis, Maria, 55
Milnes, Richard Monckton, 1009
Miloslavsky, Maria, 1072
Mince Pie Administration, 1098
Minden, battle of, 756
The Miner (Hardie), 592
Ministry of Armaments and Munitions, 641
Minorca, 1094
Mirabeau, Count (Victor Riqueti), 525, *935*, **935–40**, 1162
    chronology, 936
    de Gouge writes ode and play for, 527
    named to Assembly of Notables, 938
    physical characteristics, 936
    writes while imprisoned, 937–38
Mirabeau, Eleanor of Aquitaine, 692
"Mirabeau in the Elysian Fields" (de Gouges), 527
Mirandola, Count Giovanni Pico della, 1189
Mise of Amiens, 802
Missi dominici, 203
Mistress Lark, 1364
Miswa, Stephen, 1089
Mithridates VI, king of Pontus, 1114
Mizwa, Stephen P., 1087
Mnishek, Jerzy, 501
Moctezuma II, 300, 301
Modern Warfare (1935) (Sikorski), 1208
Modrzejewska, Madame Helena, 1029
Mohacs, battle of, 910
Mohammad Ali, pasha of Egypt, 1034
Mohammed-Amin, 661
Moirova, Varvara, 736
Moje Pierwsze Boje (My First War Experience) (Pilsudski), 1089
Mola, Emilio, 441
Moldavia, 1121
Mollwitz, battle of, 461, 861
Molotov, Viacheslav, 101, 1117, 1123–25, *1124*
Moltke, Helmuth von, 114, 682, 771, 821, *941*, **941–44**, 944, *944*
    as Chief of General Staff, 942–43
    chronology, 942
    quarrels with Bismark, 943
Monarchies, by divine right, 545
Monasteries, English, destruction of, 623
Monastic life
    Benedict of Nursia, Saint, 96–98
    Bernard of Clairvaux, Saint, 103–7
    Celtic, 96
    of Gregory (later Pope Gregory I, the Great), 535
Mongol (Tatar) tribes, 994
Mongols, 1075
    Nevsky and, 996
    strategy of, 995

Monowitz, 82
Monro, Robert, 553
Monroe, James, 759
Monroe Doctrine, 481
Monte Cassino, 95
    as Benedictine monastery, 97–98
    during World War II, 97
Montecuculi, Count Sebastian, 922
Montenegrans, 1258
Montespan, Marquise de, 807
Montesquieu, Baron Charles de, 1215
Montgomery, Bernard, *945*, **945–51**, *948*, 1173
    chronology, 946
    in India, 946
    World War I, 947
    World War II, 948–49
        leads assault at Normandy, 950
        vs. Rommel, 949
Montgomery, Comte de, 923
Montgomery, on Ireland, 947
Montigly, Lucas de, 938
Montijo, Eugenie de, 980
Montmorency, Anne de, 433
Montmorency-Bouteville, 1153
Montoire, Pétain meets with Hitler, 1071
Moore, Augustus, 1041
Moore, Sir John, 1316
Moorehead, Caroline, 1194
Moors, in Spain, 816
Moral Essays, 1203
Moralia (Gregory I, the Great), 535
Moravia, 898
Moray, 833
Moray, Andrew, 371
More, Thomas, 620, 621, 622, *952*, **952–55**, 1365
    chronology, 953
    Henry VIII and, 954–55
Morel, Edmund D., 783
Morell, Theodor, 634
Morgan, William, 1324
Moriscos, 686, 1081
Mormaers (royal officers), 833
Mornington, Lord, 1313
Morocco, 797
Morris, John, 1049
Mortier, Edouard, 753
Mortimer, Edmund (earl of March), 610
Mortimer, Roger, 375
Morton, John Cardinal, archbishop of Canterbury, 617
Morton, Thomas, archbishop of Canterbury, 952
Moscovy, 15th century, 659
Moscow
    French retreat from (1812), 976
    great fire (1547), 665
    Napoleon takes, 754
    pillage of (1571), 666
Moscow, bishop of, 499
Moscow Declaration (1943), 579
Moscow subway, 1119
Motley, John L., 402
Mountjoy, Lord, 620
"Movement against Anti-Semitism, Racial Hatred and Glorification of War," 587
Mozarabs, in al-Andalus, 2
Mudéjars. See Muslims
Muhammad, 2
Muhammad II, Emir of Granada, 37
Muirchu (chronicler), 1047, 1048

Mummolus the Prefect, 447
Munich Agreement, 845
Munich Conference (1938), 893
Munich Crisis of 1938, 891, 893
Municipal Reports (Kossuth), 745
Munro, D. C., 1225
Murat, Caroline Bonaparte, queen of
     Naples, 971
Murray, General Sir Archibald, 47
Muscovy, grand duke of (Ivan III, the
     Great), 658–62
Musketeers, Russian, 498
Muslim Spain, 1–5, 655–66, 872
     de Vivar, Rodrigo Díaz (El Cid) and,
          334, 335
Muslims
     in al-Andalus, 1–2
     Charles Martel vs., 872–73
     Crusades against, 105–6, 651
     negotiate with Frederick II, 456
     Portugese war against, 602
Mussolini, Benito, 74, 197, 365, 441, 631,
     842, 904–5, *956*, **956–61**, *960*, 1069, 1103,
     1132, 1173
     appointed prime minister, 958
     chronology, 957
     edits socialist newspapers, 957–58
     and France, 762
     joins Nazis, 961
     leads fascist movement, 904
     oratory style, 959
Mustafa Kemal (Atatürk), 700
Mustapha, Kara, Grand Vizier, 398
Mutiny Act, repeal of, 531
Muwallads, in al-Andalus, 2
My Confession (Mirabeau), 937
My Life (1930) (Trotsky), 1272
Mycale, battle of, 1055
Mysore, battle of, 1315
Mysticism, Alexander I, Tsar, 27–28

N

Na Fianna Eireann, 867
Naef, Elisabeth, 1062
Nagle, D. Brendan, 326
Nagy, Imre, 715, *962,* **962–65**
     becomes premier, 964
     chronology, 963
Namur, 689
Nanney, Hugh Ellis, 796
Nansen, Fridtjof, *966,* **966–70**, 1131
     Arctic explorations, 967–68
     chronology, 967
     works for refugee relief, 969
Nansen Kitchens, 970
Nansen Passports, 970
Nantes, Edict of, 607–8, 806–7
Naples. *See also* Kingdom of the Two Sicilies
     annexed by Ferdinand, 656
     Kingdom of, 919
     taken by Garibaldi, 1291
     University of, 456
Napoleon, (Charles) Louis. *See* Napoleon III
Napoleon I Bonaparte, 27, 185, 216, 250,
     310, 397, 526, 742, 751, 752–54, 918, 932,
     941, *971*, **971–77**, *974*, 984, 1063, 1099,
     1101, 1160, 1177, 1214, 1239, 1315
     abdicates, 976–77
     Alexander I, Tsar, 25–30, 27, 975
     becomes emperor of France, 974

captures Egypt, 984
chronology, 972
de Staël and, 1216
defeat at Waterloo, 1317–18
excommunicated, 975
exiled to Elba, 976
exiled to St. Helena, 1318
invasion of Europe, 932
Lafayette criticizes, 759
makes peace with Alexander I, 975
marries Josephine, 972
marries Marie Louise of Austria, 976
military career during Revolution, 972
Russian campaign of 1812, 753
Third Coalition against, 752–53
Napoleon III, 32, 113, 187, 268, 384, 469,
     919, 921, 943, *978*, **978–81**, 1034, 1105,
     1290, 1296
     chronology, 979
     meets with Alexander II, 32–33
     seizes power, 980
     supports Victor Emmanuel, 1291
     surrenders to Wilhelm I, 943, 981
Napoleonic codes, 974
Napoleonic Wars
     England, 1315
     England during, 1099–1100
     Ireland during, 1052
Narautowicz, President Gabriel, 1207
Narbonne, Louis de, 1215
Narodna Wola, 1088
Narodniki, 34
Narva, battle of, 1073
Naryshkin, Natalia, 1072
Nase Nynejsi Krise (Our Present Crisis)
     (Masaryk), 897
Naseby, 208
     battle of, 307
Nasjonal Samling, 1132
Nassar, Gamal Abdel, 367, 572, 965
Nation-state, development of, 545
National Assembly (France), 315, 758, 811,
     939, 972. *See also* Mirabeau, Count
     declares war on Austria, 317
     decree of voluntary tax, 526
     establishment of, 938–39
     World War II, 765
National Assembly (Spain), 1158
National Association (Irish Catholic), 312
National Bank of Sweden, 571
National Convention, 972
National Government (British), 841–42,
     844
National Health Insurance Act (British), 797
National Land League, 1044
National Liberal Party (German), 1232,
     1233
National Liberation Partisan Detachments,
     1260
National Reformer (Besant), 109
National Socialist German Workers' Party
     (NSDAP; Nazis), 77–78, 637, 641
     in Austria, 579–89
     German resistance to, 766–71
     growth of party, 632–33
     Ludendorff joins, 823
     plan "Final Solution" for Jewish popula-
          tion, 81–82
     resistance to racism of, 587
     seize power, 633
National Unemployment Insurance Act
     (British), 797

National Union of Women's Suffrage Soci-
     eties, 408
Nationalism
     19th century, 933
     socialists, 829–831
Nationalists (Spain), 1158
Nationalities Law (Hungary), 747
Nationalsozialistische Deutsche Arbeiter-Partei
     (NSDAP; National Socialist German
     Workers' Party). *See* Germany, National
     Socialist (Nazi); National Socialist Ger-
     man Workers' Party (NSDAP)
NATO, 569
Natural Questions, 1203
Nature, 1062
Naval League (German), 1255
Navarre, 3, 653
     Alfonso X, 36
     annexed by Ferdinand, 656
     Henry of (later Henry IV, king of
          France), 606
Navarre family, as Huguenots, 923
Navy
     first, 42
     first Russian, 1074
     of Germany, 1330
Nayler, James, 423–24
Nazareth, 370
Nazi Germany. *See* Anti-Nazi resistance;
     Germany, National Socialists (Nazi);
     Göring, Hermann; Hitler, Adolf; Hitler's
     generals; National Socialists
Neale, J. E., 392
Neale, John Mason, 1322
Neave, Airey, 1247
Necker, Jacques, 315, 316, 938, 1167
Nehra, Henrietta-Amélie de, 938
Nelson, Admiral, 1100
Nelson, Horatio, *982*, **982–86**
     affair with Lady Hamilton, 984
     at Battle of Trafalgar, 985
     chronology, 983
     naval career, 984
Nelson, Janet L., 446
Nemours, Du Pont de, 938
NEP. *See* New Economic Policy
Nero, 266, 559, *987*, **987–92**, *990*, 1199
     Agrippina the Younger, 14–15
     chronology, 988
     musical tour of Greece, 991
     performs, 988
     Seneca tutors, 14–15
     son of Agrippina the Younger, 11
Nero, Tiberius Claudius. *See* Tiberius
Neronia, 988
Nerva, 560, 1263
Netherlands, 16, 862. *See also* Dutch
     Netherlands; Holland
     Calvanism in, 545–46
     Don John of Austria in, 688
     historic leaders
          Grotius, Hugo, 544–47
          Wilhelmina, 1333–36
          William III of Orange, 1347–51
          William the Silent, 1342–46
     in 17th Century, 545
     under Philip II of Spain, 1343
     revolt of, 402, 403–6, 1080–81, 1343–44
     Spanish, 400–3
     vs. Spain, 1081
     World War I, 1334–35
     World War II, 1335–36

Neue Rheinische Zeitung (Marx), 878
Neuenburg, Heinrich von, bishop of Basel, 1175
"Neurasthenia," 1012
Neustria, 871
Neutrality, 546
Neville, Anne, 1146, 1148
Neville's Cross, battle of, 376
Nevsky, Alexander, *993*, **993–97**
   chronology, 994
   rules Russia, 996
"New Course," 963
New Deal for Coal (1945) (Wilson), 1353
"New Economic Mechanism," 717
New Economic Policy (NEP), 1220, 1271
   under Lenin, 734, 737, 775
   Stalin abolishes, 1220
New Hospital for Women and Children, 474
New India (Besant), 110
New Model Army, 307
New Testament, translated by Luther, 827
New World
   Columbus in, 290–92
   English exploration of, 617–18, 1136, 1138
   exploration of, 219, 824
   Pizarro in, 1107–11
   Portuguese exploration of, 601–4
   Spanish exploration of, 656, 1107–11
New York Daily Tribune (Marx), 878
Newer Ideals of Peace (Addams), 1196
Newgate Gaol (jail), 464–65
Newman: His Life and Spirituality (Bouyer), 1001
Newman, John Henry, Cardinal, 57, 244, *998*, **998–1002**, 1102
   chronology, 999
   converts to Catholicism, 999–1001
   Oxford movement, 1000
Nicholas, 387
Nicholas I, Tsar, 29, 31, 32, 139, 747, 1034
Nicholas II, Tsar, 100, 328, 720, 725, 821, 849, *1003*, **1003–7**, 1130, 1259, 1330, 1359–61
   abdicates, 1006
   chronology, 1004
   coronation of, 1004
   Russian Revolution forces abdication, 1006
Nicholas, Russian tsar, 830
Niederer, Johannes, 1064
Niekisch, Ernst, 767
Niemöller, Martin, 769
"Night of the Long Knives," 633, 640, 767
Nightingale, Florence, 362, **1008–1912**, *1008–1010*
   chronology, 1009
   continues work though bedridden, 1012
   reforms War Office, 1011
   at Scutari Hospital, 1010–11
Nightingale Fund, 1011
Nightingale Training School for Nurses (St. Thomas's Hospital), 1012
95 Theses (Luther), 218, 826, 1378
Ninety-six, battle of, 741
Ninjitsu, 1374
Nisbet, Frances, 983
Nivelle, Robert, 419, 683, 1068
Nixon, Richard, U.S. President, 1121
Noailles, Adrienne de (later Adrienne de Lafayette), 756, 758–59

Nobel Peace Prize
   Brandt, Willy, 134
   Hammarskjöld, Dag, 569–73
   Kollontai nominated for, 737
   Nansen, Fridtjof, 970
   Stresemann, Gustav, 1234
Nogueres, Henri, 921
Nomadic tribes, Huns, 59–60, 61
Nominalism, 645
Nomothetes, 1211
Non Plus Ultra, 250
None Can Harm Him Who Does Not Injure Himself, 244
Noninterference, *vs.* balance of power, 479
Nonsuch, Treaty of, 405
Nordenskiold, Nils (Swedish explorer), 967
"Nordic" cult, 823
Nördlingen, battle of, 414, 1153
Norman, Diana, 866
Normandy
   invasion of, 950, 1173
   King John, 692
Normandy, duke of (William the Conqueror), 1337–41
Normans, 1337
Norsemen, in Scotland, 832, 834
North, Lord, 1095
North Africa, 602
   World War II, 949–50
North America, 862
   French claims in, 807
   visited by Wesley, 1325
North Korea, 788
North Pole, 966
Northern Ireland, 867
Northumbria, 40, 577, 835
Norton, Thomas, 395
Norway, 857
   Canute I, 169–73
   divided (1046), 576
   Hardraade, Harald III, 575–78
   Lie, Trygve, 785–89
   Margaret (Valdemarsdottir), 857–60
   Nansen, Fridtjof, 966–70
   Olaf I Tryggvason, 1018–21
   Quisling, Vidkun, 1130–33
   Union of Kalmar, 548
   World War I, 969–70
   World War II, 786–87, 1132–33
Norway and the Union with Sweden (Nansen), 969
Norwegian-German trade, World War I, 969
Norwegian Trade Unions Federation, 786
Nostradamus, 606, 922
Note on the Usefulness of Provincial Estates to the Royal Authority (Riqueti), 936
Notebooks of grievances, 938
Notes Affecting the Health, Efficiency, and Hospital Administration of the British Army, Notes on Nursing, Notes on Hospitals (Nightingale), 1012
Notes on a Visit Made to Some of the Prisons in Scotland and the North of England in Company with Elizabeth Fry, 465
Nottingham, Sheriff of, 1143
Novatis, Annaeus, 1199
"November Criminals," 631
November Revolution, 725, 774
Novgorod
   asks for Alexander Nevsky, 996
   Ivan defeats, 660
   Nevsky, Alexander, 993, 996

Novotny, Antonin, 522
Novus homo (new man), 259
Nowak, Frank, 1027
NSDAP. *See* National Socialist German Workers' Party
Nu-Pieds, revolt of, 1154
Nuclear war, 702
Nuclear weapons, 727, 846
Nuestra Señora de la concepción, 352
Núñez de Balboa, Vasco, 1108
Nuremberg Laws, 633
Nuremberg trials, 544
Nursing, modern. *See* Nightingale, Florence
Nyers, Rezsö, 717
Nygaardsvold, Johan, 786
Nyköping, Diet of (1611), 554

O

Oakley, Ann, 407
Oates, Titus, 50, 210
Obolenski, Prince Ivan, 663
O'Brien, Donnell, king of Limerick, 691
Observations on the Visiting, Superintendence and Government of Female Prisoners, 465
O'Connell, Daniel, 310, 311, *1013*, **1013–17**, 1052
   campaigns for repeal of Irish union with England, 1016
   chronology, 1014
   Great Famine, 1016
   law career, 1015
   runs for British Parliament, 1016
O'Connell, Mary, 1015
O'Connell, Maurice, 1013, 1014
O'Connor, Ulick, 865
Octavia, 64, 988
Octavian, 791
Octennial Act, 530
"October Manifesto," 735, 1005, 1361
Odessa, siege of, 752
Odo, bishop of Bayeux, 1339
Odo of Chatillon-Sur-Marne. *See* Urban II, Pope
Oekolampadius, Johannes, 1379
Of Lettres de Cachet and of State Prisons, 937
Offensive, all-out, as war strategy, 418
Oil embargo (1973), affects Hungary, 718
Ojeda, Alonso de, 1108
Olaf I Tryggvason, king of Norway. *See* Tryggvason, Olaf I
Olaf III, king of Norway, 577
Olaf V, 858, 859
"Old Man of the Mountain." *See* ad-Din Sinan, Rashid
"Old Pam." *See* Palmerston, Lord
Oldcastle, Sir John, 610
Olid, Cristóbal de, 299, 302
Ollivier, Emile, 981
Olympias (mother of Alexander the Great), 21
On Communism: In Defense of the New Course (Nagy), 964
On Moses Mendelssohn and Political Reform of the Jews (Mirabeau), 938
On the Art of Hunting with Hawks (De arte venandi cum avibus), 457
On the Priesthood (John Chrysostom), 241, 242
"Operation Market-Garden," 950
Oprichnina, 498, 666

Optimates, 157, 1113, 1115
Opus Evangelicum (Wycliffe), 1370
Orange Free State, 481
Orange, House of, 1334
"Orange Peel." *See* Peel, Robert
Orange, Prince of
    William III, 1347–51
    William the Silent, 1342–46
Oranienburg, 78
Oratorians, 314
Oratory, of Mussolini, 959
Ordaz, Diego de, 299
Ordeal, verdict by, 598
Order of the British Empire, 409
Order of the Garter, 603, 1310
    Edward III establishes, 376
Order of Suvorov, 1239
Ordoño II of León, 3
Orellana, Francisco de, 1110
Organic Law of the State (Franco), 443
Organisation Armee Secrete (Secret Army Orga-
    nization), 486
Organization of European Economic Coop-
    eration, 571
Oriel College, 999
Orkney Islands, 832
Orkneyinga Saga, 834
Orlov, Grigori, 1127
Orosius Universal History, 43
Orsini Plot, 1035
Orthodox Christianity, 275
Orthodox Church, 996
    Russian Patriarchate, 499–500
Orthodoxy
    in Balkans, 1258
    test of, 646
Oscar II, 1196
O'Shea, Captain William, 1044
O'Shea, Katherine (Kitty), 1044–45
Osip, Metropolitan of Moscow, 663
Osterreichischer Jugendbund; OJB (Austrian
    Youth League), 587
Ostia (port of Rome), 1265
Ostpolitik (Brandt), 133
Ostrogoths, 96
Oswiecim (Auschwitz), 81–82
Otho, Marcus Salvius, 989
Otrepev, Grishka, 501
Ottaviani, Cardinal, 702
Ottawa agreements (1932), 842
Otto of Brunswick, 455, 1085
Otto the Great, 3
Otto, Holy Roman Emperor, 648, 692
Otto I, the Great, *1022,* **1022–26,** 1322
    chronology, 1023
    crowned emperor, 1023, 1025
    fights Magyars, 1025
    rebellious duchies, 1024
Otto II, 1025
Otto III, 1026
Ottokar II (Premyslid), king of Bohemia,
    1176
Ottoman Empire. *See also* Turkey
    19th century, 1034
    Russian war against, 1073
    vs. Spanish Empire, 1080
    in World War I, 47, 48
Ottoman Turks, 687
    Francis I allies with, 433–34
Ottonian era, 450
Our Corner (Besant), 109
Out of My Life (Hindenburg), 626

"Out of Weakness Were Made Strong"
    (Newman [sermon]), 1000
Ovid, 67
OVRA, 958
Owen, Margaret, 796
The Ox (Zwingli), 1377
Oxenstierna, Axel, 554, 558, 1153
Oxford Methodists, 1324
Oxford Movement, 55, 1000–1
Oxford University, 379
Ozanam, Frederic, 1102

P

Paar, Catherine, 623
Pacem in Terris (Peace on Earth) (encyclical
    letter), 702
Pacifica (cousin of St. Clare), 429
Pacification of Ghent, 1344
Pacifico, Don, 1034
Pacifism
    of Keir Hardie, 594–95
    women's movement, 1195–96
    during World War I, 1195–97
Pactus Legis Salicae, 275
Paderewski, Ignace Jan, *1027,* **1027–30,**
    1030
    chronology, 1028
    as pianist, 1028–29
    as Polish statesman, 1029–30
    reinterment of, 1030
Paderewski, Jan (father of Ignace Jan
    Paderewski), 1028
The Paderewski Memoirs, 1028
Padover, Saul K., 704
Paine, Thomas, 1168
Painlevé, Paul, 761
Painting as a Pastime (Churchill), 256
Palaeologus, Zoë (later Duchess Sophia),
    659–60, 661–62, 663
Palatinate
    annexation of, 1305
    wars with Bavaria, 910
Palermo, 469
Palestine
    annexed by Pompey, 1114
    Montgomery in, 948
    partition of (1949), 788
    during World War II, 84
Palitinate, 398
    lower, 413
Pallas, devoted to Agrippina the Younger,
    13, 14
Palmer, A. Mitchell, 1197
Palmerston, 1054
Palmerston, Lord, 56, 57, 280, 478, 490,
    1031, **1031–35,** 1296, 1297
    chronology, 1032
    in foreign office, 1033–34
    foreign policy of, 1034
    as prime minister, 1034–35
    as war secretary, 1033
Pamplona, 814–15
    battle of, 1372
Pan Germanic League, 1232
Panama, 1108
Panegyric on Theodoric (Ennodius), 60
Panegyric to Maximian, 338
Panin, Count Nikita P., 26
Pankhurst, Christabel, 409, 1037, **1039,**
    1194

Pankhurst, Emmeline, 407, 409, *1036,*
    1036–40, 1194
    begins hunger strike, 1039
    chronology, 1037
    organizes W.S.P.U., 1037–39
Pankhurst, Richard Marsden, 1037, 1038
Pankhurst, Sylvia, 409, 1037, **1038**
Panmure, Lord, 1011
Pannonia, 856, 1251
Pannonia, Lower. *See* Hungary; Yugoslavia
Pantheon, 562
Papal infallibility, 701, 1101, 1105
Papal States, 1103
    in 19th century, 1103
    Piedmontese army occupies, 920
Pappenheim, Count zu, 557
Parackeho Idea Naroda Ceskeho (Palacky's Idea
    of the Czech Nation) (Masaryk), 897
Paravas, 1373
Paris, 980
    captured by Henry V, 612
Paris, Matthew, 690
Paris National Guard, 758
Paris Peace Conference, 271, 420, 1090
Paris, siege of, by Prussia, 943
Paris, Treaty of (1259), 802, 1092
Parkes, Bessie Rayner, 408
Parlement of Paris
    lit de justice, 914
    Mazarin and, 912–15
Parliament Act (1911) (British), 797
Parliament (British), 208, 209.
    acts of. *See* specific act, e.g., Corn laws
    Ashley-Cooper, Anthony, 7th earl of
        Shaftsbury, 55–57
    Baldwin, Stanley, 70–71
    Bright, John, 278–80
    Burke, Edmund, 153–54
    Cecil, Robert (later third marquess of
        Salisbury), 478
    Churchill, Winston, 252–53
    Cobden, Richard, 278–80
    conflict with Charles I, 305
    Cromwell, 305–8
    Eden, Anthony, 365
    during Edward III, 377
    under Henry VII, 617
    James I, 672
    Lloyd George, David, 796–97
    MacDonald, Ramsey, 839
    O'Connell, Daniel, 1015, 1016
    Palmerston, Lord, 1033
    Peel, Robert, 1051–52
    Pitt the Younger, 1097
    Salisbury (formerly Robert Cecil), 479
    Thatcher, Margaret, 1247
    Wilson, Harold, 1353
Parliament (Irish), 321, 531–32, 869
    Grattan, Henry, 530–31
    Wellesley in, 1314
Parliament (Italian), 905, 958
Parliamentarianism *vs.* socialism, 829
Parliamentary Council, Adenauer elected
    chairman, 9
Parliamentary Labour Party (PLP), 594
Parliamentary Reports (Kossuth), 745
Parma, 862
Parma, duke of (Alessandro Farnese), 402–6
Parnell, Charles Stewart, 480, 491, *1041,*
    1041–45
    chronology, 1042
    fights for Home Rule, 1043

Roman Gaul, 274–75
Roman law, 562
Roman oratory, 1001
Roman peace (*pax romana*), 794
Roman Republic, 66. *See also* Roman Empire
    Cicero, 257–61
    Julius Caesar, 156–60
    restored by Augustus, 65
Romanoff, Nikita, **663**
Romanov, Alexander Nikolayevich. *See*
    Alexander II, Tsar
Romanov, Alexis Mikhaikovich, Tsar, 1072,
    1076
Romanov, Michael, 501
Romanov, Nicholas, Grand Duke. *See*
    Nicholas I, Tsar
Romanovna, Anastasia (wife of Ivan IV [the
    Terrible]), 498, 666
Romanovs, and marriage, 1075–76
Romanticism, 749
Romanus, 95
Rome
    Agrippina the Younger, 11–15
    architecture, 67
    burning of Rome, *990*
    Christina of Sweden in, 236–37
    Golden Age of, 63
    great fire of 64 A.D., *990, 991*
    under Julius Caesar, 157–58
    navy under Pompey, 1114
    sack of (1527), 432–33, 1280
Rome-Berlin Axis, 961
Rommel, Erwin, 949–50, *1170*, **1170–74,**
    1172
    chronology, 1171
Roncaglia, Diet of, 451–52
Roncalli, Angelo. *See* John XXIII
Roosevelt, Franklin D., 255, 367, 485, 1030,
    1132, *1221,* 1222, 1336
Roosevelt, Theodore, 1360
Roper, William, 620
Rosario, 353
Rosebery, Lord, 481, 796
Roselli, General Pietro, 469
Rosetta Stone, 973
Rossi, Pellegrino, 468
Rostopchin, governor of Moscow, 753
Rotholz, Lotte, 76
Rotholz, Siegbert, 81
Rothschilds, 583
Rouen, siege of, 611–12
"Rough Wooing," 882
Rousseau, Jean Jacques, 1062, 1161, 1166
Rovine, Arthur, 787
A Roving Commission: My Early Life (Win-
    ston Churchill), 256
Roxana, Princess, 24
Royal Charles, 209
Royal Irish Constabulary, 869
Royal Military College, Sandhurst, 946
Royal Sanitary Commission (British), 1011
RPF *(Rassemblement du peuple Francais,* or
    "Rally of the French People"), 486
Rude, George, 1161
Rudolf, duke of Swabia, 542
Rudolf I, of Habsburg, 37, *1175,* **1175–77**
    chronology, 1176
Rudolf II, Holy Roman Emperor, 412, 1304
Rudolph II, emperor of Germany, 499, 667
Rudolph (Rasul), 106
Ruffy, Thérèse-Richard-Sophie de (Marquis
    de Monnier), 937

Rufus, William, 1340
Rule of Benedict, 96–97, 97–98, 104
"Rule of Secretaries," 551
Rumania, 745
    Balkan Wars, 1285–86
    Ceaucescu, Nicolae, 190–94
    during Trajan's reign, 1264
Rumiantsev, Nikolai, 752, 1127, 1238
Rump Parliament, 208, 307
Runciman, Steven, 1224, 1226
Runnymede, 650, 693
Rupert, Prince, 306
Rupp, E. G., 827
Rurik, House of, 994
Rus, Principality of, 993
Russell, George ("A. E."), 866
Russell, Lord John, 1054, 1104, 1291, 1296
Russell, William Howard, 1008
Russia. *See also* Russian Revolution; Soviet
    Union
    commercial ties with England, 28
    in Diplomatic Revolution, 461–62
    domination of Balkans, 479
    ethnic groups in, 1003
    famine of 1602, 501
    revolutionary France, 1239
    Harald III Hardraade in, 575
    historic leaders
        Alexander I, 25–30, 27
        Alexander II, 31–34
        Breshkovsky, Catherine, 136–40
        Catherine II, the Great, 179–84
        Godunov, Boris, 497–502
        Ivan III, the Great, 658–62
        Ivan IV, the Terrible, 663–68
        Kerensky, Alexander, 720–23
        Kollontai, Alexandra, 734–38
        Kutuzov, Mikhail, 751–54
        Lenin, V. I., 772–75
        Mannerheim, Karl Gustaf, 848–51
        Nevsky, Alexander, 993–97
        Nicholas II, 1003–7
        Peter I, the Great, 1072–77
        Potemkin, Grigori, 1126–29
        Sakharov, Andrei, 1178–81
        Suvorov, Alexander, 1236–39
        Vladimir I, 1299–1302
        Witte, Sergei, 1357–62
    Hungarian nationalism, 747
    Industrial Revolution, 735
    industry in, 1003
    Japan, 1005, 1360
    Mannerheim and, 848–49
    Mongol rule of, 995
    Napoleonic Wars, 753–54, 975–76
    Poland, 752, 1028, 1090–91
    railroads in, 1359
    Revolution of 1905, 1005, 1361
    in Seven Years' War, 462
    society in, 1075
    subdues Hungarian uprising, 965
    Sweden, 552, 1073
    unification of by Alexander Nevsky,
        996–97
    Witte's system for industrial reform,
        1358–59
    World War I, 437, 735, 821–23, 849,
        1006, 1331–32, 1332
    World War II, 754
Russia and History's Turning Point (Keren-
    sky), 723
Russian Bible Society, 28

Russian Civil War, 774–75, 1006–7,
    1270–71
    Stalin in, 1220
Russian Communist Party, 772
Russian Orthodox Church, 1076
Russian Provisional Government (1917),
    718
Russian Revolution, 99, 773, 830, 897,
    1005–7, 1269–70, 1361
    Breshkovsky, Catherine, 137–39
    Kerensky, Alexander, 720–23
    MacDonald, Ramsay, 839
    Trotsky, Leon, 1268–72
    Witte, Sergei, 1361
    World War I, 774–75
Russkaia Pravda (Russian Law Code), 1301
Russo-Finnish War, 737
Russo-Japanese War, 46, 1005, 1360
Russo-Polish War, 1207
Russo-Turkish War, 752–53, 1238
Ruthenia, 898
Ryazan, 995
Rymnik, battle of, 752, 1238

S

SA. *See Sturmabteilung* (SA)
Sabina, Poppaea, 989
Sacheverell, Henry, 52, 1324
Sadler, Michael, 56
Saga of Magnus the Good, 577
Saint Bartholomew's Day Massacre, 606,
    924, 925
Saint Basil's Cathedral (Moscow), 665
Saint Germain, Peace of, 924
Saint Giles Cathedral (Edinburgh), 732
Saint Joan (Shaw), 678
Saint John, Henry (later Viscount Boling-
    broke), 52, 1309
Saint Martha's (Rome), 818
Saint Mary's Dispensary for Women, 474
Saint-Megrim, 925
Saint Olaf's Saga (Sturluson), 575
Saint Petersburg. *See* Petrograd
Saint Quentin, battle of, 922
Saint-Simon, Comte Henri de, 876, 877,
    980
Sainte-Chapelle, 801
Saints, Zwingli on, 1378
Sakhalin Island, 1360
Sakharov, Andrei, 512, 1121, *1178,* **1178–81**
    calls for freedom of thought, 1180
    chronology, 1179
Saladin, 1141, 1282
"Salami tactics," 963
Salamis, Persian navy at, 779
Salazar, António, *1182,* **1182–87**
    chronology, 1183
    as prime minister, 1185
    as writer and teacher, 1183–84
Salian Franks, 274
Salic Law, 275, 921
Salimbene, 455, 457
Salisbury, Lord, 1053, 1297
Salisbury, third marquess of. *See* Gascoyne-
    Cecil, Robert
Salzman, L. F., 369
Samoa, 481
Samoilova, Konkordiya, 736
Samuel, Sir Herbert, 72, 841
San Marino, 469

in Russo-Polish War, 1207
Silesia, 863, 1305, 1306
    annexed by Frederick II, the Great, 461
    invasion of, 861
Silesian War, First, 862
Silesian War, Second, 862
Silesian Wars, 461
Silvestr, Daniil, 665
Simic, Stanoje, 787
Simnel, Lambert, 615
Simony, 540, 541, 542, 655
Simpson, Sir James, 474
Sinai Peninsula, 572
Sinn Fein, 321, 866, 868, 947
Sinodik (Ivan), 667
Sir Robert Walpole (Kemp), 1311
Sisa, Stephen, 1228, 1230
Sit, battle of, 995
Sitric, king of Dublin, 834
Siward, earl of Northumbria, 835
Sizeranne, Comtesse de la (aunt of Maud
    Gonne), 508
Skaane, 858, 860
Skard, Sigmund, 970
Skeffington, Francis Sheehy, 868
Slansky, Rudoph, 518, 521–22
Slave trade, 1033
    and Children's Crusade, 1226
        Wesley on, 1326
Slavery, 489, 536
"Slavery of Negroes" (de Gouges), 526
Slavic groups, 892
Slavs, 1230, 1331
    of Austria-Hungary, 436
Slipyi, Joseph Cardinal, 702
Slovak Communist Party, 518
Slovakia, 898
Slovaks, 745, 746
Slovenes, 1258
Slovenia, 411
Sluys, battle of, 376, 405
Smallpox, 1347
    Aztecs contract, 302
Smeral, Bohumir, 516
Smigly-Rydz, marshal Edward, 1208
Smith, Adam, 1098
Smith, Denis Mack, 961, 1288
Smith, Rev. Sydney, 463
Smolensk, battle of, 754
Smyrna, 1287
Snowden, Philip, 841
So? oder So? (Harand), 586, 587
Soaemias, Julia, 709, 711
Sobibor, 81, 83
Sobieski, John III, 398, *695*, **695–98**
    chronology, 696
Sobieski, Marek, 696
The Social Bases of the Woman Question, (Kol-
    lontai), 735
Social Democratic Federation (SDF), 838
Social Democratic Party (SPD), 9
Social Democrats (German), 633
Social Democrats (Russian), 735
Social reforms
    Ashley-Cooper, Anthony, 7th earl of
        Shaftsbury, 54–58
    Besant, Annie, 108–11
    Bismarck, Otto von, 116
    in England (Cobden and Bright), 277–80
    Fry, Elizabeth, 463–66
    Pestalozzi, Johann, 1062–65
    Peter I, the Great, 1075

Socialism in England. *See* MacDonald,
    Ramsey
    Polish, 1088–89
    and Roman Catholic Church, 701, 702
Socialism and Government (MacDonald), 839
Socialism and Society (MacDonald), 839
"Socialism of the Possible," 717
Socialist Movement, The (MacDonald), 839
Socialist Party, of Hungary, 719
Socialist Party (Italian), 903, 904, 905, 957
"Socialist Realism," 717
Socialist Revolutionary movement, 721
Socialist Unity Party (SED), 1275
Socialists, Italian, 903–5, 957
Society for the Improvement of the Condi-
    tion of Factory Children, 56
Society for the Improvement of Prison Dis-
    cipline and the Reformation of Juvenile
    Reformers, 465
Society of Cogers, 1014
Society of Friends (Quakers). *See* Quakers
Society of Jesus (Jesuits), 816–18, 1371
    becomes influential in Church, 818
    founded by Ignatius Loyola, 816–17
Soderblom, Nathan, 570
"Softsword." *See* John, king of England
Sogdiana, 24
Sokolovskaya, Alexandra, 1268
Sola scriptura, 1378
Solferino, battle of, 360–61
Solon, *1210*, **1210–13**
    begins reform program, 1211
    chronology, 1211
    moves Athens toward democracy,
        1212–13
Solzhenitsyn, Alexander, 727, 1120
Somaliland (French), 762
Somerset, Protector, 731
Somme, battle of, 419, 682, 947
Somme-Py, battle of, 915
Sommes
    battle of, 844
    Haig leads forces, 567
Song of Roland, 203
Sophia, Duchess, wife of Ivan III (formerly
    Zoë Palaeologus), 659–60, 661-62, 663
Sophia, electress of Hanover, 51, 53
Sophia Dorothea, mother of Frederick II,
    the Great, 460
Sophie (Ruffy, Thérèse-Richard-Sophie de,
    marquise de Monnier), 937
Sophism, 1059
Sophists (Wisemen), 1055
Sophocles, 1059
Sorensen, Jon, 966
Sosnowski, General Józef, 740
Soubirous, Bernadette, 1105
Sound dues, 231
South Africa, 594, 846
    Boer War, 46, 481, 1297
South America, Garibaldi in, 468
South Korea, 788
South Russia Workers' Union, 1268
"Sovereign of all Russia." *See* Ivan III, the
    Great
Sovereignty, national, 622
Soviet, 1269
Soviet, Petrograd, 722
Soviet Central Committee, 1117, 1119,
    1122, 1123
Soviet Communist Party, 1117, 1121, 1179,
    1180, 1181

conservatives kidnap Gorbachev, 513
    under Gorbachev, 511–14
Soviet Occupation Zone of Germany,
    1275–76
Soviet Politburo, 1117, 1121, 1122, 1123,
    1125
Soviet Secret Police, 1274–75
Soviet Union, 570, 772. *See also* Russia;
    Russian Revolution
    atomic bomb, 1179
    and Belgian Congo, 573
    collapse of, 512
    crackdown on nationalism of satellites,
        521
    and Czechoslovakia, 356–58, 891,
        893–94
    and England, 840
    establishes Eastern European satellites,
        519
    ethnic groups in, 513
    famine of 1920, 969
    historic leaders
        Beria, Lavrenti, 99–102
        Breshkovsky, Catherine, 136–40
        Gorbachev, Mikhail, 511–14
        Khrushchev, Nikita, 724–28
        Stalin, Joseph, 1218
        Trotsky, Leon, 1268–72
    and Hungary, 714–19
    invaded by Hitler, 81
    launches *Sputnik*, 727
    and People's Republic of China, 727,
        1121
    and Poland, 505, 1090
    purge of Eastern European leaders,
        504–5
    purges of scientists, 1180–81
    relationship with Poland, 503–6
    secret police. *See* Beria, Lavrenti
    after Stalin, **1116–25**
    Suez Canal Crisis, 572
    and United States, 513, 727. *See also*
        Cold War
    World War II, 893, 1117, 1118, 1119,
        1121, 1124–25
Soviets, defined, 774
Sowinski, Peter, 1028
Space race, 727
Spain, 862. *See also* Castile, León
    as empire, 653
    conquered by Rome, 67
    Dutch revolt against, 394
    and England during Elizabeth I,
        395–96
    15th century geographic divisions,
        653–54
    historic leaders
        Abd-al-Rahman II, 1–5
        Charles III, 212–16
        Columbus, Christopher, 289–93
        de Vivar, Rodrigo Díaz, 332–35
        Franco, Francisco, 439–44
        Isabella and Ferdinand, 653–57
        Philip II, 1078–82
        Primo de Rivera, Miguel, 1155–59
    Islamic, 1–5
    John of Austria, 685–89
    Moors in, 816
    and Napoleon I Bonaparte, 975
    and Netherlands, 402, 403–6
    Netherlands ruled by, 1342–45
    New World conquests, 289–93, 1108–11

Transubstantiation, 645–46, 651, 1369, 1379

Transvaal, 481

Transylvania, 1229
  Turks attack, 399

Trapezus (Trebizond; Trabzon), 1265

Trasimunds, 648

Treatise Against the Errors of Abelard (Bernard of Clairvaux), 105

Treaty of Füssen, 862

Treaty of Lübeck, 232

Treaty of Nijmwegen, 284

Treaty of Paris, 32

Treaty of Utrecht, 53

Treaty of Westphalia, 283

Treblinka, 81, 83

Treitschke, Heinrich von, 582

Trench warfare, 568

Trent Affair, 1296, 1297

Trew Law of Free Monarchies, 671

Trialogus (Wycliffe), 1370

"Tribune of the People." *See* Mirabeau, Count

Tribunicia potestas (tribunal power), 854

Tribur, Diet of, 542

Trierarch, 324

Triple Alliance, begins World War I, 437

Triple Entente, pulled into World War I, 437

Tritton, Lydia, 723

Triumvirate, first, 64–65

Trolle, Gustav, archbishop of Uppsala, 549

Trotsky, Leon, 77, 330, 721, 722, 736, 775, 970, 1130, 1219, 1220, *1268*, **1268–72**
  chronology, 1269
  Kerensky imprisons, 722
  on Lenin, 1269
  Russian Civil War, 1270–71
  vs. Stalin, 1271–72
  theory of permanent revolution, 1269–70

Troyes, Chretien de, 390

Troyes, Treaty of, 612

Truce of God, 544, 1281

Trudovik (Workers) Party, 722

Truman, Harry, 788

Truth, as Quaker concept, 422

The Truth about Peparations and War Debts (Lloyd George), 798

The Truth about the Peace Treaties, The (Lloyd George), 798

"The Truth-Teller." *See* Alfred the Great

Tryggvason, Olaf I, 549, *1018*, **1018–21**
  chronology, 1019
  converts to Christianity, 1020
  marries Thyre, 1021

Tsar, traditional role of, 1076

Tsaritzn, 499

Tschombe, Moise, 573

Tsushima, Straits of, 1005

Tuaregs, 681

Tucker, Robert, 1219, 1223

Tudor, Mary I, queen of England (Bloody Mary), 220, 393, 731, *886*, **886–90**, 1383
  chronology, 887

Tudor, William, 610

Tudors
  Elizabeth I, 392
  Henry VII, 614–18
  Henry VIII, 619–24
  Mary. *See* Tudor, Mary I, queen of England

Tuileries Palace, 316, 811, 812, 925

Túmkes, 1108

Tunis, republic of, 688

Tunis, Emir of, 370

Tunisia, 762

Turati, Filippo, 905

Turkey, 491. *See also* Ottoman Empire
  grants asylum to Kossuth, 747–48
  Greek conflict with, 1284–85
  World War I, 1286

Turkish crisis (1922), 798

Turkish Empire, 687

Turks
  attacks inspire First Crusade, 1281–83
  in Balkans, 1258
  besiege Vienna, 697–98
  and Eugene of Savoy, 397
  Kipchak (Polovetsians), 994
  raid Austria, 909
  Seljuq, 1281
  vs. Spanish, 1080

Turner, D. H., 97

Turner, Sir Charles, 1309

Tuscany, duchy of, 975

Tuscany, Matilda of, 899–902

Tutti fratelli, 360

Tver, 659, 995

Twain, Mark, 783

"Two Acts," 1099

Two Sicilies, 213

Two Sicilies, dictator of. *See* Garibaldi, Giuseppi

Typecliffe, Righard, 395

Tyre, 23

Tyrol, 909

Tyrone's Rebellion. *See* Elizabeth I, queen of England

U

Udgorn Rhyddid (Trumpet of Freedom) (Lloyd George), 796

Uganda, 480

Ugeday, 994

Ukraine, during World War II, 725–26

Ulbricht, Walter, 357, *1273*, **1273–78**, 1274–75

Uldarick, prince of Bohemia, 1301

Ulfsdottir, Marta, 858

Ulfsson, Svein

Ulm, battle of, 753

Ulpia Marciana, 1265

Ulster, Annals of, 833

Ulstermen, Protestant, 867

Ultramontanes, 310, 312, 431, 1104

Ultraquists, 1304

Ulug-Mahmed, Khan, 659

Ulyanov, Alexander, 721, 773

Ulyanov, Ilya, 772

Ulyanov, Vladimir (V.I. Lenin). *See* Lenin

Umayyad dynasty, Abd-al-Rahman II, 1–5

Un Souvenir de Solferino (A Memory of Solferino), 361

Unemployment insurance, 797

Unemployment Insurance Fund (British), 841

UNESCO. *See* United Nations Educational, Scientific, and Cultural Organization (UNESCO)

"The Unexpected Marriage of Chérubin" (de Gouges), 526

UNICEF. *See* United Nations Children's Fund (UNICEF)

Union for Democratic Control, 839

Union of Riflemen's Clubs (Poland), 1089

Union of Socialist Soviet Republics. *See* under Russia; Soviet Union

Union(s). *See also* Trade unions
  coal miners', 592

United Irishmen, 532

United Kingdom (1801), 1099

United Nations, 442
  charter drafted for Security Council, 787
  charter of, 569
  and Hammarskjold, Dag, 569–73
  and Lie, Trygve, 785, 787–89
  peacekeeping force (United Nations Emergency Forces [UNEF]), 572

United Nations Children's Fund (UNICEF), 573

United Nations Educational, Scientific, and Cultural Organization (UNESCO), 788.

United Nations Emergency Forces (UNEF), 572

United Nations Relief and Rehabilitation Administration (UNRRA), 788

United Nations Security Council, 570

United Partisan Organization, 82

United Provinces, 402, 862, 1348

United States, 481, 892. *See also* American colonies
  after Civil War, 490
  Civil War, 1035, 1042
  and England, 846
  Harands emigrate to, 588
  Hitler declares war on, 634
  and Pankhurst, Emmeline, 1040
  and Soviet Union, 513, 569, 727. *See also* Cold War
  in space race, 727
  Suez Canal crisis, 572
  Vietnam War, 1355
  in World War I, 627, 822, 683, 1029, 1257, 1332
  in World War II, 634, 950

Universal Christian Conference on Life and Work, 571

Unofficial Committee (Russia), 27

UNRRA. *See* United Nations Relief and Rehabilitation Administration

Unterseeboot (U-boot), 1256

Untertanengebiete, 1063, 1377

UP. *See* Patriotic Union (UP)

Uppsala, University of, 555, 571

Urban, Heinrich, 1029

Urban II, Pope, 495, 901, 1224, *1279*, **1279–83**
  chronology, 1280
  and Henry IV, 1281
  launches First Crusade, 1281
  reforms church administration, 1281

Urban VIII, Pope, 913

Uruguay, Garibaldi in, 468

U.S.S.R. *See* Russia; Russian Revolution; Soviet Union

Ustasi, 1260

Utopia (More), 953, 1365

Utrecht, Treaty of, 53, 400, 808, 1345

V

Valdemar IV. *See* Waldemar IV

Valdemarsdottir, Margaret. *See* Margaret of Denmark

Valencia, 335, 653
Valentinian III, 61
Valois, Marguerite, 924
Valois monarchs, 687
Van Hoorne, count of, 1080, 1344
Van Keppel, Joost, 1350
Vandals, 61
Varangian Guard, 575
Varangians, 1300
Vasa, Gustavus I, **548–52**
  chronology, 549
Vasa, Sigismund, king of Sweden and
  Poland, 553, 555
Vasa (Wasa) family, 696
Vasili III, tsar, 663
Vassalage, 451
Vassan, Marie-Geneviève de, 936
Västerås
  battle at, 549
  Gustavus calls Estates, 551–52
  Recess of, 550
Vaterland (Vogelsang), 581
Vatican City, 959
Vatican Council
  First, 313, 701
  Second, 701–2, 1105
Vazeille, Mary, 1326
Vecinos, 300
Vedrosha River, battle of, 661
Vegetius, 246
Veimarn, General I. I., 1238
Velázquez, Diego, 299, 301
Velho, Gonzalo, 602
Venezuela, 481
Venice, 687, 910
Venizelos, Eleutherios, *1284,* **1284–87**
  chronology, 1286
  as prime minister, 1285–87
Venta Icenorum, 126
Vercingetorix, 756
Verdi, Giuseppe, 1290
Verdun, battle of, 682, 822, 1068
Verdun, Treaty of (843), 1022
Vergil, Polydore, 618, 1149
Vernadsky, George, 660, 996
Vers l'armee de metier (The Army of the Future)
  (de Gaulle), 485
Versailles
  palace at, 283
  Treaty of (1756), 462
  Treaty of (1919), 267, 268, 462, 627, 631,
    633, 761, 798, 969, 1233, 1234, 1257
Versailles Peace Conference, 1029–30,
  1286–87
Verus, Lucius, 853, 854
Verus, Marcus Annius, 852
Vespasian, 988, 991, 992
Veterim Sapientia, 701
Veuillot, Louis, 1102
Vexin, 1085
Viatichians, 1300
Viaz'ma, battle of, 754
Vibia Sabina, 560
"Vicar of Christ," 649
Vichy government, headed by Henri-
  Philippe Pétain, 1066, 1070–71
Victor Emmanuel II, 187, 470, 905, *1288,*
  1288–92
  chronology, 1289
Victor Emmanuel III, king of Italy, 958
Victor III, Pope, 901, 1280
Victor of Savoy, duke, 399

Victoria, queen of England, 114, 344, 383,
  481, 1004, 1011, 1034, 1053, 1254, *1293,*
  1293–98, *1296,* 1330, 1334
  Bedchamber Crisis, 1053–54
  chronology, 1294
  honors Florence Nightingale, 1011
  and Prince Albert, 1295, 1297
Victoria of Saxe-Coburg and Saalfeld, 1293
Victoria the princess Royal, 383
Victorie, 757
Victricius of Rouen, 1048
Victuals Brothers, 859
Vidkunnsson, Erling, 858
Vienna, 437, 589
  as cultural capital, 437
  siege of (1683), 697–98
  threatened by Turks, 398, 697–98
Vietnam, 570
Vietnam War, 1355
Viking (hunting ship), 967
Vikings, 832
  Brian Boru fights, 141–45
  Canute I, 169–73
  Harald III Hardraade, 574–78
  Olaf I Tryggvason, 1018–21
Villa Rica de la Veracruz, 299–300
Villiers, Elizabeth, 1349
Villiers, George, duke of Buckingham, 673
Villiers, Lady Harriet, 1092
Vincennes, 937
Vinchy, 871
Vindex, C. Julius, 991–92
Violante of Aragon, 38
Vipsania, 791, 792
Virgil, 67
Virginia, named in honor of Elizabeth I, 1136
Virtue, 1161
Visigoths, 61, 538
Vishinsky, Andrei, 894
Visby, city of, 860
Vistula, miracle on the, 1091
Vitalis, Orderic, 1340
Vitoria, battle of, 976
Vives, Luis, 887
Vivian Grey (Disraeli), 341
Viviani, René, 683
Vladimir, grand duke of (Alexander
  Nevsky), 993, 995–96
Vladimir I, *1299,* **1299–1302**
  chronology, 1300
  converts to Christianity, 1301
Vladimir-Suzdal, grand duchy of, 994
Vladislav, John, 1229
Vogelsand, Karl von, 581
Volga Bulgars, 994, 995, 1300
Volkogonov, Dmitri, 1218
Volpe, Gian-Battista della, 660
Voltaire, 800, 1177
Vom Erkiesen und Freiheit der Speisen
  (Zwingli), 1378
Voroshilov, Klement, 101
Voting rights. *See* Women's suffrage
Vsevolod (Big Nest), 994
Vsyakaya vsyachina (All Kings of Things)
  (Catherine II, the Great), 184
Vulgate (Latin Bible), 43
Vyshnegradsky, Ivan A., 1358

W

Wagner, Richard, 629

Waldemar IV, king of Denmark, 858, **860**
Waldensians, 434
Waldheim, Kurt, 580
Waldo, Peter, 434
Wales, 796–97
  Edward I wars against, 371–72
Wallace, William, 371
Wallachia, Russian invasion of, 752
Wallenstein, Albrecht von, 232, 413, 556,
  1303, **1303–7**
  chronology, 1304
  dismissed by Ferdinand II, 413
  murder of, 414
  removed from command, 556
Wallenstein (Schiller), 1303
Wallhof, battle of, 555
Walloons, 17, 403, 404
Walpole, Robert, 1093, *1308,* **1308–12**
  chronology, 1309
  as Whig leader, 1309–10
Walsingham, Sir Francis, 885
Walther, Irene, 80
Waltz, 437
Wandruszka, Adam, 1175
Wannsee Conference, 634, 637, 640
War and Peace (Tolstoy), 29
"War criminals," of World War II, 544
War Memoirs (Lloyd George), 798
War of American Independence, 215, 983
War of Devolution (1667), 807
War of Jenkins' Ear, 1311
War of Spanish Succession, 52, 53, 247,
  248, 249, 399–400, 808
War of the First Coalition, 527
War of the Gaedhil with the Gaill, 142
War of the Polish Succession, 400, 1311
War of the Roses, 86–89, 614–16, 1145
Warbeck affair, 617
Warfare, in trenches, 568
Warner, Geoffrey, 762
Warnsfield, battle of, 405
Warren, W. L., 694, 1143
Wars of Religion, 607
Warsaw, duchy of, 975
Warsaw Conservatory, 1029
Warsaw Ghetto, Jewish uprising, 83–84
Warsaw Pact, 570
Wasa (Vasa) family, 696
Washington, George, 740, 757
Washington, Treaty of (1871), 490
Waterloo, battle of, 933, 976, 1316–17
Waugh, Dhoondiah, 1315
Wavell, Field Marshall, 568
The Way of Perfection (Teresa of Avila), 1242
Wazo, bishop of Lietge, 540
Weber, Max, 1233
Webster, Daniel, 749
Wedgwood, C. V., 411–13, 1342, 1344,
  1345
Wedl, Irene. *See* Harand, Irene
Wehrmacht (Laval), 765
Weimar Republic, 625, 627–28, 830, 1233,
  1234, 1257
Weisskunig (Maximilian), 910
Weitling, Wilhelm, 877
Welch, Oliver, 936
Welf V, count of Bavaria, 901, 1280
Wellesley, Arthur, 1st duke of Wellington,
  55, 975, 1033, *1313,* **1313–19,** *1318*
  chronology, 1314
  defeats Napoleon at Waterloo, 1317
  hero of Peninsular War, 1316

Italy, 904, 957
last German offensive, 568
Macmillian in rifle corps, 843–44
Netherlands, 1334–35
Norway, 969–70
offensive vs. defensive strategy, 418
peace movement, 1195–97
Poland, 1029–30, 1089–90, 1206–7
Russia, 735, 774, 821–23, 849, 1006,
1331–32
and Russian Revolution, 774–75
socialist reaction to, 830
Turkey, 48, 1286
United States, 627, 683, 822, 1029,
1257, 1332
Verdun, battle of, 1068
Western Front, 419
World War II, 6, 569
Algeria, 1070
Allied invasion of Normandy, 765, 1173
and Anderson, Elizabeth Garrett, 476
beginning of hostilities, 197
cartography for, 941
Czechoslovakia, 516–17, 517–18, 893–94
Dutch occupation, 1335–36
England, 845
Finland, 850
France, 763, 1066, 1069–71
Germany, 948–51, 1172–74, 1234, 1274
navy, 1256–57
Great Britain, 634, 948–51
historic leaders
Adenauer, Konrad, 6–10
Churchill, Winston, 254–55
de Gaulle, Charles, 485–86
Hitler, Adolf, 633–35
Montgomery, Bernard, 945–51
Rommel, Erwin, 1170–74
Italy, 961
Kerensky during, 723
Netherlands, 1335–36
North Africa, 949–50
Norway, 786–87
Operation Barbarossa, 754
Poland, 1030
Portugal, 1186
rearmament for, 73
Rumania during, 192
Russia, 726
Sicily, 950
Soviet Union, 1117, 1118, 1119, 1121,
1124–25
Spain pursues neutrality, 442
Turkey, 700
Ukraine, 726
United States, 634, 950
Yugoslavia, 1260–61
Worms, Diet of, 218, 542, 826–27, 910
Writ of Mort d'Ancestor, 598

Wyatt's Rebellion, 889
Wycliffe, John, 610, 643, 1366, *1368,*
1368–70
chronology, 1369
doctrine of predestination, 645
English translation of Bible, 1370
views on transubstantiation, 1369
Wyntoun, Andrew, 375

X

Xanthippus, 1055
Xavier, Francis, 816, *1371,* **1371–75**
chronology, 1372
Loyola and, 1372
as missionary, 1373–75
Xenophon, 13
Xerxes, Persian king, 777, 1059
Xicotencatl, 301
Xuárez, Catalina, 299, 302
XXX Ulpia, 1264

Y

Yad Vashem Martyrs and Heroes Remem-
brance Authority, 588
Yalta Conference (1945), *1221,* 1276
Yaropolk of Kiev, 1300
Yaroslav, king of Russia, 575
Yaroslav II, Grand duke of Vladimir, 995, 996
Yaroslav III, 996
Yeats, William Butler, 509, 866
Yeltsin, Boris, 511, 513, 1181
Yezhov, Nikolai, 100–1
"Yilderim," 48
YMCA. *See* Young Men's Christian Associ-
ation (YMCA)
York, archbishop of, 599
York, Elizabeth of, 615
Yorks, 86
Young, Richard, 395
Young Conservatives, 844
Young Czech Party, 896, 897
Young Hegelians, 876
Young Italy, 919
Young Italy movement, 310–11
Young Men's Christian Association
(YMCA), 359
Young Plan, 841
Ypres
first battle of, 567
second battle of, 843
Yucatán, 299
Yugoslavia, 762
Jewish resistance movement, 82
Marshal Tito, 1258–62
World War II, 1260

Z

Zachary, Pope, 872
Zagreb, Tito in, 1260
Zajic, Zybnhacek, archbishop of Prague,
645, 646
Zalman, Dr. Moritz, and Irene Harand, 585
"Zamour and Mirza, or the Happy Ship-
wreck" (de Gouges), 526
Zanzibar, 480
Zapotocky, Antonin, 521
Zealots, 991
Zedong, Mao, 570
Zeeland, 1349
Zemski Sobor (a national council), 665
Zemstvo Law (Russia, 1864), 33
Zeno of Elea, 1056
Zenschina (Zemshtshina), 666
Zenta, battle of, 399
Zetkin, Clara (European socialist), 829
Zeugitai, 1212
Zhdanov, Andrei, 726, 1118
Zhukovsky, Vasily Andreyevich, 31
Zinoviev, Grigori, Russian president, 737,
840, 1117, 1220, 1271
Zionism, 77
Zlicane tribe, 1322
Zloty Wiek (Golden Age of Poland), 1381
Zoe, empress (Byzantine)
Zoë Palaeologus (later Duchess Sophia, wife
of Ivan III), 659–63 Zotto, duke of Lom-
bard, 96
Zubatov, Sergei V., 1359
Zubczewska, Helena, 1206
Zugewandte Orte, 1379
Zúñiga, Doña Juana de, 302
Zurich
and European socialism, 828–29
Pestalozzi in, 1062, 1063
Zwingli at, 1377–78
Zwiazek Strzelecki, 1089
Zwingli, Bartholomew, 1376
Zwingli, Huldrych, *1376,* **1376–80**
chronology, 1377
debates with Martin Luther, 1380
Zwyn, naval battle at, 692
Zygmunt, Holy Roman Emperor, 646
invites Hus to attend council, 646
Zygmunt I Stary, 1381–82
Zygmunt I Vasa, king of Sweden, 499
Zygmunt II Augustus, 666, 695, *1381,*
1381–83
chronology, 1382
joins Poland and Lithuania, 1383